THE
ROCKY MOUNTAIN
REGION

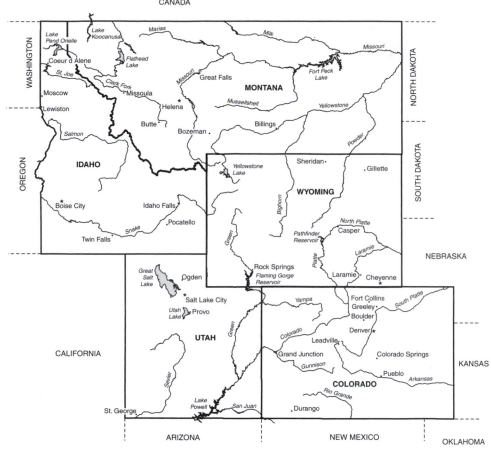

CANADA

WASHINGTON

Lake Pend Orielle
Lake Koocanusa
Marias
Milk
Missouri

Coeur d Alene
Flathead Lake
St. Joe
Clark Fork
Missoula
Missouri
Great Falls
MONTANA
Fort Peck Lake

Moscow
Lewiston
Helena
Musselshell
Yellowstone

NORTH DAKOTA

Salmon
Butte
Bozeman
Billings

Powder

OREGON

IDAHO

Boise City
Idaho Falls
Pocatello

Twin Falls
Snake

Yellowstone Lake
Sheridan
Gillette

WYOMING

SOUTH DAKOTA

Bighorn

North Platte
Casper

Green
Pathfinder Reservoir
Laramie

Platte
Laramie
Cheyenne

NEBRASKA

Rock Springs
Flaming Gorge Reservoir

Great Salt Lake
Ogden
Salt Lake City
Utah Lake
Provo

Yampa
Fort Collins
Greeley
Boulder
South Platte

CALIFORNIA

UTAH
Green
Colorado
Leadville
Denver

Grand Junction
Gunnison
Colorado Springs

KANSAS

Sevier

Pueblo
Arkansas

COLORADO

St. George

Lake Powell
San Juan
Rio Grande

Durango

ARIZONA

NEW MEXICO

OKLAHOMA

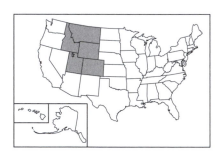

THE
ROCKY MOUNTAIN
REGION

The Greenwood Encyclopedia of American Regional Cultures

Edited by
Rick Newby

Foreword by William Ferris, Consulting Editor

Paul S. Piper, Librarian Advisor

GREENWOOD PRESS
Westport, Connecticut • London

Library of Congress Cataloging-in-Publication Data

The Rocky Mountain region: the Greenwood encyclopedia of American regional cultures / edited
by Rick Newby ; foreword by William Ferris, consulting editor.
　　p.　cm.
　Includes bibliographical references (p.　) and index.
　ISBN 0–313–33266–(set : alk. paper)—ISBN 0–313–32817–X
　　1. Rocky Mountains Region—Civilization—Encyclopedias.　2. Rocky Mountains Region—
History—Encyclopedias.　3. Rocky Mountains Region—Social life and customs—Encyclopedias.
4. Popular culture—Rocky Mountains Region—Encyclopedias.　5. Regionalism—Rocky
Mountains Region—Encyclopedias.　I. Newby, Rick.　II. Series.
　F721.R74　2004
　978'.003—dc22　　　　2004056066

British Library Cataloguing in Publication Data is available.

Library of Congress Catalog Card Number: 2004056066
ISBN: 0–313–33266–5 (set)
　　　0–313–32733–5 (The Great Plains Region)
　　　0–313–32954–0 (The Mid-Atlantic Region)
　　　0–313–32493–X (The Midwest)
　　　0–313–32753–X (New England)
　　　0–313–33043–3 (The Pacific Region)
　　　0–313–32817–X (The Rocky Mountain Region)
　　　0–313–32734–3 (The South)
　　　0–313–32805–6 (The Southwest)

First published in 2004

Greenwood Press, 88 Post Road West, Westport, CT 06881
An imprint of Greenwood Publishing Group, Inc.
www.greenwood.com

Printed in the United States of America

The paper used in this book complies with the
Permanent Paper Standard issued by the National
Information Standards Organization (Z39.48–1984).

10 9 8 7 6 5 4 3 2 1

CONTENTS

Contents

FOREWORD

Region inspires and grounds the American experience. Whether we are drawn to them or flee from them, the places in which we live etch themselves into our memory in powerful, enduring ways. For over three centuries Americans have crafted a collective memory of places that constitute our nation's distinctive regions. These regions are embedded in every aspect of American history and culture.

American places have inspired poets and writers from Walt Whitman and Henry David Thoreau to Mark Twain and William Faulkner. These writers grounded their work in the places where they lived. When asked why he never traveled, Thoreau replied, "I have traveled widely in Concord."

William Faulkner remarked that early in his career as a writer he realized that he could devote a lifetime to writing and never fully exhaust his "little postage stamp of native soil."

In each region American writers have framed their work with what Eudora Welty calls "sense of place." Through their writing we encounter the diverse, richly detailed regions of our nation.

In his ballads Woody Guthrie chronicles American places that stretch from "the great Atlantic Ocean to the wide Pacific shore," while Muddy Waters anchors his blues in the Mississippi Delta and his home on Stovall's Plantation.

American corporate worlds like the Bell system neatly organize their divisions by region. And government commissions like the Appalachian Regional Commission, the Mississippi River Commission, and the Delta Development Commission define their mission in terms of geographic places.

When we consider that artists and writers are inspired by place and that government and corporate worlds are similarly grounded in place, it is hardly surprising that we also identify political leaders in terms of their regional culture. We think of John Kennedy as a New Englander, of Ann Richards as a Texan, and of Jimmy Carter as a Georgian.

Because Americans are so deeply immersed in their sense of place, we use region like a compass to provide direction as we negotiate our lives. Through sense of place we find our bearings, our true north. When we meet people for the first time, we ask that familiar American question, "Where are you from?" By identifying others through a region, a city, a community, we frame them with a place and find the bearings with which we can engage them.

Sense of place operates at all levels of our society—from personal to corporate and government worlds. While the power of place has long been understood and integrated in meaningful ways with our institutions, Americans have been slow to seriously study their regions in a focused, thoughtful way. As a young nation, we have been reluctant to confront the places we are "from." As we mature as a nation, Americans are more engaged with the places in which they live and increasingly seek to understand the history and culture of their regions.

The growing importance of regional studies within the academy is an understandable and appropriate response to the need Americans feel to understand the places in which they live. Such study empowers the individual, their community, and their region through a deeper engagement with the American experience. Americans resent that their regions are considered "overfly zones" in America, and through regional studies they ground themselves in their community's history and culture.

The Greenwood Encyclopedia of American Regional Cultures provides an exciting, comprehensive view of our nation's regions. The set devotes volumes to New England, the Mid-Atlantic, the South, the Midwest, the Southwest, the Great Plains, the Rocky Mountains, and the Pacific. Together these volumes offer a refreshing new view of America's regions as they stretch from the Atlantic to the Pacific.

The sheer size of our nation makes it difficult to imagine its diverse worlds as a single country with a shared culture. Our landscapes, our speech patterns, and our foodways all change sharply from region to region. The synergy of different regional worlds bound together within a single nation is what defines the American character. These diverse worlds coexist with the knowledge that America will always be defined by its distinctly different places.

American Regional Cultures explores in exciting ways the history and culture of each American region. Its volumes allow us to savor individual regional traditions and to compare these traditions with those of other regions. Each volume features chapters on architecture, art, ecology and environment, ethnicity, fashion, film and theater, folklore, food, language, literature, music, religion, and sports and recreation. Together these chapters offer a rich portrait of each region. The series is an important teaching resource that will significantly enrich learning at secondary, college, and university levels.

Over the past forty years a growing number of colleges and universities have launched regional studies programs that today offer exciting courses and degrees for both American and international students. During this time the National Endowment for the Humanities (NEH) has funded regional studies initiatives that range from new curricula to the creation of museum exhibits, films, and encyclopedias that focus on American regions. Throughout the nation, universities with regional studies programs recently received NEH support to assist with the programs that they are building.

The National Endowment for the Arts (NEA) has similarly encouraged regional initiatives within the art world. NEA's state arts councils work together within regional organizations to fund arts projects that impact their region.

The growing study of region helps Americans see themselves and the places they come from in insightful ways. As we understand the places that nurture us, we build a stronger foundation for our life. When speaking of how she raised her children, my mother often uses the phrase "Give them their roots, and they will find their wings." Thanks to *American Regional Cultures*, these roots are now far more accessible for all Americans. This impressive set significantly advances our understanding of American regions and the mythic power these places hold for our nation.

William Ferris
University of North Carolina
at Chapel Hill

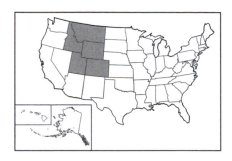

PREFACE

We are pleased to present *The Greenwood Encyclopedia of American Regional Cultures*, the first book project of any kind, reference or otherwise, to examine cultural regionalism throughout the United States.

The sense of place has an intrinsic role in American consciousness. Across its vast expanses, the United States varies dramatically in its geography and its people. Americans seem especially cognizant of the regions from which they hail. Whether one considers the indigenous American Indian tribes and their relationships to the land, the many waves of immigrants who settled in particular regions of the nation, or the subsequent generations who came to identify themselves as New Englanders or Southerners or Midwesterners, and so forth, the connection of American culture to the sense of regionalism has been a consistent pattern throughout the nation's history.

It can be said that behind every travelogue on television, behind every road novel, behind every cross-country journey, is the desire to grasp the identity of other regions. This project was conceived to fill a surprising gap in publishing on American regionalism and on the many vernacular expressions of culture that one finds throughout the country.

This reference set is designed so that it will be useful to high school and college researchers alike, as well as to the general reader and scholar. Toward this goal, we consulted several members of Greenwood's Library Advisory Board as we determined both the content and the format of this encyclopedia project. Furthermore, we used the *National Standards: United States History* and also the *Curriculum Standards for Social Studies* as guides in choosing a wealth of content that would help researchers gain historical comprehension of how people in, and from, all regions have helped shape American cultures.

American Regional Cultures is divided geographically into eight volumes: *The Great Plains Region, The Mid-Atlantic Region, The Midwest, New England, The Pacific Region, The Rocky Mountain Region, The South,* and *The Southwest.* To ensure that cultural elements from each state would be discussed, we assigned each state to a particular region as follows:

The Great Plains Region: Kansas, Nebraska, North Dakota, Oklahoma, South Dakota
The Mid-Atlantic Region: Delaware, District of Columbia, Maryland, New Jersey, New York, Pennsylvania, West Virginia
The Midwest: Illinois, Indiana, Iowa, Michigan, Minnesota, Missouri, Ohio, Wisconsin
New England: Connecticut, Maine, Massachusetts, New Hampshire, Rhode Island, Vermont
The Pacific Region: Alaska, California, Hawai'i, Oregon, Washington
The Rocky Mountain Region: Colorado, Idaho, Montana, Utah, Wyoming
The South: Alabama, Arkansas, Florida, Georgia, Kentucky, Louisiana, Mississippi, North Carolina, South Carolina, Tennessee, Virginia
The Southwest: Arizona, Nevada, New Mexico, Texas

Each regional volume consists of rigorous, detailed overviews on all elements of culture, with chapters on the following topics: architecture, art, ecology and environment, ethnicity, fashion, film and theater, folklore, food, language, literature, music, religion, and sports and recreation. These chapters examine the many significant elements of those particular aspects of regional culture as they have evolved over time, through the beginning of the twenty-first century. Each chapter seeks not to impose a homogenized identity upon each region but, rather, to develop a synthesis or thematically arranged discussion of the diverse elements of each region. For example, in turning to the chapter on music in *The Pacific Region*, a reader will discover information on Pacific regional music as it has manifested itself in such wide-ranging genres as American Indian tribal performances, Hawaiian stylings, Hispanic and Asian traditions, West Coast jazz, surf rock, folk scenes, San Francisco psychedelia, country rock, the L.A. hard-rock scene, Northwest "grunge" rock, West Coast hip-hop, and Northern California ska-punk. Multiply this by thirteen chapters and again by eight volumes, and you get a sense of the enormous wealth of information covered in this landmark set.

In addition, each chapter concludes with helpful references to further resources, including, in most cases, printed resources, Web sites, films or videos, recordings, festivals or events, organizations, and special collections. Photos, drawings, and maps illustrate each volume. A timeline of major events for the region provides context for understanding the cultural development of the region. A bibliography, primarily of general sources about the region, precedes the index.

We would not have been able to publish such an enormous reference set without the work of our volume editors and the more than one hundred contributors that they recruited for this project. It is their efforts that have made *American Regional Cultures* come to life. We also would like to single out two people for their help: William Ferris, former chairman of the National Endowment for the Humanities and currently Distinguished Professor of History and senior associate director for the Center for the Study of the American South, University of North Carolina at Chapel Hill, who served as consulting editor for and was instrumental in the planning of this set and in the recruitment of its volume editors; and Paul S. Piper, Reference Librarian at Western Washington University, who in his role as librarian advisor, helped shape both content and format, with a particular focus on helping improve reader interface.

With their help, we present *The Greenwood Encyclopedia of American Regional Cultures*.

Rob Kirkpatrick, Senior Acquisitions Editor
Anne Thompson, Senior Development Editor
Greenwood Publishing Group

INTRODUCTION

The Rocky Mountain West—made up, for the purposes of this volume, of the states of Colorado, Idaho, Montana, Utah, and Wyoming—is a decidedly diverse place. "The West is several different regions," Wallace Stegner famously wrote, "all so different in their history and ethnic compositions, that . . . trying to make a unanimous culture out of them would be a hopeless job."[1] Stegner was speaking here of the broader West, but his statement certainly rings true for the cultures to be found within the Rocky Mountain region.

Acknowledging this diversity means, of course, keeping in mind the varied physiography of the region, ranging from badlands to plains to intermontane basins and plateaus to the Rocky Mountains themselves. Montana, for example, as Larry Swanson of the O'Connor Center for the Rocky Mountain West points out, is made up of three markedly distinct regions: one west of the Continental Divide, one east of the divide but relatively close to the Rocky Mountain Front, and the third encompassing the eastern plains. These three subregions, Swanson argues, differ radically not just in landforms and climates but also in their economies, politics, and general culture.[2]

The chapters in this volume ably address this diversity and the cultural richness it engenders. They range over myriad Rocky Mountain cultural expressions: from romantic images of cowboys to postmodern artworks critiquing environmental degradation, from log cabins to modernist skyscrapers, from Native American folktales to the folklore of Basque and Hawaiian immigrants, from homesteader ballads to free-jazz excursions, from logger garb to Latino zoot suits, from rancher lingo to mountain-biker-speak. Some of the cultural manifestations they highlight are startling, whereas others reassure us as they deepen our understanding of traditional subcultures.

Almost from the moment they set eyes on the place, Euro-Americans mythologized the awe-inspiring landscapes, galvanizing opportunities, and utterly alien cultures they found in the Rockies, and a tension has long existed between the persistent myths and the insistent realities. In 1950, for example, *The Denver Post* published a book it titled *Rocky Mountain Empire*, and in the book's foreword, Palmer Hoyt noted that "this American legend . . . became in fact a wall behind which the true modern West was developing in a manner and to a degree scarcely comprehended in older parts of the nation."[3] Not only outlanders but also a good portion of Rocky Mountaineers themselves still hold tight to the legend, while plenty of other locals—writers, historians, and artists prominent among them—call for an understanding of the region that privileges what essayist and fiction writer William Kittredge calls the "actual."

This tension, both within and without the Rockies, makes for conflict between worldviews and ideologies and, it can be argued, for cultural dynamism. Although some yearn for a decline in Western Exceptionalism (the notion that the place is somehow special and therefore privileged), the sense remains that the Rocky Mountain states, with their great natural beauty, relative uncrowdedness, and apparent freedom from civilization's corruptions, are indeed unique, even within a nation that prides itself on its exceptional nature. This struggle for a Rocky Mountain identity is not over, and it may never be. As Wallace Stegner put it, he had fought the good fight against the myth of the chivalric, gun-toting cowboy, but "he is a faster gun than I am . . . too attractive to the daydreaming imagination."[4]

The authors of the chapters in this volume confront both the daydreams and the actualities, and the culture they uncover cannot be labeled bland or one-dimensional. The notion of regional culture is taken seriously in the Rockies, and institutions like the Center for the American West in Boulder, Missoula's O'Connor Center for the Rocky Mountain West, and the Charles Redd Center for Western Studies in Provo all seek to further understanding of, and help define, the place's culture, economy, and politics. In 1991, the Center for the American West hosted a seminal conference titled "A Society to Match the Scenery," and the resulting book (by the same title) offered multiple visions both of what Rocky Mountain culture is and what it might become. The present volume, while it is more purely descriptive, contributes to this ongoing dialog and, it is hoped, offers further perspectives on the society, actual and mythic, to be found in the shadow of the Rockies.

Historian Carroll Van West, who has written extensively about capitalism on the frontier and the region's built environment, traces Architecture of the Rockies from the cliff palaces of Mesa Verde and the tipis of the Plains to the distinctively Rocky Mountain "parkitecture" first developed by Robert Reamer with his Old Faithful Lodge in Yellowstone National Park and to the Government Rustic style that emerged during the Great Depression. West also surveys the building styles imported to the region, from stately Victorian mansions to modernist homes and Brutalist skyscrapers to the monotony of suburban sprawl. He addresses issues of historic preservation, land use, and architectural education within the region. On a cautionary note, he concludes that the "boom-and-bust mentality that has so shaped the region both psychologically and physically continues to play a large role in the preservation of the past and the planning for the future, built environment of the Rocky Mountains."

The Art chapter, written by Rick Newby (whose specialties include the rise of visual modernism in the Rocky Mountain West), speaks to the central role of artists in shaping the myths of the West and, more recently, in offering correctives to those myths. The arts in the Rockies are incredibly rich and diverse, and they range from ongoing and inventive Native American traditions to folks arts of a dazzling variety (including the making of fine saddles, star quilts, and Hmong embroidery) to a western art sector that shows no signs of flagging. Various modernisms have taken root, among which the strongest may be what Newby calls "Rocky Mountain ceramic modernism," which began at mid-twentieth century in Montana, and environmental art (both land-based and otherwise).

Environmental historian Chris J. Magoc, who has written an award-winning book on the creation of Yellowstone National Park, provides an illuminating and balanced look at the Ecology and Environment of the Rocky Mountain region. Magoc offers a succinct overview of the "stunningly wide range of alpine, desert, and forest landscapes and literally hundreds of ecosystems" within the region, and he presents the history of human interaction with that complex and fragile environment. This is often the story of extraction of resources and resultant degradation—from the slaughter of the great bison herds and extirpation of predators to the ill-conceived efforts to plant homesteads on arid landscapes to "cut-and-run" deforestation and mining that have poisoned whole river systems. Magoc traces the fault lines that separate those within the region who support unrestrained development and those who favor a preservationist ethic. Between these two extremes, Magoc argues, lie those who seek to bridge the gap: ranchers, recreationists, and environmentalists who are finding common ground after decades of struggle. "Since the great mineral boom of the 1970s," Magoc writes, "family ranchers and farmers have often joined with the environmental community to form state 'Resource Councils' and other organizations to contest a wide array of recent threats to the environment and the overall quality of life in the region."

In the Ethnicity chapter, archaeologist/historians A. Dudley Gardner and Laura Pasacreta examine the very real diversity of the peoples to be found in the Rockies. As they point out, even though the region is among the "whitest" in the nation (in the 2000 census, the populations in all five states were at least 80 percent white, with only Colorado and Utah under 90 percent), it possesses a diversity of peoples of European origin, together with minorities from many different cultures, including populations of Polynesians, Southeast Asians, North Africans, African Americans, Latinos, and of course, the region's original inhabitants, Native Americans, who live on numerous rural reservations as well as in the region's urban areas. Gardner and Pasacreta examine discrimination based upon race and ethnicity in the Rockies, including violence against blacks and Chinese, anti-German sentiment during World War I, and the internment during World War II of Japanese Americans in camps situated in Colorado, Wyoming, and Idaho. They also shed light on unique groups within the region such as the Métis and communal Hutterites of Montana, the Basques of Idaho, and German Russian farmers on the plains.

The Fashion chapter, written by Laurel Wilson, a leading authority on ranch dress, and Rick Newby, explores the distance between mass-culture perception and regional reality, especially in the case of the garb of the working cowboy. The authors also offer information about the dress of the many Native American groups in the Rockies; early explorers, trappers, traders, and prospectors; the U.S. military on the frontier; wagon-train emigrants; miners, loggers, and homesteaders; as well as religious communities like the Mormons and Hutterites and a number of immigrant groups, including Scandinavians, Basques, and Hmong. The chapter concludes with a look at contemporary dress, including the high-fashion western wear showcased at the annual Western Design Conference in Cody, Wyoming, and catalogs that use imagery from the Rockies to sell their apparel. In their conclusion, Wilson and Newby note that "certain fashions with global resonance, especially those related to outdoor recreation, remain closely identified with an athletic Rocky Mountain ideal, even if they are designed, manufactured, and marketed elsewhere. And of course, the cowboy and cowgirl style, the popularity of which waxes and wanes like that of the western film, remains indelibly linked with the ranching traditions of the Rockies (and the broader West)."

In the Film and Theater chapter, Simon Dixon, a specialist in film theory, describes and analyzes the central role film has played in creating and elaborating western myths and in shaping perceptions of Rocky Mountain culture. In his conclusion, Dixon sounds a theme that recurs throughout the volume: Does much film set in the Rockies (but made by outsiders) tell us anything genuine about the place itself? He answers his own question: "Film and theater in the Rocky Mountain region have seldom sought to represent the states or peoples specifically but have done so obliquely. . . . This has been especially so in the western [film]. . . . The western has its own agendas and has sought landscapes in which to tell stories, but it has been typical of the western's relation to the land to deny it particular geographical reverence." Dixon notes that in more recent films, such as *My Own Private Idaho*, 1991 (not even shot in the region), "fittingly for the age, place is not a backdrop but an idea, the site of a dream."

The Folklore chapter, written by folklorists Kristi A. Young and Ronda Walker Weaver, focuses on stories that the peoples of the Rocky Mountains tell themselves. These folktales, legends, and tall tales recount the exploits of local heroes, villains, and fellow citizens. These include such legendary figures as Coyote, John Colter, Brigham Young, Chief Joseph, the unsinkable Molly Brown, Calamity Jane, and Butch Cassidy, together with lesser-known tricksters like The Honorable Lyulph Gilchrist Stanley Ogilvy, D.S.O., a mischief-making Colorado rancher of British descent. The authors also recount stories of lost mines, fiddle-playing sheepherders, Chinese, Basque, and Latino immigrants, Idaho potato farmers, and big-game hunters. They include examples from the region's rich traditions of cowboy (and cowgirl) song and poetry, together with sometimes humorous, sometimes heartbreaking tales drawn from the diverse Native American groups in the Rockies.

Award-winning essayist Susan H. Swetnam writes about the Food of the Rocky Mountain region. Before discussing the region's foodways, she describes the challenging weather and geography, key factors in food production. She writes, "As the twenty-first century begins . . . most residents have been forced to recognize [the region's] limits, even as they love its tough beauty—and to explore ways to live (and eat) here that accommodate the land's essential nature." Richly detailed, Swetnam's chapter describes aboriginal Native American foodways, as well as those of early explorers, settlers (including Mormons, miners, and ranchers), peoples of various ethnic heritages, and contemporary residents (ranging from home cooks to restaurant chefs to source-conscious growers and consumers). She traces the history of food production in the region, discusses controversies over water, land use, and pollution, and illuminates emerging Rocky Mountain food trends. She writes, "Foodways in the Rocky Mountain region have evolved significantly over the past hundred years and are still evolving, coming full circle, one might say, back to the idea that smaller local production might be better, that whole foods are preferable, and that eating seasonally is a good idea. Those who knew the region twenty years ago will say that they are able to eat much better here now. At the same time, old-time tastes and traditions hang on."

Linguist Lamont Antieau, in his chapter on Rocky Mountain Language, presents a fascinating look at the ways in which Rocky Mountain speech differs from—and resembles—that found elsewhere in the United States. First, he offers succinct and clearly written descriptions of the diverse Indian languages to be found in the Rockies, underscoring the impact Native American languages have had on the naming of topographical features, towns, and even states (Utah and Wyoming). Though many of these languages face extinction, Antieau notes "growing interest in the study and preservation of these languages . . . from tribes themselves as they see language as a means of tribal empowerment." Antieau then examines the impact of European languages—Spanish (the first to arrive), French, and English—on the region. He discusses the specialized languages of various occupational groups, from the early explorers to homesteaders, miners, and ranchers. He takes a look at Mormon and African American contributions to regional speech, as well as those of immigrants from central and eastern Europe, the British Isles (Gaelic, Welsh, and Cornish), Finland, and the Basque region, together with numerous Asian and Middle Eastern groups who found their way to the Rocky Mountains. In many ways, Rocky Mountain English resembles that spoken elsewhere, but as Antieau concludes, "one of the greatest differences between Rocky Mountain English and the dialects of the eastern states may be in how it encodes a vastly different environment in its language."

The outgrowth of this encoding is the Literature of the Rocky Mountain West, and veteran literary scholar Ron McFarland demonstrates an encyclopedic grasp of the subject as he surveys the region's vibrant written heritage. McFarland writes, "Most residents of Montana, Wyoming, Colorado, Utah, and Idaho know they are out of it and off the beaten track, and they're glad of it. Over the years those who have given the region its literary voice have celebrated various versions of their 'tough paradise.'" Place does play an important role in Rocky Mountain literature, and whether writers use the region merely as backdrop or evidence an intimate understanding of local landscape and culture, the "landscape," in McFarland's words, "seems almost invariably to intrude on poems, memoirs, and narratives from the Rocky Mountain West, to demand what amounts to 'character rights.'" Given this regional emphasis, the Rockies have, nevertheless, long been home (at least in imagination) to nationally recognized writers, most recently such figures as Annie Proulx, Thomas McGuane, Richard Ford, Lorna Dee Cervantes, James Welch, Janet Campbell Hale, Ivan Doig, Marilynne Robinson, Robert Wrigley, Mary Clearman Blew, Gretel Ehrlich, James Crumley, and Judy Blunt. McFarland traces the development of this rich and diverse literary tradition from Native American oral traditions to pioneer journals to the first modern works to a twentieth-century flowering of what McFarland characterizes as the postmodern memoir, that "self-reflexive genre" in which emotional truth becomes paramount in the creation of Rocky Mountain identities.

In their chapter, musicologists Stephanie Baker, Sharon Graf, and Petra Meyer-

Frazier seek to uncover the actualities of Music in the Rockies, pointing out that musicians, composers, dancers, and choreographers "work with the images of the region, both on site and as 'muse' . . . , to define cultural life in the Rocky Mountain region." The authors assess those genres most associated with the prevailing myths of the Rockies, "cowboy ballads, square dancing, saloon and parlor piano music, and Native American rituals," and then offer a wide-ranging discussion of less-expected subjects, from classical compositions addressing regional themes to avant-garde composer La Monte Young (whose auditory experiences as a child in Idaho inform his later works) to the powerful modern dance traditions of Utah. They offer rich detail about the various musical and dance forms currently practiced in the region—bluegrass, rock, pop, jazz, blues, fancy dancing, and ethnic and religious musics—and identify the many festivals that lure listeners to high mountain towns.

In the Religion chapter, historian Jeremy Bonner opens with a discussion of American Indian spiritual beliefs and practices. "Perhaps nowhere in the United States," he writes, "is the enduring legacy of Native American spirituality so evident as in the Rocky Mountains. The last region of the continental United States to be subdued and settled, it contains some of the most extensive Indian reservations in the country, as well as many protected Native American religious sites." Bonner then examines the traditional role of the Rocky Mountain region as a religious refuge, describing the diversity of religious faiths that have flocked to the region, "all of whom viewed the 'irreligious' nineteenth-century West as a fit location for the saving of souls." While the Church of Jesus Christ of Latter-day Saints (Mormons) and the Roman Catholic faith have tended to dominate, many Protestant groups, Jews, Muslims, and even Buddhists have settled in the Rockies. Bonner offers an in-depth discussion of the distinctive religious culture that has emerged in Mormon Utah (and to a lesser extent, neighboring Wyoming and Idaho), and he describes the influence Catholicism has had on the region, especially in rural areas. Despite the considerable representation of Protestantism in the Rockies, Bonner writes that there is no unified "Protestant voice in the Northern Rockies, merely a denominational babble that cannot really hope to undermine Mormon hegemony or significantly erode rural Catholicism." At the start of the twenty-first century, the region grows increasingly urban and secular, leaving Bonner to conclude that "as secularism advanced . . . so religious identity receded in much of the Rocky Mountains."

In his Sports and Recreation chapter, historian E. Duke Richey—whose specialty is Rocky Mountain ski town culture—examines the role of sports in the Rockies, from precontact Native American athletic competitions to the contemporary region-wide passion for the Denver Broncos, and offers a nuanced discussion of the place as a realm to which the world retreats for leisure pursuits. This notion of the region as a restorative sanctuary is an old one, and writes Richey, "The skier's culture that developed in Aspen and elsewhere across the region was that of the athlete's bohemia, the mountaintop paradise where play and the cult of youth were celebrated more than work." Richey describes the myriad of entertainments practiced by the locals, from those related to work (rock-drilling contests, rodeo) to hunting and fishing to pursuits linked to life among the mountains and the waterways that cleave them (rock climbing, mountain biking, kayaking, rafting).

Richey might be speaking of all cultural expressions in the Rocky Mountains when he writes, "[T]here was 'a kind of magic' to the region." This magic Richey speaks of, and that the other authors in this volume ably elucidate, is the outgrowth of powerful historical forces and equally powerful myths, immense contradictions, and contrary visions. Out of these elements, multiple Rocky Mountain cultures continue to emerge, forward looking and in love with the past, fiercely independent and consciously communal, resolutely rural and increasingly urban, firmly rooted and wholly imaginary. The chapters in this volume aim to present something of this complex Rocky Mountain reality, this richness, this magic.

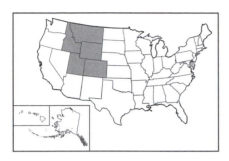

ARCHITECTURE

Carroll Van West

Think of the words *architecture* and *Rocky Mountains* and immediately images of log houses, hay stackers, headframes, grand mansions, grid-pattern cities, soaring towers, and cast-iron fronts come to mind. The Rockies of the western United States—defined for this series as including the states of Colorado, Idaho, Montana, Utah, and Wyoming—have long been recognized as the most compelling scenic landscapes in the United States. The region's soaring, craggy peaks, endless vistas of rich forests, and stark, foreboding deserts and plains are unmatched in their scenic beauty. Yet the beauty of the landscape hides the demands of living, and of building, in this country. And therein lies the architectural roots of this chapter. The climate, available resources, and patterns of settlement of the Rocky Mountains have indelibly shaped the region's architecture in both its vernacular and its more formal forms, leaving a living legacy of designed spaces that speak to the challenge of creating an existence in a demanding environment.

A second theme that informs this story is one found in other geographically distinct regions of the United States; that is, architecture may either be interjected into the region or be reflective of the region. Many important landmarks, such as the Utah State Capitol in Salt Lake City and the Broadmoor Hotel near Colorado Springs, Colorado, are extensions of larger national architectural movements into the region, or architecture *in* the Rocky Mountains. Many other places represent how residents and architects took themes and materials from the landscape and translated them into three-dimensional spaces, such as the Boise sandstone masonry of Fort Boise in Idaho or the rustic-inspired lodges of Zion National Park in Utah, or what can be described as architecture *of* the Rocky Mountains. Then, naturally, there are those few, special places that blend both national architectural movements and local traditions and materials to create designs that speak not only to the region but to the nation at large. There are no better examples of this latter category than Robert Reamer's majestic Old Faithful Lodge in Yellowstone National Park and the craggy, visual exclamation point of the Ames Monument,

Broadmoor Hotel, Colorado Springs, Colorado. Courtesy of Carroll Van West.

designed by master American architect Henry Hobson Richardson, near the Wyoming and Colorado border.

The Ames Monument is also closely associated with the third theme—architecture as a statement of power and dominance. As the region was mined, farmed, and developed from the mid-nineteenth century, great disparity existed between those who worked the land and those who owned and controlled it. The two worlds might be at odds, as when the railroad magnates of the East expressed their corporate power through the landmark depots and town plans centered on the railroad's operations. Other times the two worlds coexisted within the landscape. Take, for an example, the famous copper town of Butte, Montana, where the mansions of the mine owners—multistory architecturally distinctive brick homes—stood tall on the skyline, along with the black metal headframes of the mines themselves. Or consider the various company towns that existed in the region, such as the rather odd choice of Spanish Colonial Revival design for Sinclair in Wyoming. Then there are places where the federal government stamped its power on the region, such as the New Deal–planned communities of standardized schools and homes. The need to express power through ornate architectural style, and by placing buildings in dominant locations within the landscape, is evident in both rural and urban places of the Rocky Mountains.

The architectural legacy of the Rocky Mountains is a chronologically deep story, one of environmental and cultural adaptation and one where academically trained architects and their European-inspired design visions play a secondary role to the functionality and continuity of the vernacular landscape.

TRADITIONS OF THE DEEP PAST: NATIVE AMERICANS

Mesa Verde

The story begins in the region's thousands of extant archaeological sites. Some are internationally renowned. Mesa Verde—the words are Spanish, meaning "green table"—is near the four corners of Utah, Arizona, New Mexico, and Colorado. Over 700 years ago, a large group of Native Americans, perhaps as many as 1,300 people, lived in and around a series of mesas. They built hundreds of cliff dwellings and other structures, many interconnected into what we would call villages, from mud, stone, and wood in a manner that has become known as Pueblo architecture.

Then, in the late 1200s, drought devastated their communities and their villages; the people who had built Mesa Verde left, for unknown destinations. Soon their built environment was forgotten and stayed that way for hundreds of years. In

1859, a geologist, Professor J. S. Newberry, made the first mention of Mesa Verde, a brief observation at that, in a report he prepared from a survey of resources in the southern Utah and southern Colorado area. A generation later, a photographer working for the U.S. Geological and Geographical Survey, W. H. Jackson, became the first known white man to discover and explore the architectural wonders of Mesa Verde. But not until 1888, when a couple of local ranchers, Richard Wetherill and his brother-in-law Charles Mason, went looking for lost cattle did Americans ever discover the wonders of Cliff Palace, the largest and among the best preserved of the ancient sites. By 1906,

Butte, Montana, cityscape with headframes. Courtesy of Carroll Van West.

the U.S. government had designated thousands of acres as the Mesa Verde National Park, one of the first national parks created to preserve significant archaeological and architectural remains.

Today, within the park's 52,073 acres, the land seems tough, with few available resources and precious little water. Scholars report that the environment was different—more lush, suitable for rudimentary agriculture, and adequately watered—almost 2,000 years ago when people first moved here. The first residents are called the Basketmakers (1–400 C.E.), and little is known of their architectural traditions. But the next group—the Modified Basketmakers (400–750 C.E.)—began to erect roofed buildings, building small villages of pithouses primarily on tops of the mesas. Pithouses looked as the word suggests; they were partially underground, permanent buildings. Shaped in rough rectangles or circles, most pithouses had two rooms, the larger of which was for sleeping and for working, whereas the smaller chamber was used mostly for storage. The residents of Mesa Verde erected the pithouses with mud and stone walls, placing wood posts in the four corners to support a flat roof of wood, covered with sticks, bark, and mud to bind the materials together. Once baked in the hot sun, the roofs of pithouses—as would be true for the later and larger Pueblo dwellings—effectively kept out the elements. The result was a low-profile building, with no side entrance since a large portion was sunken into the ground. Residents entered pithouses through a wood ladder placed in a roof/ventilation opening that was directly above the firepit.

The functional considerations, resources, and available technology of crude stone and wood tools largely determined the design of the pithouse. As residents gained in numbers, and improved their own building technology, they began to construct more above-ground structures and began the process of turning pithouses into more important sacred and social spaces.

Those who lived at Mesa Verde from 750 to 1000 C.E. became the generations who evolved the design concepts underlying pithouses into a village landscape of pueblos. Experts classified these people as the Developmental Pueblo culture, largely because they were architectural experimenters. They tried different types of materials for house walls, from adobe and wood poles to stone layers and adobe and, finally, layered masonry walls. They arranged their dwellings around open courtyards, which, in turn, were dominated by a new type of evolved pithouse, called a kiva.

The kiva, according to scholars Peter Nabokov and Robert Easton, was "the most symbolic Pueblo built-form, an architectural embodiment of the collective, insular, and spiritual nature of Pueblo theocracy."[1] It was a large circular-shaped room, entered by a small, more rectangular-shaped chamber. It differed from the earlier pithouses in size, construction, interior design, and purpose. Builders made large stone or layered masonry walls to support large numbers of residents. Although they sunk kivas deeper into the ground, the exterior building profile was more massive than the pithouse due to higher walls, a much deeper ventilation shaft and roof opening, and a more elaborate roof of logs and adobe. Interiors could be painted and decorated, while furniture remained sparse, outside of low wood or mud benches that lined the walls.

Experts still debate the meaning of these sacred and social buildings. One group asserts that the growth of kivas from 1000 to 1300 C.E. suggests the emergence of clans within the pueblo villages, where groups of related, dependent, or at least like-minded peoples tended to meet together. Others conclude that the presence of multiple kivas within a pueblo village may indicate a semblance of neighborhoods, perhaps like today's neighborhood centers, within the larger built environment.

Kivas were the dominating architectural element of the Classic Pueblo Period (1100–1300 C.E.) at Mesa Verde. During these decades, residents largely stopped building on top of mesas—where land was increasingly used for low levels of agricultural production—and moved into the alcoves of the canyon walls. They erected such landmarks as the Cliff Palace, Two-Story Cliff House, Sixteen Window House, and Square Tower House. Each structure represented different forms of what is known as Pueblo architecture: groups of interconnected rooms, which rise several stories in height, with flat roofs and layered walls of masonry, stone, adobe, and wood.

The stunning architectural legacy of Pueblo culture is on public view at Mesa

Mesa Verde, Colorado. Courtesy of Carroll Van West.

Verde and many other sites in southern Colorado and in southern Utah at the Hovenweep National Monument and the Poncho House ruins. As a travel writer for the *New York Times* admitted in a July 2, 1950, story about the western parks: "[A]fter experiencing eye fatigue from gaping at peaks, gorges, waterfalls, glaciers and other natural spectacles, there is welcome mental stimulation in studying the ruins of Mesa Verde."[2] The stacked dwellings with their small rooms and ladder entrances sit nestled into the arms of the harsh southern Rockies environment, a powerful reminder of past cultures and past ideas of architectural adaptation that still speak to the modern nostalgia for the ancient and the unknown.

The Tipi

Far to the north, where the vastness of the northern plains encounters the equally commanding presence of the northern Rocky Mountains, lies the other major Native American contribution to the region's architecture: the tipi. The word *tipi* is a white derivative of the Siouan word for "used as dwelling."

When Europeans and later Americans discovered the pueblo villages, their minds' eyes, trained by culture and precedent to think of architecture as permanent, solid, and proportional, found many elements to admire. The tipis of the Plains Indians were another matter—they were impermanent, they appeared flimsy, and they were decidedly inferior as an example of the building arts. Accordingly, many whites interpreted the peoples who designed and lived in tipis as inferior to those who once inhabited the pueblos. In so doing, the commentators and writers betrayed not only their own cultural biases but also their failure to understand the design ingenuity of the tipi as an architectural response to a different climate and geography.

Tipis are tilted one-room cones of fabric (once made from animal hides exclusively, now made typically of canvas) supported by a frame of carefully prepared and arranged long, narrow wooden poles and exterior flaps that are either laid on the ground and covered by stones or connected to stakes driven into the ground. The tilted cone shape added stability and headroom, while it also followed the poles of the frame to cross at the top end of the smoke hole, protecting the interior from rain and snow.

Native Americans have used variations of the tipi for thousands of years. Once they had acquired horses between the 1500s and 1700s, they were able to move larger tipis; and sometimes they constructed large tipi lodges, with as many as thirty buffalo skins and two or three rock-lined hearths. Most lived in the tipis year-round, even as the residents moved to different areas to take full advantage of available natural resources. Women typically maintained their family's tipi and had responsibility for moving the structure and erecting it. Once they had learned the art of tipi building from their female relations, young Indian women found that putting up a tipi was quick and simple, usually taking no more than thirty minutes.

The poles were the most important parts since the number of available poles determined the size of the tipi and the proper placement of the poles kept the often high winds of the plains from toppling the structure. A tipi with a diameter of eighteen feet needed about eighteen poles, with the average length being about twenty-one feet. An American fur trader, who operated at the confluence of the

Piegan tipi, Montana. Courtesy of Carroll Van West.

Yellowstone and Missouri Rivers, noted that tipis were "stretched on poles from 12 to 20 feet in length . . . each family making one to suit the number of persons to be accommodated or their means of transporting it; therefore their sizes vary from 6 to 23 skins each . . . the common or medium size being 12 skins, which will lodge a family of eight persons with their baggage, and also have a space to entertain two or three guests. The area of a lodge of 12 skins when well pitched is a circumference of 31 feet."[3]

Northern Montana Indians often cut their poles of lodgepole pine, which is found in the Little Rocky Mountains, the Bears Paw Mountains, and the Cypress Hills of Canada. Stripped of their bark and pointed at the butt end, the poles were smooth and thin, measuring about two inches at the top and four to five inches at the bottom. A smooth, straight pole was mandatory for a tight, weatherproof structure. Locating the right pine trees and then preparing the poles took much energy and time, so Native Americans carried their poles from camp to camp and tried to keep a pole in use for at least two years. Until the late nineteenth century, tipis were covered with buffalo hides that the women had transformed into a pliable cover, usually decorated with religious or personal symbols. The decoration of tipi covers remains a significant artistic tradition among present-day Plains cultures.

The tipi was the perfect dwelling for peoples who adapted to the climate and environment of the Rockies by moving to different areas and exploiting resources at the most opportune time of the year. In the summer, the Native Americans could roll up the tipi walls from the bottom to create better ventilation. During the winter, they surrounded their tipis with snow fences and kept the flaps tight on the ground to retain heat.

Ceremonial Structures in the Northern Rockies

Tipis did not solely define the Native American architectural traditions of the northern Rockies. Ceremonial structures include the medicine lodge and the sweat lodge. The medicine lodge was a polygonal structure centered on a large wooden (usually cottonwood) pole, with forked posts placed around the center pole. The builders then used light, thin wooden poles to connect the outside forks to the center pole. Brush and animal skins were used to cover the lower exterior of the frame, creating a sense of sanctuary for the sacred rituals that took place within the medicine lodge.

The sweat lodge was used to purify the body and soul before the ceremonies of the medicine lodge. The Piegans, who lived near Glacier National Park, built sweat lodges shaped like small hemispheres. They made them by bending thin, short willow branches, placing the pointed ends into the ground and then layering the frame with buffalo robes, canvas, and other materials. Inside was a tiny space centered around a rock-lined hearth, where heated rocks and a container of water were placed in order to quickly raise the temperature and humidity to make the occupants sweat profusely. Similar in size and appearance, but quite different in function, was the menstruation lodge used by different Plains tribes. This structure, located at a distance from the camp, was used to separate women from the group during the first days of their menstrual period, after which they returned to their tipis.

Medicine Wheels

Sweat lodges were among the smallest Native American structures in the Rockies. One of the largest is high in the northern Wyoming mountains near Yellowstone National Park. The Big Horn Medicine Wheel is the southernmost known example of an architectural tradition that stretches well into the Canadian Rockies. The Big Horn wheel is a huge circle of stone, eighty feet in diameter, with twenty-eight stone spokes radiating from a central stone cairn. Once a tourist destination in a national forest, Native groups have worked with federal officials to better respect the sacred nature of the structure.

Scholars continue to debate the meaning of medicine wheels. Detailed studies in Alberta suggest that some were built to commemorate famous leaders and warriors; another site has been used for thousands of years, a pattern that suggests that the meaning and function of medicine wheels probably changed over time. Astronomer John Eddy proposed that the Big Horn Medicine Wheel was purposely aligned with the rising sun at summer solstice, suggesting that the wheel may be a celestial clock, but other astronomers discount that theory. Recent work by Matthew Liebmann concludes that the wheel clearly holds significant spiritual meanings for the native residents of the region but that these meanings have changed over time. He also emphasizes its importance as a place for individual vision quests for hundreds of years. The Big Horn Medicine Wheel is one of the best Rocky Mountain examples of how a simply conceived and executed design may still convey deep and multilayered cultural messages.

EUROPEAN AESTHETICS AND ADAPTATION

Spanish Influence

When the Spanish from the 1500s to the 1700s attempted to expand into the northern reaches of their empire, they left many enduring legacies including the introduction of European architectural traditions and construction techniques. Encountering the native peoples of present-day Arizona, New Mexico, Colorado, and Utah, they coined the word *pueblo* to describe the local built environment. They also introduced improvements in the making of adobe brick, making it stronger and more durable than those made by the Native Americans, and designed stronger roofs by improving the wooden supports for the flat-roofed pueblo houses. The housing vernacular that emerged in the Southwest became a combination of available resources, Native American design traditions, and Spanish building technology. More important, the Spanish imposed a new political landscape to replace the centuries-old vernacular landscape determined by geography, climate, and

The Big Horn Medicine Wheel, Wyoming. Courtesy of the Bureau of Land Management.

resources. In contrast, the political landscape was the opposite: Rather than reflecting the environment, it reflected the design ideas and cultural assumptions of a powerful political elite, whose etchings on maps and paper soon became boundary lines separating people from the natural environment. These abstract divisions of land boundaries took the form of various types of land grants (particularly important in southern Colorado and in the formal design of urban spaces).

The best evidence of the Spanish systematic approach to defining place through legal means may be found in 148 ordinances laid out by King Phillip II (1521–1598) in his Laws of the Indies (1573). Indeed, a group of scholars have described the king's decrees as "the most complete such set of instructions ever issued to serve as a guideline for the founding and building of towns in the Americas and, in terms of their widespread application and persistence, probably the most effective planning documents in the history of mankind."[4]

In the southern Rockies, the most important Spanish town plan was the plaza, a square-shaped village, where dwellings and buildings were interconnected, facing an open courtyard (the plaza), with their rear walls facing outward, and having no windows or doors. Such an arrangement of buildings and space created a fortified village, which offered settlers some protection from Native American attack.

Although buildings from the Spanish colonial era are scarce in southern Colorado, the Spanish presence is amply illustrated by surviving place names, such as the San Luis Valley and the towns of Pueblo, La Junta, and Trinidad. A much later, distinctly American interpretation of the Spanish colonial era architecture is quite plentiful. Spanish Revival style, one of the popular revival styles of American architecture in the early twentieth century, may be found in domestic settings, in public architecture, and in commercial buildings, too. In 1927, the Chicago-based Milwaukee Road, for example, built the Spanish Revival–styled Gallatin Gateway Inn outside of Bozeman, Montana, for its travelers headed to Yellowstone National Park. In 1919, in Idaho, architect B. Morgan Nisbet designed a stuccoed Spanish Revival–styled city hall in the small town of Buhl. Almost every town of any size had at least one Spanish Revival–style residence.

French Influence

The French presence in the Rocky Mountains landscape is not so pronounced as that of the Spanish and is typically found in nineteenth-century vernacular settings. French Canadian fur traders operated log posts in Idaho and Montana as early as the first decade of the nineteenth century and as late as 1871 when the Hudson's Bay Company finally closed its Fort Connah post in western Montana. David Thompson of the North West Company built Kullyspell House on Lake Pend Oreille in 1809, following that with the construction of Salish House on the Clark's Fork River in Montana (near the Idaho border) in November 1809. Architectural historian Jennifer Attebery believes that Kullyspell House was probably built in the French *pièce sur pièce* method since the North West Company often used this type of horizontal log construction. The Hudson's Bay Company, however, preferred the *poteaux et pièces*, or Red River frame, method of construction, where logs are tenoned into morticed corner posts. The one surviving building at Fort Connah, Montana, reflects *poteaux et pièces* carpentry.

Westward Expansion

Residents from the United States moved into the Rockies at a later date than the Spanish or French. Explorers, fur traders, and government agents came in the wake of the Louisiana Purchase of 1803. The number of American posts began to increase in the 1830s and 1840s. Then came a large colony of Mormons to Utah in 1847, a year before the Treaty of Guadalupe Hilgado of 1848 officially made the rest of the Rocky Mountains American territory.

In those early decades of the nineteenth century, neither officials of the American government nor Americans citizens made much of a lasting imprint on the landscape. The early traders and explorers left few marks in the built environment since they commonly lived in, or were dependent upon, existing Native American settlements. American military expeditions pitched their tents at many locations but always packed up and returned home. As the fur trade became more lucrative, however, larger well-capitalized firms, such as the American Fur Company, began to build permanent headquarters to control their employees and to gather the rich resources of fur-bearing animals. The American Fur Company's major post, Fort Union, stood at the confluence of the Missouri and Yellowstone Rivers. It is a National Historic Site administered by the National Park Service. Its tall log walls were commonplace, but within the stockade was one of the first English classical architectural statements in the region: a two-story residence for the "factor," or the company's chief administrator at the post, covered with clapboards and reflecting an understated interpretation of a three-part Palladian-styled dwelling.

Bent's Old Fort, near La Junta, Colorado, was built within a few years of Fort

Union, and it, too, is a National Historic Site. While the materials and design of Fort Union depict the easy availability of cottonwoods and imported building materials via steamboats for construction, the brown adobe brick walls of Bent's Old Fort reflect its very different environment and comparative isolation. William and Charles Bent of St. Louis, together with another Missourian named Ceran St. Vrain, established the post in 1833. Seven years later, visitor Matthew Field observed that the sight of the fort, rising as it did from the desert ground with its American flag flapping in the breeze, would "strike the wanderer with the liveliest surprise, as though an 'air-built castle' had dropped to earth before him in the midst of the vast desert."[5] The post's fifteen-foot-high adobe walls enclosed a complete town, with residences, offices, council room, warehouses, and a billiard room. For travelers and traders, within the walls everything—commerce, politics, diplomacy, light industry, recreation, and entertainment—took place. The fur posts were isolated settlement outposts, almost like stereotypical Wild West towns in miniature, but just as obvious they were intrusions in what was still a Native American–dominated landscape where open spaces far outnumbered the buildings, roads, and structures of "civilization."

Mormon Migration and Their Architecture

In 1847, the region's reputation for isolation helped to lure Brigham Young (1801–1877) and his fellow members of the Church of Jesus Christ of Latter-day Saints (LDS) to the Great Salt Lake and the Great Basin of Utah, one of the nation's true geological wonders where miles upon miles of salt flats are framed by the Wasatch and Uinta mountain ranges. LDS members were weary of religious persecution and looked for a land—even if it was officially part of Mexico until 1848—where they could build a nation of believers, safe from violence and reprisals. Young and his followers crossed the Mississippi at Nauvoo, Illinois, and headed for a land that surveyors and explorers for a generation had dismissed as desolate.

Young called his new land Deseret and chose the "Great Salt Lake City" as the first settlement. He handpicked the location of the future LDS temple, then announced his intention to follow the earlier "Plat of the City of Zion," developed by LDS founder Joseph Smith (1805–1844) in 1833, as the city's blueprint. Smith's original plan called for a square town grid oriented to the four cardinal directions, with streets 132 feet wide and huge blocks of ten acres in size. The middle block was reserved for the temple grounds, clearly placing God and the LDS faith at the core of the new community.

Young's plan must have seemed grandiose to the families who first moved to the Great Salt Lake, but within three months, the town counted over 2,000 residents, and by the end of the decade, in 1850, over 8,000 people lived in the LDS capital, making it one of the region's largest cities. During the 1850s, other LDS groups adapted Smith's "Plat of the City of Zion" for the plans of other towns, always placing the LDS temple at the center, in isolation from the surrounding real world. Today, it is often difficult to discern Smith's plat within the modern urban landscape of suburbs and sprawl, but the LDS temples still serve as beacons to the land once called Deseret.

The early LDS temples were intentional landmarks; their huge size, prominent location, and ornate Victorian styling dominated the surrounding landscape of shops, light industries, and farms. These distinguished buildings are excellent examples of how LDS members blended architectural ideas and images from their eastern birthplaces (most typically Gothic Revival style) with the raw materials of Utah to create compelling regional architecture. In the LDS temple at Manti, for example, Castellated Gothic walls are highlighted by twin towers more Second Empire in style. The real glory of the building, designed by self-trained architect and LDS member William Folsom, however, is in its materials of Utah-native oolite sandstone. This variety of rock is easy enough to quarry, but then it hardens once exposed to the elements.

The LDS temple in Logan also sits on a prominent rise in the center of town, but its primary material is locally quarried quartzite. LDS architect Truman O. Angell supervised a construction crew numbering in the thousands—some 25,000 members worked on the Castellated Gothic temple between 1877 and 1884. By the measure of actual man-hours, the Logan temple and the LDS temple at St. George are works of handicraft artistry, both designed by Angell, who also is credited with the largest LDS temple at Temple Square in Salt Lake City. At St. George, thousands served forty-day missions at the southern Utah town, while local men worked one day out of ten to erect this first LDS temple. The building's 17,000 tons of black volcanic stone and sandstone were hand-quarried and carried by oxen to the site where others covered it with stucco and painted it white. Gleaming in the desert sun, the St. George temple symbolizes the centrality of faith in LDS culture as well as the power of the church over most Utah institutions.

The historic LDS temples and tabernacles are architectural expressions of faith and permanence; at the same time, the more commonplace built environment of Utah from the late 1840s through the 1880s was not so ornate or distinguishable from the rest of the western agrarian landscape. Folklorist Tom Carter has recorded many of these vernacular farm buildings, finding a plethora of single-room, double-room, and central hall houses with symmetrical facades similar to most rural communities in the United States in the mid-nineteenth century. These

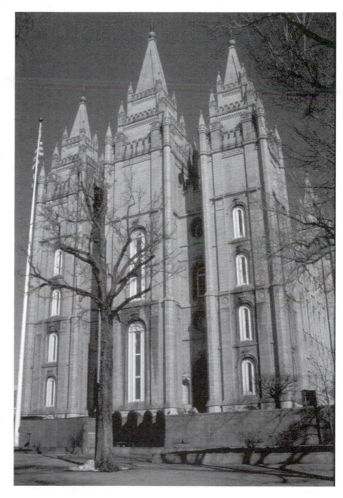

Latter-day Saints Temple, Salt Lake City. Courtesy of Carroll Van West.

smallish houses, however, could be built from various materials, from hand-quarried rock to locally fired brick to log and to heavy-braced frame houses.

Cabins of the Nineteenth Century

Thus, while LDS members lived or worked in planned cities, and worshipped in architecturally elaborate buildings, their domestic landscape differed little from other nineteenth-century farmers and ranches in the Rocky Mountains. In the Yellowstone Valley during the 1870s, for instance, some log cabins were considered substantial homes. Andrew Jackson Hunter's place at Springdale had a low-pitch roof and consisted of three connected rooms, two for his family and one as the post office. Alonzo Young was another postmaster who lived near Park City; his dwelling was a classic single-pen cabin, made of hand-hewn logs, with a steep roof creating an upstairs loft. Prosperous farmer Orson N. Newman lived near present-day Billings. His dwelling of sawn logs measured thirty feet in length, large enough to house his family of ten and to serve the community as a social center for dances and other gatherings. But most homes were single-pen dwellings at best, dugouts cut into a rise or hill at worst. William A. Allen recalled that when he built his dwelling in the Canyon Creek area in 1879, it was the first to have a shingle roof; his neighbors had used sod or dirt to keep the elements out.

Wyoming ranchers lived similarly. Architectural historian Eileen F. Starr has emphasized the connections between the state's natural landscape and its vernacular architecture. She has documented how the owners of the Stone Wall Ranch in Carbon County used a huge rock outcropping as part of their corral system, securing livestock without using so much timber and also using the height of the stone wall to protect the animals from the elements.[6] Sublette County contains an excellent example of Wyoming log construction in the Nicholas Swan Cabin, a single-room, half-dovetailed notched log dwelling carved from locally available cottonwood trees.

But long-term field research by a group of geographers concluded that common eastern vernacular forms did not dominate log construction in the Mountain West. The eastern log cabin was a single-story, rectangle-shaped, gable roof building, with entrances usually on both of the long sides of the building. What scholars label as the Anglo-Western Cabin is similar, except that the single entrance is on the gable-end (or the short side) of the building. One group of log architecture scholars asserts: "[S]o abundant and dominant is this house type that it serves as a regional symbol and icon, a way of saying 'we are westerners.'"[7]

BUILDING TOWNS AND CREATING TRANSPORTATION NETWORKS

Mining and Railroads

The vernacular landscape of the agrarian west, of the fur traders, early settlers, and initial towns, existed well into the twentieth century. Persistence and continuity, of course, are basic characteristics of vernacular design. But its dominance of numbers never quite matched the architectural impact of urban development, and concurrent architectural diversity, that came with two revolutionary developments during the mid-nineteenth century: the discovery of gold and other precious metals and the arrival of the railroads, those "metropolitan corridors" of eastern values, ideas, and institutions. The presence and use of architectural style increasingly became a way that mine owners and railroad companies distinguished their control of the landscape.

Gold fever first affected the Rockies in 1849–1850 when easterners headed overland to the California gold fields and paid princely sums for supplies and services at the new Salt Lake City. The region's first rush came in 1858, when William Green Russell struck gold at a place that is now the center of Denver, Colorado. When the news reached the East, thousands of prospectors, leaving depressed economic conditions at home, rushed to the "Pike's Peak" gold strike. Within months, a new major western city named Denver, platted by William Larimer in a grid pattern, emerged, as if by magic, on the eastern edge of the Rocky Mountains. Then, in 1859, just as the Denver gold seemed panned out, a new strike took place at Central City, and soon a string of high mountain mining towns—places such as Boulder, Golden, Breckinridge, and Fairplay—existed to the west of Denver.

In the 1860s, while the Civil War raged in the East, western prospectors eager to find that next great strike fanned out into the Rocky Mountains, searching for gold and silver. In 1862, miners found gold—eventually $24 million of precious metals over a four-year period—in the Boise Basin of present-day Idaho. So many came to the land that within a year Congress designated the Idaho Territory, and by 1863, over 6,000 residents crowded into Idaho City, which in a matter of months had become the largest city in the Northwest.

The year 1863 was also when the prospectors rushed into the mountains of present-day Montana, creating instant cities at Bannack, Alder Gulch (later Virginia City), Emigrant Gulch, and Last Chance Gulch (later Helena). Like Idaho, it only took a year for Montana to achieve territorial status, and Virginia City grew quickly as a mining camp and territorial capital.

After the Civil War, in 1867, miners found gold in Wyoming, the rich Carissa lode near South Pass City; the following year another strike took place in the Wind River region, leading to the establishment of Lander. Within another year, by 1869, Wyoming, too, was a territory.

Looking back at the boom that swept through Colorado, Wyoming, Idaho, and Montana from 1859 to 1864, historian Duane Smith concluded:

> [T]his fast-paced urbanization created the major uniqueness that characterized the mining frontier, when compared to the other waves of settlement in the trans-Mississippi West. . . . It brewed a flavor, a character, a sense of place and time, and opportunities that intrigued westerners and easterners alike. A good living, even a fortune, could be made even more easily on a dusty Main Street than it could with backbreaking digging and sluicing in the gulches.[8]

Instant Cities

Cities mushroomed across the Rockies also in response to the presence of glistening new steel tracks—those of the mighty Union Pacific Railroad and, later, the Northern Pacific Railroad, the first two transcontinental railroads to pass through the Rocky Mountains. Utah Territory was where in 1869 the two ends of the

Ames Monument, Sherman, Wyoming. Courtesy of Carroll Van West.

Union Pacific met, and that place on Promontory Summit is now preserved as the Golden Spike National Historic Site. The path of the rails opened up a new era and created waves of towns, both large and small, across the central Rockies. A similar pattern happened in the northern Rockies as the Northern Pacific completed its route between Minnesota and the West Coast in 1883.

The tracks not only brought instant cities, but many times railroads created instant architectural landmarks to symbolize their power over the landscape. Certainly, the most compelling statement is that made by the giant rock pile of the Ames Monument (1882), designed by architect Henry Hobson Richardson in honor of Union Pacific officials Oliver and Oakes Ames, who are memorialized near its apex by sandstone medallions by the famous sculptor Augustus Saint-Gaudens. Resting on a mountain summit overlooking the original route of the Union Pacific Railroad in southwestern Wyoming, the monument rises, unassisted it seems, from the ground, giving the Ames brothers unobstructed views of the land they conquered.

More typically, railroad corporations marked their space with grand passenger stations, urban gateways linking the tracks to the cities that they served. Chicago architect Henry Van Brunt designed a soaring tower for his Victorian-styled Union Pacific station in Cheyenne. Van Brunt's design for the Union Station (1895) in Denver reflected the Beaux-Arts school of classicism. The St. Paul, Minnesota, architectural firm of Reed and Stem gave Livingston, Montana, a Renaissance Revival jewel in its Northern Pacific Railway station (1902). The Union Pacific passenger station (c. 1920) in Nampa, Idaho, is a rare example of Sullivanesque design for railroad buildings, while the Denver & Rio Grande station (1910) in Salt Lake City reflects Classical Revival style, which was very popular for railroad depots in the early twentieth century.

The railroads also used their depots as corporate symbols of control and efficiency. In the Northern Rockies, for instance, the Great Northern, Northern Pacific, Burlington Route, Milwaukee Road, and the Chicago and Northwestern often built large, brick depots of recognizable architectural style at their division points and major trade centers along the lines. For the smaller rural stops, however, they devised frame buildings of standardized designs that looked the same, no matter the town, giving the open land between the major cities an undeniable corporate stamp.

Gold fever and railroad construction combined to create a region littered with urban oases. No matter the location or size, the architectural development of these instant cities followed a similar pattern.

First came irregular street patterns and impermanent architecture of tents, hastily erected log cribs, and hybrids of both canvas and wood. The random look and placement of these structures also reflected a relative equality of economic status and opportunity. Land and power were not yet concentrated but open for the taking.

Once control and power became more centralized—a few controlled most of the mines or the railroad corporation arrived with its town plat in hand—the early temporary squatters townscape disappeared. The second life of the town began, with a formally planned town plat and larger, more elaborate one- and two-story wooden buildings. Many mining towns never grew out of this phase and are now ghost towns where their frame, false-front buildings (one-story buildings with a large solid frame wall attached to

Union Station, Denver. Courtesy of Carroll Van West.

the top of the roofline to mimic the presence of a second story) and two-story frame buildings speak to the architectural pretensions of the age. At the ghost town of Elkhorn in Montana, for instance, the Queen Anne–style influence of the second-story bay of Fraternity Hall is an overt reminder that the miners, no matter the drudgery of the work, wanted some sense of normalcy in their town environments.

Public Architecture in the Nineteenth Century

The third phase was when towns and cities shed their mining or railroad camp appearance. Brick rather than wood became the dominant building material for commercial and public buildings, and suddenly the boomtowns took on the air of permanence. Architecture style, commonly applied on bland storefronts by means of imported cast-iron facades, became a method of suggesting Victorian respectability, and scores of publications full of photographs of these new buildings were sent back East to promote additional immigration and investment. Georgetown, Colorado, typifies this three-step transformation from mining camp to settled town. Identified as a National Historic Landmark for its many extant buildings associated with the mining and railroad era, local landmarks include the Gothic Revival–styled First Presbyterian Church, built out of locally available stone in 1874, and the Italianate-styled Hotel de Paris, established by Louis DuPuy in 1875. Nearby Central City features the stone masonry of the two-story, Second Empire–style influence of the Central City Opera House (1878). Several mining barons underwrote the cost of bringing high culture to their isolated mountain surroundings—such gestures suggested a touch of class and helped to boom local real estate holdings. Horace Tabor's Leadville Opera House was described as the most architecturally polished and ornately furnished theater in the West when it opened in 1879.

Idaho and Montana also have excellent examples of public architecture from the late nineteenth century, such as the Madison County Courthouse, a brick Italianate-styled building in Virginia City, Montana, and the squat, stone Assay Office, an-

Hamill House, Georgetown, Colorado. Courtesy of Carroll Van West.

other Italianate design by federal architect Alfred Mullett in Boise, Idaho.

The mining barons expressed their power and taste in their private homes as well, and many regional cities still have grandiose Victorian-styled mansions that now operate as local museums. The William A. Clark House, a huge three-story brick house of Queen Anne pretensions, still dominates the residential neighborhoods of Butte, Montana, while in Helena another Queen Anne–styled home, built by miner William Chessman, later became the Montana State Governor's Residence. In Colorado, the historic mansions open to the public include Denver's Molly Brown House, built of local lava stone in a Queen Anne fashion, and the Gothic Revival styling of Georgetown's Hamill House, transformed from a Gothic cottage to a Victorian decorative arts showplace between 1874 and 1885. The Standrod House (1901) in Pocatello, Idaho, documents how by the end of the century bankers and other civic capitalists challenged the social prominence of miners and those who got wealthy from the boom years by building their own lavish residences. The Standrod House is an excellent example of French Chateau style—scholar Jennifer Attebery counts it as one of the region's best—in its rugged stone masonry and eclectic Victorian detailing.[9]

While the mining barons, commercial leaders, and professional classes lived lavishly in the towns they controlled, most miners and workers lived in quite different circumstances. The built environment they interacted with on a regular basis was not the grand opera hall or the primary public buildings, but the headframes of the copper mine, the decorated false front of a favorite bar, the smokestacks of the factory, and the neighborhood of tightly clustered frame homes where their families resided. Once again the difference between the stylish and the vernacular underscored the difference between those who controlled and those who toiled in the Rocky Mountains.

Early Architects of the Rockies

The rise of metropolitan centers, and continued population growth, helped to create a demand for professional architectural services, especially by the last two decades of the nineteenth century. Denver's preeminent architect was Robert S. Roeschlaub (1843–1923). Born in Germany, Roeschlaub grew up in Quincy, Illinois, where his father practiced medicine. As a young man, he served in the Civil War on the side of the Union and was wounded at the Battle of Stones River in late 1862 and then again at the Battle of Chickamauga in 1863. After the fighting had ended, Roeschlaub tried different careers before settling on architecture. He lacked formal university training but received a rigorous apprenticeship from Robert Bunce, a Quincy architect who had learned the craft from Edward Burling, the skilled mid-nineteenth-century Chicago architect.

After six years with Bunce, Roeschlaub moved to Denver, where he made his mark in school architecture and the use of modern technology in public buildings. He designed several significant churches, commercial buildings, and almost 200 dwellings. In its rough-edged native stone exterior, his Central City Opera House (1878) reflected Roeschlaub's admiration for the local environment. Trinity Methodist Church (1887) in Denver reflected the influence of the Richardsonian Romanesque style of Henry Hobson Richardson, an influence repeated in Roeschlaub's design for a grand stone commercial block, the Central Block (1889), in Pueblo, Colorado. (In fact, Richardson's design influence extended across the region, from the major cities to small towns.) Roeschlaub's best adaptations of Richardsonian style are at the University of Denver, particularly the Old Main hall, and his interpretation of the Classical Revival movement, the most popular architectural style of the early twentieth century, is expressed well in the columned portico and dome of the university's Carnegie Library (1906).

According to scholar David N. Wetzel, Roeschlaub "was neither wholly an idealist nor a pragmatist, a westerner nor a cosmopolite, a traditionalist nor a radical innovator. He was at bottom a working architect."[10] That same description would apply to many Rocky Mountain architects of the late nineteenth and early twentieth centuries. Most lacked formal university training; they learned on the job. Few were strikingly original, yet they were "working architects" who shaped the western landscape, giving it forms and ideas that reflected the times and the place.

To his credit, Roeschlaub did not decry university training because he lacked it. Rather, he devoted a large part of his career to the promotion and extension of professional standards. His lasting contribution came from his twenty years as president of the Colorado chapter of the American Institute of Architects, where he helped to bring a degree of professionalism to the practice of architecture in Colorado in specific and to the region in general.

Like Roeschlaub, Richard A. Kletting, the "Dean of Utah architecture," was born in Germany in 1858. Kletting, however, arrived in the Rockies a decade later, in 1883, and decided that Salt Lake City, not Denver, was promising territory for an architect with new ideas and an ability to please a wide array of patrons. Trained in Germany and France, Kletting immediately met with success in Salt Lake City, winning commissions from the LDS church, its members, and many others not associated with the Mormons. Early Kletting landmark designs include the Richardsonian Romanesque-styled Commercial Savings Bank (1889) and the eclectic Victorian-styled Fisher House (1893) in Salt Lake City. He even found time to play a significant part in the early conservation movement in Utah, helping to organize the Utah Forestry Association in 1891. Two years later, in 1893, he secured his reputation as an architect when he completed the massive Saltair

Utah State Capitol, Salt Lake City. Courtesy of Carroll Van West.

Resort, a fantasy of western and Middle Eastern architectural traditions, outside of Salt Lake City.

Over the next two decades, Kletting designed middle-class homes, college buildings (particularly at the University of Utah), and commercial buildings. He capped his active career by winning the competition to design a new Utah State Capitol. His robust interpretation of classicism won him much acclaim upon its completion in 1916. Kletting, again like Roeschlaub, played an active role in the Utah Chapter of the American Institute of Architects, and the Utah Society of Professional Engineers, encouraging greater professionalism among Utah's architects.

In Wyoming, William DuBois arrived from the Midwest to execute a commission for a classically styled Carnegie Library in Cheyenne. The potential of the region so intrigued him that he made Wyoming his home, designing in a range of twentieth-century styles, including the Stripped Classicism of the Supreme Court and State Library Building in Cheyenne, the Classical Revival of the Masonic Temple in Laramie, and the Arts and Crafts originality of the Plains Hotel in Cheyenne. A colleague, and collaborator on the Albany County Courthouse, was Wilbur Hitchcock, who taught engineering at the University of Wyoming and then opened his own architectural practice in 1921. Hitchcock incorporated a regional feel to his campus buildings by using local stone. For the Cooper Mansion in Laramie, he adapted the California Mission style into a large, expressive residence.

Roeschlaub, Kletting, and DuBois were regionally recognized leaders, but the growth of the profession extended well beyond their personal networks. In Idaho, for example, no architects were listed in the 1880 census, and a generation later, in 1902, only eleven were working in the state. But between 1900 and 1920, at least ninety-seven architects opened or operated offices in Idaho, and once the state in 1917 established a professional licensure board, thirty-two resident architects and fifty-five out-of-state architects received licenses to practice over the next three years.

This new cadre of professional architects brought new styles, technologies, and competencies to the region's built environment. The look of Rocky Mountain cities became more similar to that of the eastern metropolises. Indeed, in their new statehouses in Montana, Idaho, and Utah, the region provided some of the nation's best examples of Classical Revival, while the new Civic Center Plan for Denver ranked the Mile High City on par with the latest trend—the City Beautiful Movement—in American urban planning and design.

THE ROCKIES, RUSTIC STYLE, AND REGIONAL DESIGN

In contrast to the classicism reigning supreme in the Rockies' major cities, a very different movement added new layers of design and meaning to the regional landscape in the first third of the twentieth century. The Rustic Movement in turn-of-the-century American architecture came about, in part, as a search for a national design aesthetic free of European precedents and, in part, as a reflection of the broader Arts and Crafts Movement in English and American culture in the last quarter of the nineteenth century.

Promoters of western tourism were the first to endorse the Rustic Style. Seattle architect Robert Reamer's Old Faithful Lodge (1902) in Yellowstone National Park contrasted sharply with earlier park buildings, such as the classical-styled Lake Hotel (1890). While in general Old Faithful Lodge may be classified as an example of Shingle style, then a popular variation for Victorian domestic architecture, Reamer used materials from the park—thick logs, large stones—in exaggerated combinations, providing "oversized roof gables and overhangs, columns, stairs, roofs, and doors. These enlarged elements," according to David Leavengood, "reached out to the visitor with protective arms, providing assurance and a feeling of familiarity." The building materials, and the oversized nature of the hotel, also helped to root it in the monumental natural landscape of the park itself, achieving a sense of harmony between the man-made intrusions into the natural world of the parks. There are few better examples of the architecture *of* the Rocky Mountains than Old Faithful Lodge.[11]

Reamer's design helped to popularize Rustic style as the perfect "parkitecture" for the Rocky Mountains. At Glacier National Park in Montana, the Great Northern Railway built a Rustic-styled passenger station and grand hotel at East Glacier, while its Lake McDonald Lodge reflected both Rustic style and the log vernacular of the surrounding ranches and logging camps. North of Denver, Rocky Mountain National Park has several excellent examples of small-scale Rustic designs in various backcountry cabins, including Twin Sisters (1914), Willow Park (1923), Fern Lake (1925), Thunder Lake (1930), Chasm Lake (1931), and Lawn Lake (1931). Gilbert S. Underwood designed the Rustic charm of Zion Lodge, in Zion National Park in Utah, during the 1920s.

The Depression Decade, however, would witness the codification of Rustic design throughout national, state, and local parks, largely due to the influence of the National Park Service's design guidelines that work crews from the Civilian Conservation Corps (CCC) and the Works Progress Administration (WPA) carried out in their park projects. In these years, the CCC promoted a more stripped-down, standardized approach to Rustic style, which has become classified as Government Rustic. By utilizing locally available materials such as stone and logs, and adopting one-story, horizontal forms, this style was meant to blend into the natural landscape as much as possible, allowing the beauty of the natural landscape to compensate for human intrusions. Ideas of simplicity, strength, and the exposed glory of craftsmanship from the earlier Arts and Crafts Movement, along with grandiose Rustic style examples from the western national parks and resorts in the Adirondacks, clearly influenced Government Rustic style.

The CCC built hundreds of Government Rustic cabins in state and national parks throughout the Rockies; it also built thousands of miles of trails in those

Old Faithful Lodge, Wyoming. Courtesy of Carroll Van West.

same parks and improved roads and other park infrastructure. Not so well recognized, however, is that the CCC also carried out many historic preservation projects at historic sites and museums. It built new museums and other interpretive tools. The Museum at Guernsey State Park in Wyoming, for instance, is an imaginative CCC building, designed by National Park Service architect Roland Pray, where a large stone wall is punctured by a stone entrance arch, giving the building a sense of weight and importance. Another impressive Rustic-style CCC museum in Wyoming is at Madison Junction in Yellowstone National Park.

The Federal Landscape

The standardization of Government Rustic style was just one way the federal government made its presence known in the Rocky Mountains. Considering the massive land grants the federal government gave to railroad companies to build through the Rocky Mountains, and the incessant grid of 640-acre sections mandated by the homestead laws, it is impossible to argue that the federal imprint on the western landscape is totally a creature of the twentieth century. Certainly, that federal imprint became deeper and more profound over the last 100 years. More important, it involved much more than the system of national parks and forests established during those decades.

The Newlands Reclamation Act of 1902, for example, reshaped huge swaths of the Rockies, not merely through the creation of the various irrigation projects and mammoth reservoirs but through reforms that were encouraged at both the farms and in rural towns. In the Yellowstone and Big Horn rivers area, local and eastern reformers viewed the Huntley Project, one of the early projects of the U.S. Reclamation Service (later U.S. Bureau of Reclamation), as the ideal way to use machines to meld agriculture and industry, and urban and rural communities, in what they envisioned as a New West, far removed from the Wild West of the late nineteenth century. The irrigation project, similar to others throughout the Rockies, would interject into the landscape a modern engineering system designed, built, and controlled by professional experts, changing thousands of acres of useless land into modern, progressive farms of forty acres.

Even the products of the land would change in this New West. Sugar beets became an agricultural mantra for thousands of farmers in Montana, Wyoming, Colorado, and Idaho, and the billowing smokestacks of sugar refineries soon competed with the mountain peaks as the prominent points of the skyline. As historian Mark Fiege has observed of the Snake River watershed, a new age of reciprocal agricultural-industrial partnerships was under way, one that redesigned a huge hunk of the valley from scattered ranches and livestock operations into one of standardized-size farms, planned communities, and the omnipresent irrigation works. Moreover, the cultivation and processing of the crop would lead to the immigration of new ethnic labor forces into the valley, from Russians to Mexicans to the Japanese. These groups, in turn, introduced new patterns in the vernacular architecture of the Rockies, such as the white-painted stucco of the *colonía*, a type of corporate housing for Mexican beet workers once commonplace from Colorado to Montana. Most of these unadorned single-story residences have disappeared, but one representative example remains at the Centennial Museum in Greeley, Colorado.[12]

Not only did the progressives in the Yellowstone and Big Horn areas create small farms that were dependent on industrial production and immigrant labor for their profits; they also tied them to several small towns designed and platted by the Reclamation Service in partnership with the railroads. In the Yellowstone Valley, for instance, the Reclamation Service opened lots for sale at Huntley, Ballantine, Worden, Osborn, and Pompeys Pillar in August 1907 and established their own headquarters at Ballantine, Montana. The Reclamation Service's buildings came right out of the type of standardized designs popularized in various agricultural department bulletins from the turn of the century to the depression era. They invariably were rectangular frame one-story buildings, with hints of Bungalow styling in the exposed rafters and porches. Public buildings—schools, civic buildings—even churches, were similar in style: white clapboard, gable-front buildings that typically lacked stylistic details. They reflected a particular industrial aesthetic that characterized many American places in the early twentieth century.

Even farmhouses expressed the new industrial aesthetic. The dwellings were small—most with a kitchen, dining area, living room, and bedrooms and a standardized-designed privy. While exhibiting traits of bungalow design, the dwellings had more in common with industrial housing, built on the quick and mass-produced at sites across the nation. In their restrained style, mass-produced materials, and general industrial aesthetic, the towns and their buildings were standardized intrusions into the western vernacular, reflecting little to nothing of the local landscape or resources. They were part of the region's new image. Agricultural progressives viewed these unadorned dwellings as model farmhouses, highly superior to the sod homes and tarpaper shacks that homesteaders were erecting by the thousands across the region in those same years. As the Reclamation Service's I. D. O'Donnell asserted, "[The] better business of the farm reaches into every item of farm life. The layout of the farm with its buildings and fields should be planned as a manufacturing plant is planned—for efficiency."[13]

The U.S. Bureau of Reclamation's mark on the Yellowstone and Big Horn valleys was replicated along the Snake River in Idaho and Wyoming, the Cache La Poudre in Colorado, and most spectacularly, along the Colorado River in southern Utah, creating the huge Lake Powell and Glen Canyon National Recreation Area. The agency's largest project was on the Colorado River—at world-famous Hoover Dam—on the border between Arizona and Nevada. While the dam is outside of the Rocky Mountain region, its architectural characteristics, as noted by historian Richard Guy Wilson, are shared by many other federal dams in the Rockies. They reflect "several key themes of modernism: efficiency, the utilization of advanced technology, the use of abstract and ahistorical images, and the emphasis on beneficial results."[14]

The Bureau of Reclamation began and controlled Hoover Dam, but the New Deal of President Franklin D. Roosevelt (1882–1945) finished the project and deepened the federal imprint on the Rocky Mountain region. Between 1933 and 1942, such federal agencies as the Federal Emergency Relief Administration (FERA), the Public Works Administration (PWA), the CCC, and the WPA gave a new look to the public architecture of the Rocky Mountains through thousands of construction projects.

Federal officials considered the region that included eastern Montana and Wyoming, for example, to be among the most desperate; therefore, they flooded the area with dollars and projects, an effort that yielded small and mammoth public works. The largest was Fort Peck Dam on the Missouri River, which remains the single largest human alteration in the Montana landscape. Through Margaret Bourke-White's later powerful photographs of the dam in the initial issue of *Life* magazine, the modernism inherent in the design of Fort Peck became a national symbol of the New Deal.

Most New Deal projects were more local in their impact, including hundreds of schools, hundreds of public buildings, and enhanced local, state, and national parks. In the late 1930s, Billings architect J. G. Link designed the Big Horn County Courthouse in Hardin, Montana, blending regional materials with more standardized New Deal design motifs. The striking stonework of the courthouse reflected the natural beauty of the Big Horn Canyon and linked the building's modern styling to the local landscape. Promoting a regional look within a national aesthetic marked other courthouses in the Rockies. For example, the Wayne County Courthouse in Loa, Utah, reflects Art Deco styling but sits on a raised basement of local rock-faced stone, while its projecting central entrance uses that same rocky look within the Art Deco motif. By enhancing the façade with quotations from the frontier past, Wyoming's Natrona County Courthouse, designed by architects Karl Krusmark and Leon Goodrich, concretely linked the past to the present.

The new courthouses symbolized more than the federal presence; they also reminded depressed residents of the national government's commitment to the region and their ever-deepening dependence on the largesse and policies of the federal government. In this manner, the courthouses symbolically confronted the much-prized "independence" of westerners because their commanding presence within the local townscape ironically spoke more of dependence than independence.

This sense of dependence was further emphasized by the thousands of new schools that New Deal agencies built in the region. In larger towns and cities, the schools were often Art Deco- and Art Moderne-styled showplaces, such as the WPA-sponsored Student Union Building at Idaho State University, the Odgen High School in Ogden, Utah, and the Helena High School in Helena, Montana. Community centers and auditoriums were another New Deal addition to the region's built environment, and they varied greatly, from small frame centers in rural areas of Montana, Wyoming, and Colorado to more stylish, multistory brick buildings, such as Helper, Utah's Civic Auditorium and Library, an Art Moderne design from the Salt Lake City firm of Scott and Welch. Outside of Denver, the CCC constructed the beautiful and still popular Red Rocks Amphitheater (1939–1941), an effective and inspiring blending of the natural landscape and man-made built environment designed by Burnham Hoyt. Great Falls, Montana, even became home to a stunning group of Art Deco buildings constructed in the mid-1930s as the new State Fairgrounds.

For decades, reformers had spoken of the need for a New West. Through dams, schools, post offices, government buildings, communities, roads, privies, housing projects, utility systems, and parks, the New Deal built a New West public landscape, with many of these buildings and structures still serving the function for which they were designed.

ROCKIES ARCHITECTURE IN THE MODERN ERA

From the 1950s to the 1980s, an oil boom of unsurpassed intensity in Rocky Mountain history reshaped the region's urban landscape. Billings, for instance, was transformed from being just one of several medium-sized towns to becoming the state's largest urban area, surpassing Butte and Great Falls, once the most powerful due to mining and railroads. Casper underwent a similar transformation in Wyoming, but nothing in the growth experienced in Montana and Wyoming could match the boom that made Denver one of the leading metropolitan centers in the nation.

Corporations have vied for dominance of the Denver skyline for a generation. Some tapped the internationally prominent New York City architectural firm of Skidmore, Owings and Merrill. Others signed on with another internationally renowned architect, I. M. Pei of Boston. Add in other important regional firms and the result is a cache of modern designs unrivaled in the region and excellent examples of the theme of architecture in the Rocky Mountains.

Pei introduced the modernist ethos of glass, steel, and the machine to Denver. Pei's first building in Denver was the Mile High Center (1956), his first major commission after creating his firm the previous year. In this commission, Pei attempted to create a new city center, with his tall buildings surrounding a sunken skating rink and a landscaped plaza—a type of Le Corbusier–influenced urban planning that Pei soon became famous for in later designs in Boston and other eastern cities. Pei's next landmark was in Boulder, with his "Brutalist"-styled campus for the National Center for Atmospheric Research (1965–1966). Here Pei paid homage to the surrounding landscape by incorporating rough concrete and a brownish aggregate that reflects the coloring of the adjacent mountains.

The early popularity of Skidmore, Owings and Merrill in Denver was undoubtedly due to the great success the firm enjoyed with their campus plan and designs for the U.S. Air Force Academy (1956–1963), outside of Colorado Springs, a complex of buildings and designed landscapes recently listed as a National Historic Landmark. Everything within the campus underscored general themes of regimentation and precision while celebrating the military role of the air force through a modernist machine aesthetic. The Chapel has become, in fact, a true national landmark of modernist style, as it uses aluminum tetrahedrons to create its walls and steeples—and each section is reminiscent of the profile of a jet fighter with the nose of the plane headed skyward.

After its success at Colorado Springs, the firm took on various commercial commissions in downtown Denver, such as the Anaconda Tower (1978), a forty-story glass skyscraper; the Denver National Bank Plaza (1980); and the Hudson's Bay Centre (early 1980s).

Frank Lloyd Wright (1867–1959) is the acknowledged American master of modernism. Wright designed seven buildings in the Rocky Mountains, mostly private residences. Near Cody, Wyoming, in 1952 he designed the Quintin Blair residence in his one-story, stone-and-wood style known as Usonian. In the same year, he incorporated the Usonian concepts of a house integrated into the landscape, with materials reflecting local resources, in the Archie B. Teater residence, a one-story studio overlooking the Snake River in Bliss, Idaho. Six years later, for the Bountiful, Utah, family of Don M. Stromquist, Wright used concrete blocks to define an imaginative modernist house jutting out from the canyon wall. It is one of his best examples of architecture coexisting with the natural surroundings in his last decade of active practice.

The best example of Wrightian style, however, was produced in 1967 by Taliesen Associates (a firm consisting largely of Wright's students) as a new headquarters for Rocky Mountain National Park. The firm's Tom Casey was the project architect. The Beaver Meadows Visitor Center is a National Historic Landmark for its very creative interpretation of the earlier park service tradition of Rustic style.

Another major name in modern American architecture, Philip Johnson (1906–   ), produced Denver's first "postmodern"-styled landmark, the United Bank Center (1979–1985). Designed in partnership with architect John Burgee, Johnson's bank complex linked Pei's earlier Mile High Center plaza by means of a half-vaulted indoor atrium.

As the masters of modern American architecture made their mark in the Rockies, so too did a more homegrown architectural profession, one not imported from the East but developed in various schools of architecture across the region in the second half of the twentieth century. In general, courses in architecture preceded the creation of full degree programs that led to professional accreditation. At the University of Idaho, for instance, university architect Rudolph Weaver was offering architectural courses and training as early as 1923–1924, and the university's Department of Art and Architecture dates to 1929. However, actual professional degrees in architecture were not offered until 1956.

The Idaho pattern is similar to the history of architectural departments and degrees at other state universities. In 2003, students could receive professional training leading to accreditation as an architect at the University of Utah, Montana State University, and the University of Colorado as well as the University of Idaho. The University of Wyoming offered studies in architectural engineering within its school of engineering. Of the region's programs, Colorado's College of Architecture and Planning was the largest, counting 900 students in a variety of degree programs, including landscape architecture and historic preservation.

The latter field of historic preservation found an important niche in the region's design traditions in the late twentieth century, and the early success of the various renovations has shaped towns both large and small throughout the Rockies, blending remnants of the past into restructured downtown districts. Denver's Lower Downtown district, known locally as LoDo, mixes converted warehouses, old hotels, and restored industrial buildings with a new baseball stadium that reflected older design motifs in its flashy exterior. Critic Stewart Brand notes: "[W]idespread revulsion with the buildings of the last few decades has been an engine of the preservation movement worldwide. Shoddy, ephemeral, crass, over-specialized, the recent buildings display a global look especially unwelcome in tradition-enriched environs."[15] Brand would only need to look as far as Denver's LoDo for an area where modern and historic design traditions build upon one another to create a lively and aesthetically pleasing urban environment.

Historic motifs also have proved popular at the region's ski resorts. Tourists long viewed the Rockies as a playground but mostly for the summer months. Winter recreation significantly expanded in the second half of the twentieth century, and large, modern-styled ski lodges became important components of the landscape. One of the most expressive—and influential in the design of later complexes in Idaho and Montana—was the Elkhorn ski lodge complex (1973–1976) in Sun Valley, Idaho. Architect Edward Killingsworth wanted to keep the feel of an Alpine village but to move away from the mere replication of a Swiss chalet look, which had been the norm for most Rockies lodges to that time. While Elkhorn was a winner aesthetically, it struggled financially. In the winter of 2003, a local zoning board approved its demolition to make way for a new complex.

A more successful story marks the West Portal Station (1980–1982), designed by the firm of Muchow, Haller, & Lawson at Winter Park, Colorado. Here the architects engaged the local mining vernacular by using materials and irregular forms to give the ski lodge the look of abandoned mine shafts. Deer Valley Resort (1980–1981) near Park City, Utah, incorporated a modern Rustic-style look, using huge Douglas fir logs and local sandstone to integrate the technologically modern complex into the mountains. Its great success—within a decade Park City became one of the nation's elite skiing centers, a reputation further enhanced by the 2002 Winter Olympics—led to the Rustic style appearing in many other ski lodge complexes by the end of the century.

CONCLUSION

Thousands of years of building in the Rocky Mountain region has left an astonishing array of architectural landmarks, from some of the most compelling archaeological properties in the nation to landmark historic districts of America's mining past to glistening monuments of modernism.

The pace of building and development in the late twentieth century, however, reached unprecedented levels of intensity, which, in turn, brought forth new concerns from many residents. As the major cities grew, and ski country became over-populated with lodges, chalets, and other tourist amenities, local as well as outside critics began to worry about the Rockies' loss of regional identity. No doubt, the sameness monotony of suburban sprawl now covers acres and acres of the West, not only around Denver and Salt Lake City but also around towns of any size, such as Billings and Bozeman, Montana. A cover story in the September–October 2003 issue of the National Trust for Historic Preservation's *Preservation* magazine worried that the return of gambling to the mountain towns of Black Hawk and Central City, two National Historic Landmarks, would eclipse the historic built environment with a new plastic glossy look suggesting easy money and plentiful fortunes. A visit to Black Hawk in the fall of 2003 was jarring—flashing lights, neon, and such odd place names as the Mardi Gras Casino assaulted one's senses.[16]

Uncontrolled growth, however, is not region wide—many communities continue to cope with population loss and a generally depressed economy. The future of places once so dependent on extractive industries, such as Butte, Montana, which is another National Historic Landmark, appear bleak. Are there new ghost towns on the horizon?

Probably. The boom-and-bust mentality that has so shaped the region both psychologically and physically continues to play a large role in the preservation of the past and the planning for the future built environment of the Rocky Mountains.

Yet compared to 100 years ago, the region is more stable and settled, with decades-old cultural institutions, architectural monuments, and expansive street plans defining distinct living environments within the much larger world that is the Rocky Mountains. As landmarks of identity, nothing from human hands has eclipsed the majesty of those mountains—indeed, it appears that the nineteenth-century quest of conquering and replacing nature has been, thankfully, forgotten. Whether traveling the Rockies by air, plane, or automobile, one cannot escape the compelling, competing landmarks, designed and built by men and women, that combine with the open skies and craggy peaks of the West to define a region.

RESOURCE GUIDE

Printed Sources

Attebery, Jennifer. *Building Idaho: An Architectural History*. Moscow: University of Idaho Press, 1991.

Carter, Thomas, and Peter Goss. *Utah's Historic Architecture, 1847–1940*. Salt Lake City: University of Utah Press, 1988.

Jordan, Terry, Jon T. Kilpinen, and Charles F. Gritzner. *The Mountain West: Interpreting the Folk Landscape*. Baltimore, MD: Johns Hopkins University Press, 1997.

Nabokov, Peter, and Robert Easton. *Native American Architecture*. New York: Oxford University Press, 1989.

Starr, Eileen F. *Architecture in the Cowboy State, 1849–1940: A Guide*. Glendo, WY: High Plains Press, 1992.

West, Carroll V. *A Traveler's Companion to Montana History*. Helena: Montana Historical Society Press, 1986.

Web Sites

Library of Congress
http://www.loc.gov

The American Memory site within this Web page contains hundreds of photographs and drawings of Rocky Mountains architecture documented by the Historic American Building Survey from the 1930s to the end of the century. Accessed June 22, 2004.

National Park Service
http://www.nps.gov

Histories, images, and some preservation plans for the many national parks and national historic sites in the Rocky Mountains. Accessed June 22, 2004.

Organizations

Colorado Historical Society
1300 Broadway
Denver, CO 80203
303-866-3682
http://www.coloradohistory.org/

Idaho State Historical Society
450 North Fourth Street
Boise, ID 83702
208-334-3863
http://idahohistory.net

Montana Historical Society
225 North Roberts
Helena, MT 59620
406-444-2694
http://www.his.state.mt.us

Utah State Historical Society
300 South Rio Grande Street
Salt Lake City, UT 84101
801-533-3500
http://history.utah.gov/

Wyoming State Parks and Cultural Resources
2301 Central Avenue
Cheyenne, WY 82002
307-777-6303
http://wyospcr.state.wy.us

ART

Rick Newby

The West *is* America, some like to say, and the Rocky Mountain region (for the purposes of this volume, the states of Colorado, Idaho, Montana, Utah, and Wyoming) might be called, as geographer Gundars Rudzitis puts it, the "unambiguous west," that place of sweeping prairies, towering mountain peaks, vast plateaus, and surging rivers most clearly identified as the West of the imagination.[1] A site of outsized dreams, perhaps more so than other American places, the Rocky Mountain region has long lured artists from elsewhere while producing a host of its own creators: painters, sculptors, photographers, weavers, ceramists, and folk artists of every description.

For millennia before contact with Europeans, American Indians in the Rockies created works of art out of local materials, embellishing rock faces and objects of use with designs that retain their power and beauty today. From the beginning of Euro-American contact, artists have traveled to the region to record the lifeways of these native peoples and to capture a landscape that continues to inspire awe and affection. With the emergence of the military and ranching frontiers, artists like Frederic Remington and Charles M. Russell did more than document the changing Rocky Mountain scene; they crafted, with considerable skill and passion, a myth of the West that refuses to die despite enormous shifts, cultural and economic, since.

With the advent of the twentieth century came incursions of both European and homegrown modernisms into the region. Despite these new influences, western art—that is, works depicting life on the frontier more or less realistically but often with a romanticizing edge—continued to dominate the scene well past mid-century. Nevertheless, modernism made inroads, gaining influence and respectability with the arrival of artists like Wyoming ranch wife Fra Dana, influenced by Mary Cassatt and the Impressionists, German modernist Winold Reiss, famous for his portraits of Blackfeet Indians, and Maynard Dixon, whose visionary approach to western scenes involved an increasing simplification of forms.

At mid-century, G.I.s returning from World War II (and enrolling in expanded arts programs in the region's universities) opened the way for true gains for modern tendencies in the visual arts, and a few artists from the Rockies—among them Montana's Peter Voulkos, Jackson Pollock, born in Cody, Wyoming, and Edward Kienholz, raised in Washington state but long associated with Idaho—went on to national prominence, bringing fresh (and brash) energies to American art.

At the start of the twenty-first century, the Rocky Mountain art scene is rich, diverse, lively, and sometimes contentious, made up of history-oriented western painting and sculpture, ongoing Native American art practices and innovations, thriving expressions of varied folk traditions, and artful depictions of landscape and wildlife. In addition, a growing population of modernist (and postmodernist) artists create works in every medium imaginable: paint and clay, bronze and photographic emulsions, barbed wire and animal collagen, computers, and the Rocky Mountain landscape itself.

NATIVE AMERICAN ARTS

The very first peoples to populate the Rocky Mountain region created works requiring great skill. To survive, these Paleoindian and Archaic people depended on their prowess at hunting, and some of their best-crafted surviving artifacts, especially projectile points, centered around that activity. As some scholars have noted, the flaked stone spear points these peoples created are among the finest found anywhere in the world. Other remnants they left behind appear to be related to ceremonies and rituals. Archaeologists have found bison skulls painted with zigzag patterns at burial sites in the Northern Plains, paraphernalia relating to shamanic practices (flutes and miniature projectile points), and even the first evidence of rock art in the region (at Whoopup Canyon, Wyoming, petroglyphs dating from 9300 B.C.E. depict communal hunting).

Rock art is among the most vivid and lasting legacies of precontact Native Americans. Almost all tribal groups found in the Rockies created petroglyphs (incised or pecked into the stone) or pictographs (painted on the surface with pigment), often in caves and other rock shelters or on sacred "medicine rocks." The imagery in these works of art varied widely, ranging from figurative depictions of people and animals (sometimes blended to create legendary creatures half human, half animal) to mostly abstracted mazelike designs to wholly abstract geometric shapes. Archaeologists have categorized the rock art of the Northern Plains, for example, into eleven traditions, among them the Biographic, Foothills Abstract, Hoofprint, Columbia Plateau, and Pecked Abstract traditions.

While the meaning of some rock art seems relatively clear (especially those narrating a hunt or battle), many pictographs and petroglyphs remain mysterious. Even some representational images are freighted with clearly symbolic imagery that is difficult to decipher. Nevertheless, these striking images retain their original sense of power and continue to fascinate those who encounter them. As James Keyser and Michael Klassen have written, rock art is complex, beautiful, and richly human, "an almost limitless variety of images throughout the landscape that represent a nearly infinite variety of ideas, experiences, and perceptions."[2]

Highly vulnerable to vandalism, Rocky Mountain rock art is a precious heritage. From the Holy Ghost pictographs in Canyonlands National Park, Utah, to snakes and turtles painted on the cliffs of Montana's Gates of the Mountains to Columbia Plateau petroglyphs of human figures along the Snake River in Idaho, rock art might be seen to underlie all future artistic efforts within the region.

Closely related to rock art are the paintings and drawings that Rocky Mountain Native Americans applied to various objects made of perishable materials. These materials include bison and other animal skins and, with the arrival of Euro-Americans, canvas, muslin, and paper (often from ledgers, hence the name "ledger" drawings). Most often these works were in the Biographic tradition; that is, they featured the exploits of warriors, winter counts (a form of calendar), or scenes of everyday life. As narrative works, they provide invaluable information about eighteenth- and nineteenth-century Native American life in the Rockies and were much sought after by early Euro-American visitors to the region.

Some "spirit robes," however, were nonnarrative and ceremonial, and their imagery related to rituals, visions, and spirit powers. In the Blackfeet tradition, men received the designs with which they decorated their bison-hide tipi covers in dreams. According to John Ewers, "[T]he original animal owner of the lodge appeared to the sleeper and promised to give him some of his power"; upon awakening, the men painted their tipis as the dream animals dictated. Although the tipi designs were beautiful, their owners, Ewers notes, "treasured them more as religious symbols than as aesthetic creations. They counted upon their painted tipis to bring them good fortune."[3] Apparently in the precontact period, only the most distinguished leaders of the tribe possessed painted tipis.

Whether they were depicting battles, recording everyday occurrences, or articulating visions, precontact painters used natural pigments: basic black and white; yellow, orange, and red ochers; and brown lignite; their paintings grew more colorful as Euro-American traders introduced commercial pigments (especially reds, blues, greens, and yellows). With the near-annihilation of the bison herds, canvas replaced the buffalo hide as the preferred material for tipi covers—and as the surface for the continuing tradition of painting sacred designs.

Ledger drawings, with their roots in Biographic painting, were first created on animal skins, but Indian artists in the Rockies found that paper acquired from missionaries, traders, and explorers was perfectly suited for making these detailed drawings. For example, Father Nicholas Point, a Jesuit missionary who traveled in the Northern Rockies in the 1840s, provided Blackfeet and Salish (Flathead) artists with paper and then collected their ledger drawings; as a tireless painter himself, Point appreciated their artistry. Speaking of Crow and Gros Ventre ledger drawings, curator Gordon McConnell writes, "Deft line quality, elegant stylization . . . a keen appreciation for telling detail, formal balance, and judicious use of color mark these drawings as works of great and enduring artistic worth."[4]

Another object that lent itself to brilliant artistic endeavor was the humble parfleche, a folded envelope constructed of rawhide and decorated by women belonging to most of the tribes living in the Rockies. Always painted with complex geometric designs of infinite and beautiful variety, the light but durable parfleches were used as containers by the nomadic peoples of the Intermountain West. Women were also responsible for another key artistic expression: decorative patterns created, first, from porcupine quills (and other natural materials like black maidenhair fern stems, various grasses, and corn husks) and then beads.

Reflecting a love of elaborate ornamentation, quillwork and beadwork are found among all of the tribes in region, but the patterns vary widely from group to group. The Crow, for example, appear to derive their patterns from the geometric designs on their parfleches, whereas the Ute use small seed beads to produce distinctive massive triangular designs, often in only blue and white or similar limited palettes. Floral designs may have entered the Northern Plains with the arrival of Great Lakes tribes, though the floral designs used by the Métis (mixed-blood offspring of French or Celtic traders and Chippewa or Cree wives), some speculate, may have had a European origin, deriving from embroidery patterns learned in mission schools. By the mid-nineteenth century, most people in the region had turned from quills to using beads imported by traders, although quillwork remains a living art among certain tribes as a way of honoring past traditions.

Beadwork certainly thrives today, and as Ralph Coe demonstrated with the impressive exhibition *Lost and Found Traditions*, Rocky Mountain Indian artistic traditions (as well as those of other regions) are alive and well and continuing to evolve—a fact long evident to Native American artisans themselves. Ethnographer James Clifford has written that Coe situated the objects in the exhibition, all by contemporary Indian artists, "in ongoing, inventive traditions" and that along with clearly traditional works "we find skillfully beaded tennis shoes and baseball caps, articles developed for the curio trade, quilts, and . . . peyote kits modeled on old-fashioned toolboxes."[5] In the Rocky Mountain region, a variety of events showcase this creativity, from the annual Native American Art show in Great Falls, Montana, to the twice yearly Colorado Indian Market and Southwest Showcase, held in Denver.

Museums in the Rocky Mountain region also hold strong collections of prehistoric and historic Native American art. The Denver Art Museum (DAM), for example, began collecting Indian objects (from the region and beyond) in the late 1920s, and until 1944, 95 percent of the objects acquired by the museum came from North American tribal cultures, resulting in a collection that today totals 16,000 objects. Moreover, DAM was one of the first museums anywhere to treat Native American artworks not just as anthropological documents but as aesthetic equals to art from all other cultures. Significant collections of precon-

The Denver Art Museum's 28-sided building was designed by Gio Ponti and opened in 1971. The museum is the largest art museum between Kansas City and the West Coast. © Denver Art Museum.

tact artifacts and Native American art and costume (for more on Indian dress, see the **Fashion** chapter in this volume) also reside at the Plains Indian Museum of the Buffalo Bill Historical Center, the University of Colorado Museum, the Chase Home Museum of Utah Folk Arts, the Museum of the Plains Indian in Browning, Montana, and the Museum of the Montana Historical Society.

EARLY PAINTERS AND PHOTOGRAPHERS OF THE ROCKY MOUNTAINS

Field sketches by Captains Meriwether Lewis (1774–1809) and William Clark (1770–1838) might be said to launch a Euro-American artistic tradition in the Rocky Mountains, but it was with the arrival of skilled artists like George Catlin, Karl Bodmer, Father Nicholas Point, and Charles Deas that the tradition truly began. These artists, arriving on the heels of the Corps of Discovery in the 1830s and 1840s, found themselves in a wholly unfamiliar world, one with fully functioning native cultures, expanses of wild country, and teeming populations of exotic wildlife. Profoundly taken with these new realities, the artists set out to chronicle them in paint and ink. Even then they sensed that, with the arrival of their own kind, the West could not remain unchanged.

In 1832, George Catlin, standing at the verge of the Rocky Mountain region, where the Yellowstone River meets the Missouri near the border of present-day Montana and North Dakota, proclaimed the need for a "*magnificent park*, where the world could see for ages to come, the native Indian in his classic attire, galloping his wild horse . . . amid the fleeting herds of elks and buffaloes. . . . A *nation's Park*, containing man and beast, in all the wild and freshness of their nature's beauty!" Catlin's anxiety about preserving the Wild West grew out of his certain knowledge that already "three-fourths of [the Native Americans'] country has fallen into the possession of civilized man." He declared that the Indians of the Upper Missouri, particularly the Blackfeet and Crow, were the "finest looking, best equipped, and most beautifully costumed of any on the Continent," and the self-taught artist painted portraits of scores of them (as many as 140 in 1832 alone). Known as Montana's first press agent, Catlin returned to the East with his drawings, paintings, and extensive journals, plus many artifacts.[6]

Accompanying a scientific expedition led by German prince Maximilian of Wied-Neuwied, Swiss artist Karl Bodmer felt a similar urge to document both the landscape and the peoples of the Northern Plains. Arriving at Fort Union a year after Catlin, Bodmer proceeded further up the Missouri, painting beautifully rendered watercolors of the rock formations along the river. Always with an eye for the telling detail, he painted Fort Mackenzie at the mouth of the Marias River (and a Blackfeet camp outside the walls), together with a number of Blackfeet, Shoshone, and Kutenai individuals arrayed in their finery and many artifacts collected by the expedition, including bison robes painted with warrior exploits, hair ornaments, pipe bowls and stems, clubs, knives and beaded scabbards, pouches and bundles, even snowshoes.

As William H. Goetzmann has written, "No less than Catlin, Bodmer felt that in his contact with the Indian he was in touch with sublime nature in all its

George Catlin, *The Author Painting a Chief at the Base of the Rocky Mountains.* © Yale Collection of Western Americana, Beinecke Rare Book and Manuscript Library.

mysterious power."[7] Products of the Romantic Age, Catlin and Bodmer were to offer easterners their first views of the opening West. Ironically, these highly charged visions of a paradise on the verge of extinction, intended to preserve a way of life, undoubtedly helped fuel Americans' desire to explore, and domesticate, this untamed land.

Less romantic in his approach, Jesuit missionary Nicholas Point, in 1840, journeyed deeper into the Rocky Mountain West, traveling with the legendary Father Jean-Pierre DeSmet. While DeSmet proselytized to the Flathead (Salish) and Coeur d'Alene Indians, Point painted miniatures of tribal scenes, depicting everything from bison hunts to family groups at rest to the gathering of camas roots to scalp dances to the Sun Dance and other ceremonies. Many of Point's scenes also recorded the conversion of tribal members to Catholicism, reflecting a crucial shift in the local culture. Other artists soon followed into the Rockies, including the painters Alfred Jacob Miller, who spent much time in present-day Wyoming, and St. Louis–based Charles Deas, who specialized in images of the fur trade. The Denver Art Museum's Institute for Western American Art claims Deas' *Long Jakes, the Rocky Mountain Man* (1844) as the single most influential image in Rocky Mountain iconography.

Many would dispute that claim, and any of several works by the artists who arrived in the next wave of exploration and settlement certainly warrant that distinction. Less concerned with ethnographic detail, these painters and photographers brought a passion for landscape to the region. Influenced by the Hudson River School, which sought to capture the majesty of the American wilderness, these accomplished artists painted what has retrospectively been labeled the American Sublime. Like Catlin and Bodmer, they brought a Romantic overlay to the landscapes of the Colorado Rockies and the wonders of the nascent Yellowstone National Park.

Albert Bierstadt, a German émigré, carried a Teutonic theatricality to the vertical wonders of the Rockies, and his first masterwork from the region, a seven-foot portrait of "Lander's Peak," excited much notice when he exhibited it in 1863. Bierstadt is credited as the founder of the Rocky Mountain Luminist (emphasizing effects of light and atmosphere) school. Another Luminist landscape painter, British-born and largely self-taught Thomas Moran was influenced by an early encounter with Catlin (who he heard lecture in London), the sublime land- and waterscapes of J.M.W. Turner, and the pre-Raphaelite painters. Even though he often traveled with expeditions intent on accurately surveying the West, Moran, like Turner, was more concerned with artistic truth than topographical accuracy.

In 1871, Moran completed a watercolor study he titled *First sketch made in the West*, and for the next forty years, he would serve as one of the greatest chroniclers of Yellowstone, the Colorado Rockies, and the Sierras. Arriving just a year before it became the world's first national park, Moran loved the Yellowstone country, calling it "the most wonderful region on the Continent,"[8] and his *Grand Canyon of the Yellowstone* (1872) can certainly be called an icon of westward expansion. Other Rocky Mountain Luminists were Denver's Henry Elkins, a protégé of Bierstadt, and Frederick Ferdinand Schafer, who, though based in San Francisco, painted scenes throughout the Rockies. John Casilear, a member of the Hudson River School, also painted Colorado landscapes.

Photographers, too, served to bring stunning images of the Rocky Mountain West to eager audiences back East. After working as photographer for the Union Pacific Railroad, William Henry Jackson came to Yellowstone with the Hayden Survey Party in 1870. Like Moran, he was entranced by the country, and after traveling and photographing widely in the West, he set up a studio in Denver in 1879. Jackson's grand images of Yellowstone's features have been credited with cementing Congress's determination to name the region a national park, and his photographs of the Colorado Rockies, especially those of the Mount of the Holy Cross, remain among the most indelible images from the age of exploration.

Timothy H. O'Sullivan, another documentary photographer who accompanied U.S. Geological Survey parties, brought a different sensibility to his images taken in Utah, Idaho, Wyoming, and Colorado. As Joel Snyder has written, O'Sullivan's photographs "do not portray nature as majestic, breathtaking, or . . . humane. O'Sullivan's interior demands heroic labor and in return gives back very little . . . it is the source of quiet, still, sometimes desperate pictures."[9] Photographers James Fennemore, John Hillers, and E. O. Beaman documented Major John Wesley Powell's Second Expedition down the Green and Colorado Rivers; San Franciscan Carleton E. Watkins also photographed in Yellowstone; and

William Henry Jackson, *On the Continental Divide*, between 1900 and 1923. Courtesy of the Denver Public Library.

Union Pacific photographer A. J. Russell did important documentary work in the region (his most famous image is of Wyoming's Citadel Rock, a key landmark for westward sojourners).

The Luminist painters and their photographic counterparts established in the American imagination images of a Rocky Mountain world that beckoned with promises of adventure and the sublimity of nature. They had laid the groundwork. It would take the following generation of Rocky Mountain artists to cement the emerging myth.

WESTERN PAINTING AND SCULPTURE: AN ART OF PLACE

Scion of a prominent St. Louis mercantile family (he was nephew to William Bent, reputed to be the first white settler in Colorado and founder of Bent's Fort), Charles M. Russell (1864–1926) came west in 1880 at age sixteen. The young city boy, eager to become a cowboy on the open range, stayed in Montana. For some eleven years, he worked as a wrangler (by all accounts, not a particularly skilled one), but very early on, he took to drawing and then painting and sculpting the western life he loved. Russell felt a powerful nostalgia for the "wild and freshness" of the frontier, and though he was too late to see bison hunts, intertribal warfare, or the men of the fur trade, he made his mark capturing scenes from those idyllic times. A late Romantic, Russell portrayed, perhaps better than anyone, a Rocky Mountain dreamscape already mythologized by the Luminists, dime westerns, and Buffalo Bill's Wild West Show.

During his thirty-three years as a professional artist, Russell produced more than 3,000 works of art. He illustrated books, sent friends and acquaintances marvelously illustrated letters, painted canvases small and large (the largest is his 1912 mural *Lewis and Clark Meeting the Flathead in Ross' Hole*, which, at twenty-five by twelve feet, takes up an entire wall in the chambers of the Montana House of Representatives), and sculpted in bronze grizzly bears, bison, and mounted warriors and cowboys. Like Catlin before him, Russell was particularly drawn to Native American life, and he spent the winter of 1888–1889 with the Blood Indians of Alberta, learning something of their language and customs. In his many paintings of Indian scenes, he sought to portray, accurately and with sympathy, a way of life that had nearly vanished.

Russell's was a narrative art immensely popular with collectors and the public, and the Cowboy Artist was, in the testimony of his friend Will Rogers, a master storyteller in words as well; this is attested to, too, by his letters and collections of stories, *Trails Plowed Under* (1927), *More Rawhides* (1925), and *Good Medicine* (1929). He was a realist—he always strove for the accurate detail—but nevertheless he clearly understood the role he played as a fabulist who, in the face of a rapidly industrializing present, fed a hunger for a more innocent and free time. He wrote in a poem, "Myth is the Mother of Romance/and I am her oldest son."[10]

Frederic Remington (1861–1909), more so than Russell, was a professional artist who never pretended to live the life he depicted, though he did for a brief period own a sheep ranch in Kansas. Trained in art at Yale and an alert observer, Remington submitted illustrations of western subjects to major magazines, and in the

Charles M. Russell, *When the Land Belonged to God*, 1915. Courtesy of the Montana Historical Society.

1880s, *Harper's Weekly* began publishing his drawings of Rocky Mountain life. Like Russell, Remington surrounded himself with artifacts of the frontier, and he prided himself on his accurate depictions of dress, topography, and equipment. By the mid-1890s, Remington found himself a successful illustrator, with extensive credits as both illustrator and reporter, but he wanted more—to be regarded as a fine artist.

Following a brutal stint as correspondent to Cuba during the Spanish-American War, Remington traveled to Montana and Wyoming to recuperate. Once again inspired by western scenes, he turned to painting oils that differed markedly from his more narrative illustrations. Perhaps colored by his firsthand experiences of the suffering of war, these later works were less romantic and more melancholy. Literally darker, they were often "nocturnes," scenes like his classic *In from the Night Herd* (1907) lit only by moonlight. These works, filled with mystery and often menace, brought him critical acclaim and strong sales at New York's Knoedler Gallery. When he died prematurely in 1909, Remington had turned his attention from narrative subjects altogether and was painting a series of unpeopled landscapes set in Wyoming. Both these almost Impressionist landscapes and his spare and anxious nocturnes, of which he painted more than seventy, revealed a turn away from the reassuring myths of the West.

As settlers rushed to the Rocky Mountain region during the latter half of the nineteenth century, more and more artists joined them. One of the most brilliant was the European-trained photographer and painter Joseph Henry Sharp (1859–1953). Although Sharp has long been identified with Taos, New Mexico, he made his first mark in the Northern Rockies. In the late 1890s, he traveled from his home in Cincinnati, where he worked as an illustrator and teacher, to the battlefield of the Little Big Horn, where he painted portraits of Plains Indians. In 1900, he exhibited these portraits in Paris and Washington, D.C., where President Theodore Roosevelt saw them. Impressed, Roosevelt commissioned Sharp to paint portraits of 200 warriors who had survived their 1876 victory over General George Armstrong Custer and the Seventh Cavalry. Sharp spent the bulk of the years 1902–1910 at Crow Agency, where the Indian Commission provided him with a cabin he called Absarokee Hut (the hut now stands on the grounds of the Buffalo Bill Historical Center, Cody). In addition to his beautifully rendered, always respectful portraits, Sharp took many photographs and painted memorable landscapes. The financial security this commission provided, plus the support of major collectors like Phoebe Apperson Hearst (1842–1919), the mother of William Randolph Hearst, allowed Sharp to devote his energies full-time to his art. Immensely productive, Sharp proved a true master of western art, and his portraits and landscapes remain highly prized today.

Plenty of others followed in the footsteps of Russell, Remington, Sharp, and the Luminists. Like many immigrants, Harry Learned came to Colorado in search of high-mountain air to cure his tuberculosis; he would paint hundreds of small paintings of the Rocky Mountain peaks and the rough-and-tumble mining towns in their midst. The German artist Charles Ostner settled in the Idaho goldfields where, failing to strike it rich, he turned to painting romanticized scenes like *Bear's Attack*, in which a valiant Indian warrior plunges his lance into a grizzly bear. French-born Henry François Farny (1847–1916), a noted illustrator, traveled the Northern Rockies, painting Indian life. John Fery led hunting parties of aristocratic Austrians to the region and was subsequently hired by the Great Northern Railway to paint monumental Rocky Mountain scenes, especially of Glacier National Park. Besides his paintings, Will James wrote and illustrated numerous books on the cowboy life, including the classic children's book *Smoky the Cowhorse*. Danish-born Olaf C. Seltzer (1877–1957), one of Charlie Russell's few protégés, continued on the master's path; in the 1920s, for example, Dr. Philip Cole, a wealthy collector with Montana roots, commissioned Seltzer to paint 275 miniatures of episodes in Montana history.

Also coming into the country were Mormon artists who helped document the emerging culture of Utah. Utah's first Euro-American artist was British-

Frederic Remington, *A Bucking Bronco*, c. 1908. Courtesy of the Library of Congress.

born William W. Major, who arrived in Salt Lake City in 1848. Major painted landscapes as well as portraits of his fellow settlers and Indian leaders. Danish painter C.C.A. Christensen was known for his scenes depicting early Mormon life and episodes from the *Book of Mormon*. Other important early painters were Danquart Weggeland and George M. Ottinger, together with Utah Luminists George Beard, H.L.A. Culmer, and Alfred Lambourne. Deseret also produced sculptors, including Cyrus E. Dallin of Springville and the noted brothers Solon (1868–1922) and Gutzun Borglum (1867–1941) of Ogden. Gutzun, born in Idaho, went on to carve the monumental heads of Mount Rushmore.

Photographers contributed mightily to the documentation of western settlement. In Utah, for example, George Edward Anderson captured the life of his state from the 1870s until the late 1920s. Headquartered in Springville, Anderson is remembered for his portraits of Mormon settlers and their Paiute neighbors, his views of growing towns, ranch life, and industrial development, and his sobering images of a mine disaster that claimed the lives of 200 miners at Scofield on May Day 1900.

In Colorado, the development of the region and the soaring Rocky Mountain peaks themselves proved compelling subjects for many photographers. In the 1870s and 1880s, twenty-odd companies produced stereo views of the state. One of the most prolific publishers, German-born Charles Weitfle, marketed stereos not only of mountain scenery but also of the state's burgeoning mining camps, tourist attractions, and boomtowns like Denver and Leadville. Besides his studio in Central City (later Denver), Weitfle also operated a branch in Cheyenne, Wyoming. In the early twentieth century, another Colorado photographer, Harry Landis Standley, gained fame by focusing on mountain scenery. An avid climber, Standley photographed all of Colorado's Fourteeners (peaks of over 14,000 feet)—and he reached all of their summits, too. From his studio in Colorado Springs, he marketed his hand-colored mountain images to tourists who fell in love with Colorado's rugged terrain.

At first headquartered in Minnesota, photographer Frank Jay Haynes (1853–1921) was hired by the Northern Pacific Railway to record the building of the railroad and document life along the line, from St. Paul to Tacoma (and the Rocky Mountain country in between). The railroad employed Haynes' beautifully crafted images to lure more settlers into the region. Eventually settling at Mammoth Hot Springs, Haynes became the official photographer of Yellowstone National Park, serving in that capacity for more than thirty years. His Yellowstone views, alongside those of Thomas Moran, remain among the most iconic images of the "Wonderland."

After apprenticing under Haynes in Minnesota, Laton A. Huffman (1854–1931) came to Miles City, Montana, in 1879. From there, Huffman documented what he termed "This Last West," the frontier world of vast bison herds, unfettered Indians, tough cowboys, and unfenced prairie. Huffman marketed his images to an America hungry for the western dream, and his widely distributed photographs—often used as illustrations by magazine and book publishers—then inspired paintings, drawings, and etchings by such western artists as Charlie Russell (a Huffman friend), Remington, and Edward Borein.[11] Among Huffman's most powerful images are shots of slaughtered bison littering the plains, unvarnished photos of cowboys at work, and a series of somber portraits of Sioux, Northern Cheyenne, and

Layton A. Huffman, *Red Sleeve, Cheyenne Scout*, Fort Keogh, Montana Territory, 1879. Courtesy of the Montana Historical Society.

Crow men and women, often in traditional dress.

Another eastern Montana photographer, Evelyn Cameron, had less commercial success than Huffman, but her images, rediscovered in the 1970s, afford quite another look at late-nineteenth- and early-twentieth-century life in the region. Cameron documented not the remnants of a romantic frontier but the ongoing activities of ranch and homesteading families, from ice cream socials and Fourth of July picnics to women kneading bread to hunting trips into the area's harshly beautiful badlands. Like Cameron, other pioneering women artists contributed important work and differing perspectives to the region's artistic heritage. Despite the male-dominated western art scene, women persisted in making art in the region's small towns and emerging urban centers and on ranches and farms.

Women artists were not wholly impervious to the myths of the West. Renowned French painter Rosa Bonheur (1822–1899), for example, known for her vivid animal paintings, loved the work of George Catlin, and in 1892, she met Buffalo Bill Cody in Paris and painted a famous portrait of the western impresario (now owned by the Buffalo Bill Historical Center). Closer to home, Sally Farnham (1869–1943), a friend of Remington's, produced bronzes of western subjects from her studio in New York. Oftentimes, though, the women on the ground in the Rockies were most interested in depicting the western landscape, the nitty-gritty of mining or ranching, or their own experiences within the domestic sphere.

In Denver and Salt Lake City, the region's two largest cities, women had greater access both to arts education and the companionship of female colleagues. Denver was a regional model for integrating the arts in public life; seen as civilizing influences, women played a vital role in this flourishing arts scene. For example, landscape painter Helena Henderson Chain founded the city's first art school, and women actively participated in the Artist's Club of Denver, founded in 1893 (the club would become the Denver Art Museum in 1923). For Denver's women, the arts offered autonomy and possibilities for influence outside the home. Among the most accomplished of Denver's women painters were Chain, Henrietta Bromwell,

Emma Cherry, and Anne Evans (Evans was central to DAM's early focus on collecting and exhibiting Native American art).

The Mormon Church had long been supportive of the arts, especially if they celebrated, as Erika Doss puts it, "God's handiwork and Zion's bounty,"[12] and in fact, Utah was the first state to establish a government arts agency, in 1899. However, while Mormon male artists received church commissions and educational support, women did not. Nevertheless, numerous Mormon women turned to the arts, creating their work as their family responsibilities and finances allowed. Prominent among them were Harriet Harwood, Minerva Teichert (considered by many to be the greatest visual chronicler of the Mormon story), Mary Teasdel, and Rose Hartwell. Teasdel and Hartwell succeeded in the larger artistic world by leaving Utah, at least for a time; both studied in Europe (where each exhibited in the Paris Salon).

Idaho artist and author Mary Hallock Foote (1847–1938) created important illustrations of development in the Northern Rockies, especially her "Pictures of the Far West," which appeared in *Century Magazine* in 1888–1889. Whether she depicted the effects of irrigation on an arid landscape (with a well-dressed young woman strolling a ditch bank) or portrayed *A Pretty Girl in the West* (1889) strumming a guitar on a veranda high above Boise Canyon, Foote brought a feminized West to a national readership.

In the turn-of-the-twentieth-century Rockies, perhaps the best trained and most prodigiously talented woman painter was Wyoming's Fra Dana (1874–1948), who had studied with Joseph Henry Sharp in Cincinnati and Impressionist Mary Cassatt in Paris. Married to a Wyoming rancher, Dana painted sophisticated domestic scenes, often of a gowned woman at leisure, reading a newspaper or sipping tea. These lovely Impressionist works introduced something to western painting that had little to do with myth or even men's work; instead they suggested that some westerners yearned for more civilization and fewer rough edges. As Dana would write in her diary in 1907, "Beauty of any kind is a thing held cheap out here in this land of hard realities and glaring sun and alkali. There are no nuances."[13]

THE RISE OF ROCKY MOUNTAIN VISUAL MODERNISM

At first, modernism found the Rockies less-than-fertile ground. Charlie Russell, as the exemplary western painter, expressed general hostility toward modernism, and after encountering an Italian Futurist exhibition in London in 1914, he lampooned the wild paintings in letters to friends, comparing them to spoiled sausages. As artists traveled to Europe and the East Coast to study, however, they picked up new techniques and new ideas; others came to the Rockies to teach the new "isms" at state universities.

Maynard Dixon brought a modern look to his paintings of traditional western subjects. Dixon's Montana paintings, such as *The Conversation* or *Picture Writing* (both 1917), with their loose, powerful brushwork, reveal him working in a post-Impressionist, almost Expressionist mode. To his landscapes set in Utah and the Desert Southwest, Dixon would introduce simplified forms that reflected Cubist influence. A key proselytizer for European modernisms in America, German artist

Winold Reiss cofounded the magazine *Modern Art Collector* (1915) and is credited with designing the first modernist restaurant interior in New York. During the 1920s, on commission from the Great Northern Railway, Reiss painted scores of vibrant Art Deco–inflected portraits of Blackfeet tribal members in Glacier National Park, where he also ran an art school for aspiring painters.

Some Rocky Mountain artists left the region young and made their mark as modernists elsewhere. Artist-designer E. McKnight Kauffer (1890–1954), born in Great Falls, Montana, ended up in Great Britain, where he became a member of the Vorticist movement and an important designer of avant-garde rugs, posters, and book jackets. Influenced by Constructivism and Surrealism, Kauffer would later return to the States, where he continued to create elegant book jackets, including that for the classic 1947 Random House edition of James Joyce's (1882–1941) *Ulysses*. (Perhaps the only Kauffer work that referred to his western roots was an advertisement for the Container Corporation of America; the 1946 ad depicted a herd of Constructivist cows on a barren hillside, with the word *Montana* stenciled on a slightly bilious sky.)

Things began to change with the end of World War II. Thousands of veterans were returning to the Rocky Mountain states, and fueled by the G.I. Bill, they sought out meaningful educations, sometimes in the arts. At the same time, new artistic ideas carried by new Americans—Europeans who had fled their homelands to escape fascism—arrived in the Rocky Mountain hinterland.

In 1945, Chicago industrialist Walter Paepcke, chairman of the Container Corporation of America, visited Aspen, Colorado, for the first time. Paepcke quickly had a vision for the old mining town—as a high-mountain center for culture. Paepcke was a firm believer in the importance of modern design and passionate about the ideas embodied by the German Bauhaus, the extraordinarily influential art school shut down as subversive by the Nazis (1933). In 1937, Paepcke had helped Hungarian Bauhaus master Laszlo Moholy-Nagy (1895–1946) found a New Bauhaus in Chicago. When that experiment failed, Paepcke and Moholy-Nagy worked together to found the Chicago Institute of Design, which carried on the Bauhaus tradition of integration of the arts. In 1949, Paepcke launched his great Aspen experiment with the ambitious Goethe Bicentennial Convocation, which brought together luminaries like Albert Schweitzer, José Ortega y Gasset, and Artur Rubinstein. The next year Paepcke turned to another Bauhaus master, the multitalented artist and designer Herbert Bayer, to launch his Aspen Institute for Humanistic Studies.

Bayer, who also served as design director for Paepcke's Container Corporation, believed in the concept of total design and was a master in architecture, painting, photography, sculpture, and typography. He brought these talents to Aspen, where Paepcke asked him to design the campus for the Aspen Institute, which Bayer did in the classic modernist International Style. Bayer also selected, with his wife Joella, the color and design standards for new homes in Aspen, and he designed the town's logo, a simplified aspen leaf. An early environmentalist, Bayer fought for an ordinance against billboards in Aspen, and in 1955, on the grounds of the Aspen Institute, he sculpted *Grass Mound*, an earthen mound forty feet in diameter, one of the first examples of Land or Environmental Art anywhere. *Grass Mound* would presage such important works of Rocky Mountain Land Art as Carl Andre's *Rock Pile* and *Log Piece* (both 1968), also at Aspen; Robert Smithson's monumental *Spiral*

Jetty (1970) in the Great Salt Lake; Nancy Holt's *Sun Tunnels* (1973–1976) in the Utah desert; and even the 3,770-ton solar salt ring Matthew Barney created on the Bonneville Salt Flats for his film *Cremaster 2* (1999).

But it was as founder of the International Design Conference (IDC), first held in Aspen in 1951, and as a world-renowned artist-designer that Bayer has had his greatest impact on Rocky Mountain culture. Instead of looking inward at regional myths, the IDC has, for the past half century, brought the world of international design to Colorado, stimulating a regional interest in design that might not otherwise have arisen. Although he left Colorado for Montecito, California, in 1974, Bayer donated his personal art collection and archive to the Denver Art Museum in 1979, and after his 1985 death, his widow Joella continued to donate further works. The 2,500 objects in the Herbert Bayer Collection and Archive, covering Bayer's career from the Bauhaus to his final years as a designer for Atlantic Richfield, draws scholars from all over the world.

While Herbert Bayer and Walter Paepcke were turning Aspen into a cultural magnet, Frances Senska (1914–   ), a young ceramics instructor at Montana State College in Bozeman, brought European aesthetic and pedagogical ideas to Big Sky Country. Senska had received her training in fine arts at the University of Iowa, but it was not until World War II, during her navy service, that Senska took her first pottery course, studying with Edith Heath at the California Labor School. In the summer of 1946, just before coming to Bozeman, she took a second pottery course, this time from Finnish potter Maija Grotell at Michigan's Cranbrook Academy of Art. Grotell believed that each potter should find his or her own approach, and she hesitated to critique her students' work, instead encouraging them to search and inquire.

Another European émigré profoundly affected Senska's thinking about design and pedagogy. He was Laszlo Moholy-Nagy, Paepcke's collaborator at the Chicago Institute of Design. Vehemently opposed to specialization (which he felt isolated people and deadened the

Aspen, Rocky Mountain Art Town

Fueled by Walter Paepcke's vision, the ski town of Aspen has grown into a vibrant cultural center and, more particularly, a hotbed for the visual arts. Home to the Aspen Art Museum, one of the finest small museums in the nation, Aspen also boasts a sophisticated array of commercial galleries that feature works by such contemporary art stars as Louise Bourgeois, James Turrell, Dale Chihuly, Peter Halley, Louise Nevelson, and Ross Bleckner. One gallery, bucking the modernist trend, features works by George Catlin, Albert Bierstadt, and other classic Rocky Mountain artists.

In 2001, when *Art & Antiques* listed the 100 top art collectors in America, they discovered that the only major collectors from the Rockies resided in Colorado. Of those 7, 5 maintained homes in Aspen, with another close by in Vail.

During the 1960s, for five memorable summers, publisher and collector John Powers ran the Aspen Center for Contemporary Art. He lured to Aspen such celebrated artists as Roy Lichtenstein, Claes Oldenburg, James Rosenquist, and Robert Rauschenberg, and in 1971, he commissioned Bulgarian artist Christo to span Rifle Gap with his *Valley Curtain*, a 1,300-foot drape made of orange nylon. Anderson Ranch Arts Center continues in Powers' tradition, drawing aspiring and established artists to Snowmass Village, ten miles west of Aspen.

Aspen isn't the only Rocky Mountain art town. Loveland, Colorado, for example, celebrates the art of bronze sculpture with public art throughout the town and is home to more than eighty sculptors. Helena, Montana, the site of the Archie Bray Foundation for the Ceramic Arts, crawls with potters and ceramic sculptors. Other ski towns, including Vail, Telluride, Jackson Hole, Park City, and Sun Valley–Ketchum, boast active gallery scenes and wealthy collectors. Resort communities like Livingston and Bozeman, Montana, Sandpoint and Coeur d'Alene, Idaho, and Cody, Wyoming, also welcome visitors with diverse visual arts offerings.

emotions), Moholy-Nagy sought to produce "many-sided amateurs with their own ideas and practical skills." The Bauhaus master also believed in granting students the freedom to fully explore their ideas, never telling them something could not be done. Studying with Moholy-Nagy only briefly, Senska embraced his pedagogical approach and aimed to apply it to her own students.[14]

Senska was fortunate in her first students after the war, especially two young veterans even more talented and focused than the rest. The two were Montanans Peter Voulkos (1924–2002) and Rudy Autio (1926–   ), soon to become among America's most revolutionary and celebrated ceramic sculptors. Together with Senska's emphasis on self-direction, artistic freedom, and broad artistic education, Voulkos and Autio—the sons of Greek and Finnish immigrants, respectively—benefited from the inauguration of another important Rocky Mountain arts institution. In 1949, industrialist Archie Bray invited the two young artists to work in his Helena, Montana, brickyard, where they would have plenty of clay to make their pots and ceramic sculpture. In 1951, Bray incorporated the Archie Bray Foundation for the Ceramic Arts, creating a place to work for ceramic artists from all over the world. Another event soon reinforced certain qualities—internationalism and elevation of ceramics to the status of a fine art—of an emerging Rocky Mountain ceramic tradition.

In December 1952, three legendary figures arrived in Helena to conduct a workshop. The men were Bernard Leach (1887–1979), the British potter and writer who ardently championed the notion of the artist-potter; Shoji Hamada (1894–1978), reputed to be Japan's leading potter; and Soetsu Yanagi, director of the Museum of Folk-craft in Tokyo. Those who attended the workshop (among them Senska, Voulkos, and Autio) came from as far away as Grand Junction, Colorado. While Leach irritated the attendees with his disdain for the American absence of a ceramic taproot, Yanagi's philosophical approach struck a chord. As Autio recalled, Yanagi spoke of "Zen and the art of gutsiness and of letting things happen. . . . And simplicity, economy, no fussing."[15] More than anything, though, it was the living example of Shoji Hamada that most affected and influenced the young ceramists. They responded immediately to the spontaneity Hamada embodied, to the freedom of the master potter's forms and the deftness of his clay handling.

No longer satisfied with making well-crafted pots, Autio and Voulkos sought their own freedom to experiment. For Voulkos, this impulse was reinforced in 1953 when he was invited to teach ceramics at North Carolina's Black Mountain College, a hotbed of the American avant-garde (and until 1949 led by another Bauhaus master, Josef Albers). At Black Mountain, Voulkos encountered dancer/choreographer Merce Cunningham, composers John Cage and David Tudor, abstract painters Jack Tworkov and Esteban Vicente, and fellow western potter M. C. Richards (she hailed from Weiser, Idaho). These young American avant-gardists inspired Voulkos with their inventiveness and expressive looseness.

A visit to New York City—which included his first time in a museum—introduced Voulkos further to Abstract Expressionism (Ab Ex); he met Willem de Kooning, Franz Kline, and other Ab Ex painters at the Cedar Bar. When he returned to Montana, Voulkos was energized, and both he and Autio began in earnest to create work in the Abstract Expressionist idiom (arguably the first in ceramic history). Ironically yet another encounter with a Bauhaus alumnus would cement the young lions' determination to transform ceramic art. At a 1954 workshop at the Archie Bray Foundation, Voulkos and Autio found Marguerite Wildenhain, a famous potter trained at the Weimar Bauhaus, arrogant and authoritarian, and her rigidity only egged them on in their drive to experiment.

Later in 1954, Voulkos, already one of the most highly regarded young American potters, received an offer to head up the new ceramics program at the Los Angeles (L.A.) County Art Institute. Once there, Voulkos proceeded on the path he'd begun in Montana. He ran his program, in the words of Rose Slivka, "in his usual style, as a free-wheeling place where energies and enthusiasms were high."[16] In L.A. and later at the University of California at Berkeley, Voulkos would generate the ceramic equivalent of the New York School of painting, becoming the most celebrated American ceramic sculptor (as early as 1960, he had a solo show at the Museum of Modern Art) and, by example and through his emphasis on total artistic freedom, influencing many others. His students included Paul Soldner, John Mason, Michael Frimkess, Henry Takemoto, and Stephen De Staebler. With immense energy and consummate skill, Voulkos ripped, pierced, slashed, and perforated clay to create ceramic works—monumental plates, vessels, and "stacks"—that rival sculpture in any other medium. Voulkos died in 2002. In 1957, Rudy Autio also left the foundation, beginning a distinguished career at the University of Montana at Missoula, where he, too, would influence generations of ceramic artists. Autio, sometimes called the Matisse of ceramics, creates slab-built forms decorated with vertiginous women and cavorting horses; these brightly colored works are objects of pure pleasure.

In 2001, the residency program at the Archie Bray Foundation celebrated its first fifty years and an ongoing tradition of Rocky Mountain ceramic modernism, which emphasizes influences from all ceramic traditions (begun by Leach, Hamada, and Yanagi), openness to a multitude of aesthetic approaches (from the beginning, Archie Bray encouraged both pottery and sculpture, though he was puzzled by those first Abstract Expressionist pots), and an assumption that ceramics is a fine art (not simply a craft). At this writing, an exhibition of works from the Archie Bray Foundation's permanent collection, *A Ceramic Continuum: Fifty Years of the Archie Bray Influence*, is touring nationally.

Almost all of the region's universities are home to graduate programs in ceramics, and the Nora Eccles Harrison Museum of Art at Utah State University holds 1,200 ceramic works, making it the largest repository in the region of modern and contemporary American ceramics. In 1966, one of Voulkos' first students in Los Angeles, master ceramist Paul Soldner, settled at Snowmass Village, near Aspen, where he started Anderson Ranch Arts Center, yet another outpost of the Rocky Mountain modernist ceramic tradition. In addition to workshops in ceramics, Anderson Ranch offers courses taught by leading artists in painting, printmaking, sculpture, photography, furniture-making, and digital imaging; it also hosts established artists for several-month residencies. For many years, Betty Woodman, another American ceramic legend, made her home in Boulder, Colorado. In good Rocky Mountain fashion, her brightly colored vessels incorporate Chinese and Italian influences; she now lives in New York and Italy.

At mid-twentieth century, many modernist artists—like Frances Senska and Rudy Autio in Montana—settled into teaching jobs at (or other affiliations with) Rocky Mountain universities. One of the earliest, and most influential, was Vance Kirkland (1904–1981), who founded the School of Art at the University of Denver

Faith and Charity in Hope: Edward and Nancy Reddin Kienholz

In the tiny northern Idaho town of Hope (next door is Beyond Hope), two of the Rocky Mountain region's most accomplished modernists staked their claim. Like Peter Voulkos a towering figure in postwar American art, Edward Kienholz, born and raised on the Washington-Idaho border, left the Northwest in the early 1950s for Los Angeles, where he sought to establish himself as an artist (without any formal training). Faced with utter indifference from the reigning galleries, the self-confident Kienholz started his own Ferus Gallery. A founder of the California Assemblage movement, Kienholz produced disturbing and controversial works assembled from the detritus of society: dolls' heads, cast-off furniture, abandoned bridal gowns, limbs from mannequins. His socially conscious works grew more and more harsh and complex, evolving into multiple-figure tableaux that had searing things to say about racism, war, American popular culture, and the art world.

With works like *Five Car Stud* (1969–1972), *The State Hospital* (1968), and *Portable War Memorial* (1968), Kienholz's fame grew, especially in Europe, and he took to spending half the year in Berlin. In 1972, he met Nancy Reddin, and they soon married. By 1973, the newlyweds had settled, for at least part of the year, in Idaho. There they became collaborators on a series of works called *The Kienholz Women* and thereafter jointly signed all of the work.

The Kienholzes opened the Faith and Charity in Hope Gallery at their Idaho studio, contributing to local culture by mounting shows of leading modern and contemporary artists, including Peter Voulkos and Alberto Giacometti. In 1994, Kienholz died of a heart attack while hiking in the Idaho mountains. He was buried in his last work of art, a 1940 Packard, laden with his corpse, a bottle of 1931 Chianti, and the ashes of his dog Smash, in a giant hole at his Idaho hunting cabin. Nancy still divides her time between Germany and Hope.

in 1929. Always restless, Kirkland moved from style to style, taking on De-signed Realism, Hard-edge Abstraction, Surrealism, and Abstract Expressionism in turn. His dot paintings, which he called Energy in Space Abstractions, are considered his most distinctive work. As a pioneering modernist, Kirkland is much honored in Colorado. The Vance Kirkland Museum and Foundation, located in Kirkland's Denver studio, is dedicated to the appreciation and preservation of his work. Another remarkable Colorado modernist was Eve Drewelowe, the first woman to receive a Master of Fine Arts from the University of Iowa. Married to political scientist Jacob von Ek, who later became dean at the University of Colorado, Drewelowe was fiercely independent. Her energetic and wildly colored Rocky Mountain landscapes often express a concern over degradation of the natural world.

Robert DeWeese, together with his painter wife Gennie, joined Frances Senska and printmaker Jessie Wilber at Montana State College (today Montana State University) in 1949. DeWeese introduced his students to the whole range of postwar art, from Abstract Expressionism to Pop Art to a return to figurative painting. His enthusiasms were infectious, but it was his and Gennie's unwavering interest in, and support of, younger artists that made the difference. They opened their home to students and fellow artists, and despite Montanans' indifference to modern art, both painters proved remarkably prolific. In Bob DeWeese's recollection, "If we were a minority, we didn't act like it."[17] At the University of Montana, beloved teacher Walter Hook applied Surrealist technique to Rocky Mountain subject matter, juxtaposing bison with kites or arrays of eggs.

Printmaker Arnold Westerlund, sculptor George Roberts, and painter Mary Kirkwood introduced University of Idaho students to modernist techniques and notions while producing distinguished work of their own. V. Douglas Snow, who studied at the Cranbrook Academy of Art and in Rome, brought his own brand of Abstract Expressionist landscape painting to the University of Utah, where he served as chair of the art department from 1966 to 1971.

ROCKY MOUNTAIN MODERN OR WESTERN MYTH?
BLURRING THE BOUNDARIES

It would be a mistake to make too much of the fact that one of America's great modernists was born in Cody, Wyoming. After all, Abstract Expressionist Jackson Pollock left Wyoming as a boy and never spent much time in the Rockies. But at mid-twentieth century, Pollock's spirit and energy did have a powerful effect on artists in the Rockies (as they did elsewhere in a nation eager to break with old models). The stories of two Rocky Mountain artists who took dramatically different paths in their careers (but both with strong ties to Abstract Expressionism) underscore the contradictions and rich ironies in the region's artistic life.

Bill Stockton grew up in central Montana, on his family's sheep ranch. Early interested in art, Stockton parlayed the G.I. Bill into study at the Minneapolis Art Institute and the École de la Grande Chaumiere of Paris. During his travels, he encountered Pollock's work, but it was not until he returned to the family ranch near Grass Range—with his French bride Elvia—that he developed a personal style. There, in the "bleak, winter landscape" of Montana, he found "inspiration for countless Avant Garde paintings."[18]

Where Fra Dana had found no nuances, Stockton saw infinite nuance. His calligraphic Abstract Expressionist works, which he called microlandscapes, are powerful evocations of a place he clearly understood and cherished. While he returned to representation, Stockton retained a modernist stance and a passion for swiftly rendered landscape. Evolving into Montana's acknowledged modernist master, Stockton experimented with sculpture, even created felt garments, but always returned to painting, using watercolors, ink, pastels, wax, and cattle markers to fashion extraordinary meditations on prairie, brush, and his favorite hill (which he dubbed the Chinese Mountain). Always working as a rancher, Stockton wrote and illustrated the classic *Today I Baled Some Hay to Feed the Sheep the Coyotes Eat* (1982). He was never sure, he said, if he was an artist who ranches or a rancher who "arts." Because he stuck close to home, Stockton received little recognition. In his last years, though, the Yellowstone Art Museum in Billings, with the assistance of patron Miriam Sample, purchased more than seventy of Stockton's paintings for the museum's Montana Collection. Stockton received the Montana Governor's Art Award just before his death in 2003.

Harry Jackson (1924–), born Harry Shapiro on Chicago's South Side, ran away to a Wyoming ranch at age fourteen. Like the young Charlie Russell, he fell in love with the cowboy life. But before becoming an acknowledged master of western realism, he took a side trip into Abstract Expressionism. Upon his return to Chicago, Jackson studied at the Art Institute of Chicago and then moved, following service in World War II, to New York, where he sought out his idol Jackson Pollock. The two painters became fast friends, and Harry Jackson adopted Abstract Expressionism, revealing considerable talent. He married fellow abstractionist Grace Hartigan and studied with Hans Hofmann, teacher of modernists.

Hartigan and Jackson divorced, and after moving to Europe in the late 1950s, Jackson began his turn to realism—and specifically to western subject matter. He spent several years in Italy, where he developed his skills as a sculptor. In 1958, collector Robert Coe commissioned Jackson to paint a pair of powerful mural-sized works, *The Stampede* and *Range Burial*, which Coe then donated to the Whitney Gallery of Western Art at the Buffalo Bill Historical Center. By 1966, Jackson had produced a body of work sufficient for a one-man show at the National Cowboy Hall of Fame in Oklahoma City. In 1970, he returned to Wyoming, settling in Cody. Unwilling to be categorized, Jackson sees himself simply as an artist. Critic Gene Thornton notes that, despite Jackson's mythic subject matter, his western works possess a "melancholy realism that is wholly of our time" as well as a keen awareness, clearly drawn from Abstract Expressionism, of the "formal values of art."[19]

Stockton and Jackson constitute two contrary poles of art in the Rocky Mountains, both powerful, complex, and persuasive voices of the region. Perhaps as Harry Jackson said of "simple luminous right and heartless evil wrong" during his seventy-fifth birthday celebration at the Buffalo Bill Historical Center in 1999, "Each and every one of us, with no exception, is an inextricable meld of both of these extremes."[20]

FOLK ARTS OF THE ROCKY MOUNTAINS

While the modernists and the western artists shoot it out, many Rocky Mountain citizens are happily engaged in creating folk or traditional arts. Some of these relate to tribal traditions (see "Native American Arts" above), while others have emerged out of regional occupations like cowboying or logging. Still others have their roots in age-old European or Asian ethnic traditions. And then there are the Rocky Mountain outsider artists, whose visionary works transcend all boundaries.

Just as it has in the fine arts, ranching in the Rockies has spawned a number of traditional crafts related specifically to the work of the cowboy. In nearly all of the states in the region, artisans make beautifully hand-tooled and hand-built saddles and boots. Saddle making, in particular, is a craft kept alive through apprenticeships, both informal and funded by state arts agencies. The western stock saddle is a complex artifact, and an apprenticeship can take several years, during which the aspiring saddle maker learns at the side of the master, often through making repairs of existing saddles and then graduating to crafting simple undecorated saddles, before taking on a fully tooled saddle. The true art of the saddle is in the tooling of the leather, and every master saddle maker has his own distinctive designs, often drawn from cowboying's earliest roots, the Moorish, Spanish, and Mexican cultures and including floral, geometric, or pictorial designs. Custom bootmakers continue to practice their craft throughout the Rockies. Again, hand tooling is important to the look of a custom boot, but equally, and perhaps more, important is the perfection of the fit and the absence of nails (many custom boots are held together with beeswax-covered pegs, giving them a much longer life than mass-produced boots). Other cowboy arts include the braiding of rawhide to create lariats, reins, hobbles, and quirts. Tightly braided rawhide with its clean lines makes for objects of elegant utility. Although handmade saddles, boots, and tack are expensive, they are still used by working men and women who prize durability and distinctiveness in their gear.

Western life also generated a need for furniture, especially in the early days when it was costly to ship chairs, tables, and beds from the coasts. In Utah, for example, this resulted in local craftsman creating furniture modeled on designs popular back East in the first half of the nineteenth century. These handsome works, however, were most often constructed of locally available woods—cedar, pine, box elder, aspen, and cottonwood—rather than the hardwoods usual elsewhere. This use of local materials sometimes resulted in pieces of furniture that were truly western in design. Especially unique were chairs crafted from elk or deer antlers, cow or bison horns, or branches and twigs; also popular were chairs carved from tree stumps or burls. While this improvised furniture functioned well, it also called up images of a Wild West that proved irresistible to collectors.

Arising out of this folk tradition came one of the most successful fusions of Rocky Mountain design and commerce. In 1931, Thomas Molesworth founded his Shoshone Furniture Company in Cody, Wyoming. With its roots in rustic Adirondack style and the simplified forms of Arts and Craft furniture, Moleworth's furniture, which he often designed for wealthy collectors with retreats in Wyoming, was evocative of life on the range. Romanticized like much western painting, the furniture combined rusticity with high style. Its exaggerated forms—taking advantage of flaws in nature: burls, twisted logs—and local materials corresponded to urban dreams of laid-back Rocky Mountain grandeur.

After a large commission for publisher Moses Annenberg for his Wyoming lodge, Molesworth found his furniture, with its massive logs and leather cushions, much in demand. He decorated hotel lobbies throughout the West, and for a time, Abercrombie and Fitch sold his furniture line throughout the world. In the years since Molesworth's death in 1977, scores of Rocky Mountain craftsmen have emulated the style he pioneered, and the annual Western Design Conference in Cody—inspired in part by Molesworth's success—always showcases the latest Rocky Mountain furniture designs, from handmade lodgepole couches to finely crafted cabinets sporting elk-antler door handles.

The young Mormon culture in Utah and surrounding states produced a remarkable array of folk symbols that conveyed the values of the faith. The all-seeing eye symbolized God's constant interest and concern, and in nineteenth-century Utah, the all-seeing eye appeared everywhere, on buildings and in publications. Another image, the beehive—official symbol of the kingdom of Deseret—was even more pervasive. Enthusiastically adopted by Mormon parishioners as an emblem of hard work, cooperation, and determination, the beehive appeared, and continues to appear, in many contexts: in business names and as decoration in masonry walls, on rings and gravestones, on Utah Highway Patrol cars, and in stained-glass windows. The various ethnicities that adopted Mormonism also incorporated Mormon imagery into their native art forms. For example, Indonesian converts create batiks depicting biblical scenes, Syrian Mormons weave carpets portraying elders of the church, and Tongan converts produce bark tapa cloths displaying images of Temple Square and Eagle Gate.

Fiber arts, especially quilting, weaving, and embroidery, flourish throughout the Rockies. Quilting is an especially beloved expression that crosses all cultural boundaries. Some claim that, in Utah, quilting is the art form practiced by more of the state's citizens than any other. While this love of quilting has its roots in pioneer traditions, when quilts were needed for warmth and worn work clothes were the materials most readily at hand, the tradition is vitally alive today, perhaps because, as folklorist Carol Edison writes, it provides "opportunity for individual creativity, the camaraderie of the quilting circle, the challenge of crafting beauty from scraps."[21] In some isolated areas in Montana and elsewhere, quilting bees were the sole community gathering during long winters.

While, as mentioned above, many American Indians keep beadwork and other traditions alive, a new tradition has emerged out of contact with Euro-American culture. This tradition is that of the star quilt, which is particularly powerful among Assiniboine and Sioux women on Montana's Fort Peck Reservation, although it has become a pan-Indian art form. At the turn of the twentieth century, Presbyterian missionaries set up quilting circles on various reservations, and the local women took to this new craft, quickly making it their own. They preferred fan quilting, which resulted in circular designs; the Sacred Circle is a key image in Plains Indian symbology. The gorgeous contemporary star quilt patterns echo an older tradition, that of diamond or starburst patterns painted on bison robes, and star quilts play an important role in giveaways, Northern Plains rituals honoring individuals with gifts during powwows, basketball games, and other community gatherings.

Every state in the Rockies has a state quilt guild, and many communities support their own guilds, often hosted by churches. The Utah Quilt Guild sponsors workshops, lectures, and displays to encourage the art of traditional quilting, and it offers classes on a variety of techniques, including hand piecing, appliqué, strip piecing, and rotary cutting. Situated in Golden, Colorado, the Rocky Mountain Quilt Museum collects quilts of all sorts, from pioneer efforts to those on the cutting edge. The museum's exhibits can range from quilts honoring jazz musicians or the victims of September 11, 2001, to quilts that address the emotions around breast cancer.

Embroidery, lacemaking, and needlepoint are other popular fiber arts in the Rockies, often reflecting the ethnic origins of the embroiderers. In Montana, for example, Hmong embroiderers in the Bitterroot Valley and Missoula produce embroidered "flower cloth," featuring complex and colorful geometric designs. New to the Hmong since their flight from Laos in 1976 are "story cloths," narratives told in embroidery about important events in the makers' lives. In Colorado, Latino women create *colcha* embroidery, which originally decorated bedspreads but now adds beauty to skirts and other garments. *Colcha* patterns are often narrative, telling stories about daily life, addressing historical and regional themes, or depicting flowers and animals. Mormon women in Idaho, often of Danish descent, have appropriated the Norwegian Hardanger embroidery and lacemaking traditions, among the most technically challenging in any culture. Greek Idahoans also keep their culture's needlework traditions alive, sometimes improvising with patterns from other cultures.

Weaving is, along with quilting, the most pervasive fiber art practiced in the Rockies. Like quilters, Rocky Mountain weavers are well organized, with weavers guilds, as they like to say in Colorado, "Interlaced/Interwoven/Interlocked" throughout the five states. This rich weaving culture can be traced to the efforts of one remarkable Rocky Mountain woman. In 1914, Mary Meigs Atwater moved to the tiny mining town of Basin, Montana, where her husband, a mining engineer, established a plant to recover zinc from mine tailings. Atwater, who had been educated at the Art Institute of Chicago and in Paris, loved the high mountains, having already lived in Telluride, Colorado. To her, Basin, "so full of sunlight and pure air and so empty of humans," was "one of the most livable spots in the world."[22]

At the same time, in this quiet place, Atwater wanted to apply her considerable energy and intellect to some artistic effort. In 1916, she began to study handweaving, and as an early feminist, she saw in weaving an opportunity to provide work for other women in the community. She bought looms and launched the Shuttle-Craft Guild and Weaving Shop, bringing a weaving instructor to Basin to teach her neighbors the art. Atwater had worked as a designer for a wrought-iron factory while in Chicago, and her design skills proved useful as she realized that few patterns existed for handweavers. She traveled to textile collections and libraries in Pennsylvania and New York, where she was able to reconstruct patterns for such lost designs as the summer-and-winter weave, the double weave, the double-face twill weave, and simple damask weaving as practiced in colonial times. Soon she was marketing blueprints of these and other unavailable designs.

After World War I, when she served as a pioneer in the use of handicrafts as occupational therapy for recuperating troops, and following the death of her husband in 1919, Atwater moved to Cambridge, Massachusetts, to further develop her weaving business. She began publishing *The Shuttle-Craft Guild Bulletin*, which quickly became the primary periodical for American handweavers. In 1928, she published the first edition of the *Shuttle-Craft Book of American Handweaving*, and homesick for the West, she returned to Basin, where she and her son started a beaver ranch. While beaver ranching proved a bust, she continued her weaving business, offering a correspondence course and, in 1937, convening a weaving institute at Palmer Lake, Colorado. She would continue to teach at conferences and institutes, including ones she sponsored at her son's dude ranch near Glacier National Park. Travels to Guatemala brought her new designs, which she duly published. In 1946, her health failing, she moved to Salt Lake City, where she was welcomed by the local weaving guild (which now bears her name). She died in 1956. From her vantage point high in the Rockies, Atwater made a difference, leading the charge to revitalize handweaving in the United States. Today, the Montana Artists Refuge keeps Atwater's spirit alive in Basin.

Outsider artists may be the only truly original creators, and those in the Rockies are no exception. For a variety of reasons, these idiosyncratic individuals pursue their personal visions with single-minded passion, and the results are often astonishing. James Castle, born in Garden Valley, Idaho, in 1900, is the most famous Rocky Mountain outsider. Profoundly deaf and autistic, Castle did not communicate by the usual means, only learning to write his name in his fifties. Instead he drew constantly. He drew on every surface available, and rather than use pens or pencils, he fashioned his own implements out of twigs, dipping them into pigments he concocted from saliva and stove soot. He hung his drawings, which often offered multiple perspectives on familiar scenes, in his workroom, and then included images of these drawings in his next drawings. Besides drawings, he produced three-dimensional constructions, sometimes of animals, as well as coats and shirts (packaged as if to be sold in his family's store) and, most powerfully, imaginary companions constructed of cardboard (these friends often appeared in his drawings). Castle also produced remarkable books, including his *Large Primer*, a 180-page work featuring 300 of Castle's illustrations that, in Tom Trusky's words, "seemingly catalogue all the items in the artist's world."[23]

In Roundup, Montana, cowboy twins Lee and Dee Steen created a similarly detailed imaginary world. The brothers elaborated on their property a maze of expressive and often humorous totemlike figures (constructed out of cottonwood limbs and applied elements like bottle caps, belts, and buttons), cages (populated with pheasants, deer, and a badger), and constructions made of automobile parts. This manipulated environment, which at first glance resembled a junkyard, soon enticed passersby with its wonderfully inventive figures and the sheer obsessiveness with which it was assembled. Lee Steen, the last surviving brother, died in 1975. Many of the Steens' figures, luckily preserved when the property was sold, are now held by the Paris Gibson Square Museum of Art in Great Falls, Montana.

Other remarkable outsider artists in the Rockies include Mormon mason Thomas Child and sculptor Maurice Brooks, who created Gilgal Garden in Salt Lake City. In this tribute to Mormonism, visitors will find a two-ton sphinx carved with the face of Joseph Smith, founder of the Mormon Church; a giant Mormon cricket; and Bible verses carved into the granite steppingstones. In southern Colorado, at 9,000 feet, Jim Bishop has created his own castle, surrounded on three sides by the San Isabel National Forest. What began as a cabin has morphed into what Bishop claims is the world's largest one-man project, an elaborate stone- and ironwork castle with 160-foot towers. Entirely improvisatory, the castle—still an empty shell—just keeps growing.

THE DIVERSE PRESENT: A DISTINCTIVE REGIONAL ART?

At the start of the twenty-first century, the visual arts in the Rocky Mountains are truly pluralistic, offering something for every art lover. Western art still reigns supreme. Some of the region's largest museums, like the Buffalo Bill Historical Center and the C. M. Russell Museum, are devoted to its preservation and exhibition. Events like the annual Western Rendezvous of Art and countless galleries ensure that the works of contemporary western artists receive their due. And from a purely financial perspective, western art has never been healthier. In 1996, Idaho's Coeur d'Alene Art Auction (which has since moved to Reno) garnered $8.2 million in sales; in 2001, the auction brought $14 million. The Buffalo Bill Art Show and Sale, the C. M. Russell Art Auction in Montana, and Denver's Coors Western Art Exhibit and Sale afford collectors other opportunities to acquire classic and contemporary western paintings and sculpture.

Contemporary art in the modernist mode also thrives in the region, though outside of the largest cities and college towns there are relatively few galleries. Still many of the region's finest museums are devoted to contemporary art, including the Yellowstone Art Museum in Billings, the Boise Art Museum, the Nicolaysen in Casper, and the Boulder Museum of Contemporary Art. Even a small town like Montana's Chester (population 2,295) has its contemporary art center. Every college and university worth its salt has an art department and often offers a master's in fine art. Every state in the region, where life is often less expensive than on the coasts, hosts a multitude of productive contemporary artists creating a dizzying array of work. Fine crafts—jewelry, ceramics, fiber art, and glass—are available widely, at craft fairs and in galleries.

The Denver Art Museum, without doubt the most powerful visual arts institution in the Rockies, is expanding yet again. Its 146,000-square-foot new building, augmenting the existing 210,000-square-foot structure, is under construction at this writing. It will be completed in 2006. The National Museum of Wildlife Art in Jackson Hole honors the region's tradition of painting and sculpting animal life, and beneath all the hoopla the region's most characteristic art, landscape painting and photography, continues to draw admirers everywhere.

Given all this diversity, is there any art of the region that can be said to truly speak to the place itself in new and important ways? Certainly landscape and wildlife art address issues of place, often directly and with considerable beauty. Traditional Native American arts are profoundly rooted in the place. Western painting and sculpture continue to convey myths about the region, telling stories and awakening powerful emotions. But two contemporary aesthetic approaches may be most truly *of* the region, offering fresh perspectives on locale in deep and resonant ways. These are Environmental Art, defined broadly, and contemporary work produced by Native American artists.

Environmental Art can take a variety of forms, from Robert Smithson's powerful and intrusive *Spiral Jetty* to minimalist paintings that meditate on the life cycles of plants to photographs that depict not sublimity but the disruption of landscape. When Smithson created his giant jetty in 1970, he intended not just to use earth and water as raw materials, but to perfectly match his construction to its site, generating a kind of dynamic harmony. Other Environmental artists reveal strains of this turn toward a more respectful relationship with locale. Anne Appleby, a painter who makes her home near Jefferson City, Montana, generates reductive paintings that, upon first glance, appear to be monochromatic Color Field works that refer to nothing other than the history of painting and the effects of light. But Appleby is up to something else altogether. Before receiving her M.F.A. from the San Francisco Art Institute, she spent ten years studying with Ojibwa holy man Eddie Barbeau. When she painted a bear under Barbeau's tutelage, he told her to depict the way a bear's spirit would feel, its essence, not its outward aspect. She brought this approach to her meditations on the plants—kinnikinnick, sweet pine, aspen, willow, sage—that surround her Montana home, painting on multiple panels the sequence of a given plant's existence from new shoot to new leaf to mature leaf to seed to decaying seed to the inevitable frosting of the leaf. The effect of Appleby's paintings, with their forty layers of underpainting, is uncanny. They somehow lead the viewer to an ever-deepening appreciation for the flora of a particular place.

Colorado photographer Robert Adam can be called an Environmental artist, too, although his black-and-white images of places in Colorado, Utah, Wyoming, and other western states suggest a decidedly anti-Romantic sensibility. Adam reveals a region that has been treated harshly by man. Not for him the serene mountainscapes of Ansel Adams (1902–1984), who photographed perfect idylls in the Rockies in the 1940s and 1950s. Instead, as the title of one of his books expresses, Adam is determined to look straight at this beautiful but ravaged place and, through his graphic testimony, help "to make it home."

The Rocky Mountain region has long been home to American Indians. *Offerings from the Heart*, a recent exhibition curated by Jaune Quick-To-See Smith, the renowned Salish-Kootenai painter and printmaker, includes art by twenty-six Native American artists from many tribes. Their works, ranging from beadwork to tapestries to photographs to oil paintings to etchings to mixed-media assemblages

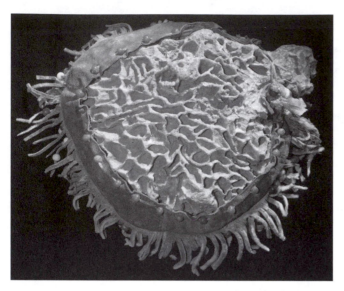

A Crow rock medicine bundle with buckskin wrapper and beads that was opened during the first sound of thunder in spring and just before the onset of winter, from Wyoming. Werner Forman/Art Resource, NY.

of resin and birch bark, tell multiple stories of North America and its original peoples. Quick-To-See Smith's own mixed-media works meditate on radical shifts in the Rocky Mountains and the broader West. These are maps that aim to trace memories or acknowledge losses, express political anger or heal the "hole in the sky." Her *State Names Map* (2001) shows only those state names that derive from Indian languages. In the artist's view, are those left blank (including Smith's native Montana) bearing illegitimate names? Or is Smith simply insisting upon the importance of Native American speech, even in this twenty-first century when the displaced, the hyperreal, and the deracinated are said to have replaced any vestige of the real? By raising difficult questions, Quick-To-See Smith and many other Native American artists of the Rocky Mountains make powerful claims for the ongoing importance of cherished places in the discourse about regional identity.

But then again, the hyperreal, mediated by digital gadgetry and distanced from any semblance of nature, may be the future of Rocky Mountain art. Matthew Barney, arguably the most famous young artist working in the United States today, grew up in Boise, Idaho. His work represents a transregional aesthetic that, at the same time, acknowledges regional differences. About personal vision but also about broader social issues, Barney's complex and idiosyncratic work, especially his series of *Cremaster* films, is almost reminiscent of outsider art, compulsively unfolding in strange and fascinating iterations, open to interpretation but ultimately mysterious.

A champion high school quarterback, Barney set a part of *Cremaster 1* (1996) (there are five films) in the Boise football stadium where he led his team to state championship glory, and in fact, some critics speculate that the stadium represents the center of the Barney universe, the still point from which he moves outward into the wider world. In *Cremaster 2* (1999), Barney returns again to the Rockies, this time to tell the story of Gary Gilmore, the Utah murderer, using elements from Mormon iconography (including beehives and swarming honeybees) as well as the vast stillness of the Bonneville Salt Flats and dancing cowboys and cowgirls. To say that Barney's films have anything to do with Rocky Mountain regional culture might seem ridiculous, but in the twenty-first century, the art of the Rockies must include, as it always has, the unexpected—whether it be the work of Matthew Barney, Fra Dana, James Castle, Mary Meigs Atwater, Herbert Bayer, or Peter Voulkos.

Luckily, no choice is necessary, between the beauty of long-held traditions like beading and saddle making and Hardanger embroidery and the new sensations that, in their turn, become cherished Rocky Mountain traditions.

RESOURCE GUIDE

Printed Sources

Cannon, Hal, ed. *Utah Folk Art: A Catalog of Material Culture.* Provo, UT: Brigham Young University Press, 1980.

Coe, Ralph T. *Lost and Found Traditions: Native American Art, 1965–1985.* Seattle: University of Washington Press; New York: American Federation of Arts, 1986.

Conn, Richard. *Native American Art in the Denver Art Museum.* Denver, CO: Denver Art Museum; Seattle: University of Washington Press, 1979.

Harris, Neil, Marlene Chambers, and Lewis Wingfield Story. *The Denver Art Museum: The First Hundred Years.* Denver, CO: Denver Art Museum, 1996.

Harthorn, Sandy, and Kathleen Bettis. *One Hundred Years of Idaho Art, 1850–1950.* Boise, ID: Boise Art Museum, 1990.

Keyser, James D., and Michael A. Klassen. *Plains Indian Rock Art.* Seattle: University of Washington Press, 2001.

McConnell, Gordon. *The Montana Collection.* Billings, MT: Yellowstone Art Museum, 1998.

McMurrin, Trudy, ed. *Utah, State of the Arts.* Ogden, UT: Meridian International, 1993.

Prown, Jules David, Nancy K. Anderson, William Cronon, Brian W. Dippie, Martha A. Sandweiss, Susan Prendergast Schoelwer, and Howard R. Lamar. *Discovered Lands, Invented Pasts: Transforming Visions of the American West.* New Haven, CT: Yale University Press, 1992.

Reber, Wally, and Paul Fees. *Interior West: The Craft & Style of Thomas Molesworth.* Cody, WY: Buffalo Bill Historical Center, 1990.

Reiter, Mary Jo, comp. *Weaving a Life: The Story of Mary Meigs Atwater.* Loveland, CO: Interweave Press, 1992.

Siporin, Steve, ed. *Folk Art of Idaho: "We Came to Where We Were Supposed to Be."* Boise: Idaho Commission on the Arts, 1984.

Swaney, Alexandra, ed. *From the Heart and Hand: Montana Folk and Traditional Arts Apprenticeships, 1992–1996.* Helena: Montana Folklife Program, 2001.

Torrence, Gaylord. *The American Indian Parfleche: A Tradition of Abstract Painting.* Seattle: University of Washington Press; Des Moines, IA: Des Moines Art Center, 1994.

Trenton, Patricia, ed. *Independent Spirits: Women Painters of the American West, 1890–1945.* Los Angeles: Autry Museum of Western Heritage; Berkeley: University of California Press, 1995.

Festivals and Conferences

Art in the Park
Boise, ID
http://www.boiseartmuseum.org/i_events_art_in_the_park.htm

C.M. Russell Auction of Original Western Art
Great Falls, MT
http://www.cmrussellartauction.com/

Cherry Creek Arts Festival
Denver, CO
http://www.cherryarts.org/asp/users/

Jackson Hole (WY) Fall Arts Festival
http://www.jacksonholechamber.com/events_fallartsfestival.htm

Utah Arts Festival
Salt Lake City
http://www.uaf.org/

Western Design Conference
Cody, WY
http://www.westerndesignconference.com/index.html

Western Rendezvous of Art
Helena, MT
http://www.westrendart.com/

Organizations

Anderson Ranch Arts Center
5263 Owl Creek Road
Snowmass Village, CO 81615
970-923-3181
info@andersonranch.org
http://www.andersonranch.org/

Archie Bray Foundation for the Ceramic Arts
2915 Country Club Avenue
Helena, MT 59602
406-443-3502
archiebray@archiebray.org
http://www.archiebray.org/

Colorado Council on the Arts
1380 Lawrence Street, Suite 1200
Denver, CO 80204
303-866-2723
coloarts@state.co.us
http://www.coloarts.state.co.us/default.asp

Idaho Commission on the Arts
2410 North Old Penitentiary Road
Boise, ID 83712
208-334-2119 or 800-278-3863
http://www2.state.id.us/arts/

Jentel Artist Residency Program
130 Lower Piney Creek Road
Banner, WY 82832
307-737-2311
jentel@jentelarts.org
http://www.jentelarts.org/

Montana Artists Refuge
P. O. Box 8
Basin, MT 59631
http://www.montanaartistsrefuge.org/

Montana Arts Council
P. O. Box 202201
Helena, MT 59620-2201
406-444-6430
mac@state.mt.us
http://www.art.state.mt.us/

Sun Valley Center for the Arts
191 5th Street East
Ketchum, ID 83340
208-726-9491
information@sunvalleycenter.org
http://www.sunvalleycenter.org/

Ucross Foundation
30 Big Red Lane
Clearmont, WY 82835
307-737-2291
ucross@wyoming.com
http://www.ucrossfoundation.org/index1.html

Utah Arts Council
617 East South Temple
Salt Lake City, Utah 84102-1177
801-236-7555
http://arts.utah.gov/index.html

Western States Arts Federation
1743 Wazee Street, Suite 300
Denver, CO 80202
888-562-7232 or 303-629-1166
http://www.westaf.org/

Wyoming Arts Council
2320 Capitol Avenue
Cheyenne, WY 82002
307-777-7742
http://wyoarts.state.wy.us/staff.html

Museums and Special Collections

Aspen Art Museum
590 North Mill Street
Aspen, CO 81611
970-925-8050
info@aspenartmuseum.org
http://www.aspenartmuseum.org/

Boise Art Museum
670 Julia Davis Drive
Boise, ID 83702
208-345-8330
http://www.boiseartmuseum.org/

Boulder Museum of Contemporary Art
1750 13th Street
Boulder, CO 80302
303-443-2122 ext. 14
http://www.bmoca.org/

Buffalo Bill Historical Center
720 Sheridan Avenue
Cody, WY 82414
307-587-4771
http://www.bbhc.org/

C.M. Russell Museum
400 13th Street North
Great Falls, MT 59401-1498
406-727-8787
http://www.cmrussell.org/

Denver Art Museum
100 West 14th Avenue Parkway
Denver, CO 80204
720-865-5000
web-mail@denverartmuseum.org
http://www.denverartmuseum.org/

Montana Historical Society Museum
225 North Roberts
Helena, MT 59620-1201
406-444-2694
http://www.his.state.mt.us/

Montana Museum of Art and Culture
Performing Arts and Radio/Television Center
University of Montana
Missoula, MT 59812
406-243-2019
http://www2.umt.edu/partv/famus/default.htm

Museo de las Américas
861 Santa Fe Drive
Denver, CO 80204
303-571-4401
http://www.museo.org/

Museum of Church History and Art
45 North West Temple Street
Salt Lake City, UT 84150-3470
801-240-4615
http://www.lds.org/churchhistory/museum/

Museum of Contemporary Art, Denver
1275 19th Street
Denver, CO 80202
303-298-7554
http://www.mcartdenver.org/#

Museum of the Plains Indian
P. O. Box 410
Browning, MT 59417
406-338-2230
http://www.doi.gov/iacb/museum/museum_plains.html

National Museum of Wildlife Art
2820 Rungius Road
Jackson Hole, WY 83001
800-313-9553 or 307-733-5771
http://www.wildlifeart.org/

Nicolaysen Art Museum and Discovery Center
400 East Collins Drive
Casper, WY 82601
307-325-5247
info@thenic.org
http://www.thenic.org/

Nora Eccles Harrison Museum of Art
Utah State University
650 North 1100 East
Logan, UT 84322-4020
435-797-0163
artmuseum@hass.usu
http://www.hass.usu.edu/%7Emuseum/

Rocky Mountain Quilt Museum
1111 Washington Avenue
Golden, CO 80401
303-277-0377
http://www.rmqm.org/

Springville Museum of Art
126 East 400 South
Springville, UT 84663
801-489-2727
http://www.shs.nebo.edu/Museum/Museum.html

Yellowstone Art Museum
401 North 27th Street
Billings, MT 59101-1290
406-256-6804
artinfo@artmuseum.org
http://yellowstone.artmuseum.org/index.html

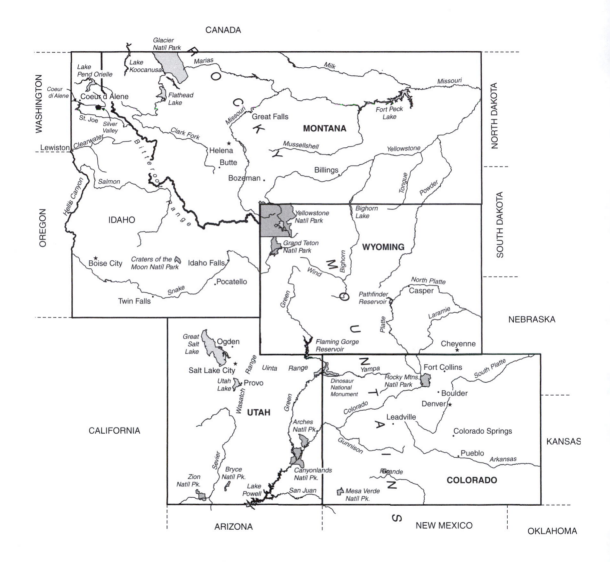

ECOLOGY AND ENVIRONMENT

Chris J. Magoc

For as long as humans have inhabited the Rocky Mountain region, they have exploited, preserved, and irrevocably altered what is at once one of the most stunningly beautiful and forbidding landscapes on the planet. After centuries of relatively modest environmental change brought by the presence of indigenous peoples, Euro-Americans, as elsewhere on the continent, dramatically reshaped and quickened the pace of environmental history. Beginning early in the nineteenth century, the forces of an industrializing civilization linked the region to a national, global economy, and consequently brought sprawling agricultural operations, bustling mining towns and cities, rising incomes, burgeoning urban populations, and other indicators of progress. The extraction of natural resources gave life to the Rocky Mountains (indeed the entire West), enriched the nation, and made possible the industrial powerhouse the United States had become by the early twentieth century. Those same instruments of modernity, however, also wrought darker ecological legacies, including befouled air and water, diminished and degraded flow of once clean and free-flowing rivers and streams, and extirpation of flora and fauna. Environmental change also wrought localized impoverishment of Native American peoples, increasingly concentrated wealth and political power, and a nonsustainable boom–bust economic cycle.

Moreover, the extractive economy that lies at the heart of the region's environmental history also defines the relationship between the American West and the eastern centers of political and economic power that has often been perceived by westerners as one of colonial subjugation. Not without merit, the idea of a powerful eastern elite lording over the land and the rugged, free-spirited people of the Rocky Mountain West has over two centuries taken on mythical proportions and defines still the general regional attitude toward the federal government. Embedded within that myth, however, as we shall see, is the truth that from the very beginning both eastern capital and the federal government have been essential, economically subsidizing forces driving the development of the West. The frontier settler has never been quite as independent as the region's mythmaking literature and political rhetoric would suggest. More than 50,000 square miles (62 percent) of land in the state of Utah, for example, is publicly owned federal property and has been the source of economic vitality in the form of tourism from the state's national parks and monuments, lower grazing fees for cattle ranchers, and federal irrigation projects. Still, rooted in the environmental history of the Rockies is the great western myth of rugged individualism—the Jeffersonian idea that here in the splendor and utter vastness of the West men would be free to wrest a living from nature, free from coercive forces of any kind. Since the late nineteenth century, the challenge to that mythology from both government regulation and corporate exploitation has provoked the central tension that courses through the environmental history of the Rocky Mountain West.

Other central themes that permeate the region's environmental story unfold here. Foremost is the large national myth of a rural and unspoiled Rocky Mountain West. Although vast stretches of remote, desolate, alternately forbidding and magnificent landscapes suggest a measure of truth in that image, in fact the Rocky Mountains are per capita the most heavily urbanized region in the nation. For well over a century western cities have developed as points of transportation for shipping resources from the region, to serve extractive industries, or as the marketplace for manufactured goods needed by rural residents. Beginning with World War II, the mushrooming size of the national security establishment gave life to still other urban centers. Beyond the cities lie vast portions of rugged wilderness that appear little different from the landscape first encountered by white men more than two centuries ago. Yet even the famed national parks, monuments, wilderness areas, and wildlife refuges that are so identified with the region bear the imprint of the culture that established them. Protected and regulated, they are monuments of an industrialized society intent on saving the last vestiges of the wild nature upon which its civilization is built.

This is a complex story with no unequivocal legacies. The taming of the Rocky Mountain region and the associated loss of ecological complexity and integrity are today celebrated by some as a clear measure of the region's prosperity and mourned by others as symptoms of a region in decline and a planet in distress. Preservation and regulation are hailed in some quarters and scorned in others. Therein lies the central political fault line of western—and American—environmental history.

ENVIRONMENTAL CHARACTERISTICS

The Rocky Mountain states embrace a stunningly wide range of alpine, desert, and forest landscapes and literally hundreds of ecosystems. Even after two centuries of significant human impact, these systems remain ecologically entwined and collectively give life to an equally rich variety of animal and vegetative life. The eastern portion of the region, encompassing nearly one-half of Colorado, the eastern one-third of Wyoming, and eastern and central Montana, constitute the western edge of America's Great Plains. Colorado's portion consists of short-grass prairie (mainly buffalo and blue grama grasses), roughly eight to twenty inches in height, compact and shallow-rooted. These are the famed "sod grasses" from which early frontier settlers constructed crude shelters. With an elevation ranging from 2,000 feet in the east to 5,000 feet in the west, the short grass prairie extends

Rocky Mountain National Park. Courtesy of the National Park Service.

into southeastern Wyoming. Precipitation here averages about ten inches annually, which comes mostly in the form of winter snow and spring rains. Temperatures fluctuate more widely here than anywhere else in the Rocky Mountain states. Since the end of the Pleistocene Age, the region's grasses and, later, invading sagebrush, cactus, and mesquite have all adapted well to short- and long-term periodic drought. This is true as well for the mixed-grass environment that dominates the northeastern quadrant of Wyoming and more than one-half of Montana. Here one finds both short and taller grasses, which can grow more than four feet.

As is true of the Great Plains region, the short and mixed-grass biomes in the eastern portion of the Rocky Mountain region were first shaped by the invasion of massive continental sheets of ice during the Pleistocene. It was then that the grasslands were shoved further and further south—so far that at one time they encompassed more acreage than any other form of vegetation on the continent; they were, Walt Whitman said, "North America's characteristic landscape." Protection of the grasslands from invading shrub and tree species was afforded not only by climate and rainfall but also by periodic human and natural fire that checked the growth of larger forest vegetation. Massive herds of deer, pronghorns (antelope), elk, and bison gorged upon the grasses, moving constantly about the region and generally keeping the grasslands from being overgrazed.

Prior to the arrival of American settlers, the grasslands biome extended more than 1 million acres, with a variety of grasses and forbs providing home to a great array of large grazing mammals, small rodents such as prairie dogs and ferrets, prairie and predatory birds, and grass and leaf-hoppers. Led by the mighty Missouri-Mississippi, the slow-moving river systems that began in the melting of mountain-top glaciers and that have coursed through the eastern prairies and more arid plains in the west have enriched the region's biological diversity. As cottonwoods and other vegetation came to line the rivers, riparian edge habitats attracted a variety of birds and smaller mammals.

Conversion of the eastern prairie and western plains to farm and ranchland, and in some areas, sprawling cities, has greatly simplified and irrevocably altered biotic life here. Although the changes were most dramatic in the tall grass prairie further east, the mixed- and short grass biomes have also been transformed. However, in part because most of the 5,000 plant species that grow in the Great Plains also exist elsewhere, the percentage of rare and endangered plant species is low (less than 3 percent in the north, as high as 15 percent in the southern portion). Similarly, because an overwhelming percentage of animals are well distributed outside the grassland biome, few faunal species are listed as rare and endangered on the plains. Only about fifteen mammal species are thought to be endemic to the prairies. Long gone, of course, are the ancient camels, horse herds, saber-toothed cats, and mammoths that roamed the plains in the Pleistocene Age. Bison and pronghorns, whose numbers once ran in the millions, have had their range and populations dramatically reduced. Grizzly bears and gray wolves that once inhabited the grasslands were driven away more than a century ago. The chief remaining mammalian predators on the plains are the red fox, the swift and common gray coyote, and the American badger.

In terms of Great Plains biodiversity, perhaps the story of greatest consequence in recent times is that of the black-tailed prairie dog. Underground prairie dog colonies once covered vast acreages (one in the 1880s was estimated at more than 2,500 square acres). Although scientists today remain unconvinced of any threats posed to cattle by the rodent, ranchers in the late nineteenth century targeted it for eradication, successfully eliminating the prairie dog from 99 percent of its historic range. Because the animal's extensive excavating work provides critical habitat and prey for a host of other species (including the critically endangered black-footed ferret), biologists have declared the prairie dog a "keystone species" in the retention of a heterogeneous, biologically diverse landscape.

To the west lies the Rocky Mountain Cordillera, a massive complex of mountain ranges extending from Alberta, Canada, to New Mexico. The broad rolling plains are abruptly met by a series of north-south-running mountains that mark the eastern boundary of the Rockies. The cordillera is often divided into two "provinces," the ranges north of South Pass, Wyoming, labeled the Canadian Rockies, and the ranges south of that corridor, the Colorado Rockies. In Wyoming, the Absoraka, Bighorn, Grand Teton, and Wind River ranges feature peaks over 13,000 feet. Separated from the main chain of Canadian Rockies to the east by the Clark Fork River, the Bitterroots run along part of the Idaho-Montana border. Central Idaho features a series of largely north-south-trending ranges with steep sides whose geologic origins are owed to an immense granite batholith (igneous rock that has melted and solidified deep in the earth) laced with veins of gold, silver, zinc, and other minerals. Utah is home to the Wasatch and Uinta ranges, the latter extending east-west and boasting many peaks between 11,000 and 13,500 feet. Many of these peaks are sharp and crisp, suggesting a relative newness (geologically speaking) of the entire region. Southern Idaho features the Craters of the

Moon National Park, where fissures in the crust of the continent allowed lava to pour out from the bowels of the earth only 2,000 years ago.

The heart of the Colorado Rocky Mountains dominates the western two-thirds of Colorado. This is the famous "top of the world," where fifty-one of the eighty peaks in North America over 14,000 feet are found. Much of the beauty here and throughout the Rockies is owed to the many steep chasms, ravines, and gorges that have been cut by ancient glaciers and the region's rivers—the Yellowstone, Colorado, Green, and Gunnison, to name but a few. Hell's Canyon of the Snake River in Idaho is the deepest river-carved canyon in the world.

Covering such a long latitudinal swath of the midcontinent and extending altitudinally from 5,000 feet to over 14,000 feet, the Rocky Mountain Cordillera offers wide fluctuations in climate and precipitation and therefore features a wide variety of biomes. The grassy meadows of lower elevations are often filled with a variety of wildflowers, with quaking aspens and scrub oaks to be found as one ascends the mountains. The subalpine forests of the Colorado Rockies feature ponderosa and limber pine, blue spruce, and white fir, while Douglas fir, Engelmann spruce, and lodgepole pine are more frequently found at the same elevations in the Canadian Rockies. The timberline in both provinces is generally well delineated, though conifers (including ancient dwarfs) reach improbably upward beyond the timberline into sheltered canyons.

West of the southern Colorado Rockies lies the broad Colorado Plateau, which stretches across 130,000 square miles of the "Four Corners" region. One of the most desolate and stunningly beautiful high desert environments on earth, the Colorado Plateau features numerous national parks such as Zion, Bryce, Canyonlands, and Arches. This remarkable landscape is in reality a large basin surrounded by mountains and mesas and littered with plateaus. Geologically speaking, it is singularly unique in the Rockies, for while the mountains themselves are the collective result of millions of years of volcanic eruption and convulsion, geologic thrusting and contorting, and glacial bulldozing, this large chunk of continental crust remained essentially intact. Great biotic contrast on the plateau results from dramatic changes in elevation: from desert shrub on the mesas of Canyonlands National Park to forests of quaking aspen and grass-forb meadows in the La Sal Mountain range, 5,000 feet higher.

Completing this land of wondrously contrasting biomes is the cold desert. There are essentially two sections of the Rocky Mountain region containing cold (or "cool") desert biome: the Great Basin and the eastern half of the Colorado Plateau. Characterized by cold and dry winters and hot, even drier summers, the main portion of cold desert is bounded on the west by the Sierra Nevada Mountains and the Colorado Rockies on the east, with the Wasatch Mountains of Utah separating the two. Precipitation is scarce throughout the year and falls mainly in the form of snow. Sagebrush, bluebunch wheatgrass, Idaho fescue grass, western juniper, and ponderosa pine dominate the lower elevations, while stunted conifers forming "pygmy forests" dot the foothills of the mountains surrounding the basin. Many species of flowering plants found nowhere else in the world permeate the Great Basin, endemically restricted by a unique combination of soil, rocky foundation, altitude, and precipitation.

The Rocky Mountains still are famously home to a rich variety of charismatic wildlife. The mountains and foothills of Glacier National Park and the Bob Marshall Wilderness Area of northwest Montana provide habitat for the largest bighorn sheep and grizzly bear populations in the nation. The Greater Yellowstone Ecosystem, encompassing Yellowstone and Grand Teton national parks, large portions of surrounding national forests, and other public and private lands, is home to the nation's largest bison herd, nearly 50,000 elk, endangered trumpeter swans, grizzly bears, and a newly reintroduced gray wolf population. The famed Yellowstone cutthroat trout, which evolved and lives only in Yellowstone Lake, has served as important prey for a host of mountain species, including ospreys, pelicans, and the endangered grizzly bear and bald eagle. The cutthroat trout itself is now in trouble, threatened by the illegal introduction of predatory (Great Lakes) lake trout into Yellowstone Lake. Further west, in the still relatively impenetrable region of National Wilderness Areas in central Idaho, live ancient cedar forests at not too great a distance from arid red rocky canyons. A great diversity of biotic life flourishes here, most notably salmon and steel head trout, which still swim from the Pacific Ocean to spawn in the stream tributaries of the Clearwater and Salmon Rivers.

EARLY INDIGENOUS SETTLEMENT AND ENVIRONMENTAL CHANGE

Human populations have been altering the environment of the American West for 28,000 years—the point in prehistoric time marking the arrival of Paleo-Indians into the region. These were the people who hunted the great mastodons and massive-sized ancient bison and contended with saber-toothed cats. They would have witnessed dramatic climate change as well as the end of massive glacial gouging and sculpting of this region.

By the late eighteenth century, the general location of indigenous tribes in the region looked like this: Utes and Apaches in the high country of the Colorado Plateau and western Colorado Rockies; Shoshone or Snake Indians in (all present-day state locations) southwestern Wyoming, northeastern Utah, and southeastern Idaho; Nez Percé in north-central Idaho; Salish (Flatheads) and Blackfeet along the rugged Montana-Idaho border; Crows in south-central Montana and northern Wyoming; on the open Great Plains there were Gros Ventre in eastern Montana, Cheyennes, Arapahos and the recently arrived Lakota (Western, Teton) Sioux in eastern Wyoming, and Arapahos, Kiowas, and Kiowa-Apaches in eastern Colorado.

Contrary to the popular myth that Indians lived in such perfectly blissful harmony with nature that they left no imprint whatsoever, all Indian tribes shaped and manipulated their environment in order to sustain themselves. As elsewhere throughout the continent, Indians in the region deliberately set fire to the vegetative landscape, here primarily to improve their hunting. Periodic Indian fire left a mosaic pattern of vegetation that did not go unnoticed by the first white explorers and travelers in the region.

A growing volume of scientific and anthropological evidence points to other strategies by which Indians altered their environment. Shoshones and Utes built rock walls in order to encircle and trap big game, or drove deer and elk into massive drifts of winter snow from which there was no escape. Throughout the northern Rocky Mountains the people employed weirs, nets, traps, and spears to catch fish. Like the Paleo-Indians who preceded them, Native Americans in the Rockies moved seasonally to take advantage of the resources available in quantity at a particular time of year, generally migrating to the mountains in the spring and summer. There, mountain meadows, streams, and their rich riparian habitats afforded a richly balanced diet of berries, nuts, roots, fish, deer, and elk.

In fall and winter, Indians generally followed the bison onto the Great Plains. The ancient tribal hunt for bison was made much easier and more efficient by the arrival of horses introduced by the Spanish. Through Indian trading and raiding, by the middle of the eighteenth century horses had made their way to virtually every Rocky Mountain people. Horses allowed Indians to move more rapidly when the herds moved, to encircle their prey more tenaciously during the hunt, and to chase down other tribes who became targets of raiding parties. The horse altered the balance of power in the West away from horticultural societies and toward nomadic hunters, resulting in the general dominance of the latter on the Great Plains. Although the degree of the bison's importance varied (it was more important to Plains Indians than those of the high country), generally the animal moved to the center of the native world following the introduction of the horse. For the Gros Ventre, Cheyenne, Lakota, Crow, Arapaho, and Kiowa peoples, the bison was all: the source of food, shelter, clothing, tools, and weapons. In addition, it held great trade value with distant tribes and whites.

It also bore enormous spiritual significance. In important ways, the sacred meanings Indians attached to the bison symbolized their larger cosmological and spiritual understanding of the natural world. Though Indians have been romanticized in the modern era as the "first ecologists," that ecological sensibility derives not (as American environmentalism does) from European romanticism, rapacious exploitation of nature, or a growing distance between society and the natural world. Rather, most native peoples saw themselves (and do) as having emerged *from* nature. They were indivisible from the natural world. Hunting was holy; the downed bison was to be revered for having given its life for the sustenance of the people. This is not to say that there were not periods of overhunting—particularly following the introduction of horses and guns into Indian culture. Indeed, growing evidence suggests that the population of bison on the southern plains suffered a fairly steep decline by the middle of the nineteenth century (in part owing to the spread of disease and competition for diminished grass)—*before* the final slaughter by white market hunters commenced. The larger story holds nonetheless: Indians generally lived in balance with bison and the larger natural world that they believed to be sacred and very much alive and the health of which very much predicated their own survival.

ANIMALS INTO COMMODITIES

The first significant chapter of environmental change in the Rocky Mountains concerns the near demise of the beaver. Because of its extraordinary ability to engineer the construction of dams on streams and rivers, the beaver provides critical riparian habitat for large numbers of a wide array of species. Unfortunately for the beaver, in the early 1800s the underside of the animal's skin also was much desired for the fashioning of felt hats, which had ruled European fashion for more than two centuries. The popularity of beaver felt hats crippled the animal's population in North America and transformed ecosystems where beaver had been important species. Although the changes were not as severe as they had been in New England, the devastation and near extinction of the beaver in a short period of time, from roughly 1810 to 1840, did alter the hydrology and biodiversity of certain locales in the Rocky Mountains.

The story begins shortly after the Lewis and Clark expedition when John Colter, who had served as a guide for the journey, went to work for Manuel Lisa, an enterprising St. Louis merchant who had organized the Missouri Fur Company. In just a few years, Colter and his trapping fraternity made Lisa a wealthy man by trapping and returning beaver pelts in great numbers. Then in the early 1820s William H. Ashley, Missouri's lieutenant governor, recruited dozens of "enterprizing [sic] young men" to go into the mountains and trap for his enterprise. Ashley's "mountain men" included many of the legendary characters of the Rocky Mountain fur trade era: Mike Fink, Hugh Glass, Jim Bridger, William and Charles Bent, and Jedediah Strong Smith. It was Smith who Indians guided through the all-important South Pass across the Rockies, in southern Wyoming, allowing American trappers to thereafter extract beaver from both sides of the continental divide.[1]

After Indians attacked Ashley's men in 1823, he devised a new method for getting the pelts to market. Avoiding the Missouri River, he sent his men directly into the mountains. From their base camps they trapped all winter long and then in midsummer converged upon a predesignated site for a "rendezvous." The mountain men would bring their mules dripping with beaver furs, while the company met them with dollars and the supplies needed for the coming year. Indians came to barter and to join in a legendary good time. The traders (though not the trappers) made themselves a handsome fortune—$85,000 worth of beaver in 1832 alone (equivalent to more than $1 million today). Two of the men ambitiously began their own enterprise aimed at the southern beaver market. After a century or more of beaver heading south to Mexico, the Bent brothers, operating from a fort on the upper Arkansas River, hired men to trap beaver from the southern Colorado Rockies and then shipped them east to St. Louis. In addition, John Astor's American Fur Company, operating from the northwest, established trading posts on the Missouri River and trapped out the northern tier of the Rocky Mountains. At the peak of the trade, more than 1,000 trappers took out who knows how many beaver from the heart of the Rocky Mountains.

It all came to an end by 1840 when two things happened: Diminishing numbers of beaver made them harder to find and the business more marginally profitable; and second, silk hats—just in time for the poor beaver—came to dominate European fashion. Suddenly ended, this mythical era in Rocky Mountain history changed the landscape. Abandoned and dried-up beaver reservoirs turned to meadow, but gone was riparian edge habitat for other species. The flow of water from beaver ponds into groundwater aquifers diminished. Beaver populations did recover somewhat by the latter part of the century (only to fall again later due to habitat destruction). More profoundly, however, the transformation of the beaver into a commodity for sale at distant markets foreshadowed larger, more widespread—and for native populations, far more devastating—environmental change in the Rocky Mountains. One harbinger: As the fur trade ended, the trappers' mountain trails became overland corridors for tens of thousands of miners and settlers to California and Oregon. South Pass would serve as the avenue for the first transcontinental railroad—the very symbol and force of industrial progress and of environmental change in the nineteenth-century American West.

Indeed, it was the railroad, combined with the need for industrial-strength leather in eastern factories, that signaled the rapid acceleration in the bison hunt. Native tribes, as noted, had long hunted for the animal. And as buffalo robes became popular in the East, demand increased and Indians were drawn into the exchange. Two factors limited the commercial buffalo hunt: The robes were most valuable when the animal's coat was thickest—in late fall. The heavy skins had to be cleaned and processed on site for transport to market. Indian women who did that work could only process about twenty robes in a winter, thereby creating a bottleneck. Approximately one-quarter of the bison killed in 1840 went to the robe market.

So it remained until after the Civil War and the arrival of the Union and Central Pacific Railroad, the first effect of which was that the animals were shot to help feed the veritable army of railroad builders constructing the line. The penetration of the railroad onto the Great Plains and into the Rockies coincided with the development in 1870 of industrial processes for tanning the hides and turning them into leather belts needed to turn industrial machinery in eastern factories. Now Indian hunters were not needed; white market hunters could take down dozens in a day. With hunters skinning the hides on the spot and industrial tanning on the other end of the rail line, Indian women similarly were eliminated from the process. And with the hide, not the robe, now the object of the hunt,

Stacked bison hides. Courtesy of the National Park Service.

hunting became year-round. It did not take many years. From 1872 to 1874, nearly 6 million bison were killed on the southern plains, wiping out the herd. The waste was appalling, as many hunters killed many more than they could skin or carry. At the peak of the slaughter perhaps one out of four dead animals actually reached market. The U.S. Cavalry, then at war with southern tribes, encouraged the slaughter as a way of hastening their demise.

The conquest of the Great Plains tribes did indeed coincide with the wholesale killing of the bison. By 1890, the year of the last violent encounter between the U.S. Army and Indians, fewer than 300 bison remained of a herd that once numbered in the tens of millions, and most of these were enclosed in a protective pen inside Yellowstone National Park; fittingly, perhaps, as the fraction of the original Indian population of the Great Plains remaining was largely contained within government reservations.

As Richard White has written, Indians, having always viewed hunting for trade value as perfectly legitimate, had readily participated in the market hunt for buffalo robes. What had been unleashed in those early years, few of them could have imagined. After the last animals from the Northern Plains herd were taken in 1883, Plains tribal leaders believed that the bison had simply gone underground because white men had killed with egregious disrespect.[2]

Supplanting bison were millions of head of Texas cattle. After the Civil War, cattlemen began driving 6 million head of cattle north from the Texas range toward stockyard towns located on the Kansas and Pacific Railroad and Atchison Topeka and Santa Fe Railroad. Mythologized in the American imagination, the era of the cowboy and the cattle drive lasted just over a decade but demonstrated the financial promise of western cattle. Slaughterhouses and railroads that controlled much of the open range aggressively worked to develop a domestic market, promoting a shift in the American diet away from pork and toward beef. Dr. Hiram Latham of the Union Pacific Railroad bullishly declared that western grasslands should be turned into forage for cattle and sheep "until every acre of grass in Colorado is eaten annually." Sensing a limitless financial opportunity, by the late 1870s men of means established vast cattle operations throughout the region. John W. Iliff, who had dreamed of striking a vein in the Pike's Peak gold rush of 1859, went bust as a miner but struck it rich feeding cattle on eastern Colorado bunchgrass prairie and selling it in western mining towns. Iliff grazed 35,000 cattle on the open, unfenced range from Julesburg to Greeley, becoming the first cattle king in the Rocky Mountain states.[3] Soon after "forage fever" akin to "gold fever" struck the region.

The shift from bison to cattle was stunningly sudden. In 1880, nearly 2 million bison and just 250,000 cattle roamed the grassy plains of central and eastern Montana. By the middle of the decade, fewer than 300 bison remained in the country, while the Montana cattle herd numbered more than half a million and was growing. Cattle populations soared in every western state: from roughly 4 million throughout the region in 1870 to nearly 40 million by 1885. The invention of barbed wire in 1874 allowed cattlemen to commandeer millions of acres of public land and fence it off from would-be homesteaders and other ranchers and to cut their labor costs. The cattle *industry* attracted big investors from the East and Europe looking to cash in. Big cattlemen also seized Indian lands, some of that activity legally sanctioned by the 1887 Dawes Act that ostensibly aimed to "civilize"

Indians as Christian farmers. The "Arkansas Division" of the XIT ("Ten in Texas") cattle corporation sprawled over 3,500 square miles of eastern Colorado.

Though vanquished tribes by then were in no position to mount serious opposition, the increasing dominance of the Rocky Mountains plains by "cattle barons" provoked severe tensions with farmers and smaller ranchers, erupting into range wars across the West, most famously the Johnson County (Wyoming) War of 1892. Western cattlemen grew enormously in their power, increasingly controlling state governments along with vast acreages of western land and access to the region's precious water resource. Violating the land laws, big cattlemen frequently filed false claims on lands to which they had no right, fraudulently seizing control of millions of acres.

The Effects of Grazing

The heavy grazing took an immediate toll on the land, an impact so severe that the cattle suffered from want of grass within the first decade. Drought struck the plains and, in 1886–1887, the worst winter in recorded history. Cattle that did not freeze to death took to eating bark from trees. Losses were devastating, as high as 90 percent in Montana. The natural limits of the plains environment had spoken.

Whether cattlemen listened is another matter. The "great die-off" of 1887 did force many from the cattle business and caused others to seriously consider the natural carrying capacity of the range. Yet the market continued to grow, and small ranchers and big cattlemen who remained continued to take advantage of free access to the grassy plains to feed the growing American appetite for beef. Although never as severe as in those first years, overgrazing of the western plains continued. Neither the establishment of the U.S. Forest Service that began in the first years of the twentieth century to regulate grazing on the new national forests nor passage of the reform-minded Taylor Grazing Act in 1934 did much to limit the temptation to put more grass-eating, cash-generating cattle on the land. On the contrary, the Forest Service, along with later the Bureau of Land Management, facilitated the increasing control of public lands by large corporate interests through the remainder of the twentieth century. At the end of the twentieth century, just 7 percent of western ranchers own 70 percent of the leases on federal grazing land.

The ecological changes in this once biologically rich "sea of grass" have been considerable. Whereas the bison's free movement about the region had allowed grazed areas to recover, fenced cattle often remained in one area too long, taking the grass down to stubble and compacting the soil, consequently increasing runoff and diminishing the capacity of the vegetation to recover. By 1990, 73 percent of public lands were being grazed by cattle or sheep, and two-thirds of those were judged to be in poor or fair condition. Scientists declared livestock grazing the number-one threat to endangered species in the West. Plants that had been important to the diets and medicinal needs of native tribes for centuries were virtually wiped out by livestock. Because cattle must stay close to water, their defecation and trampling of stream banks have damaged riparian habitats. Wetlands were drained (27 percent of Montana's original wetlands, for example, are gone). The war on western wolves commenced as soon as men began running cattle on the plains and was largely completed by the 1930s, with ripple effects through the ecosystem. For climatologists, most disturbing are the global implications: A healthy plains grassland biome produces far more vegetation than a boreal forest or even a tropical rainforest, thereby absorbing far more carbon dioxide, a leading contributor to global warming.[4]

Today, although the overall attitude of big cattlemen toward government regulation of the public domain remains wary at best—resistance remains fierce, for example, to the idea of raising grazing fees on public land to a level remotely commensurate to what ranchers pay on private land—there are signs of a more environmentally sustainable form of animal husbandry on the plains. As a way of improving their range and slumping economic fortunes, a number of small ranchers turned to the bison, returning the animal to parts of its former range. And after decades of castigating cattlemen for the destruction their herds have wrought, environmentalists have come to recognize the necessity of working with small and modestly sized ranchers in preserving open space against threats like suburban sprawl and diminished water supply.

AGRICULTURE'S EFFECTS: RAIN FOLLOWS THE PLOW

The cattle industry is not solely responsible for the condition of the plains. A regime of intensive, mechanized, and increasingly corporate agriculture that began after the Civil War has also contributed to the region's transformation. As with ranching, where control of the agricultural landscape by fewer and often distant landowners accelerated exploitation, so too did farming become an enterprise increasingly driven by geographically alien forces whose primary interest was turning natural capital into financial wealth. Although the rhetoric behind its passage promised to end monopolization of agricultural lands in the West, the Homestead Act of 1862 intensified the concentration of land and wealth in the West. The railroads alone sold more land than all that was given away to homesteaders under the law. Much of what was sold went to absentee corporate owners with no knowledge of the land or interest in its proper stewardship.

Beyond the chimerical promise of land laws, settlement of the arid plains required a shift in attitudes regarding the arid West. Part of what was popularly labeled the "Great American Desert," the plains portion of the Rocky Mountain region for decades was thought too dry to farm. Though that notion proved to be not quite true, the popular myth that supplanted it by the middle of the century was outright fiction: "Rain Follows the Plough" went the claim offered by the railroads and other western boosters. Cultivating the land would increase the humidity and consequently the level of precipitation in the region, a fantasy endorsed by some scientists. For a while it seemed true. The late 1870s and early 1880s was one of the wettest periods in the history of the plains, and farmers prospered (though those who sold them land were the real beneficiaries). But drought, as it always had, returned, and thousands went bust.

Some farmers who had turned from corn to "dryland" farming of drought-resistant strains of Russian wheat survived the lean years and in fact signaled the wave of the future: wheat—mile after golden mile of waving wheat from eastern Montana south into the plains of eastern Colorado, with wheat farms well into Idaho. In the tradition of gold and forage, the rush to wheat farming became sheer madness in the World War I era, when global demand for American wheat, along with precipitation levels, was high. Aided by larger and larger equipment, millions of acres of plains grassland were plowed under to yield big returns for wheat farmers' investments. Wheat "futures" were brighter than ever. And then, it stopped raining. The result was the Dust Bowl, one of the greatest ecological disasters in American history. Dust from the Great Plains blew all the way on to ships off the Atlantic coast. Decades of destruction of indigenous plant life and trees, compounded by the subsequent mono-cropping of wheat, exposed the soil to wind and drought and had invited this disaster.[5]

Although many of the agricultural initiatives of Franklin Roosevelt's New Deal were too little and late for many farmers, soil conservation and grazing reforms, along with federal subsidies, signaled the presence of the federal government that would only grow for the remainder of the century. Following World War II the "Green Revolution" allowed Plains farmers to produce more wheat, corn, and soybeans than ever before. But there were fewer of them doing it than ever before, as agricultural production became dominated by larger and larger corporate entities. With ever-increasing volumes of pesticides, fertilizers, and water—mined from irrigation projects hundreds of miles away and from diminishing underground aquifers—their capacity to grow ever-greater volumes of food more efficiently seemed to grow exponentially. And yet, beyond the incalculable cost of losing the family farmer as a pillar of American society, there were other costs to highly mechanized agriculture, including the fact that overproduction and overexposure of the soil have sent millions of tons of rich topsoil down the river; the average topsoil layer of the Great Plains has been reduced from twenty-one to between six and ten inches. The ultimate consequences of the latest agricultural boom are yet to be seen.

MINING

Following a familiar trajectory of individual enterprise to corporate dominance was mining. Contrary to popular myth, the era of the pick-and-shovel prospector did not last long, as corporations came to dominate western mining. Enterprising capitalists came, as they do still, to extract the valuable resources buried in this portion of earth: gold, silver, and copper most famously but also increasingly since the mid-twentieth century a host of other underground resources: molybdenum, gypsum, oil, natural gas, tungsten, lead, zinc, vermiculite, platinum, manganese, and uranium. The economic and social benefits to the region have been remarkable: Fabulous wealth accrued to the men who capitalized mining operations; generations of western miners have raised families and made good lives for themselves; ramshackle mining towns became thriving cities, regional centers of commerce and economic activity; national and global economic growth has been fueled by the mining of western precious metals and other minerals. And yet the environmental costs of this enterprise, which few considered in mining's romantic heyday, have been mounting—so much so that they now lie at the center of the increasingly polarized debate in the Rocky Mountain West over what sort of economic development will best serve the future of the region.

Soon after western mining began in the foothills of the Sierra Nevada Mountains, the enterprise moved east, into the Rocky Mountains. As in California, throughout the Rockies in places like Gold Creek, Montana, and Cherry Creek, Colorado, individual miners or groups of them arrived to "stake their claim" and dig and "pan out" all the surface (placer) gold. Generally this took just a few years, after which it became increasingly a matter of very good luck and years of perseverance in order to strike it rich. Most of the gold, silver, copper, and later other valuable minerals lay buried deep within the bowels of the earth. They would require technologies like hydraulically powered jets of water targeted at the side of a mountain in order to expose the gold-bearing ore. The environmental effects were devastating. Whole mountainsides were torn apart, with the muddy silt, rocks, and gravel flowing down mountainsides and into rivers and streams, doing damage to aquatic life and riparian habitat. One travel writer in 1881, after glowing about the wealth and rising prosperity mining seemed to have brought to western Montana, described a hydraulic operation there as a "scene of utter desolation and ruin."[6] Such were the contradictions of mechanized mining in the Rockies.

The more famous example of the mixed legacy of mining in Montana is Butte. It began as it did elsewhere: From 1863 to about 1870 prospectors mined placer gold and some silver, until the surface diggings were all gone. In 1876 Marcus Daly (1841–1900), reconnoitering the silver deposits on behalf of California "silver kings," established the first stamping mill that crushed the ore, amalgamating the silver particles with mercury. But as Daly quickly concluded, the real wealth here was less in silver than in the rich copper deposits lying beneath the silver. In the late 1870s the electrification of the nation had just commenced—a watershed development that would require endless amounts of copper. Daly saw the future. He bought up the most promising silver and copper mines in the area, built a copper smelter at Anaconda, coal mines and power plants to fuel his furnaces, and bought up (or simply commandeered) surrounding forests to supply the necessary timber. A rivalry with William A. Clark for control of the industry engulfed the region for years, as would a bitter labor struggle with his labor force. Daly effectively controlled the political machine and media of Butte and stood at the center of Montana politics and the state economy. Mining the "richest hill on earth," he became one of the richest men in America.

As Jim Robbins has written, the story of Butte and Anaconda Copper is "steeped in contradiction," embodying the history of mining in the Rockies. Butte was in its glory years, "filthy and beautiful, wealthy and dirt poor." Visitors in the 1890s saw all the expressions of individual wealth and, to an extent, community prosperity: glorious Victorian mansions, prosperous hotels, theaters, restaurants, dozens of gambling casinos, more than 200 saloons, and electric trolleys lining the streets. And yet also overwhelmingly present were the deleterious effects of this operation: "thick, pungent, acrid smoke, heavy with arsenic and sulfur from burning ore and from the smelters. . . . Streetlights had to be lit during the day, and people couldn't see across the street." Vegetation, along with human health, was severely impacted. In 1955 Anaconda ended underground mining and turned to more cost-effective open pit extraction. This continued until 1982, when the operation finally closed.[7]

Daly's enterprise, along with the labor of generations of workers, generated fabulous wealth for a few and a prosperous life for many. It helped fuel the growth of Montana and wired the nation. But the cost was high. Much of the city of Butte, Montana, is listed as a Superfund hazardous waste site, its landscape littered with the toxic waste by-products of a century of mining. Twenty-five miles west of Butte, where the Anaconda smelting operation was located, sit 185 million cubic yards of poisoned mining tailings, 27 million cubic yards of furnace slag, and 300,000 cubic yards of flue dust. The force of gravity that so effectively allowed glaciers to help sculpt the northern Rocky Mountains has also spread mining waste far beyond Butte and Anaconda. The entire watershed of the Clark's Fork River has been poisoned. Fish populations have been reduced by as much as 95 percent for a 120-mile stretch of the river.[8]

Although Butte represents one of the worst environmental legacies of mining in the Rockies, it is far from an isolated case. As with Butte, the entire 1,500-square-mile Coeur d'Alene River Basin has been contaminated with 70 million tons of oozing toxic mine waste of a century of silver, zinc, and lead mining in the Silver Valley region of northern Idaho—the largest Superfund site in the nation. In the 1980s and 1990s the Environmental Protection Agency spent more than $500 million to perform most (though not all) of the cleanup. Just as Denver's growth is owed to development of the state's gold fields, so is the Superfund site at Leadville, Colorado. More than 400,000 abandoned hard rock mining sites litter the nation, more than half of them in the Rocky Mountains. Mining has left behind 15,000 miles of polluted rivers and streams across the country—again, the majority in this region. Since the early 1980s hard rock mining has become increasingly dependent on the cyanide heap-leach method, which involves pulverizing metal-laden ore, mixing it with water to create a slurry that is then treated with cyanide and baked to draw out the gold. The mining industry is the single greatest source of environmental pollution in the Rocky Mountains.

Much of this history derives from the General Mining Law of 1872 that was signed by President Ulysses S. Grant to accelerate the development of western mineral resources. For less than $5 per acre, companies could—and still can—lay claim to mineral deposits and pay no royalties to the federal treasury on whatever they extract. Companies are responsible for the most minimal environmental cleanup of their sites. For example, developers of the 630-acre Summitville, Colorado, gold mine paid $7,000 to patent their claim. Using the cyanide heap-leach method, the operation took out more than $130 million worth of gold, but the environmental cleanup cost of the operation totals $232 million. Mining in the area adjacent to the Fort Belknap Indian Reservation in Montana has been a boon to the corporation owning the patent but a disaster for the Indians whose lands were expropriated to develop the claim and who have received no remuneration for the riches extracted and whose water supply has now been contaminated.[9] For Indians, for fiscal conservatives, and for environmentalists, the law is a disaster whose reform is long overdue.

Yet the mining industry and its many supporters in western communities and in the states continue to lobby tenaciously—and successfully—against reform. Debate over reform of the law and the challenge to raise grazing fees have become two points of tension in the debate over the future of the West. Preservers of the status quo argue that any attempt to alter these cornerstones of early western development undermines economic growth and would represent an obnoxious incursion of federal power westerners have been fighting for two centuries. Mining companies argue that the law was forged in the spirit of free enterprise, the cornerstone of American capitalism. Mining-dependent communities make the obvious point that jobs in the industry pay good wages, with benefits. Those on the other side claim that resistance to reform of both mining and grazing laws is short-sighted, slowing the inevitable movement toward a "New West" whose economy will need to be more environmentally sustainable. They point out that outdoor recreation that depends on clean and healthy watersheds sustains local businesses throughout the Rockies, whereas most of the profits of mining corporations leave the region.

LOGGING AND FOREST CONSERVATION

The environmental history of timber and logging in the Rocky Mountains states is rooted far beyond the region—in New England and the Midwest, where loggers had had their way with the forests since the beginning of European settlement. After the timber was exhausted in the Midwest at the end of the nineteenth century, timber companies turned their attention to the massive ancient forests of the Northwest—Oregon, Washington, Idaho, and western Montana. When timber baron Frederick Weyerhauser (1823–1914) began buying up hundreds of thousands of acres of land in the Northwest, the boom was on. Sawmills and logging towns pocked the landscape of northern Idaho and northwest Montana by the first decades of the twentieth century. Led by Weyerhauser, companies went aggressively after the region's conifer forests. The steam donkey engine, an "octopus of steel with several grappling arms," allowed loggers to remove larger and larger trees from the forest, but smaller trees had to be removed in order to clear the way.[10] Massive piles of vegetation from the forest understory were left on the forest floor as waste. In Utah, loggers would spend the summer burning the unwanted undergrowth of the forest, making it easier to take out the choicest tall timber during winter months. Where the moisture-trapping upper story of the forest was taken out, the forest floor was exposed to sun and wind, and the remaining litter on the forest floor became tinder for massive fires. The boom-bust cycle of mining was paralleled in timber: Once the forests were cut, the lands were largely abandoned, and soon the region was dotted with abandoned logging ghost towns.

These kinds of operations, typical of the historic national pattern of "cut-and-run" deforestation, led the first trained foresters in the United States, first Bernard Fernow and then Gifford Pinchot, to begin sounding the alarm about a possible "timber famine" if the nation did not begin to more carefully manage the resource. Heretofore, the federal government's only role in publicly owned forests was to encourage their cutting. The Timber and Stone Act of 1878 had accelerated the purchase of public lands by private individuals, ostensibly for the purpose of cutting the timber for agricultural cultivation. Farmers in the West had begun to recognize the vital importance of forests in reducing erosion and regulating the overall cycles of water flow and climate in a region.

Protection of the agricultural watersheds in the West underpinned the growing argument for timber conservation and, coupled with the growing fears of a timber shortage, led to the passage of the 1891 Forest Reserve Act that authorized the president of the United States to set aside publicly owned forests as "preserves" (later national forests) for the protection of watersheds and the long-term careful use of the timber. This was about use—a point not lost on timber magnates like Weyerhauser, who came to support the federal government's role in overseeing the development of national forests as a way of squeezing out smaller, less efficient, and less politically connected loggers, thereby consolidating their hold on the industry. Gifford Pinchot, the first head of the Division of Forestry, believed the purpose of government management forests was not to "lock up" the forests but to use them—carefully, with scientifically trained foresters overseeing their leasing to private companies in a way that would yield perpetually sustainable timber "harvests"—much as farmers harvest corn. President Benjamin Harrison established the first forest preserves in 1891 along the Wyoming borders of Yellowstone National Park (later the Bridger-Teton and Shoshone National Forests).

During his celebrated conservation-oriented administration (1901–1909), President Theodore Roosevelt added more than 100 million acres of new national forest lands to the system (an increase of 400 percent), over half of them in the Rocky Mountains. Roosevelt and Pinchot implemented policies grounded in the Progressives' conservation philosophy that forests, grasslands, and water should be scientifically managed by an independent federal government whose charge was to serve the *national, public* interest—a point contested ever since by many westerners, especially western corporate interests.

In the 1930s federal involvement in the national forests was highlighted by the presence of the Civilian Conservation Corps (CCC), which performed erosion control work and built trails, roads, and cabins. Throughout the period, up until World War II, timber in the national forests continued to be leased for logging, but at a relatively modest rate.

The direction of the Forest Service shifted dramatically with the onset of World War II and particularly with the onset of the postwar housing boom. Timber leases on the national forests soared, as the percentage of the nation's timber supply coming from Rocky Mountain forests increased. Ignoring its own previous studies, the agency threw scientifically grounded caution to the wind and intensively accelerated the cut in places like the Targhee and Coeur D'Alene National Forests in Idaho. The timber boom of the postwar era was unlike any the region had seen in decades.[11] Compared with the more time-consuming, labor-intensive selective cutting of the old days, modern logging relied on more cost-effective clear-cutting. The tools of the clear-cut—chain saws, caterpillar tractors, and logging trucks (which require logging roads)—wrought havoc on watersheds. Mile after mile of logging roads—twenty to thirty miles of logging road *per square mile* of forest in some national forests in the region—became gullies over time, washing soil down into streams and rivers. Thus in the timbering regions of the Rockies the flip side of booming logging towns and community prosperity was lost soil, degraded stream quality, diminished populations of fish and other aquatic life, and devastated habitat for creatures who depended on old-growth forests.

By the 1970s and 1980s, fierce resistance to increased clear-cutting ensued, both from environmental organizations and from increasingly important sectors of the Rocky Mountain economy—hunting, fishing, and tourism. Businesses dependent on outdoor recreation and tourism argued that they generated much broader economic vitality to the region and that these interests were being damaged with every timber sale. As with grazing fee and mining subsidies, environmentalists and fiscal conservatives complained about the financial cost in the form of massive federal subsidies provided to timber companies through the building of logging roads and below-cost timber sales. By the early 1980s the cost to taxpayers of the road-building program averaged $80 million annually. Logging communities argued that this was a small price to pay for meeting the nation's timber and paper needs and that logging was vital to the continued survival of western communities. Environmentalists pointed out the small percentage (less than 5 percent) of the nation's needs that actually came from the region's national forests and argued for new strategies that could wean logging-dependent towns from what was in truth a diminishing, exhaustible supply of valuable old-growth timber. Diversifying the economy of the Rocky Mountain region before it was too late became their rallying cry.

Increasingly destructive forest fires in the region in the 1980s and 1990s further fueled the dispute. Timbering advocates argued that the prevention of logging in some national forests through environmentalist-generated appeals to the Forest Service left the forests vulnerable to massive conflagrations. Most independent scientific studies have concluded that livestock grazing and the previous long-standing policy of the Forest Service to suppress all fire are much greater culprits than a lack of logging. Forest understories historically experienced cool burns every few years, fueled by abundant grasses and forbs. These cooler fires removed woody debris that built up on the forest floor. Moreover, grasses and forbs competed with young saplings, helping reduce the number of new trees being established in the forest. Livestock remove many of the grasses and forbs that carried these regular small, less destructive fires. Saplings that normally would be destroyed in these smaller burns or overwhelmed by the grasses and forbs between burns grow and thrive, increasing tree densities and inviting massive fires that consume whole forests. Finally, they argue, logging that extracts the choice timber accelerates the drying of the remaining forest, increasing the danger of fire.

Preservation: Yellowstone National Park

On March 1, 1872, President Ulysses S. Grant signed into law the bill creating Yellowstone National Park, the first such preserve in the United States and the world. What led to this momentous event in Rocky Mountain and U.S. environmental history was more than a growing romantic infatuation with sublime and picturesque locales in nature among the genteel classes. There was that, but given the overwhelming impulse of Americans in the second half of the nineteenth century to develop and exploit the resources of the American West, it is not surprising that the forces of industrial capitalism intrude into the story of Yellowstone's creation. The Northern Pacific Railroad, having been granted 47 million acres of public land by the federal government in 1862 (the most generous right of way given to any railroad), played a major role in the development of all the resources lying within its far-flung domain. Eying increased traffic on its line, an extension of its line (sixty miles to the north) into the park, and the control of park tourist concessions, Northern Pacific officials sponsored an unofficial exploration of the region in 1870, which led to an official expedition the following year headed by Ferdinand V. Hayden, head of the U.S. Geological Survey. Hayden confirmed the previous mountain man tall tales of hundreds of spouting geysers and other wonders. Upon his return he received the first official suggestion for the establishment of a federal reserve—written on Northern Pacific stationery. In lobbying for the bill that winter, Hayden assured congressmen that the region's volcanic geology and soils left no better practical purpose (minerals, agriculture, timber) for the area. The region's worthlessness in the extractive economy of the West—and its value as a tourist's "pleasureing ground"—softened congressional opposition and assured passage of the bill.

What followed in the first decades of the park's existence was a struggle over how the park would be managed and to what extent it would be protected. Railroad and mining interests, supported by Wyoming politicians and other regional boosters, waged a furtive battle to build a rail line across the park's northern tier that would hasten the development of the mining town of Cooke City, Montana, lying just outside on the park's northeast corner. They were bitterly fought and successfully defeated by park protectionists, led by sportsmen-conservationists including George "Bird" Grinnell, editor of *Forest and Stream* magazine, and Theodore Roosevelt. The Boone and

The Gray Wolf Project

The new law protecting wildlife did not, of course, protect wolves or any other predator in Yellowstone. The gray wolf had been part of the Yellowstone ecosystem for nearly a thousand years. But as was true throughout the Rockies and the United States, the wolf was poisoned, trapped, and shot to near extinction. Ostensibly to defend perceived threats to sheep, cattle, and tourists, park officials and hunters assaulted the Yellowstone wolf until the last one was shot in 1926. Nearly three-quarters of a century later, after decades of maturing scientific study and evolving ecological consciousness—and following more than a decade of bitterly polarized debate—the gray wolf was reintroduced into Yellowstone Park. Despite the fears of neighboring cattlemen, few incidents of wolf-cattle predation followed. Furthermore, the environment has improved as willow stands have regrown due to fewer elk eating and destroying them. Thus did Yellowstone Park make history again and set another precedent. The success of wolf reintroduction in Yellowstone inspired other efforts to return the animal to select pockets of its former vast territory. Roughly 300 wolves today live in the Yellowstone Recovery area.[12]

Crockett Club, a sportsmen's organization founded by Grinnell and Roosevelt, also waged a battle to save park wildlife, focused in part on neighboring Indian tribes. A band of Shoshones had long lived in the park, and Crows and Arapahoes were among the other tribes who had frequented Yellowstone country and, through the use of fire, had helped to shape its meadows and forests. In 1880, in the interest of quieting tourist fears, the park superintendent forbade Indians from entering the park. For more than a decade afterward, however, Grinnell's magazine was filled with the complaints of sportsmen complaining about repeated "incursions of savages" into the park in search of elk.

Park defenders also focused their efforts on a group of about 200 Yellowstone bison, the last remaining "herd" in America. In 1894 a reporter and photographer sent by Grinnell covered the capture of a bison poacher nabbed by the U.S. Cavalry, then policing and managing the park. The story made national news, and within weeks Grinnell successfully parlayed the sensation into legislation outlawing the killing of wildlife in the park—the first federal law affording protection of wildlife.

Eleven other spectacular locales of beauty in the Rocky Mountains joined Yellowstone as national parks, along with fifteen national monuments, twenty-two wildlife refuges, and ninety-three national wilderness areas in the region. Throughout these federally preserved lands, officials have contended with such issues as the historical ecological role and contemporary rights of Native Americans, fragmentation of wildlife habitat caused by private development outside park borders, and National Park Service–sanctioned activities like snowmobiles and jet skis that threaten the integrity of the parks. These issues continue to provoke de-

Wolves harass a bison in Yellowstone National Park. Courtesy of the National Park Service.

bate within the West, and between advocates of stronger, expanded protection of the Rockies' wilderness qualities and those seeking to eviscerate the presence of the federal government in the West and place land stewardship entirely in the hands of individuals and businesses.

WATER

No resource has been more central to the environmental history of this semi-arid region than water. The traditional English common-law right to use stream and river water without diminishing its flow, nor degrading its quality, had already been weakened by the time Americans moved into the West. Emerging out of battles over the damming of New England rivers to serve the textile industry was the doctrine of "reasonable use." Classically American, reasonable use emphasized individual property rights and ambitious enterprise at the expense of other considerations, including the long-term sustainability of an exhaustible and degradable resource. In the Rocky Mountains how the water was to be used and who would control its flow were central to all else that transpired, proving particularly pivotal to the expansion of the cattle industry. Early in the twenty-first century, the diminishing supply of water remains at the center of the debate over the future of the West—how it will develop, where, in what forms, to benefit whose interests, and at whose expense.

A pivotal moment in the development of western water came in the last decades of the nineteenth century when Congress briefly debated, and ultimately rejected, the recommendations of John Wesley Powell (1834–1902) on how America's arid regions should be developed. After conducting two intensive explorations of the Green and Colorado Rivers in 1869 and 1871, Powell concluded that the lands west of the one-hundredth meridian should not be developed in the grid pattern long since established by the nation's land laws. He believed that the arid region should be politically organized and developed according to its watershed boundaries. The availability of water and the shape of the land, not political considerations or arbitrary lines on the map, should govern how many people lived in the region, where they lived, and how (and how much of) the water was to be used. And, said Powell, the federal government would take the central role in building irrigation projects to deliver the water where it was most needed.

That final recommendation was about the only one of Powell's ideas the Congress incorporated into the Reclamation (Newlands) Act of 1902, the legislative blueprint for what became the hydrological engineering of the West. Over the next century, the Bureau of Reclamation established by the law constructed more than 600 projects—dams, canals, and reservoirs in seventeen western states at a cost of $22 billion. Many of those projects brought hydroelectric power to hundreds of thousands of rural residents in the Rocky Mountains, and they have fostered the explosive growth in population of western cities like Los Angeles. They have been indispensable instruments in the development of the urban West.

And yet the growing urban population has not been the primary beneficiary of the irrigation of the West. From the beginning, large agricultural operations have been the driving forces behind the law, its implementation, and its judicial interpretation when water rights have been contested. The phenomenal growth of the Idaho potato industry, for example, was made possible by hydroelectric power generated by dams on the Snake River. But the same force that made water run uphill also damaged arguably the greatest salmon runs on the planet. Other Snake River aquatic species have been listed as endangered or threatened because of the construction of dams.

More to the point, agriculture accounts for a stunningly high percentage of the water delivered by the Bureau. Less than 10 percent of all irrigated water in the Rocky Mountain region goes to sustain urban populations. Ninety-seven percent of all the water used in Montana goes to irrigate hay and pasture forage for cattle, which makes the cattle in that state, as environmentalists argue, just about the least efficient users of water on Earth (one study estimates that it takes 3,430 gallons of water to produce one steak dinner from a western cow). Irrigation canals in Montana's Bitterroot Valley have led to the decline of up to 90 percent of the young population of westslope cutthroat trout from small streams critical to their survival. Construction of dams in the Colorado River system has led to the decline of the bonytail chub, the endangered Colorado pikeminnow, the razorback sucker, and the humpback chub.

With headwaters in the Rocky Mountains of Colorado and Wyoming, the Colorado is one of the most important river systems in the world—and one of the most heavily dammed, irrigation-drained as well. The possibilities were first demonstrated with the construction of Hoover Dam—one of the engineering marvels of the twentieth century. In the euphoric glow following its completion in 1935, a cartel of six industrial corporations, in concert with western politicians, conceived a plan to open the entire Colorado Plateau to massive, federally subsidized development centered on the extraction of coal and uranium and the generation of energy through dams, power plants, oil-shale projects, and transmission lines to sustain the growth of western cities from Denver to Los Angeles. A powerful western water lobby, backed by a broad popular constituency, encountered fierce resistance in 1956 when they proposed a dam on the Green River (a tributary of the Colorado) inside Colorado's Dinosaur National Monument. The fledgling environmental movement leapt to life. Led by the Sierra Club and the Wilderness Society, project opponents galvanized a massive outpouring of popular opposition through letter writing and publications that illustrated the magnificent beauty of the obscure Echo Park area. The project was defeated, an unprecedented victory for preservationists and a watershed moment for the political maturation of the Sierra Club, which, in deliberations with politicians and officials of the Bureau of Reclamation, had agreed not to contest an alternative proposal to construct a dam on the Colorado River in Utah's Glen Canyon. David Brower, the club's president, had never seen the area; once he did, he never forgave himself. Sacred Navajo sites and a magnificent red rock canyon were lost to the flooding of what became Lake Powell. An effort led almost solely by Brower to halt the project ended in defeat (though environmentalists achieved another victory with the defeat of a subsequent proposal in the 1960s to flood the Colorado inside the Grand Canyon with additional dam projects). It seemed a Pyrrhic victory, however, as the Colorado and other important western rivers continued to be dammed and developed; the western water lobby proved to be an unstoppable political force. Perhaps the ultimate testament to their victory: By the end of the century, so much of the Colorado River was drawn off for irrigation and development that its waters failed to reach the sea.

The same general pattern applies to the largest underground aquifer in the region. On the Great Plains the Ogllala Aquifer, the great underground river that underlies the Great Plains, continues to be tapped at a rate that alarms most hydrologists. In 1950 Colorado had 350 wells that drew from the Ogllala Aquifer; by the end of the century it had more than 3,000. Between 1959 and 1975, farmers in the region pumped more than 27 billion gallons a day from the aquifer, far more than can be naturally replenished. One-fifth of irrigated cropland in the United States is serviced by the Ogllala, yet at current rates of recharge hydrologists estimate that the aquifer will be depleted by 2035.

POSTWAR ISSUES: COLD WAR, ENERGY, AND SPRAWL

Since the nineteenth century the development of the Rocky Mountain West had been anchored by the growth of its cities. Salt Lake City served as a regional model of innovative urban design and diversified economic development. Other cities such as Denver, Colorado, and Billings, Montana, flourished around the development of extractive industries or as points of transshipment on rail lines. World War II fueled the expansion of urban areas throughout the West. Although the most notable magnets for federal military spending were Los Angeles, Seattle, and Albuquerque, the Rocky Mountain states also shared in the flow of defense dollars in the form of military contracts, newly developed and expanded military bases, and of greatest long-term consequence, research and development of the nation's first atomic bomb.

The Cold War that followed brought not the end of military spending in the West but its expansion. Defense contracts were delivered to weapons makers from Colorado Springs to Idaho Falls. Major installations for the U.S. Army and especially the U.S. Air Force expanded in every Rocky Mountain state, infusing economic vitality into cities like Cheyenne, Wyoming. Situated at the foot of the Rockies near Colorado Springs, Cheyenne Mountain became the command center for North American air defense. The flow of federal dollars helped to reverse what many westerners believed was a century-old pattern of colonial exploitation of the West's extractive wealth by eastern political and economic elites. By 1962 Utah, Colorado, Wyoming, and Montana were each generating 25 percent of their state income from defense spending provided by the federal government; Idaho was not far behind. The trend would continue in the 1980s when heightened Cold War tensions spiked the military budget once more.

There were, as there had always been, environmental consequences. At Rocky Flats, a classic western tabletop mesa located between Denver and Boulder, workers for nearly 40 years built thousands of triggering devices for thermonuclear weapons from radioactive plutonium. Periodic, increasingly regular environmental problems plagued the facility, including plutonium-contaminated soil and groundwater and charges that hundreds of workers had been recklessly exposed to radioactive elements in the workplace. Two major fires in 1957 and 1969 nearly became catastrophic. Not until the early 1990s did the contractor plea bargain to its environmental crimes and a $2 million a day cleanup of the site begin. The Idaho National Engineering and Environmental Laboratory, located west of Idaho Falls, served as a research center for nuclear reactors and for many years received much of the nuclear waste generated elsewhere around the West. Independent studies of the site have concluded that plutonium has been leaching through the soil and into the Snake River aquifer.

Beginning in the second half of the twentieth century a national mission to provide for the nation's ever-expanding energy needs was centered in the Rocky Mountain states and also became a source of massive federal spending. In the early 1950s the Atomic Energy Commission launched a major effort to mine uranium to supply a growing chain of nuclear power reactors. The first federally subsidized mineral rush in American history, the uranium rush was centered on the Colorado Plateau where 800 mines pocked the landscape by 1955. By 1962 Utah alone had generated some $25 million worth of uranium. As with defense dollars, federal subsidies opened the door to the boom. By the mid-1970s, every dollar of tax revenue received by the federal government was matched by a federal investment of $1.25. Grand County, Utah, received $2,462 in federal expenditures per person in 1976—a rate 46 percent higher than the national average. The uranium boom eventually busted, and left behind were two generations of radiation-poisoned workers who contracted leukemia and other radiological diseases, along with contaminated soil and water in vast sections of rural Utah. The worst site is just outside Moab, where by the 1980s, 10,000 tons of radioactive soil were leaching

The suburban sprawl around Missoula, Montana, in 1942. © Corbis.

into the Colorado River, the waters of which feed cities from Las Vegas to San Diego.[13]

Energy development assumed renewed importance in the region during the energy crisis of the 1970s. Sitting on top of one of the deepest bituminous coal beds in the world, the Powder River Basin of northeast Wyoming became the site of intensive mining in the 1970s and 1980s. For the state on the whole, coal production increased 20 percent annually for much of the period. Gillette, Wyoming, saw its population explode from 4,000 in 1969 to 14,000 by 1980. From northeast Montana to southern Utah and southwest Colorado, coal, oil, oil shale, uranium, and natural gas were extracted in greater volumes than ever before. Economic boom brought not only prosperity but, as always, attendant social and economic upheaval and environmental disruption. Providing the required expanded infrastructure and additional social services were among the issues faced by western communities whose populations exploded overnight. And when the energy economy went bust, so did towns like Rock Springs, Wyoming, which became a decaying shell of its former boom self. Rising rates of unemployment, alcoholism, and other social problems seemed to always accompany the "bust" in the extraction-based economic cycle.

Native American tribes throughout the Rockies were caught between the need to generate income and the desire to preserve the integrity of their lands. In 1966 the Bureau of Indian Affairs persuaded the Northern Cheyenne Nation of the Tongue River section of southeastern Montana to lease 400 square miles to multinational coal mining companies. The rates of return, they soon discovered, were less than 10 percent of what such leases brought elsewhere in the West. After years of political and legal struggle, the tribe pressured the Congress to cancel the leases. This unprecedented victory was followed by the tribe's action against a powerful mining and utility conglomerate that had proposed the construction of two coal-fired power plants just west of the reservation. The Cheyennes petitioned the Environmental Protection Agency (EPA) for Class I Clean Air status, the same designation accorded national parks. In another historic agreement, the EPA agreed, and the company was forced to install state-of-the-art scrubbers at their plants.[14]

In southeastern Utah in the late 1970s a furious battle raged between environmentalists and those who favored accelerated development of the region's energy resources. Under the terms of the 1976 Federal Land Policy and Management Act (FLPMA), the Bureau of Land Management (BLM) had undertaken an inventory of the region with the goal of designating federal wilderness areas, which would prohibit extractive development in those areas. The FLPMA would also have imposed a whole new set of stiffer mining, grazing, and road right-of-way regulations on all BLM lands in the West. Squaring off against both wilderness advocates and the BLM was the Utah contingent of a broad western movement known as the Sagebrush Rebellion. Well funded by large corporate enterprises such as the Rocky Mountain States Legal Foundation, the Sagebrush Rebellion's campaign to end or severely roll back federal regulation of western lands tapped into a groundswell of frustration and economic desperation among ranchers and farmers throughout the West. Facing a wide array of other problems having to do with interest rates and prices on the global agricultural market, ordinary westerners increasingly saw the source of their economic plight to be environmentalists and the federal government and directed their ire accordingly. In the most intense period of the standoff in Utah, bulldozers were driven onto BLM study areas, death threats were delivered to BLM offices, and BLM officials were burned in public effigy. As Raymond Wheeler astutely observed, at the center of this bitter dispute was the "philosophical question: Who really owns the public lands of the West? Do they belong to the nearest small town? . . . to the federal land-managing agencies? . . . to Peabody Coal, Exxon, Tenneco, Sohio? Or do they . . . actually belong to the American public?"[15]

Growing numbers of Rocky Mountain citizens increasingly made the argument that preservation brought a greater overall economic return to the region than extractive-based development in the form of recreation and tourism. In 1986, for example, that sector of the Utah economy generated nearly $2 billion in revenue—more than twice the total that uranium, coal, and oil extraction produced that year; the disparity was even greater in the area of jobs, with six times as many jobs generated in the travel industry as in mining and twice as much wage income. In the end the Sagebrushers won the fight, as the BLM succumbed to their pressure and erased half of the previously designated wilderness-eligible areas from its final study. In the 1990s a "Wise Use" movement, descended from the Sagebrush Rebellion, began to rail against what they saw as an intrusive, obstructionist, "anti-human," anti-property rights, "un-American" environmental community, and the federal government that advanced their agenda. That debate continued into the next century.[16]

The divide between mostly urban environmentalists and more conservative longtime rural residents of the Rocky Mountains is not as impassable as it may appear. Since the great mineral boom of the 1970s, family ranchers and farmers have often joined with the environmental community to form state "Resource Councils" and other organizations to contest a wide array of recent threats to the environment and the overall quality of life in the region. The increasing dominance of large multinational energy companies on the landscape is seen perhaps most egregiously in the rise of coalbed methane development in eastern Montana and the Powder River Basin of eastern Wyoming. To extract methane gas embedded within layers of coal buried deep in the earth, enormous volumes of water are pumped out as salty wastewater. Whether contained in holding ponds or sent down the river, the process, as ranchers and conservationists see it, represents an enormously wasteful use of the most precious resource on this arid landscape. In Wyoming alone, 43 million barrels of water are pumped from ever-diminishing aquifers and dumped, depleting stock wells of family ranchers.

In addition to intensive energy development, other issues have provided common ground between environmentalists and ranchers and farmers who have long seen themselves as good stewards of the land. Between 1990 and 1995 more than one-third of the new residents in the Rocky Mountain states have concentrated themselves on the suburban perimeter of cities. Posing a threat to both ranchers and those who value green space, sprawling development has spawned an alliance of environmentalists and ranchers. The growth of "ranchette" subdivisions on the perimeter of Yellowstone National Park, for example, has brought the Greater Yellowstone Coalition—concerned about fragmented wildlife habitat and water quality—together with Montana ranchers concerned about the loss of the open range. Integrated Pest Management (an alternative to herbicides and pesticides)

Unidentified suburban sprawl. Courtesy of Corbis.

and more environmentally friendly (and economically efficient) grazing methods that can allow small ranchers and farmers to better compete in the agricultural marketplace against big growers are other issues that have advanced this dialogue.

As many environmentalists have come to understand, those who live on the land understand it as no one else can, know well through experience the ramifications of the boom-bust cycle, and appreciate what is at stake when externally driven corporate development arrives to bring prosperity. Ultimately, at the heart of this surprising alliance is a common concern for the ecological integrity of the Rocky Mountain region that, despite its radical transformation over the past two centuries, remains one of the most remarkable places on earth.

ENVIRONMENTAL LITERATURE

Most Americans had been only dimly aware of the existence of the Rocky Mountain region until the first generation or two of explorers and travelers began publishing their accounts. Read by an increasingly wider audience as the nineteenth century wore on, this genre began with the 1814 publication of the *History of the Expedition under the Command of Captains Lewis and Clark to the Sources of the Missouri, Thence Across the Rocky Mountains and Down the River Columbia to the Pacific Ocean*. The journals provided readers with a keenly detailed view of the breathtaking landscape and stunning biological diversity of the Northern Rockies and the Pacific Northwest prior to American settlement. In his delightful appreciation of the "whole face of the country . . . covered with herds of Buffaloe, Elk & Antelopes," Meriwether Lewis foreshadowed the rapturous response of generations of Americans to this region of the country. Passages in the journals inscribe the sense of sublime awe inspired by mountain landscapes that would be firmly embedded by countless romantic travelers to follow. The journals continue to offer an ecological benchmark of the romantic and biologically Edenic landscape the West once was.

A generation later, Warren A. Ferris (1810–1873), a mountain man in the employ of the American Fur Company, published one of the first and most popular accounts of the fur-trading era. Ferris' *Life in the Rocky Mountains* (1842) captured the rugged and spectacular scenery, sublime solitude, and invigorating clear air that was fast becoming associated with the region. Contemporary mountain men diarists such as Osborne Russell and Jedediah Smith further inscribed the grandeur of the Rockies in the American imagination.

Not surprisingly, the spirit of Manifest Destiny dominated much western writing at the midpoint of the nineteenth century. None were more emotionally charged than the tracts of William Gilpin (1813–1894). A onetime governor of the Colorado territory, Gilpin turned afterward to land speculation and is most famous for his vigorous promotion of America's conquest of the West. Many of his articles and speeches were gathered in *The Central Gold Region: The Grain, Pastoral, and Gold Regions of North America, with Some New Views of Its Physical Geography and Observations on the Pacific Railroad* (1860). His rhetoric of conquest, echoed by an entire generation of politicians and writers, went beyond mere boosterism. This was the language of imperialism, envisioning that the divinely inspired American mission of continental conquest—based in Colorado—would ultimately extend around the globe.

Extraordinarily popular with eastern audiences, the western dime novel rendered the mountain West a land where seemingly irreconcilable conflicts could be heroically solved by men of action. Emerging in the 1860s, this literary genre conveyed the Rockies as the dramatic stage for righting civilization's misdeeds. Celebrated buffalo hunter, guide, and Pony Express rider William F. "Buffalo Bill" Cody (1846–1917) was featured in 121 dime novels. Along with Cody's own "Wild West Show" (a highly theatrical and largely fictionalized version of western history), the Cody dime novels, as literary historian Thomas Lyon has written, "helped to solidify the West as a pageant-like realm of adventure in the popular understanding."[17]

Western photographers and painters further amplified the glories of the Rocky Mountain landscape. Like western dime novels and weekly newspapers that had earlier acquired national readership, so too with visual imagery: Thomas Moran's (1837–1926) paintings and William Henry Jackson's (1843–1942) photographs of Yellowstone became widely disseminated through reproductions and facsimiles. Charles M. Russell (1864–1926) spent much of his early life painting the Montana frontier, dramatically representing the land and people of a wild West rapidly being tamed. His works became wildly popular and remain so with enthusiasts of Rocky Mountain history and landscape. Russell later became not only a historian and storyteller of the West but also an outspoken advocate for its conservation.

Zane Grey (1872–1939), like Owen Wister (1860–1938), Theodore Roosevelt

(1858–1919), and other well-bred easterners, went west for spiritual and personal rejuvenation. For them the Rockies provided an antidote for that antimodern impulse felt by many men of this class who believed their urbanized, increasingly consumption-driven society was in danger of becoming overcivilized. Beginning with *Riders of the Purple Sage* (1912), Grey honed the western theme of wilderness as a force for reinvigorating the heroic, individualistic qualities that men seemed to be losing in the modern age. Grey vividly details the color and grandeur of the western landscape, offering it as a redemptive force to recapture the best qualities in his protagonists.

With greater nuance and piercing insight, Willa Cather's (1873–1947) *The Professor's House* (1925) took aim at modernity and materialism and spoke for the power of things wild and ancient to inspire and redeem. *The Professor's House* had been inspired by a visit to the Mesa Verde archaeological site on the Colorado Plateau—a landscape richly conveyed in the book.

Based on the real story of the Johnson County Range War of 1892, Jack Schaefer's *Shane* (1949) continued the tradition of the lone western hero driven by a personal code of honor, drawn from the mountains from whence he rides, to restore goodness to a lawless town. The 1953 Hollywood version, filmed amid the backdrop of the towering Grand Tetons of western Wyoming, became an archetypal western film and established in living color the majesty of the West.

In a thirty-year career, Louis L'Amour (1908–1988) prolifically carried the torch of the western, penning more than 100 books. L'Amour further refined the western sense of place, contributing higher levels of nuance and color, and in works like *Hondo* (1953) ecological sensitivity, imbuing that manly western landscape with a degree of fragility.

With still greater realism, Idahoan Vardis Fisher (1895–1968) in his first western novel, *Toilers of the Hills* (1928), tells a grim story of Idaho dry-land farming. The story is told through the eyes of Opal Hunter and is centered on her struggle to come to terms with the isolation and silent loneliness of the remote and rugged Idaho agrarian frontier. In the end the Hunters' farming success is tempered by their struggle to come to terms with this hard and beautiful place. Fisher's final novel, *Mountain Man* (1965), became the inspiration for Sidney Pollack's film *Jeremiah Johnson* (1972). The book and the more romanticized film version reintroduced a new generation of Americans to the historic Rocky Mountain West and seemed to resonate with popular concerns about the ecological fate of the Rocky Mountains. Indeed, the film arrived the same year that singer-songwriter John Denver (1943–1997) began inspiring millions of listeners with both his passion for the Rocky Mountain West and his environmentalism.

Threats to the aesthetic and ecological integrity of the Rocky Mountain region inspired much western writing in the postwar era. Utahan novelist and western historian Bernard DeVoto (1897–1955) contributed vigorously to the growing campaign to save public lands in the West. The fiction of Wallace Stegner (1913–1993), Norman Maclean (1902–1990), and Larry McMurtry (1936–) each infused new meanings and symbolic importance into a landscape increasingly imprisoned, as they frequently saw it, by a myth of conquest. Edward Abbey's (1927–1989) *Desert Solitaire* (1968) was both a worshipful paean to the desolate beauty of the Colorado Plateau region as well as a biting critique of its encroaching development. (See also chapter on **Literature**.)

RESOURCE GUIDE

Printed Sources

Cawley, R. McGreggor. *Federal Land, Western Anger: The Sagebrush Rebellion and Environmental Politics*. Lawrence: University Press of Kansas, 1996.

Echeverria, John D., and Raymond Booth Eby, eds. *Let the People Judge: Wise Use and the Private Property Rights Movement*. Washington, DC: Island Press, 1995.

Flores, Dan L. *The Natural West: Environmental History in the Great Plains and Rocky Mountains*. Norman: University of Oklahoma Press, 2003.

Limerick, Patricia. *The Legacy of Conquest: The Unbroken Past of the American West*. New York: W. W. Norton, 1988.

Magoc, Chris J. *Yellowstone: The Creation and Selling of an American Landscape*. Albuquerque: University of New Mexico Press, 1999.

Rostad, Lee. "The Rise of Environmentalism and Its Relation to Western Myths." In *Fifty Years after* The Big Sky: *New Perspectives on the Fiction and Films of A. B. Guthrie, Jr.*, ed. William E. Farr and William W. Bevis. Missoula: O'Connor Center for the Rocky Mountain West; Helena: Montana Historical Society Press, 2001.

Sutton, Ann, and Myron Sutton. *The American West: A Natural History*. New York: Random House, 1970.

White, Richard C. *"It's Your Misfortune and None of My Own": A New History of the American West*. Norman: University of Oklahoma Press, 1991.

Worster, Donald. *Rivers of Empire: Water, Aridity, and the Growth of the American West*. New York: Oxford University Press, 1992.

Web Sites

Lavender, Catherine. West Web. January 6, 2004.
http://www.library.csi.cuny.edu/westweb/
A great starting place for the environmental history of the American West.

Travis, William Riebsame. "Changing Federal Lands Management." December 16, 2003.
http://www.colorado.edu/geography/projects/range/brief4_history.html

Wheeler, Ray. "The Colorado Plateau Region." *Land Use History of North America*. January 3, 2004.
http://www.cpluhna.nau.edu/Places/places.htm

Videos/Films

In Our Own Backyards. Dir. Pamela Jones and Susanna Styron. Eleventh Hour Films, 1982.

Poison in the Rockies. Dir. Christopher McLeod. Environmental Research Group, Aspen, CO, 1990.

The West. Dir. Stephen Ives. Nine episodes. Florentine Films, PBS Home Video, 1996.

Organizations, Museums, Special Collections

Denver Public Library, Western History/Genealogy Department
The Denver Public Library
10 West 14th Avenue Parkway
Denver, CO 80204

720-865-1818
http://photoswest.org/email.htm

In partnership with the Colorado Historical Society, a collection of 100,000 photographs and catalog records available online. The library's western history special collections are among the best in the Rocky Mountains.

High Country News
119 Grand Avenue
P. O. Box 1090
Paonia, CO 81428
970-527-4898
http://www.hcn.org/

Award-winning regional publication covering environmental issues in the Rockies.

Museum of the Rockies
600 West Kagy Boulevard
Bozeman, MT
406-994-2251
http://www.montana.edu/wwwmor/

Preserves and interprets the natural and cultural history of the Northern Rocky Mountain region. In association with Montana State University, whose Merrill G. Burlingame Special Collections contain rich holdings of Northern Rockies history.

ETHNICITY

A. Dudley Gardner and Laura Pasacreta

The Rocky Mountains, once thought of as the "Empty Quarter," have always been home to people from numerous nations. Here vast open spaces, endless plains, jagged peaks, and deserts seemed to be the home for antelope and buffalo, not people. The truth is that for nearly 12,000 years Native Americans gathered wild plants and hunted and lived in the region. By the time Christopher Columbus (1451–1506) reached the New World, native farmers grew corn in the future states of Utah and Colorado. When Europeans first reached the area in the 1500s, on the plains Crow Indians hunted bison; in the desert Shoshones gathered seeds; and in the heart of the Rockies, Ute hunters pursued deer. The people were as diverse as the land. When, in the 1800s, Europeans, Africans, and later Asians moved into the region, they lived alongside Native Americans. Native peoples and newly arrived immigrants created a cultural landscape that matched the natural landscape: a place where diversity and contrast not only defined the land but also reflected the people who lived in the region.[1]

For many Americans, the concepts of race and ethnicity have become blurred. Race simply defined is a gift given at birth. We are Chinese or French, however, based on cultural factors. A French child is trained (socialized) to use a fork and speak French; a Chinese toddler is trained to use chopsticks and speak Mandarin. Their identity as French or Chinese has little to do with what they look like but with how they are raised (socialized). It is in their upbringing that people gain their culture and one might say their ethnicity. An ethnic group generally regards itself as distinct. This distinction is based on "social or cultural characteristics such as nationality, language and religion."[2] There are complicating factors. Variations exist within ethnic groups, and in the case of most groups, there are divisions that make generalizing difficult. What makes America so unique are the diverse races and ethnic groups that live here. This chapter looks at the various races and ethnic groups who chose to live in the Rocky Mountains, at why people immigrated, where they came from, and when they first arrived.

NATIVE PEOPLE

For at least 12,000 years, a variety of nations lived in the Northern Rockies and the surrounding environs. Mountains and basins meet in the states of Idaho, Montana, Wyoming, Utah, and Colorado. Sometimes the meeting is abrupt; in other places the different zones blend together. The places where they meet create niches rich in plants from adjoining environments. On the front range of Colorado and in the basin zones of Utah where mountains meet flat expanses, people have lived for thousands of years.

Which native groups lived in the Rocky Mountains when Europeans arrived is open to question. It is known that in present northern Idaho the Kutenai, Pend D'Oreille, and Nez Percé lived. Their homeland extended into the Northern Rockies, where they encountered Blackfeet and Crow who also claimed the mountains and plains of present Montana. Sioux, Cheyenne, Assiniboine, Métis, and Arapaho came into Montana seeking buffalo, and they fought with the Shoshone, Crow, and Blackfeet for the right to live in eastern Montana. The Shoshone ranged from southeastern Idaho to southeastern Montana, but the core of the nation lay in Wyoming. To the west of the Shoshone, in Idaho, lived the Bannock, to the south the Ute. The Ute nation controlled the mountains of Utah and Colorado. Their neighbors in Utah included the Paiute and Goshutes, but the Utes controlled the most area by far. Their control extended eastward onto the plains.

When the Europeans first reached the region in present southern Colorado, Apache and Utes lived there. To the west in southern Utah, the Navajo had settled. These three tribes hunted deer or bison and gathered seeds. There is some indication that, in addition to hunting and gathering, the Navajo and Apache cultivated corn where weather and water allowed crops to grow. Shortly after Spanish settlers arrived in Santa Fe in 1598, they came in contact with these three tribes. The effect would be profound. From the Spanish, all three gained the horse. The Apache would migrate further south; the Utes and Navajo would remain. The Navajo culture would undergo a transformation. From Spanish traders they acquired sheep and goats and plants like peach trees and watermelon. Peach orchards appeared in well-watered areas of New Mexico, and throughout the area shepherds moved their sheep from valley floors to mountainsides. The Navajo became the region's first ranchers. They also learned from Spaniards how to work silver and weave wool. In present southern Utah, Navajo herders grazed horses and sheep long before Americans reached the Rocky Mountains. Meanwhile, to the east in present southern Colorado, Ute herders raised horses.

As early as the seventeenth century, Ute Indians traveled to Spanish settlements in present New Mexico to trade. They brought deer hides and furs and even "Indian" slaves. What they wanted were horses. Utes could then trade horses to their northern neighbors, the Shoshone and Comanche. Both of these two tribes moved out of southwestern Wyoming and northwestern Colorado soon after acquiring the horse. The Comanche headed east, then south, where they became the "Lords of the Plains." The Comanche adapted quickly to living on the plains of Colorado. Hunting bison and antelope, they came to dominate the region. Living on the eastern flanks of the southern Rockies, mounted warriors kept Spanish settlers from moving into southern Colorado. The Shoshone moved out of southwest Wyoming and headed northeast and north to the present plains of Montana.

The Shoshone Indians long had lived hunting bison and antelope. They gathered a variety of wild plants and knew and understood the environment of the central Rockies. Here winters are long, and survival depended on storing enough food to carry them through the longest season of the year. On the plains of Wyoming, Montana, and southern Alberta, large bison herds roamed. These herds offered enough meat to ensure survival and even prosperity. With the horse they could range out onto the plains. Not only could they hunt bison; they could gather berries that grew in the river valleys and along the flanks of the eastern Rockies. As they moved north seeking better hunting grounds, they came in contact with the Blackfeet Indians, who lived in present Montana and southern Alberta.

The Blackfeet traded with Assiniboia, Cree, and Chippewa who lived to the east of their homeland. These traders had access to French guns. By the 1700s, French traders had reached the fringes of the Rockies. They traded knives and guns to Native Americans in exchange for furs. By the time the Shoshone reached the northern plains and mountains of Montana, the Blackfeet had acquired the gun. On the plains, in the shadow of the Rocky Mountains, guns and horses met. The collision took place on a battlefield where First Nations fought one another in a classic struggle of firepower versus mobility.

Pretty Weasel, who is pregnant, and Singing Beauty, Crow women, pose outdoors. Singing Beauty wears beaded moccasins, a belt, dress decorated with elk teeth, and bead necklaces. Courtesy of the Denver Public Library.

Both nations had great warriors. In some ways the battle ended in a stalemate. The horses circled as Blackfeet warriors opened fire. The Blackfeet, awed by the horse, held their ground but could not claim total victory. The battle affected both tribes deeply. The Blackfeet obtained the horse. The Shoshone contracted smallpox, which they carried south as they retreated from present southern Canada. The spread of disease and the horse now went hand in hand. On the positive side, the horse allowed the native peoples the mobility to hunt and travel freely from mountain to plain. The tribes grew rich trading furs for metal and horses. But their improved standard of living came at a price. Diseases, in the form of smallpox, measles, and chicken pox, cut across the land, killing thousands. Because these diseases preceded contact with Europeans and Americans, exact counts of how many died are not available. Blackfeet legends and histories indicate smallpox devastated their tribe, and it is a given that the disease affected all tribes in the mountain West.

EARLY IMMIGRANTS

Early Spanish Presence

Since their arrival in New Mexico in 1598, Spaniards had lived and worked together with native peoples. By the 1600s, the Spanish had made at least minimal contact with the Utes. Spaniards came into the mountain West slowly. In 1776, two priests, Francisco Dominguez and Silvestre Escalante, left Santa Fe and traveled north to the Uinta Mountains in present Utah. Their route took them through Ute lands in western Colorado and Utah. Spanish military expeditions also entered the southern Rocky Mountains. In 1779, Don Juan Bautista de Anza set out from Santa Fe to fight the Comanche. Traveling north, he went into the San Louis Valley before heading east toward the southern plains of Colorado. The expedition had 573 fighting men, plus Apache and Ute allies. Near the foot of present Greenhorn Mountain, Anza defeated the Comanche chief Cuerno Verde. The defeat of Cuerno Verde led to changes in the area's tribal politics, but it also gave Spain a better understanding of the region's topography.

Spain attempted to gain control of the Comanche in southern Colorado throughout the late eighteenth century. In 1787, for example, they built a short-lived settlement named San Carlos along the Arkansas River near present Pueblo. Designed to help the Comanche make a transition from hunting to farming, the settlement failed when a Comanche woman died and the Comanche considered this a sign of disapproval by their gods. Spanish efforts to suppress the Comanche met with mixed results. Possibly as a result the Spanish did not succeed in expanding their settlements north into the Platte River drainage of Colorado. The 1800s brought change to the Spanish empire. In 1803 the United States purchased Louisiana and gained control over a vast area north of Spanish America. Then in 1821, Mexico essentially achieved its independence. Mexico took an active interest in its northern frontier. The government gave land grants to encourage settlement in present southern Colorado.

These land grants provided a clear indication that Mexico intended to occupy the northern frontier, which extended all the way into southwestern Wyoming. Prior to the Mexican Revolution, trade with the United States had been restricted, but following the revolution, trade between the two countries expanded. The Santa Fe Trail, which extended from Independence, Missouri, to Santa Fe, New Mexico, passed through southern Colorado. Along this trail Mexican and American settlements emerged. The most famous of these, Bent's Fort on the Arkansas River, became a meeting place for native peoples, Mexicans, and Americans. In the 1840s, the fort's occupants included Josefa Tafoya of Taos, African Americans, Frenchmen, muleskinners from Mexico, and Native Americans. Soon the settlements of Hardscrabble, Greenhorn, and Pueblo emerged, populated by Mexican and Indian women whose husbands trapped, hunted, and traded. Small farms would emerge near these communities in present southern Colorado.

The irrigation ditches and churches built in the San Luis Valley by Mexican frontiersmen represented some of the first water works and stone buildings constructed in Colorado since the ancient Pueblo people abandoned their homes in about 1400 C.E. In 1851, the Hispanic town of San Luis became the first non–Native American village built in the San Luis Valley. While Mexican settlers moved into southern Colorado, to the north, Frenchmen trappers began to call the Northern Rockies home.

French and Métis

The first documented arrival of the French came in the early 1700s. Frenchmen had heard about the Rocky Mountains prior to reaching them. The first direct references come between 1738 and 1743 when the La Verendryes traveled into present Montana and Wyoming. By the late 1700s, French and British trappers and traders knew much about the Northern Rockies. Journals abound describing Frenchmen and their "Indian" wives living in remote corners of the Rockies. Sacajewea, the Shoshone who guided Meriwether Lewis (1774–1809) and William Clark's (1770–1838) fabled party, had married a Frenchman Toussaint Charbonneau (1767–1843). By the time the Americans arrived in the area in the early 1800s, the Métis, children of French and Native American marriages, hunted buffalo on the plains of present Montana. The world the Americans moved into had long witnessed interaction between native peoples and Frenchmen. Like their Spanish counterparts in the southern Rockies, Frenchmen had gained much from living, trading, and even battling with the Native Americans who called the mountains home.

First Nations, like the Blackfeet, Flathead, and Crow who lived along the flanks of the Rocky Mountains hunting buffalo on foot, had come in contact with English and French Canadian traders sometime in the eighteenth century. Eventually, Frenchmen became directly involved not only in trading but in trapping. Many chose to live with Native Americans. By the early 1800s, French Canadians traded with Indians along the upper Missouri, traveled south into Colorado, and became an entrenched part of the Rocky Mountain fur trade. While small in number, they left a definite imprint on the region—names like Laramie, Gros Ventres, and Nez Percé are all French names. Frenchmen settled throughout the region. They often built *piece-sur-piece* log cabins, a French Canadian specialty. In addition, the Métis, a group distinctively French and Indian, moved westward to eastern Montana, leaving a French and Indian heritage that still survives.

The Métis (from a French word meaning "mixed") owe their existence to the meeting of native peoples and French trappers and traders in the fur trade. Métis has come to mean a group that formed a common identity on the plains of western Canada, North Dakota, and Montana and proclaimed itself a "New Nation." The Métis saw themselves as different from their Indian and European heritages, and indeed they were. French-speaking and Catholic, they adhered to lifeways that had roots in Chippewa, Ojibwa, and Cree culture.

The Métis who settled in present Manitoba and North Dakota evolved out of marriages between French trappers and either Chippewa, Ojibwa, or Cree women. Moving west and north of the Great Lakes, the trappers established stable unions with native women. The French and Indian families formed kinship ties that facilitated trade. In this trade, native wives proved invaluable. They served as interpreters and trading partners. More, they performed skilled "domestic tasks such as making moccasins and snow shoes, drying meat and dressing furs."[3] On the surface it seemed their principal skill lay in translating and preparing hides, but often the women were the only bilingual negotiators in the trade process—this fact gave them power.

By around 1800 the Métis had settled along the Red River that divides present North Dakota and Minnesota. The river flows north, finding its way eventually to Hudson's Bay. Every year, from their settlements along the Red River, the Métis moved onto the plains to hunt buffalo. Bison were the cornerstone of their economy. "Traveling in their distinctive two-wheeled Red River carts pulled by horses or oxen," they sallied forth. "The carts, which were essential for transporting equipment and hauling meat, were made entirely of wood bound with rawhide." In time the hunts grew in size. One hunt, in 1840, involved 1,600 people and 1,200 carts. In winter they returned to their villages.

The Métis tended to have large families, and soon they dominated the area. Many French Métis spoke both French and English plus "Cree or Ojibwa from their mother's side. In time, a distinct composite language, usually termed 'Michif' emerged based primarily on Cree and French."[4]

The Métis arrived in present Montana in the early 1800s. In 1870 a group of Métis left the Pembina area to settle at present Lewistown in central Montana Territory. Among them was Louis Riel. Riel, the fabled leader of the Métis, initially hunted buffalo in Montana. Beginning in 1879 he worked as an agent, trader, and woodcutter near Carroll. There, he met Marguerite Monet Bellehumeur, a Métis. They were married on March 6, 1882. Riel became a naturalized citizen of the United States in 1883. The following year found him teaching at a Jesuit mission near Great Falls, Montana.

Riel's heart, however, drove him to try and improve his people's plight. Recruited by the Métis to assume a leadership role in the drive for an autonomous homeland, Riel began considering a move back to Canada. In March 1885, Riel would return to Canada, where he became enmeshed in a Métis rebellion that led to his execution in Regina, Saskatchewan, on November 16, 1885. This rebellion resulted in many Métis thinking of Montana as a refuge. Unfortunately, the great bison herds no longer roamed the Montana plains. With the buffalo herds diminishing, the Métis turned to ranching and homesteading. The Métis never acquired reservation lands.[5] Estimates vary, but in 2000, approximately 4,000 Métis resided in Montana.

African Americans

In 1538, a black soldier and servant named Estaban accompanied Fray Marcos to the flank of the Zuni mountains and died at the hands of Zuni capturers. Other black women and men also entered the western frontier relatively early. In 1598, when Juan de Onate colonized New Mexico, he brought with him three female Negro slaves and one mulatto slave. Africans on the frontier became a fixture of the western experience. Black trappers, traders, explorers, homesteaders, cowboys, and even slaves lived in the mountain West. Black trappers and explorers came west with other American explorers shortly after much of the region became part of the United States in 1803.

In 1804, William Clark's slave York accompanied the Lewis and Clark expedition up the Missouri into present Montana. Six feet tall and weighing more than 200 pounds, York attracted the attention of Plains Indians. The Gros Ventres considered him a great medicine man. According to one legend, he would return, after the expedition ended, to live among the First Nations on the plains.[6] Another account has York returning east to Saint Louis, where he ran a carting and "drayage" business. Either way York is part of early American western history.

Afro-Americans accompanied many early trapping expeditions into the Rocky Mountains. James P. Beckwourth was French and Afro-American. Along with William Ashley, he attended the first rendezvous on the Henry's Fork in present Wyoming in 1825. Among the first Americans to camp north of the Uinta Mountains, he also provided one of the first descriptions of the Green River. Beckwourth preceded a wave of African Americans who would make their homes in the West.

Caravans moving in the West in the mid-1800s brought with them black laborers. In 1847 three black men accompanied the Mormon pioneers into the Utah Valley. The westward migration headed for the California gold fields in 1849 increased the number of African Americans residing in the region. A group of Cherokee Indians who went west in 1850 brought along black slaves. By 1850, the U.S. Census indicates fifty African Americans resided in Utah Territory. There were twenty-four free blacks, and the rest were slaves. The 1860 census lists the number of blacks at fifty-nine; this time twenty-nine came under the classification of slave. Congress abolished slavery in the territories in June 1862, and shortly thereafter Utah slaveholders freed their slaves.

By the time the Civil War broke out in 1861, blacks could be found throughout the Rocky Mountain West. At Fort Union, where the Yellowstone meets the Missouri River near the present Montana–North Dakota border, one black named "George" worked as a brick maker. In 1862, Fort Union employed three blacks, two as laborers and one as a cook.[7] In Colorado, blacks worked in the mines and by the late 1860s voted in general elections in the territory. The votes cast by blacks in the 1860s went to Republican candidates. The fact that the party had championed both the emancipation of slaves and given them the right to vote created a loyal voting block.

Blacks enlisted in the military both in the East and West. Many southern-born blacks found their way into regiments stationed from Utah to Montana. First called "Buffalo Soldiers" by Plains Indians, the name stuck. An *esprit de corps* arose among the black infantrymen stationed in some of the more remote reaches of the region. They interacted with native peoples, Chinese, and white Americans and gained a reputation of being fair and fearless.

On the Ute reservation in northern Utah, native traditions describe a memorial marked by Buffalo Soldiers from Fort Duschene. The small heart-shaped mound rises north of the White River in a badlands where little grows. Atop this mound is the outline of a man made with river cobbles. It is a stick figure. The Utes say it is a memorial the Buffalo Soldiers made for a fallen comrade who died fighting them along the river in the 1880s. Another legend holds that it signifies a respectful symbol created by Ute warriors to dignify a place where black soldiers died.

Interaction between blacks and native peoples did not always end tragically. Some blacks took Native American wives. Others lived near reservations long after their enlistments ended. For black Americans, the West offered a place where they could build a life free from the memories of slavery. Hundreds of black settlers from Louisiana, for example, came north to homestead on plots offered free to settlers if they improved and farmed the land. Black homesteaders and cowboys endured the heat, dust, and biting winds along with everyone else who ever lived in the area. Immigrants and emigrants alike found the weather could be "akin" to a "curse." In Wyoming and Montana, blacks from the South and Chinese immigrants from southern China all found the cold winters too long—and not so much a season as a year-round event.

Scottish Immigrants

Scotsmen first entered the region in the 1700s. Crossing the present Canadian border, Scottish trappers entered the northen Rockies with their French counterparts in the employ of the North-West Company. Ultimately, the Hudson's Bay Company (HBC) would come to dominate the trapping industry. The HBC trappers and traders ranged wide and far over the northern plains and into the Rocky Mountains.[8] By the mid-1700s the HBC hired Scottish immigrants along with French and Indian trappers. The HBC would find a new source of competition in the form of Scottish trappers hired by American companies. When, in 1800, John Jacob Astor started his American Fur Company, he hired six Scots who had experience in the fur trade.

Near the junction of the Yellowstone and Missouri Rivers, Scot Kenneth McKenzie supervised the construction of Fort Union. The trading post, built in 1828 by Astor's American Fur Company, relied heavily on the Scotsmen's knowledge of the fur trade to run the enterprise. Throughout the Rockies, Scotsmen could be found working in the fur trade.

Scottish immigration to America spans almost the whole history of the nation. From 1750 to 1914, Scots men and women left their homeland to seek employment in the New World. Over time, 2 million left Scotland for distant shores.[9] Those who moved to the Rocky Mountain West came for a variety of reasons. Following the trapping era, a variety of gold rushes brought Scottish miners into Colorado, Idaho, and Montana. The gold strikes of the late 1850s and early 1860s also brought in a wave of Scottish women looking for opportunities or to be with their families.

In Utah the migration of the Scots came for a different reason. Mormons went to great lengths to bring Scotch immigrants west.[10] Between 1840 and 1900, some 9,200 Scots joined the Mormon Church in Scotland. About one-third of the converts immigrated to Utah. Indeed, immigrants from the British Isles played a major role in the beginning of the church. Thousands of English and Welsh people journeyed to America during the 1840s and 1850s, and they headed west as part of the Mormon migration of 1847.

Asian Immigrants

Americans reached the Rocky Mountains in waves: first the explorers, then the trappers, then immigrants headed for Oregon, Salt Lake, and California. To Oregon in 1843, Salt Lake in 1847, and then in 1849 to California gold fields, women and men from Europe and the eastern states crossed the Rockies. From Asia came

Sandwich Islanders (Hawaiians) and Chinese sojourners. The Salt Lake City census noted a "yellow man" in town in 1850. Hawaiians were noted in the Hudson's Bay Company journals.

The end of the Civil War brought almost a frenzied rush into the mountain West. Gold had been discovered in Idaho, Montana, Colorado, Utah, and even Wyoming prior to the end of the Civil War in 1865. Many of these areas witnessed gold rushes prior to and during the war. At war's end, the pace of the race to the gold regions quickened. Added to the gold rush was the construction of the transcontinental railroad. The building of the railroad and the opening of the new gold fields would forever alter the ethnic makeup of the Mountain West. From China and Japan came railroad workers. They laid rails on newly built earthen paths and erected towns at set intervals along the railroad.

Once the railroad was finished in 1869, Chinese and Japanese workers, along with other immigrants, shared the fate of losing their jobs. Chinese railroad workers found work in Idaho and Wyoming. Some of the unemployed eventually went to work on the construction of the Northern Pacific Railroad across Montana.

A miner standing next to an ore cart track deep in an unidentified mine, Cripple Creek (Teller County), Colorado. Courtesy of the Denver Public Library.

Chinese Immigrants

Chinese immigrants entered the mountain West relatively early. From 1855 to 1857, Chinese mined gold in the Boise Basin.[11] In 1857, a young Chinese boy accompanied trappers to Fort Bridger, Wyoming. New gold discoveries in Colorado in 1858, and Idaho and Montana in the 1860s, brought waves of Chinese miners into the region. Trained in the California gold fields, Chinese miners sought new areas to mine, contributing to the expansion and development of many of the Rocky Mountain gold fields. By the early 1860s, Chinese immigrants could be found from Denver to Fort Benton, Montana. Gold drew them, but their ability to make money in a variety of trades brought Chinese entrepreneurs to mining towns.

Soon Chinese immigrants found their best chance to make money was to open a business or work as a laborer. Throughout the West, laundries, restaurants, and railroads became linked to Chinese immigration. There were good reasons for this.

In the mid-1800s, a laundry could be opened for less than $200. In fact, a tub and fire to boil the water put a person in business until they could afford a more elaborate operation. Chinese cooks brought to the West the ability to create inexpensive nutritious meals. Soon Irishmen, Englishmen, Swedes, Americans, and Canadians ate Chinese food in restaurants spread from the Boise Basin to Butte.

Likewise, by the 1870s, Chinese entrepreneurs had set up shops in cities and towns throughout the region. Often they succeeded where others failed. Frugal, hardworking, and excellent managers, Chinese tailors, laundrymen, and restaurateurs owned businesses in towns like Helena, Butte, Deer Lodge, Boise, Salmon, Salt Lake City, Evanston, Cheyenne, Denver, and Rock Springs. They typified the American dream of hard work and enterprise.

Chinatowns, or in some cases villages, became a part of the Rocky Mountain landscape. While they varied in size, they met basic needs. One writer in 1883 described how Chinese and Native Americans lived side by side in northern Idaho. He noted that by the side of the road he saw "canvas villages of Indians and Chinese." The tents appeared so much alike, he added, "one must look closely to see which is aboriginal and which Asian." The Chinese laborers near the Idaho border began the day "grouped around little camp fires . . . eating from small bowls with chopsticks, drinking tea."[12] Chinese did interact with native peoples and in some cases married Indian wives. The Chinese formed self-contained mobile villages that followed the advance of railroads and the opening of mines. Like the Indians, they lived in tents and cooked over open fires.

Business success did not mean acceptance. Viewed as the "yellow peril," the Chinese faced beatings, lynchings, and riots. Like Irishmen and Jews, they were looked down on more for where they were from rather than for anything they did. In terms of hard workers, few equaled Jews, Irishmen, and the Chinese.

Japanese Immigrants

Few, if any, Japanese reached the Rocky Mountain region prior to the Meiji Restoration in 1868. While the ascension of the Meiji to the throne led to Japanese leaving the land of the Rising Sun for America, it did not result in large numbers settling in the Rocky Mountains. Settlement in the area took place in the 1890s when railroads actively recruited Japanese laborers to work on the Northern Pacific and the Union Pacific. From Havre, Montana, to Kemmerer, Wyoming, Japanese worked building or repairing the rails. By the turn of the century, they found work in the coal mines. Many came from Fukokoka Ken (Ken means Province), an area in Japan known for its coal mines. These miners arrived in the West already experienced in mining "black gold." In the 1907 coal strike in Wyoming, the savvy coal miners from southern Japan became the first Asians admitted into the United Mine Worker's Union. The integration of the union meant that for the first time collective bargaining had to occur before any labor took place in Wyoming coal mines. Japanese immigrants began to call the area home.

Japanese women often came unwillingly to the American frontier. Parents arranged their marriages, and their unseen husbands paid for the trip to the Rocky Mountains. Getting off trains, they not only met what seemed like a harsh environment, they also saw their new husbands for the first time. One woman cried for days, finding that her mountain home had few trees and even fewer women.

These women formed the core of the next generation. Working in a variety of service industries, they raised a generation of Japanese Americans (Nisei) that changed the cultural landscape. Sugar beet farmers in Colorado, shop owners in Idaho, and railroad workers in Montana all had roots in Japan but families in America.

In many ways in 1900, the region was young. In a twenty-year span, between 1876 and 1896, all of the mountain states joined the Union. As territories turned into states, they faced a new set of challenges. One of those challenges was how to attract settlers (taxpayers) to their region. Europe proved fertile ground. Asians, while not often recruited, saw the mountain states as a "land of chances," where they could improve their lot in life.

Comparing just two nations illustrates how many immigrants still come from Europe instead of Asia. England had long provided a stream of immigrants to America. In 1900, 13,575 English-born settlers lived in Colorado, 3,943 in Idaho, 8,077 in Montana, 18,879 in Utah, and 2,596 in Wyoming. In the same decade, Japanese immigrants numbered 51 in Colorado, 1,305 in Idaho, 2,427 in Montana, 419 in Utah, and 397 in Wyoming. English immigrants were desirable settlers; Japanese were needed to work in difficult jobs. Southern Europe also proved to be a large source of settlers.

Jewish Immigrants

Jewish adventurers entered the Rocky Mountains relatively early. By the 1860s, reports of Jewish merchants celebrating Yom Kippur circulated in western newspapers. Denver, Colorado, developed a thriving Jewish community, as did Salt Lake City. In Denver, synagogues and Jewish hospitals served the community. Schools and community services aided Jewish immigrants. In 1913, future prime minister of Israel Golda Meir moved to Denver to pursue an education. Jewish communities actually existed in all of the Rocky Mountain states, but Denver's was particularly strong and viable, containing immigrants from around the globe but particularly from Europe. The origins of these communities lay in the nineteenth century.

In northern Utah and southern Idaho, pioneer Jews lived along with immigrants from the Middle East and Europe. Jews and Arabs had a long history in the New World. Columbus's flotilla had an interpreter named Luis de Torres who greeted the "Indians" on the Caribbean islands in both Hebrew and Arabic. Jewish immigrants found opportunities throughout the West. The gold rush, which drew thousands to California in 1849, brought Jewish entrepreneurs onto the frontier. Traveling west over the California Trail, a few decided to stop before reaching California. Some stayed in the Salt Lake Valley. In 1851, one "Hungarian Jew" who retained his faith earned $6 a day painting window blinds in Salt Lake City.[13]

The 1850 census, one of the first conducted in the intermountain West, noted Jewish residents in Utah territory. While the census is not always clear as to Jewish versus Polish or German immigrants, assessor rolls indicate that, by 1853, Jews owned and operated businesses in Salt Lake City. By 1869, the number of Jews had climbed to fifty individuals. They prayed publicly on New Year's day and the Days of Atonement. By the standards of the day, they were considered "wealthy through their trade." They worked hard, and one 1869 account related "the Mormons honor them very much and trust them."[14]

Meanwhile, the gold fields in Idaho attracted Jewish pioneers northward. In 1861, at least two Jewish men worked in the mines. The development of Boise and Silver City in the early 1860s led to Jewish merchants opening up shops and stores in the communities. By the 1880s, Jewish entrepreneurs moved on to the "Hailey Gold Belt." A German-born Jew named Simon Itzag Friedman illustrates the movement of the Jewish pioneers in the area. In 1869, Friedman found his way to Salt Lake City. Here he found employment in the Jewish-owned "Auerbach Store." In 1870, he moved to Corrine, the jump-off point for the Montana mines. Corrine sat along the Union Pacific Railroad line, and from there, teams of freight headed north to Virginia City, Butte, and Helena. Here Friedman could gain an understanding of freighting and supplying stores in the interior. When gold was discovered in Hailey, he transferred his stock to the mining camp and set up a twenty-by-forty-foot tent. He prospered. In 1886, he returned to Salt Lake City, where he married Luscha Meyer. Friedman's success came from following mining booms in the frontier West.

Irish Immigrants

While the Chinese sailed east to California, Irishmen sailed west to New York. In 1845, the Potato Famine destroyed the primary food source the poor of Ireland relied on. Two years later, 106,000 Irish women and men sailed for America. Over the next seven years, 1.1 million more made their way to the Atlantic shores.[15] Soon they moved inland, and at the end of the Civil War, their numbers in the West swelled. Many found their way into the gold fields prior to the War between the States, but the building of the transcontinental railroad concentrated Irish railroad workers along a string of rails being laid between Omaha, Nebraska, and the Great Salt Lake. With the transcontinental railroad completed in 1869, Irish railroad workers had to find jobs elsewhere in the West.

Although deepening poverty attracted the Irish to the New World, once in the New World, they retained a nationalistic view of their homeland. Proud to be Irish, they continued their values of family, church, and country in places like Denver and Butte, Montana. The Catholic churches on the Butte skyline serve as reminders even today of the Irish love of their faith. The church and family anchored the community. By 1900, 9,436 women and men born in Ireland lived in Montana. Colorado had 10,132 Irish residents; Idaho, 1,633; and Wyoming, 1,591.[16]

Prejudice and Change

In 1876, the Sioux defeated George Armstrong Custer (1839–1876) at the Battle of the Little Horn. With Custer's defeat, the Native Americans faced confinement on reservations. Every territory in the Rocky Mountain West would have reserves set aside for the area's first inhabitants. What the reservations insured was the interaction among Native Americans, Asians, and Europeans from the end of the so-called Indian Wars to the present. The reservation system created fixed political boundaries but did not isolate native peoples from the impact of a fresh wave of immigrants sweeping into the territories that became states between 1889 and 1896. A new wave of immigrants from Europe and Asia helped create these new states, but the new states all contained Native Americans.

The first contacts with native people resulted in Europeans writing about Native Americans, but these accounts commonly contained judgmental views that contained the belief that Indians were savages. At least initially, trappers and traders treated the Indians as equals. As the numbers of Europeans and Americans grew, however, prejudice and mistreatment against Native Peoples rose. When Sitting Bull took his people from Montana to Canada in 1877, they fled to save their lives. When Chief Joseph led the Nez Percé of Idaho in 1877, they fled oppression and violence. The Utes in Colorado suffered repeated attacks, and in 1898 when Ute hunters were murdered in Lily Park, no one was prosecuted. That same year similar attacks came against Bannock hunters along the Idaho/Wyoming border. Prejudice extended to many groups. Some of the worse racial biases came against the Chinese. Fear of the outsider, or jealousy over jobs, fueled the rage against them.

Chinese encountered prejudice almost from the moment they arrived in California. People discriminated against the Chinese, and at times the discrimination became violent. Violence against the Chinese spread from California to the gold fields of Idaho, Montana, and Colorado. Beatings, boycotts, and racial slurs too commonly reflected a deep prejudice against people whose roots lay in Asia. Events in Rock Springs, Wyoming, illustrate this fact.

In September 1885, Rock Springs lay divided in two general groups: "white miners" and "Chinese miners." All mined coal. Of course there were small divisions within the two general groups. Whites consisted of Cornish, Welsh, Irish, English, and even some Swedish miners, along with "native-born" Americans. Chinese consisted of two groups, "Tongs" or clans, all from Guangdong Province in southern China. The friction between the groups erupted over a labor dispute. The source of the problem lay in multiple issues.

On September 2, 1885, the problem came to a head, and the white miners attacked, killing 28 men, injuring over 100 others, and burning Chinatown to the ground. One Chinese man, who later recalled that day, told that he crawled nearly three miles to White Mountain, where he hid in a cave. Bleeding and sick, he lay there until strong enough to walk to Green River, twelve miles to the west.

Rock Springs was not alone in race riots. In 1880 the Denver Chinatown was burned. Both in Denver, Colorado, and the 1885 "Pierce Chinese Massacre," Idaho, Chinese men lost their lives to lynchings. In Butte, Montana, the residents boycotted Chinese laundries. In Helena, Montana, they passed ordinances limiting and even banning Chinese laundries. For Indians, Chinese, and blacks, hate crimes too often came in the form of shootings and lynchings.

Attacks against Chinese immigrants would continue into the twentieth century.

Table 1. Place of Birth of Rocky Mountain Immigrants, 1900

1900 Place of Birth	China	Japan	Ireland	Pacific Islands	England	Germany	French Canada
Colorado	581	51	10,132	36	13,575	14,606	960
Idaho	1,411	1,305	1,683	24	3,943	2,974	395
Montana	1,685	2,427	9,436	26	8,077	7,162	3,156
Utah	544	419	1,516	149	18,879	2,360	128
Wyoming	424	397	1,591	10	18,879	2,146	150

Source: U.S. Census Bureau, *Abstract of the Twelfth Census of the United States: 1900* (Washington, DC: Government Printing Office, 1904), 56–63.

At Tonopah, Idaho, on September 18, 1903, the *New York Times* reported "members of Idaho Labor Union Attack Mongolians and injure several." The union members drove the Chinese out of town. Seven or eight Chinese men suffered injury. One old man nearly died, and five Chinese men turned up missing. The Chinese consul in San Francisco asked for an immediate investigation and that the government do all in its power to protect the Chinese residents of Tonopah.[17]

While the battle for control of the mountains raged between Native Peoples and Americans, Europeans from southern, northern, and central Europe came west in increasing numbers. Slowly, the interaction between Native Peoples and Europeans became one where they shared similar hardships and had to live on the lands they shared. Immigrants headed for the coal mines and got off trains in Rock Springs. Here Shoshone Indians came to town to get their meat rations. While Crow and Sioux hunted the northern plains, Scandinavians began to settle in and farm. While Sioux hunters and Norwegian farmers might not live side by side, they occupied the same sections of Montana. Both groups understood the effects of a "northern" wind whipping snow drifts across the prairie, and both knew the scorch of sand carried in summer whirlwinds. They did not necessarily join hand-in-hand to conquer the land, but they shared a topography and climate that gave them a common understanding.

LATER SETTLEMENT IN THE ROCKIES

Scandinavian Immigrants

Immigrants from Sweden and Finland found their way into Rocky Mountain forests and mines as early as 1870. Swedish coal miners found the work dangerous, low paying, and without upward mobility. Most would leave the coal mines. Work could be had in the gold and silver mines, but working the woods or raising wheat proved more to their liking. Lumberjacks and homesteaders from Sweden did well in the woods of the Northern Rockies, and farmers managed to earn a living on the plains.

Finns did work in the mines, laboring long and hard in remote corners of the region. Bringing their own sense of hard work and fair play, they joined labor unions and formed political associations bent on improving working conditions in mines and smelters. Coal mine owners in Wyoming, for example, praised the Finnish work ethic but cursed their union-organizing tendencies. Both Finnish and Swedish immigrants helped build communities in remote areas where few others would settle. Mining camps particularly benefited from their effort to improve not only labor conditions but the community as a whole.

In the 1800s, 900,000 individuals had left Norway. Outside of England, only Ireland exceeded Norway in the number of immigrants who crossed the Atlantic to seek homes in the New World. The Norwegians who settled in the Rockies shared much. First, they came from farming backgrounds. Second, they were relatively well educated and wanted to pass that legacy to their children. Third, Norwegian Americans who immigrated in the late nineteenth century tended to stay on their farms. In 1900, 1,142 Norwegians lived in Colorado, 1,173 in Idaho, 3,354 in Montana, 2,128 in Utah, and 378 in Wyoming.[18] Their Swedish counterparts had more of a tendency to move to urban areas.[19]

More than a million "Swedes" moved to the United States from the end of the Civil War to the beginning of World War I. These immigrants found the West a place where through labor and perseverance they might have a chance to own land and improve their plight. Like their Norwegian counterparts, Swedish settlers moved into the Red River Valley of North Dakota in the late 1860s. By 1900 thousands of Swedish immigrants had settled in the mountain states. Colorado and Utah attracted the most. In fact, in 1900 Colorado had 10,765 "Swedes"; Montana, 5,346; Utah, 7,025; Idaho, 2,822; and Wyoming, 199. They would move into Montana—especially along the High-Line—in large numbers in the late 1800s. Hardworking, literate, and generous, the Scandinavian homesteaders successfully turned the prairie into farms.[20]

German Russians

German Russians settled throughout the region. Most settled in Colorado, but every mountain state contained a German Russian population. By the late nineteenth century, the political turmoil in Russia made the United States attractive.[21] Among the new immigrants who came from Russia were Hutterites. The road from Russia to Montana Hutterite colonies had its beginnings in the eighteenth century.

In the early 1760s, Queen Catherine the Great (1729–1796) put forth a manifesto that invited western Europeans to settle in Russia. To any western European choosing to migrate to Russia, Catherine promised transportation, land, religious freedom, and political autonomy. Soon, western Europeans, primarily Germans, immigrated to Russia. The first groups entered the Volga in 1764. The Hutterites arrived in Russia in 1770 and the Mennonites in 1789, but Germany provided the bulk of the settlers. By the mid-nineteenth century, the Volga, Crimea, and the Caucasus had German immigrants. In all, roughly 1.8 million Germans resided in Russia in 1900. Political oppression ultimately brought many German Russians to America in the 1870s.[22]

While the census statistics are not always clear that Russian immigrants were also of German extraction, in 1900 Idaho had 124 Russians; Montana, 394; Utah, 119; and Wyoming, 90. By 1930 the numbers in Colorado had climbed to 12,979; Idaho, 1,153; Montana, 4,212; Utah, 342; and Wyoming, 1,322.

The valley and plains of the Rocky Mountain states still offered opportunities for farmers, and most of the Germans leaving Russia had been farmers. To Colorado came hardworking Mennonite immigrants. Like so many immigrant farmers, they chose to plant wheat on their homesteads. Using practices honed in Russia, the Mennonite farmers prospered, succeeding where many dry land farmers had failed. Their success came from hard work and a community structure that fostered cooperation.[23] Other immigrants from Russia had also fled and took up free lands in the West. Among those fleeing were Hutterites.

Hutterites

Hutterites are a religious sect that emerged in Moravia in 1528. They adhered to a strict belief that "absolute authority comes from God" and that war was evil. They truly believed that men and women's chief purpose in life was to serve God.

In 1536, the Austrian government chose to make an example of their leader, Jacob Hutter, and burned him at the stake. This did not deter the faithful. Clinging to High German and historic patterns of dress and church structure, they chose to separate from mainstream cultures. Believing God's law superior to man's law, they refused to take allegiance to any earthly government. This fact, and their separation from modern culture, led to their persecution. Genocide and forced assimilation reduced their numbers to nineteen in 1750. In the late 1700s, the few remaining Hutterites, like Mennonites, fled to Russia to avoid persecution.[24] They further distinguished their faith in Russia by relying on self-sufficient communal villages. This would serve them well in the New World, where they arrived in the 1870s.

In 1873, a Hutterite delegation selected South Dakota as an ideal place to settle. In South Dakota, Hutterites faced the same challenges that all homesteaders did. Hutterites in South Dakota and eventually Montana faced isolation as well as the elements, but they desired this. Decades of repression and prejudice drove them to seek isolated spots and then work hard to cultivate the land they settled. Their communal lifestyle and hard work enabled them to prosper. The outbreak of the Spanish-American War threatened the Hutterites in the Dakotas. As pacifists, the Hutterites felt they could not support the American government, and some chose to migrate to Canada. The outbreak of World War I found Canada engulfed in the deadly war. No longer could the Hutterites migrate to Canada to avoid the war, and the U.S. entry into the conflict in 1917 led to direct persecution of 2,000 Hutterites. "Their German language and their pacifism, as well as their wealth made them targets." Some had their property seized. Others had to join the military. Four men went to prison, first at Alcatraz, then to Fort Leavenworth, Kansas, where due to brutal treatment, two died. After the war, many Hutterites elected to immigrate to Canada. Nonetheless, a sizable group remained in the Dakotas, Montana, Washington, and Minnesota. Combined with those living in Alberta, Saskatchewan, and Manitoba, 23,000 Hutterites followed the faith of their ancestor. Most lived on the plains of these states and provinces.[25]

Canadian government discrimination brought Hutterites into Montana. With a high birthrate of up to ten to twelve children, the Hutterite population had grown in Alberta. Large families meant they needed to acquire more and more land for their communal colonies. In 1942 the Canadian government passed a law that stated that enemy aliens and Hutterites could not be sold land in Canada. With nowhere to turn north of the border, new colonies moved into the United States. Not only could they buy land; they also received conscientious objector status. In Montana they prospered.

The Hutterite colonies in Montana speak a dialect of Low German, share a common doctrine, and have a communal outlook toward life. The men dress in black, the women in dresses. Education ends at about the eighth grade, but because they work so hard, they own their farms outright. Pigs, horses, cows, chickens, wheat, vegetables, and a diverse agriculture system allow them to prosper in a region where many ranchers and farmers failed. As Susie Waldner from the Duncan Ranch Colony notes: "Community life is hard but you know you'll never have to peel potatoes by yourself."[26]

Basque Immigrants

In the American West, Basques gained their fame as sheepherders. They first appeared as sheepherders in Los Angeles County in the 1850s and spread north and east in the decades that followed. By the 1900s Basques in Idaho had become a part of the agricultural economy of the state. Many of the early Basque immigrants to Idaho came from rural areas in northern Spain. The Basque homeland lies in the borderland between France and Spain along the southeast coast of the Bay of Biscay. The Basques from the interior regions of Spain fit well in a region where self-reliance was practiced like a religion. They also had another quality valued by westerners: They worked hard. One of the hardest jobs was herding sheep.

Basques entered the sheep industry in the mountain West via an indirect route. The first Basques to reach the region did not draw their herding experience from Europe. Instead, they gained their knowledge of herding on the pampas of Argentina. In Idaho, Basque herders settled in and notified family and friends that prosperity could be found grazing sheep. The pattern of prosperity would be repeated in Utah and Wyoming, but Idaho witnessed the largest influx. "Since at least the 1920s, Idahoans, both Basques and non-Basques, have claimed their state the home to the largest group of Basques anywhere on earth, except in their own native country in the Pyrenees."[27] Their hardworking ways soon propelled Basques into the banking industry, education, and entrepreneurial endeavors throughout the area.

Greek Immigrants

The decades spanning the end of the nineteenth century and the beginning of the twentieth witnessed an increase in the number of immigrants from southern Europe. Greece contributed to the diverse ethnicity of the Rocky Mountain states. By 1880, only 210 Greeks found their way to the United States. In the decade between 1900 and 1910, 167,579 moved to America. Like others, they immigrated to the West seeking opportunity and work. The farther into the interior West these Greeks moved, the less likely they were to live in urban areas. In 1910, only 30 percent of all Greek immigrants living in the mountain West lived in cities. Usually they worked on railroad gangs or in coal, copper, and silver mines. They also found work in smelters and mills. An indication of where they found work can be seen in Wyoming.

In 1900, 299 Greeks lived in the mountain states. All but 69 of these immigrants lived in Wyoming. Initially, the Greeks of Wyoming worked on railroad gangs. By 1900, they lived in Rock Springs, Hanna, and Kemmerer where they worked in the coal mines.[28] Some found the danger too great and found employment elsewhere. For example, one man named Charles August left the coal mines of Hanna to open up a photography shop in Rock Springs. His partner was a Japanese man named Frank Nakako. August would not be the only Greek miner to leave the coal mines to look for work elsewhere. In addition, a new wave of immigrants increased the number of Greeks in Colorado in 1910 to 2,272, 1,843 in Idaho, 1,905 in Montana, 4,039 in Utah, and 1,915 in Wyoming.[29]

Diversity: Other Immigrants

Mining contributed to the ethnic diversity of the Rocky Mountains. In general, mining is hard and dangerous work. The pay was low, the job dangerous, and life in remote mining communities difficult. Owners often needed to find new laborers for their mines. In the 1880s and 1890s, the coal fields of Utah, Colorado, northern New Mexico, Idaho, Wyoming, and Montana all hired Welsh, Slovenian, Italian, Greek, Serbian, Croatian, Austrian, Mexican, Russian, and Polish workers. In many cases, the original coal miners came from England, Wales, and Scotland. Labor disputes and the companies' desire to pay lower wages led to mines hiring men from around the world.

From Butte, Montana, to Pueblo, Colorado, enclaves of southern and eastern Europeans created communities with distinct characteristics. Greek Orthodox churches and Catholic cathedrals emerged in places where the dominant faiths had been either Protestant or Latter-day Saints. Lebanese settlers often located in mining areas, usually opening stores for miners and their families. The mining towns reflected a mix of cultures and peoples. The buildings constructed in these communities mirrored the diverse ancestry of the town's residents.

England, long a source of immigrants to America, continued to provide large numbers of settlers to the Rocky Mountains. By the 1870s, so many wealthy English had settled in the Colorado Springs area that it was often called "Little London."

The new wave of southern European immigrants added to the diversity in the region. So-called Slovenes who immigrated to the area actually consisted of three major groups: Serbs, Croatians, and Slovenes. While it is not clear when these immigrants first arrived, by the 1880s, Slovenians appeared in the coal camps throughout the region. By 1920, Utah had 836 residents from Yugoslavia. By comparison, Colorado had 2,109 Slovenians; Idaho, 400; Montana, 3,782; and Wyoming, 1,189. In Utah, southern Slavs who turned to farming found that the sandy and alkaline soil, watered by little rain, played no favorites. Everyone struggled to make a go of it on farms and ranches. In Carbon County, Utah, and Pueblo and Trinidad, Colorado, Slovenes came to find work in the coal mines.[30] As in Wyoming, Slovenian miners in Colorado and Utah worked underground, planted a few vegetables, fed pigs, and in places too cold and dry to grow crops, dreamed of being farmers.

In the 1870s, Italians had made their way into the interior West. By 1900, Tyroleans from northern Italy found their way to the coal mines of Wyoming, Utah, and Colorado. As the coal mines closed or other opportunities presented themselves, Tyroleans moved into other crafts. Many became farmers. By the early 1900s, Tyrolean immigrants found that they could succeed at farming. In some places, men worked in the mines and women and children on the farms.

Like all farmers in the mountain West, they found the task of converting desert or prairie soils to productive cropland daunting. For example, Mary Rauze Costesso in Utah told of her family's difficulties. They purchased their farm in 1942. "Outside the [weeds] were higher than the house." All there was to eat "were jack rabbits."[31] Eventually, they succeeded, but the work took its toll. The West grew crops only when the soils, sun, water, weather, and wind were just right, and the insects did not get to the crops before harvest.

The southern and eastern Europeans, like the vast majority of immigrants, worked hard. When tragedy struck, whether it was due to a mining accident or death resulting from natural causes, the immigrant communities supported the survivors. In cases where a person lost their job, immigrants invited their countrymen into their homes, fed them, encouraged them, and helped them get the first job that came open.

PREJUDICE AND TOLERANCE DURING THE TWENTIETH CENTURY

While new immigrants arrived, old prejudices remained. African Americans homesteaded, ranched, worked in mines, and ran businesses throughout the Rocky Mountains. Yet no matter how hard they worked, they could not escape the prejudice rooted in slavery. Oftentimes prejudice was manifested in the extreme crime of lynching. Lynching occurred in every western state. From 1900 to 1920, lynchings of blacks reached epidemic proportions. One example, among many, illustrates the tragedy.

In Wyoming in December 1918, a black man named Woodson walked into a restaurant at the Green River Depot. According to accounts, he insulted a waitress. She hit him with a saltshaker. Two switchmen, Edward Miller and E.J. Curtis, stepped between the two. Woodson left the restaurant, got a gun, and waited until the two men came outside. He shot Curtis, breaking his arm. The bullet he fired at Miller killed him. He fled to the courthouse and hid in the jail. The mob entered the jail and dragged him out, taking him back to the railroad, where they threw a rope over the arms of a telephone pole and placed a noose around his neck. Hoisted aloft, he died from strangulation.[32] Seeking refuge in a jail, hoping for justice, symbolizes the prejudice blacks experienced throughout the region. In an almost ironic twist, not quite comprehensible until the Holocaust, Germans during World War I, like African Americans, felt the blind sting of prejudice.

World War I

From 1914 to 1919, when World War I engulfed Europe, immigrants from Slovenia, Croatia, Tyrolia, and Serbia built communities in America. They all had one thing in common: They came from the Austrian Empire. They were, however, very distinctive. One town, Rock Springs, Wyoming, illustrates their distinctiveness. The Tyroleans actually were more Italian than Austrian. In fact, some Tyroleans came from northern Italy. In Rock Springs, they built a separate Catholic church, Our Lady of Sorrows, that reflected their values and culture. On the north side of town, the Slovenians, Serbs, and Croatians laid down their differences long enough to raise Saint Cyril and Methodius, the northside Catholic church. In a town where less than 10,000 people lived, roughly one-third of the people attended a Latter-day Saint's church, one-third went to the two Catholic churches, and the remainder divided among several churches that included the black Methodist church, the English Anglican church, and the German Lutheran church. The churches became social centers. The Slovenians went further in forming social and political associations. Slovenski Dom became the meeting place for the Slovenian immigrants. One block from Saint Cyril and Methodius, the Dom doubled as a dance hall and political center. When the United States declared war on Germany and Austria in 1917, the Slovenian community met and voted to support American war efforts and the liberation of Yugoslavia. The so-called natives or "Americans" welcomed the support and praised the Slovenian purchase of Liberty or War bonds. Meanwhile, the "natives" plotted to paint German houses in town yellow to show their newfound contempt for Germany. Interaction between diverse immigrant groups was always complex, and the Rock Springs reaction against Germans found similar expressions in Butte, Denver, and towns throughout the area.

American entry into World War I in 1917 turned neighbors against neighbors. Germans had settled throughout the region. German farmers, merchants, and craftsmen carried into the Rocky Mountains skill and knowledge. Once considered a hardworking immigrant group, they were now viewed with suspicion. They became an object of prejudice with the opening shots fired by Americans in Europe. Labeled "Huns," they found they could not get work or shop in stores. Their houses were painted yellow. Some lied about their ancestry or changed their names. Others waited out the storm only to see it rise again during World War II. The end of World War I in 1919 led to a new wave of immigrants finding their way West. Middle Easterners such as Syrians, Armenians, and Lebanese joined the Basques, Portuguese, and Swiss immigrants who had arrived earlier.

At the end of World War I, ethnic groups whose roots ran as deep as the Spanish Empire thrived. Blacks who reached the region with the first Spaniards had a firm foundation in Denver. The Denver black community centered around churches. Black churches played a significant role in the community. As elsewhere, black churches trained the community's leadership. They served the role of sponsoring social events and providing educational opportunities.[33] The pattern of having the church at the center extended even to remote areas where black communities developed. For example, in Rock Springs, Wyoming, the "Black Methodist" and later the New Hope Baptist Church served as a community center. More, the churches prepared black leaders. In the 1920s and 1930s, the church served as one of the few places black women and men could

Black women with children in front of a doorway, Denver, Colorado, 1920. Courtesy of the Denver Public Library.

Table 2. Place of Birth of Rocky Mountain Immigrants, 1930

1930 Place of Birth	China	Japan	Italy	French Canada	Mexico	Greece	Spain (Basques included)
Colorado	148	1,386	10,670	572	12,816	1,230	210
Idaho	256	676	1,086	571	849	414	1,086
Montana	314	438	2,840	1,966	1,687	840	67
Utah	214	1,730	2,814	97	2,217	274	274
Wyoming	85	562	1,653	118	3,011	888	119

Source: U.S. Census Bureau, *Abstract of the Fifteenth Census of the United States: 1930* (Washington, DC: U.S. Government Printing Office, 1933).

gain leadership experience. It is no coincidence that later generations of black leaders came from a religious background. The most noted national example of this was Reverend Martin Luther King (1929–1968). Community alliances such as the Denver Metro Black Church Initiative contended that the black church was the preeminent institution for enabling self-sufficiency.

The 1920s did witness a change in the ethnic makeup of the region. Every state had immigrants from Syria, Latvia, Lithuania, Greece, Bulgaria, Rumania, Armenia, Turkey, and Albania. All of these areas witnessed internal or external pressures brought on by the political turmoil surrounding World War I. These immigrants joined Mexican workers in a search for employment and opportunity. Areas that had long provided immigrants continued to be a source of new waves of immigration. In the decade of the 1920s, immigrants arrived from Finland, Italy, Spain, China, Japan, Yugoslavia, Russia, Poland, Norway, Sweden, Denmark, and the United Kingdom.

Compared to European immigrants, Asian settlers accounted for a small percentage of the new arrivals, but they had become a significant part of the cultural landscape. By the 1920s, for example, 1,386 Japanese lived in Colorado, 676 in Idaho, 438 in Montana, 1,730 in Utah, and 562 in Wyoming. By the 1920s Japanese families had settled in every mountain state. These families were less prone to move, and a permanent Japanese population began to call the region home. Farmers and shopkeepers purchased land and opened new businesses, making noticeable the success of Japanese immigrants. From Denver to Salt Lake City, Japanese entrepreneurs opened a variety of businesses. Beginning in the early 1900s, Japanese farmers, photographers, retailers, and restaurant owners could be found throughout the region.

These Japanese businesswomen and -men anchored communities that contained Buddhist temples and Japanese associations, and by most measures, immigrants seemed to prosper in the New World. The end to the growing prosperity came on December 7, 1941.

World War II

With the outbreak of World War II in December 1941, "Enemy Aliens," especially the Japanese, witnessed discrimination regionwide. Following the bombing of Pearl Harbor, a national policy of removing Japanese from the Pacific coast to the interior emerged. Many Japanese in America did not support the Japanese attack on Pearl Harbor. Those who did tried to return to Japan, and a third group, while not in support of the Japanese Empire, refused to be a part of a war effort against their homeland. The Japanese immigrant community splintered while the American government took steps to seize their property and place them in relocation camps in the Rocky Mountain states. Internment camps in Utah, Colorado, and Wyoming housed Japanese residents from California, Oregon, and Washington. Due to fear, Japanese lost jobs and businesses. The Union Pacific Railroad, for example, fired its hundreds of Japanese railroad workers based on the threat of sabotage. They replaced them, in many cases, with Mexican laborers.

A Japanese family on their way to the Granada Relocation Center, Camp Amache, Prowers County, southeastern Colorado, 1942. Courtesy of the Denver Public Library.

The Union Pacific termination dealt a double blow. Japanese railroad workers were required by the railroad to live in company housing. In Wyoming, there was a section camp every six miles. These camps housed the repairmen for the railroad. From Laramie to Evanston, a stretch of nearly 300 miles, Japanese workers and families lived. While most section camps housed only single males, a few Japanese families also lived in the camps. On February 11, 1942, workers and wives received notice that they had two days to pack all they had and leave. Since there had been no evidence of sabotage and since, in towns like Rock Springs, Japanese continued to live right along the railroad tracks, the firing proved more tragic than logical. People buried, sold, or destroyed belongings in their haste to leave. Where to go proved to be the next problem. Some went to Rock Springs, where the Union Pacific Coal Company (owned by the Union Pacific Railroad) employed Japanese workers. Others went to the West Coast, where they found they were unwanted. Discrimination abounded. The internment camps symbolized the depth of the discrimination.

The U.S. government placed Japanese internment camps and Italian and German prisoner-of-war camps in the interior West due to the remoteness of the region. Still sparsely populated, the region offered vast stretches of open space. In the basins of Utah, the plains of Colorado, and the valleys of Wyoming, there appeared camps designed to isolate Japanese. The fear was that the Japanese would land on the western shores, and Japanese Americans would assist in the invasion. The invasion never materialized, but the policy of removal became fact. Taken from their homes, Japanese Americans became prisoners. The internment camps held thousands of people who never committed a crime.

Forty percent of the camps were set in the basins, plains, and mountains of the Rocky Mountain states. Amache, Colorado, held at its peak 7,318 internees; Minidoka, Idaho, 9,397; Topaz, Utah, 8,130; and Heart Mountain, Wyoming, 10,767. After their closing in 1945, a hue and cry went forth, calling for justice for the citizens confined in the camps. Not until later in the twentieth century would Japanese receive financial compensation for their internment and loss of property. For many, money could never compensate for the loss of dignity. The end of World War II meant the closure of the camps.

Like the end of World War I, the end of World War II brought a new wave of immigration to the region. By 1950, the region's diversity could readily be seen in place names like Germania, China Butte, Shoshone, Gros Ventres Mountains, and others. With integration of public schools in the 1950s and 1960s, black, Hispanic, Chinese, Russian, Jewish, and Native American children learned alongside "white" students. The decades of immigration from around the world created diverse classrooms. In Montana, children whose grandparents came from Sweden went to school with kids whose relations lived in China, Germany, Hungary, and Bulgaria. Basque children in Idaho went to school with Mexican, Bannock, Chinese, and Japanese children. The region's pulse and energy grew out of diversity.

The 1950s to the Present

The 1950s, long heralded as a decade of prosperity, witnessed not only the integration of public schools but also the troubling shadow cast by the Cold War. The war in Korea and later Vietnam directly contributed to the rise in the number of Koreans and Southeast Asians who migrated to the region. The interesting thing about the Rocky Mountain region is that the immigration of Europeans and Americans from what the locals call "back east" put a distinct mark on the region. A look at the 1940 census clearly illustrates this fact. In that year the census claimed that 98.5 percent of Coloradans, 98.9 percent of Idaho residents, 96.6 percent of Montanans, 98.7 percent of Utah residents, and 98.3 percent of Wyomingites were what the census takers called "white." The label "white" masked the diversity of the people's homelands and ethnicity. As we shall see, in the later half of the twentieth century, the percentages of those classified as white dropped.

In the last half of the twentieth century, immigrants to the Rocky Mountain states came from Africa, Asia, Europe, Southeast Asia, South and Central America, and Polynesia. While Sandwich Islanders, or Hawaiians, had reached the Rockies in the nineteenth century and "Filipinos" arrived shortly after the United States acquired the Philippines, the new wave of Pacific Islanders and Asians came from areas little known to western Americans before World War II. Koreans were among the first to arrive in large numbers in the second half of the twentieth century.

Koreans initially were frequently mistaken for Japanese or Chinese. By 1900 some Koreans worked in the mines and on the railroads. Not until after the Korean War did their numbers increase dramatically. It is not clearly known when

Koreans entered the mountain West, but tombstones in Asian sections of cemeteries indicate Koreans had reached the region by the late nineteenth century. Korean coal miners in Wyoming and possibly Korean railroad workers at Havre, Montana, worked alongside Japanese workers. The Hope Cemetery in Havre and the Rock Springs cemeteries have inscriptions in Japanese characters that indicate Korean immigrants lived in both towns.

After the Korean War, immigrants fleeing the effects of the war moved to the West Coast and the interior West. They worked in a host of jobs but moved quickly into private ownership of businesses. Colorado, especially the Denver Metroplex, gained the most. Meanwhile, places like Boise and Salt Lake City had Korean churches. Some of these churches blended Protestant doctrines with Eastern philosophies, but many Koreans also chose to worship in Buddhist temples.

In both Salt Lake City and Denver, Buddhist temples appeared in the twentieth century. The Salt Lake Buddhist temple served nearby Wyoming. From Salt Lake, the priest organized the maintenance of Japanese graves in southwest Wyoming. While the Japanese population in Wyoming diminished, the one in Utah grew. Two Buddhist temples, one Japanese and one Vietnamese, now operate in Salt Lake City. Likewise, the Denver Japanese Buddhist community built a temple downtown, and there are followers spread throughout the Metroplex. While Korean and Japanese communities evolved, Polynesians increasingly began to find the cities of the region attractive.

Pacific Islanders were drawn to the area because they could easily find jobs. Essentially, every major Polynesian group is represented in the mountain West. Most native-born Guam and Micronesian immigrants moved to Colorado, with a scattering settling in Idaho and Utah. Tongans and Samoans, however, chose Utah over other mountain states; they came in the nineteenth century and remain to the present. By the late twentieth century, Rapi Nuis (Easter Islanders), Tahitians, Fijians, Filipinos, and Maoris (New Zealanders) resided in the area. The Filipino population is not considered part of the Polynesian count in the census. This is due to the unique historical relation of the Philippines as a colony of the United States. Nonetheless, Filipinos and Polynesians often found themselves working in agriculture, menial labor, or more recently, the service industry, all low-paying jobs that provided money for food and housing but little else.

Filipinos and Asian Indians

When the United States purchased the Philippines from Spain, following the Spanish-American War in 1898, Filipinos immigrated legally to America. The Filipino immigration came in two waves: circa 1900 to 1934, when the Philippines obtained conditional independence, and from 1965 to the present, when a 1965 immigration law abolished discriminatory national origins quotas, which had banned Asian immigration.

Filipinos were valued as agricultural and railroad workers. After passage of the "Gentleman's Agreement" in 1907 curtailed Japanese immigration, Hawaiian plantation owners recruited Filipino "Manong" immigrants, who quickly headed for the Pacific Coast. In 1920, 5,603 Manong had arrived on the mainland. Ten years later, there were 30,470 in California. Most Manong were young, single, uneducated men. Initially, Filipinos were not racially classified "Mongolian." Mongolians in California and elsewhere in the West had been barred from leasing and owning farmland. Later, some western states defined Filipinos as members of the Malayan race, forbidding them from marrying whites and barring them from leasing and owning farmland. Although Filipinos were "Malay" and Christian, they experienced discrimination. Categorized as "little brown brothers" and stigmatized as violent and sexual predators, they worked as house servants, in restaurants and hotels, as railroad laborers, and in the fields. In 1934, Congress granted the Philippines transitional independence in order to end Filipino immigration and to eliminate the potential for naturalization. The next year Congress allowed free transportation to Filipinos traveling to the Philippines on the condition the repatriated person did not return. After the 1965 Immigration Act, thousands of Filipinos joined the military to gain entry into the United States. They were joined by family members. Other immigrants came from the medical profession, particularly doctors and nurses. The 1965 act led to an increase in the number of Filipinos settling in the region.[34] By 2000, 15,973 Filipinos lived in the five mountain states. Filipino laborers still worked in the fields, but recent immigration has brought a high number of professionals into the region.

In 1897 the first Asian Indians arrived in Canada. Two years later the first Sikhs from the Punjab landed in San Francisco. Their numbers steadily climbed, but immigration from India slowed due to bans placed on Asian Indian immigration. At the end of the twentieth century, the number of Asian Indian immigrants arriving and settling in the United States climbed significantly. In 2000, 16,998 Asian Indians lived in the Rocky Mountain states. Many of the immigrants had come as professionals or as businessmen with money to invest in restaurants or motels. Like other immigrants they brought their own faiths. Hindus, Buddhists, and Jains (followers of Jainism) could be found in many Asian Indian communities.

Middle Eastern Immigrants

The end of World War I, in 1919, led to a new wave of immigrants finding their way West. Many came from the Middle East. Often the census takers simply listed their nationality as Arab, but because of the diversity of the Middle East, there became an insistence, on the part of the various ethnic groups, to be recognized according to their ancestry. By the end of the century, Syrians, Lebanese, Afghans, Iraqis, Palestinians, and Jordanians lived in the region. In 2000, 10,109 Arabs lived in Colorado alone. In addition to what the census classified as "Arabs," Colorado had 3,504 Lebanese and 643 Palestinian residents. All mountain states had Middle Eastern populations in 2000, with Utah coming in second behind Colorado in the total number of Middle Eastern inhabitants. The Utah population, like that of Colorado, consisted of Palestinians, Iraqis, Jordanians, Syrians, and Egyptians. Idaho and Montana had residents from most Middle Eastern countries, while Wyoming contained primarily "Arabs," Lebanese, and Egyptians.

Throughout the region Middle Eastern immigrants have brought with them their Muslim faith. The Islamic Society of the greater Salt Lake City area has two mosques: the Khadeeja Islamic Center in West Valley and the Masjid Al-Noor, in Salt Lake City. Most major Colorado cities, especially along the Front Range, have Islamic societies and sometimes several mosques. In Boise, Idaho, the Islamic Center of Boise provides religious and social support for the Muslim community.

Cinco de Mayo

Cinco de Mayo celebrations are now held throughout the area. In Denver in 2003, an estimated 350,000 people went to the Cinco de Mayo celebration in Denver's Civic Center Park. In Idaho, Governor Dirk Kempthorne proclaimed May 5, 2000, Cinco de Mayo, a celebration of diversity. In Salt Lake City, Cinco de Mayo festivals bring the community together. In May 2003, Midvale, Utah, held its sixteenth annual Cinco de Mayo Parade. Cinco de Mayo commemorates the defeat of Emperor Napoleon III's army by a much smaller Mexican force on May 5, 1862. The battle at Puebla became a symbol of pride to the Mexican nation and is celebrated annually in many western states. The celebration reflects pride in traditions and culture.

Hispanics

As noted above, Spaniards were the first Europeans to reach the Rocky Mountains. For generations they controlled the region, and they never did completely leave. In fact, at the start of the twenty-first century, Hispanics figure prominently in the culture of the Rocky Mountain region. In 1900, 274 "Mexicans" lived in Colorado, 28 in Idaho, 47 in Montana, 41 in Utah, and 58 in Wyoming. That same year Spanish residents numbered 41 in Colorado, 77 in Idaho, 20 in Montana, 8 in Utah, and 5 in Wyoming. One hundred years later, the region had changed. In 2000, Hispanics (the term has come to mean all Spanish speakers in both the literature and popular culture) numbered 1,086,572 in the five mountain states. This figure represented 11.8 percent of the area's total population.

CONCLUSION: CITIES AND DIVERSITY

The ethnic diversity of the Rocky Mountain region in the twenty-first century has roots in the nineteenth and twentieth centuries. The evidence of diversity exists in the region's two largest cities. In 2000, the Denver-Aurora Metroplex contained 1,984,887 people—385,005 Hispanic, 61,177 Asian, and 111,545 African American. Denver County, which was essentially the core of the Denver Metroplex, contained 554,636 people—175,704 Hispanic, 15,611 Asian, and 61,649 African American. Salt Lake City had 181,743 individuals—3,433 African American, 6,579 Asian, and 34,254 Hispanic. In fact, blacks and descendants of Spanish-speaking immigrants dominate the Denver landscape. Boise and Salt Lake City

Table 3. Comparison of Populations of Selected Ethnic Groups, by State, 2000

2000	Colorado	Idaho	Montana	Utah	Wyoming	Totals
Total Pop	4,301,261	1,293,953	902,195	2,233,169	493,782	9,224,360
White Alone	3,558,579	1,176,568	817,604	1,991,560	454,095	7,998,406
African American	159,279	5,244	2,359	16,150	3,126	186,158
South American	7,190	1,319	308	9,620	261	18,698
Spaniard	2,263	411	136	859	132	3,801
Hispanic (all)	735,099	101,594	18,490	200,005	31,384	1,086,572
Mexican	458,847	80,152	12,058	135,904	20,046	707,007
Puerto Rican	13,772	1,220	814	4,155	708	20,669
Central American	9,991	1,391	235	6,893	188	18,698

Source: Table based upon data from U.S. Census Bureau, *United States Census 2000*, American Fact Finder, http://factfinder.census.gov/home/saff/main.html?_lang=en. Note: *American Fact Finder* is a statistically based program that at times generates conflicting data.

Table 4. Comparison of Urban Populations of Selected Ethnic Groups, 2000

2000	Alaska Native and Native Americans	Pacific Islanders	Foreign Born	Hispanics	Asians	African American
"Salt Lake City"	7,892	3,437	33,252	34,254	6,579	3,433
"Denver County"	7,290	648	96,306	175,704	15,611	61,649

Source: Table based upon data from U.S. Census Bureau, *United States Census 2000*, American Fact Finder, http://factfinder.census.gov/home/saff/main.html?_lang=en. Note: *American Fact Finder* is a statistically based program that at times generates conflicting data.

have also grown into communities where English and Spanish speakers mingle on the city streets, but in Denver, minorities represent 40 percent of the population.

Regionwide, a different picture appears. In Colorado the 2000 census indicates 82.7 percent of the state's population was "white"; Idaho, 90.9 percent; Montana, 90.6 percent; Utah, 89.1 percent; and Wyoming, 91.9 percent. Denver and Salt Lake attracted people from around the world, but the region as a whole showed a distinct European heritage.

At the same time, the 2000 census reflected exactly how diverse the region had become. Denver had immigrants from nearly every Asian and Polynesian nation. Salt Lake City, however, could boast of the largest Polynesian population, a fact due in part to the Latter-day Saints' mission efforts in the Pacific. With the fall of Saigon in 1975, Southeast Asian refugees from Vietnam, Laos, and Cambodia fled to Thailand and safe havens in the region. For many, their ultimate destination was the United States, and in the 1970s, Southeast Asians began to enter America in increasing numbers. Members of hill tribes from Laos, known as the Hmong, left Southeast Asia out of fear for their lives. Likewise, Cambodians fled a holocaust of major proportions. This political turmoil provided a new source of immigrants to the Rockies, many of these political refugees.[35]

There is a contradiction: Some cities and places in the intermountain West have far less diversity than the rest of the nation. Compared to Denver and Salt Lake City, Boise, Billings, and remote towns in the area have fewer ethnic groups. Butte, Montana, traditionally a diverse mining community, in 2000 had 34,606 citizens; of these 32,998 were classified as "white." Boise, a considerably larger city, has 185,787 residents—8,410 Hispanic, 1,437 African American, and 3,870 Asian. Billings had 89,847 people in 2000. Of that number, in the city along the Yellowstone River, there were 495 African Americans, 533 Asians, and 3,758 Hispanics. Havre and Helena exhibited similar trends. In 2000, 9,621 called Havre City, Montana, home. Only 11 African Americans lived there, as did 47 Asians and 169 Hispanics. Helena, the capital of Montana, had 25,563 residents in town. Of this number, 59 were African Americans, 201 Asians, and 534 Hispanics. But when you analyze the census figures for the states as a whole, a broader picture emerges.

In 1700, essentially only native peoples lived here, but the population was not homogeneous. Shoshone, Bannocks, Lemhi, Navajos, Apache, Comanche, Crow, Blackfeet, Nez Percé, Utes, and other nations called the Rocky Mountains home. In 2000 the population of the region was essentially what census takers called "white," but it was not homogenous. In that year, those labeled white included Germans, French, Hutterites, Greeks, Italians, Portuguese, Spaniards, Russians, Slovenians, Croatians, Ukrainians, and people from a host of countries. Labels defy the reality

Table 5. Comparison of Native American Tribal Populations by State, 2000

2000	Blackfeet	Chippewa	Crow	Shoshone	Sioux	Ute
Colorado	430	894		139	3,018	2,648
Idaho	219	409		394	499	
Montana	10,105	2,665	6,944		5,003	
Utah	138	222		589	665	2,940
Wyoming	106	230	165	2,132	702	
Totals	10,998	4,420	7,109	4,254	9,877	5,588

Source: Table based upon data from U.S. Census Bureau, *United States Census 2000*, American Fact Finder, http://factfinder.census.gov/home/saff/main.html?_lang=en. Note: *American Fact Finder* is a statistically based program that at times generates conflicting data.

of diversity. On the surface the region's population appears homogenous, but Greek Orthodox churches, Native American "sweat lodges," Jewish synagogues, and Sun Dance poles dot the landscape, illustrating the true diversity of the region's people.

In 2000, Native American populations still lived on traditional lands but also in cities and towns, adding further diversity to the urban mix. Rarely do reservations exist in urban areas in the Rocky Mountain region. A reservation like Rocky Boy (home to the Chippewa-Cree) is relatively remote, with some of the tribal members living in nearby Havre. Havre, for example, has 867 Native Americans inside the city. This reflects the largest single minority in town. Throughout Montana, a similar demographic trend is evident. Within the city limits, Billings has 3,088 Native Americans, Helena has 541, and Butte has 675. Larger cities like Denver, Salt Lake City, and Boise contain 7,290, 7,892, and 1,300 Native Americans, respectively.

Today the region contains vibrant native cultures. Though the Sioux possibly outnumber all other groups in the region, reservations in each of the mountain states are home to Crow, Chippewas, Bannocks, Lemhi, Navajo, Arapahoe, Shoshone, Blackfeet, Cheyenne, Coeur d'Alene, Nez Percé, Gosute, Paiute, Sioux, and Utes.

Poverty among Native Americans remains a challenge. In southern Utah, members of the Navajo Nation live just to the west of the Utes in Colorado. In 1970, these Navajos residents were among the poorest in the nation. Their unemployment rate stood at 60 percent. The median family income was less than $3,000. Sixty percent of the adult population had no schooling. By 1999, much had changed. The median household income on the Navajo Reservation was $20,005. The number of students dropping out of high school had fallen to 31 percent. Prospects for higher education had improved. And while residents of the reservation had a way to go to reach the living standards of Denver, Salt Lake, or Boise, the evidence of an improved standard of living gave hope to many. Unfortunately, too many living on the reservations still live below the poverty level. The old and young on the reservation remained in homes where the median income fell below $11,500.[36]

The ethnicity of the region cannot be discussed without considering the continuity of diversity. Sometimes the immigrants came in small numbers, but always they came from around the world. Today these diverse peoples are raising children in places where centuries before Arapaho and Comanche hunters traveled. Immigrants from Bangladesh, Taiwan, the Philippines, Indonesia, Korea, Pakistan, Sri Lanka, Thailand, and Polynesia now live where Utes once camped. Indians from India, called Asian Indians by census takers, live where "American Indians," or First Nations, laid blankets and traded with the first Europeans to reach the area.

A distinctive quality of the mountain states is that First Nations still claim land in all five states. Newly arrived immigrants learn that American Indians are not part of the region's past but instead part of its future. The states whose spines are made from rocks rising to the horizon have their core nationalities whose roots lie in all continents. But the taproot of this country lies in the arrival of the Native Americans who came here more than 12,000 years ago.

RESOURCE GUIDE

Printed Sources

Bieter, John, and Mark Bieter. *An Enduring Legacy: The Story of Basques in Idaho*. Reno: University of Nevada Press, 2000.

Chan, Sucheng, Douglas Henny Daniels, Murio T. Garcia, and Terry P. Wilson, eds. *Peoples of Color in the American West*. Lexington, MA: D. C. Heath, 1994.

Daniels, Roger. *Asian America: Chinese and Japanese in the United States since 1850*. Seattle: University of Washington Press, 1988.

Emmons, David M. *The Butte Irish: Class and Ethnicity in an American Mining Town, 1875–1925*. Urbana: University of Illinois Press, 1990.

Frey, Rodney. *The World of the Crow Indians*. Norman: University of Oklahoma Press, 1993.

Knoll, Tricia. *Becoming Americans: Asian Sojourners, Immigrants, and Refugees in the Western United States*. Portland, OR: Coast to Coast Books, 1982.

Mackey Mike. *Heart Mountain: Life in a Concentration Camp*. Casper, WY: Mountain States Lithographing, 2000.

Melendy, H. Brett. *Asians in America: Filipinos, Koreans and East Indians*. Boston: Twayne, 1977.

Muzny, Charles C. *The Vietnamese in Oklahoma City: A Study in Ethnic Change*. New York: AMS Press, 1989.

Oliver, Mamie O. *Idaho Ebony: The Afro-American Presence in Idaho State History*. Boise: Idaho State Historical Society, 1990.

Papanikolas, Helen Z. *The Peoples of Utah*. Salt Lake City: Utah State Historical Society, 1981.

Petrik, Paula. *No Step Backward: Women and Family on the Rocky Mountain Mining Frontier, Helena, Montana, 1865–1900*. Helena: Montana Historical Society Press, 1987.

Rosier, Paul C. *Rebirth of the Blackfeet Nation, 1912–1954*. Lincoln: University of Nebraska Press, 2001.

Taylor, Quintard. *In Search of the Racial Frontier: African Americans in the American West, 1990*. New York: W. W. Norton, 1999.

Taylor, Quintard, and Shirley Ann Wilson Moore, eds. *African American Women Confront the West: 1600–2000*. Norman: University of Oklahoma Press, 2003.

Simmons, Virginia McConnell. *The Ute Indians of Utah, Colorado, and New Mexico*. Niwot: University of Colorado Press, 2000.

Singh, Jane, et al., eds. *South Asians in North America: An Annotated and Selected Bibliography*. Berkeley: University of California, Center for South and Southeast Asian Studies, 1988.

Stamos, Henry E. IV. *People of the Wind River: The Eastern Shoshones, 1825–1900*. Norman: University of Oklahoma Press, 1999.

Wegars, Priscilla, ed. *Hidden Heritage: Historical Archaeology of the Overseas Chinese*. Amityville, NY: Baywood Publishing, 1993.

Wilson, Laura. *Hutterites of Montana*. New Haven, CT: Yale University Press, 2000.
Zhu, Liping. *A Chinaman's Chance: The Chinese on the Rocky Mountain Frontier*. Niwot: University Press of Colorado, 1997.

Web Sites

African-Americans on the Frontier
No Date
Accessed February 2004
http://lili-z.boisestate.edu/farrit/Bibs_AfricanAmerican.htm

A resource guide for African American influences on the American frontier.

American Historical Society of Germans from Russia. Northern Colorado Chapter
2003
Accessed February 2004
http://www.ahsgr.org/conorthe.htm

The official site for the American Historical Society of Germans from Russia.

Anasazi Heritage Center
No Date
Accessed February 2004
http://www.co.blm.gov/ahc/index.htm

Web site for the Anasazi Heritage Center in Delores, Colorado.

Buffalo Bill Historical Center
2004
Accessed February 2004
http://www.bbhc.org/exhibitions/windRiver.cfm

The official site for the Buffalo Bill Historical Center. The site features an online exhibition of the Arapaho and Shoshone of the Wind River.

Montana-Wyoming Tribal Leaders Council
Assiniboine and Sioux Fort Peck Reservation
No Date
Accessed February 2004
http://tlc.wtp.net/fortpeck.htm

This Web site offers specific information on the Assiniboine and Sioux Fort Peck Reservation.

Blackfeet Nation
2003
Accessed February 2004
http://www.blackfeetnation.com/

The official site for the Blackfeet nation. The site provides information on the history and current status of the Blackfeet Nation.

People's Center
1999–2000
Accessed February 2004
http://www.peoplescenter.org/

This site has information on the Peoples' Center Museum and the history of the tribal alliance of the Salish, Kootenai, and Pend d'Oreille Tribal Nations.

Apsaalooke Nation (Crow Nation)
No Date
Accessed February 2004
http://www.crownations.net/

This Web site documents the history and current status of the Crow Nation.

Heart Mountain Digital Preservation Project
1998
Accessed February 2004
http://chem.nwc.cc.wy.us/HMDP

The Web site displays photos and the history of the Japanese Internment Camp in the Heart Mountain. The collection is from the John Taggart Hinckley Library.

Hutterian Brethren: Living in Community in North America
No Date
Accessed February 2004
http://www.hutterites.org/

Homepage for the Hutterite Brethren in North America. The site provides information on the history and structure of the Hutterite community.

Idaho Black History Museum
No Date
Accessed February 2004
http://www.ibhm.org/History.htm

The official site for the Idaho Black History Museum—a museum that holds collections from the history of the African Americans in Idaho.

Japanese-Americans Internment Camps: During World War II. Special Collections Department, J. Willard Marriott Library, University of Utah
1996
Accessed February 2004
http://www.lib.utah.edu/spc/photo/9066/9066.htm

An online photographic exhibit from the Marriott Library at the University of Utah. The exhibition features historic photographs from the Topaz Japanese Internment Camp in Utah and the Tule Japanese Internment Camp in Northern California.

Minidoka Internment Camp
2003
Accessed February 2004
http://www.lib.washington.edu/exhibits/harmony/Exhibit/minidoka.html

Online exhibit from the University of Washington Library on the World War II Japanese Internment Camp Minidoka in southeastern Idaho.

Minidoka Internment Camp National Monument
No Date
Accessed February 2004
http://www.nps.gov/miin/

The National Park Services official Web site. Offers information on the Minidoka Internment Camp Monument in Idaho.

Navajo Nation
1999
Accessed February 2004

http://www.navajo.org/
Official site for the Navajo Nation.

Nez Percé Tribe Web Site
No Date
Accessed February 2004
http://www.nezperce.org/Main.html
Official Web site for the Nez Percé Tribal Group.

Northern Arapaho Tribe
No Date
Accessed February 2004
http://www.northernarapaho.com/
Official site for the Northern Arapaho Tribe.

Montana-Wyoming Tribal Leaders Council
Rocky Boy Reservation: Chippewa Cree Tribe
No Date
Accessed February 2004
http://tlc.wtp.net/chippewa.htm
Information on the Rocky Boy Reservation of the Chippewa Cree Tribe.

Volga Germans
2004
Accessed February 2004
http://www.webbitt.com/volga/index.htm
Details and genealogical records on the Germans who settled in the Volga Valley settlement in Russia.

Shoshone Bannock Tribe
2004
Accessed February 2004
http://www.shoshonebannocktribes.com/
Official Web site for the Shoshone Bannock Tribe.

Skull Valley Goshutes
No Date
Accessed February 2004
http://www.skullvalleygoshutes.org/
The Web site contains information on the Skull Valley Goshute Reservation. The reservation is now a testing ground for chemical and biological weapons.

Southern Ute Tribe
No Date
Accessed February 2004
http://www.southern-ute.nsn.us/
Official Web site of the Southern Ute Tribe.

Topaz Museum
2000–2003
Accessed February 2004
http://topazmuseum.org/index.html
The official site for the Topaz Museum, which features detailed information on the World War II Japanese Internment Camp in Utah.

Ute Indian Tribe
No Date
Accessed February 2004
http://www.utah.com/tribes/ute_main.htm

The State of Utah information on the Ute Tribe.

Documentary Films

Ancestors in the Americas. Prods. Loni Ding and PBS, 2000.

This in-depth television series looks at the Chinese immigrant experience in the West and focuses a portion of the series on Wyoming. It looks at Asian immigration from the 1700s to the 1900s.

Bicycle Corps, The: America's Black Army on Wheels. Prod. PBS, 2000.

In the 1890s, the U.S. Army thought it could replace the horse with the newly developed and highly popular "safety bicycle." Testing this theory, the army sent 20 African American soldiers on a ride from Fort Missoula, Montana, to St. Louis, Missouri—2,000 miles away.

The Buffalo War. Prod. PBS, 2001.

A documentary about the conflict over the killing of bison that wander outside the boundaries of Yellowstone National Park.

Conscience and the Constitution, the Story. Prods. Frank Abe and PBS, 2000.

This film looks at the civil liberties violated by the internment of Japanese in the internment camps of the region during World War II.

A Rising Voice: Hispanic Utah. Prods. Colleen Casto and KUED Production, 1991.

This is a documentary that describes the legacy of Utah's 100,000 Hispanics.

The West
Fight No More Forever: Episode Six (1874 to 1877). Prod: PBS, 2001.

Part 6 of an 8 part documentary series on the history of the West. This episode deals with the tragedy of the Nez Percé's flight to Canada.

Imagining Indians. Prod. Victor Masayesva Jr., 1992.

The film crew visited tribal communities in Arizona, Montana, New Mexico, South Dakota, Washington, and the Amazon to produce this film.

Indian Self-Rule: A Problem of History. Prod. Selma Thomas and KWSU-TV, 1985.

This film deals with the experiences of the Flathead Nation of Montana, the Navajo Nation of the Southwest, and the Quinault people of the Olympic Peninsula.

Politics and Growth in the Southwest. Prod. Rock Melnick and PBS, no date.

This film by Rob Melnick, based out of the Morrison Institute for Public Policy, Arizona State University, takes a look at the change and ethnic make up of the southwest region.

Recordings

Basque Oral History Project Index
Basque Museum
611 West Grove Street

Boise, ID 83702-5971
208-343-2671
http://www.basquemuseum.com/oralhistory/

Center of Southwest Studies
Oral History Collection
Fort Lewis College
Durango, CO 81301-3999
http://swcenter.fortlewis.edu/inventory/SWOH.htm

Idaho Oral History Center, Idaho State Historical Society
450 North Fourth Street
Boise, ID 83702
208-334-3863 (phone)
208-334-31989 (fax)
http://home.rmci.net/dyingst/oralhist.htm

The Montana Historical Society Oral History Collection
225 North Roberts
P. O. Box 201201
Helena, MT 59620-1201
406-444-2694
http://www.his.state.mt.us/

The Utah Oral History Consortium
University of Utah Marriott Library
295 S1500 E
Salt Lake City, UT 84112
801-581-8558
http://utahoralhistory.org/

Western Wyoming Community College
Oral History Archives
2500 College Drive
Rock Springs, WY
307-382-1700
http://www.wwcc.cc.wy.us/

Festivals or Events

Basque Jaialdi
http://www.jaialdi.com/

The event is held in Boise, Idaho, and in 2005 will be held from July 7–31. Dancing and emphasis on Basque culture mark the event.

Cinco de Mayo
Civic Center Park, Denver, CO
May 5th every year
http://cincodemayo.denverfanatic.com/

Annual Cinco de Mayo festival is a traditional celebration of Hispanic culture and includes eating, music, and politics. An estimated 350,000 people enjoy the two-day festival in Civic Center Park.

Evanston, Wyoming, Chinese New Year Celebration
Evanston Depot Square, Evanston, WY

307-783-6319

http://www.evanstonwy.org/events/annual-chinese-new-year.asp?id=145

Involves festivities and rickshaw rides.

Organizations

American Historical Society of Germans from Russia
Northern Colorado Chapter
22409 Weld County Road 46
Lasalle, CO 80645
Chapter President: Mary Lauck
970-284-5301
Email MELauck@aol.com
http://www.ahsgr.org

A nonprofit corporation providing information and assistance on research and genealogical services for Germans from Russia.

Asian Association of Utah
1588 South Major Street
Salt Lake City, UT 84115-1631
Phone 801-467-6060
http://www.aau-slc.org/

Founded in 1977, the AAU aids Asian Americans in Utah with facets of immigration, education, and community building.

Basque Center
601 Grove Street
Boise, ID 83702
208-342-9983
http://www.basquecenter.com

The Basque Center is a social club founded in 1949 and is an important center for preserving the heritage of Basques in Idaho.

Denver Buddhist Cultural Society
2530 West Alameda Avenue
Denver, CO 80219
303-935-3889 (phone)
303-935-1196 (fax)
http://www.denverbuddhism.org/

The society helps to join the Buddhist community and to strengthen the beliefs and cultivate the spiritual growth of the Asian community in Colorado.

Latin American Educational Foundation
930 West 7th Avenue
Denver, CO 80204-4417
http://www.laef.org/

The foundation aids Hispanics in attaining higher education in Colorado.

Mi Casa Resource Center for Women
571 Galapago Street
Denver, CO 80204
303-573-1302

http://www.micasadenver.org/

This center provides support and self-sufficiency to low income women and youth in Colorado.

Montana-Wyoming Tribal Leaders Council
207 North Broadway Suite BR-2
Billings, MT 59102
http://tlc.wtp.net/index.html.htm

This council is composed of representatives from 10 tribal councils in the Rocky Mountain area. The group provides resources on education, culture, politics, and economic development of different reservations throughout the area.

Urban League of Metro Denver
5900 East 39th Avenue
Denver, CO 80207
303-388-5861
email info@denverurbanleague.org
http://www.denverurbanleague.org/default.asp

The society, which was established in 1946, encourages low income and disadvantaged African Americans to gain social and economic equality and self-reliance.

Museums and Special Collections

Anasazi Heritage Center
2750 Highway 184
Dolores, CO 81323
970-882-5600
http://www.co.blm.gov/ahc/

This museum holds collections from archaeological excavations in the four corners region of the Southwest. The museum grounds are also the site for the Canyons of the Ancients National Monument.

Basque Museum and Cultural Center
611 Grove Street
Boise, ID
208-343-2671
http://www.basquemuseum.com

This museum holds valuable information on the immigration movement of Basques into Idaho.

Black American West Museum and Heritage Center
3091 California Street
Denver, CO
303-292-2566
http://www.coax.net/people/lwf/bawraus.htm

This museum houses an extensive collection on the history of the African American influence in the American West.

Fremont Indian State Park and Museum
3820 West Clear Creek Canyon Road
Sevier, UT
435-527-4631

http://www.utah.com/stateparks/fremont.htm

The museum is situated on the Clear Creek Canyon archaeological site and exhibits the extensive collection acquired from archaeological excavations of the Five Finger Ridge Valley.

Josh House Chinese Museum
Evanston Depot Square
Evanston, WY
307-783-6319

This museum is located in a replica of the Chinese Josh House in Evanston and features an interesting collection of Chinese artifacts excavated from the Evanston Chinatown.

Idaho Black History Museum
In the historic St. Paul Baptist Church
Julia Davis Park
508 North Julia Davis Road
Boise, ID
208-433-0017

This nonprofit museum was established to provide educational resources on the history of African Americans in Idaho.

Minidoka Internment Camp National Monument
Contact Park Headquarters at 208-837-4793 before visiting.
http://www.nps.gov/miin/

Minidoka Internment National Monument in Jerome County, Idaho, is a National Park Service Site that provides information on Japanese internments during World War II.

Montana Historical Society
225 North Roberts
Helena, MT
406-444-2694
http://www.his.state.mt.us/

The society holds information on the history of Montana, with a particular focus on the Lewis and Clark expeditions.

Topaz Museum
10000 West 4500 North
Delta, UT
http://topazmuseum.org/

The museum displays the history of the Topaz Japanese Internment Camp.

Western Heritage Center
2822 Montana Avenue
Billings, MT
406-256-6809
http://www.ywhc.org/

The Western Heritage Center houses information on the history of the Yellowstone River Valley.

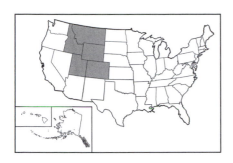

FASHION

*Laurel Wilson and
Rick Newby*

Environment, which includes climate, and especially weather, can be said to be the most important factor influencing dress in the Rocky Mountain region. Winter was, and is, the most important season for creating specific fashions in the region since it not only causes people to wear heavy winter outerwear but also continues to influence activities like skiing and snowmobiling that allow people to take advantage of the beauty of the Rocky Mountain landscape. Traditional occupations such as mining, ranching, and the timber industries remain important in the way people dress in the Rockies. Since the Rockies are noted for their beauty, it comes as no surprise that tourism—which includes shopping for articles of clothing that remind tourists of the places they have visited—is an important economic activity.

Despite—or perhaps because of—this emphasis on utility, much of the clothing associated with the region has taken on a certain cachet elsewhere. In *The Fashion System*, Roland Barthes might have been talking about rough-and-ready Rocky Mountain fashions when he wrote that a particular outfit possessed a "mixed essence of country and labor [that] will be looked upon as a rather exotic spectacle."[1] At the same time, through the mediation of spectacles—Wild West shows, films, rodeos—cowboy fashions, for example, have grown increasingly distant from their utilitarian roots, colorful, wildly exaggerated, more purely exotic. In turn, the locals, after first disdaining these innovations, have embraced them, thus closing the circle between mass culture and regional identity.

The resources for making dress in the Rockies were most important during the period before ready-made fashion became widely available to the region's dwellers, and by the 1960s, many of the region's apparel manufacturers, such as Jack Frost Woolen Goods of Salt Lake City, had succumbed to competitors outside the region. Today, a small fashion industry survives in the Rockies, mostly centered in Denver, with annual western fashion shows also held at the Western Design Conference in Cody, Wyoming, and with a few diehard clothing manufacturers still producing garments within the region.

Nevertheless, Rocky Mountain dress can still be said to exist, at least as a reflection of recreational pursuits important to the region, of particular occupations, especially that of the cowboy, and of Native American clothing traditions. More important, as image or ideal, the Rocky Mountain lifestyle—and by extension the clothing worn while practicing it—continues to resonate nationally and globally. Clothing retailers, whether within the region or beyond its borders, continue to draw customers with garments that might adorn firm-jawed cowboys, wind-burnt mountain climbers, wild-eyed kayakers, or just urban refugees lucky enough to own a little place in the shadow of the Colorado Rockies, the Tetons of Wyoming, or Montana's Front Range.

PREHISTORIC DRESS

A number of prehistoric cultural groups lived in the Rocky Mountain region, but while they probably used dress in different ways, little evidence of what they wore survives, given that most clothing was made of perishable materials like leather and plant and animal fibers. Despite the absence of clothing remains, some archeological sites, particularly burials, provide information about the materials early peoples used to make and decorate clothing and accessories. The most common remains are the tools used to prepare animal skins for use. In burial and village sites, archaeologists have found stone scrapers used to clean hides and bone awls and needles used to sew clothing. Archaeologists speculate that early peoples made their thread from sinew (animal tendons) and twine from plant fibers.

At prehistoric sites like Pictograph Cave State Park, near Billings, Montana, archaeologists unearthed jewelry—pendants, plaques, bracelets, and rings—crafted from ocean clams and other seashells acquired from people on the Pacific coast, indicating significant trade beyond the region. Prehistoric people in the Rockies also made pendants, incised with markings of bird shapes or simple line patterns, from local materials, including bone and the teeth and claws of animals, particularly bears and beaver. They also wore tinklers that made sound when the wearer moved. Archaeological evidence shows that people of all ages and both sexes wore jewelry and decorated clothing. Pigments found in burial sites may have been used for funerary purposes or to decorate hair and skin. Since Native Americans used face paints, it is likely that prehistoric people did as well.

NATIVE AMERICAN DRESS

Three broad groupings of aboriginal Native Americans made their homes in the Rocky Mountain region (today's Colorado, Utah, Wyoming, Montana, and Idaho): Plains Indian tribes, the people of the Great Basin, and Plateau tribes. Significant differences in dress existed among these three groupings, and further, every tribe within each group had its own style of dress that reflected the materials used to make clothing and accessories, the physical environment in which the dress was used, and the artistic influences that shaped the style and form of decorations. Because trade had long been important to Native Americans, even those articles of precontact dress collected by early explorers include elements manufactured in Europe or eastern America; however, these manufactured elements, such as beads and ribbons, were used completely differently from the way they would be by Europeans. Europeans had introduced horses to Southern Plains tribes in the sixteenth century; this new means of transport then spread to the Northern Plains tribes by the beginning of the nineteenth century. This meant that information and material culture could move among tribes even more easily. Although the traditional practices of each cultural group showed distinct regional or tribal characteristics, most tribes continued to add manufactured elements such as beads or metal tinklers to their dress. This fact was confirmed in the 1830s by artists Karl Bodmer

Note the beadwork and elk's tooth decoration on these Piegan children's clothing, c. 1910. Courtesy of the Library of Congress.

(1809–1893) and George Catlin (1796–1872), among the first Euro-Americans to provide images of Plains Indians.

Indians of the Plains

The Plains Indians who make their homes within the Rocky Mountain region include the Arapaho, Assiniboine, Blackfeet, Crow, Cheyenne, and Northern and Eastern Shoshone. Ranging over the prime buffalo range of eastern Montana, Wyoming, and Colorado, these tribes embodied the image of the American Indian that captured the popular imagination in Catlin's and Bodmer's paintings, Wild West shows, and western films. Although the dress of the various tribes certainly differed, it is often difficult to discern those differences because of the extent of trade and gift giving among the tribes. In general, the clothing of the Plains Indians, as scholar Josephine Paterek has written, was a "costume of movement and sound—feathers and fringes streaming in the wind, tinklers and bells jangling, beads and shells rattling."[2]

Plains Indian men generally wore a buckskin breechclout. The breechclout was a symbol of sexual prowess, and though some were unadorned, many were decorated with fringe or quillwork. Men also wore thigh-length leggings of tanned hide, held together with sinew. These, too, could be decorated with fringe and quillwork. Men wore shirts made of deer, elk, or pronghorn skin. These beautiful shirts, in white or tan (with some smoked brown or dyed black) were variously decorated, often with bands of quillwork, fringe, strips of ermine, or locks of hair.

Plains Indian women generally wore skirts or dresses made of skin. These ranged from a basic wraparound skirt held up with a belt (and worn with a poncholike top) to dresses of various designs. The most complex was the "three-skin dress," which included a skirt made of two skins sewn together and the top fashioned from a single skin folded in half and then sewn to the skirt, resulting in a large yoke with a neck opening. Women also wore knee-length leggings held up with bands of otter fur or leather thongs. The women decorated their clothing even more elaborately than the men's shirts, adding seashells and rows of elk teeth as well as quillwork and fringe, and sometimes retaining the tail of the deer, elk, or antelope from which the garment was made.

Both men and women wore moccasins, either a soft-soled one-piece design or a hard-soled two-piece version with the sole fashioned from thick bison hide. Some moccasins sported cuffs, which could be turned up and tied off during winter, to prevent snow from reaching the wearer's feet. Also, for winter, some moccasins were worn extra large so they could be stuffed with insulation, often buffalo hair, fur scraps, or grass.

A robe made of bison skin was the standard for winter outerwear, for both men and women. These robes were remarkably warm but could weigh close to ninety pounds. For warmth, the skin was turned fur side in, and the outside was generally decorated with paints, in a variety of designs, depending on the wearer's tribe and role. Women's designs tended to be geometric, while men's often featured pictographic depictions of their exploits in war. For less cold weather, Plains Indians wore lighter robes made of elk, pronghorn, or deer hides.

Remarkably, year round, most Plains Indians did not wear headgear, except for fur caps sometimes in winter. But headgear played a key role in their cultures, particularly feathered headdresses worn on ceremonial occasions. These dramatic objects were constructed of a skullcap made of leather to which feathers (primarily golden eagle wing feathers) were attached. More feathers were attached to a long strip of buckskin that trailed behind. A band on the forehead was decorated with quill- or beadwork and strips of ermine fur. The bison horn headdress, often extensively decorated with shells, braided horse tails, and other precious materials, was worn only by the most distinguished men and symbolized great power.

Both men and women wore their hair in two braids, though men's hairstyles varied from tribe to tribe. Some people wrapped their braids in otter or other fur, and men often wore feathers in their hair, along with various objects attached to their scalplocks (long thin locks hanging from their crowns); these might include beads, bones, or animal claws.

Plain Indians prized adornment highly, and they wore beautifully crafted necklaces, chokers, earrings, armbands, and bracelets. Among the most remarkable (and most powerful) were grizzly bear-claw necklaces. With the advent of Euro-Americans, Plains Indians also highly valued peace medals made of silver. Some men wore breastplates made of rows of hair pipe beads (made from the shell of the queen conch from the Caribbean, introduced by Euro-American traders). In addition to jewelry, Plains Indians adorned their bodies and faces with paint. Painting was not simply adornment but often had spiritual significance, as when both men and women used paint to call upon the support of spirit beings in times of war.

As more manufactured trade goods reached the region, Plains Indians actively and inventively incorporated new materials into their dress. These included glass beads, and by the 1830s, beads had mostly replaced porcupine quills in the decoration of garments. Manufactured cloth began to replace buckskin, and woolen Hudson's Bay blankets, sometimes made into hooded jackets called capotes, slowly took the place of the bison robe for winter wear. Plains Indians also adopted the white man's vest, decorating it with beadwork. Metals provided new opportunities for decoration. Metal tinklers, worn on dresses and shirts, added new sounds to Plains Indian dances, and silver disks became essential elements in "hair plates," strips of rawhide attached to the hair and trailing down the wearer's back. The tall, black felt "Indian" hat was adopted late in the nineteenth century, as the U.S. government resettled Plains Indians, often forcibly, on reservations.

Indians of the Great Basin

The Great Basin tribes within the Rocky Mountain region included the Western Shoshone, Bannock, Southern Paiute, and Ute. Their homeland was the arid basin country of Colorado, Utah, and southern Idaho (and extending into Nevada and California).

Because this region was hotter than the Northern Plains or the Columbia Plateau, Great Basin people tended to wear less. Quite often, men and boys went naked in the summers, while in winter they wore leggings and breechclouts or a kind of kilt, made of buckskin or woven of bark or grass. Some groups also wore rabbit-skin tunics. In summer, women wore an apron in the front, and in the cool seasons, two aprons, front and back, plus a poncho. These garments could be fabricated from skins or from sagebrush, juniper bark, or yucca. They also wore long dresses made of buckskin decorated with magpie feathers and seashell pendants.

Most Great Basin people went barefoot, at least part of the year, but they also wore sandals (made of sagebrush or yucca fibers) or leather moccasins in a variety of styles. In winter, they wore robes, most often made of rabbit skins (or more rarely bison hides). A rabbit-skin robe required as many as 100 pelts. Some robes were also made of other small mammal hides, including those of woodchuck, beaver, and even meadow mouse sewn together.

Great Basin people generally went bareheaded, except for fur caps in cold winters. The Ute and Bannock wore their hair in braids, but in most other groups, the men let it hang free, while women brought theirs forward and simply tied it with cords. Great Basin jewelry included necklaces and ear pendants reflecting trade with the West Coast (including abalone and other shells); they also employed turquoise from the Southwest. Compared to Plains tribes, their decoration—created from shells and feathers—was simple, though the Shoshone and Ute were skilled beadworkers.

Indians of the Columbia Plateau

The Columbia Plateau is a land of sagebrush desert, high plains, and mountain valleys, with some wetlands and forested slopes. The plateau extends from the Rocky Mountains in Idaho and Montana to the Cascades of Washington and Oregon, and north into British Columbia. The Eastern Plateau tribes are those found within the Rocky Mountain region, and these include the Flathead (Salish), Interior Salish to some extent (in Idaho), Kutenai, and Nez Percé.

The Flathead, Kutenai, and Nez Percé adopted aspects of Plains Indian culture, including costume. There were, however, significant differences. Plateau men's breechclouts were rarely decorated, then only with fringe. Plateau men's shirts tended to be shorter than those worn on the plains, only waist-length, and they were decorated with the characteristic Plateau rows of holes in the buckskin, made with an awl.

Plateau women, beginning early in the nineteenth century, wore ankle-length two-skin dresses constructed from mountain goat, black-tailed deer, or elk hides left in their natural shapes. Cotton soon supplanted these materials, and the cotton Plateau dress was T-shaped with the seams of the square-cut sleeves left unhemmed. The women wore belts or sashes at the waist and sometimes a cotton blouse under the dress.

Plateau people generally wore one-piece deerhide moccasins, often with the hair left inside for warmth. Like Plains Indians, they favored buffalo robes for outerwear, along with lighter buckskin or rabbit skin robes. Imported blankets eventually replaced these robes. Both sexes wore their hair loose or in a pair of braids. They preferred the war bonnet identified with the Blackfeet, though some scholars believe that these eagle feather bonnets originated with the Kutenai and were then adopted by the Plains tribes. Plateau men wore rawhide sunshades, while women made basketry hats without brims that they decorated with painted or "false" embroidery (false because created during the weaving process). Women used cornhusk bags, decorated with elaborate nonobjective designs. Plateau jewelry, especially necklaces and chokers, included seashells, copper tubes, and beads. They preferred red paint for body and face decoration but used yellow, black, and green pigments as well.

Native American Dress in the Twenty-first Century

At the start of the twenty-first century, Native Americans in the Rockies have not abandoned their traditional dress. Nevertheless, their costumes have evolved to make use of modern technology and changes in Native American culture. Because traditional dress is time-consuming to make and leather garments are not as comfortable to wear in hot or very cold weather as clothing made of cloth, most American Indians in the region wear contemporary fashions in their daily lives. However, during Native American ceremonies and the many powwows in the Rockies, members of all tribal groups continue to wear traditional leather garments decorated with beads and quills.

Men wear feathered dance bustles and porcupine guard hair roaches that originated among the Plains tribes. Men's grass dance outfits are a modern phenomenon. These consist of cotton shirts and trousers trimmed with brightly colored yarn fringes that sway with the dancer's movements. Leather- and cloth-clad women wear fringed silken shawls to dance the Fancy Dance, more flamboyant than traditional women's dances. Women dancers also wear jingle dresses that include tinklers made of tobacco can lids bent into cones and hung from thongs that allow them to jingle against one another. At giveaways, tribal members offer Pendleton blankets as tributes to honored individuals and as thanks for special favors.

Skilled craftswomen still practice quillwork and pass this craft on to younger generations. Beadwork has grown ever more complex as Native Americans have leisure time to devote to creating beadwork masterpieces; these include beaded vests, moccasins, leggings, dresses, shirts, and cradle boards but also such innovations as beaded athletic shoes and expand-a-back "gimme" caps. Although some traditional leather tanning still exists, most leathers used by Native Americans come from leather suppliers who sell domestic and imported leathers.

EARLY SETTLER AND NATIVE AMERICAN DRESS

Lewis and Clark

Captains Meriwether Lewis (1774–1809) and William Clark (1770–1838)—and their Corps of Discovery—were among the first Euro-Americans to travel deep into the Rocky Mountain region, though French Canadian explorers had ventured there in the late eighteenth century. As they assembled their gear for the journey, the intrepid American explorers had to consider appropriate clothing for Rocky Mountain conditions since they could not rely on resupply posts once they entered the uncharted region.

Made up of volunteers from the U.S. Army, the Corps of Discovery were subject to military law and discipline. This was apparent in the clothing they wore. Each of the enlisted men was issued linen shirts that were usually white, although Sgt. John Ordway wore a red shirt while hunting buffalo.[3] Shirts were considered underwear to be covered with vests that buttoned nearly to the neck and with high-collared fatigue jackets or dress coats of red and blue. Each of the men also received white wool overalls, white linen trousers, coarse linen trousers, and gaiters tarred to make them waterproof to protect the men's lower legs. The officers wore cocked hats also known as *chapeau bras* or bicorns, while the enlisted men wore round hats that resembled top hats, especially in formal encounters with Native Americans. Members of the Corps also wore fatigue hats resembling watch caps or stocking caps as well as low-crowned, wide-brimmed hats made of felt.

Footgear presented the biggest problem. Although the men initially had cobbler-made shoes, these soon wore out, and they were forced to make moccasins for the rest of the journey. Since cold weather can occur any month in the Rockies, cold weather clothing was essential. The men had hunting frocks made of heavy linen and having elbow-length capes that provided some additional warmth and helped to shed rain and snow. Woolen surtouts (overcoats) with hoods and belts provided even more warmth. The men wore the clothing they were issued as long as it could be repaired, then replaced it with leather only when necessary. Scholars believe that this did not happen until they came close to the Rocky Mountains. By the time they reached the Rockies, they were probably wearing a combination of cloth and leather clothing they made themselves.[4]

Fur Trappers

Oddly enough, it was fashion that brought the first significant influx of Euro-Americans into the Rocky Mountain region. Stylish dressers in the East and on the European continent clamored for beaver hats, and trappers had already, by the first decade of the nineteenth century, decimated beaver populations elsewhere on the continent. Immediately following the return of the Lewis and Clark expedition, trappers headed into the Rocky Mountain country, eager to capitalize on the demand for pelts.

Fur trappers and traders were not themselves fashionable dressers, but they developed their own sense of style that was a result of several factors. The first, a lack of white women, profoundly affected the dress worn by fur trappers since none of the trappers brought Euro-American women with them. Traditionally, women of almost every culture are those who are responsible for making and mending ordinary clothing (though dress clothing for men, on the other hand, was often made by male tailors). Other factors included the kind of dress they commonly wore in more settled regions of the country, the environmental conditions they encountered in the Rocky Mountains, and once their Euro-American clothing wore out, the dress they adopted that reflected Native American culture. Additionally, many of the trappers stayed in the mountains during the winter, facing the challenges of keeping warm in often inhospitable conditions.

Many of the men married Native American women, and once the garments on the trappers' backs wore out, their Indian wives fashioned new garments according to the traditions of dress practiced by the wives' various tribes. In addition to making clothing, women native to the Rockies often knew of food sources not familiar to the trappers, and they knew the trails to good trapping country.

One of the first people to record images of Rocky Mountain fur trappers was Alfred Jacob Miller, who traveled to the mountains in 1837. His drawings and paintings show leather-clad men wearing broad-brimmed hats and carrying long rifles. They were generally clean-shaven except for mustaches and wore their hair past shoulder length. Some of the pictures show fringed leather shirts trimmed with beadwork or quillwork, and Miller pictured nearly all the trappers wearing moccasins. Other images show the trappers wearing brightly colored shirts that were probably cotton calico shirts, part of the trade goods sold to Native Americans. An illustration titled *A 'Bourgeois' of the Rocky Mountains* shows Captain Joseph Rutherford Walker wearing a broad-brimmed hat and fringed leather shirt and trousers and carrying a long rifle. He is also wearing a bandolier bag decorated Native American style, and he has a pistol tucked under a sash at his waist. He wears a beard, and his hair is longer than shoulder length. William Gray in his *History of Oregon* describes Joe Meek, another fur trapper, as a "tall man, with long black hair, smooth face, dark eyes . . . a harum-scarum, don't care sort of man, full of life and fun in the mountains."[5] A photograph taken somewhat later shows that Meek grew a beard. Osborne Russell wrote a complete description of the dress and gear he used while a trapper in the Rocky Mountains between 1834 and 1843:

> A Trappers equipments is generally one Animal upon which is placed one or two Epishemores [a buffalo fur pad made of several pieces sewn together] a riding Saddle and bridle a sack containing six Beaver traps a blanket with an extra pair of Mocasins his powder horn and bullet pouch with a belt to which is attached a butcher Knife a small wooden box containing bait for Beaver a Tobacco sack with a pipe and implements for making fire with sometimes a hatchet fastened to the Pommel of his saddle his personal dress is a flannel or cotton shirt (if he is fortunate enough to obtain one, if not Antelope skin answers the purpose of over and undershirt) a pair of leather breeches with Blanket or smoked Buffaloe skin, leggings, a coat made of Blanket or Buffaloe robe a hat or Cap of wool, Buffaloe or Otter skin his hose are pieces of Blanket lapped round his feet which are covered with a pair of Moccassins made of Dressed Deer Elk or Buffaloe skins with his long hair falling loosely over his shoulders complets his uniform. He then mounts and places his rifle before him on his Saddle. Such was the dress equipage of the party myself included.[6]

Leather trousers found in museums show that they were styled in Euro-American fashion with front button closures at each side or in the center front crotch seam and having waistbands rather than resembling the leggings and breech cloth normally worn by Native American men. Often the pants are decorated with beads, stroud (woolen cloth in red or blue), and quillwork that were part of Native American tradition. Museum collections also include leather frock coats made European style but trimmed with quillwork and beadwork. These coats illustrate that Native American women were skilled at adapting European styles in leather and embellishing them with the designs of their own cultures. Assumption sashes were typically worn by French Canadian trappers but were also worn by some Rocky Mountain trappers. The sashes were made of woolen yarns in reds, blues, yellows, and greens finger woven into lightning-bolt patterns.

The period of the free trappers ended about 1845 when European fashion had shifted from fur-felt hats using beaver pelts to silk hats. Also, because of extensive trapping, beaver had grown too scarce for free trappers to make a profit. In addition, fur-trading companies found that they could increase their profits by trading with Native Americans who trapped beaver and killed buffalo for their hides. Although there were some trading posts deep in the Rocky Mountains, most were located on the Great Plains where buffalo could be found in abundance. By the 1850s, the fur trade had shifted irrevocably from beaver skins to buffalo robes.

The Métis

On the frontier, the offspring of the French Canadian and Scots trappers who married Indian women—often Chippewa and Cree—became known as Métis (French for "mixed blood"). The Metis, though their greatest numbers were in Manitoba, Saskatchewan, and North Dakota, ranged down into Montana and were among the first Euro-Americans to settle at Spring Creek, later Lewistown, and along the Front Range. As a natural outgrowth of their hybrid heritage, Métis people sported the flamboyant hybrid dress that had suited their fathers so well. William Keating wrote of a band of Métis hunters he encountered in 1825: "Their dress is singular, but not deficient in beauty; it is a mixture of the European and Indian habits."[7]

The Assumption sashes brought into the country by French Canadian trappers became a symbol of Métis identity. Like the "many strands, many patterns, many colors" of the sash, one Métis priest would note, Métis culture was "woven together from a variety of cultures, traditions and beliefs." Another item from the fur trade frequently worn by the Métis was the capote, a hooded parka fashioned from woolen Hudson's Bay blankets.[8]

From the Indian side of their heritage came leather garments embellished with bead- and quillwork, often in floral designs that may have emerged from European floral embroidery patterns taught in mission schools. Métis women were celebrated for the fringed and beaded buckskin jackets—such as those worn by George Armstrong Custer (1839–1876) and Buffalo Bill Cody (1846–1917)—they made for sale in the emerging cash economy.

The singular Métis way of dressing also influenced the apparel of certain non-Métis. The painter Charles M. Russell, for example, frequently wore an Assumption sash as an emblem of his solidarity, speculates folklorist Nicholas Vrooman, with his mixed-blood neighbors in central Montana, who often found themselves accepted by neither the white nor Indian cultures. Three Russell drawings, held by the C. M. Russell Museum in Great Falls, Montana, depict a Métis scout, a Métis trapper, and a "French Half-Breed," each dressed in some variant of classic Métis garb, including the Assumption sash, buckskin leggings and shirts (beaded in floral designs), and a capote constructed from a Hudson's Bay blanket.[9]

Métis people still wear Assumption sashes at celebrations of their culture, like the annual Spring Creek Métis gathering at Lewistown, and contemporary artisans, like Gary Johnson of Lodge Grass, Montana, keep Métis beadwork traditions vibrantly alive.

NINETEENTH CENTURY

Immigrants in the Rocky Mountains

Immigrants heading to Utah and Oregon in the 1840s, Colorado in the 1850s, and the Montana and Idaho gold fields in the 1860s made up another important early group of Euro-Americans to pass through the Rocky Mountain region. These travelers on the dusty and often dangerous trails had to bring the goods they needed for the journey, together with the materials and supplies required to establish homes in a relatively unsettled region of the country. They did encounter army forts along the way, where they could get supplies including fabrics and some articles of clothing. In these forts, the average Oregon Trail migrant, for example, spent nearly $4,000 on foodstuffs, dry goods, and other necessities.[10] This was a goodly sum that required careful planning to reserve for the westward migration.

The men, women, and children who traveled the westward trails were civilians, and all needed clothing that withstood the rigors of Rocky Mountain travel. Handbooks listed the kinds of clothing needed for the journey; these included underwear, outerwear, and overcoats. Men were advised to have flannel shirts, woolen trousers, woolen undershirts, thick drawers, woolen and cotton stockings, and stout shoes. Rainproof ponchos, broad-brimmed hats, and lined coats were among the clothing recommended.

Less advice was available for women, and many of them relied on the conventions in dress of more settled places. At the beginning of the trip, some women wore "traveling dress"; these consisted of styles made of dark-colored woolen or worsted fabrics and cut somewhat more simply than "at home" dresses. However, they were floor length, designed to be worn on smooth floors or paved sidewalks and were clearly not suited for walking on rocky, dusty trails. Most women soon abandoned this confining costume and wore cotton work dresses instead. By the time the migrants reached the Rockies, women shortened their skirts to above the ankle so they could walk over uneven ground without lifting their skirts to keep from tripping. A very few women decided to wear the new bloomer costume consisting of knee-length skirts and long loose pants of matching fabric gathered at the ankles. Although this would seem to be very practical clothing for the arduous journey, propriety nearly always reigned supreme, and even women who had bloomer costumes wore them only when their other clothing was not fit to wear. In 1866, one Bozeman Trail traveler did mention encountering an immigrant train from Iowa in which "the women were all dressed in bloomers." In the same year, another Bozeman Trail immigrant described the garb of her immediate party: "Chell has got on her Debarge dress, tucked up short, a large calico apron, and her buff [color] sunbonnet and water-proof sacque. . . . Will has on his old short coat and Scotch plaid pants and vest and broad-brimmed hat. . . . I have my calico wrapper in the wagon, a large bib apron . . . and a new green gingham sunbonnet, so you can see I am armed and equipped."[11]

Since pale skin was valued as a symbol of upper-class status, women and girls wore sunbonnets with very deep brims and long capes in the back to protect them from the sun's rays. Shawls were the most common form of outer wrap for women during the 1850s, but they also had lined coats to protect them from the cold. Sturdy shoes were necessary in a place that had plenty of hazards for bare feet.

Children who traveled the trails west wore cotton clothing that in another place might have been considered play clothing. Although illustrators whose work appeared in *Frank Leslie's Monthly* and *Harper's Weekly* often pictured children barefooted, the photographic record shows that children, like their parents, wore sturdy shoes or boots. Boys wore hats and girls wore bonnets to protect them from the sun.

The Military in the Rocky Mountains

The U.S. Army established its first posts in the Rockies to protect the immigrants traveling the Oregon Trail and the other trails to the Rocky Mountain mining camps. Fort Laramie, originally a fur trading post in Wyoming, and Fort Hall in Idaho both served the needs of weary migrants as they traveled the Oregon Trail. With the discovery of gold in the Rocky Mountains, the United States established additional forts to guard routes that carried goods to the camps and brought gold from the mines. These included Fort Collins in Colorado and Forts Fetterman, Casper, Reno, McKinney, and Phil Kearney in Wyoming, and Fort C. F. Smith in Montana. After the government confined Native Americans on reservations, it established army posts to make sure they stayed there. Those forts included Fort Washakie in Wyoming and Forts Custer, Keogh, Maginnis, Assiniboine, and Missoula in Montana. Today, there is still a military presence in the Rockies, most notably in Colorado Springs, Colorado, where the Air Force Academy is located.

Soldiers were often recruited among recent immigrants to America, and so a variety of ethnicities were represented in the ranks. Most dominant among the new immigrants were the Irish and Germans. Among the most distinctive soldiers on the Northern Plains were African Americans known as Buffalo Soldiers. Serving in the Ninth and Tenth Cavalries and the Twenty-fourth and Twenty-fifth Regiments of infantry organized just after the Civil War, the black troops were known as "Buffalo Soldiers" because Native Americans thought their hair resembled the curly coats of buffalos. The men accepted the name as a badge of honor and even used the buffalo as part of their regimental insignia. Much of the Ninth and Tenth Cavalries service took place in the Rockies, including at Fort Assiniboine and Fort Missoula. Nineteenth-century soldiers in the Rockies faced very cold conditions during the winters and had to make do with uniforms left over from the Civil War. These uniforms were not suited to the rigors of frontier use, and new uniforms were slow to arrive due to poor supply routes and the distance from suppliers. The men despised the hats that had been developed for the cavalry because they blew off easily and got in the way of the rifles. The troops preferred forage caps since they were easier to wear in windy conditions. The men put aside the heavy-skirted frock coats that were regulation dress in favor of loose fatigue sack coats; the sack coats better accommodated physical motion and were less expensive to make than frock coats. Blouses made of lightweight wool (what we would call shirts today) were even more practical for the work done at forts in the Rockies. Soldiers wore flannel shirts and drawers under their blue uniforms.

During very cold weather, the men wore as many layers as they could and still move, and many men bought their own nonregulation buffalo-hide coats. The army did not provide special winter headgear, so soldiers devised a number of ways to keeps their heads warm, including tying the overcoat cape over their heads as a hood. Unfortunately, this reduced the needed layers over the body but prevented their ears from freezing. Often men bought their own fur or woolen caps with earflaps or made their own earflaps to be worn with forage caps. The Quartermaster General did not include gloves as part of winter wear for troops stationed in the West, so frostbitten fingers were often a reality. Soldiers pulled their cuffs over their hands or bought or made their own mittens. The best mittens were made of fur, with buffalo hide the most common, and had wide gauntlets to accommodate the bottom of the coat sleeves.

Soldiers wore regulation uniforms at the fort but were free to adapt their clothing for the conditions they found in the field. Consequently they sometimes wore cotton shirts with their wool campaign blouses that could be easily removed during the day as the temperature rose from the chill of nighttime. Since soldiers carried only one blanket into the field, they also used woolen blouses for an extra layer of warmth when needed.

Buffalo soldiers of the 25th Infantry, some wearing buffalo robes, Ft. Keogh, Montana, 1890. Courtesy of the Library of Congress.

In 1872, the army authorized and distributed new uniforms, at least to enlisted men, since officers had to purchase their own uniforms. In most ways the uniforms resembled earlier ones but with some additions. The fatigue blouse was of a completely new design, with a pleated front and skirt designed to go over two to three layers of underclothing; it could also be worn alone. The pleats concealed bag pockets, one at the breast and two in the skirt. The blouse was available in lined and unlined versions. The only change made to pants was to add a saddle piece in the seat and the inside legs to provide another layer of fabric for wear and comfort. The pleated blouse was a failure since the pleat flapped in the wind and snagged easily, so men often stitched down the pleats, changing its function back to a blouse with no pleats.

In 1873 the army considered the need for warm footgear when it issued overshoes made of buffalo hide with the hairy side in. These worked just fine for foot soldiers during the very cold, dry conditions often part of Rocky Mountain winters; however, they did not fit into stirrups and so were useless for mounted men. It was not until the winter of 1876 that the army authorized below-the-knee, double-breasted buffalo coats with high collars for winter use.

In 1878 the army developed additional outer clothing for conditions found in the West. The most important was a blanket-lined overcoat, but it was sent only to soldiers posted north of forty-two degrees latitude. This included most of Wyoming and part of Utah and all of Montana and Idaho, but Colorado was excluded in spite of conditions that were often very cold because of the altitude. Soldiers who could afford it bought their own buffalo-hide coats or, lacking money but having sewing skills, made their own. The army provided knitted wool gloves, but these were not adequate for keeping hands warm. Again, men bought or made warm fur or wool mittens and headgear.

The army added new garments after soldiers made numerous complaints. One of the first was a new campaign hat made of good-quality wool that had a ventilated crown. A new blouse that had no waistline seam or pleats and was available lined or unlined replaced the hated pleated blouse. Shirts with a breast placket were made in two weights to serve the needs of troops in cold as well as hot weather. All-wool stockings were made fourteen inches tall; this helped to keep troops a little warmer.

The best thing to happen, however, was that special winter outerwear was developed for use on the frontier. The first consisted of sealskin hats with earflaps, back cape, and visor. The army also provided gloves that had gauntlets at least five inches long to accommodate the sleeves of the coat. In 1878, the Quartermaster authorized muskrat caps designed like the sealskin caps and muskrat gloves lined in lamb's fleece and the gauntlets lined in flannel.

At the end of the nineteenth century, cavalry uniforms changed from blue to olive drab, the color still most prevalent in army uniforms. By the end of the twentieth century, technology radically changed military uniforms. Now synthetic fibers such as polyester are used to make it easier for soldiers to care for their clothing as well as to meet standards for appearance. Synthetic linings and fabrics such as Gor-Tex make it more comfortable for soldiers to serve in cold weather.

OCCUPATIONS AND DRESS

Miners in the Rocky Mountain West

Surface Mining

With the discovery of gold in Colorado in the late 1850s, thousands of would-be miners headed west. How these miners did their work affected what they wore. At first, most mining was done along streams where the gold had been deposited over time. Miners separated the gold from the surrounding "dirt," using water sloshed through gold pans with flat bottoms and slopping sides. A new development, the cradle, allowed miners to wash the gold from the other material; then sluices—long boxes that had riffle bars placed crosswise—made separating gold from the dirt even more efficient. Finally, when the claims were cleaned of most of the gold, miners used hydraulic hoses filled with high-pressure water to tear apart the earth, which was then fed into sluices to separate the gold from surrounding material. Even dredges used water to separate the gold from baser materials. Miners did much of this work during spring, summer, and fall when water was available; frozen water is of no use to miners. Gold mining was wet work.

Since gold mining was such wet work, most miners used rubber boots to keep their feet dry. Broad-brimmed hats shielded them from the sun. A few photographs of Rocky Mountain miners show that some wore bib overalls over long underwear or waist-high trousers. Although rubber boots were most practical, some men wore leather work boots either for comfort or because they did not own rubber boots. Some miners used waterproofed slickers, especially desirable during hydraulic mining operations.

The Beginnings of Levi Strauss and Company

The first miners in the Rockies wore cotton work shirts and trousers supported by braces; these were worn over long-sleeved and long-legged underwear usually called union suits because they were all-in-one garments united at the waistline. Some of the men may have worn Levi "Waist High Overalls" since these pants were developed in the gold mining fields of California about 1855. Levi's added rivets to these sturdy pants made of cotton duck and sailcloth, heavy weight cotton fabrics, in 1873 when Levi Strauss and Company and a Carson City, Nevada, tailor named Jacob Davis patented the process, which evolved into today's blue jeans. The work shirts made of heavy cotton or wool flannel typically had placket fronts and attached collars. Shirt jackets, looser shirts that opened from neck to hem, provided another layer of warmth for the miners as they worked their claims.

It would seem that this would complete the discussion of mining dress, but the photographs of mining camps show yet another picture. Some of the most remote mining camps in the Rockies offered surprising amenities that extended beyond the expected saloons and brothels. Virginia City, Montana, had the Planter House Hotel that hosted balls and theater performances. Leadville, located at 10,188 feet in the Colorado Rockies, boasted of the Tabor Opera House where Oscar Wilde (1854–1900) lectured on the ethics of art. Although not all of the men who rushed to the gold fields achieved their dreams of great wealth, those who did gladly indulged their sophisticated tastes for fine dining, fine accommodations, and fine entertainment.

They also expected to wear fine clothing. General stores sold all the tools needed by miners, but they also carried good-quality woolen and worsted frock coats, vests, and trousers. Photographs show that when the miners were not at their claims, they wore sack coats (loosely fitted jackets styled like the business sports coats worn today) over their work clothing or with dress trousers and vests, if they did well enough at their claims. This concession to eastern conventions shows that the camps were not completely wild, wooly places. The men who struck it rich hired laborers to work their claims, thus freeing themselves to participate in the rich social life available in the camps. Wealthy miners wore white shirts with removable collars and silk ties under well-made frock coats, matching trousers, and silk or woolen vests. This sartorial elegance displayed the wearer's success and set him above the men still laboring on claims.

Underground Mining

Underground copper mines required other kinds of gear, especially lighting gear. The first lighting for underground miners consisted of candles inserted into candleholders with horizontal points shoved into the wall. Miners used these primitive lighting devices even after better forms of lighting became available. Safety lamps, developed in 1815, were enclosed lanterns carried into the mine. By 1886 portable electric safety lamps came into use in underground mines, and finally, in 1909, electric cap lamps were developed in Scotland. This lamp had a bulb inside a casing that was attached to the miner's cap, with a wiring cord attached to an acid battery suspended by a belt. By the 1920s, miners began wearing hard hats with built-in lanterns attached to batteries. Today, these are still in use but vary in style and material. The hard hats miners wore in the 1950s were made of fiberglass, while the hard hats of today are usually made of aluminum.

Underground mines tend to be warm, and the deeper the mine, the warmer the air. The miners who work the stopes (actively mined tunnels) deep in the mine need protective clothing; the combination of metal and water creates slightly acidic conditions that are hard on the skin and clothing. Jerry Dolph, reminiscing about his mining days, wrote that Butte, Montana, copper miners cut the hems from their pants with pinking shears because copper-contaminated water would collect in the hem layers and the "bottoms of the pant legs would rot, drop down on one side, and trip us up."[12] The pants he described were denim jeans or bib overalls.

In addition, underground miners wore plaid flannel work shirts that they could shed to long underwear tops that had button plackets at the neck. They also wore steel-toed work boots or, if the mine was very wet, steel-toed rubber boots. Hard

A miner stands next to a box of explosives in a tunnel at the Wolf Tongue Mine, a tungsten mine, in Nederland (Boulder County), Colorado. The man wears a hard hat with a head lamp, holds a stick of dynamite, and stands beside a wooden box that reads: "Hercules Powder." Dynamite sticks are stuffed in crevices in the rock. Courtesy of the Colorado Historical Society.

rock miners have changed their clothing very little since the 1950s. They have added clothing made of synthetic fibers that are comfortable in a broad range of temperatures and comfortable when wet, but the styles of the clothing have not changed very much. Today, t-shirts are more common than button-placket underwear, but jeans, flannel shirts, and hard-toed work boots or rubber boots still remain part of the miner's wardrobe.

Social activities were also part of hard rock mining life, but few mining towns had as many wonderful recreational opportunities as Butte, Montana. In 1899, copper king William Andrews Clark bought about sixty-nine acres at the trolley car turnaround, and there he built the finest amusement park west of the Mississippi. It included a Parker Scenic Railway; a forerunner of a movie house; a Parker Ferris Wheel; a Parker Miniature Locomotive; and the centerpiece of the Gardens, a Parker "Carry Us All," the first permanent merry-go-around in Montana.

When miners and their families went to Columbia Gardens, they dressed in the latest fashions. At the start of the twentieth century, women wore white waists (blouses) and long dark skirts over tightly laced corsets, piles of underwear, and high-button shoes. Over their Gibson Girl–styled hair, they wore fancy straw hats in summer and wool hats in the fall. The men wore three-piece sack-coated or frock-coated suits over stiff-collared shirts. They wore straw boaters or felt bowlers. Little boys wore short pants and bolero jackets over lace-collared shirts, and the little girls wore ruffled collared dresses over white stockings and high-buttoned shoes. Columbia Gardens closed in 1973 but remains a fond memory for the families that dressed up to ride the carousel or the Ferris wheel.[13]

Cowboy and Cowgirl Dress

Much of cowboy culture originated in Salamanca, Spain, a region of open plains much like those found in North America, and the clothing worn for herding cattle in the Rocky Mountain states (Colorado, Utah, Wyoming, Montana, and Idaho) reflects those origins. According to C. J. Bishko, the cattle herders of twelfth-century Spain wore low-crowned hats, bolero jackets, tight-fitting trousers, sashes, and boots with spurs.[14] In Mexico, the vegetation where cattle were raised, unlike that found on the open plains of Spain, included grass but also thorny shrubs that ripped riders' clothing and tore their flesh as they raced after the half-wild cattle that grazed the unfenced range. The first solution was to wear *armas*—slabs of leather tied to the saddle, then folded over the rider's legs—a cumbersome means of protection. *Chaparejos*, leather leggings worn over pantaloons, were the next solution. These eventually evolved into shotgun chaps that extended from waist to ankle. Other items of clothing also changed to reflect the culture of the men who herded cattle in a variety of environments, including the Rocky Mountains.

As North Americans, whose clothing traditions originated in northern rather than southern Europe, became dominant players in cattle culture, cowboy dress became less Spanish in appearance. The most important piece of the cowboy outfit illustrating the origins of the men who wore them was the vest. In the more settled regions of the United States, shirts were considered underwear, and decent men covered them with vests and suit coats. Cowboys used vests in a different way. These useful garments added another layer of warmth in the cool mountain air, and their pockets could be used to store cigarette papers and tobacco, among other things.

In their reminiscences, cowboys recall that they wore work shirts made of "hickory," described in an 1894 dry goods dictionary as "a particular style of coarse shirting known for its . . . alleged hickory-like toughness, or superior wearing quality."[15] Photographs show that cowboys also wore dress shirts without the button-on collars that were characteristic in more civilized places. Cowboys wore a variety of types of pants; these included woolen pants that were intended for dress. They were more comfortable to wear than Levi's. The denim pants, though they wore well, were stiff. An advertisement in the *Yellowstone Journal* of Miles City, Montana, shows that Levi's were marketed in the region.

Stetson hats were familiar all over America, but those worn by cowboys were often distinctive because of the way they shaped the crowns and brims. John Rollinson, Wyoming cowboy, wrote that in the 1890s "all wore Stetson hats of the high-crowned pattern—most of which looked like they had seen plenty of service, as indeed they had, for those hats had fanned many an ember into flame for a fire; had served to dip into a creek or water hole to drink from; had been used to spook a horse along side the head, or to slap him down the rump."[16]

Working men of all descriptions used bandanas, but those worn by cowboys brought real style to their outfits, even if only incidentally. These bandanas had a number of uses, including filtering out the choking dust churned up on cattle drives. John Barrows wrote that "a gaudy silk handkerchief was used . . . not for decoration but to protect a sensitive part of his body from flying ants and other stinging insects."[17]

Boots were another article of dress that distinguished cowboys, both in how they looked and how they walked. John Rollinson said that most of the boots worn by cowboys were made by a bootmaker named Hyer who lived in Olathe, Kansas. Spurs in a wide range of styles were also part of cowboys' outfits. John Barrows wrote, "The heavy hand-wrought spurs were serviceable as accelerators and were also useful when hooked into the handmade goat-hair cinch, a short of sheet anchor which has kept more than one man in the saddle when he otherwise would have been thrown."[18]

Chaps were probably the most important part of the cowboy's outfit because they carried symbolic weight. They were the article of dress that differentiated the occupation of cowboy from all other outdoor occupations. This was most important to the youngest cowboys who wanted to show their new adult status. Firearms, in particular six shooters, were another part of the cowboys' outfits that proved they were men.

The next category of cowboy gear was the result of the cold climate of the Rocky Mountains. Most cowboys were employed from spring roundup to fall roundup, a period of the year that might have some cold, wet weather but not the bitter cold of winter. Those who stayed on to open frozen waterholes and keep an eye on the cattle preferred the fur and fur-lined coats advertised in the *Yellowstone Journal* during the 1880s, but these were expensive. Most cowboys had to settle for blanket-lined work coats made of cotton or wool. They also wore fur hats and glove/mitt combinations that had wide gauntlets, which can be seen at the Grant-Kohrs Ranch National Historic Site near Deer Lodge, Montana.

Some cowgirls also rode the Rocky Mountain ranges in the late nineteenth century. They were usually the daughters of ranchers who had no sons and so relied on their women folks to help with outdoor work. These early cowgirls wore long divided skirts with fitted waists (blouses) that met the requirements for propriety. They wore wide-brimmed hats and boots with spurs as they went about their ranching chores. Photographs indicate that they even wore fitted corsets under their cowgirl outer clothing since corsets were also required of moral women at that time.

Because it had been developed for functional reasons, the dress worn by working cowboys and cowgirls changed slowly. The emergence of new kinds of cowboys at the end of the nineteenth century and beginning of the twentieth brought more rapid change. The first of these new cowboys were those who toured the world with Wild West shows. Because these shows occurred in open-air arenas, with the audience seated on the perimeter of the action, some elements of the cowboys' outfits needed to be exaggerated. Photographs of the performing cowboys reveal that they wore very large hats with extrawide brims and extratall crowns; this ensured that the cowboys' heads were visible from a long distance. The other form of exaggeration was the shift from fringed shotgun chaps (worn by most working cowboys) to very hairy woolie chaps. Wild West cowboys did not introduce these chaps; they had been part of the vaquero tradition since the eighteenth century and were part of Northern Plains gear since the 1870s. The woolie chaps appeared on the show circuit simply because they made the cowboys' legs look much larger.

Quite a few women performed shooting and horseback riding tricks in Wild West shows. They, too, wore exaggerated hats, but instead of chaps, they sported heavily fringed divided skirts. The fringes on the skirts swirled wildly as they performed their cowgirl tricks.

Actors who appeared on stage and screen around the turn of the twentieth century became an important influence on cowboy goods sold in catalogs. The first stage cowboys appeared in the 1880s, and the first American feature film, *The Great Train Robbery* of 1903, was a western. Movie cowboys superficially resembled real cowboys, but with important differences, as shown by this 1911 description of Bronco Billy Anderson who starred in *The Great Train Robbery*. "He was dressed like a Wild West Show cowboy, with such extravagant extras as brass-studded wrist guards, fringed gauntlets, and a bandanna worn full in front like a lady's big bertha collar, instead of tied tight around the neck to keep dust out and sweat from running all the way down into your boots."[19]

Most movie cowboys of the 1910s, 1920s, and 1930s wore variations of this costume, along with very wooly woolies, silver embellished leather vests by Hollywood saddler Ed Bohlin, and highly decorated boots made visible because movie cowboys usually tucked their pants into their boots, a practice not commonly used by working cowboys. Although real cowboys looked upon actors playing the part of cowboys with incredulity and disdain, the fictionalized cowboys made a distinct impression on boys who dreamed of being cowboys.

Soon apparel companies that targeted working cowboys started making clothing based on the movie model, introducing new fabrics, especially rayon (which was less expensive than silk), to produce flashy fashions. Movie-influenced shirt makers like Rodeo Ben and Nudie Cohn also introduced the smile pockets and shaped yokes now recognized as distinctly western, and Rodeo Ben put the first snaps on western shirts in 1933.

Professional rodeo performers, like the Wild West and movie cowboys, also used dress to enhance their appearance. In 1910 rodeo cowboys were pictured wearing various styles of woolies. By the mid-1910s, batwing chaps were the preferred style, and with that, the types of embellishment changed from year to year so that the fashion-conscious rodeo rider could purchase the latest color and embellishments.

Fanny Sperry Steele, of Mitchell, Montana, was among the first women to perform in rodeos. She and other female bucking bronco riders wore long wool or leather divided skirts. By the 1910s, a few women wore athletic bloomers with their cowboy boots and spurs, but most stuck to the more proper divided skirts. It wasn't until the 1920s that rodeo cowgirls began wearing jodhpurs and trousers in the arena. They dressed up these practical garments with bright sashes and embroidered vests and the usual hats, boots, and spurs.

Rodeo is still an important form of entertainment in the Rockies, and new developments in technology have an impact on the clothing worn by cowboys today. Chaps now have very long fringes that flap dramatically as cowboys ride bucking horses and fishtailing bulls. The chaps are fastened from hip to knee so that the bottoms of the chaps also flap. Chaps are further embellished with Mylar films in very uncowboylike shocking pinks and bright chartreuses. Performers now buckle Kevlar vests over their bright cowboy shirts to prevent broken ribs and reduce the bruises that are among the hazards of rodeo performing. Most bull riders use a gauntlet-style glove that includes their initials at the cuff. Most cowboys still wear Stetsons jammed tight to their heads, blue jeans, slant-heeled or straight-heeled cowboy boots, and spurs since those are part of the cowboy tradition. Some more safety-conscious bucking bull and bronc riders wear riding helmets. Rodeo cowgirls still perform, but very few ride bucking stock. Instead they do barrel racing and pole bending to show off their horseback riding skills. They wear fancy western-cut blouses and pants in bright metallic colors that flash as they streak around the arena. Their hats are often trimmed with metallic hatbands as well.

There is yet another form of cowboy that developed in the Rockies in the early twentieth century—the dude ranch cowboy. The oldest dude ranches are located in Wyoming and Montana; the Eaton Ranch of Wolf, Wyoming, established in

Dudines at Valley Ranch Dude Ranch, Valley, Wyoming, c. 1933. Courtesy of the Buffalo Bill Historical Center.

1905, is still operating. By the 1920s, many dude ranches catered to wealthy dudes who wanted adventure with some creature comforts. Those who operated the ranches created a setting that met the expectations of easterners influenced by images of screen cowboys wearing huge hats, chaps, and fancy shirts and boots. The dudes themselves dressed in styles they had seen in the movies. They wore red satin shirts with woolen frontier pants tucked into fancy boot tops.

Guest ranches remain a part of Rocky Mountain life today, but those who visit them usually wear baseball caps and athletic shoes when they go horseback riding. Still others succumb to fancy western duds, including ten-gallon Stetsons, fancy boots, and fringed leather coats still available at western retailers.

Loggers

The forest products industry has played a key role in the economies of western Montana and northern Idaho since the late nineteenth century. The loggers who worked there dressed much like their counterparts in other U.S. lumbering regions (the adjacent Pacific Northwest and the North Woods around the Great Lakes). Often faced with cold, wet weather, loggers in the Rockies wore stout leather boots and thermal underwear coupled with heavy wool clothing. In the summer, they wore sturdy cotton outerwear and striped cotton hickory shirts.

Norman Maclean, in his memoir "Logging and Pimping and 'Your Pal Jim,'" noted, "Clothes that would stand [loggers'] work and the weather had to be something special." Of an early-twentieth-century Montana lumberjack, Maclean wrote, "He was dressed all in wool—in a rich Black Watch plaid shirt, gray, short-legged stag pants, and a beautiful new pair of logging boots." Special boots were essential to a logger's outfit, and as elsewhere, the Rocky Mountain loggers wore what are called caulk (pronounced "cork") boots. These sturdy boots featured heavy leather soles and steel caulks (short spikes) for traction on the logs. Though a number of boot makers served loggers' needs, White's Boot Company in nearby Spokane, Washington, was the one preferred by Montana and Idaho timber workers (at this writing, White's continues to supply its boots to loggers and other outdoor workers). The White boot, wrote Maclean, "was shaped to walk or 'ride' logs. It had a high instep to fit the log, and with a high instep went a high heel."

One less savory aspect of "corks" was that loggers sometimes employed them in their fights. When one fighter fell to the ground, the other would rake him with the steel caulks. "This treatment," wrote Maclean, "was known as 'giving him the leather,' and when a jack got this treatment, he was out of business for a long time and was never very pretty again."[20]

In the early twenty-first century, loggers' clothing focuses on issues of durability and safety, especially for those operating chainsaws, log splitters, and trimmers. Safety apparel includes hard hats or special helmets, safety glasses, boots with steel toes, and chaps or double-thickness saw pants.

DISTINCTIVE DRESS FROM SETTLERS

Many of the settlers in the Rocky Mountains were drawn there by the lure of gold and silver, but even those who did not achieve their dreams of wealth often stayed on to make their living in other ways. Some established ranches, while others worked in the mines, became involved in the lumber industry, or lived in growing towns where they operated businesses or worked as teachers, preachers, and public servants. The dress they wore was similar to the clothing they wore in the places they had come from. Some of the people who eventually settled the Rocky Mountains had lived in America for generations, while others were new immigrants, all feeling the influence of fashion with a few exceptions.

Homesteaders

The Homestead Act of 1862 made 160 acres of land available to settlers who gained title for a small fee once they made prescribed improvements and lived on the land for five years. The Timber Culture Act of 1873 increased acreages to 480, and in 1916, homesteaders could obtain 640 acres for grazing livestock. Homesteaders claimed land in the Rocky Mountain region in hopes of making good livings for themselves and their families. Part of the definition of making a good living was to have a good house that was furnished with fine furniture and to be able to dress in the latest fashions. Magazines like *Godey's Ladies Book*, *Peterson's Magazine*, and *Harpers Bazaar*—delivered to post offices throughout the Rockies—carried the latest news about current fashion. Even the Montgomery Ward and Sears and Roebuck catalogs brought information about fashion—and the fashions themselves—to Rocky Mountain settlers.

Following the rules of propriety was as important as following the dictates of fashion. Women, in particular, were expected to wear clothing that showed they were decent, moral women. This meant that they wore breath-constricting corsets along with cumbersome layers of petticoats and other underwear even while doing physical chores on their homesteads. In addition, they wore long cotton stockings held up by garters attached to the corsets. Shoe styles included slip-on pumps and high-buttoned or laced styles. By the late nineteenth century, women wore house-dresses known as Mother Hubbards; these one-piece, cotton dresses were gathered from a yoke at the shoulder and fell to the floor without the constriction of a waist seam. The dresses had long sleeves that could be rolled up and matching belts to take in the fullness at the waist. These garments allowed women to wear their corsets a bit looser or, in some cases, not at all while doing household chores. Mother Hubbards were not considered appropriate for public view, however, so when women left their houses to shop, they tightened their corsets and put on two-piece walking dresses or skirts and waists (what we call blouses today) along with hats and whatever overcoats were required for the weather. Most women also wore gloves for propriety, since decent women covered their hands, for warmth and to keep their hands clean.

Men did not escape notions of propriety either. They wore long underwear with long legs and long sleeves under long-sleeved shirts, also considered underwear and therefore not seen in public without vests and jackets. Work shirts had attached collars that laid flat at the neckline, whereas dress shirts had collar bands to which were attached very stiffly interfaced and starched collars. Vests that matched coats and pants or that were contrasting in color went over shirts. Pants were cut very long in the crotch and were supported by braces (suspenders). Men's shoes included low oxford types and high laced or pull-on boots. Men wore hats outdoors but removed them indoors and in the presence of women. Since the Rockies have long, cold winters, men wore coats made of fur or blanket-lined coats in addition to fur caps and gloves.

Children also wore the fashions considered appropriate for propriety. Little boys wore dresses until they were three or four years old. They then got their first short pants that extended to the knee. They got their first long pants about age twelve to fourteen, when they were also considered old enough to have adult responsibilities. Little boys wore two-piece underwear consisting of sleeveless cotton tops that buttoned to short underpants. Until they wore long pants, they wore stocking suspenders that consisted of cotton straps worn over the shoulders and ending in garters to which stockings were attached. Their footwear usually consisted of high-buttoned shoes. As they graduated to long pants, they also graduated to underclothing like that of their fathers, and tied shoes or boots replaced the high-buttoned shoes.

Little girls' underclothing was like that worn by little boys, although many girls were also put into corsets by the time they were eight or ten years old—some even younger. All girls wore dresses with petticoats, even when they did the same kinds of outdoor chores as their brothers. Their stockings were attached to stocking suspenders, and they, too, wore high-buttoned shoes. When girls reached the age of fifteen or sixteen, they lengthened their skirts to the floor and were also considered old enough for adult responsibilities. It was not unknown to find teachers in Rocky Mountain schools who were only fifteen or sixteen years old, although most completed normal school, which lasted one year, once they had graduated from high school at seventeen or eighteen.

Dress in the Rocky Mountains began to change after World War I. Styles for women and girls, in particular, grew less constrictive. Even magazines like *Good Housekeeping* and *Ladies Home Journal* were beginning to show practical jodhpurs for gardening and some other outdoor tasks. Most housewives, however, were more comfortable wearing housedresses cut very straight from the shoulders to below knee length. Although there is a myth that women threw away their corsets, they only shifted to breast reducers and girdles to shape their figures into the boyish silhouettes that were fashionable from the end of the 1910s into the early 1930s. Women's dress-up clothing was also cut straight from shoulder to hip and was embellished with slightly gathered or pleated skirts. They, like their fashionable big-city sisters, wore tightly fitted cloches over their cropped hair. In other words, Rocky Mountain women followed fashion as closely as any East Coast woman did.

Men's clothing did not change as radically as women's dress did. The vest was the one garment not seen as often from the 1910s on. Men still wore three-piece suits, but more casual men's dress did not include vests. Farmers, miners, and railroad laborers more commonly wore bib overalls, whereas other laborers preferred denim overalls (now called jeans). By the 1930s, even dress shirts had permanently attached collars since mechanical washing machines made it easier to keep clothing clean.

While most settlers in the Rocky Mountain region followed the dictates of eastern fashion, with some differences due to weather and the character of work in the region, other Rocky Mountain settlers dressed in truly distinctive ways based upon their religious beliefs or the sartorial traditions of their cultures of origin. From Mormon settlers in the 1840s to Hmong immigrants in the late twentieth century, these settlers have added richness and texture to the fashion landscape of the Rockies.

Mormons

Mormons carried with them to their Rocky Mountain sanctuary unique clothing traditions mandated by their religion. More even than most nineteenth-century Americans, Mormons were concerned with modesty in dress. They believed—and continue to believe—that dressing modestly shows respect for God and for themselves. Modest dress serves to prevent immoral behavior. Neatness and cleanliness are also high values in Mormon dress.

Because the body, in Mormon theology, is a temple for an eternal spirit, all Mormons who have received their temple endowment wear "temple garments," an outward expression of an inward covenant. These white undergarments, signifying that they have been washed by the blood of Christ, are to be worn twenty-four hours a day, except under certain circumstances (like bathing, participation in athletic events, doctor's visits, etc.), and each Mormon's regular clothing should completely cover the temple garments, further emphasizing the importance of modest dress.

Today, the emphasis on modesty remains a value among practicing Mormons. In the guidebook for Mormon teachers and parents, *For the Strength of Youth*, the section on "Dress and Appearance" advises young people to avoid any revealing attire (short shorts or skirts, tight clothing, midriff-baring tops) as well as disfigurements like tattoos and piercings; if a young woman wants pierced ears, she should wear only a single pair of modest earrings. The booklet asserts, "When you are well groomed and modestly dressed, you invite the companionship of the Spirit."[21]

Hutterites

One Rocky Mountain group not affected by fashion is a sect of Mennonites called Hutterites. The Hutterites believe in communal ownership of property, which differentiates them from the Amish and the General Conference Mennonites. Hutterites, named for the Mennonite leader Jakob Hutter (d. 1563), emigrated from Europe to found three colonies in South Dakota during the 1870s. They subsequently established many colonies in Montana where they are distinctive in the way they own property as well as how they live and dress.

Each member of the community is allotted a set amount of yardage from which to make clothing. This has resulted in styles of clothing, especially for women, that have remained nearly unchanging for generations. The women and girls wear stiffly starched polka-dotted scarves and dresses made of colorful flower prints, stripes, and plaids. The dresses consist of skirted jumpers worn over blouses with collars and short or long sleeves and nearly ever-present aprons. Although the garments have changed very little for women, the shoes they wear today vary in style from running shoes to loafers. When they work in the sun, Hutterite women still wear slatted bonnets like those worn by pioneer women in the nineteenth century.

While at one time Hutterite men's shirts and pants were probably made at home, now they wear ready-made plaid or printed shirts made of combinations of synthetic and natural fibers, together with black jackets and pants held up by braces. They wear black broad-brimmed cowboy hats except during the summer when they turn to light-colored straw cowboys hats. Boys sometimes wear caps with stiff, straight-sided crowns, much like those their ancestors wore in Russia. Boys in some Hutterite colonies also wear expand-a-back "gimme" caps, often given to tractor-buying farmers. Men and boys wear loafers and laced work boots, and boys sometimes wear running shoes. All married men have beards.

Norwegians

Few Norwegians settled in the Rocky Mountains until the end of the nineteenth century, a period after fashion had found its way even to Norwegian subsistence farms. Most people of Norwegian ethnicity wore the same fashions as settlers whose ancestors were longtime Americans, but some immigrants did wear clothing that marked them as Norwegian. The practice of wearing aprons for dress occasions as well as for work remained part of Norwegian American culture, even when most American women used them only for functional reasons. These aprons often included open-work embroidery or colorful embroidered patterns, but Norwegian women also wore woven or printed aprons as well. When fashionable dress was called for, Norwegian women wore brooches called *sølje* that were made of silver and had small dangles that sparkled with movement; they also wore chains presented to them as part of traditional wedding dress. Although virtually all the photographs of Norwegian immigrants show them wearing fashionable American dress, older women wore theirs without the body-shaping corsets considered necessary for decency by most women.

Men, too, retained aspects of the dress of Norway. Some wore the standing collars that were part of traditional style on coats, vests, and jackets. Their Norwegian-style vests featured silver, brass, or pewter buttons that ran from waist to nearly chin height. Many men preferred wearing silk neck scarves without the stiffly starched collars that were part of American men's fashion during the nineteenth and early twentieth centuries. Some men wore soft, brimless caps typical of traditional Norwegian dress. Some men and women retained wooden shoes for dirty farm work, and hand-knitted stockings continued to be a tradition among Norwegians in America.

Basques

Found throughout the Rocky Mountain region, but especially in Utah, Idaho, and Wyoming, Basques brought their distinctive dress with them, and even today, when dancing their liturgical dances, Basques sport their traditional costumes. For example, in Boise, Idaho, during the annual Boise Basque festival on the Feast of Corpus Christi, Basque men perform the *Korpus dantzak* as it has been danced for centuries in the town of Onati, Spain (there is considerable variation in the dances from locale to locale within the Basque region).

All dancers but the leader wear red berets, red skirts, and red sashes, together with white pants and shirts; the leader's beret, skirt, and sash are blue. In Basque tradition, white signifies purity, while red means the earth or soil; blue stands for the heavens. Other Basque dance companies in the region, such as the Utah'ko Triskalariak Basque Dancers of the Utah Basque Club, help keep Basque dance and costume traditions alive in the Rockies.

Hmong

Hmong people arrived in western Montana in 1976 as refugees from the conflict in Vietnam and Laos. They have since made their homes in the area around Missoula, making important contributions to the culture of the area in part as masterful truck gardeners and restaurateurs and in part through their crafts, especially embroidery and appliqué. Though the Hmong in Montana tend to wear standard American clothes in their workaday lives, some of them still create and wear traditional clothes for New Year's celebrations and such rites of passage as weddings, baby blessings, and funerals.

In Laos, the Hmong wove cloth from the fibers of the hemp plant and dyed the cloth with natural dyes, especially indigo (*nkaj*), which they grew. In Montana, they tend to use factory-made cotton cloth in creating their ritual clothes. Family members often give Montana Hmong infants "baby hats" at birth. These brightly colored, embroidered hats—sometimes also decorated with amulets, coins, beads, and sequins—are saved for special occasions, especially New Year's celebrations and cultural performances.

New Year's is a time of courtship for young Hmong, and young women craft beautiful costumes for the celebrations. If they lack the time or skills to make their own costumes, they buy them from relatives or from Hmong refugee camps in Thailand. Montana Hmong women also make their own wedding costumes for traditional ceremonies at home, but they may wear American wedding gowns for a separate wedding celebration open to the larger Hmong community.

"Old people's clothes," beautiful and complexly embroidered collars, sashes, coats, jackets, and pants, are among the most remarkable costumes created by Hmong craftspeople. It is traditional that family members give these garments to their elders well before their deaths. At their funerals, elders are then dressed in these elaborate outfits, sometimes in many layers. Montana Hmong send boxes of these costumes to their loved ones back in Laos or Thailand, purchasing the garments if they lack the skills to make them. At Montana funerals, some Hmong now place American clothes on the bodies of their elders, perhaps reflecting the loss of traditional skills and adaptations to a new culture.

ROCKY MOUNTAIN FASHION IN THE TWENTY-FIRST CENTURY

At first glance, with the start of the twenty-first century, it might appear that Rocky Mountain dress is beginning to lose any distinctiveness it once possessed (except in certain ethnic or religious enclaves). For example, rancher and writer Ralph Beer (a Montana native now living in Colorado) writes that, when autographing books with rodeo cowboy and poet Paul Zarzyski, "Darned if Paul and I didn't seem to be the only two guys in Bozeman [Montana] wearing western hats and boots. The whole place looked to have been outfitted by J. Crew and the folks at Lands' End."[22] Still, though Beer and Zarzyski only encountered New Westerners that day, it is true that some rural Rocky Mountain communities still take cowboy dressing seriously, and not just at rodeo time. Nearly every Rocky Mountain town of any size has at least one western wear shop, and the Denver Western and English Apparel & Equipment Market, held five times a year, serves buyers from throughout the nation, offering western wear retailers a chance to order merchandise from approximately 1,000 manufacturers.

Within the region, western wear companies like Denver's Rocky Mountain Clothing Co. continue to produce clothing lines with names like Rockies, Cinch, and Cruel Girl, competing with better-known outlanders like Wrangler and Levi. (Following the national trend, Rocky Mountain Clothing recently closed its jeans manufacturing plant in Rocky Ford, Colorado, choosing to work with contractors rather than employ the sixty-four Coloradoans who worked in the plant.) Rockmount Ranch Wear of Denver, started by Jack A. Weil in 1946, also remains in business, producing high-end cowboy apparel, including many vintage shirt styles from its extensive catalog and western-tailored leather garments. Weil's grandson Steve joined the company in 1981 and introduced a number of innovations, including looser fitting shirts (the classic cowboy shirt was cut slim, making it less likely to get caught on barbed wire or brush) and garments made of 100 percent cotton, especially the gabardines that had gone out of vogue in the 1960s with the introduction of polyester fabrics.

Designer Ralph Lauren (1939–   ) is a master of creating seductive atmospheres around clothing styles, and through his ownership of the 16,000-acre Double RL Ranch near Ridgway, Colorado, his personal style of casual dressing (worn jeans, frayed chambray shirts, battered cowboy hats), and certain of his clothing lines, Lauren has helped imagine what Lauren biographer Michael Gross calls "a new, luxurious frontier, one on which women wore shearling coats, suede fringed jackets, silver-buckled cowgirl belts and luxe chamois blouses."[23]

Helping keep this imaginary frontier alive is the Western Design Conference in Cody, Wyoming, which nurtures "couture" western fashion with its annual fashion show. Each September, the runway in Cody features, in the words of the conference's Web site, a "kaleidoscope of shimmering silk, soft chamois, sparkling silver, rugged denim, thick fringe, sleek leather and antique lace." Designers from Colorado, Wyoming, Idaho, and Montana (and elsewhere in the West) vie for awards for Best Collection, Best Adaptation of Materials (in 2003, a New Mexico designer won for her deerskin bags and clothing), and Best New Designer. Dramatically abstracted from any semblance of use, these sleek and often sexy designs offer clear evidence of the continuing fascination for things western.

Another fashion scene, less concerned with regional traditions, thrives in the Rockies. As the region's largest metropolis, Denver is home to a number of talented designers. Perhaps the best known is Sarah Siegel-Magness, proprietor of So Low (based in Los Angeles), noted for its lines of low-riding underwear and jeans worn by movie stars. The Denver chapter of Fashion Group International holds an annual awards show, honoring local designers; other fashion shows are held as fund-raisers for worthy causes. A longtime Cherry Creek/Denver couture designer, in fact, told the *Denver Post* that much of her market for custom "special-occasion clothing," besides weddings, is fund-raisers. "Denver is a big benefit town," she noted, and her "clients are loath to show up . . . where another woman might be wearing the same dress."[24]

Serving the more daring among Denver's Latino population is Suavecito's Apparel Co., the self-proclaimed "World's Leader in Zoot Suits and Latino Fashion" dedicated to preserving the "history and culture associated with the *pachuco* [Zoot suiter] way of living." Besides its "Suits of Action" and Zoot tuxedo, Suavecito's offers two-tone shoes, brightly colored Zoot shirts, chains, and hats—even pheasant feathers to decorate the hats.[25]

A variety of small manufacturers use images of an idealized Rocky Mountain region to sell their wares. Founded on Old Buffalo Trail in Bozeman, Montana, H. S. Trask markets high-end shoes made of buffalo and elk hide. Even the shoes' names evoke Rocky Mountain places (Gallatin, Sun Valley, Elk Horn) and western icons (War Horse, River Guide, Saddle Bronc). Another footwear manufacturer, Chaco of Paonia, Colorado, dominates the specialty outdoor retail market with its sport sandals made locally and offers purchasers a chance at a life of Rocky Mountain perfection: "Wear [your Chacos] to stroll through the farmers market, climb a fourteener, barefoot or with socks." Mountain Sprouts, situated in Grand Junction, Colorado, creates fleece garments for children; the Mountain Sprouts mission statement reads, in part: "to heartily clothe the youth of the world in FUN-ctional mountainwear, inspired by our collective experiences with . . . the wilderness, and the wild adventures therein!"[26]

Clothing catalog retailers, from both within and without the Rocky Mountain region, frequently rhapsodize about the region's beautiful, relatively unspoiled scenic qualities—and the lifestyle, leisurely *and* hardworking, that goes with the spectacular views. *The Territory Ahead* catalog, for example, lauds its Laramie Denim Jacket as perfectly suited to Wyoming's "close-knit culture of rugged pragmatism," while its Hi-Liner Jacket, named for Montana's Hi-Line—frigid "wheat and cattle country rolling east from the Rockies"—will help the purchaser "shoulder off the cold." Robert Redford's (1937–   ) Sundance catalog touts its home "nestled in a cradle of rock, forest and meadow high in the Wasatch Mountains," implying that by purchasing its "products of discovery" (clothing, jewelry, and house wares) outlanders can share this fictive "home."

Coldwater Creek's Northcountry catalog, which originated in Sandpoint, Idaho, celebrates "Western styling," though many of its products have little to do with the region. Patagonia until recently ran its catalog business out of Bozeman, Montana, and though it embraces the active outdoor life wherever it's enjoyed, a recent Patagonia fishing catalog fixates, in text and image, on the flyfisher's paradise of the Greater Yellowstone ecosystem. The GoLite camping supply company in Boulder, Colorado, creates lightweight clothing and camping equipment for hikers and other outdoor enthusiasts who do not want to be weighed down by heavy gear.

Granted, as Ralph Beer noted that day in Bozeman, much of Rocky Mountain fashion mimics the casual dress found in the rest of the country. After all, Rocky Mountain residents see the same programs on television, read the same magazines and clothing catalogs, and commonly travel outside the region. It is true that trends in fashion are accepted more slowly in some Rocky Mountain communities than they are in larger urban centers (even Denver).

At the same time, certain fashions with global resonance, especially those related to outdoor recreation, remain closely identified with an athletic Rocky Mountain ideal, even if they are designed, manufactured, and marketed elsewhere. And of course, the cowboy and cowgirl style, the popularity of which waxes and wanes like that of the western film, remains indelibly linked with the ranching traditions of the Rockies (and the broader West). And within the region, a visitor is certain to spot touches of regional color: men wearing dress boots and bolo ties with their sport coats, plenty of folks in their Wranglers and pearl-snapped cowboy shirts, bearded Hutterites dressed all in black, fancy dancers at a powwow, mountain bikers in spandex and fleece, flyfishers in monotone vests and long-billed caps, and even the occasional couture-draped matron heading to the latest Denver fundraiser.

RESOURCE GUIDE

Printed Sources

Beard, Tyler. *100 Years of Western Wear*. Salt Lake City, UT: Gibbs-Smith Publisher, 1993.

Brown, Mark H., and W. R. Felton. *L. A. Huffman Photographer of the Plains: The Frontier Years*. New York: Bramhall House, 1955.

Colburn, Carol. "'Well, I Wondered When I Saw You, What All Those New Clothes Meant': Interpreting the Dress of Norwegian-American Immigrants." In *Material Culture and People's Art among the Norwegians in America*, ed. Marion John Nelson. Northfield, MN: Norwegian-American Historical Association, 1994. 188–155.

Emmet, Boris, and John E. Jeuck. *Catalogues and Counters: A History of Sears, Roebuck and Company*. Chicago: University of Chicago Press, 1950.

Jeffrey, Julie Roy. *Frontier Women: The Trans-Mississippi West 1840–1880*. New York: Hill and Wang, 1979.

Lucey, Donna M. *Photographing Montana, 1894–1928: The Life and Work of Evelyn Cameron*. New York: Alfred A. Knopf, 1990.

McChristian, Douglas C. *The U.S. Army in the West, 1870–1880: Uniforms, Weapons, and Equipment*. Norman: University of Oklahoma Press, 1995.

Miller, Susan Lindbergh, Bounthavy Kiatoukaysy, and Tou Yang. *Hmong Voices in Montana.* Missoula, MT: Art Museum of Missoula, 1993.

Paterek, Josephine. *Encyclopedia of American Indian Costume.* New York: W. W. Norton, 1993.

Peavy, Linda, and Ursula Smith. *Frontier Children.* Norman: University of Oklahoma Press, 1999.

Quartermaster General of the Army. *U.S. Army Uniforms and Equipment, 1889, Specifications for Clothing, Camp and Garrison Equipage, and Clothing and Equipage Materials.* Lincoln: University of Nebraska Press, 1986.

Rickey, Don. *$10 Horse, $40 Saddle: Cowboy Clothing, Arms, Tools and Horse Gear of the 1880s.* Ft. Collins, CO: Old Army Press, 1976.

Wilson, Laura. *Hutterites of Montana.* New Haven, CT: Yale University Press, 2000.

Wilson, Laurel E. "American Cowboy Dress: Function to Fashion." *Dress* 28 (2001): 40–52.

———. "'I Was a Pretty Proud Kid': An Interpretation of Differences in Posed and Unposed Photographs of Montana Cowboys." *Clothing and Textiles Research Journal* 9 (1991): 3.

Young, Otis E., Jr. *Western Mining.* Norman: University of Oklahoma Press, 1970.

Web Sites

Onata Dantza Taldea, Boise, ID
Basque dance and dress.
http://www.ysursa.com/onati.htm
Accessed June 22, 2004.

Mormon Modesty in Dress
http://www.lightplanet.com/mormons/daily/modesty.htm#eom
Accessed June 22, 2004.

The Western Design Conference Fashion Show, Cody, WY
http://www.westerndesignconference.com/fashion.html
Accessed June 22, 2004.

Museums and Special Collections

Bannock County Historical Museum
P. O. Box 253
3000 Alvord Loop
Pocatello, ID 83204
http://www.museumsusa.org/data/museums/ID/67795.htm

Basque Museum
611 Grove Street
Boise, ID
208-343-2671
http://www.ohwy.com/id/b/bbasqmcc.htm

Buffalo Bill Historical Center
720 Sheridan Avenue
Cody, WY 82414
307-587-4771
http://www.bbhc.org/

Fort Bridger Historical Association
P.O. Box 112
Fort Bridger, WY 82933
307-782-3842
http://www.wyoparks.state.wy.us/bridger.htm

Fort Hall Replica
3002 Alvord Loop
Parks and Recreation Department
Pocatello, ID 83201
208-234-1795
http://www.forthall.net/

Grant-Kohrs Ranch National Historic Site
266 Warren Lane
Deer Lodge, MT 59722-0790
406-846-2070 ext. 230
http://www.nps.gov/grko/

Montana Historical Society
225 North Roberts
Helena, MT 59620-1201
406-444-2694
http://www.his.state.mt.us/

Museum of Church History and Art
45 North West Temple
Salt Lake City, UT 84150-3810
801-240-4615
http://www.lds.org/placestovisit/location/0,10634,1880-1-1-1,00.html

Museum of the Fur Trade
6321 Highway 20
Chadron, NE 69337
308-432-3843
museum@furtrade.org
http://www.furtrade.org/

Museum of the Mountain Man
Sublette County Historical Society
P. O. Box 909
Pinedale, WY 82941
877-686-6266 or 307-367-4101
museummtman@wyoming.com
http://www.pinedaleonline.com/mmmuseum/

Museum of North Idaho
P. O. Box 812
Coeur d'Alene, ID 83816-0812
208-664-3448
http://www.museumni.org/

Museum of the Plains Indian
P. O. Box 410
Browning, MT 59417
406-338-2230
http://www.doi.gov/iacb/museum/museum_plains.html

Museum of the Rockies
Textiles Collection
Montana State University
600 West Kagy Boulevard
Bozeman, MT 59717-2730
406-994-6622
http://www.montana.edu/wwwmor/

National Cowboy and Western Heritage Museum
1700 Northeast 63rd Street
Oklahoma City, OK 73111
405-478-2250
http://www.nationalcowboymuseum.org/

National Mining Hall of Fame and Museum
P. O. Box 981 (120 West 9th)
Leadville, CO 80461
719-486-1229
http://www.leadville.com/miningmuseum/

Pro Rodeo Hall of Fame and Museum of the American Cowboy
101 Pro Rodeo Drive
Colorado Springs, CO 80919
719-528-4764
http://prorodeo.org/hof/

World Museum of Mining and Hell Roarin' Gulch
155 Museum Way
P. O. Box 33
Butte, MT 59703
406-723-7211
http://www.miningmuseum.org/

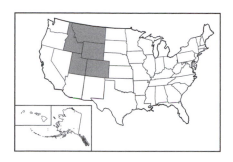

FILM AND THEATER

Simon Dixon

Michael Apted's film *Continental Divide* (1981) presents a lighthearted yet insightful look at the unbridgeable gap between urban American reality and the fragile yet symbolic wilderness of the American West. In this film, John Belushi plays Ernie Souchak, a tough investigative reporter for the *Chicago Sun-Times* with a knack for revealing political graft. He is a city man through and through; he smokes constantly and claims "fresh air makes me nauseous." Souchek has a dangerous job, but his courageous reporting earns him plenty of respect on the street, even from muggers. However, a beating by corrupt police officers in the pay of city officials lands him in the hospital, and his newspaper editor suggests that he should get out of town and write a very different story. Writing this story would, improbably, send him to the Rocky Mountains to cover the work of naturalist Nell Porter (Blair Brown), a specialist on eagles. Porter, who has lived alone for four years high in the Rockies, has never been interviewed and is leery of reporters. Seeing Porter as a professional challenge, the dedicated journalist Souchak (who at first thinks he will find the Rockies in Nebraska) finally heads for Wyoming and the mountains, taking plenty of cigarettes and a brand-new orange backpack as big as himself. He survives an intrusion by brown bears—who steal his cigarettes— and, with the help of a weatherbeaten local guide, finally makes it to Porter's lonely cabin. Thus begins an improbable and often prickly romance between the city newspaperman and the solitary mountain ornithologist. When Souchak refers to the mountains as "a godforsaken place like this," Porter responds by taking him to see a breathtaking view of the mountain range near her cabin. Tellingly, she refers to the wilderness mountains as a "church, the oldest one in America."

The representation of the Rocky mountain region in *Continental Divide* speaks volumes about America's limited knowledge of, and ambivalent attitudes toward, the region and the region's history, which is dominated by the picturesque yet forbidding Rocky Mountain range, historically a barrier to westward expansion, sometimes a site of natural wonder but just as often an arid zone of easily extracted mineral resources. To the film's merit, it doesn't try to turn Souchak into a mountain man, nor does it ask Porter to give up her career and the environment she loves to become a Chicagoan. But at the same time it leaves the romantic couple and the audience in a kind of limbo between two vastly different lifestyles and apparently irreconcilable attitudes to place. This uncertain divide (the title is apt) between extremes of pristine wilderness and grimy urban civilization might be considered the constant condition of the film spectator's understanding of the Rockies: Even in a contemporary realist narrative like this (directed by a famous English documentary filmmaker), the region remains a place more mythologized than real, somewhere between godforsaken and heavenly and sometimes both at the same time.

This chapter treats the representation and the cultural presence in the Rocky Mountain region of two flourishing dramatic forms: theater and film. The place of these artistic forms in the Rocky Mountain region is diverse and complex; on the one hand, the life of dramatic performance might be considered, relative to the theatrical culture of New York or Chicago, rather thin; on the other, the representation of the region's rural life and history in film has been startlingly rich and abundant. Film representation of Colorado, Idaho, Montana, Utah, and Wyoming is implicit or simply accidental in the western, the major American film genre whose fictional treatment of the region's history has often challenged the facts while mythologizing the pioneer experience. Indeed, an initial problem in treating the representation of the region in films that treat these states is that historically the western must often treat indeterminate or nascent territories rather than states proper (which is also to say, vague sites for dramatic and often belligerent action) and also that the geographical vagueness of "the West," or the Frontier, means that the western will just as likely take place in Oklahoma or Texas, or between Texas and Missouri (Hawks' *Red River*, for example), as it will the historical events of pioneering settlement, gold prospecting, and ranching in the Rocky Mountain region. That said, a large number of films that fit the generic category of the western evidently take place in the Rocky Mountain region, and it is through these films that an overall image of the region, one composed of quite disparate shards, slowly emerges.

THEATER IN THE ROCKY MOUNTAIN REGION

The history of theater in the region is part and parcel of the history of development and urbanization. The ubiquity of small-town western opera houses is a measure less of the power of Giacomo Puccini (1858–1924) than that of burgeoning civic pride, a sense that the future of each city would depend upon active cultivation of the arts. The local opera house is thus a gesture of confidence in the city's promise. At the same time, theatrical life, from vaudeville to William Shakespeare (1564–1616), from college production to touring troupe, can be considered a secular opportunity for communal and, above all, cultural gathering. A high school or college football game might provide a recreational community event, but the region's theater audiences have sought a more reflective dramatic experience, one of enactment.

When Judy Garland in *A Star Is Born* (1954) sings her curious line, "I was born in a trunk in the Princess Theater, in Pocatello, Idaho," the effect is slightly comical. Pocatello in this context is a city far away from the Hollywood stardom she aspires to, a city whose citizens are very unlikely to have attended a play on Broadway, or off Broadway, or indeed anywhere near New York City. One imagines a rather humble theater showing vaudeville acts, and Pocatallo here is Peoria or Dubuque, only more so—a city far away from the centers of metropolitan glamour. In fact, the Princess began life as the Lyric Theatre in 1905, changed its name to the Grand in 1909, and to the Princess in 1912. Like many theaters in the region, it became a motion picture theater in 1916 and now exists only as the ground floor of the Whitman Hotel. A small reference in a Hollywood song is thus the germ of a history that speaks of vaudeville struggles in anonymity and the radical shift from live theater to film that would change the life and function of theaters across the United States, just as it would lead Garland's character away from itinerant performances in provincial anonymity and toward a different insecurity, that of Hollywood stardom. Specifically, however, Garland's line suggests that theater in Pocatello, as in many

Oscar Wilde at the Tabor Opera House

The Tabor Opera House was the site of a visit by Irish playwright and aesthete Oscar Wilde (1854–1900). Of his visit to Leadville, Wilde noted, "They are miners—men working in metals, so I lectured them on the Ethics of Art. I read them passages from the autobiography of Benvenuto Cellini and they seemed much delighted. I was reproved by my hearers for not having brought him with me. I explained that he had been dead for some little time which elicited the enquiry 'Who shot him?' . . . Then they asked me to supper, and having accepted, I had to descend a mine in a rickety bucket in which it was impossible to be graceful. Having got into the heart of the mountain I had supper, the first course being whisky, the second whisky and the third whisky."[1] The story of Wilde's visit to the Rockies specifically contrasts his decadent and effeminate aestheticism with the rough-hewn character of the miners; it's also a story with a subtext about the relation between money and culture, for while the Rockies were poor in art and education, in this period they were also spectacularly wealthy and could invite even an expensive exotic like Wilde.

Among the many opera houses in Colorado are Central City Opera House in Denver, Telluride Opera House, Wright's Opera House in Ouray, and the Trinidad Opera House. The last of these may have been typical, offering not opera but instead a broad range of social events and entertainments, including, said one local newspaper editor, "some of the rottenest, barnstorming aggregations that ever escaped scalping."

regional towns, is a stop on a tour (hence the trunk) rather than itself a source of theatrical art. The place of theater in the region is significant or not depending on one's view of theater. Histories of theater in America routinely overlook entire states as they focus on Broadway and Boston and New Haven, and even a book on American provincial theater, which might be expected to give each state its due, glances at Denver before moving swiftly to San Francisco. In this respect, then, the region does not produce plays, nor does a theatrical culture flourish, on a par with New York and Chicago and other metropolitan hubs. However, to take this view denies the importance of theatrical performance in Rocky Mountain communities and the support that theater in some form or other—from mining boom-town saloon vaudeville to comic opera, from farce to itinerant Shakespeare companies—has often enjoyed.

The history of the Wheeler Opera House in Aspen, Colorado, is exemplary of the link between theatrical culture and mineral wealth. The Gala Grand Opening of the Wheeler Opera House was in 1889, six years after the arrival of wealthy New York entrepreneur J. B. Wheeler and only ten years after the first prospectors entered the Roaring Fork Valley in 1879. The opera house, described at the time as "a perfect bijou of a theater," opened not with an operatic classic but a lesser known English comic opera *The King's Fool*. Like the Wheeler, the Tabor Opera House in Leadville, Colorado, was built with the proceeds of mining, this time by Horace Austin Warner Tabor. Typically, the Tabor Opera House does not boast of visiting sopranos but of popular entertainers like Harry Houdini (1874–1926) or the composer John Philip Sousa. Theater performances in the region mix entertainment and edification, but in contrast with the dramatic staging of western life in the filmed western, or the fictional accounts of western derring-do in dime novels, the plays that bring dramatic culture on tours from the East outnumber those by local authors.

It would be wrong, however, to represent all western theatrical performances as light or paltry entertainment. The passion for opera houses coincides with the popularity of opera in the 1880s and 1890s, and the opulence associated with the European opera houses certainly underscored the appeal of theatergoing as a sign of civilized society, the apotheosis of the settlement project that imposes European culture on Indian land. The building of the opera house, the "grand temple of amusement" in Rocky Mountain cities, suggests a lack of compromise with indigenous culture, an unwillingness to forego European lifestyles in the face of Indian traditions and therefore a stern rejection of the lives of the early trappers whose relation to the Indians was much more intimate and respectful. In her study "On the Western Stage: Theatre in Montana, 1880–1920," Leslie Noelle Sullivan suggests that "important indicators of social status for many patrons were the physical manifestations of art in theaters: marble floors, gilded arches, and ornate scrollwork. Montana playhouses from 1880 to World War I illustrated this material glory. Only the smallest houses paid no attention to decoration; most theaters imported fine fabrics, sculpture, stained glass, and hired painters to create elaborate frescoes."[2] Sullivan's account of theater life in Montana reminds us of the enormous popularity of theater in the era before both film and television. Theater at this time met the demand for both the lowest level of amusement and the highest degree of dramatic merit, so inevitably the reviews of theater as a whole are likely to be mixed. Just as Oscar Wilde graced Colorado, so French actress Sarah Bernhardt visited Butte and delivered her lines in French, thereby causing a rift in local critical debate about whether the performance was either pretentious or uplifting. Before film, the works of Shakespeare were common currency among the educated classes, and in the period of Sullivan's study, many performances of the major Shakespearean plays, along with Molière (1622–1673) and Richard Sheridan (1751–1816), graced the boards of Montana's small theaters. For each classic, however, there were as many minor works of melodrama and comedy. Next to Henrik Ibsen's (1828–1906) *Ghosts* and *A Doll's House*, or George Bernard Shaw's (1856–1950) *Arms and the Man*, were to be found comic works like *The Truant Spouse*, *The Talk of New York*, *King of the Opium Ring*, *A Trip to Chinatown*, *The Marble Heart*, and so on. The common experience of these plays is to see otherness on stage and to be therefore taken out of one's own life. However, the fashion for realism indicated by Ibsen's work, along with a growing nostalgia for the days of the western frontier, did lead to a theater that treated life in the region and prompted performances of such plays as *The Cowboy and the Lady*, *The Squaw Man* (later filmed), *The Girl of the Golden West*, and *The Great Divide*. That said, many of these plays were written back East and were hardly valued as realist reflections on western life.

A key figure in western history, and one whose career characterizes the complex relation between actuality and make-believe that shadows the western theater and film's reinscription of history for artistic purposes, is William Frederick Cody (1846–1917), known as Buffalo Bill. Cody was the agent of his own mythology, and the gap between the performance of Bill Cody in life and the performance of Buffalo Bill by various actors on screen is often small—rather like the gap between Samuel Clemens (1835–1910) and Mark Twain. Edward Buscombe agrees with Cody's biographer Don Russell that Cody's appearance, essentially as himself, an army scout, in a Chicago play, *The Scouts of the Prairie*, on December 16, 1872, signals the birth of the western.[3] This pivotal moment concerns not the western subject matter but the presentation of that subject matter as worthy of the stage, inherently dramatic. Acting as a bridge between theater of the West and the West itself, Cody spent his winters on the stage and his summers back in the West, so he can be seen as the western mythmaking process personified. Indeed, a press release for his show in 1887 describes it as "The Romantic West Brought East in Reality."[4] Cody's itinerant show *Buffalo Bill's Wild West*, a cross between circus and vaudeville performance that responded to the western environment, employed acts of bravado and derring-do, such as famed crackshot Annie Oakley (1860–1926) and Native Americans recently involved in armed conflict were now presented as feature attractions. The important quality of *Buffalo Bill's Wild West* is that it engaged less in historical reenactment (although it did do this, too) than a kind of contemporary restaging *as theater* of the western expansionist project. Thus Sitting Bull (c. 1831–1890) was killed after he had appeared in the show, and the show had already been running seven years and had already included Indians when the 7th Cavalry massacred 150 Sioux at Wounded Knee. The further connection between Cody's theatrical career and the cinema is established in surviving kinetoscope footage of the company from 1894 and a subsequent series of Thomas Alva Edison (1847–1931) kinetoscope films that begin in 1897 and continue through 1917 with the Essanay production *The Adventures of Buffalo Bill*. These documentary films are supplemented by numerous fiction films beginning with *In the Days of Buffalo Bill* (1922) and including *Annie Get Your Gun* (1950) and *Buffalo Bill and the Indians or Sitting Bull's History Lesson* (1976).

Touring Shakespeare: Cultural Outreach

The culture of theatergoing in the Rocky Mountain region has been as diverse as the communities that did or did not support it. Theater performances for Colorado miners or those in Butte, Montana, were generally popular entertainments, leaving theatrical avant-gardes to bigger cities and more enthusiastic audiences. For all the changes brought about by the changing economies of the New West, the same is essentially true today: Denver, the largest metropolis in the region, is well endowed with theater life. Here are the Denver Performing Arts Complex, home of the Denver Center Theatre Company, the Colorado Ballet, and Opera Colorado. Also in Denver is the repertory Changing Scene theater. College towns such as Boulder, Missoula, Fort Collins, Provo, Laramie, and Moscow have theatrical performances allied to theater departments as well as small resident companies. One measure of theater's reception in the region is the vibrant touring Shakespeare troupe, including Montana Shakespeare in the Parks, founded in 1972; the Idaho

Shakespeare Festival, founded in 1977; the Utah Shakespearean Festival, founded in 1961; and in Colorado, both the Colorado Shakespeare Festival, founded in 1958, and the Theatreworks Shakespeare Festival, founded in 1976.

Of these, the Colorado Shakespeare Festival also claims a heritage as far back as 1897, when Shakespeare was performed on Class Day on the campus of the University of Colorado at Boulder. Subsequent performances drew over 1,000, with many of the audience making the trip from Denver for the occasion. In the late 1930s, in honor of the university's first woman professor and under the auspices of the Works Progress Administration (WPA), an outdoor amphitheater, the Mary Ripon Theatre, was constructed, and performances of Shakespeare plays were performed there annually for fourteen years, beginning in 1944, until the founding of the Colorado Shakespeare festival in 1958. Since then, the festival has grown and developed both its repertoire and its projects. As one of only two university-affiliated theaters to perform the entire Shakespearean canon, the Colorado Shakespeare Festival has also produced plays by other leading dramatists, and a Young People's Shakespeare program, thereby adding to the diversity of theater in the region. Nominally based in Bozeman, Montana Shakespeare in the Parks is a regional touring theater whose brief is to take Shakespeare on the road to communities that would otherwise be denied the opportunity of seeing any performances. Founded by Bruce C. Jacobsen, director of theater at Montana State University, to "enrich the cultural environment of the state," Montana Shakespeare in the Parks travels thousands of miles every summer and performs both Shakespeare and Restoration comedies to eager audiences in the sparsely populated state. The Idaho Shakespeare Festival, which began as a single 1977 performance of *A Midsummer Night's Dream* in the courtyard of a restaurant, has responded to rapid growth in its home city of Boise, moving several times to more permanent venues, and has—unlike the university-based companies in other states—received a mix of corporate and government sponsorship for its popular summer season. It, too, has a touring outreach component, Shakespearience, which takes performances to schools throughout Idaho. State Shakespeare festivals might be considered a celebration of summer, as much as of the Bard, offering an attraction to tourists and generally permitting audiences to combine play attendance with picnic gatherings on summer evenings. The Utah Shakespearean Festival, in Cedar City, supported by Southern Utah University, was founded in response to the annual visit of thousands of tourists to neighboring national parks but has now developed into one of the most prosperous companies with a year-round schedule of performances in its Adams Memorial Shakespearean Theatre, a near-replica of Shakespeare's Globe. Consistent with the theater building, and perhaps with the state's conservatism, Utah performances have stressed historical accuracy rather than radical or modern reinterpretations of the play text. Like other state Shakespeare companies in the region, the Utah festival conducts auditions throughout the nation, and it also produces plays outside the Shakespearean canon, such as Shaw's *Misalliance* and Arthur Miller's (1915–) *Death of a Salesman*.[5]

Local Theater

On titles alone it is tempting to read Anthony Mann's classic western *The Man from Laramie* (1955), with its story of revenge and family drama, as a way of understanding the homophobic brutality that led to Moises Kaufman's collage-structured play *The Laramie Project* (1999) and the subsequent film. *The Laramie Project* is based on the murder of twenty-one-year-old gay student Matthew Shepard in Laramie, Wyoming, in 1998. Shepard was lured out of a straight bar by two men who drove him to a lonely place, tied him to a fence, and beat him. He died in hospital a few days later. This Wyoming city connection suggests that the generic, routine representation of male violence in the western might have permeated American culture. At the very least, the mention of Laramie proposes a comparison and makes us wonder how much, and with what awkwardness, the region has changed from West to New West, from frontier values to those determined strongly by media images (not just film but also television, music videos, computer games, and so forth) generated on either coast. As a play, *The Laramie Project* was produced by the Tectonic Theater Project of New Jersey, who arrived in Laramie and set about interviewing the townspeople. The thirty characters in the play are the product of over 200 interviews that sought common reactions to Shepard's death. Built from interviews with the people of Laramie (rather than written at a safe distance in New Jersey), the play seeks answers to a death that seems not just insensibly brutal to residents of large cities, in which gay subculture is just one part of the rich fabric of life, but strangely motivated, the product of a mental state in the murderers that might have cause in the increasingly anachronistic cowboy culture of Wyoming, or roots in the violent making of the state. In many respects, the arrival of the Tectonic Theatre Project in Laramie replays the role of theater historically in the region, which is that, notwithstanding the numerous local playwrights and performances in each state, it is a thing that also visits and tours, leaving an atmosphere of sophisticated urban cultural otherness. This play suggests that theater was not the natural response of Wyoming to the death but the response of other Americans who saw in Matthew Shepard's murder a local tale of great national significance, larger than itself. In this respect the writing of the play resembles the western genre itself: Though they may not visit it, other Americans know that they have a stake in it.

A key question in the Shepard affair was the implicit indictment of the people of Laramie for the crime of two men. The relation between a community and the theater it produces has been especially problematic in Utah, a state whose population is 70 percent Mormon and in which individualism of the playwright is in conflict with the collective mentality of the church. In "Behind the Mormon Curtain," an even-handed yet ultimately critical article in an *American Theatre* issue devoted to theater and place, David Pace examines the tension between individual artists and the church in a state that is 70 percent Mormon but in which the church is a consistent supporter of the arts. Pace's article portrays a culture in which the censoring power of the church can produce such oddities as Noel Coward comedies at Brigham Young University, "produced without cocktails and cigarettes," but also says that plays more critical of the Mormon church, such as Tom Rogers' *Heubner*, based on the true story of a Mormon in Nazi Germany who was excommunicated by the church before being killed by the SS for distributing anti-Nazi leaflets, can now be performed after a fifteen-year moratorium.[6] The Pioneer Theatre Company is essentially a state theater in Utah, but it is joined by the Salt Lake Acting Company, and Theatre Works West, among others, in Salt Lake City. Each has varying degrees of conflict with the dominant church culture in terms of production denials, threats of excommunication, and pressure to avoid criticism of the church. Pace notes also that the Salt Lake Acting Company has focused on courting the considerable minority of non-Mormons and has staged several Broadway plays, including *The Heidi Chronicles*, and David Henry Hwang's *M. Butterfly*, whose scope extends far beyond the Mormon church's sphere of influence.

FILM

Film: The Earliest Images

The earliest filmed images of the region appear soon after the invention of the medium in 1895, and immediately the issue of representation becomes complex, as some films provide a documentary recording of the West, while others, belonging to the genre Scott Simmon calls the "Eastern Western," provide a staged representation of the West that was shot in New York or New Jersey, close to the studio. Film pioneer D. W. Griffith's (1875–1948) first western *The Redman and the Child* (1908) is set in Colorado but was shot in New Jersey. Edison's *Serving Rations to the Indians* of 1898, thought to have been shot in Utah, might be considered an example of ethnographic observation, while *Cripple Creek Bar Room Scene* of 1899, again supposedly shot in Colorado, has been described as "theatrically staged."[7] Significantly, some early film images of the region are linked to both tourism and specifically to the railroad, which like film will alter forever the experience of western time and space. One such primitive film is *Tourist Train Leaving Livingston, Mont.*, of 1897; its title does not hint at a plot but simply describes the scene in words that the film will show in moving pictures. Other films of this kind are Edison's *Cattle Fording a Stream* (1899) and *Lassoing Steer* (1898). The association between railroad and film is consolidated by an entire series of short films, *Hale's Tours and Scenes of the World*, which first appeared in 1904 at the St. Louis Exposition and featured a stationary railway car from whose seats the paying public could watch a short travelogue film that had been shot at the front of a train. In his study of primitive American cinema, *Film before Griffith*, Raymond Fielding cites a contemporary description of one of Hale's tours in the Colorado Rockies: "The scene starts at Divide on the Colorado Midland and runs down the pass until Pike's Peak, covered with snow, is seen just ahead. Then the camera is taken to the caboose and the freight train is seen ahead winding around the tortuous curves into tunnels and rounding steep crags. The background is sublime. The entire picture is filled with hypnotic views that make the beholder steady himself to catch the motion of rounding curves. It is impossible not to imagine that you are actually on the train. The scene closes at Manitou."[8] Captured here is early evidence of the photogenic appeal of the Rocky Mountains, but there is also a hint at the longer history of depicting mountains that takes us back to the era of the Hudson River School, and the Californian mountain sublime of Albert Bierstadt, whose Sierras owe more to a state of mind than the measurements of a surveyor. The sublime has a special currency in the logic of the picturesque: It suggests a landscape more forbidding than appealing, but there is a neo-Gothic appeal in the awe it invokes in spectators. Even General George Armstrong Custer (1839–1876) resorted to a painterly analogy when describing "the view spread out before us, worthy of the brush of a Church, a Bierstadt."[9] The logic of this western imaginary is profound and far-reaching, since it suggests that even before it is filmed, the Rocky Mountain region is subject to a taught mode of seeing whose optical framework, established in the tradition of landscape painting, is one of wonder, of sublimity of scale, yet also of artistic control. To see the landscape according to the dictates of this essentially historical condition of perception is to *subject it* to pictorial organization.

A notable early filmmaker from the region, one whose narratives certainly organize space for her own artistic purposes, is Nell Shipman, whose works have been archived at the Hemingway Western Studies Center in Boise, Idaho. Originally from Alberta, Canada, Shipman has also been claimed by Idaho as a filmmaking pioneer. Indeed, Shipman's numerous Idaho films include several shot near Lookout Mountain and Priest Lake, notably *The Grub-Stake* (1923), *Trail of the North Wind* (1923), *The Light on the Lookout* (1923), *White Water* (1924), and a film discovered in 2003, *Wolf's Brush* (1924). Shipman has been described by Idaho Film Collection curator Tom Trusky as "proto-suffragette, or feminist" for her consistent depiction of heroic and resourceful women who protect their men and save the day. Her filmmaking methods were direct and realist, often putting considerable stress on actors when harsh winter conditions were not allowed to interfere with the shoot. Shipman was an independent filmmaker in an era before the studio system took over, and in this respect her approach provides a model for women independent filmmakers today.

The West by Reputation

Although the West on film is exhaustively and problematically treated in the western, other films also contribute to the western imaginary by making reference to the region or portraying characters who are associated with it. The centrality of the Rockies to the American experience is best expressed in the work many scholars consider the great masterpiece of American film art, Orson Welles' (1915–1980) *Citizen Kane* (1941). We first meet protagonist Charles Foster Kane as a boy in Colorado, a child with no particular hopes of riches until he inherits vast wealth from a former boarder in his mother's boarding house, in the form of mineral rights, and is packed off East by his guardian for an expensive education. The significance of this story is that Kane, in the mold of F. Scott Fitzgerald's (1896–1940) Jay Gatsby, or the mythical rags-to-riches stories of Horatio Alger, is an exemplary American figure whose entire career is sustained by a wealth that comes to him not just easily but mysteriously and randomly, paradoxically denying Kane the healthy pursuit of hard-earned wealth. Such must have been the unsettling experience of the first gold miners in Colorado, those who passed up millions for just a few thousand dollars—and even these to be squandered on whisky. Kane's Colorado roots become central to our understanding of his and America's mania for corporate expansion, and it is fitting that his dream career for mistress Susan Alexander (who cannot sing a note) is that of opera star. It's as if the older Kane remembers from childhood a small town Colorado "opera house" like the Wheeler Opera House in Aspen or the Leadville Opera House, with its own pretensions to the vastness of New York's Metropolitan, or even the opulence of Milan's La Scala, so that when he is able, with mineral wealth, to build big, he builds big.

A comparable rendering of the region in a film whose subject matter seems far removed is Frank Capra's (1897–1991) political morality play *Mr. Smith Goes to Washington* (1939). It was and is widely thought that Jefferson Smith, a junior senator from Montana, would be read as Montana Senator Burton K. Wheeler, but the film's Washington premiere, at which the senator sat with Capra, caused an uproar for its cynical treatment of the U.S. Senate and the corrupt (but finally redeemed) senior senator from Montana, played by Claude Rains. The plot of this film concerns the callow Smith (James Stewart), an admirable and ethical figure whose idealism threatens the corrupt and cosy relationship between a state manipulator (like Kane, another media magnate) and the state's representatives in Washington. The image of Montana is rather condescending (it has produced corrupt officials, but it has also produced the heroic Jeff Smith), but ultimately Capra's intention of making the state look good, with solid values and old-fashioned idealism, is successful.

True West and Mythical West in the Classical Western

Look at a map of the United States of America, and the West seems to begin with the Rockies: a change of landscape as the prairies give way to vertiginous peaks. The paradox of the Hollywood western is that the genre deals with states of mind whose best embodiment seems to be in Texas or Oklahoma: an earlier West that is born of a discomfort with the South and especially with the mark of slavery. The urge, as Huckleberry Finn says, to light out for the territories, is a sign of optimistic risk taking, and at the time, to head from Texas to Kansas City with hundreds of cattle is essentially an adventure in movement. The chirpy and peppy Calamity Jane (c. 1852–1903) played by Doris Day may be felt to be inaccurate, but the dearth of documentary accounts of the historical figure Calamity Jane leaves film viewers with few alternatives; and thus the only representation becomes the dominant representation of record, the core of the myth. The geographical and natural facts of the American West have long maintained an uncomfortable relation with the cultural forces of myth and symbol. Motion pictures did not begin the construction of American myths about the Rocky Mountain West, but the representation of the region in American film is a fundamental element in the myth-building process. Is the American West a pristine reserve with clear mountain trout streams and hot spring resorts, with abundant wildlife and limitless wildlands, or is it a region of limitless natural resources to be exploited by extractive industries? The drama of the contest between the dual urges to exploit minerals or instead to celebrate the libertarian possibilities of the landscape has found consistent expression in the western film.

In Edward Buscombe's exhaustive *BFI Companion to the Western*, we find the comment that although "[t]he real history of much of the West is . . . the history of its agriculture . . . agriculture does not loom large in Westerns."[10] Numerous films, for example, provide an account of the journey west, such as John Ford's story of Mormon settlers in *Wagon Master* (1950), Anthony Mann's *Bend of the River* (1951), and Andrew V. McLaglen's version of A. B. Guthrie's novel *The Way West* (1967). While the entire western film genre might be considered at odds with the facts, it stands as the dominant representation of the Rocky Mountain region and contributes not just to the mythology of the West but to the mythology of the entire United States, as the grandiose ambitions of motion picture distributors find a perfect match in the grandeur of the western landscape. Specifically, the locations of westerns are often ambiguous, since the action often takes place in the territories, before incorporation as states, but Buscombe provides statistics that indicate (albeit in the form of a "rough guide") a clear preference for some states over others. In the sound period, Texas features as a location for 198 films, while the states of the Rocky Mountain region fare much less well. Idaho, with 3 films listed, matches the midwestern state of Nebraska; 10 films are located in Utah, 16 in Montana, 27 in Colorado, and 58 in Wyoming. These figures suggest that, for example, the Oregon Trail, which passes through southern Idaho, is considered hardly worthy of film treatment or that the ranching story set in Wyoming is much more consistent with the western story of ranching conflict than Idaho's modest mining operations and farming. Of primary consideration here is the status of the western as a genre, which means that repeated locations and repeated references to such places as Cheyenne, Wyoming, often have more to do with the demands of genre than the desire to represent a particular community or state. At the same time it is important to note that while the western frequently takes place in the

1880s or before, many territories only acceded to statehood after this, with Colorado first in 1876, followed by Montana in 1889, Idaho and Wyoming both in 1890, and Utah in 1896. This explains why so little attention is paid to statehood and so much to the establishment of the rule of law in a territory constantly at the edge of lawlessness and uncertain of definition.

A notable example of the historical creation of semifictional characters whose identity is then ripe for film exploitation is Calamity Jane. Calamity Jane, who was known to have lived in Virginia City, Montana, was the nickname of Martha Jane Cannary, a woman who dressed—and swore—like a man and who appeared on stage as "the Famous Woman Scout of the Wild West." Calamity Jane is perhaps less interesting as a historical figure than as a site of ambiguous representation in fiction and then in film. She was fictionalized in the dime novels of Edward L. Wheeler and then in such films as *Will Bill Hickock* (1923), *Custer's Last Stand* (1936), and two versions of *The Plainsman* (1936 and 1966). The best-known screen portrayal, however, is that of Doris Day in the musical *Calamity Jane* (1953). As

Calamity Jane, c. 1895. Courtesy of the Library of Congress.

Film still of Doris Day as Calamity Jane in the 1953 production. Courtesy of Photofest.

might be expected of a musical, Calamity Jane's foul language and heavy drinking are removed, her dubious morals are papered over, her buckskins are clean, and her character is reduced to, well, Doris Day: perky and full of vim. This gesture of simplifying and cleaning up history for the sake of the plot is common to Hollywood, but the case of Calamity Jane and the eponymous film gives us a measure of the Hollywood film's unreliability as a historical account. *Calamity Jane* suggests that film, whether documentary or fiction, drama or musical, treats and represents the Rocky Mountain region, but always at an aesthetic or rhetorical remove, so that we have to read between the lines or look for mythic structures hidden in the stories that are told and in the images that are re-presented.

Among the most canonical westerns are those of John Ford (1894–1973). Ford's films returned so frequently to Monument Valley in southeast Utah that other film directors avoided it. In classics like *Stagecoach* (1939), *My Darling Clementine* (1946), *The Searchers* (1956), and *Cheyenne Autumn* (1964), Ford set his stories in a space that isolates them and makes their stories timeless. Buscombe has said the use of

Monument Valley, on the border between Utah and Arizona, "gave his work a visual signature unmatched by any other director. No other place evokes, so unambiguously and resonantly, the West. And perhaps no other landscape in the cinema is so quintessentially American. Ford, more than any other director, defines what is American about the Western."[11] Ford's use of Monument Valley, it might be argued, may make his films especially American, but typically for the classical western they do so at the expense of local color. We hardly detect the actuality of historical life in Utah here, and the more Ford returns to his personal location, the less relevant does geography appear to him.

By contrast, Howard Hawks' *The Big Sky* (1952), which follows a group of traders up the Missouri River on their boat the *Mandan*, and into the territory that would become Montana, is determined precisely and literally by the course of the river, which leaves little room for dehistoricizing their journey. Indeed, the claim to historical accuracy of *The Big Sky* requires Indians to speak in their native tongue, and the French to speak in theirs, so the journey depicted is not to be allegorized as American so much as local and entrepreneurial. Set in the era before settlement, when Indian tribes were still in control of their lands and white visitors could distinguish between the friendly Blackfeet and the unfriendly Crow, *The Big Sky* presents a story of encounter that eschews simple conflict in favor of delicate negotiation. The only true villains are in fact whites, in league with the Crow, and we see the latter only in a brief skirmish. A key element in the plot is the *Mandan*'s task of returning a Blackfeet woman (the love interest, who remains unmolested for weeks as the only woman on the boat) to her tribe, and the film ends in approval of miscegenation, proposing that harmony could be achieved between Europeans and Indians by a process of trade and intermarriage in which the indigenous tribes remained, fundamentally, in control of the land and the terms of encounter. In this respect it anticipates the prelapsarian yearnings of trapper Johnson (Robert Redford) in Sydney Pollack's *Jeremiah Johnson* (1972). The *Mandan* may not travel through an edenic garden, but certainly from the Indian point of view, there was still hope of reconciliation with the Europeans.

A cycle of films in the 1940s and 1950s were devoted to the figure of the cattle baron, usually a tyrannical figure greedy to grab more land and expand his personal empire. Buscombe has also noted that the cattle baron film provides an opportunity for family melodrama, especially popular in 1950s Hollywood. Among these are *The Man from Laramie* (1955), *The Big Country* (1958), and *Shane* (1953). Wyoming is the preferred site for several cattle baron films, and two historical figures from Wyoming, Alexander Swan and John Clay, provided models for such stories of imperial ambition and family conflict. *Shane*, directed by George Stevens, is also exemplary of the classic western, and its backdrop of the Teton mountain range in western Wyoming lends grandeur to the story. Shane (Alan Ladd) is a retired gunslinger and former soldier in the Civil War, while homesteader Stonewall has come from Alabama, and the narrative of escape from the South is specifically linked to the image of the snowy peaks, the pristine preserve that stand like an unchanging backdrop to the action. But such an escape will not be easy. Shane is a solitary traveler who befriends the Starrett family of homesteaders who are being threatened by a tough neighboring ranching family, the Rikers, who routinely attack the homesteaders and destroy their crops. Typically, the hero is challenged to

Film still from the 1953 movie *Shane*, with Alan Ladd and Brandon De Wilde. Courtesy of Photofest.

be courageous in the face of intimidation, but here it is the Starretts' little boy Joey who offers the challenge, suggesting that Shane might leave because the Starrett homestead is too dangerous.

Realizing that he has walked into danger, Shane has, according to the logic of the classic western, only one option: to stay and fight. At the local saloon, Shane buys farming clothes to replace his buckskin, then orders soda pop rather than whiskey, a sign of his peaceful, civilizing intentions. *Shane* uses iconography of both clothing and music to make clear the division between good and evil. In its portrayal of the saloon, of a figure who plays the harmonica, of a gunslinger (Jack Palance) wearing black (including a black hat, the sure mark of badness), of townsfolk who fear violence yet stand to benefit from the courage of the good hero, *Shane* bears all the marks of the classic of the genre. The Rikers are initially presented as outlaws, while the homesteaders are specifically dissociated from violence (they do not wear guns); but this insistence on peacefulness leads to a major fistfight when Shane is outmanned and decides to take on the Riker clan singlehandedly. Shane's leadership brings the homesteader Joe Starrett into the fray, and the two, in a victory of righteousness over cowardice, win the day. Shane's heroism is impossible to ignore, but the arrival of gunslinger Wilson (Palance) from Cheyenne ups the ante and requires the former gunslinger Shane to strap on his revolver once more.

A significant element of *Shane* is its representation of the conflict as one between gun-wearing ranchers and unarmed farmers, with farming specifically linked to a gun-free and law-abiding future. With the marshall over a hundred miles away (also described as "three days ride" and therefore present in principle while absent in fact), the homesteaders are defenseless, but they are resolutely peaceful. When Marian Starrett finds Shane teaching Joey how to use a sixgun, she pulls her son away, saying that "guns aren't going to be my boy's future." But Shane compares the gun to any farm implement and replies that "a gun is as good or as bad as the man using it." One homesteader voices what the logic of the classic western holds to be an untenably pacifist view, that gunslinging is another name for murder; but for Shane, violence, though sometimes necessary, is used only as a last resort, by a courageous man who has right on his side. This is the fundamental lesson of the classic western: that in American history, the principle of right is the basis of law, and any violence performed in the name of that principle is both acceptable and historically necessary. The arrival of the hired gunslinger Wilson is a guarantee of a showdown with Shane, but throughout the film scenes of conflict are interspersed with peaceful family life, celebrations of the fourth of July, even country dancing. Significantly, the Riker clan is all male and adult, and the absence of both women and children from their group is an indication of both their uncivilized, undomesticated nature and the passing of their sole dominion over the land. Nonetheless, Riker's view is voiced, providing a historical explanation for the conflict. When he says that "we made this country . . . we made a safe range" and that the homesteaders have moved in to ruin the ranchers' work, his point is taken, but Joe Starrett notes that trappers had preceded Riker, and so there is no original claim to the land. Significantly, no Native American voice is heard here; the conflict is one of priority between whites, between those who run cattle and those who settle in larger numbers on small claims provided by a government whose distance from the conflict is a measure of its tenuous authority.

A significant subtheme is that of the recently ended Civil War, which causes the first death, of the Alabama native Stonewall at the hands of Wilson. The homesteader vision, expressed at Stonewall's funeral when the choice between flight and fight is fully made, is one of a town, schools, a place to raise families, essentially one of community—indeed, it is a vision of Wyoming, and the Rocky Mountain region, as it "will be," the very principle of Manifest Destiny. But the fact that Shane departs the town and that his solitary status is maintained at the end are key to the film's status as a classical western. This divergence from the logic of history, whereby he should marry and settle down to an ordinary life of pioneering hard work on the land, or helping to build a church and a schoolhouse, marks the classic western as a tale less about history than about an ethical condition, the possibility of heroism. This explains the tension between such films and the historical record of the region in which they are set. They cannot, finally, be trusted to document the regional history and are a more useful gauge of the moral landscape of the time in which they were made. In this respect, *Shane* teaches us as much about America in the early 1950s as it does the historical conditions of Wyoming in the 1870s.

The Revisionist Western and the Claim of Historical Accuracy

The Rocky Mountain states belong and do not belong to American film. Belonging to the American West, they do not exhaust the western genre, which boasts, among others, Texas, Missouri, Arkansas, Oklahoma, Arizona, New Mexico, and even, in *How the West Was Won* (1963), upstate New York in the mental geography of the West. The cattle drive in Howard Hawks' classic western *Red River* (1948) takes us from Texas to Missouri. John Ford's late masterpiece *Cheyenne Autumn*, with the name of a Wyoming city in its title, does not take place in Wyoming so much as toward Wyoming, away from Oklahoma, and tells the story of the Cheyenne people, led by Chief Dull Knife, who surrendered in Nebraska and were eventually placed on reservations in Montana. By comparison with the representation of Native Americans in Ford's earlier films, notably *Stagecoach* (1939), *Cheyenne Autumn* stands as a mea culpa; it now offers an account of Native Americans as the victims of white violence, and in this respect it earns the title of revisionist western. Ford's *The Searchers*, which returns to the Utah and Arizona setting he made his own, Monument Valley, is less overtly revisionist, although it might be said that John Wayne's final change of heart, from overt racism to troubled uncertainty, is a step in the right direction. There is a significant sign of revisionism in the pro-Indian film of the 1950s, such as Delmer Daves' *Broken Arrow* (1950) and Robert Aldrich's *Apache*, but the revisionist western of the Vietnam era is less a western than a western-as-allegory, establishing a direct link between the U.S. "imperialist" actions in the West and in American foreign policy in Southeast Asia. Several such films have regional connections to the Rockies.

The revisionist western proper appears at a specific moment in American history when American foreign policy in Vietnam was recast by many at home and abroad as racist warmongering. Among revisionist westerns, *Soldier Blue* (1969), generally considered a flawed film, is the most blatant example of staging a western as a commentary on contemporary political conditions. Set in Colorado, *Soldier Blue* makes a brutal show of the 1864 Sand Creek massacre, which killed nearly 200 Arapaho Indians, mostly women, children, elderly, and infirm. Director Ralph Nelson specifically claimed a link to the My Lai massacre of 1968, establishing an allegorical link between the supposedly historical account of early Colorado and the Vietnam War.

Arthur Penn's *Little Big Man* (1970) takes the western out of its mythical mode and places it in history, making the western both ordinary (it can be remembered by one old man who is found in a nursing home, far away from the legendary and mythic landscape of the genre) and callously factual rather than heroic. The battle of the Little Big Horn on June 25, 1876, was simply an event that happened on a given day in what is now eastern Montana, and its violence, known mythically as Custer's Last Stand, and featured in film as *They Died With Their Boots On* (1942), is now specifically presented as racist, at one with the racist violence of the Vietnam War. Likewise, Robert Altman's *McCabe and Mrs. Miller* (1974), whose location is vaguely Pacific Northwest (and is therefore in thrall to historical conditions rather than a simplified mythic art form), deliberately eschews the common iconography of the western and recasts the action to counter the audience's expectations of moral simplicity. *Little Big Man* was a watershed in the representation of Native Americans in film, as it provided an account of Custer as a murderous psychopath, the U.S. military as criminals. A crucial step in the reimaging of Native Americans, and one that film easily allows, is the construction of a framework of audience identification with Indian otherness through point of view, something repeatedly provided in *Little Big Man* as Jack Crabb's identity shifts back and forth between Indian tribe and Cavalry regiment. However, only when Indians are given complete control of the process of western film image making can the misrepresentation begin to be fully reversed.

A film that begins this process is Cheyenne-Arapaho director Chris Eyre's *Smoke Signals* (1999), a lighthearted character study based on Sherman Alexie's novel, which allows the audience to identify with the lead characters Thomas and Victor and thereby see the European settlers in a different light. That said, a consideration of Native American pictorial representation reminds us of the complicity of the motion picture camera in an essentially European, Renaissance system of depiction. The process whereby Indians could take back the image of themselves that the western had produced is complex indeed.

The Missouri Breaks (1976), set in eastern Montana among the Missouri River tributaries, is exemplary of the revisionist western's treatment of historical circumstance. Penn's film eschews the mythologizing practice of the genre—its employment of stark simplicity in characterization and iconography—and substitutes a range of quirky atypical props, such as a bartered clarinet and a pair of binoculars. Marlon Brando's psychopathic murderer wears a range of costumes that seem specifically tailored to upset the audience's expectations of codified western garb, from a Chinese straw hat to a woman's sun bonnet. In many respects *The Missouri Breaks* does follow the standard format of the western, with a horse rustler who considers ways to give up his criminal lifestyle, a wealthy rancher, a hanging, a figure taking a bath, a whorehouse and a civilized woman who could become a schoolteacher in the yet-to-be-built one-room schoolhouse, and even a regiment of cavalry. But this film incorporates these stock figures from the western only to reverse them: The wealthy rancher reads rather urbane, dandyish comic English

Marlon Brando (right) and Jack Nicholson are just two of many stars in *The Missouri Breaks*, 1976. Courtesy of Photofest.

literature (Laurence Sterne's *Tristram Shandy*); the bath tub is marble, not copper, and is full of modesty-preserving bubble bath and a "lavender-smelling" Brando; the civilized woman is sexually rapacious and forward and is on familiar terms with the local whores; and the cavalry, John Ford's stalwarts, are here the victims of horse theft as they sing "Bringing in the Sheaves." Indeed, the fact that we never see the cavalry is a full measure of their impotence. Penn's deliberate strategy of revising the western and making it "more real" is still put at the service of drama rather than documentary, and *The Missouri Breaks*, with its sexual and bodily frankness (not only do we see an outhouse; one character is shot from long range while using it) and long-haired heroes in Brando and Nicholson, seems like a film from the 1970s rather than a true account of life in this part of Montana. The closing credits note, however, that certain parts of the film were shot near Nevada City, Montana, and since this is the only location credited, the attempt to link history and fiction film seems conscientious.

Jeremiah Johnson (1972), starring Robert Redford and directed by Sydney Pollack, was shot entirely on location in Utah, in the Wasatch and Uinta National Forest, the Ashley National Forest, Zion National Park, and Snow Canyon State Park. This film is key in developing an association between the actor (who had also appeared in New York City films such as *Barefoot in the Park* [1967]) and the state of Utah. Set in the era before massive migration from the East, and before the gold rush that sparked the sudden attraction of the Rockies, *Jeremiah Johnson* presents the Rocky Mountain region as an essentially idyllic interlude in history rather than an idyllic place on the map. Unlike the settlers, Johnson has come to the mountains to escape the force of civilization, and unlike historical figure Jim Bridger, a mountain man who established a fort on the Oregon Trail and worked as a guide during the Mormon War of 1857–1858 and on Union Pacific railroad projects, Johnson carefully avoids white company. The old trapper who teaches Johnson the ways of the mountains advises that "the mountain's got its own ways" and "whatever you learned down on the flat will serve you no good up here, you got some work to do," suggesting that trappers have to conform to the ways of both the mountains and the indigenous tribes that live there, rather than conquering and controlling them. As with *Shane*, the protagonist here has left war behind (this time the Mexican-American War), but Shane has come to a ranch in the valley, whereas here Johnson is in the mountains, living in delicate balance with the Crow Indians on whose land he hunts. The mere fact that the Crow are given names and speak their own language already marks the respect for Native American culture *as* a culture that distinguishes the revisionist western from the classic of the genre. Here the old trapper, Johnson's guide, himself speaks the Crow language, and Johnson realizes that he must make payment in furs for the taking of an elk on Crow lands. The Blackfeet are presented as practitioners of that barbaric enterprise, scalping; but then, in a reversal characteristic of the revisionist western, so are the English. "London is wallpapered with Indian scalps," we are told. The film's treatment of the Indians is also more subtle than that of the classic western, a division into tribes, with the Flatheads, for example, French-speaking, practicing Christians, and the Crow are specifically contrasted with the Apaches. When Johnson is given the Flathead chief's daughter in marriage, the complex and often mutually misunderstanding relationship between the white trappers and Indian tribal culture is examined in greater depth. Nonetheless, the story is Jeremiah

Johnson's, not that of his Flathead wife, and the film gives us an Indian point of view only as Johnson develops one himself.

Johnson and his wife and adopted son build a cabin and settle, and they are visited by members of the Third Cavalry, including one Reverend Lundquist. When Johnson says that they are on Crow territory, the Reverend replies, "Well, this is the department of Colorado." Thus the renaming of the land is signaled as the first step in its appropriation and annexation by the American government. The star of the film is the Utah landscape, as the viewer is provided frequent interludes to simply take in the grandeur of the snowcapped peaks or the high desert. This incorporation of touristic spectatorship is more for the film viewer's benefit than a characterization of Johnson's worldview. Significantly, however, the camera often pans the forests, and these are intercut with reverse shots of an attentive Johnson, as if to suggest that the forests are full of invisible Indians, watching his every move. This is especially so when Johnson is persuaded to lead the cavalry through a Crow burial ground. There is no indication that the company has been seen, and no military engagement, but as Johnson passes back through the burial ground, he has a premonition that the Crow were watching all the time and have exacted revenge by killing his wife and son. It is Johnson's loquacious, sometimes travel partner Daryl who characterizes the Rockies as "the marrow of the world" and "God's finest sculpturings," and Johnson agrees; but when asked about his future, Johnson says that he might go north to Canada, a sign that he senses the inevitable passing of the mountain man's time and that he, like the Crow, is living on borrowed time.

The representation of the Rocky Mountain region as a place of asylum from the forces of government, but a place that is ultimately incapable of escaping the forces of history, is also the theme of *Legends of the Fall* (1994). In this film Colonel Ludlow brings his three sons Samuel, Alfred, and Tristan to Montana, to be free of the civilizing constrictions of eastern life and, significantly, of women. But the distant call of war, and the possibility of battlefield glory, dashes his hopes of protecting his sons; and the arrival of Susanna, the fiancé of one son, leads to jealousy among the three brothers. Released at a time when Idaho and Montana in particular were developing reputations as refuges for the disaffected and Radical Right (although only a 1996 television movie was made about Unambomber Ted Kaczynski), *Legends of the Fall* punctures the myth of the West as safe haven, a place of refuge from human frailties that are dramatized in domestic jealousy and the glorification of war.

Robert Redford's association with the Sundance Institute and the Sundance Film Festival recognizes the importance of his role as the Sundance Kid, playing opposite Paul Newman as the Utah-born Butch Cassidy, in *Butch Cassidy and the Sundance Kid* (1969). Redford of all Hollywood stars is most closely associated with a process of selling the region by producing engaging stories and images that celebrate the Rockies. This film glamorizes the lives of two western outlaws who robbed banks and trains up and down the Rockies, from Montana down to Colorado. Eventually they headed south to Bolivia to escape the interest of the Pinkerton agents, where they were killed in a failed bank robbery. *Butch Cassidy and the Sundance Kid* is only one among numerous filmed accounts of their exploits, including *Cheyenne* (1947), *Wyoming Renegades* (1954), and the comedy *Cat Ballou* (1965), but it might be considered a revisionist apologia for the western at a time of revisionist criticism and a wrenching war in Vietnam. A loving portrayal of two charming outlaws, it works strenuously and successfully to place the bank robbers in a kindly light while paying little attention to the historical circumstances of armed robbery.

The Neorevisionist Western

A notable example of this subgenre is Clint Eastwood's Oscar-winning *Unforgiven* (1992), whose action takes place in 1888, chiefly in the small community of Big Whiskey, Wyoming, whose sheriff Little Bill (Gene Hackman) has decided to ban firearms within the city limits. Immediately the pacifist setting establishes a classic conflict between the urges of armed lawlessness and peaceful civilization. The action begins in a whorehouse, with the mutilation of one of the prostitutes by her client in response to her laughter at his meager endowment. As the prostitute lies bleeding, the local sheriff agrees that a wrong has been done, but only to the male owner of the whorehouse, and he orders the perpetrators, two cowboys, to repay this wronged man in horses—which, come spring, they duly do, all in disregard for the injured woman. As a group, the prostitutes recognize that they are held in less esteem than horses (which is literally the case) and decide to take summary action. Thus begins the neorevisionist plot and agenda. The revisionism here is that the plot is overtly feminist, since the women in the whorehouse pool their savings and advertise to hire a killer and avenge their young colleague's injuries. If the 1970s revisionist western recasts the classic western as violently imperialist, *Unforgiven* presents us with a Wyoming experience of latter-day feminist consciousness raising. Even though the film follows the classical format, focusing on the lives of men, its plot is driven by an injury to women that will be avenged by the women. Here, then, the men are employees of the women, proxy actors in a drama that the classic western would center on male agency. Eastwood plays a reformed killer, William Munny, whose deceased wife Claudia, another strong woman, is repeatedly credited with getting him off whisky and away from crime. As in so many classic westerns, Munny is forced out of retirement (by the unfortunate coincidence of a failing hog farm and the arrival of a young gunslinger with the promise of $1,000) for one more killing that will supposedly give his young motherless children a better start in life. *Unforgiven* also features the hardly generic figure of English Bob (Richard Harris), an outspoken monarchist and cool assassin who is also on the trail of the prostitutes' money. English Bob, we are told, was hired by the railroad to kill the Chinese, and he is presented as both psychotic and theatrically entertaining in the mold perhaps of Oscar Wilde, a fish out of water. English Bob, however, is an experienced killer, and he travels with his own bookish biographer, Beauchamp, who has written dime novels that immediately mythologize the still-living assassin as the "Duke of Death." The fact that English Bob is racist is now taken by other characters as acceptable (the Chinese are not mentioned further), but the film's agenda is clearly postimperial and insistently critical of the violence to both women and minorities in the frontier West. Significantly, the race of African American partner Ned (Morgan Freeman) is not made verbally an issue but only iconically, as he is whipped and finally killed by Little Bill (supposedly by accidental zealotry rather than premeditation) in order to extract information. Ned's wife, a Native American, is wisely convinced that the

Clint Eastwood stars in the 1992 film *Unforgiven*. Courtesy of Photofest.

arrival of Munny in her quiet pastoral life with Ned can only be bad news. Indeed, nothing good comes of the Wyoming adventure, except that Munny survives to go back to the Midwest and grieve all the more.

A key characteristic of the neorevisionist western is that, unlike the original revisionism of the 1970s, historical research has a chance of impinging on the plot. Here, for example, the Kid, who claims to have killed five men, finally confesses to having killed none, and when he does finally make his first killing, the trauma and guilt involved convince him that he will never kill again. The Kid is also extremely shortsighted; so the scene in which the Kid and Ned find their quarry the cowboys and decide to pick them off from a distance—which would be common practice in the classic western, thereby establishing the fundamental role of the firearm as a device for the control of distance—is here bungled and messy, with the cowboy victims, who have been humanized in an early scene where they try to make amends for their violence toward the prostitute, now suffer agony and a desperate fear of their imminent death. People may take indoor baths in classic westerns, but here the Kid's sole victim dies while using the outhouse. Gone, then, is the stylization of death; here it is ordinary, or marked by sickness, and bereft of glamour, just as it must have been. In *Unforgiven*, this Wyoming that stands in for the West is a place that might be the site of western mythology but proves altogether too ordinary, and the gory particulars of this story are never allowed to transcend the sense that here is a historical and geographical backwater that witnessed messy settlement. The immediate recognition that this film received is a measure of its intelligent and, above all, mature handling of a film genre in the context of a real place that had a real history so very much at odds with the myth.

Heartland (1979), set in Wyoming in 1910, and shot in Wheatland, Fergus, and Meagher counties, Montana, is an independent release that achieved major critical success and festival awards but received little mainstream publicity. Starring Rip Torn and Conchetta Ferrell, *Heartland* was written by Beth Ferris (also writer and producer of the documentary *Contrary Warriors: A Film of the Crow Tribe* [1985]), and it revises the Hollywood formulaic western in two respects: in its realistic account of life in turn-of-the-century Wyoming and in its focus on the experience of a small-time ranching family from the point of view of a woman. So we hear the accents of first-generation immigrants from Europe, and the camera takes us into the kitchen to observe the mundane conditions of domestic life. While the western gives us iconic kitchenware, *Heartland* lingers longer on things we might find only in a museum of western history: the stove, the pots and pans, the laundry mangle, all of which are essential to the portrayal of Elinore and of her life as a housekeeper and homemaker. Essentially a documentary reenactment, since *Heartland* is based on the diaries of frontier woman Elinore Randall Stewart, this film lacks the conflictual gunplay that we expect from male-dominated westerns, but there is death and suffering and above all hardship attendant upon the Stewart family's lonely independence. Answering a classified advertisement, Elinore Randall accepts a job as housekeeper for a solitary, stoical rancher in Wyoming, a man of few words, Clyde Stewart. In less than a year, Randall decides that she wants to start a homestead on some neighboring land but is persuaded by Clyde that she would be better off, in a practical sense, if she married him. And so she does. This marriage, apparently born of necessity, evolves into a taciturn, hardworking life of mutual support and companionship. Stewart says little, but he is no villain; indeed, the only villain is misfortune, chiefly in the form of the climate. As winter comes, Elinore gives birth to a son, but the child soon dies, leaving Elinore grief stricken and Clyde all the more stoical. A notable anomaly in *Heartland* is the treatment of animals, which is bluntly documentarian, direct, and necessarily cruel (a hog is shot and slaughtered, calves are branded, many cattle die in the cold); so while the classic western is marked by violence between cowboys and Indians, or depicts conflict simply between heroes and villains, *Heartland* denies such formulaic dramatic play and structure. As such, it is an especially telling measure of the theatrical stakes in the western, its relative disregard for frontier actuality, with its mix of privation and winter boredom rather than lawlessness and violent retribution (here the Stewarts play dominoes by oil lamp, whereas the classic western gives us, conventionally, only poker and usually only that as a pretext for cheating and conflict). Employing such documentary techniques as hand-held camera, *Heartland* suggests that this is how the West really was, with dramatic violence replaced by a less picturesque struggle. The placement of the action in Wyoming also removes this film from the classical conflict of Texan or Arizona westerns, suggesting, first, that this is a marginal territory whose attractions are by no means certain and then that this is a film set in the West but not to be confused with the genre. At the film's close, as Elinore and Clyde assist in the birth of a heifer, the miracle of new life is allowed to make up for all the months of death, and the film therefore does conform, albeit in a muted way, to the hopeful Hollywood ending: After a long winter, spring will surely come.

Filming the West and the New West

Beyond the western proper, with its instantly recognizable iconology, and the revisionist western, which might look right but which systematically recasts the old stories in a new light, there are, simply, all the other films that provide a measure of the region, from documentaries to films of natural history, and fiction films whose location is here in the Rocky Mountains but whose concerns are other than those of the pioneering past. As we have seen, Apted's *Continental Divide* is exemplary of such a treatment, but there are others. The various states have their film commissions, and each one boasts that major motion pictures were made in that state. Some such films, like Idaho's *Breakfast of Champions* (1999), or southern Utah's *Octopussy* (1983), make no particular claim on regional history; filmmaking conditions, including incentives, made the state an attractive place to shoot. This explains the logic whereby the Montana depicted in *Legends of the Fall* (1994) proves to be not Montana at all but Canada, that the northern California of *Pale Rider* is Idaho, and that the Wyoming of *Heartland* is Montana; but for the most part, films shot in a region do make some claim of historical connection.

A constant cable television option to guests at Idaho's Sun Valley Lodge is the film in which the lodge itself features, *Sun Valley Serenade* (1941). Sun Valley, the ski resort founded near Ketchum, Idaho, was conceived as an image and a touristic mise-en-scène, based on a possible mapping of the culture of the European Alps onto the western American landscape. The project was conceived by railroad magnate Averell Harriman, who hired Count Felix Schaffgtosch to scout the Rocky Mountains for a ski resort site that would match the best in Switzerland or Austria. With this preconception at its heart, Sun Valley naturally became the haunt of Hollywood actors, whose photographs still line the corridors of the lodge. *Sun Valley Serenade* was a vehicle for Norwegian Olympic skating star Sonja Henie and featured the performance of the Glenn Miller Orchestra, but it clearly fits the commercial agenda of publicizing the resort and provided a rare opportunity for moviegoers in the golden age of film stardom to live out a star fantasy by staying at the actual hotel and skiing on the selfsame slopes. *Sun Valley Serenade* is symptomatic of the inclusion of the Rocky Mountain region in an economy of desirable images that separates film star work from a stable location and allows them to stage themselves in exotic environments. It is this logic that makes Hollywood producers and actors flock to Sundance every year or to spend time in Aspen or similar resorts. Some movie stars are widely known to have homes in the region, such as Dennis Quaid or Peter Fonda in Montana, Harrison Ford in Jackson Hole, Wyoming, Bruce Willis in Hailey, Idaho, and most famously, Robert Redford in Utah. While the region for these stars means escape from Los Angeles, it also brings cachet to the communities that they choose to grace. As a result, small ranching towns become exotic and too expensive for the locals. This, too, is part of the complex equation of film image and place in the Rocky Mountain region.

A key film in the representation of Montana as a pristine paradise is Robert Redford's *A River Runs through It* (1992), which combines stunning cinematography of pure rivers and sunny meadows with an essentially nostalgic story about a Montana childhood. Crucially, author Norman Maclean's nostalgia is for a time not entirely unlike our own, a time already somewhat modernized. The motor car has arrived, the railroad is no longer being built but has become a common form of transportation, and this Montana is aware of the world beyond the Rockies. It seems to be a place in which one could expect wildness as a recreational opportunity, and that wildness could be relied upon to nourish the characters' ethical makeup, as if good land could, contrary to the lessons of countless westerns, guarantee good people. In this respect the film's account of the relation between the region's landscape and its people is an echo of Jeff Smith in *Mr. Smith Goes to Washington*, whose purity of heart stems from his rural Montana background. The unexpected effect of the film was simply to sell the state, and to some extent the region in general, as an idyllic site where an innocent American past could still be found and purchased. Set during an apparently endless summer, *A River Runs through It* creates an image of Montana that amounts to an advertisement for it, and in this respect it might be considered the obverse of the eternal winter of *Heartland*, which is set in a similar era and also filmed in Montana.

As a measure of the region's contrasts once we leave the generic security of the classic western, Travis Wilkerson's *An Injury to One* (2002) is a historical documentary about the never-solved murder of union organizer Frank Little in 1917. *An Injury to One* treats the gritty actualities of the region (specifically Montana here, but these are certainly mirrored in Colorado mining country) and stands in stark contrast to the classic western, whose adherence is divided between historical reality and the demands of story. Butte, Montana, was dominated by the Anaconda Mining Company, and during World War I Butte produced 10 percent of the world's copper. However, working conditions were poor, and mining accidents were common. Little, a socialist "Wobbly" organizer, was widely believed to have been killed by "capitalist interests" for his all-too-effective union organizing: Eight thousand people attended his funeral. Rather than focusing on Little alone, *An Injury to One* places Little's story in the broader context of Butte's rise and decline and the destruction of the natural environment by capitalist mining and smelting industries.

By further comparison with the common products of Hollywood, even those like Eastwood's *Unforgiven* that revise the western genre and take a much more liberal line with the western's treatment of history, *An Injury to One* is fundamentally marginalized. First, it is a documentary, and documentaries are outside the mainstream of American movie culture, and second, its agitational agenda seems designed for an audience of the already convinced. We might think that a Left-leaning documentary has no chance of exposure and that the story of Frank Little would remain overlooked—his battle supposedly lost and his death put down to political misadventure. There are, however, liberal documentaries (in practice the term may be a tautology) on the region with mass appeal. Among these, *Bowling for Columbine* (2002) is exemplary, an astute reckoning of the relation between the region and the nation, and its thesis encourages a thoroughgoing reappraisal of the place of violence in the region. David Hamilton Murdoch commented that "[t]he ultimate appeal of the Western film may well be, as the critic Robert Warshow long ago suggested, that it is the only genre in any medium which seriously suggests that violence solves problems."[12] In this Oscar-winning documentary, filmmaker Michael Moore visits Denver suburb Littleton, Colorado, to investigate the roots of the Columbine High School massacre that left thirteen dead and dozens critically injured on April 20, 1999. Moore's film is necessarily about the Denver locality of the massacre, but he sees the events of that morning in Colorado as symptomatic of a broader malaise in American society, one whose main symptom is the lack of gun control. Moore detects a connection between the Columbine massacre and the proximity of the world's largest weapons manufacturer, Lockheed Martin, the proximity of Rocky Flats plutonium weapons factory, which he describes as "a massive radioactive dump," and the Norad missile control center, also in Colorado. A corollary to this story, one that Moore is keen to explore, is the success of the television cartoon series *South Park* and its feature-length film version *South Park: Bigger, Longer & Uncut* (1999). South Park was conceived and written by two former Columbine students, Trey Parker and Matt Stone. For Moore, the events of that morning have national resonance; he sees the violence as symptomatic of an American state of mind that is irrationally fearful and that leads to Americans being therefore excessively armed, either with handguns or with intercontinental ballistic missiles. In the context of prior representation of the Rocky Mountain region, chiefly in the Hollywood western, we see here both continuity and rupture. The region is not accidentally but historically agonized and violent; it is also rhetorically pristine and attractive. Montana, for example, can boast of being "the last best place," but the tourist brochure images of snowy peaks and just-hooked trout or idyllic putting green hardly constitute a culture. When the hidden historical culture comes to the surface, it proves to be neither heroic nor picturesque but local and ordinary.

A further case of New West disruption of long-cherished images of the region is *SLC Punk* (1999), directed by James Merendino. Deliberately contradicting every image of Utah's ultraclean, caffeine-free lifestyle, *SLC Punk* is set in the heart of the Mormon capital, Salt Lake City (SLC). The incongruity of punk rock culture in Utah is not lost on the film's narrator Stevo, who delivers occasional tirades (in a play they would be called soliloquies), one of which explains the existential trap that a Utah punk find himself in. As a subculture, punk is English, from the late 1970s, vehemently antiestablishment, and equally opposed to the hippie counterculture that seems to have lost its rebellious credentials. Punk rebellion in Salt Lake City suffers from a lack of authenticity: While its motivations are logical, given the Mormon dominance in both city and state, the appropriation of a distant and essentially foreign subculture feels superficial, a fashion rather than a life. Stevo lambastes punk fashion, recognizing in it the seeds of market-driven conformity that punk sought to undermine, but the blue hair, razor blade jewelry, and Gothic garb suggest a major historical rupture in the culture of the region. Indeed, like *Bowling for Columbine*, with its mix of local and national focus, *SLC Punk* puts the very issue of regionalism to the test. The Utah fashion punk tries too hard, is rootless in his or her rejection of the local culture, and belongs to an era of global capitalism (the image of Ronald Reagan [1911–2004] is frequently seen) that encourages high-tech industry, suburban growth spurts based on property speculation, and the prospect of a newer, cleaner, crime-free California. This is the other side of the New West, and *SLC Punk*, like *South Park*, is specifically designed to satirize and expose the Mormon ideal of family, cleanliness, and purity of conduct as culturally vacuous. Stevo's tirade is compellingly rational and calmly delivered, as if written by a Ph.D. in sociology, so when he explains a fistfight between two punks (himself included) and two police officers as a result of "this complex world of fascism that was Utah state policy" it seems to make sense.

Like *South Park*, *SLC Punk* initially comes across as a student project, but this proves to be a disarming strategy, making the astute observations on Utah society all the more biting. Paradoxically, Salt Lake City's punk transgression is not opposed to the cultural norm but the inevitable counterpart to the dominant culture. In this respect the Utah punk looks back not just to its English roots but to those of Jack Kerouac's (1922–1969) disaffected Beat Generation in the 1950s, in another era of guilt-free family consumerism and willful innocence that finally collapses when the Vietnam War comes home to roost. The opening of *SLC Punk* now bears chilling resemblance to the 1998 beating death of young gay student Matthew Shepard in Laramie, Wyoming. Moisés Kaufman's play *The Laramie Project*, which was released as an HBO film in 2002, is tellingly linked to commentary in *SLC Punk* about the common practice of "fag bashing" in the state. Indeed, the commentary is delivered as Stevo and friends drive to Wyoming, a state that has the benefit of unadulterated beer but in which the punks look, by comparison with the local cowboy fashion, entirely alien. As if in direct commentary on the post-Shepard scrutiny of Wyoming, the liquor store Wyoming characters are depicted here as both simple-minded and religiously excessive. So in this beer run to rural Wyoming, the Utah punk phenomenon reveals another paradox: that it is really an urban, Salt Lake City subculture (with the emphasis on "city") that is allowed to exist only to the extent that it remains part of the urban life, very much as Jack Kerouac's Colorado Beat experience in *On the Road* focuses on Denver, not on small-town or even suburban life. In this respect the contrast between the normalcy of punk culture in the city and its oddity in the country is another echo of the murder of Matthew Shepard, since he was taken out of the tolerance of the city to be victimized in the solitude of mere landscape. A strange twist of plot in *SLC Punk* has Stevo reenter the conservative fold by taking up, rather improbably, a place at Harvard Law School and claiming that he can do more punk anarchic damage within the system than by being punk outside it. The spuriousness of the claim is mitigated by the wisdom of Stevo's commentary on punk and the predictability that youthful rebellion will generally dissolve into some degree of conformity. This ending shirks the film's prior confrontation with the conservatism of the New West, but it also responds effectively to advice given by South Park cocreator Trey Parker in Michael Moore's *Bowling for Columbine* that high school will eventually end and that another and saner world awaits. For Stevo, Cambridge, Massachusetts, awaits, a location that embodies difference, indifference to punk styles, and that, necessarily, beckons adulthood.

THE ROCKY MOUNTAIN FESTIVALS: FILM CULTURE FLOWN IN

Sundance Film Festival might be considered the jewel in the region's film culture crown: An annual gathering of ambitious filmmakers gather to screen their new work for an audience of sophisticated filmgoers and astute Hollywood producers looking for the next big thing. Held every January in Park City, Utah, Sundance began at Trolley Corners Theaters in Salt Lake City in 1978 with the ambitious title of the United States Film Festival. Since then the title has become more humble, while the festival itself has matched the original ambition, as Sundance clearly ranks as the premier film festival in the United States, a place to see great independent films and to be seen as a player in the industry. In 1981, at the behest of director and actor Sydney Pollack, the festival was moved to Park City, Utah, and organizers responded to the burgeoning popularity of the contemporary independent films by scaling back the number of retrospective screenings. The year 1985 saw the film festival sponsored by Robert Redford's Sundance Institute (though the festival was to retain its title of United States Film Festival until 1990) and the screening of numerous films that have since established major reputations, including Jim Jarmusch's *Stranger than Paradise* (1984), the Coen brothers' *Blood Simple* (1984), and Woody Allen's *Hannah and Her Sisters* (1986). Subsequent years have seen a combination of retrospective celebrations (Richard Lester, Powell and Pressburger, Robert Altman, Arthur Penn, Rainer Werner Fassbinder) and restorations of classics. As with the Academy Awards, the famous names that appear at Sundance obscure the festival's encouragement of documentary film, cinematography, and independent film acting, and the range of prizes has grown from the Jury Awards to include prizes for Screenwriting, Freedom of Expression, Latin American Filmmaking, an Audience Award, and a World Cinema Audience Award. Located in the Rocky Mountains, the Sundance Film Festival has continued to attract Hollywood producers who hope to sign the most promising newcomers. This growth and popularity explains the establishment of an alternative film festival for smaller-scale and lower-budget films that are not necessarily seeking an entry into the Hollywood industry.

The Slamdance Film Festival, which runs concurrently with Sundance every January, claims to present serious filmmakers without the glitz of Hollywood and is conscious of maintaining a distinction between its agenda and that of its now-famous parent. Colorado's Aspen Filmfest and its highly regarded Shortsfest are less well known than Sundance (even though Aspen is well known as a resort for Hollywood's rich and famous) and have a global catchment of independent films. Aspen Filmfest, which was founded in 1979, has been described as "one of the film world's best kept secrets," while Shortsfest is acknowledged as "one of the nation's top short film festivals." Telluride Film Festival, which runs annually in early September, has less press than Sundance and boasts excellent screenings, yet denies much of the transplanted Hollywood glamour. Other notable film festivals in the region include the Big Sky Documentary Film Festival, held annually in Missoula, Montana, and the Banff Mountain Film Festival, which tours throughout the region from its base in Canada and presents a series of recreational films on mountain themes, such as skiing and mountaineering.

An important addition to the documentary representation of the Rocky Mountain region, the Banff films put the stress on mountains as a paradise for mountain sports. In this respect, it offers a more positive view of the possibilities of the New West, a reply to the unexpected nihilism suggested by *SLC Punk* or *Bowling for Columbine*. The representation of the Rocky Mountain region as pure and idyllic hardly suffers from the foul-mouthed, albeit telling, satire of *South Park: Bigger, Longer, and Uncut* (1999). The dominant film image of the region remains one of clear rivers, snow-capped mountains, and fresh air recreation. State governments remain convinced that having a film crew in the state is a promise of tourist revenue, and their advertisements in such professional journals as *American Cinematographer* clearly beckon the film industry as an arm of tourism.

A consideration of the function of the state film commissions in concert with their advertising to industry professionals speaks volumes about the perceived place of film as a commercial, revenue-enhancing representation of the state. Here the question of representation takes on a practical commercial quality, and the process is prescriptive and constructive rather than retrospective and interpretive. We might look at the role of the Tetons in *Shane* as a contribution to the story of frontier ranchers; that the Tetons are a geographical feature in Wyoming is a mere footnote to the film's story; but the film commission agenda is much more knowing today about the construction of a state's image around the world and a sense of state's self-worth, both morally and financially.

An exemplary case here is Redford's *A River Runs through It*, whose representation of Montana over a period of twenty-one years in the early part of the twentieth century mixes nostalgic memoir based on Norman Maclean's book with stunning images of an unsullied landscape. The film, based on a remarkable memoir by a professor at the University of Chicago, had a major impact not just on tourism but on relocation to Montana, as if Redford had conceived the project as an advertisement of the pleasures of a trout-blessed "Montana lifestyle." A contributing factor is the refusal of Paul (Brad Pitt), the charismatic younger brother, to consider departing for the sophisticated East. A trout fisherman who seems to live on the river in a state of grace, fully at home, Paul has always been attractive, courageous, and confident, and Norman's nostalgia for Montana is inextricably linked to his memories of his brother and their times on the river. While Norman sees himself as artificial, self-conscious, too thoughtful, Paul is natural, a good dancer, and at home in the Montana landscape.

The fact that the film takes place entirely in the brief summer months of an otherwise notoriously cold state says much about the theme of nostalgia but also about the role of film in misrepresenting the reality of the region for the sake—quite legitimately, from the filmmaker's point of view—of its art. In this respect the representation of the region as gloriously and breathtakingly beautiful, rather than, say, scarred with racism and violence, is a potential further chapter in the debate about the difference between screen violence and real violence: Is film essentially realistic or is it essentially artistic? And what does such a debate bode for the representation of a geographical space like the Rocky Mountains, which we want to be pure and "high" in the John Denver sense (energized by the beauty of nature) but which may prove to be false and temporary filmic opiates, ending in unforeseen nightmares like the one in Littleton, Colorado, or Laramie, Wyoming? The Montana of *A River Runs through It* is not all sweetness and light, of course. Paul, the younger brother, develops a drinking and gambling problem, and his liaison with a Native American woman puts them in peril; but tellingly their life contrasts with that of the rising (but actually failing) Hollywood star, whose sense of self is superficial, denied as he is the nourishment that the combination of Presbyterianism and rugged summer landscape has given the Maclean boys.

CONCLUSION: SELLING THE IMAGE

The Web site of the Colorado Film Commission advertises "big water, sophisticated cityscapes, vast farms (yes, we do mean *flat*), and neighborhoods you'd swear were . . . well, somewhere else," while the Wyoming Film Commission and the Idaho Film Bureau offer filmmakers a searchable photographic database of possible locations, so that production designers can see a range of possibilities—cabins, churches, canyons, and so on—at a glance. The effect of such a compendium is to organize films less according to their stories than to particular articulate spaces whose natural or human and historical architecture is the locational starting point to a film. Films become, from this point of view, images of determining place (the place comes first and helps engender or at least qualify the story) rather than a backdrop to a prescribed drama. Montana has one central film commission, but Utah has several regional commissions, each with its own landscape to offer. The Moab and Monument Valley Commission, for example, describes the local landscape as part of sixty years of film history, thereby layering the landscape with historical film value as well as its natural aesthetic value.

Film and theater in the Rocky Mountain region have seldom sought to represent the states or peoples specifically but have done so obliquely, unknowingly, as directors have told their stories and the question of place has been hardly acknowledged. This has been especially so in the western, a major current in film history and a central genre in American film history. The western has its own agendas and has sought landscapes in which to tell stories, but it has been typical of the western's relation to the land to deny it particular geographical reverence. Even in the work of John Ford in Monument Valley, the familiar landscape is employed chiefly for a pictorial quality, and the details of the actual location have fallen into obscurity behind a general artistic agenda. Typical of this removal from actual geography and toward an imaginary linkage of place and longing are the titles of two independent films that seem to be all about location. But neither the Polish brothers' *Twin Falls, Idaho* (1999) nor Gus Van Sant's *My Own Private Idaho* (1991) take us on a journey to Idaho. *Twin Falls, Idaho* was shot entirely in Los Angeles, and *My Own Private Idaho* was shot in Portland and Seattle. In these films, fittingly for the age, place is not a backdrop but an idea, the site of a dream.

RESOURCE GUIDE

Printed Sources

Buscome, Edward. *The BFI Companion to the Western*. New York: Atheneum, 1988.
Fielding, Raymond. "Hale's Tours: Ultrarealism in the Pre-1910 Motion Picture." In *Film Before Griffith*, ed. John L. Fell. Berkeley: University of California Press, 1983. 116–130.
Lusted, David. *The Western*. Harlow, England: Pearson, 2003.
Pace, David. "Behind the Mormon Curtain." *American Theatre* 9.6 (October 1992): 42.
Simmon, Scott. *The Invention of the Western Film: A Cultural History of the Genre's First Half Century*. Cambridge: Cambridge University Press, 2003.
Trusky, Tom, ed. *Letters from God's Country: Nell Shipman: Selected Correspondence and Writings*. Boise: Boise State University Press, 2003.

CD-ROM

Farmer, Walt. *Wyoming: A History of Film and Video in the 20th Century*. 2001.

Selected Films

The Big Sky. Dir. Howard Hawks. Winchester Pictures. 1952.
Bowling for Columbine. Dir. Michael Moore. International co-production. U.S. producer: Dog Eat Dog Films. 2002.

Cheyenne Autumn. Dir. John Ford. Warner Brothers and Ford-Smith Productions. 1964.
Continental Divide. Dir. Michael Apted. Universal Pictures. 1981.
Heartland. Dir. Richard Pearce. Filmhaus. 1980.
An Injury to One. Dir. Travis Wilkerson. First Run Features and Icarus Films. 2002.
Northfork. Dir. Michael Polish. Polish Brothers Construction, Departure Entertainment, Romano Shane Productions, and Prohibition Pictures. 2003.
A River Runs through It. Dir. Robert Redford. Allied Filmmakers. 1992.
The Searchers. Dir. John Ford. Warner Brothers and C. V. Whitney Pictures. 1953.
Shane. Dir. George Stevens. Paramount Pictures. 1953.
SLC Punk. Dir. James Merendino. Beyond Films, Blue Tulip, and Straight Edge. 1999.
Smoke Signals. Dir. Chris Eyre. Shadowcatcher Entertainment. 1998.
Sun Valley Serenade. Dir. H. Bruce Humberstone. 20th Century Fox. 1941.

Web Sites

http://www.coloradofilm.org
Colorado Film Commission website, "established for marketing purposes."

Extensive site, with location database, production guide; also links to information on weather, film permits and regulations, and Colorado film festivals. Accessed June 14, 2004.

http://www.filmandhistory.org
Film & History: An Interdisciplinary Journal of Film and Television Studies.

Accessed June 14, 2004. Web site for a scholarly journal, with links to "controversial films," and "film and book reviews."

http://www.imdb.com
Internet Movie Database.

Extensive capacities for search by location and state, information on production companies, stars, other films by the same director, and production details such as art direction, cinematography, and sound.

http://www.filmidaho.org
Idaho Film Bureau.

Official state Web site with links to "crew, equipment and support services," extensive illustrated location guide, accommodations, permits, climate. Lists recent films made in Idaho. Accessed June 17, 2004.

http://www.montanafilm.com
Montana Film Commission.

State Web site offering "a better brand of locations," including a searchable database of locations, advice for crews, and still photo examples of Montana locations for *Forrest Gump* and *A River Runs through It*. Accessed June 17, 2004.

http://www.film.utah.gov
Extensive Utah Film Commission website.

Links to information on the local film culture and the Utah film incentive program. Accessed June 17, 2004.

http://www.wyomingfilm.org
Wyoming Film Commission.

Offering Wyoming's "pristine scenery, financial incentives, and small towns full of character," to prospective filmmakers, this Web site offers details on weather reports, film shoot regulations, and links to information on local crew recruitment. Accessed June 17, 2004.

http://www.boisestate.edu/hemingway/ifc/nell.html
Site specifically devoted to the work of Nell Shipman. Accessed June 17, 2004.

http://www.boisestate.edu/hemingway/index.html
Site of Hemingway Western Studies Center.

Link to Howard Anderson Idaho Film Archive, listing and describing films shot in Idaho. Accessed June 17, 2004.

Selected Film Festivals

Aspen Filmfest
110 East Hallam Street, Suite 102
Aspen, CO 81611
tel: 970-925-6882
fax: 970-925-1967
http://www.aspenfilm.org

September 29–October 3, 2004. Announcing a goal "to enlighten, enrich, educate and entertain through film," this illustrated film festival Web site provides links to an archive of prior years, descriptions of films for the current year, laudatory press reviews, such as the *New York Observer's* "one of the film world's best kept secrets," information on educational outreach, and links to the companion festival, the *Aspen Shortfest* (April 6–April 10, 2005), and the *Aspen Academy Screenings* (December 19, 2004–January 1, 2005).

Big Sky Documentary Film Festival
131 South Higgins Avenue, Suite 201
Missoula, MT 59802
tel: 406-728-0753
http://highplainsfilms.org/festival/index.htm/

February 17–February 23, 2005. Features links to films exhibited and to their production company Web sites, a list of award winners, a call for entries, and press releases for the current year.

Slamdance Film Festival
Park City, UT
2633 Lincoln Blvd. #536
tel: 310-285-8496.
http://www.slamdance.com/

January 22–29, 2005. Links to information on the film festival, screenplay competition. *Anarchy Film Competition* and *$99 Specials* provide numerous short films viewable online.

Sundance Film Festival
Park City, UT
225 Santa Monica Blvd.
8th Floor
Santa Monica, CA 90401
tel: 310-204-2091
fax: 310-204-3901
http://institute.sundance.org/

January 20–30. Provides full program listing of this major independent film festival under such feature categories as Drama, World Cinema, Documentary, Premiere, Native Forum, American Spectrum, and a program of shorts. Also provided for festival-goers are the important links *How to Sundance* and the *Insiders' Scoop*, with details of ticket availability and screening sites.

Jackson Hole Wildlife Film Festival
P.O. Box 3940
Jackson Hole, WY 83001
http://www.jhfestival.org/

September 19–25, 2005. Homepage includes general information on the festival, historical background, a mission statement, links to a related wildlife film tech symposium, information for participants on lodging and travel, and a link to prior year's participants and competition winners.

Telluride Film Festival
Telluride, CO
http://www.telluridefilmfestival.com/

September 3–6, 2004. Peppered with compliments from film industry stalwarts, this site provides links to a useful page of FAQs and film entry protocols, email links for the press, pdf downloads for volunteer applications, a helpful guide on attending the festival on a budget, and information on the festival's heart in Telluride's Sheridan Opera House.

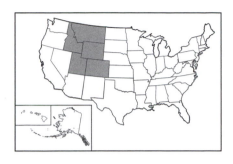

FOLKLORE

*Kristi A. Young and
Ronda Walker Weaver*

"This is the West sir. When fact meets legend, print the legend," asserts a character in John Ford's *The Man Who Shot Liberty Valance* (1962). Ford was right. When fact meets fiction, it is generally the half-truths—or what many consider the folklore—that document the era. While the folklore of the Rocky Mountains is rich and diverse, the visual images tend to be stereotypical—a lonely log cabin, a cowboy riding the range, miners hitting a mother lode. In reality, the folklore of the Rocky Mountain region allows us to begin separating the lore and the legend from the factual and the future. There is no question that folklore has shaped the Rocky Mountains, but how much of the early folklore is relevant now? How has folklore changed and adapted along with the region? These questions will be addressed in this chapter.

NATIVE AMERICAN LORE

Despite proof to the contrary, the West is often viewed in terms of the childhood game of cowboys and Indians. This does a disservice to both groups. Arising out of complex and beautifully diverse cultures, Native American customs and traditions deserve recognition for their complexity. A variety roamed the Rocky Mountain region. This list includes the Utes and Navajos of Utah and the Métis and Gros Ventre of Montana. From the Arapaho of Wyoming to the Blackfeet of Idaho, the Rocky Mountains are home to varied cultures that possess unique oral heritages. Yet, despite their differences, throughout the tribes' tales run common threads or themes that unite them in the human experience.

One such common thread is the coyote whose exploits pop up in tribes not only throughout the Rocky Mountain region but also in Native American populations in other areas. Barre Toelken, a noted scholar of Native American lore who has a great familiarity with coyote tales, warns that it is impossible for an outsider to ever completely comprehend the story the way members of the tribe would. Reading the tales presents a problem in itself since these tales are generally shared orally and always during the winter months. Placing them in a written form removes them even further from their naturally occurring context. However, Toelken, in his introduction to Barry Lopez's *Giving Birth to Thunder, Sleeping with His Daughter*, writes:

> Small details of geography, seemingly minor references to the color of a feather, the direction of the wind, the smell of grass or water, are all signals which awaken memories, trigger recognition, and allow for the re-experiencing of the texture and quality of a life locally known as it becomes a context for Old Man Coyote's universal adventures.[1]

Texture becomes important in understanding that coyote tales are very different from the typical European folk and fairy tales on which many North Americans are raised. While these tales once carried more social significance, many now fulfill one of American anthropologist William Bascom's four functions of folklore—entertainment. But no matter how entertaining a coyote tale may be, there is no doubt that it is also meant to instruct. While we might not be able to discern the particular tribal significance of the tale because of the universality inherent within the escapade, there is something to be gleaned.

A selection of coyote tales from Rocky Mountain tribes shows that other animals are generally prominent in the stories and that the stories tend to deal with the basic needs of food, sex, and creation. While often considered a trickster figure, the coyote frequently is the one being tricked. Take the Southern Ute tale of coyote and spider. Coyote is hungry and spider looks like a pretty good solution to his problem. Unfortunately for coyote, the two spiders he approaches separately are very wily and use their brains to remove themselves from danger. Coyote remains hungry.

The Blackfeet tell of coyote's futile attempts to recover the berries from the stream. Only after reaching the point of exhaustion does he notice the bountiful berry bushes near the bank of the stream. All of his work goes toward obtaining the unobtainable—a reflection—while, all the while, the real thing was within his grasp if he would just have looked up.

The Arapaho recount a tale of bear/women and coyote. When coyote first comes upon their camp, the inhabitants appear to be four women who are caring for their children. Notice the use of different numbers in Native American tales versus the European standard number three. Coyote tricks them into fetching him plums and uses their absence to kill their children and boil their bodies. After telling the women that he has killed and boiled wolves, they eat their own children. Coyote then gleefully tells them what they have done, and at this point the women assume the roles of bears. It is only through trickery that the coyote corners the bears in a magic tunnel and smokes them to death. At this point he consumes the bears. "I was very lucky to find these bears like this," he says to himself. "I like bear meat. You don't find this kind of food laying around. It's work."[2] The irony is obvious.

While coyote's appetites cause him to literally devour the bear/women, at times he is satisfied with merely conquering the opposite sex sexually. The Crow tell of coyote's willingness to exchange his ample sexual organ for the tiny one possessed by a mouse in order to get the girl who says she will only have relations with the one with the smallest member. The Gros Ventre speak of how, by hiding in an elk skull, coyote is able to force intercourse upon several maidens before escaping from his disguise and escaping from the tribe through open trickery.

While sexual acts may result in the creation of another being, coyote's own shaping comes through his mishaps. One such tale is the Navajo account of how coyote's eyes became yellow. Unhappy with the limitations of his own eyes, he unwisely begs the birds—his cousins—to give him their eyes so that he can see as far as they do. After being beseeched four times—there's that number again—the birds remove his eyes, and he stumbles around until he finds juniper pitch to fill his sockets. Thus were the coyote's yellow eyes created.

The coyote plays a cunning and sacred role in the Nez Percé account of how human beings were created. A monster from the North comes and consumes coyote's friends. After rescuing his fellow animals, coyote cuts the monster into pieces that become human beings. After throwing the pieces to the four winds, the tribes filled the land except for in one area. Then, "Coyote said, 'Here on this ground I make the Nez Percé. They will be few in number, but they will be strong and pure.'"[3]

It is no surprise that creation stories are found in tribes throughout the Rocky Mountain West. Humans seem to have an innate need to know where they come from and what their purpose is on this earth. The Navajo creation story involves male and female beings of colored light who use song to protect the male as he ascends the noisy mountain and brings back the first child. It is around this child that the woman orders her life through the use of words and the stories and tales they create. For Navajos, creation involves words.

One creation myth told by the Blackfeet of Montana shares similarities with the Judeo-Christian creation story of Adam and Eve. Created by man, woman asks what state she was in before she was alive. The man replies that she was dead. Curious, the woman asks if she will always be alive. The man suggests that they throw a buffalo chip into the water, and if it floats, humans will always be alive. In her ignorance of natural laws, she chooses to attempt to float a stone instead. Like Eve and the forbidden fruit, woman's choice irrevocably introduces death into the world.

Another tale of origins comes from the Utes. Derived from the Shoshones, the Utes share cultural traits with Plain Indians. They opted to live in tipis, and one of their native dances is the sun dance. They were also friendly with white settlers. Now they make their living primarily from raising sheep. A dependence on animals for food is illustrated by the folktale "Blood Clot." A young warrior is born from the blood clot of a buffalo. As a young man he is able to provide his adoptive parents with ample buffalo. As a last act, he sends a whirlwind of buffalo that feeds not only his parents but also the tribe for many days to come. Like the folktales of other Native American tribes, there are several layers to this seemingly entertaining tale. The importance of honoring both parents and food sources are underscored.

The Utes' account of an old medicine man, Smoking Waters, is a story of origin that explains the source of mountain hot springs rather than dealing with life and death. The Utes live in peace until a restless young brave, Many Feathers, convinces them to seek adventure and glory. Choosing to stay behind, Smoking Waters later sees in a vision the disasters that befell his people. Sitting on the stream bank by the fire he builds, Smoking Waters cries for his people until he dies. His tears, warmed by the fire and the love for his people, fall into the water and continue to warm the mountain hot springs.

The nomadic nature of many tribes leads to splinter groups like the Northern Cheyenne of the Lame Deer Reservation in Montana. Originating in the Great Lakes region as buffalo hunters, they lived in tipis and became proficient on horses and in battle. In fact, they fought alongside the Sioux against George Armstrong Custer (1839–1876) at Little Bighorn. Eventually the Cheyenne were confined to an undesirable section of Indian Territory. While the majority of Cheyenne remained in Oklahoma, the Northern Cheyenne made their way back to Montana. Given their history, it is not surprising that they needed the legendary character Sweet Medicine to bring order to their tribe. Born of a mortal mother and a magical father who came unseen in the night, Sweet Medicine is found among the brush. His great powers were apparent early, and he brings the sacred arrows to his tribe and begins to teach them and bring them order. They are grateful for the four lives he has been granted. But Sweet Medicine is mortal, and when the time comes for his death, he prophesies about the coming of the white men who will bring nothing good to his people.

Like the Utes, the Nez Percé had a reputation for befriending the white man that dated from when they saved Meriwether Lewis (1774–1809) and William Clark (1770–1838) from starvation. Like the Métis and the Cheyenne, their name is French. It means "pierced noses," after their practice of wearing a piece of shell through their noses. They were good traders and horse breeders, and the women were known for their basketry.

Perhaps the most famous Nez Percé was Chief Joseph (1840–1904). He represented the view that the land belonged neither to the tribe nor to the white settlers. Rather, it was the domain of Him who created it. The Nez Percé cared for the land in His behalf. Originally located in Washington, Oregon, and Idaho, the Nez Percé were forcibly removed to Fort Leavenworth, Kansas, following their famous flight from the U.S. Army in 1877. After malaria greatly reduced their numbers, the Nez Percé were split into two groups and relocated in Washington and Idaho.

One of Chief Joseph's favorite legends was the serpent of Wallowa Lake. Both the Blackfeet and the Nez Percé made use of the rich hunting and fishing ground, but eventually discord grew and the tribes used the winter to prepare for war. It was only through the bravery of a Nez Percé chief's daughter, as she put herself in harm's way to prevent battle and even gave herself in marriage to the son of the Blackfeet chief, that disaster is averted. Similarly, Chief Joseph worked for harmonious use of the land between a variety of groups.

"The ancestors of the Métis Nation of the Northern Plains, including northern Montana, were," in the words of Lawrence Barkwell and Ed Swain, in their introduction to *Métis Legacy: A Métis Historiography and Annotated Bibliography*, "the children of the unions between North American Aboriginal mothers and European fathers," primarily French and Scots men with mostly Cree and Ojibwa women.[4] While some full-blooded Europeans felt that these "half-breeds" were superior to full-blooded Indians, others saw the first generation of Métis women as possessions of their husbands rather than wives in the European sense. In Spring Creek or Lewistown, Montana, the Métis struggled for survival. At first their children were accepted into the schools, but as time went on, the Métis were marginalized due to the influx of non-Métis settlers. But it is not clear that this diminishment was the result of racial discrimination or because few Métis spoke, wrote, or read English. Eventually a number of the Spring Creek Métis departed for economic reasons. It is important to note that people of Métis heritage remain in Montana, especially in the Milk River/Lewistown/Glasgow triangle and along the Front Range. And Lewistown holds annual celebrations honoring the Spring Creek Métis and their contributions.

Because of their mixed European/Native American heritage, Métis tales contain elements of both traditions. A good example is the story of the hairy little man. As in many European folktales, the unlikely hero is a wanderer and an adventurer; he possesses superior intellect and common sense and attains magical powers that allow him to defeat larger foes and win the love of beautiful women. But in good Native American tradition, he maintains his powers through his connection to nature's creatures and keeps the women he woos happy through his sexual prowess, rather than through a magical transformation into a handsome prince.

TRAPPERS, EXPLORERS, AND MILITARY MEN

Many of the early non–Native Americans in the Rocky Mountain area were not settlers at all. Trappers led a nomadic life that led to an extensive knowledge of the geography of the Rocky Mountains. As the need for fur decreased, many of these men turned into guides for explorers. The Lewis and Clark expedition brought some of the first mountain men into the Northern Rockies.

When President Thomas Jefferson called upon them to explore the interior of the United States, both Lewis and Clark were military men. Jefferson charged them with mapping and describing in detail everything they saw—in fact, Lewis nearly poisoned himself by tasting an unknown ore. Lewis and Clark used waterways whenever possible, with Clark mathematically charting currents and recommending the best routes. Lewis was experienced in diplomacy and used his skills to communicate with various individuals and groups the explorers encountered.

At Fort Mandan near modern-day Bismarck, North Dakota, Toussaint Charbonneau joined the expedition, bringing along his sixteen-year-old pregnant wife, Sacajawea. Charbonneau's role was that of interpreter, and Lewis and Clark thought that if they needed to buy horses from Sacajawea's native people, the Shoshone, she would be of assistance. While her role in the expedition was not as dramatic as legend indicates, Sacajawea appears to have been a remarkable young woman. It was her quick thinking that saved documents and specimens from a sinking boat—with her young babe slung across her back as she worked. Sacajawea did help the expedition find her people and barter for the horses Lewis and Clark needed to reach Oregon.

John Colter, a member of Lewis and Clark's Corps of Discovery, became one of the first mountain men, spending two years in the primitive West immediately following the expedition. An extraordinarily strong man, Colter was able to endure physical hardship that would have conquered most men. Legend says that when captured by the Blackfeet and told to strip naked and run for his life, Colter was able to outrun his captors despite the prickly pears that his raw feet traversed. Pulling out of sight, he was able to hide in a beaver dam until his pursuers gave him up for lost. Colter spent the next eleven days covering 300 miles to the nearest trading post while subsisting on roots and bark. Such feats correspond to the western myth of the invincible frontiersman at one with nature and capable of conquering every obstacle.

Another larger-than-life character was Jedediah Smith, who is credited with making Jackson Hole well known. Mauled by a bear, Smith nevertheless survived with little more than a torn ear that he carefully covered with hair slightly longer than the norm. While perhaps not the most lucrative trapper, Smith actively sought new trapping grounds. He was part of a small group of men that first reached the Pacific Ocean overland.

Smith also participated in the annual rendezvous begun in 1825. The rendezvous provided trappers and traders with a time to meet and do business. Liquor flowed freely, knowledge was exchanged, and tempers flared; the rendezvous served as enculturation for both the experienced and inexperienced regarding the practices and traditions of a difficult and dangerous profession.

In 1822 James Bridger came west and never looked back. At first he adopted the life of a trapper and was very successful in his chosen field. He worked hard and played hard, never missing a rendezvous if he could help it. Not content to trap in one area, Bridger ranged over Wyoming and Utah. One of the first men to see Yellowstone, his tales of natural wonders seemed suspect to listeners in the mid-1820s. Finally, Bridger, in desperation that anyone would ever believe him, decided that if no one was going to believe his tales, he might as well make them as fantastic as possible. It wasn't until 1863 that Yellowstone was "officially" discovered, Bridger vindicated, and the National Park concept introduced to the world.

While Bridger was a consummate mountain man, his shrewdness in the business world left something to be desired. In 1830 Bridger and four other men purchased from Jedediah Smith, David Jackson, and Bill Sublette a trapping and fur company, which became the Rocky Mountain Fur Company. Unfortunately for Bridger and his partners, John Jacob Astor (1763–1848) became involved in the western fur trade. Using the shrewd business tactics that he was known for, within a few years Astor dominated the fur and trapping business, and the Rocky Mountain Fur Company ceased to exist.

Rendezvous are still popular in the Rocky Mountain region with both men and women donning the garb of the nineteenth century and engaging in competitions centered on trapping skills. These weekend trappers enter wholeheartedly into the experiences that were once necessary for survival but now function as ritualized nostalgia. One noticeable adaptation is that rather than receiving payment for a year's work, participants pay organizers for the opportunity to participate.

While not a part of the traditional lore of the West, African Americans also embraced the life of a trapper. One notable example, Jim Beckwourth, was the son of an aristocratic Southern planter and a black woman. Beckwourth's coloring made it easy for him to blend in with the Crow tribe, where he was accepted as a full tribal member. Happy with a life that provided him with an abundance of wives to serve him—Beckwourth claimed that he had eight wives at one time—he also gained a reputation as a warrior. In addition to trapping, he was involved in dispatch riding, saloon keeping, prospecting, and gaming. Mountain men tended to value a man by his skills and not by the color of his skin; this allowed Beckwourth equality unheard of in other sections of the country at that time.

While Jim Bridger and another legend, Kit Carson (1809–1868), crossed paths during their trapping years, Carson tended to work farther south and resided in Colorado for many years. Unlike Bridger, Carson was known for his honesty. Involved in many professions, Carson gained his greatest notoriety as John Charles Frémont's (1813–1890) guide through the West. While working for Frémont, Carson became involved in military service and eventually rose to the rank of brigadier general. Carson spent much of his life among the Native Americans, both as their friend and foe. His first two wives were Native American. However, the majority of his military battles were with the Navajos, and he presided over the infamous "Long Walk," which resulted in the virtual imprisonment of 8,000 Navajos.

Jim Beckwourth, the son of an aristocratic Southern planter and a black woman, who lived with the Crow tribe as a mountain man. © Bettmann/Corbis.

In retrospect, it should not come as a surprise that George Armstrong Custer (1839–1876) led the most famous defeat of the military in the history of the Indian Wars. Custer's lackluster career at West Point where he graduated last in his class only began because of the Civil War and the need for trained Union officers. If the war hadn't broken out, Custer's career would have ended with court martial before he even graduated.

As a Civil War officer, Custer was dashing and daring and won a fair number of battles. At that point it didn't seem important that his number of casualties ran higher than other commanders. Following the Civil War, Custer's ineptness finally resulted in his court martial. After appealing that the decision was based on personal prejudice against him, General William Tecumseh Sherman (1820–1891) reinstated him. At this point Custer was sent to Montana to fight the Lakota. Returning home after a successful campaign, Custer eventually made his way back west with Generals John Gibbon (1827–1896) and George Crook (1828–1890). The plan was that the three would converge upon the Lakota and Cheyenne at the same time and quickly defeat them.

However, Custer traveled ahead of schedule, and Gibbon and Crook ran into delays. Custer, seeing an Indian village, divided his men into threes and immediately attacked. All 219 of his men were killed. The times being what they were, Custer became a martyr. It didn't matter that he had initiated the attack—and a poorly thought-out one, to begin with. The nation saw him as a slain hero, and songs, poems, and a book lauding his accomplishments written by his widow turned him into a popular icon. Only time and changing views have shattered the once-heroic status of General Custer.

With the demise of the Rocky Mountain Fur Company, Bridger was on the look-out for a new profession. He and a partner built a trading post known as Fort Bridger. The life of a merchant was a little confining for Bridger, and he often joined military exploration parties as a guide. Despite being ideally located for those traveling west and selling supplies to groups from the Donner Party to the Mormons, Bridger and his partner eventually sold Fort Bridger to the Mormons.

To say that Bridger didn't like the Mormons would be something of an under-statement. Legend has it that Bridger told Brigham Young (1801–1877) that he would never be able to grow anything in the arid desert surrounding the Great Salt Lake. In fact, Bridger is reported as saying that he would pay Young $100 for the first bushel of wheat grown in the Salt Lake Valley. There are no reports as to whether Bridger bought his bushel, but it is known that he sued the Mormons for what he viewed as taking over his fort. It is historically documented that Bridger received his portion of money from the Mormons years before his partner did. And ironically, the buildings that Bridger claimed were appropriated by the Mormons were actually built by them.

MORMONS AND FOLKLORE

The most famous polygamist of the mid-nineteenth century was Brigham Young (1801–1877). More than a century ago, Tom Thumb (1838–1883), an interna-tionally famous diminutive performer of the day, came to Salt Lake City. Young courteously showed Thumb around his homes, the Lion and Beehive Houses. While conducting the tour, Young explained the tenets of the Church of Jesus Christ of Latter-day Saints (LDS). Tom Thumb replied, "Well, now I understand about you Mormons. But there is one thing that I just can't see, and that's how a man can cope with more than one wife."

Swiftly Young countered, "Well, when I was your size I didn't either."

The Tom Thumb story can be taken at least two ways. Perhaps Young was quite rude to his miniature guest. Another possibility is that Young was tired of ques-tions about his numerous wives and was trying to cleverly put an end to Thumb's inquiries. The Tom Thumb legend demonstrates how important context is for un-derstanding individual folklore items.

Before plural marriage in the LDS church was abolished, federal officers tried to arrest church officials. Although they never succeeded, the officers often tried to take Young into custody. One day, one of Young's wives warned him that fed-eral officers were on the way to capture him. Young quickly threw a slouch hat on his head, turned his collar up, grabbed his cane, and exited the Lion House into a cornfield behind the house. Suddenly a shot rang out, and Young felt the whoosh of a bullet as it passed through the top of his hat. Knowing there was no way to escape, Young decided to meet his foes head on. Not recognizing Young, the of-ficers inquired if he knew where Young was. Rising to the bait, Young replied, "I'm looking for the darn fool myself." Young sauntered back into the Lion House. The federal officers were unsuccessful in their search. Soon after that, Young was able to escape to southern Utah.

Folklorists like to look at the stories told about an individual and what these stories indicate about the person. The stories of the personalities of settlers color our comprehension of the forces behind successful colonization. It is indisputable that Young put his stamp upon Utah; he was a multifaceted man.

Young determined the locations of towns, which settlers would live there, and often the name of the community. Usually things worked smoothly, but that was not always the case. When Scipio was founded, the inhabitants refused to follow Young's directions. Actually, the pioneers thought they were following the prophet's advice. They built their town and gave it the last name of a friend of Young's. Nevertheless, he was displeased. It seems the town was not in the right place. Despite Young's directions, the good citizens of Scipio had no desire to build their town again. After all, they had already put considerable time and labor into their little city.

Young was not always patient. He told the citizens of Scipio that, because they had failed to comply with his wishes, Scipio would never be a large town. Young's curse is supposedly the reason that Scipio has remained so small.

Moroni City was more obedient to Young's counsels. Every spring Moroni found itself under floodwaters. One day Young rode through the struggling town. He wisely advised the citizens of Moroni to move their city to the hills above the valley. The residents complied and were no longer troubled by floodwaters.

At one point, Young concerned himself with the welfare of the citizens of Springville. Three families left Springville and returned to England. Young was concerned about so many people leaving. He called a meeting to determine why others thought the families had left. One man cited unreasonably low wages as the problem, and Young agreed to look into the matter. Another man stated that Springville families were tired of eating dry bread. With wry humor, Young replied, "Dry bread? Is anyone here eating dry bread? No one should have to eat dry bread. Go soak it in the City Creek."

One story from southern Utah indicates Young's literal concern with the bread the Mormons ate. Evidently, Young devoted an entire discourse to the subject of making bread correctly and efficiently.

Despite the demands on his time, Young was available to members of the church. As a result, he very seldom finished a meal. One mealtime a woman who was having difficulties with her husband interrupted him. The woman told President Young that her husband had even told her to go to hell! Amused, President Young asked, "You didn't do it, did you?"

While Mormons encountered problems common to settlers of the Rocky Mountain region, their religious traditions shaped their responses to their experiences and the ways in which legends and narratives were transmitted. Pioneers in early Utah settlements, like those throughout the West, often lost children to death. At times there were tragic accidents. There was a young family with two beautiful, little daughters. One morning the parents woke to find their youngest child dead. Overcome with grief, the parents found the source of their daughter's death outside. A kerosene container had inadvertently been placed near the water. Thirsty in the night, the girl drank kerosene instead of water. She died of asphyxiation. Fatal accidents reinforced the parents' need to be watchful. Death was always at the doorstep. Along with being careful, parents must listen to promptings and dreams.

A mother, an early settler of Utah, dreamed three nights in a row that her son would die. The dreams did not prevent her son's death but provided perhaps a measure of comfort and purpose. After having three dreams, she went into town. Returning to her property, she could not find her son, so she organized search parties. Eventually her child was found dead at the bottom of a well. It is not known if she shared her dream before the boy's death. But since his death, it has become a sacred family story.

Many narratives exist that underscore the dangers and death present during the trek to Utah. One family carefully preserves a pair of scissors that are handed down from generation to generation. On one particularly frigid night on the plains, two girls huddled together for warmth. The next morning it was discovered that one girl had frozen to death. The other girl was connected to the dead child—the living girl's hair had frozen to the other girl's back. The only way to separate the children was to cut the living girl's hair. The antique scissors are the pair used to accomplish the task. The scissors may remind the family of the fragility of life. They also underscore the fact that their progenitor was saved and that they are the result.

A poignant story is told about a young mother whose baby died while crossing the plains. The child was placed in a shallow grave, and the company moved on. The mother was inconsolable and felt strongly that something was amiss. Under the cover of darkness, she returned to her baby's grave. She was rewarded when she discovered her baby was still alive. The baby was nursed back to health. One Springville woman about twenty years ago told the story and added the fact that the baby was her grandmother.

MINING FOLKLORE

Mining offering its possibilities of untold wealth figured prominently in the development of the Rocky Mountain area. While many tried their hand at prospecting, the percentage that struck it rich was small. But the rich claims depended on cheap labor to mine the ore. Men and women from various parts of the world made their way to the mining camps. Among those represented were Swedes, Afghans, Poles, Finns, Serbians, Turks, Greeks, Chinese, Italians, Welsh, Spanish, Cornish, Austrian, English, and French Canadians. With them they brought their rich cultural heritages of language, beliefs, cooking, and other folk practices. During the 1930s, Works Progress Administration (WPA) projects produced valuable documentation of how these diverse people worked and lived together. Books like *Copper Camp* (1943) and *An Ornery Bunch* (1999), both of which are a result of the Montana WPA efforts, make these valuable documents of Rocky Mountain heritage readily available.

Each state in the Rocky Mountain region has at least one account of a lost mine of untold wealth. Montana's WPA project collected two tales of missing mines:

A Great Falls man, who was known to drink too much, was urged by his friends, for his own good, to accompany them on a deer hunt. The company made camp in the northern part of Fergus County. The man in question refused to take part in the deer hunting; having just recovered from a "party," he preferred to wander around the hills himself. He picked up some specimens of Agates and what he considered fool's gold.

After returning to Great Falls he showed his specimens to a dentist in

Great Falls and the ones which he called fool's gold were assayed and proved to be very valuable pure gold. He returned to the hills but searched in vain for the mine. He made his home with Charley Kelley while searching and when later he was killed in a train wreck, the lost mine was left to Kelley and it still remains a lost mine.

And a second mining tale went like this:

The early mining business was quite a spicy game, every one for himself. A gentleman once found some float ore on the lower end of a stream near his ranch. On his way to the western coast he left it at Helena to be assayed. It proved to be very valuable, and when he was asked where he found it, he airily replied: "In the West."

As he resided in the Judith Mountains, the assayer suspected the ore was from there and had him watched for the purpose of finding the mine. But this gentleman had no more idea where it was than his rivals and neither of them ever located it. So it still remains among the Mystery Mines.[5]

In another lost-mine story Dora Cyre came as a young bride with her husband to Golden, Colorado. A year later Dora was a young widow alone in a place that scared her somewhat. Desiring the protection of a man, she jumped into a hasty marriage with a prospector named Clem Tucker. Taking his new bride out into the mountains, Clem began looking for gold. He forced Dora to look for gold, too, and beat her when her efforts at gold digging and traditional women's chores weren't satisfactory. One day Clem literally stumbled upon a rich vein of gold. He told Dora that in a month they would accumulate enough to visit Golden and cash in their loot. Another month with Clem was more than Dora could bear. Despondent, Dora tried sneaking away while Clem slept, only to be hunted down and beaten. Finally as Clem slumbered, Dora, half out of her mind with despair, grabbed Clem's gun, shot him in the head, and hightailed it back to Golden.

The good women of Golden took one look at her and took her into their homes. They'd always had their doubts about Dora's hasty marriage. Gradually Dora's tale came out, and the men of Golden ran for the hills. They never found Clem's rich gold vein. By the time they returned to Golden, Dora had entered an insane asylum, and the location was locked in the recesses of her mind.

Dora's story is more than a traditional lost mine story, however. The precarious role of the western woman is center stage. Dora's inability to share the location of the strike with gold-hungry men and her willingness to eliminate her abusive husband create almost a cautionary tale.

Not all frontier women were as fragile as Dora. Take Ella Watson of Wyoming, for example. Not a fan of hard work in the mines, Ella found another profitable venture. However, the proceeds did end up underground. "For several years before she was hanged one summer afternoon in 1899, Ella Watson had buried approximately fifty thousand dollars in gold and silver near her residence in the Sweetwater River Valley in southwestern Wyoming. Watson's fortune, the proceeds from selling cattle, has remained lost since that time."[6]

In Idaho the Chinese played an integral part in the mining story. Written by Sister Mary Alfreda Elsensohn in 1970, *Idaho Chinese Lore* documents the contributions of the Chinese while revealing the hatred and persecution they encountered in the late 1800s.

> In 1869 the miners voted to admit the Chinese to Florence, the first county seat of Idaho County. Those who favored admitting the Chinese argued that the best deposits were exhausted and that white men could no longer work them profitably and that the Mongolians ought to be able to mine the residue. The permission was received with enthusiasm by the Chinese, who came into camp in a body, protected against those who were hostile to them by an adequate guard of white people. Their coming was the signal for others to come and in 1870 there were several thousand in the different mining districts. They seem to have infused new life into the district. Though it was generally thought that a Chinese lived on a few cents a day and sent the rest of his earning back to China, these Chinese are said to have spent their money freely whenever fortune favored them.[7]

Words like "Tartar" and nicknames such as "China Dick" and "Goon Dick" reveal the attitudes of the mainstream population. The need for security guards and stereotypical folk beliefs about spending habits reveal more about the lore of the dominant settlers and their prejudices.

LEGENDS OF THE WEST

In the Rocky Mountain West, folk heroes and the tales told about them are as broad and expansive as the West itself. Legends of heroes such as Jim Bridger, Sacajawea, Lewis and Clark, Kit Carson, General George Custer, Frank and Jesse James, Calamity Jane, and Buffalo Bill Cody paint pictures of a rough-and-tumble West where guns and outlaws and outlandish actions were the norm. In these stories harsh words and harsh ways seem to be the way of winning the West. However, each hero becomes a multifaceted character as one begins to read and better understand the mythical proportions of these people. And not all of these mythic heroes were men.

Cissy Patterson was a newspaper heiress and by marriage a Polish countess. Beloved by her neighbors in Jackson Hole, Patterson was a liberated woman completely at home with horses. "Jackson Holers liked Cissy for being the woman she was, unafraid to live and speak as she saw fit."[8] The women of the West were a varied, mythic lot.

And not all men came from rough-and-tumble backgrounds. A rancher in a remote section of Colorado, Captain the Honorable Lyulph Gilchrist Stanley Ogilvy, D.S.O., hailed from London and was the son of the Eighth Earl of Airlie. Despite his breeding and upbringing, Ogilvy was at home in the West. Like a little boy he was constantly getting into mischief, and his fame spread far and wide. Any true Colorado resident would know better than to let Ogilvy near their horses. It was a fearful thing what that man could do with horses.

> When Lady Maud, Ogilvy's sister, came to visit, she was met at the depot. Ogilvy used a couple of unbroken two-year-old horses to pull the surrey. When Lady Maud climbed aboard, the horses bolted into a dead run. Dur-

ing the whirlwind trip to Ogilvy's ranch, Lady Maud didn't say a word. Near the ranch, the vehicle careened madly, and one of the wheels splintered. The surrey almost turned over and came to rest against a tree. Lady Maud stepped serenely down and remarked to her brother, "What a charming place you have, Lyulph."[9]

While cowboys and Indians may be the stereotypical groups most associated with the West, there was also a third prominent contingent—the bad guy. The dubious honor of being the most famous homegrown outlaw from and in the Rocky Mountain region belongs to Butch Cassidy (1866–1908?). Born in Beaver, Utah, Butch practiced his trade in Utah, Wyoming, Colorado, and Idaho, among other locales. Many legends focusing on Butch's propensity to take from the rich and give to the poor are similar to those attached to Jesse James (1847–1882) and Robin Hood. One tale about Butch relates that he went to see an old couple living in Utah. Consumed with worry, the couple revealed that tomorrow the banker would be coming to collect their mortgage. Unable to pay, the elderly man and woman faced eviction. Cassidy asked when the banker was due to arrive, gave the couple the money to pay the note, and went on his way.

The next day the couple paid their debt, much to the surprise and dismay of the banker who had been anticipating foreclosure with great glee. As the shocked banker rode back to town, Butch and the boys gladly relieved the banker of the heavy moneybags. C. W. Sullivan III attributes a similar story to Jesse James and then writes, "[A]n almost identical story is told of Robin Hood, his friend Sir Richard of Lee, and the Abbot of St. Mary's. . . . Whether English or American, then the legendary outlaw hero is responding to or the result of 'a recurrent social situation, namely, one in which the law is corrupt.'"[10]

But Butch's escapades paled in comparison to those of another less-known lawbreaker. Rumored to have held up sixteen stagecoaches in one day, Ed Trafton made his mark in Montana. As an outlaw he did everything in a big way. "Not only did he serve two sentences for horse theft, another for robbing his mother of ten thousand dollars, but late in his long career he is said to

Molly Brown

In 1964 Metro-Goldwyn-Mayer produced a movie starring Debbie Reynolds titled *The Unsinkable Molly Brown*, based on the life of a woman never called Molly. In 1886, at the age of nineteen, Margaret Tobin left Hannibal, Missouri, for Leadville, Colorado. She met and married James Joseph (J. J.) Brown, and they moved to a cabin in Stumpftown, a small community near the Colorado mines. J. J. Brown became a mining superintendent, and the Browns became wealthy.

In defending the enormity, opulence, and apparent richness of her home in Leadville, known as the House of Lions, Brown declared, "Some people smirked when I brought home ancient statuary from Egypt and decorated up a few acres of the Rocky Mountains for my home, but I am sure that those who know the place will agree that culture knows no boundaries, and that fine arts are international." In 1914, Margaret, while traveling in Egypt, learned that her grandson was ill. She booked passage on a ship back to America. During the sinking of this ship, the *Titanic*, Margaret helped people into lifeboats and commandeered, along with several other women, a lifeboat. She used her fluency in several languages to assist the survivors and helped to later erect a memorial to the *Titanic* victims. The *New York Times* declared her the "Heroine of the *Titanic*."

Margaret was described as an "Amazonian" woman, a woman who could swear like a miner, a refined woman who could speak five languages, a woman born into poverty but who pulled herself up the ranks of society by her bootstraps, and was praised by kings and princes for her graciousness. She continued to be a folkloric figure in Colorado.

Buffalo Bill, William Frederick Cody, full-length portrait, in buckskin clothing, with rifle and handgun, c. 1870. Courtesy of the Library of Congress.

have been apprehended before he could carry out a cherished plan to build an armored car and use it to kidnap the head of the Mormon Church."[11] Trafton was definitely not of the Robin Hood variety of outlaw.

Until Butch Cassidy found his way onto the silver screen, perhaps the best-known outlaw was Jesse James. He and his brother Frank, along with Cole Younger, headed up the infamous James Gang. The James Gang is known for wandering the Midwest and Southwest, committing a variety of complicated robberies. However, they did venture into Colorado during the course of their career. Originally from Missouri, the James Gang favored banks but also honed their skills on trains and stagecoaches. Robin Hood–type legends circulated about them, and residents of their home state often sheltered them from the law. It is rumored that during their 1876–1879 hiatus from crime they spent time in Colorado prospecting.

Two of the most colorful figures in western lore—Buffalo Bill Cody (1846–1917) and Calamity Jane (c. 1852–1903)—were friends who lived lives of adventure. Both served as army scouts, and in fact it was in this capacity that they initially became acquainted. Despite his many adventures, Buffalo Bill was more concerned with business and showmanship than actually living the life of a legend. Ironically, while serving as a symbol of all that embodied the Wild West to easterners, he paved the way for the development of the modern West where commerce and tourism, rather than danger and adventure, flourish.

The Buffalo Bill Historical Center in Cody, Wyoming, contains many items from Cody's world-famous Wild West Show. Cody treated the women he employed with the same respect and benefits as the men. All of them were extremely competent, and many, like Annie Oakley (1860–1926), were crack shots.

While Calamity Jane was as talented as any of Cody's employees, she didn't get into the performing business until later in life—when she joined several different Wild West shows, including Buffalo Bill's. Calamity Jane received her name from a Captain Egan. During a battle with Indians, an arrow struck Egan, and Calamity Jane turned around, put Egan's body across her horse, and delivered him to safety. Upon waking, Egan humorously nicknamed the former Martha Cannary, Calamity Jane.

During her time in the Rockies, Calamity Jane served with several military units as a scout but also as a participant in numerous battles. Known for wearing men's clothes and her hard drinking, she rode one of the most dangerous Pony Express routes, encountering little opposition, and she saved a coach filled with six men, all too timid to grab the reins when their driver was killed. She is buried in Deadwood, South Dakota, next to Wild Bill Hickock, with whom she is said to have been in love.

For every legendary hero claimed by the Rockies, many Rocky Mountain communities, ethnic groups, and families have their own heroes. Every society carries a philosophical outlook that in turn produces characters that become the worldview bearers that are distinct to the culture. These archetypical heroes assist in the perpetuation of the myths surrounding the larger myth of the Rocky Mountains.

Vern H. Petersen, from Brigham City, Utah, a legend in his own family and community, wrote the narrative below many years after the experience. This story has been told by Petersen and his family throughout the years. Petersen's ability to put his own experiences into words and embellish them with vivid details allows this story to be remembered and retold, with the tellers at least getting the major points in the right order!

In 1940, Vern drove to Denver and the wilds near Laramie looking for sources of wool for a business venture. He met an old sheepherder who shared his supper with him. Noticing a violin on the wall of the sheep wagon, Vern asked the man about it and was told that he needed to be able to hear a perfect "A" to put it back in tune. He had played since he was a boy and missed the music:

> I guess, forty years went by and it was in 1994 or 1995, when I was living in Brigham City when the following happened. I was listening to a television rebroadcast of a talk given by a leader from The Church of Jesus Christ of Latter-day Saints. In the speech he told this story in order to bring out his theme. He said, "I want to tell you a story which originated in Laramie, Wyoming many years ago. A sheepherder wrote to the maestro of the New York Philharmonic Orchestra. Here's a copy of the letter he wrote him,
>
> "Dear Maestro, I'm a sheepherder out in east Laramie, Wyoming. The only real enjoyment that I appreciate deeply is the concert you play every Sunday morning. I have a battery-operated radio, but my batteries are just about dead. I have a violin I haven't played in several years because I haven't been near a piano to tune it. Maestro, if you would be so kind, would you have your orchestra, or at least your first violinist play a perfect 'A' for me? I only have enough power in my batteries for maybe five minutes of playing, so I can listen to you for about five minutes.
>
> "The maestro said during that Sunday morning session, 'Ladies and gentlemen, I'm going to have the orchestra hit a perfect "A" for this grand old man who is ten miles east of Laramie, Wyoming who has made this request. We won't hit a perfect "A" with just one violin, but we'll have all of the violins and the rest of the orchestra hit this "A" together.' Then the maestro waved his baton and the large Philharmonic Orchestra hit an 'A' and held it out for possibly a minute."[12]

Petersen's story reflects the worldviews held by himself, his family, and his community. Hard work, perseverance—regardless of the lack of glamour—and developing one's talents are only a few of the values apparent in this story. Perhaps Petersen is saying, to himself and those who hear this story: Don't be too quick to judge. The continual telling and retelling of stories such as this reinforce the values and beliefs of the man and the community. As Petersen's children, grandchildren, and great-grandchildren hear this story, they will most likely remember the main points, but they will definitely remember the caliber of man Vern Petersen is, because of the stories he tells.

Journals and letters become keepsakes that tie one's personal history to that of the larger settling of the West. Communities and families take great pride in having heroes in their own social groups who are equally as legendary as Kit Carson and Margaret Brown. These heroes become the mirror from which we see ourselves, and the window, regardless of the clarity, from which those outside best can peer through in an attempt to understand the West.

Westerners are also capable of contributing to the collective Rocky Mountain lore. In doing this, a community can laugh at itself and quite obviously tell the difference between an "insider"—one who knows the truth—and an "outsider"—one who believes all they see and hear. Examples of such are almost initiation stories—told to jovially explain the culture—and then, once the listener gains the respect of the teller, he or she is introduced to the truth, or the facts behind the lore. Commercialism comes into play here as a particular image is marketed to the "outside" consumer. What is for sale in the Rocky Mountain West? Bigger, better, more—these abundances were enticing not only to those easterners and immigrants traveling west in the 1800s but also to tourists today who are looking for unique and interesting places for their next family vacation. An enticing commodity means a curious onlooker and, farther down the road, a tourist who needs to be initiated into the local culture.

However, this lore does carry a germ of truth. Such exaggerations are often based on the tales told by hunters, fishermen, farmers, and ranchers when competing for the bigger, better, and more embellished story. There is playfulness in the telling or viewing, which brings about a sense of oneness: "We know our friend here didn't really catch a nine-foot trout, but only 'we' know that."

Tall tales seem to somehow belong to the open spaces of the Rocky Mountains. Consider the following tale:

> We didn't have much money and all I had was 7 shells to go hunting with. My father-in-law told me that I better have more shells than that and I told him, "No this will be fine." So we went hunting and we hunted all day and we never saw a thing. Then on the way home I saw this coyote and he was real close so I shot him, but missed him. Then I said, "Did you see that coyote?" and my nephew said, "No, all I saw was that buck." Then I saw the buck and I shot at it and two more jumped up and I shot them. They were all four points. So I had shot three deer, missed one coyote, and still had three shells left over.[13]

Evoking the same bravado as the little folktale tailor who advertised killing seven in one swat, the hunter underscores the uniqueness and difficulty of his accomplishment. Often tall tales incorporate humor:

> After shooting a deer one season, Paul's father reached it and found it not actually dead, but rather unconscious from an unclean shot. As he straddled the deer and reached forward to pull its head back and slit the throat, the deer stood and headed downhill with Paul's father on his back. Eventually while trying to hang on for life, he cut the deer's throat with the knife he

had in his hand, and killed it. As he stood to assess where he was and what had happened, he found the deer had taken them very near the car and eliminated most of the hiking it would have taken to pack the deer out.[14]

Portrayed as one of the last bastions of true masculinity, hunting is often confined to the men in the family or group or friends. The exploits that they share with the women in their life are selectively chosen and may slightly exaggerate the hardships encountered. Here is one example:

A man came back from a weekend of hunting, and after a hot bath and storing of his gear, he sat down to tell his wife of the hardships of the bush. He spent a good half hour explaining why he had not been able to get a deer, all the while making himself out to be a hero of sorts. At the conclusion of his narrative, he told his wife how miserable he had been during the entire trip because his foolish wife had forgotten to put in any extra socks for him. As a result he had spent the entire trip in the same wet dirty socks. To this his wife calmly replied, "I put them in your gun case, dear."[15]

The ability of the western woman to handle any situation with understated calm lives on.

RANCHING AND FARMING LEGENDS

The lure of the land is as responsible for the making of the Rocky Mountain region as those who came to the West looking for a place to call home, or at least a place to make home. Americans have always been goal-oriented, but moving West was not a goal in the traditional manner, not one of working communally for the highest good but being independent, taking care of oneself, conquering the rock-hard ground of the West. Tackling an obstacle and conquering it—this lure was often called "end in view." Those hoping to carve a place where the old way of life could be retained quickly learned that moving West also meant moving on. Old ways were soon transcended as a new land called for a new plan. Adapting the ways of the old world to fit the landscape and the livestock of the West kept many old traditions alive. In addition, adopting the ways of other immigrants and then melding them with traditions of one's own culture meant that westerners were always ready to be innovative.

Regions where the economy is so entrenched in the environment have a certain sense of pride and robustness about them. The people of the area may be hardened on the outside, but working with the land brings a particular sensitivity and gentleness that is not always apparent when listening to workingman humor or looking at a farmer's rough hands. Small communities must stick together, whether it is through tough economic times, times of environmental peril, or times of reevaluating their future. The ecosystem is as much a part of one's culture as are the traditions and folkways. One sees this when reading a local newspaper, listening to the local commodity report on the radio station, or overhearing a conversation at a potato warehouse where women are sorting spuds in order to allow their husbands and families to remain on family farms and ranches.

The plight of the farmer in the Rocky Mountain West is a typical story of battling beetles, bandits, and bureaucracy. Farmers trust other farmers; they trust the tried and true, regardless of whether it is founded in science or folk belief. Water is still king in the West, and much value is placed on having a well or a spring on one's land. Canal and irrigation boards are manned by the most honest and God-fearing men in the community, those with diplomatic skills, those who know the laws of the land, with a water-master leading, one who has the respect of the entire community. During the taming of the West, there were numerous stories about men whose lives were lost over irrigation disputes—stealing water was a crime often punishable by death—with or without the law's involvement. Even today there are attorneys who specialize in water rights litigation.

Because of the scarcity of water, one valued skill in the Rockies is water witching:

> Joseph Hatch was twenty-five years old when his mother told him about his grandfather's ability to witch the land to locate under ground water for a well. At this time she took him outside and showed him his father's method of dowsing, and to Joseph's surprise it worked for him.
>
> Irven Hatch first learned of his water witching ability when he was only 12 or 13 years old. One day Joseph, his father, took his 4 sons out to see if any of them had the ability of himself and his father. Out of the 4 boys Irven was the only one whom it worked for. Irven still uses the first method his father taught him, but Joseph has researched it out more and has adopted new methods of dowsing.
>
> Both Irven and Joseph considered their witching ability to be a gift rather than a talent. Irven said "If you've got it, you've got it, if you don't, you don't. It's as simple as that."[16]

Just as the scarcity of water inspired folkways like water witching, so did the presence of certain crops generate folk traditions particular to the Rockies. In Idaho, for example, time is often given off from school for the potato harvest, and young people who do not live on farms often join work crews bringing in the harvest. Their experiences become part of the lore of their life, like this account collected by Marianne Day:

> It was the harvest of our junior year, so it was extra-double muddy. The muddiest harvest ever. It was so muddy that the spuds were all sticking together in the back of the truck. So our boss came and sent us up there with shovels to push the potatoes down to the bottom of the truck and creating a kind of hollow dome in the back of the truck. . . . We went up front by the cab, that's not where we were supposed to be, but we figured out that if we stepped in the spuds up there, it would create kind of a suction that pulled all the potatoes down. We would wait till our shin was sucked under about half way, then we'd climb out. Well, on this one truck, I was letting my shin get suck down, and I got stuck. Another guy saw me and he asked if I was okay and I told him I was stuck, so he came and tried to pull me out, but he couldn't. So he went and told them to stop the combine, but they didn't. The potatoes kept pouring in till I was stuck above my waist

in potatoes and mud. The guy went and got Corey and Justin to dig me out, but the boss said they couldn't use shovels because it would hurt the potatoes. So they had to dig me out by hand. It took them thirty to forty-five minutes, and my legs were behind me twisted around all weird and stuff. By the time they got me out my legs were numb. It was cold and painful.[17]

Vernal H. Jensen, whose parents farmed in Ucon, Idaho, and whose brother still lives on that Centennial Farm, often talked about the "spare" time he had as he waited for his watering turns; waited to lift the canal gates changing the water from one irrigation channel to another; wandered the fence line, mending the barbed wire fences; sat on the combine waiting at the potato warehouse to dump his load of spuds; or sat on his horse, or later in his pickup, as he rounded up the cattle or the sheep from their summer pasture. He said that his hands were busy doing the duties of the every day, but his mind took him places neither his hands nor his feet could. Jensen's words are typical of those referred to as cowboy poets. Although Jensen's work was never published, his letters and jokes make him a legend in his own family:

[Sung to "Auld Lang Syne"]
It may be so
I do not know
It sounds so very queer
You'll have to tie your bull outside
Your B.S. don't go here[18]

Colen Sweeten, of Malad, Idaho, and now living in Springville, Utah, received the Idaho Governor's Millennial Award for Excellence in the Arts with the focus in Literature in 2000. This cowboy poet has been active reciting his poetry since 1985 when Hal Cannon and the Western Folk Life Center, in Elko, Nevada, initiated the revival of the genre. Sweeten and other cowboy poets write about what they know and love best—life on the farm or the ranch and family. This is based on a true event that occurred in the early 1950s:

Rural Hospitality

Half afraid, I put my knuckles
To that weathered ranch house door;
The clouds were sendin' down the rain
Like it had never rained before.

Our truck stood in a mudhole,
The gears completely gone.
We'd had to walk to get to talk
On someone's telephone.

The door opened and roast beef smell
Hit me like a train.
Then he smiled as only a farmer can
When the skies are pourin' rain.

"Sorry, there is no telephone
But don't you have a doubt.
We can't work in a storm like this,
And it's a pleasure to help you out.

"But it's dinner time, and you're not home
And we've lots of spuds and meat.
So, come on in and out of the rain,
Sit down with us and eat."

So we sat down like we belonged,
And when the meal was done,
He said, "I think we'll solve your problem,
With our tractor and my oldest son.

"He'll tow you to the highway,
It's five miles, or maybe four,
And by the time the roads are dry again
You'll have your truck repaired once more.

"No, put your purse away, boys,
We're not for hire today,
The One who sent this rain to us
Would want it done this way."[19]

Sweeten's poem reminds the listener that someone both raised the potatoes and the roast and someone cooked that meal. That someone most likely was the wife of that farmer or rancher. Women of the West are as in love with their life as the men that are so heroically discussed. When it comes to ranching and farming, women work right next to the men and keep up, neck and neck. Cowboy (yes, that's how they prefer to be labeled) poet Marie W. Smith writes about the benefits that come with being a cowboy's wife. Smith's poem "If" begins with the assertion that, if she had not married a cowboy, she would have never seen the magical glow of lights on snowdrifts. She continues her poem talking about raising farm animals and associating with wild animals—and the peace she finds in doing so. She discusses the beauty of a summer night and the blessing of a rainstorm. Smith concludes "If" with the assertion that she is grateful to have married a cowboy because, through the experience, she had grown to cherish the "joys and trials of western life."[20]

A ranch woman's life, or the life of a farmer's wife, differs from that of her city-slicker counterpart. But if asked to trade the country life for that of the town, most would answer that living an unconventional life in a day filled with conventionalities makes for a life that is never dull.

IMMIGRANT GROUPS AND ETHNIC FOLKLORE

In many of the western states, there are communities of Basque people. The Basques originally came from Spain and are widely known for their sheepherding skills. Today many Basque are prominent men and women in commercial and political enterprises of the states. Every fifth year, in July, a Basque festival, "Jaialdi," is held in Boise, Idaho. Basques from the United States, as well as from the homeland of Spain, attend this festival. Here this prominent ethnic group has the opportunity to showcase their culture, to each other and to those interested in learning about the culture. The festival usually begins with a parade through downtown Boise. Musicians playing traditional music and dancers dressed in traditional dress and dancing long-honored dances are a part of this parade. The festival then moves to the fairgrounds, where vendors are set up to sell Basque foods, Basque crafts, mementos, books, and traditional clothing. Jaialdi is not complete without the traditional Basque games. These games include hoisting weights, up to 250 pounds, throwing weights, javelin throws, log sawing, alone and in teams, and log chopping, singly and in teams. This festival gives the Basque an opportunity to celebrate their heritage and showcase it for others. Interestingly, the Basque community in the United States is known worldwide for its ability to keep the culture and ways of the Old World pure, with many Basque families from Spain sending their children to American Basque families to learn the ways of their Basque culture.

In addition to the roles the Basque traditionally held and now continue to hold as they adopt American ways, many other ethnic groups call the Rocky Mountain states home. These groups straddle two cultures and two cultural mind-sets—to maintain pride in one's ethnicity and to become American.

A Basque festival, "Jaialdi," is held in Boise, Idaho, in July. © Buddy Mays/Corbis.

The many ethnicities that are a part of the Rocky Mountain region include Latinos whose visibility, both in the economic and political arenas, provides an awareness of their presence in the West. While some Latinos embrace American culture completely, others seek to combine their new traditions with the lore of their native country. Many young women of Mexican descent still enjoy having a *Quincianera*. This is a party given for young women with ties to Mexico when they turn fifteen. Attending the party are family and close friends. The girl, generally dressed in pink, chooses a young man to be her escort and introduce her formally to society. An important transitional event, the party includes dinner and dancing. It is an event that is reminisced about and the stories are shared between friends and families.

The Latinos also brought with them their rich oral heritage. One popular tale with mainstream counterparts is the tale of La Llorona. The original tale contains a weeping woman in white who walks along the banks of a river at night, crying for her dead children. A mistress of a prominent man, she went crazy when her lover returned to his wife and she drowned all three of their children. She was then overcome with grief at her horrendous act. Young children are taught to be wary of La Llorona, lest she drown them as well. Thus an important rule—children must stay away from rivers, especially when alone at night—is taught through a memorable cultural tale. It is interesting to note that the tale has been modified and updated by some tellers:

> There once was a lady who had three kids. She came to be known as La Llorona because she cried and cried for her kids who had died. They were killed in a car accident. She spent the remainder of her life trying to steal kids to replace the ones she had. Any kid that went outside, La Llorona would immediately know about it. She had an all knowing power. She could only come out at night. That is when she rounded up children to replace her own. She was known to have stolen many kids. She wore a long white gown and sounded like the wind. Sometimes she transformed herself into different animal parts. At first, while her kids were alive, she was a good person, then after their death that is when she became evil and bitter.[21]

So a danger that was once prominent—drowning in rivers—is replaced by a more modern concern: kidnapping. But both stories serve the same purpose—shaping children's behavior.

El Chupacabra is a more recent legendary figure. Translated, his name means "goat sucker," and while everyone agrees that he is hideous and two legged, his height and color are points of debate. But there is no doubt that he is to be feared. His favorite pastime is sucking the blood of agricultural animals. Undoubtedly a variant of similar contemporary legends, El Chupacabra is an ethnic-specific creature whose activities endanger the livelihood of an already economically marginalized people.

Pockets of Polynesian people representing a diverse group of islands—New Zealand, Tonga, Samoa, and even Hawaii—call the Rocky Mountain West home. Probably the first Polynesians in the area were Mormon converts from Hawaii who settled Iosepa near Tooele, Utah, in the late 1800s. While the desert of Utah was a far cry from the tropical paradise where they were born, residents of Iosepa strived to make their homes beautiful. One woman whose grandparents lived in Iosepa reports:

> Our family was very careful when they planted their gardens and flowers. They would plant vegetable gardens underneath the flowers so that when time came to water the plants, they were using the water for two purposes. Grandma and great grandma just loved their flower garden and kept it up all the time.[22]

Once the Mormon church decided to build a temple in Hawai'i, the majority of residents returned home, and the colony disbanded. Perhaps the spirit of Iosepa is well stated in an article from the *Herald Republican*, September 5, 1915, written just a few months before the colony was disbanded:

A few days ago a large party of Salt Lake men and women went in autos out into the great Skull Valley and spent a day at Iosepa, mingling with Hawaiians, Samoans, and Maoris; listening to speeches and song in the liquid language . . . and dining with grizzly old Maoris who have startling records as warriors in New Zealand, and with pretty, dimpling, twinkling Hawaiian and Samoan girls, who showed the unsophisticated whites how to eat poi in the approved manner of their beloved countries. The entire picturesque community was clothed in smiles, garlands, flowers, characteristic dresses and unlimited welcome for the visitors, many of whom had never heard of this, perhaps the strangest, most appealing and interesting community in this country.[23]

CONCLUSION

Despite the wide diversity and varied lore of the Rocky Mountain region, the folklore will probably be marked forever by the movie cowboy. And while singing cowboys like Gene Autry and Roy Rogers might seem highly fanciful, their vocal abilities might have stood them in good stead in the real Old West. While movie cowboys sang to their sweethearts, the true cowpuncher, so goes the tale, sang to their little dogies to keep them in line. Folklorists seldom try to determine truth since they are more concerned with the "why" of the lore. Perhaps for the treasure of lore of the Rocky Mountains, the "why" is as deep as the verdant valleys, as tall as its peaks, as broad as the windswept plains.

RESOURCE GUIDE

Printed Sources

Cannon, Hal, ed. *Cowboy Poetry: A Gathering*. Salt Lake City, UT: Gibbs-Smith Publisher, 1985.

———, ed. *Old Time Cowboy Songs*. Salt Lake City, UT: Gibbs-Smith Publisher, 1988.

Elsensohn, Sister M. Alfreda. *Idaho Chinese Lore*. Cottonwood: Idaho Corporation of Benedictine Sisters, 1970.

Erdoes, Richard. *Legends and Tales of the American West*. New York: Pantheon, 1998.

Erdoes, Richard, and Alfonso Ortiz. *American Indian Myths and Legends*. New York: Pantheon, 1984.

Hiller, Megan, Rick Newby, Elaine Peterson, and Alexandra Swaney, eds. *An Ornery Bunch: Tales and Anecdotes Collected by the W.P.A. Montana Writers' Project*. Helena, MT: TwoDot Books/Falcon Publishing, 1999.

Jameson, W. C. *Buried Treasures of the Rocky Mountain West: Legends of Lost Mines, Train Robbery Gold, Caves of Forgotten Riches, and Indians' Buried Silver*. Little Rock, AR: August House, 2003.

Jessen, Kenneth. *Bizarre Colorado*. Loveland, CO: J. V. Publications, 1994.

Lomax, John A. *Cowboy Songs and Other Frontier Ballads*. New York: Macmillan, 1966.

Stewart, Polly, Steven Siporin, C. W. Sullivan III, and Suzie Jones, eds. *Worldviews and the American West: The Life of the Place Itself*. Logan: Utah State University Press, 2001.

Workers of the Writers' Program of the Work Projects Administration in the State of Montana, comps. *Copper Camp: The Lusty Story of Butte, Montana, the Richest Hill on Earth*. 1943. Helena, MT: Riverbend Publishing, 2001.

Videos/Films

Cowboy Poets. Los Angeles, CA: Direct Cinema Films, 1988.

Festivals

Montana

All Web Sites accessed June 22, 2004.

Ashland—Ashland Labor Day Powwow
http://travel.state.mt.us/categories/moreinfo.asp?IDRRecordID=13363&SiteID=1

Bannack—Bannack Days
http://travel.state.mt.us/categories/moreinfo.asp?IDRRecordID=8784&SiteID=1

Bigfork—Tamarack Time!
http://travel.state.mt.us/categories/moreinfo.asp?IDRRecordID=8792&SiteID=1

Big Timber—Montana Cowboy Poetry Wintercamp
http://travel.state.mt.us/categories/moreinfo.asp?IDRRecordID=12640&SiteID=1

Big Timber—Sweet Grass Fest
http://travel.state.mt.us/categories/moreinfo.asp?IDRRecordID=12856&SiteID=1

Billings—Billings Jaycees Western Days
http://travel.state.mt.us/categories/moreinfo.asp?IDRRecordID=8954&SiteID=1

Billings—Clark Days
http://travel.state.mt.us/categories/moreinfo.asp?IDRRecordID=9830&SiteID=1

Billings—Festival of Cultures
http://travel.state.mt.us/categories/moreinfo.asp?IDRRecordID=9135&SiteID=1

Bozeman—Historic Preservation Days
http://travel.state.mt.us/categories/moreinfo.asp?IDRRecordID=13582&SiteID=1

Butte—An Ri Ra Montana Irish Festival
http://travel.state.mt.us/categories/moreinfo.asp?IDRRecordID=13783&SiteID=1

Chinook—Bear Paw Commemoration
http://travel.state.mt.us/categories/moreinfo.asp?IDRRecordID=13796&SiteID=1

Colstrip—Festival of Living History
http://travel.state.mt.us/categories/moreinfo.asp?IDRRecordID=13785&SiteID=1

Dillon—Cowboy Poetry and Music Rendezvous
http://travel.state.mt.us/categories/moreinfo.asp?IDRRecordID=13771&SiteID=1

Great Falls—16th Annual Lewis & Clark Festival
http://travel.state.mt.us/categories/moreinfo.asp?IDRRecordID=8901&SiteID=1

Hardin—Little Bighorn Days
http://travel.state.mt.us/categories/moreinfo.asp?IDRRecordID=8995&SiteID=1

Missoula—Germanfest
http://travel.state.mt.us/categories/moreinfo.asp?IDRRecordID=10836&SiteID=1

Polson—Live History Day
http://travel.state.mt.us/categories/moreinfo.asp?IDRRecordID=11785&SiteID=1

Virginia City—The Virginia City Gathering
http://travel.state.mt.us/categories/moreinfo.asp?IDRRecordID=11183&SiteID=1

West Yellowstone—Burnt Hole Rendezvous/Historical Reenactment
http://travel.state.mt.us/categories/moreinfo.asp?IDRRecordID=8851&SiteID=1

Whitefish—Big Mountain Summer Festival
http://travel.state.mt.us/categories/moreinfo.asp?IDRRecordID=13514&SiteID=1

Wisdom—127th Commemoration of the Battle of the Big Hole
http://travel.state.mt.us/categories/moreinfo.asp?IDRRecordID=9264&SiteID=1

Utah

All Web Sites accessed June 22, 2004.

Blanding—5th Annual Winter Storytelling Festival
http://www.utahfolkarts.com/cgi-bin/folklife_events.pl?RecordNumber=10

Clarkston—Clarkston Pony Express Days
http://travel.utah.gov/Events.pdf

Ephraim—Old Ephraim's Mountain Man Rendezvous
http://travel.utah.gov/Events.pdf

Ephraim—Scandinavian Festival
http://www.utahfolkarts.com/cgi-bin/folklife_events.pl?RecordNumber=2

Kanab—Western Legends Round-Up
http://travel.utah.gov/Events.pdf

Little Cottonwood Canyon—Annual Oktoberfest
http://travel.utah.gov/Events.pdf

Moab—Moab Bighorn Sheep Festival
http://travel.utah.gov/Events.pdf

Moab—Moab Folk Music Festival
http://travel.utah.gov/Events.pdf

Mount Pleasant—Spring City Pioneer Days
http://www.utahfolkarts.com/cgi-bin/folklife_events.pl?RecordNumber=3

Mt. Pleasant City—Black Hawk Mountain Man Rendezvous
http://travel.utah.gov/Events.pdf

Ogden—Ogden Pioneer Days
http://travel.utah.gov/Events.pdf

Promontory—Golden Spike National Historic Site Railroader's Festival
http://travel.utah.gov/Events.pdf

Promontory—Joining of the Rails–Golden Spike Anniversary Celebration
http://travel.utah.gov/Events.pdf

Salt Lake City—Folk Masters At The Utah State Fair
http://www.utahfolkarts.com/cgi-bin/folklife_events.pl?RecordNumber=4

Salt Lake City—Greek Festival
http://travel.utah.gov/Events.pdf

Salt Lake City—Living Traditions Festival
http://www.utahfolkarts.com/cgi-bin/folklife_events.pl?RecordNumber=8

Spanish Fork—Fiesta Days
http://travel.utah.gov/Events.pdf

Sterling—Mormon Miracle Pageant
http://travel.utah.gov/Events.pdf

Vernal—Outlaw Trail Ride
http://travel.utah.gov/Events.pdf

Wellsville—Frontier Christmas Eve
http://travel.utah.gov/Events.pdf

West Valley City—International Folk Festival
http://travel.utah.gov/Events.pdf

Colorado

All Web Sites accessed June 22, 2004.

Colorado Springs—Territory Days
http://www.jerrysings.com/territory/index.html#start

Denver—A Taste of Colorado
http://www.atasteofcolorado.com/

Littleton—Colorado Dance Traditions
http://www.littletongov.org/museum/events/details.asp?ID=19

Littleton—Colorado Scottish Festival
http://www.scottishgames.org/

Littleton—Harvest Festival
http://www.littletongov.org/museum/events/details.asp?ID=4

Littleton—Plowing and Planting at the Museum
http://www.littletongov.org/museum/events/details.asp?ID=15

Littleton—Sheep to Shawl
http://www.littletongov.org/museum/events/details.asp?ID=14

Littleton—Western Welcome Week
http://www.westernwelcomeweek.com/

Wyoming

All Web Sites accessed June 22, 2004.

Afton—Historical Summer Theater
http://www.wyomingevents.com/

Basin—Pioneer Expo & Festival
http://www.wyomingevents.com/

Buffalo—Battle of the Brands Powder River Ranch Rodeo—June 18
http://www.wyomingevents.com/

Buffalo—Powder River Days—June 18
http://www.wyomingevents.com/

Cheyenne—Cheyenne Frontier Days
http://www.cfdrodeo.com/indianvillage.cfm

Saratoga—14th Annual Platte Valley Festival of the Arts
http://www.plattevalleyarts.com/

Idaho

All Web Sites accessed June 22, 2004.

American Falls—Portneuf Mountain Man Rendezvous
http://www.pocatelloidaho.com/

Boise—Annual Soul Food Extravaganza
http://www.boisesoulfood.com/

Caldwell—Fourth Annual Mariachi Festival
http://www.hccidaho.org/

Custer—Custer Days
http://www.idahoparks.org/parks/yankeefork.html

Ketchum—Trailing of the Sheep Festival
http://www.visitsunvalley.com/

Montpelier—Oregon Trail Rendezvous Pageant
http://www.bearlake.org/

Nampa—Fiesta Idaho
http://www.hccidaho.org/

Rexburg—Idaho International Folk Dance Festival
http://www.rexcc.com/

Sandpoint—North Idaho Timberfest
http://www.sandpointchamber.com/

Weippe—Weippe Camas Festival
http://www.weippe.com/LewisClark.htm

FOOD

Susan H. Swetnam

Those who live in and love the Rocky Mountain region often think of it as a place of abundance: abundant light, abundant sky and space, abundant horizons, abundant mountains and rivers, abundant possibilities for privacy and reflection. In some respects and at some periods, *abundance* is also a word that might have been applied to the region's food-producing capabilities. Horses are reported to have shied from central Idaho's Redfish Lake in the nineteenth century, for instance, because spawning salmon were so dense that they formed a writhing crimson mat across the water's surface.

In fact, however, Rocky Mountain foodways have been more typically shaped by accommodation to finite resources. This region, whose landscape seemed rich and nearly inexhaustible to many early travelers and settlers, is actually a delicate place, even a place of scarcity in some respects. In the early twenty-first century, many of the resource management issues that have always sparked debate here are more volatile than ever. Questions of water management, of wildlife conservation, of development and land use can still lead to hard words in the region's cafes, its bars, its city halls, and its public school meeting rooms. Such questions are inextricably linked to the region's foodways—for whenever people eat or drink food found or produced in the region, they are inevitably participating in choices about how the land's limited capacity is being managed. Citizens of the Rocky Mountains tend to have strong opinions about their home region and their relationship to it, and their foodways—prodigal, conservation-minded, or ingenious—have always reflected those opinions.

CLIMATE AND GEOGRAPHY

The Rocky Mountain West—here defined as Montana, Wyoming, Idaho, Colorado, and Utah—varies widely in terms of climate and geography. Its elevations range from 738 feet at the confluence of the Clearwater and the Snake in Idaho to over 14,000 feet in Colorado's mountains; it encompasses huge plains, sheltered valleys, deep canyons, broken mesa country, and jagged mountain ranges; it has areas of abundant rainfall and true desert; it includes temperate valleys and places in which no month is frost free.

Some generalizations can be made about most of the region, though, generalizations that have important implications for food production and foodways. Most important, the Rocky Mountain region is arid compared to the rest of the United States. Many sections receive less than twelve inches of rain a year, including Idaho's Snake River Plain and lower southwestern valleys and much of Utah. Some parts of eastern Colorado, Wyoming's Red Desert, and extreme southern Utah receive less than ten inches a year, the amount necessary for successful dryfarming. Very low relative humidity is typical, so whatever moisture does fall quickly evaporates.

The Rocky Mountain region is also subject to temperature extremes. Because of the high average elevation of the area—6,800 feet in Colorado, 6,700 feet in Wyoming, above 3,000 feet in Utah, Idaho, and Montana—winter temperatures can be frigid. In the hardest winters, temperatures of minus fifty have been recorded in all Rocky Mountain states—and not just on the mountain tops. In the coldest valleys, agriculture is practically impossible. "For tender plants there is practically no growing season in such areas as the upper Green River Valley, the Star Valley, and Jackson Hole," reports the National Oceanic and Atmospheric Administration (NOAA) about western Wyoming.[1] Even in more average years, many parts of the region are gardeners' climate zones 3–4, and growing seasons of 125 days are typical. Extremely hot summer temperatures are also the norm: All sections of Utah, the NOAA reports, can experience summer temperatures over 100; Colorado has seen 115; Montana, 117; Idaho, 118.

Harsh weather phenomena also occur. Deep snow cover and blizzards are common in many areas, with wind-driven snow particularly dangerous on the eastern plains. In 1984, for instance, five- to six-feet drifts closed all roads to Cheyenne. Hail can be severe: One storm in Wyoming in 1972 left five inches on the ground in forty-five minutes. Winds can reach 80 to 100 miles per hour occasionally; warm down-sloping chinooks can trigger flooding runoff, as temperatures suddenly rise twenty-five to thirty degrees in late winter or early spring. Tornados and lightning storms are common in some areas.

The region is also remote from major U.S. markets and thinly populated. It is full of natural barriers to travel—the high ranges of the main Rocky Mountain chain; the interior ranges, like the Wasatch and the eighty named ranges in Idaho; deep river canyons like the Black Canyon of the Gunnison and Hell's Canyon; vast arid deserts, including the Great Western Desert beyond Salt Lake City and Idaho's Arco Desert. Denver is the only city over 500,000; the next two largest, at about 180,000, are Salt Lake City and Boise. Idaho's population did not top 1 million until 1985; Wyoming's is still less than half of that. Population density in Montana is 6.2 people per mile.

All of these factors have influenced the region's foodways. An arid climate subject to temperature extremes dictates what can and cannot be grown, even with technological help. Distance from markets and difficult topography influence food distribution. Small markets can affect availability and variety.

Residents' attitudes have also been shaped by the region's geography in respects that impact foodways. Many believe that the landscape breeds independence and individualism; many believe that those who have settled here are entitled to use this land freely, since they rise daily to its demands and population is relatively thin. Many have family traditions of so using it. Some have labored to make this land act like it was somewhere else; some want to preserve it, frozen in time, as an idealized version of itself. As the twenty-first century begins, though, most residents have been forced to recognize its limits, even as they love its tough beauty—and to explore ways to live (and eat) here that accommodate the land's essential nature.

TRADITIONAL NATIVE AMERICAN FOODWAYS AND THE LAND

Historically, Native American tribes that inhabited the Rocky Mountain region drew on a broad repertoire of foodstuffs. Depending on what was available, foodways were somewhat different among the Plains tribes of eastern Montana, Wyoming, and Colorado than they were among the Plateau tribes of northern Idaho and Montana, or among the Shoshone-Bannocks of southern Idaho and western Wyoming, or among the numerous branches of Utes that inhabited the Great Basin and Colorado Plateau. Still, all tribes ate a variety of foods that supplied balanced nutrition, including berries, roots, and meat. Those who inhabited ground well watered and rich in game could find true abundance, like the Kootenay, who lived near the Canadian border. Such was not the case with most Rocky Mountain tribes, however. Like hunter-gatherers worldwide, they spent a large proportion of their time seeking and preparing food, and many were threatened with starvation if a key crop failed or if food stored for winter was inadequate. Early spring, in particular, could be a time of shortage, and many tribes held festivals to welcome the year's first crops. Most tribes also migrated to seek seasonal foodstuffs—not an aimless, vagrant migration, as some early Anglo observers assumed, but a regular, orderly migration governed by strict tradition. Food was not to be taken for granted in this region, even in precontact days.

The Plateau tribes of the northernmost Rocky Mountain region had perhaps the widest available variety of foodstuffs. The Kootenay ate game, including deer, elk, and bison. One man (such as a "Deer Chief") was given responsibility to orchestrate each hunt. Bands sometimes combined to hunt caribou, though in this case little organization was needed, since caribou were said to be too tame to really require communal effort. Plateau tribes also ate waterfowl, especially duck, fresh or dried.

Native Americans also fished in the lakes and rivers of the far northern Rockies. They caught trout, bull trout, and other stream fish using woven funnel weir traps, lines, and hooks. They sometimes went ice fishing. The Kootenay speared salmon at night from boats on rivers, using torchlight to draw the fish. Coeur d'Alenes speared them from banks, built fish traps, or netted them. Salmon were roasted fresh or dried on rectangular racks around a fire, or in the sun.

These Plateau tribes, who lived in Idaho and western Montana, also ate a wide variety of plant foods, including roots, berries, and barks. Camas was the most important staple food of precontact Nez Percé and Coeur d'Alene, in particular. Camas grows in damp ground and displays a vivid blue flower in spring; in the nineteenth century, some important camas grounds, like the Weippe Prairie in Idaho, were so rich that they looked like a sea. Camas was harvested in late summer by women. The harvest began with a crier's announcement, and all bands began the journey together, to arrive at the same time. Each band had its own traditional digging area, and within each area, each family had its designated spot, within which it was expected to work. Camas was dug with a two-pointed stick whose end had been fire-hardened. The work was reportedly labor-intensive, but in a two-week digging season, it was possible to harvest five 100-pound sacks. After peeling, camas was dried in pits, a multiday process involving slow fires. So prepared, camas would keep for years. It tastes musky and sweet—rather like tobacco smells—and is extremely filling, full of insulin that bakes into fructose. Camas was sometimes ground into flour, which was then made into camas bread and dried, or mixed in stews, cooked in tightly-woven bags, into which hot rocks were dropped. Kouse ("biscuit root," a member of the carrot family) was another staple, also dried and made into cakes. Bitterroot, nodding onion, and wild carrots were also harvested.

Plateau tribes valued berries, including blackberries, raspberries, dewberries, buffalo berries, and elderberries. Berries were dried; they were also pounded fresh, along with seeds and pits, and mixed with melted animal fat, fish, or meat into pemmican bricks that could sustain a man for a day. Flatheads especially relied on service berries, sprinkling powdered horse mint or field mint over drying berry patties to keep flies away; or mixing dried berries with flour and water for sweet puddings. After contact, sugar was used in such puddings, but before, black tree lichen, reportedly "a sweet and delicious food,"[2] was baked underground like camas, yielding a sweet, gelatinous substance. Another sweet treat was the inner bark of Ponderosa and lodgepole pines. This bark was so enduringly popular that officials on the Flathead reservation issued edicts against its consumption in 1908 "because it was deemed injurious to commercial species of timber."[3]

Plains tribes of eastern Montana, Wyoming, and Colorado used many of the same foods as Plateau tribes—berries, roots, onions, other plants, and meats. Camas did not grow on the plains so other roots assumed prominence in the cuisine of the Cheyenne, Arapaho, Blackfoot, Crow, and others. Indian breadroot ("pomme blanche," "white apple," "Indian turnip") was gathered in June and boiled or roasted. Explorer Lamare-Picquot, who visited the plains before Meriwether Lewis (1774–1809) and William Clark (1770–1838), thought that breadroot had such potential as a food crop that he sent samples back to France for cultivation. Box elder trees—true maples—were tapped by the Cheyenne to make syrup, collected in birch bark pails or young deer stomachs, then boiled or allowed to freeze and separate, and made into candy. Some plains tribes also did limited farming, including the Cheyenne, who cultivated land for corn along the North Platte.

Indigenous Tribes and Game Hunting

Above all, plains tribes relied on game. They hunted buffalo throughout the year, moving camps with the herd. Strict tribal laws governed buffalo hunting. When buffalo were plenty, hunts could only be conducted communally, and those who hunted independently could be punished by corporal punishment or property confiscation. Hunters on foot surrounded buffalo; the animals were pursued on horseback, then driven into pens built under cut banks or bluffs and fenced with bushes or branches. Antelope were also an important food source. Plains Indians constructed long winged chutes of brush, then drove antelope into pits. Such tactics could be extremely effective: When the Cheyenne who accompanied William Bent's party in 1858 held an antelope hunt, they were so successful that each of the 600 Cheyenne lodges had its own antelope, and the expedition itself had all that it could use. Hunts for both antelope and buffalo had ritual characteristics, including special dress or body painting, purpose-made arrows, and specific songs.

The Shoshone and Bannock peoples who lived in eastern Idaho and western Wyoming were divided into many bands, and their foodways were so varied that some bands were known by their dominant foods, such as "sheepeaters," and "fisheaters." Depending on where a band lived, it might migrate east of the mountains to hunt buffalo, travel to a river at salmon migration time, or gather roots in high meadows. Overall, though, foodways were similar to those of surrounding tribes—Shoshone/Bannocks ate berries, wild plants, and game as staples of their diet.

George Catlin, *Buffalo Chase with Bows and Lances*, 1832–33. Smithsonian American Art Museum, Washington, DC/Art Resource, NY.

The Ute tribe, which inhabited Utah and Colorado, was the most diverse group of Rocky Mountain Native Americans. The Eastern Utes, who lived in the mountainous areas of the Colorado Plateau, were comparatively rich in resources, including deer, elk, pronghorn, and bighorn sheep, along with sage grouse and other birds. In the autumn, extended family groups traveled to harvest pine nuts, which women roasted by placing in baskets with hot coals, then tossing the mixture in the air. They also ate acorns, sunflower seeds, berries, sego lilies, and small game.

The Southern Paiutes of the Great Basin in southern Utah inhabited some of the region's most rugged land, high desert (3,000–5,000 feet) cut by red-rock canyons and topped by steep mesas. In this arid land, life could be difficult, and some early settlers considered them a pathetic race, but the Southern Paiute had foodways well adapted to available resources. Southern Paiute bands made their homes for much of the year near semipermanent springs in lower elevations, favoring sites along the Paria Plateau and the Vermillion Cliffs. Some Paiute bands raised corn, squash, and sunflowers by digging irrigation ditches from the Virgin and Santa Clara Rivers. These groups were in fact carrying on a Native American tradition: Between 900 and 1200 C.E., Pueblo people had grown corn, squash, and other crops, building prosperous villages before deserting the region. If one travels in Canyonlands National Park, one may still find their granaries deep in remote canyons and even discover tiny corncobs that they produced, preserved by the desiccating climate.

Large game was rare in Paiute territory, but small game was common. Pauites hunted rabbits, marmots, and squirrels with throwing sticks; they ate locusts and caterpillars in spring. Seeds were a diet staple, especially grass seeds. Some bands ate pine nuts (particular women claimed particular trees year after year); some ate yucca, mescal, and cactus.

Each of the Rocky Mountain tribes thus had foodways well adapted to its particular subregion. While spring could be "starving time," these peoples had long-established seasonal routines that insured that each available food source would be harvested in its season, routines that typically involved travel to various sites as crops ripened, as the high country opened for hunting, as fish returned.

The Effects of Westward Expansion on Native American Food Cultures

The coming of immigrant settlers forever disrupted tribal life. The Utes' story is typical. After the United States acquired the region in 1848 and settlement began in Colorado's San Luis Valley and western slope, immigrants began to demand that Ute land be available for homesteading and mining. Settlers squatted illegally on lands that had been promised to the tribe. "They are a dissolute, vagabondish, brutal and ungrateful race and ought to be wiped from the face of the earth," the *Rocky Mountain News* proclaimed in 1863. A series of treaties diminished the Utes' land base, then they were threatened with removal to southeastern Utah. "How shall we farm if we have no water," one asked. "What are we going to eat there? Are we going to eat stones?"[4]

Even sadder, perhaps, is the fate of the Southern Paiute. From the time that the Old Spanish Trail cut through their homeland, they were no longer able to maintain their careful husbandry. Large stock drives and immigrant trains poured through their territory, quickly depleting it. One group of 200 men trailing 4,000 horses camped at the headwaters of the Santa Clara for several weeks, laying waste to grasses and fouling the water; another group, a train of more than 100 wagons, 400 people, and 1,000 cattle, blithely decimated Paiute agriculture. "We packed up and to the cornfield intending to lay by and let our animals rest and eat fodder," one immigrant noted matter-of-factly in his journal. Beginning in the 1860s, permanent Mormon settlement in the region further disrupted Paiute resources. One Latter-day Saint sympathetic to the Paiute, Jacob Hamblin, described their plight:

> The great numbers of animals brought into the country by the settlers, soon devoured most of the vegetation that had produced nutritious seeds. . . . When, at the proper season of the year, the natives resorted to those places to gather seeds, they found that they had been destroyed by cattle. With, perhaps, their children crying for food, only the poor consolation was left them of gathering around their campfires and talking over their grievances.[5]

Conflicts were inevitable in such situations, but where the Indians fought back—as they did from Nez Percé country to Cheyenne country to Colorado to Utah—they were inevitably defeated and sent to reservations.

Today, the tribes of the Rocky Mountains have adopted foodways of the larger American culture—though, given the poverty on most reservations, not always the healthiest or most abundant of mainstream eating habits. Some traditional foods have been adapted to fit modern tastes and resources: Wild carrot roots are eaten with sugar and cream, for instance, and berries are canned and frozen. Some elders do work to keep old foodways alive, informing the young about their heritage, incorporating traditional foods into community festivals and family gatherings. Where possible, seasonal harvest traditions have been maintained. Weippe Prairie is now farmland, the camas long gone, but Nez Percé travel to Musselshell Creek, on national forest land, where they have been given digging rights. Flathead and Kootenay still fish for salmon; Utes, Shoshone, and Cheyenne still hunt parts of their traditional grounds. Some families carefully maintain rituals associated with food gathering: In a 1996 interview, a Coeur d'Alene told how his father would make the family wait at the car until he returned, singing, with two huckleberry bushes, then rub the bushes over his children and give his wife the year's first berries. "We would stand there and watch as my mother would eat them, and he would talk in Indian, and he would talk about reproducing human beings and the powers of mothers, the power and the spirit of the mothers being like Mother Earth, needing nourishment," the informant reported.[6]

With members of various tribes traveling on the powwow circuit, pan-Indian foodways are frequently adapted and marketed to outsiders today. The Shoshone-Bannocks of southeastern Idaho, for instance, now commercially raise buffalo in the Fort Hall Bottoms, where no buffalo ever lived before, and one can buy southwestern-style fry bread and Indian tacos at their yearly festival.

THE FOODWAYS OF EXPLORATION AND IMMIGRATION

The first whites to see the Rocky Mountain region were missionaries, trappers, and explorers. Undertaking long journeys, they lived off the land, supplementing their beans, bacon, flour, and whiskey with game and indigenous foodstuffs that they learned about from Native Americans. When Lewis and Clark traveled through the region in 1805–1806, Sacagawea dug Jerusalem artichokes and prairie turnips; the expedition's hunters procured buffalo, antelope, and bear. Foods new to the expedition were bent to familiar uses: Sacagawea's French husband made boudin blanc, the traditional "white sausage" of France, from buffalo. The expedition did face hunger in Idaho's "tremendous mountains" during September 1805, as it moved down the Lochsa River, using snow for cooking and eating colts and candles, finally. When its members came to Nez Percé territory at the end of that month, they were grateful for the abundance that they found. Salmon reassured them that they "were on the waters of the Pacific Ocean," and Clark described a feast in which he indulged too freely: "roots, dried roots made in bread, roots boiled, on Saumon, berries of red hawes some dried . . . those roots are like onions, Sweet when Dried, and tolerably good in bread. I eate much and am Sick in the evening."[7] On the expedition's return trip in 1806, members continued to experiment with local resources. Lewis enjoyed rosy spring salmon, while Clark whimsically tried to cook meat in what is now called Jackson Hot Springs.

Mountain men followed Lewis and Clark into the Rocky Mountain region, including Osborne Russell, who trapped in the Yellowstone/Snake River country in the 1830s. They, too, depended on the land to provide their food. Russell's diet seems to have consisted mainly of meat; one night, his memoir notes, he and his companions returned to camp to find that their Camp Keeper "had prepared an elegant supper of Grizzly Bear meat and Mutton nicely stewed and seasoned with salt and pepper." The journal also mentions eating buffalo, elk, and venison. When wild produce was available, trappers did eat it avidly: Russell describes a stand of plum trees "loaded and breaking down to the ground with the finest kind as large as Pheasants eggs and sweet as sugar the'l almost melt in yo mouth." Despite such summer bounty, explorers who were unlucky or careless could quickly be reminded of the Rocky Mountain region's harshness. When John C. Frémont's (1813–1890) party insisted in pressing through the Sangre de Cristos and San Juan mountains in southern Colorado in winter 1848, they were stopped by fierce blizzards. The Christmas menu at their "Camp Desolation," one expedition member recalled, consisted of "mule tail soup, baked white mule, and boiled gray mule." Not all members of the party survived.[8]

Immigrant travelers on the Oregon Trail were less able and willing to adapt to indigenous foods of the Rocky Mountains than most explorers or mountain men— their unfamiliarity with what might be found along the way and the sheer number of people traveling the same route dictated that they could not depend on living off the land. Immigrants brought large stores of provisions, including flour, bacon, dried apples, sugar, and whiskey. They baked bread daily, leavened with saleratus or with yeast powder. Travelers also relied on bread and bacon, dried apples, beans, and rice. To supplement their diets, hunters might provide game birds, venison, or buffalo. Killing one of the latter was a major event, and trains would pause so that the meat could be cut up, jerked, and strung onto wagon covers to dry, "gay red fringe" decorating them for the next several days.

By the time that immigrants arrived in eastern Wyoming, they were jettisoning excess baggage, including food, aware that the mountains lay ahead. One train left behind a ton of bacon and several barrels of hardtack; some people even discarded rolling pins. On the trip over the Rockies, such travelers relied more on the land, and hunting was taken up in greater earnest. Some gathered wild greens, including chard, mustard, and onions; nearly all gathered berries to replace the now-tedious dried apple pies. Parties finding themselves short of staples could restock (at high prices) at the region's forts, including Fort Laramie and Fort Hall.

Depending on the time of year, crossing the Rockies could signal scarcity for Oregon Trail pioneers. Still, some found compensations. Many diarists remarked that they were glad of the Sweetwater River's "cold mountain water," which, after the Platte, "seems to give us a new lease on life."[9] When trains reached naturally carbonated springs, travelers were happy for the novelty. Nearly every diarist notes the alkaline water at Soda Springs, Idaho; some mixed it with sugar and vinegar and proclaimed it equal to the best commercial soda water. Equally ingenious were the men who, when their train reached Wyoming's Ice Springs, made mint juleps in the heat of summer.

Overall, though, immigrants found travel difficult and the region itself uninviting. One Oregon Trail diarist concluded that southern Idaho's Snake River Plain "looked like Desolation brooding over Despair," and even official observers were pessimistic. In 1853, James Cowden, sent by the federal government to examine the potential of the interior West, reported that it seemed "good for nothing but to hold the rest of creation together."[10] In the first decades of westward migration, thus, almost nobody imagined that the Rocky Mountain West could consistently feed a civilized human being.

Permanent Anglo-European settlement in the Rocky Mountain West began only when particular resources beckoned. For the region's earliest settlers, the Mormons, those were resources of buffering space; for those who followed, they were mineral resources or land that might be exploited for grazing or farming. Fortunes *were* made in the region, and comfortable permanent settlements established, despite the skepticism of earlier visitors. Still, those who came to live in the Rocky Mountain region quickly learned that bad luck or ignorance might mean dashed hopes and empty bellies.

Mormons and Rocky Mountain Food

The Mormons were first, moving west to escape persecution. After their first leader, Joseph Smith, was murdered by a mob in Missouri, Brigham Young (1801–1877) led the Latter-day Saints (LDS) west to the Salt Lake Valley, which they reached in 1847. While remote from enemies and declared "promised," their new home was inauspicious as a place to grow food, a barren, alkaline desert. Mountain man Jim Bridger is said to have told Young that he would give $1,000 if he heard that an ear of corn ripened there. With high hopes, though, the Saints plowed ground, planted potatoes, and diverted water from City Creek to the fields within days of arriving. Hampered by lack of knowledge of the region and harassed by insects, however, the pioneers found their first year's grain crop a failure and harvested only a few potatoes. Rationing was instituted and, according to Daughters of Utah Pioneers, "by the next spring the pioneers were subsisting on 'crows, wolf meat, tree bark, thistle tops, sego lily bulbs, and hawks.' "[11] The next year, June frost killed most of the crops. Even in the mid-1850s, grasshopper infestations and severe cold threatened famine.

Despite these trials, the Latter-day Saints did, as they would say, "make the desert bloom." The keys to their success were cooperative effort and population control. In the Mormon model, families built houses together in a village and farmed perimeter land; church leaders allotted twenty to forty acres to each family, and villagers held water and timber in common. They dug cooperative irrigation ditches and established community storehouses. As population pressure built near Salt Lake City, church leaders directed their followers to spread out. The Cache Valley in northern Utah and Provo in central Utah were settled in 1859; in the early 1860s, settlement reached further north, to Franklin, in what would become Idaho, and further south, into Utah's "Dixie," reaching down to St. George and then beyond into Arizona.

Lack of sufficient water and climate extremes could still lead to hunger, but, thanks to planned settlement that limited population demands, within a decade most Mormons found themselves with sufficient food. LDS pioneer autobiographies suggest that meals were not fancy, but they were filling. Sourdough or salt-rising bread, corn bread, stew and dumplings, potatoes and other root vegetables, and apple desserts (supplied from trees grown from seeds that the pioneers brought west) formed the backbone of their cuisine. In the summer, fresh vegetables and fruits supplemented this diet. Some areas were especially propitious for growing such crops, like the bench lands just south of Brigham City, an area to which pioneer women traveled to buy fruit in summer. Mormons canned and dried foods; they stored enough food to last for two years, as their church directed. Most important, they cooperated, thus not overtaxing the area's limited resources.

Food in Mining Camps and Towns

Miners, the second large population wave to settle the Rocky Mountain region, were much less willing to organize their settlement or to adapt to the land's demands. They were thinking primarily about riches, not food, planning on moving on as soon as they found wealth. The earliest gold strikes were in Colorado, where "59ers" found gold near present-day Denver. Though the initial strikes were not as rich as miners hoped, major finds deeper in the Colorado mountains—up and down the range and further west in subsequent years—made the territory boom. Miners came to Idaho also in the 1860s, rushing to the Clearwater/Salmon region, then to Idaho City. They flooded to Montana's Last Chance Gulch (Helena) in 1864; they rushed to Wyoming's South Pass City. Even Utah saw its rushes, first in Bingham Canyon in 1863 and, in the early 1870s, to Park City, to the Tintic region, to Little Cottonwood Canyon/Alta, and to Silver Reef/American Fork. Silver drew miners to Leadville, Colorado; silver and copper to Butte, Montana. Coal mines were established in Durango and Pueblo; in Rock Springs, Wyoming; and in Carbon County, Utah.

Mining booms generated enormous influxes of immigrants; the silver rush to Leadville in 1877–1878, for instance, drew 15,000 people. With such sudden pressure on previously unsettled areas, food was an instant problem. Most mining areas were remote and mountainous, extremely cold in winter, and liable to be isolated by deep snow. In the first weeks or months, food shortages could be extreme and prices exorbitant. Before farmers began bringing potatoes and vegetables to Montana's Hellgate Ronde district near Missoula, for instance, wild lamb's quarters sold for $1.50 a gallon in gold dust. Winters could be especially difficult. "There is no food for sale in the camp," miners heading to Thunder Mountain, Idaho, were warned. "One must carry in his food, or stay away until spring."[12] Some miners starved; one doctor in Florence, Idaho, told of a hungry miner who begged for a cow's head frozen on the roof for four months. Montana's Virginia City saw a bread riot in 1864, when snow closed the camp to freighting, and miners seized hoarded flour. In the most climatically extreme areas, even summer could be difficult. Rock Springs, established in 1875 in the Wyoming desert, did not even have adequate water. For twelve years, until a water main was built, Rock Springs residents paid 25 cents a barrel for water imported on a daily train from Green River.

Opportunistic merchants quickly recognized camps' needs. Florence soon had twenty eager capitalists competing for miners' dollars; a store in Auraria, Colorado, stayed open twenty-four hours a day and accepted gold dust for food. Boarding houses provided regular meals, and restaurants and saloons also fed customers. The latter offered "free lunches," food available to any drinking customer. Butte's Council Bar became especially famous for its "merchant's lunch," a half-block-long bar loaded with bologna, pig's feet, liverwurst, anchovies, cheese, breads, pickles, onions, kippered fish—anything salty to increase customers' thirst.

Some price gouging did occur, but merchants also faced risks. When miners heard of new strikes in Idaho City in the spring of 1862 and rushed away from Florence, for instance, dropping the town's population from 8,000 to 2,000 in one week, merchants were left with $40,000 worth of unsold inventory. That year, the miners who remained in Florence spent only 5 percent of their income on their diet.

Other speculators were tied to the land itself—farmers who came to raise vegetables and meat for the camps. In Idaho, opportunistic farmers took up the closest flat land, along the Boise, Payette, and Weiser Rivers; Montana's Prickly Pear Valley near Helena was also quickly filled with farms and ranches.

The food available in camps varied widely. At first, miners might have only hardtack, bacon, beans, and coffee. As camps prospered, miners might be able to take meals in luxurious restaurants: Georgetown, Colorado's Hotel de Paris maintained its own trout farm and a large wine cellar. In towns with diversified populations, eating establishments sometimes offered options literally stratified by class. Butte's California Music Hall, for instance, provided private upstairs rooms for "elegant parties," where five- to six-course meals with champagne were served; while on the main floor (where ladies were not permitted, outside of an all-girl orchestra) beer cost 5 cents a glass, along with a free lunch of frankfurters, cheese, and crackers.

Despite flashy prosperity, mining towns were subject to boom and bust cycles, dependent on their mineral resources and on market prices. The silver crisis of the 1890s, in particular, crippled many. Some are now ghost towns, their once-opulent restaurants open to the winds. Others, though, have found new life as ski resorts or diversified cities; some have even managed to continue as mining centers. One can still visit storied bars in such places and can see the boarding houses or even stay in them, reincarnated as beds and breakfasts, now plating apple-hazelnut French toast instead of beef stew and oyster pie.

Rancher Foodways

Though Mormons, mining town residents, and other settlers raised livestock for local sustenance, commercial ranching began in earnest in the Rocky Mountain West in the 1880s. By then, stockraisers had realized that cattle turned out to winter returned "sleek and fat" on prairie grass in the spring; buffalo, largely exterminated, no longer competed for grazing land; the "Indian problem" had been solved; and rail lines provided routes to markets. By the early 1880s, thousands of cattle, driven north from Texas, filled the ranges of eastern Montana, Wyoming, and Colorado; they grazed in southwestern Idaho and in parts of Utah. Montana alone had 660,000 head by 1885. Huge ranches, often owned by English investors, dominated the landscape—one in Colorado covered 2,240,000 acres.

Food for such cattle barons could be quite extravagant, finding its zenith in such venues as Wyoming's Cheyenne Club, where banqueters one night consumed sixty-six bottles of champagne and twenty of red wine. Cuisine for cowboys, in contrast, was basic but filling, prepared by cooks who worked from well-organized chuckwagons. Sourdough bread and pancakes were staples, as was, naturally, beef. Cowboys liked their steaks fried; they also enjoyed organ meats. A favorite dish was a beef stew that included "everything except the horns, hoofs, and hide." They also enjoyed steamed suet pudding called "son-of-a-bitch-in-a-sack" (which Mormon settlers also ate but called "son-of-a-gun-in-a-sack," at least in their reminiscences). Vegetables were largely represented by canned tomatoes, and coffee was consumed black. Dried beans were another staple, soaked and baked for many hours in a buried "bean hole." That custom was so universal that Elinor Pruitt Stewart, who homesteaded in western Wyoming, tells of a cattle-camp cook chiding his employer, who had chided *him* when she arrived and found nothing to eat. "How iss it," this German cook retorted, "dat you haf not so much sense as you haf tongue? How haf you lived so long as always in de West und don't know how to hunt up a bean-hole when you reach your own camp?"[13]

Sheep ranching was also practiced on a large scale. In this case, ranchers would send hired herders, often Basque or Mexican, to work alone or in pairs on the range, grazing bands of sheep and protecting them from predators. These herders were supplied with provisions, staple, long-keeping food like canned corn and tomatoes, beans, salt pork, and coffee. For holiday celebrations, though, employers might send care boxes. Stewart describes how she and a neighbor who ran a sheep operation prepared geese, hens, meatloaf, hams, sausage, rye bread, iced cakes, doughnuts, fruitcakes, butter, and jelly and delivered the boxes to twelve pairs of isolated sheepherders on Christmas Eve morning.

In the late 1880s, ranchers suffered terrible blows. During the winter of 1886–1887, blizzards and extreme cold decimated the herds. When the snows stopped, more than 60 percent of the free-ranging cattle and many sheep were dead, and the industry never again grew to the same scale. Competition also troubled the cattle industry, as homesteaders fenced their land, limiting free range. Big cattle operations, like those that made up the powerful Wyoming Stock Growers Association, discovered that they no longer had absolute domain. Wyoming's Johnson County War swung public opinion further against large ranching operations, as did tales of fence-cutting and illegal land use. Violence occurred between cattlemen and sheepmen: In one incident in Idaho, shepherds tied to trees by cattlemen were forced to watch as their herd was "rimrocked," driven over a cliff. In the twentieth century, ranchers had to deal with new limitations: facing, after the Taylor Grazing Act of 1934, what they considered the indignity of paying to use public land.

Still, ranching could provide a viable living, even in the hardest times: Grace Jordan and her husband, later Idaho's governor Len B. Jordan, took up a sheep ranch just downriver from Idaho's Hell's Canyon during the 1930s depression, and they succeeded. Jordan's memoir documents the backbreaking labor required to keep their venture fed and afloat: One year, this former college professor canned 300 quarts of fruit, she reports, and she figured out how to butcher a deer on her own when her husband was gone trailing their sheep. Most of the clichés of Rocky Mountain pioneer life do have their basis in fact, and hard work is certainly one.

Farmers

Jordan was fortunate, for her canyon home sat at low altitude, and fruit and vegetables grew easily there, irrigated from the little stream that came down a side canyon to the Snake River. Outside of such protected valleys and river bottoms, agriculture in the Rocky Mountain region has always been an especially difficult proposition.

The earliest farmers in the Rocky Mountain region were Hispanics who migrated north from New Mexico to till the mild, fertile San Luis Valley in southern Colorado; they dug the first irrigation ditches in the state and raised corn, beans, peppers, fruit, and other crops in abundance. The first Anglo-European farmers took up land along the region's streams and rivers; they came to supply food to the mines but stayed as their farms prospered. In western Montana, small irrigated farms raised wheat, potatoes, and fruit in the Bitterroot, Deer Lodge, Jefferson, Madison, Ruby, Prickly Pear, and Gallatin Valleys. By the territory's first census in 1870, western Montana had 851 farms, watered by 1,269 miles of main irrigation ditches. In Colorado, farmers took up land along the South Platte, on the western slope, along the Gunnison and the Colorado; in Idaho, they farmed near Boise; in Utah, they farmed along the benches of the Wasatch Mountains and the banks of the Sevier, Santa Clara, and other rivers. Before railroads crisscrossed the region, farmers might use wagon-freight lines to transport their goods to markets. The most famous freighting center was Utah's "gentile capital," Corrine, which supplied Montana and Idaho mining towns.

Mormons were not the only cooperative farmers in the region, for Colorado also saw some organized experiments in communal agriculture. Greeley was originally founded as one of these, the inspiration of Nathan Meeker, agricultural editor for Horace Greeley (1811–1872) of the *New York Tribune*. In 1869–1870, after an organizational meeting in New York City, Meeker established the colony on land purchased from the Denver Pacific Railroad. Cooperative irrigation works were soon in place, and the colony prospered. Longmont and Fort Collins also began as successful planned agricultural colonies. It soon became clear that irrigation was essential in the success of both communal and independent farmers, and Colorado passed water rights legislation, guaranteeing that the first to use a source held permanent rights. This "Colorado system" was quickly adopted by other western states.

Farming was much more risky away from perennial streams. Explorer John Wesley Powell had noted the climate's aridity and warned that the American West could not support dry farming, but his words were ignored in a rush of propaganda. In 1865, the Montana Commissioner of Immigration proclaimed that the territory "could hardly be excelled in any country" as a farming region; as railroads built into eastern Colorado, they endorsed the belief that "rain follows the plow" and urged settlers to take up homesteads along their routes. "So much rain now falls in the eastern portion of the arid lands of Colorado," a Burlington promoter claimed, "that it is no longer fit for a winter range for cattle."[14]

During the relatively wet decades of the 1880s, homesteaders trusted these words, and they came to eastern Colorado, Montana, and even Wyoming. Soon, however, the climate returned to its customary aridity, and by 1889, many farms failed. Among the casualties were several ill-advised colonies, including a

---

Wild Buffalo Berry Catsup

(A pioneer recipe from Wyoming)

1½ quarts of berry pulp
1 pint vinegar
1 quart sugar
1 T cinnamon
1 T allspice
½ T cloves
½ tsp salt
⅛ T cayenne pepper

Cook over slow heat until it thickens.

group of sixteen Polish/Prussian Jewish families in eastern Colorado. The Hebrew Aid Society finally gave each family $100 toward a new start somewhere else.

Dry farming was pursued more successfully in other areas, especially north-central Montana and northern Idaho's Palouse region. After the railroad came to the latter in the 1880s, farmers began experimenting with dry-farmed wheat and were soon shipping their crop to Portland via river steamboats. "An army of itinerant laborers, a parade of reapers and combines . . . and smoking and puffing steam-powered threshing machines" traveled around the Palouse to harvest the wheat, which was then lowered to landings 2,000 feet below plateau level via aerial trams and inclined railroads.[15]

Enabled by the 1894 Carey Act and 1902 Newlands Act, government-supported irrigation projects opened much more land in the Rocky Mountain region to farming. The Minidoka Project on Idaho's Snake River Plain, for instance, brought water to the volcanic soil east and northeast of Twin Falls; dams on the Milk, Lower Yellowstone, Huntley, and Sun Rivers in Montana opened rolling land to grain production. Some of the projects were astounding, like the 1910 construction in western Colorado of a tunnel that brought Gunnison River water *through* Vernal Mesa to the Uncompahgre Valley. News that irrigation was imminent could spark inflation in land prices, and communities trumpeted such reports to "boost" their areas. Hamilton, Montana, for instance, grew enormously in 1906–1915 during the "Big Ditch" or "Apple" Boom in the Bitterroot Valley, which promised an eighty-mile canal.

As irrigation improved, new food-based industry arose in the Rocky Mountain West. Sugar beets became big business in Idaho, Utah, and Colorado; the first sugar beet refinery opened near Idaho Falls in 1903 and was quickly followed by plants in northern Utah and eastern Colorado. Nearly every state in the region has a place named "Sugar City." Lentils and peas, melons and strawberries, barley and hops—all became profitable where the climate allowed.

Not all farmers found success in the region, however. Everyone knows about the drought of the 1930s, when Dust Bowl farmers in eastern Colorado lost their land on a scale not seen since the 1890s, but other, less-celebrated tragedies occurred elsewhere. Some advertised land was simply not suitable for cultivation by small farmers, too rocky or sage-covered, subject to grasshopper or rabbit depredation or temperature extremes, too alkaline. Some irrigation projects—like the Apple Boom itself—went bust before they were completed or even before they began. Some never delivered the amount of water that they promised or delivered it only to part of the projected region. Some farmers complained that banks and irrigation companies took advantage of them. In some districts, like Idaho's North Side Project, nearly all of the original homesteaders lost their land.

In good times and in hard times, the families that farmed the Rocky Mountain region relied on home production. Putting food on the family's table involved a great deal of planning and work for women, in particular. Louise K. Nickey, whose family homesteaded in northeastern Montana, remembers that her mother stored 600 to 800 pounds of flour and sugar each fall; other pioneer reminiscences speak of canning hundreds of jars of fruit, vegetables, and meat every autumn and of baking a dozen loaves of bread every few days. Settlers smoked hams; they made sausage and dried beef; and they pickled vegetables that they had raised, making "mountains of sauerkraut." They churned butter, made cottage cheese, and rendered lard. In hard times, frugal cooks might turn to their root cellars and fill their families with such dishes as rutabaga loaf. They hunted and gathered wild foods. Nickey remembers that she and her sister were often sent out to find mushrooms after rain; the family also ate sage hens, frogs' legs, and carp eggs. Her mother did not waste anything, Nickey reports, remembering rhubarb wine and carrot preserves. Some families incorporated plants that Native Americans had used; pioneer recipe collections include cottage cheese bread that substitutes kouse seed for the traditional dill, wild rose-hip jelly, buffalo berry catsup, and dried huckleberry pudding.

Harvest time, when dozens of neighbors might gather with hired workers, was a particular challenge for cooks. Annie Pike Greenwood, who homesteaded near Twin Falls, describes planning eight meals at a time, "twenty for bread," soaking two quarts of dried beans with "slabs of ham," chopping three quarts of chopped cabbage, and cooking "raisin pies, cream pies, fresh-prune pies, apple pies, and Jeff Davis pies" until she was exhausted. She loved to hear the threshing machine being shut down on the last day of harvest, she reports, as did most women whom she knew.[16]

> ## Venison Pasties
>
> **(Adapted from the *Butte Heritage Cookbook*)**
>
> *Dough:*
>
> Cut 2 C shortening into 4½ C flour until crumbly. Then mix 1 egg and 1 tsp vinegar in a measuring cup and add cold water to fill the cup. Stir into flour just till dough holds together.
>
> *Filling:*
>
> Mix 10 medium potatoes, diced; 5 lbs diced raw venison, ¼ C finely chopped salt pork; 3 medium onions, chopped; 1 tsp thyme; and salt and pepper to taste.
>
> Roll out dough on a floured board and cut into smaller or larger circles, as you wish. Put a scoop of filling in the center of each circle (not so much that you can't fold it over and pinch the edges but enough to fill the pasty generously), then fold each pasty into a half circle and pinch edges shut. Bake at 350 degrees on a lightly greased baking sheet for 1–1½ hours, depending on the size of your pasties, until dough is brown and filling is done.

ETHNIC FOODWAYS

While the Rocky Mountain region has perhaps been less ethnically diverse than other parts of the country, it has always included lively pockets of distinctive ethnic cultures, as immigrants came to take up specific occupations.

Many came as miners. Cornish "Cousin Jacks" brought their pasties—meat turnovers easily carried in pockets—to the diggings of Colorado, Montana, and Idaho, then adapted them by substituting elk or venison for the beef typical in their homeland. Italians, mostly from southern Italy, also came to work the mines and coal fields of Montana, Wyoming, and eastern Utah and on the railroad. They raised backyard gardens of tomatoes, eggplants, peppers, fava beans, and figs; they patronized old-country-style butchers and bakers. They also ordered railroad cars full of California grapes at harvest time; in one year alone, Butte's Italians imported 186 carloads. Eastern European workers joined them, men from Poland, Yugoslavia, Czechoslovakia, and Hungary. In their homes and through their lodges, they prepared horseradish and beets, nut and poppy-seed rolls, sausages, and sour turnips. Greeks also came to mining districts and railroad towns, raising lambs and large gardens, making cheese, kourambeithes (cookies), and baklava, establishing sociable coffeehouses.

Other immigrants came to work with livestock and in the fields. Basque shepherds came early to the Rocky Mountain region. Basque boarding houses catered to them with roast lamb, beans, bacala, vegetable soups, hearty red wine, and picon punch. Mexicans/Hispanics also herded sheep, along with working in the fields; in the twentieth century they became the dominant ethnic group in the region. They brought tortillas, beans, enchiladas, tamales; they grew the region's first hot peppers and tomatillas.

Soon after Utah was settled, Mormon missionaries traveled to the British Isles and northern Europe seeking converts, and their success brought waves of immigrants from that region to the Rocky Mountain West. In 1860, 22 percent of Utah's population was British born; 30,000 converts came from Sweden, Denmark, and Norway in the second half of the nineteenth century. Many of these immigrants settled to working the land. Scandinavians and Swiss began the dairy business in northern Utah; they settled, also, in central Utah, in Sanpete County, bringing their potato cakes, their holiday pastries. Northern Europeans who were not Mormons also brought their foodways to the region, like the Finns who settled Idaho's Long Valley, and Montana's Irish.

Other immigrant groups congregated in the region's towns and cities. Cheyenne, Denver, and Boise, for instance, have substantial numbers of Jewish immigrants. Lebanese and other Middle Eastern groups came to Salt Lake City, among other places; African Americans to Denver.

One of the largest ethnic groups to come to the Rocky Mountain West, the Germans, engaged in many different occupations. Germans farmed and ran ranches in the prairies; they worked in the mines; they kept stores and were professionals. Some parts of the region were dominated by German immigrants, as with northern Idaho's Camas Prairie/Palouse, where German remained the dominant language until World War I, and where towns have names like Keuterville. Germans brewed beer in Evanston and Rock Springs, Wyoming; they made sausage; they cured sauerkraut. Ethnic Germans who had lived for a century in Russia also came to work in the beet fields; Hutterites established colonies in Montana; Mennonites settled in Aberdeen, Idaho.

Asian immigrants came to the Rocky Mountain region at first to work on the railroads and in the mines. Some opened restaurants where homesick men could eat familiar food; Butte's China Alley once had seven noodle parlors that "did a standout business." Japanese moved to farming as quickly as they could and often found success. One Utah man, Daigoro Hashimoto, was instrumental in establishing the Clearfield Canning Company for the Utah-Idaho Sugar Beet Company; another, Taijiro Kasuga, bred and patented the everbearing Twentieth Century Strawberry (along with Sweetheart and Jumbo Celery) and made millions. Even internment during World War II did not stop many Japanese from working the land: at the Minidoka Camp in Idaho, they raised victory gardens.

Some accounts have these varied nationalities living together harmoniously. In Wyoming's Sunrise-Hartville district, for instance, the annual area picnic was run by the Dante Alighieri Society and featured Italian sausage and homemade wine; the "many nationalities" who are said to have attended enjoyed singing opera tunes and dancing tarantellas. Butte, in particular, has been celebrated as a place where almost fifty nationalities lived and got along. Other studies, however, suggest that relations weren't quite so harmonious everywhere and at all times. The Chinese, of course, faced great prejudice. But Eastern Europeans, too, met with suspicion. In southern Utah's Carbon County, for instance, Greeks, Italians, and other Eastern Europeans were seen as violent and superstitious, their participation in labor activities anti-American. Foodways could be crucial as symbols of group identity under such circumstances: Once, when a group of Italians in Price was arrested during a strike, their first action when locked in a bullpen was to cook spaghetti in coffee cans.

Visitors lucky enough to be invited to family meals or celebrations today can still find time-warp glimpses of ethnic traditions in the midst of what appear to be white-bread districts. One can find middle-aged Basque women visiting and laughing in a kitchen as they prepare wedding feasts in places like Shoshone, Idaho; one can eat lutefisk at Danish Christmas Eve celebrations; or enjoy sweet potato pie made by celebrated local African American cooks; rellenos made with chilis roasted on a backyard fire; or homemade dolmades. And that's just in southern Idaho.

Ethnic foodways are shared more generally with the public during annual festivals. Greek churches hold public celebrations, with whole lambs roasting on spits over out-of-doors fireplaces and spanokopita and ouzo for sale in social-hall basements. Basque festivals occur annually, including Boise's St. Ignatius Festival, and a picnic in honor of the Assumption of the Virgin Mary in the Big Horn Mountains, which draws Basques from all over Wyoming. In the region's larger cities, ethnic markets sell specialty goods; Salt Lake City and Colorado Springs both hold fine Italian groceries, for instance. Some specialty-produce farmers have enthusiastically embraced ethnic diversity: One eastern Idaho pick-your-own operation owned by an Anglo man and his Japanese wife has signs in Spanish announcing poblanos, habaneros, and zucchini blossoms.

Though "railroad Chinese," fast-food Mexican, and franchised Italian operations dominate Rocky Mountain ethnic restaurants in sheer numbers, one can find more interesting options. Boise's Bar Guernica is a holdout for Basque food; Cedars of Lebanon in Salt Lake City also manages to stay authentic. The region holds dozens of good Mexican restaurants, ranging from very traditional hole-in-the-walls to Denver's Tamaya, at this writing nationally acclaimed for its inventive renditions of classic dishes. Swiss and German restaurants flourish in ski towns; Aurora offers Korean barbeque; a dining room in Mesa Verde National Park serves modern versions of Southwestern Native American cuisine, including smoked duck tamales. Ethnic gems sometimes appear in unexpected places: Lava Hot Springs and Twin Falls, Idaho, both have credible Thai restaurants. Boulder's Dushanbe Teahouse may well be the region's most beautiful ethnic restaurant, assembled by forty artisans from elaborate, colorful components hand carved and painted in the town's sister city in Tajikistan. Besides an enormous variety of teas, it serves a pan-world menu including Tajik plov, a rice, meat, and vegetable specialty from Tajikistan.

CONTEMPORARY MAINSTREAM FOODWAYS

During the twentieth century, Rocky Mountain mainstream foodways have become largely indistinguishable from those nationwide. Food distribution networks and supermarket chains have brought home cooks and restaurants the goods available from coast to coast. Food supplies no longer depend on local climate. Some populations *are* still hungry—the Food Bank of the Rockies provided 2,000 meals in its Denver Kid's Cafés in one day in November 2002; and the Food Distribution on Indian Reservations program, which serves over 1,300 families on Montana's seven reservations, noted that six out of ten families relied on it as their main or only source of food. Still, scarcity is not a problem for most residents. Fast-food chains line major streets; national trends are evident. One can find espresso stands, for instance, in remote, working-class towns like Kooskia, Idaho, pickup trucks with gun racks waiting patiently.

Sometimes, however, this homogeny can be depressing. Many cafes in the state with "Famous Potatoes" on its license plate serve only slabs of frozen hash-browns, dripping with grease, for breakfast, not fresh spuds; it is possible to eat a flavorless piece of beef imported on a truck from somewhere else while watching cows out the window; commercial "air bread" appears in all-too-many breadbaskets of wheat-growing-region restaurants. A survey of picnic tables in campgrounds will inevitably reveal bags of potato chips, store-brand hot dogs, Coke, and Budweiser. No longer an outback in terms of food, the Rocky Mountain states have embraced the national diet with a vengeance.

State and county fair foodways provide a telling glimpse of the gap between what residents sentimentally believe about the region's food and what their eating habits have become. If one looks at the premium books, one sees nostalgia for the pioneer past, competitions in bread and pie baking, canning, vegetable growing. One *can* find beautiful loaves of bread, impeccably packed jars where every bean, every carrot is the same size, and perfectly aligned, lovely strawberries and huge pumpkins in those exhibit halls. Some fairs even run competitions in local foodways: the North Idaho Fair, held in traditionally German- and Scandinavian-settled country, has a homemade beer contest with *sixteen* carefully differentiated categories. Even in the food competitions, though, the dreary influence of junk foodways surfaces: The Eastern Idaho State Fair has begun to sponsor a Spam recipe contest. Generic junk food rules outright on the midways, a few boiled corn-on-the-cob and trout concessions aside. One can eat French fries—straight, curly, or "tornado"—or deep-fried "Tiger Ears," generic Mexican and Greek and Italian, hamburgers and corn dogs, snow cones, industrial fudge. All of this can taste good, of course, outdoors in the summer, in the company of friends. But distinctive food it is not. Still, it is possible to find some regionally specific foodways, if one knows where to look, and several of the most prominent are discussed below.

Home Cooking

One of the most distinctive foodways of the Rocky Mountain West involves residents' enduring affection for game and other hunted/fished/gathered indigenous products. In the fall, a slow stew of elk or other game simmers in many households. Even people who don't hunt may find friends knocking on their doors, sharing this year's take of venison, elk, moose, mallard ducks, and trout—even wild bison, antelope, and steelhead. One may find oneself the sudden recipient of wild geese or pheasants, complete with heads, feathers, and guts. In autumn, woodlands, mountains, marshes, and prairies in the Rocky Mountain region swarm with hunters. The Wyoming Game and Fish Commission proclaims that 52 percent of the *total* state population hunts or fishes; in Montana, the figure is not far behind,

43.5 percent. Opening day is madness, with shots echoing in the canyons from first light. Most hunters do bag their game, sooner or later.

What cooks often do, ironically, is to disguise the wild game. Regional cookbooks abound with recipes designed to mask the taste, which to many is superb, or simply to substitute game for beef, preparing such dishes as elk chili, venison-tater-tot casserole replete with canned cream soup, or moose burritos. Sausage is a default treatment for many home cooks. Most local cookbooks contain appalling game recipes; one of the worst invites readers to take a jackrabbit, put it in a crock-pot with a bottle each of catsup and teriyaki sauce, then cook the dickens out of it.

Fortunately, some home cooks treat game with reverence, and recipes exist for lovely roasts and stews flavored as Native Americans might have done, if they'd had a Wild Oats market down the street. Elk stew might, under the best of circumstances, include winter squash and leeks from the farmer's market, culinary sage, mint, and garlic from the garden, dried cranberries, and a splash of cognac, a tip of the crockpot lid to Lewis and Clark's whiskey. Those good cooks and some regional restaurants, like The Fort, near Denver, have shown the way, using game so as to respect its essential nature. In some states, though, the selling of wild game is forbidden, a hedge against poachers. So, in game-rich Idaho, for instance, one can dine out on elk and venison—but it is farm-raised, imported from Texas. Fish is less protected, and diners who have good timing can enjoy sweet trout in restaurants ranging from the Old Faithful Inn in Yellowstone to modest corner cafes. Chico Hot Springs, Montana, offers a particularly lovely setting for eating local fish, along with bison.

Beyond meat products, residents also love to gather the region's wild berries. Huckleberries are especially beloved in northern Idaho and Montana; blackberries, elderberries, and even the tiny stone-bearing chokecherries have their fans. Some families plan annual camping trips to the same locations to pick each summer, replicating Native American migrations; others buy their berries at the stands that proliferate in the parking lots of the region's shopping centers, roadside pull-offs, and farmers markets for a few weeks each year. A jar of homemade huckleberry or chokecherry jam is a sacred gift, in some circles.

Another feature that distinguishes Rocky Mountain cooking is the popular embrace of the Dutch oven. Dutch ovens are lidded iron pots, often with legs. One fills the oven with raw materials, covers it, and places glowing briquets on the lid and/or underneath, adjusting the temperature by the number of briquets. People make astounding things in Dutch ovens, not just stews and casseroles but roasts and bread, cobblers and cakes. Cookbooks, festivals, and catering companies feature Dutch oven cooking, and

Autumn Elk Stew

4 strips bacon
2 lbs elk stew meat
2 acorn squash, peeled, seeded, and chopped into medium chunks
3 leeks, sliced
1 garlic clove, minced
¼ C dried cranberries
2 cans beef broth
3 garden sage leaves, chopped
2 T fresh mint, chopped
2 T cognac, or to taste
salt and pepper

Brown bacon in a skillet and remove, then brown elk in the rendered fat. Put elk in a crock pot, leaving bacon fat behind. Crumble bacon into the crock pot, then add all the other ingredients and cover pot. Cook on slowest heat setting for 5–6 hours.

Steamed Huckleberry Pudding with Chunky Huckleberry Syrup

(A fancier, modern version of a pudding that pioneers or Native Americans might have eaten)

Pudding:

¼ C shortening
⅔ C sugar
1 egg
1½ C flour
½ tsp salt
3 tsp baking powder
⅔ C milk
1 C fresh huckleberries
1 tsp grated lemon zest
½ tsp cinnamon

Cream shortening and sugar; add egg. Mix in the rest of the ingredients; pour into a greased and sugared 1-quart baking dish. Cover. Bring 1 inch of water to boiling in a large covered pot that a rack fits inside; put baking dish on the rack and reduce heat to simmer. Cover the large pot and steam the pudding, adding water as necessary, 1½ hours or until done.

Syrup:

1 lb fresh huckleberries
1 C sugar

Combine in a pan and stir; cook over medium heat until berries melt into syrup, stirring often. Serve warm over warm pudding.

Utah is said to buy the most in the nation. People cook in Dutch ovens in their backyards, not just on camping trips, and every Girl Scout or Boy Scout leader is assumed to know how to use them. Part of the enthusiasm comes from romance—the pioneers did cook in Dutch ovens (though not with commercial briquets, of course)—and so a Dutch oven dinner is a link to the past. Also, though, if one *is* going camping, Dutch ovens broaden the repertoire of what can be prepared. Some outfitters who run expensive multiday trips down wild rivers like the Salmon in Idaho use Dutch ovens to provide elaborate cuisine for their clients, as do commercial hunting guide operations.

In farming communities and on ranches, another distinctive regional food practice continues: the groaning-board harvest feast. Such "feeds" feature stick-to-your-ribs foods, including large servings of whatever is being harvested or rounded up. Young women who come to college in eastern Idaho report that it seems odd to them, along about mid-September, not to be paring spuds all one weekend in anticipation of thirty for potato salad, to be served out of doors on plank and sawhorse tables, just as Annie Pike Greenwood would have served it. An American Studies scholar in Wyoming who visited a roundup feed reports that pie is still a huge draw there; he tells of cowboys digging into pie as soon as they sat down and being chided by the cooks.

Mormon foodways also constitute a distinctive subcultural presence in the region. Mormons live by "The Word of Wisdom," principles set down a hundred years ago, including instructions not to drink alcohol, coffee, or tea. Mormons tend to have very large families, and they frequently gather in large groups for social activities connected with church. They are also instructed to tithe, so working-class or middle-class Saints who take their religion literally must be frugal. Out of these factors have come distinctive food practices, which Mormons themselves acknowledge and tease about. Women are told that homemaking and care for their family is a sacred duty, that home-cooked food is a symbol of industriousness. Mormon cookbooks are thus full of recipes for bread, for thrifty casseroles that use leftovers efficiently, and for home-canned products. Given contemporary pressures on LDS women's time, however, the ideal of homemade seems to be increasingly honored in appearance: Utah is the second largest market in the nation for Rhodes Frozen Bread Dough. Mormons are also famous for their consumption of jello—a cheap food easily expandable for large groups—and for their sweet tooths. Ice cream parlors abound in Utah ("It's the only vice we're allowed to have," one Mormon woman explained), and sweet drinks are popular. Nearly every Mormon gathering offers red or green punch, and Salt Lake City consumes the most canned soda pop in the country.

Drinking and Eating Out

Though the Mormon church does forbid alcohol, Utah's laws concerning alcohol have changed in recent years, due in part to Salt Lake City's bid for the Olympics and in part to gentile immigration and pressure. Twenty years ago, if one ate in a restaurant where liquor was available, one had to leave the table and go to a small, speak-easy-like "liquor store" window to buy alcohol. Now, liquor by the drink can be ordered from the wait-staff if one is ordering food. To drink hard liquor in a bar, though, one must still join an individual "private club"; short-term "memberships" are available for a price. Low-alcohol 3.2 can be had in bars without such requirements; these range

Cook lifting lid full of coals from dutch oven used for baking bread in Montana, 1937. Courtesy of the Library of Congress.

from abysmally depressing lounges in downtown Salt Lake City to upscale establishments in ski towns. Brew pubs can sell beer produced on the premises; the airport in Salt Lake City and resorts/convention centers follow yet other regulations. Although hard liquor by the bottle is only available in state-run stores, microbreweries are a booming business in Utah these days. These include the amusingly named St. Provo Girl, and Polygamy Porter ("Why have just one?" the billboards proclaim).

Most Rocky Mountain states have much simpler alcohol sales laws. While all but Colorado have embraced tougher federal standards for drunk driving (Colorado's holdout seems to be inspired more by states' rights sentiment than by tolerance for booziness), alcohol consumption practices in some parts of the Rocky Mountain West might surprise those from other regions. Wyoming, for instance, has drive-through liquor stores. In Montana, small children can go into bars (though not, of course, drink alcohol); one sees them merrily shooting pool, playing hide and seek around the tables, or even (though this is forbidden) slyly slipping nickels into slot machines, as their parents talk with neighbors. Somehow, this scene usually seems companionable, and in the tiniest towns, such bars appear to serve as community centers that happen to serve alcohol. Things used to be even looser; twenty years ago, an establishment in southwestern Montana featured a natural hot springs pool under the same roof as a full bar, and one could stroll across the Astroturf, grab a beer, and take it into the water. It called itself a "bar and plunge."

As suggested above, brewpubs have come to the Rocky Mountain West; nearly every ski town has one, as do most towns of any size. They frequently include local references in their business names, like Bozeman's Spanish Peaks Brewery. Wine bars are not as numerous, but more appear every year, especially in resort towns like Coeur d'Alene and Jackson Hole.

Restaurants

Sad to say, generic "American" food, pizza, and fast food still dominate regional dining options. Many medium-sized towns do have "bistros," but they are typically pretentious, eager to tell the rubes who dine there about every ingredient, while serving clichéd, mediocre food. Some large sections of states are nearly devoid of what a foodie might consider worthwhile restaurants: The recent guidebook *Culinary Colorado*, for instance, completely omits eastern Colorado from its chapter headings. Still, some very good restaurant dining is available, and the scene is improving. Restaurant options tend to be best, as one might expect, in the region's largest cities; the Denver/Boulder area, in particular. There, besides steakhouses, wild game restaurants, seafood places, and ethnic restaurants of many stripes, one can find the best of "fancy" dining: inventive cuisine that pays attention to ingredients, prepared by talented, skilled chefs who take chances. Kevin Taylor and The Fourth Story in Denver and Q in Boulder are among such places. Boulder also includes those rarest of restaurants in this meat-loving region, vegetarian.

Other Rocky Mountain cities, too, have their gems, and one can find inventive cooking in places like Missoula, Boise, Salt Lake City, and even Livingston, Montana. Ski towns hold some of the region's best dining rooms, like Aspen's Conundrum, Vail's The Wildflower, Deer Valley, Utah's Mariposa, and Sun Valley's Ketchum Grill. Some of the most endearing restaurants are in old hotels, like the Gallatin Gateway Inn, near Bozeman, and Red Lodge's The Pollard. Good, solid supper club–style steakhouses distinguish themselves from the horde, like Laramie's Cavalryman, with its wagon-bed salad bar, giant cuts of beef, and creme-de-menthe-drizzled ice cream sundaes. Even some cafes that look ordinary from the outside can serve up delicious food, especially at breakfast.

Retail Stores and Farmer's Markets

Raw-material food availability is becoming better in the region—though it, too, is stratified by place, and one shouldn't count on walking into a supermarket in, say, Burley, Idaho, or Beaver, Utah, and finding fresh fish or arugula. Some stores are changing that, however, where the market will bear variety. Wild Oats, Whole Foods, and Real Foods Markets offer organic meat, fabulous produce, and deli salads worth eating in some cities, including Missoula and Salt Lake City; Boise's twenty-year-old Co-op has moved well beyond the diet-for-a-small-planet stage to include an extensive olive oil, vinegar, meat, imported food, and wine selection. One can spend many happy hours in Denver's Cook's Fresh Market and Marczyk Fine Foods. Even outside of the region's hippest towns, demand for better raw ingredients is apparently growing: Some ordinary Albertsons now stock such things as radicchio and blood oranges.

Denver's farmer's market, c. 1882. Courtesy of the Denver Public Library.

Specialty stores also exist, pilgrimage sites to regional foodies. Fine international and local cheeses, for example, are available at Longmont, Colorado's Cheese Importers store, where one can ogle whole wheels and graze samples as long as one can stand the temperature in the giant cooler; a more homey but equally delicious selection is available at Logan, Utah's Gossner Foods. Specialty produce markets, like Salt Lake City's Liberty Heights Fresh, have appeared in the Rocky Mountain region. Fine butcher shops have a much longer tradition here, in Denver, but also in places like Ennis, Montana, as do ethnic bakeries, like Joe's Pasty Shop in Butte.

Food Producers

The Rocky Mountain region today supports extensive food production, with the region's traditional products forming the industry's backbone. Potatoes dominate commercial food production in Idaho, with 413,000 acres under cultivation, and communities near processing plants smell like French fries. Among the largest potato-processing corporations is the J. R. Simplot Company, named for its founder, who dehydrated potatoes during World War II, then began freezing them for the fast-food industry. Wheat and other grains are also big business, with nearly 65 million bushels of wheat produced in Montana in 2003. Coors, in Golden, Colorado, is the largest brewery centered in the region, but Anheuser Busch also maintains plants. Lentil and dried pea production has prospered in Idaho, which now holds more than a quarter of the land devoted to lentil production nationwide. Though demand for beet sugar has slackened somewhat, the business is still viable in the Rocky Mountain region; in 2002, a group of 120 growers and investors from the Big Horn Basin and Fremont County in Wyoming were feeling bullish enough about the market to buy a plant in Worland with the capacity to process 3,250 tons of sugar beets a day and rechristen it with its original 1916 name, Wyoming Sugars.

The region is also full of livestock concerns—15,000 beef producers in Colorado alone, according to the Colorado Beef Council. Lamb is an important retail product in the Rocky Mountain West, and ranchers have been working aggressively to find markets for their meat. The producer-owned Mountain States Lamb and Wool Cooperative recently announced a partnership with B. Rosen and Sons, the largest supplier of lamb meat and products in the United States. Several operations in the region raise farmed buffalo, including the Montana-Wyoming Buffalo Company and the Jackson Hole Buffalo Company.

Farm-raised fish are also important, particularly in Idaho's Thousand Springs area. Several enormous concerns and some smaller ones market fresh, frozen, and smoked trout, including the Idaho Trout Company, in business for fifty years and with a capacity to process 30,000 pounds of fish a day, and Silver Creek Farms, whose smoked trout has been acclaimed by *U.S.A. Today*.

Some businesses reflect subregional particularities. Utah's Agricultural and Food Directory lists more than four dozen producers of candy and other sweets ("2 Moms in a Kitchen" in Hurricane and "Grandma Leahs" in Hooper make especially direct appeals to LDS values); the state also has many bottled-water companies, taking advantage of the state's reputation for clear mountain streams; and twenty honey farms appropriate in this official "Beehive State."

Hundreds of family businesses, indeed, produce food products throughout the region. Many use local produce. Every farmer's market, nearly every gift shop, and many crafts shops sell local jams and jellies, salsa, and flavored vinegars. Local honey is sold from northern Montana Pleasant Valley Apiaries, near Glacier National Park, to Durango's Honeyville. Even remote Dove Creek grows celebrated popcorn. Some previously small businesses have become successful enough that they have franchised themselves, like Montana's Great Harvest Bakery, which has stores from Tampa to Anchorage. Others have preferred to stay local, like Grandrud's Lefse Shack in Opheim, Montana, which produces twenty tons of flat breads from locally grown potatoes each fall and winter season.

As is true in much of the nation, wineries have proliferated in the Rocky Mountain region in recent years. Some of these are located in places where growing grapes is extremely difficult, including Missoula and Dayton, Montana; Moab, Utah; and Cheyenne. Paonia, Colorado, boasts the nation's highest elevation winery, Terror Creek, at 6,400 feet. Most wineries cluster in the region's temperate belts, however. The relatively low elevation valleys of western Idaho hold most of that state's eighteen wineries (though people are making wine in Sandpoint and Moscow). Ste. Chapelle is the largest of them and has won numerous gold and silver medals. Colorado holds about forty wineries, with concentrations on the western slope in the Grand Valley, especially near Palisade, and on the front range, encircling Denver.

FOOD FESTIVALS

Rocky Mountain residents can celebrate local products and local traditions at a daunting variety of food festivals—if one wished, one could visit a different festival nearly every weekend of the year and not leave the region. Most of these are sweet old-timey celebrations of locally famous types of produce, complete with queens, small parades, and homemade food for sale. Bear Lake, on the Idaho-Utah border, for instance, has an annual raspberry festival, as do the Sisters of St. Gertrude up north in Cottonwood, Idaho; Shelley, Idaho, holds a potato festival; Palisade, Colorado, a peach festival. Utah may be the most food festival–rich state; its offerings include Payson's Onion Days, Green River's Melon Days, Moroni's Turkey Days, and Richmond's Black and White Days (named for the markings of the Cache Valley's dairy cows).

Some towns in the region offer festivals of a different sort. Telluride holds an annual mushroom festival, which draws both countercultural throwbacks, the extremely rich, actual mushroom specialists, and those who simply like to eat. The August event includes foraging sessions, classes, a parade where participants dress as their favorite mushrooms, and a grand concluding feast. Vail holds a pro-am duck confit cook-off in August and the extravagant festival Taste of Vail

Contestants eat pies without using their hands during an Independence Day pie-eating contest at the Center Creek Meeting House in Utah. © James L. Amos/Corbis.

in March–April. Aspen counters with the three-day *Food and Wine* Magazine Classic in June, one of the most important culinary events in the nation. One of the odder of the region's conspicuous-consumption festivals takes place in Keystone, Colorado, where every Christmas a master chocolatier creates Chocolateville, a carved mountain and alpine village constructed from hundreds of pounds of chocolate. On a much rowdier note, Butte's St. Patrick's Day party is long running and famous; an hour away on the same day, Wolf Creek, Montana, holds its Wild Game Feed, where one can sample bear meatloaf and mountain lion strips along with more mundane offerings.

The region also includes festivals celebrating beverages. Beer festivals, like Steamboat Springs Brewfest and Snowbird, Utah's Oktoberfest, have proliferated. Wine festivals exist, too. The oldest of them is Telluride's, which began in 1981 and has grown to feature more than seventy wineries, talks with master sommeliers, and classes by distinguished chefs. The newest as of this writing began in 2003, when eight wineries in Colorado's Grand Valley collaborated to host that region's first spring barrel tasting event.

THE FUTURE OF ROCKY MOUNTAIN FOODWAYS: CONTROVERSIES AND TRENDS

All appearances suggest, thus, that modern distribution systems, industrial agricultural practices, and increased population density and disposable income have banished the issue of scarcity from Rocky Mountain foodways. For most people (the hungry poor aside), this is true in terms of daily eating habits. But several controversies have continued to spark debate in the region, and an observer will find that they are rooted, if he or she looks closely enough, in questions about management of limited resources. Water rights and dam construction, grazing allotments, chemical pollution and poor farming practices, issues of wildlife management—all have forced many citizens of the Rocky Mountain region to consider how they are using their land. In the last few decades, some residents have begun to respond to that challenge, and their efforts—to use land-friendly agricultural practices, to consume locally grown food, to maintain regional identity in the face of national homogenization—are among the most encouraging and interesting trends in the foodways of the Rocky Mountain region.

Water

Irrigation has been crucial to food production in the Rocky Mountain West, and it has spawned many of the region's hardest-fought battles. Local historical lore suggests that prior appropriation water laws were frequently end-run, even in small ditch systems. Family histories tell of men sitting on headgates with guns, making sure that their neighbors did not shut them; they report angry confrontations when people waited their turns, then found no water coming because neighbors had taken more than their share. Even when farmers did not cheat, those downstream sometimes had no water in dry years. Currently, agricultural water users are facing new criticism from recreational interests. Southern Idaho's Snake River, for instance, has renowned stretches of rapids like the Murtaugh section that in recent years have often been unrunnable, all year long, because of agricultural diversion. It seems only a matter of time before the hard words now being said become more formal challenges.

One of the most volatile battles in water use has concerned the region's Native Americans. Treaties that sent Indians to reservations noted that they were to become "pastoral and agricultural" peoples, but when government-sponsored irrigation projects began, water was diverted away from reservations. The first case to test this practice came in northern Montana in the first decade of the twentieth century; to the amazement of "apoplectic settlers," the Indians won. Appeals blunted the effect of the decision, however, and though the Bureau of Indian Affairs (BIA) has planned numerous irrigation works to benefit tribes, funds have never been sufficiently appropriated. "We began our first irrigation project in 1867, and we've never finished one yet," a BIA official told a U.S. Senate Select Committee on Indian Affairs in 1990.[17] Some tribes have succeeded in finding justice, as the Shoshone-Bannocks did with the 1996 Fort Hall Water Rights Settlement, but more have found injustice, as did the Utes, who agreed to the Central Utah Project on the stipulation that they would benefit from one of its dams, then were told that part of the project was too expensive. That case is still being contested; the Utes were given a settlement payment and decisions have suggested that they have rights to the water from the project, but water continues to flow into the Central Utah Project. If the tribe decides to, say, sell the water to the highest bidder (and officials have met with the city of Las Vegas), irrigated agriculture in some parts of Utah could be in big trouble.

The debate over what to do about the region's depleted salmon runs is another water-based issue. In the nineteenth century, salmon swam up the undammed Columbia River and its tributaries into Idaho, spawning by the thousands in areas like the Sawtooth Mountain country, turning lakes and streams red. Pioneers tell of gathering fish with their hands, they were so numerous—who needed a hook and line? By the 1970s, though, only a few salmon were returning to the high mountain lakes where thousands had once congregated. The reason was the dams lining the Columbia and Snake, biologists said, along with pollution from farms and logging. Dam-breaching became a hot topic in the region; farmers argued that they would be bankrupted; environmentalists called for immediate action; Native Americans were arrested as they fished out of season, insisting on ancestral rights. What has happened is a compromise, a work-in-progress involving fish ladders that seems to be at least partly successful, for more salmon runs are up somewhat.

Grazing and Animal Rights

Another controversy with implications for food production involves grazing on the region's public lands. Ranchers have always used public lands in the West, at first running their stock on unsettled, unregulated lands in the nineteenth and early twentieth centuries, then paying fees under the 1934 Taylor Grazing Act, which allowed them to use rangelands for a per-animal-unit price.

Today, many people are unhappy about public lands grazing. Recreationists complain about cows fouling land and crowding the trails even of high peaks. Biologists document riparian damage, where cattle congregating at streams strip vegetation and cause crumbling banks. Water flows more slowly, temperatures rise, and fish die; wildlife that depends on stream-side vegetation finds no food. On too heavily grazed land, too, biologists warn, natural movement toward plant diversity is halted, and pest populations like grasshoppers can thrive. The grazing program doesn't even pay for itself, some critics have noted: In 1989, the Forest Service earned $11 million from grazing fees and spent $35 million to manage the range.

Challenging public land grazing is vexing, however, because ranchers argue that they could not afford to raise stock if they had to pay for grazing on private land, raise all feed themselves, or pay higher fees. They point to small operations going out of business and say that family ranches are the real endangered species. Feelings run high about the issue: A few years ago, Wyoming ranchers closed their lands to hunters from Georgia, Massachusetts, and Oklahoma, home states to congressmen who favored increased grazing fees. Speaking out publicly against public grazing can also can be dangerous: A southern Idaho forest ranger who suggested to the *New York Times* that the number of cattle on public lands be reduced received death threats. More radical critics, like Earth First activists, have cut fences and vandalized water supplies in an effort to sabotage the cattle industry. To say that the issue is volatile is to understate vastly.

Another regional controversy related to stock raising has received national press in recent years: the brucellosis debate. Cattlemen fear brucellosis, a disease that can cause cows to abort their calves, decimating herds. In the 1980s, it was discovered that some bison living in Yellowstone National Park were infected with brucellosis. Everyone who lived on the park's borders knew that bison roamed outside the official boundaries, and ranchers panicked, fearful that their cows would catch the disease. They convinced officials to let them destroy the wandering buffalo. It was never proven that bison could transmit the disease to cows, and elk (which can carry the disease) were coming and going freely, but between 1985 and 1990, 700 bison were shot. Public outcry against the practice led to its curtailment, but not before much anger on both sides.

Even more incendiary is the issue of wolf reintroduction. Wolves are back in Yellowstone, and they have also been reintroduced in other areas remote from human concerns. Wolves *will* get around, however, and they have been spotted killing stock. Ranchers shoot them when this happens, setting off the predictable debate. "If it gets in the way, shoot it, poison, or trap it—that's the Cowboy Way," opponents sneer. "Our livelihood is at stake," the ranchers insist.

Now and then, small groups of residents in the Rocky Mountain West will advance that most radical idea in the region, the assertion that one should not eat any meat at all. In Boulder, among cohort groups in some college towns and more liberal circles, this is accepted, but to the larger population it seems like sedition. In Pocatello, Idaho, for instance, during the summer of 2003, someone painted "Moo! Please don't eat us!" on a butcher-shop highway sign. As soon as the slogan was noticed, a local radio station featured a call-in rally to register public indignation, and sentiment was lively, to say the least.

Pollution and Damaging Land-Use Practices

During the early years of settlement in the Rocky Mountain region, virtually no one worried about pollution or damaging land-use practices. The country seemed just too big, too rich in resources, too tough; if damage was done, one could always move on. In the twentieth century, however, residents have had to face the fact that the region does have finite resources and that misuse can have long-range effects on food-producing capacity.

Mining has had particularly serious consequences. Placer mining, which plowed up stream beds, disrupted fish populations from the 1860s in places like Idaho's Yankee Fork. Some individual mines have caused ongoing problems: Above Cooke City, Montana, the McLaren Mine, which drained red iron-laden water, has sterilized Soda Butte Creek in Yellowstone National Park for nearly 100 years. Bigger operations have caused wider-ranging consequences. Arsenic, lead, cadmium, and mercury from Butte's mines have sterilized long sections of the Clark Fork River and Silver Bow Creek; the town's Berkeley Pit, filling up steadily, is predicted to contaminate the area's aquifer within ten years if corrective steps are not taken.

Some agricultural practices, too, have damaged habitat. Agricultural chemicals have killed birds and wild food plants; they have leached into streams and destroyed fish. In places, too, agricultural practices have ruined farmland itself. In some fields in eastern Montana, for instance, saline seeps have appeared, caused when land with an impenetrable underground shale layer is farmed by crop rotation. Shallow-rooted crops cannot reach deeply, and water gathers above the shale, absorbing soluble salts, then moves along the layer to pool in toxic concentrations. New agricultural techniques are being developed to prevent such problems, but the reminder is clear, as it was when 1920s plowing caused horrific erosion in Colorado: This land is delicate, and one treats it cavalierly at one's own peril.

One land-use practice rooted paradoxically in infatuation with the region also has troubling implications for its food production: residential subdivision. In pockets of the region with glamorous scenery—most famously western Montana but also the Wood River Valley and Jackson Hole—wealthy people are building expensive homes on what could be food-producing land. The twenty counties that form the Greater Yellowstone region were the fastest-growing part of the United States between 1969 and 1989, and the trend is continuing. Farmers and ranchers in such places say that they were marginally making livings in the best of times and that, as land values and taxes have risen, they cannot afford to make livings now. Homesteads and vast ranches are thus being sold off. The same thing is happening on the outskirts of many western communities, where new developments cluster, often without review, since they are beyond city limits; an estimate puts 90 percent of suburban growth around Missoula in that category. "The West is up for grabs," one environmental historian has declared.[18] Beyond farm- and ranch land availability, new developments tax water resources and may involve pollution, contributing to larger problems in resource management.

Trends in Food Production

Despite the controversies and difficulties facing food production in the Rocky Mountain region, the past few decades have seen some encouraging trends. One of these is the movement toward locally grown and produced food. Montana is a leader in this respect: AERO (Alternative Energy Resources Organization, a grassroots, nonprofit organization concerned with fostering the development of sustainable communities in the rural Rocky Mountain West and Northern Plains) is headquartered in Helena. Its "Abundant Montana" directory lists dozens of state producers committed to careful land stewardship and local marketing. "Local," of course, is relative in this vast area ("If it's grown in Montana, it's local," one article about the state's "food renaissance" remarked). Still, the riches available—organic lamb, Highland beef, spearmint, lentils in many colors, mushrooms, cherries—are amazing. Producers in other areas are also committed to organic farming: Colorado is among the top states nationwide in acreage devoted to the practice, and Idaho has an enthusiastic organization beginning to spread the word in that state. Numerous small businesses in the Rocky Mountain region are committed to small-batch production and careful land stewardship, and some have won national fame for their work, like Fort Collins' Bingham Hill Artisan Cheeses.

Much of this locally produced and organic food is showing up in farmers' markets, one of the nicest trends for the region's residents. Food availability and variety have been transformed in some places by such markets: In high, dry Laramie, for instance, the farmer's market on a frigid Labor Day weekend in 2003 offered sweet peaches and cherries from the western slope of Colorado, boutique goat cheese, and peppers roasting to order in a New Mexico–style drum over an open flame. Farmers' markets are places to "meet the producer," as slogans say; they can also be celebrations of very local essence. Almost every stall in Boulder offers organic produce, while Butte's market is held on a closed-off city block among the bars and shops, like a weekly market in an Italian town.

Another trend is for restaurants and markets to use local produce. Montana is, again, a self-conscious leader in this movement; besides the hip towns where one would expect such a thing to happen, the AERO directory lists many less-predictable resources, including Rueb's Super Value, in Plentywood. Up and down the Rockies, fine restaurants are being joined by modest cafes in their commitment to eating regionally.

CONCLUSION

Foodways in the Rocky Mountain region have evolved significantly over the past hundred years and are still evolving, coming full circle, one might say, back to the idea that smaller local production might be better, that whole foods are preferable, and that eating seasonally is a good idea. Those who knew the region twenty years ago will say that they are able to eat much better here now. At the same time, old-time tastes and traditions hang on, and those who prefer well-done meat and potatoes, jello, spanokopita, lefsa, or railroad Chinese can be happy, too.

The region is going to be in for trouble, though, if residents continue to act as if this were a place like every other. The climate can still threaten food production: Severe drought in 2003 had the Montana Agricultural Statistics Services reporting that 70 percent of the state's farmland was very short of moisture; 59 percent of its range and pastureland was rated in "poor" or "very poor" condition, with just 12 percent "good" and 1 percent "excellent." Residents' own practices can deplete our food resources, killing fish, destroying wildlife habitats, closing potentially productive land.

As those who love the region and call it home raise a glass of regionally produced Pinot Noir over a supper of garden chard and organic lamb—or a Budweiser over elk chili and Jiffy-mix cornbread—all must vow to pay attention to the lovely place that feeds them, this tough and fragile place that is their home.

RESOURCE GUIDE

Printed Sources

Adams, Ramon F. *Come and Get It: The Story of the Old Cowboy Cook*. Norman: University of Oklahoma Press, 1952.

Alternate Resources Energy Organization (AERO). *Abundant Montana*. Helena: AERO, 2003.

Conlin, Joseph R. *Bacon, Beans, and the Galatines: Food and Foodways on the Western Mining Frontier*. Reno: University of Nevada Press, 1986.

Daughters of Utah Pioneers. *The Mormon Pioneer Cookbook*. Salt Lake City, UT: Northwest Publishing, 1995.

Hart, Jeff. *Montana Plants and Early Peoples*. Helena: Montana Historical Society Press, 1992.

Idaho Historical Auxiliary. *Historical Treasures from Idaho Kitchens*. Boise: Idaho Historical Auxiliary, 1967.

Julander, Paula, and Joanne Milner. *Utah State Fare: A Centennial Recipe Collection*. Salt Lake City, UT: Deseret Book Co., 1995.

McGrath, Jean, ed. *Butte Heritage Cookbook*. Butte, MT: Ashcraft Printers, 1976.

Nickey, Louise K. *Cooking of the Prairie Homesteader*. Beaverton, OR: Touchstone Press, 1976.

Rawlings, Marla. *Favorite Utah Pioneer Recipes*. Bountiful, UT: Horizon Publishers, 2000.

Robbins, Jim. *Last Refuge: The Environmental Showdown in Yellowstone and the American West*. New York: William Morrow, 1993.

Scrimsher, Leda Scott. "Native Foods Used by the Nez Percé Indians of Idaho." Master's thesis, University of Idaho, 1967.

Sublette County Learning Centers. *1890–1990 Wyoming Centennial, a Lusty Legacy Commemorative Cookbook*. Pinedale, WY: Sublette County Learning Centers, 1990.

Voight, William, Jr. *Public Grazing Lands: Use and Misuse by Industry and Government*. New Brunswick, NJ: Rutgers University Press, 1976.

Walter, Claire. *Culinary Colorado*. Golden, CO: Fulcrum Publishing, 2003.

Williams, Jacqueline. *Wagon Wheel Kitchens: Food on the Oregon Trail*. Lawrence: University of Kansas Press, 1993.

Wyoming Recreation Commission. *Cooking in Wyoming* (Women's Suffrage Centennial Edition 1869–1969). Casper, WY: Bighorn Book Co., 1969.

Web Sites

Colorado Farm Fresh Directory
State of Colorado Department of Agriculture, accessed June 22, 2004
http://www.ag.state.co.us/mkt/farmfresh/welcome.html

Colorado state government–supported site listing farms and other agricultural producers in that state.

Farmers Markets Directory by State
Chef2Chef Culinary Portal, accessed June 22, 2004
http://marketplace.chef2chef.net/farmer-markets/

Site listing farmers' markets nationwide, including the Rocky Mountain region.

Festivals
epodunk: the power of place, accessed June 22, 2004
http://www.epodunk.com/festivals/

Web site organized by a group of journalists that provides information about 25,000 communities nationwide, with a listing of festivals by state and month.

Utah Agriculture and Food Directory
Utah Department of Agriculture and Food, accessed June 22, 2004
http://www.ag.utah.gov/mktcons/AgDirectory2003.pdf

Utah state government–supported site listing small businesses in the state that are food related.

Utah Events Calendar
Utah Division of Travel Development, accessed June 22, 2004
http://travel.utah.gov/festivalsevents.html

Utah state government—supported site listing the state's major events and festivals, including food-related events.

Videos/Films

Heartland. Prod. Beth Ferris and Michael Hausman. Dir. Richard Pearce. Perf. Rip Torn, Conchata Ferrell. Filmhaus. 1979.

Events

Bear Lake Raspberry Festival
Greater Bear Lake Valley Chamber of Commerce
Garden City, UT 84028
1-800-448-BEAR
http://www.bearlake.org/calendar.html

Held annually in August.

Black and White Days
Cache Valley Chamber of Commerce

Richmond, UT 84333
435-258-0510

Held annually in May since 1913.
Stock show, parade, quilt show, dairy foods contest.

Butte St. Patrick's Day Celebration
Butte-Silver Bow Chamber of Commerce
1000 George
Butte, MT 59701
800-735-6814

Held annually March 17.
Parade, corned beef and cabbage, beer.

Food and Wine Magazine Classic at Aspen
1120 Avenue of the Americas
New York, NY 10036
212-382-5600
http://www.foodandwine.com/ext/classic/index.html

Held annually in mid-June.
Seminars, dinners, tastings, chef demonstrations, awards.

Grand Valley Spring Barrel Tasting
Grand Valley Winery Association
P. O. Box 99
Palisade, CO 81526-0099
970-464-5867
http://www.winebarreltasting.com/

Two-day May event begun in 2002.

Palisade Peach Fest
c/o Palisade Chamber of Commerce
319 Main St.
P. O. Box 729
Palisade, CO 81526
970-464-7458
http://www.palisadepeachfest.com/

Three-day event held annually in August.

Payson Onion Days
Payson, UT 84651
435-465-5200
http://www.payson.org/OnionDays.shtml

Held annually in September.

St. Gertrude's Raspberry Festival
Monastery of St. Gertrude
Cottonwood, ID 83522-9408
http://www.StGertrudes.org/

One-day event held annually in early August.
Homemade raspberry shortcake with berries from the monastery garden.

St. Ignazio Festival (St. Ignatius)
Basque Center

601 Grove St.
Boise, ID 83702
208-342-9983
http://www.basquecenter.com/

Weekend event held annually in late July.

Shelley Spud Days
Shelley, ID 83274

Held annually in September.
Parade, free baked potatoes, world championship potato picking contest.

Taste of Vail
P. O. Box 5663
Vail, CO 81658
888-311-5665
http://www.tasteofvail.com/

Held annually in March–April.
Founder's dinner, Grand Tasting, seminars related to food and wine.

Telluride Mushroom Festival
Fungophile
P. O. Box 480503
Denver, CO 80248-0503
http://www.shroomfestival.com

Held annually in late August.
Includes foraging expeditions, meals, parade, workshops.

Organizations

AERO (Alternative Energy Resources Organization)
432 North Last Chance Gulch Street
Helena, MT 59601
406-443-7272
http://www.aeromt.org/

Basque Museum and Cultural Center
611 Grove Street
Boise, ID 83702
208-343-2671
http://www.basquemuseum.com/

Colorado Organic Producers Association
Jim Dyer
2727 CR 134
Hesperus, CO 81326
970-588-2292
http://www.organiccolorado.org/

Huntley Project Museum of Irrigated Agriculture
770 Highway 312
P. O. Box 353
Huntley, MT 59037
406-967-2881
http://www.huntleyprojectmuseum.org/

Idaho Farm and Ranch Museum
220 North Lincoln
Jerome, ID 83338
208-324-5641

Living history and exhibits.

Idaho Organic Alliance
Rebecca Mirsky
P. O. Box 8625
Boise, ID 83707
208-440-7161
http://www.idahoorganicalliance.com/

Idaho World Potato Exposition
130 N. W. Main Street
Blackfoot, ID 83221
208-785-2517
www.potatoexpo.com/main.htm

Museum devoted to the history of potatoes and potato growing, with "free [baked] taters to out-of-staters."

Wyoming State Museum
2301 Cheyenne Avenue
Cheyenne, WY 82002
307-777-7022
http://www.wyomuseum.state.wyo/

Had a traveling exhibit titled "It Takes Weather, Water, and Work: Farming in Wyoming" (2002).

LANGUAGE

Lamont Antieau

As a part of the American West, the Rocky Mountain region has differed from the eastern regions of the United States in many ways, and among these differences has been its linguistic situation. The region has been home to numerous Native American languages of the Rocky Mountains and the Great Plains (some of which are still spoken on reservations scattered throughout the region); speakers of Spanish have inhabited the region longer than they have most other areas of the United States; and speakers of some languages, notably Basque, have populated the region in much greater numbers than they have the eastern states. Furthermore, the relatively recent introduction of American English to the region, and its use by some groups that are perhaps more characteristic of the West than the eastern United States, such as ranchers, miners, and Mormons, has created a variety of American English reflecting the diversity and the ongoing development of the Rocky Mountain region.

NATIVE AMERICAN LANGUAGES

Background

Long before the European colonization of North America, various Native American tribes inhabited the Rocky Mountain region. By 1500 B.C.E., the Anasazi had developed a complex society in the Four Corners region of southwestern Colorado. North of the Anasazi settlement, the Fremont people lived in Colorado and Utah from about 1 C.E. Both cultures disappeared in the fourteenth century. It is believed that the Anasazi abandoned their dwellings and migrated to the south, joining tribes of Zuni and Pueblo in what is now New Mexico and Arizona, while the Fremont were assimilated into the Ute and Shoshone tribes that had entered the area searching for food. Although a great deal of study has been done on these groups and is being conducted today on the cultural artifacts they left behind—

Native American Linguistic Studies

The recording and analysis of Native American languages began with French and Spanish missionaries in the early 1500s and has continued to be an important part of linguistic work, especially in the early twentieth century with the work of such linguists as Leonard Bloomfield, Franz Boas, James Crawford, Mary Haas, Edward Sapir, and Morris Swadesh. Work continues in the documentation and analysis of Native American languages, for instance, by Pamela Munro and her students at the University of California, Los Angeles, as well as in the classification of Native American languages. The indigenous languages of the Americas have been some of the most difficult to categorize according to this method, due to their great number, the complexity of relations between tribes, and the paucity of written data.

most notably in the cliff dwellings of Mesa Verde—little is known about the languages they spoke.

By the time of European exploration of the Rocky Mountains, many tribes inhabiting the region had only recently migrated to the area in search of buffalo on the western plains and as a reaction to persistent westward migration by Anglo-Americans. Warfare among various Native American tribes also contributed to the movement of various tribes into the region.

This section will provide a sketch of the more significant Native American languages that have inhabited, and some that continue to inhabit, the Rocky Mountain region. The discussion will largely follow popular classifications of Native American languages and will also include a discussion of languages that are considered "genetic isolates" because of the lack of evidence for any historical relationship between them and other languages of the area.

Algonquian

Distributed throughout the eastern and central United States and Canada, and comprising such tribes as the Cree, Fox, and Ojibway, the Algonquian (or Algonkian) family forms one of the largest groups of Native Americans and includes many of the first Native Americans encountered by early French and British explorers of North America. In the Rocky Mountain region, the Algonquian family was primarily represented by the Arapaho, Blackfoot, Cheyenne, and Cree. The Arapaho and the Cheyenne originally inhabited Minnesota and formed an alliance before being uprooted by tribes of Sioux and Ojibway and moving first to North Dakota and then to the eastern plains of Colorado and Wyoming. The Blackfoot occupied the Snake River country in Idaho, as well as the Three Forks of the Missouri River in Montana and Wyoming, and the Cree inhabited parts of Montana, North Dakota, and central Canada. Not to be confused with the Hidatsa people of North Dakota, a Siouan tribe with which they share the same French name, the Gros Ventre, or Atsina, is an Algonquian tribe that apparently split from the Arapaho in the early eighteenth century and is now settled in Montana.

Like many other Native American languages, languages of the Algonquian family are considered to be polysynthetic, capable of affixing many small grammatical or semantic units (called morphemes) to root words to convey in a single word what in English and many other languages would require an entire sentence. For example, the Blackfoot word *nitáakahkayi* translates into "I'm going home." Algonquian languages use suffixing to distinguish between two grammatical genders of nouns—animate, which comprises humans, animals, plants, and spirits, and inanimate; they also employ suffixes in a phenomenon called obviation, which serves as a way to distinguish whether third-person referents are being used for the first time in a conversation or have been mentioned in previous discourse.

The greatest number of Algonquian speakers in the Rocky Mountain region are speakers of Cheyenne, with just over 1,700 speakers.[1] They reside primarily in western Oklahoma and on the Northern Cheyenne Reservation in southeastern Montana. Approximately 1,000 speakers of Arapaho live in Wyoming, where they share the Wind River Reservation with the Shoshone, and Oklahoma, where they live with the Cheyenne. There are just over 1,000 speakers of Cree living in Montana, but another 30,000 live in Canada, and approximately 1,000 Blackfoot speakers reside primarily on the Blackfeet Reservation in Montana. There are about 200 speakers of Shawnee, most of them living in Oklahoma. About 100 speakers of Atsina live with the Assiniboine at Fort Belknap Reservation in Montana. Although primarily a language of central Canada and midwestern United States, Ojibway (or Chippewa) is also spoken to some extent on the Rocky Boys Reservation (which they share with the Cree) in Montana. Both Plains Cree and Ojibway, as well as a Plains Indian sign language, were at one time used as *lingua francas* among various tribes of the Plains region.

Athapascan

Of the Native American language families of the Rocky Mountain region, only the Athapascan is not considered a member of the large Amerind family proposed by linguist Joseph Greenberg, who instead classifies it as part of the Na-Dene family of languages. The Athapascan family comprises Tlingit and other languages of the Pacific Northwest, as well as Apache and Navajo, which is by far the most commonly spoken Native American language with approximately 150,000 speakers throughout the Southwest. Originating in Canada, Navajo apparently began moving in the 1400s, traveling along the edge of the Great Plains and arriving in southwestern Colorado, where they raided Pueblo villages for food and slaves. Eventually the Navajo learned to farm from the Pueblo Indians and to raise livestock from the Spanish. Apache is another Athapascan language spoken in the Rocky Mountain region and includes the Jicarilla Apache in Colorado.

Athapascan languages are characterized as tonal because they use contrasting tones to create differences in meaning in a manner similar to such languages as Chinese and Vietnamese. Navajo has a complex verbal morphology and primarily uses prefixation rather than suffixation to derive new words. Syntactically, Athapascan languages are considered subject-object-verb, but they allow for movement of any noun phrase to the beginning of the sentence, a phenomenon known as *topicalization* and exemplified by an English sentence like "Dogs, I like."

Nearly 150,000 speakers of Navajo live in Arizona, Utah, and New Mexico, including over 7,500 that are monolingual. The language is noteworthy in having been used as a military code by the U.S. Army in World War II due to structural complexities in the language that would make it difficult to decode; perhaps partially due to its importance in American history, a great deal of effort has gone into preserving the language and culture. Speakers of Jicarilla Apache number about 800 and live primarily in New Mexico. Fewer than 20 Kiowa Apache live in western Oklahoma, but about 12,000 Western Apache live on reservations in Arizona.

Sahaptin

The Sahaptin language family is a family of the Pacific Northwest that includes Nez Percé, which at one time was a relatively common Native American language with a geographical distribution from the Blue Mountains in Oregon to the Bitterroot Range in northern Idaho. They also lived sporadically in Montana and Wyoming.

Reduplication in Nez Percé is frequent and is typically used to convey distributive properties, as in the partial reduplications *háma*/"man"—*háham*/"men"; *hácwal*/"son"—*hahácwal*/"sons," or diminutive properties, as in the total reduplications *témul*/"hail"—*temultémul*/"sleet."

Although still comprising the greatest number of speakers among related tribes of the Sahaptin languages, only around 700 speakers of Nez Percé remain, primarily in northern Idaho.

Salish

A large family of languages in the Pacific Northwest, the Salishan family includes Bella Coola and Kalispel. The languages furthest east are called Interior Salish and include a group of related dialects called Kalispel-Spokane-Flathead, which are distantly related to Algonquian. The Flatheads were named for the custom among some Salishan tribes to engage in head flattening.

Salishan languages are known for having elaborate consonant inventories that include a variety of pharyngeal consonants but a relatively small inventory of vowels. Morphologically, the languages are characterized by a heavy use of affixation, particularly in their extensive use of suffixes. Reduplication is common in the Salishan languages to show such things as plurality, repetition, intensity, and diminution. Salish languages also use an affixation process called *infixation*, in which a morpheme, in this case a single reduplicated consonant, is inserted into a word rather than being added onto the beginning or end of it. Syntactically, Salishan languages are verb-initial languages.

Although there are about 6,800 Kalispel–Pend d'Oreille (1997 census), only about 200 of them are first-language speakers. Many tribe members live on the mountainous Flathead Indian Reservation outside Missoula, Montana.

Siouan

One of two major families of the Great Plains of the United States, the Siouan family, which includes Assiniboine, Sioux (also known as Dakota or Lakota), and Winnebago, have a distribution from the provinces of Alberta and Saskatchewan in Canada to Montana and the Dakotas and are also spoken in Arkansas, Mississippi, and the Carolinas. Although they typically made their homes on the Plains, some Siouan tribes lived and hunted in the Rocky Mountain region. The Sioux, for instance, relocated from Minnesota and Wisconsin to the Dakotas and hunted in the eastern plains of Montana and Wyoming. The Crow were originally a tribe of Siouan farmers in the Missouri River valley but moved west to Montana in the early eighteenth century and by the early nineteenth century were based in Wyoming's Bighorn Mountains. Eventually becoming buffalo hunters, the Crow began calling themselves "bird people" to reflect their nomadic lifestyle.

One of the traits shared by languages of the Siouan family is a complex phonology that observes distinctions between consonants based on the absence or presence of aspiration, glottalization, and nasalization, as well as distinctions between vowels based on length. Siouan languages are considered agglutinating languages, and compounding is a productive means of word formation.

The Crow moved onto a reservation in southern Montana in 1868, and there are now about 4,200 speakers. Assiniboine is spoken mostly in Canada but also on the Fort Belknap and Fort Peck Reservations of Montana. There are about 15,000 speakers of Dakota and 6,000 Lakota speakers in the United States.

Tanoan

The Tanoan languages have historically been spoken among the pueblo dwellers of Arizona and New Mexico, but the northernmost of these people, the Tewa, may have lived in southern Colorado at one time as well. Most scholars also classify Kiowa as a Tanoan language, the speakers of which opted to live on the Great Plains rather than in pueblos, living in Montana prior to 1700 before moving south into the area between the Arkansas and Red Rivers.

Tanoan languages are marked by a complex system of sounds. There are distinctions between consonants on the basis of absence or presence of voicing, aspiration, and glottalization; length and nasality are distinguishing features of vowels. Tanoan languages use a great deal of affixation, and reduplication and compounding are productive word-formation devices. Kiowa has a number of differences with other Tanoan languages; for instance, it uses switch-reference anaphora; linguists are divided as to whether these differences are due to historical divergence or merely to the adaptation of the Kiowa to the culture of the Great Plains.

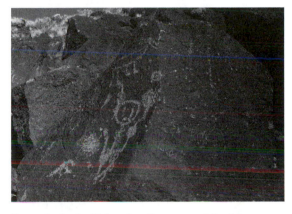

Petroglyphs in Colorado. Courtesy of Corbis.

Today, Tanoan speakers live primarily south of the Rocky Mountain region with about 1,200 Tewa (1980 census) living in Arizona and New Mexico and about 900 Northern Tiwa (1980 census) living in New Mexico; about 1,600 speakers of Southern Tiwa (1980 census) also live in New Mexico. Kiowa is spoken by about 1,000 speakers, mostly living in Oklahoma.

Uto-Aztecan

The Uto-Aztecan language family is distributed over a broad area from Oregon to Central America and includes such families as Nahuatl (or Aztec). Members of the Uto-Aztecan family in the Rocky Mountain region include Ute, who occupied the Colorado Plateau in Colorado and Utah since the 1300s before moving east onto the Plains, Northern Southern Paiute in southwestern Utah, Comanche in Colorado, Hopi, speakers of which at one time inhabited Utah but now reside primarily in Arizona, and Shoshone, who inhabited Idaho, as did the Paiute, after apparently migrating there from Nevada or Utah during the sixteenth century.

Uto-Aztecan languages are polysynthetic and have a complex verbal morphology. Reduplication and compounding are productively used in the word-formation process. For instance, in Southern Paiute, partial reduplication of an initial syllable is used to indicate that nouns or verbs are repetitive or distributive (a grammatical concept similar to plural), as exemplified by *qa'ŋ*/"house"—*qa'qa'ŋ*/"houses." Shoshone reduplication is used to show plurality in nouns and is usually initial syllable, as in *potso*/"drip"—*potsotso*/"drips." With respect to compounding, Uto-Aztecan languages primarily use noun-noun and modifier-noun compounds to derive new words. For instance, Comanche combines the nouns *puhihwi*/"money" and *kahni*/"house" to create *puhihwi-kahni*/"bank" and combines the modifier *pia*/"big" and the noun *huutsu*/"bird" to form *pia-huutsu*/"eagle."

About 5,000 Hopi reside mainly in northeast Arizona with smaller numbers in Utah and New Mexico. There are about 2,000 speakers of Shoshone, primarily on reservations at Fort Hall, Idaho, and Wind River, Wyoming. Speakers of Northern Paiute number just over 1,600 (1999 Summer Institute of Linguistics) across several western states. There are about 2,000 (1977 SIL) speakers of Ute–Southern Paiute with the Ute in Colorado and Utah, and the Southern Paiute in Utah, Arizona, and Nevada. About 850 Comanche speakers live in Oklahoma.

Isolates

Among the Native American languages of the Rocky Mountain region, at least two are considered isolates. One of these languages is Zuni, a language used at one time in southwestern Colorado and now spoken by about 6,000 (1980 census). Although generally accepted as an isolate, some scholars have classified Zuni as a Penutian language with such languages as Chinook, Nez Percé, and Choctaw, while other scholars consider it to be related to the Tanoan languages.

Another language typically characterized as an isolate is that spoken by the Kootenai (also spelled Kutenai), which comprises approximately 100 speakers who live primarily with the Salish in Idaho and on the Flathead Reservation in western Montana.

LINGUISTIC INFLUENCE OF NATIVE AMERICANS

While limited in their influence, Native American languages have had a long history of contact with European languages, and since before the British colonization of North America, Spanish and Portuguese were borrowing words from various indigenous languages throughout Mexico, the West Indies, and South and Central America. These borrowings typically pertained to foods and other goods used by indigenous peoples that Europeans were interested in commercially, such as *chocolate*, *cocoa*, and *potato*; and many of these words were later borrowed by the English language.

Since early colonists were forced to rely on Native Americans for their survival during the first years of colonization, and Americans have had prolonged and intimate contact with these people, the influence of Native American languages has come to bear more heavily on American varieties of English than on British English. As is often the case in situations of lexical borrowing, many Native American borrowings refer to the introduction of new material goods to American culture, including such words as *toboggan*, *canoe*, and *moccasin*. Many of these borrowings originally came from languages of the eastern United States, especially any of a number of Algonquian languages, which had the greatest impact on early American English due to their wide geographical distribution throughout the continent and their importance in the areas of early colonial settlement. Nevertheless, some words were apparently borrowed from the Plains Indians that later inhabited the Rocky Mountain region. For instance, the word *tepee* (also spelled *teepee* or *tipi*) was borrowed from the Sioux, as this type of temporary dwelling was typically used among Siouan and other tribes of the Great Plains. Other words that have been attributed to Native American tribes associated with the Rocky Mountain region include *wapiti* (Shawnee for a type of North American deer) and *pemmican* (Cree for a food made with dried meat and fruit).

The historical significance of indigenous languages in the United States is most obvious in the numerous place names of Native American origin found throughout the nation, and these are apparent in the Rocky Mountain region as well. The state names *Utah* and *Wyoming*, for instance, are both derived from Native American words, the former meaning "those who dwell up high" or "mountaintop dwellers" (in reference to the Utes who inhabited some of the highest altitudes in North America), and the latter a shortening of *mecheweamiing*/"at the big plains," a word used earlier by the Delaware people in the eastern United States to refer to the Wyoming Valley in Pennsylvania. The etymology of the state name *Idaho* is more controversial, however; while some scholars have claimed it to be a Native American word meaning "gem state," it is now more commonly identified as a word coined by an eastern politician in the 1800s.

Native American words, including the names of chieftains, used as names for communities throughout the region include *Chama*, *Cochetopa*, *Cotopaxi*, *Manitou Springs*, *Niwot*, *Ouray*, *Pagosa Springs*, *Yampa*, and *Yuma* in Colorado; *Kooskia* and *Weippe* in Idaho; *Ekalaka*, *Moccasin*, *Nashua*, *Peritsa*, and *Yaak* in Montana; *Kanosh* and *Ouray* in Utah; and *Oshoto* and *Washakie* in Wyoming. Although they are not all Native American in origin but were instead used by early European explorers to designate indigenous groups, many tribal names serve also as the names of communities and counties in the Rocky Mountain region, including *Arapahoe*, *Cheyenne*, and *Kiowa* in Colorado; *Blackfoot*, *Nez Percé*, and *Shoshone* in Idaho; *Bannack*, *Blackfoot*, and *Kalispell* in Montana; *Paiute* in Utah; and *Arapaho*, *Cheyenne*, and *Shawnee* in Wyoming.

In addition, a great number of topographical features in the region are designated by Native American words and tribal and chieftain names, including *Arikaree River*, *Uncompahgre Plateau*, and *Wahatoya* ("breasts of the earth" or "twins"; also known as the *Spanish Peaks*) in Colorado; *Coeur d'Alene Lake*, *Kootenai River*, and *Lake Pend Oreille* in Idaho; *Flathead Lake* and *Sioux Pass* in Montana; *Ibapah Peak*, *Uintah Mountains*, *Wah Wah Mountains*, and *Wahweap Creek* in Utah; and *Togwotee Pass* in Wyoming.

Because they include sounds and combinations of sounds not typically used by speakers of English, many Native American words, particularly place names, have undergone significant changes in pronunciation when borrowed by English.

Elimination of one or more syllables in multisyllabic words is common, most typically syllables at the beginning or end of a word, as in the pronunciation of *mecheweamiing* as Wyoming. Not all changes in pronunciation are as orderly or as obvious, however, and many words are subject to highly variant pronunciations. For instance, a small town in the San Luis Valley of Colorado named *Saguache* ("blue earth" or "water at the blue earth" in Ute) is typically pronounced as *Sawatch* or *Swatch* by residents of the community, but pronunciations from outside the community also include such variant pronunciations as *Sagwachie*, *Sagwach*, and *Sagoochie*. Occasionally, variation in the pronunciation of place names has been perceived as such a problem that Native American names have been changed, or they have simply been replaced by the names of significant events or of more recent town leaders. However, the town of Kooskia, Idaho, provides a counterexample to this trend. Shortened from the Nez Percé reduplication *kooskooskia*/"where the waters meet," *Kooskia* replaced the previous name of the town, *Stuart*, in the early twentieth century.

Although the Rocky Mountain region was at one time home to a great variety of Native American languages, many of the languages once spoken in the area are nearing extinction, and some rather quickly. Although bilingualism is sometimes practiced among Native Americans, many younger Native Americans have eschewed the language of their ancestors in favor of English or Spanish. Interest in preserving these languages has traditionally been great among linguists if only for the linguistic evidence they provide for the study of universals and typology. More recently there has been growing interest in the study and preservation of these languages, as well as Indian English, from tribes themselves as they see language as a means of tribal empowerment and as an influx of Native Americans have entered academic programs in such fields as linguistics and anthropology.[2]

THE LANGUAGES OF EUROPEAN EXPLORATION

Beginning in the eighteenth century, speakers of European languages began to explore and subsequently settle in the Rocky Mountain region. Two Romance languages were particularly well represented during the exploration of the area west of the Mississippi River—Spanish and French—with later exploration by speakers of English.

Spanish

Of the numerous European groups that would eventually settle in the Rocky Mountain region, the Spanish were apparently the first, as explorers from New Mexico entered southern Colorado as early as the mid-1500s, formally claiming the region for Spain during the eighteenth century. Expeditions also went into Utah and possibly Wyoming. Although their early visits were purely exploratory, Spaniards began settling in southern Colorado in the 1700s and established San Luis—recognized as Colorado's first town—in 1851.

The linguistic influence of Spanish on the Rocky Mountain region is realized in a number of ways, particularly in the southern areas of the region, where they have had the greatest presence. Like the influence of the Native American languages, Spanish influence may be greatest in the various place names of the region. For instance, the Spanish first applied the name *Colorado*/"reddish-colored" to a major river in the area; the word was later used as the name of the territory and then the state where the river was located. Although the name *Montana*/"mountainous" is also Spanish, it was suggested as the state name by an eastern politician and does not reflect the influence of early Spanish explorers. Towns with Spanish names in the region include the oldest settlement of Colorado, *San Luis*, and other towns in the surrounding San Luis Valley, including *Alamosa*/"cottonwood grove," *Conejos*/"rabbits," *La Jara*/"rock rose," and *Las Mesitas*/"little tables." Elsewhere in Colorado, coal-mining camps were named according to their order from the nearby city of *Trinidad*/"trinity"—*Primero*/"first," *Segundo*/"second," and *Tercio*/"third." Other Colorado towns with Spanish names include *Aguilar* and *La Junta*/"junction." In Utah, Spanish place names are typically the names of early Spanish explorers and include *Castilla*, *Escalante*, and *Salina*.

Spanish influence is also reflected in the names of topographical features in the region, and many of these names reflect not only the national origin of the explorers who named them but their religious orientation as well. For instance, two of the mountain ranges in southern Colorado are the *Sangre de Cristo*/"blood of Christ" and *San Juan*/"Saint John." A number of rivers were given Spanish names in the early days, including the *Rio Grande*/"big river," which flows from south-central Colorado to the Texas-Mexico border, and the *San Juan* and *San Rafael* in Utah. A lone hill in southern Colorado some distance from the Front Range was given the label *Huerfano*/"orphan," a name later extended to the county it resides in. The Anasazi ruins in southwestern Colorado were named *Mesa Verde*/"green plateau."

Aside from place names, Spanish has had a great influence on American English in a number of ways. Early Americans encountering unfamiliar landforms in the Rocky Mountain region found ready-made Spanish labels in such words as *arroyo*, *canyon*, and *mesa*. As Americans found themselves occupied in western-style ranching, they learned the Spanish vocabulary already in use in what had at one time been largely a Spanish activity, including *alfalfa*, *burro*, *chaps*, *cinch*, *lariat*, *lasso*, *mustang*, *palomino*, *pinto*, *rodeo*, *stampede*, and *wrangler*.

Although some are no longer restricted to the Southwest but are now pervasive in American society, Spanish influence is also found in foods that have been popular in this region for a great time, including *enchiladas*, *frijoles*, and *tacos*. Other Spanish words for food and drink include *jerk(y)*, *tamale*, *tequila*, and *tortilla*. Other words for cultural items that have come into the region were *adobe*, *cafeteria*, *desperado*, *fiesta*, *gringo*, *loco*, *patio*, *plaza*, *poncho*, *pueblo*, *sombrero*, and *tornado*. The word for Mexican jails—*calabozo*—was borrowed into American English but was subsequently pronounced *calaboose* and then *hoosegaw*.

As is the case with Native American words, Spanish words have often undergone pronunciation changes when borrowed into English, especially with respect to place names. For instance, locals of the central Colorado town *Buena Vista*/"beautiful view" often pronounce the first word of the name as [byuna] or even [byuni] (rhyming with *puny*) rather than using the traditional Spanish pronunciation [bwena]. Other corruptions are more semantic in nature, stemming from misunderstanding of the borrowed word and often involving redundancy. The *Rio Grande*/"big river" is often, for instance, called the *Rio Grande River* by Americans, even in published form. Other Spanish phrases were shortened considerably. For instance, the *Rio de Nuestra Senora de los Dolores* is now simply called the *Dolores River*, and *El Rio de Las Animas Perdidas en Purgatoria* is now officially the *Purgatoire River*, although it is typically called the *Purgatory River* by locals and *Picketwire* by some old-timers. In Utah, *El Sierra Blanca de los Timpanois* simply became *Mount Timpanogos*. Other names were literally translated from Spanish to English, as in *Cuerno Verde*/"green horn," now called the *Greenhorn* Mountains.

Aside from place names, a number of other terms current in the region have been simplified from the original Spanish pronunciation or have been misinterpreted with respect to their meaning. For instance, the word *lariat* is derived from the Spanish noun phrase *la reata* and became *lariat* by fusing the article and the noun together and dropping the ending, and the word *vamoos*/"go" has become *mosey*. The word *galon*/"braid" in *ten-gallon hat* was used in reference to the number of braids on a hat, but the word's similarity to the English term of measurement and the large size of the hat created confusion and, consequently, the new meaning of the phrase. Although there is some debate, most scholars recognize the word *buckaroo* as a corruption of the Spanish word *vacquero*/"cowboy."

As in other parts of the United States, Hispanic populations have increased greatly in recent years in the Rocky Mountain region, particularly in places that have traditionally had large Hispanic populations, and laws regarding bilingual education and bilingualism in the workplace are a hot topic of debate. The effect that large populations of Spanish speakers will have on the lexicon and pronunciation of English in these areas is yet to be studied in great detail.

French

The French had an interest in the Rocky Mountain region relatively early. In 1682, the French explorer René-Robert Cavelier, Sieur de La Salle (1643–1687), claimed the entire region between the Allegheny Mountains and the Rocky Mountains for the French, naming the vast region Louisiana, after King Louis XIV (1638–1715). Although La Salle never went west of the Mississippi River himself, French trappers and traders ventured into the region during the mid-eighteenth century. In 1743, the sons of the French trader-explorer Pierre Gaultier de Varennes, Sieur de la Vérendrye, Louis-Joseph and François, probably became the first Europeans to enter Montana and may have also reached present-day Wyoming, as there is mention in their journals of "Shining Mountains," perhaps in reference to the Bighorn Mountains of Wyoming.

A great many French terms were used in the Rocky Mountain region at one time, and some are preserved as place names, including *Bellvue*, *Florissant*, and *Platte* in Colorado; *Boise*, *Bruneau*, *Coeur d'Alene*, and *Dubois* in Idaho; *Butte*, *Choteau*, and *Rivulet* in Montana; *Duchesne*, *La Sal*, and *La Verkin* in Utah, and *Bonneville*, *Dubois*, *Fontenelle*, and *La Barge* in Wyoming. French names for topographical features are also prevalent, as in the *St. Vrain River* in Colorado and the *Grand Teton Mountains* in Wyoming. The word *cache* from the verb *cacher*/"to hide" was used as a label for a hiding place for goods and is now found in such place names as *Cache Valley*, Utah; *Cache la Poudre Creek*, Colorado, which is simply called the *Poudre River* and sometimes pronounced [putr] (rhyming with *scooter*) by those familiar with the river. There were also a number of French words and phrases that were literally translated and borrowed by mountain men as in *Rouchejaune*, or

Yellowstone (a county in Montana, a lake in Wyoming, and a river throughout the region), and *Bayou Salade*, or *Salt Marsh*, which has since been renamed South Park, Colorado. The names of French Canadian trappers used as place names in the region include *Ogden* and *Provo* in Utah.

Aside from the term *butte*, which is a generic term used to describe flat-topped hills in the area, French terminology that was used at one time but has since largely passed on is *herbe salee*/"salt grass," a type of grass cows refused to eat; *bois de vache*, of which the literal translation still survives in *buffalo chips*/"animal excrement"; and *shivaree* from the French *charivari* for a party in which people played pranks on a newly married couple that often went by the name *serenade* in other regions of the United States.

As in the case of contact between the early Spanish explorers and indigenous people, close relations existed between the French and various Native American tribes, which led to the borrowing of a number of Native American words into English via French, including *caribou* from Micmac *galipu*/"scraper or pawer (of snow)." Some of the names of Native American tribes in the region are French in origin, including the *Gros Ventre*/"great belly," *Coeur d'Alene*/"heart of awl" or "sharp-hearted," and *Nez Percé*/"pierced nose."

Perhaps the greatest impact the French language has had on the Rocky Mountain region comes as the result of its role in the creation of a mixed language used by some Native Americans in the area. Spoken by the Métis, a group of people descended from European fur trappers and traders (usually French along the St. Lawrence Seaway, and English, Scottish, or Scandinavian near the Hudson Bay) and Native American women (typically of Cree or Ojibway origin), the Michif language combines elements of French and Cree (and to a lesser extent, elements of Ojibway and English). The vocabulary of Michif is a mixture of French and Cree, but almost all nouns are French and almost all verbs are Cree, with particle words being a mixture of the two. Michif has gender agreement between nouns and verbs, with French nouns conforming to the gender assignments made on Cree nouns that share the same referent. The word order of the language is also more characteristic of Cree than French. Identity plays an important role in the Métis nation as Métis do not consider themselves French or Indian; nevertheless, Michif is in danger of extinction, as young Métis take English as their native language. Some Métis also speak more mainstream varieties of French and Cree.

English

The third European linguistic group to enter the Rocky Mountain region comprised speakers of English; however, neither the speakers of British and Scottish English who worked in the fur trade nor the Americans who traveled through as part of the Lewis and Clark expedition settled in the area. Even after the Louisiana Purchase of 1803 gave the United States the rights to the region between the Mississippi River and the Rocky Mountains, including the eastern Plains region of Colorado, Wyoming, and Montana, and allowed for westward expansion, boundary disputes with the Spanish and conflicts with various Native American tribes in the area kept many Americans from venturing there. Stephen Long's expedition to the region in 1820, after which he called the Plains region of the United States the "Great American Desert," probably did nothing to help expansion, and aside from the Mormon migration to Utah in 1847, it wasn't until gold was discovered in Colorado in the late 1850s that significant numbers of people began going to the region. The Homesteading Act of 1862 gave people the chance to own land and also encouraged westward expansion.

The varieties of English spoken by the first Americans to enter the Rocky Mountain region came from the eastern United States, where Hans Kurath, who oversaw the creation of the *Linguistic Atlas of the United States*, used Linguistic Atlas methodology to provide evidence for three major dialect regions in the eastern United States: Northern, Southern, and Midland. For Kurath, the North included the northeastern United States starting from a point north of Philadelphia and south of New York City and including the northern portion of Pennsylvania. The Midland region began in Philadelphia and spread westward and then southward into the Ohio Valley, Kentucky, and the Appalachian Mountains. The South began on the eastern shore of Maryland and Virginia, went westward to the foothills of the Appalachians, and southward to include the Virginia Piedmont and most of the Carolinas, before sweeping through the piedmont of Georgia and through the Deep South toward Texas. All three of Kurath's dialect regions ended at the Mississippi River.

Kurath found several linguistic features to be characteristic if not unique to each of these regions, especially with respect to vocabulary. Since the publication of Kurath's work, many scholars have studied his distinctions and have arrived at similar conclusions about the dialect regions at various levels of language, including pronunciation and syntax.[3]

According to these studies, features associated with the Northern dialect of English include the use of *pail*/"a container used to collect water" as opposed to *bucket* elsewhere; the pronunciation of *roof* and *root* with the /U/ of *book*; and a pattern of raising vowels called the Northern Cities Vowel Shift. Midland characteristics include the merger of the vowels of /a/ and open o, also known as the *cot/caught* merger; use of positive *anymore*, as in "All the kids have cell phones anymore"; and the use of lexical variants such as *roasting ears* and *slop bucket*. Characteristically Southern features are the identical pronunciation of the vowels in words like *pin* and *pen* and the pronunciation of words like *tire* and *fire* as *tar* and *far*. Grammatical features include the acceptability of double modals, for example, *might could*, as in "I might could do that"; perfective *done*, as in "He *done* fixed the flat tire"; and the use of *fixing to*/"preparing to," as in "He's fixing to drive to town." Words associated with Southern American English include *yonder*/"a distance"; *carry*, in the sense of "to take someone somewhere"; the use of the brand name *Coke* as a generic term for carbonated, nonalcoholic beverages, known as *pop*, *soda*, and *soda pop* elsewhere; and the use of the second-person plural pronoun *y'all*.

Compared to the eastern United States, little is known about the variety of English spoken in the western United States. All dialects of American English have had currency in the Rocky Mountain region, but unlike in the eastern United States where there are clearly differences between the North, Midland, and South dialect regions, there is no tripartite division in the Rocky Mountain region. Most scholars attribute this to dialect mixture, but some have also suggested that many settlers migrated from areas of the United States where a dialect mixture was already in place, such as the Midwest region. In general, however, many linguists assert that the Rocky Mountain region is primarily Northern in character, particularly in the northernmost states of the region and especially with regard to vocabulary.[4]

Some scholars, however, argue that the entire West is an extension of the Midland dialect—at least with respect to pronunciation—as western speakers of American English generally use the same vowel in the pronunciation of such words as *cot* and *caught*, but with its own unique phonological system.[5] A number of other Midland features can also be found in the area, including the use of positive *anymore* and some of the lexical variants associated with the Midwest, such as *roasting ears*/"corn on the cob."

Perhaps owing to the cattle culture of the Rocky Mountain states, especially Colorado, Wyoming, and Montana, and their relationship with Texas, some Southern influence can be found in the region. One is the pronunciation of the words *tire* and *fire* as *tar* and *far*.[6] Other features that have often been associated with Southern speech in the past that are attested in the region are a-prefixing, as in "I'm a-going home now"; and the occasional double modal construction, as in "I might could do that." Furthermore, there is some r-lessness among old-timers of the region in words like *hoss*, *cuss*, and *podnuh* for *horse*, *curse*, and *partner*, which linguists believe reflect the influence of Southern American English.

Several features can also be found in the region, primarily among older speakers, that were used in various areas of the East at one time but are now considered relic pronunciations. These include the pronunciation of *crick* for *creek*, as well as *deef* for *deaf* and *drouth* for *drought*. Contrasts between the sound /w/ as in *well* or *war*, and /hw/, or *voiceless w*, in words such as *which* and *whip*, can also be found among older populations.

Although dialect mixture is the norm for the region, there do seem to be some generalizations that can be made based on settlement patterns. In general, early groups of settlers from the eastern United States migrated due westward, so that the northernmost areas of the Rocky Mountain region, such as Montana, Wyoming, and northern Colorado, were primarily settled by migrants from Kurath's Northern region, as well as from parts of the Inland North, such as Michigan, Minnesota, and the Dakotas. However, the southernmost areas of the West were more likely to attract settlers from Kurath's Midland and Southern regions. Linguistic Atlas data collected in Colorado in the 1950s provides some evidence of patterns of migration into the state.[7] In general, they found evidence in historical records as well as in the linguistic data that speakers of Northern American English tended to follow the Platte River into the state and that Southern and Midland speakers followed the Arkansas River into the state. However, they also reported that the settlement patterns and demographics of the region made it difficult for them to make strong generalizations about the speech of the area, a finding supported to some extent by others.[8]

OCCUPATIONAL GROUPS

Several occupational groups were instrumental in the settling of the Rocky Mountain region, particularly the early mountain men, miners, ranchers, and farmers. The major linguistic contribution of these groups to the region was in the specialized vocabulary that each of the occupations required. Furthermore, opportunities in each of these occupation were instrumental in attracting people of various languages, as well as dialects of American English, to the region.

Mountain Men

The first Europeans to reach the northern Rocky Mountain region, the mountain men were attracted to the area due to reports of an abundance of beaver, a fur that was highly sought after in Europe at the time. Several factors contributed to an interesting linguistic situation for the mountain men. First, some of these men spoke a dialect of English they had brought with them from other mountain ranges, notably the Ozark and Appalachian Mountains. Mountain men also found themselves in the company of Spanish, French, and Native Americans and incorporated words, phrases, and pronunciations into their own language. Finally, mountain men needed to give names to a great number of objects with which they were unfamiliar but would need to be able to discuss.

In order to label the species of plant and animal life they encountered in their new environment, many mountain men resorted to compounding two or more words they already knew, which is a productive word-formation process in English. For instance, of words found in the journals of the Lewis and Clark expedition that had not previously been recorded in American English, the majority were such combinations as *ground squirrel*, *bull snake*, and *copperhead*.[9] The name for the *prairie dog* has been attributed to mountain men, with the synonyms including *prairie squirrel* and *prairie marmot*. Also, a number of phrases have been attributed to mountain men, including *up to beaver* to refer to a trapper not good enough to catch beavers made cautious by the death of other beavers in its family; *the horse has stopped* to mean tired; and *water scrape* to indicate a trip in which water is hard to come by, probably not an uncommon experience for explorers in the arid West.

Miners

Perhaps because it was the first state in the region to experience a mining boom, Colorado is often thought of for its mining activity, but mining was vital to the growth of all the states in the Rocky Mountain region. Montana, for instance, saw a population explosion that began with fewer than 100 settlers in 1860 and increased to more than 20,000 by 1870, mostly due to the influx of prospectors from the eastern United States and Irish, Cornish, and other immigrants attracted to opportunities in the silver and copper mines in and around Butte. Mining played a significant role in the ethnic diversity of the region in that it attracted a great number of ethnic groups to the region who might not have come otherwise, including the Finnish, Lebanese, and Welsh.

Another way in which mining impacted the language of the region was in the specialized vocabulary that mining requires. Although they were certainly not unique to the region but were also used in other places where mining is an important economic activity, words and phrases like *bonanza*, *boom*, *boomtown*, *croppings*, *laggings*, *leavings*, *lode*, *pay dirt*, *placer*, *played out*, *prospect*, *shaft*, *sluice*, *strike*, *tailings*, *trace*, *tunnel*, and *vein* took on great importance in the Rocky Mountains during the years of heavy mining activity. Although many of the words and sayings associated with mining have been lost due to the abandonment of mining as a major economic activity, many have gone on to take on new meaning via metaphorical extension. For instance, a term like *pay dirt* can be used for any sort of financial gain, be it mining related or not.

Place names in the Rocky Mountain region reflect the historical importance of mining, and every state in the region has several communities with names relating to the minerals or mining activities of the area. In Colorado these include *Basalt, Boulder, Bonanza City, Carbondale, Coalcreek, Coaldale, Cokedale, Copper Mountain, Gold Hill, Granite, Gypsum, Leadville, Marble, Silver Cliff, Silver Plume* and *Tin Cup*; in Idaho, *Cobalt, Placerville, Silverton,* and *Smelterville*; in Montana, *Coalwood, Goldcreek,* and *Mill Iron*; in Utah, *Bonanza, Carbonville, Coalville, East Carbon, Minersville,* and *Silver City*; and in Wyoming, *Cokeville, Diamondville, Granite Canon, Iron Mountain, Marbleton, Nugget,* and *Opal*.

The colorful characters who played a part in the various mineral rushes in the Rocky Mountains, as well as the many superstitions that surround mining in general, contributed numerous expressions to the speech of the region, many of which deal with failure or potential success rather than realized success. These included *Pikes Peak or Bust, I'll strike it rich next summer,* and *Gold is where you find it*.

Ranchers

As elsewhere in the western United States, ranching has traditionally been an important activity in the Rocky Mountain region, and the activity has influenced the language of the region in several ways: One is that it attracted speakers of languages to the region who might not have been there otherwise, for example, the Basque; another is that ranching is a specialized activity that relies on its own vocabulary, or jargon, for communication; and finally, the importance of ranching in the area meant a greater influx of ranchers and ranch hands who spoke Spanish or a variety of American English spoken in Texas, as well as the borrowing of words and ideas from these areas.

As mentioned previously, the importance of ranching in the region has meant the use of Spanish words associated with the activity. Aside from words borrowed from Spanish via ranching that have been accepted into standard American English, some nonstandard terms also prevail. One example is the

Spanish American ranchers, such as these in Pagosa, Colorado, had a great deal of influence on the English language. Courtesy of the Library of Congress.

word *penco/*"motherless lamb," which is variantly denoted by such words as *bum*, *dogie*, or *orphan lamb*.[10]

Particularly in the days of the great cattle drives, ranching was a colorful activity with numerous expressions conveying the dangers associated with it. *In spite of hell and high water*, for instance, refers to the determination ranchers must have had as they drove cattle on overland trails through the deep waters of rivers and the scorching temperatures and aridity of the high plains. A number of euphemisms for dying have been attributed to ranchers, including *crossed over the range* and *down grade with no brakes*. Additionally, ranchers have been attributed with several colorful euphemisms for killing, presumably animals, including *eased them of their blood*, *frightened a few out of their skins*, and *rubbed from the earth*.

Like mining, ranching has contributed words and sayings to American English that are now used metaphorically in other domains, include *branding*, *corral*, and *stampede*.

Homesteaders/Farmers

Enacted by Congress in 1862, the Homestead Act enabled settlers without capital to acquire land in the public domain not exceeding 160 acres, provided they met certain conditions in respect to age and American citizenship. Homesteaders were obligated to settle on or cultivate the land for a period of five years after the land was granted to them. Since much of the eastern third of the United States, particularly along the Eastern Seaboard, was privately owned by the time of the act, many potential homesteaders looked westward, and the first claim under the newly established act was made in Nebraska on January 1, 1863. With the decline of suitable public lands, homesteading ended in 1935.

An important part of the development of the West, homesteading created its own vocabulary, including words associated with homesteaders traveling to their new homes, such as *stone boat*, *chuck wagon*, and *covered wagon*. Once reaching their destination, homesteaders went about *driving their stakes* to mark their claims. Attempts to further delineate and protect their property required different homesteaders to erect different types of fencing than the stonewalls and split rail fences that had been used elsewhere in the United States. For instance, the use of split rail fencing in the West was quickly deemed impractical due to the scarcity of lumber and the great size of farms and ranches in the region. Instead, homesteaders in the West relied on *barbed wire*, which was invented in the late 1860s and was alternately pronounced *barb wire* or *bob wire*. However, the ranchers who had made their living with the open range system and now faced the formidable obstacle of fenced property may have joined with the Native American who called the innovation the *devil's rope*.

Once settled, homesteaders of the western United States accustomed to farming in the East found far different conditions west of the ninety-eight-degree meridian, particularly with respect to average yearly rainfall, which was typically less than the twenty-two inches required by traditional farming methods. This new type of agriculture, called *dryland farming*, or *dry farming*, required some of the latest technology, including the *spring-tooth harrow* and the *disk weeder*. Irrigation also played a greater role than it had in the East, and systems comprising ponds, reservoirs, and ditches had to be constructed to take advantage of the little moisture available for farming.

Other Cultural Groups

In addition to groups that migrated to the West for economic opportunity, two groups of Americans went westward in pursuit of freedom: the Church of Jesus Christ of Latter-day Saints, which migrated to Utah and other areas of the West to escape religious persecution, and African Americans, who went westward to flee the oppression of slavery and, later, various Jim Crow laws enacted in parts of the eastern United States.

Mormons

After the death of the founder of the Church of Jesus Christ of Latter-day Saints, Joseph Smith (1805–1844), Brigham Young (1801–1877) of Whitingham, Vermont, led the persecuted followers of the faith, or Mormons, on what is now known as the Mormon Trail from Ohio to Missouri and back to Illinois before heading out to the Great Basin. After originally claiming most of the southwestern United States, including parts of present-day Utah, Nevada, and Arizona, as well as large portions of Colorado, Wyoming, Idaho, New Mexico, and the southern coast of California, and naming the entire area the State of Deseret, the Mormons eventually settled in Utah with smaller branches in Nevada, Idaho, Wyoming, and Colorado. Many of the place names of Utah are drawn from the Book of Mormon, including *Alma, Lehi, Manti, Moroni,* and *Nephi,* and some from the Old Testament of the Bible, including *Eden, Jericho, Moab, Paradise,* and *Zion.* In fact, the entire state of Utah was nearly named *Deseret*/"honey bee," from the Book of Mormon, now used in the name of the mountain *Deseret Peak. Bountiful* is a city in both Utah and in an area heavily populated by Mormons in the San Luis Valley of Colorado; *Manassa* and *Sanford* are small Mormon communities in southern Colorado.

Due primarily to the isolation of Mormon communities, both geographically and socially, several features of their speech have evolved, which has led to the creation of the label "Utahnics" for the distinctive speech of the area. For instance, Utah English pronunciation includes a merger of the vowel sounds /a/ and /o/ before /r/, a linguistic phenomenon sometimes called the *card/cord* merger. Grammatically, the Mormon community has adopted positive *anymore*, reflecting the affiliation of Utah with the Midland dialect region of the East. Another grammatical feature noted among the Mormon population is the use of propredicate *do,* as in sentences like "I may have done" and "I haven't done in ages."[11] One reason suggested for the presence of this form is the settlement of a great number of British speakers with the Mormons, as well as the migration of Americans from British-influenced areas of the Northeast United States. Scottish and Welsh ancestry is also common among Mormons, which may have also had an influence on the speech.

Although few if any words can be considered uniquely Mormon, some lexical phenomena are characteristic of Mormons. The word *gentile,* for instance, is sometimes used by Mormons to refer to non-Mormons. When a member engages in behavior the church considers inappropriate, the offending Mormon is sometimes referred to as a *jack(leg) Mormon*. Because of the strong religious orientation of the Mormons, the use of obscenities is avoided and sometimes replaced by euphemisms generally used by other speakers of American English, if not in quite the same frequency or the same situations.

Several quotes are well known in the Mormon Church, particularly those attributed to Brigham Young, the leader of the Mormon church during the migration to Utah and the early settlement of Salt Lake City. Perhaps the most famous of these quotes is Young's proclamation upon first seeing the Valley of the Great Salt Lake in 1847: "This is the place." Other quotations attributed to Young are: "Keep still and mind your own business" and "Never let a day pass that you will have cause to say, 'I will do better tomorrow.'"

African Americans

One of the most widely studied varieties of American English, African American English is a variety that originated among the slave population centered in the southern United States in the eighteenth and nineteenth centuries and was spread during the exodus into other parts of the country and the world. Among those who migrated to the American West were a group of 20,000 African Americans that migrated to form a colony in Kansas in 1879, cowboys who worked across the range, and the Buffalo Soldiers, who were African American soldiers comprising several infantry and cavalry units in the U.S. Army stationed in the West. The African American population in the Rocky Mountain region has been relatively small; perhaps the greatest areas of concentration were in the Five Points community of Denver, a historically African American community on the edge of the downtown business district; Billings and other cities of Montana; and Deerfield, which was an African American colony created in the northeastern part of Colorado near the turn of the century.

The origins of African American English have been debated by linguists for many years with arguments ranging from its derivation from a creole spoken in the southern United States to it being derived from earlier (and often nonstandard) dialects of English used by overseers on the plantations of the South. African American English has several characteristics that belie its history in the southern United States, including the use of double modals, for example, *might could*; the use of perfective *done*, as in "He *done* finished the work"; the use of *fixing to* in the sense of "preparing to," for example, "We are fixing to go to town"; and the merger of the vowels /I/ and /e/ (as in *pet*), particularly before nasal sounds like /n/ and /m/, so that words like *pen* are often confused for *pin* by speakers of other American dialects. Perhaps one of the most discussed, and stereotyped, features of African American English is the use of *be* in a habitual sense, as in the use of a sentence like "John be working" to refer not to the whereabouts of John at the moment but to indicate that he has a job. Little research has been done on the use of African American English in the Rocky Mountain region or in other western states aside from work done in various communities in California, including Los Angeles and Palo Alto.

IMMIGRANT LANGUAGES

The great waves of immigration to the United States from various parts of the world during the nineteenth and early twentieth centuries impacted the Rocky Mountain region as well. Many immigrants arrived in the United States seeking economic opportunity or to avoid religious persecution or famine. The westward expansion of the United States offered them a way to take advantage of recent opportunities provided by mining, including the various services that miners needed, such as restaurants, laundries, and transportation. Homesteading laws gave more recent arrivals to the United States a chance to obtain their own property. Still other groups were attracted to the West because the environment reminded them of the homes they had left behind in Europe and Asia.

Languages of Europe

Of the immigrants who arrived in the Rocky Mountain region in the late nineteenth century, various European groups were probably the best represented due to economic and social conditions in Europe during the nineteenth and early twentieth centuries that forced Europeans of many nationalities to go abroad, and many arrived in the United States. The previous mining experience of members of some of these groups made them desirable in the Rocky Mountain region.

Germanic Languages

German

Although there were some German miners, many German immigrants came to the Rocky Mountain region to take advantage of the homesteading laws and make their living in grain farming. As one of the largest foreign-speaking populations in the United States during the late nineteenth century, significant populations of Germans inhabited the Rocky Mountain region, and their presence was reflected in the spread of German cultural and recreational centers, or *Vereine*, throughout the region. There were also numerous German newspapers throughout the area, including the *Montana Argus* and *Montana Freie Press*, which were published in Helena in the 1880s.

The German language is a close relative of English, which is considered a West Germanic language, as English was created in Britain by West Germanic tribes. Years of relative isolation from one another and independent changes in pronunciation, grammar, and meaning have caused English and German to differ from one another, yet they are alike in significant ways. For instance, a majority of the most commonly used words in English are Germanic in origin. Words that the English language has borrowed from German in recent times include *angst, frankfurter, kindergarten, noodle,* and *sauerkraut.*

German is reflected in some of the place names of the Rocky Mountain region, for example, *Nederland* and *Walsenburg* in Colorado. The *German Gulch* outside of Butte, Montana, was an area of gold mining in the 1860s.

With the general assimilation of Germans into American society, the largest German-speaking populations are now found in the Hutterite colonies scattered throughout the region. Although religious services and readings in these colonies are typically in German, English is usually the language used at school and in conducting business in other communities.

Scandinavian

Various groups of Scandinavians began settling in the region during the mining years, bringing with them their vast experience in hard-rock mining, as well as working in the lumber industry and as farmers. Many were second-stage immigrants, migrating from such places as Minnesota or the Upper Peninsula of Michigan and settling in communities throughout the region.

Scandinavian languages are classified as northern Germanic languages. They were quite influential during earlier periods of the English language, when Britain was vulnerable to invasions by the Vikings, but their influence has been relatively slight since, and speakers of Scandinavian have largely assimilated to the English of the Rocky Mountain region.

Slavic Languages

Speakers of several Slavic languages migrated to the Rocky Mountain region, especially in the early twentieth century. For instance, many Czech, Slovak, and Polish immigrants came to the region to work in the coal mines and smelters of Colorado and Montana, and there have also been several Polish farming communities in the region. The Rocky Mountain region also drew a number of Serbo-Croatian people, mostly to work as miners but also to work as stonemasons and as laborers in smelters throughout the region. The town of *Kolin* in Montana was named after a city in Bohemia, and *Belgrade*, Montana, was named by a Serbian immigrant near the beginning of the twentieth century.

Celtic Languages

Cornish

Mostly due to their expertise in mining, the region attracted Cornish immigrants, especially to Butte, Montana, and several mining towns in Colorado. Like the Scandinavian miners, some Cornish had not traveled directly from Europe to the Rocky Mountains but had already lived in the eastern United States, particularly in mining towns in Michigan, Minnesota, and Wisconsin. Although the Cornish language is extinct, one word that has come into the mining regions of the United States attributed to the Cornish is *pasty* (rhyming with *nasty*), a meat and vegetable pie that was carried into the mines and eaten as lunch by Cornish miners. The food and its name were apparently introduced to other ethnic groups working in the mines, such as the Norwegian and Finnish, who introduced them to cities like Detroit, Green Bay, and Butte after the mines closed. One other linguistic artifact of Cornish immigration was the designation of Cornish males as *Cousin Jack* and females as *Cousin Jenny*.

Gaelic and Welsh

Due to religious and political persecution and the failure of their major crop during the Great Potato Famine, many Irish immigrants began arriving in the United States during the mid-1800s, settling in New York City, Boston, and Philadelphia, as well as western Pennsylvania and the piedmont region of the Appalachian Mountains. At about the same time as their arrival, opportunities were developing in the mines of the West and attracted Irish in numbers. Welsh coal miners also began arriving in the region.

Although most Irish and Welsh immigrants spoke a variety of English by the time of their arrival in Colorado, the Irish language (or Gaelic), as well as Scots-Irish, can be heard in other varieties of American English, especially Appalachian English and other Midland varieties of English. Gaelic and Welsh are endangered languages, but steps are being taken in some parts of the British Isles to preserve the languages, and festivals are held in various parts of the United States, including the Rocky Mountain region, to preserve Gaelic and Welsh.

Other European Groups

Basque

The Basque began arriving in the Western Hemisphere in the eighteenth century when they migrated to South America. The first Basques in the United States came primarily from South America as part of the California gold rush in the mid-1800s. While some stayed in mining even after the booms, many Basque became sheepherders in California and Nevada and from there migrated into Oregon, Idaho, Montana, and Wyoming, where they were eventually joined by Basques from the Old World who were looking for economic opportunity and avoiding warfare in Europe. After first entering Idaho in the 1880s, the Basque population increased rapidly after the Spanish-American War.

Although the Basque language, or Euskara, is considered an isolate because of its dissimilarities with other languages spoken in Europe, some similarities have been noted between it and various Asian languages. Linguistically, Basque has a relatively simple sound system, but it is a highly agglutinating language with most of its affixation occurring as suffixing. Its case system for the declension of nouns is considered highly complex.

The Basque population in Idaho lives primarily near Boise and are mostly descendants of European immigrants who tend to isolate themselves from others, thereby managing to retain their distinctive customs. Shepherds were discouraged from learning English as their employers assumed this would bring knowledge of other jobs, and good sheepherders were scarce. The Basque have only slowly assimilated to mainstream society and have not eagerly gone into other occupations.

Finnish

The majority of Finnish immigrants came to the Rocky Mountain region to work in mines and in the timber industry, and like other Scandinavians, they often migrated from elsewhere in the United States, particularly Minnesota and Michigan. Although typically associated with the Scandinavians culturally, the Finnish language is not related to the Scandinavian languages and is, in fact, one of a very few languages spoken in Europe that is not a member of the Indo-European language family. Finnish is exceptional in comparison with the world's languages in its complicated case system.

Greek and Italian

Although not closely related linguistically, Greek and Italian are the native languages of speakers from two Mediterranean countries in close proximity to one another, and many speakers of these languages immigrated to the United States, and later to the Rocky Mountain region, at approximately the same time and for similar reasons. Greeks arrived in towns throughout the Rocky Mountain region to work on the railroads or in coal mines and smelters, creating communities in such cities as Denver, Colorado, and Butte, Montana. Today, there are still monolingual speakers of Greek, which is classified as a Hellenic language, throughout the region.

Aside from the languages of the explorers from France and Spanish, the only Romance language to be represented by a significant population was that used by the Italian immigrants who came to the Rocky Mountain region primarily for railroad work or to work in the coal mines and smelters scattered throughout the region.

Languages of Asia

Sino-Tibetan Languages

Chinese

The first Chinese in the region were primarily employed in railroad construction but also worked in mining towns, typically in laundries and restaurants rather than mines. When they did work in the mines, it was often after being hired as strikebreakers for which they would meet with great public hostility. The Chinese of the Rocky Mountain region were mostly concentrated in Colorado, Wyoming, and Montana.

Considered a tonal language because of the semantic importance of tones, Chinese has the most speakers of any language in the world. Morphologically, it is considered an isolating language because separate words are used to make such distinctions as tense, number, and gender, which would be indicated by affixes in a synthetic language.

Hmong

Due to the war between the United States and Vietnam, many of the Hmong people of Southeast Asia fled their homeland and arrived as refugees in the United States between 1975 and 1994. Although they primarily settled in California, Minnesota, and Wisconsin, many also settled in Montana's Bitterroot Valley. Like many other Asian languages, including Chinese, Hmong is considered to be a tonal language.

Independents

Japanese

Japanese people first entered the Rocky Mountain region in significant numbers in the early twentieth century, and their main economic activities during this period were as laborers in railroad construction, in the sugar beet industry, in the smelters, or in coal mines. During World War II, Japanese were also relocated from the West Coast to various sites in the Rocky Mountain region, including the Amache Relocation Center near Lamar, Colorado. Denver attracted a great number of Japanese during the war due in part to Colorado governor Ralph Carr's stand against the deportation of Japanese Americans, and about 2,000 of the more than 7,000 Japanese interned at Amache moved to Denver after the war ended.

Japanese is an isolate with no apparent relationship to any other languages. Although it has borrowed some words from Chinese, as well as one of its writing systems, Japanese is not related to Chinese. However, the observation of the characteristics held in common between Korean and Japanese has prompted some scholars to propose that the two languages are related. This relationship has yet to be proven and may simply be the result of language contact rather than a genetic affiliation.

Vietnamese

With the fall of South Vietnam to North Vietnam in 1975, many Vietnamese fled to the United States, including the Rocky Mountain region and especially Colorado. Like Chinese, Vietnamese is an isolating language; that is, inflectional endings are not usually affixed to words to show differences in tense or number, but a speaker must use an additional word to make those distinctions. Unlike other Asian languages, Vietnamese uses a form of the Roman alphabet in writing, but it makes extensive use of diacritics to show differences in tone.

Languages of the Middle East

Arabic

Many speakers of Arabic in the Rocky Mountain region are Lebanese, a nationality that historically had had strong associations with coal-mining towns throughout the United States, where Lebanese typically served as merchants and peddlers rather than as mineworkers. In the Rocky Mountain region, Lebanese lived and worked a great deal in the early coal-mining camps of Montana and along the Front Range of southern Colorado. With the end of coal mining in southern Colorado, many Lebanese went on to own businesses in larger towns and cities of the area, such as Trinidad.

Hebrew

The first Jewish immigrants arrived in North American in the seventeenth century, but large-scale Jewish immigrations began in the mid-1800s and continued until just before World War II, as Jews fled Germany, Russia, and other eastern European communities to escape religious persecution. Although many Jewish people set-

Dialectology

The study of language variation, particularly with an emphasis on geographical variation, began in Europe, under the guidance of early scholars like Georg Wenker and Jules Gillieron. The methods developed by Gillieron were largely used in creation of the *Linguistic Atlas of the United States and Canada* in the 1930s under the direction of Hans Kurath of Brown University. These methods incorporated a fieldworker trained in phonetic transcription to conduct interviews with native, often rural and elderly, informants of various communities in a region. Fieldwork was conducted throughout the eastern United States with much of this work being published in a variety of forms, but work in the West faced several challenges. The methodology required some modification to account for sociohistorical differences between the East and the West, and funding for fieldwork and publication was diverted to other areas of linguistics in the 1950s, particularly the generative framework that was then being developed under the direction of Noam Chomsky.

Work on a *Linguistic Atlas of the Western States* is now under way under the direction of Lee Pederson of Emory University, taking advantage of recent technological advancements in audio recording and personal computing. As in earlier Atlas interviews, worksheets revolve around the topics of daily life. Interviews are typically three hours long, rather than the eight or more hours required to complete earlier Atlas interviews in order to reflect the active lives of potential informants. Fieldwork has been completed in the Rocky Mountain states of Wyoming, Utah, and Colorado, and nearly all the Colorado interviews have been transcribed in standard orthography in their entirety.

Other dialectology projects that include data from the Rocky Mountain region are the *Dictionary of American Regional English* (DARE), which collects data using postal questionnaires, and the *Phonological Atlas of North America*, which collects data via telephone interviews.

tled in large cities like New York City, Philadelphia, Boston, and Chicago, with later populations arriving in San Francisco and Miami, some settled in towns scattered throughout the Rocky Mountain region, including Denver, Colorado, and Billings and Butte, Montana. There were some attempts at creating Jewish colonies in such places as Atwood and Cotopaxi, Colorado, and a significant Jewish population also gathered in the San Luis Valley of Colorado.

Although the Jewish population of the Rocky Mountain region is relatively small, Hebrew is used in the region for several purposes. First, communities with Hebrew names are scattered throughout the region, especially in Utah, primarily due to the strong influence of the Mormon church. Another is that it is used in some of the Jewish ceremonies held throughout the region. Finally, Hebrew characters are used in the writing of Yiddish, a Germanic language with some Hebrew vocabulary that is perhaps a second or third language to older residents of the region.

Although immigrants of many different nationalities have arrived in the Rocky Mountain region since the mid-1800s, their linguistic influence has been relatively small for a number of reasons. One is that those who came strictly for mining often stayed in the region only temporarily; more important, many immigrants already knew English, if not by the time they arrived in the United States, then by the time they migrated westward from the eastern cities. Aside from some speakers of Spanish, most speakers of immigrant languages were assimilated into the mainstream English-speaking society of the region rather quickly, and their languages had relatively little influence on the linguistic community as a whole.

ROCKY MOUNTAIN ENGLISH

Rocky Mountain English is not only a dialect mixture of the three eastern varieties of American English but has also been influenced by American Indian tribes, early Spanish and French settlers, and the various occupational groups that have settled in numbers in the region. To a lesser extent, it has also been influenced by the great variety of immigrants who came to the area as well as other groups. However, one of the greatest differences between Rocky Mountain English and the dialects of the eastern states may be in how it encodes a vastly different environment in its language.

Language and Environment

The greatest differences in the English of the Rocky Mountain region and the eastern United States may be differences in the vocabulary used to describe the physical environment of the two vastly different places. Early settlers in the region encountered unfamiliar plant and animal life and landforms that demanded the creation or borrowing of new vocabulary. Although many of the words used to talk about the physical environment of the Rocky Mountains has since been adopted by general American English, the frequency and familiarity with which these vocabulary items are used constitute one of the primary differences between the speech of the eastern and the western United States.

Topography

Topography acts as an important difference between the eastern and western United States that is reflected in differing terminology as well.[12] For instance, in the Rocky Mountain region, the word *hole* is used to refer to a geological basin, as in *Jackson Hole* in Wyoming and *Brown's Hole* and *Pierre's Hole* in northwestern Colorado. Due to the connotation of the *hole* in the history of the American West as places in which outlaws would hide, some of the place names that included the word *hole* have been changed, for example, *Mace's Hole* in central Colorado is now known as *Beulah*. Another name for a topographical feature used in the Rocky Mountain region is the word *park* when used to refer to a clearing in the mountains, as in *North Park* and *South Park* in Colorado. This is a use of the term largely unknown in the eastern United States and, for that matter, in the eastern plains of Colorado, at least in the 1950s.[13] Many of the topographical features are also of Spanish and French origin, as discussed previously.

A number of terms, especially in Colorado, commemorate the altitudes of the Rocky Mountains. For instance, the term *fourteeners* is used in Colorado to celebrate the state's fifty-four mountain peaks measuring over 14,000 feet high. The status of Denver being over 5,280 feet above sea level (at least, in some places) is a point of pride reflected in its nickname as the *Mile High City* and names for places within the city such as the recently razed *Mile High Stadium*, the former home of the Denver Broncos football team and the Colorado Rockies baseball team. The term *Rocky Mountain* is also used as part of several other terms, notably in *Rocky Mountain spotted fever* and *Rocky Mountain tick fever*.

Altitude is also reflected in the Rocky Mountain use of *up* and *down* to refer to changes in elevation rather than for northerly and southerly, as someone in Leadville (which is over 10,000 feet above sea level but southwest of Denver), for example, would typically say they were going down rather than up to Denver. There also seems to be a tendency among people, especially along the Front Range, to give directions in terms of north, south, east, and west, rather than in terms of right and left turns, presumably because one can always use the mountains as a reference point.

A great number of place names reflect the topography and the terrain of the region, including *Boulder, Crested Butte, Mesa,* and *Two Buttes* in Colorado; *Twin Falls* in Idaho; *Cutbank, Great Falls, Greycliff,* and *Whitewater* in Montana; *Bluff, Gusher;* and *Whiterocks* in Utah; and *Basin* and *Point of Rocks* in Wyoming. Unusual geographical formations in the Rocky Mountain region, particularly in Utah, have resulted in numerous descriptive names, including *Chimney Rock* in Colorado; *Arches National Park* and *Rainbow Bridge National Monument* in Utah; and *Needle Mountain* in Wyoming.

Vegetation

The topography of the Rocky Mountain region has made for a variety of plant species not found elsewhere in the United States. These include the *bitterroot*—a daisy found in Montana that serves as its state flower and is commemorated with the *Bitterroot Mountains.* Many of the state flowers and trees in the region are particular to the region including *Columbine* (Colorado), *Syringa* (Idaho), *Ponderosa Pine* (Montana); *Sego Lily* (Utah), and *Indian Paintbrush* and *Cottonwood* (Wyoming). Some parts of the Rocky Mountains serve as tourist destinations due to the spectacular sight of aspens in the fall; these trees are also called quaking *aspen, quaking asp, quakers,* and *quakies.* A number of place names commemorate the vegetation of the area, including *Aspen, Cedaredge, Evergreen,* and *Larkspur* in Colorado; *Cottonwood* and *Yellow Pine* in Idaho; *Big Timber, Box Elder, Highwood, Plentywood,* and *Poplar* in Montana; *Cedar City* in Utah; and *Wheatland* in Wyoming.

Weather

A number of weather-related terms are commonly found in the region that are uncommon elsewhere, typically relating to aridity or wind. For instance, a *chinook (wind)* is a term derived from the name of the Chinook Indians of the northwest coast denoting a warm, moist wind along the coast; however, in the Rocky Mountain region, the term denotes a warm wind that has lost much of its moisture in passing over the mountains and is often responsible for unseasonably warm temperatures contributing to the melting of snow in the winter. *Blue northers,* or *blue northerners,* on the other hand, designate cold, northern winds. *Dust devil* denotes a small whirlwind of dust.

Transportation

An important aspect of the settlement of the West was innovations made in transportation. Early settlers used the term *stone boat* or *skid* to refer to a crude transportation device made of logs and rocks to transport people some distance; *covered wagons* were also a big part of the settlement of the region. *Bullboats* were framed vessels covered with bison hide that were used by the Flathead Indians. The development of railroads was also important to the region if only for the various ethnic groups of people it brought to the region, particularly in those people who worked for the railroads such as the Chinese, Italians, Greeks, and others.

Roadways through the mountains, or *passes*, continue to be crucial to travel throughout the regions, as do the *shelf roads* for more local routes. Finally, the Pony Express and Overland Stage are responsible for some place names in the region, including *Overland Canyon* and *Overland Pass*, both in Utah.

Recreation

Many of the people of the Rocky Mountain region are concerned with living healthy lifestyles with a great emphasis on outdoor recreational activity. While few of the activities they engage in are exclusive to the Rocky Mountain region, and in fact, much of the terminology used in these activities originated elsewhere in the eastern United States, California, or even Europe, the topography of the region, especially the mountains of Colorado, and the ensuing tourism industry in the region, lends itself to a treatment of this terminology in a report on Rocky Mountain speech.

Alpine skiing has obviously made a great economic impact on the region with the popularity of such places as Aspen and Vail, Colorado; Jackson Hole, Wyoming; and others. The first single chairlift was introduced in Sun Valley, Idaho, in 1936, and the first competitive snowboarding meet was held in Leadville, Colorado, in 1981. Linguistically, some terms have originated with snow sports, or at least are commonly associated with them, including *powder* for a type of snow good for skiing, *bunny slope* for a hill for novice skiers, and *ski bunny* for a female skier. The University of Colorado at Boulder, often designated by the acronym *CU*, is alternately referred to as *Ski U* due to its attraction to students who head for the mountains on the weekend or at any other opportunity. From Union Station in Denver, one can take the *Ski Train* to Winter Park during ski season. There are also a number of places throughout the region with *snow* in their names, including *Snowmass Mountain* in Colorado, *Snowyside Peak* in Idaho, and *Snowshoe Peak* in Montana.

Hunting and fishing in the Rocky Mountain region are popular among natives of the region as well as visitors. Although there is probably little in the way of everyday speech that is affected by these activities, the Rocky Mountain region has a considerable number of places named after game animals and fish, including *Elk Springs* in Colorado; *Bear City, Elk City, Elk River,* and *Salmon* in Idaho; *Antelope, Bearcreek, Buffalo, Deer Lodge, Fishtail, Four Whitetail,* and *Whitefish* in Montana; *Beaver* in Utah; and *Moose* in Wyoming. Designations for topographic features are also found that include animal names including *Elkhead Mountains* and *Trout Creek Pass* in Colorado; *Caribou Range, Grizzly Mountain,* and *Grouse Creek Mountain* in Idaho; *Grouse Creek* in Utah; and *Elk Mountain* and *Wapiti Ridge* in Wyoming. Several places in the region are named after tools used for hunting and fishing, including *Rifle* in Colorado; *Bow Park* and *Silver Bow* in Montana; *Gunlock* in Utah; and *Fishing Bridge* in Wyoming. There are also a number of animals not typically associated with hunting serving as place names in the region, testifying to the great interest in wildlife in the region; these place names include *Eagle* in Colorado and in Idaho; *Squirrel* in Idaho; *Black Eagle, Crane, Heron,* and *Wolf Point* in Montana; and *Hawk Springs, Horse Creek,* and *Wolf* in Wyoming.

Finally, there are a great number of natural hot springs in the area for those people whose idea of recreation is more on the relaxing side. Some of the hot springs of the region are *Glenwood Springs, Hot Sulphur Springs*, and *Pagosa Springs* in Colorado.

FUTURE RESEARCH ON LANGUAGE IN THE ROCKY MOUNTAINS

The linguistic situation in the Rocky Mountain region is an interesting one for many reasons, not least of all in the apparent differences it has with other areas of the United States. Its characterization by linguists as a region in formation is another, especially since migration into the region began relatively recently and the details of this settlement have perhaps been recorded better than earlier settlement in the United States. Furthermore, in a time when Spanish-speaking populations are expanding greatly in communities throughout the United States, and as issues like bilingual education and cultural assimilation begin to emerge as a result, parts of the Rocky Mountain region may offer answers in communities that have been dealing with the same issues and others for many years.

Despite good reasons for doing it, however, relatively little work has been done on the language of the Rocky Mountain region. This chapter has provided brief descriptions of a number of areas where research has been conducted, but in many ways the Rocky Mountain region is an unexplored linguistic territory open to future scholarship.

RESOURCE GUIDE

Printed Sources

Bakker, Peter. *A Language of Our Own: The Genesis of Michif, the Mixed Cree-French Language of the Canadian Métis*. New York: Oxford University Press, 1997.

Bieter, John, and Mark Bieter. *An Enduring Legacy: The Story of Basques in Idaho*. Reno: University of Nevada Press, 2000.

Carver, Craig. *American Regional Dialects: A Word Geography*. Ann Arbor: University of Michigan Press, 1987.

Cassidy, Frederic G., et al., eds. *Dictionary of American Regional English*. Cambridge, MA: Harvard University Press, 1985.

Cutler, Charles L. *Tracks That Speak: The Legacy of Native American Words in North American Culture*. Boston, MA: Houghton Mifflin, 2002.

Di Paolo, Marianna. "Propredicate *Do* in the English of the Intermountain West." *American Speech* 68 (1993): 339–356.

Hankey, Clyde Thomas. "A Colorado Word Geography." Ph.D. dissertation, University of Michigan, 1960.

———. "Semantic Features and Eastern Relics in Colorado Dialect." *American Speech* 36 (1961): 266–270.

Kimmerle, Marjorie. "Bum, Poddy or Penco." *Colorado Quarterly* 1 (1952): 87–97.

———. "The Influence of Locale and Human Activity on Some Words in Colorado." *American Speech* 25 (1950): 161–167.

Kimmerle, Marjorie, Raven I. McDavid, Jr., and Virginia G. McDavid. "Problems of Linguistic Geography in the Rocky Mountain Area." *Western Humanities Review* 5 (1951): 249–264.

Kurath, Hans. *Word Geography of the Eastern United States*. Ann Arbor: University of Michigan Press, 1949.

Labov, William. "The Three Dialects of English." In *New Ways of Analyzing Sound Change*, ed. Penelope Eckert, 1–44. New York: Academic Press, 1991.

Leap, William L. *American Indian English*. Salt Lake City: University of Utah Press, 1993.

Marckwardt, Albert H. *American English*. Oxford: Oxford University Press, 1958.

Metcalf, Allan. *How We Talk: American Regional English Today*. Boston, MA: Houghton Mifflin, 2000.

Pederson, Lee. "Dialects." In *The Cambridge History of the English Language, Volume VI: English in North America*, ed. John Algeo, 253–290. Cambridge: Cambridge University Press, 2001.

Poulsen, Richard C. *The Mountain Man Vernacular: Its Historical Roots, Its Linguistic Nature, and Its Literary Uses*. New York: Peter Lang, 1985.

Thybony, Scott. *Dry Rivers and Standing Rocks: A Word Finder for the American West*. Albuquerque: University of New Mexico Press, 2000.

Web Sites

Atlas of North American English
William Labov, University of Pennsylvania. May 17, 2004.
http://www.upenn.edu/phono.atlas

This Web site provides the results of an ongoing linguistic survey conducted with speakers in communities throughout the United States via telephone.

Cassidy, Frederic. *Dictionary of American Regional English*.
March 23, 2004.
http://polyglot.lss.wisc.edu/dare/dare.html

The main page of one of the *DARE* projects, which was compiled under the direction of the late Frederic Cassidy, from fieldwork carried out in 1965–1970. Harvard University Press/Belknap has already published four volumes of the dictionary, which should soon be completed.

Ethnologue
Summer Institute of Linguistics (SIL). May 17, 2004.
http://www.ethnologue.com/

SIL provides information on the world's languages, including proposed classifications of language families and bibliographies for many of these languages.

Labov, William. TELSUR.
The Atlas of North American English. March 23, 2004.
http://www.ling.upenn.edu/phono_atlas/

The Web site through which one can access the TELSUR Project, a survey of linguistic changes now under way in North America, which seeks to systematically describe the phonology of the United States and Canada. Contains a Labov paper titled "The Organization of Dialect Diversity in North America" as well as maps.

Linguistic Atlas Projects
Linguistics Program, University of Georgia at Athens. May 17, 2004.
http://www.atlas.uga.edu

This Web site provides linguistic data, particularly that dealing with pronunciation and vocabulary, to scholars of American dialects; future plans for the site include posting texts and sound files from interviews recently conducted in Colorado, Wyoming, and Utah.

Varieties of English (with sound samples).
http://www.ic.arizona.edu/%7Elsp/

This dialect site has a good overview of general linguistics (phonology, IPA, etc.). Features information on African American English, American Indian English, British English, Canadian English, Chicano English, Northeast United States English, and the Southern English.

Organizations

Bohua Chinese School
Hellems Building
University of Colorado at Boulder
Boulder, CO 80309
http://www.geocities.com/bohuaboulder

A school devoted to the teaching of Chinese culture to adults and children in the Boulder area. The school is housed in the Hellems Building at the University of Colorado at Boulder.

Colorado Welsh Society
7832 S. Garfield Way
Centenniel, CO 80122
http://home.att.net/~coloradowelsh/CWSmain.html

An organization dedicated to the preservation of Welsh culture in the Rocky Mountain region, offering lessons in language, music, and dance. Most meetings of the organization are held in metropolitan Denver.

Gabriel Dumont Institute
121 Broadway Avenue East
Regina, Sasketchewan
S4N 0Z6
http://www.gdins.org/index.html

Offers studies in Métis culture in conjunction with several universities in Canada.

Rocky Mountain Chinese Association
5589 Arapahoe Avenue, Suite 208
Boulder, CO 80303
http://www.coloradochinese.org/

An association serving the growing Chinese community of Denver and its surroundings.

Rocky Mountain Irish Community Center
2401 East Second Avenue #300
Denver, CO 80206
303-320-9480
http://www.irishcommunity.org/

A center devoted to the preservation of Irish culture in the Rocky Mountains. There are plans to move to a renovated building at 16th Street and Gaylord that will house various programs in Irish culture, including language classes.

Museums and Special Collections

Basque Museum and Cultural Center
611 Grove Street

Boise, ID 83702
208-343-2671
http://www.basquemuseum.com/

Offers exhibits on local Basque history, as well as classes in the Basque language.

Blair-Caldwell African-American Research Library/Denver Public Library
2401 Welton Street
Denver, CO 80205
720-865-2401
http://aarl.denverlibrary.org/

Contains materials on the history of African Americans in the western United States.

Vietnamese Collection, Ross Barnum Branch/Denver Public Library
3570 West First Avenue
Denver, CO 80219
303-935-1891
http://www.denver.lib.co.us/

Includes approximately 800 Vietnamese texts.

LITERATURE

Ron McFarland

WRITING FROM THE ROCKIES

In his *The Pacific Northwest: An Interpretive History* (1989), Carlos Schwantes suggests that the early literature of the region, which includes Idaho and Montana, "reflected its status as a cultural hinterland."[1] A hasty review of the contents of mainstream anthologies of American literature or of modern or contemporary prose or poetry will confirm this premise. The conditions have moderated somewhat, albeit slightly, in recent years, but anthologies like McGraw-Hill's *The American Tradition in Literature* (10th ed., 2002) and the *Heath Anthology of American Literature* (4th ed., 2002) are indicative. The former includes only Lorna Dee Cervantes as a writer from the Rockies, while the latter goes all ethnic with Cervantes (Hispanic), James Welch (Blackfeet/Gros Ventre), and D'Arcy McNickle (Flathead). John Edgar Wideman (African American) has Wyoming connections but teaches at the University of Massachusetts in Amherst.

The two-volume edition of *The Norton Anthology of Modern and Contemporary Poetry* (3rd ed., 2003) includes work by only three poets who might be classified as connected with the Rockies in any way: May Swenson (1913–1989), who was born to a Mormon family in Logan, Utah, and graduated from Utah State but "escaped" to New York during the Great Depression; Seattle native Richard Hugo (1923–1982), who taught at the University of Montana for nearly twenty years; and Lorna Dee Cervantes, born in San Francisco in 1954, who has taught at the University of Colorado in Boulder since the 1990s but maintains a home address in California as well as in Boulder. The poems in her two books *Emplumada* (1981) and *From the Cables of Genocide: Poems on Love and Hunger* (1991) speak to the politics of feminism and lash out against racism, but they do not speak to the region specifically. In effect, it is as though the editors, and perhaps the literary agents and publishers, have leapfrogged the Rockies.

A simple and perhaps too obvious explanation for this state of affairs is that writers and artists tend to congregate in large cities, where the political climate is progressive and where nonconformity may be welcomed, or at least more easily concealed. With the exceptions of Salt Lake City and Denver, the Rocky Mountain West continues to be a region of small towns and relatively small universities, many of which are located in small towns. Laramie, Wyoming, for example, has a population of about 27,000, and the University of Idaho, Idaho State University, Utah State University, the University of Montana, Montana State University, and Colorado State University are all located in towns with a population considerably under 100,000. Boise State University, the University of Utah, and Brigham Young University are in cities in the 100,000 range. The University of Denver and the University of Colorado, located a couple of dozen miles up the interstate, along with Colorado College, the Air Force Academy, and a University of Colorado branch campus all located in or near Colorado Springs, a city of some 360,000, are the only institutions of higher education in the Rockies located in what most easterners and westerners on the coast would recognize as a metropolis. The bulk of the U.S. population is elsewhere, so the odds simply favor other regions: More people equals (most likely) more writers. The five-state area that constitutes the Rocky Mountain West numbers a little over 9.2 million in the 2000 census, with some 4.3 million of that number residing in Colorado; at under 500,000, Wyoming is the least populous of the fifty states. The Rockies, although state and local business boosters insist they are being "discovered," remain the hinterlands.

The five states that comprise the Rocky Mountain region have in common not only the mountains with their beauty and potential for tourism (for better or worse) but also such factors as extensive, flat, nearly barren areas that escape being described as "ugly" only by those whose aesthetic generosity transcends that of the common citizen; serious land and water issues, some of which relate to the large percentage of federally owned acreage; and a conception of distance that applies not only to their hinterland status but also to the psychology of the majority of their inhabitants. Most residents of Montana, Wyoming, Colorado, Utah, and Idaho know they are out of it and off the beaten track, and they're glad of it. Over the years those who have given the region its literary voice have celebrated various versions of their "tough paradise." The Idaho Humanities Council adopted the phrase for its state-focused programs in 1994, echoing trapper Andrew Garcia's journals published as *Tough Trip through Paradise, 1878–1879*.

In his essay, "Writing in the Rockies," first published in 1937, Colorado poet Thomas Hornsby Ferril suggests an unusual drawback writers from the Rockies faced in what James C. Work has described as the "Neomythic Period" (1890–1914) and that some writers from the region still struggle with: "a low-grade mysticism dictated by landscape."[2] The mountains, in effect, overwhelm the imagination. Work goes on to examine how this impulse undermines the efforts of writers from the Rockies, particularly poets, by leading them into vague or cliché abstractions or into fatuous personification. Whether writers glamorize or romanticize the landscape, or whether they simply feel themselves obliged to account for it as scenery or environment, they struggle not to yield to it. Or, perhaps more often, they do yield to it. The landscape seems almost invariably to intrude on poems, memoirs, and narratives from the Rocky Mountain West, to demand what amounts to "character rights."

Although Idahoans sometimes like to claim Ezra Pound (1885–1972) (just as he sometimes liked to claim Idaho), the founder of modernism left the state at age two and never returned. At least Ernest Hemingway (1899–1961), although he never wrote anything of consequence about the state, wrote from the Sun Valley–Ketchum area, reflected his love of the Rockies in a few stories and passages in his novels, and is buried in Idaho. And then there are the sojourners, those who came and stayed for a few months (sometimes less) and then wrote of the Rockies, often from the comfortable vantage point of a condo in California or an office at Harvard. Should they be counted, or not? Does that decision have mostly to do with the quality of their writing? For example, one might disregard the writer of popular westerns, Jack Schaefer, whose best known novel, *Shane* (1949), is set in Wyoming, although he had never been west of Ohio when he wrote it (he settled in New Mexico in the mid-1950s). But Wallace Stegner, even though his sojourn in the Rockies covered no more than fifteen or sixteen years of his eighty-four, is generally considered a Rocky Mountain writer. Or what of Ivan Doig, born in White Sulphur Springs, Montana, in 1939 but leaving the state in the late 1950s? Doig has lived in Seattle since 1965, but nearly all of his six novels and three books of nonfiction are located in Montana.

Novelist Denis Johnson, who lives near Bonners Ferry, Idaho, and who teaches part of the year at Iowa, has lived in the Rockies for years but has written little so far that speaks to the region. On the other hand, many writers who have migrated to states in the Rocky Mountain region have in effect been transformed into spokespersons for their new homes. Rick Bass, for example, has become a vocal proponent of wilderness, and particularly of the Yaak Valley, in the northwestern corner of Montana, and Annie Proulx's (1935–) recent collection of short stories departs from her long love affair with New England and the Canadian Maritime provinces in favor of her new home in rural Wyoming. For other writers the migration has reversed. Marilynne Robinson, who grew up in Sandpoint, Idaho, where her lyrical novel *Housekeeping* (1980) is set under the name of Fingerbone, has lived and taught in Iowa City for many years, and her writing interests have turned elsewhere. Similarly, Richard Ford, whose novel *Independence Day* won the 1995 Pulitzer Prize, taught for several years at the University of Montana and has a novel, *Wildlife* (1990), and a collection of short stories, *Rock Springs* (1987), most of which are set in Great Falls, but he was born and raised in Mississippi, teaches at the University of Mississippi, and is now often regarded as a "Mississippi writer."

In the Nez Percé cemetery in Spalding, Idaho, one tombstone is inscribed: Born Nez Percé, Lived Nez Percé, Died Nez Percé. Very few writers could be associated in that manner with the Rockies: Born in the Rockies, Lived in the Rockies, Died in the Rockies. Even those writers most intimately connected with the Rocky Mountain West tend to have been born elsewhere (often in the Midwest), and many left at an early age. Through his visits to the family's summer cabin, Norman Maclean (who grew up in Montana but was born in Iowa) was able to maintain his ties to the Rockies during his years of teaching at the University of Chicago, but writers like Ivan Doig live hundreds of miles away from what might be called not only the geographical and personal but also the spiritual source of their writing.

EMERGENCE WRITING (TO ABOUT 1850)

To reject temporary residents of the Rockies as Rocky Mountain writers would be to reject, among others, the writings of Meriwether Lewis (1774–1809) and William Clark (1770–1838), whose *Journals* may be regarded as the region's literary genesis. The Corps of Discovery crossed and recrossed the eventual states of Montana and Idaho in 1805 and 1806. To claim the journals of Lewis and Clark as the region's primal literary utterance, however, may be inadvisable in other ways. First, there is the question of whether to include Native American "oral literature." One might avoid that issue simply by considering the oxymoronic nature of the phrase itself, inasmuch as "literature" is written by definition. Moreover, there is the increasingly touchy matter of whether informants who talked to such ethnographers as Franz Boas and Alfred Kroeber, or even more recent anthropologists like Rodney Frey, trespassed on sacred ground in the process. (Frey's *Stories That Make the World*, published by the University of Oklahoma Press in 1995, is subtitled "Oral Literature of the Inland People of the Inland Northwest.") Setting aside such narratives (Frey's renditions are drawn from the Crow, Coeur d'Alene, Kootenai, and Nez Percé, among other tribes) is one of those decisions one makes by erring on the side of caution. Second, one might begin with accounts from Spanish explorers that go back to the sixteenth century. James Work includes passages from Pedro de Castañeda's (1510?–1554?) *The Coronado Expedition* (1542) in his anthology. The third and more important issue concerns, given their obvious historical significance, the ostensible "literary value" of such materials. Certainly Lewis and Clark's intentions were not literary but documentary in nature; however, the current enthusiasm for nonfiction has opened the literary canon considerably.

Work includes early Native American legends and tales along with journals of explorers like Lewis and Clark and trappers like Jedediah Smith in what he calls the "Emergence Period," which he dates between 1540 (accounts of Spanish explorers) and 1832, but a good case might be made for extending the latter date at least to 1848, when the United States acquired what would become the states of Colorado and Utah as a result of war with Mexico. Some of these writings do appear to involve something more than merely denotative or expository accounts. Among them are Osborne Russell's *Journal of a Trapper*, published in 1955 with extensive editing, from his trek through Wyoming, Montana, and Idaho between 1834 and 1843. Russell's syntax is often loose and rambling, and his paragraphs seem nearly endless, but that he had some literary pretensions is implicit in such passages as the following: "Poets have sung of the 'meeting of the waters' and fish climbing cataracts but the 'parting of the waters and fish crossing mountains' I believe remains unsung as yet by all except the solitary Trapper who sits under the shade of a spreading pine whistling blank-verse and beating time to the tune of a whip on his trap sack whilst musing on the parting advice of these waters."[3] At least equally self-consciously "literary" is trapper Warren Angus Ferris's diary entries between 1830 and 1836, published by his brother Charles in the *Western Literary Messenger* in 1843–1844: "On the fourteenth, hurrah, boys! we saw a buffalo; a solitary, stately old chap, who did not wait an invitation to dinner, but toddled off with his tail in the air."[4] Ferris' buoyant nonchalance alters considerably about ten pages later, when they come across the bodies of three Indians, including that of a boy about four years old, "horribly maimed and disfigured."

The literature of the early nineteenth century is, for the most part, expository, nonfiction prose, but sometimes it does not sound very "literary." Consider, for example, the following passage from Zebulon Pike's (1779–1813) account of his expedition to the Rocky Mountains in 1806–1807: "The perpendicular height of this mountain [Pike's Peak], from the level of the prairie, was 10,581 feet, and admitting that the prairie was 8,000 feet from the level of the sea, it would make the elevation of this peak 18,581 feet; equal to some and surpassing the calculated height of others for the peak of Teneriffe, and falling short of that of Chimborazo only 1,701 feet."[5] But on the previous page, Pike writes, "The storm still continuing with violence, we remained encamped; the snow by night was one foot deep. Our horses were obliged to scrape it away to obtain their miserable pittance, and to increase their misfortunes the poor animals were attacked by the magpies, which, attracted by the scent of their sore backs, alighted on them, and in defiance of their wincing and kicking, picked many places quite raw." Most of the travel accounts mingle the dully denotative with the sometimes dramatically descriptive. The thirty-two volumes that comprise Reuben Gold Thwaites's *Early Western Travels, 1748–1846,* published between 1904 and 1907, offer numerous examples of early exploration of the Rockies.

Certainly the most renowned American literary figure to write of the Rockies during the Emergence Period was Washington Irving (1783–1859), but his own travels to the Far West, in 1832, took him no farther than present-day eastern Oklahoma. His contributions to the literature of the Rocky Mountain West are to be found in books he wrote based on the accounts of John Jacob Astor (1763–1848), *Astoria* (1836), and of Captain Louis Bonneville, *The Adventures of Captain Bonneville* (1837), originally titled *The Rocky Mountains: Or, Scenes, Incidents, and Adventures in the Far West* (1837). It should relieve admirers of his "Legend of Sleepy Hollow" and "Rip Van Winkle" to know that Irving's account of the Blackfeet, whom he describes as "the most dangerous banditti of the mountains," does not reflect his own prejudices but is some version of Captain Bonneville's observations. "They are extremely fond of spirituous liquors and tobacco," Bonneville/Irving adds, "for which nuisances they are ready to exchange, not merely their guns and horses, but even their wives and daughters." He concludes that the "treacherous race . . . have cherished a lurking hostility to the whites" since the expedition of Lewis and Clark. Predictably, perhaps, Bonneville/Irving is better disposed toward the compliant Nez Percés, who "evince strong and peculiar feelings of natural piety," "abstract notions of morality," and "a respect for the rights of their fellow-men."[6]

Later responses to the Rockies are anticipated in some ways in the reports and memoir of John C. Frémont (1813–1890), whose expeditions in the early 1840s took him from Fort Laramie through the Great Salt Lake. Accompanied by the renowned Indian fighter and guide Kit Carson (1809–1868), Frémont records some memorable encounters with hostile Cheyenne and Sioux, but he is more inclined to fuss over his barometers and to celebrate soil samples:

[W]e left the [Platte] river, which makes a bend to the south, and, traversing an undulating country, consisting of grayish micaceous sandstone and fine-grained conglomerates, struck it again, and encamped, after a journey of twenty-five miles. Astronomical observations placed us in latitude 42° 32' 30", and longitude 108° 30' 13".

Frémont is decidedly less interested in the beauties of landscape than he is in promoting settlement: "The bottoms [of the Bear River area near the Great Salt Lake] are extensive, water excellent, timber sufficient, the soil good and well adapted to the grains and grasses suited to such an elevated region."[7] His modern editor indicates that such passages greatly influenced Mormon leaders in their decision to migrate to Utah where, in 1847, Brigham Young (1801–1877) would look over their new Zion and pronounce, "This is the place." Probably the most readable account of the early visitors is Francis Parkman's *The Oregon Trail*, first published in 1849, which records his eighteen-day stay with the not-yet-hostile Sioux. The Harvard graduate, whose particular interest was the Indians of the region, visited Fort Laramie and the Front Range of the Rockies.

WRITERS OF THE "OLD WEST": THE FIRST GENERATION (1850–1910)

The second half of the nineteenth century witnessed the settlement period buoyed by such factors as gold and silver strikes, the Civil War, the coming of the transcontinental railroads (the last spike ceremony for the Northern Pacific took place in Garrison, Montana, in 1883), and the end of the various western Indian wars, marked by the engagement at Wounded Knee in 1890. Work describes the writing of this "settlement generation" as that of the "Mythopoeic Period," accounts, stories, and poems that created what might be called a new myth of the Old West, as the fur trapper and mountain man were replaced by the miner and rancher, the schoolmarm and the dancehall girl, the cavalryman and the cowboy. Rugged and independent individuals retained top billing, but as Work observes, the new western character was to be connected to society and its values. Moreover, Work notes, the new era was delineated by steel: rails and barbed wire.

Included in this period are what seem even a century and a half later to be historic exploits of mythic dimension: covered wagons rolling along the Oregon Trail, the settlement of Salt Lake City by the Latter-day Saints (Mormons), gold discoveries in 1858 in Colorado and 1860 in the Idaho panhandle, the driving of the golden spike in Utah in 1869, George Armstrong Custer's (1839–1876) cataclysmic defeat at the Battle of the Little Bighorn in 1876. All of this was rounded up and brought to some sort of conclusion in Frederick J. Turner's enunciation of his "frontier thesis" in 1893. John Wesley Powell's accounts of his expeditions on the Colorado River and elsewhere in the Rockies (among the Utes, in the Uintas, and on the Green River in Wyoming, for example) in 1869 and later are among the last of what might be called "exploration journals" to be written about the region.

Work designates a "Neomythic Period" running from 1890 till the outbreak of World War I in 1914, but most of the writers he anthologizes under that rubric, including A. B. Guthrie, Jr. (1901–1991), Wallace Stegner (1909–1993), and Dorothy Johnson (1905–1984), while born in 1914 or earlier, made their mark during the years following World War II. The writers from the Rockies surveyed in this section will be, for the most part, those whose work appeared during the settlement period, between about 1850 and 1910. This entails a conflation of Work's Mythopoeic and Neomythic periods into a "First Generation" of writers (obviously not adhering to the dictionary definition of "generation" as a period of twenty to thirty years). In both fiction and nonfiction, then, this includes not Wallace Stegner but Mary

Hallock Foote (1847–1938), the writer whose novels helped define the western as a genre and whose reminiscences, published in 1972 as *A Victorian Gentlewoman in the Far West*, were the source of Stegner's Pulitzer Prize–winning novel *Angle of Repose* (1971). Also included in the nonfiction of this era are such accounts as Helen Hunt Jackson's (1830–1885) essays pertaining to Colorado, most of which appeared in two books published in 1878, and Andy Adams' (1859–1935) *The Log of a Cowboy* (1903), which is a fictionalized reminiscence of events occurring in the early 1880s. During this First Generation, events occurred historically that were to be converted into the myths and lore of the Old West.

Again, what material to "count" in the canon of writing from the Rockies is problematic. Should pertinent chapters from Mark Twain's *Roughing It* (1872) be included? He passed through the Rockies, after all; he was a legitimate sojourner, and anthologizers eager to increase the marketability of their books tend to favor the "name" author. But where does one draw the line? Does any visitor to the five Rocky Mountain states who also happened to be a writer who left some account of his or her experiences there, by that fact, qualify? The massive anthology of Montana writing *The Last Best Place* (1988) has been criticized, particularly outside of the state, for including writers whose sojourn in Montana was significant for its brevity. It considers writing by "frequent visitors" like Hamlin Garland, although he never spent more than a few months in the Rocky Mountains at any one time. That is, he does not really count as even a "temporary resident." On the other hand, he wrote about the Rockies at considerable length, and he did more than simply pass through Colorado and Utah on the way to or from the gold fields of California, as did Joaquin Miller, who came to the Idaho Territory in 1862 as a miners' advocate.

The anonymous writer for the Wyoming Writers' Project's *Wyoming: A Guide to Its History, Highways, and People* (1941) asserts the issue from the adversarial point of view: "The flowering of romantic and historical fiction during the 1890's and early 1900's brought a boom in Western romances, done mostly by casual visitors from the East who exploited the Wyoming scene for its color."[8] The key word here is *exploited*. Seen from such a perspective, sojourners like Isabella Lucy Bird, Hamlin Garland, Mary Hallock Foote, George Frederick Ruxton, and even Wyoming's own Edgar Wilson (Bill) Nye, who edited newspapers in Laramie for about half a dozen years starting in 1876, take on something of the opprobrium of "interlopers." In more recent years such writers have set themselves up in the Rockies for whatever season or seasons are most amenable to them (summer and backpacking for some, winter and skiing for others) while living the remainder of their lives elsewhere, perhaps teaching a term or two at the University of Iowa's renowned Writers Workshop, perhaps wintering in sunny California. But such a contrary perspective may be excessive. Unlike miners or clear-cutting loggers, the writer, whose infatuation with the region is at least as genuine as his or her lust for profit, returns something to the region. Significantly, the anonymous writer cited above devotes more space to Bill Nye than to any other Wyoming writer.

In their nonfiction, First Generation writers usually turn away from stories or accounts of encounters with grizzlies, slaughtering buffalo, and trading or fighting with Indians to stories or accounts of life in the mining camps, adventures on cattle drives or ranches, or experiences on marginal farms. Andrew Garcia's memoir of his experiences in western Montana and parts of the Wyoming and Idaho terri-

Portrait of writer Andrew Garcia, by James Todd, 1988. Courtesy of Dover Pictorial Archives.

tories in 1878–1879, however, should remind us that outside of towns like Denver and outposts like Fort Hall in the Idaho Territory, the Rocky Mountain West remained much like the world depicted in Osborne Russell's *Journal of a Trapper*, which covers the years between 1834 and 1843. Perhaps the greatest difference between Garcia's account and that of Osborne Russell concerns the intimacy between the narrator and the Indians he encounters. The "Squaw Kid," as Garcia calls himself about a third of the way through his memoir, finds himself falling in love with the Blackfeet woman Le-oh-hee. But this romance comes to naught, and Garcia eventually marries the remarkable Nez Percé woman In-who-lise (he calls her Susie), a survivor of the Battle of the Big Hole. An unschooled writer, as his editor Bennett H. Stein describes him, Garcia died in 1943 without seeing any of his work in print. Stein discovered his manuscript in 1948, and his edition was published in 1966. Garcia's memoir is fascinating to the very end, when he foolishly participates in a horse-stealing raid against the Blackfeet in which his wife is mortally wounded.

Isabella Lucy Bird may have been the shortest of the First Generation's short-termers, her visit to the Estes Park region lasting only about three months, between mid-September and mid-December 1873, but her seventeen letters, published in 1879 as *A Lady's Life in the Rocky Mountains* in her native Britain (she came from Edinburgh) as well as in the United States, was immensely influential, running through four London editions by 1881. Bird's most recent editor Ernest S. Bernard (1999) argues the case for her book as an important contribution to the growing mass of prose furthering preservation politics. At the time, however, the reading public was more taken with her descriptions of the sublimity of the mountains and for her daring climb up Longs Peak. Her prose tends toward the predictable purple of the age: "Then came the glories of the afterglow, when the orange and lemon of the east faded into gray, and then gradually the gray for some distance above the horizon brightened into a cold blue, and above the blue into a broad band of rich, warm red, with an upper band of rose color; above it hung a big cold moon." When it comes to the mines she encounters around Boulder, however, Bird's impassioned prose is anything but "purple": "Agriculture restores and beautifies, mining destroys and devastates, turning the earth inside out, making it hideous, and blighting every green thing, as it usually blight's man's heart and soul."[9]

Mary Hallock Foote's impact on the literature of the Rockies is both direct and indirect, as she is contemporary both with the First Generation (she was born in 1847 and died in 1938) and, thanks to Wallace Stegner's novel *Angle of Repose* (1971), with the Third Generation as well (Stegner quotes from Foote's letters in *Angle of Repose*). Born in New York, Molly, as she was known, came west with her mining engineer husband Arthur in 1876. Her first novel, *The Led-Horse Claim* (1883), draws on her years in Leadville, Colorado, a mining boomtown. Following a stay in Mexico, the Footes moved to southern Idaho, where Arthur worked on an elaborate irrigation project. Despite her reservations about life in the isolated Boise River basin, she produced several short stories with Idaho locations and two novels, *The Chosen Valley* (1892) and *The Desert and the Sown* (1902), dealing with the ill-fated irrigation projects. The 1890s found the family more happily settled in Grass Valley, California. Foote's memoir offers about as different a picture of life in the Rocky Mountain West from that of Andrew Garcia as one could imagine. Hers is a world of raising her children and waiting for telegrams to inform her of the acceptance of her drawings by various eastern magazines like *Scribner's Monthly*.

Helen Hunt Jackson's observations on life in Colorado Springs, where she lived between the winter of 1873 and her death in 1885, are even more domestic in nature than those of Foote. The writings of both Foote and Jackson illustrate the coming of law and order to the Rockies, of towns and families, of schools, churches, and courts of law. Indeed, the myths of the Old West are to a large degree dependent on its civilization, for it was the civilized townie living east and west of the Mississippi that

Author and illustrator Mary Hallock Foote. Courtesy of Dover Pictorial Archives.

295

cherished those myths. Best known to the literary world as a friend of Emily Dickinson (1830–1886), with whom she corresponded for several years, Jackson made her mark on western history with her scathing study of the government's treatment of the Ponca (of California) and other tribes in *A Century of Dishonor* (1881). Her romantic novel *Ramona* (1884) takes place in California and New Mexico, so it is not pertinent here, but her lesser known children's novel, *Nelly's Silver Mine* (1878), is subtitled "A Story of Colorado Life" and is somewhat reminiscent of novels and stories written by Foote. The Colorado Historical Society has published some of Jackson's nonfiction pertaining to Colorado in *Westward to a High Mountain* (1994), most of the pieces drawn from essays published in *Bits of Travel at Home* (1878).

Among other nonfiction texts of this First Generation with some claim to literary quality is Thomas J. Dimsdale's *The Vigilantes of Montana* (1866), the first book to be published in Montana. An Oxford educated Englishman who came to Virginia City in what was then the Idaho Territory in 1863, Dimsdale taught at a private school and became the first editor of the *Montana Post*. He came west for his health but died of tuberculosis not long after his book on the notorious Plummer gang appeared in print. Dimsdale signs on to the evolving myth of the goodness of the Rockies miners: "Every one does what pleases him best. Forms and ceremonies are at a discount, and generosity has its home in the pure air of the Rocky Mountains." But his thesis is, "Finally, swift and terrible retribution is the only preventive of crime, while society is organizing in the far West." Dimsdale's accounts of the crimes and punishments of the territorial outlaws are as dryly unflappable as the following: "William Palmer was coming across the Stinkingwater Valley, near the scene of the murder, ahead of his wagon, with his shotgun at his shoulder. A grouse rose in front of him, and he fired. The bird dropped dead on the body of Tbalt."[10]

At the opposite end of the spectrum from dark to light, or from serious to comic, are Bill Nye's columns, published during the 1880s as books of satiric essays or, to appropriate Nye's words from his "Piazza to the Third Volume" (*Baled Hay*, 1884), "trite and beautiful sayings." Nye offers in one piece to preserve the easterner's "lovely vision of copper-colored grace and smoke-tanned beauty," which is "the Indian maiden": "Let her dwell there ['in the rose-hued chambers of fancy'] as the plump-limbed princess of a brave people. Let her adorn the hat-rack of his imagination—proud, grand, gloomy and peculiar . . . while the true Indian maiden eats the fricasseed locust of the plains and wears the cavalry pants of progress."[11] The best of Nye's writings have just such a waspish edge to them, and they are blissfully free of any tincture of political correctness.

First Generation Fiction

The fiction of the First Generation writers is amply represented by the novels and stories of Mary Hallock Foote, Hamlin Garland, George Frederick Ruxton, and Andy Adams, each of whom resided at least briefly in Colorado—and of course, one hastens to add, Owen Wister's groundbreaking epic *The Virginian* (1902), which resulted from a summer visit to Wyoming for his health in 1885 and more than a dozen subsequent visits to the West. Ruxton's *Life in the Far West* appeared in book form in England and the United States in 1849, a year after his death from dysentery at age twenty-seven. A former lieutenant in the British army, Ruxton was an adventurer who spent only a year in the Rockies, but he left a loosely historical novel about fur trappers that set the paradigm for such later writers as Vardis Fisher and A. B. Guthrie, Jr. Ruxton's intent appears to have been to present the trappers as "true pioneers of that extraordinary tide of civilization" that "opened to commerce and the plow the vast and fertile regions of the West."[12]

Miners, cowboys, and even a stray forest ranger abound in First Generation fiction. Hamlin Garland drifted from the Midwest, where he had made his reputation primarily as a writer of short stories, notably in *Main-Travelled Roads* (1891), and turned out a dozen books of western fiction, particularly after his visits to Arizona, New Mexico, and Colorado in the fall of 1899. The titles include such regional novels, or more accurately "romances," as he had strayed from his earlier "Veritist" stance, as *Her Mountain Lover* (1901), *The Long Trail* (1907), and *Cavanagh, Forest Ranger* (1910). Garland's western short stories, published in *They of the High Trails* (1916), cover practically every stock character of the First Generation, from "The Grub-staker" and "The Cow-boss" to "The Outlaw" and "The Forest Ranger." His novel *The Captain of the Gray-Horse Troop* (1902), published the same year as Wister's *The Virginian*, sold nearly 100,000 copies. The stories collected in Garland's *The Book of the American Indian* (1923) are considered among the first to depart from traditional Indian stereotypes.

Three novels that might be described as "definitive" of the genre of the western appeared within three years of each other: Garland's *The Eagle's Heart* (1900), Wister's *The Virginian* (1902), and Adams' *The Log of a Cowboy* (1903), which reads enough like a trail journal that some have taken it to be nonfiction. James C. Work, in his *Prose & Poetry of the American West* (1990), describes Wister's *The Virginian* as the model for such "characterizations as the strong silent cowboy, the villainous backshooter, the comic sidekick, and the supercilious schoolmarm."[13] The showdown between the Virginian and Trampas initiated the tradition of the gunfight sustained in movies and television. After he shoots Trampas in the streets of Medicine Bow, Wyoming, the concerned Virginian confesses to his sweetheart Molly, the schoolteacher from Vermont, but she is clearly more relieved than offended. Civilization, in effect, shrugs off her concerns about savagery and expresses her gratitude to the West's male code-hero. The novel sold 50,000 copies in its first two months.

First Generation Poetry

No poetry of consequence appears to have been written and published from the Rockies during the latter years of the nineteenth century or the first decade or so of the twentieth. In fact, the Rocky Mountains' foremost poet of the Second Generation, Thomas Hornsby Ferril, went to some lengths in an essay published in the *Saturday Review of Literature* in 1937 to lambaste one of the few pertinent poems by a noted writer, Walt Whitman's (1819–1892) "Spirit That Form'd This Scene," which was written at Platte Canyon. Curiously, it is Whitman's poem that represents the state of Colorado in the recent anthology *Across State Lines: America's 50 States as Represented in Poetry* (2003). Much of the verse published from the Rockies during the First Generation period appeared in local newspapers, often anonymously. For example, in a poem titled "The Rustic Miner," from the *Idaho Avalanche* (1877), a poet who called himself Darby lashes out at the "lazy fops"

Writer William Kittredge in St. Malo, 1991. © Bassouls Sophie/Corbis Sygma.

from the city who "lounge on downy pillows." His concluding stanza catches the ethos of the First Generation miner, and perhaps of the rancher and homesteader as well, given some adjustments for their occupations, as he lashes out against "These growling, lazy, crawling elves, / Known to all men as whiners" and urges them to "step out and help themselves, / And work like honest miners."[14]

Doggerel or not, such verses give voice to a spirit of independence and self-reliance and to a work ethic, at the same time asserting an angry disapprobation of those who might think or behave otherwise. This attitude remains alive and well in the Rockies today, and it has become the primary target of writers like Montana's William Kittredge, who asks, "Who Owns the West?" Ideally, one might suppose, the answer is "No one," or perhaps "All of us." "Many of us," Kittredge writes, "like to imagine ourselves as honest yeomen who sweat and work in the woods or the mines or the fields for a living. And many of us are," he agrees. But, and in this "but" lies Kittredge's thesis, we must "revise our dominant mythology" because that myth has turned out to be "too simpleminded."[15] Of course the fact that Kittredge (among others) has eloquently argued for a new mythology for the West in books ranging from *Owning It All* (1987) to *The Nature of Generosity* (2000) does not mean that that new myth has been established.

WRITERS OF THE NEW WEST: THE SECOND GENERATION (1910–1970)

James C. Work identifies a "Neowestern" period that stretches from 1915 to the present. The first half of this period saw two world wars and the Great Depression, and as Work notes, westward migration continued at an unprecedented level. As early as 1941 the anonymous writers of the Wyoming Writers' Project guide observed that while the population density of the state was just 2.1 persons per square mile, only a third of that population of about 250,000 lived on ranches or farms. On the other hand, at that time only four cities could boast a population in excess of 10,000, and of the 275 "settlements," 151 had populations of 100 or less. Colorado's guidebook suggests only a slight contrast at the opposite end of the population figures for the five Rocky Mountain states, although its 1,035,791 inhabitants were four times those of Wyoming. Most Coloradoans were distributed among the state's eight cities of more than 10,000, with more than a quarter of them living in Denver. The 2000 census shows that Wyoming's population has not yet doubled, and it can boast of only eight cities with more than 10,000 inhabitants. Meanwhile, Colorado has more than quadrupled in population (4,301,261). Denver alone, at 554,636 persons, outnumbers the population total for Wyoming.

It is not these population figures alone that prompt a revision (not merely a re-division) of Work's Neowestern period. Presumably, writers between about 1910 and 1970, intentionally or otherwise, were carrying regional writing in different directions, sometimes enriching, sometimes repudiating certain traditional elements of the Old West myths, or at least of the genre western. The old myths had been codified, rigid with ritual. Have writers during the past thirty or so years succeeded in defining a different West distinct from that which emerges in the writings of such giants as Wallace Stegner, Vardis Fisher, A. B. Guthrie, Jr., and Dorothy M. Johnson? If so, as may be inferred from the organization of this chapter, perhaps the current Third Generation may be denominated "Postwestern." In the introduction to *Talking Up a Storm* (1994), his collection of interviews with contemporary writers from the West, Gregory L. Morris proclaims, "These are flush and wondrous times" for fiction in the American West, and he celebrates the "emergence of distinctive and *new* Western voices, voices that are at once literary and political, that seek both to demolish myth and to create myth anew."[16] Morris distinguishes these writers (including Mary Clearman Blew, Ivan Doig, and William Kittredge) from "an older generation of Western writers" like Stegner, Johnson, and Guthrie. Some writers and scholars, then, have detected trends in the past thirty or so years that suggest the need to reconsider the broad period that Work describes as Neowestern.

First, however, the considerable achievements of that Neowestern double-generation of sixty years should be summarized. Writers during the age of the Neowestern variously embrace and repudiate the traditional (perhaps "formulaic") genre western that started with Zane Grey's (1872–1939) *Riders of the Purple Sage* (1912), which some consider the quintessential western. While most of the writers during the Emergence and First Generation periods are sojourners, one distinguishing aspect of the Second Generation writers is that most of them could make some claim to resident status in one of the five Rocky Mountain states. Writers who may be more appropriately assigned to other regions, like Oregon's Ernest J. Haycox or Nevada's Walter Van Tilburg Clark, should be considered elsewhere, even though they may have set this or that novel in the Rockies or may have taught for some time at a university in one of those states. It seems most unlikely, after all, that Jack Schaefer (1907–1991), born and raised in Ohio, would have considered himself a Wyoming resident just because he set *Shane* (1949) in that state.

Universities and Regional Literature

By 1910 most of the region's state universities had been in operation for at least twenty years. The Universities of Colorado and Wyoming opened in 1887, the University of Idaho in 1889, and the Montana State University system was under way by 1893. The University of Utah, formerly the University of Deseret, began offering degrees in 1884; Utah State University opened its doors in 1890; Brigham Young became a university in 1903. Colorado State University preceded all of these, opening in 1879. These academies fostered literary interests, promoting literary societies, guilds, and clubs, and by the 1920s most of them sponsored campus literary magazines, but Professor Merriam's *Frontier* was to hold center stage as a serious literary magazine welcoming (and refereeing) contributions from outside campus for at least two decades before the University of Utah's *Western Humanities Review* began publication in 1947. But most of the surviving, and occasionally flourishing, literary magazines in the Rockies are products of the 1960s and 1970s. *The Denver Quarterly* and *The Colorado Review*, run out of the Center for Literary Publishing, started up in 1966, the same year as the inaugural issue of *Western American Literature*, the scholarly organ of the Western Literature Association. Editors of these magazines generally favor serious prose and poetry, and they refuse to consider genre fiction of the Zane Grey or Louis L'Amour variety. Chief among these magazines, considering only those that have survived for at least twenty years (founding dates indicated parenthetically) are Wyoming's *Owen Wister Review* (1978), Utah's *Weber Studies* (1984) and *Quarterly West* (1976), Montana's *CutBank* (1973), and Idaho's *Rendezvous* (1966) and *Cold-Drill* (1970).

And although Zane Grey's first successful novels, beginning with *The Heritage of the Desert* in 1910, are set in Utah, his focus moved mostly to the Southwest. He migrated to California in 1918.

By 1927 Harold G. Merriam, a professor of English and creative writing at the University of Montana (then the State University of Montana), was editing the literary magazine *Frontier* (after 1933, *Frontier and Midland*), which historian Carlos Schwantes notes "goaded Northwest writers to rise above the region's reputation for literary mediocrity."[17] The awareness of that low reputation surfaces in various ways, suggesting something of a regional inferiority complex. "No literary master has yet arisen to portray in adequate and lasting words either the magnificent scenery of the Rocky Mountain West or the colorful life that has existed in this region," declared the editors of *The Literature of the Rocky Mountain West, 1803–1903* in 1939.[18] Regional and state anthologies began to appear, often accompanied with apologetic disclaimers by the editors. "There is some terrible writing in this book," confesses Joseph Kinsey Howard in his introduction to *Montana Margins: A State Anthology* (1946). Author of the highly regarded popular history *Montana: High, Wide, and Handsome* (1943), the Great Falls journalist proposed that his was not an anthology in the "classical sense" of a collection of "flowers": "Much of this book is grass."[19]

Second Generation Fiction

For whatever reasons, and these would include a shift in poetic sensibility that writers in the culturally isolated Rockies were slow to recognize or to adopt, the prose writers of the Neowestern period have suffered a better fate than the poetry (see poetry section). It may well be that prose is simply less susceptible to stylistic conventions than poetry. In any event, both the fiction and the nonfiction from the region published between 1910 and 1970 are rich and varied, and the writing of Wallace Stegner (1909–1993) figures powerfully in both genres. Generally regarded as the "Dean of Western Writers," Stegner's career as a writer of important fiction and nonfiction began, respectively, with *Mormon Country* (1942), which often reads like fiction, and the novel *The Big Rock Candy Mountain* (1943), which draws heavily on his own family's history. Born in Iowa, Stegner grew up in Saskatchewan and Utah, taught at the University of Wisconsin, at Breadloaf in Vermont, and at Harvard and Stanford (from 1945). He lived most of his years in California, but the best of his more than two dozen books are those that look back to his boyhood in the Rockies region. This includes not only the two titles indicated above but also many of his short stories, the memoir *Wolf Willow* (1955), and the Pulitzer Prize–winning epic novel of the West, *Angle of Repose* (1972). In the sixteen essays that make up his later book, *Where the Bluebird Sings to the Lemonade Springs* (1992), subtitled "Living and Writing in the West," Stegner lashes out at the "boomer" mentality that persists in the West, the dangerous atmosphere of "transience" and "deficiency of community." The westerner, Stegner argues, "is less a person than a continuing adaptation," and "The West is less a place than a process." "We are in danger of becoming scenery sellers," Stegner warns in his essay "Thoughts in a Dry Land," and "tourists can be as destructive as locusts."[20] Such political sentiments are very much the stuff of the Postwestern period.

Most of Stegner's writing, however, is representative of the Neowestern period, which witnessed a huge increase in sophisticated authors who wrote with serious literary intent. The problem with such terms as *sophistication* and *serious literary intent*, however, is that they are inescapably subjective. Critics often speak slightingly of cowboy poetry and genre westerns (for example, the novels of Zane Grey and Louis L'Amour) as escapist or as mere popular entertainment, whereas novels like Mildred Walker's [Schemm's] *Winter Wheat* (1944) and D'Arcy McNickle's *The Surrounded* (1936) and Dorothy Johnson's stories "The Man Who Shot Liberty Valence" and "A Man Called Horse" (both from *Indian Country*, published in 1953) are "serious literature." If pinned down, critics, scholars, and teachers are inclined to insist that such texts are better written (the appeal to quality) and that they show greater thematic density or depth (the appeal to conceptual profundity). From a slightly different perspective, the argument is that writers like Stegner, Walker, McNickle, and Johnson appeal to more sophisticated and demanding readers. "Literature," perceived conventionally, withstands the test of time, although just how much time is involved is rarely stated. Perhaps the critic Roland Barthes was as close as anyone on the matter when he described literature as "what gets taught."

Most of the novels from this period are written in the Realist tradition. Mildred Walker [Schemm] (1905–1998) moved to Great Falls, Montana, with her physician husband in 1933, but her first novel, *Fireweed* (1934), which won the Avery Hopwood Award, is set in the timber country of northern Michigan. The protagonist, Ellen Webb, of *Winter Wheat* (1943), set on a Montana wheat farm in the early days of World War II, goes away to college and falls in love but must return to the farm because of hard financial circumstances and eventually takes a job teaching in a one-room school. D'Arcy McNickle (1904–1977) was born on the Flathead Reservation in St. Ignatius, Montana. A member of the Confederated Salish and Kootenai Tribes, he was to become a distinguished anthropologist. Thirty years before N. Scott Momaday's *House Made of Dawn* (1968) gained a wide audience for Indian or Native American writers, McNickle's first novel, *The Surrounded*, introduced the tensions on the reservation between traditional ways and the values and laws imposed by the dominant Anglo culture. Dorothy Johnson's

(1905–1984) reputation has been sustained to some degree by the successful movies based on her stories. *The Hanging Tree* (1959), with Gary Cooper, George C. Scott, and Karl Malden, is based on her novella published in 1957, *The Man Who Shot Liberty Valance* (1962) features James Stewart, John Wayne, Lee Marvin, and Vera Miles (directed by John Ford), and *A Man Called Horse* (1970) stars Richard Harris. Johnson lived most of her life in Whitefish and Missoula, Montana.

Two novelists of the Neowestern period have also benefited from movies based on their books, Montana's A. B. Guthrie, Jr. (1901–1991), whose *The Big Sky* (1947) was made into a film directed by Howard Hawks and starring Kirk Douglas in 1952, and native Idahoan Vardis Fisher (1895–1968), whose *Mountain Man* (1965) was released under the title of the historical character upon whom his protagonist (Sam Minard) was based, *Jeremiah Johnson* (1971, directed by Sydney Pollack, starring Robert Redford). Guthrie was to win the Pulitzer Prize for *The Way West* in 1950. He wrote three additional novels to complete his chronicle of five generations of settlement in the Rockies, concluding with *Fair Land, Fair Land* in 1982. Guthrie also wrote the screenplay for the movie *Shane* (1953). The cantankerous Fisher has attracted less notice than Guthrie, although his controversial historical novel on the Mormons, *Children of God* (1939), was awarded the Harper Prize and finished second to John Steinbeck's (1902–1968) *Grapes of Wrath* for a Pulitzer Prize. The epic novel opens with fourteen-year-old Joseph Smith in Palmyra, New York, and ends in 1890 with the outlawing of plural marriages. In addition to an autobiographical tetralogy (Fisher names his protagonist Vridar Hunter), the two early novels, *Toilers of the Hills* (1928) and *Dark Bridwell* (1931), deal with homesteading in the Idaho Territory. Fisher's early novels are characterized by the dark, deterministic vein of literary Realism known as Naturalism.

Among other writers of fiction worthy of mention are Colorado-born Frank Waters (1902–1995), whose first four books are set in his native state: *The Wild Earth's Nobility* (1935), a novel based on his family history; *Midas of the Rockies* (1937), a biography of Winfield Scott Stratton, who prospered in the Cripple Creek gold rush; *Below Grass Roots* (1937), which picks up where his first novel left off and covers the birth and boyhood of March Cable, whose life is based on Waters'; and *The Dust within the Rock* (1940), which completes the fictional trilogy. Waters' best-known novels, however, concern the Southwest (he moved to Taos, New Mexico, in 1938). Similarly, short story writer Damon Runyon (1884–1946), although he is associated with eccentric New York City gangsters and molls, wrote several stories that take place in Colorado (he grew up in Pueblo). In his *Vintage Colorado Short Stories: When Past Meets Present* (1997) James B. Hemesath anthologizes Runyon's memorable comedy "My Father," first published in 1911. Novelist Jean Stafford (1915–1979), whose career as a writer is also firmly associated with the East (she was poet Robert Lowell's [1917–1977] first wife), was born in Boulder, Colorado, and turned out several stories and one novel, *The Mountain Lion* (1947), set in her native state. But while such writers are worthy of mention, they are somewhat like shirttail relatives alongside Guthrie and Fisher.

There are many others. Artist Charlie Russell (1864–1926) turned out two collections of cowboy short stories during the 1920s. Renowned literary and cultural critic Bernard de Voto (1897–1955) was born in Ogden, Utah, and attended the University of Utah for a year before heading east to Harvard. Although he is best known as a literary and historical scholar, author of such volumes as *Mark Twain's*

America (1932), *The Year of Decision: 1846* (1943), and *Across the Wide Missouri* (1947), de Voto wrote three novels set in the Rockies, beginning with *The Crooked Mile* in 1926. Carol Ryrie Brink (1895–1981) is best known for her children's books, including the children's classic *Caddie Woodlawn*, which won the John Newbery Medal in 1936, but she also wrote three novels set in her native Idaho, the best known being *Buffalo Coat* (1944), which concerns small-town politics, ambitions, murder, and romance in the 1890s. Florence Crannell Means (1891–1980), who lived much of her life in Boulder, wrote some forty children's books, mostly concerning minorities, and she traveled the continent to do her research. Her novel on Japanese internment camps, *The Mover-Outers*, won a Newbery Medal in 1946. Born in Provo, Utah, Virginia Sorenson (1912–1991) was a successful writer of juvenile fiction, winning the Newbery award for *Miracles on Maple Hill* (1956), but she also wrote important novels dealing with Mormon issues, starting with *A Little Lower Than the Angels* (1942), which draws on the life of her mother-in-law's grandmother. And [Maxwell] Struthers Burt (1882–1954), who left a teaching job at Princeton University to homestead in Wyoming in 1908 and to set up a dude ranch, turned out five novels and three books of short stories of some note, beginning with *John O'May, and Other Stories* (1918).

It is impossible to make a sweeping statement that would do justice to the variety of characters, settings, incidents, and themes dealt with in the fiction mentioned above, but in the most general terms these writers examine the process of settling in. At one extreme of a hypothetical spectrum, novels like *The Big Sky* and *Mountain Man* are well-written literary reenactments of the Western Myth: Lone, rugged individualists overcome hostile elements, Indians, and outlaws. Guthrie's Boone Caudill, Fisher's Sam Minard, and Dorothy Johnson's Bert Barricune are more sophisticated characters than those one encounters in genre westerns, and as James C. Work has observed, Guthrie creates heroes of mythic dimension; he also commends the psychological complexity of Guthrie's protagonists. At the other end of that hypothetical spectrum, however, are characters whose lives, although often hard, are associated with the settlement of the Rocky Mountains region and with the development of the modern West as a place composed of families, farms and ranches, and communities: Margaret Walker's Ellen Webb, for example, and Stegner's memorable couples Bo and Elsa Mason and Susan and Oliver Ward and Fisher's Dock and Opal Hunter.

Second Generation Nonfiction

Not surprisingly, the nonfiction of the Second Generation focuses almost altogether on this latter end of the thematic spectrum, what one might describe as the Domestication of the West. A notable exception is James Willard Schultz's (1859–1947) autobiography of his years living with the Blackfeet (1883–1903) in *My Life as an Indian* (1907), but much of this book concerns his domestic life after he married a Pikuni (Piegan) woman. Schultz was to write nearly forty books, including *With the Indians in the Rockies* (1912) and numerous titles intended for juvenile readers. But the myth of the domesticated West clearly dominates the nonfiction of the Second Generation, as one can tell from *Letters of a Woman Homesteader*, by Elinore Rupert [Pruitt] Stewart (1878–1933), a widow who left Denver in 1909 with her young daughter to become a housekeeper for a rancher in

Wyoming: First published in 1914, her book served as material for the movie *Heartland* (1979).

The can-do attitude permeates the nonfiction of the Second Generation, which might seem to take its cue from Mary Hallock Foote's reminiscences. A similar memoir is Annie Pike Greenwood's (1879–1956) *We Sagebrush Folks* (1934), which chronicles their years on an irrigated farm in southern Idaho: "A clean kitchen one moment, and bits of sagebrush and dirt from the door to the woodbox the next." Greenwood's lyric rhapsody might represent nearly any such memoir from the Rockies: "I loved the vast, unspoiled wilderness, the fabulous sunsets, lakes of gold, and the dreamy, purple mountains. . . . It was not all beautiful. Idaho's wild winds raged for days at a time, lifting the earth in great clouds of dust." Greenwood's final chapter begins, "Yes, we lost the farm. Thank God! It had become a case of our losing the farm or the farm gobbling us up," a familiar lament during the Great Depression.[21] Similar accounts of settlement in Idaho are Grace Jordan's (c. 1900–1985) *Home Below Hell's Canyon* (1954), which concerns sheep ranching in the primitive Snake River gorge during the early 1930s, and Nelle Portrey Davis's (1901–1986) *Stump Ranch Pioneer* (1942), perhaps the most overtly "domestic" of the titles mentioned. The setting is Boundary County in northern Idaho, where the family moves in 1936 after losing their sheep ranch in Colorado.

Standing somewhat apart from the memoirs connected to such occupations as farming and ranching is Frank C. Robertson's (1890–1968) *A Ram in the Thicket* (1950). Born in Moscow, Idaho, Robertson, despite having only an eighth-grade education, was to become a prolific writer of genre westerns, seeing more than 130 titles in print. Roughly the first half of Robertson's memoir takes place in the Palouse country of the Idaho panhandle, where his occasionally abusive father rambles from job to job until he converts to Mormonism, after which the family moves to Chesterfield, a Mormon community in southeastern Idaho, where their fortunes improve considerably. The book, which moves swiftly through the 1920s and 1930s in the last chapters, is something of a tribute to Robertson's father. In *The Life of an Ordinary Woman* (1929) Colorado's Anne Ellis (1875–1938) describes her father as charming, good-looking, and cheerful but disinclined to work and provide for his family. In fact, her father deserts the family, so the early pages of Ellis' memoir of growing up in Colorado mining towns become something of a tribute to her mother. Mostly, however, her book is a straightforward account of her life as a miner's wife and a mother during the 1890s and the first two decades of the twentieth century.

More poignant than Anne Ellis' memoir is that of Margaret Bell (1888–1982), who, as Mary Clearman Blew observes in her introduction, grew up "poor and female in a frontier world controlled by men," particularly by her abusive, sadistic stepfather, who is given the name of Hedge.[22] Like Mary Hallock Foote's memoir, *When Montana and I Were Young* (2002) was not published until after the author's death and many years after the events recorded in its pages. Bell's memoir ends when she is about eighteen, so technically it belongs with the writing of the First Generation, but at the same time it might be said to belong with the memoirs of the Postwestern period, as its perspective involves a new version of western writing, and as Blew's introductory comments make clear, the memoir is the product of multiple authorship and of a feminist perspective that would have been alien to Bell when she began writing in the 1940s.

Second Generation Poetry

Writing of the 300 or so poems he collected in his *Northwest Verse: An Anthology* (1931), H.G. Merriam predicted the start of a literary movement in Washington, Oregon, Idaho, and Montana, but he noted that most of the verse was still at the descriptive as opposed to the interpretive stage, and he found the forms overly imitative and the subjects and themes too conventional. Few of the ninety-four poets whose works are represented would be familiar today, even to students of regional writing from the Pacific Northwest or the Rocky Mountains: Idaho's Vardis Fisher, Montana's Dorothy M. Johnson and Grace Stone Coates, and Oregon's H.L. Davis are better known as writers of fiction; other featured poets include John C. Frolicher, Gwendolen Haste, Ben Hur Lampman, Elliott C. Lincoln, Norman MacLeod, and Lew Sarrett, most of them hailing from Montana. That same year Idaho's Bess Foster Smith, one of whose poems appears in Merriam's volume, edited *Sunlit Peaks: An Anthology of Idaho Verse*, some 160 poems of even lesser distinction. Included in her anthology are poems by Irene Welch Grissom (1873–after 1950), who wrote of irrigation, ranching, and farming in the Idaho Falls area and was named Idaho's first poet laureate in 1923.

The single nationally prominent poet from the Rockies during the Second Generation period (that is, a poet whose work matured prior to 1970) was Thomas Hornsby Ferril (1896–1988), born in Denver and a lifelong resident. Coeditor of *The Rocky Mountain Herald* from 1939 to 1972, Ferril was named the Colorado state poet laureate in 1979, but his half dozen books of poetry date back to 1926, when he won the Yale University young poets competition with *High Passage*. Yale also published his second collection, *Westering*, in 1934. His new and selected poems appeared in 1952. Most of Ferril's poems, like "High-Line Ditch," which finds the first-person speaker riding "a quiet broncho, mountain bred / Along a prairie irrigation ditch," celebrate the region. The Rockies are "standing as if some child / Had cut the mountains out of purple cardboard, / And propped them far and cool behind the hayfields." The cottonwoods make "a silver tunnel for blue herons / That fly too slowly to be plausible."[23] Gwendolen Haste (1889–1979) spent about ten years in Billings and wrote poems reflecting on the lives of Montana's ranch women between 1927 and 1946, even after she moved East. More influential as a teacher than as a poet, Brewster Ghiselin (1903–1996) began teaching at the University of Utah in 1929; he founded and for many years headed the university's Utah Writer's Conference. His best-known work is *The Creative Process* (1952), a collection of essays from a symposium on invention in the arts.

To say that Thomas Hornsby Ferril is the only poet from the Rockies to have gained national prominence during the long Neowestern period entails at least two significant gestures. First, poets like Seattle-born Richard Hugo (1923–1983), who started teaching at the University of Montana in 1964, are placed among writers of the Postwestern period; that is, although some of their books were published earlier, they achieved prominence after 1970. Second, the hundreds of minor poets and poetasters, among whom are surely some accomplished versifiers whose efforts fill the pages of anthologies like *Northwest Verse* and *Sunlit Peaks*, both published in 1931, and *Rocky Mountain Reader* and *Montana Margins*, both published in 1946, are being set aside. While certain diamonds in the rough are thereby overlooked, the majority of the poems encountered in those regional anthologies are thick with cliché. In the popular imagination, perhaps as fed by poets themselves, heartless editors and publishers cruelly ignore thousands of worthy poems every day. The fact is that scores of books written by versifiers from all five Rocky Mountain states appeared in print between 1910 and 1970, but most of them are justifiably consigned to oblivion.

THE POSTMODERN ROCKIES (1970–2000)

Postmodern Fiction

Most writers from the Rockies distinguish between their nonfiction and their fiction. In fact, one might speculate that after having written one or two memoirs, most writers are compelled to turn elsewhere for their next books. Norman Maclean's (1902–1990) striking novellas *A River Runs through It* (1976) and *USFS 1919: The Ranger, the Cook, and a Hole in the Sky* (1976) are so pointedly autobiographical and memoirlike that he goes out of his way in the preface to advise the reader that they are fictional. Casual readers of Ivan Doig's novel *English Creek* (1984) may find themselves confusing the first-person speaker Jick McCaskill with the narrator of the memoir *This House of Sky*. Autobiographical fiction from the region can be traced back at least to Stegner.

Of course not all of the recent fiction from the Rockies has been autobiographical, and not all of it pertains to the region, but only that which does qualify as "regional" is of particular significance here. For various reasons, numerous writers from the region live there only part-time, and many writers whose fiction

Thomas McGuane, 1996. © Bassouls Sophie/Corbis Sygma.

continues to have settings in the Rocky Mountain states are recent or former residents, so deciding just who "belongs" is hard to judge. Pocatello native Tom Spanbauer, for example, located his first two novels, *Faraway Places* (1988) and *The Man Who Fell in Love with the Moon* (1991) in Idaho, but he has lived for years in New York City, and his most recent novel *In the City of Shy Hunters* (2002) concerns AIDS and the gay culture in Manhattan. Kent Haruf (1943–) has lived most of his adult years outside of Colorado but has relocated to Salida, Colorado, and much of his fiction is located in fictional small-town Holt, Colorado, where his novels *Where You Once Belonged* (1991) and *Plainsong* (1999) are set. *Plainsong* was a National Book Award finalist. Haruf's Holt, Colorado, in some respects parallels Thomas McGuane's (1939–) Deadrock, Montana, which first appears in his novel *Nobody's Angel*

(1982) and reappears in such novels as *Something to Be Desired* (1984) and *Nothing But Blue Skies* (1992). A Michigan native, McGuane's novels have varied in setting from his home state in *The Sporting Club* (1969) to the Florida Keys in *Ninety-two in the Shade* (1973), but his later novels, stories, and essays speak to his adoptive state (he raises cattle and horses on his 2,500-acre ranch near Livingston, Montana).

McGuane's career has led him in various directions, including work as a screenwriter on such films as *Rancho Deluxe* (1975), *Missouri Breaks* (1976), and *Tom Horn* (1980). "In essence," writes Dexter Westrum, "McGuane depicts the West's inability to fulfill its own frontier myths."[24] His recent books include thirty-three essays, sometimes meditative, sometimes humorous, on angling from the Florida Keys and Ireland to Montana, published as *The Longest Silence: A Life in Fishing* (1999), and his ninth novel, *The Cadence of Grass* (2002), which has been described as "wildly unsettling," "quirky," "complex and dark," and "a masterpiece of savage comedy." Reviews have remained mixed, however, throughout McGuane's career, and if some have celebrated his unrelenting comedy, others have complained of it. Novelist Larry McMurtry has expressed concern over the "grim marital feuding" in all five of the Deadrock novels.[25]

Kent Nelson's (1943–) novel *All Around Me Peaceful* (1989) and many of his short stories are set in Colorado. Although he lived for several years outside of the Rockies, Nelson grew up in Colorado Springs, and like Haruf, he now lives in Salida. His most recent novel *Land That Moves, Land That Stands Still* (2002), features three women who run a large ranch in South Dakota, and in a recent interview he explains that he finds women "more interesting than men," whom he characterizes as "jerks" who "start wars." Women's roles in the fiction of the Postwestern period have expanded considerably, owing largely to the significant increase in the number of women writing from the region. Marilynne Robinson's (1943–) lyrical novel *Housekeeping* (1980) is set in Fingerbone, her fictional name for Sandpoint, the town where she grew up in northern Idaho. A successful movie based on the novel came out in 1987, starring Christine Lahti. Judith Freeman (1946–), although she no longer considers herself a Mormon and no longer lives in her native Utah, has drawn heavily on Mormon culture in her fiction, which includes the novels *The Chinchilla Farm* (1989), *A Desert of Pure Feeling* (1996), and *Red Water* (2002). Although she now lives in northern Idaho, Claire Davis's novel *Winter Range* (2000) is set in the Montana cattle country where she grew up. In *Rima in the Weeds* (1991), Deirdre McNamer (1950–) lashes out against development on the Montana Hi-Line. Montana-born novelist Melanie Rae Thon (1957–), who teaches at the University of Utah, sets most of her stories and novels in the Rocky Mountain West, including *Iona Moon* (1993), which is set in rural Idaho, and *Sweet Hearts* (2000), which is set in Montana.

The numerous writers of short fiction in the region range from quondam residents like Patricia Henley (1947–), who was living in Bozeman when her first book, *Friday Night at the Silver Star* (1986), won the 1985 Montana Arts Council's First Book Award for fiction, to Wyoming newcomer Annie Proulx's (1935–) *Close Range: Wyoming Stories* (1999). Proulx is best known for her novel *The Shipping News* (1993), set in Newfoundland. Pam Houston's (1962–) stories in *Cowboys Are My Weakness* (1993) won a Western States Book Award. She lives on a ranch in southwestern Colorado. Rick DeMarinis (1934–) maintained dual residence in Missoula, Montana, where he received his B.A. and M.A. degrees in the 1960s and studied with poet Richard Hugo, during most of the years he taught at the University of Texas in El Paso. Although his novel *The Year of the Zinc Penny* was a *New York Times* Notable Book, DeMarinis is perhaps less known for his half a dozen novels than for the black humor of the stories in his five collections, beginning with *Under the Wheat* (1986). David Long (1948–   ), who lived many years in Kalispell, Montana, but now lives in Olympia, Washington, may be the premier writer of short fiction from the Rockies, featuring his adoptive state throughout his three collections, *Home Fires* (1982), *The Flood of '64* (1988), and *Blue Spruce* (1995). Rick Newby includes writers like Pete Fromm, McNamer, and Long among those who make up a "third wave" in Montana fiction in his anthology *The New Montana Story* (2003).

Among writers of what might qualify as "literary" mysteries from the region are Manuel Ramos (1948–   ), a Denver lawyer whose detective Luis Montez figures in four novels beginning with *The Ballad of Rocky Ruiz* (1993). Ramos' thrillers generally include social commentary on the Chicano experience. James Crumley's (1939–   ) half dozen detective novels featuring hard-boiled detectives C. W. Sughrue and Milo Milodragovitch, fashioned in the antiheroic Raymond Chandler tradition, take place in the West, often, like *Dancing Bear* (1984), in Montana. *The Mexican Tree Duck* (1993) won the Dashiell Hammett Award for Best Literary Crime Novel. His most recent novel is *The Final Country* (2002). His 1996 novel *Bordersnakes* pairs up his detectives and is set in his native Texas. Tim Sandlin (1950–   ) plays it fast and loose in a half dozen novels set in Wyoming featuring an often bizarre, zany humor reminiscent of Washington's Tom Robbins (*Even Cowgirls Get the Blues*). Sandlin's trilogy, *Skipped Parts*, *Sorrow Floats*, and *Social Blunders*, follows twenty years in the lives of a couple who grow up in a small Wyoming town. His most recent novel is *Honey Don't* (2003). Gino Sky (1935–   ), who lives in Boise, sets his bizarre Cowboy Buddha novels, *Appaloosa Rising* (1980) and *Coyote Silk* (1987) in a distinctly far-out West. He is also the author of several books of poetry and a book of autobiographical fiction, *Near the Postcard Beautiful* (1993).

Unlike the harsh urban world depicted in Coeur d'Alene writer Janet Campbell Hale's *The Jailing of Cecilia Capture* (1987), Salish-Kootenai novelist Debra Magpie Earling's (NA) *Perma Red* (2002) takes place on the Flathead Indian Reservation of Montana and is rich with the kind of visionary experience reminiscent of James Welch's (1940–2003) novels. Earling's novel won both a 2003 Spur Award and a Medicine Pipe Bearer Award. Welch's writing helped define Native American writing in the decades following N. Scott Momaday's Pulitzer Prize winning *House Made of Dawn* (1968). Welch, of Blackfeet and Gros Ventre heritage, began his literary career with a volume of poems, *Riding the Earthboy 40* (1971), noted for its surrealistic qualities and showing the strong influence of his mentor at the University of Montana, Richard Hugo. He followed the book with five powerful novels: *Winter in the Blood* (1974), *The Death of Jim Loney* (1979), *Fools Crow* (1986), *Indian Lawyer* (1990), and *The Heartsong of Charging Elk* (2000). In *Fools Crow*, a historic novel of epic dimensions that culminates in the Marias River Massacre of 1870, Welch captures the idiom and vision-laden culture of the Blackfeet in their last years as one of the most powerful plains tribes. Visionary moments in his other novels lend them something of the texture of surrealistic fantasy infused in contemporary, realistic settings.

Postmodern Nonfiction

Memoirs

In her introduction to *When Montana and I Were Young*, Mary Clearman Blew (1939–) refers to readers "seasoned by the memoir decade of the 1990s" (xxiv). Certainly the 1990s saw a blossoming of this self-reflexive genre, but while its origins may be traced in accounts of discovery and exploration dating back to Lewis and Clark and to journals of fur trappers like Osborne Russell and Andrew Garcia, and then in the writings of visitors like Isabella Lucy Bird and Helen Hunt Jackson, and then again in the memoirs of residents like Mary Hallock Foote, Annie Pike Greenwood, and Frank C. Robertson, there is something different about many of the memoirs written in the years following the success of Ivan Doig's (1939–) *This House of Sky* (1978). In a short essay titled "The Art of Memoir," published in *Bone Deep in Landscape* (1999), Blew writes of her struggle with the "literal" or "exact" truth, as opposed to the "emotional truth" of the story as she experienced it, and she concludes, "The boundaries of creative nonfiction will always be as fluid as water."[26]

The opening paragraph of Judith Blunt's (1954–) *Breaking Clean* (2002) might be paradigmatic for Rockies memoirs. She describes a ranch on "hardpan and sagebrush flats" that goes back four generations, "a country so harsh and wild and distant that it must grow its own replacements, as it grows its own food, or it will die."[27] Teresa Jordan's (1955–) *Riding the White Horse Home* (1993) reflects on her girlhood on the family ranch in the Iron Mountain country of southeastern Wyoming: "I was raised to be Western," Jordan writes, "which is to say stoic."[28] Typically, the location of such memoirs is an hour or more from the nearest town, which is most often a burg of just 2,000 or so population. Jordan's other books include a collection of more than a hundred interviews with ranch and rodeo women, *Cowgirls: Women of the Rural West* (1982, 1992) and two volumes of *Field Notes* containing her own watercolors of the Grand Canyon (2000) and Yosemite (2002). Doig's memoir and most of his novels are set around White Sulphur Springs in central Montana, the Rocky Mountain Front. *English Creek* (1984) introduces the McCaskill family and probably remains his most admired fiction, but he has produced three additional novels pertaining to Scottish homesteaders and sheepherding families in central or eastern Montana. Mary Blew's first memoir, *All But the Waltz* (1991), also takes place in central Montana, and her short fiction, the most ambitious of which is in *Sister Coyote* (2000), is most often set on cattle or sheep ranches in that vicinity. Events in her second memoir, *Balsamroot* (1994), occur in northern Idaho, where she currently resides, but it looks back to her favorite aunt's earlier days in Montana.

Certainly one important aspect of the Postwestern memoir is its critique of the life and values, largely patriarchal, into which the writers were born. Mary Blew sees her great-grandfather Abraham, a surveyor in the early 1880s, as a man whose job was "to convert landscape into property," and she struggles to deal with her father's embracing of the romantic myths of the Old West.[29] Judith Blunt struggles against the patriarchal system that aimed at marrying her off to a rancher before she had an opportunity to define her own life. Mark Spragg's (1952–) memoir from Wyoming, *Where Rivers Change Direction* (1999), also involves the world of horses, and it, too, concerns the necessity of being tough and measuring up to the physical demands of the outdoors. Like Doig's *This House of Sky*, Spragg's book at least begins as a tribute to his father, who runs the oldest dude ranch in Wyoming, but by the end of the memoir, his parents have divorced, and his mother is dying from cancer. Throughout these and other memoirs from the Rocky Mountains one gets the impression that something has gone wrong. In Kim Barnes's (1958–) memoir of growing up in northern Idaho, *In the Wilderness* (1996), the author struggles with her father's traditional patriarchal attitudes heightened by his conversion to Pentecostalism, and in *Hungry for the World* (2000) the rebellious Barnes ironically finds herself dominated and exploited by her abusive lover.

William Kittredge is not alone in arguing that the new stories of the West must involve an increased sense of community and responsibility, a "taking care" and a new generosity, and also a revised version of relations between the genders. Terry Tempest Williams's (1955–) *Refuge* (1991), a combination of natural history and memoir, culminates in a visionary dream of women circling a fire in the desert and speaking of change. As mothers they speak of a new contract being drawn up by women who connect the fate of the earth with their own. Her book involves connections in the world between her own life and that of the birds in the Bear River Migratory Bird Refuge, threatened by the rising Great Salt Lake, connections between the 1950s nuclear tests and her mother's death from breast cancer, and connections between her personal political views and her Mormon faith. A more apt term might be that of nineteenth-century French Symbolist poet Charles Baudelaire: "correspondences." Williams' other books include *Pieces of White Shell* (1984), *Desert Quartet: An Erotic Landscape* (1995), and *Red: Passion and Patience in the Desert* (2001). Chris Cokinos, who teaches at Utah State University, has also contributed to environmental nonfiction of the Rockies with his award-winning *Hope Is a Thing with Feathers: A Personal Chronicle of Vanished Birds* (2000). He edits the journal of nature and science writing, *Isotope*. Although his writing generally connects him with the Southwest, Edward Abbey's (1927–1989) first important work was *Desert Solitaire* (1968), a memoir and ecological testament set in the Arches National Monument of southeastern Utah.

Numerous other works of nonfiction from the Rockies move between memoir and environmental commentary, as do some of those mentioned above. Pete Fromm's (1958–) *Indian Creek Chronicles* (1993) concerns his seven months' initiation in Idaho's Selway-Bitterroot Wilderness area, where he tended salmon eggs. Fellow Montanan Rick Bass' (1958–) *Winter: Notes from Montana* (1991), a journal of his first winter in the primitive Yaak Valley of northwestern Montana, is one of several titles he has devoted to his personal drive to save a wilderness region from exploitation and development, among them *The Nine Mile Wolves* (1992), *The Book of Yaak* (1996), and *The Roadless Yaak* (2002). Both Fromm and Bass have also produced several books of fiction that feature stories set in the Rockies. Annick Smith's (1936–) *Homestead* (1996) and *In This We Are Native* (2001) are Montana memoirs written from the perspective of a newcomer who was to raise four sons on her own after her husband died at the age of forty-one. Like Fromm and Bass, and in fact like many writers of memoir from the Rocky Mountain region, Smith is an environmentalist, an identity that does not necessarily endear her to some longtime residents.

What separates the writer from the rancher/farmer in the region, even when the writer is herself or himself a rancher/farmer, or more often a former rancher/farmer, is what might be described as the rancher/farmer's pragmatic attitude toward land and water. Like Annick Smith, Gretel Ehrlich (1946–) discovered the Rockies, in her case a sheep ranch in Wyoming, only after having lived in a wholly different world. Smith was born in Paris to an artistic Hungarian Jewish family, and she grew up in Chicago; Ehrlich was born and raised in Santa Barbara, California and attended Bennington College, UCLA Film School, and the New School for Social Research. Ehrlich's memoir *The Solace of Open Spaces* (1985) recounts her adaptation to the region following the death of her lover, David, at the age of thirty. She grapples with the Wyoming character as much as with the rigors of its cold and wind: "People are blunt with one another, sometimes even cruel, believing honesty is stronger medicine than sympathy, which may console but often conceals."[30] She finds herself adopted by the sheepherders she lives among, and she continues to live in Shell, despite being struck twice by lightning, as described in *A Match to the Heart* (1994).

It could be argued, however, that despite their sense of fitting in, such writers inevitably find themselves outside the world of ranchers and farmers whose livelihood depends on the hard, dry, windy world the writers so eloquently depict. And the writers' politics are often at odds with those of the longtime residents, which tend to be strongly conservative, isolationist, and almost paranoid about government (federal in particular). In fact, many of the memoirists are or have been college professors of creative writing, employed by the state—for example, Kittredge, Blew, and Barnes. And most of the memoirists and other nonfiction writers from the region maintain close contacts with one academic community or another. Their present lives are not ranch lives, no matter how they might lament the passing of what they knew when growing up (Doig, Blunt, Spragg, Jordan). Similarly, Idaho's John Rember (1951–), although he subtitles his memoir *Traplines* (2003) "Coming Home to the Sawtooth Valley," went off to Harvard and currently lives in Caldwell, where he teaches at Albertson College.

There are many ways to subcategorize the varieties of memoir that reflect life in the Rocky Mountains. Those of Kittredge, Doig, Spragg, Fromm, Bass, and Rember, for example, could be described as "gendered male," just as those of Blew, Barnes, Blunt, Smith, Jordan, and Ehrlich could be described as "gendered female." Janet Campbell Hale's (1946–) memoir *Bloodlines* (1993), subtitled "Odyssey of a Native Daughter," traces her family's roaming away from and back to the area in the Idaho panhandle where the Coeur d'Alene tribe has its reservation. Hers is a painful account of alienation from her family and of coming to grips with her native heritage. Although he was born in Seattle, mixed-blood Gros Ventres writer Sidner J. Larson (1949–) speaks mostly of his years in Montana in his first book *Catch Colt* (1995). These might be described as "ethnic memoir."

Although memoir has dominated the nonfiction of the Postmodern Rocky Mountain West, it is not the exclusive subgenre. Mary Clearman Blew's *Bone Deep in Landscape* (1999) is a collection of essays on writing, reading, and place (namely, Montana), and most of Rick Bass' and Terry Tempest Williams' nonfiction is environmental writing. Colorado native James Galvin (1951–), who presently lives part of the year in Wyoming and part of the year in Iowa, where he teaches at the University of Iowa's Writers' Workshop, has created in *The Meadow* (1992) a book that might be described as part memoir, part local history (both of people and of a place), part fiction, and part poetry. Montana's David Quammen is a renowned science writer of the kind known as a "naturalist," which means that he writes with scientific accuracy and authority for a readership mostly of nonscientists, or at least of nonspecialists. His accessible and, in effect, "literary" books of essays include *Natural Acts: A Sidelong View of Science and Nature* (1985) and *Wild Thoughts from Wild Places* (1998), both drawn from his columns in *Outside* magazine. Similarly, Ann Zwinger (1925–), who lives in Colorado Springs, has written nearly twenty books of natural history, including *Beyond the Aspen Grove* (1970), *Wind and Rock: The Canyonlands of Southeastern Utah* (1978), *The Nearsighted Naturalist* (1998), and most recently, *Shaped by Wind and Water: Reflections of a Naturalist* (2000). C. L. Rawlins' nonfiction includes *Sky's Witness* (1992), drawn from a year he spent monitoring air pollution for the Forest Service in the Wind River range in Wyoming, and *Broken Country* (1996), a memoir of the year 1973 spent in the Salt River mountains herding sheep.

In the Postmodern age of professional writers, whether they sustain themselves by teaching, as do most of the poets, or by other means, including spousal income, crossing genres is more the rule than the exception. C. L. Rawlins, for example, is also a poet, whose most recent book, *In Gravity National Park* (1998), is said to celebrate "the ferocity and majesty of nature." James Galvin's published work also includes a novel, *Fencing the Sky* (1999), and half a dozen books of poetry, including his collected poems *Resurrection Update* (1997). William Kittredge, David Quammen, Gretel Ehrlich, Rick Bass, Janet Campbell Hale, Mark Spragg, Mary Blew, and Kim Barnes—indeed *most* writers of nonfiction from the Rocky Mountain West—have all turned out creditable fiction, both stories and novels. Particularly with the memoir, the subgenres of prose have blended. Australian writer Jill Ker Conway asks in the opening sentence of *When Memory Speaks: Reflections on Autobiography* (1998), "Why is autobiography the most popular form of fiction for modern readers?"[31]

Postmodern Poetry

Poet Richard Hugo's (1923–1982) name has been invoked on several occasions in this chapter in part because the nearly twenty years he spent teaching at the University of Montana in Missoula, starting in 1964, provided identity to what has become one of the premier M.F.A. programs in creative writing in the country. His influence has been considerable, not only on such poets as James Welch, Sandra Alcosser, and Robert Wrigley but also on writers of fiction as diverse as Rick DeMarinis and David Long. More significantly, however, Hugo set the benchmark for regional poetry in the Rocky Mountain West, and it is doubtful whether any poet has come close to that standard. Beginning with *The Lady in Kicking Horse Reservoir* (1973), Hugo visited dozens of Montana sites by name: "Helena, Where Homes Go Mad," "The Only Bar in Dixon," "Missoula Softball Tournament," "Driving Montana." In "Degrees of Gray in Philipsburg," which features Hugo's recurring color, the speaker comes "on a whim" because his life has broken down: "The principal supporting business now / is rage. Hatred of the various grays / the mountain sends, hatred of the mill, The Silver Bill repeal, the best liked girls / who leave each year for Butte."[32] Montanans will catch the joke: Butte is hardly the big time.

Edward Dorn (1929–1999) started his life as a poet studying with Charles Olson and Robert Creeley at Black Mountain College in North Carolina, and between 1961 and 1965 he taught at Idaho State University in Pocatello. One product of that stay is the longish poem "Idaho Out," from *Geography* (1965). By 1977 he was teaching at the University of Colorado, where he continued his prolific output, some thirty books of poems and a dozen other books, mostly through such small presses as Fulcrum and Black Swallow, which published his mock-epic *Gunslinger* poems starting in 1968. His poems, many of which are set in the West, show the experimental "open" style promoted in Olson's manifesto *Projective Verse*, which appeared in 1950, and are rigorously antiestablishment and countercultural in sentiment. Also out of Boulder, but more devoted to regional focus in his work, Reg Saner (1931–) began his long teaching career at the University of Colorado in 1962. His first collection of poems, *Climbing into the Roots* (1976), won the Walt Whitman Award, and his second, *So This Is the Way* (1981), was selected in the open competition for the National Poetry Series. He has written half a dozen books, poetry and prose, on the American West.

It may be that most poets believe the best poems transcend regional identity. Apparently writers of nonfiction are the most likely to mine the region. But surely a good case can be made for the premise that good poems achieve the universal through, or by means of, images born of the region. Ron McFarland (1942–), named Idaho's first state writer-in-residence in 1984, reflects on his adoptive state in a generally light and playfully ironic vein in several poems from *Stranger in Town* (2000): "Idaho Requiem," "Bad Lunch in Cottonwood, Idaho," "At the Regional Hospital," and "An Idaho Perspective." Native Idahoan William Studebaker (1944–) records his lifelong fascination with the state in such poems as "The Bruneau Desert," "In Hells Canyon," and "The Big-Sky Map of Idaho" in *Travelers in an Antique Land* (1997), a book illustrated with black and white photographs by Russell Hepworth. Studebaker and McFarland collaborated in editing *Idaho's Poetry: A Centennial Anthology* (1988), which gathers poems from Native American oral tradition and gold rush versifiers as well as contemporaries. Studebaker's most recent collection, *Passions We Desire* (2002), reflects his enthusiasm for kayaking.

Idaho's best-known poet, and probably the only contemporary with a national reputation, is Robert Wrigley (1951–), who won a Kingsley Tufts Award in 2000 for *Reign of Snakes*. The images, and particularly the fauna, of the inland Northwest began to figure prominently in Wrigley's poems with *Moon in a Mason Jar* (1986), which followed receipt of his M.F.A. degree from the University of Montana. He transforms his love of music into rich lyricism reminiscent of Theodore Roethke, Hugo's mentor at the University of Washington. In his most recent book, *Lives of the Animals* (2003), Wrigley reveals the natural world infused with the passion of love and death, from horseflies, snakes, and swallows to deer, moose, coyotes, and bear. Domestic animals (dogs, cats, horses) are also part of this world, and in "Snake in the Trough," he brings the domestic and the wild together with deadly results, as is also the case in his poems on encounters between deer and automobiles, "The Other World" and "Highway 12, Just East of Paradise, Idaho."

Montana's successors to Richard Hugo, with the exception of his former student and onetime bronc-rider Paul Zarzyski, have not generally gravitated toward their adoptive state with his enthusiasm. Greg Pape (1947–), for example, scatters only a few poems specific to Montana in his books, including *Storm Patterns* and *Sunflower Facing the Sun*, both of which appeared in 1992. While Pape's poems reflect the nature of the West, it is most commonly that of the Southwest (he received his M.F.A. from the University of Arizona). This is not to say that Pape never writes of Montana. "To a Woman on the Local News" follows a demented woman's flight from the police from Florence to Lolo to Missoula, and poems like "Wading the Bitterroot" and "Photograph of Richard Hugo" speak to the region and reflect Pape's fondness for trout fishing. Patricia Goedicke (1931–) has taught for many years at the University of Montana, but the intimate world of human relationships dominates her dozen books, and a poem like "Mountainside Farm" could be located anywhere. Goedicke's disinclination to embrace Montana in her poems may be implicit in the poem "Time Zones," from her most recent book *As Earth Begins to End* (2000). Speaking on the phone with her sister in Virginia, whose husband is dying, the Boston-born poet writes, "out here in the West taking the long view / it's the emptiness I can't stand, the prairie grass blowing, / miles and miles of it between one town and another."[33]

Less renowned than Pape or Goedicke, Paul Zarzyski is the rare poet who can sustain a following among readers of both "serious literary poetry" and "cowboy poetry," but most of the poems in his first book, *The Make-Up of Ice* (1984), did not focus on either cowboys or rodeos. The lead poem, however, has become the title of his recent collection, *All This Way for the Short Ride: Roughneck Sonnets* (1996), which captures the mingled humor and pathos that dominates the genre, from Baxter Black to Waddie Mitchell. Zarzyski is a popular performer at the annual cowboy poets gathering in Elko, Nevada. The book is illustrated with ranching and rodeo photographs by Barbara Van Cleve. Similarly skating the thin ice that separates the literary from the popular is Greg Keeler, who teaches at Montana State University in Bozeman and whose humorous poems on fishing (or misfishing) he often performs to the twang of his guitar. His books include *American Falls* (1987) and *A Mirror to the Safe* (1997); his CD *Trout Ball* features such unlikely tunes as "Whitefish Blues," "Neoprene Waders," and "Little Bitch Creek," a trout fly (nymph) named after a Beach Boys song. David Lee (1944–), who chairs the English Department at Southern Utah University, has been known familiarly as "the pig poet" ever since the publication of *The Porcine Legacy* (1974), noted for its broad western humor and redneck dialect. Named Utah's first poet laureate, Lee's most recent book is *A Legacy of Shadows* (1999). In effect, it is quite possible to be at the same time a college professor and a populist poet, as opposed to an "academic" poet.

From the foregoing one may deduce that there is a sort of hierarchy in poetry, and perhaps in all art. Folk poems, light verse, and most cowboy poetry represent the popular tier, defined largely by the nature of the audience, which often responds most readily to performance. Dialect (generally what one might describe as Standard American Redneck) and slang, often (but not always) intentionally erroneous grammar, simple diction and syntax, and cliché or transparent metaphors predominate. At the other end of this hypothetical spectrum are the poems read closely and intently by the apparently ever-dwindling number of those who consider themselves to be readers of serious poems. While the voices and styles of the poets who write for this largely academic audience vary considerably, the poems generally deal with complex ideas and reject folksy usage, including dialect. The poets employ generally sophisticated diction and syntax, often striving for nuances of meaning that should (at least) send even serious readers to their dictionaries, and they reach for freshness and ingenuity, sometimes for intentional complexity, in their images and metaphors, often taking considerable risks in the process. Such poets tend to pursue publication of their work aggressively, aiming for the most selective and competitive literary magazines, contests, and publishers: Hugo, Wrigley, Goedicke, and most of the others mentioned in this chapter exemplify these poets. Zarzyski, Keeler, and Lee are what might be considered exemplary types of the popular end of the spectrum.

Massed perhaps uneasily somewhere between the ends of the spectrum are a large number of poets of what might be called "middling reputation." Typically, they seek out what Renaissance commentators then called a "middle style." They tend to find only rare acceptance in the more prestigious literary magazines, and their books are generally published by small presses and achieve minimal marketing and distribution. There are literally thousands of good but less selective literary magazines and hundreds of small presses. Alan Swallow's (1915–1966) Swallow Press, which dates back to 1940, was one of the most notable pioneers among such presses. Himself a middle-tier poet, Swallow taught for several years at the University of Denver before devoting himself full-time to his press, for which he did it all (edit, design, print, and market). His output eventually expanded to some thirty titles a year. McFarland and Studebaker number among the midway poets mentioned above.

Bin Ramke (1947–), who has directed the creative writing program at the University of Denver for a number of years, is among the poets of the first tier. Perhaps these poets might be described as those whom other poets read and admire; they are the poets' poets. While his earlier books look back to his boyhood in the Southeast, featuring many poems set in Louisiana, Ramke rarely centers his poems in the Rockies. In his most recent book, *Airs, Waters, Places* (2001), his poems move from the cerebral to the downright esoteric. Both conceptually and stylistically they are beyond the reach of what one might think of as a popular audience or a casual reader of poems. Pattianne Rogers (1940–), who lives near Colorado Springs, may be the most environmentally aware poet of the day; certainly her understanding of science distinguishes her from most poets, although her biological field of reference is that of the naturalist rather than the professional zoologist or botanist. The most recent of her ten books is *Song of the World Becoming, New and Collected Poems, 1981–2001* (2001).

Sandra Alcosser (1944–), who divides her time between San Diego, where she teaches creative writing at San Diego State University, and Florence, Montana, received her M.F.A. from the University of Montana in 1982, and several poems in *A Fish to Feed All Hunger* (1986) involve women in Montana settings. Her most recent collection is *Except by Nature* (1997). Denver-born Linda Hogan (1947–) has taught at the University of Colorado since 1989. She writes frequently of her Chickasaw heritage, setting many of her poems on tribal lands in Oklahoma, and her first novel, *Mean Spirit* (1994), which was a finalist for the Pulitzer Prize and the National Book Award, is set there during the 1920s. Her sixth and most recent collection of poems is *The Book of Medicines* (1993). Seattle-born Paisley Rekdal (1970–) taught for several years at the University of Wyoming but has recently begun teaching at the University of Utah. To date, her poems, including those in her most recent book, *Six Girls without Pants* (2002), have been largely concerned with issues of gender and sexuality. From the foregoing one may derive one other identifying feature of first-tier poets; that is, most of them teach poetry writing courses at the university (M.F.A.) level. Utah's current poet laureate, Kenneth Brewer, taught for thirty-two years at Utah State University. His books include *To Remember What Is Lost* (1982) and *The Place in Between* (1998). Poetry may not pay, but teaching it does. The most prominent Mormon poet of this period was native Utahan Clinton F. Larson (1919–1994),

Rocky Mountain Newspapers

While the hundred-odd newspapers listed from the five Rocky Mountain states have not produced a bumper crop of Pulitzer Prize winners since the award was initiated in 1917, journalists often flirt with literature, sometimes intentionally and sometimes not. Among the writers mentioned in this chapter, several have turned out journalistic pieces first published in newspapers or mass-circulation magazines that subsequently appear in books that are regarded as "literature": William Kittredge, David Quammen, and Rick Bass are three cases in point.

Among the half dozen journalists or newspaper staffs to win Pulitzers for writing are Dave Curtin (*Colorado Springs Gazette Telegraph*, 1990), Eric Newhouse (*Great Falls* [MT] *Tribune*, 2000), Robert D. Mullins (*Deseret News*, Salt Lake City, 1962), and staff of *The Denver Post* (1986 and 2000). Historically, newspapers offered pioneers and settlers a dash of literature via patented inside short stories and poems, sometimes by local writers, but the days when towns of 10,000 or so population could boast two or three rival newspapers are long gone. And gone, too, are some of the towns that fostered frontier newspapers like Fort Bridger, Wyoming's *Daily Telegraph* (founded in 1863); Lewiston, Idaho's *Golden Age* (1862); Silver City, Idaho's *Owyhee Avalanche* (1865); and Virginia City, Montana's *Montana Post* (1864). A few of the frontier newspapers have survived, however, including Salt Lake City's *Deseret News* (1850) and Denver's *Rocky Mountain News* (1859).

The "flagship" paper of the Rockies is the *Denver Post*, the motto of which is "Voice of the Rocky Mountain Empire," but in a recent article Ray Ring of the *High Country News*, an independent biweekly out of Paonia, Colorado, noted for its environmental advocacy, insists that "only a few" of the West's 240 English-language dailies "do their work well."[34] Ring observes that only the *Durango* [CO] *Herald* was noted for excellence by the Institutes for Journalism and Natural Resources, and he connects the decline of quality in news reporting to the spread of national newspaper chains like Gannett. Each of the five states covered in this chapter can boast of one or two leadings newspapers. In addition to the Colorado papers mentioned above, to which one might add Boulder's *Daily Camera*, for Idaho those would be the *Idaho Statesman* out of Boise, the *Lewiston Morning Tribune*, and the Idaho edition of Spokane, Washington's *Spokesman-Review*; for Montana, *The Missoulian* and the *Billings Gazette*; for Utah, in addition to the *Deseret News*, the *Salt Lake City Tribune*; for Wyoming, the *Casper Star Tribune*, the *Sheridan Press*, and the *Wyoming Tribune-Eagle* out of Cheyenne. From the literary viewpoint, perhaps the most important periodical in the Rockies is the *Bloomsbury Review*, which has been published bimonthly for the past twenty-three years out of Denver and specializes in reviews of books from the region.

who taught for thirty-five years at Brigham Young University; his *Selected Poems* appeared in 1988.

Mary Crow (1933–   ), who began her second four-year term as Colorado's poet laureate, a governor's appointment, in 2000, has taught at Colorado State University (CSU) since 1964. She has translated several poets from the Spanish and has written five books of her own, the most recent being *I Have Tasted the Apple* (1996). Laura Mullen also teaches at CSU, her most recent books being a collection of postmodern Gothic stories, *The Tales of Horror*, and a book of poems, *After I Was Dead*, both published in 1999. Donald Revell (1954–   ) teaches at the University of Utah. The most recent of his eight books is *My Mojave* (2003). Robert Roripaugh (1930–   ), the current Wyoming poet laureate, taught at the University of Wyoming for some thirty-five years, starting in 1949. His western novel *Honor Thy Father* (1963) won recognition from the National Cowboy Hall of Fame. His books of poetry are *Learn to Love the Haze* (1976) and *Ranch: Wyoming Poetry* (reprinted 2001). His daughter Lee Ann Roripaugh teaches at the University of South Dakota. Her first book, *Beyond Heart Mountain* (1999), was a National Poetry Series selection. It deals with the Japanese Americans who were interned at Heart Mountain, Wyoming, during World War II. Gretel Ehrlich's novel *Heart Earth* (1988) is also drawn from that historical event.

Not all poets are teachers. Wyoming's Charles Levendosky (1936–   ) is an editor and award-winning columnist for the *Casper Star-Tribune*, but he has produced eleven books and chapbooks of poetry, beginning with *Perimeters* (1970) and including *Wyoming Fragments* (1981) and most recently *The Peeping Tom Poems* (2003). Vietnam veteran David Romtvedt (1950–   ), who lives in Buffalo and teaches part-time at the University of Wyoming, combines music and poetry and has also written both fiction, *Crossing Wyoming* (1992), and nonfiction, *Windmill: Essays from Four Mile Ranch* (1997). His CD *Ants on Ice* was released in 2000, and his books of poems include a 1991 National Poetry Series selection, *A Flower Whose Name I Did Not Know*, and *Certainty* (1996).

All of the foregoing, one might ask, amounts to what? One would like to say simply that the whole amounts to more than the sum of its parts. This sprawling chapter touches on writers who write or have written from the five Rocky Mountain states over the past 200 years, and its focus is on those who write of and for the region. Virtually no poet writes *only* of the region he or she lives in and cares about; Richard Hugo's early books in particular speak to his years in Seattle and to his experiences as a bombardier stationed in Italy during World War II. Few writers of fiction or nonfiction set all of their books in the same site. For writers like Hamlin Garland and Frank Waters, the books they set in the Rockies are an important part of their achievement, but not necessarily the part for which they are best remembered. Like other citizens of this restless nation, writers come and go. The early literary response to the Rocky Mountain West was largely the work of visitors, sojourners at best. Only with the Second Generation (1910–1970) do we encounter significant numbers of residents who lived many years and occasionally all of their lives in the region. The surge in population since 1970 has left the region with writing scenes of all sorts, but particularly in the larger cities and university towns. Writers, like other artists, tend to congregate, as the recent memorial service for James Welch (August 27, 2003) in Missoula, Montana, demonstrated dramatically. Ivan Doig, Mary Blew, Rick DeMarinis, Robert Wrigley, Gretel Ehrlich, James Crumley, William Kittredge, Annick Smith, Judith Blunt, Paul Zarzyski, and many other writers named in this chapter attended.

How cohesive, though, is the literary world of the Rocky Mountain West? Some writers speak jokingly of a Montana Mafia. Others would argue that the proper literary capital of the Rockies is not Missoula but Denver—or perhaps Salt Lake City. All five states have arts councils funded mostly through the National Endowment for the Arts, and these offer a similar array of programs for writers, including state poets laureate or writers-in-residence, fellowships and writing grants, annual conferences and workshops, and readings. Writers congregate at such events as the BookFest in Boise and the Festival of the Book in Missoula, both usually held in September, or the Rocky Mountain Book Festival, the most recent being in Denver in April 2002. Moreover, most of the states have independent writers' leagues like the Idaho Writers League, the Colorado Authors League, and the League of Utah Writers.

The Western States Arts Foundation (WESTAF), organized in 1991, administers a community-based literature program called "TumbleWords: Writers Rolling Around the West" that covers the five states from the Rockies along with Nevada, Arizona, and New Mexico. The *TumbleWords* anthology, edited by William L. Fox and published by the University of Nevada Press in 1995, gathers writing from participating poets and authors who give readings and run workshops throughout the region. These programs reflect the awareness that the states of the interior West have been culturally isolated and, as WESTAF director Donald Meyer observes, "underserved." The goals of such programs, and of the arts councils so far as they are involved with literature, have been to develop new audiences and readers, particularly for regional and local writers. The three states initially involved, presumably those most isolated and underserved, were Utah, Idaho, and Wyoming. The intent has been to provide connections for and among writers and between writers and communities. The literary communities of the Rocky Mountain region remain distinct in most ways, but certainly they are more interconnected today than they have been at any time in the past, and there is likely to be even greater identity and cohesion in the future.

RESOURCE GUIDE

Printed Resources

The Western Literature Association has sponsored two hefty volumes that provide an invaluable starting point: J. Golden Taylor and Thomas J. Lyon, eds., *A Literary History of the American West* (Fort Worth: Texas Christian University Press, 1987); note particularly Levi S. Peterson's essay "The Rocky Mountains," 822–848. Thomas J. Lyon, ed., *Updating the Literary West* (Fort Worth: Texas Christian University Press, 1997); note particularly Gregory L. Morris's essay "The Rocky Mountains," 731–752. Both of these essays are accompanied by selected bibliographies.

An invaluable research and ready reference tool is the collection of booklets in Boise State University's Western Writers Series, which now numbers more than 150, dealing with writers ranging from Vardis Fisher and Mary Hallock Foote to Gretel Ehrlich and William Kittredge.

Fox, William L., ed. *Tumblewords: Writers Reading the West*. Reno: University of Nevada Press, 1995.

Kittredge, William, ed. *The Portable Western Reader*. New York: Penguin, 1997.

Kowaleski, Michael, ed. *Reading the West: New Essays on the Literature of the American West*. New York: Cambridge University Press, 1996.

Lyon, Thomas J., ed. *The Literary West*. New York: Oxford University Press, 1999.

Meldrum, Barbara Howard, ed. *Old West–New West: Centennial Essays*. Moscow: University of Idaho Press, 1993.

Morris, Gregory L. *Talking Up a Storm: Voices of the New West*. Lincoln: University of Nebraska Press, 1994.

Work, James C., ed. *Prose and Poetry of the American West*. Lincoln: University of Nebraska Press, 1990.

Festivals and Conferences

Flathead River Writers Conference
Whitefish, MT 59937
http://writing.shawguides.com/FlatheadRiverWritersConference/

Held annually in the fall.

Features speakers, panel discussions, and one-on-one workshops; aimed at improving writing skills in a variety of areas.

Great Salt Lake Book Festival
Salt Lake City
http://www.utahhumanities.org/bookfestival/bookfestival2003.php

High Plains Bookfest
Billings, MT
http://www.msubillings.edu/library/bookfest/bookfest1.htm

Idaho BookFest
Boise, ID
http://www.logcablit.org/Bookfest03/2003%20BookFest%20Schedule.htm

International Ezra Pound Conference
Sun Valley, ID
http://www.isu.edu/departments/pound/index.html

Montana Festival of the Book
Missoula, MT
http://www.bookfest-mt.org/

Rocky Mountain Book Festival
Denver, CO
http://www.coloradocenterforthebook.org/

Wyoming Writers, Inc. Conference
Cody, WY
http://www.wyowriters.org/

Organizations

Colorado Center for the Book
2123 Downing Street
Denver, CO 80205
303-839-8320
ccftb@compuserve.com
http://www.coloradocenterforthebook.org/

Colorado Council on the Arts
1380 Lawrence Street, Suite 1200
Denver, CO 80204
303-866-2723
coloarts@state.co.us
http://www.coloarts.state.co.us/default.asp

Idaho Center for the Book
Hemingway Western Studies Center
Boise State University
Boise, ID 83725
ttrusky@boisestate.edu
http://www.lili.org/icb/

Idaho Commission on the Arts
2410 North Old Penitentiary Road
Boise, ID 83712
208-334-2119 or 800-278-3863
http://www2.state.id.us/arts/

Montana Arts Council
P. O. Box 202201
Helena MT 59620-2201
406-444-6430
mac@state.mt.us
http://www.art.state.mt.us/

Montana Center for the Book
311 Brantly Hall
University of Montana
Missoula, MT 59812-7848
406-243-6022 or 800-624-6011 (in Montana)
lastbest@selway.umt.edu
http://www.montanabook.org/

Utah Arts Council
617 East South Temple
Salt Lake City, UT 84102-1177
801-236-7555
http://arts.utah.gov/index.html

Utah Center for the Book
Salt Lake City Public Library
210 East 400 South
Salt Lake City, UT 84111
801-524-8200
http://www.slcpl.lib.ut.us/details.jsp?parent_id=15&page_id=59

Western States Arts Federation (WESTAF)
Literary Arts Programs
1743 Wazee Street, Suite 300
Denver, CO 80202
888-562-7232 or 303-629-1166
http://www.westaf.org/prog-literaryarts.php

Wyoming Arts Council
2320 Capitol Avenue
Cheyenne, WY 82002
307-777-7742
http://wyoarts.state.wy.us/staff.html

Wyoming Center for the Book
Wyoming State Library
Lesley Boughton, State Librarian
2301 Capitol Avenue
Cheyenne, WY 82002
lbough@state.wy.us
http://www.wsl.state.wy.us/slpub/cenbook/

MUSIC

Stephanie Baker, Sharon Graf, and Petra Meyer-Frazier

The Rocky Mountain West is one of the most mythologized regions in the United States. The identity of the region relies on the dichotomy of heavy tourism contrasted with bristling locals interested in preserving a remote character. Such contradictions lead to successful enterprises, such as Cheyenne's popular Frontier Days Festival. Historian Patricia Limerick notes, "Tourists do not need any assistance in defining frontierland." The list of images includes, without dissension: "mountain men, cowboys, prospectors, pioneer wives, saloon girls, sheriffs, and outlaws. Teepees, log cabins, and false-front stores; coonskin hats, cowboy hats, bandannas, buckskin shirts . . . moccasins . . . sunbonnets or calico dress . . . canoes . . . covered wagons, and stagecoaches."[1] One only has to look at a rerun of *Dr. Quinn, Medicine Woman* or the movie *Unforgiven* (1992) to see how ubiquitous this historical vision of the West is. Similarly, the modern concept of the region as an outdoor playground with grand vistas and powdered slopes is equally mythologized, as seen prominently in ads by the Coors Brewing Company. These images are successful in part due to their accompanying sonic characteristics: cowboy ballads, square dancing, saloon and parlor piano music, and Native American rituals, to name a few.

Music and dance are two primary iconic carriers of culture, and the Rocky Mountain region is "booming" with the sounds and sights of artistic pursuit. Today one can choose among regional rock band String Cheese Incident, Telluride's bluegrass festival, Cleo Parker Robinson's dance troupe, Ballet West, Central City Opera, Berlioz at the Aspen Music Festival, the Lionel Hampton Jazz Festival, or a concert of the Mormon Tabernacle Choir. Inclusive within the events constantly taking place in the region are myriad uses of the mythology of the region to create an "American" sound or image within a work of art, including Charles Ives' "Charlie Rutlage," Libby Larson's *Songs from Letters*, John Denver's recording of "Rocky Mountain High," and Aaron Copland and Eugene Loring's *Billy the Kid*. Music and dance work with the images of the region, both on site and as "muse" to the American artist, to define cultural life in the Rocky Mountain region.

NATIVE AMERICAN MUSIC IN THE ROCKY MOUNTAIN STATES

Before the nineteenth century, the Rocky Mountain states were largely populated by what ethnographers identify as Plains cultures and by Great Basin and Plateau cultures. While these culture areas differ in languages shared, patterns of subsistence, political organization, religious beliefs, and manufacturing specialties, they share a central idea about music making that is distinct from general western notions: Music is intimately connected to its context.

Alan Merriam points out in his landmark study of Plateau Flathead Indians in northwestern Montana that the western aesthetic is different from the Native American in that native culture does not have any comparable quality of psychical distance. Traditional galleries and concert halls display objects or musical pieces as things in and of themselves, separate from function or creator. In contrast, Native American art and music is so complexly linked to its context that it cannot be displayed and analyzed this way. Flathead consultants who worked with Merriam unanimously agreed that each of their songs had a specific purpose or context and should never be used for another. "People who do so are either ignorant to an unbelievable degree or, more likely, are drunk, or perhaps trying to be funny. . . . As one informant phrased the matter, 'Any song made for one kind of doings, that's where you sing it.'"[2] The categories of songs Merriam collected include life cycle, social, war complex, ceremonial, and miscellaneous, including songs of joy and animal dances. Merriam's stress on the importance of song context among the Flathead applies to Plains, Plateau, and Great Basin people's music alive, which is usually performed in connection with some event such as a religious ceremony, a game, an everyday chore, or a social occasion.

In both historic and modern Plains tribal life, self-inflicted suffering is the major feature of a widespread ritual known as the Sun Dance. Dancers participate in this ceremony seeking health and well-being for themselves, family members, and others. The hardship one must endure to receive blessings has changed over time and varies among Plains tribes. On the Wind River Reservation, contemporary Shoshones practice fasting, which usually lasts three days (Friday evening to sometime on Monday). Music is an integral part of the ceremony, and dancing is performed intermittently throughout the fasting period, accompanied by drumming and singing. The Sun Dance Chief also performs a Sunrise song and a special set of Morning Prayer songs at the beginning of each of day. The ceremony commonly concludes with "Forty Nine" songs, a genre in which comical English texts appear suddenly in contrast to the sung syllables or "vocables" that make up the rest of the song. One of the few detailed studies of Native American musical traditions in the Rocky Mountain region is Judith Vander's study of five Shoshone women.[3] All five could sing Sun Dance songs and said these songs played a meaningful role in their lives.

Handgames, featuring pairs of bones hidden by players' hands, have been historically popular among many tribes including the Plains Shoshone of the Wind River Reservation in central Wyoming. Two equal-sized teams sit facing each other behind two parallel logs three feet apart on the ground. Each team tries to guess which of two of the opposing team members' hands hold the unmarked bones. The hiding team usually begins singing a Handgame song just after the bone is hidden and ends when the other team guesses the correct hand with the unmarked bone. Singers accompany themselves with a stick tapping a light steady pulse. Singing the Handgame song serves both to distract the opposing team and to entertain the team waiting for the guessing to take place. Often the songs are accentuated at wrong guesses as a form of taunt, further distracting the competition. A similar Flathead version of this game is called Stick Game. Merriam observed these games in the 1950s and collected a number of songs. The Flathead and their Kootenai neighbors still enjoy hand games as part of social events, and they use songs to bring them gambling luck.

By the late nineteenth century, U.S. governmental policy confined Native Americans to reservations, simultaneously dislocating tribes from their homelands and uniting them with other tribes with whom they formerly had no common interests. As a result, North American natives began to see themselves as a national "race" of people. Music and dance has proven to be a powerful tool for cultural, psychological, and social survival of Native Americans. In the Rocky Mountains, as in greater North America, tribe-specific musical genres persist as well as pantribal traditions.

The Ghost Dance was one of the first widespread pantribal ceremonies among Native Americans. The Ghost Dance movement and related songs originated in the Great Basin Area (Utah, Arizona, New Mexico) and by the 1880s had spread rapidly. Indians performing the Ghost Dance believed a spirit would send the oppressive government and settlers back to where they came from. They also believed their deceased great Indian leaders would be resurrected and the buffalo would return to provide them with their former way of life. Because performance of the Ghost Dance was aimed at exorcising non-Indians, the U.S. Army declared the dance illegal. The Wounded Knee massacre in South Dakota was the result of a misunderstanding related to the Ghost Dance and resulted in 146 Indian deaths and 51 wounded. Vander found Ghost Dance songs in the repertory of four of the five women she worked with and suggests those who sing Ghost Dance have strong connections to the generation of Wounded Knee. The one woman who did not sing Ghost Dance songs was more than fifteen years younger and more removed from the strong beliefs associated with these songs. Perhaps even more important, she belonged to a family who had witnessed the failure of the songs to produce their intended healing effects and so chose to sing other, more rewarding, types of songs.

Since the nineteenth century, many American Indians have practiced Native American Church musical traditions to foster physical, psychological, and social healing and well-being. While this religious movement has roots in ancient Mexico, it became popular in North America in the wake of the Ghost Dance movement and, because of U.S. government restrictions, has often been practiced underground. The rituals performed by members of this church are based on the use of hallucinogenic buttons of the peyote cactus. The ingestion of peyote produces a sense of well-being and an intense feeling of commitment to both ceremony and community. Songs in the Native American Church frequently incorporate elements of both Indian spiritual practices and Christian religion and are sung in a soft, introspective manner accompanied by a peyote rattle specifically designed for this purpose.

The Navajo, who occupy parts of southern Utah and Colorado, practice common Native American Church rituals including holding meetings in a large Plains Indian teepee. Within the teepee a sacred fire and crescent-shaped altar is built on the earth floor. Meetings last through the night, beginning with prayers, followed by each member in turn singing four songs accompanied by a rattle and the water drum, a midnight water break, more singing, and finally a fellowship breakfast in the morning. The water drum consists of an iron pot half filled with water with a wet buckskin drumhead. This instrument resonates strongly, helping the singers to communicate their pleas for help in life to spirits including Jesus and Father Peyote.

Another example of a new musical style resulting from contact with European culture is Métis music. When Métis settlers arrived in central Montana in 1879, they brought a tradition of songs and dances combining native traditions with Anglo and Franco folk musics. The Métis (*métis* is a French word meaning "mixed") are descendants of Cree and Ojibwa women who married early European explorers, trappers, and traders in the Canadian territory. The Métis have adapted numerous songs from the French chanson repertory to express their own perspective and perform Scots-Irish dance music in a manner resembling native song and dance traditions. Ann Lederman has documented the latter adaptations in her study of Métis fiddle tunes. Scholars long assumed Métis fiddlers continued to play tunes the way Scots-Irish fiddlers had taught them 250 years ago, but upon closer examination, Lederman found the structure of Métis versions resemble older native Cree and Ojibwa song forms. She suggests that government bans on native music and dance in the late 1800s and early 1900s contributed to the development of a native expression through European instruments and musical forms, such as the chanson and the fiddle tune.[4] While five years ago these traditions in Montana had declined, currently they are being rejuvenated by the annual Métis Festival held in September in Lewiston and by the efforts of individuals like young Fort Belknap fiddlers Vincent and Jamie-Lee Fox who study with master Métis fiddlers from Saskatchewan.

Native American music is growing and changing with the world. Contemporary Native American artists make commercial recordings that are aired on the radio, streamed from satellites to Web-based stations, and nominated for Grammy Awards. In 2001 the National Academy of Recording Arts and Sciences awarded the first Grammy for Best Native American Music Album. Artists in the running perform traditional music with modern innovations, like the Denver-based musicians Calvin Standing Bear and James Torres who call their musical duo "Red Tail Chasing Hawks." Standing Bear is an accomplished Native American flutist who sings and plays a variety of hand percussion. Torres complements Standing Bear with his expertise on the piano. Such a synthesis of western and Native American religious beliefs, including musical performance practice, is common; scholars of culture describe the process as "syncretism." Both musicians feel music is a powerful way to communicate their spirituality, sharing messages of peace and hope with their audience.

The most common setting for traditional Native American music and dance today is the powwow. The term *powwow* seems to come from one of the Algonquian languages (in northeastern America), where it originally referred to actions used by healers. While the expression was adopted in the East in the seventeenth century by non-Indians to describe medicinal conjuring, it was transported to the

West in the nineteenth century and early twentieth century by way of traveling medicine shows. Now the term is used throughout North America to describe a place where Indians sing and dance.

Today a powwow is essentially a social gathering at which people from several tribes dance together, using a few basic patterns all the tribes recognize. The music is highly stylized, with dancing throughout the afternoon and evening. Dancers rest occasionally while particular groups (young men or older women, for example) compete for prize money. From time to time, groups demonstrate a particular dance from their own tribe, while other participants watch. According to participants, the most significant features of an intertribal powwow include dancing, singing, ground blessing, sharing, honoring, Indian tacos, Indian fry bread, preservation of heritage, meeting old friends and making new ones, dance contests, Indian flags, and Indian Time (one can forget clocks and live for the moment). Powwows range in size and length, lasting one afternoon or held in conjunction with another event such as a rodeo. Two of the largest regular powwows held in the Rocky Mountain region are the Denver March Powwow, held in the month of March (as the name implies), and the Plains Indian Museum Powwow, held annually in June at the Buffalo Bill Historical Center in Cody, Wyoming.

PIONEERS AND MUSIC IN THE ROCKY MOUNTAIN TERRITORY

It is impossible to mark the moment any type of musical entertainment begins in a place. When settlers arrived in the region in the late 1840s, two centers of development arose: one around the Denver area and the other in the Salt Lake City area. The reasons for development are very different. Colorado was a product of the trappers and explorers and, later in the 1850s, the miners. Social and musical activities were established as these prospectors and settlers made the Rocky Mountains home. Utah was the chosen settlement of the Latter-day Saints (LDS), who migrated from the East and founded Salt Lake City in 1847. Music was an important part of their life, a need and value clearly outlined by LDS leaders, and choruses and bands were quickly formed. These urban centers solidified as hubs of social and musical developments when they became main stops for the transcontinental railroad.

An example of a grand party and musical Christmas celebration (in December 1858) has been preserved from Camp Spooner, "3 miles below Denver City." The menu included oyster soup, buffalo tongue, sage hens, grizzly bear "a la Mode," mountain rat, sandhill crane, several kinds of pie, nuts, raisins, prickly pear, whiskey, Taos lightning, Madeira, champagne, and sherry. The party sang "The Girl I Left behind Me," "Rosalie, the Prairie Flower," and "The Home of My Boyhood." The final song of the evening was written especially for the occasion by A. O. McGrew and was called "A Hit at the Times."

Instruments were not listed in the above account, but there likely were fiddles, banjos, or harmonicas. After all, Meriwether Lewis (1774–1809) and William Clark's (1770–1838) Corps of Discovery included a fiddler, and the miners who came to the mountains often carried various forms of portable music, ranging from jaw harps, concertinas, "squeeze boxes," ocarinas, and harmonicas. The pioneers who crossed the prairie brought fiddles and banjos, harmonicas, and songs. Saloons in the new cities offered entertainment of various kinds, including music and theater. By at least 1859, bands were formed in the region, as illustrated by the band from Council Bluffs who performed for Independence Day. Established by 1864, the First Regimental Band of the Colorado Volunteers began a series of concerts led by Alexander Sutherland, immortalized in Alfred Tennyson's (1809–1892) "Charge of the Light Brigade." The series began on May 4 with thirteen members playing the "Anvil Chorus," "Gunmaker of Moscow Overture," and "On to the Field of Glory."

The family of Julia Lambert brought the first piano to the territory. As an adult, in 1916, she wrote about the journey in *The Trail*, a monthly publication by the Sons of Colorado. The square Brown and Allen instrument was boxed and laid flat in the wagon, and the family piled everything imaginable on top of it, including beds, clothing, pillows, dishes, utensils, shovels, and "boxes of mother's treasures." West of the Missouri River, it became obvious some of the furniture had to go to make room for more provisions. However, "we girls begged our parents to keep the piano, so other things were disposed of and we bought flour, corn meal, sugar, coffee, tea, bacon, and molasses." When they reached Denver, men were anxious to assist Mr. Lambert just so they could see the piano, and a crowd quickly appeared at the Lamberts' upstairs without invitation. Julia writes, "When [the piano] was set up every man that could play took his turn and, at supper-time, some were still there."[5] Pianos kept coming to Denver, and they were a sought-after luxury, maintaining their high value. By 1865, a Steinway shipped from the Missouri River is documented as costing $200 freight. The piano was later sold for $200 cash plus thirty-two lots in a Denver addition. Half of the block of lots later netted the owner $15,000.

From 1859 to 1881 people heard music in saloons in the Rocky Mountain West. In Denver, Denver Hall featured a small orchestra that was frequently interrupted by gunfire; fortunately, the hall owners did have the foresight to build a low iron-plated enclosure around the stage. The orchestra played favorites like "Old Susannah," "Lilly Dale" and "Sweet Betsy" and probably consisted of a piano and a fiddle or two. According to the *Rocky Mountain News*, Denver's founder General William Larimer, Jr. remarked that the "musicians were usually of the class that took up their wages at the bar." Another local watering hole, the Criterion Saloon, was remodeled in 1862, turning the upper floor into a theater. The *Rocky Mountain News* also reported:

> The Criterion Minstrels will throw themselves on the latest movements and melodies of the day. Banjo and tambourine solos, comic and sentimental songs by the renowned Gus Shaw and others—*La Sylphide* and *Militaire* dancing by the fascinating Mad'lle Carlista. The farce of the "barbershop" and the after piece of "Barnum in Trouble."[6]

Ten years later, the Cricket Saloon received an orchestrion from Berlin at a cost of $10,000. It took a week to assemble the machine's horns, reeds, drums, xylophone, and keyboard. It stood eleven feet high and was played with interchangeable, pinned cylinders. Each cylinder had six to eight pieces of music on it: *Der*

Wacht Am Rhein, *Rose Waltz*, *Moonlight Sonata* (Beethoven), *Traumerie* (Schumann), *Serenade* (Schubert), *Yode hi Lee Hi Loo* (Schweitzer).

Music was an important part of church life in the West. Instruments such as the melodian, standard orchestral instruments, and organs were used in most local Catholic and Protestant churches. By 1872, pipe organs were being built in the region in Central City, Colorado.

Visiting Performers

Significant musical contributions in church and secular life were also occurring in Utah (see "Music in the Church of the Latter-day Saints" below). In 1862 conductor C.J. Thomas emigrated from London and became the director of the Tabernacle Choir and the Salt Lake Theater Orchestra. The Salt Lake Theater was dedicated on March 6, 1862, with an orchestra of twenty members and the Tabernacle choir. By 1869, Salt Lake City was also a primary stop on the railroad to California and soon became a desired stop for traveling music and theater groups. These included, over the years, the English Grand Opera Company, the Gilbert and Sullivan Opera Troupe, and Carlotta Patti.

In 1878, the region was visited by tours of two famous musicians of the day: Camilla Urso, a French violinist, and the "Divine Patti." Carlotta Patti was a star in every way, playing the role of the diva on stage and off, traveling across the country in a luxury, private train car. Patti was known for her talent but also for her temperament, her jewels, and her high fees. In Denver, she played in Turner Hall, and her visit spurred Denver residents to demand a hall to match the performers they were attracting.

Opera houses sprang up, serving not only for opera but also for concerts, speeches, plays, and important gatherings. In Denver, the Tabor Grand Opera House presented its first season in 1881 and had a resident orchestra of five strings, flute, clarinet, cornet, and percussion. When the Tabor opened on September 5, 1881, it featured a performance by Emma Abbott and her Grand English Opera Company. Abbott not only opened the Tabor Grand but also dedicated twenty-five theaters, from Springfield, Ohio, to Ogden, Utah.

In Boise, the Sonna Opera House opened in 1889, and within six months, renovations and improvements were being made to the house. By June 1889, it could seat 800 and had inclined seating, so that views were not obstructed. Boise gained another theater in 1892 with the opening of the Columbia Theater, which was built at a cost of $30,000 and could seat 1,000 people. The Philharmonic Orchestra was engaged for this theater, which was lit by 450 incandescent lamps and beautifully decorated with frescos and portraits of William Shakespeare, Ludwig van Beethoven, Franz Liszt, Alfred Tennyson, Johann Goethe, Richard Wagner, and Wolfgang Amadeus Mozart.

By the late nineteenth century, the Rocky Mountains were a standard stop for national tours. In 1872, Mlle. Marie Aimme, one of the most popular stars in the United States, and the French Opera Buffe Company came to Denver. Prices at the Denver Theater went up to $3.00 for reserved seats. The year 1876 saw the Oates Comic Opera Company touring San Francisco, Salt Lake City, and Denver with an orchestra of violin and piano. In 1877 the Richard-Bernard Company made its western debut with *The Bohemian Girl, Martha*, and *Il Trovatore*. Clara Louise Kellogg and Annie Louise Cary visited with the Kellogg and Carey Opera Company in November 1877 and gave operatic concert performances. Bands continued to be popular. In 1888, Patrick Gilmore's band played, and in 1892, John Phillip Sousa (1854–1932) made his first visit to Denver with the U.S. Marine Band.

Touring circuit theaters lured even more musical entertainment to the region. Guaranteeing a company more than one performance in different cities assured a profit since cost and distance were major factors in bringing attractions. The "Silver Circuit," a loose organization of theaters across Colorado, created circa 1881, provides an example. The Tabor Grand, Colorado Springs Opera House, Tabor Opera House at Leadville, Central City Opera House, and Georgetown Opera House were the original houses; by November 1884 opera houses in Fort Collins, Canon City, Salida, and Pueblo were added. The house in Cheyenne, Wyoming, was added in July 1885. Cheyenne was an important addition because it was the terminal junction of the Union Pacific Railroad, and the majority of traveling companies going to and from California passed through. The railroad proved to be the impetus for adding theaters to the circuit; as the rail reached more towns, the circuit included them in its route. At its peak in 1888, the Silver Circuit included thirteen large theaters in Denver, Leadville, Aspen, Salida, Pueblo, Trinidad, and Colorado Springs, Colorado; Ogden, Salt Lake City, Park City, and Provo, Utah; and Evanston and Rawlins, Wyoming. It also included smaller theaters across Colorado, Utah, and Wyoming. The circuit failed within fifteen years but was a major factor in bringing opera and music across the West.

In 1899, the Metropolitan Opera traveling company was on tour in Idaho. In Pocatello, the company was the victim of a fire that destroyed $2,500 worth of costumes and scenery, but the show went on. They traveled to Boise for an engagement at the Columbia Theater, where they played to an ice-cold house because the furnace was broken. On April 16, 1899, the *Idaho Daily Statesman* reviewed the performance, without stating which opera was performed, and said that there were very few good voices in the company.

Symphony Orchestras

The earliest professional symphony orchestra in the region was a summer orchestra at Elitch Gardens Amusement Park in Denver. Mary and John Elitch opened the park in 1890, and outdoor symphony concerts were one attraction. The concerts eventually moved inside to the Elitch Theater, and in 1897 an Italian, Raffaelo Cavallo, was conducting. The group proved to be very popular and was an impetus for a permanent winter orchestra.

The examples above instruct us that music of the pioneers, in the mountains, on the plains, in the rural setting and the urban city, in the home, lodge, saloon, or concert hall, was, by and large, the same music as that heard across the country: parlor songs, popular band music, excerpted opera selections from Bellini, Donizetti, and more. However, finding the time and or place for the music oftentimes required a bit more effort than one might have to exert in New Orleans, Charleston, Chicago, Boston, or New York. In addition to the Anglo-European repertory, the influence of the Latino population as well as other folk traditions (Métis and Basque, to name just two) moving into the region is what begins to give the region its distinctive flavor.

POSTFRONTIER POPULAR MUSIC

By the 1890s change was in the air. Although musicians and entertainers strongly cultivated the myth of the western frontier for audiences, the Rocky Mountains were no longer a "frontier" but a settled land. Legally, to qualify as "frontier" an area had to have 1.8, or less, persons per square mile, whereas most of the region had at least double that. An increase in population was accompanied by a financial crisis that affected many people of the West—the Silver Panic of 1893. When the government devalued silver, fortunes were lost. Among those affected was H.A.W. Tabor, and the demise of the Tabor Grand can be traced directly to 1893. Unions came to the mines, and labor strikes dominated many towns; with the strikes came economic problems. Nationwide, by the time of World War I, theaters were converted to movie houses, which were less expensive and where tickets were cheaper to come by.

While "art" music was actively being cultivated at the turn of the century (for example, the Denver Symphony Orchestra began in 1900 with forty musicians), the use of the already established myth of the "frontier" was also being actively pursued for its entertainment value. Buffalo Bill's Wild West Show brought a new concept of the western frontier to both the American East Coast and to Europe. It fostered and perpetuated the concept of "The West" as a place to be conquered and civilized. This depiction of American culture not only provided fictional entertainment filled with adventure and romance, but it also spun a dream of a freer way of life in the wide-open Great Plains. The Wild West Show was filled with rugged images including Plains Indian costumes, equestrian tricks, and mock battles between cowboys and Indians as well as between free westerners and encroaching civilization. Buffalo Bill's Cowboy Band made the Wild West experience complete by filling the aural space on the event canvas.

Buffalo Bill kept the band members busy, having them play not only afternoon and evening shows but also morning parades to drum up business for the main presentations. The band had around twenty members, midsize for the times. They dressed in cowboy attire rather than military uniforms, adding to the western mystique of the show and giving each member the appearance that he had been hired off of a western ranch (which most of them were not). The band played music common to the era: marches, polkas, patriotic tunes, popular song arrangements, dance music including cakewalks and waltzes, medleys of opera tunes, and transcriptions from orchestral literature. The band played "The Star Spangled Banner" at the opening of each show, the de facto national anthem, although it was 1931 before Congress decreed the song as the United States' official anthem.

The function the band performed in the Wild West Show is dictated by the action, similar to circus musicians. Action in the arena called for lively music; contemplative scenes needed more tender music to engage the audience. Music was also played as entertainment as the stage props were being arranged. Several musicians from circus bands were hired including the last director, Merle Evans, from Ringling Brothers Barnum Bailey Circus. Although there are no recordings of this

Buffalo Bill's Wild West Band. Courtesy of the Buffalo Bill Historic Center.

band, there were a number of positive reviews. In the July 25, 1887, *London Evening News*, a reporter described the band's playing as "really beautiful music . . . a musical treat . . . and a musical combination worth listening to,"[7] pointing to a high level of musicianship that went beyond the purely functional aspects of their job.

Cowboy Songs

The "Cowboy Ballad" is a major musical component of the "Wild West" mythology and regional heritage. The repertory was created on the frontier between 1870 and 1920, as pioneers ventured west to settle the untamed land. Cowboys were the conquerors of extreme terrain (vast prairies, steep mountains, snow, drought, and flood) and animals (bison, grizzly bear, mountain lion, and even other people). They accomplished all of this with the help of their trusted horses. Today machines like pickup trucks, all-terrain vehicles, railroads, and airplanes perform much of the work on the western cattle ranch. The ranchers take pride in the heritage and mythology of cowboy life, still sporting the cowboy hat, boots, and equine mount; and many of them enjoy cowboy ballads, songs commemorating the courage and resourcefulness of the cowboys past and present, and the premechanical era of pure horsepower.

Immigrants from a wide variety of cultural backgrounds brought song material with them to the region. Unfortunately, many early songs that were not in English have been lost, while a wealth of songs stemming from the British ballad tradition has survived. In one of the most well-known cowboy ballads, "The Cowboy's Lament," an eighteenth-century soldier ("The Unfortunate Rake") dying of syphilis is transposed to a dying young cowboy wrapped in white linen on the streets of Laredo after a barroom fight. While the young man's request for the military funeral custom to "beat the drum slowly and play the fife lowly" seems somewhat out of place in the cowboy song, the earlier versions explain the origin of this line. Similarly, cowboys adapted other songs from the ballad tradition including "Gypsy Davy" (from the British "Gypsy Laddie") and "Bury Me Not on the Lone Prairie" (from "Bury Me Not in the Deep Blue Sea").

Cowboys composed new songs, in addition to adapting the old ones, and some have been around since the 1860s when cattle ranching became lucrative for baron capitalists who bought and sold cattle and hired transient cowboys to tend them. "The Old Chisolm Trail" originated in oral tradition during this time period. It commemorates Jesse Chisolm's wagon road, along which cattle were driven north from Texas to the Kansas railroads bound for the eastern markets, and to Colorado, Wyoming, and Montana, where the livestock matured before being shipped east. Along with the cattle, songs and stories traveled from state to state along the trunk line trails like the Chisolm and its cowpath tributaries. As a result, the Rocky Mountain region shares a rich western music and poetry tradition with other cattle industry states including Arizona, Arkansas, Kansas, Missouri, Nebraska, New Mexico, Oklahoma, and Texas.

Ranching is a thriving industry in the Rocky Mountain states, and many cowboy ballads have been composed about landmarks and happenings specific to the region. D. J. O'Malley, who spent many years cowboying on the open ranges of Montana, wrote two well-known songs about stampedes: "When the Work's All Done This Fall" and "Charlie Rutledge." In the 1880s Owen Wister (1860–1938) began spending his summers on a ranch in Wyoming where he became so inspired by the cowboy lifestyle that he abandoned his careers in music and law to write cowboy fiction, including the classic *The Virginian* (1902). When a stage version of this novel opened in New York, Wister decided the play needed a theme song and penned what was to become a popular cowboy ballad, "Ten Thousand Cattle." The ballad about the cowboy "Utah Carroll," who gave his life saving a little girl from the stampede, is sung in many states; not surprisingly, its most detailed and lengthy versions were collected in Utah. Finally, "The Colorado Trail" is a song collected by a doctor, T. L. Chapman, tending an injured cowboy recuperating in a hospital. Carl Sandburg (1878–1967) learned the song from the doctor and published it in his *American Songbag* (1927). The song is about the cattle route that branched off of the main Western Trail in southern Oklahoma and angled northwest toward Colorado.

Today, many active cowboy poets and ballad singers belong to state chapters of The Western Music Association. This organization's mission is to "support the music of the American Cowboy and the Code of the West." Near Colorado Springs, the Flying W is a working cattle ranch that features a band of cowboy balladeers that entertains while guests dine. These musicians have built a reputation, earning them an invitation to perform at Carnegie Hall. Each year in early spring the Buffalo Bill Historical Center in Cody, Wyoming, sponsors a weekend of cowboy songs and poetry performed by cowboys from the Wyoming, Montana, and Idaho area. In addition, the gathering features national headliners in western music.

Salt Lake City, Utah, is the home of Hal Cannon, folklorist, accomplished cowboy balladeer, writer, and the founding director (in 1980) of the Western Folklife Center in Elko, Nevada. The Center hosts the annual Cowboy Poetry Gathering, an event that has fostered new interest in this old art form. Cowboys and cowgirls travel to Elko from all over the United States, Canada, and other countries to recite and sing their poetry. The Center also coordinates research and documentation efforts, media projects, exhibits, and educational programs about the rich heritage and contemporary culture of the people of the West.

Latino Musical Communities

The Rocky Mountain region is home to a sizable number of Latino communities, particularly Colorado, which has the ninth largest Hispanic population in the nation. The oldest of these communities trace their ancestry to the first permanent Spanish settlers who came to the area in 1598, and some music continues to be performed today that dates back to colonial times. There are a number of ritual genres surviving using very old music, including the Comanches' Captive commemoration ceremonies; the *alabado*, a type of religious folksong sung in free meter by congregations in the Southwest since the sixteenth century; and the *Matachines*, a Southwestern American Indian spiritual music and dance performance complex first introduced to Pueblo people by Spanish colonists.

In addition to people with colonial ancestors, the region's Latino population includes immigrants who have moved to the region within the last fifty years. Denver has a sizable ratio of Latino inhabitants, approximately 15 to 20 percent of the city's population of 2.5 million, and many of these came from Mexico. Although the communities are not as dense as in Denver, Mexican immigrants also live in Utah, Wyoming, Idaho, and Montana and have long provided labor for agriculture and various service industries throughout the Rocky Mountain region. Among them the Mexican mariachi tradition continues to thrive, a popular form of Latino music associated with community celebrations. Latin dance bands that perform a variety of old and new music are popular, too. There are over twenty mariachi groups performing in the Denver area alone. Many of the musicians are seasoned performers who have spent some of their careers with famous Mexican groups. Often they travel around the United States and teach at mariachi workshops including one of the most popular ones held in the summer in Albuquerque, New Mexico. Coloradans are becoming more and more involved in mariachi music as new bands form, including several sponsored by high schools as a sophisticated alternative to mainstream classical music ensembles. Two well-known venues for excellent Mexican food coupled with mariachi music in Denver are El Tejado, with live bands on Wednesdays and Sundays, and El Paraiso, featuring the mariachi Colorado Friday through Sunday evenings. A similar venue in Boise, Idaho, the Acapulco Mexican Restaurant, regularly features the mariachi Sol de Acapulco.

Bluegrass

Bluegrass is a musical genre that grew out of Kentucky string band traditions. The music uses traditional idioms including ballads and dance tunes in combination with blues, jazz, gospel, and ragtime influences to form a contemporary style. Bill Monroe, credited with creating bluegrass, experimented with many instrument combinations, eventually settling on an acoustic string combination added to his "high, lonesome" vocals. Today bluegrass bands commonly include bass, guitar, banjo, fiddle, and Monroe's instrument of choice, the mandolin; and people all over the world enjoy it, including large audiences in the Rocky Mountains.

Bluegrass music is eclectic in nature and consequently adaptable. Much of the mountains and plains of the Rocky Mountain region is sparsely populated, and one finds few of the dense ethnic communities common in other parts of the country. For example, Wyoming's immigrant settlers included Basques, Hispanics, Russian Germans, Eastern Europeans, and Scandinavians. Musicians from these various backgrounds play bluegrass music with one another and carry on some of their musical traditions within new contexts. For example, La Verne Billingsly of Douglas, Wyoming, grew up playing a variety of dance music on the fiddle including Russian German "Dutch Hop" music, British Isles fiddle music, ragtime, and country western. He feels at home playing the bass in bluegrass bands because it features a little of each of these musics and more.

The range of events appearing on the Idaho Bluegrass Society's calendar illustrates Rocky Mountain bluegrass fans' eclectic interests. Roughly half of the calendar consists of bluegrass "jam sessions" (informal music making) and a few bluegrass concerts; the other half consists of old-time square dances, contra dances, Celtic groups, Scottish Highland events, and western cowboy music. The trend appears in Utah as well where a look at the Intermountain Acoustic Music Association calendar lists a healthy number of bluegrass events along with Celtic and old-time events.

Bluegrass fans not only like to listen to music; they like to play music. A U.S. Senate resolution designates May as Worldwide Bluegrass Music Month (S.J. Res. 228, 1989) stating, "Bluegrass is a music which since 1946 has encouraged fans to play as well as listen to it and stresses both teamwork and individualism which mirrors the American character." Amateur musicians looking for others to play with often belong to state bluegrass organizations like the Idaho Bluegrass Society mentioned above or the Colorado Bluegrass Music Society (CBMS). These groups publish newsletters and post Web sites with informative articles and schedules of music happenings. The CBMS sponsors regular jam sessions including Thursday Jams at Whitefence Farm and Tuesday jams in cooperation with Swallow Hill Music, a folk music association based in Denver. Jam sessions need not be formally scheduled, though; they occur regularly in private homes, restaurants, bars, on college campuses, and at campgrounds.

In the 1980s the bluegrass band Hot Rize became popular in Colorado. This band featured the late Charles Sawtelle (d. 1999) on guitar, Tim O'Brien on vocals, mandolin, and fiddle, Nick Forster on bass, and Pete Wernick on banjo. The band cultivated a strong base of interested bluegrass fans in the Rocky Mountain region, was eventually recognized nationally as a top bluegrass band, and is one reason bluegrass festivals remain a top draw in the region. The group represented bluegrass abroad on a world tour of countries including Australia, Japan, France, Holland, Scandinavia, Ireland, England, Belgium, and Canada.

Hot Rize made their last recording together in 1990, but they often perform reunion shows around the country. O'Brien moved from his native Boulder to Nashville, where he is active as a performer and songwriter. His performances and recordings of fresh versions of old-time music have been seen and heard all over the world. Currently he is the president of the International Bluegrass Music Association (IBMA) and has made numerous recordings with a variety of musicians.

Wernick, founder of the IBMA, lives in the Boulder, Colorado, area and teaches banjo workshops both nationally and locally. Forster and his wife, Helen, host and play music in the weekly National Public Radio program *E-Town*. The show is taped in front of a live audience, usually at the historic Boulder Theater, a restored art-deco movie house from the 1930s.

Rock in the Rockies

Popular music in the Rocky Mountain region does not vary significantly from that which is found on the national music scene. In the age of mega concerts, concert tours, and national radio programming, the spawning of "regional" sounds is more and more of a distant occurrence. At least four cities (Salt Lake City, Denver, Laramie, and Colorado Springs) in the region have large event facilities and vie for standard stops on national tours. Types of music brought into the region include the controversial rap of 336 or Eminem, alternative of Linkin Park, urban rock of U2, southern rock of the Dave Matthews Band, country sounds of the Dixie Chicks, Clint Black, or Trisha Yearwood, and rock legends from the mellow sounds of James Taylor to the constantly reinvigorated sounds of Mick Jagger and the Rolling Stones.

Outside of large-scale productions, bars and coffeehouses are filled every weekend with local bands, especially in the expected breeding grounds of college towns. These bands survive doing the standard rock music covers mixed in with some truly innovative work. Local performers often maintain high regional profiles with recordings and local engagements. The only true description of the "locals" scenes throughout the region is eclectic. Performers, who maintain constant scheduling, tend to perform in college towns, such as Boulder, Missoula, and Moscow. Local bands and soloists run the gamut in terms of style. They include Moscow thrash band Gunt and The Minds, a garage rock/punk band, now in Portland, the hard-core punk tendencies of Oblio Joes from Missoula, funk/jazz fusion of the Motet, and the return of bluesman Chaz Leary, both from Boulder, Irish band Colcannon, originally from the Boulder-Laramie corridor, and the Denver-based singer-songwriter Matthew Moon. Such diversity speaks volumes about the demand for live music in the region's vibrant college towns, particularly Moscow and Missoula, where regional and local music are booming. The larger, cosmopolitan cities (and their nearby college centers) maintain some local bookings in small venues. The tendency in urban areas is to have lineups of midlevel national bands attracting college-age audi-

John Denver performs at a concert in New York to benefit the Wildlife Conversation Society. © Corbis Sygma.

ences, including a recent Club 156 concert in Denver of Engine Down and From Autumn to Ashes or lineups in Salt Lake City including Something Corporate and Death Cab for Cutie.

National artists who either are from the region or have made the region their home are well known. They include, starting in the 1970s, the very commercial Osmond family, who lived and recorded from Salt Lake City. Perhaps most remembered for their TV-variety shows, *The Donny and Marie Osmond Show* with its signature duet "I'm a Little Bit Country, I'm a Little Bit Rock and Roll" and the ensuing *Osmond Family* show solidified the Osmond family in 1970s popular music history. Donny and Marie have continued in more solo veins—Donny in a career revival in the 1990s on Broadway and then a talk show with his sister, and Marie in her newest endeavor, a radio show. The original brothers group currently performs most frequently in their Branson, Missouri, Osmond Family Theater. Grassroots folk singer Judy Collins hails from Colorado and began her career as a child prodigy classical pianist. She was soon drawn to the music of Woody Guthrie and Pete Seeger and began her own career as one of the 1970s' most successful female folk singers. Continuing her career with popular PBS specials and a recent memoir, Collins is perhaps best known for her diversity, often including "Amazing Grace," "Send in the Clowns," and "Both Sides Now" from her ever popular *Wildflowers* (1967) album, in the same concert. John Denver, the famous balladeer from Colorado, was best known for his songs "Rocky Mountain High" and "Take Me Home Country Roads."

More popular and mainstream are the alternative/rock sounds making it into the national spotlight from the region. In the 1980s Boulder-based Big Head Todd and the Monsters emerged with its mixture of classic rock, blues, and funk. Leftover Salmon, also out of Boulder in the early 1990s, terms their own music "Polyethnic Cajun Slamgrass," mixing bluegrass instrumentation with southern rock vocals and some jazz and cajun influences. The String Cheese Incident began in Crested Butte, Colorado, in 1993 and then

Red Rocks Amphitheatre

The most popular regional venue of international renown is the Red Rocks Amphitheatre in Denver. A stunning natural setting, surrounded on three sides by towering boulders of red rocks, the venue features exceptional natural acoustics. Although concerts began there as early as 1910, including a visit by opera singer Mary Garden in 1911, the modern stage and amphitheater was constructed in 1941. A relatively small setting by modern concert standards, Red Rocks Park began an annual concert series in 1947 and has featured premier musicians ever since. In the late 1940s and 1950s, the lineup consisted primarily of classical musicians and opera singers, including Lily Pons, Claudio Arrau, and Igor Stravinsky, as well as ballet and square dancing. In the 1960s ballet continued to be a frequent event, including visits from the San Francisco Ballet, then under the direction of the Christensens, as was the Koshare dance troupe (see "Music and Dance in the Rocky Mountains" later in this chapter). Other notable performers of the time included Ray Charles, Ella Fitzgerald, and Nat King Cole. However, as early as 1960 the Kingston Trio performed at the venue, and folk and rock music were more and more frequent by the end of the decade, including Peter, Paul, and Mary, The Mamas and the Papas, Simon and Garfunkel, and Jimi Hendrix. The trend of rock and folk continued in the 1970s with a who's who of the next two decades, including Judy Collins, Jethro Tull, Pat Boone, Joan Baez, Pete Seeger, John Denver, Joni Mitchell, Gladys Knight and the Pips, the Eagles, Willie Nelson, Chuck Mangione, B. B. King, Herbie Hancock, Charlie Daniels, Jimmy Buffett, and Bruce Springsteen. Acts of international caliber have often performed at Red Rocks early in their careers including U2, whose June 1, 1983, concert provided the basis for their *Live at Red Rocks* album. Since then, artists ranging from Tom Petty, Laurie Anderson, Ziggy Marley, Blues Traveler, Metallica, Tool, The String Cheese Incident, and Coldplay have played Red Rocks.

Jello Biafra, singer for the punk rock group Dead Kennedys, performs at a concert in San Francisco, 1984. © Roger Ressmeyer/Corbis.

moved to Boulder. Their unique blend of improvisation-based instrumental music has found national success through such local venues as the Telluride Bluegrass Festival and is paired with good causes, which they call the Gouda projects, such as the food drives in Colorado, South Dakota, and Australia. Jello Biafra (of Dead Kennedy's fame) hails from Colorado, and he runs an independent record label in San Francisco, Alternative Tentacles; the bands that Biafra currently records include Denver's Slim Cessna's Auto Club, who played the 2004 South by Southwest Festival.

Jazz

Jazz was originally a product of American sociological and cultural forces east of the Mississippi in the early twentieth century; however, when the genre gained popularity on the East and West Coasts, musicians began traveling regularly between these two points. They necessarily made stopovers in the Rocky Mountain region, attracting listeners and discovering a frontier setting where jazz could flourish. One of the region's most important early contributions to jazz music on a national level was bandleader Paul Whiteman, born in Denver in 1890. Whiteman was a violist with the Denver Symphony Orchestra from 1907 until 1914, when he joined the San Francisco symphony. During World War I he served in the navy as a bandmaster, performing marching and dance music. In 1918 he created a dance band in San Francisco, featuring jazz melodies performed in a lush orchestral style. He settled in New York in 1920 and became well known with two major hit recordings, *Whispering* (1920) and *Japanese Sandman* (1920), and later toured the British Isles (1923) and Europe (1926), spreading the sound of highly polished jazz to eager listeners there. Whiteman commissioned *Rhapsody in Blue* (1923) from George Gershwin (1898–1937), to be performed on his first extended concert tour of the United States. Although Denver's son Paul Whiteman has been criticized for diluting the character of jazz for commercial purposes, he was a key figure in American popular music and professed a high, personal respect for original African American jazz innovators.

Violinist George Morrison studied music in Denver with Paul Whiteman's fa-

Red Rocks Ampitheater in Colorado. Courtesy of Corbis.

ther, Wiberforce J. Whiteman, and went on to earn a national reputation with his dance orchestra. Like many classically trained African American musicians in his generation, Morrison performed a wide variety of music that included the classics, popular songs, and "syncopated" styles like ragtime and jazz. Morrison's band "The 12 Rigadooners" toured extensively throughout the region and in Europe. He was often referred to as the "Colored Paul Whiteman." Jimmie Lunceford and Andy Kirk, two musicians who had also studied with the senior Whiteman and refined their skills playing in Morrison's orchestra, went on to form their own nationally known jazz orchestras. When Morrison was not on tour, he gave lessons in his Denver home on Gilpin Street, including those who could not afford to pay him. He also volunteered as an assistant to many of the elementary and secondary school music programs in the Denver area.

More recently, Denver's multiple Grammy Award winner Diane Reeves has delighted audiences around the world with her rich vocal jazz. Born in Detroit, she grew up in Denver where her father was a singer, her mother was a trumpet player, and her uncle, Charles Burell, played the classical double bass. Jazz and rhythm and blues (R&B) recording artist George Duke is her cousin. Reeves performed with her high school big band at the National Association of Jazz Educators' convention in Chicago, where jazz trumpet great Clark Terry discovered her.

Reeves' experiences in Colorado include one she describes as "life saving" and another that was part of an innovative jazz venue that originated in Denver. In 1971, while a junior in high school, Reeves participated in one of the first programs to integrate school buses. "There was a lot of tension between blacks and whites—many people felt we were an intrusion to their neighborhood—and we all gave a concert to show some kind of unity," she said. During a rehearsal for this concert the school music director, Bennie Williams, discovered her vocal talent. Not only did the concert begin the tedious process of fostering goodwill between races, but it launched Reeves into a music career. Colorado performances soon to follow included guest performances with Clark Terry at the Colorado Jazz Party.[8]

Dick and Maddie Gibson's Annual Jazz Party was a private jazz festival held annually from 1963 to around 1993. Its organizer, Denver investment banker Dick Gibson (d. 1998), became a full-time jazz promoter in the early 1980s. Starting in 1986, he put together thirteen more jazz parties at various locations around the world. The Colorado Jazz Party was held successively in Vail, Aspen, and Colorado Springs and, starting in 1982, took place annually at the Fairmont Hotel in Denver. Lasting three days in September, it was essentially a series of jam sessions in which over sixty jazz musicians participated and was attended by about 600 guests. The Colorado Jazz Party gained national recognition when it was featured in the film *The Great Rocky Mountain Jazz Party* in 1977 and later in 1998 when in New York the JVC Jazz festival included a tribute to Gibson entitled "The First Ever NYC Jazz Party."

Denver's contemporary music scene is a rich mixture of mainstream, Latin jazz, swing, acid jazz, and freeform. One of the most popular venues for jazz music standards is El Chapultapec, owned by music aficionado Jerry Krantz. The club has been around since the 1950s and is known internationally as "the place to go in Denver for jazz." It features house band The Max Wagner Quartet and top regional musicians like pianist and vocalist Ellyn Rucker. Another popular club is The Mer-

Portrait of Bennie Moten's Victor Recording Orchestra, 1926. Leader Bennie Moten is seated at the piano (far left). Frank Driggs Collection/Getty Images.

cury Café, a smoke-free establishment that offers lessons in ballroom dancing. Favorite big bands performing at the Mercury include Denver's Hot Tomatoes Dance Orchestra and Joel Kaye's Neophonic Big Band (a twenty-four-piece ensemble). The 9th Avenue West offers an array of musics including blues and swing, acid jazz on Tuesdays, and Thursday night salsa lessons with the band Conjunto Colores. Creative Music Works is a devoted jazz promoter, consistently presenting not only top local musicians but also cutting-edge national jazz performers.

Jack Walrath's witty trumpet playing is one of Montana's significant contributions to the national jazz scene. Walrath, born in 1946 in the tiny ranching community of Edgar, claims he "developed a healthy perception of music from lack of negative peer pressure which so often happens in cities."[9] He began playing trumpet at age nine, completed his composition diploma at Berklee College of Music in Boston in 1968, and launched into a performance career including joint leadership with the groups Change (with Gary Peacock) and Revival (with Glenn Ferris), a year-long tour with Ray Charles' band, and working with Charles Mingus. Additionally his talents have been utilized by Miles Davis, Quincy Jones, Gunther Schuller, and Bobby Watson. He has released twenty-two albums and has appeared on innumerable others. While Walrath's home is in New York City, he maintains contact with Montana jazz players. Walrath appeared on albums by the group Montana, which included Kelly Roberti, the state's finest jazz bassist and a key organizer, and Bob Nell, an award-winning composer and pianist. Nell and Walrath recorded the album *Injury or Malpractice* (1989) together.

Contemporary jazz thrives throughout Montana in several lively pockets. Missoula and Bozeman are active scenes, as are Billings and Butte, and the Flathead Lake region has several fine players. The state capital Helena hosts the annual Sleeping Giant Swing 'n Jazz Jubilee and is the home of the internationally known cutting-edge jazz presentations sponsored by the Myrna Loy Center for Performing and Media Arts. Montana's sole jazz-only nightclub is Indigo in Great Falls, though a number of restaurants around the state program jazz regularly.

Although most of the major universities in the Rocky Mountain region offer jazz music training, one school stands out for its devotion to the art of jazz. In 1987 the University of Idaho became the first to name its school of music in honor of a jazz artist and an African American, Lionel Hampton. The University of Idaho has been exposing high school and college students to jazz since they first sponsored a jazz festival in 1967. In 1984, Hampton appeared at the festival and was impressed by the number of young people attending. He told Dr. Lynn J. Skinner, festival director, "When I travel I [usually] see more people over than under thirty. If I can help you in any way . . . I'd like to help."[10] After exclaiming this, Hampton immediately wrote Skinner a check in the amount of $15,000 to establish an endowment. The endowment has grown and with it the university's jazz resources. In addition to sponsoring the annual Lionel Hampton Jazz Festival, plans now include establishing the Lionel Hampton Center to house a jazz museum and performance facilities.

CHURCH-RELATED MUSIC

Religious and spiritual music can be found at virtually every church, synagogue, and mosque in the region. From these spaces emanate sounds ranging from chanting and cantoring, hymns, anthems, and organ music to electric guitars, African drums, and Buddhist prayer wheels. There are significant inroads in the region in gospel music, notably the influence of nationally recognized authority Horace Boyer and the festivals he has inspired, including one at Mt. Calvary Lutheran Church in Boulder.

In large part, the Rocky Mountain region retains a socially conservative character, and the prevailing musical/religious activities reflect this. Therefore, most traditional churches, Protestant and Catholic, include a standard list of full- or part-time musicians on staff: choir/music director, organist/keyboardist, and some paid soloists and/or paid section leaders. The choirs are largely volunteer and range from small (10 to 15 members) to large (over 100). Such groups provide two basic services: music during weekly worship services and occasional special performances of cantatas, oratorios, or other large-scale religious piece. Many churches (both traditional and evangelical) also include a "contemporary" service in which a different type of music is featured: using a standard rock and roll grouping (electric guitar, electronic keyboard, and drums) to incorporate Christian rock, and the occasional interpretive dance, within a nonliturgical worship setting.

Latino community churches (Catholic and Protestant) feature sacred music using Spanish language and Latin American instrumentation. St. Joseph's Catholic Church in Cheyenne, Wyoming, maintains a choir performing a variety of traditional Latino hymns and songs as well as contemporary Mexican American compositions. Their performances include Sunday Mass, weddings and funerals, and special occasions such as the 100th anniversary of the Casper (Wyoming) Catholic Church (in 1988). They also perform special Christmas plays featuring a mixture of traditional Mexican beliefs and Catholic liturgy. In northwest Denver, mariachi musicians began performing in the 1960s for the Sunday Mass and other church events at Our Lady of Guadalupe Parish. This local tradition has contributed to a wider regional movement of musicians who have adapted the mariachi style and other genres of Latino music to the purpose of religious and spiritual expression.

Music in the Church of the Latter-day Saints

Few religious institutions can claim the lasting regional/musical impact of the Church of the Latter-day Saints. Formed in the early 1830s by Joseph Smith (1805–1844), the LDS (also commonly known as the Mormon Church) has a long and rich history of including music in its worship services and social activities. Following social injustice and persecution in the East and Midwest, the Church of the Latter-day Saints began a mass exodus to the Rocky Mountain region, settling in Salt Lake City in 1847. Here the group created a successful, if insular, community in an area that also became a major stop on the railroad to California.

From the beginning, music played an integral role in the foundation of the church's worship and community activities at large. One of Smith's first revelations was that his wife, Emma, should "make a selection of sacred hymns," which became the first hymnal (1835), made up of contemporary tunes with new texts. Early texts for LDS hymnals focused on the divine authority of the church, building Zion, courage in the face of persecution, and other church doctrines, including the most controversial one allowing polygamy. Examples include Eliza Snow's (1804–1887) "O My Father" and her hymn with the refrain "Shout! Shout! O camp of Israel," a hymn about Smith, "A Church without a prophet is not the church for me," Parley Pratt's "The Morning Breaks, The Shadows Flee," or William Clayton's "Come, Come Ye Saints," concerning the trek to Salt Lake. The current hymnal, *Latter-day Saints Hymns*, was published in 1927 and has undergone various updates to incorporate modern and traditional hymns.

Outside of the expected hymnody, the early church included a band for musical entertainment. Brigham Young (1801–1877) was clear about the role of music for the Latter-day Saints, saying, "Music belongs to heaven to cheer God, angels, and men."[11] Indeed, the earliest settlers brought their band instruments with them (trumpets, trombones, clarinets, horns, cornets and drums, and even the bell of the temple at Nauvoo), even when the space could easily have been filled by some other necessity or luxury that would have made daily life more bearable. Before moving to Salt Lake City, the LDS band numbered twenty-five and performed in the worship service, occasionally including Baroque selections from Handel or Bach. The bands were also used, of course, for social occasions and celebrations and to lead dancing.

The insular nature of the LDS community meant its participants learned music of all types under the umbrella of the church and its music schools. In 1849, John Parry was appointed leader of the choir, a date that is generally seen as the beginning of the acclaimed Mormon Tabernacle Choir. In 1867, the actual Tabernacle and its organ were completed. The organ was made of white pine from Parowan and Pine Canyon, 300 miles from Salt Lake City. It was reported that as many as twenty wagons, carrying organ parts, each drawn by three yoke of oxen, traveled between the mountains and the city. The organ had thirty-five stops and 2,000 pipes, the largest at thirty-two feet long, and was built by Joseph Ridges. The Tabernacle serves multiple purposes: as worship space, auditorium, and concert hall. The building's unusual shape and domed roof allow for intense amplification of mass choral and organ sonorities.[12]

Today the Mormon Tabernacle Choir maintains 340 members and is an all-volunteer choir. The choir is available to sing at not only general conferences and Sunday services but also for international tours and standard concerts. Also, *Music and the Spoken Word*, a radio broadcast on air since 1929, features the choir. The choir also has made many recordings, including a Grammy-winning recording of "Battle Hymn of the Republic."

CLASSICAL MUSIC IN THE ROCKY MOUNTAIN REGION

On any given day in the Rocky Mountain region, innumerable concerts and arts events are presented featuring traditional and new classical music. Examples might include the internationally known concerts of the Mormon Tabernacle Choir, Mark O'Connor's *Double Fiddle Concerto* under Marin Alsop and the Colorado Symphony, small chamber concerts at the University of Wyoming at Laramie, a concert of the Percussion Ensemble at Montana State University in Bozeman, and concerts using the Robert Morton organ at the University of Idaho Music Auditorium. True to most regions of the United States, today's performers and composers find the bulk of their employment through the academic centers. Only occasionally, however, do those composers profess an interest in composing "from the region" or, rather "about the region." In this section, a few major composers who are either from the region or have lived and worked for an extended time in the region are highlighted with a specific eye to the question of whether the region has affected their compositions.

Regional Composers

Internationally recognized as one of the founders of minimalism, La Monte Young (1935–) was born in Bern, Idaho. As each of Young's biographers points out, this is the site of one of Young's most influential and earliest musical memories—the tone of wind whistling across the gaps of his family's log cabin at the early age of two. Young's subsequent interest in tone and pitch are lifelong, particularly the resonance of sustained tone. Jeremy Grimshaw observes, "Virtually all of Young's compositions, in their explorations of long tones and sustained harmonies, defy normal conceptions of teleology and temporality."[13] Young recounts that his famous piece *Composition 1960* is "based on an experience I had when I still lived in the cabin. I walked from the house over to, I guess, Aunt Emma's house, and all these grasshoppers were all over the place. I have vivid memories."[14]

While Young's later fascination with Eastern philosophy and its connection to his musical ideas has been well explored, Young points out that his physical surroundings in Idaho were profoundly important, as was his upbringing in the Mormon church. Some degree of conflict between his current spiritual thought and his Mormon history can be found in his comments. In one interview he professes the church had only a "vague influence on my overall outlook" but quickly expands the comment, stating that "being born a Mormon was also extremely significant because they have this concept of Eternal Life, and there's no doubt but what that had something to do with my interest in the concept of extended time structures."[15] Recently, Grimshaw explored the connection between Young and the Mormon Church:

> Young's efforts to raise the soul "to a higher state of evolution" through aural lessons in universal structure—that is, microcosmic lessons in macrocosmic principles—aspire to a distinctly divine pedagogy. Young thus sees himself just as he had been taught as a child to see Joseph Smith: as a prophet chosen by God to restore eternal truths that had been hidden during a long period of apostasy—truths with the potential to transform the mortal into the divine.[16]

On a distinctly different path, Normand Lockwood (1921–1996) was a late arrival in the Rocky Mountain region. He studied with Nadia Boulanger in Paris and had already pursued a long career in freelance composition and academia, including stints at Oberlin, Columbia, and in Texas when, in 1955, Lockwood took a two-year leave from teaching and arrived in Laramie, Wyoming, as an already established composer. Lockwood lived in Wyoming and Colorado from 1955 until his death in 2002, the largest part of his adult life. He returned to teaching in 1958 and eventually began a thirteen-year association with the University of Denver. Some of Lockwood's many compositions include the regionally based works *Return of the Spirits*, performed at Mesa Verde; his opera, *The Hanging Judge*; and a multi-movement choral work, *Land of Promise A Dramatic Portrait of Rocky Mountain Methodism*.

Cecil Effinger (1914–1990) stands between Young and Lockwood philosophically. A more traditional composer than Young, Effinger chose consciously to create music with a regional feel, unlike Lockwood. Effinger's biographer, Larry Worster, observes, "His works reflect the spirit of the Rocky Mountain Region with their texts, programmatic titles, or pastoral style, which the composer often associated with explicit western or naturalist themes."[17] Born in 1914 in Colorado Springs, Effinger was educated at Colorado College, where he joined the faculty in 1936. After a brief stint studying with Boulanger in 1939, Effinger returned to Colorado College. He was heavily influenced by both Boulanger and the music of American composer Roy Harris, with whom he worked at Colorado College from 1941 to 1948. Effinger's regional interest was already well established by this time, as the titles to his works *Western Overture* (1941) and *Variations on a Cowboy Theme* (1945) suggest.

Effinger used traditional forms and harmonies to evoke specific images from nature and the region. In his most popular choral work, *Four Pastorales* (1962), Effinger uses verbal imagery—from the poetry of Colorado poet laureate Thomas Hornsby Ferril—of the American West within a four-movement (fast, slow, fast, fast) form using modality, traditional four-part harmony, unisons, chromaticism, and obbligato instrumentation. The poems are "No Mark," "Noon," "Basket," and "Wood." Of Effinger's work, Ferril said; "Our land was so rich in subject matter I used to wonder if America needed poets at all, so great was the need for simple stenographers merely to take down what the land was saying."[18]

Composers Using the Myth of the West

The musical works of these composers illustrate different styles, images, and philosophies all coming from the Rocky Mountain region and recognized nationally and internationally in the twentieth century; however, the draw of the mystique and myth of the Rocky Mountain West does not limit itself to regional composers. Most often using repetitive gestures, emphatic and syncopated rhythms, open harmonies, wide intervals, and droning minor harmonies so often associated with the sonic image of the American West, composers from Charles Ives to Libby Larsen repeatedly evoke the region as an underpinning of Americana. As early as 1921, Charles Ives composed his song "The Indians" (later to become Movement 1 of Chamber Orchestra Set No. 2) and "Charlie Rutlage." Ives accomplishes his western sound via a "slow tempo, multiple meters, blurred rolling attacks, and durations that seem free of any regular pulse" in "The Indians" and recitation, powerful rhythmic momentum, and repeated pitches and pitch patterns in "Charlie Rutlage."[19] Aaron Copland (1900–1990) turned to sounds of the open range, square dances, and cowboys in his ballet *Rodeo* (choreographed by Agnes de Mille) in 1942, composed specifically to return to a sense of nationalism and pride during World War II. The sonic imprint of the piece has become so synonymous with American pride and the West that it is instantly recognizable and has been frequently used in large shows of patriotism (Fourth of July, inaugurations, etc.) and more recently in ad campaigns ("Beef, it's what's for dinner"). Copland's earlier work the ballet *Billy the Kid* (1938, choreographed by Eugene Loring) incorporated cowboy tunes from trail drives.

Women from the region have also inspired major works, including one of the most successful American operas, *The Ballad of Baby Doe* (1956), by Douglas Moore. More recently, Libby Larsen's *Songs from Letters* (1989) celebrates the life of Calamity Jane (c. 1852–1903), using texts from Jane's own letters to her daughter, Janey, at the turn of the century. Insistent rhythm, extensive word painting, alternating wide leaps, intense chromaticism, and shifting tonal centers are present in this five-movement piece. The texts depict one of the region's most interesting nineteenth-century women, her relationship with Wild Bill Hickok (1837–1876), her daughter, her various jobs (including stagecoach driver and Bill Cody's Wild West Show), and her own encroaching death. Larsen notes that her interest in the texts, which were published in *Between Ourselves* by Karen Kane, was their graphic portrayal of a woman who was irrefutably unconventional[20]—highlighting another

The Denver Symphony Orchestra

Aside from the music and composers, the day-to-day drama of the financial struggle for classical music organizations is played out in communities throughout the nation. Relying on ticket sales, foundation grants, and patron support, professional organizations squeak by to meet, at the bare minimum, union scale for their performers. Garnering international attention, the history of symphonic music in Denver is one such story.

After several early symphonic enterprises, the Denver Symphony Orchestra (DSO) was founded in 1934 (around which time two other large-scale musical organizations were functioning: the Denver Municipal Band and the Effinger Army Band). Early controversy erupted in the symphony over conductors, when Antonia Brico and Saul Caston were vying for the position. In 1945, Saul Caston received the conductorship, whether due to gender or Brico's admittedly brusque manner.

By 1983, the DSO had been struggling with finances and labor disputes for a decade. Protracted musician lockouts occurred in 1973–1974, 1977, and 1980. In 1983, the DSO restructured its administration to include the BUMM (board, union, musicians, and management) committee. The organization was optimistic when a three-year contract was achieved; however, disputes continued. In September 1988 the Denver Symphony Association canceled all performances. The musicians, having refused to cut their wages by 70 percent, re-formed as a workers co-op. The new Colorado Symphony Orchestra began a virtually sold-out season on October 27, having hired Barry Fey, rock promoter, as producer. Despite surviving for two years solely on ticket sales, the orchestra entered into a successful merger discussion with the Denver Symphony Association. The old DSO board resigned, and a new board and by-laws were created, including stipulations that the board and every board committee consist of one-third musicians. The benefits of the merger included budget revisions, a stronger salary negotiating voice for musicians, a link to existing government grants, endowments, and physical property (library and pianos). The resulting international model for successful cooperation between management and musicians put the Colorado Symphony Orchestra on the map.

In the 1993–1994 season, the Colorado Symphony Orchestra made headlines again, this time for the hiring of Marin Alsop as its principal conductor and music director. A winner of the Koussevitzky Conduction Prize and Leopold Stokowski Conducting Competition, Alsop is a conductor with international stature who also happens to be female. The orchestra in Denver now runs as a solvent, professional orchestra with a full season including masterworks, pops, and Cultural Convergence series and more.

myth of the region. The women who settled here are viewed as tough women forced to defy convention for the sake of survival, often enduring untold hardship.

MUSIC AND DANCE IN THE ROCKY MOUNTAINS

Classical Dance

Historically, classical dance in the Rocky Mountain region can be attributed to a few key characters. Leading among these are the Christensen brothers: Willam (1902–2001), Harold (1904–1989), and Lew (1909–1984), from Brigham City, Utah. The Christensen family emigrated from the Netherlands in 1854. Lars, the brothers' grandfather, taught social dancing and formed a traveling orchestra in Brigham City. Their father and uncles (four sons in total) all became professional teachers of social dance. In turn, all three of the Christensen brothers became national figures in classical and modern dance and pioneers in the extremely vibrant dance culture in current Utah and Idaho. That such a long commitment to dance grew out of the Mormon culture is no curious accident. Brigham Young frequently noted the benefits of both music and dance. Trained in music and social dance by their father and uncles, the brothers also studied classical technique. In the late 1920s and early 1930s, the brothers began their performing careers in vaudeville as both Russian character dancers and in a stunt ballet act. Initiated by Willam and Lew, Harold took over Willam's spot when the latter married and moved to Portland, Oregon, to teach in schools established by his uncle.

In 1934, Lew and Harold debuted on Broadway in the cast of *The Great Waltz*. They began simultaneously studying with George Balanchine and Pierre Vladimiroff at the recently formed School of American Ballet. Both dancers eventually joined Balanchine's company and worked with the progressive Ballet Caravan (a company "designed to nurture young American choreographers and generate repertory based on American themes"[21]). Lew was both ballet master and one of several emerging choreographers in the company, creating both *Pocahontas* (1936) and *Filling Station* (1938). Choreographed to a score by Virgil Thompson, *"Filling Station* . . . reflected Lew's vaudevillian roots, incorporating acrobatics, deadpan humor, allusions to social dance, and tap dancing into its episodic structure."[22] Lew also created the role of Pat Garrett in *Billy the Kid* by Eugene Loring.

While Lew was earning a national reputation as both dancer and choreographer, Harold was dancing and working as stage manager for Ballet Caravan. Willam, who had remained in Portland, was hired in 1937 as lead dancer for the San Francisco Opera Ballet. In 1938 he became director of the company. In this capacity, he became the first American to set and present the complete *Coppelia*, *Swan Lake*, and *Nutcracker* (in 1939, 1940, and 1944, respectively), putting San Francisco on the national map in dance.[23] Maintaining frequent contact with his brothers, Willam's works echoed similar goals of combining classical and social forms of dance within American themes. From 1942 to 1946, Lew was engaged in military service. In 1948, he joined Harold and Willam in San Francisco, taking over directorship in 1951 and working simultaneously as ballet master of the New York City Ballet until 1954.

Willam maintained his association with the San Francisco Opera and, later, the independent San Francisco Ballet (and ballet school) until 1975. Meanwhile, in

1951, he also began working with the University of Utah to establish a ballet program in the conservatory tradition (versus the more popular current trend of modern dance programs through physical education programs). Willam was in charge of the student dance company, created within the Department of Theater, and choreographed theater and opera productions. The student dance company turned professional in 1963 and created the prestigious Ballet West, so named in 1968. The brothers all garnered immense administrative respect in 1963 when both the San Francisco Ballet and the soon-to-be Ballet West were awarded Ford Foundation Grants, giving both companies enviable financial freedom. All three brothers were recipients of the Dance Magazine Award (in 1973, alongside Rudolf Nureyev [1938–1993]) and the 1984 Capezio Dance Award.

The Christensen brothers are significant not only for their national visibility with roots in the Rocky Mountain region but also for creating an enormous legacy of superior technique, innovation, and the creation of dance opportunities in the West at large and the Rocky Mountain region. The legacy of Willam's work with the university of Utah is a thriving department of dance that currently houses departments in both Modern Dance and Ballet within the College of Fine Arts, where the Virginia Tanner Creative Dance Program and Children's Dance Theatre also reside. The university also houses a 333-seat facility designed specifically for dance productions. Similarly, there are four dance programs at Brigham Young University: the Ballroom Dance Company, The Dancer's Company, Theatre Ballet, and the International Folk Dance Ensemble. Ballet West, so named because most of its extensive touring is in the intermountain region of the West, continues to have a respected reputation and is nationally and internationally recognized, as evidenced by recent mentions in the *New York Times*.

Outside of this impressive list of dance activities, two other professional dance companies of note exist in Salt Lake City. The Ririe-Woodbury Dance Company, founded in 1964, is dedicated to contemporary dance. Utah's Repertory Dance Theatre, a fully professional modern dance company, founded in 1966, considers itself "a living museum representing one hundred years of dance history, preserving the largest and most significant collection of American dance in the world" as well as commissioning new works.[24]

The legacy of the Christensen brothers on the national dance scene and the Rocky Mountain region cannot be overstated. However, one fact of geography and two other figures loom large in the history of classical dance in the region: the railroad, Erick Hawkins (1909–1994), and Hanya Holm. As pointed out previously, the Colorado Front Range was a frequent stop on the transnational rail service between New York, Chicago, and San Francisco, bringing innumerable companies (both musical and dance) to the region. Nijinski danced in Denver as early as 1916. Martha Graham danced in Colorado Springs in 1936.

Erick Hawkins (1909–1994) was born in Trinidad, Colorado. He discovered dance during his studies at Harvard and sought out Native American ceremonies in his travels throughout the West. Hawkins debuted in 1934 in Balanchine's White Plains Concert. A contemporary of Lew and Harold Christensen, Hawkins was also active in the American Ballet and a founding member of Ballet Caravan (1936–1939), performing leading roles in *Pocahontas*, *Filling Station*, and *Billy the Kid*. He studied with Martha Graham and became her partner in 1938 (two years after Graham was presented in the inaugural year of the Colorado Springs Fine

Arts Center). They married in 1948 and danced together until 1950. In 1952, Hawkins created his own company based on his philosophy in which "he saw dance as motionless and deeply sensed floating as well as in speed through space," putting on equal level "doing" and "non-doing" in dance. By 1979, Hawkins was known for "his Native American, pure dance style.[25] In the same year, he was also awarded the Dance Magazine Award.

While Hawkins was working and creating a national reputation based out of New York, Hanya Holm, premier dance teacher and choreographer of *Kiss Me, Kate*, *My Fair Lady*, and *Camelot*, among others, was busy with her long association with the Colorado College Summer School of Dance in Colorado Springs. Having previously taught at the Perry-Mansfield School in Steamboat Springs, Holm, a German immigrant in 1931, taught in Colorado Springs from 1941, at the age of forty-eight, until 1983. Designed as an eight-week summer intensive, Holm's program was based on stringent technique, often using exercises she had developed in conjunction with Joseph Pilates, and was seen nationally as significant in the world of dance. In the early years of her association, Holm used the Colorado College program as a time for intense collaboration and major innovation. During World War II she worked with Roy Harris on *What So Proudly We Hail* and the *Walt Whitman Suite*. In 1949, she worked with Nicolas Slonimsky on his *Little Suite*, Igor Stravinsky's *History of a Soldier*, and Edgar Varese's *Ionisation*. This early ground for new works changed in the 1950s as Holm became ever more popular on Broadway. By 1956 she also began an association with the Central City Opera Company for the premier of *The Ballad of Baby Doe*. Under the patronage of Colorado College president Thurston Davies and, later, Dean Gilbert Johns, Holm helped pinpoint Colorado Springs as a regional leader in dance recognized on a national level. In 1978 Holm received the Capezio Dance Award and in 1981 choreographed Béla Bartók's *Cantata Profana*.

With its legacy in dance, it is no surprise that the Rocky Mountain region currently supports a number of dance companies, outside of the above-mentioned Utah troupes. The professional dance company Idaho Dance Theatre is based in Boise. Colorado is home to several companies including Colorado Ballet, begun as a school in 1951 and professional company in 1961 and now home to thirty-seven professional dancers. Cleo Parker Robinson founded the Cleo Parker Robinson Dance Theatre (and school) in 1970, a primarily African American troupe dedicated to bringing new audiences to dance. Nationally recognized, Robinson has served on the National Endowment for the Arts and the Lila Wallace Foundation. Also in Colorado is The David Taylor Dance Theatre founded in 1979 as a professional contemporary dance company and the Kim Robards Company. Jackson Hole, Wyoming, is home to the recently formed Contemporary Dance Wyoming, a modern dance troupe founded in 1996 with permanent residence in Dancers' Workshop, an overarching nonprofit organization involved with a junior company and the Vista 360° festival. Montana, one of the least populated states in the region, is home to the thriving University of Montana modern dance program, where the Montana Transport Dance Company resides. In addition, the Montana Ballet Company, a preprofessional classical troupe, produces several works each season.

Folk and Social Dance

Groups settling in the area for over 150 years brought various national dances to the Rocky Mountain region. In the absence of movie theaters, bowling alleys, and television sets, dancing was a popular form of entertainment. In many regions, homesteads were isolated. To create an opportunity for socializing, civic groups, such as women's clubs, organized dances. The locations were often the schoolhouse or a community hall, which, like the homesteads, stood by itself miles away from another human structure. One such meeting place, in Woods Landing, Wyoming, was built by Scandinavian tie-hacks who balanced the dance floor on railroad boxcar coils to get more "spring" in their step. Overall, such occasions were a time to relax and forget for an evening the hard work required by such occupations as rancher, tie-camp worker, and miner.

Music was performed live, and these states abounded with musicians to perform it. The most popular dance tunes performed all over the region included the Heel and Toe Polka and the Rye Waltz. There were generic types of dances too, such as the waltz, varsouvienne, schottische, and polka, to name the most popular. A number of different instrumentalists accommodated these requests. They included accordionists, pianists, fiddlers, and banjo players. Later when the foxtrot and jitterbug became the craze, small bands with big band sound composed of saxophones, brass, and percussion played for enthusiastic dance crowds. Coal miners in Hannah, Wyoming, formed a number of bands that traveled the area to play for dances. One of the most popular halls was a first-class Octagon building in nearby Elk Mountain. In addition to local bands, touring bands like Lawrence Welk's (1903–1992) also played there.

Although country dances in isolated communities continue today, they became fewer with the onslaught of modern technology after World War II. First, the big band craze and then phonographs and radios displaced the local stringed instrumentalists from the dance scene. Fiddlers in particular refused to give up fiddling regardless of dwindling dance audiences. Instead, they organized fiddle contests to provide an atmosphere where tunes could be learned and performed for an appreciative audience, and where healthy competition stimulated their fiddling technique and style. Old-time music contests, especially fiddle contests, are popular throughout the country today and are a means by which old-time dance tunes have been perpetuated from one generation of musicians to the next.

Competition is organized so that the fiddler must play at least three different styles of dance music. The first tune is a "hoedown," a lively tune to which a fast-moving line or square dance could be danced. The second tune, a waltz, gives the fiddler the opportunity to demonstrate her ability to play long, sustained notes beautifully. The third category is called "tune of choice." Any danceable tune may be played, with a few exceptions. Hoedowns or waltzes should not be repeated for the third tune, and in most contests, the "double-shuffle" bowing, as heard in the famous tune "Orange Blossom Special," is not allowed because it is "modern" and "hard to dance to." Possible "tunes of choice" include rags, polkas, jigs, schottisches, marches, and two-steps.

The movement to create a series of state old-time fiddling organizations originated in Weiser, Idaho. In 1953, the Weiser Chamber of Commerce hosted their first annual National Oldtime Fiddlers Contest, and at the same time the Idaho

Old Time Fiddlers Association was formed. Surrounding states followed suit, and now each of the Rocky Mountain states has a fiddling organization and hosts a state championship. Since 1973 Wyoming's state contest has been held in the small town of Shoshone over Memorial Day Weekend, while the other contests tend to move around their relative states. The winners of the state contests take each other on for the national title every third week of June in Weiser, Idaho. Montana is the home of Dick Barrett, who has won the national contest numerous times, and Métis Mary Trotchie (1911–1982) in the Fiddler's Hall of Fame, while Danita Harz, the first woman fiddler to win the Grand Champion title in old-time dance fiddling, was born and reared in Idaho.

The continuing legacy of modern social dance can be traced in large part to the work of Lloyd Shaw of Colorado Springs. A dance educator, Shaw began collecting dance patterns and calls in the 1930s and took them on tour as "cowboy dances." While he used the traditional western square dance as a framework, he manipulated the dances for formal display and "introduced the idea of all four couples dancing throughout the dance, with no inactive time." During World War II many of Shaw's dance specialists were hired to teach square dancing at home and to the troops. "Square dancing became further entrenched in the popular consciousness as the archetypal American folk dance" (part of the reason it is the state dance of both Idaho and Colorado). Shaw's work helped spark an interest in organized western square dancing, and clubs subsequently formed all over the country. Highlighting this trend is the Rocky Mountain Dance Roundup Week, occurring annually near Colorado Springs and providing sessions in contra, traditional, and modern square dance, as well as Scottish, English, and folk dancing. The Colorado Friends of Old Time Music and Dance are active in Fort Collins and Denver. The Boulder Chautauqua house also sponsors contra dance, as well as innumerable classical music concerts, every summer. Contra dance groups abound throughout Wyoming and Montana. Of note are the Steam and Stomp in Boulder Hot Springs, hosted by the Helena, Montana, Contra group, and the Wintergreen Dance Weekend in inner-city Bozeman. Irish and Scottish dance is also lively in the region with five well-known teachers in Denver alone and students sent annually to place in the national Irish Dance competitions.

Not surprisingly, country dancing is a frequent dance pastime in the region with virtually every community hosting its own favorite Country/Western dance bar. Two of the most renowned in the region are The Cowboy Bar in Laramie, Wyoming, and The Grizzly Rose in Denver. The form is so popular that the University of Wyoming has a cowboy dance class for credit through their physical education department. Dance (jazz, ballet, dance as cultural expression) is still offered at Montana State University through the Health and Human Development Department as well.

Social dancing has always been popular among Latinos, and there are a variety of bands performing music to satisfy dancers. New Mexican native Roberto Griego has a national reputation and performs often in southern Colorado and the Denver area. The secret of his captivating performances is his ability to set original songs carrying special messages of Hispanic community pride and solidarity to an irresistible danceable beat, winning the hearts of his followers. Denver Latinos of various nationalities also enjoy Afro Latin beats including salsa and cumbia provided by the group Conjunto Colores. In Green River, Wyoming, members of the Luceros family perform both older and newer styles of Latino dance and song traditions.

Native American Dance

Native American dance is also of significance in the region, as pointed out above. Perhaps most unique, however, is the long-standing Koshare Dance Troupe/Boy Scout Troop No. 232 presenting Native American dance throughout the region. Using a model similar to the modern powwow, meaning that interpretations and/or short versions of traditional dance are presented, the group, based out of La Junta, Colorado, performs around sixty shows a year. Typical inclusions in the show are the Koshare War Dance, Ghost Dance, Comanche Dance, Eagle Dance, Oaxaca Plume Dance, Kiowa Shield Dance, and the Aztec Dance of the Shield. Begun in 1934, modeled on a similar program in the Colorado Springs area (no longer functioning), James F. ("Buck") Burshears used dance to focus his scout troop. In doing so, he has created a renowned group of dancers often held up as one of the "foremost interpretive" groups of Native American dance. Burshears points to several factors for the success and longevity of his program. In his words:

Here's an opportunity for a kid to do all the handicraft work he can do (building costumes). And he's building something for a purpose, not just making something for nothing, just to do something. He's got a reason for making it. This is important. He's got all the exercise he can stand in learning the dances. But the climax is putting on a show. That's the secret.[26]

The group is so well thought of that they have presented shows for important feast days at the Santa Clara Pueblo and regularly attend the Gallup Ceremonials.

FESTIVALS IN THE ROCKY MOUNTAIN REGION

Classical Festivals

The Rocky Mountain region is an enormous winter playground and hiking/biking summer activity center. Although the tourist industry often appears to be focused on the snow pack and powder statistics, an explosion of the national music scene is transported to the Rocky Mountains in the summer via music festivals. Blessed with a temperate climate, beautiful scenery, and a reputation for a more "laid-back" atmosphere, the area attracts thousands of artists each year in both the "classical" and "popular" music areas.

Festivals in the region began at least as early as 1895 when the Festival of Mountain and Plain was initiated. Part of the festival was a band competition for nonprofessional bands, which proved to be successful and profitable for some years. Such premier festivals continue today. Foremost among the modern classical festivals is the Aspen Music Festival. Dating back to 1949 the festival includes both professional music series and the Aspen School of Music for a duration of nine weeks (June to August), plus some other events year-round. The schedule ranges from large-scale productions of Berlioz to intimate chamber concerts. In 2003 alone, premier artists included Joshua Bell, Sarah Chang, James Conlon, James DePriest,

Vladimir Feltsman, Leon Fleisher, Stephen Hough, Joseph Kalichstein, Lang Lang, Cho-Liang Lin, Robert McDuffie, Midori, Nadja Salerno-Sonnenberg, Gil Shaham, and Michael Stern. Historically the Aspen Music Festival has been heavily influenced by the participation of such notable names as Darius Milhaud, Lillian Fuchs, Leonard Slatkin, and the Emerson String Quartet, to name only a few.

With an even longer history, dating back to 1932, Central City Opera in Central City, Colorado, forty miles west of Denver, presents three operas each summer in continuing rotation, two from the standard repertory and one American opera or operetta. Performed in the 1878 Opera House, the season lasts approximately five weeks (July and August). Notable in the opera's history is the commission of *The Ballad of Baby Doe* by Douglas Moore and *The Face on the Barroom Floor* (Henry Mollicone). Also in the Colorado mountains is the renowned Telluride Chamber Festival focusing on the performances of the Telluride Chamber Players; this festival lasts only two weeks every summer (August). Also of note are the Colorado Music Festival and Boulder Bach Festival.

Nestled at the foot of the Grand Tetons in Wyoming, the Grand Teton Music Festival takes place in July and August. Here large-scale symphonic concerts take place on the weekend, and chamber music rounds out the weekdays. Included in the festivities is "Music in the Present Tense," giving voice to both performances and discussions with such contemporary composers as Joan Tower and George Crumb.

Multi-Arts Festivals

Utah is home to the only state-sponsored festival in the country. The Utah Arts Festival occurs in June in Salt Lake City and features music, dance, and the visual arts. Musical offerings include all genres from classical and jazz to blues, pop, funk, and folk. Audiences in 2003 saw the participation of such diverse dance ensembles as The Repertory Dance Theatre and the Ririe-Woodbury Dance Company. Other festivals in the region presenting classical and popular music and dance include the newly formed Vista 360° Mountainfest in Jackson Hole, Wyoming. Sponsored by the Center for the Arts, Vista is a multivenue festival focusing on an international theme alongside "traditional mountain culture." Thus, in its inaugural year (the third weekend in June 2003), the presentation of the music of Krygyzstan, by theatrical troupe Ordo Sakhna, coincided with concerts by Darol Anger and his American Fiddle Ensemble and the dance group Project Bandaloop. The festival also features film, crafting, demonstrations, and traditional exhibits at the National Museum of Wildlife Art. Another festival incorporating both classical and popular art is the annual Cherry Creek Arts Festival in Denver. Cordoning off blocks of the Cherry Creek District the first weekend in July, the festival presents a large market of visual artists interspersed with staging of classical, popular, and folk music and dance. Similarly, but specifically celebrating music and dance of the Basque culture, is the three-day San Inazio Festival in July at and around the Basque Center in Boise, Idaho.

Popular and Folk Festivals

Bluegrass Festivals

A number of firmly established bluegrass festivals exist in the Rocky Mountain region, including the Bitterroot Valley Bluegrass Festival held since 1990 in Hamilton, Montana. At the festival, favorite Montana bands, including Leftover Biscuits, Mountain Groan, Lang Creek, and Kane's River, appear along with nationally known bands like the Grasshoppers and Fragment, a band originally from Czecholslavakia. Utah boasts a nationally known performer, Ogden native Ryan Shupe & the Rubberband. Shupe's family founded the Utah Oldtime Fiddlers association and has been active in keeping bluegrass alive by supporting regional events like the Moab Folk Festival. Another Utah festival featuring bluegrass is the Founders Title Company Founders Bluegrass festival in Salt Lake City, presented by the Intermountain Acoustic Music Association.

One of the earliest Wyoming bands to experiment with the sounds of bluegrass is the Chugwater Philharmonic String Quartet from the southeastern part of the state. The band performs regularly for the Cheyenne Frontier Days Rodeo events in late July and early August and at the Happy Jack Mountain Music Festival in July. In northeast Wyoming the Annual Grand Targhee Bluegrass Festival takes place in mid-August, and in the central area the High Plains Country Music Show happens each spring in Douglas, Wyoming. The Laramie Peak Bluegrass Festival Association is held at the state fairgrounds in September. Bands who participate in these festivals include Big Hollow of Laramie, Turtle Creek of Gering, Nebraska, and Shelley and Kelly of Jackson, Wyoming.

Colorado has a number of annual bluegrass festivals that attract large audiences. In 1973 the Rocky Mountain Bluegrass Festival was created by the CBMS when Bill Monroe, "the father of Bluegrass music," volunteered to support the festival for three years. Monroe was looking for a place to feature his band in the Rocky Mountain region on tours between the East and West Coasts. This festival has grown into what is now known as "Rockygrass," a major festival in July that includes the "Rockygrass Academy," a week of instructional sessions with the experts before the official performance begins. Presently Rockygrass is owned by Planet Bluegrass, the same corporation that puts on the internationally famous Telluride Bluegrass Festival. The Telluride Bluegrass Festival, in its thirtieth year, is a four-day event in June in the Town Park and attracts national talent, including Doc Watson, John McKuen, Edgar Meyer, Sam Bush, and many others. The Midwinter Bluegrass Festival held in February at the Northglenn Holiday Inn has become a long-standing tradition for the CBMS. Missouri native Ken Seaman, a member of the popular Bluegrass Patriots, originally founded the festival in Fort Collins in the 1980s. The festival, which was moved south to Northglenn to attract a wider audience, remains an annual destination for bluegrass fans. The indoor event takes the chill off the long winter between summer festivals.

One unique aspect of bluegrass festivals is that many bluegrass music fans play music themselves; the festivals, therefore, are not only extended concerts but also venues for the transmission of the music. After hearing an inspirational band perform a memorable tune, a festival attendee may return to her RV, parked in the campground along with the vehicles of hundreds of others, pull out her guitar, and start learning that song, often supplementing the memory with hand-held cassette recorders. As is usually the case, she may join together with other musicians in the lot for an informal "jam" or "picking session." Such musicians often actively participate in scheduled sections of the festival, competing in instrumental contests or volunteering to accompany dance workshops featured on smaller stages adjacent to the main attractions.

Jazz and Blues Festivals

A number of major jazz festivals of national repute take place in beautiful mountain settings in Colorado including Jazz Aspen Snowmass, the Vail Jazz Festival, and Jazz in the Sangres. In 1997 Denver hosted the first festival in the nation to celebrate jazz music captured on film. Every February since, music fans have been enjoying jazz movies at the Denver Jazz on Film Festival. In August, Telluride returns to the festival scene with the Telluride Jazz Festival, a multivenue festival (incorporating local bars, the historic Sheridan opera house, and the Town Park). Just as with the bluegrass festival, the jazz festival, which began in 1977, attracts national attention and musicians, from Wynton Marsalis to Larry Coryell.

In Idaho, of significance is the Lionel Hampton Jazz Festival at the University of Idaho. In its thirty-fifth year, the festival takes place in February and incorporates workshops, competitions, and concerts. The 2004 festival presenters include the Roy Hargrove quintet, Slide Hampton, and the Lionel Hampton New York Big Band. More recently added to the festival scene, à la Memphis in May, is the Denver Blues and Bones Festival celebrating local and national blues artists alongside a barbeque competition. In its seventh year, Blues and Bones takes place for two days in June.

Folk Festivals

More diverse in their focus are two of the region's folk festivals. The McCall Summer Music Festival in McCall, Idaho, began in 1979 and occurs for three days in July. In 2003, presentations incorporated everything from bluegrass, jazz fusion, acoustic dance, and gospel to Brazilian world music. Much smaller in scope, and brand new to the festival circuit, is the Moab Folk Music Festival, mentioned above, begun in 1993. The festival takes place in downtown Moab in early November. In addition, the National Oldtime Fiddler's Contest and Festival is held every third week in June in Weiser, Idaho. The festival is so popular that the small population, circa 4,000, doubles during the weekend.

Dance Festivals

Last, but certainly not least, are the festivals of dance. The Idaho International Folk Dance Festival, based out of Ricks College in Rexburg, Idaho, began in 1986 and sponsors teams from Africa, Asia, Europe, South and North America, and so on. Inclusive in the program is dance instruction, cultural sharing, and innumerable performances. Similarly, the tradition of summer instruction thrives with Dance IDAHO!, a series of six-day workshop intensives in ballet and jazz. Vail Festival presents national and international companies for two weekends each summer. The Aspen Festival began as a summer residency for Ballet West and now presents a select few companies in four performances each throughout the summer months.

CONCLUSION

In addition to the representative music and dance examples highlighted above, there are innumerable programs throughout the region that have not been discussed. Among the latter are the myriad music and dance activities and courses in the elementary and secondary schools, and colleges and universities, where both performers and audience receive not only their initial but continuing musical/movement experiences throughout adolescence and into adulthood. Significant contributions to such academic settings by individuals are ongoing. Of particular note is Alan Merriam, from Montana, who almost single-handedly renewed comparative musicology into a new, and deeply influential, discipline termed *ethnomusicology*. The region's academic performance and scholarly communities are active and prospering.

The immense diversity of this large region, with important Native American, Latino, Basque, Métis, Anglo, Middle Eastern, Asian, and other communities living together, creates an area full of traditional, classical, and fused activities. Diverse in ethnicity and western in geography, the region has a relatively recent history (a century and a half), rich in scenery and minerals, and sparse in moisture and population. These realities, together with the remarkable myths they have spawned, have done much to shape the region's general culture, including music and dance.

RESOURCE GUIDE

Printed Sources

Duckworth, William. "La Monte Young and Marian Zazeela." In his *Talking Music: Conversations with John Cage, Philip Glass, Laurie Anderson, and Five Generations of American Experimental Composers*. New York: Schirmer Press, 1995.

Fife, Austin. "'Tying Knots in the Devil's Tail' and Other Cowboy Songs." In *Exploring Western Americana*, ed. Alta Fife. Ann Arbor, MI: UMI Research Press, 1988. 217–237.

Gitelman, Claudia. *Dancing with Principle: Hanya Holm in Colorado, 1941–1983*. Boulder: University of Colorado Press, 2001.

Grimshaw, Jeremy. "The Sonic Search for Kolob: Mormon Cosmology and the Music of La Monte Young." *Repercussions* 9.1 (Fall 2001): 77–120.

Johnson, Lynn M. "The Co-op Alternative: Revisiting Symphony Orchestras in New Orleans, Oakland, and Denver." *International Musician* 91 (April 1993): 4–5+.

Kroeber, Alfred L. *The Arapaho*. Lincoln: University of Nebraska Press, 1983.

Kroeger, Marie. "The Federal Music Project in Denver: 1935–1941." *American Music Research Center Journal* 3 (1993): 50–64.

Lederman, Anne. "The Drops of Brandy: Several Versions of a Métis Fiddler Tune." *Canadian Folk Music Bulletin* 24.1 (June 1990): 3–11.

Marini, Stephen. *Sacred Song in America: Religion, Music, and Public Culture*. Urbana: University of Illinois Press, 2003.

Norton, Kay. *Normand Lockwood, His Life and Music*. Metuchen, NJ: Scarecrow Press, 1993.

Peake, Thomas. "Denver, Colorado." *Down Beat* 66.11 (November 1999): 21.

Rabin, Carol Price. *The Complete Guide to Music Festivals in America: Classical, Opera, Folk, Country, Pops, Bluegrass, Jazz, Oldtime Fiddlers.* Great Barrington, MA: Berkshire Traveller Press, 1990.

Romero, Brenda. "Latino Musical Communities in Colorado and New Mexico." *American Musical Traditions*. Vol. 5, *Latino and Asian American Music.* New York: Schirmer, 2002. 49–58.

Schuller, Gunther. *Early Jazz: Its Roots and Musical Development.* New York: Oxford University Press, 1968.

Sowell, Debra Hickenlooper. *The Christensen Brothers: An American Dance Epic.* Australia: Harwood Academic Publishers, 1998.

Stoll, Dennis Gray. *Music Festivals of the World: A Guide to Leading Festivals of Music, Opera, and Ballet.* Oxford: Pergamon Press, 1963.

Swan, Howard. *Music in the Southwest: 1825–1950.* San Marino, CA: Huntington Library, 1952.

Tinsley, Jim Bob. *He Was Singin' This Song: A Collection of Forty-eight Traditional Songs of the American Cowboy, with Words, Music, Pictures, and Stories.* Orlando: University Presses of Florida, 1981.

Titon, Jeff Todd, ed. "North America/Native America." In *Worlds of Music.* Belmont, CA: Wadsworth Group, 2002.

Titon, Jeff Todd, and Bob Carlin. *American Musical Traditions.* Vol. 3, *British Isles Music.* New York: Schirmer, 2002.

Vander, Judith. *Songprints: The Musical Experience of Five Shoshone Women.* Chicago: University of Illinois Press, 1988.

von Glahn, Denise. "Charles Ives, Cowboys and Indians: Aspects of the 'Other Side of Pioneering.'" *American Music* (Fall 2001): 291–314.

Worster, Larry. *Cecil Effinger: A Colorado Composer.* Lanham, MD: Scarecrow Press, 1997.

Web Sites

Morrison, George, Sr. Papers. 2002.
Blair-Caldwell African American Research Library, Denver Public Library. May 19, 2004.
http://www.aarl.denverlibrary.org/archives/morrison.html

Prendergast, Alan. "The Brico Requiem: One of the World's Great Conductors Battle Fate—and Denver Society—for Almost Fifty Years; Guess Who Won." November 1, 1995.
http://www.Westword.com/

Recordings

Songs and Stories of Wyoming Settlement. 2nd ed. Accompanying booklet by Dennis Coelho. ". . . you know that Wyoming will be your new home." Cheyenne: Wyoming Council on the Arts, 1986.

Wild West Music of Buffalo Bill's Cowboy Band. Accompanying program notes by Michael Masterson. C Museum Selections, Buffalo Bill Historical Center, Cody, WY, 1996.

Festivals

Bluegrass

Bitterroot Valley Bluegrass Festival
Hamilton, MT

http://www.bluegrassfestival.org/

Grand Targhee Bluegrass Festival
Grand Tetons, Alta, WY
http://www.grandtarghee.com/summer/festival.html

Happy Jack Mountain Music Festival
Laramie, WY
http://www.happyjackfestival.com/

High Plains Country Music Show
Douglas, WY

Laramie Peak Bluegrass Festival Association
Laramie, WY
http://www.laramiepeakbluegrass.com/

Midwinter Bluegrass Festival
Denver, CO
http://www.seamanevents.com/midwinter/schedule.html

Rockygrass
Lyons, CO
http://www.planetbluegrass.com/

Telluride Bluegrass Festival
Telluride, CO
http://www.planetbluegrass.com/

Classical

Aspen Music Festival
2 Music School Road
Aspen, CO 81611
http://www.aspenmusicfestival.com/
Held every summer since 1949.

Boulder Bach Festival
Boulder, CO
http://www.boulderbachfest.org/

Central City Opera
Central City, CO
http://new.centralcityopera.org/

Colorado Music Festival
Boulder, CO
http://www.coloradomusicfest.org/

Grand Teton Music Festival
Jackson Hole, WY
http://gtmf.org/home

Park City International Music Festival
Park City, UT
http://www.pcmusicfestival.com/

Telluride Chamber Music Festival
Telluride, CO
http://www.telluride.com/chamber.html

Utah Music Festival
Park City, UT
http://www.utahmusic.org/

Dance

Aspen Dance Festival
Aspen, CO
Dance IDAHO!
Moscow, ID
http://www.festivaldance.org/

Idaho International Folk Dance Festival
Rexburg, ID
http://www.rexcc.com/festival/index.html

Vail International Dance Festival
Vail, CO
http://www.vvf.org/dance.cfm

Folk Music

Cheyenne Frontier Days
Cheyenne, WY
http://www.cfdrodeo.com/

McCall Summer Music Festival
McCall, ID
http://www.mccall-idchamber.org/visiting/music/1themusic.html

Moab Folk Music Festival
Moab, UT
http://www.moabfolkfestival.com/

National Oldtime Fiddler's Contest and Festival
Weiser, ID
http://www.fiddlecontest.com/

Rockygrass Folks Festival
http://www.planetbluegrass.com/

San Inazio Festival (Basque)
Boise, ID
http://www.basquecenter.com/SanInazio/SanInazio.html

Jazz and Blues

Denver Blues and Bones
Denver, CO
http://www.denverbluesandbones.com/

Denver Jazz on Film Festival
Denver, CO
http://www.jazzfilmfestival.org/

Jazz Aspen Snowmass
Aspen, CO
http://www.jazzaspen.org/

Jazz in the Sangres
Westcliffe, CO
http://www.jazzinthesangres.com/home.asp

Lionel Hampton Jazz Festival
Moscow, ID
http://www.jazz.uidaho.edu/

Telluride Jazz Festival
Telluride, CO
http://www.telluridejazz.com/

Vail Jazz Festival
Vail, CO
http://www.vailjazz.org/

Multi-arts

Cherry Creek Arts Festival
Denver, CO
http://www.cherryarts.org/

Utah Arts Festival
Salt Lake City, UT
http://www.uaf.org/

Vista 360°
Jackson Hole, WY
http://www.vista360.org/

RELIGION

Jeremy Bonner

The notion of the West as a religious refuge is an abiding one. It was here that the Mormon refugees of the 1840s revived the New England Puritan model of theocratic governance, safely isolated from the currents of mainstream American life, and here that the Roman Catholic enclave of Butte, Montana, emerged, though Butte's identity was defined as much by its Irishness as by its Catholicity. Outside the Mormon heartland of Utah, eastern Idaho, and western Wyoming, Catholics represented the largest religious community but, except for southern Colorado and western Montana, did not exercise the complete dominance that they enjoyed further south. Rather, they were obliged to share their region with a multiplicity of Protestant groups, all of whom viewed the "irreligious" nineteenth-century West as a fit location for the saving of souls. Such a setting was far removed from either the Northeast—with its burgeoning urban Catholic population and clearly defined denominational boundaries—or the South—with its heavily rural Protestant ascendancy. Catholics and Jews, who found their opportunities for public service greatly curtailed in the East, had much less trouble influencing and participating in public affairs in the trans-Mississippi states. Protestants, with often weak connections to their respective denominational hierarchies, proved to be much more reliant on their neighbors for material and spiritual sustenance, and transdenominational initiatives were consequently much more advanced in the Northern Rockies at the beginning of the twentieth century than in many other parts of the United States.

That the West was a haven for many religious minorities has been fairly well understood. Of arguably equal importance has been the transitory nature of many of its religious communities. From the mining rushes of the 1850s to the dot-com bubble of the 1990s, the West has been a crucible of the "instant community." During the nineteenth century, many towns sprang up, only to vanish into obscurity within a matter of years.

Westerners today continue to display an economic mobility second to none, and community roots are even more fragile than in the past. During the nineteenth-century settlement of the West, Protestant pastors and Catholic priests were viewed as agents of stability. Today, many of the residents of the northern Rockies' urban frontier—suburban Denver, Salt Lake City, and to a lesser extent, Boise—themselves often migrants from the secularized states of the Pacific Rim states, have, at best, an ambivalent attitude toward organized religion. The most enduring forms of religious culture in the Northern Rockies—outside the Mormon heartland—are in those rural areas that are losing population rather than gaining it.

The bifurcation of the Northern Rockies into a monolithic Mormon religious culture and a more pluralistic religious setting in which Roman Catholicism must compete with an emerging secular ethos informs the shape of this chapter. We begin by tracing the nature of indigenous religious expression by various Native American groups in the Northern Rockies, explore the cultural clash that followed the arrival of missionaries and settlers during the 1840s, and then examine the West during its formative years from around 1890 until 1920. The discussion then shifts from a chronological approach to a thematic one, with examination of the internal operations of the leading religious groups in the Northern Rockies, the role of religious organizations in sustaining and upholding the social needs of the local community, and the part played by the various denominations in the public policy process. The chapter concludes with selective consideration of the role of the churches in the urban life of the region, an analysis that inevitably focuses on Denver and Salt Lake City.

PRE-1848 NATIVE AMERICAN RELIGION

Perhaps nowhere in the United States is the enduring legacy of Native American spirituality so evident as in the Rocky Mountains. The last region of the continental United States to be subdued and settled, it contains some of the most extensive Indian reservations in the country, as well as many protected Native American religious sites. A very distinct pattern of spiritual behavior, however, separates the tribes of the northern Rocky Mountains from their counterparts in the Southwest. The northern tribes inhabiting the Plateau (the region between the Rocky and Cascade Mountains), the Great Basin, and the western Plains all display a very individualistic spirituality, with few ceremonies intended for community observance and a distinct lack of ritual.

The great diversity of Indian religious belief and practice was one of the key characteristics of Native American culture prior to 1865, yet common to all was a unifying sense of the inseparable relationship between the natural world and the spiritual world. Religious life was at its simplest among the tribes of the Great Basin such as the Ute, who emphasize the interdependence of man and nature and the role of the various tribes in helping to maintain the cosmic balance. For such communities, the role of the shaman—or medicine man—was of critical importance because he was in contact with the most powerful spirits. A shaman's powers were generally acquired through dreams, and his principal role was that of a healer: determining the cause of an illness and helping to alleviate it. Rites of passage among the Great Basin tribes, such as a puberty rite for girls or ceremonies for the dead, were extremely simple and usually limited to the immediate family.

Apart from some form of first fruits ceremony, to ensure a good growing season, there were few instances of group rites.

A slightly more sophisticated pattern prevailed among Plateau Indians, like the Flatheads (Salish), Nez Percé, or Coeur d'Alene, who resided in Idaho and western Montana. Here, the role of the shaman was still important, but he was not considered to have the same connection with peculiarly powerful spirits as his Great Basin counterpart. While healing remained his principal function, a shaman could also have responsibility for predicting the future, locating lost objects, and performing death rites. The Plateau Indians placed great emphasis on an individual's search for his or her personal spirit guardian through a vision quest between the ages of six and twelve. Children would be dispatched to a suitable location—often a mountain—where they fasted for three or four days until their animal guardian appeared to teach them their sacred song and assure them of protection from danger and special skills. The central position of the vision quest emphasized the extent to which personal spirituality transcended a community's religious observances. Plateau residents did have one community rite that distinguished them from the inhabitants of the Great Basin, the Winter Spirit Dance, which brought the tribes together for up to two months in winter. This was the time when novices performed their own songs for the first time as a rite of initiation and when shamans would receive visions. Most Plateau tribes also had first fruits ceremonies and practiced more sophisticated naming ceremonies for newborn infants, puberty rites for girls, and death rites, which included the ceremonial expulsion of evil spirits from the corpse by a shaman and a feast and distribution of the deceased's possessions after the burial.

The individualist outlook was most strongly defined on the western Plains among the Crow of Montana and the northern Cheyenne of Wyoming and Colorado. While the Plateau and Great Basin Indians were as much gatherers as hunters and for the most part peaceful, the Plains Indians were generally warlike societies, dependent upon the buffalo for subsistence. Like their Plateau counterparts, the Plains Indians ascribed a central role to the vision quest but regarded it as a means of spiritual renewal throughout life, rather than a once-in-a-lifetime search for a spirit guardian. Both the Crow and the Cheyenne were known to use self-mutilation in addition to seclusion and fasting to try and enhance the supernatural experience. Unlike other Indian communities, the centrality of the vision quest tended to reduce the authority of the shaman, who became merely someone who had received enhanced spiritual training.

The Great Plains was also the setting for the Sun Dance, a practice most highly developed among the Cheyenne, held in the early summer for one week to reanimate and recreate the world of plants and animals. Rituals were undertaken to renew the earth, as various tribal societies performed sacred dances and songs. On the fifth day an altar was erected, and certain Indians would perform dances while tethered through the skin as a means of obtaining supernatural power. The ceremony concluded with a general dance, after which the chief priest and sponsor smoked a final sacred pipe.

One counterweight to Great Plains religious individualism was the presence of tribal societies, some of them explicitly religious. Typical was the Crow *Bacusa* or Tobacco Society, concerned with the cultivation of what they viewed as a sacred plant and with medicine. New candidates were initiated in the spring in a ceremony that included dancing, the smoking of tobacco, and a sweat bath, the latter practice used by all the Plains tribes both for healing and for purification. At such times, a dome was erected over a fire pit and hot stones placed on the ashes; a priest then censed the area, sang sacred songs, and poured water in a prescribed fashion over the stones. As tribal members exposed themselves to the steam, songs were sung and more water was gradually added. Plains Indians had a variety of life cycle observances, including rites for newborns, puberty rites for girls, and death rites that were more elaborate than those of the Great Basin and Plateau Indians and reflected, at least among the Cheyenne, a fear of ghosts. Wailing and hair cropping were common as the body was prepared for burial, and as with the Plateau Indians, the property of the deceased was distributed and their tipis dismantled. Plains Indian religion was the most elaborate of the three discussed here, but it was also the most individualistic. Shamans did not, except perhaps at the Sun Dance, enjoy the same authority as they did further west and certainly did not enjoy the political authority of their counterparts in the Southwest.

NATIVE AMERICAN RELIGION TODAY

Given the attachment of Native American religious practices to the land, it is unsurprising that their gradual loss of territory during the 1850s and 1860s was a time of spiritual crisis. The 1870s and 1880s were marked both by the confinement of Native Americans to reservations and by the concurrent effort of successive American governments to undermine the cultural and religious bases of Indian life. From the 1860s to the 1930s, the federal government ceased to recognize the tribes as sovereign entities and turned over management of the reservations to the mainstream Protestant churches, particularly the Episcopalians, Methodists, and Presbyterians and many missionaries traveled west to serve in this capacity. Welsh-born John Roberts (an Episcopalian) came to the Wind River Reservation in Wyoming in 1873, where he remained for fifty years. There he learned the Arapahoe and Shoshone languages, opened a girl's boarding school that used bilingual education, and baptized the Arapahoe chief Washakie and many of his followers into the Episcopal Church. That same year, Scottish-born Susan Mcbeth (a Presbyterian) began work in Idaho with the Nez Percé. Although a fierce opponent of mixing Indian customs with Christianity, Mcbeth established close relations with the Nez Percé, learning the Saheptian language and compiling a grammar in 1879. She also trained many preachers and established an annual camp meeting that continued to meet until the 1930s. Many Indians joined the Protestant denominations during this period, and missionaries helped preserve Indian languages, artifacts, and folklore. Nevertheless, a strong strain of resistance to assimilation remained, revealed in separatist Indian Christian churches, such as the Indian Presbyterian Church of Kamiah, Idaho.

The exposure of the tribes to the work of Protestant missionaries and the suppression of outward manifestations of indigenous religious expression had an effect, though not one necessarily anticipated by the reformers. By the 1890s, a new religious phenomenon had begun to emerge, which ultimately gave rise to a pan-Indian religious body—the Native American Church—and the Tipi and Cross Fire peyote ceremonies, the latter the more overtly Christian of the two. Peyote use began among the tribes of Oklahoma but spread to the Northern Arapahoe, the

Cheyenne, and the Crow in the 1890s. By the 1920s, it had also been adopted by the tribes on Idaho's Fort Hall Reservation and by most of the tribes in the Great Basin.

Peyote ceremonies require both a sacred fire (with the embers arranged in a particular pattern) and a sand altar and are generally conducted on a Saturday night. Peyotists sit on the floor in a circle, peyote buttons are distributed and consumed by the participants, and the organizer sings four songs before surrendering the floor to the next participant. Most of the meeting is occupied by singing, and the rest devoted to individual public prayer. At dawn, a breakfast of corn, meat, and fruit is consumed, and the participants have an opportunity to socialize. Significantly, the Cross Fire ceremony is a syncretic observance that is viewed as an extension of the Christian faith and may include a Bible reading. Peyote is seen as a gift from God that cures and heals and provides the user with a more acute sense of the transcendent. "Generally speaking," one anthropologist was informed in 1938, "there is no conflict internally when the same person is a good Episcopalian, a good Peyotist and a leader of the Sun Dance."[1] Despite this outlook, the non-Indian establishment has generally looked with disfavor on peyote use. Between 1917 and 1925, all the states in the Rocky Mountains banned peyote use off the reservation, to which Native Americans responded by incorporating state Native American churches, such as the 1925 Montana charter that brought the former rivals, the Crow and the Cheyenne, into one religious body. In 1955, they established the Native American Church in North America, headed by Frank Takes Gun, a Crow Indian from Montana. While some tribes today continue attempts to revive the old religious traditions of their particular tribes, the future of Native American spirituality is much more evident in syncretic pan-Indian religion than in the plethora of tribal practices that existed in the Northern Rockies before 1848.

MISSION AND SETTLEMENT

The Northern Rockies were largely settled by individual initiative before 1862, and until the 1840s there were few resident Christian missionaries. Although Idaho's Flathead and Nez Percé Indians sent a request for "black robes" as early as in 1831, the Roman Catholic Church at first ignored them, and it was the Presbyterian Henry Spalding and his wife Eliza who first brought Christianity to the region. Not until 1841 did Father Pierre Jean de Smet, S.J., arrive in Montana's Bitterroot Valley, where he established St. Mary's Mission. Unlike their southwestern counterparts, the Catholic missions to Montana and Idaho did not follow in the wake of Spanish imperial power, nor did they precede Protestantism into the region. They did, however, provide a contribution to the region's economic and social development. St. Mary's Mission boasted flour and lumber mills, raised cattle, and cultivated wheat, and its resident physician, Father Anthony Ravalli, was Montana's first doctor. Subsequent missions included the St. Ignatius Mission (1845), which became a model for seminaries in the United States and Europe, and the Cataldo Mission (1847). The religious order priests who served here helped lay the groundwork for regular parish life for Catholic immigrants in the 1860s.

With one exception, white settlement of the Northern Rockies only really began at the conclusion of the Civil War. That exception was the Church of Jesus Christ of Latter-day Saints (LDS). For twenty-four years, beginning with his famous vision at Palmyra, New York, in 1820, Joseph Smith (1805–1844) had helped build up America's first enduring indigenous white religious tradition. As they grew in numbers and power, the Mormons encountered rising hostility on their journey from Ohio to Missouri and ultimately to Nauvoo in Illinois. Smith's murder at Carthage in 1844 persuaded the Mormon leadership, headed by future president Brigham Young (1801–1877), to leave territories under U.S. suzerainty for a western refuge. Although consideration was given to Texas, the Mormons ultimately settled on the Great Basin, and a pioneer company departed Winter Quarters, Nebraska, on April 14, 1847. On July 22, Young's party reached the Valley of the Great Salt Lake.

The Mormon migration constituted a fundamental shift in religious outlook for the Latter-day Saints. At Nauvoo, despite their peculiar religious practices, they had been full participants in the civic and economic life of America. The communities that were established in Utah, by contrast, were driven by a religious zeal and theocratic mind-set that subordinated the individual's freedom of action to the needs of the wider church community. Conditions in the Great Basin, at least in the early days, demanded that agriculture be on a subsistence model, but the church also expected its members to devote their labors to religious upbuilding. This proved all the more attainable during the 1850s, as a steady stream of American and European converts made their way to Utah (a process that came to be known as the Gathering of Zion), partially funded by the church. The church combined civic and religious authority in one institution, allocating land and water rights, the latter being a break with American tradition by being cooperative in nature. It was also under the auspices of the LDS Church that Utah's first educational and health societies emerged. Unlike the region's Protestant and Catholic missionaries, the Mormons did not give high priority to proselytizing the local Indian population. Although Native Americans occupied a special position in Mormon theology, as descendants of the Lamanites described in the Book of Mormon with whose redemption the Latter-day Saints were charged, missionary work in Utah and surrounding states tended to focus more on the erection of physical outposts of the Mormon empire than on wholesale conversion.

The cession of Mexican territory under the Treaty of Guadalupe Hidalgo (1848) led the Mormon leadership to seek territorial status from the U.S. government in 1849, and Utah became a territory under the Compromise of 1850. Over the next thirty years, an increasingly bitter battle was waged between anti-Mormon federal appointees and a shadow government dominated by the LDS Church hierarchy. Between 1857 and 1858, indeed, the territory was in a state of war with the American government. One source of conflict was the issue of polygamy, which Joseph Smith had instituted as a sacramental rite of the church before his death. Fiercely condemned by reformist Republicans in Washington, polygamy became the touchstone issue of religious controversy in the 1870s and 1880s. Of comparable significance was the rise of church-sponsored cooperative marketing institutions—the most famous being Zion's Cooperative Mercantile Institution—which ensured the LDS Church economic dominance in state affairs. As development of Utah's mineral wealth increased and more non-Mormons moved to settle in Utah, they began to voice objections to such an all-encompassing religious state. An alliance of Protestants, Catholics, Jews, and apostate Mormons founded the Liberal Party in 1870, and Utah politics were conducted largely on religious lines until the 1890s. Aided by favorable Supreme Court rulings against polygamy, the Liberals in-

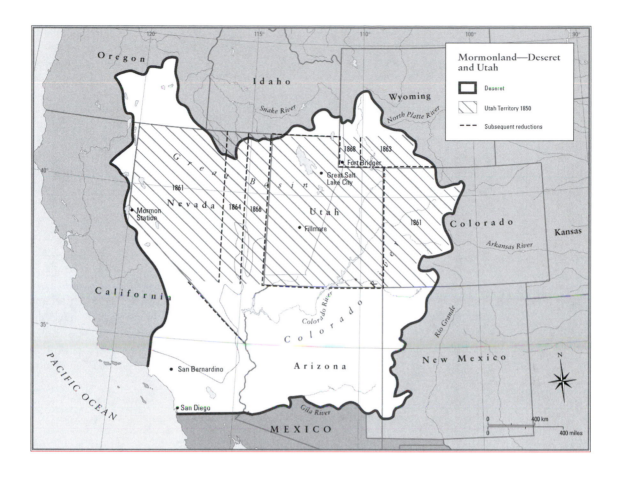

creasingly took the field against church opposition, seeking to deny the suffrage to anyone who endorsed the latter's stance. In Salt Lake City, Protestant missions were set up and schools founded in an effort to wean Mormons from their "heresy," while the first Catholic church—St. Mary Magdalene—was dedicated in 1871. The threat of the Edmunds-Tucker Act of 1887 to deprive the church of all its temporal property led President Wilford Woodruff to issue a Manifesto on September 24, 1890, in which the church repudiated plural marriage and endorsed American notions of secular governance in the public sphere.

The opening of the Mullan Road from Fort Benton, Montana, to Walla Walla, Washington, in 1860 and the Homestead Act of 1862 both served as a spur to the settlement of the Northern Rockies, as did the mining rushes that swept the region during the 1860s. Almost overnight, instant communities took shape, many of them inhabited by large numbers of Roman Catholics who looked to their church to provide them with spiritual services. Although lay Catholics often took the lead in erecting places of worship, such as Denver's St. Mary's Cathedral, they expected priests to perform the real leadership role, unlike their Hispanic counterparts in the Southwest. In Montana and Idaho, the Jesuit missions provided some support to immigrant Catholics, but the greatest burden fell on the secular priests, many of whom were obliged to undertake extensive circuit riding to scattered Catholic communities. The uncertain state of the mining industry further hampered their efforts, but the parishes the new priests created helped to establish a degree of social order.

Although Catholics and Mormons dominated the local landscape, it should be remembered that many Protestant ministers also went west between 1870 and 1890, inspired by the writings of Congregationalist ministers Josiah Strong and E. P. Tenney. Some of the most successful were Colorado's Episcopal Bishop John Spalding, Methodist minister William Van Orsdel of Montana, and Presbyterian minister Sheldon Jackson, whose "planting" activities throughout the region between 1869 and 1883 were among the most successful of all. Many congregations began by meeting in private homes or public buildings, and when a church building was erected—often at considerable financial sacrifice—it generally followed the architectural style of the parent denomination in the East. Local communities took pride in their new churches and would sometimes subscribe to their erection, even if they were not themselves members. For the frontier ministers, serving in the West could be a wearing occupation. Trans-Mississippi postings lacked the glamour of a congregation in the East or even a foreign mission assignment, and constant circuit riding was the order of the day. Protestant ministers also challenged the cultural mores of the West, as when Congregationalist Josiah Strong backed a crusade to save prostitutes in Cheyenne, Wyoming, and attacking the saloon was a popular gambit. Attempts by the churches to discipline their members on moral grounds, however, proved to be of limited value in the Intermountain West, where a fairly tolerant moral tone prevailed.

THE GROWTH OF THE WEST

By 1892, all the states of the Northern Rockies had been admitted into the Union, and the settlement phase was largely over. Where an earlier generation of clergymen had been involved in church planting and morality crusades, those who resided in the region from 1890 to 1920 had a much wider range of functions. Counseling, both spiritual and practical, remained very much a pastoral function, particularly regarding the abuse of alcohol, and clergymen were often the distributors of relief funds and front-line relief workers at times of natural disaster. Often, they were also the first librarians in a town, providing free literature to those who sought it and offering lectures on issues of religious and public interest. Martin Hart, dean of Denver's St. John's Episcopal Cathedral, was the author of articles on chemistry and mineralogy, helped bring the first smelter to Colorado, and directed Denver's principal charity organization, in association with Roman Catholic priest William O'Ryan and Rabbi William Friedman. Presbyterian William Boone, who came to Caldwell Presbyterian Church in 1887, helped establish the College of Idaho in 1893 and eventually became its president. Rabbi William Friedman of Denver's Temple Emmanuel was the driving force behind the city's National Jewish Hospital, which opened in 1899 to treat tuberculosis sufferers, and is now—as the National Jewish Medical and Research Center—one of the top hospitals in the United States for treatment of respiratory, immune, and allergic disorders. Friedman frequently delivered sermons on public policy that were reprinted in the press and helped explain Jewish customs to Denver's Christian community.

By the 1890s, churches were sufficiently established to sell off the lands they had initially acquired in the central business districts of many western cities for a profit and move to new neighborhoods, where they could erect massive—and expensive—edifices. Denver's Trinity Methodist Church, erected in 1886, cost $173,000, and First Presbyterian Church, erected in 1892, cost $165,000. Smaller cities also experienced this phenomenon, with Cheyenne's First Methodist Church costing $30,000 in 1890, and First Presbyterian Church, Helena, costing $50,000 in 1913.[2] In 1893, moreover, the Church of Jesus Christ of Latter-day Saints dedicated its temple in Salt Lake City. Many of the new western churches drew upon the Romanesque style and, by virtue of their size, dominated the urban landscape in a fashion that had not previously been experienced in the Intermountain West.

The physical presence of the churches was not confined to ecclesiastical structures. "Unlike their northern or southern counterparts," notes Ferenc Szasz, "from the 1890s to the WW I era the forces of organized religion in the West essentially created the institutional infrastructure for their subregion."[3] Foremost in the field of education was the Episcopal Church, which had established an academy in every diocese in the region by 1900. These academies focused on character formation, which the church feared would be neglected in the public schools, but they also provided a rigorous academic grounding that enabled many non-Episcopal westerners to attend college in the East. Other Protestant denominations set up a plethora of tertiary colleges in the West. Despite numerous failures, institutions that survived included Colorado College in Colorado Springs (Congregational), the College of Idaho in Caldwell (Presbyterian), Westminster College, Salt Lake City (Presbyterian), and Rocky Mountain College, Billings (Methodist). The University of Colorado and the University of Wyoming both owe their origins to the Methodists, while Boise State University began its existence as an Episcopal academy. One religious university that has subsequently achieved a high academic standing while retaining its religious identity is Brigham Young University in Provo, a Mormon foundation. Although church-related schools remained significant until the 1930s, many colleges collapsed during the depression of the 1890s. Theological seminaries also sprang up, most notably the Methodist Iliff Seminary in Denver, a leading Protestant seminary in the West during the nineteenth century.

Although the public presence of the churches in the West acquired a new urban gloss in the early twentieth century, rural churches continued to form an important source of culture and entertainment. Ladies Aid Societies and women's guilds played an essential role in organizing the dramatic productions, Shakespeare readings, public addresses, church suppers, and in some denominations, church dances, found in so many towns in the West. Such events almost always had a fund-raising component and sought to attract as many nonmembers from the immediate community as possible, as support from the various Home Mission Boards declined after 1890.

While the scattered communities of the 1870s were more connected by the 1890s, the vast distances involved still demanded application of the circuit-riding approach. Itinerant preachers also distributed large numbers of religious periodicals and other literature throughout the region. As technology improved, the innovation of the chapel car—and later the auto chapel—came to be employed in the rural West, as when the Baptists sent their "Glad Tidings" car to tour

Wyoming. Inevitably, some transdenominational forms of religious education emerged, the most influential being the Sunday School program, whose printed lessons plans enabled the unordained men (and even women) to lead religious discussions. Many church congregations in the West grew out of a Sunday School class.

The Intermountain West also experienced the rise of the Social Gospel, a nationwide phenomenon in mainstream Protestantism that called for greater ecclesiastical attention to the material needs of the underprivileged. Certain features of this peculiar to the region included language classes and special missions to immigrant Chinese communities in Denver and Salt Lake City and the development of medical care for the treatment of tuberculosis in Colorado. Denver was the region's strongest bastion of the Social Gospel, boasting such figures as Thomas Uzzel, who headed the Methodist People's Tabernacle from 1885 to 1910, where he helped establish a free dispensary, unemployment bureau, summer camp, night schools, and language classes. Myron Reed of First Congregational Church (1884–1894) became a spokesman for organized labor on issues such as mine safety and workmen's compensation, and he later helped organize a nondenominational church because of the antipathy of his former congregation for his views. Baptist Jim Goodheart established an unemployment bureau and free food and lodging for transients at the mission that he ran, before becoming city chaplain (director of public welfare) of Denver in 1918. Together with reformist Jews and Roman Catholics, such Protestant ministers helped develop Denver's social welfare system between 1900 and 1920.

BELIEF SYSTEMS AND CHURCH ORDER

Despite a great variety of religious groups in the Northern Rockies, two denominations, the Church of Jesus Christ of Latter-day Saints and the Roman Catholic Church, stand out, although certain Protestant groups (Lutherans in Montana and the United Methodists and Southern Baptists in Wyoming and Colorado) have enclaves in the region.[4] Participation in any church organization, however, correlates positively with the presence of the Latter-day Saints. In Mormon Utah, a staggering 74.7 percent of the population belonged to a church in 2000, while in Idaho and Wyoming, the figures were a still respectable 48.5 percent and 46.7 percent, respectively. In Catholic Montana, by contrast, the figure was 44.7 percent, while increasingly secular Colorado managed only 39.5 percent.

In the Mormon heartland, the LDS Church retained a clear advantage, with 88.9 percent of the churchgoing population (Roman Catholics accounted for only 5.8 percent). In Idaho, the Mormons have expanded beyond their original settlements in the East, with 49.6 percent of the churchgoing population, compared to 20.9 percent for Roman Catholics, 3.0 percent for the Assemblies of God, 2.8 percent for the United Methodists, and 2.5 percent for the Southern Baptist Convention. Mormons are strong throughout southern and eastern Idaho, while Roman Catholics are strongest in the northwestern panhandle.

Wyoming's religious geography reflects the diverse pattern of settlement during the nineteenth century. Although 34.9 percent of the churchgoing population were Catholics in 2000, the LDS Church claimed 20.4 percent, and the Southern Baptist Convention claimed 7.4 percent. Mainline Protestant groups included the

Table 6. Religious Adhesion in the Northern Rockies, 2000

Denomination	Number	Percentage of total adherents
Church of Jesus Christ of Latter-day Saints	1,967,464	42.5%
Roman Catholic	1,230,108	26.6%
Evangelical Lutheran Church in America	146,815	3.2%
Southern Baptist Convention	146,216	3.2%
United Methodist	131,165	2.8%
Lutheran Church-Missouri Synod	91,688	2.0%
Assemblies of God	89,476	1.9%
Jewish congregations	78,830	1.7%
Presbyterian Church in the United States of America	78,152	1.7%
Episcopal Church in the United States of America	64,216	1.4%
Other	603,459	13.0%
TOTAL	4,627,589	100.0%

Source: Dale E. Jones, Sherri Doty, Clifford Grammich, James E. Horsch, Richard Houseal, Mac Lynn, John P. Marcum, Kenneth M. Sanchagrin, and Richard H. Taylor, *Religious Congregations and Membership in the United States 2000: An Enumeration by Region, State and County Based on Data Reported for 149 Religious Bodies* (Nashville, TN: Glenmary Research Center, 2002).

United Methodist Church with 5.0 percent, the Episcopal Church with 3.8 percent, and the Presbyterian Church in the United States of America with 2.9 percent. Lutheran groups included the Lutheran Church–Missouri Synod with 4.8 percent and the Evangelical Lutheran Church in America with 4.4 percent. Catholics are generally strong throughout the state, while the Latter-day Saints have an advantage in western Wyoming.

In Montana, Roman Catholics maintain something of their historical advantage with 41.9 percent of the churchgoing population, compared to 12.5 percent for their rivals in the Evangelical Lutheran Church in America and 3.8 percent for the Lutheran Church–Missouri Synod. Steady mission work has pushed up the numbers of Mormons, who represent 8.1 percent of the population. Other groups with significant representation are the United Methodists (4.5 percent) the Assemblies of God (4.1 percent), and the Southern Baptist Convention (3.8 percent). Catholics are strongest in the old mining communities of western Montana, while the Evangelical Lutheran Church in America is strongest in the northeast, close to the North Dakota border, marking the extreme edge of Scandinavian settlement.

While Colorado boasts a larger proportion of Roman Catholics than Montana (37.3 percent), it also has a greater denominational diversity overall. Protestant groups include the United Method-

Church of Jesus Christ, Aryan Nations

One piece of religious notoriety that most Idahoans could well do without is the presence in Hayden Lakes, near Coeur d'Alene, of the Church of Jesus Christ, Aryan Nations. Originally founded by Wesley Swift in California in the 1940s, the church was reorganized by Richard Butler in Idaho in 1974. Part of the Christian Identity movement, which views whites of Anglo-Saxon and Germanic descent as the chosen people, the United States as the new Israel, and the Jews as children of Satan, the sect is avowedly white supremacist. Increasingly associated with the Ku Klux Klan and the American Nazi movement, it hosted the first World Aryan Congress in 1982. In 1988, however, Butler was indicted for sedition, and in the late 1990s, after a court action accusing his followers of harassment, the church lost title to its property in Idaho.

Religion in Montana: The Traditional and the Esoteric

Montana attracts both traditional communitarians and more exotic sects to its vast open spaces. An example of the former is the Anabaptist Hutterite community that settled in Yankton, South Dakota, during the nineteenth century. Their first Montana colony was organized at Spring Creek in 1911, but the bulk of the Hutterites migrated to the state after 1945. In 1992, there were forty-one colonies (about 4,000 people) living a communal life and eschewing personal adornment, television, and dancing.[5] Montana's Hutterites account for a sizable portion of the state's agricultural production and maintain a school within the public school system in northern Montana. They remain a very closed community, however, with little interaction with the outside world.

A more esoteric body is the Church Universal and Triumphant, located in Livingston, Montana, since 1986. Originally Summit Lighthouse, formed by Mark L. Prophet in 1958, the church seeks to publicize and disseminate the teachings of the "Ascended Masters," who have mastered the circumstances of their lives, including such persons as Jesus, Moses, Zarathustra, and Buddha, and is headed by the founder's widow, Elizabeth Clare Prophet. Although it affirms a Judeo-Christian perspective, it is concerned with the eternal truths found in Eastern *and* Western traditions and urges on its followers the need to purify the soul to become one with God. Summit University in Corwin Springs provides instruction to members of the Keepers of the Flame fraternity, who form the inner core of the movement and may ultimately become baptized communicants who tithe their income.

ists at 7.1 percent, the Southern Baptist Convention at 6.3 percent, the Latter-day Saints at 5.4 percent, and the Evangelical Lutheran Church in America at 4.8 percent. The Catholic presence extends to every corner of the state, with Catholics enjoying a majority in ten counties and a plurality in another thirty-eight. The heart of Catholic power lies in two distinct regions: ten counties in and adjacent to the Denver-Boulder suburbs and another eleven in the central south and southwest of the state, centered on Pueblo. The Southern Baptist Convention boasts majorities in three counties and pluralities in another three, including three in the southwest and two south of Denver, while the United Methodists have a majority in one and pluralities in three, including three adjacent counties in northeastern Colorado.

The Church of Latter-day Saints

Mormonism remains the dominant religion in the Northern Rockies. While professing itself Christian and avowing a belief in the Trinity, it is truly a faith unto itself. Part of the family of religious groups termed "Restorationist," it has attempted to return to the primitive Christianity of the early Church. Unlike bodies like the Disciples of Christ, however, the Latter-day Saints assert a theology considerably removed from mainstream Christianity that includes reliance on the Book of Mormon as a historical and theological text of equal weight with that of the Bible. The church practices baptism by immersion and the laying on of hands to convey the Holy Spirit. Proxy baptisms are also performed by devout Mormons for deceased relatives who died without ever being exposed to the message of the Gospel. Of equal importance in a denomination that prizes marriage and childbearing are the ceremonies employed to bind spouses together, not only for their mortal lives but throughout eternity. Both "baptisms for the dead" and marriage "sealings" can only be conducted in temples, of which there were few outside Utah until the 1960s. Today, fifteen of the sixty-two temples in the United States are located in the Northern Rockies, eleven of them in Utah.

The organizational nature of the church reflects, at one and the same time, a strongly hierarchical structure and a great dependence on lay activism. Divine revelation is understood to be something that comes directly from God to the president of the church, who is viewed as a prophet comparable with Abraham or Moses. The president is assisted by two counselors and a Council of Twelve Apostles, but both are ultimately subordinate to his direction. At the local level are the ward (or parish) presided over by a bishop and the stake (roughly equivalent to a diocese) composed of around five wards and presided over by a three-man stake presidency. The Mormon priesthood is universal, and all males in good standing can expect to be called to it. Bishops and stake presidents are appointed by leaders at the next level of the hierarchy, usually for a limited period of time, since all local church positions are held by men (and women in some of the auxiliaries) while they are otherwise employed and are not remunerated. Auxiliary organizations include educational groups like Primary (children's religious education) and Sunday School (adult religious education) and the Relief Society (a women's auxiliary concerned with a variety of family and social service activities within the Church).

The twentieth century has also seen the flourishing of a more modern bureaucratic structure in the LDS Church, including Zion's Security Corporation (which manages church property), the Social Welfare Department, Children's Primary Hospital in Salt Lake City (completed in 1922 and now one of America's leading pediatric hospitals), and in more recent years, the Church Historian's Office. Although the church largely divested itself of its network of schools and colleges dur-

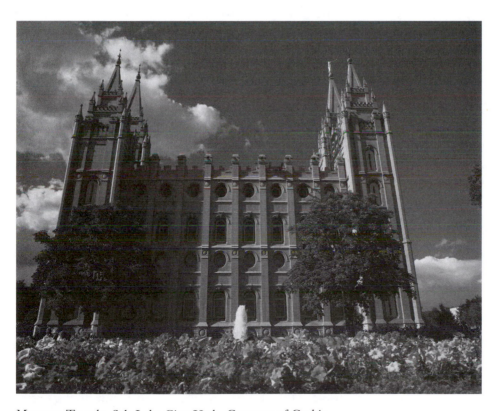

Mormon Temple, Salt Lake City, Utah. Courtesy of Corbis.

ing the 1920s, its remaining educational establishments like Brigham Young University and Ricks College in Idaho now have an international reputation. In place of church-run schools, the church has created a network of high school seminaries, which provide a religion-centered education program either before or after school.

Roman Catholic Church

At first glance, some distinct parallels can be drawn between Mormon and Roman Catholic ecclesiastical structures in the West. During the nineteenth century, both represented religious cultures generally condemned by American Protestants, and both acknowledged a vertical chain of religious authority. While Mormonism established itself in Utah and steadily expanded into adjacent areas, Roman Catholicism came into the region by stages, through mission work and ministry to the communities created by the mining frontier. The Roman Catholic Church has more direct claim to participate in the family of Christian churches, as the embodiment of Catholic Christianity in the West. As a product both of the Tridentine reforms of the sixteenth century and of the more recent changes effected by the Second Vatican Council (1962–1965), it stresses the sacramental life: baptism, frequent reception of the eucharist, confession and unction, veneration of the saints, especially the Virgin Mary, and an all-male celibate priesthood.

The Spanish influence can easily be seen in the architecture of this Catholic church east of Harlem, Montana. © Michael S. Lewis/Corbis.

There are currently eight dioceses in the region, including two in Montana and three in Colorado. While the bulk of ordinary parishes remain very rural, urban growth led to the creation of the Diocese of Colorado Springs in 1983. The parish remains an essential unit of Catholic identity, but its focus, especially in urban areas, has been transformed. Until the 1920s, parishes were often strongly associated with a particular ethnic group—the Irish of Butte or the Poles and Germans of Denver—and were largely self-contained. Today, most parishes provide specialist services based on the geographical community that they serve. The old emphasis on parish jurisdiction is also declining, particularly in university settings where the local Newman Center (the Catholic agency charged with ministering to students) has become an effective parish.

Rural parishes, meanwhile, have been affected by the massive population decline in effect throughout the rural West.

The liturgical changes wrought by Vatican II have resonated throughout the West. In a structure that had traditionally demanded a high level of priestly leadership, there has been considerable growth in lay participation. During the 1960s, Bishop Raymond Hunthausen of Helena, a participant in Vatican II, established a Priests' Senate, an Association for Women in Ministry, and a Diocesan Pastoral Council with clerical, religious, and lay representatives to determine diocesan pastoral priorities and provide advice to parish councils. The problem of a declining number of priests led to the increased employment of women religious to minister to the needs of parishes in eastern Montana on a day-to-day basis, with a priest present only on Sunday to celebrate mass. Parish staffs are now more likely to include permanent deacons and members of the laity, and there has been a rise in the number of parish councils intended to help set priorities and act as a clearinghouse for parish organizations. Such bodies, however, can only be as effective as the priest is willing to allow them to be, since they do not have ultimate authority over the conduct of church policy. Parochial schools have been on the wane, especially as Catholic mining communities contract, and have only really endured in the Salt Lake City area, where they serve as a defense mechanism against the encroachment of Mormon culture.

Protestant Churches

Despite the great expenditure of resources by the mainline Protestant denominations during the nineteenth century, their share of the churchgoing population today is far from impressive. The Episcopal Church accounts for only 1.7 percent of the region's believers, and the Presbyterians claim 2.4 percent. The United Methodist Church enjoys the largest representation at 4.0 percent. The United Methodists are a product of the 1939 reunion of the northern and southern branches of American Methodism and owe their origins to John Wesley and his American disciple Francis Asbury. Methodism was historically distinguished by its espousal of Arminianism—the belief that Christ died for all, not just for the elect, and that man is a free moral agent with the ability to choose or reject God—and pietism—a movement that began among seventeenth-century Lutherans, that emphasized a devotional life for the laity and private study of the Bible. It affirms the sufficiency of the Bible for salvation and recognizes the sacraments of baptism and the Lord's Supper. During the 1960s, liturgical reforms led to a reorientation of liturgical focus from the pulpit to the altar and permitted the use of clerical vestments. The largest American Protestant denomination, the Methodists had a distinguished record of social service during the twentieth century but have in recent years voiced an increasingly liberal theological perspective. The church is organized around district and annual conferences, which form a hierarchy of authority, with the quadrennial general conference being the church's highest legislative and policymaking body.

In the Northern Rockies, the United Methodist Church has played an influential role, particularly in Denver. Since the beginning of the twentieth century it has operated Goodwill Industries, which incorporated in Colorado in 1931. In 1956, it established an old people's home in the Rocky Mountains. Iliff School of

Theology remains an influential seminary, which hired faculty in the 1950s who changed the emphasis of the institution to reflect the relationship of psychology to religion and the application of theological questions to real-life situations. Urban ministries like the Crossroads Urban Center in Salt Lake City for Hispanics and Denver's High Street Center for African Americans have also been a feature of Methodism since World War II.

While Mormons, Catholics, and Methodists all came to the Northern Rockies before 1900, the emergence of the Southern Baptist Convention (SBC) in the region has come since the 1950s. At the heart of Baptist belief is an essential need to convert the world to Christ. Structurally, the SBC has traditionally left individual congregations free to determine their own budgets, ministries, and theological emphasis. Above the congregation comes the regional association (also autonomous) and the state and national conventions, which meet annually and to which every congregation is entitled to send "messengers." In recent years, the national bureaucracy has grown apace, and there has also been a decline in the idea that a pastor derives his authority from his congregation. As the ministry has become professionalized, the congregation's role in fiscal affairs has diminished, and fundamentalists have sought to elevate the status of the pastor relative to his congregation.

The final group with significant regional representation is the Evangelical Lutheran Church in America (ELCA). Although most Lutherans reside in the Great Lakes region, they constitute a significant minority in Montana and, to a lesser extent, in Wyoming and Colorado. Lutheranism in America traces its heritage to the Reformation of the sixteenth century in Germany and northern Europe, stressing justification by faith and the sacraments of baptism and the eucharist. A series of synodical mergers during the early 1960s left American Lutherans with three theological bodies: the Lutheran Church in America (LCA; progressive and based in the Northeast), the American Lutheran Church (ALC; moderate and based in the Midwest), and the Lutheran Church–Missouri Synod (conservative and based in the Midwest). Because of the large numbers of Norwegian-descended Lutherans in the Rocky Mountains, the ALC was dominant in Montana and had a narrow advantage in Wyoming and Colorado. In 1987, the ALC and LCA united to form the Evangelical Lutheran Church in America, now one of the largest Protestant groups in the country. Despite its overall size, almost half the ELCA's congregations are located in rural or small town settings, and 15 percent are linked with at least one other congregation. The proportion of the baptized congregation who attend is, on average, lower than for other Protestant denominations, and the median age is higher. Structurally, the ELCA is organized in synods, specifically the Montana Synod in the northwestern District One and the Rocky Mountain Synod in the southwestern District Two.

SOCIAL LIFE AND ACTIVITIES

It is often overlooked in contemporary culture how important church life may be to ordinary people, and this is, if anything, more true in the Northern Rockies than elsewhere. Again, it is the Mormon case that provides the most comprehensive example, for church work represents a considerable portion of the Latter-day

Saint's working hours. In one respect, matters have been simplified in that all religious services (sacrament and priesthood meetings, Sunday School, Primary and Relief Society) are now held over the course of three hours on a Sunday, instead of extending throughout the working week. Mormonism tends to stress the active over the contemplative life, demanding high levels of participation and commitment. Holders of the priesthood are charged with making monthly visits to families in their community and becoming personally acquainted with their needs and concerns. Ward councils form a supportive apparatus for organizing ward functions and identifying individuals who may need special help. All Latter-day Saints in good standing are expected to observe periodic fast days, with the money raised going to provide emergency relief for those suffering from famine or natural disaster and to follow the Word of Wisdom, the church ordinance barring the use of drugs, alcohol, tea, and coffee. Perhaps the two most overt symbols of Latter-day Saint commitment are the tithe and missionary service. The church requires the commitment of one-tenth of a member's income to the support of church work and calls on all unmarried young men and women to undertake missions, mostly abroad, a process that they or their families must finance themselves.

Family life is an essential component of the Mormon experience, with "celestial marriages" solemnized in a temple ceremony. To keep family life uppermost, the church launched the family home evening program in 1965—a weekday night devoted to a family meal and recreational activities. For this purpose, Monday evenings are kept clear of church-sponsored activities and, in a region where Mormons are often a local majority, many school and town administrators avoid scheduling athletic or community events on a Monday. The LDS Church has enjoyed a close relationship with the Boy Scout movement, adopting the national program in 1952 as a further reinforcement to family life. The church also sponsors many cultural events that benefit the region as a whole. Athletic and dance programs have long been featured and have, since 1971, been more overtly regional and less oriented to bringing contestants from all parts of the church to Salt Lake City. The annual dance festival is a major event in the Intermountain West. Utah enjoys the presence of the world-renowned Mormon Tabernacle Choir as well as the Salt Lake City Youth Symphony and Youth Choir, while the Mormon Festival of Art has been a key feature of Brigham Young University life since 1968. The Latter-day Saints have also made great use of the pageant (embodied in such forms as *The Mormon Miracle* performed in Manti, Utah) to retell the Mormon story in music and drama. Finally, an important cultural event in Mormon communities is the celebration of Pioneer Day (July 24)—commemorating the entry of Brigham Young's company into the Salt Lake Valley in 1847—although in recent years attempts have been made to acknowledge the contributions of other pioneers, particularly Hispanic and non-Hispanic Catholics.

While Rocky Mountain Catholics once enjoyed a community life comparable to that of the Latter-day Saints, today the region's Catholics tend to be better educated and more oriented to specialist ministries. The descendants of European immigrants have been strongly affected by the new importance accorded by Vatican II to the ministry of the laity. Given the current shortage of priestly vocations, there has been a marked rise in the number of permanent deacons (often older men) as well as greater involvement by women in a variety of church functions.

As the Catholic population has become increasingly well educated, so the focus on Christian education at the parish level has grown, particularly the Rite of Christian Initiation for Adults and family-based programs that have proved particularly popular in the new urban Colorado parishes. In Montana, Cursillo and the Genesis Program (for married couples) were both set up during the 1960s and continue to be very popular, as is the Renew Program in eastern Montana—a parish-based program devoted to prayer, spiritual meditation, and discussion. Lay ministry has also grown in scope, with services to church youth, the sick, and the dying, such as the Emmaus Grief Ministry. This represents a marked shift from 100 years ago, when most lay ministries focused on the maintenance of the church building and interior. As noted above, many lay Catholics now serve on parish councils, giving them a sense of involvement in decision making, though their impact varies from parish to parish. The parish church, however, is less the integrated and self-contained community that it was at the beginning of the twentieth century, a change epitomized by the erection of family centers adjacent to churches that are viewed more as community resources (and rented to non-Catholic groups) than as part of a wider Catholic social fabric. The Vatican II changes have had a lesser impact on the Hispanic parishes of the region, which remain closer in style to the ethnic parishes of the nineteenth century. The existence of a Hispanic culture and the enduring power of family life put Hispanic Catholic religious life in a slightly different category.

Where the Mormon and Catholic communities have sizable local populations, Protestant groups remain perpetual minorities. Since 1945, the response of the Methodists has been to stress social outreach through groups such as the Women's Society of Church Service and the Methodist Youth Fellowship. One early example was Ada Duhig's Utah Protestant Mobile Mission (1932–1960), which tried to keep an isolated community together with a mix of skating parties, basketball games, arts and crafts, Bible study, and well-baby clinics. The church operated a youth center at Pine Crest, Colorado, from 1926 onward, which has been well attended by students and sponsors. The 1950s witnessed a steady decline in the denomination's hostility to social dancing, though not in its advocacy in favor of temperance. While this was also a time of crisis for the rural part of the Methodist church, many suburban congregations were organized around Denver. During the 1960s, the Methodists began to develop new forms of evangelism to resorts, recreational centers, and apartment buildings.

By contrast, the Southern Baptist Convention's post-1952 emergence has been driven by a desire to create a separate evangelical enclave. Southern Baptist belief in the need for every Christian to have a personal evangelical encounter with Christ demands that every individual strengthen their relationship with God through private devotion, personal morality, and evangelism, achieved through regular church attendance and participation in Bible study and midweek prayer meetings. Sunday worship is supplemented by morning Sunday School and evening Training Union, which provides instruction in Baptist doctrine, history, ethics, and Christian citizenship. Training is also provided in evangelistic technique, particularly how to witness for Christ and "give testimony" as to one's own experience. There is little interest in the social justice approach of the United Methodists, and the round of church-sponsored events, including church socials, revival meetings, the Women's Missionary Union, and the Men's Brotherhood, tend to be very focused on the internal life of the church.

Lutheran church life in the Northern Rockies reflects a blend of the Baptist and Methodist approaches. Traditionally, Scandinavian Lutheranism fostered the inner life through instruction in doctrine and catechesis rather than the revivalist techniques associated with other Protestant denominations, and parish education has always been important. In 1958, a new Lutheran service book and hymnal were adopted, and in 1967, forty Lutheran congregations adopted the Bethel Bible study course. The 1960s gave rise to new experimental ministries and conferences on the problems of town and country living. Bible camps became more popular, and there was also a rise in support for old people's homes in Montana during the 1960s. Many women's church groups also switched their focus from raising money for mission work to working in educational and charitable institutions or social action programs. With the emergence of the Evangelical Lutheran Church in America, the social liberalism of eastern Lutheranism has come to inform the behavior of Lutherans in other regions.

THE CHURCHES AND THE WIDER WORLD

The idea of churches promulgating their views in the public sphere has always been more controversial in the West than in the Northeast or the South, particularly since 1945. Indeed, the 1920s were marked by an upsurge in support for the Ku Klux Klan in Utah and Colorado that, in part, reflected local resentments at the perceived influence of the LDS and Catholic hierarchy over public affairs. Between 1920 and 1945, LDS Church leaders worked tirelessly to convey a positive impression to the world outside, making use of the mass media whenever possible (a church-owned radio station was dedicated as early as 1922). Church presidents from Heber J. Grant to David O. McKay continually stressed that Mormons belonged to both political parties and that the church had no preferences in such matters. During the Great Depression of the 1930s, the church launched its own faith-based initiative to care for unemployed Latter-day Saints, the Welfare Plan, providing supplies to the needy from a network of bishops' storehouses in exchange for work by all the able-bodied unemployed. The Welfare Plan caught national attention and won approval for the church from many non-Mormons, including President Franklin Roosevelt (1882–1945).

The 1930s witnessed dramatic clashes between liberals like Senator Elbert Thomas of Utah and conservatives like Reuben J. Clark, a former ambassador and member of the First Presidency, but devout churchmen continued to be divided between the parties. Beginning in the 1950s, however, the church leadership shifted to the political Right, a trend reflected in the appointment of Ezra T. Benson (1899–1994) as secretary of agriculture by President Dwight Eisenhower (1890–1969). Moderates like Hugh Brown, member of the First Presidency from 1961 to 1970, continued to exert an influence on church policy, but as cultural issues began to supersede economic ones in the political dialogue, the church moved to take a more public stand on issues that it considered important. In 1968, it opposed liquor by the drink in Utah (just as it had fought repeal of national Prohibition thirty-five years before) and supported Sunday closing and right-to-work laws. In recent years, it has spearheaded or supported campaigns against abortion, gambling, homosexual rights, and pornography. More controversial was its successful campaign in Utah to defeat the Equal Rights Amendment, though church leaders emphasized that they still wished to remedy injustices to women. By contrast, the civil rights revolution of the 1960s took the church at a disadvantage, since a revelation of Joseph Smith had barred the universal priesthood to men of African descent. During the 1960s, the church argued that it endorsed civil equality and equal rights for African Americans but that the priesthood was a matter of revelation and could not simply be changed at will. It fell to President Spencer Kimball (1895–1985) to receive a prophetic revelation in 1978 that the priesthood was now open to all worthy males regardless of race. One untypical action by a denomination that generally endorsed the agenda of social conservatism was LDS resistance to the deployment of the MX missile system in Utah in 1981. In recent years, Thomas Alexander has argued, the old religious divisions in Utah have reemerged, with observant Mormons being mostly Republican and nonobservant Mormons and non-Mormons dominating the minority Democratic Party.

The Roman Catholic hierarchy in the Northern Rockies has generally avoided direct political involvement, although the Helena Diocesan Synod of 1988 affirmed the importance of working for peace and economic justice, and Bishop Elden Curtiss of Helena (1976–1993) was a strong pro-life advocate. By contrast, the United Methodists of the Rocky Mountains, though comparatively few in number, have spoken out vocally on social justice issues. Unhampered by the problems faced by their southern counterparts, they challenged segregation in Denver during the 1960s, and Maurice Mitchell of the University of Denver served as chairman of the mayoral council administering the bussing program to integrate the city's public school system. During the same period, Bishop Marvin Street was a vocal critic of the Vietnam War, visiting students camped out on the University of Denver campus to protest the invasion of Cambodia. The Rocky Mountain Conference was also active in ecumenical endeavor in Colorado, helping create Columbine United Parish in Littleton with the Presbyterians in 1972 and Mountain View Parish in Aurora with the United Church of Christ.

While the United Methodist Church has moved to the Left in recent years, the Southern Baptist Convention has moved to the Right. In 1979, Adrian Rogers was elected the first fundamentalist president of the SBC, and fundamentalists have controlled the national organization since that date. The triumph of the fundamentalists had implications for the SBC activities in the world. In 1984, they sought to reduce the role of women in the ministry by denying aid to congregations with female pastors, while in 1988 they passed a resolution affirming the role of the pastor as the shepherd of his flock, reflecting the increasing dominance of the pastors of urban mega-churches in the decision-making process. Perhaps most significant was the SBC's strong endorsement of the social policies of the Reagan administration on abortion, family life, and school prayer. In contrast with its antipolitical past, the SBC now boldly endorses the conservative agenda in support of Israel and school prayer and opposition to the Equal Rights Amendment.

Like the Baptists, Lutherans have also entered the public sphere, but more often on the liberal side of social issues than on the conservative side. Until the 1960s, the Lutheran churches were preoccupied with Lutheran unity, but since then they have been active in liberal causes. Increasingly, there has been a redefinition of the public role of the church by Lutheran theologians, though they still stress personal redemption through grace, not works. Such has not been the case with the Missouri Synod, which has continued to follow its own course and avoid ecumenical contact with other Protestants or even other Lutherans. Since 1987, the ELCA has issued a series of position papers on social and political problems that are generally liberal in outlook, in contrast with the Missouri Synod, which generally takes a conservative attitude on moral issues. The year 1996 saw the creation of Lutheran Services in America—an inter-Lutheran organization for 280 Lutheran social service organizations—and in 2000, the ELCA signed a concordat with the Episcopal Church that allowed their clergy to minister to members of either church.

RELIGION AND THE CITY

The rise of the urban frontier during the late nineteenth century produced one of the most profound revolutions in the history of the American churches. The "urban problem" that exercised the minds of secular reformers also suggested to religious leaders that they must adapt their mission to deal with ethnic and religious minorities who flooded into the urban environment during the nineteenth century and implement new types of outreach ministry to assist the downtrodden. In the West, the idea of the Social Gospel was not new, but the metropolitan centers that nurtured it in the East were far from visible west of the Mississippi until the 1950s.

The "Mormon Divide"

The story of the cities in the Rockies reflects the region's Mormon-Catholic divide.[6] Salt Lake County, with 74.7 percent participation in any religious organization and with Mormons constituting 86.0 percent of churchgoers, is scarcely different from the more rural communities around it. By contrast, Ada County, Idaho (Boise), where the Latter-day Saints have made significant gains in recent years to claim 36.9 percent of the churchgoing population, compared to only 17.7 percent who are Roman Catholic, has only 42.8 percent religious participation, a reflection of the recent influx of migrants from the Pacific Rim. The urban character of the Northern Rockies is, however, largely defined by Colorado. Here, in a curious inversion, urban religious participation is generally higher than the statewide average, with Pueblo County at 49.7 percent and Denver County at 46.3 percent. Only El Paso County (Colorado Springs) is more typical of the state as a whole, with participation at 38.9 percent. Pueblo is the banner Catholic city with 56.3 percent of its churchgoing residents claiming Catholicism, although there is significant support for United Methodism (6.1 percent), the Southern Baptist Convention (5.4 percent), and the Assemblies of God (5.3 percent). Denver remains the heartland of ethnic and racial minorities, being 38.6 percent Catholic but also containing communities of Black Baptists (7.2 percent), Episcopalians (5.9 percent), Jews (5.3 percent), American Baptists (5.1 percent), and United Methodists (5.0 percent). Colorado Springs is more secular, less Catholic (31.1 percent) and more appealing to a variety of Protestant groups than the other cities. These include the Southern Baptist Convention (12.6 percent), the United Methodists (7.3 percent), the Presbyterians (5.4 percent), the Latter-day Saints (5.3 percent), and the Black Baptists (5.1 percent).

Until the 1950s, cities rarely played an important part in the daily life of residents of the Northern Rockies. Compared with the Southwest, the Rockies continue to remain relatively free from urban sprawl. Indeed, the only two genuinely metropolitan clusters are greater Denver and the urban corridor north and south of Salt Lake City. Both have a sizable presence of high-tech industries and a large number of relatively new residents relocating from other parts of the nation, yet culturally they are distinctly different. Denver's new residents have helped to shift it from its former status as the most northerly city of the Hispanic Catholic region to a heavily contested marketplace of religious ideas, in which popular trust in a secular culture seems to have won out. Salt Lake City, despite some erosion of the dominance of the LDS Church, remains the headquarters of a worldwide religious entity, in which one religious ethos continues to inform the lives of many of its residents. From such contrasts has the urban religious history of the region been formed.

Religion in Denver

Early Denver represented a mélange of religious cultures. The Catholic diocese (later archdiocese) was headquartered here, as was one of the Intermountain West's largest Jewish communities. Protestant leaders Thomas Uzzel, Myron Reed, and Jim Goodheart helped advance the Social Gospel. After weathering the Great Depression and World War II, Denver entered upon a period of dramatic expansion during the 1950s. During the 1960s and 1970s, instant suburbs were the order of the day as out-of-state migrants flowed into Colorado to take up well-paying, white-collar jobs in the heart of the pristine American West. Yet the suburban environment by no means fulfilled all the expectations of those who promised that the "new" cities would be spared urban blight. During the late 1960s, Our Savior's Reformed Church in the western suburbs of Denver suddenly found itself the only Protestant church ministering to a community of over 7,000 people. In a population without much in the way of municipal services and in which both parents in many families worked, Our Savior's found itself obliged to address issues of middle-class juvenile vandalism caused by a lack of parental supervision and a general lack of social interaction, even between near neighbors, problems that had little to do with inner-city poverty. Nevertheless, suicide rates were high, one marriage in two ended in divorce, and only one child in seven had a relationship with any church body. Our Savior's responded with a drop-in center for school-age children that offered food and games. At the same time, the church's pastor sought to use his church as an instrument to strengthen social cohesion. He himself served on the Chamber of Commerce's Community Action Committee and made the church building available to local community organizations during the week. He saw socialization and community involvement as crucial for the church as it dealt with a diverse community, many of whose residents were from different religious traditions or none. In a certain sense, Our Savior's had, in the 1970s, returned to a model practiced by churches in the West during the nineteenth century.

While the approach of Our Savior's served to ameliorate the problems of the suburbs, Frank Tillapaugh, a graduate of Conservative Baptist Seminary in Denver and pastor of the city's Bear Valley Baptist Church, faced a different dilemma: how to save an inner-city parish. In 1970, his church had a membership of 100 and an income of $17,763; by 1982, it had grown to 1,000 members and $500,000 in income. Tillapaugh subsequently published an account of his successful formula for "unleashing" the power of the urban church. Critical of the evangelical churches for what he termed their "fortress" mentality and their pursuit of growth at all costs, Tillapaugh argued that they should learn from parachurch organizations like Campus Crusade for Christ. The local church was too often tied to its rural past, while the parachurch organizations better understood the needs of the city. "Any Bible-believing church can have an effective ministry in the city," Tillapaugh insisted, but it had to arise more from the initiatives of the laity and address the problems of target groups in the local community.[7] The administrative structure of an urban church should be ruthlessly streamlined to minimize the number of standing committees. Ministries should be structured around the skills of new members rather than trying to "plug" the latter into the existing organization, and the professionalization of church staffs should be minimized in favor of recruiting qualified candidates from within the congregation. Tillapaugh's formulation was not a liberal one with regard to theology or morals, but it did seek to awaken evangelicals to the dangers of an excessive focus on the needs of middle-class family members. They were unaware, argued Tillapaugh, of the peculiar features of the urban environment: rapid change, diversity, and social mobility. The Bear Lake congregation certainly applied the formula to the operation of their congregation and the needs of the wider community.

During the 1970s, the church found sponsors for refugees from war-torn Laos and, at one time, included around sixty Laotians in their worship services. It also operated the Genesis Center, a communal home for fifteen to thirty street people that incorporated opportunities for work and witness. International students, many of whom studied at universities in the Denver area, were also seen as a potential target of church ministry. Even traditional church work offered the potential for expansion to a more far-flung audience. The Singles Ministry sought to address the problems of a large unmarried community that resided in Denver, while the Seniors' Ministry hoped to target the "gray ghetto" in inner-city Denver in conjunction with Denver Social Services. There was no need, Tillapaugh concluded, for churches to flee to the

Non-Christian Faiths in Denver

Although the above discussion of Denver is Christocentric, the city has been a popular destination for other religious groups. Guru Maharaj Ji launched his Divine Light Mission here in 1972 with a program of meditation and vegetarianism as paths to truth that appealed to antiwar activists and political radicals. Mainstream Buddhism is represented by thirty-four study centers (most of them in Denver, Boulder, and Crestone) including the Tri-States Buddhist Temple in Denver and the Great Stupa of Dharmakaya at the Rocky Mountain Shambhala Center, built to honor Chogyam Trungpa Rinpoche, the first spiritual leader to extensively translate Buddhist teachings into English and who founded Naropa University in Boulder in 1974.[8] Denver's Jews, meanwhile, are the only sizable Jewish community in the region, though their growth has not matched that of the general population. Like other western Jewish communities, the Reform tradition has generally prevailed, particularly in the prestigious setting of Temple Emmanuel. Denver Jews helped create many city institutions, including the Jewish National Home for Asthmatic Children, National Jewish Medical and Research Center, and Beth Israel Hospital. Since the 1940s, many Jews have moved into the city suburbs, serving further to dilute the religious intensity of their community.

Rocky Mountain Shambhala Center (Buddhist). Courtesy of the Rocky Mountain Shambhala Center.

suburbs, and there were some powerful reasons for not doing so. The Bear Lake model, then, had potential application to a far wider audience than just the Intermountain West.

Ministries Outside of Parishes

By the late 1970s, some denominations and individuals were also operating ministries outside the framework of the traditional parish. One such was the Reformed Church in America's Native American Urban Transition Program (NAUTP), headquartered in a lower-middle-class suburb of Denver. Recognizing both the peculiar problems faced by Native Americans in the city and the attraction of Denver for residents of reservations as far away as South Dakota, NAUTP provided short-term accommodation for families and single mothers, donations of food, clothing, and furniture, advice on obtaining housing, food stamps, and medical care, and locating a church community. It also had a contract with the federal government to conduct classes on job survival skills and urban community living. Caseworkers worked, lived, and worshipped with their Native American clients, and there was an emphasis on hiring qualified Native Americans to work in the program and recruiting former clients to serve on its board of directors.

If NAUTP is a denominational ministry devoted to a target group, Hope Communities, founded in Denver in 1980, is a parachurch body devoted to renovating apartments for low-income families, the brainchild of Ray Stranske, a graduate of Denver Seminary, and his wife Marilyn, a youth counselor and former volunteer for Campus Crusade for Christ. They noted how gentrification of inner-city Denver had forced out many families or obliged them to double up in tiny apartments. Beginning with the about-to-be-condemned Booker T. Washington apartment complex (which now provides homes for thirty-three families), Hope Communities had completed 107 projects by 1989, as well as providing support, encouragement, and resources and helping people to enter job readiness and training programs. It is a Bible-based, nondenominational ministry that encourages its members to participate in daily prayer and witness and often attracts workers formerly employed in well-to-do white-collar jobs.

Colorado Springs

Denver is the principal city of Colorado with the attendant urban problems, but Colorado Springs is a more traditionalist and conservative city. Home to the Christian and Missionary Alliance, a nineteenth-century interdenominational missionary fellowship, now a church with over 250,000 members in the United States in 1991, it also plays host to one of the more influential conservative Christian groups, Focus on the Family, a nondenominational agency. Founded by Dr. James Dobson, a child development specialist at the University of Southern California until 1977, Focus on the Family moved to Colorado in 1991, where its four buildings occupy half a million square feet. The heart of Dobson's ministry is a daily half-hour broadcast, supplemented by topical programs on children, teenagers, women, and public policy. The ministry has no ties to a particular denomination but takes an aggressive culturally conservative stance and has had great influence in the Reagan and both Bush administrations. It supports parachurch groups like Bill McCartney's Promise Keepers and the Family Research Council. Focus on the Family receives 36,000 pieces of mail every week, for which a staff of 100 are employed to write personal replies, and receives 200,000 visitors every year. The choice of topics for the radio broadcasts is generally based on the mail received, but sometimes matters of public concern are addressed. The institute also produces a magazine, *Citizen*, which encourages people to become involved in city, state, and national political issues. The presence of Focus on the Family in Colorado Springs reflects the conservatism of the host community but is also a source of tension for Colorado liberals who view it as defying their belief in the necessity of the separation of church and state.

Salt Lake City

Perhaps the most interesting urban religious story is that of Salt Lake City. "Many people who move to Salt Lake City," writes Thomas Alexander, "are not used to a culture in which religion is central to the lives of intellectuals, professionals and business people."[9] Despite the rise in the non-Mormon population, the LDS Church, if only by virtue of its status as a major landowner, continues to influence urban life. The church donated the land that was used to build the Salt Palace—a civic auditorium and arts complex—in 1961, and church leaders have remained constantly in touch with the city authorities, so much so that former mayor Ted Wilson (first elected in 1973) paid an annual visit to the Church Office Building to show them details of the budget. Members of the First Presidency were strong advocates of downtown development, and the church aggressively demanded action on pornography and liquor by the drink. The church also sponsors theater performances in the Promised Valley Playhouse, and Temple Square and the ZCMI Shopping Center are great tourist attractions. While LDS leaders do participate in the Utah Conference of Christians and Jews, many gentiles continue to feel a sense of alienation from the prevailing culture, and there are often clashes in "neutral" groupings like PTAs. Nevertheless, while Focus on the Family is attempting to change the culture around it, the LDS Church enjoys much more effective control over civic institutions in its metropolis.

CONCLUSION

Religious culture in the Northern Rockies reflects the dramatic socioeconomic changes that have transformed the West in the last fifty years. Where once the majority of the region's residents lived in small mining and farming towns, today they reside in ever-expanding metropolitan corridors, whose high-tech jobs and unspoiled environment serve to bring in many people who grew up outside the region. Unlike the immigrants of a century ago, however, few bring with them a faith community or even a coherent religious identity. Priests and pastors who, in times past, could at least count on an acquaintance with Holy Scripture and religious iconography now face an often spiritually illiterate populace. The secularization that is already considerably advanced in the Pacific Rim states has begun to make its way eastward.

As we have seen, not all urban churches have stood still since the 1960s. Frank Tillapaugh's formula for church growth, with its reliance on allowing initiatives for church ministry to arise from within the existing faith community, demonstrates that church growth can be fostered through application of the principle of the priesthood of all believers. Tillapaugh's approach, while pursued in a western city, is obviously one that churches throughout the United States would do well to apply. There is also a growing acceptance that the parachurch model speaks much more readily to younger Americans for whom the institutional church seems unapproachable. The success of Hope Communities reveals another way in which Denver Christians are working out the imperatives of their faith.

We began this chapter by noting the role of the West as religious refuge, and so it has remained for the dominant force in the region—the Church of Jesus Christ of Latter-day Saints. The difference is that today the Mormon presence in the Northern Rockies is merely as an outpost for a worldwide church. More Mormons now live in places where they are in a decided minority, and the church's numerical dominance in Utah and eastern Idaho has, at times, a surreal quality. Nevertheless, this part of the Northern Rockies is a religious fiefdom in which public and private life intersect. Freed from the national opprobrium heaped on them a century ago, the region's Mormons may often be unconscious that things could be any different. Even in metropolitan Salt Lake City the LDS Church still wields great authority on issues that it considers of importance. If anyone can claim an intact religious culture in America today, it is the Latter-day Saints.

Mormon religious hegemony stands in stark contrast with other parts of the Northern Rockies. Although the Roman Catholic Church is supposedly the other cultural force in the region, it has been constantly engaged in a delicate balancing act, since its local majorities are confined to sections of Montana and Colorado and even here are eroding. Catholic culture, moreover, is split between the family-centered religion of the Hispanics of southern Colorado and the white, better-educated Catholics of the region. The latter have increasingly challenged the authority of the church's leaders and demanded a greater share in its administration, even as the ethnic communities that used to sustain Catholic identity have almost all dissolved. Providing a coherent message will be an essential objective for the church in the twenty-first century.

If the region's Catholics face an uncertain future, the outlook for the many

Protestant groups in the region seems no more assured. The one-third of church-goers who are neither Mormon nor Catholic are fractured into a plethora of denominations, all of them comparatively small. Some, like the Southern Baptists, the Lutheran Church–Missouri Synod, or the Assemblies of God, preach conservative theology and an enclave identity, others; like the United Methodists, the Evangelical Lutheran Church in America, or the Presbyterians, preach liberal theology, social justice, and political activism. Except for the Lutherans, most are largely urban phenomena and try to recruit from the pool of new arrivals to the region rather than evangelizing the older rural communities as their nineteenth-century predecessors were willing to do. There is no Protestant voice in the Northern Rockies, merely a denominational babble that cannot really hope to undermine Mormon hegemony or significantly erode rural Catholicism.

For over a century, the churches were a fundamental part of daily life in the Northern Rockies. They converted and educated a sizable portion of the Native American population, provided teachers and scholars for frontier communities, and contributed to the erection of a social welfare system in many states. Contrary to popular belief that the frontier lacked a religious sensibility, the regional evidence suggests that priests and pastors, as well as believing Christians, were key players in the transformation of the West from frontier to settled society. As skepticism about organized religion slowly gained ground after 1920, however, many of the region's churches discovered they rested upon unsound foundations. There was no cultural bedrock for the Protestant churches in the way that there was for the Latter-day Saints or Hispanic Catholics, and as secularism advanced in the West, so religious identity receded in much of the Rocky Mountains. Attempting to create such a cultural bedrock from scratch in the forthcoming decades will be no small task.

RESOURCE GUIDE

Printed Sources

General Sources

Alexander, Thomas G. "The Emergence of a Republican Majority in Utah, 1970–1992." In *Politics in the Postwar American West*, ed. Richard Lowitt. Norman: University of Oklahoma Press, 1995. 260–276.

Allen, James B., and Glen M. Leonard. *The Story of the Latter-day Saints*. Salt Lake City, UT: Deseret Book Company, 1992.

Almen, Lowel G. *One Great Cloud of Witnesses: You and Your Congregation in the Evangelical Lutheran Church in America—A Guide to Our Life Together in Mission*. Minneapolis, MN: Augsburg Fortress Press, 1997.

Bradley, Martin B., Norman M. Green, Jr., Dale E. Jones, Mac Lynn, and Lou McNeil. *Churches and Church Membership in the United States 1990: An Enumeration by Region, State and County Based on Data Reported for 133 Church Groupings*. Atlanta, GA: Glenmary Research Center, 1992.

Carriker, Robert C., "Joseph M. Cataldo, S.J.: Courier of Catholicism to the Nez Percés." In *Churchmen and the Western Indians, 1820–1920*, ed. Clyde A. Milner II and Floyd A. O'Neil. Norman: University of Oklahoma Press, 1985. 109–139.

Collins, John J. *Native American Religions: A Geographical Survey*. Lewiston, NY: Edwin Mellen Press, 1991.

Jensen, Carol L. "Deserts, Diversity and Self-Determination: A History of the Catholic Parish in the Intermountain West." In *The American Catholic Parish: A History from 1850 to the Present*, ed. Jay P. Dolan. Mahwah, NJ: Paulist Press, 1987. 2:137–276.

Jones, Dale E., Sherri Doty, Clifford Grammich, James E. Horsch, Richard Houseal, Mac Lynn, John P. Marcum, Kenneth M. Sanchagrin, and Richard H. Taylor. *Religious Congregations and Membership in the United States 2000: An Enumeration by Region, State and County Based on Data Reported for 149 Religious Bodies*. Nashville, TN: Glenmary Research Center, 2002.

Melton, J. Gordon. *Encyclopedia of American Religions*. 6th ed. Detroit, MI: Gale Research, 1999.

Miller, Jay. "Basin Religion and Theology: A Comparative Study of Power (Puha)." *Journal of California and Great Basin Anthropology* 5.1–2 (1983): 66–86.

Quinn, D. Michael. "Religion in the American West." In *Under an Open Sky: Rethinking America's Western Past*, ed. William Cronon, George Miles, and Jay Gitlin. New York: W. W. Norton, 1992. 145–166.

Small, Lawrence F. *Religion in Montana: Pathways to the Present*. 2 vols. Billings, MT: Rocky Mountain College, 1995.

Stewart, Omer C. *Peyote Religion: A History*. Norman: University of Oklahoma Press, 1987.

Swierenga, Robert P. "The Little White Church: Religion in Rural America." *Agricultural History* 71.4 (Fall 1997): 415–441.

Szasz, Ferenc M. *The Protestant Clergy in the Great Plains and Mountain West, 1865–1915*. Albuquerque: University of New Mexico Press, 1988.

———. *Religion in the Modern American West*. Tucson: University of Arizona Press, 2000.

Szasz, Ferenc M., and Margaret C. Szasz. "Religion and Spirituality." In *The Oxford History of the American West*, ed. Clyde A. Milner II, Carol A. O'Connor, and Martha A. Sandweiss. New York: Oxford University Press, 1994. 359–391.

Templin, J. Alton, Allen D. Breck, and Martin Rist, eds. *The Methodist, Evangelical and United Brethren Churches in the Rockies, 1850–1976*. Denver, CO: Rocky Mountain Conference of the United Methodist Church, 1977.

Urban Sources

Alexander, Thomas G., and James B. Allen. *Mormons and Gentiles: A History of Salt Lake City*. Boulder, CO: Pruett Publishing, 1984.

Collins, Rebecca. "When Native Americans Move to the City." *Church Herald* 39.15 (August 20, 1982): 16–17.

Focus on the Family: Celebrating Twenty-five Years of God's Faithfulness. San Diego, CA: Tehabi Books, 2002.

Joice, Lois M. "The Shack at Our Savior's." *Church Herald* 27.8 (February 20, 1970): 12–13.

Orsi, Robert A. "Introduction: Crossing the City Lines." In *Gods of the City: Religion and the American Urban Landscape*, ed. Robert A. Orsi. Bloomington: Indiana University Press, 1999. 1–78.

Scheele, Christine. "Mile-High Hope." *Christian Herald* 112.5 (May 1989): 10–12, 14–15.

Tillapaugh, Frank. *The Church Unleashed*. Ventura, CA: Regal Books, 1982.

Web Sites

Brigham Young University
http://www.byu.edu/
Accessed June 21, 2004

Catholic Archdiocese of Denver
http://www.archden.org/
Accessed June 21, 2004

Catholic Diocese of Helena
http://www.diocesehelena.org/
Accessed June 21, 2004

Church of Jesus Christ of Latter-day Saints
http://www.lds.org/
Accessed June 21, 2004

Rocky Mountain Conference of the United Methodist Church
http://www.rmcumc.org/
Accessed June 21, 2004

Festivals

Mormon Miracle Pageant
South Temple Hill, Manti, UT 84642
888-255-8860
http://www.mormonmiracle.org/

Held annually in June.
Recounts Mormon struggles from 1830 and their migration to Utah in 1849.

Organizations

Cathedral of the Immaculate Conception
1530 Logan Street
Denver, CO 80203
303-831-7010
http://www.denvercathedral.org/

Focus on the Family Welcome Center
8685 Explorer Drive
Colorado Springs, CO 80902
719-531-3328
http://www.family.org

Garden of the Rockies Museum
1071 Terrace Lake Road
Ronan, MT 59864
406-676-5210

Mormon Handcart Visitors' Center
47600 West Highway 220
Alcova, WY 82620
307-328-2953

Museum of Church History and Art
45 North West Temple
Salt Lake City, UT 84150
http://www.lds.org/churchhistory/museum

St. Mary's Mission
P. O. Box 211
West end of 4th Street
Stevensville, MT 59870
406-776-5734

Temple Square
50 West North Temple
Salt Lake City, UT 84150
800-537-9703

SPORTS AND RECREATION

E. Duke Richey

In early 1991, in the week following its notorious annual swimsuit issue, *Sports Illustrated* (*SI*) ran two separate stories—both profiles of high school athletes—that spoke volumes about twentieth-century American culture, sports, and recreation and the daily reminders of regional history in the Rocky Mountain states of the West. In the story of Justin Armour, a suburban Colorado Springs three-sport athlete, and that of Jonathan Takes Enemy, a basketball player from the Crow Reservation in Montana, the readers of the nation's largest sports weekly were treated to two abbreviated examples of what scholar Patricia Nelson Limerick discussed several years earlier in her influential book *The Legacy of Conquest: The Unbroken Past of the American West* (1987). The story of Armour, "almost too good to be true," according to *SI*, was the classic account of the all-American kid that Hollywood and *LIFE* magazine helped shape in the American imagination a half century earlier: He was white, with short hair; had a perfect grade-point average; was Student Council president; Christian; sober; and bound for Stanford University.

Takes Enemy was, literally and figuratively, an altogether different story. His was a narrative that followed the predictable script of the "challenged reservation Indian" genre—a Jim Thorpe-ian tale of the Native American gifted with ability but plagued by alcoholism and poverty. In fact, "Shadow of a Nation" was a story told in the past tense, beginning seven years earlier when Takes Enemy was named Montana's Outstanding Athlete of 1984 after leading Hardin High School to its third consecutive state championship in basketball. By *his* senior year, Takes Enemy had turned to the moonshiner's bottle many times ("to say no was to mark oneself as an alien" among Crow peers), gone on reckless joy rides down rural dirt roads, fathered two children out of wedlock, and hung around the gym long enough to know that Indians who left the reservation for college basketball scholarships risked being called an "apple"—red on the outside, white on the inside. Crows risked a loss of identity if they took their athletic skills beyond the high school level, beyond the line that demarcated the reservation from the wide and largely non-Indian cultures beyond it. As *SI* made clear, Crow culture celebrated staying put, staying Indian; but staying put usually meant staying down and out. Seven years later in 1991—at age twenty-five—Takes Enemy had seen several of his teammates from the not-so-distant championship years buried under empty cans, broken bottles, and mangled automobiles. He had apparently seen enough. *SI*'s story was painful to digest, but it was equally a story of despair and a story of hope in that it ended with Takes Enemy—now with a new girlfriend and two more young children—clean and sober, living in a small apartment in Billings, Montana, while taking classes and playing basketball at Rocky Mountain College.

Armour's and Takes Enemy's stories reflected larger legacies of the region's history and culture in a number of ways. Armour was the son of a lawyer and a successful restaurateur, the latter-day beneficiaries of Anglo pioneers who had removed from the Front Range of Colorado many of its native inhabitants by the 1870s. When Armour graduated from one of the nation's top universities at Stanford, he was one of the millions of white men and women who had inhabited—and benefited from—a conquered Rocky Mountain West. In 1998, seven years after his own high school graduation, when Armour—at age 25—took to the field at Mile High Stadium as a member of the National Football League's (NFL) World Champion Denver Broncos, he was of a decidedly elite group of men. When he ran onto that manicured grass, Armour traversed hallowed ground for Denver's fans; however, it was also ground that Cheyenne, Arapahoe, and other native peoples had moved across just 150 years earlier in chase of bison, elk, and other wild animals. "Progress" in the mid- to late nineteenth century, which lay the groundwork for regional towns and cities from Boise, Idaho, and Butte, Montana, to Provo, Utah, to Casper, Wyoming, and perhaps especially to Denver, meant Indian removal—by death or by wagon trail to government-managed reservations. Takes Enemy, the son of a recovering alcoholic father, who worked as a custodian at the Crow Reservation hospital, and the son of a mother ravaged with diabetes, was a legacy of that same story of "Progress" that produced the all-American

Armour. Yet Takes Enemy was an important reminder that America's vanquished still survived in the region, beyond the grassy hills, out of sight of the big city's television cameras and stadium tailgate parties, and beyond the ski lifts, the winding bicycle paths, the hiking trails, or the rivers that laced together much of the region.

The stories of Armour and Takes Enemy reflected long histories, but they also spoke to the present cultures of the region, to Limerick's "unbroken past." In the Rocky Mountain states of Colorado and Montana (as well as in Idaho, Utah, and Wyoming)—imagined nationally and internationally more for their national parks and national forests, trout streams, and ski resorts than for

Tailgaters at Mile High Stadium. Courtesy of www.tailgating.com.

how the lives of high school athletes reflected history, geography, and culture—history is often shadowy across a landscape that is nearly as horizontal as it is vertical and where cultures are plural. The Crow Reservation is on the flat-to-rolling grasslands of the Great Plains, just on the edge of where Gen. George Armstrong Custer (1839–1876) lost his scalp at Little Bighorn in 1876. Colorado Springs, like Denver, lies where the plains rise gradually to the red sandstone rocks that, like cathedrals, form the first escarpments of the Rocky Mountains. In fact, much of Montana and large portions of Wyoming and Colorado are considered plains environments, just as a great deal of Utah and Idaho are desertlike landscapes. This geography usually means that people recreate somewhat differently in those places than people recreate in the high country and the mountain valleys. Just as important, the region is home to two very large, sprawling urban areas in Denver and Salt Lake City. In a region where the vast majority of inhabitants live in urbanized settings—while the remaining minority live in rural areas—the ways in which people live and play in particular sections of the region are very diverse, yet often more similar to the sporting and recreational lives of the rest of the United States than not. This chapter seeks a broad understanding of how human beings play today in the Rocky Mountains states, how they have recreated in the past, and how recreation in the region has evolved over time. What is unique to the Rocky Mountain states, and what is not? As important, how and why did the region become so well identified with the games people play there?

More than any other region in the United States, the states surrounding the various ranges of the Rocky Mountains are thought of as the nation's playground. From the trails and roadways through the grizzly bear country of Montana's Glacier National Park, south through the fishy waters of the Yellowstone River in Wyoming, and into Utah's red rock canyons and onto bike-tracked sandstone, and beyond to Colorado's famous ski towns, when Americans and the rest of the world speak of "the American West," they usually refer to the mountainous states of the wider region; and they often speak (mostly ambiguously) of the opportunities there for fun, freedom, and even magic. While it is certainly true that activities such as hiking, hunting, skiing, mountain biking, fly-fishing, mountaineering, canyoneering, rock and ice climbing, and whitewater boating are sports that often are associated with both outdoor gear mail-order catalogs *and* the expansive public lands of the Mountain West, simplifying how people play in the region is no easy task. It must be remembered that the region's inhabitants—sometimes as different in background and opportunity as Justin Armour and Jonathan Takes Enemy—are just as likely to throw around footballs on a field, or basketballs in a gymnasium, as they are to throw a dry fly through the rarified air above a mountain trout stream or to throw themselves (whether on a sled, skis, or snowboard) down snow-covered hills.

NATIVE GAMES, NATIVE SURVIVAL: THE NATIVE AMERICAN AT PLAY

In 1904, a remarkable group of young women traveled from the Fort Shaw Indian Boarding School outside of Great Falls, Montana, to St. Louis, Missouri, for the World's Fair. St. Louis was the starting point 101 years earlier for the Lewis and Clark expedition into the interior West of the new Louisiana Purchase. The official title of the fair—the Louisiana Purchase Exposition—was therefore a proposed celebration with the world of Thomas Jefferson's (1743–1826) great land purchase, the "discoveries" of Meriwether Lewis (1774–1809) and William Clark (1770–1838) in places such as Great Falls, and what it all meant for America and the world a century later. Included in this celebration was the Model Indian School, designed to showcase the assimilationist programs of the U.S. government's Indian boarding schools. For months on end, visitors to the fair might tour the school and see model classroom exercises and other displays of Indian "success" stories in the form of poetry recitals, musical and theatrical presentations, and most surprisingly, perhaps, in the skill and grace of a champion girl's basketball team from Fort Shaw.[1]

The nascent form of the game of basketball that we know today had its origins in a Young Men's Christian Association (YMCA) gym in Springfield, Massachusetts, circa 1891. It was there that graduate student James Naismith, trying to embody the ideas of "Muscular Christianity" (which espoused the notion that strong bodies equaled strong spirits), drew up rules for a game to be played indoors during the dark and cold winter months. Due in part to a proliferation of YMCAs in cities and towns throughout North America, the game spread quickly. In 1895, Naismith took over management of Denver's YMCA, while he worked on a medical degree in the city, claiming later that Denver had the first high school basketball league in the nation. With the game's inventor and the game's first high school league in the Rocky Mountains, news of basketball—namely, the basics of how to play it—reverberated from Denver throughout the Mountain West like the ripples from a ball tossed into a pool of water. It was no wonder that basketball took with such force among boys *and* girls, especially when one considers Naismith's opinions of female athletes. The *Rocky Mountain News* noted in 1896 that Naismith " 'evidently believes in the new woman, for he says the ideal woman is possessed of a sound mind, in a sound body, and is able to take care of herself.' "[2]

The Fort Shaw Indian Boarding School girl's team took care of itself quite well. Coached by Fred Campbell, a graduate of the University of Kansas, where Naismith became chaplain and basketball guru after leaving Denver, the girls became famous in Montana after winning an unofficial state championship in 1902–1903, including one win against the women of Montana Agricultural College in Bozeman, where more than 800 fans watched the game. One study of the team noted that when Campbell brought the game to Fort Shaw, he inherited an Indian cultural tradition in which women had always been welcomed on the fields of play. In addition, basketball was reminiscent of several games Indian women knew well. "Double ball," for example, was played among many Native American cultures in the Rockies and was often known as "woman's ball." The object of the game, like basketball, was to advance an object through, or across, the opponent's goal. Players used sticks to catch and pass two balls tethered together with a cord. In the Wind River area of Wyoming, both men and women attempted to pass the double ball (the two bags were made of sand-filled buckskin, ten inches in length with the tether) between goals set fifty yards apart in a field.[3]

On their way to St. Louis, the Fort Shaw team played several "whistle stop" exhibition games at train stops, beating one all-star team 34–0. Once they arrived in St. Louis, the girls played mostly intrasquad games as a display of "progress" made by the Indian schools. When they faced non-Indian opponents, Fort Shaw continued their winning ways. They traveled away from the fair grounds to play Missouri and Illinois high school teams, and they beat St. Louis Central High's state champion team again and again. They were crowned Exposition champions, and the press called them "World Champions." As many of the team members' children said years later, their mothers felt that their experiences in St. Louis in 1904 served as shining moments of brilliance throughout the rest of their lives. Basketball became an important cultural institution thereafter on Indian reservations throughout the region.

Other Native Americans in the region had for centuries found glory and spiritual sustenance in any number of endeavors that appear to some modern-day observers as athletic, or sporting. Many of these activities were linked closely with tribal cosmologies. For example, in the hoop and pole game, played by nearly all of the region's boys and men, participants threw arrowlike poles through a hoop rolled along the ground. The game coupled together the rituals of fertility and the buffalo hunt, while it also served as a practical way for hunters to practice the hand-and-eye coordination necessary for throwing a spear at a moving object. Women often played a game called "shinny," which closely resembled the modern-day game of field hockey. The Crows played men against women in the game, while among the Utes, both sexes played, but never together. Long-distance running has a deep-rooted tradition among native peoples. Tribes needed messengers to carry information between distant groups in times of both war and peace. Races, therefore, became an important test by which Indians discovered those runners best suited to the task.

Horse racing, swimming, wrestling, and marksmanship contests exemplified forms of play that were also important to Indian people's continued existence. Hunting and fishing (which often required important whitewater-canoeing skills) were absolutely necessary for survival, but it is impossible to imagine that the region's native hunters did not also enjoy their searches for fish, bison, elk, deer, and other animals. The line between native games and native survival was never an easy line to draw because it was often a blurred one. Clearly, however, not all Native American recreational activities were embedded with life-and-death importance or with the intention of training boys and girls for their later work roles as adults. Very often, of course, Indians at play in the Rocky Mountains simply wanted to have fun. In the long winters, Blackfeet children in what is now Montana, for example, made sleds from buffalo hides and rib bones and "tried to see who could coast the greatest distance down the slope and into the valley." They slipped and slid in their leather moccasins while racing in circles on frozen rivers. Blackfeet children played another game whereby the players started river stones spinning on the ice, with the winner being the boy or girl with the stone that stopped spinning last.[4] Lewis and Clark noted that both the Nez Percé of Idaho, as well as other groups of natives across their long route from Missouri to the Pacific Coast and back, played a game in which they hid a stick or a small bone "in their hands which they frequently changed accompanying their operations with a song." As the players danced and made music, switching the sticks from hand to hand, observers gambled on where the stick might be found at the end of the song.[5] It was in such acts of gambling where Anglos, Indians, and other peoples in the region found some of their most common ground when it came to recreation and leisure.

WORK AND PLAY IN THE ROCKIES: EURO-AMERICAN EXPLORATION AND SETTLEMENT

At some point in nearly every western film or television program ever made, a man wearing a leather vest and cowboy hat (picture John Wayne, Gary Cooper, Clint Eastwood, or Kevin Costner) walks into a saloon where other men—and occasionally women—play cards and gamble. Gambling—usually with the card games faro, poker, or 21—was, in fact, a very popular pastime in the nineteenth-century West and is still today. From Las Vegas, then east and north through various Indian reservation casinos, and old mining towns in the Rockies, all the way to the Canadian border, casinos and poker bars are a part of the western landscape. Contemporary observers noted that Native Americans and Euro-Americans in the Rockies gambled often, whether as to the outcome of a stick game, a race, or some other contest combining luck and skill. At the fur-trapper gatherings known as the "rendezvous," beginning in the summer of 1824 at Green River, Utah, "mountain men" (often of mixed Indian and European ancestry) gathered for fun and games that almost always included betting. They jumped, they ran, they shot guns at targets, and they wrestled, but they also played checkers, dominoes, and cards. Although the fur trappers often wintered together with fellow company men—and played card games night and day—by the summer they were still no match for the professionals at the rendezvous. One observer "lamented the fact that 'gamblers would come there, and lay for the beaver catchers just as they had laid their traps for the beaver.'"[6] These "gamblers" were likely the infamous card sharks and confidence men who had plied their trades for years in port towns like New Orleans, then spread throughout the plantation country of the Mississippi Valley, where they picked clean the bulging pockets of cotton kings in the 1830s before heading toward the Rockies to get at the fur trappers, and later, the region's cowboys and miners.

By the late 1870s and into the last decades of the nineteenth century, as the mining camps in the Rockies lured thousands of men and women from around the world, gamblers had some old games (Denver had 200 gambling halls in 1885) and some new games on which to wager their hard-earned dollars. Like the Indians and fur trappers before them, the newcomers to the region developed sports that mirrored what they valued most in their day-to-day lives. As one historian has written, rock drilling was the skill in which miners took the most pride. Drilling—the practice of using a hammer and a sharpened drill bit to

Trappers' Grisly "Sports"

The fur trappers were a decidedly dangerous crowd and therefore not to be taken lightly by gamblers or anyone else. One account mentioned two men who—for sport and the display of their skills as riflemen—liked to shoot cups full of whiskey off each other's heads. One of them eventually caught a bullet between the eyes. Other trappers played a game of cards while using the dead body of a fallen comrade for their table, and in another account—more bizarre and disturbing than the rest—one man lit another man on fire for fun. Trappers also taunted and tortured wild animals. Calling it "sport," one mountain man told the tale of two fellow trappers who, after deliberately leaving their rifles behind in their camp, mounted horses and encircled a nearby grizzly bear. They galloped around the bear, their horses hard to control as the bear turned in circles to fend them away. They shot more than fifty arrows into the bear—none of them deep enough to kill it—and may have shot more, had a Ute man from their camp not intervened and killed the anguished animal. In light of such unsettling forms of play, a trapper gambling away a year's worth of beaver pelts at a game of checkers seems downright charming.

make a deep hole in rock so that dynamite might blast away the rock at its
core—became a huge test of skill both
underground and in the town squares
above the mines. July 4th celebrations
usually pitted teams from various mines
against one another for yearlong brag-
ging rights. Drilling clearly became
sport when towns matched their best—
often ringers imported from out of
state—against another town's best to see
who might drill the deepest hole in a
large boulder in an allotted amount of
time. At Denver's Festival of the Mountain and Plain in 1899, first prize for a
team of two men garnered $750. In
1916—long after air drills had replaced
hammers and made hand-drilling obsolete—the sport lived on. That year,
nearly 4,000 drillers competed for prize

Rock drilling contest. Courtesy of the Denver Public
Library.

money in Nederland, Colorado's contest. Today, rock drilling competitions continue
to draw contestants to Ol' Timers Days and Mining Day celebrations across the
Rockies, but the prize money is less than it was more than a century ago.

Early Skiing

Men and women in the mining camps also skied, or as they usually described it,
they used "Norwegian snowshoes." Miners and their wives and children used long,
often homemade wooden skis with simple straps to hold their boots to the boards.
In deep snows, especially, the use of skis became a practical means of transport
around and between towns. Circuit preachers and mailmen of the mining era used
skis to deliver messages of faith, and letters or packages, respectively, in places like
the rugged San Juan Mountains of southwestern Colorado. Swede Swan Nelson,
for example, carried the mail on skis between Silverton and San Miguel (now a
ghost town west of Telluride) over the imposing Ophir Pass in the 1880s. Scandinavian immigrants like Nelson had used skis in their work and at play in their home
countries, then brought their skills to California's mines after 1849. It was largely
through northern European immigrants that skiing grew from a simple means of
travel into sport in both the Sierras and the Rockies. In what is easily imagined as
a precursor to the modern-day freestyle-skiing events at the X Games, as early as
1882 skiers in Snowmass City near Aspen, Colorado, built jumps and launched
themselves willy-nilly over log cabins. By the end of the decade, cross-country ski
races were frequent events in the Aspen area and elsewhere in the region. While
many preferred the slower pace of ski touring on the flat lands and valley floors,
others preferred the thrills of skiing fast downhill. In 1891, one of the region's newspapers noted that it was not an uncommon sight in the mining towns to see a
woman, dressed in a petticoat, race down a mountainside on skis, then hit a jump
that carried her over a wide road at the bottom of the run. For decades to come,

Myrtle Stedman poses outdoors on skis near American City (Gilpin County), Colorado. Courtesy of the Denver Public Library.

ski jumping became as popular in the region as any other form of skiing. In the early years of the twentieth century, Steamboat Springs, Colorado, built its famed Howelson Hill—named in honor of Norwegian Carl Howelson; and as late as the 1920s, Ogden, Utah, held one of the largest professional ski jumping competitions—dominated by men like Alf Engen and Halvor Bjorngaard—in the nation.[7] As will be discussed in detail later, the economies and cultures of towns like Aspen and Telluride, Sun Valley, Idaho, and Jackson Hole, Wyoming, eventually revolved around skiing as a leisurely activity.

Early Rodeos

Although they would have never recognized it as such, grizzly bear–taunting mountain men were also engaged that bloody day in a perverse form of another sport—rodeo—that is often identified with the Rocky Mountain states. Much of rodeo—a word that evolved from the Spanish *rodear* (to surround)—involved encircling and catching other animals from horseback. In other words, rodeo is a sport that evolved unmistakably from the work of cowpokes in their roundups of livestock and in breaking wild horses so that they might be put to work on the range. Although cowboys most certainly created contests of skill in riding and roping among their cohorts while on the job, official rodeos as distinct sporting contests have fuzzy origins. Although several regional towns in the mountain states claim to have organized the first rodeo (the plains community of Deer Trail, Colorado, claims 1869 as the date for the first rodeo in the region, while Cheyenne, Wyoming, argues that the first official rodeo took place there in 1872), rodeo contests were staged much earlier—some accounts mention rodeos in the late eighteenth century—to the south and west in the Spanish lands of New Mexico and California. Today, in places as urban and urbane as Boulder County, Colorado, one rite of summer remains the rodeo at the county fair, which in 2003 included a "Mexican bull riding competition," where the bulls were not necessarily of Mexican origin, but many of the riders were.

Regardless of rodeo's origins, the annual event at Cheyenne's Frontier Days celebration, which began in 1897 and continues today, is the oldest continuous competition in the United States. As one magazine put it, it is "the daddy of 'em all" and, with a purse of $1 million in prize money, ranks second only to the professional-level National Finals Rodeo in Las Vegas. But unlike the event in Vegas or anywhere else, rodeo in Cheyenne is unique in that—in addition to bull riding, steer wrestling, bareback riding, saddle bronc riding, and other events—Frontier Days offers rookie amateurs a saddle bronc competition that uses horses that have never been saddled. One veteran professional noted that such an event with "range" horses was something even the most seasoned rodeo cowboys rarely had the opportunity to witness.

With the sport of rodeo and the valor of the cowboy so well represented in both regional and national mythologies (the bucking horse on the Wyoming license plate—since 1935—is the infamous Cheyenne rodeo bronc "Steamboat" that Teddy Roosevelt [1858–1919] saw perform when he attended Frontier Days in the early twentieth century), it is no wonder that many people forget that rodeo—and all of the cultural trappings of a cowboy, or "western" *style*—has its origins in the work of early settlers on the plains and in the mountain valleys. Like other sports mentioned above—hoop and pole, rock drilling, and skiing, for example—rodeo is rooted historically in the work and the economies of men and women who have lived in the Rocky Mountains over centuries. Lest one forget, the rodeo held each year in Miles City, Montana, serves as a reminder that horses and the cowboys who ride them are—albeit less and less—workers in a region that retains much of its agrarian culture. At Miles City, ranchers with old horses enter them in what is known as the Bucking Horse Sale. If a horse performs well in this rodeo—if it throws a rider or gives a rider a hard fight—then it might save itself from slaughter and become a regular horse used on a rodeo circuit. If a horse shows no fight, and is not bought by a rodeo's animal buyer, it is auctioned to the highest bidder, who usually represents a meatpacking firm. Reflecting a long-held belief in the rural West that killing old horses is simply a part of life on the ranch or farm, the observers at Miles City see their rodeo as entertainment, but they also see it as one part of the multiple processes that connect humans and animals with the land.[8]

THE GREAT OUTDOORS: HUNTERS, BOATERS, MOUNTAIN BIKERS, AND CLIMBERS MOVE THROUGH IT

In August 1883, President Chester Arthur (1830–1886) headed west on a train from the suffocating heat and humidity of Washington, D.C., for a well-publicized summer vacation in the mountains of Wyoming. Once there, Arthur and his entourage rode horses through the country around Crow Heart Butte between the Wind River and Shoshone Mountain ranges, visited the town of Jackson Hole, and eventually entered the eleven-year-old Yellowstone National Park. The *New York Times* noted that the president spent considerable time fishing for trout in mountain lakes and that the group's hunters killed antelope, grouse, and other game to complement the president's dinner table. Perhaps as a titillating reminder to eastern readers that the West was still very much wild in character, the *Times* noted that one of the hunters, known as Shoshone Dick, was "a white member of the tribe" who was kidnapped from an "emigrant train" at a young age and had lost all memory of that earlier life (except, perchance, that his name was Richard). As "one of the Indian party," the story read, Shoshone Dick had "gone to look for signs of game." Toward the end of the nineteenth century, presidential recreation in the West involved fishing, riding horses through rugged country, and hiring out an "Indian party"—of which at least one member had a tantalizingly vague biography—to hunt for the evening's table fare.

More than 100 years later, in 1995, President Bill Clinton (1946–) and his family vacationed for seventeen days in Jackson Hole. Although the White House said prior to the trip that the president planned to hike, camp, raft, and ride horses—typical forms of recreation the public might expect in such a famous western locale—when asked, Clinton said only that he planned to play golf and relax. Although the president's spokesman hinted that the First Family might actually camp in Yellowstone, one wry reporter noted that it would likely be not under the stars but "in accommodations secure enough for better-than-average bears." The reporter then went on to describe the 8,000-square-foot "villa"—owned by West Virginia Senator John D. Rockefeller IV (1937–)—where the Clintons planned to stay. The correspondent then made reference to several social events on the president's agenda, including a party at the home of the head of the World Bank and an "intimate" dinner at movie star Harrison Ford's house.[9]

Tourist Destinations

Between 1883 and 1995, the ways in which Americans—including their political leaders—played in the Rocky Mountains clearly evolved a great deal. When Chester Arthur passed through Jackson Hole, he was as unlikely to consider a round of golf there as Bill Clinton was to consider hiring a group of Indian hunters to kill his dinner. Both men were products of their own time and place; and of course, Jackson Hole was a different place in 1883 than it was more than a century later. To begin with, in 1883, Jackson Hole had no golf course. Critics of New West meccas such as Jackson—where elites ski and golf, network, socialize, and buy elk antler chandeliers for their mansions that look out on the Tetons—might grab hold of this comparison of Arthur and Clinton as a perfect example of a vanished hard West gone soft. They might lament that the development of luxury second homes, condominiums, spas, and exclusive clubs have pushed out "natives"—both humans and animals—and turned the Rockies into a national playground for outsiders practicing elite and expensive sports better suited for the Hamptons or Switzerland. Critics might also note that the Arthur/Clinton example exemplifies perfectly how elites today would rather play golf—usually a less-than-strenuous sport, especially when played with the use of a gasoline, or battery-powered golf cart—than do something as manly, as wild (*wild* like Shoshone Dick!), as truly western, and as politically incorrect—for many Americans—as to stalk and kill animals.

In the case of Jackson Hole, particularly, the critics would neither be right nor wrong. Like many tourist hot spots in the Rockies, the history that Jackson sells is not quite the history that actually happened. Likewise, the argument that Old West pastimes (for example, "native" forms of "sport" such as hunting) have passed the way of Shoshone Dick, just as golf carts have replaced horses, is not an entirely legitimate claim, either. Jackson's first Anglo settlers arrived just a few years ahead of President Arthur's hunting group, and most of the town's pioneers did not settle there until after his trip in the mid-1880s. Furthermore, as early as the 1890s, struggling ranchers in Jackson Hole actually courted eastern hunters as guests. The ranchers acted as hired hunting guides and charged the visitors to house and feed them in their own homes in order to make ends meet. Owen Wister (1860–1938), a Philadelphian and a Harvard graduate who wrote *The Virginian* (1902), considered widely as the archetypal western cowboy novel, loved the area so much that he built his own cabin there, becoming Jackson's first celebrity second-home owner. The money that they earned from guiding eastern hunters was so important to the local economy that Jackson's ranchers made certain that elk and other game in the valley were reserved for them and their clients. Although guaranteed the privilege to hunt there by treaty, Bannock Indians from the Fort Hall Reservation across the mountains in Idaho were banned by the Supreme Court in 1896 from laying claim to their traditional hunting rights. Jackson's rancher-guides welcomed the ruling.[10]

All of this is to say something very simple about Rocky Mountain culture and sports and recreation: Much of—and Jackson is a wonderful example—the region's economy and culture has been intertwined with the desires of elites (and the locals' attempts to market to and gain from that desire) for most of the region's Anglo history. In the 1920s and 1930s, John D. Rockefeller, Jr. (1874–1960), the grandfather of the man who later loaned President Clinton his vacation home, bought up much of the valley floor around Jackson and gave the land to the federal government. The donation helped establish Grand Teton National Park, which served as a refuge from hunters for Jackson Hole's famed elk herds and as a sister-park to Yellowstone. As historians have made clear, Rockefeller, and many full- and part-time time residents—namely, dude ranchers (ranch owners who offered horseback riding and other activities to visitors) who saw elk herds as a profitable part of the scenery, as part of the overall experience that their clients desired and expected—helped make it harder for local sportsmen to hunt in the valley.

Hunting

Although the hunting of elk and other game in the Jackson Hole valley—and in the immediate areas surrounding the numerous destination resorts in the Rockies—may have, in fact, diminished substantially as different forms of tourism grew in the twentieth century, hunting thrives today in other parts of the region. In 2001, the total economic impact of all types of hunting (deer, upland game, and all variety of birds and waterfowl) on the economies of Colorado, Wyoming, Montana, Idaho, and Utah amounted to roughly $3 billion. A good portion of this money was generated by hunters after pheasant, Hungarian partridge, sharp-tail grouse, and quail in and around small plains or foothills communities. Meanwhile, most of the elk, deer, bear, and big horn sheep hunting took place deeper in the mountains. That same year—2001—one hunting industry report noted delightedly that Americans spend more annually on their hunting dogs than they spend on ski equipment.[11] Yet when one considers that in Colorado alone, skiing (and most important the real estate transactions that are considered as part of skiing's economic "multiplier effect") generates $4 billion, then comparing dogs, which eat, and skis, which do not eat, does not seem to work out so well for the hunter in an argument that attempts to pit hunting's worth against the recreational pursuits that dominate in the high country.

Fishing

When one begins to consider how the Rocky Mountain region has been imagined as a national playground, it is perhaps most important first to note that although a sizable number of men and women in the region—and visitors—hunt, even more of them fish. In Montana, for example, a state with the highest percentage of residents (24 percent) in America who hunt, still more residents (31 percent) fish. This number includes fly-fisherman, as well as lake and reservoir fisherman pursuing pike and other species, although most of Montana's biggest spenders use fly rods and stalk colorful river trout. Fishermen, both resident and nonresident, generate annually $20 million more than hunters for Montana's economy.[12] Such statistics become important when we recognize that fishing in the Rocky Mountains—fly-fishing for trout, specifically—has been romanticized into a multibillion-dollar industry and helped make the sport synonymous with the region. The watershed year was 1992, when a little-known book—a 1976 memoir with a cult following among fly-fisherman—titled *A River Runs through It*, hit the big screens across America. The critically acclaimed book was written by Montana native and University of Chicago English professor Norman Maclean, who died in 1990. The film version, starring Brad Pitt, with Montana (and more broadly, the Rockies) as his backdrop, had a story line about family and fly-fishing that pulled at the heart strings. The movie also had an undeniable visual appeal, and it hooked millions on a new sport, while reminding them that the West was the best place to practice it. Five years after the film, 7.7 million people—or, twice as many as in 1992 when the film was released—went fly-fishing in America. And most of them came west, hired guides, enrolled in instruction programs, stayed in hotels and lodges, and left with good memories of specific places and people. More than a decade after the movie's release, very few fly-fishing travel stories in major newspapers or periodicals fail to make reference to the film. As the producer and director of a documentary that chronicled the making of the movie said later, "No one had any idea of the impact of the movie at the time it was being made. The book was obscure, we thought the title was unwieldy. But during the shoot we knew that we had something special. There was a kind of magic."[13]

There was a kind of magic, indeed: the magic of American popular culture and the sudden prestige that came with having experienced a sport that Pitt (and director Robert Redford) made look sexy, sensitive, and exciting all at once. As others have noted, the romanticizing of fly-fishing in the West had a long history that built slowly toward the 1992 flood of popularity. Before the advent after World War II of monofilament fishing line, fiberglass rods, and open-faced spinning reels—all of which made catching big river fish faster and easier—the leisurely sport of fly-fishing for trout had been largely the domain of elite easterners who plied western waters while on extended vacations. The region's fly-fishing legends—Dan Bailey (who dropped out of a Ph.D. program at New York University to open his fly shop and guide service in Livingston, Montana, in 1937), West Yellowstone's Bud Lilly, Idaho's Ted Trueblood (an editor at *Field and Stream* magazine), and others—knew that their own success depended on helping supply a unique experience to wealthy eastern fisherman who could afford the expense of traveling to the remote West, hiring guides, and buying equipment. As soon as he opened up his shop, for instance, Bailey printed catalogs and sent them to friends in New York City; then the old boy network among the city's fishermen commenced. By the 1950s and 1960s, Lilly made speaking tours around the country in which he told of the splendors of fishing in and around Yellowstone National Park. By the time that Ohio native Leigh Perkins bought the Vermont-based Orvis Company in 1965—and began marketing expensive fishing trips to the Rockies—

the fly-fisherman's catch-and-release ethic that Bailey, Lilly, and Trueblood had advocated for years seemed to go hand in hand with what appeared to be a Mountain West region that was more pristine than many of the eastern states that their clients called home.[14] Indeed, easterners tend to become very upset when their ideas of an untouched, or pristine, "catch and release" West are spoiled. One New Yorker, who made no effort to hide his belief that fly-fisherman were superior to spinning-rod-and-bait-fishermen, noted on a trip to a remote section of Wyoming's Gros Ventre River that he "was sickened to find Styrofoam worm containers on the best pool." Disregarding the notion that some Wyomingites might enjoy the inexpensive nature of fishing with worms or live crickets, the New Yorker then called for a law in Wyoming that would outlaw bait other than the pricey hand-tied artificial lures with which he fished.[15]

The "Pristine Rockies"

The image of a pristine Rocky Mountain West may be explained any number of ways. First, the region has more publicly owned lands than much of the rest of the nation. More than half of the ground in Idaho and Utah is owned and managed by the federal government, while Montana, Colorado, and Wyoming range from 28 percent to 36.3 percent and 48.9 percent public lands, respectively. Compared to the much smaller states of the Northeast, for example, where only New Hampshire reaches into the double digits with 12.7 percent, the Rocky Mountain states are—to a large extent—vast expanses of land owned by an American people who see their holdings as *preserved* remnants of America, as part of what Montanans often refer to as "the last best place." When easterners visit the West—or when westerners visit the East—they often notice the differences immediately since most public lands are relatively undeveloped (although by no means *preserved* in most cases) compared to the predominantly privately owned states, such as Massachusetts or New Jersey. For the average American, the very words *national forest* and *national park* are antonyms for *city* and synonyms for *vacation, freedom*, and *pure*. Most Americans also understand that these "national" places are predominantly in western America, in the snowy mountains and deep canyons where generations have gone to cleanse their souls and thrive while at play.

Americans understand that their national playgrounds are western through their own travels, through word-of-mouth, through stories in the newspapers, books, and magazines they read, and through the images they see on their televisions and on movie screens. Often, these stories and pictures explain how recreation on the public lands of the West is a transforming experience. Chester Arthur's journey through Wyoming on horseback—and even Bill Clinton's downtime within *view* of Grand Teton National Park (and the *suggestion* of a visit to Yellowstone)— needed little explanation for Americans who have had it ingrained in them by popular culture since the nineteenth century that the West is a magical place. Take, for example, the New Yorker who was upset by the worm container on the Gros Ventre River. In describing the Tetons, he said that he had "the happy sense of being time-warped onto the set of a John Ford movie." For younger readers who are not so familiar with Ford's classic western films (many of them starring John Wayne), perhaps the picture of Brad Pitt with the bent fly rod or the image of Meryl Streep—whacking Kevin Bacon across the head with an oar—comes to mind when one thinks of the rugged "set" of the Rockies. Streep certainly came to mind for the Glacier Raft Company of West Glacier, Montana—located just outside Glacier National Park—which advertised its Middle Fork of the Flathead River trip with the following: "[T]here's a special magic. . . . You'll be able to see exactly where Meryl Streep guided her family on the river in the exciting Universal film *The River Wild*." As historians have noted, the work of Hollywood in prolonging a mythic image of the West as the rugged frontier—where Americans come to become American through a magical process—has had an impact on the region that is nearly impossible to measure but certainly impossible to ignore.

Many long sections of several rivers in the Rockies are not dammed and are, therefore, considered "wild." In fact, outside of Alaska, the longest stretches of federally managed Wild and Scenic waters in the United States are in Idaho, mostly on the Clearwater and the Salmon, and in Montana, on the Flathead and the Missouri. Recreation on these rivers usually involves rubber rafts, wooden dories, or plastic canoes and kayaks. Part of the definition for Wild and Scenic usually means that roadways can not be within one-quarter mile of the river on either side and that motorized craft are illegal. Limited access to the rivers often forces boaters to enter a river out of the designated area and float into the "scenic" section. These trips gain their "wild" flavor due to the nature of the trip—once in the river, there is no turning back.

River Sports

For many of the region's outdoor athletes—climbers, skiers, canyoneers, hikers, and certainly boaters—many of whom play largely, if not exclusively, on public lands, not turning back is a sort of mantra. Perhaps nowhere is this idea expressed more plainly than in Idaho, where the Frank Church River of No Return Wilderness covers more than 2 million acres of what is widely considered the wildest of the National Wilderness areas south of Alaska. The vision of not turning back in modern Rocky Mountain recreational pursuits may also be studied closely in the book *Never Turn Back: The Life of Whitewater Pioneer Walt Blackadar* (1994). Born in the East and educated at Dartmouth College and Columbia University, Blackadar represents tellingly the story of the rise of new forms of recreation to a firm position at the cultural forefront in the Rocky Mountains after World War II. In 1949, just graduated from medical school, Blackadar ran an advertisement in the American Medical Association's journal declaring his goal of practicing family medicine in a place where he might hunt and fish as often as possible. Blackadar and his family soon moved to the small town of Salmon, Idaho, where the young doctor found a job and eventually became a legend in whitewater boating after his time fishing on the waters of the lower Salmon gave way to simply being in—and challenging himself against—rough river rapids. Featured on Wyomingite Curt Gowdy's ABC television show *American Sportsmen* in the early 1970s, Blackadar became quite famous for running wild stretches of churning Rocky Mountain whitewater (often more brown than white during the big water of spring runoff when Blackadar and others liked it best). His fame grew when, in 1974, as millions of television viewers watched, Blackadar plucked Evil Knievel (a native of Butte, Montana) from the Snake River after the daredevil crashed a "Sky Rocket" into the Snake River Canyon. Although his biographer paints Blackadar as a cowboy in a kayak ("he proved to himself that he was worthy of manhood—and a revered place in the West," he writes in an early chapter), it is clear that Blackadar's values—putting risky play that was not associated with work above everything else—were not characteristic of most people in the rural hamlet of Salmon. Many residents questioned Blackadar—as a medical expert for the isolated town, as a father, and as a husband—for playing in a manner they found to be reckless. When he died in his kayak in 1978, well into his fifties, many of Blackadar's neighbors likely questioned the final costs of proving one's "manhood" while gaining a hard-won western identity through play.[16] Today, however, the folks of Salmon may at least measure the economic impact of whitewater rafting on their local economy. Although a town of only 3,000, Salmon has at least four whitewater rafting companies that help pump thousands of dollars into the local economy each year.

Blackadar was an early prototype for a "river rat." These serious boating enthusiasts, who spend much of their time in various human-guided boats on the region's rivers, are a subsubculture within a broader American subculture of outdoor enthusiasts. Not relegated just to the Rockies (the rain-drenched southern Appalachians are considered a river rat Shangri La, as well), boaters often live out of their trucks—usually covered with a camper top and topped with a beefy rack that is piled high with their open canoes, C-1s (closed-deck canoes resembling kayaks), kayaks, skirts (the neoprene devices that keep water from splashing into the small entry holes of closed-deck boats), and paddles—chasing one big runoff after another. Occasionally, the river rats plaster their boats and/or trucks with insider-joke bumper stickers, such as "Hayduke Lives." In reference to Edward Abbey's river rat character George Hayduke, from the 1975 cult-classic novel *The Monkey Wrench Gang* (and a follow up-novel, *Hayduke Lives!*, in 1990), the sticker often acts as a unifying cryptogram between river runners and environmentalists (sometimes one and the same) who would love nothing more than to see countless western rivers freed from behind the dams that contain them. Although most of them may not be willing to actually blow up Utah's Glen Canyon Dam—as Hayduke and his partners do in Abbey's earlier novel—river rats in the Rockies are often players in a broader cultural clash that pits New West "fun hogs" against a more traditional core of locals with different ideas about appropriate forms of play. Those who see the newer forms of recreation, and the economies and people that come with them, as going against an older, more traditional rural western way of life are very often "locals" who were once seen as invaders themselves. One of the best examples of this may be seen at the ski area at Alta, Utah, where "old-timer" skiers do not allow younger snowboarders to ride on their mountain.

Boating enthusiasts were not and are not today always outsiders in the Rockies. One of the original river rats was Utah native Bus Hatch. Hatch and his group of family and friends—known as the "Dusty Dozen"—took their homemade wooden boats down the Green River through Colorado and Utah beginning in the 1920s. When folks said that they were senseless to try such antics, Hatch simply reminded them that John Wesley Powell had done the same thing in the same type of boats in 1869, so why should he not try? Following World War II, when the easy access to military surplus rubber rafts made river expeditions less prone to disaster (wooden boats are harder to patch than rubber boats), Hatch figured he could make river running a career. In 1953, he received a permit to run river trips in Colorado's Dinosaur National Monument, and today his family still operates Hatch River Expeditions out of Vernal, Utah. Part of the success of the river trip is that it often combines together in one place a number of the recreational pursuits that outdoor enthusiasts love. When not maneuvering through rapids, or floating languidly through slow water, river runners often pull off to a rocky or sandy shore and explore narrow side canyons. Known as canyoneering, this sport often requires technical rock-climbing skills and proper equipment, but more often on river trips it simply requires a sturdy pair of hiking boots and the ability to scramble over boulders, to pull oneself up by grabbing a tree's roots, or the courage to wade or swim through creeks and pools. River runners on overnight trips also camp. For many backcountry travelers—namely, hikers—the whole point of being outside is to get to a campsite, pitch the tent—or throw the sleeping bag on the ground and sleep under the stars—cook a meal, and enjoy being away from the city, the job, the house, and the television. On a river trip, one can float, swim, hike, climb, and camp, or at least pull over to the side of a river on a day-trip and have lunch. Across the region, the industry that Hatch started has become vital to local economies—in 2000, for example, more than half a million whitewater rafters contributed over $122 million into Colorado's economy—but perhaps nowhere is this so obvious as in the canyon country of Utah from Vernal to Moab. In Moab, for instance, more than ten companies base their operations for the Green and Colorado Rivers, which converge near the town in the deep rock gorges of Canyonlands National Park.

Mountain Biking

Surrounded by Canyonlands and Arches National Park, as well as thousands of acres of other public lands (managed mostly by the Bureau of Land Management), the southeastern Utah town of Moab has one of the most fascinating late-twentieth-century histories of any town in the Rocky Mountain region. Founded in the 1880s, by the 1920s Moab's economy centered on agriculture and the mining of uranium and manganese. Beginning in the 1950s, uranium mining in the area boomed for roughly a dozen years, but then crashed. By the 1970s, following the 1968 release of Abbey's book *Desert Solitaire*, which chronicles beautifully his years spent in the backcountry of Arches National Monument before it became a National Park, Moab evolved into a tourist town—a gateway to the public lands and the recreational opportunities people sought there—where river rafting, hiking, Jeep tours, and motorcycling along the Slickrock Trail helped fill motels and restaurants with visitors. Around the same time in California, a small group of men began to gather on the weekends to ride their converted street-cruiser bicycles down mountain roads. Over time, these "mountain bikers" began building lightweight aluminum bike frames, hand-operated brake systems, and resilient rubber tires more suitable to their new sport; some of them traveled to other parts of the country to ride up and down other mountain trails. By the early 1980s, a number of mountain bike enthusiasts lived in Crested Butte, Colorado, several hours east of Moab. In 1985, one Crested Butte man—Hank Barlow—began publishing *Mountain Bike* magazine. The first issue featured Moab's Slickrock Trail, and later that same year, the owners of Moab's Rim Cyclery bike shop organized a Fat Tire Festival for the town, which celebrated the bikes with fat knobby tires that ski bums, river rats, and other fun hogs in the region were increasingly riding at break-neck speeds on trails near the town. As one historian has noted, the mass production of mountain bikes, beginning in the early 1980s, allowed the sport to boom. Between 1983 and 1993, mountain bike sales in the United States rocketed from 5 percent of all bikes sold to 95 percent of all bikes sold. As baby boomers helped increase the popularity of the sport—mountain biking grew 500 percent between 1987 and 1998—the word *Moab* became as synonymous with the sport as *Aspen* was to skiing. Of course, this also meant that Moab itself changed—a fact that some locals (the owners of Rim Cyclery, for example, who had worked earlier in the mining industry before realizing Moab's potential for bikers) welcomed, while others cringed. In 1990, one real estate company reported that 90 percent of its sales were to bikers and other outdoor enthusiasts looking to relocate to Moab or to own second homes there.[17]

Outdoor Schools and Adventure Training

As noted earlier in the example of Idaho kayaker Walt Blackadar, and as will be examined below in the section of this chapter on skiing and ski towns, many of the outdoor enthusiasts in the Rockies—hikers, fly-fishermen, river rats, mountain bikers, climbers, and skiers—have come to the region from other parts of the country, usually defined broadly as "the East." One of the institutions—Outward Bound—that initially brought many adventurers to the region over the last forty years has its roots very far to the east of the Rocky Mountains, in Germany, Scotland, Wales, and New Hampshire. After being run out of Germany in 1934 because of his criticism of Adolf Hitler (1889–1945), educator Kurt Hahn started the Gordonstoun School in Scotland, where he put great emphasis on each student being challenged in both the classroom and in athletics. This school was the genesis of Outward Bound, founded by Hahn in 1941 at Aberdovey, Wales, which sought to challenge male British youth—by sending them both literally and metaphorically into rough waters like a ship leaving the safety of port and going "outward bound." Once the students returned home from their experience outdoors—swimming, sailing, climbing the riggings of ships—the philosophy went, they would be more physically fit, stronger mentally, bolder, and more compassionate for their fellow man. They might also be able to survive in a lifeboat after being torpedoed at sea by a German submarine. In 1950, American Joshua Miner, a Princeton graduate who taught at New Hampshire's Phillips Exeter Academy, went to Gordonstoun to teach for Hahn. When he returned to the States in 1952, Miner was convinced that American youth might benefit from Outward Bound. After years of planning, Miner's dream came true in 1961, when the first Outward Bound school in the Western Hemisphere opened in Colorado. With the decidedly Westernized-myth mission of offering young men (sixteen and over) a "unique and challenging opportunity to prove themselves in a rugged contest" against the wilderness and against themselves, it made sense that the first courses in America were offered in the Rocky Mountains. After all, the Rockies had been where Americans went for challenges for more than a century. By 1965, young women and adults also enrolled in the programs at the Colorado Outward Bound School (COBS), and by 1969, courses were coed and offered in several other regions of the country. By Miner's death in 2002, the schools had more than 600,000 alumni. In 2003, COBS and the Pacific Crest Outward

Bound School—based in Portland, Oregon—merged to become Outward Bound West in Golden, Colorado. "Our instructors," the school's website explains, "are chosen primarily because they are adventurers and educators in their own right—self-made individuals who have lived their dreams both in and out of the wilderness."[18] For many of Outward Bound's students over the years—who have backpacked in Montana, rafted in Utah, climbed rock in Wyoming, and bagged hundreds of Colorado's peaks—living their own dreams after a course sometimes meant returning to live and work in the region where they experienced profound personal transformations.

The National Outdoor Leadership School (NOLS), based in Lander, Wyoming, turned thousands more onto the beauty and the power of the Rocky Mountains. Founded by Paul Petzoldt—one of the first Outward Bound instructors, who felt that there needed to be a school that focused more on hard outdoor skills rather than on personal growth—NOLS graduates often became Outward Bound's instructors. In describing legends in the culture of outdoor and adventure recreation in the Rocky Mountains, Petzoldt has few equals. In 1924, at age sixteen, he set out from his family's Idaho farm with a friend to climb the Grand Teton near Jackson Hole. In the ascent, Petzoldt wore cowboy boots, bib overalls, and a cotton shirt. After being stranded overnight in a snowstorm, Petzoldt learned that surviving in the wilderness required skills. "We had little sense," Petzoldt said later. " 'Hypothermia' wasn't in the dictionary then, and the only reason we lived is we didn't know we were supposed to die." For the remainder of his life, Petzoldt honed "good judgment" skills for the outdoors, and he taught them to others, including the soldiers of the 10th Mountain Division, based at Pando, Colorado, during World War II.[19] In 1941, Petzoldt gained fame when he climbed Devil's Tower, in Wyoming, to rescue a stranded parachutist who had landed atop the high volcanic spire.

Climbing

The rock walls of the region—from the Petzoldt Ridge and the Exum Route on the Grand Teton to The Diamond on Long's Peak in Colorado's Rocky Mountain National Park—have long been noteworthy proving grounds for America's climbers. But perhaps nowhere in the region is the test of a climber's mettle and skill so starkly obvious as at Devil's Tower, which rises from the plains in the northeastern corner of Wyoming like a large brown petrified tree stump and which appears on the state's license plate alongside Steamboat, the bucking bronco. Formed millions of years ago, Devil's Tower is the 867-feet-tall hardened lava core of an eroded volcano. In 1906, thirteen years after two ranchers used a 350-feet ladder, hammers, and spikes (an early form of what climbers today refer to as "aid" climbing) to reach the top as a thousand spectators watched, President Theodore Roosevelt decreed the striated massive rock America's first National Monument. Petzoldt's maneuvers there with the parachutist in 1941 brought more headlines. In 1977, when Steven Spielberg used the tower as a central prop to his story line in the hit film *Close Encounters of the Third Kind*, the strange and beautiful rock became something to see for both the recreational vehicle (RV) set, as well as for climbers, whose numbers had grown with the advent of better equipment and with the skills learned through programs like Outward Bound and NOLS. In the 1990s, reflecting larger trends of conflict in the region—conflicts that pitted people against one another around questions of culture, sports, and recreation—Devil's Tower became a battle ground between climbers, Native Americans, and administrators at the National Park Service. The Lakota Sioux call the tower *Mateo Tepee*, which means "Bear's Lodge," and they—and Cheyenne and Arapahoe people—consider the rock a sacred place of spiritual power. Each summer, Native Americans come there to perform religious ceremonies, and it pains them that climbers are able to look down upon them from high on the rock or make noise from the tower with their yells and screams of fear and joy, the banging of hammers, or the use of bolt-drills and other actions the Indians find disrespectful. After years of meetings with the Park Service, most climbers (there is an 85 percent compliance rate) now honor the requests of Native Americans and do not climb in June, when the monument is used for religious ceremonies. Still, as one astute historian has shown, many climbers also see climbing as a spiritual activity that is much more a part of their life—their fabric—than it is a recreational diversion or sport.[20]

The region's climbers were, in fact, the first to proclaim that their forms of play constituted a way of life—a distinct outdoors-oriented culture—in the Rockies. The Rocky Mountain Club, founded in Denver in 1896, led an expedition to the Grand Teton two years later. The Rev. Franklin Spalding led the first verified ascent, then lowered a rope to his teammate, Owen, thus establishing the famed Owen-Spalding route in 1898. Rock climbing, which evolved from mountaineers' uses of ropes to get over vertical sections of rock in their attempts to scramble to a summit, came very much into play in the high Tetons. Other climbers set out to climb long stretches of rock with no large mountain summit in mind. As early as 1906, climbers inched up Boulder, Colorado's Third Flatiron using ropes and other "technical" climbing skills, such as the placement of fixed anchors that might catch them (or slow their descent) if they fell. By the time the Colorado Mountain Club (CMC) was founded in 1912, getting to the tops of rocks and mountains was a favorite pastime for a select crowd in the Rockies. By 1917, CMC had 200 members, and today it has 10,000, many of whom still gather together to climb Fourteeners (Colorado has more than fifty mountains over 14,000 feet), ski, hike, snowshoe, or do other activities in the mountains on club-sponsored "outings." Today, the CMC, Outward Bound West, the American Alpine Club (the leading national organization of climbers), the American Mountain Guides Association, the Colorado Fourteeners Initiative, and Climbing for Life, a group that works with youth-at-risk, all share office space in Golden, Colorado's old brick high school, known now as the American Mountaineering Center.[21]

Climbers in the Rockies today are very often the same people who spend time in kayaks or on skis. They may be found in the remote canyons of the Bitterroot Valley of western Montana or on Potash Road, in Moab, climbing so close to the highway that an observer can park and watch them through the sunroof of an automobile while eating a Big Mac; or they may be seen in the winter in Ouray, Colorado's ice park, where water pipes and cold temperatures help develop frozen faux-waterfalls that men and women scale with spiked crampons and ice axes. Although a climber will often throw his or her rope and chalk bag into the back of a car loaded down with skis and paddling gear, like river rats or ski bums, climbers also seem to have their own distinctive subculture. A number of magazines are devoted to the sport in all its manifestations, which includes everything from climbing with ropes on sixty-feet-tall plastic walls indoors to climbing unroped across thousands of feet of exposure (vertical drop) in the high mountains. Regardless of the type of climbing one does, there is always some element—bigger at times than at others—of challenge. The 1999 death of a forty-eight-year-old St. Louis man in the Tetons served as a reminder that American climbers still come to the Rockies to seek challenge. Echoing what Petzoldt had said of his own trip up the Grand Teton in 1924, park officials noted that the climber's party was not prepared with proper clothing or equipment and that hypothermia likely played a role in some bad decision making that resulted in the tragedy. In the Rockies, the tragic and the magical often came together to form the singular emotion of awe.

SKIING AND SKI TOWNS: NOT JUST A SPORT BUT A WAY OF LIFE

The ski towns of the Rocky Mountains are often important centers for many of "the great outdoors" sports—fishing, whitewater boating, mountain biking, hiking, and climbing—discussed in the previous section. But one point should be made clearly: These forms of recreation take place predominantly in the warmer months of late spring, summer, and early fall. In the winter months—from November through mid-April in the high country—skiing is the most obvious collective pastime for many Rocky Mountain residents and visitors alike. This fact, combined with the unique modern histories of ski towns (most of them evolved from extractive industries to tourism due mainly to skiing), helps explain why places such as Whitefish, Montana, Jackson Hole, Wyoming, Aspen, Colorado, Ketchum, Idaho, and Park City, Utah, are known today mainly as "ski towns" and not as "fishing towns" or as "hiking towns." Today, the Rocky Mountains are known internationally as America's ski country.

As seen earlier in the chapter, the history of skiing in the West has mining-era roots in the late nineteenth century. While Coloradoans, for example, continued to ski throughout the first half of the twentieth century—due in large part to the efforts of organizations like the CMC, which operated a bus from Denver to Berthoud Pass in the winter—it was largely not until the years following World War II that skiing in the state and elsewhere in the region developed into an industry recognizable to skiers today.[22] In Idaho, the corporate-financed form of skiing that is exemplified today in the region by companies such as Vail Associates and Intrawest had its origins at Sun Valley before the war. Built north of the town of Ketchum, which at one point was the largest sheep and lamb shipping station in the United States, the Union Pacific Railroad opened the resort at Sun Valley in 1935, hoping to bring in skiers on the rails that had once carried livestock to market. During World War II, Ketchum's gaming houses prospered from Sun Valley's gamblers—the waves of soldiers who convalesced at the resort after it was converted to a hospital for wartime use. At the same time in Colorado, other soldiers thought of a different type of a gamble—the development of ski resorts in Colorado after the war. Austrian-born Friedl Pfeiffer and additional members of the 10th Mountain Division ski troopers, based outside of Leadville at Camp Hale in Pando, saw in Aspen the possibility for recreational skiing along the lines of Sun Valley. After the war, Pfeiffer gained the financial backing of Chicago's Walter

Paepcke and other investors to build the world's longest chairlift in Aspen in 1946. By the 1950s, Aspen was well known among American skiers.

Skiing Culture

The skier's culture that developed in Aspen and elsewhere across the region was that of the athlete's bohemia, the mountain-top paradise where play and the cult of youth were celebrated more than work and the commitments that came with maturity in the "real world" below. One could not help but to notice in Aspen—as visitors did from the 1940s through the 1990s—that men and women wore blue jeans, or later, running shorts and sneakers, to work, that Ivy League graduates tended bar and worked as custodians, and that locals skied better than everyone else. It was a culture—like many tourist cultures—that sucked people in and never let some of them go for years, if at all. When Peggy Clifford moved to Aspen in 1953, she wrote that she felt superior to the rest of America. "Men were moonbound," she wrote, "but we still sat around wood stoves on cold evenings." In 1980 Clifford left Aspen, disgruntled because it had, in her opinion, grown too much and had become crowded with people who had lost the vision of Aspen as a haven for mavericks and misfits. It was no longer a skier's town. Aspen had conformed to a world Clifford had tried to escape. She returned, after twenty-seven years away, to her hometown of Philadelphia.[23] When the writer Ted Conover moved to Aspen in the late 1980s to work as a cab driver and to research life there, he felt himself—almost against his will—being sucked into the town's culture of leisure that he described as being akin to life on a cruise ship far at sea from the rest of the world. He described a t-shirt popular in Aspen in the 1970s that summed up the town's recreational ethos: ASPEN: SOFT POWDER, HARD DRUGS, CASUAL SEX.

Aspen's distinctiveness stems in large part due to its *role* as a place. Aspen is a town where people come to play and where individual forms of play take on greater meanings than they might in most other American towns. Aspen has no factories, no interstates running through the middle of town, and more hotels, real estate firms, and bars than it has convenience stores or schools. It also has ski slopes that drop right into its downtown. Over the years, numerous self-described "ski bums" in Aspen described skiing as not just a sport but "a way of life." The title to a *National Geographic* article about the town echoed the idea in 1973: "A Town . . . A Mountain . . . A Way of Life." Ski bums in other towns reflected the same notion: that there was something different about the people and the places at the center of the sport. The parents of one Sun Valley child in 1974, for example, were so out of the ordinary that they decided to let their daughter name herself when she was good and ready. At age three, prior to a family trip to Mexico that required a passport, the baby's name went from "Little Girl" to "Picabo" in honor of both her favorite game, "Peek-a-boo," and the hamlet of Picabo nearby her hometown of Triumph, Idaho. Years later, the little girl had a new game she liked to play. In 1998, Picabo Street won the gold medal in the thrilling Super G at the Nagano Olympics. Although snowboarders spoke often about their sense of "community," some skiers did not consider snowboarders as equals. Alta, Utah, for example, does not allow snowboarders access to its lifts. Aspen Mountain only allowed snowboarders be-

Picabo Street takes to the air as she skis the Women's Downhill course during the third training run in Lake Louise, November 28, 2001. © Reuters/Corbis.

ginning in April 2001. Although scholars have noted how communities, entire regions, and nations can gain identities associated with particular sports—for example, Canada and ice hockey—Aspen and the other ski towns are somewhat unique in that their entire economies and cultures are founded on recreation, whereas recreation in most other places evolved as one aspect of the broader culture and economy.

In Colorado—the Rocky Mountain state with the most ski areas (twenty-five) and most skiers (11.6 million skier visits in 2002–2003, or nearly ten times the number of skier visits as second-place Utah)—a skiing culture akin to Aspen's is pervasive from Nederland's Eldora Mountain, 45 miles from downtown Denver, to Telluride, more than 350 miles from the capital city. The term "skier visit"—a phrase meaning a skier (or snowboarder) who visits a ski area for all or part of a day—reflects the notion that skiing today in the West, and especially along Colorado's Interstate 70 corridor, often takes place on slopes developed and managed by large corporations. Much of modern skiing reflects an industry with as many technical terms, divisions, and accountants as it has ski bums. Although there are no precise numbers—only the empirical data of the weekend traffic jams of skiers that clog the 65 miles of I-70 from Denver to Summit County during the winter, and of "price wars" that have sent Front Range season pass prices spiraling downward since the late 1990s—it is safe to say that the ski industry in Colorado depends to a significant degree on Coloradoans who ski.

Big corporate-backed resorts (for example, Vail Associates, which owns several other ski resorts, is a publicly traded company) are the antithesis of the majority of the region's ski areas, many of them small "mom and pop" areas (family owned businesses with only a few lifts) that do not cater to tourists. From Missoula's Montana Snobowl to Eldora (with the advertisement campaign "Just Say No to I-70"—which seems to say that Eldora's skiers shun more than traffic when they choose to ski at a smaller, yet still challenging mountain), many of the turns made on the snow by the region's skiers and snowboarders are made at areas where glitz and glamour are shunned for what hardcore locals refer to as "true" skiers' mountains.

SPORTS AND THE CITY: BRONCOS, MAGGOTS, SCORCHERS, AND MORE

Professional Sports

The most nationally recognizable team sports in the Rockies involve professional athletes drawn together less by regional loyalty than by contracts, stadiums, and cultlike followings of team fanatics or fans. Of all of the region's favorite teams, the Denver Broncos of the NFL have the widest appeal across the Mountain West. Although there are thousands of individual exceptions to the rule, most Montanans, Utahans, Idahoans, or Wyomingites are as likely as a native Coloradoan to wear the orange and blue of the Broncos and to travel to home and away games. The Broncos, led by legendary quarterback John Elway, satisfied their eager fans (the club had lost in the 1977, 1986, 1987, and 1989 Superbowls) with back-to-back world championships in 1997 and 1998. Simply put, most of Denver's major professional teams—the Broncos, the National Hockey League's (NHL) Avalanche, and major league baseball's Rockies—tend to be regional favorites in a region with only one other major sports franchise. The Avalanche, formerly the Quebec Nordiques, set off a hockey frenzy in the Rockies when they won the Stanley Cup in their first year in Denver in 1996, then won it again in 2001. Although Salt Lake City's Utah Jazz of the National Basketball Association (NBA) has traditionally been more popular in the region than Denver's perennial loser, the Nuggets, the retirement of Jazz point guard John Stockton and Karl Malone's signing with the Los Angeles Lakers in 2003, combined with the arrival of superstar Carmelo Anthony in Denver that same year, seemed to indicate a shift in fan interest toward the revived Nuggets. A recent poll between Wyomingites corroborated these general trends in favorite regional teams: They said that their favorite baseball team was the Rockies, favorite football team the Broncos, the Avalanche in hockey, and the Jazz in basketball. Denver also has a major league soccer team (the Colorado Rapids), while Salt Lake has a Women's National Basketball Association team (the Utah Starzz).

Denver's and Salt Lake's teams are not the only professional sports squads in the region. A number of minor league baseball and hockey teams are scattered across the Rockies. The all-rookie Pioneer League fields four minor league baseball teams in Montana, two in Utah, and one each in Wyoming and Idaho. Colorado Springs is conveniently home to the Colorado Rockies' AAA affiliate, the Sky Sox, while Salt Lake's AAA team, the Stingers, is part of the Anaheim Angels' organization. The America West Hockey League (which started in 1992 as the American Frontier Hockey League) merged in 2003 with the North American Hockey League. The league has "Junior A" hockey teams in the Montana towns of Billings, Bozeman, and Helena. Junior A players typically go on to play college hockey, although some get drafted directly into the NHL. The Professional Golf Association (PGA) also makes an annual stop at Castle Pines Golf Club, south of Denver, for The International each summer. The Modified Stableford format, which awards points for great shots—so that unlike a normal golf tournament, the high score wins—makes the International one of the most unique stops on the PGA tour.

Amateur Sports

Golf

Over the last decade, golf has grown in popularity in the region as it has in other parts of the country, but contrary to what one might expect, the sport has been popular in the Rockies for many years. Montana, for example, had a number of courses before 1910, and at one point, Wyoming was home to nearly as many PGA players per capita as any other state. Cherry Hills Country Club in Denver hosted the 1960 U.S. Open and the PGA Championship in both 1941 and 1985—important feathers in the cap for any golf course or golf-crazed town. Although most of the ski towns built golf courses over the years to draw summer tourists—and Rocky Mountain National Park had a golf course at one time that has since been removed—other parts of the region have only recently focused on golf as a tourist attraction. When the busted smelter town of Anaconda, Montana, hired Jack Nicklaus to design a championship golf course on the town's recovered slag dump in the 1990s, the town's philosophy was akin to that of the main character in the film *Field of Dreams* (1989): "If you build it, they will come."

Team Sports

A great number of team sports, of course, are played throughout the region. The residents of ski towns show their athleticism in sports other than skiing. Telluride, for example, has thriving leagues in summer softball and winter broomball (akin to ice hockey played without skates and with duct-taped brooms instead of hockey sticks). Aspen's well-known rugby team, the Gentlemen of Aspen Rugby Football Club, was established in 1968. Due to a roster that is loaded with New Zealanders, Australians, South Africans, and others from rugby-rich cultures, it stands to reason that the "Gents" are contenders each year for the national championship. Considering that the other American "Super League" teams represent major metropolitan areas (the Denver Barbarians are the only other team from the Rocky Mountain region), Aspen's presence among teams from New York, Chicago, and San Francisco in the nation's premier rugby league adds to the aura of the small town's enormous athletic image. Although many other towns and cities around the region have rugby teams—Missoula, Montana's All-Maggots Rugby Club may be one of the most distinctively named teams—team sports in the Rockies, with only an occasional odd twist, are usually the same sports played by teams in other regions of the country, from small town to big city.

The best example of an "odd twist" in team sports in the region is six- and eight-man high school football. In rural communities of the region—notably, but not exclusively, on the plains—where populations are small and the total number of students at a high school may number well under 100, it is often difficult to field the eleven players required for regulation football. Invented during the depression on the Great Plains, when thousands of families left their small communities for larger regional cities, depleting high schools of students—and with the strongest traditions in Colorado, Texas, and Nebraska (before six-man play ended in 1998)—six- and eight-man teams in the region thrive today in all of the Rocky Mountain states. Six-man football operates quite differently from the version with eleven players. First, the field is 80 yards long, as opposed to 100, and 10 yards less wide.

Touchdowns count as six points, as in regular football, but on conversions, a good kicker is worth more than on average. Extra points that are kicked count for two points, and only one point if the ball is carried over the goal line. A field goal counts for four points instead of three. Also, teams must go 15 yards, instead of 10, for a first down, and—like rugby—once the ball crosses the line of scrimmage, it can be reversed (thrown or handed off to a player behind the ball) as many times as possible. In this high-scoring sport, any team with a forty-five-point lead automatically wins. Discussing the wide-open aspects of the game, one Idaho eight-man coach noted, "It's hard to hide a weak player. The kids have got to be able to make a tackle." As it is harder to trick the defense and screen the ball with fakes, the tackles in six- and eight-style football are often bone-crushing because they involve one-on-one collisions at considerable speeds. In a statement that at once imparted reverberations of the Old West and of the physical nature of small-town football in the region, one six-man player from Colorado described the rough nature of his game: "I took a hit in a game last year against Kit Carson from their running back, who was over 200 pounds. I made the tackle but I didn't make it through the rest of the game."[24]

Ovid, Colorado, native Keith Miller, who played six-man high school ball against teams from Kit Carson High while at Revere High, eventually made it to the big time. After walking on at the University of Colorado at Boulder (CU), Miller received a scholarship and won praise from his Buffalo teammates for the rough-nosed style of play he learned in the stripped-down version of the game on the plains. Although CU's shared national championship with Georgia Tech in 1990—and its strong teams throughout the 1990s and early 2000s—make it one of the Rocky Mountain region's top college football programs, it is by no means clear each year whether the Buffaloes—who represent the region's largest university—are even the best team in the state. The Rams of Colorado State University (CSU) are generally a thorn in the side for every team they play, including Colorado, while the Air Force Academy (AFA) has also fielded nationally ranked teams. The University of Wyoming (UWY)—which had the only undefeated regular season football team in the nation in 1967—has wavered of late, as have Utah's two major college football programs at the University of Utah and at Brigham Young University (national champions in 1984). Meanwhile, the University of Montana, which competes in Division I-AA (a divisional notch below the schools mentioned above) is a national powerhouse at their level, having won National Collegiate Athletic Association (NCAA) championships for I-AA in 1995 and 2001; and the University of Northern Colorado, after having won two national football championships in Division II in the 1990s, moved to Division I-AA in 2003.

Although football is certainly the most followed collegiate sport in the region, with men's and women's basketball second in popularity (Utah is consistently the best-ranked Rocky Mountain men's team, while Colorado is a consistent winner among women), a few of the more notable collegiate sports teams in the region are the nationally ranked Division I hockey programs at the University of Denver (DU) and at Colorado College, and the powerhouse coed skiing programs at DU, CU, and Utah (Montana State also has a Division I ski team). A number of colleges and universities in the region also field intercollegiate rodeo teams. In 2003, the College of Southern Idaho, Weber State (of Ogden, Utah), and Montana State finished highly ranked. Although baseball and women's softball, swimming, wrestling, and soccer are popular at all school and club levels in much of the region, none of the region's colleges normally field top-ranked teams. However, this is not to say that the region or its schools do not produce an occasional champion in any of these sports. Denverite and Olympic swimming gold medalist Amy Van Dyken (the first American woman to win four gold medals) transferred from the University of Arizona to Colorado State, where she became NCAA swimmer of the year in 1994. Van Dyken then moved to Colorado Springs and the U.S. Olympic Training Center, where she prepared for the Atlanta Games and her four triumphs there. Wyomingite wrestler Rulon Gardner, also an Olympic champion, began his collegiate career at tiny Ricks College in Rexburg, Idaho, before winning a scholarship to Nebraska.

"Scorchers" and Snowmobilers

Sometimes the roads and trailways in the region become battlegrounds between various sporting enthusiasts. As early as 1899, Denverites worried about "scorchers," the packs of "hoodlums" who rode their bikes at high speeds on Denver's streets and bicycle paths. Similar debates continued in the city 100 years later, when runners, dog-walkers, and noncyclists complained about the speeds at which cyclists looped around urban parks as if in training for the Tour de France. At one time or another, some of the riders in the region were in training for big European races. Three of the six Americans to win stages at the Tour de France either live or have lived in Boulder. Andy Hampsten lives in Boulder today, while Davis Phinney was born there but resides in Italy. Current standout Tyler Hamilton attended the University of Colorado.

The loudest debates in the region about how the assorted playgrounds ought to be shared are between snowmobilers and those who believe the loud and fast machines have no place in the region's backcountry. Based on a decision made by Park Service officials in the Clinton administration, snowmobiling was to be banned in Yellowstone and Grand Teton National Parks beginning in the winter of 2003. Opponents of snowmobiles had argued for years that the machines were an environmental hazard. Yet after George W. Bush became president, he reversed the policy and directed that 35 percent more of the machines might enter the park. Some of Yellowstone's rangers, who were issued respirators due to the poor air quality in the snowmobile areas, may have disagreed with the policy. The entire controversy—which made headlines for years—was yet another reminder that the ways in which people played in the Rocky Mountains seemed like important news on a national scale and a cause worth fighting for or against.

Olympic Training Center

Several years after Colorado voters voted against holding the 1976 Winter Olympics in Denver—for fear that it would burden taxpayers and bring unwanted growth—the Olympic Training Center opened in Colorado Springs in 1978 on the grounds of a closed air force base. The center offers unique facilities—such as the International Center for Aquatic Research, which studies how humans operate at different speeds in a "swimming treadmill"—for more than 500 athletes at any given time. Weight rooms, gymnasiums, tracks, and training tables piled high with foods prepared by expert nutritionists, in addition to Colorado Springs' elevation (6,035 feet) and the thinner air that comes with it, make the center an ideal place for athletes in training. In fact, the lower levels of oxygen in the higher reaches of the Rockies make much of the region a desirable place to train for many endurance athletes. Once their lungs adapt to working out at the lower oxygen levels of high altitude, racing at lower altitudes where oxygen levels are greater means less strain on the body. Boulder, Colorado, is home to a number of world-class runners, cyclists, and triathletes. When runner Frank Shorter moved there in 1970—leading the migration—he said that he had done so because it was the only place in America over 5,000 feet that also had a synthetic indoor track. Although he claimed that Boulder was "not a magic place"—but simply a good place to train if one was willing to work hard—following his victory in the marathon at the 1972 Olympics, other athletes wanted to test Shorter's theories about magic. Today, dozens of elite athletes from around the world live and train in Boulder. Many of the runners compete each year in The Bolder Boulder, one of the nation's most popular ten-kilometer road races.

CONCLUSION: MAGIC, BEAUTY, POWER, AND A REGION AT PLAY

Some antisnowmobiling advocates may have thought "I told you so" when Rulon Gardner wrecked his machine in the Wyoming wilderness and lost a toe to frostbite in February 2002. For Gardner, there was more at stake than the image of recreational snowmobiling as dangerous; the loss of a toe put at risk his chance to defend a title as Olympic champion in a sport that required precisionlike balance, as well as brute strength. When Gardner—who had become America's favorite lovable country-boy-made-good on late night talk shows and in one of the ubiquitous milk-mustache magazine advertisements—returned to championship form a year

Frank Shorter runs at the 19th Bolder Boulder in Boulder, Colorado, on the 25th anniversary of his winning of the 1972 Gold Medal in the Munich Olympics Marathon, May 26, 1997. © Getty Images.

later, however, few were surprised. After all, Gardner was a *western* hero, simply a burlier version of another Rocky Mountain sports icon—Picabo Street—who overcame a ski wreck that mangled her leg to race again in the Olympics. When the Super G came to her adopted hometown of Park City, Utah, as part of the Salt Lake games in the winter of 2002, Street was rehabilitated and ready. By the time she strapped on her skis—nicknamed "the Earnies" for the late racecar driver Dale Earnhardt—Americans adored Street for her commercial smile, but they respected her for her guts, which, as a Rocky Mountain native, seemed to go hand in hand with her image as a carefree spirit sprung from a mountainside like a wildflower with wings. Gardner's and Street's images as resilient fun-hogs who, when it came time to do battle, were front and center, ready for action, had a long tradition in the Rockies. Americans have come to expect as much from a place that produced mountain men, rodeo riders, Native American basketball champions, rock-drillers, river rats, climbers, six-man football players, Tour de France stage winners, and more. To make use of what one man said of *A River Runs through It*, there was "a kind of magic" to the region, its people, and their games. The magic—a combination of beauty and power that awed—produced and produces heroes with hearts on scales comparable to the region's mountains and rivers. Where else other than the Rockies was it possible that a major college football player—Colorado's Jeremy Bloom, at five feet nine and 165 pounds—might also be an Olympian in a sport (mogul skiing) that had nothing in common with football other than rapid leg movement and a heavy ration of nerves? It also seemed appropriate to observers that Bloom had a little bit of the happy-go-lucky, lovable outlaw aspect of the mythical cowboy when he sued the NCAA as a freshman, then drafted a Student-Athlete's Bill of Rights as a sophomore that called for a reasonable approach to a by-law that did not allow him to have product sponsors in skiing, to work as a model, or to have a television show on MTV—all activities that seemed to have little or nothing to do with catching a football. Again, where else but the Rockies might another man climb into a remote and spectacular Utah canyon, get his hand stuck under a rock for days, then commonsensically amputate his arm (the other sure option was starvation) with a pocketknife, before walking calmly to a trail-head for help. When Aspen's Aron Ralston did this very thing in the spring of 2003, it was virtually impossible to imagine something similar happening anywhere else but the Rocky Mountain West. Finally, when blind climber Eric Weihenmayer stepped onto the summit of Mount Everest in 2001, it made perfect sense to the world that his journey without sight to the top of the world had started from a home in Golden, Colorado.

Americans have come to expect that, regardless of the sport, the mountains will always be a force in the Rocky Mountain region's games. Altitude and lack of oxygen are favorite topics of television sports announcers, visiting hunters, golfers, and distance runners in the area. The perception of the Rockies as a national playground is sometimes reflected through bizarre intersections of sport. The ski industry and airlines, for example, noted decades ago that any nationally televised Denver Broncos game—in which a snowstorm blew even briefly—resulted in increased reservations at resorts throughout the mountains. In addition, stories like those of basketball player Jonathan Takes Enemy, Rulon Gardner, Picabo Street, Jeremy Bloom, Aron Ralston, and Eric Weihenmayer—twenty-first-century champions of the region—help us understand images of the Rocky Mountain playground that have been persistent since the region's Native Americans and earliest Anglo explorers challenged themselves there. The Rockies are a playground of natural wonders and unparalleled tests—still the mythic frontier in the American mind—a magical place where men and women live up to the trials of life and to the challenges of the games that make for better living.

RESOURCE GUIDE

Printed Sources

Abbey, Edward. *Desert Solitaire: A Season in the Wilderness*. New York: McGraw-Hill, 1968.
———. *Hayduke Lives! A Novel*. Boston, MA: Little, Brown, 1990.
———. *The Monkey Wrench Gang*. Philadelphia, PA: Lippincott, 1975.

Clifford, Peggy. *To Aspen and Back: An American Journey*. New York: St. Martin's Press, 1980.

Conover, Ted. *Whiteout: Lost in Aspen*. New York: Random House, 1991.

Limerick, Patricia Nelson. *Legacy of Conquest: The Unbroken Past of the American West*. New York: W. W. Norton, 1987.

Nicholas, Liza, Elaine M. Bapis, and Thomas J. Harvey, eds., *Imagining the Big Open: Nature, Identity, and Play in the New West*. Salt Lake City: University of Utah Press, 2003.

Rothman, Hal. *Devil's Bargains: Tourism in the Twentieth-Century American West*. Lawrence: University Press of Kansas, 1998.

Street, Picabo, and Dana White. *Picabo: Nothing to Hide*. Chicago: Contemporary Books, 2002.

Watters, Ron. *Never Turn Back: The Life of Whitewater Pioneer Walt Blackadar*. Pocatello, ID: Great Rift Press, 1994.

Web Sites

Colorado Mountain Club
http://www.cmc.org/

National Collegiate Athletic Association
http://www.ncaa.org/

National Outdoor Leadership School
http://www.nols.edu/

National Park Service
http://www.nps.gov/

Outward Bound West
http://www.outwardboundwest.org/

Films

Aspen Extreme. Prod. Leonard Goldberg, 1993.

A River Runs through It. Prod. Robert Redford and Patrick Markey, 1992.

Fire on the Mountain: The Story of the Men of the 10th Mountain Division. Prod. George Gage and Beth Gage, 1995.

The River Wild. Prod. David Foster, 1994.

Museums

Colorado Ski Museum and Ski Hall of Fame
231 S. Frontage Road East
Vail, CO 81657
800-950-7410
http://www.skimuseum.net

Rocky Mountain Elk Foundation Wildlife Visitor Center
P. O. Box 8249
Missoula, MT 59807
800-CALL-ELK
http://www.rmef.org/

ProRodeo Hall of Fame and Museum of the American Cowboy
101 ProRodeo Drive

Colorado Springs, CO 80919
719-528-4764
http://www.prorodeo.org/hof

Mountain Bike Hall of Fame
P. O. Box 845
Crested Butte, CO 81224
800-454-4505
http://www.mtnbikehalloffame.com/

TIMELINE

60 million B.C.E.	Last period of flooding of the region by a vast inland sea stretching from the Arctic to the Caribbean.
11,000 B.C.E.	Evidence that early Paleo-Indians live on the Plains and in the Rockies along with mastodons and mammoths.
9000 B.C.E.	Increase in abundance of grasses and extensive herds of bison.
2000 B.C.E.	Bow and arrow technology revolutionizes Plains hunting.
1400s C.E.	Large areas of the Plains abandoned by native peoples due to increasingly arid summers, dust storms, and the like.
1540–1541	Francisco Vásquez de Coronado searches for the "Seven Cities of Cibola" on the Great Plains and is the first European to reach the Continental Divide.
1600s	Indian tribes of the southern Plains, including those in southern Colorado and Utah, acquire horses from Europeans.
Early 1700s	Indians of the northern Plains acquire the horse and firearms.
1743	Pierre and François de la Verendrye, French adventurers, sight the eastern reaches of the northern Rocky Mountains, possibly the Bighorns of Wyoming.
1803	President Thomas Jefferson signs the Louisiana Purchase, bringing the Rocky Mountain region into the United States.
1805	Meriwether Lewis and William Clark and the Corps of Discovery explore the region.
1806	John Colter leaves the Corps of Discovery early and heads back west. The fur trade begins in earnest.
1830	Jedediah Smith and William Sublette bring full-sized wagons as far as the Rocky Mountains.

1832	Painter George Catlin arrives at Fort Union and begins documenting the Indians of the northern Plains.
1834	Fort Hall, established in present Idaho, becomes hub for trails to western part of the United States. Also, first party of missionaries heading to Oregon passes through northern Rockies.
1841	Jesuit Father Pierre-Jean de Smet arrives in Montana's Bitterroot Valley and establishes St. Mary's Mission.
1843	Heavy traffic on the Oregon Trail during this "Year of the Great Migration."
1847	Members of the Church of Jesus Christ of Latter-day Saints (Mormons) begin to settle in Utah.
1849	California gold rush draws thousands of prospectors, some of whom pass through the Rockies.
	The precursor to the Mormon Tabernacle Choir founded (the Tabernacle itself was completed in 1867).
1850	Utah Territory created.
1858	Gold found at Dry Creek south of present Denver. Colorado gold rush ensues.
1859	Geologist J.S. Newberry makes first known mention of the ruins at Mesa Verde, in southwestern Colorado.
	John W. Illiff, the first cattle king of the Rocky Mountain region, arrives in Colorado.
c. 1860	First piano arrives in Colorado.
1860	Mullan Road opened between Fort Benton, Montana, and Walla Walla, Washington.
1861	Colorado Territory created.
1862	Gold discovered in the Boise Basin, Idaho, and at Grasshopper Creek in southwestern Montana. Thousands rush to the new goldfields.
1863	Idaho Territory created, including parts of present Montana and Wyoming.
1864	Montana Territory created.
1867	The Mormon Tabernacle completed in Salt Lake City, replacing the Old Tabernacle built in 1851.
1868	Wyoming Territory created.
1869	Golden spike driven at Promontory Point, Utah Territory, to mark completion of transcontinental railroad.
	Wyoming Territory passes first law in U.S. history granting women the right to vote.

1872	Yellowstone National Park, world's first national park, founded.
	President Ulysses S. Grant signs the General Mining Law to facilitate development of western mineral resources.
1876	Colorado achieves statehood.
	George Armstrong Custer and the 7th U.S. Cavalry lose their lives to an overwhelming force of Sioux and their allies on the Little Big Horn.
1880	Artist Charles M. Russell arrives in Montana, at the age of sixteen.
1883	Buffalo Bill Cody starts his Wild West Show, bringing Rocky Mountain culture to the rest of the world.
1885	White miners burn the Chinatown in Rock Springs, Wyoming, to the ground.
1886–1887	Severe winter devastates livestock industry on northern Plains.
1889	Montana and Idaho achieve statehood.
1890	Wyoming achieves statehood.
1893	Silver Panic brings economic depression to the region. The Artists Club of Denver, precursor to the Denver Art Museum, founded.
1896	Utah achieves statehood.
1899	Utah Arts Institute established, the first state arts agency in the nation, "the object being to advance the interest of the fine arts."
1901–1909	President Theodore Roosevelt adds 100 million new acres to the country's national forest system, more than half of them in the Rocky Mountain states.
1902	President Theodore Roosevelt commissions Joseph Henry Sharp to paint portraits of 200 Native American survivors of the Battle of the Little Big Horn. Architect Robert Reamer designs and builds Old Faithful Lodge, Yellowstone National Park. Mary Teasdel is first Utah artist to exhibit in the Paris Salon.
1904	Girl's basketball team from Fort Shaw Indian Boarding School, Montana, travels to the St. Louis World's Fair, where they are crowned Exposition champions.
1909	Congress passes the Enlarged Homestead Act, which brings thousands of aspiring farmers into the region.
1910	The first concert is held at the Red Rocks Amphitheatre near Denver (the modern stage was built in 1941).
1916	Montana first state to elect a woman, Jeanette Rankin, to U.S. Congress.

1919	Drought and a decline in farm prices bring an end to the homestead boom, launching twenty years of depression in the region.
c. 1920	Pioneering woman filmmaker Nell Shipman sets up a film studio, LionHead Lodge, at Priest Lake, Idaho.
1923	Denver Art Museum incorporated.
1927	Buffalo Bill Historical Center founded, Cody, Wyoming. Harold G. Merriam launches *The Frontier*, a journal devoted to the literature of the region.
1930s	The federal Civilian Conservation Corps performs erosion control and builds trails, roads, and structures throughout the Rockies while the Works Progress Administration funds literary and visual arts projects in the region.
1935	The Union Pacific Railroad opens the region's first world-class ski resort at Sun Valley, Idaho.
1936	D'Arcy McNickle publishes the novel *The Surrounded*, a seminal text in modern Native American literature.
1945	End of World War II brings influx of returning veterans and their families into the Rocky Mountain states.
1946	The ski resort at Aspen, Colorado, opens the world's longest chairlift.
1947	A. B. Guthrie, Jr., publishes the fur trade novel *The Big Sky*.
1951	Founding of International Design Conference, Aspen, Colorado, and Archie Bray Foundation for the Ceramic Arts, Helena, Montana.
1953	Film version of *Shane* released, with Academy Award–winning script by A. B. Guthrie, Jr. Dorothy Johnson publishes *Indian Country*, which includes the classic stories "The Man Who Shot Liberty Valance" and "A Man Called Horse."
	Weiser, Idaho, hosts the first National Oldtime Fiddlers Contest.
1955	At the Aspen Institute, Herbert Bayer creates his *Grass Mound*, thought to be among the first works of contemporary Environmental Art anywhere.
1956	Architect I. M. Pei designs Denver's Mile High Center. Environmentalists successfully defeat a proposal to dam Colorado's Green River.
1958	The United States Air Force Academy opens in Colorado Springs.
1962	At the peak of the uranium boom, Utah generates $25 million worth of uranium.
1964	Poet Richard Hugo begins teaching at the University of Montana.

1965	Publication of Ed Dorn's long poem "Idaho Out" in his collection *Geography*.
1970	Artist Robert Smithson completes his *Spiral Jetty*, 1,500 feet of limestone and black basalt curling into the Great Salt Lake. Painter Harry Jackson, having abandoned Abstract Expressionism and embraced Western Realism, moves full-time to Wyoming.
1974	Publication of *Winter in the Blood* by Blackfeet–Gros Ventre author James Welch.
	Arthur Penn's *Little Big Man* takes the film western out of its mythical mode and places it in history.
1976	Publication of Norman Maclean's *A River Runs through It and Other Stories*.
	Hmong immigrants arrive in western Montana as refugees from the conflict in Vietnam and Laos.
1981	Robert Redford founds Sundance Film Institute, Park City, Utah.
1988	The worst forest fires in the history of Yellowstone National Park engulf 1.4 million acres in and around the park.
1991	Utah author Terry Tempest Williams publishes *Refuge*, a meditation on 1950s nuclear tests and her mother's death from breast cancer.
1995	The Northern Rocky Mountain Wolf Recovery Team reintroduces wild wolves to Yellowstone National Park, after a sixty-year absence.
2000	Nearly 123,000 separate forest fires, several of the largest and most catastrophic in Idaho and western Montana, burn 8.5 million acres of forest. In a normal year, fires burn only 3.8 million acres in the United States.
2002	Salt Lake City, Utah, hosts Winter Olympics.
2003	Construction begins on 146,000-square-foot addition to Denver Art Museum; to be completed in 2006, the addition is designed by Daniel Libeskind, the architect whose design was selected for the new World Trade Center, New York City.
2004	Drought continues to plague the Rocky Mountain region.

NOTES

Introduction

1. Quoted in David M. Wrobel and Michael C. Steiner, *Many Wests: Place, Culture, and Regional Identity* (Lawrence: University Press of Kansas, 1997), v.

2. See Gary Jahrig, "Economics 101: Expert Helps Leaders Understand State's Diverse Economy," *Research View* (Winter 2003), http://www.umt.edu/urelations/rview/winter2003/economic.htm (accessed May 5, 2004).

3. Palmer Hoyt, foreword to Elvon L. Howe, ed., *Rocky Mountain Empire* (Garden City, NY: Doubleday, 1950), vii.

4. Wallace Stegner, *The American West as Living Space* (Ann Arbor: University of Michigan Press, 1987), 79.

Architecture

1. Peter Nabokov and Robert Easton, *Native American Architecture* (New York: Oxford University Press, 1989), 356–357.

2. *New York Times*, July 2, 1950.

3. The tipi description is by Edwin Denig, cited in Carroll V. West, *A Traveler's Companion to Montana History* (Helena: Montana Historical Society Press, 1986), 41.

4. Dora P. Crouch, Daniel J. Garr, and Axel I. Mundigo, *Spanish City Planning in North America* (Cambridge, MA: MIT Press, 1982), 2.

5. Field as quoted in Jerry C. Dunn, Jr., *The Smithsonian Guide to Historic America: Rocky Mountain States* (New York: Stewart, Tabori & Chang, 1989), 79.

6. Eileen F. Starr, *Architecture in the Cowboy State, 1849–1940: A Guide* (Glendo, WY: High Plains Press, 1992), 24–31.

7. Terry G. Jordan, Jon T. Kilpinen, and Charles F. Gritzner, *The Mountain West: Interpreting the Folk Landscape* (Baltimore, MD: Johns Hopkins University Press, 1997), 17.

8. Duane A. Smith, *Rocky Mountain West: Colorado, Wyoming, & Montana, 1859–1915* (Albuquerque, NM: University of New Mexico Press, 1992), 26.

9. Jennifer Attebery, *Building Idaho: An Architectural History* (Moscow, ID: University of Idaho Press, 1991), 62.

10. Francine Haber, Kenneth R. Fuller, and David N. Wetzel, *Robert S. Roeschlaub: Architect of the Emerging West, 1843–1923* (Denver: Colorado Historical Society, 1988), 1.

11. David Leavengood, "A Sense of Shelter: Robert C. Reamer in Yellowstone National Park," *Pacific Historical Review* 54 (November 1985): 502.

12. Mark Fiege, *Irrigated Eden: The Making of an Agricultural Landscape in the American West* (Seattle: University of Washington Press, 1999), especially 115–179.

13. I. D. O'Donnell, *Better Business, Better Farming, Better Living: Hints from a Practical Farmer* (Washington, DC: Government Printing Office, 1918), 7.

14. Richard Guy Wilson, "Machine-Age Iconography in the American West: The Design of Hoover Dam," *Pacific Historical Review* 54 (November 1985): 466–467.

15. Stewart Brand, *How Buildings Learn: What Happens After They're Built* (New York: Penguin Books, 1994), 92.

16. Gillian Klucas, "High Stakes Game in Colorado," *Preservation* 55 (September/October 2003), 46–51.

Art

1. Quoted in Wendy McClure, "'The Unambiguous West': Town Morphology as a Factor in Sustaining Regional Identity," in *Borderlands: Contested Terrain*, Proceedings of the 2001 Western Region ACSA (Association of Collegiate Schools of Architecture) Conference (Bozeman: Montana State University, 2001), 159.

2. James D. Keyser and Michael A. Klassen, *Plains Indian Rock Art* (Seattle: University of Washington Press, 2001), ix–x. See also A. Dudley Gardner, *Architecture of the Ancient Ones* (Salt Lake City, UT: Gibbs-Smith Publisher, 2000), which features rock art from the Great Basin.

3. John C. Ewers, "Painted Tipis of the Blackfeet Indians," 1975, http://libmuse.msu.montana.edu/epubs/nadb/ewers-doc.html (accessed June 8, 2004).

4. Gordon McConnell, *Balancing Accounts: Crow and Gros Ventre Indian Ledger Art* (Clearmont, WY: Ucross Foundation Gallery, 2002), 3.

5. James Clifford, "Of Other Peoples: Beyond the 'Salvage Paradigm,'" in *Discussions in Contemporary Culture*, ed. Hal Foster (Seattle, WA: Bay Press, 1987), 128. See also Ralph T. Coe, *Lost and Found Traditions: Native American Art 1965–1985* (Seattle: University of Washington Press; New York: American Federation of Arts, 1986).

6. George Catlin, *North American Indians*, ed. Peter Matthiessen (New York: Viking, 1989), vii, 3, 18.

7. William H. Goetzmann, introduction to *Karl Bodmer's America* (Omaha: Joslyn Art Museum; Lincoln: University of Nebraska Press, 1984), 22.

8. Nancy K. Anderson, *Thomas Moran* (New Haven, CT: Yale University Press, 1998), 51.

9. Joel Snyder, *American Frontiers: The Photographs of Timothy H. O'Sullivan, 1867–1874* (Millerton, NY: Aperture, 1981), 37.

10. Quoted in Brian W. Dippie, *Looking at Russell* (Fort Worth, TX: Amon Carter Museum, 1987), 94.

11. See Larry Len Peterson, *L. A. Huffman: Photographer of the American West* (Tucson, AZ: Settlers West Galleries, 2003).

12. Erika Doss, "'I *Must* Paint': Women Artists of the Rocky Mountain Region," in *Independent Spirits: Women Painters of the American West, 1890–1945*, ed. Patricia Trenton (Berkeley: University of California Press, 1995), 216.

13. Quoted in Doss, ibid., 222.

14. Krisztina Passuth, *Moholy-Nagy* (New York: Thames and Hudson, 1985), 205–206.

15. Rudy Autio, interview by Chere Jiusto and Rick Newby, Missoula, MT, November 3, 1998, Archie Bray Foundation for the Ceramic Arts Archives, Helena, MT.

16. Rose Slivka, "The Artist and His Work: Risk and Revelation," in *The Art of Peter Voulkos*, by Rose Slivka and Karen Tsujimoto (Oakland, CA: Oakland Museum, 1995), 39.

17. Quoted in Gordon McConnell, *The Montana Collection* (Billings, MT: Yellowstone Art Museum, 1998), 35.

18. Bill Stockton, "Paris 1948—The End of an Era," in *The Arts in Montana*, ed. H. G. Merriam (Missoula, MT: Mountain Press Publishing, 1977), 7.

19. Gene Thornton, *Harry Jackson: A Retrospective Exhibition* (Cody, WY: Buffalo Bill Historical Center, 1981), 9.

20. Harry Jackson, "Harry Jackson Celebrated," *Points West Online*, Fall 1999, Buffalo Bill Historical Center, http://www.bbhc.org/pointsWest/PWArticle.cfm?ArticleID=10 (accessed June 8, 2004).

21. Trudy McMurrin, ed., *Utah, State of the Arts* (Ogden, UT: Meridian International, 1993), 136.

22. Mary Meigs Atwater, *Weaving a Life: The Story of Mary Meigs Atwater* (Loveland, CO: Interweave Press, 1992), 132.

23. Tom Trusky, "Autism, Physiognomy & Letter Forms: The Faces of James Castle," *Journal of Artists' Books* 18 (Fall 2002): 3.

Ecology and Environment

1. Robert V. Hine and John Mack Faragher, *The American West: A New Interpretive History* (New Haven, CT: Yale University Press, 2000), 150–151.

2. Richard White, "Animals and Enterprise," in *The Oxford History of the American West*, ed. Clyde A. Milner II, Carol A. O'Connor, and Martha A. Sandweiss (New York: Oxford University Press, 1994), 244–245.

3. Ibid., 253–254.

4. John Perry, "America's Grasslands: A History of Our Common Sod," http://www.terrain.org/articles/5/perry.htm (accessed June 22, 2004); and The Nature Conservancy, "The Status of Biodiversity in the Great Plains," http://www.greatplains.org/resource/biodiver/biostat/ecologic.htm (accessed June 22, 2004).

5. Donald Worster, *Nature's Economy: A History of Ecological Ideas* (New York: Cambridge University Press, 1994), 221–255.

6. Quote in Chris J. Magoc, *Yellowstone: The Creation and Selling of an American Landscape* (Albuquerque: University of New Mexico Press, 1999), 42.

7. Jim Robbins, *Last Refuge: The Environmental Showdown in the American West* (New York: HarperCollins, 1994), 44–45.

8. Ibid., 55–56.

9. Robert McClure and Andrew Schneider, "More Than a Century of Mining Has Left the West Deeply Scarred," *Seattle Post-Intelligencer*, June 12, 2001, 5–7; and Thomas J. Stohlgren, U.S. Geological Survey, "Rocky Mountains," http://biology.usgs.gov/s+t/SNT/noframe/wm146.htm (accessed June 22, 2004).

10. Quoted in Anthony N. Penna, *Nature's Bounty: Historical and Modern Environmental Perspectives* (Armonk, NY: M. E. Sharpe, 1999), 44.

11. Paul W. Hirt, *A Conspiracy of Optimism: Management of National Forests since World War II* (Lincoln: University of Nebraska Press, 1994).

12. Douglas W. Smith, "Wolf Behavior: Learning to Love in Life or Death Situations," in *Encyclopedia of Animal Behavior*, ed. Marc Beaoff (Westport, CT: Greenwood Press, forthcoming).

13. Raymond Wheeler, "The Boom," in *Reopening the Western Frontier*, ed. Ed Marston (Washington, DC: Island Press, 1994), 139–140; and Jerry D. Spangler and Donna Kemp Spangler, "Uranium Mining Left a Legacy of Death," *Deseret News*, February 13, 2001, 11–12.

14. Stephen Hendricks, "Small Wonder," *Sierra* (January–February 2004): 18–19.

15. Wheeler, "The Boom," 23–24.

16. See, for example, William Norman Grigg, "Sunset on the West?" http://www.the-newamerican.com/tna/1996/vo12no03/vo12no03_sunset_west.htm (accessed June 22, 2004); and Tim Findley, "Nature's Landlord," *Range Magazine* (Spring 2003): 1–24.

17. Thomas J. Lyon, "The Literary West," in *The Oxford History of the American West*, ed. Clyde A. Milner II, Carol A. O'Connor, and Martha A. Sandweiss (New York: Oxford University Press, 1994), 712.

Ethnicity

1. The literature on ethnicity in the West has grown by leaps and bounds since the end of World War II. By far the greatest number of works center around Native Americans, but currently books describing the lives of Basques, Chinese, Japanese, and other minority groups have expanded the body of data we have about ethnic groups in the region. The most significant change in the literature comes in the form of native-born members of minority groups writing their own accounts of what they have experienced. Native writers describing their past in both histories and novels have greatly expanded understanding of ethnic groups' lives in the mountain West.

2. John E. Farley, *Majority-Minority Relations*, 4th ed. (Upper Saddle River, NJ: Prentice Hall, 2000), 526. The definition of *ethnicity* is complex. So here we are defining an ethnic group as distinct based on "social or cultural characteristics such as nationality, language and religion." We also follow the definition used by David Gradwohl and the theoretical stance of George DeVos, "Ethnic Pluralism: Conflict and Accommodation," in *Ethnic Identity: Cultural Continuities and Change*, ed. George DeVos and Lola Romanucci-Ross (Palo Alto, CA: Mayfield Publishing, 1975), 5–41.

See David Mayer Gradwohl, "Intra-Group Diversity in Midwest American Jewish Cemeteries: An Ethnoarchaeological Perspective," in *Archaeology of Eastern North America: Papers in Honor of Stephen Williams*, ed. James B. Stoltman (Jackson: Archaeological Report No. 25, Mississippi Department of Archives and History, 1993), 364–382.

For excellent discussions of different ethnic groups in the regions, see Liping Zhu, *A Chinaman's Chance: The Chinese on the Rocky Mountain Mining Frontier* (Niwot: University of Colorado Press, 1997); John Bieter and Mark Bieter, *An Enduring Legacy: The Story of Basques in Idaho* (Reno: University of Nevada Press, 2000); Laura Wilson, *Hutterites of Montana* (New Haven, CT: Yale University Press, 2000); Henry E. Stamos IV, *People of the Wind River: The Eastern Shoshones, 1825–1900* (Norman: University of Oklahoma Press, 1999); Virginia McConnell Simmons, *The Ute Indians of Utah, Colorado, and New Mexico* (Niwot: University of Colorado Press, 2000); Helen Z. Papanikolas, *The Peoples of Utah* (Salt Lake City: Utah State Historical Society, 1981). See also Paula Petrik, *No Step Backward: Women and Family on the Rocky Mountain Mining Frontier, Helena, Montana, 1865–1900* (Helena: Montana Historical Society Press, 1987); Sara Deutsch, *No Separate Refuge: Culture, Class, and Gender on an Anglo-Hispanic Frontier in the American Southwest, 1880–1940* (New York: Oxford University Press, 1987); Quintard Taylor, *In Search of the Racial Frontier: African Americans in the American West, 1990* (New York: W.W. Norton, 1999); Quintard Taylor and Shirley Ann Wilson Moore, eds., *African American Women Confront the West: 1600–2000* (Norman: University of Oklahoma Press, 2003); Peter Iverson, *Dine: A History of the Navajos* (Albuquerque: University of New Mexico Press, 2002); and Roger Daniels, *Asian America: Chinese and Japanese in the United States since 1850* (Seattle: University of Washington Press, 1988).

3. Alan D. McMillan, *Native Peoples, and Cultures of Canada* (Vancouver: Douglas and McIntryre, 1988), 273–278. All quotes regarding the Métis come from McMillan's *Native Peoples*. This excellent work is often overlooked but provides great insight into the plains and Rockies of the United States and Canada.

4. Ibid.

5. Jacquelyn Peterson and Jennifer S. H. Brown, eds., *The New Peoples: Being and Becoming Métis in North America* (Winnipeg: University of Manitoba Press, 1985), 119–127.

6. William Loren Kutz, *The Black West*, 3rd ed., rev. and expanded (Seattle, WA: Open Hand Publishing, 1987), 11–13.

7. W. Sherman Savage, *Blacks in the West* (Westport, CT: Greenwood Press, 1976), 7–9. Savage notes that possibly York lived with the Crows in the 1830s (9).

8. Howard Palmer and Tamara Palmer, *Peoples of Alberta: Portraits of Cultural Diversity* (Saskatoon, Saskatchewan: Western Producer Prairie Book, 1985), 108–109.

9. T. M. Devine, ed., *Scottish Emigration and Scottish Society: Proceedings of the Scottish Historical Studies Seminar University of Strathelyde* (Edinburgh: John Donald Publishers Ltd., 1992), 15–17.

10. R. A. Cage, ed., *The Scots Abroad: Labor, Capital, Enterprise, 1750–1914* (London: Croom Helm, 1985), 94–95.

11. Zhu, *A Chinaman's Chance: The Chinese on the Rocky Mountain Mining Frontier*, 27–28.

12. *New York Times*, September 23, 1883, 6.

13. Juanita Brooks, *History of the Jews in Utah and Idaho* (Salt Lake City, UT: Western Epics, 1973), 1, 2–3, 13.

14. Ibid., 14, 54, 55.

15. David M. Emmons, *The Butte Irish: Class and Ethnicity in an American Mining Town, 1875–1925* (Urbana: University of Illinois Press, 1989).

16. Matshen Frye Jacobson, *Special Sorrows: The Diasporic Imagination of Irish, Polish, and Jewish Immigrants in the United States* (Cambridge, MA: Harvard University Press, 1995), 24.

17. *New York Times*, September 18, 1903, 3.

18. U.S. Census Bureau, *Abstract of the Twelfth Census of the United States: 1900* (Washington, DC: Government Printing Office, 1904), 56–63.

19. Francìe M. Berg, *Ethnic Heritage in North Dakota* (Hettinger, ND: Attiyeh Foundation, 1983), 95.

20. Ibid., 100, 101.

21. D. Jerome Tweton and Theodore B. Jelliff, *North Dakota: The Heritage of a People* (Fargo: North Dakota Institute for Regional Studies, 1976), 114–115.

22. American Historical Society of Germans from Russia, "Villages," http://www.ahsgr.org/villages.htm (accessed June 8, 2004).

23. Royden K. Loewen, *Family, Church, and Market: A Mennonite Community in the Old and New Worlds, 1850–1930* (Urbana: University of Illinois Press, 1993), 71, 118.

24. Palmer and Palmer, *Peoples of Alberta*, 349–351, 354; Wilson, *Hutterites of Montana*.

25. Palmer and Palmer, *Peoples of Alberta*, 348, 355–356.

26. Wilson, *Hutterites of Montana*. Wilson's work is the primary source for the section on Hutterites.

27. John Bieter and Mark Bieter, *An Enduring Legacy. The Story of Basques in Idaho* (Reno: University of Nevada Press, 2000), 26.

28. Louis James Cononelos, "Greek Immigrant Labor" (master's thesis, University of Utah, 1979), 117–119, 120.

29. Department of Commerce, *Statistical Abstract of the U.S. 1913* (Washington, DC: Government Printing Office, 1914), 49.

30. Joseph Stipanovich, "The South Slav Experience in Utah" (master's thesis, University of Utah, 1973).

31. Amanda L. DeLucia, "Tyrolean-Italian Heritage in West," Weber, UT (master's thesis, University of Utah, 1991), 40.

32. *Rock Springs Rocket [Miner]*, December 13, 1918, 1. This is a Friday the 13th editorial.

33. Lynda F. Dickson, "African American Women's Club in Denver, 1890–1920," in *Peoples of Color in the American West*, ed. Sucheng Chan, Douglas Henry Daniels, Murio T. Garcia, and Terry P. Wilson (Lexington, MA: D. C. Heath, 1994), 226.

34. Benny Joseph Andres, "Power and Control in Imperial Valley, California: Nature, Agribusiness, Labor and Race Relations, 1900–1940" (Ph.D. diss., University of New Mexico, 2003); Ronald T. Takaki, *Strangers from a Different Shore: A History of Asian Americans* (Boston: Little, Brown, 1989); H. Brett Melendy, *Asians in America: Filipinos, Koreans, and East Indians* (Boston: Twayne, 1977). Andres' efforts have provided insight into the historic and present nature of Filipino immigration into the United States. Dr. Andres graciously provided the background data regarding Filipinos in the United States.

35. Mee Her, Ge Lor, Sirathra Som, and Salouth Soman, "Hmong and Cambodian Voices, 1970s–Present," in *Peoples of Color in the American West*, ed. Sucheng Chan, Douglas Henry Daniels, Murio T. Garcia, and Terry P. Wilson (Lexington, MA: D. C. Heath, 1994), 576.

36. Jeffrey Holt Bork, "Income and Employment Status of the Navajo Indians in San Juan County, Utah" (master's thesis, University of Utah, 1973), 1–2; *United States Census 2000*, Utah; Elizabeth A. Brandt, "The Navajo Area Student Dropout Study: Findings and Implications," *Journal of American Indian Education* 31.2 (January 1992).

Fashion

1. Roland Barthes, *The Fashion System*, trans. Matthew Ward and Richard Howard (New York: Hill and Wang, 1983), 247.

2. Josephine Paterek, *Encyclopedia of American Indian Costume* (Denver: ABC-CLIO, 1994), 84.

3. Robert J. Moore and Michael Haynes, *Tailor Made, Trail Worn: Army Life, Clothing, & Weapons of the Corps of Discovery* (Helena, MT: Farcountry Press, 2003).

4. Ibid.

5. Bernard DeVoto, *Across the Wide Missouri* (1997; Boston: Houghton Mifflin Company, 1975), 256–257.

6. Osborne Russell, *Journal of a Trapper*, ed. Aubrey L. Haines (1955; Lincoln: University of Nebraska Press, 1965), 82–83.

7. Quoted in Sherry Farrell Racette, "Beads, Silk and Quills: The Clothing and Decorative Arts of the Métis," in *Métis Legacy: A Métis Historiography and Annotated Bibliography*, ed. Lawrence J. Barkwell, Leah Dorion, and Darren R. Préfontaine (Winnipeg, Manitoba: Pemmican Publications, 2001), 181.

8. Quoted in "The Métis Sash," Métis Culture and Heritage Resource Centre, http://www.metisresourcecentre.mb.ca/history/sash.htm.

9. Nicholas C.P. Vrooman, "Charlie's Sash: The Métis and Montana Cattle Culture," *Russell's West. The C.M. Russell Museum Magazine* 8.2 (2001): 3–10.

10. David Michael Delo, *Peddler and Post Traders: The Army Sutler on the Frontier* (Salt Lake City: University of Utah Press, 1992).

11. Samuel Finley Blythe Diary, *Journeys to the Land of Gold: Emigrant Diaries from the Bozeman Trail, 1863–1866* (Helena: Montana Historical Society Press, 2000), 2: 642; Ellen Gordon Fletcher Diary and Letters, *Journeys to the Land of Gold*, 2: 491.

12. Jerry Dolph, *Fire in the Hole: The Untold Story of Hardrock Miners* (Pullman: Washington State University Press, 1994), 10.

13. Chuck Kaparich, "How Copper Killed Forty Horses (A History of the Columbia Garden Carousels)," http://www.carousels.com/copper.htm (accessed June 22, 2004).

14. C.J. Bishko, "The Peninsular Background of Latin American Cattle Ranching," *Hispanic American Historical Review* 32.4 (November 1952): 491–515.

15. George S. Cole, *A Complete Dictionary of Dry Goods* (Chicago: J.B. Herring Publishing, 1894), 191.

16. John K. Rollinson, *Pony Trails in Wyoming* (1941; Lincoln: University of Nebraska Press, 1968), 33.

17. John R. Barrows, *U-Bet: A Greenhorn in Montana* (1934; Lincoln: University of Nebraska Press, 1990), 153.

18. Ibid., 153.

19. Quoted in Dianna Serra Cary, *The Hollywood Posse* (Boston, MA: Houghton Mifflin, 1975), 17.

20. Norman Maclean, "Logging and Pimping and 'Your Pal Jim,'" in *A River Runs through It and Other Stories* (Chicago: University of Chicago Press, 1976), 108, 109–110.

21. "Dress and Appearance," in *For the Strength of Youth*, The Church of Jesus Christ of Latter-day Saints Web site, http://library.lds.org/ (accessed June 22, 2004).

22. Ralph Beer, *In These Hills* (Lincoln: University of Nebraska Press, 2003), 127.

23. Quoted in "Ralph Lauren: Fashion, Furnishings Titan Gets Contrasting Portrayals in New Bios," *Denver Post*, January 21, 2003.

24. Suzanne S. Brown, "A Space to Create: Fashion Designer Finds Her Niche in LoDo Loft," *Denver Post*, December 8, 2002.

25. Suavecito's Apparel Co: The World's Leader in Zoot Suits and Latino Fashion Web site, http://www.suavecito.com/ (accessed June 23, 2004).

26. Epic Adventures Web site, http://www.epicadventures.com/trips/chaco-sandals-shoes-2 shtml (accessed June 23, 2004); Mountain Sprouts Web site, http://www.mountainsprouts.com/about.php?PHPSESSID=1a380be51d44dbb1112c84d563a8b10a (accessed June 23, 2004).

Film and Theater

1. Oscar Wilde, *Impressions of America* (1882), http://www.catbirdpress.com/firstchaps/usa.pdf; quoted in Bryan Zug, "Jaffa Brothers built one of the first auditoriums in Trinidad," http://www.trinidadco com/WalkingTour/OperaHouse.asp.

2. Leslie Noelle Sullivan, "On the Western Stage: Theatre in Montana, 1880–1920." (master's thesis, University of New Mexico, 1990).

3. Edward Buscombe, ed., *The BFI Companion to the Western* (New York: Atheneum, 1988).

4. David Hamilton Murdoch, *The American West: The Invention of a Myth* (Reno: University of Nevada Press, 2001), 24.

5. Ron Engle, Felicia Hardison Londré, and Daniel J. Watermeier, eds., *Shakespeare Companies and Festivals: An International Guide* (Westport, CT: Greenwood Press, 1995).

6. David Pace, "Behind the Mormon Curtain," *American Theatre*, 13, no. 3 (March 1996): 49.

7. Scott Simmon, *The Invention of the Western Film: A Cultural History of the Genre's First Half Century* (Cambridge: Cambridge University Press, 2003), 8.

8. Raymond Fielding, "Hale's Tours: Ultrarealism in the Pre-1910 Motion Picture," in *Film Before Griffith*, ed. Raymond Fielding (Berkeley: University of California Press, 1983), 127.

9. Simmon, *Invention of the Western Film*, 48.

10. Buscombe, *BFI Companion*, 55.

11. Ibid., 344.

12. Murdoch, *American West*, 119.

Folklore

1. Barre Toelken, introduction to Barry Holstun Lopez, *Giving Birth to Thunder, Sleeping with His Daughter* (New York: Avon, 1977).

2. Ibid., 83.

3. Ibid., 7.

4. Lawrence J. Barkwell, Leah Dorion, and Darren R. Préfontaine, eds., *Métis Legacy: A Métis Historiography and Annotated Bibliography* (Winnipeg, Manitoba: Pemmican Publications, 2001), 1.

5. Megan Hiller, Rick Newby, Elaine Peterson, and Alexandra Swaney, *An Ornery Bunch: Tales and Anecdotes Collected by the W.P.A. Montana Writers' Project* (Guilford, CT: TwoDot, 1999), 177.

6. W. C. Jameson, *Buried Treasures of the Rocky Mountain West* (Little Rock, AR: August House, 1993), 182.

7. Sister M. Alfreda Elsensohn, *Idaho Chinese Lore* (Cottonwood: Idaho Corporation of Benedictine Sisters, 1970), 41.

8. Robert B. Betts, *Along the Ramparts of the Tetons: The Saga of Jackson Hole, Wyoming* (Niwot: University Press of Colorado, 1978), 221.

9. Kenneth Jessen, *Bizarre Colorado* (Loveland: J. V. Publications, 1994), 141–142.

10. C. W. Sullivan III, "Jesse James: An American Outlaw," in *Worldviews and the American West: The Life of the Place Itself*, ed. Polly Stewart, Steven Siporin, C. W. Sullivan III, and Suzie Jones (Logan: Utah State University Press, 2001), 108.

11. Betts, *Along the Ramparts of the Tetons*, 165.

12. Collected by Ronda Walker Weaver, n.d., collection of Ronda Walker Weaver and Vern H. Petersen family, used by permission.

13. Collected by Jeff Bake, "Have I Got One for You, Deer Hunting Folklore" (Wilson Folklore Archives, L. Tom Perry Special Collections, Brigham Young University, 1991).

14. Collected by Lezlie Andrus, "Deer Hunting: The Truest Tall Tales" (Wilson Folklore Archives, L. Tom Perry Special Collections, Brigham Young University, 1986).

15. Ibid.

16. Bonnie Marie Vance, "The Gift of Water Witching" (Wilson Folklore Archives, L. Tom Perry Special Collections, Brigham Young University, 1979), 7.

17. Collected by Marianne Day, "Potato Harvest Traditions" (Wilson Folklore Archives, L. Tom Perry Special Collections, Brigham Young University, 1995), 12.

18. Vernal H. Jensen, "Untitled," unpublished, collection of Alice Jensen Walker and Vernal H. Jensen family, used by permission.

19. Colen H. Sweeten, Jr., "Rural Hospitality," *Back at the Ranch* (Springville, UT: Colen H. Sweeten, Jr., 1992); poem used by permission.

20. Marie W. Smith, "If," *New Cowboy Poetry: A Contemporary Gathering*, ed. Hal Cannon (Salt Lake City, UT: Gibbs-Smith, 1990), 137.

21. Collected by Emely Arroyo, "Hispanic Legends La Llorona El Chupacabra" (Wilson Folklore Archives, L. Tom Perry Special Collections, Brigham Young University, 1998).

22. Collected by Shazzelma Murray and Susan Richards, "Folklife and Material Culture of Iosepa Colony" (Wilson Folklore Archives, L. Tom Perry Special Collections, Brigham Young University, 1986).

23. Ibid.

Food

1. National Oceanic and Atmospheric Administration, *Climates of the States*, 3rd ed. (Detroit, MI: Gale Research, 1985), 866.

2. Jeff Hart, *Montana Native Plants and Early Peoples* (Helena: Montana Historical Society Press, 1992), 11.

3. Ibid., 50.

4. These are Buckskin Charlie's words, quoted in William Wroth, *Ute Indian Arts and Culture: From Prehistory to the New Millennium* (Colorado Springs, CO: Colorado Springs Fine Arts Center, 2002), 79.

5. Hamblin is quoted in *Nuwuvi: A Southern Paiute History* (Reno, NV: Inter-Tribal Council of Nevada, 1976), 82.

6. Quoted in Rodney Frey's book produced in cooperation with the Coeur d'Alene tribe, *Landscape Traveled by Coyote and Crane: The World of the Schitsu'umsh (Coeur d'Alene) Indians* (Seattle: University of Washington Press, 2001), 152.

7. Quoted in Mary Gunderson, *The Food Journals of Lewis and Clark: Recipes for an Expedition* (Yankton, SD: History Cooks, 2003), 109.

8. Osborne Russell, *Journal of a Trapper* (Lincoln: University of Nebraska Press, 1953), 64, 48; the comment about the Fremont expedition's Christmas dinner is cited in Virginia McConnell Simmons, *The San Luis Valley: Land of the Six-Armed Cross* (Boulder, CO: Pruett Publishing, 1999), 51.

9. Jacqueline Williams, *Wagon Wheel Kitchens: Food on the Oregon Trail* (Lawrence: University of Kansas Press, 1993), 91.

10. Cowden is quoted in Jim Robbins, *Last Refuge: The Environmental Showdown in Yellowstone and the American West* (New York: William Morrow, 1993), 180.

11. Daughters of Utah Pioneers, *The Mormon Pioneer Cookbook* (Salt Lake City, UT: Northwest Publishing, 1995), xiii.

12. Joseph R. Conlin, *Bacon, Beans, and Galatines: Food and Foodways on the Western Mining Frontier* (Reno: University of Nevada Press, 1986), 105.

13. Elinor Pruitt Stewart, *Letters of a Woman Homesteader* (Lincoln: University of Nebraska Press, 1961), 165.

14. The commissioner is cited in Duane A. Smith, *Rocky Mountain West: Colorado, Wyoming, and Montana 1859–1915* (Albuquerque: University of New Mexico Press, 1992), 40; the Burlington promoter in Carl Ubbelohde, *A Colorado History* (Boulder, CO: Pruett Publishing, 1972), 202.

15. Carlos Schwantes, *In Mountain Shadows: A History of Idaho* (Lincoln: University of Nebraska Press, 1991), 97.

16. Annie Pike Greenwood, *We Sagebrush Folks* (Moscow: University of Idaho Press, 2003), 174.

17. Quoted in Daniel McCool, *Native Waters: Contemporary Indian Water Settlements and the Second Treaty Era* (Tucson: University of Arizona Press, 2002), 21.

18. Robbins, *Last Refuge*, 227.

Language

1. All population numbers for Native American language speakers are from the 1990 census as reported by the Ethnologue Web site, unless noted otherwise: http://www.ethnologue.com/; SIL stands for Summer Institute of Linguistics, which runs the Ethnologue Web site.

2. For more on these programs and the challenges facing them, see William L. Leap, *American Indian English* (Salt Lake City: University of Utah Press, 1993).

3. See, for example, William Labov, "The Three Dialects of English," in *New Ways of Analyzing Sound Change*, ed. Penelope Eckert (New York: Academic Press, 1991), 1–44.

4. See, for example, Allan Metcalf, *How We Talk: American Regional English Today* (Boston, MA: Houghton Mifflin, 2000).

5. See, for example, Labov, "The Three Dialects of English."

6. As noted in Metcalf, *How We Talk: American Regional English Today*.

7. See Marjorie Kimmerle, Raven I. McDavid, Jr., and Virginia G. McDavid, "Problems of Linguistic Geography in the Rocky Mountain Area," *Western Humanities Review* 5 (1951): 249–264.

8. See, for example, Clyde Thomas Hankey, "A Colorado Word Geography" (Ph.D. diss., University of Michigan, 1960).

9. For more, see Albert H. Marckwardt, *American English* (Oxford: Oxford University Press, 1958).

10. See Marjorie Kimmerle, "Bum, Poddy, or Penco," *Colorado Quarterly* 1 (1952): 87–97, for a detailed discussion of the proposed etymology of *penco* and the geographic distribution of variants denoting orphaned lambs.

11. See Marianna Di Paolo, "Propredicate *Do* in the English of the Intermountain West," *American Speech* 68 (1993): 339–356.

12. For a more in-depth analysis on this topic, see Marjorie M. Kimmerle, "The Influence of Locale and Human Activity on Some Words in Colorado," *American Speech* 25 (1950): 161–167; and Clyde T. Hankey, "Semantic Features and Eastern Relics in Colorado Dialect," *American Speech* 36 (1961): 266–270.

13. See Hankey, "A Colorado Word Geography."

Literature

1. Carlos A. Schwantes, *The Pacific Northwest: An Interpretive History* (Lincoln: University of Nebraska Press, 1989), 233.

2. Thomas Hornsby Ferril, "Writing in the Rockies," *Saturday Review of Literature* 15 (March 20, 1937); reprinted in James C. Work, ed., *Prose & Poetry of the American West* (Lincoln: University of Nebraska Press, 1990).

3. Osborne Russell, *Journal of a Trapper*, ed. Aubrey L. Haines (Lincoln: University of Nebraska Press, 1965), 44–45.

4. Warren Angus Ferris, *Life in the Rocky Mountains*, ed. Paul C. Phillips (Denver, CO: Old West, 1940), 25.

5. Zebulon Pike, *The Expeditions of Zebulon Montgomery Pike*, ed. Elliot Coues (New York: Francis P. Harper, 1895), 2: 461.

6. Washington Irving, *The Adventures of Captain Bonneville: The Complete Works of Washington Irving*, ed. Robert A Rees and Alan Sandy (Boston, MA: Twayne, 1977), 16: 35, 36, 62.

7. John C. Frémont, *Narratives of Exploration and Adventure*, ed. Allan Nevins (New York: Longmans, 1956), 158–159, 258.

8. Wyoming Writers' Project, *Wyoming: A Guide to Its History, Highways, and People*, American Guide Series (New York: Oxford University Press, 1941), 131.

9. Isabelle Lucy Bird, *Isabelle Lucy Bird's "A Lady's Life in the Rocky Mountains": An Annotated Text*, ed. Ernest S. Bernard (Norman: University of Oklahoma Press, 1999), 134, 203.

10. Thomas J. Dimsdale, *The Vigilantes of Montana*, Western Frontier Library (Norman: University of Oklahoma Press, 1953), 18, 13, 95.

11. Bill Nye, *Baled Hay* (Chicago: Donohue, 1899), 5, 107–108.

12. George Frederick Ruxton, *In the Old West [Life in the Far West]* (Cleveland, OH: International Fiction Library, 1915), 95.

13. Work, *Prose & Poetry of the American West*, 213.

14. Ronald E. McFarland and William Studebaker, eds., *Idaho's Poetry: A Centennial Anthology* (Moscow: University of Idaho Press, 1988), 38, 39.

15. William Kittredge, *Owning It All* (St. Paul, MN: Graywolf, 1987), 63.

16. Gregory L. Morris, *Talking Up a Storm* (Lincoln: University of Nebraska Press, 1994), ix.

17. Schwantes, *The Pacific Northwest*, 355.

18. Levette Jay Davidson and Prudence Bostwick, eds., *The Literature of the Rocky Mountain West, 1803–1903* (Caldwell, ID: Caxton, 1939), 6.

19. Joseph Kinsey Howard, *Montana Margins: A State Anthology* (New Haven, CT: Yale University Press, 1946), vii.

20. Wallace Stegner, *Where the Bluebird Sings to the Lemonade Springs* (New York: Penguin, 1992), xvi, 55.

21. Annie Pike Greenwood, *We Sagebrush Folks* (repr., Moscow: University of Idaho Press, 1988), 25, 26, 451.

22. Mary Clearman Blew, ed., *When Montana and I Were Young* (Lincoln: University of Nebraska Press, 2002), xxi.

23. Robert C. Baron, Stephen J. Leonard, and Thomas J. Noel, eds., *Thomas Hornsby Ferril and the American West* (Golden, CO: Fulcrum, 1996), 42.

24. Dexter Westrum, *Thomas McGuane* (Boston, MA: G.K. Hall, 1991), 53.

25. Larry McMurty, Rev. of *The Cadence of Grass, New York Review of Books* 49.11 (June 27, 2002): 22.

26. Mary Clearman Blew, *Bone Deep in Landscape* (Norman: University of Oklahoma Press, 1999), 7.

27. Judith Blunt, *Breaking Clean* (New York: Knopf, 2002), 3.

28. Teresa Jordan, *Riding the White Horse Home* (New York: Vintage, 1994), 13.

29. Mary Clearman Blew, *All But the Waltz* (New York: Penguin, 1991), 22.

30. Gretel Ehrlich, *The Solace of Open Spaces* (New York: Penguin, 1985), 11.

31. Jill Ker Conway, *When Memory Speaks: Reflections on Autobiography* (New York: Knopf, 1998), 3.

32. Richard Hugo, *Making Sure It Goes On: The Collected Poems* (New York: Norton, 1983), 216.

33. Patricia Goedicke, *As Earth Begins to End* (Port Townsend, WA: Copper Canyon, 1999), 81.

34. Ray Ring, "The Big Story Written Small," *High Country News*, October 13, 2003, 8.

Music

Our deepest gratitude to the following people for their input and suggestions: Glenn Giffen, William Kearns, and Larry Worster.

1. Patricia Limerick, *Something in the Soil: Legacies and Reckonings in the New West* (New York: W.W. Norton, 2000), 75–76.

2. Alan P. Merriam, *Ethnomusicology of the Flathead Indians* (Chicago: Aldine, 1967), 43.

3. Judith Vander, *Songprints: The Musical Experience of Five Shoshone Women* (Chicago: University of Illinois Press, 1988).

4. Anne Lederman, "The Drops of Brandy: Several Versions of a Métis Fiddler Tune," *Canadian Folk Music Bulletin* 24.1 (June 1990): 3–11.

5. Julia Lambert, *The Trail* (Sons of Colorado, 1916), 3–6.

6. *Rocky Mountain News*, March 10, 1862, 5.

7. J.J. Watson, *London Evening News*, July 25, 1887, quoted by Michael Masterson, "Buffalo Bill's Famous Cowboy Band," program notes to accompany the CD *Wild West Music of Buffalo Bill's Cowboy Band* (Museum Selections, Buffalo Bill Historical Center, Cody, WY, 1996), 21.

8. Zan Stewart, "Diane Reeves: Aligned with Her Allies," *Down Beat* 64.2 (February 1997): 28–31.

9. Jack Walrath, http://www.jackwalrath.net/bio.htm (accessed May 19, 2004).

10. Matty Reichenthal, "University of Idaho Stays on Beat with Lionel Hampton," *New Crisis* 108.2 (March–April 2001): 40.

11. Howard Swan, *Music in the Southwest: 1825–1950* (San Marino, CA: Huntington Library, 1952), 26, quoting from Susan Young Gates and Leah D. Widstoe, *The Life Story of Brigham Young* (New York: Macmillan, 1930), 263.

12. Roger Miller, "Church of Jesus Christ of Latter-day Saints," in *The New Grove Dictionary of American Music* (New York: Grove's Dictionaries of Music, 1986), 1: 443.

13. Jeremy Grimshaw, "The Sonic Search for Kolob: Mormon Cosmology and the Music of La Monte Young," *Repercussions* 9.1 (Fall 2001): 82.

14. William Duckworth, "La Monte Young and Marian Zazeela," in *Talking Music: Conversations with John Cage, Philip Glass, Laurie Anderson, and Five Generations of American Experimental Composers* (New York: Schirmer Press, 1995), 218.

15. Ibid., 214–215.

16. Grimshaw, "The Sonic Search for Kolob," 98.

17. Larry Worster, *Cecil Effinger: A Colorado Composer* (Lanham, MD: Scarecrow Press, 1997), xiv.

18. Larry Worster, "Cecil Effinger und die Amerikanische Schule der Komponisten" (lecture for the Schwarzwald Musik Festival, Schomberg Kurhaus, Germany, May 2002).

19. For more information on both pieces, see Denise von Glahn, "Charles Ives, Cowboys and Indians: Aspects of the 'Other Side of Pioneering,'" *American Music* (Fall 2001): 291–314. The poetry for Charlie Rutlage is based on an event at a Texas ranch called the XIT, though the poet, D.J. O'Malley, is from Montana.

20. Susan Wheatley, "Music by Libby Larsen—Songs from Letters: Calamity Jane to Her Daughter Janey, 1880–1902. Overture for the End of a Century," *IAWM Journal* 2.3 (October 1996): 30; Karen Kane, ed., *Between Ourselves: Letters between Mothers and Daughters, 1750–1982* (Boston, MA: Houghton Mifflin, 1983).

21. Debra Hickenlooper Sowell, "Christensen Brothers," *International Encyclopedia of Dance* (New York: Oxford University Press, 1988), 2: 160.

22. Ibid.

23. This predated Balanchine's *Nutcracker* by ten years and established the tradition of presenting the work at Christmas. See ibid., 160.

24. Repertory Dance Theatre, http://www.rdtutah.org/ (accessed May 19, 2004).

25. David Sears, "Erick Hawkins," in *International Encyclopedia of Dance* (New York: Oxford University Press, 1988), 349.

26. Glenn Giffen, unpublished interview with James F. Burshears, January 3, 1976.

Religion

1. Demitri Shimkin, in Omer C. Stewart, *Peyote Religion: A History* (Norman: University of Oklahoma Press, 1987), 193.

2. Church costs in Ferenc M. Szasz, *The Protestant Clergy in the Great Plains and Mountain West, 1865–1915* (Albuquerque: University of New Mexico Press, 1988), 53.

3. Ferenc M. Szasz, *Religion in the Modern American West* (Tucson: University of Arizona Press, 2000), 21.

4. Unless otherwise stated, all percentages are derived from Dale E. Jones, Sherri Doty, Clifford Grammich, James E. Horsch, Richard Houseal, Mac Lynn, John P. Marcum, Kenneth M. Sanchagrin, and Richard H. Taylor, *Religious Congregations and Membership in the United States 2000: An Enumeration by Region, State and County Based on Data Reported for 149 Religious Bodies* (Nashville, TN: Glenmary Research Center, 2002).

5. Figures for the Hutterites in Richard Waltner, "The Hutterites: An Historical Overview of a Unique People," in *Religion in Montana: Pathways to the Present*, ed. Lawrence F. Small (Billings, MT: Rocky Mountain College, 1995), 2: 324.

6. Urban percentages derived from Jones et al., *Religious Congregations and Membership in the United States 2000*.

7. Frank Tillapaugh, *The Church Unleashed* (Ventura, CA: Regal Books, 1982), 61.

8. Buddhist information derived from BuddhaNet's Buddhist America's Colorado Directory, United States of America, http://www.buddhanet.net/americas/usa_co.htm (accessed May 19, 2004).

9. Thomas G. Alexander and James B. Allen, *Mormons and Gentiles: A History of Salt Lake City* (Boulder, CO: Pruett Publishing, 1984), 306.

Sports and Recreation

1. Linda Peavy and Ursula Smith, "World Champions: The 1904 Girls' Basketball Team from Fort Shaw Indian Boarding School," *Montana: The Magazine of Western History* (Winter 2001): 2–25.

2. James Whiteside, *Colorado: A Sports History* (Niwot: University Press of Colorado, 1999), 307.

3. Stewart Culin, *Games of the North American Indians* (Lincoln: University of Nebraska Press, 1992), 652; published originally in *Twenty-fourth Annual Report of the Bureau of American Ethnology* (Washington, DC: Smithsonian Institution, 1907).

4. John Ewers, *The Blackfeet: Raiders on the Northwestern Plains* (Norman: University of Oklahoma Press, 1958), 151–153.

5. Frank Bergon, ed., *The Journals of Lewis and Clark* (New York: Penguin Books, 1989), 387, 406.

6. George Eisen, "Amusements and Pastimes of the Fur Hunters in the Rockies," in *Sport in the West*, ed. Donald J. Mrozek, (Manhattan, KS: Sunflower Press, 1983), 39.

7. See Whiteside, *Colorado*, 29–40; Jack A. Benson, "Before Aspen and Vail: The Story of Recreational Skiing in Frontier Colorado," in *Sport in the West*, ed. Donald J. Mrozek (Manhattan, KS: Sunflower Press, 1983), 52–61; and Lee Sather, "It's All Downhill from Here: The Rise and Fall of Becker Hill, 1929–1933," in *Red Stockings & Out-of-Towners*, ed. Stanford J. Layton (Salt Lake City, UT: Signature Books, 2003), 179–198.

8. James F. Hoy, "The Origins and Originality of Rodeo," *Journal of the West* (July 1978): 17–32; E. M. Swift, "Bucking Tradition," *Sports Illustrated*, July 28, 2003, 32–34; and Dirk Johnson, "Buck High, Old Paint, or Goodbye," *New York Times*, June 3, 1994, A12.

9. "The President in Camp," *New York Times*, August 15, 1883, 1; Todd S. Purdom, "'Tired' Clinton in Tetons for a 17-Day Vacation," *New York Times*, August 16, 1995, B10.

10. Lawrence Culver, "From 'Last of the Old West' to First of the New West: Tourism and Transformation in Jackson Hole, Wyoming," in *Imagining the Big Open: Nature, Identity, and Play in the New West*, ed. Liza Nicholas, Elaine M. Bapis, and Thomas J. Harvey (Salt Lake City: University of Utah Press, 2003), 163–176.

11. International Association of Fish and Wildlife Agencies, *Economic Importance of Hunting in America* (Washington, DC: Author, 2002), 8.

12. Sherry Devlin, "Count Your Blessings," *The Missoulian*, July 26, 2003, 1.

13. "'A River Runs through It' Stands Test of Time," MSU News, http://www.montana.edu/news/0985713422.html (accessed May 20, 2004).

14. Ken Owens, "Fishing the Hatch: New West Romanticism and Fly-Fishing in the High Country," in *Imagining the Big Open: Nature, Identity, and Play in the New West*, ed. Liza Nicholas, Elaine M. Bapis, and Thomas J. Harvey (Salt Lake City: University of Utah Press, 2003), 111–119.

15. Howell Raines, "Casting for Trout in Western Waters," *New York Times Magazine*, May 19, 1991, 44.

16. Ron Watters, *Never Turn Back: The Life of Whitewater Pioneer Walt Blackadar* (Pocatello, ID: Great Rift Press, 1994), 35.

17. Michael A. Amundson, "Yellowcake to Singletrack: Culture, Community, and Identity in Moab, Utah," in *Imagining the Big Open: Nature, Identity, and Play in the New West*, ed. Liza Nicholas, Elaine M. Bapis, and Thomas J. Harvey (Salt Lake City: University of Utah Press, 2003), 151–159.

18. Outward Bound West website, www.cobs.org/about/instructors/ (accessed August 1, 2003).

19. Roberta Scruggs, "The 'Old Man of the Mountains': Admirers of Paul Petzoldt mourn the loss of one of the pioneers of outdoor leadership education," *Portland Press Herald* (Portland, ME), October 9, 1999, p. 1B.

20. Wendy Rex-Atzet, "Narratives of Power and Place: Laying Claim to Devil's Tower," in *Imagining the Big Open: Nature, Identity, and Play in the New West*, ed. Liza Nicholas, Elaine M. Bapis, and Thomas J. Harvey (Salt Lake City: University of Utah Press, 2003), 45–63.

21. William M. Bueler, *Roof of the Rockies: A History of Colorado Mountaineering* (Golden: Colorado Mountain Club Press, 2000).

22. Anne Gilbert Coleman, "Culture, Landscape, and the Making of the Colorado Ski Industry" (Ph.D. diss., University of Colorado at Boulder, 1996).

23. Peggy Clifford, *To Aspen and Back: An American Journey* (New York: St. Martin's Press, 1980), 72.

24. Mark Jones, "Oakley names Erickson as new football coach," *South Idaho Press*, August 8, 2003, found on the Web at www.southidahopress.com/articles/2003/08/08/sports/top_story/oakleycoach.txt; and Glen Matson, "On the plains, six-man football is name of game/Jarring hits, high scores spark interest," *Colorado Springs Gazette-Telegraph*, November 5, 1991, p. C-5.

BIBLIOGRAPHY

Allen, James B., and Glen M. Leonard. *The Story of the Latter-day Saints*. Salt Lake City, UT: Deseret Book Company, 1992.

Barkwell, Lawrence J., Leah Dorion, and Darren R. Préfontaine, eds. *Métis Legacy: A Métis Historiography and Annotated Bibliography*. Winnipeg, Manitoba: Pemmican Publications, 2001.

Beard, Tyler. *100 Years of Western Wear*. Salt Lake City, UT: Gibbs-Smith Publisher, 1993.

Beck, Warren A., and Ynez D. Haase. *Historical Atlas of the American West*. Norman: University of Oklahoma Press, 1989.

Campbell, Suzan, and Kathleen E. Ash-Milby. *The American West: People, Places, and Ideas*. Corning, NY: Rockwell Museum of Western Art; Santa Fe, NM: Western Edge Press, 2001.

Coe, Ralph T. *Lost and Found Traditions: Native American Art 1965–1985*. Seattle: University of Washington Press; New York: American Federation of Arts, 1986.

Collins, John J. *Native American Religions: A Geographical Survey*. Lewiston, NY: Edwin Mellen Press, 1991.

Conlin, Joseph R. *Bacon, Beans, and the Galatines: Food and Foodways on the Western Mining Frontier*. Reno: University of Nevada Press, 1986.

Conn, Richard. *Native American Art in the Denver Art Museum*. Denver, CO: Denver Art Museum; Seattle: University of Washington Press, 1979.

Flores, Dan L. *The Natural West: Environmental History in the Great Plains and Rocky Mountains*. Norman: University of Oklahoma Press, 2003.

Foxley, William C. *Frontier Spirit: Catalog of the Collection of the Museum of Western Art*. Denver, CO: Museum of Western Art, 1983.

Goetzmann, William H., and William N. Goetzmann. *The West of the Imagination*. New York: W. W. Norton, 1986.

Harris, Neil, Marlene Chambers, and Lewis Wingfield Story. *The Denver Art Museum: The First Hundred Years*. Denver, CO: Denver Art Museum, 1996.

Holthaus, Gary. *Wide Skies: Finding a Home in the West*. Tucson: University of Arizona Press, 1997.

Holthaus, Gary, Patricia Nelson Limerick, Charles F. Wilkinson, and Eve Stryker Munson, eds. *A Society to Match the Scenery: Personal Visions of the Future of the American West*. Boulder: University Press of Colorado, 1991.

Howe, Elvon L., ed. *Rocky Mountain Empire*. Garden City, NY: Doubleday & Company, 1950.

Jordan, Terry, Jon T. Kilpinen, and Charles F. Gritzner. *The Mountain West: Interpreting the Folk Landscape*. Baltimore, MD: Johns Hopkins University Press, 1997.

Keyser, James D., and Michael A. Klassen. *Plains Indian Rock Art*. Seattle: University of Washington Press, 2001.

Kowalewski, Michael, ed. *Reading the West: New Essays on the Literature of the American West*. New York: Cambridge University Press, 1996.

Lamar, Howard R., ed. *The New Encyclopedia of the American West*. New Haven, CT: Yale University Press, 1998.

Larson, T. A. *History of Wyoming*. Lincoln: University of Nebraska Press, 1978.

Leonard, Steve, Carl Abbott, and David McComb. *Colorado: A History of the Centennial State*. Boulder: University Press of Colorado, 1994.

Limerick, Patricia. *The Legacy of Conquest: The Unbroken Past of the American West*. New York: W. W. Norton, 1988.

Magoc, Chris J. *Yellowstone: The Creation and Selling of an American Landscape*. Albuquerque: University of New Mexico Press, 1999.

Malone, Michael P., Richard B. Roeder, and William L. Lang. *Montana: A History of Two Centuries*. Seattle: University of Washington Press, 1991.

Murdoch, David Hamilton. *The American West: The Invention of a Myth*. Reno: University of Nevada Press, 2001.

Nicholas, Liza, Elaine M. Bapis, and Thomas J. Harvey, eds. *Imagining the Big Open: Nature, Identity, and Play in the New West*. Salt Lake City: University of Utah Press, 2003.

Paterek, Josephine. *Encyclopedia of American Indian Costume*. New York: W. W. Norton, 1993.

Prown, Jules David, Nancy K. Anderson, William Cronon, Brian W. Dippie, Martha A. Sandweiss, Susan Prendergast Schoelwer, and Howard R. Lamar. *Discovered Lands, Invented Pasts: Transforming Visions of the American West*. New Haven, CT: Yale University Press, 1992.

Robbins, Jim. *Last Refuge: The Environmental Showdown in Yellowstone and the American West*. New York: William Morrow, 1993.

Rothman, Hal. *Devil's Bargains: Tourism in the Twentieth-Century American West*. Lawrence: University Press of Kansas, 1998.

Schissel, Lillian. *Black Frontiers: A History of African American Heroes in the Old West*. New York: Aladdin Paperbacks, 1995.

Schwantes, Carlos. *In Mountain Shadows: A History of Idaho*. Lincoln: University of Nebraska Press, 1991.

Simmon, Scott. *The Invention of the Western: A Cultural History of the Genre's First Half Century*. Cambridge: Cambridge University Press, 2003.

Smith, Duane. *Rocky Mountain West: Colorado, Wyoming, and Montana 1859–1915*. Albuquerque: University of New Mexico Press, 1992.

Stegner, Wallace. *The American West as Living Space*. Ann Arbor: University of Michigan Press, 1987.

Stewart, Polly, Steven Siporin, C. W. Sullivan III, and Suzie Jones, eds. *Worldviews and the American West: The Life of the Place Itself*. Logan: Utah State University Press, 2001.

Szasz, Ferenc M. *The Protestant Clergy in the Great Plains and Mountain West, 1865–1915*. Albuquerque: University of New Mexico Press, 1988.

———. *Religion in the Modern American West*. Tucson: University of Arizona Press, 2000.

Truettner, William H., ed. *The West as America: Reinterpreting Images of the Frontier, 1820–1920*. Washington, DC: Smithsonian Institution Press, 1991.

White, Richard C. *"It's Your Misfortune and None of My Own": A New History of the American West.* Norman: University of Oklahoma Press, 1991.

Wilkinson, Charles F. *The Eagle Bird: Mapping a New West.* New York: Pantheon, 1992.

Wrobel, David M., and Michael C. Steiner. *Many Wests: Place, Culture, and Regional Identity.* Lawrence: University Press of Kansas, 1997.

Wyckoff, William, and Larry M. Dilsaver. *The Mountainous West: Explorations in Historical Geography.* Lincoln: University of Nebraska Press, 1995.

Zhu, Liping. *A Chinaman's Chance: The Chinese on the Rocky Mountain Frontier.* Niwot: University Press of Colorado, 1997.

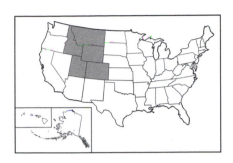

INDEX

ABOUT THE EDITOR AND CONTRIBUTORS

Poet and editor RICK NEWBY is a member of the National Coalition of Independent Scholars. Most recently, Newby compiled and edited *The New Montana Story: An Anthology* (2003). He has also served as editor or coeditor of *A Most Desperate Situation: Frontier Adventures of a Young Scout, 1858–1864* (2000) by Walter Cooper (illustrations by Charles M. Russell); *An Ornery Bunch: Tales and Anecdotes Collected by the W.P.A. Montana Writers' Project* (1999); and *Writing Montana: Literature under the Big Sky* (1996). A regular contributor to *Black & White* magazine and other arts journals, Newby is coauthor of the museum catalogs *A Ceramic Continuum: Fifty Years of the Archie Bray Influence* (2001); *The Most Difficult Journey: The Poindexter Collections of American Modernist Painting* (2002); and *Humor, Irony and Wit: Ceramic Funk from the Sixties and Beyond* (2004). A founding board member of the Montana Center for the Book, Newby makes his home in Helena, Montana.

LAMONT ANTIEAU is a Ph.D. candidate in linguistics at the University of Georgia, and he is currently writing a dissertation on the speech of rural Colorado. His latest article on the subject is "Colorado Plains English," which appeared in *American Speech* (2003). He has received an National Science Foundation (NSF) Doctoral Dissertation Research Grant, a University of Georgia Dean's Research Award, and an American Dialect Society Presidential Honorary Membership.

STEPHANIE BAKER teaches music appreciation at AIMS Community College, Greeley, Colorado, and is a member of the Longmont Symphony Orchestra. She received her master's degree from Claremont Colleges and her bachelor's from the University of Denver.

JEREMY BONNER holds a Ph.D. in American history from the Catholic University of America in Washington, D.C., and is currently an independent scholar in Baltimore, Maryland. He has published on political and religious history in such journals as the *Journal of Mormon History* and *Anglican and Episcopal History*. He is currently working on a biography of Victor J. Reed, the Catholic bishop of Oklahoma City and Tulsa from 1958 to 1971.

SIMON DIXON teaches theater and film studies at Montana State University, Bozeman. He received his master's in English from Clark University and his Ph.D. in film studies from the University of Iowa. His publications include "Ambiguous Ecologies: Stardom's Domestic Mise-en-Scène" on Hollywood star discourse, and he is currently at work on a book titled *Film Praxis: Film Theory and Production*.

A. DUDLEY GARDNER is division chair of the Social Science–Fine Arts Department at Western Wyoming Community College. He earned his Ph.D. from the University of New Mexico and his M.A. from Colorado State University. He is a professional historic archaeologist and historian who specializes in ethnic and social history. He has published several books and articles, including *Forgotten Frontier: A History of Wyoming Coal Mining* (1989), which he coauthored with Verla Flores.

A native of Wyoming, SHARON GRAF holds a Ph.D. from Michigan State University in ethnomusicology with emphasis on American folk music. A former staff member of the Wyoming Folk Arts Program, she taught throughout the Denver area before accepting an assistant professor position at the University of Illinois at Springfield. She is currently writing a book on the National Oldtime Fiddlers' Contest, an event held in Weiser, Idaho, in which she competes every year.

CHRIS J. MAGOC is assistant professor of history at Mercyhurst College in Erie, Pennsylvania. Among his works are *So Glorious a Landscape: Nature and the Environment in American History and Culture* (2002) and *Yellowstone: The Creation and Selling of an American Landscape, 1870–1903* (1999), chosen by *Choice* as an Outstanding Academic Title of the Year.

RON McFARLAND is a professor of English at the University of Idaho. His scholarly publications include booklets in the Western Writers Series on David Wagoner, Tess Gallagher, Norman Maclean, and most recently, William Kittredge. His book *Understanding James Welch* was recognized by the Association of American University Presses as one of the Best Books from the University Presses in 2000. His stories and essays from Idaho, *Catching First Light*, were published in 2001 by Idaho State University Press. He is currently working on a book about recent memoirs from the Rockies. He won the University of Idaho Award for Excellence in Research and Creative Achievement in 2002.

PETRA MEYER-FRAZIER holds a Ph.D. in musicology from the University of Colorado at Boulder with an emphasis on nineteenth-century American music. She has taught at the University of Tennessee at Knoxville and throughout the Denver area. She is currently doing freelance research and working on a book about women and parlor music in America.

LAURA PASACRETA is adjunct professor in anthropology at Western Wyoming Community College. She has recently completed her M.A. in archaeology from

Simon Fraser University in Vancouver, British Columbia, with a specialization in overseas Chinese communities on the Canadian and American frontiers. Her current research focuses on Chinese in North America and the South Pacific.

E. DUKE RICHEY is a native of Chattanooga, Tennessee, and a graduate of the University of the South. He holds master's degrees in environmental studies and history from the University of Montana. His University of Colorado doctoral dissertation, in progress, reflects both his love of skiing and his passion for twentieth-century American history and Western American studies. His dissertation is titled "Living It Up in Aspen: Cold War America, Ski Town Culture, and the New Western Dream in Colorado, 1945–1990."

SUSAN H. SWETNAM is professor of English at Idaho State University, where she has been named Distinguished Teacher, Distinguished Public Servant, and Outstanding Researcher. She is a former chair of the Idaho Humanities Council. Her main areas of scholarly interest are Intermountain West literature and culture, fiction and nonfiction narrative, and the personal essay. Her collection of essays *Home Mountains* was honored by the Idaho Library Association in the Idaho Book of the Year 2000 competition. Her work has appeared in a variety of magazines, including *Gourmet*, *Journal of the West*, and *Rendezvous*, and in several anthologies, including *Ring of Fire: Writers of the Greater Yellowstone Region* (2000).

RONDA WALKER WEAVER received her master's degree in American studies/folklore from Utah State University. She teaches folklore courses and writing classes at Utah Valley State College in Orem, Utah. Her areas of interest include Mormon women's studies, foodways, and interpreting culture in relation to the landscape. Walker has presented papers at numerous conferences, including the American Folklore Society's annual conferences.

CARROLL VAN WEST is director of the Center for Historic Preservation at Middle Tennessee State University, director of the Tennessee Civil War National Heritage Area, and senior editor of the *Tennessee Historical Quarterly*. His books include: *Capitalism on the Frontier: The Transformation of the Yellowstone Valley in the Nineteenth Century* (1993), *The Tennessee Encyclopedia of History and Culture* (1998), *The New Deal Landscape of Tennessee* (2002), and *A History of the Arts of Tennessee* (2004).

LAUREL WILSON is associate professor of textile and apparel management at the University of Missouri at Columbia, where she received the Kemper Fellowship for Excellence in Teaching in 2002. She serves as associate editor of the *Clothing and Textiles Research Journal* and as a reviewer for *Dress*, published by the Costume Society of America. She has presented her research on American cowboy dress to conference audiences at the National Cowboy and Western Heritage Museum and the International Textile and Apparel Association.

KRISTI A. YOUNG is the curator of the Wilson Folklore Archives in the L. Tom Perry Special Collections at Brigham Young University. She has published book reviews in the *Journal of American Folklore* and *BYU Studies*. She is also the author of several courtship-related entries in the forthcoming *Encyclopedia of American Folklife*.

The Greenwood Encyclopedia of American Regional Cultures

The Great Plains Region, *edited by Amanda Rees*

The Mid-Atlantic Region, *edited by Robert P. Marzec*

The Midwest, *edited by Joseph W. Slade and Judith Yaross Lee*

New England, *edited by Michael Sletcher*

The Pacific Region, *edited by Jan Goggans with Aaron DiFranco*

The Rocky Mountain Region, *edited by Rick Newby*

The South, *edited by Rebecca Mark and Rob Vaughan*

The Southwest, *edited by Mark Busby*

STRATEGIC MANAGEMENT AND ORGANIZATIONAL POLICY
TEXT AND CASES

Third Edition

James M. Higgins
Crummer School
Rollins College

Julian W. Vincze
Crummer School
Rollins College

The Dryden Press
Chicago   New York   Philadelphia   San Francisco
Montreal   Toronto   London   Sydney
Tokyo   Mexico City   Rio de Janeiro   Madrid

To
Tracy, Laura,
Linda, Jerry, and Chris

Acquisitions Editor: Joan Resler
Project Editor: Nancy Shanahan
Managing Editor: Jane Perkins
Design Director: Alan Wendt
Production Manager: Claire Roth/Diane Tenzi
Permissions Editor: Doris Milligan

Copy Editor: Beverly Goldberg
Compositor: G & S Typesetters, Inc.
Text Type: 10/12 Times Roman

Library of Congress Cataloging-in-Publication Data

Higgins, James M.
    Strategic management and organizational policy.

    Rev. ed. of: Organizational policy and strategic management. 2nd ed. 1983.
    Includes bibliographies and index.
    1. Strategic planning.   2. Management.   I. Higgins,
James M. Organizational policy and strategic management.
II. Vincze, Julian W.   III. Title.
HD30.28.H512   1986   658.4′012   85-20660
ISBN: 0-03-002418-8

Printed in the United States of America
678-016-987654321

Address orders:
383 Madison Avenue
New York, NY 10017

Address editorial correspondence:
One Salt Creek Lane
Hinsdale, IL 60521

CBS COLLEGE PUBLISHING
The Dryden Press
Holt, Rinehart and Winston
Saunders College Publishing

PREFACE

Strategic Management and Organizational Policy is intended to increase the student's knowledge of strategic management and related organizational processes, to improve the skills necessary for carrying out the work of the strategist, and to enhance the appreciation of the general management attitude. The title has been changed slightly from the first and second editions to reflect the increasing emphasis on strategic management in the business policy course.

Objectives

This text is designed around the commonly recognized objectives of a course in strategy and policy. It develops the student's general management perspective, including an understanding of the role of the general manager-strategist, in a variety of domestic and international strategic situations.

It also integrates the functional business disciplines (marketing, finance, operations, human resources management, and information systems) with the management process to illustrate their interdependencies. The environment of business and its multiple roles within society, especially in regard to external constraints, are considered.

The student's analytic and research skills are applied in a decision-making setting. This text teaches the student how to make decisions, how to identify major issues in complex situations, and how to propose alternative solutions. Through cases, the student will learn to determine appropriate choices from among these alternatives and to defend those choices.

A fourth objective is to acquaint the student with concepts in strategic management—its formulation and the resulting strategy content, policy, implementation, and control—and the incorporation of these concepts into practice. The student will be able to recognize the role of policy in the organization. Finally, this text is intended to relate the purposes of functional activity and to encourage the student to be objective-oriented as opposed to activity-oriented.

Special Features of the Third Edition

As in earlier editions, the third edition is based on current conceptual and research literature. The text features four models that explain organizational strategic management. The first model, shown in Figure 1.1, portrays the strategic process in five steps: mission determination, establishment of objectives, strategy formulation, implementation, and control. The chapters in this book follow the order of this model, as do the cases. The second model, portrayed in Figure 1.2, examines in detail the processes of objective determination and master strategy formulation. This model is the basis for discussions in Chapters 1 through 7. The third model, shown in Table 3.2, defines the contents of the master strategy. Much of Chapters 3, 4, and 5 expand on the information in this model. The fourth model, Figure 8.2, is used for discussing materials in Chapters 8 and 9.

In conjunction with the master strategy model as portrayed in Table 3.2, basic action strategies and grand strategies (for example, growth through diversification, retrenchment, stabilization, niche, concentration, and takeover defense and combination) are explained in sufficient detail to enable the student first to understand and then to use these terms.

The process of determining strengths, weaknesses, opportunities, and threats (SWOT) is discussed at length throughout. Organizations and their environments are analyzed to determine SWOT, and social issues are integrated into these analyses. Information is presented to help the student forecast SWOT.

Each chapter contains key terms and concepts to guide the student. Information Capsules (anecdotes describing specific situations to illustrate major points in the text) are presented in all chapters.

The third edition contains several significant changes over the second edition.

1. Updated Information Capsules are included in each chapter.

2. International and nonprofit situations are now each treated in separate chapters.

3. Implementation is discussed in two chapters instead of one as formerly, reflecting the emphasis on this topic in the strategic management arena—especially the increased interest in organizational culture.

4. Single-business (SBU) and functional strategies are discussed in a separate chapter as are behavioral and contingency strategies.

5. Competitor analysis receives extensive treatment, including discussion of Porter's major models.

The Cases

All of the cases used in this edition are current ones, many of them involving companies with which students will be familiar—Muse Air, Playboy, Wall Drug, Eastern Air Lines, Walt Disney Productions, Holiday Inns, Marriott Hotels, Club Mediterranean, John Hancock companies, Union Carbide, Bendix, Martin Marietta, IBM, Apple Computers, and Manville. In addition, six popular cases have been retained from the second edition. There are cases to illustrate each major part of the strategic management process. Important improvements in cases include the following:

1. A continuing emphasis is placed on including comprehensive and integrative cases that involve as many major strategy components as possible.

2. Twenty-eight new cases are included, increasing the number of cases from 30 to 34.

3. A concentrated effort has been made to include cases that cover the full spectrum of organizational size.

4. Four new cases and three industry notes deal with "competitor analyses and strategy formulation."

5. The number of "implementation" cases has been increased to four.

6. Two new cases—Bendix/Martin Marietta and Manville—deal with ethical and social interfaces.

7. One case about a nonprofit organization—in the arts—has been included.

Additional Materials

1. The four appendixes at the end of the book are designed to increase the student's ability to analyze strategic situations. Appendix 1 discusses the case method. Appendix 2 provides a strategic audit, including questions to analyze organizations and their en-

vironments. This audit is based primarily on the master strategy shown in Table 3.2. Appendix 3 further defines and discusses the ratios presented in Table 9.1. Appendix 4 contains economic and news data for 1980 through 1985. A separate Appendix to Chapter 2 provides a list of information sources.

2. An extensive *Instructor's Manual* with test bank accompanies this text. Transparency masters and other support items are included.

3. Some of the cases have accompanying videotapes to aid in their discussion. (See *Instructor's Manual* for details.)

4. An IBM PC compatible floppy disk containing up to five years of data in spreadsheet format for Lotus 1-2-3 is available to adoptors from the authors upon request.

Use of the Text

Strategic Management and Organizational Policy is intended primarily for use in the capstone policy course by senior-level undergraduate students and by second-year MBA students. This book can be employed in an instructional situation using several different pedagogical approaches. It can stand alone for the policy course, or it can be used with an instructor's own cases or lectures, or with simulations or field exercises. It can also be used with analyses of real-life organizations, such as those that appear in each issue of *Business Week*.

This text may also be used by managers in management development courses or by any manager individually as a means of "getting up to speed" in this area. The state-of-the-art of strategy and policy is reviewed, with a focus on both research and concepts in the rapidly expanding field of strategic management.

Any opinions, praise, criticisms, or other comments in regard to this text are welcome. Please write to the authors at the following address:

James M. Higgins or Julian W. Vincze
Crummer Graduate School of Business
Rollins College
Winter Park, FL 32789-4499

Acknowledgments

Many persons contributed to this book. First, we would like to thank those who examined the second edition for areas of improvement: Art Sharplin, *Northeast Louisiana University*; Richard R. Merner, *University of Delaware*; and James B. Thurman, *George Washington University*.

Our gratitude also goes to those who reviewed the third edition: Gordon C. Inskeep, *Arizona State University*; Edward F. Thode, *New Mexico State University*; Manab Thakur, *University of Texas–El Paso*; Keith L. Fay, *Arizona State University*; Daniel G. Kopp, *Southwest Missouri State University*; Dale R. McKemey, *University of Nebraska–Omaha*; Stuart R. Monroe, *Northern Arizona University*; Denise G. Jackson, *Texas Tech University*; Robert H. Howard, *Loyola University of Chicago*; and Peter Goulet, *University of Northern Iowa*.

Thanks go to the Harvard Case Service and to the Case Research Association for their service in the development of cases and to the companies and managers examined in the cases for their cooperation. The scholars whose works are cited herein are to be commended for their efforts. Special thanks are offered to the dean of the Crummer School, Marty Schatz, who has provided an excellent environment in which to work. Thanks also go to Susan Crabill who typed portions of the manuscript and of the *Instructor's Manual*.

Special thanks go to the authors who generously contributed cases to this edition: Frank C. Barnes, *University of North Carolina, Charlotte*; Mark Blankenship, *Virginia Polytechnic Institute*; Pamela R. Buckles & Juan Carlos Torrealba, *Crummer School, Rollins College*; James J. Chrisman & Fred L. Fry, *Bradley University*; Robert P. Crowner, *Eastern Michigan University*; David M. Currie, *Crummer School, Rollins College*; Lincoln W. Deihl, *Kansas State University*; David L. Daughtry, *Auburn University at Montgomery*; Sandra Foster, Steve Keith, & Cathy Shields, *Crummer School, Rollins College*; Jacques Horovitz, *IMEDE (International Management Development Institute)*, David B. Jemison & Chris Cairns, *Stanford University*; Raymond M. Kinnunen, *Northeastern University*; Tom Kosnik, *Stanford University*; Carla Litvany, *Crummer School, Rollins College*; Benjamin M. Oviatt & Alan D. Bauerschmidt, *University of South Carolina*; Robert McGlashan & Tim Singleton, *University of Houston, Clear Lake*; Arthur Sharplin, *Northeastern Louisiana University*; Donald W. Scotton, Allan D. Waren & Bernard C. Reimann, *Cleveland State University*; James D. Taylor & Robert L. Johnson, *University of South Dakota*; John Taylor, *Manhattan*; Marilyn L. Taylor & Kenneth Beck, *University of Kansas*.

Joan Resler, the editor on this project, provided outstanding support, as did her assistant, Teresa Chartos. Special thanks are due to the project editor, Nancy Shanahan, for without her this book could not have been completed on time nor in such a satisfactory manner. Alan Wendt, the designer, has done an outstanding job on this book. The copyeditor, Beverly Goldberg, deserves praise for her great efforts.

Our wives and children are greatly appreciated for their patience in enduring another project.

James M. Higgins
Julian W. Vincze
Winter Park, Florida
September 1985

CONTENTS

TEXT

Chapter 11 Strategic Management in the Not-for-Profit Organization   267

CASES

▪ Strategy Formulation ▪

APPENDIXES

The Dryden Press Series in Management

Arthur G. Bedeian, Consulting Editor

1

Strategic Management Begins with Mission, Policy, Information, and Strategists

Effective business strategy is an essential requirement for an outstanding company. Of all the contrasts between the successful and the unsuccessful business, or between the corporate leader and its followers, the single, most important differentiating factor is strategy.

▪ *J. Thomas Cannon* ▪

Whether an organization will succeed or fail ultimately hinges upon the appropriate administration of the subjects of this book: strategic management and organizational policy. IBM, General Electric, Xerox, and Mazda all shared, in 1985, at least three common factors—success, competent strategic management, and viable organizational policy. Conversely, International Harvester, Osborne Computers, and Braniff Airlines, at the time of their decline or demise, also shared three common factors—failure, inadequate strategic management, and dysfunctional organizational policy. In the short run, any firm with a strategic advantage can survive and even prosper; but in the long run, only the organizations that practice sound strategic management and that have viable policies will continue to possess that strategic advantage and will therefore be able to survive and prosper!

Fortunately, many organizations have begun to realize the importance of strategic management and organizational policy. One book in particular, *In Search of Excellence* by Thomas J. Peters and Robert H. Waterman, Jr., has stimulated many executives to improve their organizations' strategic management practices. As never before, organizations are searching for the synergistic combination of factors that Peters and Waterman suggest are critical to corporate excellence.[1] This is no easy task, nor is strategy alone sufficient, as both their book and this one advise. There is more to strategic management than just strategy. All of the strategic management concerns must be addressed for excellence to occur. Hence *Strategic Management and Organizational Policy* addresses not only strategy formulation, but policy and strategy implementation and control as well.

We are not managing this company for the next quarter.
We are building it for the next generation.

▪ *Sam Johnson, Chairman and CEO, S. C. Johnson & Son Inc. (Johnson's Wax)* ▪

---

[1] T. J. Peters and R. H. Waterman, Jr., *In Search of Excellence: Lessons from America's Best-Run Companies* (Harper & Row: New York, 1983).

1

Strategic management is the process of managing the pursuit of organizational mission while managing the relationship of the organization to its environment.

Strategic management is principally concerned with executive actions that involve

1. The determination of the organization's mission, strategic policies, and strategic objectives.

2. The formulation of a master strategy to accomplish those objectives. This strategy is most often based on a grand strategy combining basic actions and marketing considerations.

3. The formulation of policies to aid in the implementation and control of the master strategy.

4. Managing, through subordinates, the process of implementation, which translates strategic plans into action and results.

5. The practices of evaluation and control to determine whether the mission and objectives have been achieved and whether the plans and policies for reaching them are functional.

Mission is the organization's purpose, its reason for being. Mission statements should describe the organization's major areas of interest, its scope of intended actions, the basic market needs it intends to satisfy, and its primary values.

Strategic management stresses managing the organization's relationship with its environment as a means to mission accomplishment. Historically, organizational strategic management has revolved around basic action strategies and competitive marketing actions. Currently, more and more organizations recognize that the strategic process is much more complex; they therefore focus their efforts on virtually all key environmental and internal factors, not just on customers, suppliers, and the competition. Furthermore, strategic management recognizes that most organizations operate in increasingly volatile and often hostile environments. Strategic management must therefore be constantly concerned with managing in changing environments. Organizations such as Texas Instruments and Hewlett-Packard, often showcased in the 1970s as firms with sound strategic management, have unfortunately found in the early 1980s that their chosen strategies were not suited to the demands of their changing environments. As of early 1985, neither has yet completely appropriately responded to their environments.

Organizational policy comprises broad forms of guidance established to aid managers in determining strategic objectives and in formulating, implementing, and controlling the master strategy.

The guidance given by organizational policy ranges from very broad statements to somewhat more specific constraints that set out allowable or intended courses of action. Such guidance is necessary if the actions taken by organization members are to be consistent with the organization's mission. Policy provides a framework within which organization members can function, and within which the master strategy can be formulated, implemented, and controlled.

The master strategy is the group of strategic plans formulated to achieve the organization's strategic objectives as it manages the organization's relationships with

the major constituents of its internal and external environments affected by its actions, known as environmental stakeholders.

Strategic objectives are major, comprehensive objectives for accomplishing mission. They define mission in more specific, achievable terms.

Strategic plans are major, comprehensive, and usually long-term plans for accomplishing strategic objectives and, hence, mission.

All organizations' master strategies have four common components: societal response strategies, mission determination strategies, primary mission strategies, and mission-supportive strategies. In business, these strategies are referred to respectively as the enterprise strategy, the corporate strategy, the business strategy, and the functional strategy. The societal response strategy tells how the organization plans to relate to its external societal constituents. The mission determination strategy defines the organization's fields of endeavor and how it plans to conduct itself in those endeavors in very broad terms. The primary mission strategy indicates how the organization plans to achieve its primary mission. The mission-supportive strategies tell how the organization plans on supporting its primary mission strategy. The content of the master strategy varies principally with the mission strategists, and with the type of organization. (See Table 3.2 in Chapter 3).

Business organizations can be placed in two primary groups. The first group includes organizations that sell a single product or few products, largely in a single industry. This type of organization is known as a strategic business unit (SBU). Examples of single-SBU firms include Delta Air Lines, individual McDonald's franchises, the maker of Arrow shirts, and most accounting firms. The second group is made up of organizations that market their products in many industries and have many SBUs. General Mills, Westinghouse, IBM, General Electric, Mitsubishi, Xerox, and Sears Roebuck are examples of multiple-SBU firms.

When formulating strategy at the SBU, or business level, strategists are most concerned with developing a strategic advantage through the choice of an appropriate grand strategy.

The grand strategy is that combination of strategies that defines the driving force of the organization—that central-action character attribute to which all else should adhere—growth through price competition or quality competition, for example.

This strategy will focus on elements of the primary mission strategy, often marketing (although some organizations may emphasize other areas such as production and cost controls), and on the choice of basic corporate strategies, such as the decision to compete or find a niche, grow or stabilize, and so forth, which are part of the mission determination strategy.

Successfully competing in the marketplace is the aim of SBU strategy. Critical to the achievement of a competitive advantage are: supportive strategies in the economic functional areas of finance, operations/production, and human resources management; and supportive strategies in the managerial functional areas, such as planning, organizing, implementing, and controlling.

In multiple-SBU firms, the overall organizational master strategy focuses on a grand strategy aimed at obtaining a strategic advantage over other similar firms, usually conglomerates, by achieving a synergistic balance among all the SBUs. The techniques employed to achieve this balance are known as portfolio management. These emphasize corporate strategies. In addition, the master strategy at this level must examine the same fundamental issues as those portrayed in Table 3.2 (Chapter 3). That is, all major components of the master strategy must be addressed from the total organizational perspective, albeit if only from a policy viewpoint, in terms of informing major divisions of total organizational objectives and plans in those areas to which divisions would be expected to adhere, and/or negotiate for their individual differences.

In addition to strategies for corporate, SBU (business), and functional areas, the master strategy component for coping with the total organizational environment, known as the enterprise strategy, is a critical ingredient in the successful organization's master strategy. Chapter 3 discusses all of these types of strategies in much greater detail.

The wise leader considers the days that are yet to come.

▪ *Persian proverb* ▪

Strategic Management in the Organization

The role of strategic management in the organization can be examined through the use of a strategic management process model such as that presented in Figure 1.1 and an objectives determination and master strategy formulation model such as that presented in Figure 1.2, which provides more detailed information about the processes portrayed in the second and third steps of Figure 1.1. While Figures 1.1 and 1.2 (areas highlighted are covered in this chapter), as well as much of the accompanying narrative, portray the processes as sequential, they do not always occur as shown. Many times, objectives are established without exhaustive examination of information. Many times, objectives change after strategies have been formulated. Many times, objectives remain the same, but the strategies to achieve them are reformulated. However, most of the time, the processes shown in the figures occur sequentially at least once a year as organizations complete their annual planning process.

How these models are actually put into operation varies from organization to organization. Although specifics may vary, the strategic management process model contains the principal components of the effective organization. Numerous studies have indicated the

Figure 1.1   The Organization—a Strategic Management Process Model

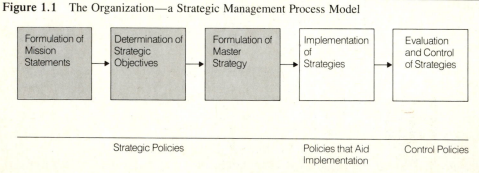

Figure 1.2   Objectives Determination and Master Strategy Formulation

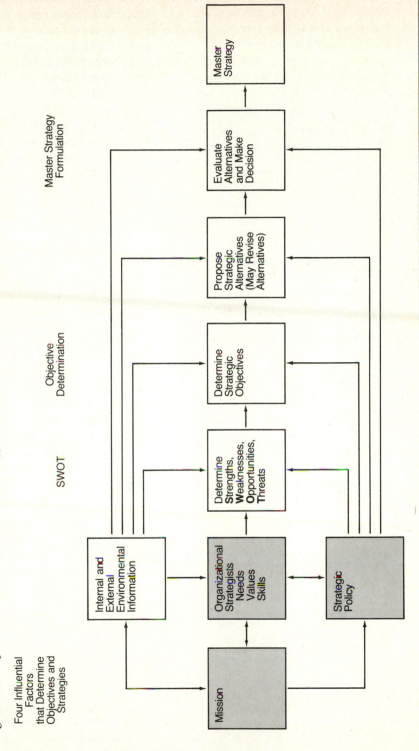

Four Influential
Factors
that Determine
Objectives and
Strategies

importance of this strategic management approach and the processes depicted in the figures.[2] Not all are supportive, but most are, and most of those that are not can be explained by methodological reasons. However, planning alone does not insure success. Implementation and control are critical. Furthermore, the size of the organization may dictate, somewhat, whether strategic planning will be appropriate or not. Essentially, there is some question as to how effective formal planning is for the smaller firm.

The contents of the model in Figure 1.1 are as follows:

1. **Formulation of Mission Statements.** Organizations exist to accomplish a mission. Mission is the organization's reason for existence. Successful organizations have well-defined missions and function in accordance with them.

2. **Setting of Organizational Policy.** Broad, general guidance must be available for the entire strategic management process: strategic policies guide the objective setting and strategy formulation processes; additional policies derived from strategy and these strategic policies guide the ensuing actions, which lead to implementation of strategy; finally, selected policies guide control actions.

3. **Determination of Strategic Objectives.** Strategic objectives for achieving organizational mission in a complex environment must be determined. These objectives are simply more definitive statements of what constitutes mission accomplishment.

4. **Master Strategy Formulation.** Successful organizations establish strategic plans for reaching strategic objectives while managing relationships in a complex environ-

---

[2]H. I. Ansoff et al., "Does Planning Pay? The Effect of Planning in Success of Acquisitions," *Long Range Planning*, December 1970, pp. 2–7; J. S. Armstrong, "The Value of Formal Planning for Strategic Decisions: Review of Empirical Research," *Strategic Management Journal*, July–September 1982, pp. 197–211; D. Burt, "Planning and Performance in Australian Retailing," *Long Range Planning*, June 1978, pp. 62–66; J. Eastlack, Jr. and P. McDonald, "CEO's Role in Corporate Growth," *Harvard Business Review*, May/June 1970, pp. 150–163; C. S. Guynes, "An Analysis of Planning in Large Texas Manufacturing Firms" (Ph.D. dissertation, Texas Technical University, 1969); H. W. Hegarty, "The Role of Strategy Formulation on Corporate Performance," *Proceedings: Midwest American Institute of Decision Sciences*, 1976; D. M. Herold, "Long Range Planning and Organizational Performance: A Cross Validation Study," *Academy of Management Journal*, March 1971, pp. 91–102; R. J. Kudla, "The Effects of Strategic Planning on Common Stock Returns," *Academy of Management Journal*, March 1980, pp. 5–20; W. M. Lindsay and L. W. Rue, "Impact of the Organization Environment on the Long Range Planning Process: A Contingency View," *Academy of Management Journal*, September 1980, pp. 385–404; Z. A. Malik, "Formal Long Range Planning and Organizational Performance: A Study" (Ph.D. dissertation, Rensselaer Polytechnic Institute, 1974); M. A. Najjar, "Planning in Small Manufacturing Companies: An Empirical Study" (Ph.D. dissertation, Ohio State University, 1966); L. C. Rhyne, "The Impact of Strategic Planning on Financial Performance" (Paper presented to the Academy of Management, August 1983); R. B. Robinson, Jr. and John A. Pearce II, "The Impact of Formalized Strategic Planning on Financial Performance in Small Organizations," *Strategic Management Journal*, July–September 1983, pp. 197–207; L. W. Rue, "Theoretical and Operational Implications of Long Range Planning on Selected Measures of Financial Performance in U.S. Industry" (Ph.D. dissertation, Georgia State University, 1973); L. W. Rue and R. M. Fulmer, "Is Long Range Planning Profitable?" *Proceedings: Academy of Management Meetings*, 1973, pp. 66–73; S. Schoeffler, R. D. Buzzell, and D. F. Heany, "Impact of Strategic Planning on Profit Performance," *Harvard Business Review*, March/April 1974, pp. 137–145; R. Stagner, "Corporate Decision Making," *Journal of Applied Psychology*, February 1969, pp. 1–13; "The New Breed of Strategic Planner," *Business Week*, September 17, 1984, pp. 62–68; P. H. Thurston, "Should Smaller Companies Make Formal Plans," *Harvard Business Review*, September/October 1983, pp. 162–188; S. S. Thune and R. T. House, "Where Long Range Planning Pays Off," *Business Horizons*, August 1970, pp. 81–87; S. C. Wheelwright, "Japan—Where Operations Really Are Strategic," *Harvard Business Review*, July/August 1981, pp. 56–66; D. R. Wood, Jr. and R. L. LaForge, "The Impact of Comprehensive Planning on Financial Performance," *Academy of Management Journal*, March 1979, pp. 81–87.

ment. In setting strategic objectives and in formulating strategy, organizational strategists examine mission, policy, and information. The evaluation of alternatives is a vital part of the strategy formulation process.

5. Implementation. Four primary critical issues are involved in implementation: how the organization is organized, having appropriate implementation systems, the proper management of human resources, and the management of organizational culture. The components and relationships among these factors are revealed in Figure 8.2 (Chapter 8). Implementation is now recognized as being very critical to the success of strategic management.

   a. **Structuring, Organizing.** The tasks required by objectives and plans must be specifically defined, with objectives distributed to combinations of tasks known as jobs; and the authority to accomplish these tasks must be granted in order for implementation to occur satisfactorily. Jobs must also be grouped into departments. Choosing the primary macro structure can have a major impact on the success of the strategy and is a decision which must be carefully made. The structure must be appropriate to the strategy.

   b. **Implementation Systems.** Integrated planning and control systems are necessary to insure that strategies are converted into individual and work group objectives and actions, and that results occur. Leadership, motivation, and communication systems are necessary to insure that individuals and groups know and understand their tasks and objectives, and are motivated to accomplish them. Human resource management systems are necessary to insure that human resources are properly managed from the total organizational perspective. Concerns include personnel practices such as recruitment and selection, training and development, compensation, and performance appraisal. The organization's culture must be designed to be compatible with strategy if strategy is to succeed.

   c. **Management of Human Resources.** One of the major concerns of successfully implementing strategy is the manner in which managers motivate and lead subordinates, and how they communicate to them. Of special interest in the top management levels is the nature of compensation. Furthermore, politics and understanding of organizational behavior are fundamental requirements to arriving at successful implementation.

   d. **Organizational Culture.** One of the most important realizations of the 1980s has been that organizational culture impacts significantly upon productivity. An organization's culture may be defined in various ways, but perhaps is most easily defined as that set of characteristics of purpose and action that separates one organization from another in a given time frame. Development of the appropriate culture is essential to organizational success. The various characteristics must be sufficiently synergistic or there will not be as effective or efficient an organization as management seeks. A vital component of the organization's culture is a series of shared values.

6. **Evaluation and Control.** Strategists must determine whether the master strategy was or will be successful and take appropriate actions based on their findings.

In quite simple terms, the contents of the model address three basic issues common to all strategic situations:

1.   **Where are we now?**

2.   **Where do we want to be?**

3.   **How do we get there?**

The Plan of This Book

The remainder of this text examines in more detail the two processes introduced in Figures 1.1 and 1.2. In Chapters 1 and 2, the objectives determination and strategy formulation processes are reviewed. The remainder of Chapter 1 discusses mission, strategic policy, and organizational strategists and how these three factors affect the processes outlined in Figure 1.2. Chapter 2 discusses the critical role of the fourth major influential factor in master strategy formulation—strategic information. Chapter 3 continues this discussion, concentrating on the steps in setting objectives and formulating strategy and on various techniques for improving the results of these processes. Chapter 4 reviews major functional strategies and discusses the principal contents of the master strategy at the SBU level, while Chapter 5 focuses on the major content of the master strategy and on the strategy formulation process in multiple-SBU firms. Chapter 6 examines the major behavioral aspects of the objectives setting and strategy formulation processes. Chapter 7 continues the discussion of the strategic management process model, focusing on the organizational elements of implementation. Chapter 8 concludes the discussion of implementation, reviewing implementation systems, human resources management, and shared values and culture. Chapter 9 completes the material on the strategic management process with a review of how evaluation and control are carried out.

In Chapters 10 and 11, the international and nonprofit applications of the topics examined are presented. The business organization is most often used to illustrate the concepts presented in the text, but nonprofit examples are also employed.

Related comprehensive cases, grouped according to the primary components of the Strategic Management Process Model (Figure 1.1), follow the textual material and are followed by four appendixes. The first appendix, "The Case Method," tells you how to approach cases and how to learn from them. The next is a strategic audit for your use in analyzing cases and actual organizations. The third is a review of how to interpret financial statements. The fourth contains key information on the economy and major news events during the period of the cases.

The following pages in this chapter and Chapter 2 examine the four factors that most strongly influence the setting of objectives. These same four factors and the strategic objectives determined from them also greatly affect strategy formulation. The role of these factors in that process is also discussed in this and the next chapter.

Purpose is the unifying principle around which human
energy clusters in the organization.

▪ *Robert R. Blake and Jane S. Mouton* ▪

Mission

Mission, or purpose, is the organization's raison d'etre, its reason to be. Mission is the primary consideration upon which organizational objectives, policies, and strategies are based. Classifying organizations into various typologies is useful in understanding and predicting organizational strategy. Classification factors which might be expected to have an impact on strategy include

- The organization's size—small, medium, or large.
- Its geographic scope—local, national, or multinational.
- The number and diversity of businesses it comprises—single-SBU or multiple-SBU organization.

However, mission exerts the most basic influence on strategy composition. The most obvious segmentation of organizations according to mission uses categories of profit and nonprofit. More definitively, Peter M. Blau and W. Richard Scott have identified four major types of organizations according to the group which receives the greatest benefit from the organization's existence. This classification scheme is essentially based on mission and the classifications are not mutually exclusive; an organization may, in fact, be appropriately classified into more than one category. The typologies are[3]

1. The business concern, which benefits the owners (and, it might be added, the employees and most of those who transact with it)—for example, General Motors.

2. The mutual benefit association, which benefits the members themselves—for example, a union or a club.

3. The service organization, which benefits its clients—for example, United Way and the U.S. Department of Health and Human Resources.

4. The commonweal organization, which benefits society in general—for example, the U.S. Department of Defense.

One would anticipate that these differing basic missions would result in varying strategies. But these simple statements of purpose alone are insufficient to distinguish one organization's mission from another when both have the same primary beneficiary. For example, all members of the business organization classification seek profit, so profit alone cannot be an organization's complete definition of purpose. Rather, as Phillip Kotler and John A. Pearce II suggest, an organization's mission is viewed as its broadly stated definition of basic business scope and operations which distinguishes it from other organizations of similar types.[4] The primary thrust of this mission statement is external, focuses on markets and customers, and typically notes current fields of endeavor. In addition to these characteristics, many mission statements include descriptions of additional basic concerns. Among them are such factors as product quality, location of facilities, important aspects of perceived strategic advantage, and so forth. The mission statement often reveals not only purpose but business philosophy as well.

Profit obtained by satisfying a societal need is the overriding purpose of all business organizations. Mission statements simply further identify how one business intends to achieve profit as opposed to how another similar firm might do so. These statements must be carefully worded, since they provide direction for policy, objectives, and strategy. Information Capsule 1.1 contains examples of mission statements abstracted from several

[3]P. M. Blau and W. R. Scott, *Formal Organizations* (New York: Chandler, 1962), pp. 250–253.

[4]Phillip Kotler, *Marketing Management: Analysis, Planning, Control* (Englewood Cliffs, N.J.: Prentice-Hall, 1980), pp. 50–54; John A Pearce II, "The Company Mission as a Strategic Tool," *Sloan Management Review*, Spring 1982, p. 15.

"We are gathered here today, gentlemen, to make money."

Source: Drawing by Opie; © 1977 *The New Yorker Magazine*, Inc.

organizations' annual reports or philosophies. Note the diversity in the statements and also the approaches to mission taken by the "new" AT&T, and one of its former subsidiaries.

Mission statements change for numerous reasons; the appearance of opportunities or threats is a common reason. New management often introduces changes. For example, when Roy E. Winegardner was elected chief executive of Holiday Inns, he made major changes in the firm's mission. As he declared, "We are in the process of reshaping Holiday Inns into a different company . . . a hospitality company." The principal result was to limit the company's scope to food, lodging, and entertainment, moving the company out of some businesses (Trailways) and into an active casino gambling position.[5]

Note the variations, and also the similarities and common components, among the mission statements in Information Capsule 1.1. As you can see, not all mission statements address each of the issues felt to be appropriate for inclusion. The basic question these statements seek to answer is "What business are we in or do we want to be in?"

In fact, it [mission] must lie in society since business enterprise is an organ of society.

▪ *Peter Drucker, 1974* ▪

[5]R. E. Winegardner, as reported in "Holiday Inns: Refining Its Focus to Food, Lodging—and More Casinos," *Business Week*, July 21, 1980, pp. 100, 104.

===== **INFORMATION CAPSULE 1.1** =====
Mission Statements

Zale Corporation

Our business is specialty retailing. Retailing is a people-oriented business. We recognize that our business existence and continued success are dependent upon how well we meet our responsibilities to several critically important groups of people.

Our first responsibility is to our customers. Without them we would have no reason for being. We strive to appeal to a broad spectrum of consumers, catering in a professional manner to their needs. Our concept of value to the customer includes a wide selection of quality merchandise, competitively priced and delivered with courtesy and professionalism.

Our ultimate responsibility is to our shareholders. Our goal is to earn an optimum return on invested capital through steady profit growth and prudent, aggressive asset management. The attainment of this financial goal, coupled with a record of sound management, represents our approach toward influencing the value placed upon our common stock in the market.

We feel a deep, personal responsibility to our employees. As an equal opportunity employer, we seek to create and maintain an environment where every employee is provided the opportunity to develop to his or her maximum potential. We expect to reward employees commensurate with their contribution to the success of the company.

We are committed to honesty and integrity in all relationships with suppliers of goods and services. We are demanding but fair. We evaluate our suppliers on the basis of quality, price, and service.

We recognize community involvement as an important obligation and as a viable business objective. Support of worthwhile community projects in areas where we operate generally accrues to the health and well-being of the community. This makes the community a better place for our employees to live and a better place for us to operate.

We believe in the Free Enterprise System and in the American Democratic form of government under which this superior economic system has been permitted to flourish. We feel an incumbent responsibility to insure that our business operates at a reasonable profit. Profit provides opportunity for growth and job security. We believe growth is necessary to provide opportunities on an ever increasing scale for our people. Therefore, we are dedicated to profitable growth—growth as a company and growth as individuals.

This mission statement spells out the creed by which we live.

Source: John A. Pearce II, "The Company Mission As A Strategy Tool," *Sloan Management Review*, Spring 1982, p. 16.

The "New" (Deregulated) AT&T

Defining Our Business

This new AT&T is in the business of meeting customer needs, worldwide, for the electronic movement and management of information.

We will provide modern, nationwide telecommunications facilities, offering a range of services unmatched by other long distance carriers.

We will develop and manufacture equipment and systems for our own and other networks, domestically and internationally.

We will design, produce and market communications and information products, systems and services for customers whose requirements are large and complex as well as for those whose needs are relatively few and simple.

We will design and produce electronic components, computers and software systems for use within our own organization and outside it.

We do not take a narrow view of the opportunities open to us—or of the market we are in. We see that market as a global one, and we will approach the various aspects of our business—research and development, manufacturing, marketing, distribution and service—from that global perspective.

We will not try to be all things to all people, but in everything we do we intend to be the best.

Customer Satisfaction

Our overarching goal will be customer satisfaction. All that we do will have meaning and purpose only as it serves that goal. And, by continuously striving to achieve customer satisfaction, we will ensure not only that we enhance the value of our shareowners' investment but that we retain the valued attributes that have distinguished our past.

From our past we bring with us impressive strengths: highly skilled and experienced people; an acknowledged proficiency in science, technology and engineering; a deserved reputation for service excellence; an emerging professionalism in marketing; and our experience in organizing resources and managing operations and systems on a very large scale.

We bring with us, as well, a sense of responsibility to conform our policies to what we believe to be the public interest.

And, finally, we bring with us fond memories of the many people whose dedication to service quality made this company so successful in the past and whose untiring efforts went into restructuring it for the future.

Source: AT&T, *Annual Report*, 1983, p. 3.

BellSouth

In short, our mission is to secure an attractive return for shareowners, provide high-quality service to our customers, and give our employees good opportunities now and into the future.

The telecommunications business is what we know best, and it will be the focus of our efforts in these early years. For the immediate future, BellSouth's primary mission will be to provide information distribution services in the local exchange and exchange access markets through the regulated subsidiaries of Southern Bell and South Central Bell.

But to prosper in the long term, we believe BellSouth must diversify. Thus, within our regulatory and legal framework, the corporation will also aggressively seek and create promising new markets for other products and services. Likely, new ventures will draw on the company's inherent strengths from existing technology and from the knowledge and training of its employees.

Related Description of the BellSouth Business

BellSouth has a lot of good things going for it. It operates in a growth area of the country, the Sunbelt. Population in the nine-state area served by its operating companies is expected to increase by 14 million by the year 2000.

Telecommunications, which is the focus of BellSouth's business, is considered by many experts to be *the* growth industry for the rest of the century.

Our two operating companies—South Central Bell and Southern Bell—were among the best earning companies in the Bell System. Both have networks that are among the most technologically advanced in the nation, and they have a legacy of 100 years of excellent service behind them.

We have about 99,000 employees, two-thirds of whom have at least 10 years of service, and many have worked together in the past when South Central Bell was part of Southern Bell. They have a strong background in innovative technology, having participated in many AT&T field trials of new products and services over the past 15 years.

Source: BellSouth, *Annual Report*, 1983, pp. 6–7.

CBS

CBS Inc. is a broad-based entertainment and communications company which operates one of the country's three commercial broadcast television networks and two nationwide radio networks. In addition, CBS owns five television stations and six AM and seven FM radio stations. The Company is the world's largest producer, manufacturer and marketer of recorded music and a leading music publisher; a major publisher of magazines and books for educational, consumer and professional markets; and a major manufacturer and distributor of toys and musical instruments. CBS also operates a unit which produces theatrical feature films, and is involved through joint ventures in additional motion picture production activities and in the marketing of videocassettes and videodiscs.

Source: CBS, *Annual Report*, 1984, p. 8.

Hewlett-Packard Company

Hewlett-Packard Company is a major designer and manufacturer of precision electronic equipment for measurement, analysis and computation. The interactive capabilities of HP instruments and systems enable its customers—decision makers in business and technical fields worldwide—to gain access to essential information, put it into meaningful form and use it effectively to improve their productivity.

HP makes more than 6,400 products that have broad application in the fields of science, engineering, business, industry, medicine and education. Principal product groups include computers and computer systems, handheld calculators and computer/calculator peripheral products; test and measuring instrumentation and solid-state components; medical electronic equipment; and instrumentation for chemical analysis.

Source: Hewlett-Packard, *Annual Report*, 1983, p. 1.

Delta Air Lines

Delta Air Lines, Inc., is a major trunk air carrier providing scheduled air transportation for passengers, freight, and mail over a network of routes throughout the United States and abroad. Delta's route structure crisscrosses the entire eastern half of the nation and connects much of it with the Southwest and the Far West. In addition, Delta operates flights to Canada, Bermuda, the Bahamas, Puerto Rico, England, and Germany. Service over most of Delta's routes is highly competitive. As an air carrier, Delta is subject to federal regulation pursuant to the Federal Aviation Act of 1958, as amended, as well as many other federal, state, and foreign laws and regulations.

Source: Delta Air Lines, *Annual Report*, 1984, inside cover.

Allegheny International

Allegheny International, Inc. (AI) is a global corporation, serving worldwide markets for utilitarian consumer goods and high-technology industrial specialties. Our operations extend from the corporate headquarters in Pittsburgh, Pennsylvania, to almost 400 regional headquarters, operating locations, sales offices, and distribution points on six continents.

Source: Allegheny International Inc., *Annual Report*, 1984, inside cover.

It is critical to organizational success that this question of business engagement be answered properly. In 1975, W. T. Grant, a retail chain with almost $2 billion in sales and 1,000 stores, went bankrupt. One of the major underlying causes of its failure was that it overlooked this basic question. One W. T. Grant executive commented that the company could not make up its mind whether it wanted to be a full-service store like JCPenney and Sears Roebuck or a discounter like K mart. The company compromised and "took a position between the two and consequently stood for nothing"[6]—and also consequently went bankrupt.

Similarly, Braniff Airlines, in 1979, decided that it wanted to be a national airline, not just a regional one. The results were disastrous. The company lost $131 million in 1980.[7] The president resigned and eventually the airline declared bankruptcy. As of early 1985, it has yet to successfully recover from this strategic error, despite reorganization and capital infusion. The mission statement must always reflect capabilities, but Braniff's choice of mission overlooked its managerial, aircraft, and professional flight staff capabilities. It simply did not have enough managers, enough airplanes, or enough pilots and host personnel to meet the demands of rampant growth. Nor could it obtain planes or personnel, or train personnel quickly enough, to meet these demands.[8] Its future was predictable.

Practically as well as conceptually speaking, all organizational activity derives from its mission. Without a proper mission statement, the organization may ultimately be doomed

---

[6] J. G. Kendrick, as quoted in "How W. T. Grant Lost $175 Million Last Year," *Business Week*, February 24, 1975, p. 75.

[7] Braniff Airlines, *Annual Report*, 1980, p. 4.

[8] This is the authors' personal analyses.

to failure. Most commercial banks are struggling with this very issue. They wonder if they shouldn't be financial services institutions, not "just banks."

Undertaking the definition of a company mission is one of the most easily slighted tasks in the strategic management process. . . . But the critical role of the company mission as the basis of orchestrating managerial action is repeatedly demonstrated by failing firms whose short-run actions are ultimately found to be counterproductive to their long-run purpose.

▪ *John A. Pearce II* ▪

Organizational Policy

The term *policy* is used here to designate broad guidance created to ensure the successful establishment of objectives and the successful formulation, implementation, and control of strategy. Most policies have a broad and major impact on the organization, but some have a more limited impact and are designed to guide decisions through the use of more specific constraints. Policies provide organization members, primarily managers, with a framework within which they can make decisions. Examples of policies include the following:

1. Only products with at least a 15 percent return on investment (ROI) will be considered as additions to existing product lines.
2. Only products with high quality will be chosen for inclusion in the product line.

Because of these policies, this firm's corporate, business, and division managers will not select products which do not provide at least this rate of return and which do not have high quality. Because the managers do not have to determine what level of ROI is appropriate or what level of product quality is sought, the policies save time and effort.

As with the term *strategy*, the usage of the term *policy* varies greatly. The student of strategic management should recognize this fact and should not allow semantic problems to interfere with organizational analysis. The term is often employed to describe what is defined—here and often elsewhere—as strategy. Or the term may be used to describe very specific rules, such as "no smoking" or "employees retire at age 65." Often, policy is considered a component of strategy. In various contexts, strategies have a way of shading into policies, and vice versa.

Regardless of what we call them, however, an organization must have major plans of action in order to accomplish its mission. The organization must also have some form of broad guidance for formulating, implementing, and controlling these plans. These components of effective organizations are labeled here as *strategy* and *policy*, respectively.

Business policy has a tendency for jargon that delineates and isolates the field from the uninitiated.

▪ *Milton Leontiades* ▪

You will note that Figure 1.1 identifies three major types of policies: strategic policies, policies that aid implementation, and control policies. Let us now examine the first of these—strategic policies—in more detail.

Organizational Policy at the Strategic Level

The master strategy derives from the organization's mission and from the policies which exist to provide guidance in formulating it. These policies, which are called strategic policies here, are usually created by the owners, the board of directors, the chief executive officer (CEO), top line and staff personnel, top SBU managers, or professional planners; however, other organizational members may aid in their formulation. Some organizations refer to these policies as "basic assumptions." Others designate them "primary intents." Still others refer to them as "master policies." But regardless of its designation, certain guidance must be available to the organization's strategists as they determine strategic objectives and formulate the master strategy. In the business organization, this guidance normally relates to the following issues, although exact policies vary from firm to firm:

1.   The return on investment desired and other performance criteria.
2.   The scope of the strategy.
3.   The basic actions in which the organization may engage; competition, growth, diversification, and so on.
4.   The industries to be entered.
5.   The qualifications of products to be offered.
6.   The organization's climate and management philosophy.
7.   The geographic location of the basic actions.
8.   The role of the organization in the total society.

Based on the issues above and on consideration of mission and internal and environmental information, the organization's strategists determine objectives and formulate strategies. After considering information related to internal and external environmental factors, the organization's strategists may, from time to time, redefine the basic policies which guide the formulation of strategic objectives and of the master strategy and its component strategies. For example, examination of internal factors may reveal critical inabilities which preclude diversification. Or exploration of the external environment may reveal that new industry opportunities are available. Strategic policies must remain flexible if the organization is to be successful. Conceptually, strategic policies constitute a body of statements different from strategic objectives and strategies. In practice, however, the three are often intermingled. Policies exist at every level of the organization. At the highest level, strategic policies guide the formation of strategic objectives and the master strategy. Lower-level policies should be subordinate to those at higher levels of the strategy. Information Capsule 1.2 contains the strategic policies for a highly successful firm—the Coca-Cola Company. Note that these policies contain some objectives that are so specific as occasionally to constitute a strategy.[9]

Once strategic, or master, policies are established, the organization literally lives or dies by them. Both implementation and control policies, discussed in later chapters, are based on the outcomes of these strategic policies. All three types of policies are critical. The title of this book stresses the importance of both strategic management and one of its principal components, policy. Neither can be overlooked. Since all actions will follow the

---

[9]Most of the early strategic management writings, which came from the Harvard School of Business, defined strategy as that "set of major policies which defined what the organization wanted to be or become."

INFORMATION CAPSULE 1.2
Coca-Cola's Strategic Policies

Our Challenge

In order to give my vision of our Company for 1990, I must first postulate what I visualize our mission to be during the 1980s. I see our *challenge* as continuing the growth in profits of our highly successful existing main businesses, and those we may choose to enter, at a rate substantially in excess of inflation, in order to give our shareholders an above average total return on their investment. The unique position of excellence that the trademark Coca-Cola has attained in the world will be protected and enhanced as a primary objective.

Our Business

I perceive us by the 1990s to continue to be or become the *leading force in the soft drink industry* in each of the countries in which it is economically feasible for us to be so. We shall continue to emphasize product quality worldwide, as well as market share improvement in growth markets. The *products of our Foods Division* will also continue to be the leading entries in those markets which they serve, particularly in the U.S. *The Wine Spectrum* will continue to be managed for significant growth with special attention paid to optimizing return on assets.*

In the U.S. we will also become a stronger factor in the *packaged consumer goods business*. I do not rule out providing appropriate *services* to this same consumer as well. It is most likely that we will be in industries in which we are not today. We will not, however, stray far from our major strengths: an impeccable and positive image with the consumer, a unique franchise system second to none; and the intimate knowledge of, and contacts with, local business conditions around the world.

In choosing new areas of business, each market we enter must have sufficient inherent real growth potential to make entry desirable. It is not our desire to battle continually for share in a stagnant market in these new areas of business. By and large, industrial markets are not our business.

Finally, we shall tirelessly investigate services that complement our product lines and that are compatible with our consumer image.

Our Consumers

Company management at all levels will be committed to *serving* to the best of its ability our Bottlers and our consumers, as well as the retail and wholesale distribution systems through which these consumers are reached. These are our primary targets. The world is our arena in which to win marketing victories as we must.

Our Shareholders

We shall, during the next decade, remain totally committed to our shareholders and to the *protection and enhancement* of their investment and confidence in our Company, its character and style, products and image.

---

*In implementing our strategy, the sale of The Wine Spectrum to Joseph E. Seagram & Sons, Inc., was completed in November 1983.

Our "Bottom Line"

My financial vision is not complicated, but it will require courage and commitment to attain financial goals consistently and effect growth in real profits, most especially during uncertain and fast changing economic times.

Our strong balance sheet and financial position will be maintained so that the Company can withstand any economic windstorm, as well as enable us to take advantage of expansion opportunities which complement our existing business and that offer acceptable earnings growth and return on investment.

It is our desire to continue to pay ever-increasing dividends to our shareholders. This will be done as a result of rapidly increasing annual earnings while of necessity reducing our dividend pay-out ratio, in order to reinvest a greater percentage of our earnings to help sustain the growth rate which we must have. We shall consider divesting assets when they no longer generate acceptable returns and earnings growth. *Increasing annual earnings per share and effecting increased return on equity* are still the name of the game—but not to the extent that our longer term viability is threatened.

Our People

Finally, let me comment on this vision as it affects our "life style"—or business behavior—as a viable international business entity. I have previously referred to the *courage* and *commitment* that will be indispensable as we move through the 1980s. To this I wish to add *integrity* and *fairness*, and insist that the combination of these four ethics be permeated from top to bottom throughout our organization so that our behavior will produce leaders, good managers, and—most importantly—entrepreneurs. It is my desire that we take initiatives as opposed to being only reactive and that we *encourage intelligent individual risk-taking*.

As a true international company with a multicultural and multinational employee complement, we must foster the "international family" concept which has been a part of our tradition. All employees will have equal opportunities to grow, develop and advance within the Company. Their progress will depend only on their abilities, ambition and achievements.

Our Wisdom

When we arrive at the 1990s, my vision is to be able to say with confidence that all of us in our own way displayed:

- The ability to see the *long-term consequences* of current actions;
- The willingness to sacrifice, if necessary, short-term gains for *longer-term benefits*;
- The sensitivity to *anticipate and adapt to change*—change in consumer life styles, change in consumer tastes and change in consumer needs;
- The commitment to manage our enterprise in such a way that we will always *be considered a welcomed and important part of the business community* in each and every country in which we do business; and
- The capacity to *control what is controllable* and the wisdom not to bother what is not.

Source: Roberto C. Goizueta, Chairman, Board of Directors and Chief Executive Officer, The Coca-Cola Company, in a 1983 update of a March 4, 1981, endorsement by the Board of Directors, "Strategies for the 1980s."

guidance provided in policy, proper policy formulation is critical to organizational suc-cess. W. T. Grant had very few policies, and most of those it did have were inappropriate. It went bankrupt. Firms such as Martin Marietta and K mart have highly functional poli-cies based on mission and information. Such policies allow firms to survive and prosper.

> *Most battles are won—or lost—before they are engaged,*
> *by men who take no part in them; by their strategists.*
>
> ▪ *K. von Clausewitz* ▪

The Organizational Strategists

In concept, organizational strategists, those involved in general management, include the owners, the board of directors, the CEO, and the top corporate and SBU line and staff officers, including professional planners. However, the evidence suggests that in reality an organization's strategic decision processes are dominated by an entrepreneurial chief exec-utive, a coalition of high-ranking corporate or SBU officers, or other strategists. For ex-ample, top-level line managers are becoming more and more involved in the strategic pro-cess as "intrapreneurship" increases in U.S. corporations. Some professional planners in certain organizations also determine strategy. The strategic decisions of all of these strat-egists are affected by their needs, values, and skills. Each of these may in turn be substan-tially affected in their strategic decisions by the inputs from corporate professional plan-ners. Before we examine the roles of the dominant strategists noted above, let us review the impact of boards of directors on strategic management.[10]

The Board of Directors and Strategic Management

Management does 90 percent to 95 percent of the talking. Outside board members, who are not part of the management, sit there and listen; then they go to lunch, and then go home and open the envelopes that contain their fees. . . . It is well known and accepted that only those men and women who can "get along" are elected to the board and stay on it.

> ▪ *Harold S. Geneen, Former President, ITT, 1984* ▪

Research reveals that the board of directors has historically performed few of the classic functions conceptualized for it, such as strategic decision making. While the board may have passively approved the organization's objectives and strategies, normally it has had very little impact on their formulation and has not scrutinized them in very great detail. Furthermore, the evidence indicates that most board members have been ill-prepared to make such decisions. However, during the 1970s, failures of several major boards to take appropriate actions combined with lawsuits and proxy actions by disgruntled stockholders and citizens' groups resulted in the board's becoming much more professional, diverse, and responsive, at least in major corporations.

---

[10] H. Mintzberg, "Strategy Making in Three Modes," *California Management Review*, Winter 1973, pp. 45–46, identified three primary strategists: the CEO, the coalition, and the planning department. Recent evidence sug-gests that planning departments have lost much of their power and are now principally advisory in nature. See "The New Breed of Strategic Planner," *Business Week*, September 17, 1984, pp. 62–66.

The role of the board of directors, while historically not well understood and not followed operationally as outlined conceptually, has in recent years become of major concern to corporations. The result has been an emphasis on increasing the board's role in making strategic decisions, monitoring executive performance and compensation, assuring the soundness of budgeting, and determining the soundness of policies. The number of outside directors has significantly increased, and a definite trend toward use of professional board members has become apparent. While the actions of boards naturally vary from firm to firm, we can anticipate continued efforts by boards to take a more active part in the organization's strategic process.

The coalitions which may develop on the board are very important, since the board must finally approve the chosen strategies. Research reveals that top management often controls the board rather than vice versa, as is normally conceptualized.[11] The behavioral aspects of the strategic decision process are examined in detail in Chapter 6, with special attention given to the coalition process. Let us now examine in more conceptual terms how each of the major groups of strategists may influence the strategic management process.

The principal function of the strategists in determining objectives and formulating strategy is to consider mission, strategic policies, and information and then determine objectives which best match the needs of the organization, given the information available about strengths, weaknesses, opportunities, and threats. Then the strategists look at these same three factors in determining plans to reach the desired objectives. How the major types of strategists—the entrepreneurial CEO, the coalition, and the top-line managers—go about their tasks may vary, however.

The Chief Executive Officer as Strategist

The CEO clearly dominates strategy formulation in practically all smaller firms, in most medium-sized firms, and in many, if not most, large firms. Within multiple-SBU com-

[11]K. R. Andrews, Replaying the Board's Role in Formulating Strategy," *Harvard Business Review*, May/June 1981, pp. 18–20, 24–25; K. R. Andrews, "Corporate Strategy as a Vital Function of the Board," *Harvard Business Review*, November/December 1981, p. 175; W. W. Wommack, "The Board's Most Important Function," *Harvard Business Review*, September/October 1979, pp. 52–62; "The Board: It's Obsolete Unless Overhauled," *Business Week*, May 22, 1971, pp. 50–58; W. Boulton, "The Evolving Board: A Look at the Board's Changing Roles and Information Needs," *Academy of Management Review*, October 1978, pp. 827–836; M. Chandler, "It's Time to Clean up the Boardroom," *Harvard Business Review*, September/October 1975, pp. 73–82; N. C. Churchill, V. Lewis, and C. Ramsay, "Changing Strategic Requirements of Boards of Directors as Companies Develop and Grow" (Paper presented to the Strategic Management Society Conference, Paris, October 1983); W. D. Clendenin, "Company Presidents Look at the Board of Directors," *California Management Review*, Spring 1972, pp. 60–66; "End of the Director's Rubber Stamp," *Business Week*, September 10, 1979, pp. 72–77; S. M. Felton, Jr., "Case of the Board and the Strategic Process," *Harvard Business Review*, July/August 1979, pp. 19–22; P. B. Firstenberg and B. G. Malkiel, "Why Corporate Boards Need Independent Directors," *Management Review*, April 1980, pp. 26–28; J. A. Groobey, "Making the Board of Directors More Effective." *California Management Review*, Spring 1974, pp. 25–34; J. W. Henke, Jr., "Making the Board of Directors' Involvement in Corporate Strategy Work" (Paper presented to the Strategic Management Society Conference, Paris, October 1983); S. L. Jacobs, "A Well-Chosen Outside Board Gives Owners Peace of Mind," *The Wall Street Journal*, January 21, 1985, p. 25; M. Launstein, "Preserving the Importance of the Board," *Harvard Business Review*, July/August 1977, pp. 36–47; M. S. Mizruchi, "Who Controls Whom? An Examination of the Relation Between Management and Board of Directors in Large American Corporations," *Academy of Management Review*, July 1983, pp. 426–435; J. Montgomery, "New Direction: Citizens and Southern Shakeup Underscores Evaluation of Boards," *The Wall Street Journal*, March 21, 1978; R. Mueller, *New Directions for Directors* (Lexington, Mass.: Lexington Books, 1978).

panies, total organization strategies are determined by corporate CEOs or other strategists, with the SBU corporate strategies being determined by SBU CEOs or other strategists. CEOs who affect strategy may be either owner/entrepreneurs or professional managers who take risks and who seek the power that such positions and decisions involve.

Almost all U.S. corporations were begun or made successful by entrepreneurially oriented owner/managers: Sears (Richard W. Sears), Xerox (Joseph Wilson), Eastern Airlines (Captain Eddie Rickenbacker), Jim Walters Corporation (Jim Walters), Eckerd Drugs (Jack Eckerd), the Coca-Cola Company (John Woodruff), Ford Motor Company (Henry Ford), Mary Kay Cosmetics (Mary Kay), Wendy's (R. David Thomas), George E. Johnson Company (George E. Johnson), Marriott Corporation (J. Willard Marriott), and McDonald's (Ray Kroc), to name a few. Many firms, including some of those just mentioned, have also been tremendously affected in their strategic courses of action by professional managers who took risks and acted as entrepreneurs—General Motors (Alfred P. Sloan), the Coca-Cola Company (J. Paul Austin), Miller Brewing Company (John A. Murphy), and Radio Shack (Charles Tandy), for example.

Look around your town or city. How many businesses are there run by a CEO or a family dominated by one person? Almost all businesses are headed by one person, aren't they? These managers are the backbone of the system of free enterprise, which rewards the investor, the innovator, and the risk taker.

In recent years, substantial concern has been expressed that this entrepreneurial motivation is missing from large, dominant corporations. Indeed, this concern appears to be well founded; and as a result, the ability of U.S. firms to compete in the international arena has been significantly reduced. This is especially true with respect to competing with Japanese firms, which actively seek to further the success of their organizations in the long run, not the short run. Consequently, many firms are now sponsoring entrepreneurship programs where managers run divisions as if they were their own businesses, thus becoming "intrapreneurs." [12]

As you progress through this text, the importance of taking the strategic management viewpoint will be further emphasized. U.S. firms do seem to have realized their overemphasis on the short term and do seem to be responding to the challenge of international competition. One of the biggest keys to success in international competition is to correlate the strategist's compensation to long-term successes and not to short-term successes such as those indicated by current profits and ROI. Information Capsule 1.3 discusses Japanese management systems and how they stress the strategic view.

Coalitions as Strategists

The business organization, whether a single- or multiple-SBU type, is a formal authority system composed of subsystems. Within this system and within these subsystems, informal social systems develop. These informal relationships often play a major role in strategy formulation.

Studies of the objectives-setting and strategy formulation processes have revealed that one or more powerful informal groups of top managers may emerge within the formal

[12]For example, in the "Productivity" issue of *Business Week* see the article entitled "Managers Who Are No Longer Entrepreneurs," June 30, 1980, pp. 74–75.

====== **INFORMATION CAPSULE 1.3** ======
Japanese Management and the Strategic View

Examining the Japanese success story shows that several factors have contributed to the enormous strides the Japanese have made economically in the last 15 years. Careful examination of the evidence reveals that the following five factors have especially contributed to this success:

1. *Cooperation between Government and Business.* Japan's government steers firms in the proper strategic direction, toward areas in which potential profits appear highest. Tax incentives, subsidies, import quotas, and R&D funding are used to this end.

2. *Cooperation between Labor and Business.* The confrontation which characterizes the U.S. labor/business interaction is largely absent in Japan.

3. *Management Style.* Employee participation in decision making, recognition of employees' performance and human needs, and employee job security are key ingredients in the Japanese management style which have clearly contributed to Japanese successes. These considerations are typically absent in U.S. managerial actions, but are increasingly being adopted as U.S. firms seek to become more competitive.

4. *Management Development and Education.* Japanese managers continually receive training on how to manage, especially interpersonal relationships. U.S. companies, in contrast, invest relatively little in such endeavors.

5. *Management Systems—Strategic and Quantitative.* Japanese managers take the strategic view. Their marketing actions, production actions, and personnel actions reflect a concern for the long-run viability of the firm. For example, they may stress market share more than profits; but in the long run, market share will lead to profits. This contrasts with U.S. management objectives, which often emphasize short-run results, such as annual profit. Because Japanese managers know their firms will be competitive in ten years, and that they will still be employed by the same firm, they are willing to sacrifice now for that future success.

   Statistical analysis is employed at every stage of the production or service process to measure the quality of inputs, to make certain that the process is as it should be, and to measure the quality of outputs. This emphasis on statistics and quality control was suggested by an American consultant, William Deming of Washington, D.C., a prophet not recognized, until recently, in his own land. The Japanese success story has, however, brought recognition to his work.

planning group. These informal groups, referred to as coalitions, may, in fact, establish an organization's objectives and strategies, depending on the nature of the entrepreneurial leadership characteristics of the organization's formal leader, and the ability of one coalition to dominate the others.

Bargaining often determines organizational objectives, strategies, and policies. Members of the dominant coalition negotiate strategic matters among themselves, with other powerful individuals, or with other coalitions which may develop inside or outside the organization. At the center of this bargaining process is the conflict which exists between, on the one hand, the manager's desire to accomplish his or her particular subunit's objectives and to protect its interests (and his or her own) and, on the other hand, the requirement of the organization to accomplish organizational objectives. Because managers must seek to improve subunit performance in organizations with scarce resources, they must compete with other managers for those resources. But total competition would be detrimental to the firm; thus, bargaining and tradeoffs in strategy and policy matters occur. The result is often suboptimization and failure to accomplish the mission. Nonetheless, negotiated solutions are often necessary and often efficient and effective. (It is interesting to note that coalitions play a very prominent role in the government and other nonprofit organizations.)

While many of the ideas presented here oppose the traditional view of the all-powerful chief executive officer, significant empirical support substantiates them. The evidence is reviewed in more detail in Chapter 6.

Other Strategists

The "other strategists" group is comprised of two principle subgroups: top-line management and professional planners. Occasionally, outside influences, such as strategic management consultants or various board members, may also be active participants in strategic decision making. Most typically, however, top-line managers of both business and functional areas are becoming more and more involved in the strategic process.

Top-Line Managers.   Influenced by many factors (recessions and changing management philosophies for example), organizations and their top managers (Chief Executive Officers, CEOs and Chief Operating Officers, COOs) have begun to realize the importance of involving those who are closest to the problem or opportunity in its solution. These same individuals are also those who are most likely to have to implement strategic decisions. One of the changes occurring in management philosophy is to delegate the decision making to the closest link to the situation. Another change is to eliminate many staff and middle-management positions in the organization (even those between upper levels of management) to make the organization "lean and mean." There is also a trend to involve the implementers in the process.

Thus, we see more and more top-line managers actively engaged in strategic decision making. For example, the plant manager has much more input into strategic decisions than he or she did five years ago. Operations are of much greater strategic concern than they were in the late 1970s and early 1980s. Furthermore, those who have both profit and loss responsibility within the organization have become "intropreneurs" in that they have gained control over their divisions as if these were their own businesses.[13] These and other related trends are noted throughout this text. Now let us examine the role of professional planners in strategy formulation, both as staff advisors and occasionally as actual decision makers.

---

[13] "The New Breed of Strategic Planner," *Business Week*, September 17, 1984, pp. 62–68.

Planning Departments—Professional Planners as Strategists.   When the duties associated with strategy formulation become too extensive for the CEO to accomplish alone, he or she normally delegates many of these duties to a planning committee of top managers or, in larger organizations, to a professional planning department. The role of the professional planning unit usually involves collecting and analyzing data and making them available, and generating and evaluating alternatives. Professional planners and planning units exist most commonly in larger business organizations. The size of these planning units vary from the planner and his or her secretary to a staff of fifty or more in the largest corporations. The professional planner should be the manager and designer of the strategy formulation system. The planner influences top and lower levels of management in their planning efforts. He or she provides information, establishes planning rules, and consults on and integrates the various plans submitted. The planner's role in most firms is not so much that of a planner but rather that of a planning coordinator and information provider—a monitor, a controller, and a critic of subsystem plans and the planning process.

Another dimension of the planning function involves the professional futurist. While strategists might be concerned with five-year forecasts, futurists peer twenty years or more into the future to attempt to define major economic, social, governmental, and technological trends. One of their primary functions appears to be to ask discerning, "what-if" questions about the outputs of traditional forecasting techniques. For example, population forecasts using traditional extrapolative techniques overlook the impact of possible changes in birth control practices. The futurist's duty is to query, "What if the use of birth control devices increases or decreases by x percent?" Even more dramatic questions that could impact on an organization can be asked by futurists, such as: "What if the government of a certain country is overthrown by leftists (or by rightists)?" or "What if there is another Arab oil embargo?"[14] Although a futurist's primary role is to question, he or she must also draw some implications from the suggested answers. Not all organizations would benefit from a futurist's predictions; but for many, it would be folly to ignore the areas in which the futurist deals.

Finally, from time to time, the professional planning department may in fact decide future courses of action for the organization. The power to do so results from its knowledge of and skill in strategy formulation and from its control of the information needed to make strategic decisions. Note that this role often leads to conflict with line managers.

The Future of the Professional Planner.   The evidence indicates that organizational environments are becoming more variable and more volatile with each passing year. Businesses' major environmental concerns—society, government, technology, competition, labor, the economy, suppliers, creditors, customers, the industry, the international environment, and natural resource availabilities—are increasingly unpredictable. As a result, organizations may depend more on professional strategists to provide information on these changes. Computer simulations will become necessities because, as the environment becomes more turbulent, the need to ask "what-if" questions becomes even greater. The time horizon of the objectives and strategies may be compressed, but objectives and strategies must nonetheless be formulated. In fact, numerous alternative contingency strategies will be developed to cope with numerous possible situations. Many firms are

---

[14]L. R. Galeese, "The Soothsayers: More Companies Use 'Futurists' to Discern What Is Lying Ahead," *The Wall Street Journal*, March 31, 1975, pp. 1, 8.

currently generating multiple strategies, each designed to be employed given a certain set of circumstances.

I hardly need to point out that it is more difficult and demanding to be a successful business manager today, in our international environment, than ever before. Nevertheless, a basic component of management's job is to adapt effectively.

▪ *James E. Lee, then President, Gulf Oil Corporation* ▪

Summary

Failing to plan is planning to fail.

▪ *Robert M. Fulmer* ▪

This chapter examined the basic concepts of strategic management, organizational policy, and the master strategy, and introduced two models which form the basis for this chapter and for the remainder of the text. Strategic management emphasizes the relationship of the organization to its environment as it attempts to accomplish its mission. Strategic management differs from traditional policy and strategy concerns, because these areas are primarily concerned only with a narrow vision of mission accomplishment, with virtually no attention given to the total environment. The strategic management process begins with mission, which leads to the formulation of strategic objectives. Subsequently, a master strategy is determined to accomplish those objectives. Intermediate planning, organizing, and implementation and operational planning occur to carry out the master strategy. Finally, evaluation takes place to see if the mission was accomplished. Organizational policy guides the entire process from the setting of objectives to evaluation and control.

The objectives-setting and strategy formulation processes depend upon four factors. One factor is the organizational strategists. There are three primary groups of strategists—the chief executive, the coalition, and top-level line managers. These strategists view the other factors—mission, strategic policy, and internal and external environmental information—and then determine strategic objectives and organizational strengths, weaknesses, opportunities, and threats (SWOT). Next they generate alternative strategies to achieve strategic objectives, and finally they choose a master strategy from among these alternatives. They may be advised by professional planners in these endeavors.

Key Terms and Concepts

Key terms and concepts with which you should be familiar include: strategic management, organizational policy, master strategy, the principal concerns of strategic management, the single-SBU organization, the multiple-SBU organization, the enterprise strategy, the corporate strategy, the business strategy, the supportive strategies, the major parts of the strategic management process model, the major parts in the objectives-setting and strategy formulation model, mission statements, the four types of mission according to benefit, the three major types of organizational policy, the common strategic policies, the historical and evolving role of the board of directors in strategic management, the three major types of strategists, and the role of the professional planner.

Discussion Questions

1. What is the major concern of strategic management? How does strategic management differ from traditional approaches to strategy and policy?

2. Locate two recent issues of *Business Week* and examine the "Corporate Strategies" section of each. Determine if the main topic discussed in each issue was really a strategic topic. Explain your reasoning.

3. Apply the strategic management process model to a profit and a not-for-profit organization with which you are familiar. What differences are there? What similarities?

4. Now apply the objectives-setting and strategy formulation model to any organization for which you can gather the information necessary to complete this model.

5. Explain how the strategists use information, mission, and policy in setting objectives and in formulating strategy.

6. What impacts on objectives setting and strategy formulation might result from the control of these processes by each of the three major types of strategists?

7. Where does Coca-Cola's 1985 decision to change Coke's formula fit in its strategic policies?

References

Ackoff, R. L. "The Meaning of Strategic Planning." In *Business Planning and Policy Formulation*, edited by Robert J. Mockler. New York: Appleton-Century-Crofts, 1972.

Ansoff, H. I. "The Concept of Strategic Management." *Journal of Business Policy*, Summer 1972.

Biggadike, E. Ralph. "The Contributions of Marketing to Strategic Management." *Academy of Management Review*, 1981, Vol. 6, No. 4, pp. 621–632.

Blass, Walter P. "Ten Years of Business Planners." *Long Range Planning*, 1983, Vol. 16, No. 3, pp. 21–24.

Bracker, J. "The Historical Development of the Strategic Management Concept." *Academy of Management Review*, April 1980, pp. 219–224.

Carroll, A. "Strategic Planning for Boundary Spanning Relations." *Managerial Planning*, January/February 1976, p. 1; "Corporate Planning Piercing Corporate Fog in the Executive Suite." *Business Week*, April 28, 1975, p. 47.

Cyert, R. M., and J. G. March. *A Behavioral Theory of the Firm*. Englewood Cliffs, N.J.: Prentice-Hall, 1963.

Frankenhoff, W. P., and C. H. Granger. "Strategic Management: A New Managerial Concept for an Era of Rapid Change." *Long Range Planning*, April 1971, pp. 7–12.

Geneen, Harold S. "Why Directors Can't Protect the Shareholders." *Fortune*, September 17, 1984.

Ginsberg, Ari. "Operationalizing Organizational Strategy: Toward an Integrative Framework." *Academy of Management Review*, 1984, Vol. 9, No. 3, pp. 548–557.

Hofer, C. W. "Research in Strategic Planning: A Survey of Past Studies and Suggestions for Future Efforts." *Journal of Economics and Business*, Spring/Summer 1976, p. 281.

Jemison, David B. "The Contributions of Administrative Behavior to Strategic Management." *Academy of Management Review*, 1981, Vol. 6, No. 4, pp. 633–642.

Jones, Thomas M., and Leonard D. Goldberg. "Governing the Large Corporation: More Arguments for Public Directors." *Academy of Management Review*, 1982, Vol. 7, No. 4, pp. 603–611.

Leontiades, Milton. "The Confusing Words of Business Policy." *Academy of Management Review*, 1982, Vol. 7, No. 1, pp. 45–48.

Mintzberg, H. "Policy as a Field of Management Theory." *Academy of Management Review*, January 1977, pp. 88–103.

Newman, W. H. "Shaping the Master Strategy of Your Firm." *California Management Review*, 1967, No. 3, pp. 77–88.

Porter, Michael E. "The Contributions of Industrial Organization to Strategic Management." *Academy of Management Review*, 1981, Vol. 6, No. 4, 609–620.

Robinson, Richard B., and John A. Pearce II. "Research Thrusts in Small Firm Strategic Planning." *Academy of Management Review*, 1984, Vol. 9, No. 1, pp. 128–137.

Schendel, D. E., and Hofer, C. W., eds. *Strategic Management: A New View of Business Policy and Planning.* Boston: Little, Brown, 1979.

Schlueter, John F. "Good Things are Happening in the Boardroom." *Director's Monthly: Official Newsletter of the National Association of Corporate Directors*, October 1984, Vol. 8, No. 9.

Shuman, J. C. "Corporate Planning in Small Companies." *Long Range Planning*, October 1975, pp. 81–90.

Springer, C. "Human Resource Strategy." *Journal of Business Strategy*, Fall 1980, pp. 78–83. This article profiles the strategic planner.

Steiner, G. A. *Top Management Planning.* New York: Collier Macmillan Ltd., 1969.

Steiner, George A., and Harry and Elsa Kunin. "Formal Strategic Planning in the United States Today." *Long Range Planning*, 1983, Vol. 16, No. 3, pp. 12–17.

Thurston, Philip H. "Should Smaller Companies Make Formal Plans?" *Harvard Business Review*, September/October 1983.

2

Internal and External Environmental Information

Nothing is permanent, except change.

▪ *Heraclitus* ▪

Change. The world is constantly changing. Business must be able to strategically adapt to ever-changing internal and external environments in order to survive and prosper. Furthermore, the pace of change is accelerating and firms are confronted with "megatrends" and "future shock" every day, making their strategic management tasks more difficult. 256K personal computers, gourmet frozen food dinners, video disks, paper bottles, natural soda, lightning storm lamps, the People's Express, Reunite, and the space shuttle all became prominent products in the period from 1980 to 1985. In the same period we also saw a prime rate ranging from 21 percent to 10 percent, a federal debt of $2 trillion-plus, devastation followed by recovery in the housing and domestic auto industries, national recognition of the need for improved quality and increased productivity, major changes in energy supplies (from rationing to surplus), an annual inflation rate ranging from 13.5 percent to 4 percent, supply-side economics, havoc in the bond markets, a dollar that once was weak and became strong again, and the People's Republic of China deciding to try capitalism instead of continuing to focus on former economic beliefs.

These and numerous similar events and facts illustrate that business currently faces an external environment that is more changeful and more demanding than anything business has previously encountered. And unfortunately, the future holds little promise of a more stable situation.

Furthermore the internal organizational environment is also changing rapidly. As employee education levels and expectations rise, as computers provide more information-processing capabilities, as the mix of employees changes, as the emphasis in management changes toward quality—and the quality of life—the internal environment must change. And it must also change as the organization adapts to its external environment. As with changes in the external environment, changes in the internal environment of the organization necessitate changes in the master strategy.

It can be argued that if a business is not growing, not changing, not meeting the current needs of society, and preparing to meet its future needs, it is declining. To the unaware, strengths too soon become weaknesses, and opportunities too soon become threats.

Just ask Joseph E. Seagram & Sons Inc. Once masters of the hard-liquor industry, they must now diversify as hard-liquor sales plummet in a more health-conscious America, an America where consumers now prefer the "light" liquors and wines to the formerly domi-

Figure 2.1   The Organization—a Strategic Management Process Model

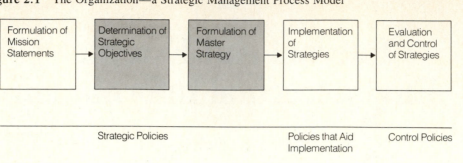

nant "brown" liquor blends, bourbons, and scotches.[1] Or query a major airline about the impact that small airlines with fuel-efficient airplanes for shorter flights have had on its profits since deregulation.[2] Or investigate the fortunes of the Victoria Station restaurant chain. That firm faces dire problems caused by the invasion by others into its niche, the theme restaurant.[3] The examples are numerous and are readily found in the bankruptcy courts or in reports of management terminations and corporate takeovers.

Organizational strategists must make themselves aware of the changing world and of the organization's internal situation as well. The basis of successful strategic action is information. Chapter 1 discussed mission, strategic policy, and strategists, three of the four major influences on the determination of strategic objectives and the formulation of the master strategy. Information is the fourth major factor, and it is information about reality and not the reality itself that causes strategies to be formulated in one way or another.

A danger facing all organizations is that top management's understanding of the environment can become obsolete.

▪ *R. T. Lenz and Jack L. Engeldow* ▪

This chapter reviews internal and external environmental information and how this information can be gathered and used in the strategic management process. (Figures 2.1 and 2.2 show which components of this process are examined in this chapter.) The objective of obtaining strategic information is to ascertain organizational strengths and weaknesses and organizational opportunities and threats in order to better determine objectives and strategy. This chapter first defines strengths, weaknesses, opportunities, and threats (SWOT) in order to provide the necessary background regarding what information is necessary. The discussion then moves to strategic information systems and the sources of information. The information sought at both the internal and the external level is reviewed. Special emphasis is given to external environmental events and their impacts on

[1] "How Seagram is Scrambling to Survive the Sobering of America," *Business Week*, September 3, 1984, pp. 94–95.

[2] W. M. Carley, "Some Major Airlines Are Being Threatened by Low-Cost Carriers," *The Wall Street Journal*, October 12, 1983, pp. 1, 23.

[3] James Higgins's personal analysis.

Figure 2.2   Objectives Determination and Master Strategy Formulation

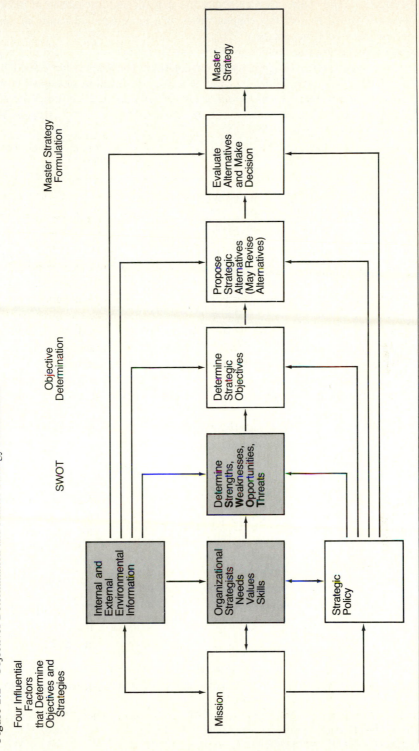

the organization. The chapter then examines the analysis and forecasting of information. The appendix which follows this chapter provides a more detailed listing of sources of external environmental information.

   As you analyze any cases which might be used in a course on strategic management, you will use such external environmental information. The knowledge gained from this chapter is important to you in class, as well as being important to strategists in business organizations. *The second appendix to this book provides an extensive checklist similar to what organizations use in determining SWOT. You should use this "strategic audit" in examining any cases assigned to you.*

SWOT

The organization's strategists observe mission, strategic policies, and current and forecasted information and then determine current and future organizational strengths, weaknesses, opportunities, and threats in order to determine where they are, where they want to be, and how they plan to get there—the essence of strategy. Strategists then perform their most important roles by determining strategic objectives and formulating the strategic plans to accomplish those objectives.

Organizations have certain characteristics—strengths—which make them uniquely adapted to carry out their tasks. Conversely they have other features—weaknesses—which inhibit their ability to fulfill their purposes.

▪ *Howard H. Stevenson* ▪

What Are SWOT?

Identifying SWOT is essential if the organization is to be successful. The process is complicated; and there are no simple solutions, as you will see in later chapters. First, though, exactly what are SWOT?

Strengths.   Strengths are positive internal abilities and situations which might enable the organization to possess a strategic advantage in achieving its objectives.

   At the business level, strengths are defined in terms of how the SBU can market its products competitively. There are five primary variables in marketing strategy: target market, product, promotion, price, and distribution. The strategies developed in these five areas are essential to success; but functional strategies, both economic and managerial, can make important contributions to a successful marketing effort. For example, in 1984, General Motors purchased 10 percent of Phil Crosby Associates, the nation's leading quality consulting firm.[4] Why? Because in the automobile industry, price and product quality are essential ingredients in successful competition, especially against the highly efficient and highly productive Japanese firms. This investment will help GM remain competitive in the future because it guarantees GM the necessary quality management training and development programs it needs to maintain and improve the quality of its products.

---

[4] Authors' personal knowledge plus see, "GM Moves into a New Era," *Business Week*, July 16, 1984, pp. 48–54; and S. Crawford, "GM Invests $4 Million in Quality," *The Orlando Sentinel*, May 16, 1984, p. D-1.

Strengths at the corporate level for multiple-SBU firms are defined most often in terms of the synergy and balance among the SBUs within the firm. Synergy is the degree to which SBUs reinforce each other in pursuit of objectives. For example, an organization such as General Electric is considered to have very strong synergy among its SBUs. All are essentially technologically based and have more than adequate profit margins or potentials. Balance refers to the relative cash requirements of the SBUs. The balance among GE's SBUs is also satisfactory; some are growing, some are stable, and some have strong cash flows that can support the total company's growth efforts.

Weaknesses. Weaknesses are internal inabilities and situations that might result in or have resulted in the firm's not achieving its objectives. Weaknesses are the opposite of strengths.

At the business level, marketing is still the principal concern. Even successful firms such as McDonald's have weaknesses. In 1984, McDonald's found itself very vulnerable to competition because its product line is limited in a time of changing consumer tastes. Sales growth has declined. One market analyst suggests that complacency may be McDonald's most significant weakness.[5]

At the corporate level in the multiple-SBU firm, weaknesses are again a function of synergy and balance. For example, McGraw-Edison, a major U.S. electrical equipment manufacturer, finds itself making money with its U.S. operations but losing money in total, thanks to its overseas operations' losses in currency transactions. The balance is absent.[6]

Opportunities. Opportunities are external factors and situations which will assist the organization in achieving or exceeding its objectives. At the business level, they, too, are almost always expressed in terms of market potentials. The founders of Apple Computers saw a need for a personal computer at a low price. They created one and made a fortune. At the corporate strategy level in multiple-SBU firms, opportunities usually involve acquisitions or mergers. The Coca-Cola Company acquired Columbia Pictures because it saw that the corporation should become less dependent on soft drinks—and on its single most important product, Coke—and move into an often-profitable industry. It was correct in its evaluation of the opportunities, at least in 1984, as Columbia's "Ghostbusters" grossed some $220 million as the year's number one box office attraction.

> *"When I came out of [Columbia's] Ghostbusters, I thought,*
> *'Gee, we're going to lose our shirts.'"*
>
> ▪ *Roberto C. Goizueta, 52, board chairman of Coca-Cola* ▪

Threats. Threats are external factors which might result in or have resulted in the firm's not achieving its objectives. Historically, threats have been defined in terms of the firm's

---

[5] "The Fast-Food War: Big MAC Under Attack," *Business Week*, January 30, 1984, pp. 44–46; Sue Shellenbarger and Jeffrey Zaslow, "Fast-Food Chains Improve Menus to Tap Big Change in Public Tastes," *The Wall Street Journal*, October 27, 1983, pp. 33, 45.

[6] Carol J. Loomis, "How Companies Are Coping with the Strong Dollar," *Fortune*, November 26, 1984, pp. 116–124.

competitors, but more recently the focus has expanded to include government, unions, society, and other stakeholders. At the business strategy level, an example of a threat is a technological innovation introduced by a competitor. Within a few months of the introduction of the digital watch, time had begun to run out on the Bulova Watch Company as a dominant force in the industry. It still depended upon pin-lever watches. Digital watches quickly captured Bulova's traditional markets. An example of how government can be a threat to business is the safety and environmental legislation which has placed extensive demands on the U.S. auto industry. An example of a societal threat is the successful campaigns of environmental groups to keep real estate developers from turning natural areas into suburbia in numerous areas in states such as Florida, California, Oregon, and the Carolinas.

At the corporate strategy level in multiple-SBU firms, threats are often the same as at the SBU level. Additional threats involve acquisitions and mergers. Rival multiple-SBU firms may compete to acquire the same SBU. A threat also exists in an unfriendly takeover attempt. In 1983 and 1984, for example, Disney was embroiled in an unfriendly takeover battle with "greenmailer" Saul Steinberg. Though the attempt was thwarted, both the CEO, Ron Miller, and the Chairman of the Board, Ray Watson, were deposed as a consequence of the ultimate resolution of this takeover attempt.[7]

At any time many businesses are confronted with a host of external technological threats. Managements of threatened firms realize that many threats may not materialize, at least in the short run. However, one or more of those potential threats may develop in ways that will have devastating impact.

▪ *Arnold C. Cooper and Dan Schendel* ▪

How Managers Define SWOT.   H. H. Stevenson studied 50 managers in six diverse business organizations to find out how they defined organizational strengths and weaknesses. He found that while the steps for defining strengths and weaknesses were essentially the same, the specific factors examined and the criteria used in judging these factors varied, and many factors modified the exact definitions. Strengths tended to be relatively well known and based on historical data; but weaknesses were less well known, and often little relevant data about them was available. Further, interpretation of data by the managers was partly a function of the managers' positions and responsibilities in their organizations, their personalities, and their perceived roles in the organizations.[8]

The implications of this study are important. Stevenson notes that in conducting an internal evaluation, managers should: View the evaluation as an aid to task accomplishment; develop areas of examination tailored to the responsibility and authority of each manager; make criteria explicit to provide a common framework; understand the differences in use of identified strengths and weaknesses; and recognize the strategic importance of defining these attributes. In addition, it also seems possible that having the evaluation conducted by an external consultant would alleviate most of the problems mentioned above.

---

[7]Discussed in detail in Case 17 (Project Fantasy: A Behind-the-Scenes Account of Disney's Desperate Battle Against the Raiders) of this text.

[8]H. H. Stevenson, "Defining Corporate Strengths and Weaknesses," *Sloan Management Review*, Spring 1976, pp. 51–66.

Omar A. El Sawy, in interviewing 37 executives from small- and medium-sized high-tech firms, found that scanning of the external environment was an ongoing process characterized by at least three stages: initial detection, threshold attainment, and confirmation. Various cues were used to verify threats and opportunities, strengths and weaknesses, and very importantly high levels of intuitive input to the identification if SWOT occurred. In short, SWOT identification was less rational than we have conceptualized here.[9]

On the basis of two research studies, one can hardly discount the rationality of all evaluations of strengths and weaknesses, threats and opportunities. However, these studies point out the need to be aware of the human variable in the strategic decision process. While this chapter is devoted to the techniques involved in strategic decision making, Chapter 6 concentrates on this human variable. As will be seen, the strategic decision process is extremely complex, much more so than the models which describe it usually depict. In fact, much of the rationality desired and built into the decision system through techniques is negated by the human variable.

Information

To manage a business well is to manage its future;
and to manage its future is to manage information.

▪ *Marion Harper, Jr.* ▪

Information has two primary strategic roles—in objective setting and in strategy formulation. Information on the strengths and weaknesses of the organization in relation to external environmental opportunities and threats is used to set objectives and formulate strategies. Strategists generate and evaluate alternatives based on this information.

Information systems indicate the existence of many strengths, weaknesses, opportunities, and threats. Most of them will not require the reformulation of the master strategy, but they often cause strategic objectives to be changed. Most threats are resolved and most opportunities taken advantage of at lower levels of planning, control, and implementation. Occasionally strategic information systems may indicate the need to formulate or reformulate the master strategy and cause the strategic decision process to be pursued.

Strategic Information Systems

Getting an idea from one place to another is as important as getting an idea.

▪ *Advertisement by TRW, 1985* ▪

It is the function of the strategic information system (SIS) to provide the informational inputs required in the strategic decision process. Any decision, and specifically the strategic decision, can be only as satisfactory as the information upon which it is based. An information system which provides accurate, timely, and relevant information for use in

---

[9]O. A. El Saury, "Undertaking the Process by Which Chief Executives Identify Strategic Threats and Opportunities," *Academy of Management Proceedings*, ed. John A. Pearce II and Richard B Robinson, Jr. (Boston, 1984), pp. 37–41.

194505

Source: Drawing by Modell; © 1983 The New Yorker Magazine, Inc.

the strategic decision process is an important organizational resource, because executives can be virtually overwhelmed by information. Various structural arrangements exist in organizations to provide strategic information. In larger organizations, elaborate management information systems (MIS) may provide this information. In smaller organizations, the CEO may scan the environment and assess his or her organization in an attempt to collect information to help determine where the organization is and where it ought to be. Numerous variations exist between these two extremes. The personal computer and its related software have provided smaller organizations with scanning, analysis, and forecasting capabilities that only larger firms used to enjoy. In addition to providing strategic information, major functions of the MIS include communication of objectives and plans and provision of information related to performance control.

Gathering information is not always easy as Information Capsule 2.1 illustrates. And information doesn't always ensure success—especially when not enough is gathered, or when it is contradictory as this chapter's cartoon reveals. Strategic information systems can be either formal or informal. Both types play a vital role in strategy formulation. The formal SIS is a component of the formal MIS. Of special concern to SBU strategic planning are demand forecasts for products and services balanced against the capacity and capabilities to produce them. Ultimately these balances are reflected in the operating plan and the operating budget. Also appearing in the operating budget are resource distribution actions and actual production commitments.

INFORMATION CAPSULE 2.1
The Intelligence Function

In the past few years, competition has intensified; for many it has become global. Finding out what your competitor is doing isn't always easy, but it's a lot easier than most people think. Companies like to tell others a lot about themselves, and if they don't, their employees do. It is this latter source of intelligence information that is becoming much more widely exploited. True, companies rightfully still subscribe to clipping services, and analyze competitors' annual reports, advertisements, job-opening announcements, and other potential information sources, but there is apparently no substitute for listening to your competitors' current or former employees.

Among the many strategies for gathering intelligence from competitors' employees are: probing potential employees who just happen to work for or who have worked for competitors in real or phony job interviews; picking the brains of competitors' employees at conferences and trade shows; and hiring competitors' employees and then debriefing them. But one of the most interesting ways is simply to sit in a popular restaurant or bar frequented by members of your competitors' staffs, and listen to them. For example, the Silicon Valley has several popular night spots, any of which may provide the astute and educated listener with numerous tactical and often important strategic bits of information. Known to have been leaked several weeks to several months in advance of product release were accurate descriptions of the Hewlett-Packard portable PC and Apple's MacIntosh. Other common secrets that have been uncovered in such evening spots are: the existence of joint venture agreements, the strengths and weaknesses of competitor-customer relationships, circuit diagrams, and software capabilities. It pays, so it appears, to become an eavesdropper. It's all quite legal, although there are some "accepted" rules to the game as to what's fair.

Sources: Steven Flax, "How to Snoop on Your Competitors," *Fortune*, May 14, 1984, pp. 28–33; Erik Larson, "Many Top Secrets in the Silicon Valley Are Spilled at Tables," *The Wall Street Journal*, June 29, 1984, pp. 1, 26.

Most organizations plan strategy on an annual, cyclical basis. For such purposes, routines for data storage and reporting should exist. Since strategic decision making may occasionally be crisis oriented, however, there are few predictable boundaries as to the types of information which might be needed. It is therefore necessary to store almost all conceivable types of information, often in a "raw" form, in order to meet the demands of various situations.

As shown in Figure 2.3, a centralized formal data bank stores the data necessary for generating both routine and nonroutine reports on internal and external environmental phenomena. Internal information is presented in this figure as being reported on a functional basis. It could be sorted on a divisional/functional or other basis if necessary. Much of the strategic information routinely exists in reports and reporting formats already in use in the firm, especially formal internal data such as financial statements, cost control reports, quality control reports, inventory level reports, division performance reports, absenteeism and turnover reports, and the like.

Figure 2.3   Strategic Information Systems

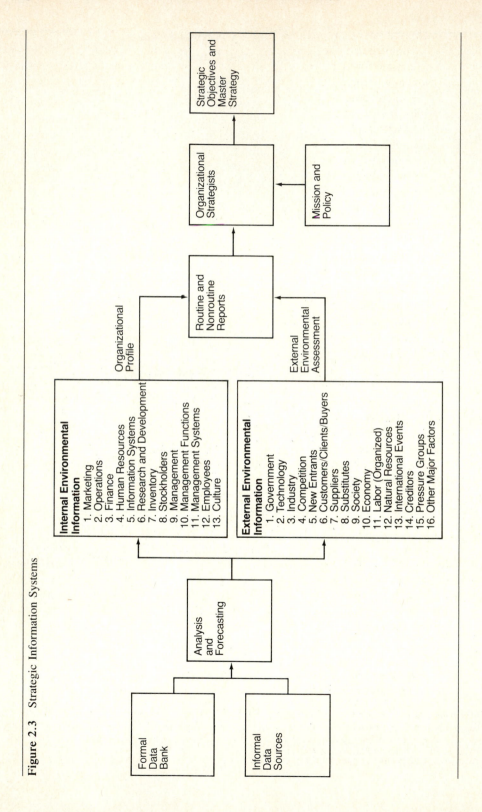

One manifestation of the computerized information system is the corporate "war room" with comprehensive computer-linked visual data display systems. While "war rooms" have existed for many years, in the past they used hand-printed charts on limited subjects. Now any corporate information can appear instantaneously on large television screens.[10] The microcomputer, which functions as a "smart" terminal, further increases the capabilities of such systems, providing top-line managers and staff with strategic information, and with sophisticated analysis and forecasting capacities.

To this point the discussion of the SIS has stressed the formal information system. But the importance of informal information should not be overlooked. Many times, personal contacts with individuals inside or outside the organization produce significant information related to the future. For example, tips on federal government legislation may prove extremely beneficial. Or rumors about a competitor's strategy may, when investigated, prove to be an important indicator of profitable strategic actions. The evidence strongly suggests that, while the formal system may be proposed as the critical element, the informal system is the most consistently used basis for many top management decisions. Research indicates that 40 to 75 percent of the information used by top managers comes from informal sources.[11]

Finally, a pragmatic note: management must make strategic decisions based on forecasts—not simply based on past history. Normally, this necessity is understood with respect to the external environment, the information about which often has already been changed in time horizon before it reaches top management. Strategists, however, often overlook forecasting when dealing with internal strengths and weaknesses. Even though the decisions must be made now, it is future as well as current strengths and weaknesses that must be compared with future as well as current threats and opportunities in the strategic decision process.

In the very large organization, the processes of information gathering and analysis described above would be accomplished in the formal information system under the direction of members of the professional planning group. At the opposite extreme, the CEO of a small organization may occasionally find it necessary to search for information or perform analyses personally.

Sources of Internal and External Environmental Information

As suggested earlier, information related to the internal strengths and weaknesses of the organization should be available in the organization's MIS. This information may also be gathered through informal sources. Typically, this type of information will be found in annual, quarterly, and monthly financial reports; in cost analyses; in capital budget statements; in cost/benefit analyses; in personnel reports on major human resource concerns;

[10] "Corporate 'War Rooms' Plug into the Computer," *Business Week*, August 23, 1976, pp. 65–67.

[11] C. R. Adams, "How Management Users View Information Systems," *Decision Sciences*, April 1975, pp. 337–345; J. Dearden, "MIS Is Mirage," *Harvard Business Review*, January/February 1972, pp. 90–99; R. E. Linnemann and J. D. Kennell, "Shirtsleeve Approach to Long-Range Planning," *Harvard Business Review*, March/April 1977, pp. 141–150; P. Lorange, "The Planner's Dual Role—a Survey of U.S. Companies," *Long Range Planning*, March 1973, pp. 12–16; K. S. Ringbaak, "Organized Corporate Planning Systems: An Empirical Study of Planning Practice and Experiences in American Big Business" (Ph.D. dissertation, University of Wisconsin, 1968); R. N. Taylor, "Psychological Aspects of Planning," *Long Range Planning*, April 1976, pp. 66–74.

in marketing reports on sales and related information; and so forth. Few problems should exist in obtaining relevant internal information if the MIS is properly designed and implemented (a big "if"). However, the human resource and cultural information contained in most systems is limited in nature. Organizations are only beginning to recognize the need for and application of this type of information. While organizations usually collect data on absenteeism, tardiness, turnover, and so forth, seldom do they measure organizational climate, satisfaction, leadership style, and the like—important ingredients in explaining human resource productivity.

In addition to standardized control reports, nonroutine control activities may be desirable. These activities include organizational climate surveys, management audits, social audits, operational audits (of any subsystem), productivity audits, financial audits, strategic audits, and so forth. Both routine and nonroutine control activities are discussed at greater length in Chapter 9.

The strategic purpose of obtaining information on internal strengths and weaknesses is to compare them with perceived external environmental threats and opportunities and to make decisions based on these comparisons. F. J. Aguilar has described four modes of scanning the external environment for information about threats and opportunities: [12]

1. Undirected viewing—general exposure to information with no purpose other than exploration.

2. Conditioned viewing—directed exposure to, but not active search for, specific kinds of data, which will be assessed as they are encountered.

3. Informal search—search for specific information carried out in a limited and relatively unstructured manner.

4. Formal search—active, deliberate, structured search for specific information undertaken with a purpose in mind.

Most organizations use all four types of scanning, depending on the cost benefit of each. These four approaches form a continuum from general exposure to information to active and deliberate search for specific information. Every firm must remain alert to the general environment and to its own operations. As bits and pieces of information obtained in this scanning indicate changes in factors relevant to the formulation of strategy, then other, more directed types of scanning should begin. Conducting formal searches is desirable any time specific information is needed for strategy formulation.

Information on environmental factors can be obtained through various sources: for example, *The Wall Street Journal*; *Fortune*; *Business Week*; *Harvard Business Review*; numerous scholarly, popular, and trade journals; and newspapers are important sources. Any number of government, industry, news media, research, and reporting services provide additional information. The appendix to this chapter lists sources for each of the major environmental factors identified in Figure 2.3.

The various information sources vary in validity and reliability, as well as accessibility and timeliness. Much of the information used is gathered from secondary sources, but primary data gathering through research may be undertaken if the organization can afford the cost. While internal information sources may allow the organization to approach a real-time (or up-to-date), on-line MIS, constraints on environmental sources make a real-

[12] F. J. Aguilar, *Scanning the Business Environment* (New York: MacMillan, 1967).

time environmental MIS unlikely. The informal information system may be used more than the formal system. Information sharing among organizations is useful and has proven to be successful.

We've named some sources of information and how we find them and what we want them for, but we have not yet examined exactly what types of information we seek. Internal information regarding existing situations and external environmental information related to government, technology, competition, society, the economy, labor, natural resources, international events, and other major variables are critical to the success of the organization. First, let us examine the internal information needed.

The Internal Information Sought

Whatever information can be gathered regarding strategic strengths and weaknesses is important. Each business unit should concern itself with identifying the results of its efforts and its strengths and weaknesses, both current and potential, with respect to:

- Functional areas such as marketing, finance, operations, human resources, information systems, R&D, and inventory.
- Management values and capabilities.
- Performance of management functions.
- Performance of management systems.
- Stockholder orientations.
- Employee perspectives.
- Organizational culture.

Organizational Assessment

This information is best obtained through a total management audit covering every facet of the business, performed annually in conjunction with routine control reports. What the unit wants to know is where it is; and, if it is not where it wants to be, why it isn't there and how it can get there. Such an audit follows as part of the strategic audit in Appendix 2 to this text and is useful in analyzing cases or other organizational situations. However, more typically this information is "put together" from existing sources. Turn now to this audit and review the major issues which are to be addressed in an internal analysis.

The External Information Sought

At one level, environment is not a very mysterious concept. It means the surroundings of an organization; the "climate" in which the organization functions. The concept becomes challenging when we try to move from simple description of the environment to analysis of its properties.

▪ *William R. Dill* ▪

External information that will have a direct impact on opportunities and threats or provide inputs for defining strengths and weaknesses should be sought. Typically, this includes information in the following areas:

- Government.
- Technology.
- Competition.
- The industry.
- New entrants.
- Customers/clients.
- Substitutes.
- Suppliers.
- Society.
- The economy.
- Labor (organized).
- Natural resources.
- International events.
- Pressure groups.
- Creditors.
- Other factors.

The purpose of seeking this information is to assess the environment and determine the fit between this environment, its opportunities and threats, and the organization's strengths and weaknesses as revealed in the organizational profile above.

Now let us examine in more detail the types of information sought and the reasons for seeking this information in each of these areas.

Government

During the 1960s and 1970s, government dominated the external business environment. While competition was of concern, businesses probably spent as much time complying with governmental requirements as they did worrying about competition, perhaps more time.

Table 2.1 presents a list of major federal laws in several vital areas. Some were recently passed; some have been enforced more stringently in recent years. As can be seen by this table, in each of several major categories, business has had many of its strategic alternatives limited. These laws have served to increase business's social responsibility. Alternatives may be limited additionally through the enforcement of these laws, since enforcement varies from law to law and geographic area to geographic area. For example, the operations of almost all manufacturing organizations have been affected by the environmental protection requirements, resulting, in numerous situations, in significant additions to production costs. Also, virtually all organizations of any size have had to make comprehensive changes in their personnel practices as the result of equal opportunity laws. For many organizations, personnel practices have been dictated by federal agencies as the result of these laws. The consumer issue has resulted in numerous recalls of automobiles to Detroit and of other products to other manufacturers in other cities. And the energy problem and related laws have caused U.S. automakers to completely redesign their automobiles, making them lighter, smaller, and more fuel efficient.

Table 2.1   Laws That Affect Business

RECENT LAWS

Environment

Federal Insecticide, Fungicide, and Rodenticide Act of 1947
Federal Water Pollution Control Act of 1956
Clean Air Act of 1963
Solid Wastes Disposal Act of 1965, as amended
Water Quality Act of 1965
A federal court broadly interprets the provisions of the Refuse Act of 1899 in 1966
Air Quality Act of 1967
National Environmental Policy Act of 1970
Noise Abatement and Control Act of 1970
Resource Recovery Act of 1970
Clean Air Act Amendments of 1970

Equal Employment Opportunity

Equal Pay Act of 1963 as amended by the Education Amendments of 1972
Title VII of the Civil Rights Act of 1964 as amended by the Equal Employment Opportunity Act
   of 1972
Presidential Executive Orders 11246, 11375, 11478, 11758 (1967–1975)
Age Discrimination in Employment Act of 1967
Sections 500 and 503 of the Rehabilitation Act Amendments of 1974
Veteran's Employment and Readjustment Act of 1972, as amended

Consumerism

Meat Inspection Act of 1906
Federal Food, Drug and Cosmetic Act 1938, as amended by presidential executive order: The Office
   of Consumer Affairs, 1964
National Traffic and Motor Vehicle Safety Act of 1966, as amended
Fair Packaging and Labeling Act of 1966
Federal Cigarette Labeling and Advertising Act, 1967
Consumer Credit Protection Act, 1968
Toy Safety Act, 1969
Truth in Lending Act of 1969
Consumer Product Safety Act of 1972
Fair Credit Billing Act of 1974
The Equal Credit Opportunity Act of 1974
Consumer Product Warranties Act of 1975
Consumer Goods Pricing Act of 1975
Fair Trade Laws repealed, 1977
Fair Debt Collection, 1978
Revised Trademark Laws, 1985 (probable)

Energy

Federal Energy Administration Act of 1974
Energy Reorganization Act of 1974 (establishes ERDA)
Energy Supply and Environmental Coordination Act of 1974
Energy Policy and Conservation Act of 1975

Economics

Chrysler Loan Guarantee Act of 1979
Revised Bankruptcy Act of 1980 (used to avoid major economic catastrophies by some firms)
Tax Act of 1981
Deregulation of airlines, trucking, 1979–1981
FCC allows AT&T to sell nonregulated services, 1979
The Federal Reserve Bank permits banks to pay interest on checking accounts, 1980
The Economic Recovery Act of 1981
Tax Act of 1984
Tax Act of 1985
AT&T divests itself of its local telephone companies, 1984

Labor

Occupational Safety and Health Act of 1970
Employee Retirement Income Security Act, 1974

continued

Table 2.1 *continued*

OTHER LAWS

Interstate Commerce Act of 1887
Sherman Act, 1890
Pure Food and Drug Act, 1906
Sixteenth Amendment, 1913 (income tax)
Clayton Act, 1914
Federal Trade Commission Act, 1914
Federal Communications Act, 1934
Social Security Act, 1935
Wagner Act, 1935
Robinson-Patman Act, 1936
Fair Labor Standards Act, 1938 (Wage and Hour Act)
Taft-Hartley Act, 1947
Anti-Merger Act, 1950
Automobile Information Disclosure Act of 1958
Landrum-Griffin Act, 1959

But these laws are not the only government constraints on business. There are regulatory agencies whose primary functions involve the observation and control of business. Indeed, the number of agencies and individuals at the federal level whose function is to regulate business is extremely high. In addition, there are state regulatory agencies, which control, for example, all public utilities; state environmental protection agencies, which are the primary enforcement mechanisms of the federal environmental law; state consumer protection agencies; various state agencies related to the building of houses; and various licensing and permit-granting organizations—state, federal, and local. These agencies, as well as various pressure groups such as the NAACP, the Sierra Club, and Ralph Nader and his group, have significant impact upon the strategy formulation of many businesses. As can be seen in some of the cases presented in this book, it is often necessary to change the major plans of action known as strategies in order to accommodate the demands of these organizations. The courts, especially the U.S. Supreme Court, may also greatly influence business activity through interpretations of laws and regulations.

The future holds some promise of less constraint; in 1985, public attitudes and the Reagan administration seemed to favor fewer constraints. But the task of control is not simple. Business's future appears to be one of continued regulation and control by federal, state, and local governments, especially the federal government. Because of these constraints and the frequent changes in them, business must continually monitor the environment and adapt to it or change it. Legal, ethical, and socially responsible political actions and lobbying are important strategic actions. All strategic actions depend on awareness.

Technology

Many, if not most, businesses depend on some type of technology for a competitive advantage or for products to sell. The American way of life has come to involve consuming more and more of the latest and greatest, and that involves technological advances. Since business is so dependent on technology, it must be ever mindful of technological surprises from competitors.

There are few major industries in this country which do not depend on technology. Television, computers, calculators, airplanes, pacemakers, Corningware, lasers, and photocopy machines are just a few of the many examples of major industrial products which are technology-based. When a major technology comes into existence, an entire new industry may be created, such as occurred with the microcomputer industry or the photocopying industry.

Businesses must first of all concern themselves with new technology in the particular industry—that is, with the technological developments of their competitors. This concern has often led to industrial espionage. Moreover, the rapid changes occurring in the business technological environment have resulted in an increase in business' efforts to forecast technology. This process involves using many judgmental forecasting techniques. Technological forecasting is not easy, nor is it very accurate. The management of strategic surprises is at best difficult. Most competitors' technologies are unknown until their products are brought to the market. This is one major reason that environmental scanning for "weak signals" of change is so critical.

In an interesting study of responses to technological threats, A. C. Cooper and others found that traditional firms encounter great difficulty in responding successfully to major technological innovations introduced into their industry, especially during maturity or saturation stages of the product life cycle. While their sample was small, virtually no well-established firm studied was able to launch a successful counterthreat to the introduction of a new technology into its industry. This finding suggests that even when firms know about new technologies and respond to them, the response strategy may be ill-advised.[13] When we consider the product life cycle, we can see that when new technology is introduced, the introducer gains a distinct strategic advantage over those who lack the technology. If the new technology captures a considerable share of the market, then the competitor who previously had the market has no advantage over any other firm coming into the market for this new product. J. M. Utterback and M. J. Abernathy found that firms in early stages of growth tended to introduce more technological innovations than did firms which were very large and complex in nature. This suggests that as firms mature, they may stagnate.[14]

In sum, these studies suggest that technological innovation may be difficult to counteract for a firm in the mature stage of the product life cycle although certainly numerous firms have prolonged their products' life cycles through technological innovation or adaptation. The available information also suggests that technology is the source of product innovation, and that new firms and new industries can be successfully based on such innovation.

The Japanese have been quite successful in adapting to someone else's technology and underpricing their international competitors through highly productive operations and other management and marketing systems strategies. However, only a few U.S. and Canadian firms have been able to achieve the high levels of productivity which allow firms to take advantage of others' technological advances. Clearly, technology is an advantage, and so is information. The firm that does not keep pace is destined for decline, as Information Capsule 2.2 indicates.

[13] A. C. Cooper et al., "Strategic Responses to Technological Threats," *Proceedings, Academy of Management*, 1974.

[14] J. M. Utterback and M. J. Abernathy, "The Test of a Conceptual Model Linking States in Firms' Process and Product Innovation," Working Paper No. 74-23, Harvard School of Business, 1974.

INFORMATION CAPSULE 2.2
New Home-Computer Design
May Revive Japanese Market

Microsoft Corporation of Bellevue, Washington, previewed its new MSX computer at the preeminent Japan Electronics Show in Osaka, Japan, in October 1983. By all measures of success, the MSX promises to be the dominant type of personal computer in the next five years. The MSX incorporates a new computer design that allows it to handle programs written for most other personal computers—something unheard of previously. In addition, the MSX is inexpensive, is the only computer to operate while several memory cartridges are plugged into it, and is expected to be able to incorporate disk-drive features currently under design—making it superior to computers such as Coleco's Adam* which incorporate less desirable tape memory systems.

The MSX incorporates a new master control program, the MSX-DOS to control the flow of information to and from magnetic disks. The program is quite similar to the popular CP/M control program used on IBM's personal computer. As a result, software firms should be able to readily adapt current programs to the new system. The MSX computer will be sold first as a game system, but will move rapidly into the personal computer line. Earlier MSX systems are to be manufactured to accommodate readily later modifications to the system. The MSX will be sold first in Japan for approximately one year, but after that, it is likely to be introduced into the U.S. market by a number of manufacturers. Industry experts estimate that the MSX system will cause computer prices to drop significantly.

*Note: the Adam computer is no longer produced.

Source: Excerpted from "New Home-Computer Design May Revive Japanese Market," by Richard A. Shaffer, *The Wall Street Journal*, October 14, 1983, p. 33. Reprinted by permission of *The Wall Street Journal*, © Dow Jones & Company, Inc., 1983. All Rights Reserved.

While technology plays an important role in business success, it also poses problems for many companies. The unexpected consequences of a new technology can sometimes result in damage to the physical environment. All organizations, not just business, must engage in ongoing assessment of the impacts of technology on the physical environment. Nuclear waste (governmental and commercial), oil spills, DDT's effects on the food chain, acid rain, and PCB contamination are all examples of the use of technology getting out of control. Even the less-dramatic wastes and products of industry and government can, in mass, damage the environment. For example, in Louisiana, the waste material from oil and related chemical by-product industries have significantly polluted the environment. In affected areas, health problems are much greater than would be considered normal; cancer and other major illnesses abound. Many feel it is the pollution that caused these diseases.[15] Such is also the case with automobile exhaust fumes, waste water, and garbage. From a strategic viewpoint, therefore, industry must be responsive not just to the profit

---

[15] Thomas Petzinger, Jr. and George Getschow, "In Louisiana Pollution and Cancer are Rife in the Petroleum Area," *The Wall Street Journal*, October 23, 1984, pp. 1, 24.

motive, but also to the greater needs of the society and to the quality of life. This is not only a moral position, but also hard reality. Where business has not been responsive to these needs, it has in the past often been forced by society and by government to respond in a manner that may be ultimately more costly and less profitable.

Technology assessment recognizes that within the ecosystem, all systems are inter-related and what affects one ultimately affects another. Technology assessment requires environmental surveillance. Business must chart a careful course of technological action. Indeed, the Environmental Protection Agency and other federal and state agencies require that such plans be made and recorded in environmental impact statements for areas of obvious impact. Business and other organizations must be ever alert to the less obvious impacts of their actions as well. The activities of various pressure groups must also be monitored. The attitudes of society should be determined. Governmental responses should be anticipated. All of this requires a satisfactory strategic information system.

Competition, Industry, New Entrants, Customers/Clients, Substitutes, Suppliers

In recent years, considerable interest has been shown in what has come to be known as "competitor analysis." The subjects of this section of the chapter—competition, industry, new entrants, customers/clients (buyers), substitutes, and suppliers, are all related to the subject of competitor analysis through the works of Michael E. Porter. You can apply this material directly to several cases that follow the text portion of this book.

Porter's Competitor Analysis.   M. E. Porter proposes that the intensity of competition is the most critical element in the firm's environment. Porter suggests that the level of this intensity is a function of five basic competitive forces as depicted in Figure 2.4. Porter contends that "The collective strength of these forces determines the ultimate profit potential in the industry, where profit potential is measured in terms of long-run return on invested capital."[16]

According to Porter, a corporation must carefully monitor its environment to determine the impact of these five factors on the firm's potentials for success.[17]

1. *Threat of New Entrants.* New entrants typically
    - have substantial resources.
    - pursue actions that increase industry capacity.
    - attempt to increase their market share.

    As a consequence
    - prices often go down.
    - incumbents' costs may become inflated.
    - incumbents' profits may therefore go down.

Because of the above factors, new entrants must be viewed as threats to incumbents. Miller's entry into the beer industry is a classic example of this type of situation.

Porter identifies seven major sources of barriers to entry into an existing industry. These barriers assist incumbents because they reduce the number of potential new entrants:

[16]M. E. Porter, *Competitive Strategy* (New York: Free Press, 1980), p. 3.

[17]The sections on Porter's model are taken from *Competitive Strategy*, pp. 3–33.

Figure 2.4   Forces Driving Industry Competition

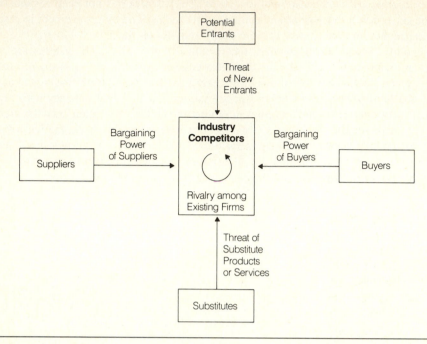

Source: Reprinted with permission of The Free Press, a Division of Macmillan, Inc. from *Competitive Strategy* by M. E. Porter, p. 4. Copyright © 1980 by The Free Press.

- economies of scale—to obtain these requires high-entry investment.
- existing product differentiation which leads to customer loyalty.
- capital requirements.
- switching costs—for buyers switching from incumbent's product to the new entrant's product.
- access to distribution channels.
- cost disadvantages independent of scale.
- government policy.

2. *Intensity of Rivalry among Existing Firms.* Porter views rivalry as a process of move and countermove among existing, mutually dependent competitors employing tactics such as price competition, advertising, new products, and so forth. He sees intense rivalry as resulting from any number of critical industry factors which can and do change:
- numerous or equally balanced competitors.
- slow industry growth.
- high fixed or storage costs.
- lack of differentiation or switching costs.
- capacity augmented in large increments.
- diverse competitors.
- high strategic stakes.
- high exit barriers.

3. *Pressure from Substitute Products.* "All firms in an industry are competing, in a broad sense, with industries producing substitute products." [18] These substitutes result in a price lid on industry products.

- The key to identifying substitutes is to look for those products that perform the same "function" as the product of the industry even though they may not appear to be obvious substitutes.
- Firms should pay attention to those products whose price-performance tradeoff with the industry's products is improving.
- Furthermore, the higher the industry's profits, the more likely that substitutes will be sought.

A good example of substitution is the problem faced by the security guard industry. Electronic alarms are a strong substitute. They are cheaper to operate and effective. Their advantage should increase in the future as labor costs increase and the cost of the electronic devices decreases.

4. *Bargaining Power of Buyers.* Customer/clients (buyers) compete with the industry in the sense that they are able to force prices down, bargain for higher-quality or more goods and services, or play one competitor in the industry against another. A particular buyer or group of buyers is powerful in the industry if:

- it purchases a large portion of the seller's total sales.
- its purchases from the industry are a significant portion of its cost of goods sold.
- its purchases from the industry are standard or undifferentiated.
- switching costs are low.
- it earns low profits.
- it has the potential for backward integration.
- the industry's product is unimportant to the quality of the buyer's product.
- the buyer has full information.

5. *Bargaining Power of Suppliers.* Suppliers can impact on an industry through their abilities to control prices and product/service quality. The conditions making suppliers powerful tend to mirror those that make buyers powerful. A supplier group is powerful if:

- it is dominated by a few companies, and is more concentrated than the industry to which it sells.
- there are few substitutes.
- the supplier's products are differentiated or switching costs are high.
- suppliers pose a threat of forward integration.
- labor, by the way, is a supplier group.

With respect to obtaining the information necessary to determine the characteristics about the industry and its competitors, suppliers, new entrants, substitutes, and buyers, Porter suggests the sources depicted in Figure 2.5. An additional list of general information sources is provided as an appendix to this chapter. Furthermore, W. E. Rothschild has prepared a more detailed list of sources and concerns specifically with regard to competitors, and his approach is discussed in the next section. One final note: Porter recom-

---

[18] Ibid., p. 23.

Figure 2.5   Sources of Data for Industry Analysis

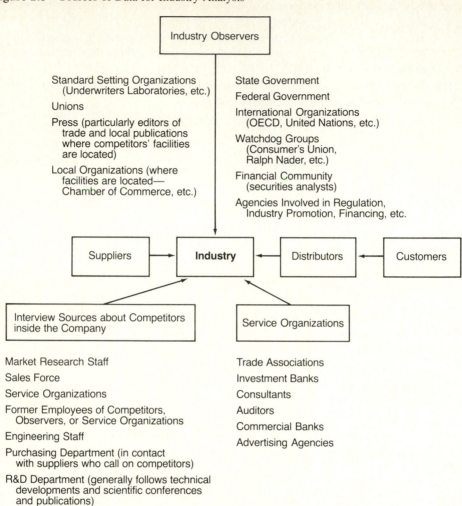

Source: Reprinted with permission of The Free Press, a Division of Macmillan, Inc. from *Competitive Strategy* by M. E. Porter, p. 378. Copyright © 1980 by The Free Press.

mends certain types of "generic" strategies for competing, and these are reviewed in more detail in Chapter 4.

Induce your competitors not to invest in those products, markets, and services where you expect to invest the most. That is the most fundamental rule of strategy.

▪ *Bruce D. Henderson* ▪

Competitor Analysis: Another Perspective.   At the business level of strategy formulation, competition is of critical concern. Any business must know what its competition is doing and is going to do and how these actions will affect it. William E. Rothschild, author and integrative strategist for General Electric, suggests that the following key questions must be answered if a firm is to be successful: [19]

- Who is the competition now and who will it be in the future?
- What are the key competitors' strategies, objectives, and goals?
- How important is a specific market to the competitors, and are they committed enough to continue to invest?
- What unique strengths do the competitors have?
- Do they have any weaknesses that make them vulnerable?
- What changes are likely in the competitors' future strategies?
- What are the implications of competitors' strategies on the market, industry, and one's own company?

As Rothschild suggests, these questions boil down to "Who are they?" and "What are they up to?"

Although these questions seem rather straightforward, answering them, according to Rothschild, is complicated by three problems:

1. Many managers are overconfident. They have won the previous battles and assume they'll win the next ones. Laxity results.

2. Many strategists do not know what they need to know or how to obtain information.

3. Many strategists are concerned that it may be necessary to act unethically to obtain the necessary information.

In response to problems 2 and 3, Rothschild assures strategists that the environment abounds with information. To help them find it, he provides a table indicating the information required and another giving sources for this information. These tables appear here as Tables 2.2 and 2.3.

The inputs from competitor analysis contribute to the identification of SWOT. Without such inputs, management is operating as would the captain of a ship without charts of the waters.

Society

Until the 1960s, business most often considered itself a closed system, one which operated without having significant transactions with those outside. But the demands placed on business by society primarily through government legislation in the 1960s and the 1970s convinced business that society did not hold the same view. Society was concerned with the impact business had on it. Government responded to society's concerns and created numerous laws which affected the operation of business. (See Table 2.1.) The perceived role of business was expanded to include much more than the mere production of goods and services. Business is now expected to contribute to the society in other ways, for example, through the employment of the economically and culturally disadvantaged. Information search must be continually maintained in order that no surprises occur in the

---

[19] W. E. Rothschild, "Competitor Analysis: The Missing Link in Strategy," *Management Review*, July 1979, pp. 22–39.

Table 2.2   Information Needed for Competitor Analysis

Conceptive Design	Physical Resources	Market	Finance	Management
Technical resources	**Capacity**	**Sales force**	**Long-term**	**Key people**
Concepts	**Plant**	Skills	Debt/equity ratio	Objectives and priorities
Patents and copyrights	Size	Size	Cost of debt	Values
Technological sophistication	Location	Type	**Short-term**	Reward systems
Technical integration	Age	Location	Line of credit	**Decision making**
Human resources	**Equipment**	**Distribution network**	Type of debt	Location
Key people and skills	Automation	**Research**	Cost of debt	Type
Use of external	Maintenance	Skills	**Liquidity**	Speed
technical groups	Flexibility	Type	**Cash flow**	**Planning**
Funding	**Processes**	**Service and sales policies**	Days of receivables	Type
Total	Uniqueness	Advertising	Inventory turnover	Emphasis
Percentage of sales	Flexibility	Skills	Accounting practices	Time span
Consistency over time	**Degree of integration**	Type	**Human resources**	**Staffing**
Internally generated	**Human resources**	**Human resources**	Key people and skills	Longevity and turnover
Government supplied	Key people and skills	Key people and skills	Turnover	Experience
	Work force	Turnover	**Systems**	Replacement policies
	Skills mix	**Funding**	Budgeting	**Organization**
	Unions	Total	Forecasting	Centralization
	Turnover	Consistency over time	Controlling	Functions
		Percentage of sales		Use of staff
		Reward systems		

Source: Reprinted by permission of the publisher, from, "Competitor Analysis: The Missing Link in Strategy," W. E. Rothschild, *Management Review*, July 1979, © 1979 by AMACOM, a division of American Management Association, p. 26. All rights reserved.

Table 2.3   Sources of Information for Competitor Analysis

	Public	Trade/Professionals	Government	Investors
What competitors say about themselves	Advertising Promotional materials Press releases Speeches Books Articles Personnel changes Want ads	Manuals Technical papers Licenses Patents Courses Seminars	Security and Exchange reports FIC Testimony Lawsuits Antitrust	Annual meetings Annual reports Prospectuses Stock/bond issues
What others say about them	Books Articles Case studies Consultants Newspaper reporters Environmental groups Consumer groups Unions "Who's Who" Recruiting firms	Suppliers/vendors Trade press Industry study Customers Subcontractors	Lawsuits Antitrust State/federal agencies National plans Government programs	Security analyst reports Industry studies Credit reports

area of societal demands. Business has learned that it must respond to the demands of the society, especially the demands of those groups which can bring significant pressure on business.

This responsiveness can lead to a reduction of strategic alternatives. In fact, E. A. Murray, Jr., has suggested that for many businesses, especially those who are regulated to a great extent by the federal government or against whom significant action has been taken by large pressure groups, decisions are more negotiated than formulated from within. Murray has proposed the following:[20]

1.   The less the effective power of the firm relative to that of other institutions in its environment with which it must interact, the more the change in strategy of the firm over time will be disjointed and incremental rather than integrated and comprehensive, irrespective of nature and environmental opportunities and threats facing the firm.

2.   The greater the degree of fragmentation of decisions of strategic significance to the firm yet external to it, the more the change in the strategy of the firm over time will be disjointed and incremental rather than integrated and comprehensive, irrespective of nature and environmental opportunities and threats facing the firm.

The concept of incremental decision making and coalition bargaining will be discussed in Chapter 6. While that chapter stresses internal coalitions, Murray's comments relate to planning that results from the need to adapt to powerful external influences. Murray examined a public utility and its frustration in attempting to comply with requirements of its environment—specifically, environmentalists and the federal government. His examination of this utility and its problems supported both of his propositions. He also found that many organizations must often comply with what seem to be irrational or contradictory regulations and requirements of different groups—or more commonly, requirements levied upon them by different agencies of the federal government. Often even the same agency of the federal government may issue contradictory requirements. Murray has raised an important issue as to whether strategy under these circumstances—circumstances which are increasingly common—can be described as having been formulated.

Many times, companies have abandoned plans or strategies because of the demands of society's pressure groups. For example, Walt Disney Productions Inc. abandoned a ski resort project at King's Mountain, California, because of pressure from environmentalists. Similarly, many nuclear power projects have been halted as a consequence of pressure from environmentalists. Finally, numerous steel plants have been shut down because of the cost of adding environmental protection equipment. It should be noted that the demands of these external organizations are appropriate, given the greater requirements of the society. Sometimes some businesses take actions which are highly questionable with respect to overall benefit to society. Regardless of the moral perspective, however, these external forces act as constraints on business, and business must have strategies for coping with them.

Businesses must continually explore the issues of social responsibility to better determine the impacts they have on society. No surprises should occur. Again, information is critical.

---

[20] E. A. Murray, Jr., "Limitations to Strategic Alternatives," *Proceedings, Academy of Management*, 1976. pp. 140–144.

The Economy

Significant changes in the economy are often caused by the actions of the federal govern-ment, either through its fiscal policies or through the monetary policies of the Federal Reserve Board. It is often argued that deficits in federal spending with "easy" money (high money supply), have been the main contributors to past double-digit inflation; that the monetary policies of the Federal Reserve have increased unemployment; and that its high interest rates have, in the early 1980s, devastated the housing and banking industries. Furthermore, presidential economic strategies, such as President Reagan's "supply-side economics," clearly move the economy in certain directions. Whatever the specific causes, the results of federal action have often dictated the level and composition of business activity.

The nature of federal expenditures, which has been changing in recent years, also clearly impacts on the economy. For example, direct benefit payments to individuals, al-most nonexistent 20 years ago, accounted in 1984 for 42 percent of the federal budget, and expenditures by the Department of Defense (DOD), which not too many years ago constituted almost 60 percent of the total federal budget, in 1984 accounted for 29 percent of the budget. Within departments, expenditures have also changed in nature, and these changes have greatly affected the economy. For example, a few years ago, procurement accounted for nearly 60 percent of the DOD allocation. In 1984, procurement accounted for only 30 percent of the DOD's budget (but this was up significantly from the Carter administration years when procurement hit a low, and military pay and benefits accounted for over 50 percent of the DOD budget) as opposed to their 1984 combined level of about 33 percent.

Another major impact of federal spending in these two major areas, transfer payments and the DOD, is the manner in which these expenditures are funded. In 1984, the national debt will require $103 billion in current expenditures for debt service. This constitutes slightly over 12 percent of the federal budget, significantly higher than past years.[21] It is no secret that the huge deficits in current federal budgets are a matter of major concern to all because of their impact on the long-term viability of the economy. At the very minimum, these deficits raise interest rates in the business money markets and tighten the supplies of monies available for business expansion.[22]

Businesses must respond to these changes. Firms must gear up to produce the military hardware to be procured, and/or to enter basic industries that typify the spending of trans-fer payments. They must also be prepared for the changing monetary conditions and be able to respond accordingly. Change is the name of the game. And to keep on top of change, businesses must have information.

Labor

Organized labor has made significant strides over the years in securing increased wages and benefits for workers; and in its efforts to organize both blue-collar and white-collar workers, especially in the South, can be expected to continue. Organized labor has an

---

[21] *The Budget of the United States Government, Fiscal Year 1984* (Washington, D.C.: Government Printing Office, 1984), MS.2, 3-38, 5-1 to 5-16.

[22] "Ballooning Deficits—What the Real Danger Is," *U.S. News & World Report*, August 13, 1984, p. 73; "A Beastly Question," *Time*, October 15, 1984, pp. 88–89.

extremely powerful influence on the national economy and on the supportive strategies
and policies of the businesses which operate within that economy. Labor's impact on the
presidential as well as gubernatorial and mayoral races has historically been significant,
but labor's impact on government and on the economy appears to be lessening, and business must be attuned to that change.

Changes in employees' attitudes also affect business. Significant changes in the attitudes of all employees, whether organized or not, occurred during the 1960s and 1970s.
These changes are primarily related to the work ethic and to the extent to which lower-
level employees help the organization's management make decisions, sometimes strategic
as well as operational.

One factor often cited as significant in the much-discussed decrease of productivity in
the United States in the 1970s and early 1980s was a change in workers' attitudes toward
work. In 1985, the evidence indicates that the "Protestant work ethic" is strengthening.
An apparent shift from emphasis on equality of opportunity to equality of reward regardless of effort was seen in the United States in the 1970s, but the country now appears
to be moving away from this approach. Workers at all levels of the organization have also
begun to expect more personal satisfaction from their work and more participation in decision making.

These and other factors make the successful implementation of strategy difficult, because they make motivation difficult. The manager today who must motivate employees is
highly constrained by numerous conditions, many of which he or she cannot control.
Since many businesses must increase productivity to survive, they must pay close attention to the attitudes of workers.

Natural Resources

Energy is not the only resource in questionable supply in the United States. Government
studies have revealed that several major metals and other primary manufacturing materials
are in short supply. Living space in large cities, clean air and water, and natural areas of
beauty are also scarce. And, on a worldwide basis, food is in extremely short supply for
most of the population. In short, the earth's inhabitants face an ever-increasing population
with a limited amount of supplies with which to support this multitude. This creates great
problems for businesses and for governments. The resource-shortage problem will be further compounded in the future as developing nations seek to emulate industrialized nations. The United States depends upon many developing nations for the provision of
scarce materials, a situation which has led and will continue to lead to a bargaining advantage for the providing nations.

While stockpiles of some of the metals and other materials which are needed may be
created, stockpiling of some resources—for example, energy—is rather difficult. And
while the United States has made significant strides toward energy independence, this
goal will probably not be achieved until the late 1980s. Yet the tremendous positive
changes in energy supply caused by reduced consumption led in 1985 to a short-term energy glut. This oversupply has caused problems for certain businesses and opportunities
for others. Business must be prepared to react quickly to changing conditions. This requires information!

While material shortages appear to be the key resource problems of the United States,
the inadequate supply of food is the most critical resource shortage for most other nations.
And while the United States is able to produce a great deal of food, its food technology is

highly energy-dependent. It is clear that the nations of the world must come to grips with the reality that the supply of materials is not inexhaustible and that the number of people who are to live upon this planet must be somehow limited if each of the individuals in the world is to enjoy a desirable quality of life. The impact upon business of these worldwide problems includes expropriation, import or export quotas, higher prices, and political power demonstrations by the underdeveloped nations who possess natural resources. Again, the needs for materials change and supplies diminish. Astute strategists observe and predict such changes. More importantly, they anticipate them, preparing their organizations for these events.

International Events

There appears to be one major factor in the international situation which business must recognize, and that is the change taking place in economic, political, and social power structures.

Immediately after World War II, the United States was clearly the most powerful nation in the world, since it alone possessed the atomic bomb and it had the most successful economy. Now, however, several European nations, the U.S.S.R., China, India, Brazil, Canada, the OPEC nations, and Japan, among others, have economic or military power significant enough to create major spheres of influence which can counteract the efforts of the United States both economically and militarily.

Furthermore, many nations are undergoing internal social change to achieve redistribution of wealth. Frequently, this change is accomplished through violence and under the banner of communism. The ability of businesses to engage in trade with communist countries is limited. Why? Because many communist nations are unwilling or unable to trade with the United States or Canada on a large scale, especially the new emerging nations. Furthermore, trade with communist countries is sometimes reduced to barter, since some of their currencies have little value outside of the communist bloc countries. These factors restrict both the number of potential consumers and the sources of raw materials for U.S. businesses.

Other problems in doing business in foreign countries include cultural differences, lack of local managerial talent, double taxation, monetary translations, tariff and trade barriers, and lack of infrastructure. As a result of the difficulties of coping with various problems in foreign countries, many firms are reassessing the need to operate in many of these countries.

Yet, the world is full of consumers. The problem is finding them and meeting their needs. Wealth changes drastically. The newly wealthy OPEC countries consume. Business need only find out what these countries want to consume and whether it can supply the goods. If people in the United States and Canada seek fuel-efficient cars, are U.S. and Canadian firms content to let the Japanese supply them? Where are the international markets? What are the needs of international consumers? Without information, a company will never know the answers to such questions. Chapter 10 reviews these issues in more detail.

Other Significant Factors

Numerous other factors affect individual businesses; perhaps the most significant remaining factor affecting most businesses is demographics.

Demographic Changes.   Perhaps the most significant demographic changes which will affect businesses are increases in population, geographic shifts in population, and changes in the composition of the population by age group. In the United States, the median age of the population has increased as the "baby-boom" generation has aged and the birthrate has fallen. (Information Capsule 2.3 profiles the baby-boomers.) It is also expected that many people who currently live in the North, Northeast, and Midwest will move to the South and the West.

INFORMATION CAPSULE 2.3
The Baby Boomers

The "baby-boomers" are that group of persons born in the period from 1946 to 1962. Since the "leading edge" of this group is now entering their forties and hence their peak ages of consumption, the baby-boomers will greatly influence the economy in the next 30–40 years. These 68 million people, nearly one-third of the U.S. population, are being closely observed by marketers for the latest trends in their consumption patterns. They are also being closely watched by government, especially as they age and require increased government services, for example, Social Security.

As they enter their peak buying years, these industries will be bouyed by the "boomers": housing, furniture and appliances, automobiles, specialty foods, clothing and cosmetics, travel, financial services, and possibly children's goods and services as the boomers themselves reproduce. However, not all industries have fared well from their consumption patterns. As they have aged, they have left behind them several markets which have consequently been significantly reduced in size—baby foods, education, soft drinks, candies, and beer, for example. Due to their aging past these products, you will notice the increased use of older persons in most of these industries' advertisements as they try to prolong the life of their product and increase their traditional target markets.

The baby-boomers are also going to have a significant effect on the organizations in this country, and on U.S. politics as well. Many of them have already arrived in positions of power with business and government and have been able to alter substantially the strategies and policies of their organizations. Politically, their votes seemed to go mostly to Reagan in the 1984 election, but their attitudes are mixed, and do not at this time seem to favor either party's long-term platforms. Because of their better educations and higher expectations than those of their predecessors, they expect more from organizations and their jobs, and these expectations are causing changes in the way business and other organizations must be managed. Conflicts between old and new values within organizations and within the society will not always be easily resolved. Because of the more structured environments in which they work, blue-collar boomers have been called the most frustrated boomers of them all.

The "yuppies" (young urban professionals) as they are often called (technically only about one-third of the boomers), have come to symbolize the boomers, but there are many other boomers who are unskilled, poorly educated, and who are likely to be drains on the economy in the future.

Sources: Geoffrey Colvin, "What the Baby-Boomers Will Buy Next," *Fortune*, October 15, 1984; "Baby-Boomers Push for Power," *Business Week*, July 2, 1984, pp. 52–62; "Here Come the Baby-Boomers," *U.S. News & World Report*, November 5, 1984, pp. 68–73.

On an international basis, the most significant demographic factor is the sheer increase in population, especially in the developing nations. In 1979, the world's population was more than 4.4 billion. Some estimate that the world population could double by the year 2000, and most believe that it will certainly reach 7 billion by then. The consequences of this enormous population growth have not even begun to be fully imagined. For example, many feel that the thousands dying of starvation in Ethiopia in 1984 and 1985 will turn into millions worldwide by the year 2000. One current negative impact on the United States has been an increase in the entrance of illegal aliens into this country. On the other hand, the increasing population represents a huge potential market if the developing nations can achieve economic success. Businesses must continue surveillance of these critical population changes if they are to take advantage of the opportunities created and negate the threats involved.

Other demographic changes are expected to occur. For example, more white-collar jobs will be created in proportion to those in the blue-collar occupations. Incomes may rise, but it is difficult at this time to determine the impact that inflation will have upon this rise. Several economists are concerned that the future mix of jobs may significantly reduce the size of the middle class.[23] The shifts in market areas, as well as the shifts in the composition of the market, will provide both growth opportunities and problems for the business community.

Making Use of the Data: Analytical and Forecasting Techniques

Forecasting is difficult, especially about the future.

▪ *Chinese proverb* ▪

Once strategic data have been accumulated, they must be transformed into information that will enable decision makers to make appropriate choices of objectives and alternatives, and that will aid in their determination and formulation. These decisions, while made in the present, relate to future events. Techniques designed specifically to provide inferences about the future are called *forecasting techniques*. Other methodologies, labeled *descriptive techniques*, provide information about current situations; decision makers can draw inferences about the future after examining the information provided by these methodologies. Some forecasting methods with which you may be familiar include regression, correlation, Delphi, Box-Jenkins, seasonal trend, and expert opinion. Simulation, one of the most important forecasting techniques, is reviewed later in this section.

The role of forecasting in strategic management is to reduce uncertainty and aid in decision making. In strategic decision situations, uncertainty can never be totally eliminated. Ultimately, decision makers attempt to quantify the uncertainty that remains. This process is usually referred to as risk analysis.

Compounding the problem of reducing uncertainty, there is evidence that the amount of uncertainty is increasing as the environment becomes more volatile and previously unknown strategic problems confront organizations. These events are made more pronounced because of the long time horizons present in most strategy formulation sit-

---

[23] V. F. Zonana, "Is the U.S. Middle-Class Shrinking Alarmingly?" *The Wall Street Journal*, June 20, 1984, pp. 1, 26; "Is Middle-Class Really Doomed to Shrivel Away?" *U.S. News & World Report*, August 20, 1984, p. 65.

uations. Three or more years frequently may transpire from conception to the actual marketing of a new product or the acquisition or divestment of an SBU. During this time the assumptions (premises) upon which the strategy was based may change significantly. But rapid change is compressing these time horizons.

However, much uncertainty can be reduced, and the strategic manager should become familiar with those uncertainty-reduction techniques at his or her disposal. Put simply, forecasting is vital. While it is assumed as given in most planning models, forecasting is not an easy task.[24]

> *We look at the present through a rear-view mirror.*
> *We march backwards into the future.*
>
> ▪ *Marshall McLuhan* ▪

Simulation Modeling and Other Uses of the Computer

One of the most significant analytical/forecasting techniques is simulation modeling. Simulation allows the strategist to ask what-if questions—for example, "What if the price of raw material rises 1 percent?"; "What if the union negotiates a 10-percent increase in benefits?"; "What if our firm raises prices by 5 percent?" The answers to these and many other vital questions can be rendered quickly and accurately if the organization possesses a valid simulation model of its operations.

Simulations are computerized models which aid management in decision making. Simulation models abstract reality—normally an organization's internal flows—in terms of logically arranged equations, expressed symbolically. These models are interactive; that is, they allow managers to "talk" with them. The normal use of simulations is to assume a change in one or more inputs to the system and view the resulting changes in the system as portrayed by the model. Simulations have evolved over a period of years but have been important only since 1970, when appropriate systems-oriented software packages were developed and time-sharing became feasible.

The more complex simulation models are expensive, so not every organization can afford one. For those who can, such models are becoming a necessity, not a luxury. To date, only complex simulations of internal operations are available; environmental simulations, with the exception of models of the national economy, are not widely available. However, such simulations are in the developmental stages. Conversely, spreadsheet programs for microcomputers offer the smallest of firms the opportunity to ask what-if questions for some fairly complex issues.[25] The complex simulations commence with an exhaustive analysis of the actual interrelationships of the organization, its subsystems, and

[24] J. C. Chambers, S. K. Mullick, and D. D. Smith, "How to Choose the Right Forecasting Technique," *Harvard Business Review*, July/August 1971, pp. 45–74; W. Bouton, "The Changing Requirements for Managing Corporate Information Systems," *MSU Business Topics*, Summer 1978, pp. 1–12; W. K. Hall, "Forecasting Techniques for Use in the Corporate Planning Process," *Managerial Planning*, November/December 1972, pp. 5–10, 33; D. Lebell and O. J. Krasner, "Selecting Forecasting Techniques from Business Planning Requirements," *Academy of Management Review*, July 1977, pp. 373–383; S. Makridakis and S. Wheelwright, "Integrating Forecasting and Planning," *Long Range Planning*, September 1973, pp. 53–63; J. Utterback, "Environmental Analysis and Forecasting," in *Strategic Management, A New View of Business*, eds. Charles Hofer and Dan Schendel (Boston: Little/Brown, 1979).

[25] "How Personal Computers Are Changing the Forecasters' Jobs," *Business Week*, October 1, 1984, pp. 123–124.

the subsystems components. Most simulations use a modular approach. They develop models for each of the major structural divisions, functions, or subsystems, combining them at an interface point into a total corporate model. The modules comprising the total model are usually at the business or functional level.[26] Eventually, every quantifiable internal resource, event, or flow is incorporated into a modular model. Modules are then combined and interrelationships interfaced. Spreadsheets for microcomputers typically analyze only major variables, but as their memories increase in capacity, spreadsheets will be able to handle these more complex analyses. *Lotus 1-2-3* and other similar programs already do, especially IFPS Personal (Interactive Financial Planning Systems).

The evidence indicates that the number of business firms employing complex simulations is large and growing. Numerous types of simulations are utilized, but few totally integrated corporate models exist. That is, few firms have combined simulations of various aspects of their operations to develop a model of the total corporation. Firms most frequently employ models in the areas of financial analysis and planning and evaluation of policy alternatives. Virtually any firm can employ a spreadsheet package and indeed most probably do.

In addition to simulation modeling, uses of the computer in strategic management include the provision of timely information at lower levels, which should eventually improve strategic decision making; the provision of more common models for financial analysis, forecasting, descriptive statistical analysis, capital budgeting, and so on; and even the training of executives to ask the right questions in strategy formulation. The future seems to lie in a mainframe tied to PC terminals, thus allowing the SIS to be utilized by affected personnel throughout the organization. For smaller firms, stand alone micros will serve this function.

It is important to remember that the computer only aids the strategist; it does not and cannot replace him or her. The strategist must use a certain amount of intuition as well as science in the strategic management process. It is this ability to meaningfully interpret and relate the scientifically derived information and to make appropriate strategic decisions that separates the successful strategist from the unsuccessful one.

The Micro Advances Our Ability to Forecast

Information and information processing have become accessible to a much larger segment of the management population than ever before possible with the advent of the microcomputer. This computer has given access to many who were previously financially or technologically denied the opportunity to employ the computer in managing their organizations. Of critical importance are the numerous software programs available to assist individuals and corporations in managing strategically. For example, the above referenced spreadsheet analyses, which allow managers to forecast the impacts of selected changes in financial and operating performance, enable even the smallest organizations and their managers to make more sophisticated, more rational decisions with respect to their strate-

---

[26] "Breakthrough in Management Planning" (Chicago: Planmetrics); "'What If' Help for Management," *Business Week*, January 21, 1980, pp. 73, 74; E. R. McLean and G. L. Neale, "Computer-Based Planning Models Come of Age," *Harvard Business Review*, July/August 1980, pp. 46–48; both EPS (Environmental Planning Systems) and IFPS (Interactive Financial Planning Systems) are computer-simulation software packages which use this approach.

gies. Numerous manipulations of balance sheets, income statements, and cash flows are also available. And, quite frankly, for the first time many smaller organizations will now consequently develop such fundamental planning statements as budgets, which, while apparently simple, are time consuming and much more readily accomplished using appropriate software packages. Similar advances have been made in word processing, in ratio analyses, in capital needs forecasting, in sales forecasting, and so forth. Even some of the more sophisticated programs, such as those employing Box Jenkins, Interactive Financial Planning Systems, or Environmental Planning Systems are available for microcomputers. Even the very complex econometrics models of the U.S. economy have been placed on personal computers.[27] The ability to crunch numbers better and faster does not guarantee that improved decision making will occur, but the improvement in both hardware and software does suggest, at least, that better decisions are possible, if not more likely.

Analytical Techniques: A Comment

Numerous forecasting techniques exist. For example, virtually hundreds of methodologies have been suggested for societal and technological forecasting; but there is not space to discuss all of them here. The important points to remember are these:

1.   Numerous techniques exist, some better than others for a particular situation.
2.   Using more than one technique should improve forecasting.
3.   The output of a technique is no better than its inputs and its assumptions.
4.   Cost-benefit analysis should be performed before expensive techniques are undertaken.
5.   The techniques should be evaluated.
6.   Regardless of the amount of time and money invested, the environment is uncertain and is undergoing an increasing amount of change. Forecasting failures will occur. Flexibility must be maintained.
7.   Somebody has to put it all together. Someone must make the decision as to what the information means. That person is not always right.

Summary

Change typifies the environment of all organizations, but the pace of change seems to be accelerating. The purpose of obtaining internal and external environmental information is to determine strengths, weaknesses, opportunities, and threats in order to better establish objectives, formulate strategic alternatives, and decide upon courses of strategic action. Strengths and weaknesses, threats and opportunities are not always perceived in the same ways or determined in the same ways. Differences in approaches to managing them consequently result.

The strategic information system is a critical element in achieving success. Both formal and informal sources are used to identify and determine the nature of internal and external factors. Strategists must continually scan the environment for information which

---

[27] "How Personal Computers Are Changing the Forecaster's Job," *Business Week*, October 1, 1984, pp. 123–124.

could necessitate changing strategies. The internal information sought relates at the corporate level to SBU performance, and at the SBU level to functions such as marketing, operations, finance, human resources management, R&D, management systems and functions, and so forth. Externally, the organization monitors information related to government, technology, competition, the industry, competitor-analysis factors, society, the economy, labor, natural resources, pressure groups, and international situations.

It must be remembered that strategic decisions are based on forecasts related to current information. Any number of forecasting techniques exist, each better in some situations than in others. Modeling through the microcomputer seems to offer much hope for the future, especially in terms of helping strategists understand how changes will affect the organization.

Key Terms and Concepts

After completing this chapter, you should be familiar with the following terms and concepts: how change affects the need for information; why information is critical to strategy formulation; how information is used in the strategic decision process; the definitions of strengths, weaknesses, opportunities, and threats; how SWOT are defined operationally; strategic information system (SIS); management information system (MIS); major sources of internal and external environmental information; scanning; the internal information sought; the external information sought, including major factors involved in each; the importance of forecasting; modeling; the impacts of the microcomputer on forecasting.

Discussion Questions

1. Why is information critical to strategy formulation?

2. M. E. Porter proposed that the intensity of competition is the most critical element in the firm's environment. He then suggests five basic competitive factors that should be monitored. What are these five factors? Show how they apply to an organization.

3. What is the role of forecasting in strategic management?

4. Discuss any organization and its strategic situation with regard to the contents of this chapter and the key terms and concepts noted above.

5. Now that you have examined all four of the primary formative factors in the strategy formulation process, which do you believe is the most critical, and why?

References

"Ballooning Deficits—What the Real Danger Is." *U.S. News & World Report*, August 13, 1984.

"Battling It Out in the Skies." *Time*, October 8, 1984, pp. 54–58.

"Behind Big Oil's Slide from the Peak to the Pits." *U.S. News & World Report*, December 17, 1984.

"Business is Turning Data into a Potent Strategic Weapon." *Business Week*, August 22, 1983, pp. 92–95.

"The Recovery Comes." *Fortune*, August 20, 1984, pp. 176–181.

Dearden, John. "SMR Forum: Will the Computer Change the Job of Top Management?" *Sloan Management Review*, Fall 1983, pp. 57–60.

Engelmayer, Paul A. "Food Concerns Rush to Serve More Quality Frozen Dinners." *The Wall Street Journal*, October 20, 1983, pp. 33.

Hall, Trish. "Industry Headache—Americans Drink Less, and Makers of Alcohol Feel a Little Woozy." *The Wall Street Journal*, March 14, 1984.

Hofer, C. W. "Research on Strategic Planning: A Survey of Past Studies and Suggestions for Future Efforts." *Journal of Economics and Business*, Spring/Summer 1976, pp. 261–272.

"How Seagram is Scrambling to Survive 'The Sobering of America.'" *Business Week*, September 3, 1984, pp. 94–95.

"How Xerox Speeds Up the Birth of New Products," *Business Week*, March 19, 1984, pp. 58–59.

"Is Middle Class Really Doomed to Shrivel Away?" *U.S. News & World Report*, August 20, 1984, pp. 65–66.

"It's a Wine Party: Bring Your Own Box." *The Orlando Sentinel*, December 9, 1984.

Klein, Harold E., and Newman, William H. "How to Integrate New Environmental Forces into Strategic Planning." *Management Review*, July 1980, pp. 40–48.

"Look, Ma, No Dials: More Major Appliances Go Digital," *Business Week*, November 12, 1984, pp. 97–101.

MacGregor, John M. "What Users Think About Computer Models." *Long Range Planning*, 1983, Vol. 16, No. 5, pp. 45–57.

Makridakis, Spyros. "If We Cannot Forecast How Can We Plan?" *Long Range Planning*, 1981, Vol. 14, No. 3, pp. 10–20.

Mintzberg, H. "Planning on the Left Side and Managing on the Right." *Harvard Business Review*, July/August 1976, pp. 49–58.

Naisbitt, J. *Megatrends*. New York: Warner Books, 1982.

"Natural Soda: From the Health-Food Fad to Supermarket Staple." *Business Week*, January 14, 1985, p. 72.

Nulty, Peter. "A Champ of Cheap Airlines." *Fortune*, March 22, 1982, pp. 127–134.

"'Paper Bottles' Are Coming on Strong." *Business Week*, January 16, 1984, pp. 56–57.

Ramanujam, Vasudevan. "An Empirical Examination of Contextual Influences on Corporate Turnaround." Paper submitted to the Business Policy and Planning Division for the Academy of Management National Meeting, Boston, August 1984.

"The Recovery Comes." *Fortune*, August 20, 1984, pp. 176–181.

"Securities Risk—Wall Street Is Finding Its Trusty Computers Have Their Dark Side." *The Wall Street Journal*, December 4, 1984.

Sherrid, Pamela. "Good News on the Productivity Front." *Forbes*, October 10, 1983, pp. 124–126.

"A Shrinking Market Has Beermakers Brawling." *Business Week*, August 20, 1984, pp. 59–63.

Steiner, G. A. *Pitfalls in Comprehensive Long-Range Planning*. Oxford, Ohio: The Planning Executives Institute, 1972.

Steiner, George A., and Kunin, Harry and Elsa. "Formal Strategic Planning in the United States Today." *Long Range Planning*, 1983, Vol. 16, No. 3, pp. 12–17.

Summer, C. E. *Strategic Behavior in Business and Government*. Boston: Little/Brown, 1980.

"Times, Tastes Are Changing Liquor Business." *U.S. News & World Report*, September 3, 1984, p. 56.

Tipgos, M. A. "Structuring a Management Information System for Strategic Planning." *Managerial Planning*, January/February 1975, pp. 10–16.

"When Inflation Takes a Breather." *U.S. News & World Report*, August 27, 1984, pp. 32–33.

"Which Inflation Rate Should Business Use?" *Business Week*, April 7, 1980, pp. 94–97.

Winston, Jim. "Could Spherical 'Lightning Storms' Turn into This Year's Lava Lamps?" *The Wall Street Journal*, September 19, 1984.

Woutat, Donald. "Yuppie Love—Detroit Auto Makers Try to Increase Sales to Young Professionals." *The Wall Street Journal*, September 27, 1984, p. 1.

APPENDIX TO CHAPTER 2
Sources for Environmental Information

1. Government.
   a. *Code of Federal Regulations, Federal Register*, other federal publications.
   b. Various publishing house services—Commerce Clearing House (CCH), Bureau of National Affairs (BNA), Prentice-Hall (PH), and the like.
   c. Lobbyists.
   d. *Kiplinger Washington Newsletter*.
   e. *Monthly Catalog of United States Government Publications*.
   f. Monthly checklist of state publications.

2. Technology.
   a. *Statistical Abstract of the United States*.
   b. *Applied Science and Technology Index*.
   c. Scientific and Technical Information Service.
   d. Congressional hearings, university reports, "think-tank" reports.
   e. Department of Defense and military department publishers.
   f. Industrial reports.
   g. Computer-assisted information searches.
   h. National Science Foundation, *Annual Report*.
   i. *Research and Development Directory*.
   j. Industry contacts, salespeople, professional meetings.
   k. Patents.

3. Industry and competition.
   a. Annual reports of companies in question.
   b. Securities and Exchange Commission—"10-K Report."
   c. *Fortune 500 Directory, Forbes, Wall Street Transcript, Barrons*.
   d. Investment services and directories: Dun & Bradstreet, Standard & Poor's Value Line, Moody's, Starch Marketing.
   e. Trade association publications.
   f. Professional meetings, salespeople, industry contacts.
   g. Espionage.
   h. Surveys, for example, market research.
   i. *County and City Data Book*.
   j. *County Business Patterns*.
   k. Standard and Poor's *Industry Surveys*.

4. Society.
   a. Pressure-group publications and pronouncements.
   b. Books which might affect societal attitudes.
   c. Government (see section 1 in this list).
   d. Surveys.
   e. Judgment, opinion, scenario forecasting (Delphi).
   f. The media, especially television and newspapers.
   g. Articles in sociological, psychological, and political journals.
   h. Various institute and foundation reports such as the Ford Foundation's and the Brookings Institute's.

5. Economy.
    a. National economy.
        i. U.S. Department of Commerce.
            (a) Bureau of Census—*Survey of Manufacturers, Statistical Abstract of the United States, Current Population Reports*, census reports on various industries, housing, population, and so on.
            (b) Office of Business Economics—*Survey of Current Business*.
            (c) Bureau of Economic Analysis—*Business Conditions Digest*.
            (d) Business and Defense Services Administration—*U.S. Industrial Outlook*.
        ii. Council of Economic Advisors—*Economic Indicators, Annual Report*.
        iii. Securities and Exchange Commission—"Quarterly Financial Reports," "Quarterly Report of Plant and Equipment Expenditures of U.S. Corporations," "Quarterly Report of Working Capital of U.S. Corporations."
        iv. St. Louis Federal Reserve Bank—"Quarterly Report."
        v. The Conference Board.
        vi. Trade association publications.
        vii. Federal Trade Commission.
        viii. U.S. Chamber of Commerce/American Manufacturers Association.
        ix. University of Michigan Survey Research Center.
        x. *Federal Reserve Bulletin*.
        xi. Econometric Models—Chase Econometrics, Michael Evans Econometrics, Wharton Econometrics.
    b. International economic conditions.
        i. U.S. Department of Commerce.
            (a) Bureau of Census—"Guide to Foreign Trade Statistics."
            (b) Bureau of International Commerce—"Overseas Business Reports," "Foreign Economic Trends and Their Implications for the United States."
        ii. OECD—*Economic Outlook and Main Economic Indicators*.
        iii. United Nations—*Statistical Yearbook*.
        iv. OIT; International Labor Office—*Yearbook of Labor Statistics*.
        v. Business International newsletters.
        vi. St. Louis Federal Reserve Bank.
        vii. National plans of European countries.
        viii. INSEAD (The European Institute of Business Administration); IMEDE (Management Development Institute, Lausanne).

6. Labor.
    a. *Labor Law Journal* and other related journals, including law school journals.
    b. Various publishing house services, such as CCH, BNA, PH.
    c. Various labor union publications.
    d. U.S. Department of Labor publications, *Monthly Labor Review*.
    e. U.S. Department of Commerce.

7. Natural resources.
    a. U.S. Department of the Interior, Bureau of Mines—*Minerals Yearbook, Geological Survey*.
    b. U.S. Department of Agriculture—*Agricultural Abstract*.

   c.   Federal Power Commission statistics of electric utilities/statistics of gas pipe companies.
   d.   Publications of various institutions: American Petroleum Institute, U.S. Atomic Energy Commission, Coal Mining Institute of America, American Steel Institute, Brookings Institute.

8.   General information.
   a.   Indexes and periodical directories.
   b.   Bibliographies and special guides.
   c.   Other basic sources.

Sources: C. R. Goeldner and Laura M. Kirks, "Business Facts: Where to Find Them," *MSU Business Topics*, Summer 1976, pp. 23–76; Francois E. deCarbonnel and Roy G. Donance, "Information Sources for Planning Decisions," *California Management Review*, (Summer 1973), pp. 42–53; and A. B. Nutt, R. C. Lenz, Jr., H. W. Lanford, and M. J. Cleary, "Data Sources for Trend Extrapolation in Technological Forecasting," *Long Range Planning*, February 1976, pp. 72–76.

3

Determining Strategic Objectives and Formulating the Master Strategy

The thing to do with the future is not to forecast it, but to create it. The objective of planning should be to design a desirable future and to invent ways to bring it about.

▪ Russell Ackoff ▪

This chapter continues to examine, primarily from a conceptual perspective, the major issues involved in a situation that requires strategy formulation:

1. **Where are we? (current performance; SWOT)**

2. **Where do we want to be? (future objectives; forecasted SWOT)**

3. **How do we get there? (master strategy; forecasted SWOT)**

The chapter focuses on the processes involved in determining strategic objectives and in formulating the master strategy and discusses the corporate strategy in particular. In the first half of the chapter, the discussions include: the objective determination process; objectives as integrative mechanisms; and management by objectives, results, and rewards (MBORR), a management planning and control system as well as a management philosophy. Most of the second half of the chapter examines the master strategy, especially corporate strategy alternatives. Finally, some of the important characteristics of all plans are noted. Figures 3.1 and 3.2 show what subjects are presented in the chapter.

Figure 3.1 The Organization—a Strategic Management Process Model

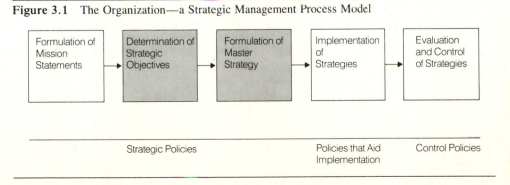

Formulation of Mission Statements	Determination of Strategic Objectives	Formulation of Master Strategy	Implementation of Strategies	Evaluation and Control of Strategies

Strategic Policies	Policies that Aid Implementation	Control Policies

Figure 3.2   Objectives Determination and Master Strategy Formulation

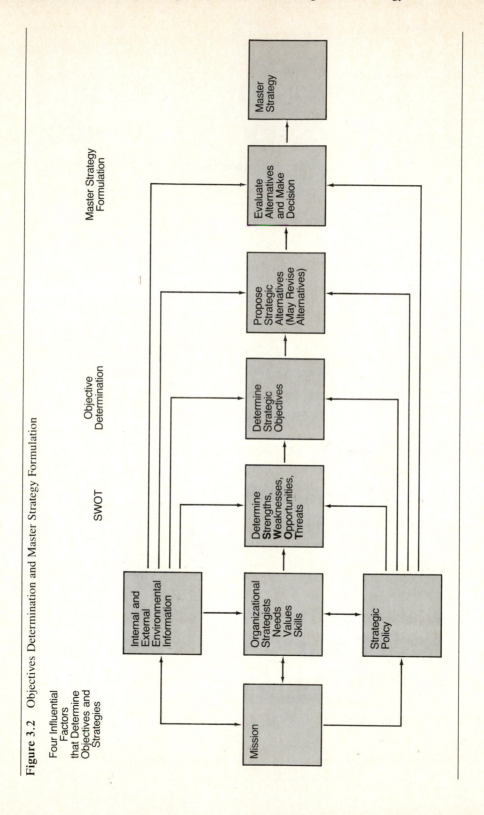

Figure 3.3 Some Typical Business Objectives

Possible Attributes	Possible Indices	Targets and Time Frame		
		Year One	Year Two	Year Three
Growth	$ sales	$100 mil	120 mil	140 mil
	Unit sales	× units	1.10 × units	1.20 × units
Efficiency	$ profits	10 mil	12 mil	15 mil
	Profits/sales	.10	.10	.11
Utilization of resources	ROI	.15	.15	.16
	ROE	.25	.26	.27
Contribution to owners	Dividends	$1.00/share	$1.10/share	$1.30/share
	Eps	$2.00/share	$2.40/share	$2.80/share
Contribution to customers	Price	Equal to or better than competition	Equal to or better than competition	Equal to or better than competition
	Quality			
	Reliability			
Contributions to employees	Wage rate	$3.50/hour	$3.75/hour	$4.00/hour
	Employment stability	< 5% turnover	< 4% turnover	< 4% turnover
Contributions to society	Taxes paid	$10 mil	$12 mil	$16 mil
	Scholarships awarded	$100,000	$120,000	$120,000
	Etc.			

Source: C. W. Hofer, "A Conceptual Scheme for Formulating a Total Business Strategy," Dover, MA: Case Teacher's Association, #BP-0040, p. 2. Copyright 1976 by C. W. Hofer. Reproduced by permission.

"Would you tell me, please, which way I ought to go from here?" said Alice.
"That depends a good deal on where you want to get to," said the Cheshire cat.

▪ *Lewis Carroll,* Alice's Adventures in Wonderland ▪

Determining Strategic Objectives

To fulfill the promise of the mission statement, strategic objectives—the results intended—must be identified. Without objectives, the organization is assured of eventual failure. Objectives, which depend on mission, policy, the strategists, information, and SWOT, state "where we want to be."

The Objective-Setting Process

All objectives possess four components:

1. The attribute sought.
2. An index for measuring progress toward the attribute.
3. A target to be achieved or hurdle to be overcome.
4. A time frame within which the target or hurdle is to be achieved.[1]

Figure 3.3 portrays these components for several typical objectives. Typical strategic business objectives include concerns for the impacts of operations on both the organiza-

[1] C. W. Hofer and D. Schendel, *Strategy Formulation: Analytical Concepts* (St. Paul, Minn.: West, 1978), pp. 20–22.

====== **INFORMATION CAPSULE 3.1** ======
Hewlett-Packard's Strategic Objectives

The following is a brief description of the Hewlett-Packard objectives in 1985:[a]

1. Profit Objective: To achieve sufficient profit to finance company growth and to provide resources we need to achieve our other corporate objectives.

2. Customer Objective: To provide products and services of the greatest possible value to our customers, thereby gaining and holding their respect and loyalty.

3. Fields of Interest Objective: To enter new fields only when the ideas we have, together with our technical, manufacturing, and marketing skills, assure that we can make a needed and profitable contribution to the field.

4. Growth Objective: To let growth be limited only by our profits and our ability to develop and produce technical products that satisfy real customer needs.

5. Our People Objective: To help Hewlett-Packard people share in the company's success, which they make possible; to provide job security based on their performance; to recognize individual achievements; and to help them gain a sense of satisfaction and accomplishment from their work.

6. Management Objective: To foster initiative and creativity by allowing the individual great freedom of action in attaining well-defined objectives.

7. Citizenship Objective: To honor our obligations to society by being an economic, intellectual, and social asset to each nation and each community in which we operate.

[a] As depicted in internal corporate documents and described to J. W. Vincze by Hewlett-Packard personnel in 1985.

Source: Hewlett-Packard Company, Inc., 1983 Statement of Objectives.

tion and the external environment. But looking at Figure 3.3, you can see that fundamental internal concerns of the organization include the attributes of efficiency (profits, profits in relation to sales), growth (sales), utilization of resources (return on investment, ROI), contribution to owners (earnings per share), and contribution to employees (wages, employee development). Externally, the organization must be concerned with contribution to customers (quality, price) and contribution to society (taxes paid, corporate citizenship). It has also been observed that contribution to other major stakeholders—those on whom the actions of the organization have a direct impact—is also of vital concern. Similar objectives exist for nonbusiness organizations, but not in profit terms.

Objectives steer the organization in the direction its mission has pointed out, as Information Capsule 3.1 illustrates. As has often been said, "If you don't know where you are going, any road will get you there." Without objectives, "there" is usually "nowhere"! The Cheshire cat was right. First you must decide where you are going, then you can decide what road to take. Objectives provide direction and motivation. The objective-setting process also provides valuable communication within and among organizational subunits.

Levels of Objectives

There are three major levels of planning within the organization: strategic, intermediate, and operational. Hence, there are three major levels of objectives and plans, although the compression of time horizons rapidly results in only two levels: strategic and operational.

The objectives toward which strategic plans are directed should be specific. For example, a firm might set objectives of a 15-percent return on investment, a 20-percent penetration of the product market, a 10-percent increase in sales per year, and so forth. However, at the strategic planning stage, the plans need not be stated so specifically; in fact, these plans are usually broadly stated. But as planning progresses through the next two stages, intermediate and operational, the plans set out more specifically how objectives will be accomplished. Intermediate plans translate strategy into more specific courses of action for major organizational subsystems. Operational plans translate intermediate plans into very specific courses of action for lower-level subsystems and for individuals. Usually, the planning process includes a series of increasingly complex and detailed subobjectives, subplans, subpolicies, and so forth, until objectives and actions are parceled to individual workers. Again, as with most management terminology, there are no generally accepted definitions which describe the various levels of plans established to accomplish the master strategy. Differences in terminology should be allowed for in the examination of strategy and in the practice of strategic management.

Organizational Objectives as Integration Mechanisms—MBORR

Let us now examine a program for establishing effective objectives and then consider types of objectives that organizations establish. The program is called management by objectives, results, and rewards—MBORR—with emphasis on the need for specific objectives. Vague objectives, at the very least, lead to misinterpretation and a lack of accountability for performance. It is precisely to deal with such problems that MBORR-type programs were established. MBORR as used here embodies specific objective-setting programs and does not focus on the more behavioral concepts of subordinate development often associated with such programs.

MBORR: Concepts and Implications for Strategy

Management by objectives, results, and rewards is a management planning, control, motivation, communication, and subordinate development system. This type of program in its various forms—MBO, management by objectives; MBR, management by results; and MBC, management by compensation; as well as MBORR—is probably the most frequently discussed management practice in the last 30 years. Few can agree on specific contents, but most would agree that four common dimensions should be considered:

1. Establishment of objectives.
2. Employee participation.
3. Evaluation and control of performance.
4. Rewards for results.

The normal MBORR process involves the establishment of specific objectives by top management in all performance areas. These objectives are then communicated to the next lower level of management, which may or may not have participated in their development. At each level, objectives may then be distributed to the appropriate managers for their acceptance or rejection. Or these managers may submit to their superiors proposals which state their commitments to the accomplishment of the objectives. What evolves is a negotiation meeting between a manager and his or her superior manager involving give and take with respect to the subordinate's objectives. Once agreement is reached, the process shifts to the next lower level of management and continues until objective distribution reaches the supervisory level. The process usually terminates at this level, since first-line positions often cannot properly utilize this technique.

MBORR-type techniques were first introduced to the public as MBR by Peter Drucker, who had observed the method's successful functioning at General Motors. Since that time, countless studies and reviews of its effectiveness and ineffectiveness have been reported, variations in its methodology suggested, and corrective actions for its weaknesses proposed. George Odiorne popularized the concept as MBO. J. Higgins has added the RR to emphasize the importance of measuring results and rewarding them.[2] Just a few of the major findings regarding MBORR-type programs are listed below. Positive results include the following:

1. Performance—both quantity and quality—are improved.
2. Communications and understanding are improved.
3. Job satisfaction is improved.
4. Individual growth is enhanced.
5. Role prescription is clarified.

Negative results include the following:

1. Managers may become more critical.
2. Managers may use MBORR objectives as a "whip."
3. Establishing objectives entails all sorts of problems: scale-unit bias may exist, objectives may be set too high or too low, may not be accepted, may be inflexible, or may be difficult to set for nonquantifiable areas.
4. The process may be too short-run-oriented.
5. The process seems to lose its effect over time.
6. Monetary rewards are sometimes insufficient and hence fail to maintain performance.
7. The process often takes too much time.
8. Group dynamics are usually not taken into consideration.
9. There are physical and mental limitations for the individual.
10. Goals established become maximums even where they could be exceeded.

The negative results reported here far outnumber the positive effects, and at least 20 more could have been listed. However, studies of the technique's effectiveness have been performed in widely varying situations, causing results to vary. More importantly, many have reported that the technique's implementation, not the technique itself, was the problem. It

[2]J. M. Higgins, *Human Relations Concepts and Skills* (New York: Random House, 1982), Chapter 13.

appears that when an appropriate implementation procedure is followed and top management is involved and concerned, MBORR is effective.

Latham and Yukl, in reviewing published and unpublished field research, report that, whether or not MBORR-type programs were specifically used, the setting of objectives led to superior performance.[3] Some have suggested that specific objectives are not necessary in every situation, and indeed M. B. McCaskey's "directional planning," which does not require objective setting, may be sufficient for certain limited situations.[4] In general, though, John Mee's "Principle of the Objective" is relevant: "Before initiating any course of action the objectives must be clearly determined, understood and stated."[5] In summary, without specific objectives, the strategy eventually fails to elicit performance.

The Objectives Established

Objectives are needed in every area where performance and results directly and vitally affect the survival and prosperity of the business.

▪ *Peter Drucker* ▪

Organizations establish many types of objectives. Some are specific, some are not. Many organizations set no specific objectives; some establish only a limited number; others establish objectives for many areas of operating performance. The following section reports on three research studies which deal with the nature of business objectives.

Les Rue, reporting on a survey of 400 predominantly large firms in several major industries, found that most firms have multiple, quantitative, written objective statements. He found that more firms established earnings and sales objectives than return objectives and that many organizations established capital growth, market share, and sales/earnings objectives. Rue also examined financial analyses associated with the objectives established and found that profit (the income statement) was of primary concern but that most firms were also concerned with balance sheet and cash flow analysis.[6]

J. W. Dobbie, in an examination of 50 large California-based firms (all with over $100 million in annual sales), found that the firms tended to express objectives according to the type of strategy they employed. His strategy classifications included: personal (the aims of the chief executive); opportunity; geographic expansion; financial growth; and business (for planning or diversified firms). The types of objectives examined were: various return methods; growth in sales or earnings; and pro forma financial statements or resource control. Dobbie observed that managerial style and the position of the planning unit within the organizational structure affected the type of objectives chosen. While Dobbie's sample size limits generalization, his study at least suggests that as complexity of operations and

---

[3]G. P. Latham and G. A. Yukl, "A Review of Research on the Application of Goal Setting in Organizations," *Academy of Management Journal*, December 1975, pp. 827–832.

[4]M. B. McCaskey, "A Contingency Approach to Planning: Planning with Goals and Planning without Goals," *Academy of Management Journal*, June 1974, pp. 281–291.

[5]J. Mee, "The Principle of the Objective," in "Management Philosophy for Professional Executives," *Business Horizons*, December 1956, pp. 5–11.

[6]L. W. Rue, "Tools and Techniques of Long Range Planning," *Long Range Planning*, October 1974, pp. 61–65.

Table 3.1   Range of Corporate Goals for 82 Firms

Category	Number	Percent[a]
Profitability	73	89
Growth	67	82
Market share	54	66
Social responsibility	53	65
Employee welfare	51	62
Product quality and service	49	60
Research and development	44	54
Diversification	42	51
Efficiency	41	50
Financial stability	40	49
Resource conservation	32	39
Management development	29	35
Multinational enterprise	24	29
Consolidation	14	17
Miscellaneous other goals	15	18

[a]Adds to more than 100 percent because most companies have more than one goal.

Source: Y. K. Shetty, "New Look at Corporate Goals," *California Management Review*, Winter 1979, p. 73. © 1979 by the Regents of the University of California. Reprinted from the *California Management Review*, Volume XXII, no. 2, p. 73, by permission of the Regents.

experience in strategy formulation increase, the number of objectives and their diversity also increase.[7]

Y. K. Shetty, in a study of 82 companies, found a wide range of corporate objectives, as indicated in Table 3.1. Most companies had five or six goals. However, one company had only one objective, while another had 18. As the table indicates, economic objectives dominated corporate concerns. Shetty found that objectives varied by industry; for example, social responsibility was the second most frequently cited objective in the chemicals and drugs group of companies, but the fifth most frequently cited objective in the electrical and electronics group. Finally, Shetty concluded that as organizations grow, their environments tend to become more turbulent; and as they become more responsive to stakeholders outside the immediate economic constituency, their objectives change.[8]

As you can see from these studies, objectives employed by organizations in their strategies are dominated by, but not limited to, economic objectives. Other types of objectives include employee development and social responsibility. And while it is apparent that most business organizations are today primarily concerned with mission objectives, other issues are expected to become increasingly important as society (and government) continue to demand more of business. Interestingly, Thomas J. Peters and Robert H. Waterman, Jr., found early in their research that organizations with only financial goals were not as financially successful as companies whose goals were concerned with broader issues and values. And while no other research we've found to date discusses similar relationships, the comments of Peters and Waterman are certainly worth noting and suggest that an overall

[7]J. W. Dobbie, "Guides to a Foundation for Strategic Planning in Large Firms" (Paper presented to the 34th Annual Meeting of the Academy of Management, Seattle, Washington, August 1974).

[8]Y. K. Shetty, "New Look at Corporate Goals," *California Management Review*, Winter 1979, pp. 71–79.

philosophy of "total excellence," not just financial excellence, may in fact be most appropriate. Intuitively, that philosophy is sensible.[9] Certainly, one key to successful planning is the process of establishing specific objectives at each succeeding level of the organization. Objectives tie the organization together.

Prioritizing Objectives

One of the most perplexing problems confronting the strategic manager is the prioritizing of objectives. Many seem important, and in the hectic day-to-day crisis-management environment, it's easy to forget that the swamp still needs draining. Even during the cyclical or periodic planning process, the task of establishing priorities for objectives is not an easy one. There exist certain natural conflicts among objectives. For example, in observing the objectives in Figure 3.3, one would expect that contributions to society and employees might be in conflict financially with returns to owners (short-term at least), and perhaps customers. Conflicts also often arise between corporate and business, or business and functional, objectives. There are almost always conflicts between certain strategic and operational objectives. And the problem of prioritizing is further compounded when one realizes that objectives are normally to some degree interdependent, and often reciprocally causal. Also, there are power centers that demand attention to their objectives in every organization. Finally, one's personal objectives may in fact be in conflict with appropriate organizational priorities. How then does the strategist determine which objectives are most important?

First, there are few proven decision rules for determining appropriate priorities. Instead, certain rules of thumb guide many managers. To begin, managers may simply react to problems as they arise, establishing the solution to the most current issue as having the major priority. Granted, this does not seem the proper action for a strategic planner, but it happens. And in fact, sometimes it's necessary to be flexible and recognize that something very current is very critical and strategic and needs to take priority. Indeed, one must recognize that major decisions are not as infrequently made on the spur of the moment, in a reactive mode, as one would like to think. For, even though we would like strategists to initiate action and be proactive, many times they need to react to situations. Thus, general managers also respond to crises as they evolve. For example, when Bendix attempted the takeover of Martin Marietta, it was imperative for the CEO of Martin to be reactive, to launch an immediate defense of the company and seek to satisfy those objectives that were dominant at the moment. Normally, urgency, and the order in which problems attract the attention of the strategist, should not determine the order in which objectives are prioritized.

More desirable is a rational approach to the prioritizing of objectives. Certainly in the periodic strategic planning process, participants have the opportunity to critically evaluate and weigh alternative objectives and assign them levels of priority. The preponderance of evidence suggests a participative approach involving the key managers affected—here, strategists. The utilization of simple ranking, paired-comparisons ranking, nonparametric statistics, or any other generally organized fashion of ranking objectives, when supported by appropriate information, and as long as implementers are participants, would seem to

[9]T. J. Peters and R. H. Waterman, Jr., *In Search of Excellence*, Harper and Row: New York, 1983, p. 103.

move the organization in the right direction. Often, several objectives will be viewed as equally important, and accomplishment of all of these will be anticipated.

Every enterprise needs a central purpose expressed in terms of the services it will render to society. And it needs a basic concept of how it will create these services. Since it will be competing with other enterprises for resources, it must have some distinctive advantages—in its services or in its methods of creating them. Moreover, since it will inevitably cooperate with other firms, it must have the means for maintaining viable coalitions with them. In addition, there are the elements of change, growth, and adaptation. Master strategy is a company's basic plan for dealing with these factors.

▪ *William H. Newman* ▪

The Master Strategy

Once strategic objectives have been determined and prioritized, organizational strategists formulate the master strategy. Strategies tell "how we get to where we want to be."

The term *strategy* derives from the ancient Greek word for general, *strategos*. Until the nineteenth century, the term related to the plans of action used by a military force in battle. More recently, *strategy* has taken on new meanings and is frequently used to refer to the endeavors of various organizations, primarily business organizations, to anticipate, respond to, and generally survive in their environments. As mentioned in Chapter 1, the term *strategy* is defined differently in the various organizational contexts in which it may be encountered; however, there is general agreement that a strategy is a major organizational plan of action to reach a major organizational objective.

An Overview of Strategy

Historically, most organizations have concentrated their strategic efforts on the development of either of two primary strategies (or sometimes both in combination): a focal basic action strategy, such as internal growth, conglomerate diversification, or retrenchment; and/or a focal marketing strategy. They have viewed strategy largely as simply requiring some basic action, perhaps internal growth, towards which the organizations would direct their remaining efforts. And/or, they have focused on some element of the marketing strategy, such as a high-quality product. This focal basic action strategy or marketing strategy, or combination of the two, has come to be known as the "grand strategy." (This grand strategy is discussed in more detail near the end of this chapter.) And while most organizations have established a grand strategy, they have not typically formulated a true, all-encompassing master strategy. But that is changing. For example, as the importance of managing environmental relationships became evident, more firms, both single- and multiple-SBU organizations, incorporated enterprise strategies into their master strategies. (In contrast, most nonbusiness organizations have historically lacked objectives and strategies, until recently, as Chapter 1 reveals.)

Most firms have yet to appreciate fully the importance to strategic success of functional strategies, although the events of the late 1970s taught most business firms the need to pay greater attention to these strategies. For example, finance strategies have become critical in periods of high interest rates and tight money. Operations strategies are also receiving substantive attention in many industries (such as electronics and automobile manufacturing) in order to meet foreign competition (especially from the Japanese). In fact, American manufacturing firms are undergoing tremendous changes with the increased utilization of computers, robots, zero-inventory approaches, quality circles, and other techniques.[10] Finally, human resources management (along with all of the management skills) have become vital to the reindustrialization efforts of U.S. and Canadian business in both manufacturing and service industries.

Typical of master strategy statements based largely on the corporate and business strategy components is the Heublein experience. In 1965, Heublein's stated only three strategic objectives:

1. To make Smirnoff the number-one liquor brand in the world.
2. To continue a sales growth of 10 percent a year through internal growth, acquisition, or both.
3. To maintain a return on equity above 15 percent.

The essence of its strategic plans of action to accomplish these objectives involved the following elements:

1. Substantive advertising.
2. Certain types of distribution.
3. Careful selection of products and acquisitions with high cash flows (to allow substantive advertising).

In these statements, Heublein succinctly captured what it perceived its objectives to be and how these objectives would be accomplished. Note that Heublein did not embellish its master strategy with any considerations not associated directly with its focal basic action or focal competitive activity.[11] There has, of course, been renewed interest in competitive strategies, as the works of Michael Porter (discussed in Chapters 2 and 4) and others in the field, have become more widely known.

In contrast to the Heublein example, firms such as IBM, GM, and Xerox take a broader approach to master strategy formulation. Their master strategies contain concerns for all of the elements of enterprise, corporate, business, and functional strategies. Annually, these firms review their master strategies as SBUs and support functions (for example, production facilities) establish objectives and plans for the year. This process occurs within the framework of corporate policies established for strategy formulation, since certain corporate strategy considerations, such as diversification and divestment (when necessary), are constraints to business and functional strategies. Strategic issues may be managed separately.

In summary, the master strategy is an umbrella beneath which specific strategies for coping with society, with the business choice decision, with competition, and with func-

---

[10] J. Nakane and R. W. Hall, "Management Specs for Stockless Production," *Harvard Business Review*, May–June, 1983, pp. 84–91; S. C. Wheelwright and R. H. Hayes, "Competing through Manufacturing," *Harvard Business Review*, January/February, 1984, pp. 99–109. "The Revival of Productivity," *Business Week*, February 13, 1984, pp. 92–100.

[11] G. A. Smith, Jr., C. Roland Christensen and N. A. Berg, *Policy Formulation and Administration* (Homewood, Ill.: Irwin, 1968).

Table 3.2   The Master Strategy for Business

Enterprise Strategy (Societal Response)

Strategies to ensure that the firm acts properly as a corporate citizen.

Corporate Strategy (Mission Determination); (What many call "The Grand Strategy")

Strategies to determine what business or businesses the firm is in or should be in and how the business or businesses should be conducted.

1. Is there some business in which the organization has a natural strategic advantage or an innate interest?
2. Does the company want to compete or find a niche?
3. Does the company want or need to grow, stabilize, engage in investment reduction, or turn around company fortunes?

Basic action strategies available to single-SBU or multiple-SBU corporations (relate to questions 2 and 3 above):

   A. Competing or finding a niche
   B. Concentration or multiple products
   C. Growth
      1. Intensive, integrative, or diversified
      2. Regional, national, or international
      3. Internal, by acquisition, by merger, by joint venture
      4. Speed
   D. Stabilization
   E. Investment reduction
      1. Retrenchment
      2. Divestment (for multiple-SBU firms only)
      3. Selected asset reduction
      4. Cost cutting
      5. Liquidation
      6. Selling out
      7. Profit extraction
   F. Turnaround
   G. Takeover Defense
   H. Combination

tional operations may be found. One vital principle underlying the master strategy concept is the belief that strategy must "fit" the environment. (See Table 3.2.)

> *We must plan for the future, because people who stay in the present*
> *will remain in the past.*
>
> ▪ *Abraham Lincoln* ▪

Whether or not they are consciously determined, all organizations have master strategies. Many business firms and other organizations can be quite successful in the short run without consciously formulating strategic objectives or plans to reach those objectives. Almost never, however, is any firm successful in the long run without first determining what it wants to be (mission and objectives) and how it plans to achieve that vision (strategy and policies).

Table 3.2 *continued*

Business (SBU) Strategy (Primary Mission; Focus of many "Grand Strategies")
Competitive strategies.
Economic functional strategies
  A. Marketing
    1. Target market
    2. Product
    3. Promotion
    4. Distribution
    5. Price

Functional Strategy (Mission-Supportive; Focus of some "Grand Strategies")
Strategies that support other strategies.
  A. Economic functional strategies
    1. Operations—production or service generation
    2. Finance
    3. Personnel/human resources management
    4. Information systems
    5. R&D, market research
    6. Other significant areas
  B. Management-functional strategies
    1. Planning
    2. Organizing
    3. Implementing
    4. Controlling
    5. Staffing
    6. Leading
    7. Motivating
    8. Communicating
    9. Decision making
    10. Representing
    11. Integrating
  C. Strategic issues strategies
    1. Known contingencies (energy)
    2. Surprises (competitor changes strategy; major economic changes; etc.)

Levels of Strategy

As we saw in Chapter 1, organizations have four major components in their master strategies. The terms this book has used for the levels of strategy for business—enterprise, corporate, business, and functional—were first used by Dan Schendel and Charles Hofer.[12] (See also Table 3.2.) These levels are described in this text as follows:

- Enterprise—the societal response strategy; how the organization relates to society.

- Corporate—the mission determination strategy; criteria for defining the organization's fields of endeavor; and how it will fundamentally conduct itself.

[12] D. E. Schendel and C. W. Hofer, eds., *Strategic Management: A New View of Business Policy and Planning* (Boston: Little/Brown, 1979), pp. 11–14.

- Business—the primary mission strategy; how the organization will achieve its mission within a chosen field of endeavor.

- Functional—the mission-supportive strategy; how the organization will support its primary mission strategy.

The main difference between the way Schendel and Hofer use these terms and the way the authors of this text uses them is that, while they include marketing under functional strategies, we include it in business strategies.

Enterprise Strategy

Organizations need an enterprise strategy to cope with their largely uncontrollable external governmental and societal environment. This strategy does not deal with product/market concerns per se, but rather with the broader issues of corporate citizenship, thus integrating the organization with society.

As Chapter 2 pointed out, the events of the 1960s and 1970s taught business leaders an important lesson—business is an open system. It has transactions not only with customers, suppliers, creditors, and unions but also with society, government, and members of pressure groups such as environmental groups and minority-interest organizations. And, contrary to the opinions of some, business does not act solely in accordance with its own self-interests in search of profit, but also considers the demands of other systems. It must consider them if it is to accomplish its mission in the long run. Business today faces many severe problems as a result of these demands, but it is learning to cope with them. Meeting these challenges is the function of the enterprise strategy.

Social power requires social response.

- *Keith Davis and Robert L. Blomstrom* -

One of the major problems facing business is its inability to define exactly what constitutes corporate social responsibility. Numerous pressure groups, such as the NAACP, the Sierra Club, the state and federal governments, and Ralph Nader's Raiders, have made varying demands on the organization. Many times these demands are contradictory, trapping the organization in a dilemma: To whom does it respond? Clearly, it must respond to the law and will also likely respond to those who can exert the most pressure upon it or who have defined their demands the most explicitly. Still, business cannot react to all of the demands with which it is confronted, nor should it.

Society's major demands have been fairly well-defined—at least legally. The law requires business to: protect the natural physical environment, provide equal employment opportunity, treat the consumer fairly, maintain satisfactory relations with government, and operate in an ethical manner. In addition, business—and the nation as a whole—has shouldered the important responsibility of maximizing energy conservation. But ironically, many individuals are now more concerned that business renew its efforts to produce goods and services at a profit, and more specifically to increase productivity and provide jobs. Interestingly, the demands on business seem to have come full circle.

While not all contingencies can be anticipated, business usually has sufficient warning of pressing social issues to be able to develop more than "do-good" statements. Nonetheless, many corporate social policies are not as specific in content as they should be, and many firms have been noticeably deficient in planning to meet external societal pressures. To formulate appropriate corporate social strategies and policy, business should apply the same sort of rigorous analysis required of other anticipated corporate interactions affecting the accomplishment of organizational goals. For, while social pressures change, so do other elements in the corporate environment. Change must be accepted and adapted to; otherwise, the costs to the firm will be high, both in terms of immediate measurable dollars and of those nebulous factors that eventually will affect profits, such as image, morale, and productivity.

With proper planning and control, corporate social problems can be realistically and satisfactorily solved. Business leaders must consider value orientations other than those economic values traditionally held, and emphasize a responsive approach to societal demands and ethical considerations. Most importantly, business must remember that the consequence of social power is social responsibility.

Corporate Strategy

Corporate strategy focuses on two questions: "What business(es) are we in or should we be in?" and "How shall we fundamentally conduct that business(es)?" The answer to the first question is derived directly from mission, and is in fact often identical to it. A correct answer to this question is critical, because being in the wrong business is usually fatal. The railroads, for example, decided at the turn of the century to stay out of the automobile industry, and later to stay out of the air travel industry. To their ultimate misfortune, they saw themselves as being in the railroad business, not the transportation business. Sears, on the other hand, has seen itself as being a provider of consumer services, not just a durable goods retailer. And, partly because of improved consumer marketing and partly because of this perspective, Sears is consequently finding itself on a prosperous road to financial success.[13] (See Figure 3.4.)

Because basic actions position a firm in an industry or across industries, the answer to the second question is also critical. A poorly positioned firm has little or no chance of long-term success. For example, at one time GE's SBU alignment included a computer division but GE's decision to compete head on with IBM was unsound, and it eventually sold this SBU. (Interestingly, GE has since reentered a portion of the computer market because it needs this capacity for its other products.)[14]

The answers to the two questions above depend in turn on the firm's answers to the three basic questions listed below. The first question concerns what business or businesses the firm will enter. The second and third concern how the firm will engage in its business or businesses—what its action strategies will be.

1.   Is there some business in which the organization has a natural strategic advantage or an innate interest?

2.   Does the company want to compete or find a niche?

---

[13] "Sears' Sizzling New Vitality," *Time*, August 20, 1984, pp. 82–90.

[14] "The Opposites: GE Grows While Westinghouse Shrinks," *Business Week*, January 31, 1977, pp. 60–66; "General Electric: The Financial Wizards Switch Back to Technology," *Business Week*, March 16, 1981, pp. 110–114.

Figure 3.4   Basic Action Strategies

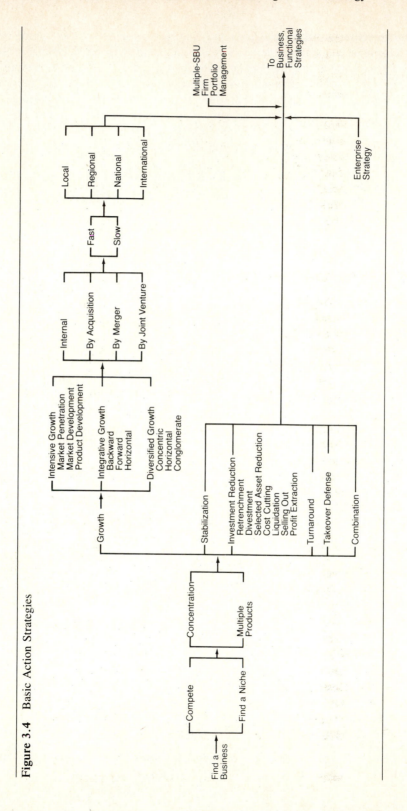

3. Does the company want or need to grow, stabilize, engage in investment reduction, defend against a takeover attempt, or turn around company fortunes?

How a firm's corporate strategy is affected specifically by its answers to these three questions varies with many factors. The following paragraphs provide some insights into these specifics.

Clearly, whether a firm has a single business or whether it is a multiple-SBU organization has a major bearing on the details of strategy. The single-SBU organization is primarily caught up in competition—the business strategy—and is much less concerned with many of the available basic actions strategies than are multiple-SBU firms. Many firms engage in only one business and have no intention of leaving that field of enterprise. But, for many, that should not be their intention. Similarly, how the organization conducts its business often follows a set pattern; but for many, following a set pattern is not the best course.

1. Natural Strategic Advantage or Innate Interest

Many companies enter a field of endeavor because a perceived customer need exists that no one is satisfying. The founder of Federal Express, Frederick W. Smith, saw the need for overnight package deliveries between major cities. He believed that a fleet of small jet airplanes could do what no other mail service could. And he was right. Other examples of natural strategic advantages include Fuddrucker's movement into the high-priced gourmet hamburger field, the sale of various forms of technology to developing countries, and the gas mileage advantage that Japanese cars had over U.S.-manufactured autos during the 1970s.

Many businesses, on the other hand, are formed simply because the owner or top manager wanted to be in that business: or in the case of small businesses, because of the founder's area of expertise. For example, many people start restaurants because they have always wanted to own one, or service stations because they are good mechanics. Similarly, the top manager of a larger organization may move the firm into new ventures simply because of a personal desire to own a publishing house, a foundry, a restaurant chain, etc.

2. Competition or Niche

Organizations, whether single-SBU or multiple-SBU, must decide whether to compete directly with others or to find a niche. Of course, all businesses always compete with other businesses (or nonprofits) in some way. The question is whether the firm chooses to compete head-on with other firms in the same business or to seek a niche—a market that no other firm has chosen to enter directly. Most businesses do compete head-on with others; for example, Sears, J. C. Penney, and Montgomery Ward historically have competed directly with each other. On the other hand, Gibsons, a loosely federated group of discount stores franchised to several different ownership groups, seeks primarily to locate in small towns where there is no competition. It does not usually choose to compete head-on with K mart or other discount stores. Another firm that employs a niche strategy is Armstrong Rubber Company, which seeks markets the dominant firms ignore.[15] Nordstrom's (or Nor-

---

[15] G. Breckenfeld, "The Niche Pickers at Armstrong Rubber," *Fortune*, September 6, 1982, pp. 100–105.

"Don't laugh—he was doing that the day he figured out how to
scoop up Trans-American Romex, Inc."

Source: Drawing by D. Reilly: © 1979 *The New Yorker Magazine*, Inc.

dies, as it is affectionately known to its customers) has a unique way of niching its market in apparel: it provides excellent service at high prices.[16] And few of its clientele balk. In fact Nordstrom's has been so successful in the northwestern United States that it's now expanding to California. Finally, in the highly competitive semiconductor industry, only firms with distinct niches have been able to raise venture capital in recent years.[17]

However, niches are not always secure; successful niche-finding strategies tend to provoke competition. Such was the case after sales of the Excalibur specialty car (a replica of a 1933 Mercedes Phaeton, priced in 1985 at about $50,000) showed that there was a market for high-quality, high-priced, unusual cars; a half-dozen or so competitors jumped into the same market. Occupying a niche can involve other disadvantages; Wendy's had the high-priced hamburger niche all to itself but found that its high prices made it vulnerable to chicken and seafood competitors.

---

[16]P. A. Bellew, "Nordstrom Strategy of Coddling Shoppers Facing Challenge in California Expansion," *The Wall Street Journal*, May 10, 1984, p. 37.

[17]R. A. Schaffer, "Start-Up Semiconductor Firms That Have Niches, Find Funds," *The Wall Street Journal*, September 21, 1984, p. 33.

Still, niche strategies are a good way for the smaller firm—the firm with fewer financial resources—to make a good return on its investment. For example, one plastic extrusion firm which makes plastic trash bags and refrigerator containers distributes its products only in the southeastern United States and has primarily established a market based on its prices being lower than those of national brands. (This form of niche strategy involves a geographic niche rather than a product-related one.) The firm considered going national but decided against it. As the production manager related, "If we went national, the big boys would notice us and could wipe us out if our market share got too big. Right now, they consider us to be a minor nuisance. But if we began to get too big, then they might consider us a threat and take action to eliminate us."

3. Concentration or Multiple Products/Businesses

Concentration is the focusing of the organization on one product, in essentially one market, using primarily one type of technology.[18] It is by far the most frequently encountered grand strategy, as most businesses are concentrated in one field. ("Kentucky Fried Chicken only does one thing," and therefore they "do it right.") There are obvious reasons for choosing a concentration strategy. First, most entrepreneurs begin this way because it is in their field of innate interest and/or expertise. Second, there is less risk, at least in terms of resources, for starting up an enterprise. In addition, the competition can be more readily identified and more carefully analyzed. And, as the firm grows, the expertise required to manage it properly remains essentially the same. Such a firm's competitive advantage comes from employing a highly developed focal marketing strategy. The contents of this strategy vary, but most frequently include product quality and/or price, sensitivity to the demands of the customer or client, and some element of recognition in the marketplace. Firms using a concentration strategy would, at the next level of choices in Figure 3.4, choose those strategies which would allow them to grow, but only through this one product or service.

However, there are problems associated with this strategy as well. Concentration exposes the organization to the vagaries of the marketplace, the economy, and to changes in technology. After all, people tire of products, (even computer games, as ATARI has discovered). Furthermore, growth reaches its peak once the market is saturated; investment opportunities are fewer; and long-term profit potentials decline as new entrants emerge in the industry (watch out KFC, here come: Bo Jangle's, Brown's, Popeyes, and a host of others). Thus, firms may choose to pursue the types of growth that result in multiple products in the next basic action choice stage.

4. Growth, Stabilization, Investment Reduction, Takeover Defense, Turnaround, or Combination

Once the firm has decided whether to compete or find a niche and whether to be concentrated in one product area or pursue multiple products—whether the answer applies to a particular SBU or to several—the next major issues are whether the firm wants to grow, stabilize, reduce investment, protect against a takeover, turn around company fortunes, or

---

[18]J. A. Pearce II, "Selecting Among Alternative Grand Strategies," *California Management Review*, Spring 1982, pp. 23–31.

pursue a combination of these goals. At the corporate level for multiple-SBU firms, answering these questions is the crux of the corporate strategy. The primary techniques used are known as portfolio techniques and are explored further in Chapter 5. At the single-SBU level, these critical decisions depend on a multitude of SWOT factors.

Growth.   Growth involves four primary considerations: type of growth—intensive, integrative, or diversified; where it will be geographically focused—at the regional, national, or international level; how it will take place—internally or through acquisition, merger, or joint venture; and how fast it will take place.

Types of Growth.[19]   The choice of type of growth—intensive, integrative, or diversified—is critical. Intensive growth is appropriate for the firm that has not fully exploited the existing opportunities in its current products and markets. There are three types of intensive growth—market penetration, market development, and product development.

Market penetration consists of seeking increased sales for present products through a more aggressive marketing effort. Market penetration is characteristic of the mature industry with homogeneous products. When Phillip Morris acquired the Miller Brewing Company in 1970, Miller management immediately employed a market penetration strategy. It significantly expanded the advertising budget and changed advertising themes. The now-famous "Miller time" ads depicted Miller beer as the drink of he-men. The results have been almost unbelievably successful.

Market development involves taking existing products into new markets. When Disney created Disney World, it was, as many commentators noted, creating a Disneyland East; it was taking its product, Disneyland, to a new market, the East Coast. When the Miller Brewing Company successfully introduced the 7-ounce container (others had tried but failed), it was taking its product to new markets—primarily to women who preferred a smaller container and were less likely to drink a lot of beer at one time than were men. Thus, the market development strategy is especially important to firms whose products, while sound, have not reached all markets.

Product development consists of developing improved products for current markets. When you see Colgate toothpaste in a pump, you are witnessing this strategy in action. Product development is extremely important to maturing products because of the need to extend the product life cycle. The Datsun 240Z became the 260Z which became the 280Z which became the 280ZX which has become the 300 ZX ("awesome," "driven," and a "major motion"). Why? Because of competition in a maturing industry—the high-performance sports car industry.

The second type of growth, integrative growth, can move in three directions—backward, forward, and horizontally. In backward integration, the organization attempts to acquire control over its suppliers. Sears has historically followed a pattern of acquiring its suppliers—for example, J. C. Higgins. A business typically follows this acquisition strategy for the purpose of reducing costs and making the firm's sales and distribution functions more cost competitive, or more responsive to the needs of the acquiring company. This strategy is particularly important to the firm in a mature industry in which price becomes a major strategic weapon.

---

[19]Philip Kotler, *Marketing Management* (Englewood Cliffs, N.J.: Prentice-Hall, 1980), pp. 48–53.

In forward integration, the firm attempts to acquire control of its distributors. When Royal Crown purchased Arby's in 1976 (a conglomerate diversification effort), one of its first acts was to arrange for long-term markets for Royal Crown Cola through its wholly owned Arby's locations, thus assuring the company of increased distribution for its products. As IBM established its consumer retail stores in 1984, it too was seeking to assure control of distribution for its current and future computer-related products. Interestingly, the major oil companies began a program of divesting their forward integration instruments—service stations—in the late 1970s, apparently because of the low profit margins involved in distribution of their products.

When a firm attempts to acquire its competition, it is praticing horizontal integrative growth. For instance, both Humana and Hospital Corporation of America have acquired several hundred hospitals each as they seek to dominate the health care industry.[20]

The final major type of growth is diversified growth. Diversification becomes an important alternative when an organization has "all of its eggs in one basket" and has the internally generated expertise and the extra cash flow to expand into other areas. Diversification can be used to smooth out corporate revenues; this strategy is desirable for highly seasonal businesses—for example, areas that specialize in providing recreational snow skiing, such as Vail, Colorado. Diversification is also advisable where current businesses or products are in mature or decline stages of the product life cycle and revenues will ultimately be threatened. Diversification may also be desirable when external opportunities are significant. Information Capsule 3.2 indicates just how important diversification can be.

There are three types of diversification—concentric, horizontal, and conglomerate. With concentric diversification, the business seeks to add new products that are technologically related to current products. These products will normally be marketed to new customers. When Texas Instruments added personal computers to its product lines, it was practicing concentric diversification. When Levi Strauss added women's clothing to its men's line, it, too, was practicing concentric diversification.

Horizontal diversification also involves adding new products to the firm's product line, but these products are not technologically related to existing ones and are aimed at current customers. Over the years, AMF has added pleasure boats, bicycles, snow skis, and other athletic equipment to its original offerings in order to provide new products for its current customers.

Conglomerate diversification involves both new products or businesses and new customers. The firm usually enters into conglomerate diversification to offset some deficiency, but it may also pursue this strategy to take advantage of a significant opportunity. Technically, of course, once a firm enters into more than one business, it ceases to be a single-business firm. Organizations such as InterNorth, GE, EXXON, and Beatrice are conglomerate companies.

Where to Grow.   Most firms start in a particular geographic region, may then move to a national sales effort, and may even eventually attempt to repeat domestic successes in foreign countries. Naturally, geographic growth is highly desirable because it increases total market size. But, of course, not all firms can be national. King's, a regional restau-

---

[20]*Industry Surveys*, Standard & Poor's, p. H.

INFORMATION CAPSULE 3.2
Expanding the World of Hallmark

When you think of greeting cards, you probably think of Hallmark, because the $1.5-billion company has 40 percent of the greeting card market. But it is not without competition; American and Gibson greeting card companies (numbers two and three respectively in industry sales) are constantly pressuring for increased market share of their own. Consequently, Hallmark's new executive vice-president, Irvine O. Hockaday, Jr., with the blessings of CEO Donald J. Hall, is steering the company down the road to diversification. Since assuming his new role in 1983, Hockaday has made three major acquisitions, two of them outside the "social expression" business that Hallmark has dominated since it was founded in 1910 by Joyce C. Hall.

Hockaday first negotiated the acquisition of Binney & Smith Inc., maker of Crayola Crayons for $203 million; and then a joint buyout, with Pincus and Company, of Chicago-based SFN, a publishings and broadcasting company, for about $470 million. His lone industry-related purchase was his third acquisition, a British greeting card firm, W. N. Sharpe Holdings, which Hallmark acquired for $52 million. Hockaday studies the market carefully for opportunities which might occur, looking for signs that a buyout would be acceptable to targets. He is fond of saying that "Chance favors the prepared mind."

It would appear that Hockaday's two nonsocial expression acquisitions, while diversifying the firm's sales by 10 percent, is not the end, but just the beginning of Hallmark's diversification efforts. Hockaday suggests that Hallmark's next move may be into financial services, and that he foresees the day soon when 40 percent of Hallmark's earnings will come from nontraditional revenue sources.

Sources: "Irv Hockaday Is Leaving his Mark on Hallmark: Diversity," *Business Week*, November 12, 1984, pp. 73–74.

---

rant chain prominent in the northeastern United States, has stated that it does not believe it should go national and attempt to compete with other major chains. It intends not to grow, at least not geographically. But for most firms, geographic growth and success go hand in hand. What is imperative is that such growth not come too quickly. International growth, in particular, involves many difficulties. It is not simply an extension of domestic efforts, but requires an understanding of numerous complex cultural, logistical, social, economic and political differences.

How to Grow.   The organization can grow in four basic ways—internally, by acquisition, by merger, or by joint venture. Internal growth offers many advantages; one of the most important of them is continuity of management style. Internal growth also has its limitations. It takes much longer to become larger and more diverse through internal growth than through the three external forms of growth. Nonetheless, many firms have grown to substantial size primarily through internal growth—the Coca-Cola Company, Radio Shack (Tandy), the Anheuser Busch Brewing Company, and Trans World Airlines, for example. On the other hand, firms such as PepsiCo, Allegheny Industries, Trans-America, and First Northern Bank have grown externally, primarily through acquisition.

Recently, Coca-Cola has become more acquisition-oriented in an effort to become less dependent upon one major industry, the soft drink industry. Its 1981 acquisition of Columbia Pictures was a major step toward that end.

Typically, businesses begin as single-SBU firms, commonly with one product. As they grow, normally internally, and if they are successful, they begin to look for growth into new markets; new products; or areas of supply, distribution, or competition. At this point growth often ceases to be internal and is stimulated primarily through external sources. Nonetheless, innovation carries many firms for many years before external growth strategies are required. Innovation is a vital grand strategy for numerous organizations including American Airlines, Apple Computer, Campbell Soup, Intel, 3M, GE, Merck, and Phillip Morris.[21]

Both acquisition and merger involve combining organizations; they differ mainly in the nature of the remaining organization. In acquisition, one firm retains its identity as the dominant firm, while the other becomes subordinate in authority to that dominant firm. For example, when Heublein acquired Kentucky Fried Chicken, top management at KFC began to report to Heublein top management. Typically, acquisitions occur for the purpose of diversification. In mergers, however, a new organizational entity emerges. When Nabisco and Standard Brands merged, a new entity, Nabisco Brands, resulted. A new management structure was formed, with members of top management of both organizations taking various positions in the new management hierarchy.

Joint ventures are temporary partnerships formed for one specific purpose. For example, Blount Brothers Construction Company joined with the French construction firm Bouygues to land one of the biggest single construction projects in history—the University of Riyadh's new campus in Saudi Arabia. In all likelihood, neither firm could have obtained the contract alone, much less have completed the project. Entering the joint venture allowed both firms to overcome these problems.[22] Historically, firms outside the United States and Canada have utilized the joint venture much more than firms from these two countries; but in recent years, even U.S. and Canadian firms have made increasing use of this mechanism.

Speed of Growth.   One of the greatest mistakes a firm can make is to grow beyond its capacities. Such a mistake was one of the major causes of the downfall of the W. T. Grant Company. It takes time to develop the managers and management systems necessary to cope with the problems of increasing size. W. T. Grant simply did not foster this development. Different problems are encountered at various stages of growth and with various types of growth. Organizations must manage their way through these problems before further growth is advisable.

Stabilization.   Some organizations are satisfied not to grow (or to grow very little). Many owners of smaller businesses, such as restaurants, insurance agencies, small manufacturers, and so forth, are satisfied to make only a certain amount of profit and do not wish to grow beyond a certain size. Understandably, the president of a large bank with a 46-percent market share in a major, highly competitive metropolitan area told author J. Higgins, he would be quite happy just to maintain that market share.

[21] S. P. Sherman, "Eight Big Masters of Innovation," *Fortune*, October 15, 1984, pp. 66–84.

[22] Blount: Building More than Buildings to Broaden Its Base," *Business Week*, April 23, 1979, pp. 108–110.

While stabilization provides an opportunity to "catch one's breath" between growth periods or during turnaround periods, it leaves the organization open to competition as a long-term strategy.

Investment Reduction.   Firms may choose to follow a program of investment reduction, which simply means reducing the amount of capital investment in the organization or a specific SBU. This move may be necessitated by financial difficulties or, as in the case of profit extraction, may be an intentional program of removing assets from a successful business to create cash flow for other parts of the business or for distribution to owners. Several types of investment reduction exist.

Retrenchment is a major, across-the-board effort to reduce cash outflows in order to reduce the scope and size of the business, to lessen the exposure of the firm to risk, to concentrate on what the company does well in order to become more profitable, or simply to survive. It is generally viewed as a temporary measure. One company recently forced to retrench substantially in order to survive is International Harvester. Two others, Kroger Food Stores and Control Data, have recently undergone retrenchment in order to ensure satisfactory profitability.[23]

At the corporate level in multiple-SBU firms, divestment—selling or liquidating individual SBUs—is the primary means of retrenchment. Often firms acquire businesses that do not continue to provide sufficient ROI. When products fail to meet the goals established by the organization to help it accomplish its mission, then these products should be eliminated, perhaps sold to others. Again, this process is known as divesting. Occasionally, losses must be taken; but long-term losses that might result from failure to divest must be estimated and balanced against short-term losses from divestment. For instance, after its disastrous bankruptcy in the early 1970s, Equity Funding eventually became Orion Capital, with only two of the six original major SBUs remaining.[24] The company thus survived and even became profitable largely by eliminating unprofitable SBUs.

At the single-SBU level, selected asset reduction is the type of investment reduction that most often occurs. For example, a firm might decide not to build a new plant, thus limiting the number of markets it can serve. Another common form of asset reduction is the decision not to give raises. Cost cutting is also often emphasized; for example, a manufacturer might cut costs by moving corporate headquarters from its plush rental facility back into the plant. Such a move might allow more markets to be served.

The next two options, liquidation and selling out, represent the ultimate in investment reduction, since the amount of investment is reduced to zero. At the single-SBU level, these options signify the ultimate disaster; but for the multiple-SBU firm, the cash received from these processes can be used to purchase other, more desirable SBUs.

Profit extraction is a strategy commonly followed by multiple-SBU firms for business subunits that are in profitable, usually mature industries in which growth is either not possible or is not desirable for some reason. By reducing investment and extracting profits, the firm can utilize cash flows for the benefit of other SBUs. Typically, the SBU from which profits are heavily extracted will be sold to another organization. Commonly, an

---

[23] J. B. Solomon, "Aggressive a Century, Kroger Is Retrenching to Stem Fall in Profits," *The Wall Street Journal*, May 31, 1984, pp. 1, 20; "Control Data Starts a Painful Retrenchment," *Business Week*, October 22, 1984, pp. 94–96.

[24] "Orion Capital: A Shady Ancestry Shapes an Insurer's Future," *Business Week*, July 1, 1980, pp. 102–106; "Orion Capital: Born Again," *Financial World*, July 1, 1979, pp. 26–27.

entrepreneur might also follow the profit extraction strategy prior to selling the firm to an acquiring organization.

Takeover Defenses. A number of takeover defense strategies exist. In 1984 a very popular one was to add a provision to the corporate charter known as the "fair price" provision, which required that all stockholders receive the same price for stock in a take-over. This defense prevented takeover attempts from occurring in tiers, typically with the first purchase at lower prices. Many firms also have provisions in their charters that require very high levels of stockholder approval of takeovers; 80 percent is a common figure. Other firms rely on very large stockholders to prevent their being taken over. Still others attempt to buy back voting stock for more control, or to stagger board of director terms, thus making it difficult for dissident stockholders to gain control of the board. Some companies attempt to issue new stock. Others, such as Martin Marietta, employ what is known as the "PAC-Man defense"—attempting to acquire the company that is attempting to acquire you. Yet another tactic is to provide special voting requirements when certain levels of "unfriendly" stock purchases have occurred. Many firms defend themselves by closely guarding their cash positions, reinvesting quickly to avoid having large amounts of cash on hand; diversification is a sound way of using this cash. Many seek the help of third parties—"friendly" individuals or companies with large amounts of cash who will in fact control the company. (This might be known as the "lesser-of-two-evils" approach.) Some seek high levels of debt. Most experts provide advice on how to determine a company's vulnerability and how then to prepare a defense. In case their defenses fail, however, most managements prepare "golden parachutes" for themselves. Finally, Congress is soon likely to intervene in this arena.[25]

Turnaround. Turnaround strategies refer to efforts to reverse company fortunes when the firm has encountered a period of poor sales, poor revenues, or losses. A turnaround strategy usually involves some type of investment reduction, an attempt to stabilize, followed by a growth strategy of some type. CBS, for example, under Chairman Tom Wyman, has turned its earnings around substantially, partly through cost effectiveness and a new management style, and also perhaps through diversification.[26] One study by Vasudevan Ramanujam suggests that contextual factors play an important role in the success of turnaround strategies. The firm may not succeed at turnaround unless, for example, its industry fortunes change. Another study, by Dan Schendel and A. C. Patton, suggests that some firms are better at implementing strategies than others, although a number of complex additional variables are noted. One final study by Donald C. Hambrick and Steven Schecter suggests that for certain types of firms, successful turnaround is a function more of cost control than marketing strategy.[27] In sum, we have some

[25] J. A. Unruh, A. V. Bruno, and J. Leidecker, "Orchestrating Your Own Takeover," *Journal of Business Strategy*, Fall 1983, pp. 87–93; "Girding for the Proxy Wars," *Business Week*, April 16, 1984, pp. 46–47; P. W. Bernstein, "Taking on Takeovers," *Fortune*, September 3, 1984, p. 96; M. A. Siegel, "How to Foil Greenmail," *Fortune*, January 21, 1985, pp. 157–158.

[26] "Tom Wyman's CBS: Is the Turnaround Here to Stay," *Business Week*, December 24, 1984, pp. 46–47.

[27] D. Schendel and A. C. Patton, "Strategic Responses to Technological Threats," *Business Horizons*, February 1976, pp. 61–69; V. Ramanujam, "An Empirical Examination of Contextual Influences on Corporate Turnaround" (Paper presented to the Academy of Management, Boston, August 1984); D. C. Hambrick and S. Schecter, "Turnaround Strategies for Mature Industrial Product Business Units," *Academy of Management Journal*, June 1983, pp. 231–248.

clues as to what leads to successful turnaround, but as yet are uncertain as to specific strategies for specific situations.

Combination.   Not all the strategies are mutually exclusive. Firms, either at the SBU or corporate level, normally employ a combination of the basic actions described above as they pursue their missions. By examining Figure 3.4, you will see that several can occur simultaneously.

Business Strategy

Once the organization has determined its strategy for coping with its environment—its enterprise strategy—and once the organization has determined what businesses it wants to be in and how it will conduct each business—its corporate strategy—then it must determine how it will compete within each business—its business strategy. This strategy, in both profit-seeking and not-for-profit organizations, can be termed the primary mission strategy. In business, we could also entitle it the mission competitive strategy, because a single business's major concern is to develop a strategic advantage which allows the firm to beat the competition in the marketplace. This strategy is discussed in considerable detail in Chapter 4.

Functional Strategy

Organizations perform certain functions critical to the successful accomplishment of all other strategies. They are designated *functional strategies*. There are two major types of functional strategies. The economic functional strategies include those concerned with marketing, operations, finance, personnel, information, research and development, and others. The management functional strategies include those related to planning, organizing, implementing, controlling, staffing, leading, motivating, communicating, and decision making. In addition, functional strategies include a third, but important type, the strategic issues strategies. With the exception of marketing, which is here considered part of the primary mission strategy, these functional strategies are labeled as mission-supportive strategies. Functional strategies support enterprise, corporate, business, and other functional strategies. These strategies, too, are discussed in more detail in Chapter 4.

The Grand Strategy

A number of authorities in strategic management have employed the term *grand strategy*. Although subtle differences exist in the various definitions, they are usually similarly operationalized by their authors in terms of the basic action strategies enumerated in this chapter. In a representative definition, John A. Pearce II described the grand strategy as "the comprehensive, general plan of major actions by which a firm intends to achieve its long-term objectives within its dynamic environment." Pearce suggests that 12 such major strategies exist: concentric diversification, conglomerate diversification, product development, market development, concentration on current activities, joint ventures, horizontal integration, vertical integration, innovation, retrenchment, liquidation, and divestiture.[28]

[28] J. A. Pearce II, "Selecting Among Alternative Grand Strategies," *California Management Review*, Spring 1982, pp. 23–31.

What Pearce is suggesting here is that these appear to be the 12 most commonly utilized basic action strategies, but even more, that these strategies drive the remainder of the firm's master strategy (our words, not his). Others, such as Charles Hofer and Dan Schendel, have identified "generic (basic action) strategies" which they suggest should be used in various stages of the product life cycle depending on the firm's relative competitive position. Their six strategies are share-increasing, growth, profit, market concentration or asset reduction, turnaround, or liquidation or divestment.[29]

As the definition of grand strategy in Chapter 1 indicates, it is our belief that grand strategies include more than basic action strategies. They may include marketing or other economic functional strategies; for the large conglomerate, they may include portfolio strategies. What constitutes that driving force of the organization—that characteristic to which all else must adhere is the primary issue. For example, Porter has developed three generic strategies: cost leadership, differentiation, and focus (discussed in more detail in Chapter 4). These strategies are marketing strategies.[30] At the business level, what very often drives the organization is the marketing strategy.

Given this more inclusive perspective, the above-referenced strategies are but a few grand strategies currently under study in the field of strategic management. The next chapter examines a number of these as identified in various studies of firms and industries in specific types of situations. It is apparent that grand strategies exist and that they drive the supportive efforts of the organization. For example, Beatrice Foods has chosen the path of conglomerate diversification. That single grand strategy drives all else that it does as a company (not necessarily, however, what its individual strategic business units do). As many as 20 acquisitions and/or divestments have occurred in a single year as Beatrice attempts to improve its profits by improving its portfolio.

This observation is not limited to anecdotal evidence. Michael A. Hitt, R. Duane Ireland, and K. A. Palia, in examining relationships in 93 industrial firms, found that depending on the type of (basic action) grand strategy employed by the firm, various of seven different economic functional areas (marketing, finance, etc.) are more critical, more focused on than are others.[31]

Because of the large number of such strategies and their combinations, the limited research evidence to support various contentions, and the infancy of the research, it would seem best at this point simply to recognize their existence and the way in which they affect the remainder of the organization. In addition, individual, industry-based, research-supported grand strategies, such as those discussed in the next chapter, might also be viable considerations in formulating strategies in similar situations. Beyond that, one must be quite careful in placing too much faith in unverified recommendations. An organization must always choose among the basic action strategies and/or marketing strategies, making one the most central thrust of the master strategy, and hence, the grand strategy. But exactly which one is most appropriate to choose is as yet an unknown in most circumstances.

---

[29] C. W. Hofer and D. Schendel, *Strategy Formulation: Analytical Concepts*, (St. Paul, Minn.: West, 1978), pp. 104, 162–177.

[30] M. E. Porter, *Competitive Strategy* (New York: Free Press, 1980), Chapters 1 and 2.

[31] M. A. Hitt, R. D. Ireland, and K. A. Palia, "Industrial Firms' Grand Strategy and Functional Importance: Moderating Effects of Technology and Uncertainty," *Academy of Management Journal*, 1982, Vol. 25, No. 2, pp. 265–298.

Preemptive Strategies

Ian MacMillan has proposed that preemptive strategies are appropriate mechanisms for firms wishing to secure advantages over competitors. A preemptive action is defined as "a major move by a focal business ahead of moves by its adversaries, which allows it to secure an advantageous position from which it is difficult to dislodge because of the advantages it has captured by being the first mover." He offers a common example of such a move in the firm that expands capacity far ahead of industry demand, anticipating the gaining of market share through discouraging competitors from expanding.[32] Preemptive moves are based on the strategists' assumptions about the marketplace. If these assumptions are inaccurate, then the preemptive moves may leave strategists vulnerable. MacMillan provides the characteristics of an ideal preemptive move:[33]

- "It should be possible to rapidly occupy 'prime' positions, at any advantageous point, along the entire industry chain.

- "Once the move is made, it should be difficult for most of the adversaries to follow into these positions.

- "Conditions should exist that slow down the response rate of any competitors who can respond.

- "It should be relatively easy for the preempting business to reverse its move, if it so desires."

He feels that there are two basic classes of preemptive opportunities which a firm should seek:[34]

- "Those opportunities that exploit rival weaknesses or its lack of commitment."
- "Those opportunities that exploit rival strengths or its strong commitments."

In terms of exploiting a rival's weaknesses, MacMillan suggests the following:[35]

- "Reshape the industry infrastructure—that which is necessary to ensure a smooth flow from raw materials to finished goods."

- "Occupy prime positions—geographically, key accounts, distributors, service organizations, suppliers, government contracts."

- "Secure critical skills—secure these across all functions."

- "Preempt a psychological position—develop an appeal to the customer that is hard for competitors to overcome."

In terms of exploiting a rival's strengths, MacMillan suggests the following:

- "Cannibalize competitive advantages—make moves that force the opponent to have to cannibalize current advantages in order to respond. An opponent is not likely to do this."

---

[32] I. C. MacMillan, "Preemptive Strategies," *Journal of Business Strategy*, Fall 1983, p. 16.
[33] Ibid., p. 18.
[34] Ibid., pp. 18–19.
[35] Ibid., p. 19.

- "Damage the opponent's image, company tradition, or strategy."

- "Threaten a major investment—for example in the competitor's production capacity, distribution system, or supply system."

- "Force competitors to antagonize powerful third parties—by choosing preemptive moves which necessitate the competitor's upsetting powerful third parties, it is likely that the competitor will offer no response."

MacMillan suggests that major opportunities for preemptive strategies exist in the areas presented in Table 3.3.

MacMillan's preemptive strategy approach seems intuitively sound. There is, in fact, evidence from a host of research to suggest that such actions generally (not necessarily those he specifically suggests) are quite sound. One must always keep in mind the situation, and be cognizant of the SWOTs involved.

Table 3.3   Sources of Preemptive Opportunities

Supply Systems

1. Secure access to raw materials or components
2. Preempt production equipment
3. Dominate supply logistics

Product

1. Introduce new product lines
2. Develop dominant design
3. Position
4. Secure accelerated approval from agencies
5. Secure product development and delivery skills
6. Expand scope of the product

Production Systems

1. Proprietary processes
2. Aggressive capacity expansion
3. Vertical integration with key suppliers
4. Secure scarce and critical production skills

Customers

1. Segmentation
2. Build early brand awareness
3. Train customers in usage skills
4. Capture key accounts

Distribution and Service Systems

1. Occupation of prime locations
2. Preferential access to key distributors
3. Dominance of distribution logistics
4. Access to superior service capabilities
5. Development of distributor skills

Source: I. C. MacMillan, "Preemptive Strategies," reprinted by permission from the *Journal of Business Strategy*, Fall 1983, Copyright © 1983, Warren, Gorham & Lamont Inc., 210 South Street, Boston, Mass., p. 20. All Rights Reserved.

Some Important Characteristics of Plans

It is relevant to note that all plans should have certain characteristics and that the contents of strategy should reflect them. A few of these characteristics are listed below.

Flexibility.   In today's volatile environment, organizations must remain flexible in their planning processes so that as changes arise, the organizations will be able to adapt. Some organizations have developed numerous contingency plans and multiple strategies for the purpose of coping with the changing requirements of the environment. Having already developed alternative strategies, the firm can implement the proper one immediately upon the occurrence of various events. For instance, the bank that has an inflexible strategy today will be out of business tomorrow, because banks operate in very volatile environments.

Contents.   Any plan should include, to the appropriate degree, specification of

- Who will be involved—organization levels and individuals.
- What will be required—resources.
- Where action will occur—geographically and by organization level.
- When action will occur—time horizon, implementation date.
- Why action will occur—the objective.
- How the objective will be accomplished—what actions are necessary (which is indicated somewhat by who, what, and where, the means of implementation).
- Control—some provision for evaluation.

Consistency.   Plans developed within a strategy should be consistent with one another, and strategies should be consistent within an organization. The objectives of the master strategy must be included in the development of intermediate and operational plans. These plans must also be consistent with organizational structure. Such considerations are especially important to the functional area division plans. These objectives often suboptimize the total strategy because functional area or product division needs are included without the proper analysis of their impact on overall organizational-objectives accomplishment.

Timeliness.   To be effective, a plan must be timely. Even the Edsel might have succeeded had it been introduced just two years sooner or later. Although some believed it unattractive, its main failing was that it was a big car introduced when the consumer was looking for a small car.

Risks.   Risk is many things to many people. To some, it is the probability of return. To others, it may be this probability in combination with the severity of consequences. Risk has often been defined in several other ways, among them in terms of the variability of returns over time. We believe that, to have a high probability of success, the strategy must have the proper level of risk however it may be defined and measured. Inga S. Baird believes that managers should consider the numerous facets of this definition when attempting to measure risk. She advises them to consider virtually all the aspects of risk, its many definitions and measurements, and then develop a summary estimate of this strategy input.[36] We agree. We also recognize that this may not always be possible, nor always necessary.

Acceptance by Society and Government.   Business's social responsibility is so important that every plan must be specifically concerned with societal impact analysis. If society and government do not accept an organization's actions as appropriate, profit may suffer. In addition, sanctions may be levied against the firm so that it will eventually be forced to change.

Summary

The major strategic objectives which exist in virtually all business organizations include: growth, efficiency, utilization of resources, contribution to owners, contribution to customers, contribution to employees, and contribution to society. Objectives serve not only to direct but also to integrate the organization. MBORR as a management system and philosophy has been shown to be highly related to organizational success.

The master strategy has four major components: a societal response strategy, a mission determination strategy, a primary mission strategy, and a supportive strategy. In business, these strategies are known as the enterprise strategy, the corporate strategy, the business strategy, and the functional (support) strategy. Each of these major strategies is composed of numerous subcomponent strategies. The enterprise strategy is concerned with how the organization functions as a member of the overall society. The corporate strategy is concerned with the business or businesses the firm is in and the basic action strategies that naturally follow. The business strategy is concerned primarily with marketing (and occasionally with other functional strategies). Business strategies are the primary driving force behind the organization's ability to compete. Finally, the supportive strategies focus on the efforts of both economic functional strategies—such as production, finance, and human resources management—and managerial functional strategies—such as planning, organizing, implementing, and controlling—to support the business strategy.

Plans, and hence strategies, have important intrinsic characteristics, including flexibility, contents, consistency, timeliness, risk, and acceptance by society and government.

Key Terms and Concepts

By the time you have completed this chapter, you should be familiar with the following key terms and concepts: the objective-setting process; typical business objectives and their major characteristics; the levels of objectives; the major MBORR processes; the positive and negative features of MBORR; the importance of objectives to performance; the four major levels of strategy for all organizations and for business in particular; the major component substrategies of the corporate strategy, including definitions and examples; the grand strategy; and the major characteristics of plans.

[36] I. S. Baird, "What Is Risk Anyway? The Treatment of Risk in Strategic Management" (Paper presented to the Academy of Management, Boston, August 1984).

Discussion Questions

1.   Describe how each of the objectives from Figure 3.3 might be operationalized.

2.   Why do organizations function better if they have objectives than if they do not?

3.   What are the major processes in MBORR?

4.   List at least three positive and three negative features of MBORR.

5.   Give examples of each of the major strategies discussed in this chapter, including the subcomponent strategies of the corporate strategy.

6.   Discuss as many strategic mistakes of well-known large firms as possible, categorizing each of these mistakes in terms of the strategies outlined in Table 3.2.

7.   Explain each of the following takeover defenses: "fair price"; "golden parachute"; "PAC-man defense"; and "lesser of two evils."

References

Ansoff, H. I. "Managing Strategic Surprise by Response to Weak Signals." *California Management Review*, Winter 1975, pp. 21–33.

Buzzell, Robert D. "Is Vertical Integration Profitable?" *Harvard Business Review*, January/February 1983, pp. 92–102.

Cochran, Philip L., and Robert A. Wood. "Corporate Social Responsibility and Financial Performance." *Academy of Management Journal*, 1984, Vol. 27, No. 1, pp. 42–56.

Davis, Bob. "Divining Defense Plans Is Art for Military Electronics Firms." *The Wall Street Journal*, September 20, 1984, p. 33.

"Did It Make Sense to Break Up AT&T?" *Business Week*, December 3, 1984, pp. 86–100.

"D'Lites: The Pioneer of 'Healthy' Fast Food Goes on a Growth Binge." *Business Week*, September 10, 1984, pp. 136–140.

Gutmann, P. M. "Strategies for Growth." *California Management Review*, Summer 1964, pp. 81–86.

Harrigan, Kathryn Rudie. "Formulating Vertical Integration Strategies." *Academy of Management Review*, 1984, Vol. 9, No. 4, pp. 638–652.

Hitt, Michael A., R. Duane Ireland, and Gregory Stadter. "Functional Importance and Company Performance: Moderating Effects of Grand Strategy and Industry Type." *Strategic Management Journal*, 1982, Vol. 3, pp. 315–330.

Odiorne, G. *Management by Objectives*. New York: Pitman Publishing, 1965.

Pearce, John A. II, "An Executive-Level Perspective on the Strategic Management Process." *California Management Review*, Fall 1981, Vol. 24, No. 1, pp. 39–48.

Ramanujam, Vasudevan. "An Empirical Examination of Contextual Influences on Corporate Turnaround." Submitted to the Business Policy and Planning Division for the Academy of Management National Meeting, Boston, August 1984.

Shaffer, Richard A. "Start-Up Semiconductor Firms that Have Niches Find Funds." *The Wall Street Journal*, September 21, 1984.

Tosi, H. "Effective and Ineffective MBO." *Management by Objectives*. 1975, Vol. 4, pp. 7–14.

Venkatraman, N., and John C. Camillus. "Exploring the Concept of 'Fit' in Strategic Management." *Academy of Management Review*, 1984, Vol. 9, No. 3, pp. 513–525.

4

The Master Strategy at the SBU Level

Never follow the crowd.

▪ *Bernard Baruch* ▪

Most business organizations engage in only one line of business. Your local auto dealer or flower shop; a wholly owned national restaurant chain such as McDonald's; a subsidiary of a major conglomerate, such as Sylvania of GTE; or a retail grocery organization, whether it be Kroger, Safeway, A&P, or Grand Union, are all examples of business organizations with essentially one line of business. The master strategies of such organizations are the subject of this chapter.

The principal concern of most single-business organizations is establishing a strategic advantage which allows them to beat the competition in the marketplace. At the business level, the organization's mastery strategy focuses primarily on basic action strategies in conjunction with marketing strategy. But the roles of supportive functional-area strategies are critical to the firm's grand strategy and indeed may be the focal point upon which the grand strategy is based.

This chapter reviews major contingency theory and behavioral theory approaches to the formulation of grand strategy. Also discussed are the business-level strategies of marketing or other functional strategies, such as operations, human resources management, or finance, which are the primary thrust of the grand strategy, or which support the primary mission strategy. And since the stage of the product life cycle is of special importance to the development of successful business and supportive functional strategies, its impacts on strategy formulation are noted as well. Figures 4.1 and 4.2 indicate which portions of the strategic process are examined in this chapter.

The Corporate Strategy for the Single-Business Enterprise

"What business are we in or should we be in?" As you have learned, all business firms must answer that question. In Chapter 3, we saw that the choice of business depends on the answers to three questions:

1. Is there some business in which the organization has a natural strategic advantage or an innate interest?

2. Does the company want to compete or find a niche?

3. Does the company want or need to concentrate, grow, stabilize, engage in investment reduction, defend against a takeover, or turn around company fortunes? A number of

Figure 4.1   The Organization—A Strategic Management Process Model

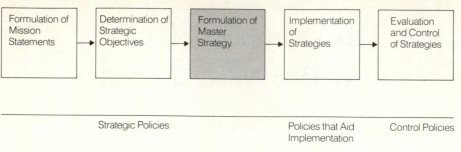

basic strategy options exist. While strategies such as diversification have been ruled out, at least for the time being, single-business firms still have numerous basic action strategies from which to choose. These basic action strategies will lead to the formulation of the grand strategy as per the discussion in the previous chapter. Often, at the business level, the marketing strategy drives the organization as part of a concentration grand strategy.

Even after these questions have been answered, the single-business organization must always be alert to the possibility of redefining the business. After all, the business changes over time; or more accurately, it should change with changes in strategic variables.

The owner of a medium-sized distribution company, when first asked what his business was, replied, "We distribute electronic components." Later, he realized that he was in the source business. This realization opened many new product horizons to the firm; but just as importantly, it caused him to realize that his primary competitive strength lay in providing service, the real central focus of his competitive effort. He saw then the need to manage inventories better than he had been.

In defining the business (determining basic action grand strategies) in a single-business firm, important points for any top manager to remember are to be flexible, to anticipate change, and to be responsive to changes, both internal and external.

The Business Strategy for the Single-Business Enterprise

Competition is the name of the game. For most single-business companies, marketing plays the most critical role in strategic business success, but selected basic action and functional-support strategies play integral roles; they may even be the driving force of the grand strategy.

The business strategy addresses the issue of how the firm is to compete in one business or in a particular product market segment. The objective of a business firm is to obtain a strategic advantage over the competition by: doing something that no other firm does; doing something better than its competition, or at least convincing people it does; or doing something in a location in which no other firm does the same thing. Any of these alternatives must be accomplished by use of the basic action strategies available, in combination with a sound marketing strategy based on the fundamental marketing components: target market, product, promotion, distribution, and price. The business strategy inte-

Figure 4.2   Objective Determination and Master Strategy Formulation

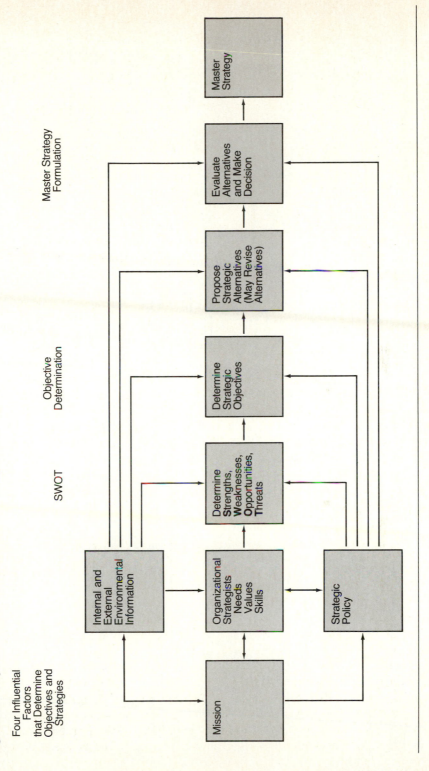

Figure 4.3   Relationships among Strategies in Single-SBU Firms

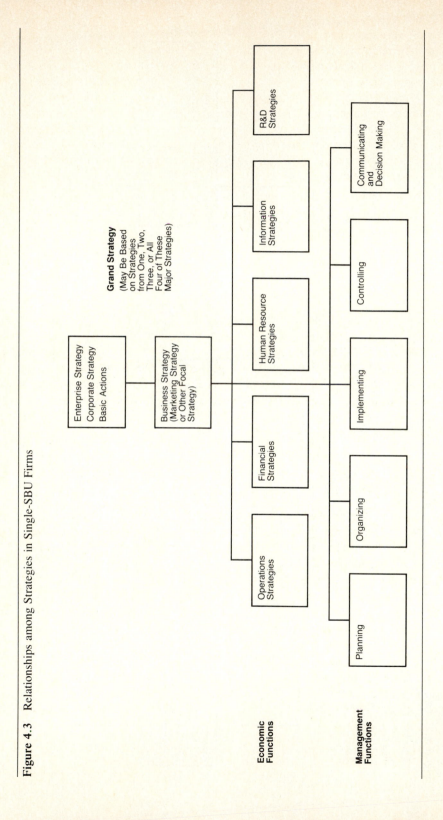

grates the various functional strategies which support the competitive effort. Figure 4.3 portrays the relationships among the various strategies in the single-SBU firm.

But how does a firm know what strategy to use? One approach to solving this problem is the contingency approach, which suggests that for a given set of circumstances, a "best" strategy exists. The contingency approach is concerned with grand strategies—basic action, marketing, and other functional strategies. And though the approach is currently in a formative stage, the related research is increasing. Thus far the approach has been applied only to profit-oriented organizations, but it may be extended to nonprofit organizations in the future. This approach to strategy formulation and alternative generation is examined next.

The Contingency Approach to Business-Level and Corporate Strategy Formulation—The Grand Strategy

One does not plan and then try to make the circumstances fit these plans.
One tries to make plans fit the circumstances.

▪ *George Patton* ▪

The science of strategic management has not yet reached the degree of sophistication that will allow executives to know the exact strategy which should be followed for every situation. However, research and theory have pointed toward a set of environmental and organizational variables that have significant impact on the content of strategy, at least with regard to strategy for a single-product line. Furthermore, for some specific situations, appropriate strategies have been identified, most of them also for a single-product line. In the following pages, major strategic variables will be reviewed and the few variable strategy combinations that have been identified will be discussed.

Strategic Contingency Variables—Factors to Be Considered When One Product or Business Is Involved

After reviewing the research and the theories mentioned previously, C. W. Hofer concluded that the most important single variable in the determination of strategy is the life cycle stage of the product for which the strategy is being formulated.[1] Table 4.1 portrays the key variables that his work has suggested are appropriate to each stage of the product life cycle. The table is arranged so that the first factor listed in each cell is the most important, the second is the second-most important, and so on.

A business could use Table 4.1 in this manner: for a product in a particular stage of the product life cycle, it would consult the table to determine what key variables should be considered in the formulation of strategy. For example, suppose a firm has a product in the maturity stage of the product life cycle. The firm's strategic managers would review information related to each of the factors listed under the maturity stage for each of the types of variables listed. Of the market and consumer behavioral variables, for example, market segmentation is considered to be the most influential factor. Of course, buyer

---

[1]C. W. Hofer, "Toward a Contingency Theory of Business Strategy," *Academy of Management Journal*, December 1975, pp. 784–810.

Table 4.1   Environmental and Organizational Variables That Are
Strategically Significant at Different Stages of the Product Life Cycle

Types of Variables[a]	Life Cycle Stages Introduction	Growth
Market and consumer behavior variables	Buyer needs Purchase frequency	Buyer needs Buyer concentration Purchase frequency
Industry structure variables	Uniqueness of the product Rate of technological change in product design	Type of product Rate of technological change in product design Number of equal products Barriers to entry
Competitor variables		Degree of specialization within the industry
Supplier variables		
Broader environmental variables	Interest rates Money supply	GNP trend Money supply
Organizational variables	Quality of products	Market share Quality of products Marketing intensity

[a] Within each category, the specific variables identified have been ranked in terms of their degree of significance for formulating viable business strategies. For instance, in the maturity stage of the life cycle, only two competitor variables are considered to be significant for the formulation of a business strategy: namely, the degree of specialization in the industry and the degree of capacity utilization. Of these, the degree of specialization is thought to be more important.

needs, purchase frequency, and buyer concentration also influence strategy. The firm's strategic managers would gather information on these and the other factors listed for each of the other variables. Based on these factors, strengths and weaknesses would be assessed.

Note that no strategy is recommended in the table. That is left for the individual organization to determine. Strategies such as those presented in Table 4.2 or Table 4.3 might

Table 4.1 *continued*

Maturity	Saturation	Decline
Market segmentation Buyer needs Purchase frequency Buyer concentration	Market size Market segmentation Elasticity of demand Buyer loyalty Seasonality Cyclicality	Market size Buyer loyalty Elasticity of demand
Type of product Rate of technological change in process design Degree of product differentiation Number of equal products Transportation and distribution costs Barriers to entry	Degree of product differentiation Price/cost structure Experience curves Degree of integration Economics of scale	Degree of product differentiation Price/cost structure Marginal plant size Transportation and distribution costs
Degree of specialization within the industry Degree of capacity utilization	Degree of seller concentration Aggressiveness of competition Degree of specialization in the industry	Degree of specialization within the industry Degree of capacity utilization
Degree of supplier concentration	Degree of supplier concentration Major changes in availability of raw materials	Major changes in availability of raw materials
GNP trend Antitrust regulations	Growth of population Age distribution of population Regional shifts of population Lifestyle changes	Interest rates Age distribution of population
Market share Quality of products Value added Degree of customer concentration Marketing intensity Discretionary cash flow/gross capital investment	Market share Quality of products Length of the production cycle P/S newness Relative wage rate Marketing intensity	Market share Quality of products Length of the production cycle Relative wage rate Degree of customer concentration

Source: Charles W. Hofer, "Toward a Contingency Theory of Business Strategy." *Academy of Management Journal* 18 (December 1975): 800–801. Reprinted by permission of the *Academy of Management Journal*.

be employed. However, research suggests that certain actions are more successful than others, regardless of the situation; these actions will be discussed later.

The conceptualization presented in Table 4.1 is extremely important and highly contributive to strategy formulation. Actual strategic decisions as well as their simulations in the classroom, such as are required by case analyses, can be improved through the use of this table. Some caution is necessary, however. These factors have not been tested, as pre-

Table 4.2   Strategies for the Product Life Cycle

Strategic Area	Phase I Introduction	Phase II Growth	Phase III Maturity	Phase IV Decline
Objective	Introducing the customer to the product; promoting initial adoption by trade, customers	Increasing trade channels; establishing brand, franchises	Maintaining trade support; leveling production; lowering costs; maintaining market share by competitive pricing	Monitor contribution to total product offering and profit
Characteristics	Learning and development in the market and the product	Demand exceeds supply; competition enters market	Sales saturation; low product differentiation	Competitors leave the market
Product	Limited line; adaption to initial adopters	Addition of variations, improvements	Cost considerations; uniformity for mass production	Simplification of the line
Promotion	Personal selling; missionary selling; awareness, interest; advertising, if any (usually introductory offers)	Awareness; interest, evaluations; brand stress; personal selling decreases; advertisement	Mass advertisements as reminder; trade promotion	Minimal
Distribution	Exclusive or direct	Selective	Extensive	Customer option
Price	Introductory, high discounts to facilitate initial adoption by trade, customers	High unit margins or competitive for high market share	Highly competitive	Profit maintenance
Profit margin	Low	High initially to recover R&D, introductory cost, investment; lower as competition enters	Normal to low, as volume stabilizes	High to compensate for lower and declining sales

Source: Henry E. Metzner, Jerry L. Watt, and William F. Glueck, "Product Life Cycle and Stages of Growth, an Empirical Analysis," *Proceedings: Academy of Management*, 1975, Table 1, pp. 61–63. Reprinted by permission of The Academy of Management.

sented, in actual corporations. Furthermore, some very limited evidence suggests that product life cycle strategies are not appropriate to every product. Nonetheless, at this point, the stage of the product life cycle appears to be the single most important factor in determining strategy.

The Contingency Theory Applied

As mentioned earlier, contingency theories are based on the assumption that for a given set of factors in a situation, a best series of actions exists. In a situation where the given set of factors is predominant, the manager—here the strategist—should act in a certain way. The advantages of establishing contingency actions for a given set of circumstances are obvious: performance should improve.

As an example of how contingency theory is applied in strategy formulation for a single product, let us look again at C. W. Hofer's work. Hofer has suggested seven contingency strategy propositions for the maturity stage of the product life cycle. Two of these propositions are listed below as illustrations. Each defines a specific situation in terms of the key variables in Table 4.1 and then suggests an appropriate strategy.[2]

N²   When the degree of product differentiation is low, the nature of buyer needs primarily noneconomic, the degree of market segmentation slight, the degree of specialization within the industry low, the marketing intensity high, the manufacturing economies of scale medium, and the ratio of distribution costs to manufacturing value added high, businesses should

1.   Use universal rather than specialized marketing appeals;

2.   Reduce their geographic scope or increase their marketing expenditures sufficiently so that their per capita marketing expenditures within their geographic service area are in excess of the industry average;

3.   Attempt to keep their degree of capacity utilization high and their fixed assets relatively modern; and

4.   Withdraw from the industry if their market share falls to less than 20 percent of that held by the industry leader within their geographic service area.

N³   When the degree of product differentiation is high, the nature of the buyer's needs primarily noneconomic, the degree of market segmentation moderate to high, the product complexity high, the purchase frequency low, and the barriers to entry in the distribution or technology areas, businesses should

1.   Focus their R&D funds first on modifying and upgrading their existing product line, second on developing new products, and last on process innovations;

2.   Allocate substantial funds to the maintenance and enhancement of their distinctive competencies, especially those in the marketing area;

3.   Develop a strong service capability in their distribution systems; and

4.   Seek to expand the geographic scope of their operations, if possible.

Observing these propositions should make the difficulties in formulating contingency statements increasingly clear. Obviously, one of the major barriers to the formulation of a usable contingency theory is the large number of variables to be considered. Hofer suggests that more than 50 major variables exist which could affect strategy on a contingency basis. He admits that this list is probably incomplete in terms of other explanatory variables such as management techniques or social responsibility. Nevertheless, taking only his variables into account gives us some 18,000,000,000,000,000 combinations of circumstances to consider. This means that in order to have a truly inclusive contingency variable theory, an almost infinite number of contingency statements would have to be formulated. Approaching the task from a life-cycle-stage basis, as Hofer has done, allows the number of situations to be reduced substantially. Even with these limitations, however, the number of possible situations that could exist is very high. This suggests that the fu-

---

[2] Charles W. Hofer, "Toward a Contingency Theory of Business Strategy," *Academy of Management Journal*, Vol. 18, (December 1975), pp. 803–805. Reprinted by permission of the *Academy of Management Journal*.

Table 4.3   Appropriate Business Strategies over the Product Life Cycle

	Functional Focus	R&D	Production	Marketing	Physical Distribution
Pre-commercialization	Coordination of R&D and other functions	Reliability tests Release blueprints	Production design Process planning Purchasing department lines up vendors and sub-contractors	Test marketing Detailed marketing plan	Plan shipping schedules, mixed carloads Rent warehouse space, trucks
Introduction	Engineering: debugging in R&D production and field	Technical corrections (engineering changes)	Subcontracting Centralize pilot plans; test various processes; develop standards	Induce trial; fill pipelines; sales agents or commissioned salespeople; publicity	Plan a logistics system
Growth	Production	Start successor product	Centralize production Phase out subcontractors Expedite vendors' output; long runs	Channel commitment Brand emphasis Salaried sales force Reduce price if necessary	Expedite deliveries Shift to owned facilities
Maturity	Marketing and logistics	Develop minor variants Reduce costs through value analysis Originate major adaptations to start new cycle	Many short runs Decentralize Import parts, low-priced models Routinization Cost reduction	Short-term promotions Salaried salespeople Cooperative advertising Forward integration Routine marketing research; panels, audits	Reduce costs and raise customer service level Control finished goods inventory
Decline	Finance	Withdraw all R&D from initial version	Revert to subcontracting; simplify production line Careful inventory control; buy foreign or competitive goods; stock spare parts	Revert to commission basis; withdraw most promotional support Raise price Selective distribution Careful phase-out, considering entire channel	Reduce inventory and services

Source: Reprinted by permission from *Atlanta Economic Review* (now *Business* Magazine). "Operational View of a Product Life Cycle," exhibit from "A Framework for Functional Coordination," by Harold W. Fox, November/

Table 4.3   *continued*

Personnel	Finance	Management Accounting	Other	Customers	Competition
Recruit for new activities Negotiate operational changes with unions	LC plan for cash flows, profits, investments, subsidiaries	Payout planning; full costs/revenues Determine optimum lengths of LC stages through present-value method	Final legal clearances (regulatory hurdles, patents) Appoint LC coordinator	Panels and other test respondents	Neglects opportunity or is working on similar idea
Staff and train middle management Stock options for executives	Accounting deficit; high net cash outflow Authorize large production facilities	Help develop production and distribution standards Prepare sales aids like sales management portfolio		Innovators and some early adopters	(Monopoly) Disparagement of innovation Legal and extralegal interference
Add suitable personnel for plant Many grievances Heavy overtime	Very high profits, net cash outflow still rising Sell equities	Short-term analyses based on return per scarce resource		Early adopters and early majority	(Oligopoly) A few imitate, improve, or cut prices
Transfers, advancements; incentives for efficiency, safety and so on Suggestion system	Declining profit rate but increasing net cash inflow	Analyze differential costs/revenue Spearhead cost reduction, value analysis, and efficiency drives	Pressure for resale price maintenance Price cuts bring price wars; possible price collusion	Early adopters, early and late majority, some laggards; first discontinued by late majority	(Monopoly competition) First shakeout; still many rivals
Find new slots Encourage early retirement	Administer system, retrenchment Sell unneeded equipment Export the machinery	Analyze escapable costs Pinpoint remaining outlays	Accurate sales forecast very important	Mainly laggards	(Oligopoly) After second shakeout, only few rivals

December 1973, pp. 10–11. Copyright 1973 by the College of Business Administration, Georgia State University, Atlanta.

ture of contingency theory probably lies in identifying the major factors that should be considered, as has been done in Table 4.1, and combining them with hypothesized strategies such as those of Metzner, Watt, and Glueck (Table 4.2) or Fox (Table 4.3). These are behavioral-type strategies which will be defined later.)

The Directional Policy Matrix

One contingency business strategy technique (developed by Shell and used primarily in Europe) employs a nine-cell matrix as a means for determining product investment strategies within a particular industry. The matrix approach is quite common in evaluating resource allocations among multiple businesses within the same firm (as you will see in Chapter 5), but has not been used that frequently in determining strategies within a particular industry. As you examine Figure 4.4, you will see that one of this matrix's axes characterizes the Prospects for Sector Profitability, while the other characterizes the Company's Competitive Capabilities. Each of these two critical dimensions is viewed as having three levels of desirability. The prospects for sector profitability are unattractive, average, and attractive. The company's competitive capabilities are seen as either weak, average, or strong. The combinations of these three levels of the two critical dimensions then lead to eight advisable strategies (phased withdrawal appears twice on the matrix). In using this matrix, a firm would compare its prospects for sector profitability with its competitive capabilities, and then choose the indicated strategy at the intersection of the determined levels for each dimension. The resultant eight strategies are portrayed as follows:

1. *Disinvest.* These products are losing money in their long-term average performance, and should be eliminated from the product line.

2. *Phased Withdrawals.* Slowly, but surely, the business should eliminate these products from the product line. They may be earning money, but only a marginal amount. Any profits derived from these products is not justifiable in terms of relative investment.

Figure 4.4   Directional Policy Matrix

Prospects for Market Sector Profitability

		Unattractive	Average	Attractive
Company's Competitive Position	Weak	Disinvest	Phased Withdrawal Proceed with Care	Double or Quit
	Average	Phased Withdrawal	Proceed with Care Growth	Try Harder
	Strong	Cash Generation	Growth Leader	Leader

Source: Adapted from D. E. Hussey, "Portfolio Analysis: Practical Experience with the Directional Policy Matrix," *Long Range Planning*, Vol. 11 (August 1978), p. 3. Reprinted by permission.

3. *Cash Generator.* This product or service has no long-term future. Normally such products are in the late maturity stage of the product life cycle. No further investment should be allowed.

4. *Proceed with Care.* Two average levels on the two critical dimensions suggest caution in terms of future investment.

5. *Growth.* Where the company is strong and the industry averagely attractive, the firm should continue to support growth in this product or service. The business's position should allow the product or service to be self-financing.

6. *Double or Quit.* If the firm is weak in an attractive industry situation, it should either invest heavily in the product or service, or withdraw from the marketplace.

7. *Try Harder.* Where the firm finds itself in an attractive industry, but is only average in that industry, it should increase investment or withdraw from the marketplace.

8. *Leader.* At this intersection of the levels of the two dimensions, the business should attempt to maintain its leadership position in the market by investing, even though necessary investment funds may not be self-generating, because earnings will be above the average.[3]

This matrix seems to offer some very prudent, logical advice. But, as with any concept of strategic management, there are a number of factors to consider further: Are there only two major sets of variables to consider? What are the specific product life cycles of the various products, and what are their impacts? Are there more than three levels of desirability characterizing the two dimensions noted? Are the recommended strategies the most satisfactory? Are there assumptions to this model which are not met in every situation? Is it always best to be the leader, or can one make substantial profits as a follower? The point is that this model is only one approach to the determination of a business-level strategy, and should not be taken as a recommended approach. Rather, it should be considered as a starting place.

An additional consideration should be used in determining an appropriate strategy. The behavioral theory of grand strategy formulation, which has often been labeled as part of the contingency theory, identifies certain behaviors which have been employed by the more successful firms in most, if not all, circumstances. The following paragraphs discuss some of the postulates of this grand strategy formulation theory.

The Behavioral Theory of Grand Strategy Formulation

There is no such thing as a growth industry. . . . There are only companies organized and operated to create and capitalize on growth opportunities.

▪ *Theodore Levitt* ▪

In the past few years, several studies utilizing regression analysis and other analytical techniques have demonstrated that successful firms engage in definite patterns of behavior in order to increase return on investment. While this research uncovered some surprises

---

[3]D. E. Hussey, "Portfolio Analysis: Practical Experience with the Directional Policy Matrix," *Long Range Planning*, August 1978, pp. 1–9.

and some contradictions, most of its findings involved factors which theory would have identified as appropriate. The following paragraphs review some of these studies to determine which factors are of primary interest.

Descriptive Characteristics and the Search for Excellence

One approach to analyzing why a firm is successful is what one might call the descriptive characteristics approach. A number of authors have attempted to determine what characterizes the successful firm, but none have received such overwhelming acceptance as have Thomas J. Peters and Robert H. Waterman, Jr. In their book, *In Search of Excellence*, Peters and Waterman identify eight descriptive characteristics that their research led them to believe are common denominators of the best-run companies. These denominators are business management practices that seem to enable the successful companies to be successful. During a two-year period, Peters and Waterman examined, through interviews and questionnaires, and through an examination of secondary information, the common characteristics of 36 successful, large, single-industry U.S. firms. These firms were part of an original sample of some 75 firms, which was shortened on the basis of various performance criteria, or on representativeness in the case of 13 European firms. A number of standard performance criteria were employed. The resulting eight common characteristics are highlighted in Information Capsule 4.1.[4] Not without its critics,[5] many company presidents nonetheless swear by the book, encouraging and often requiring their executives to read it.

Daniel T. Carroll provides us with a critical profile of the methodological and conceptual problems in Peters and Waterman's book. Carroll explains that their sample is not truly representative of American business, and is small. Perhaps most tellingly, the sample does not contain a group of unsuccessful companies for comparison. Thus, there is no guarantee that unsuccessful companies are not also characterized by these same eight common denominators. Nor is there a detailed description of how these characteristics were derived or of how each firm was analyzed. Depending heavily on secondary data, the study also focuses primarily on management practices, and fails to truly examine the impacts of other factors, both internal and environmental, which might affect the success or failure of a firm. For example, technology, market share, and competitor actions are not considered. Finally, Carroll states that Peters and Waterman attack the rational model with, unfortunately, somewhat biased and unsystematic arguments.[6]

In balance, *In Search of Excellence* must be considered a major contributor to management thought, perhaps intuitively sound, but limited in a number of critical ways in terms of research design. Its findings are suspect and its commentaries on the need for improvement in the rational model, though perhaps well founded, are not sufficiently supported by hard evidence. (The latter may, of course, be more difficult to come by than rationally and empirically oriented researchers would admit. We personally feel that Peters and Waterman make a good point about the need to be more concerned with the human aspects of the organization as opposed to what seems to be a penchant for number crunch-

---

[4] Thomas J. Peters and Robert H. Waterman, Jr., *In Search of Excellence* (New York: Harper and Row, 1982).

[5] S. Benner, "Peter's Principles: Secrets of Growth," *INC*, July 1983, pp. 34–38.

[6] D. T. Carroll, "A Disappointing Search for Excellence," *Harvard Business Review*, November/December 1983, pp. 78–88.

═══════ **INFORMATION CAPSULE 4.1** ═══════
The *In Search of Excellence* Excellence Characteristics

1. *A Bias for Action*–for getting on with it. Even though these companies may be ana-lytical in their approach to decision making, they are not paralyzed by that fact (as so many others seem to be). In many of these companies the standard operating proce-dure is "Do it, fix it, try it." Says a Digital Equipment Corporation senior executive, fo example, "When we've got a big problem here, we grab ten senior guys and stick them in a room for a week. They come up with an answer *and* implement it." More-over, the companies are experimenters supreme. Instead of allowing 250 engineers and marketers to work on a new product in isolation for 15 months, they form bands of 5 to 25 and test ideas out on a customer, often with inexpensive prototypes, within a matter of weeks. What is striking is the host of practical devices the excellent com-panies employ, to maintain corporate fleetness of foot and counter the stultification that almost inevitably comes with size.

2. *Close to the Customer.* These companies learn from the people they serve. They pro-vide unparalleled quality, service, and reliability—things that work and last. They succeed in differentiating—*à la* Frito-Lay (potato chips), Maytag (washers), or Tupperware—the most commodity-like products. IBM's marketing vice president, Francis G. (Buck) Rodgers, says, "It's a shame that, in so many companies, whenever you get good service, it's an exception." Not so at the excellent companies. Everyone gets into the act. Many of the innovative companies got their best product ideas from customers. That comes from listening, intently and regularly.

3. *Autonomy and Entrepreneurship.* The innovative companies foster many leaders and many innovators throughout the organization. They are a hive of what we've come to call champions; 3M has been described as "so intent on innovation that its essential atmosphere seems not like that of a large corporation but rather a loose network of laboratories and cubbyholes populated by feverish inventors and dauntless entrepre-neurs who let their imaginations fly in all directions." They don't try to hold everyone on so short a rein that he or she can't be creative. They encourage practical risk tak-ing, and support good tries. They follow Fletcher Byrom's ninth commandment: "Make sure you generate a reasonable number of mistakes."

4. *Productivity Through People.* The excellent companies treat the rank and file as the root source of quality and productivity gain. They do not foster we/they labor atti-tudes or regard capital investment as the fundamental source of efficiency improve-ment. As Thomas J. Watson, Jr., said of his company, "IBM's philosophy is largely contained in three simple beliefs. I want to begin with what I think is most important: *our respect for the individual.* This is a simple concept, but in IBM it occupies a major portion of management time." Texas Instruments' chairman Mark Shepherd talks about it in terms of every worker being "seen as a source of ideas, not just acting as a pair of hands"; each of his more than *9,000* People Involvement Program, or PIP, teams (TI's quality circles) does contribute to the company's sparkling productivity record.

5. *Hands-on, Value Driven.* Thomas Watson, Jr., said that "the basic philosophy of an organization has far more to do with its achievements than do technological or eco-nomic resources, organizational structure, innovation and timing." Watson and H-P's

William Hewlett are legendary for walking the plant floors. McDonald's Ray Kroc regularly visits stores and assesses them on the factors the company holds dear, Q.S.C. & V. (Quality, Service, Cleanliness, and Value).

6. *Stick to the Knitting.* Robert W. Johnson, former Johnson & Johnson chairman, put it this way: "Never acquire a business you don't know how to run." Or as Edward G. Harness, past chief executive at Procter & Gamble, said, "This company has never left its base. We seek to be anything but a conglomerate." While there were a few exceptions, the odds for excellent performance seem strongly to favor those companies that stay reasonably close to businesses they know.

7. *Simple Form, Lean Staff.* As big as most of the companies we have looked at are, none when we looked at it was formally run with a matrix organization structure, and some which had tried that form had abandoned it. The underlying structural forms and systems in the excellent companies are elegantly simple. Top-level staffs are lean; it is not uncommon to find a corporate staff of fewer than 100 people running multi-billion-dollar enterprises.

8. *Simultaneous Loose-Tight Properties.* The excellent companies are both centralized and decentralized. For the most part, as we have said, they have pushed autonomy down to the shop floor or product development team. On the other hand, they are fanatic centralists around the few core values they hold dear. 3M is marked by barely organized chaos surrounding its product champions. Yet one analyst argues, "The brainwashed members of an extremist political sect are no more conformist in their central beliefs." At Digital the chaos is so rampant that one executive noted, "Damn few people know who they work for." Yet Digital's fetish for reliability is more rigidly adhered to than any outsider could imagine.

Source: *In Search of Excellence: Lessons from America's Best-Run Companies* by Thomas J. Peters and Robert H. Waterman, Jr. Reprinted by permission of Harper & Row, Publishers, Inc.

---

ing, although they should have made a more research-based argument.) As a consequence of these arguments and similar ones made by other critics, those who would use these eight characteristics must do so with caution. Interestingly, however, a 1984 follow-up to the *Excellence* theory by *Business Week* supported their findings. When 14 of the original sample firms were found to no longer be excellent, in each case, one or more of the eight criteria proved to have been violated.[7]

PIMS and Related Studies

Profit Impact on Market Strategies, or PIMS, was a project organized in 1972 by the Market Science Institute, a nonprofit research organization affiliated with the Harvard School of Business. This project was a strategic information-sharing experience among 57 major North American corporations. The project had two initial phases. In Phase One, only 36 corporations supplied information on some 350 businesses. In Phase Two, 57 companies provided information on 620 businesses.

[7] "Who's Excellent Now," *Business Week*, November 5, 1984, pp. 76–88.

The original intent of the program was to determine the profit impact of market strategy. In addition, the project sought a basis upon which to estimate ROI for organizations in varying situations. Determining such a basis could help the organization to select businesses in which to diversify, projects in which to invest, and projects in which to divest and with which, in general, to balance the corporation's investment portfolio. Information relating to 37 major variables from these corporations was regressed against the ROI of the organizations. The intent was to determine which of these variables was the most explanatory. Some of the more significant contributory variables found included the following:

1. *Market Share*—the ratio of dollar sales by a business in a given time period to total sales by all competitors in the same market.

2. *Product (Service) Quality*—quality of each participating company's offerings appraised on several bases.

3. *Marketing Expenditures*—total cost for sales force, advertising, sales promotion, market research, and marketing administration.

4. *R&D Expenditures*—total cost of prior development of process improvement.

5. *Investment Intensity*—ratio of total investment to sales (has a high negative impact on sales).

6. *Corporate Diversity*—ratios which affect the number of different industrial categories in which most corporations engage.

7. *Other Company Factors*—characteristics of a company that owns a business; the primary concern here is organizational size.[8]

B. A. Kirchhoff believed that the interorganizational analysis used in the PIMS project was subject to methodological problems, caused primarily by the difficulty of equating measurements contained in the different accounting systems employed by the PIMS project firms.[9] Therefore, he analyzed one organization through intraorganizational analysis, choosing two of four major divisions of a capital-intensive manufacturing firm within a mature industry. The firm manufactured separate but technologically similar products. In total, some 50 geographically separate profit centers existed.

Kirchhoff chose 17 factors, several of which were not used in the PIMS project—for example, personnel factors, which he believed would be important for division analysis. He found gross profit per unit and total profit per unit to be important in explaining ROI. These factors were surrogates for market price; therefore, market price was isolated as a major determinant of ROI. Several labor attitude and productivity variables were also shown to be significant. (These are extremely important findings; personnel factors have been given little treatment in strategic literature, but Kirchhoff's results clearly suggest that these factors have a great impact on ROI.) Production also emerged as a significant variable. To summarize, the most important factors can be described as cost control and price factors.

[8] S. Schoeffler, "Profit Impact on Marketing Strategy" (Internal memorandum, Marketing Research Institute, November 1972); S. Schoeffler, R. D. Buzzell, and D. F. Heany, "The Impact of Strategic Planning on Profit Performance," *Harvard Business Review*, March/April 1974, pp. 137–145.

[9] B. A. Kirchhoff, "Empirical Analysis of Strategic Factors Contributing to Return on Investment," (Proceedings: Academy of Management), 1975, pp. 46–48.

"So much for Plan A. Now . . ."

Noticeably absent was the market share variable reported as most important by the PIMS project. Kirchhoff suggests that the PIMS findings were a result of a very high demand in the market for the products of most organizations at the time of the study, including all businesses of the organization he examined. Market share had limited impact at that time. Less favorable economic conditions would probably have caused market share to be more important.

With respect to the total corporation, the number of variables was reduced to eight because of inability to find common measurements for these variables across all four divisions. The inventory to sales ratio exerted the greatest influence on ROI; the less inventory a profit center had, the higher its ROI. Collection period had the second greatest influence; the longer the collection time, the lower the ROI. Sales revenue per salesperson, a measure of salespeople's productivity, was the third major variable. Absenteeism affected the total organization as it had Division A. The three variables that did not have a significant impact were capacity utilization, marketing expenses as a percent of sales revenue, and labor turnover.

The major contribution of Kirchhoff's study is in showing the importance of internal variables as opposed to the external variables emphasized by the PIMS project. The study's finding that the market share variable is not universally important is also significant.

A number of additional studies, across a wide variety of industries has provided general support for the original PIMS behavior.[10] But substantiation for the view that certain behaviors are applicable to all firms is limited empirically. As with any preliminary research, these findings are limited in their applicability until additional supporting research is reported. Furthermore, correlation/regression techniques such as those used in the PIMS project do not truly explain but rather indicate the strengths of relationships. Further, the variables mentioned above have several exceptions. Some are more applicable in certain situations than in others.

For example, these "universal truths," as the PIMS result are sometimes referred to, do not apply to all industries, nor to all firms in all industries, given factors such as market variables, the economy, and market position. Indeed, earlier and later in this chapter, various strategies for those in different positions within the market are noted. Indeed, it is possible that the PIMS results would not be true in some other time period other than that examined (although the few later studies support the PIMS results). Furthermore, there is also a high probability of statistical methodological problems—multicollinearity to be specific. In addition, PIMS assumes only one performance objective.[11] Other explanatory variables exist that either were not included in the PIMS project or did not prove to be sufficiently explanatory in this particular study. Nevertheless, this project has shown that for large, multifaceted business corporations, in varying industries and in differing situations, some common ROI indicators can be found. But the choice of a strategy is at least partially a function of industry. Additional research should isolate commonly successful behaviors for certain industries and for groups of firms within those industries. Finally, implementing the knowledge gained from such research is very difficult. For example, knowing that market share is critical is one thing; gaining it is another.

The meek shall inherit the world, but they'll never increase market share.

▪ *William C. McGowan, then Chairman of MCI Communications* ▪

Porter's Competitive Strategies

Michael Porter has suggested that three major business-level strategies exist for outperforming other corporations engaged in similar activities: overall cost leadership, differ-

---

[10] K. J. Hatten, "Strategic Models in the Brewing Industry" (Ph.D. dissertation, Purdue University, LaFayette, Ind., 1974); "Strategy, Profits, and Beer" (Paper presented at the Academy of Management Meetings, New Orleans, August 1975); The Boston Consulting Group, *Perspectives on Experience* (Boston: The Boston Consulting Group, 1968); the Boston Consulting Group, *Perspectives on Experience* (Boston: The Boston Consulting Group, 1970); W. E. Fruhan, Jr., *The Fight for Competitive Advantage: A Study of U.S. Domestic Trunk Air Carriers* (Boston: Division of Research, Harvard Business School, 1972); W. E. Fruhan, Jr., "Pyrrhic Victories in Fights for Market Share," *Harvard Business Review*, September/October 1972, pp. 100–107; C. R. Anderson and F. T. Paine, "PIMS—A Reexamination," *Academy of Management Review*, July 1978, pp. 602–612; M. Lubatkin and M. Pitts, "PIMS: Fact or Folklore?" *Journal of Business Strategy*, Winter 1983, pp. 38–43.

[11] T. Naylor, "PIMS: Through a Different Looking Glass," *Planning Review*," March 1978; M. Porter, "Market Structure Strategy Formulation and Firm Profitability: The Theory of Strategic Groups and Mobility Barriers," in *Marketing and the Public Interest*, J. Cady, ed. (Cambridge, Mass.: Market Science Institute, 1978); C. R. Anderson and F. T. Paine, "PIMS—A Reexamination," *Academy of Management Review*, July 1978, pp. 602–612; M. Lubatkin and M. Pitts, "PIMS: Fact or Folklore?" *Journal of Business Strategy*, Winter 1983: 38–43; Vasudevan Ramanujam and N. Venkatraman, "An Inventory and Critique of Strategy Research Using the PIMS Database," *Academy of Management Review*, January 1984, pp. 138–151.

entiation, and focus. These "generic" strategies are to be utilized in coping with the five competitive forces related to his competitor analysis approach discussed in Chapter 2.[12]

1. *Cost Leadership*—employs a set of functional policies to achieve the basic objective. This strategy "requires aggressive construction of efficient-scale facilities, vigorous pursuit of cost reductions from experience, tight cost and overhead control, avoidance of marginal customer accounts, and cost minimization in areas like R&D, service, sales force, advertising, and so on. . . . Low cost relative to competitors becomes the theme running through the entire strategy; though quality, service, and other areas cannot be ignored."[13] By having the lowest cost, satisfactory returns will still accrue to this firm even after meeting the costs of competition. Competitors will not be able to make satisfactory levels of return.

2. *Differentiation*—involves creating a product or service that is perceived as being unique throughout the industry. Differentiation allows the firm to have sizable profit margins because of brand loyalty by customers, and their subsequent lower sensitivity to price. Entry barriers are created by customer loyalty. Fewer substitutes are possible than for competitors' undifferentiated products.

3. *Focus*—the thrust of this strategy is to serve a particular target market very well, be it a specific buyer group, a segment of the product line, or a geographic market. The underlying assumption is that by focusing, the firm can provide better service or a better product, and can do so more efficiently. The consequences of this strategy will be either lower cost or differentiation, or both. The narrow target market is the vehicle to achieve these ends.

Successfully implementing these three strategies requires differing skills, resources, and other common organizational requirements. Porter's perspectives on these requirements are contained in Table 4.4.

"Generic" strategies are of modest help, at best. Most businesses consist of complex collections of product-market units which share production and/or marketing functions. The most profitable strategy for the business will depend on the relationships between product market units, market segment economics, competitive position, and the behavior of rivals.

▪ *James M. McTaggart, Marakon Associates* ▪

Porter's strategies are first of all behaviorally based, meaning that they are suggested as appropriate in all situations rather than on a contingency basis (although he does allow for assessment of the situation to see which is most relevant). But many of the complexities of each particular situation are overlooked by generic approaches. For that matter, many of the general criticisms made about PIMS could be applied to Porter's generic strategies and all other behavioral strategies. On the other hand, Porter's strategies are conceptually and intuitively sound. In examining the research, we find one study which lends support to Porter's cost and differentiation strategies. Roderick E. White examined 69 business units and found, not surprisingly, that firms with both cost and price advantages had the highest ROI. The highest sales growth was achieved by those businesses employing a pure differ-

---

[12]M. E. Porter, *Competitive Strategy* (New York: Free Press, 1980), pp. 34–46.
[13]Ibid., p. 35.

Table 4.4   Requirements for Generic Competitive Strategies

Generic Strategy	Commonly Required Skills and Resources	Common Organizational Requirements
Overall cost leadership	Sustained capital investment and access to capital Process engineering skills Intense supervision of labor Products designed for ease in manufacture Low-cost distribution system	Tight cost control Frequent, detailed control reports Structured organization and responsibilities Incentives based on meeting strict quantitative targets
Differentiation	Strong marketing abilities Product enginnering Creative flair Strong capability in basic research Corporate reputation for quality or technological leadership Long tradition in the industry or unique combination of skills drawn from other businesses Strong cooperation from channels	Strong coordination among functions in R&D, product development, and marketing Subjective measurement and incentives instead of quantitative measures Amenities to attract highly skilled labor, scientists, or creative people
Focus	Combination of the above policies directed at the particular strategic target	Combination of the above policies directed at the regular strategic target

Source: M. E. Porter, *Competitive Strategy* (New York: Free Press, 1980), pp. 40–41. Copyright © 1980 by The Free Press, a division of Macmillan Publishing Co., Inc. Reprinted by permission.

entiation strategy. White also examined the relationship of the environmental context to these strategies and firm performance, and found that, indeed, a positive relationship appears to exist.[14]

Additional research by Gregory G. Dess and Peter S. Davis also supports the view that having generic strategies leads to higher performance than not having generic strategies on an intraindustry basis. Employing questionnaires, they examined 22 firms in the same industry.[15] However, not all research is supportive. Carolyn Y. Woo and Karel O. Cool reported that the preliminary analysis of their data was not supportive of Porter's generic strategies. They question whether "generic" strategies are viable descriptions of the strategic process.[16] Obviously more research is necessary in this field before conclusions may be drawn.

Additional Behaviorally Derived Grand Strategies

Several authors have recommended strategies for firms in specific situations. Among them are: P. Varadarajan's[17] strategies for firms seeking intensive growth; R. G. Hamer-

[14] R. E. White, "Generic Business Strategies, Organizational Context and Performance: An Empirical Investigation" (Paper presented to the Academy of Management, Dallas, 1983).

[15] G. G. Dess and P. S. Davis, "Porter's (1980) Generic Strategies as Determinants of Strategic Group Membership and Organizational Performance," *Academy of Management Journal*, September 1984, pp.

[16] C. Y. Woo and K. O. Cool, "Generic Competitive Strategies: Performance and Functional Strategy Complements," (Paper presented to the Strategic Management Society, Paris, October 1983).

[17] P. Varadarajan, "Intensive Growth Strategies," *Atlanta Economic Review*, November/December 1978, pp. 4–11.

Table 4.5   Strategic Guidelines as a Function of Industry Maturity and Competitive Position

	Embryonic	Growing	Mature	Aging
Dominant	All-out push for share	Hold position	Hold position	Hold position
	Hold position	Hold share	Grow with industry	
Strong	Attempt to improve position	Attempt to improve position	Hold position	Hold position or harvest
	All-out push for share	Push for share	Grow with industry	
Favorable	Selective or all-out push for share	Attempt to improve position	Custodial or maintenance	Harvest
	Selectively attempt to improve position	Selective push for share	Find niche and attempt to protect	Phased withdrawal
Tenable	Selectively push for position	Find niche and protect it	Find niche and hang on or phased withdrawal	Phased withdrawal or abandon
Weak	Up or out	Turnaround or abandon	Turnaround or phased withdrawal	Abandon

Source: From Peter Patel and Michael Younger, "A Frame of Reference for Strategy Development," *Long Range Planning*, April 1978, p. 8. Reprinted by permission of Pergamon Press Ltd., Oxford, England.

mesh, M. J. Anderson, Jr., and J. E. Harris's [18] and Philip Kotler's [19] strategies for low-market-share firms; R. G. Hamermesh and S. B. Silk's [20] strategies for firms competing in stagnant industries; Philip Kotler's [21] suggestions for dominant firms; and R. R. Harrigan's [22] suggestions for firms in declining industries. These additional behavioral strategies, and some 200 to 300 more that have been suggested by various authors, are based on the successes of a limited number of firms. This is not to discount their validity but only to remind you that, because of the sample size upon which the recommendations are based, these strategies are worthy of consideration even though they are not steadfast rules for action.

Strategic Recommendations According to Strength and Product Life Cycle Stage

Finally, Peter Patel and Michael Younger have developed a model, shown in Table 4.5, that suggests certain strategies as a function of product life cycle stage and the relative strength of the company. [23]

[18] R. G. Hamermesh, M. J. Anderson, Jr., and J. E. Harris, "Strategies for Low Market Share Businesses," *Harvard Business Review*, May/June 1978, pp. 95–102. Also see C. Y.Y. Woo and A. C. Cooper, "Strategies of Effective Low Share Businesses," *Strategic Management Journal*, April–June 1981, pp. 301–318.

[19] R. G. Hammermesh and S. B. Silk, "How to Compete in Stagnant Industries," *Harvard Business Review*, September/October 1979, pp. 161–168.

[21] P. Kotler, *Marketing Management*, pp. 273–281.

[22] K. R. Harrigan, "Strategy Formulation in Declining Industries," *Academy of Management Review*, October 1980, pp. 599–604.

[23] P. Patel and M. Younger, "A Frame of Reference for Strategy Development," *Long Range Planning*, April 1978, pp. 6–12.

Behavioral Theories: A Commentary

You have been exposed to a number of behavioral strategy formulation theories. Considered in total, they may seem somewhat bewildering. Indeed, there are overlaps and even contradictions among them. The various strategies were presented to provide you first with a feel for the alternatives and second with some ideas for your own strategy formulation as you do case work. The actual decision process is discussed in more detail in the next chapter.

Functional Supportive Strategies as Focal Points of the Grand Strategy

Functional strategies are designed to support the competitive effort of business strategies. There are three types of functional strategies:

1. *Economic Functional Strategies*—involving the functions which allow the firm to exist as an economic entity, such as marketing, and the functions that support marketing and the basic action strategies, such as finance, operations, human resources management, information systems, research and development, and the like. These are vital to many "generic" or "behavioral" strategies.

2. *Management Functional Strategies*—involving the management functions of planning, organizing, implementing, controlling, staffing, leading, motivating, communicating, decision making, representing, and integration.

3. *Strategic Issues Strategies*–used to monitor the environment. There are two major types. One functions to help the organization contend with known contingencies; the other is designed to help the organization overcome surprises. The latter normally involves the creation of several contingency strategies, which have become increasingly popular as the operating environment has become more turbulent and should continue to increase in popularity.

It might be helpful to mention here again that, while marketing is an economic function, it is included as the main part of the business strategy because it is basic to the SBU's central focus—to compete. The other economic functions are grouped here with the functional strategies because their purpose is to support the competitive effort of the business strategy.

Marketing is so basic that it cannot be considered a separate function. . . . It is the whole business seen from the final result, that is, from the customer's point of view.

▪ *Peter Drucker* ▪

It is important to think of the management functions as integrative rather than as separate from the economic functions. As Figure 4.5 reveals, the management functions are performed across all functions of the organization. Thus, marketing, finance, operations, human resources, and the like must all be managed—there must, for example, be marketing planning, financial organizing, operations implementing, and human resources control. Similarly, the management functions must be managed—planning, organizing, implementing, and controlling must be planned, organized, implemented, and controlled.

In examining the role of functional strategies, this text will not define and describe each of the functions. That has been done in other courses. Rather, a few examples of how

Figure 4.5   The Managerial Matrix

Economic and Managerial Functions

Managerial Functions	Marketing	Finance	Operations	Human resources	Information	Research and development	Planning	Organizing	Implementing	Controlling	Staffing	Leading	Motivating	Communicating	Decision making	Representing	Integrating
Planning																	
Organizing																	
Implementing																	
Controlling																	
Staffing																	
Leading																	
Motivating																	
Communicating																	
Decision making																	
Representing																	
Integrating																	

these strategies contribute to business success will be presented to illustrate how important they are. In each of these cases, marketing is not the only driving force for either the grand strategy or the business strategy. Rather another functional strategy fulfills those roles. Extensive information as to the principal components of each of these areas is provided in the strategic audit, Appendix 2.

How Delta Combines Sound Financing and Good People Management

The excellent companies live their commitment to people.

▪ *Thomas J. Peters and Robert H. Waterman, Jr.* ▪

Delta Airlines is, by measure of continued profit, the most successful airline in the United States and has apparently even managed to recover from its slight profit problem resulting from deregulation. There are many reasons for this success. In terms of marketing strategies, "Delta is ready when you are." Delta has a product—a flight—available at the times people need it most. The airline also stresses service. Its planes are on time, its employees are courteous, and it strives to make the customer feel important. Behind its ability to succeed in these areas are two critical factors—its debt structure and its people strategy.

Delta purchased the right airplane fleet for its schedules. That was an operational consideration and an important factor in Delta's success. But perhaps more importantly, Delta purchased this fleet of airplanes at the right price, at the right time, and on the right terms. Eastern Airlines, which competes virtually head-on with Delta in every major market, has to earn millions more than Delta just to break even, because Delta's debt maintenance is so much lower. This gap in debt maintenance has existed for almost ten years, although it has not always been so large. Delta can use this difference in net available cash to pay dividends, improve employee benefits, and improve capital assets.

The second key factor in Delta's success has been its people strategy. Delta attempts to maintain a "family feeling" among members of its work force to encourage employee loyalty and productivity. Despite, and perhaps partially because of, the difficulties it has encountered, Delta's employees are so loyal to the firm that in 1983 they purchased a $30 million plane for the company to show their appreciation for the way the company treated them.[24]

Donnelly Mirrors' Low Prices and High Quality Depend on Productivity, Innovation, and People Management

Donnelly Mirrors dominates what was once a highly competitive, virtually entry-proof industry, the automotive mirror industry. They succeeded by achieving lower prices and higher quality than their competition through management techniques and systems that emphasized productivity, quality, and innovation while rewarding the individual and providing job security. Donnelly encourages its workers to find new ways of saving money, and to do the job faster or cheaper, or to eliminate the job altogether. Its encouragement includes bonuses tied to productivity and guaranteed employment. Allowing employees to participate in decisions that affect the individual or group also plays an important role in its success. Without these strategies, Donnelly could not have been so competitive.[25]

Bank of America Emphasizes Open Communication to Improve Service

The Bank of America has created what it calls "people advocacy programs." In order to improve service and make the bank a better place to work, the bank has opened up communication between managers and their subordinates. The results indicate that the programs have been phenomenally successful. Like Delta's people policies, these programs show that employees are more committed to organizational goals when they perceive corporate concern for them to be high. Included in the six people advocacy programs are the following three:

- *Employee Assistance Department.* If work-related problems cannot be solved through routine company channels, an entire department is available to devote its time and energy to solving these problems.

[24] L. Lawrence, "Thank You Delta Airlines," *Readers Digest*; "Airline Woes Catch up with Delta," *Business Week*, November 8, 1982, pp. 131–132.

[25] "Participative Management at Work: An Interview with John F. Donnelly," *Harvard Business Review*, January/February 1978, pp. 117–127.

Figure 4.6   Major Strategic Choices—a Decision Tree

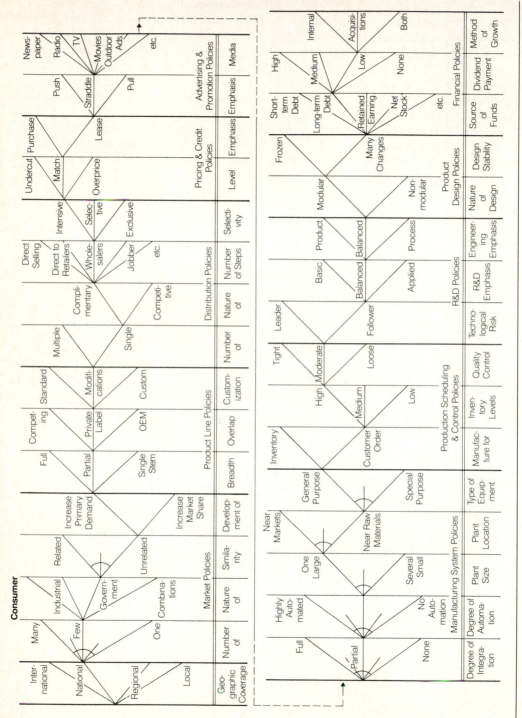

Source: C. W. Hofer, "Conceptual Constructs for Formulating Corporate and Business Strategy," Dover, MA: Case Teacher's Association, #BP-0041, p. 14. Copyright © 1971 by C. W. Hofer. Reproduced by permission.

- *Let's Talk It Over.* A six-step formal problem-solving process through the bank's officers is another alternative.
- *Open Line.* A telephone system is available to receive employees' questions. The person who asks the question receives a written answer in a short time.[26]

The Rediscovery of Production

> *We cannot afford to become a nation of video arcades*
> *and drive-in banks and McDonald's hamburger stands.*
>
> ▪ Lee Iacocca (speaking of the need to strengthen American industries–1984) ▪

American industry had neglected its production operations for some time, but Japanese competition in the late 1970s and early 1980s reawakened its concern for production strategies. If you walk through an American manufacturing firm today, you will notice several striking factors. First, there are fewer people actively involved in the process than there were a few years ago. Much of this change can be attributed to technology-robotics, computers, and "old-fashioned" automation. Secondly, those individuals who remain are more personally involved in the decision-making process. Third, there is an all-encompassing concern for quality. The consumer demands it, and because much of the competition is providing it, so must the American organization. (This is also true in service organizations.)

We have witnessed a virtual revolution in the production function of industry. There exists an entirely new attitude about the importance of operations, and there are new approaches for managing production including: lower levels of inventories—often zero in what is referred to as stockless production; a reexamination and redesign of work flows, job structures, and production schedules. Even "smokestack" firms have been made profitable. This is no easy task, and it requires capital. Nevertheless, substantial progress has been made.[27]

The Supportive Strategies

In each of the above cases, the supportive strategies were essential to the success of the marketing effort. They were so important, in fact, that they became the grand strategy, the mission-competitive strategy. Thus, support strategies and basic action strategies are often integral components of the business strategy, and often more important than that.

Charles Hofer has provided a vital perspective regarding selected functional strategies and their relevance to the business strategy. This perspective is revealed in Figure 4.6.

---

[26] A. W. Clausen, D. W. Ewing, and P. M. Banks, "Listening and Responding to Employees' Concerns," *Harvard Business Review*, January/February 1980, p. 101.

[27] J. Nakane and R. W. Hall, "Management Specs for Stockless Production," *Harvard Business Review*, May/June 1983, pp. 83–91; S. C. Wheelwright and R. H. Hayes, "Competing through Manufacturing," *Harvard Business Review*, January/February, 1985, pp. 99–109; "The Revival of Productivity," *Business Week*, February 13, 1984, pp. 92–100; H. C. Meal, "Putting Production Decisions where They Belong," *Harvard Business Review*, March/April 1984, pp. 102–111; and L. P. Ritzman, B. E. King, and L. J. Krajewski, "Manufacturing Performance—Pulling the Right Levers," *Harvard Business Review*, March/April, 1984, pp. 143–152.

This figure may be utilized as a resource in determining the types of functional strategies that a business organization should develop. Note also his guidance on marketing and certain basic action strategies.

Summary

The contingency theory of strategy formulation is conceptually appropriate but difficult to utilize because of the numerous variables involved. Several behavioral theories offer sound alternatives to the contingency theory. The behavioral strategies are based partly on research and partly on experience and suggest that, in most situations or in selected situations, certain strategies are best. The key to most contingency and behavioral theories is the life cycle stage of the particular product or service.

Supportive functional strategies are extremely critical to the success of the organization. For a few firms, these strategies do not just support the competitive effort but may become the critical components of that effort. There are two major types of supportive strategies: the economic functional strategies and the management functional strategies. A third type is strategic issues functional strategies. All strategies, including the management strategies, must be managed, as the management matrix reveals.

Most but not all of the strategies reviewed in this chapter are grand strategies founded on basic action strategies—corporate-level, mission-determination strategies. Several of those discussed concentrated on marketing (business-level, primary mission strategies) and on other functional strategies (mission-supportive strategies).

Key Terms and Concepts

By the time you have completed this chapter, you should be familiar with the following key terms and concepts: the contingency approach to business-level strategy formulation, major contingency variables, the behavioral theory of strategy formulation, major behaviorally derived strategies, the impacts of the product life cycle on strategy formulation, functional supportive strategies, economic functional strategies, management functional strategies, and strategic issues strategies.

Discussion Questions

1. Hofer's Contingency Theory of Business Strategy represented in Table 4.1 relates six organizational variables that are significant at different stages of the product life cycle. Are these six variables the only variables of importance? Suggest any additional variables which may be important.

2. Examine the Directional Policy Matrix represented in Figure 4.4. One of the strategies, "Phased Withdrawal," appears twice. Why? Is this a typing error?

3. Peters and Waterman in their 1982 book, *In Search of Excellence*, identified eight descriptive characteristics which they believe to be common denominators in the best-run companies. What are these eight characteristics? Are they still valid in today's business environment?

4. What was the original intent of the PIMS project? How has this changed over the years since 1972?

5. What are the three "genesis" strategies as proposed by M. E. Porter?

6. Provide examples of the importance of functional-supportive strategies for both economic and management functions. Can you name firms where their strategists are the focal point of the grand strategy?

7. Peters and Waterman have said that "the excellent companies live their commitment to people." Analyze a firm such as Hewlett-Packard, where this concept has been implemented and is vital to the firm's success. Why does it work? If it is so successful, why don't more firms employ a "people orientation"?

8. Choose a well-known firm such as IBM, Burroughs, or Xerox and determine how it has varied the four components of its human resources strategy for one of its SBUs as it progresses through the various stages of maturity.

References

Bussey, John. "Smokestack Managers Moving to High Tech Find the Going Tough." *The Wall Street Journal*, January 10, 1985, 114.

DeSanto, John F. "Work Force Planning and Corporate Strategy." *Personnel Administrator*, October 1983: 33–36.

Galosy, Julia Reid. "Meshing Human Resources Planning with Strategic Business Planning: One Company's Experience." *Personnel*, September/October 1983: 26–35.

Guyon, Janet, "AT&T Says Job Reductions Will Yield up to $500 Million in Annual Savings." *The Wall Street Journal*, October 8, 1984, p. 7.

Hall, William K. "Survival Strategies in a Hostile Environment." *Harvard Business Review*, September/October 1980, pp. 75–85.

Harrigan, Kathryn Rudie. "Strategic Planning for Endgame." *Long Range Planning*, Vol. 15, No. 6, 1982, pp. 45–48.

Koten, John. "New Generation—PepsiCo Gambles Big On an Ad Campaign with Michael Jackson." *The Wall Street Journal*, February 28, 1984, pp. 1 and 6.

Lubatkin, Michael, and Pitts, Michael. "PIMS: Fact or Folklore?" *The Journal of Business Strategy*, Winter 1983, pp. 38–43.

Mahon, John F., and Murray, Edwin A., Jr. "Strategic Planning for Regulated Companies." *Strategic Management Journal*, Vol. 2, 1981, pp. 251–262.

Misa, Kenneth F. and Stein, Timothy. "Strategic HRM and the Bottom Line." *Personnel Administrator*, October 1983, pp. 27–30.

Neidich, Daniel, and Steinberg, Thomas M. "Corporate Real Estate: Source of New Equity?" *Harvard Business Review* July/August 1984: 76–83.

O'Boyle, Thomas F. "Steel Companies Give Their Finance Staffs More Prominent Role in Solving Problems." *The Wall Street Journal*, August 8, 1984, pp. 33–34.

Sibson, Robert E. "Strategic Personnel Planning." *Personnel Administrator*, October 1983, pp. 37–40.

Smith, Eddie C. "Strategic Business Planning and Human Resources: Part I." *Personnel Journal*, August 1982, pp. 606–610.

Winslow, Ron. "Union Carbide Mobilizes Resources to Control Damage from Gas Leak." *The Wall Street Journal*, December 10, 1984, p. 29.

5

The Master Strategy in Multiple-SBU Firms

Destiny is not a matter of chance, it is a matter of choice; it is not a thing to be waited for, it is a thing to be achieved.

▪ *William Jennings Bryan* ▪

In the previous chapter, the master strategy of the individual business unit was examined. This chapter identifies the ways in which multiple-SBU organizations can combine the strategic efforts of various component businesses to achieve organizational objectives. The master strategy in multiple-SBU organizations focuses primarily on portfolio management techniques in combination with a limited number of master policy guidelines and a philosophy of substantial decentralization. Growth through diversification is a typical grand strategy. In the conglomerate or other multiple-SBU firm, each SBU usually operates as an independent company with only limited guidance from above.

The principal tasks that multiple-SBU firms' strategists must accomplish are:

1. Establishing strategic objectives.
2. Determining whether current businesses are helping achieve those objectives and, subsequently, determining what actions to take regarding those businesses.
3. Determining what objectives remain to be accomplished.
4. Determining what actions to take to achieve the remaining objectives of the total organization.
5. Establishing support functions and master policies for SBUs.

Establishing strategic objectives was discussed in Chapter 3. This chapter reviews the processes involved in answering questions 2, 3, 4, and 5 above, focusing primarily on the portfolio management matrix technique. In addition, this chapter discusses policies, functional support, and decentralization as key elements in the successful strategic management of multiple-SBU firms. Finally, it presents a brief commentary on the differences in perspectives between organizational and divisional strategists.

Figures 5.1 and 5.2 indicate which portions of the major strategic processes are examined in this chapter. Figure 5.3 illustrates the relationships between the various types of strategies in a multiple-SBU firm.

Corporate Strategy at the Level of the Total Organization

The corporate strategy at the total organizational level for the multiple-SBU organization is comprised of the components in Table 3.2 in a somewhat different fashion than is the strategy for the single-SBU organization, which parallels Table 3.2 almost precisely. The

Figure 5.1   The Organization—a Strategic Management Process Model

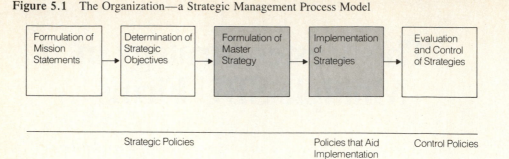

Strategic Policies		Policies that Aid Implementation	Control Policies

multiple-SBU corporation acts primarily as a coordinating unit, providing direction and service to individual SBUs. It establishes policy guidelines for the enterprise strategy. Corporate headquarters also provides certain functional services and related policies for common areas of need—typically finance, personnel, and planning services. And it provides policy in virtually all business strategy and functional and economic strategy areas. But the primary concern of the multiple-SBU firm headquarters is the corporate strategy.

For multiple-SBU firms, the essence of the corporate strategy, and hence master strategy, at the level of the total organization is portfolio management. Just as an investment counselor seeks synergy and balance in an individual's personal investment portfolio, the strategists for a multiple-SBU firm attempt to achieve these ends in terms of businesses in the total organization portfolio. But the same basic issues prevalent in any strategic situation must be addressed:

1.   **Where are we now?**

2.   **Where do we want to be?**

3.   **How do we get there?**

Portfolio Management Techniques

The portfolio matrix is only one of several portfolio techniques used by multiple-SBU firms, but a vital one. There are several major types of portfolio matrices. Historically, the most important of these include: the Boston Consulting Group (BCG) business portfolio matrix (Figure 5.4), the General Electric business screen (Figures 5.5 and 5.6), and the product/market/industry evolution portfolio matrix (Figure 5.7). Their applicability depends on the circumstances in which they are to be used.[1] Of the three, the BCG matrix is not used very much anymore because more sophisticated techniques exist, and because the variables it examines are not viewed to be as critical as they once were. A GE-type matrix can be used where the products and market segments involved are diverse, and the product/market/industry evolution matrix should be used where the products and market segments involved are limited in type.[2]

[1] Y. Wind and V. Mahajan, "Designing Product and Business Portfolios," *Harvard Business Review*, January/February 1981, pp. 155–165; M. B. Coate, "Pitfalls in Portfolio Planning," *Long Range Planning*, June 1983, pp. 47–56.

[2] "The Future Catches up with a Strategic Planner," *Business Week*, June 27, 1983, p. 62.

Figure 5.2 Objective Determination and Master Strategy Formulation

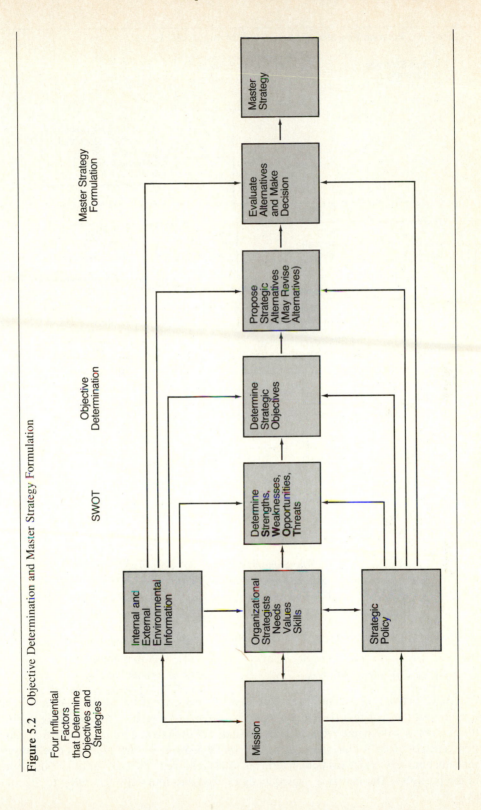

Figure 5.3   Relationships among Strategies in Multiple-SBU Firms

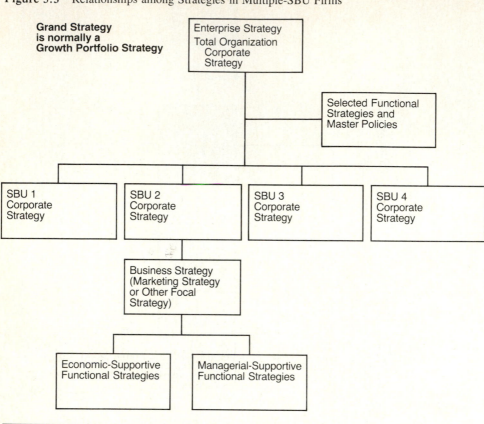

Using any of the strategic matrices involves plotting two factors against one another on a grid in order to arrive at some appropriate strategy. Understanding how these grids function will aid your insight into why they are used.

> *From 1981 to 1983, the number of large U.S. corporate acquisitions*
> *grew at a rate roughly double that of the 1970s and even exceeded the*
> *one realized during the famous merger wave of the 1960s.*
> *The drama . . . has generated an enormous amount of criticism.*

▪ *Michael C. Jensen,* Harvard Business Review, *November–December, 1984, p. 109.* ▪

The BCG Business Matrix

The BCG matrix is shown in Figure 5.4. To use it, the strategist plots the business's relative competitive position (horizontal axis) as expressed by relative market share against the business's growth rate (vertical axis), the industry growth rate for the business in question. The company is represented as a circle on the matrix, and the size of a circle represents that business's size (usually in terms of sales) relative to the sizes of other businesses in the portfolio. The matrix is subsequently divided into four cells according to the rela-

Figure 5.4   The BCG Business Matrix

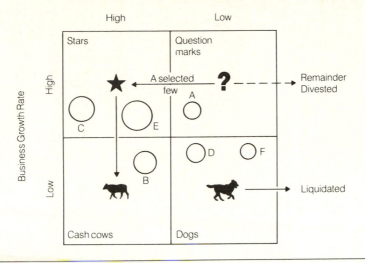

Source: Adapted from Barry Hedley, "Strategy and the Business Portfolio," *Long Range Planning* (February 1977), p. 10. Reprinted by permission of Pergamon Press Ltd., Oxford, England.

tive desirability of four combinations of competitive position and growth, which are symbolized by stars, question marks, cash cows, and dogs. Once the firm is positioned in the matrix, the strategic actions that should be employed can be identified. The basic assumptions underlying this matrix are that market share in growth markets leads to profitability, but that in slow-growing markets, obtaining market share takes too much cash. Thus, firms in slow-growing markets should either be invested in, or be "milked" of cash and divested.

Stars represent the best profit and growth potentials. These businesses show rapid growth and are self-sustaining with respect to cash flow. The company that owns such a business should continue full steam ahead. Acquiring such businesses—at the right price—is also vital.

Question marks usually have the poorest cash flows. They require large amounts of cash because they are growing; however, they are not self-sustaining because their market share is low. As their title indicates, their progress must be monitored closely. The organization that owns the business naturally hopes it will grow into a star; but if it does not, it should be divested. If a firm believes a business it does not already own may grow into a star, acquisition at the right price is desirable.

Cash cows have low growth and high market share. They also have large cash flows, because their market shares are high. They require little investment, and thus can be milked of their cash to support other businesses, especially new enterprises—for example, question marks. If market share declines and cash flow consequently subsides, they may be divested. Or the firm may choose to invest in them once again. But the firm must be careful lest they become dogs. Seldom do cash cows become available for acquisition; however, if the opportunity for acquisition at a good price presents itself, it should be taken advantage of.

Figure 5.5   General Electric's "Stoplight Strategy" for Planning

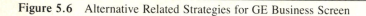

The Stoplight

G   Growth

Y   Borderline

R   No-Growth

Figure 5.6   Alternative Related Strategies for GE Business Screen

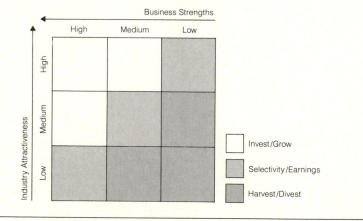

Dogs are not desirable investments. They require large cash flows but have poor competitive positions and are therefore either unprofitable or, at best, have low profitability. The owning firm should divest. Dogs are, obviously, not suitable targets for acquisition.[3]

The BCG matrix was an important development in multiple-SBU strategic planning because it determined three key factors in strategic success for such organizations—cash flow, market share, and industry growth. However, like most single management systems, the matrix oversimplifies many of the critical factors involved. For example, high and low positions on the two axes are simplistic. And, the dimensions of growth rate and market

[3]B. Hedley, "Strategy and the 'Business Portfolio,'" *Long Range Planning*, February 1977, pp. 9–15.

Figure 5.7   A Product/Market/Industry Evolution Portfolio Matrix

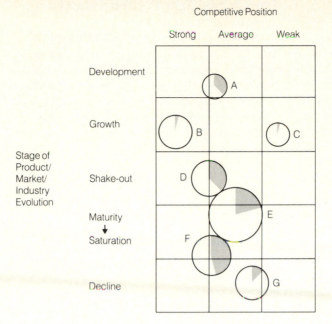

share are only one aspect of industry attractiveness and competitive position, respectively.[4] The GE business screen forces strategists to consider more of these variables.

The GE Business Screen

Most of the weaknesses inherent in the BCG matrix are eliminated in the General Electric business screen (Figures 5.5 and 5.6). The GE matrix employs composite measures of both business strength and industry attractiveness. These composites are essential additions. They allow nine possible positions or types of firms with advisable strategies to be identified, instead of four. Information Capsule 5.1 briefly summarizes the important points of the GE business screen.

The Product/Market/Industry Evolution Portfolio Matrix

As you can see in Figure 5.7, using a product/market/industry matrix involves plotting the firm's competitive position against the stage of product/market evolution in the product or industry life cycle. Various businesses are shown as pie slices (market share) of total industry (circles). The size of the circles indicates the relative size of the industries.[5] It is generally believed that conglomerate and other multi-SBU organizations should seek to have businesses in all stages of respective industry/product life cycles, with the largest

---

[4]C. W. Hofer and D. Schendel, *Strategy Formulation: Analytical Concepts* (St. Paul, Minn.: West, 1978), pp. 31–32.

[5]C. W. Hofer, "Conceptual Constructs for Formulating Corporate and Business Strategies," #9-378-754 (Boston: Intercollegiate Case Clearing House), 1977.

INFORMATION CAPSULE 5.1
The GE Stoplight Portfolio Matrix

The General Electric Company has pioneered the development of an advanced portfolio matrix to determine which SBUs or major products it wishes to retain in its portfolio, which it wishes to delete, and how it wants to treat those that it retains. With minor adjustments in the criteria employed, this matrix can also be used to evaluate potential acquisitions, mergers, or new product developments. The GE Strategic Business Planning Grid, or "stoplight strategy" as it is known, employs the use of different colored cells in a nine-cell matrix to indicate which strategies it should follow for various businesses. SBUs or products are located on the grid based on an evaluation of the attractiveness of the industry in which these are found and upon GE's strengths in that business. Both industry attractiveness and GE business strength are rated as either high, medium, or low. The term "stoplight strategy" is applied to this matrix because of the green, yellow, and red color coding employed to identify various classifications of businesses or products according to their desirability. Those firms which turn up in the green (G), are to be invested in and will employ growth strategies. Those SBUs which turn up in the red (R) will no longer be invested in and may become cash cows and/or divested. Those which end up in the yellow (Y) are monitored for progress, for change in either industry attractiveness or business strengths. Large SBUs may have products that fall into each of these three categories.

In Figure 5.5, stoplight grid A indicates that the subject organization has medium business strengths but high industry attractiveness. Since the evaluations intersect in a green box, the business would receive an invest and grow strategy treatment. Stoplight matrix B portrays a business in which the business strength is low and the industry attractiveness is low. As a result, the business is in a red zone, and will be harvested and ultimately divested, with reduced or no investment occurring, and with cash extraction occurring where possible before divestment. Stoplight grid C characterizes a firm with low business strengths but high industry attractiveness. Consequently, the firm lands in a yellow cell of the matrix and will thus be monitored for progress. Those firms that prove worthwhile from a potential earnings standpoint will be selected for invest and grow strategies. Those that do not will be divested.

One intriguing point about the grid is that it allows the firm to compare apples and oranges using the same system. With some 50 SBUs, GE needs just such an ability. Perhaps more importantly, the grid allows GE to evaluate factors such as social responsibility and employee loyalty as well as such quantitative factors as return on investment, market share, and cash flow. Each SBU or major product is evaluated during the annual planning review. A consensus is almost always reached by those present. Final strategic decisions are made by the corporate policy committee which consists of several members of top management.

Typical criteria include:

For business strengths/competitive position:
- Size
- Growth
- Share
- Position

For industry attractiveness:
- Size
- Market growth, pricing
- Market diversity
- Competitive structure

- Profitability
- Margins
- Technology position
- Image
- Pollution
- People

- Industry profitability
- Technical role
- Social factors
- Environmental factors
- Legal factors
- Human factors

Note that the factors considered include not only competitive and supportive factors, such as sales, profit, and loss, but also factors more difficult to quantify, such as technology needs, social responsibility, and employee needs.

Like the BCG matrix, the screen is used primarily to manage the current or prospective businesses of the organization, especially in balancing the investment portfolio. GE uses the grid to determine the type of strategy it should employ based on the assessment of factors illustrated in Figure 5.5. Figure 5.6 shows the alternative related strategies. For current or potential businesses judged to be in the green sectors of the matrix, a growth strategy will be followed. For those positioned in the yellow sectors of the matrix, a selective strategy based on earnings will be pursued. For those in the red sectors, a harvest/divest strategy will be employed. The matrix can be used to reevaluate investments as the environment changes; the strategists simply change the criteria (the factors considered) and the relative weights given to the criteria.

The matrix technique has been commonly used by large organizations for business project and product selection, although the color coding is perhaps unique to GE. For example, the PIMS (Profit Impact of Marketing Strategy) Project organizations, some fifty of them, have employed this type of matrix for several years for market share analysis and project selection. McKinsey & Co. has also employed a similar nine-cell "business assessment array" matrix in its strategic consulting practice.

One of the major criticisms of nine-cell matrices is that they do not provide sufficient information on market growth. The following matrix attempts to overcome this deficiency.

and most profitable firms being in the maturity stage or the late growth stage. This is, of course, similar to the classic marketing strategy of having products in various stages of the product life cycle within the same industry. Arthur D. Little Inc., has devised a modification of the product/market/industry evolution matrix which incorporates recommended strategies. This modification is shown in Figure 5.8. (Note that the axes have been rotated in the ADL version.) Their strategies are essentially the same as those employed in the GE Business Screen or the McKinsey nine-cell business assessment array.

It is probably best to use all three of the matrices discussed above in the assessment process. Similar information can be used for all three; and the sophistication of the results is greatly enhanced when all three are used. However, while the underlying concepts of the matrices appear to allow for substantial precision, the actual mechanics of their use often involves a considerable amount of subjective estimation, as the following description of the assessment process reveals. Furthermore, the matrices provide only one approach, albeit an important one.

Figure 5.8   The ADL Portfolio Planning Matrix

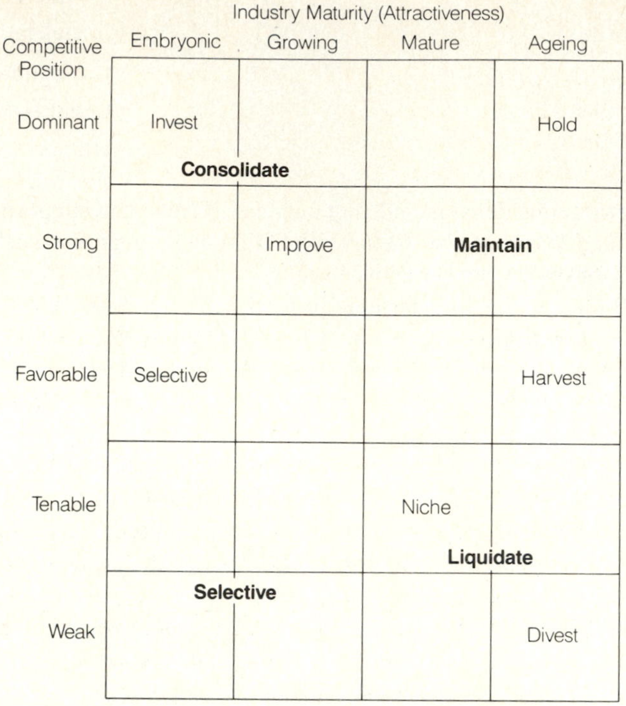

Industry Maturity (Attractiveness)

Competitive Position	Embryonic	Growing	Mature	Ageing
Dominant	Invest			Hold
		Consolidate		
Strong		Improve	Maintain	
Favorable	Selective			Harvest
Tenable			Niche	
			Liquidate	
		Selective		
Weak				Divest

The Assessment Process

Like business strategy and corporate strategy for single-business organizations, the corporate strategy for multiple-SBU firms focuses on evaluating SWOT. Assessing competitive position (what GE refers to as business strengths) requires a thorough analysis of business strengths and weaknesses. Assessing industry attractiveness requires a thorough analysis of opportunities and threats. The matrices merely combine these factors in an organized fashion. Using the GE business screen as an example, we will now examine how a business's position on the matrices is determined. Note how both the questions of "where we are" and "where we want to be" are addressed in the information provided by the matrix.

The process begins with some statement of criteria for both business strengths (competitive position) and industry attractiveness. Developing these criteria is, of course, a complex and highly subjective process, although research, such as the PIMS project mentioned in Chapter 4, and experience can help. The information sources cited at the end of Chapter 2 should be used in this process.

As noted earlier, criteria often evaluated for business strengths include size, growth, share, position, profitability, margins, technology position, image, pollution, and people. The criteria believed to determine success vary from industry to industry; but as we saw in the PIMS results, some common criteria, such as market share, seem to be determinants of success in almost all businesses. Industry attractiveness criteria might include size, market growth and pricing, market diversity, competitive structure, industry profitability, technical role, social factors, environmental factors, legal factors, and human factors. The company using these criteria has determined that any business it chooses to enter must score well on them. These criteria also vary from company to company, depending on numerous variables—risk propensity, top-management values, and so forth.

The actual mathematical calculations involved in the assessment process vary. Firms typically create checklists of the above factors and then note each of the factors according to some scale for measuring excellence. Firms often assign nonparametric values—checks, pluses, minuses, and zeroes—as a scale description. For example, a firm might assign strong plus, plus, neutral, minus, and strong minus to each line item in a strategic factors checklist: strengths and weaknesses, threats and opportunities. Or ordinal values such as $+2, +1, 0, -1, -2$ might be assigned. Various techniques are employed to interpret the meanings of these checklists. Normally, simple scanning or mathematical summation of assigned values is employed. Also, some descriptive or mathematical cut-off point is usually established which will indicate the desirability of a strategic action, for example, investment. This is an extremely complex process and one which requires careful consideration. Frequently no value is assigned; executives may simply vote based on their perceptions of each item's worth. Following is an example of how the mathematical computation process typically occurs.

"There's a gentleman here with $643 million.
He'd like to discuss a takeover."

Table 5.1   An Industry Attractiveness Assessment Matrix

Attractiveness Criteria	Weight[a]	Rating[b]	Weighted Score
Size	.15	4	.60
Growth	.12	3	.36
Pricing	.05	3	.15
Market diversity	.05	2	.10
Competitive structure	.05	3	.15
Industry profitability	.20	3	.60
Technical role	.05	4	.20
Inflation vulnerability	.05	2	.10
Cyclicality	.05	2	.10
Customer financials	.10	5	.50
Energy impact	.08	4	.32
Social	GO	4	—
Environmental	GO	4	—
Legal	GO	4	—
Human	.05	4	.20
	1.00		3.38

[a] Some criteria may be of a GO/NO GO type. For example, many *Fortune* 500 firms probably would decide not to invest in industries that are viewed negatively by our society, such as gambling, even if it were both legal and very profitable to do so.

[b] 1: very unattractive.
5: high attractive.

Source: Reproduced by permission from *Strategy Formulation: Analytical Concepts* by Charles W. Hofer and Dan Schendel. Copyright © 1978 by West Publishing Company. All rights reserved.

Assessing Industry Attractiveness

According to Hofer and Schendel, there are four steps in assessing industry attractiveness once the attractiveness criteria have been chosen:[6]

1.   The firm attaches priorities to the criteria factors in the form of weights.

2.   Each industry in which the firm currently competes or might compete is rated according to these factors, typically on some scale—say, a scale of 1 to 5.

3.   A weighted score is calculated for each industry.

4.   The weighted scores are evaluated against some experience-based standard, against other industries, or both.

Table 5.1 illustrates this process.

The weights assigned to industry attractiveness criteria directly reflect how important top management perceives each to be in accomplishing objectives. The sum of all weights must add to 1. Because of the possible differences among executives in how they perceive the importance of these criteria, several iterations of assigning weights may be necessary before the 1 is reached. Often, using GO or NO GO, instead of using a weight, may suf-

[6] C. W. Hofer and D. Schendel, *Strategy Formulation: Analytical Concepts* (St. Paul, Minn.: West, 1978), pp. 72–75.

fice. For example, where negative social factors exist, the firm may decide on a NO GO position regardless of other factors.

Rating individual industries simply involves evaluating how well that industry is doing. Other industries should be kept in mind as this process occurs, as should the overall state of the economy. Once a weighted score is obtained, then the firm may be plotted on the matrix. The choice of a scale is important to where a firm ends up on the matrix; this issue will be discussed shortly.

Assessing Competitive Position

Like assessing industry attractiveness, assessing competitive position, according to Hofer and Schendel, involves identifying success criteria and then following a four-step process:[7]

1.   For each industry, the firm must weight the relative importance of the various success factors to the specific industry in question.

2.   For each of its businesses, the firm must rate the competitive position of that business in that industry for each factor.

3.   A weighted average must be computed.

4.   Comparisons with standards and other businesses must be made.

Table 5.2 illustrates the steps in this process.

Key success factors have two main characteristics: management can influence them; and changes in them could, at least theoretically, have a significant impact on the firm's competitive position. The weighting process may once again involve several iterations before the desired sum of 1 is reached. In highly segmented markets, weights may vary significantly among market segments.

Placing the SBU on the Matrix

Once a total weighted score for both competitive position (business strengths) and industry attractiveness have been calculated, the location of these numbers on the matrix must be plotted. A key question involves what the scales of the two axes should be. Firms set these scales based on experience. The authors have found that few firms ever score below 1.5 or above 4.5 on either axis; so setting a low point of 1.5 and a high point of 4.5 for each axis seems reasonable. Exceptions can be placed on the axis itself. This scaling yields a 1-by-1 interval per square on the matrix. Utilizing this method, Figure 5.9 portrays the firm (A) characterized in Tables 5.1 and 5.2 as well as several other firms.

Gap Analysis

Often, a gap exists between SBU performance and corporate objectives. Gap analysis involves determining the contribution that current businesses are making or can make to present and future organizational strategic objectives. The various business matrices are good indicators of what is occurring and what may be expected to occur in the way of

[7] Ibid., pp. 75–79.

Table 5.2   A Competitive Position Assessment Matrix

Key Success Factors	Weight	Rating[b]	Weighted Score
Market share	.10	5	.50
SBU growth rate	X[a]	3	—
Breadth of product line	.05	4	.20
Sales distribution effectiveness	.20	4	.80
Proprietary and key account advantages	X	3	—
Price competitiveness	X	4	—
Advertising and promotion effectiveness	.05	4	.20
Facilities location and newness	.05	5	.25
Capacity and productivity	X	3	—
Experience curve effects	.15	4	.60
Raw materials cost	.05	4	.20
Value added	X	4	—
Relative product quality	.15	4	.60
R and D advantages/position	.05	4	.20
Cash throw-off	.10	5	.50
Caliber of personnel	X	4	—
General image	.05	5	.25
	1.00		4.30

[a]For any particular industry, there will be some factors that, while important in general, will have little or no effect on the relative competitive position of firms within that industry. It is usually better to drop such factors from the analysis than to assign them very low weights.

[b]1: very weak competitive position
  5: very strong competitive position

Source: Reproduced by permission from *Strategy Formulation: Analytical Concepts* by Charles W. Hofer and Dan Schendel. Copyright © 1978 by West Publishing Company. All rights reserved.

Figure 5.9   Placing the SBU on the Matrix (Using the GE Business Screen)

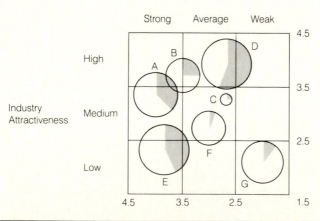

contribution. Contingency strategies recommended for each business are also portrayed by the matrices.

The most desirable portfolio of businesses obviously contains no money-losers. Certainly, having no more than one or two SBUs awaiting divestment is advisable. Meanwhile, the organization's largest and most profitable businesses should be growing in sales or profit areas. All this portrays an ideal but infrequently obtainable profile. It is also possible that a firm may prefer a different type of portfolio—for example, one that focuses on long-term growth at the expense of current profit.

If current businesses are not contributing sufficiently to organizational objectives or are expected not to contribute in the future, then six possibilities for fundamental action exist, as identified by Hofer and Schendel:[8]

1. Change the investment strategies of some or all of the SBUs.
    Change the level of resources allocated to an SBU.

2. Change the business strategies of one or more SBUs.

3. Add some new SBUs to the corporate portfolio.

4. Delete some existing SBUs from the corporate portfolio.

5. Change the way the organization relates to external environmental stakeholders—for example, suppliers, consumers, government, and so on. This involves political strategies.

6. Change strategic objectives.

Most businesses overpay significantly for their acquisitions, and then they have the nerve to wonder why ROI declines.

■ *James M. Higgins* ■

Closing the Gap

The choice of which of these six actions to take is not based strictly on the portfolio matrix results. The portfolio is part of a broader group of considerations, including the mix of businesses in the current portfolio; recent portfolio actions; the ability to integrate new firms into the portfolio; cash position; major potential environmental threats and opportunities; current resource allocation policies; the value orientations of top management, especially their risk propensities; corporate objectives; and the existing strategies of the SBUs themselves.

In selecting the businesses in which the organization will engage, strategists look for synergy and balance among existing and future businesses. Synergy, you may recall, is the degree to which SBUs reinforce each other in pursuit of objectives. The strategist may consider whether the organizations' managerial skills are transferable; whether the firms are technologically similar; whether the businesses have some common theme, such as markets; whether compatability in distribution exists; and so forth. Information Capsule 5.2 reveals some of the intricacies involved in achieving synergy.

---

[8] Ibid., Chapter 7.

INFORMATION CAPSULE 5.2
The Elusive Synergy

A firm chooses to become a conglomerate or a multi-SBU, single-industry firm for any number of reasons. Some seek protection from the vagaries of the economic cycle or an industry cash flow cycle. Others are attempting to counterbalance product and industry life cycles. Still others do so to prevent being taken over themselves, while others aim to improve funds utilization. Whatever the cause, diversifying, acquiring, and merging, whether conglomerate or otherwise, is an extremely popular grand strategy for many firms in the 1980s. Research by Royal Little, founder of Textron, indicates that conglomerates financially outperformed nonconglomerate firms (in return on stockholders equity) for the period from 1980 to 1983. Such news continues to encourage many firms to jump on the acquisition or merger bandwagon. Some, such as Monsanto, which found itself with a late-maturity core business of petrochemicals, feel they have no choice but to diversify, and quickly. In certain industries, such as petroleum and foods, diversification, often conglomerate but also along industry lines, is an accepted practice for long-term survival. For example, in 1984 the three biggest mergers were Chevron's acquisition of Gulf, Texaco's acquisition of Getty Oil, and Mobil's acquisition of Superior Oil. In the food industry, Beatrice gobbled up Esmark, among others. But for some, finding that critical synergy, that balance so vital to success, is an elusive objective. And for many of those who survive a takeover or merger, the adjustment process is difficult at best. Four firms which typify the problems that one may encounter in going the conglomerate route are Exxon, General Motors, Raytheon, and Gulf.

Exxon found conglomerate diversification a dissatisfying experience. It dropped a bundle on the Reliance Electric acquisition, abandoning efforts to compete in the office-of-the-future market after losing $500 million or more on Qyx. It also found its oil shale acquisitions to be nonproductive. Now, it's in the petroleum business with a tough new financial strategy, and that's where it intends to focus its future efforts. Similarly, Raytheon found its acquisition of Lexitron and its intrusion into the high-tech office market to be a big disappointment. It never seemed to understand that market. None of its product entries succeeded. Raytheon even found difficulty recruiting engineers for the data systems division because Lexitron's main business was defense. Raytheon finally gave up on the strategy, and sold its data systems division in 1984 at a substantial loss.

In a different vein, some at GM wonder who acquired whom as its $2.5 billion acquisition of Electronic Data Systems has proven to many that the organizational culture of the parent firm does not always dominate that of the acquired firm. EDS employees "have come on like gangbusters." GM's automatic pay raises for white-collar employees have been eliminated for those 10,000 transferred to the EDS division, whose philosophy is pay for performance. Furthermore, there is evidence that GM may adopt this EDS pay/performance philosophy, if not companywide, then at least for some divisions. Other EDS policies and cultural phenomena may wear off as well. Gulf employees, caught in another situation, have found the spartan Chevron lifestyle unpleasant. Of real concern to managers is the highly centralized decision process. It is anticipated that many former Gulf managers will leave their new employer, Chevron, because even small decisions are made at the top, and Gulf managers formerly had considerable autonomy. A real underlying problem is that 15 percent of the jobs may disappear from the new combined entity, and early indications are that it will be former Gulf employees who bite the dust.

The bottom line is that while it may appear easy from the material presented in this chapter to buy and sell companies, it's not. The results are not always positive, and in some cases, they are detrimental.

Sources: Richard I. Kirkland, Jr., "Exxon Rededicates Itself to Oil," *Fortune*, July 23, 1984, pp. 28–32; Ken Wells and Carol Hymowitz, "Gulf's Managers Find Merger into Chevron Forces Many Changes," *The Wall Street Journal*, December 5, 1984, pp. 1, 22; Damon Darlin and Melinda G. Guiles, "Some GM People Feel Auto Firm, not EDS, Was the One Acquired," *The Wall Street Journal*, December 19, 1984, pp. 1, 20; Laurie P. Cohen, "Raytheon Is among Companies Regretting High-Tech Mergers," *The Wall Street Journal*, September 10, 1984, pp. 1, 18; H. J. Steinbreder, "Deals of the Year," *Fortune*, January 21, 1985, pp. 126–130; Royal Little, "Conglomerates are Doing Better than You Think," *Fortune*, May 28, 1984, pp. 50–60; "Monsanto's New Regimen: Heavy Injections of Drugs and Biotechnology," *Business Week*, December 3, 1984, pp. 64–65; "The New Food Giants," *Business Week*, September 24, 1984, pp. 132–138.

Balance refers to the degree to which business cash flows support one another. For example, firms in growth markets usually require more cash investment than do firms in older, more mature industries. The profits from the latter can be used to support the former. Similarly, a firm with strong summer revenues, such as a soft-drink firm, can be balanced against a firm with stronger winter revenues, such as a restaurant chain, to provide the total corporation with strong year-round cash flows.

Where necessary, prospective businesses can be plotted on matrices to help identify suitable investments. Of special concern are forecasted major environmental changes, both competitive and noncompetitive. Projected political events; expected changes in laws; forecasted major economic factors (GNP, interest rates, wages, controls, and so forth); and societal response to particular investments (for example, in chemicals or energy) must all be monitored for their potential impacts on the desirability of certain businesses as members of the portfolio. Table 5.3 lists some of the major external factors which should be considered.

Table 5.3   Some Strategically Significant Broad Environmental Variables

Economic Conditions	Demographic Trends	Technological Changes	Social and Cultural Trends	Political and Legal Factors
GNP trends	Growth rate of population	Total federal spending for R&D	Lifestyle changes	Antitrust regulations
Interest rates	Age distribution of population	Total industry spending for R&D	Career expectations	Environmental protection laws
Money supply	Regional shifts in population	Focus of tech-nological effort	Consumer activism	Tax laws
Inflation rates	Life expectancies	Patent protection	Rate of family formation	Special incentives
Unemployment levels	Birth rates			Foreign trade regulations
Wage/price controls				Attitudes toward foreign companies
Devaluation/ revaluation				
Energy availability				

Source: Reproduced by permission from *Strategy Formulation: Analytical Concepts* by Charles W. Hofer and Dan Schendel. Copyright © 1978 by West Publishing Company. All rights reserved.

Pitfalls in Portfolio Utilization

From the mid 1970s through 1981, portfolio analysis was a major new concept in strategic planning. It became very popular quite rapidly as major U.S. industries pursued avid programs of merger and acquisition, to which the portfolio techniques were highly suited. However, as experience with these techniques progressed, certain doubts about them began to arise. Malcolm B. Coate has proposed that several major pitfalls exist in the portfolio approach. He suggests the following concerns:

1. They are based on certain assumptions that must be examined in each particular situation:
    a. Each firm is divisible into independent business units. Coate questions the ease of defining these in the real world.
    b. The dominant firm earns the highest profits in each market. Coate suggests this is not necessarily true. (Other research cited elsewhere in this book suggests that his objection is correct.)
    c. Industries are more or less attractive based on their life cycle. This tends to ignore differences in capital intensities between industries.
    d. Investment funds are limited, and these must be allocated among all businesses in the organization. This tends to ignore the long-term perspective, where funds will not be limited as they are in the short run.

2. In addition to pitfalls with assumptions, Coate observes that portfolio models tend to overlook additional considerations that should be incorporated in an "optimal investment planning model":
    a. The funds invested in various SBUs should be allocated in such a way as to equate marginal rates of return.
    b. It is possible that where tacit collusion exists, firms would need to alter strategies recommended by these techniques and reduce investment in order to take advantage of market power.
    c. The liquidation value of the SBU is a better measure of its value than the more commonly used cost basis. In that light, liquidation becomes a much more acceptable strategy.
    d. Risk is given very little quantitative attention in portfolio models.

Coate then proceeds to identify the pitfalls which exist in the application of a portfolio model:

1. The actual process of business unit definition is quite complex, and something more akin to an art than a science.

2. Actually using the matrix involves considerably more time and attention than the conceptual perspective would allow. After all, a large number of value judgments must be made about some very tenuous numbers and measurements are often vague. Detailed information on each unit is vital to the success of the portfolio approach.

3. There is a question related to the validity of the strategies which are recommended by the model. Since some assumptions of the model noted earlier may not be true, there can be serious problems of pursuing these strategies. The availability of resources—

financial, human, and others—always affects the ability of any business to implement strategy.[9]

Others have also pointed to the problems associated with using portfolio techniques. Philippe Haspeslagh surveyed the *Fortune* 1,000. Among the 345 respondents, he found a wide variance in the degree to which these approaches were utilized, the rate of successful utilization, and the degree to which the individual SBUs involved adhered to recommended strategies. He indicates that these approaches were perceived by respondents to be useful in these primary ways: by generating better strategies through a more selective resource allocation process, and by adding a more differentiated approach to managing specific SBUs. He points out, however, that there are "complex realities" that face the user of these strategies when it comes time to implement them. For example, problems were reported involving the defining of a business. Since a large conglomerate might technically have 100 to 500 "businesses," no one could be expected to comprehend the issues involved with that many simultaneously. Therefore, SBUs are typically grouped in similar categories for analysis purposes. This then causes all sorts of difficulties in terms of implementing strategies due to the differences among businesses within each group. Another problem with resource allocation is the power associated with these resources. Haspeslagh implies that power distribution or redistribution is going to be accompanied by behavioral adjustment. (We suspect resistance is what is most frequent.) He also found that, while in theory portfolio techniques should be used to allocate all resources, most firms focused singly on capital investment.[10]

While Haspeslagh did not discuss in depth additional implementation problems related to such factors as motivation, budgets, leadership, communication, and so forth, Walter Kiechel III, in an article in *Fortune*, has indicated just how critical these aspects of implementation can be. Kiechel, as have other authors, pointed to the fact that strategic planning can carry the organization only so far. Ultimately, the strategies deriving from the strategic management process have to be implemented.[11] His sentiments are supported by an analysis by H. K. Christensen, A. C. Cooper, and C. A. DeKluyver.[12] This means that proper structures must exist; that programs and budgets must be derived in support; that motivation, leadership, and communication be properly conducted; that operational planning systems be effective; and that the culture must be receptive. There are, in short, many ifs in the process. These difficulties with implementation will have more meaning as you read Chapters 7 and 8. Similarly, Chapter 6 indicates the numerous types of behavioral problems associated with all stages of strategy: formulation, implementation, and control. You have already learned in this chapter that much of what transpires involves imprecision.

[9]M. B. Coate, "Pitfalls in Portfolio Planning," *Long Range Planning*, June 1983, pp. 47–56.

[10]P. Haspeslagh, "A Survey of U.S. Companies Shows How Effective Portfolio Planning Could Be but Often Isn't," *Harvard Business Review*, January/February 1982, pp. 58–73.

[11]W. Kiechel III, "Corporate Strategists Under Fire," *Fortune*, December 27, 1982, pp. 35–39.

[12]H. K. Christensen, A. C. Cooper, and C. A. Dekluyver, "The Dog Business: A Reexamination," *Business Horizons*, November/December 1982, pp. 12–18.

Multiple Point Competition

For a very few, large, select conglomerates, the central strategic question is how to compete with the other few, large, select conglomerates. This issue is raised in this text primarily to alert you to its existence. There are *very few* strategists involved in such concerns, but pragmatically, their endeavors do control a relatively significant number of corporate resources. Hofer and Schendel, and Karnani and Wernerfelt, among others, have provided their guidance to those involved in such competition.[13] Both sets of these authors offer suggested strategies for responding to competitors or for initiating competition.

Difference in Perspective:
Divisional versus Corporate Strategists

In the large business organization with numerous businesses (SBUs) or products, divisions are usually established based on these businesses or products. Normally, these divisions develop their own objectives and plans, choosing among new products, new marketing strategies, and new research and development projects as points of investment. All are subject, however, to the approval of top corporate management. To the division, these plans constitute strategy, but to the corporation, they are forms of intermediate planning. Strategic perspective at the division level differs significantly from that at the corporate level. The most obvious difference is that the division must respond to corporate objectives and policies, while the corporate top management establishes those objectives and policies. Furthermore, corporate-level strategy emphasizes portfolio techniques while division-level strategies emphasize the business strategy of marketing.

Because of this problem, the role of the division manager usually involves great responsibility with less than commensurate authority. The divisional general manager must translate objectives into action and action into measurement. He or she must satisfy superiors; compete and cooperate with peers; and lead subordinates—usually organization function managers, product managers, or geographic area managers. The division manager operates in a highly political environment. He or she is, in fact, a person in the middle. The division manager's position is most often filled by a former functional specialist. The transition to generalist is often too great, the viewpoint too different, for many who have been appointed to this position. The corporate general manager, in contrast to the division manager, acts primarily as a superior, as an objectives and policy setter, and as a resource allocator.

Peter Lorange suggests that, as a result of the lack of appreciation of the differences in these perspectives, the resulting divisional strategies are perhaps too conservative, given the total corporate investment portfolio. He believes that for a very large organization, a risky venture could be "averaged out." Often, divisional managers believe they cannot accept a product with high risk, because their performance is measured on return and their compensation is based on performance. The result is often the forfeit of considerable gain. Lorange has proposed that the business strategy (industry attractiveness/competi-

[13]C. W. Hofer and D. Schendel, *Strategy Formulation: Analytical Concepts* (St. Paul, Minn.: West, 1978), Chapter 7; A. Karnani and B. Wernerfelt, "Multiple Point Competition" (Proceedings: Academy of Management, August 1983), pp. 27–31.

Figure 5.10 Matrix for Determination and Evaluation of Business Line Product Strategy

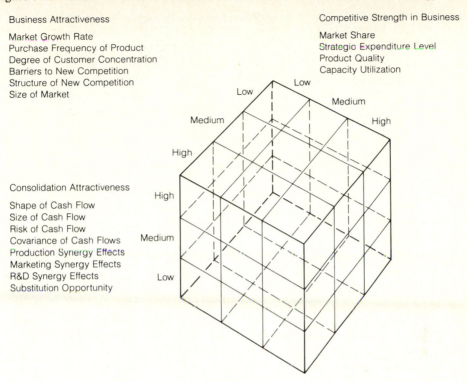

Business Attractiveness

Market Growth Rate
Purchase Frequency of Product
Degree of Customer Concentration
Barriers to New Competition
Structure of New Competition
Size of Market

Competitive Strength in Business

Market Share
Strategic Expenditure Level
Product Quality
Capacity Utilization

Consolidation Attractiveness

Shape of Cash Flow
Size of Cash Flow
Risk of Cash Flow
Covariance of Cash Flows
Production Synergy Effects
Marketing Synergy Effects
R&D Synergy Effects
Substitution Opportunity

Source: Reprinted from "Divisional Planning: Setting Effective Direction," by Peter Lorange, *Sloan Management Review*, Vol. 17, No. 1, Fall 1975, p. 87. Reprinted by permission of the publisher. Copyright © 1975 by the *Sloan Management Review* Association. All rights reserved.

tive strength) matrix be made three-dimensional to allow firms to account for the attractiveness of investment opportunities on a consolidated corporate basis. Figure 5.10 portrays this three-dimensional approach.[14]

The motivational scheme for divisional managers must be designed to incorporate the difficulty of the task and the need for attention to corporate as well as divisional interests. One such motivational scheme is that of General Electric. Both its choice of managers for various businesses (Table 5.4) and the motivational scheme for these managers (Figure 5.11) incorporate key factors related to the type of investment category (strategy). Such approaches are vital if the division-level manager is to be of the utmost utility to the corporation. If the division or product manager is not motivated to support corporate efforts, then mission is not likely to be accomplished.

Note how GE's approach accounts for the differing environments confronting managers. Too few firms appreciate these differences. Many critics point to the compensation

[14]P. Lorange, "Divisional Planning: Setting Effective Direction," *Sloan Management Review*, Fall 1975, pp. 77–91.

Table 5.4   GE Criteria for Choice of Business Managers

Investment Category	Manager's Key Strengths
Invest/grow	Entrepreneur/leader
Selectivity/earnings	Sophisticated/critical
Harvest/divest	Solid/experienced

Source: Michael G. Allen, Vice-President, General Electric Co., "Strategic Problems Facing Today's Corporate Planner" (Paper presented to the Academy of Management, Kansas City, August 1976). Reprinted by permission of General Electric Company.

Figure 5.11   Bonus Matched to Business

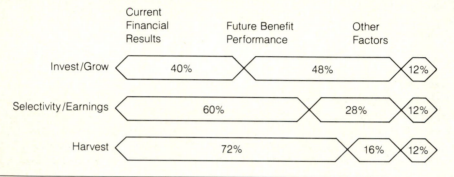

Source: Michael G. Allen, Vice-President, General Electric Co., "Strategic Problems Facing Today's Corporate Planner" (Paper presented to the Academy of Management, Kansas City, August 1976). Reprinted by permission of General Electric Company.

system as a major reason why strategic managers in most companies have a short-term outlook. General Electric has largely overcome that problem with this compensation system.[15]

Summary

In the multiple-SBU firm, the principal tasks of the strategist include establishing strategic objectives, determining the extent to which current and future businesses are helping or can help accomplish those objectives, examining what remains to be accomplished, determining strategies to accomplish those objectives, and establishing support functions and policies to accomplish those objectives. These activities center around portfolio management techniques.

The Boston Consulting Group matrix is a mechanism for relating two key factors—business or industry attractiveness and the firm's competitiveness within that industry—to help select businesses to enter or businesses in which to remain. The BCG model has

[15] M. G. Allen, "Strategic Problems Facing Today's Corporate Planner" (Paper presented to the Academy of Management, Kansas City, August 1976).

given way to other, more sophisticated matrices. As an example, the General Electric business screen has proved to be even more useful than the BCG matrix, because it isolates more specific considerations. A third matrix, the product/market/industry evolution matrix allows strategists to consider the additional critical variables related to product life cycle. A number of criteria exist to help the strategist assess both industry attractiveness and competitive position. Often, gaps exist between SBU performance and corporate objectives. As a result, corporate strategists may be required to adjust investment strategies or business strategies, add or delete SBUs from the portfolio, change enterprise strategies, or change strategic objectives. One should always keep in mind that a number of limitations exist with respect to both the concept of and implementation of portfolio approaches.

A difference in perspective often exists between the corporate and the divisional executive. Divisional managers often tend to be either function- or product-oriented. The corporate executive must be a generalist. It is often difficult for the specialist to make the transition to generalist.

Key Terms and Concepts

By the time you have completed this chapter, you should be familiar with the following key terms and concepts: contents of the master strategy at the corporate level, BCG business matrix, GE stoplight strategy, business screen, business strength and business attractiveness, assessment process, placing the SBU on the matrix, product gap analysis, product/market/industry evolution portfolio matrix, and the difference in strategists' perspectives.

Discussion Questions

1. Select a conglomerate and describe its major SBUs in terms of the BCG matrix, the GE business screen, and the product/market/industry evolution matrix. Utilize the major concepts discussed in this chapter.

2. Describe how the objectives-setting and master strategy formulation processes differ at the SBU and corporate levels.

3. If you were describing the differences between the BCG matrix and the GE business screen to a person who was unfamiliar with them, what elements would you highlight as different?

4. Provided you have successfully answered Question 3, then how would you now explain the differences between the GE business screen and the product/market/ industry evaluation matrix to the same person?

5. List the limitations that exist with respect to both the concept and the implementation of portfolio approaches.

References

Beard, Donald W., and Dess, Gregory G. "Corporate-Level Strategy, Business-Level Strategy, and Firm Performance." *Academy of Management Journal*, 1981, Vol. 24, No. 4, pp. 663–688.

Bettis, Richard A., and Hall, William K. "The Business Portfolio Approach—Where It Falls Down in Practice." *Long Range Planning*, Vol. 16, April 1983.

Campbell, N. C. G., and Roberts, K. J. *Science to Win the Competition: PIMS Analysis of Lanchester Strategy*. Paper presented at the Strategic Management Conference, Paris, October 1983.

Chakravarthy, Balaji S. "Strategic Self-Renewal: A Planning Framework for Today," *Academy of Management Review*, 1984, Vol. 9, No. 3, pp. 536–547.

Charlier, Marj. "Pabst Accepts Sweetened Offer of G. Heileman." *The Wall Street Journal*, December 7, 1984, p. 12.

Jensen, Michael C. "Takeovers: Folklore and Science." *Harvard Business Review*, November/December 1984.

Little, Royal. "Conglomerates Are Doing Better than You Think." *Fortune*, May 28, 1984, pp. 50–60.

Marshuetz, Richard J. "How America Can Allocate Capital." *Harvard Business Review*, January/February 1985.

Morrison, Ann M. "Betting the Barn at Stroh." *Fortune*, May 31, 1982, pp. 118–121.

Stahl, Michael J., and Zimmerer, Thomas W. "Modeling Strategic Acquisition Policies: A Simulation of Executives' Acquisition Decisions." *Academy of Management Journal*, 1984, Vol. 27, No. 2, pp. 369–383.

Steinbreder, H. John. "Deals of the Year." *Fortune*, January 21, 1985, pp. 126–130.

Wiener, Daniel P. "Deals of the Year." *Fortune*, January 23, 1984, pp. 54–61.

6

The Strategic Decision Process— Behavioral Perspectives

All decision is compromise.

▪ *Herbert Simon* ▪

Decision making is the most important of all of the activities in which managers engage. It is through decision making that the other functions of management are accomplished. A decision is a choice among alternatives, but decision making also involves problem or opportunity recognition, identification, implementation, and control. In earlier chapters, the strategic decision process was viewed as it is normally conceptualized, and some of the techniques which may be employed in that process were noted. This chapter focuses on the behavioral aspects of strategic decision making, including discussions of specific components of the strategic decision process, especially the solution component. This chapter is concerned with those portions of the planning models indicated in Figures 6.1 and 6.2.

The Complexity of Organizational Decision Making

As shown in Figure 6.3, decision making is normally portrayed as a five-step process: recognition, identification, solution, implementation, and control. In the recognition phase, decision makers become aware of a problem or an opportunity. A problem exists

Figure 6.1 The Organization—a Strategic Management Process Model

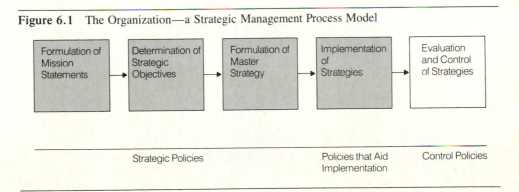

Figure 6.2   Objective Determination and Master Strategy Formulation

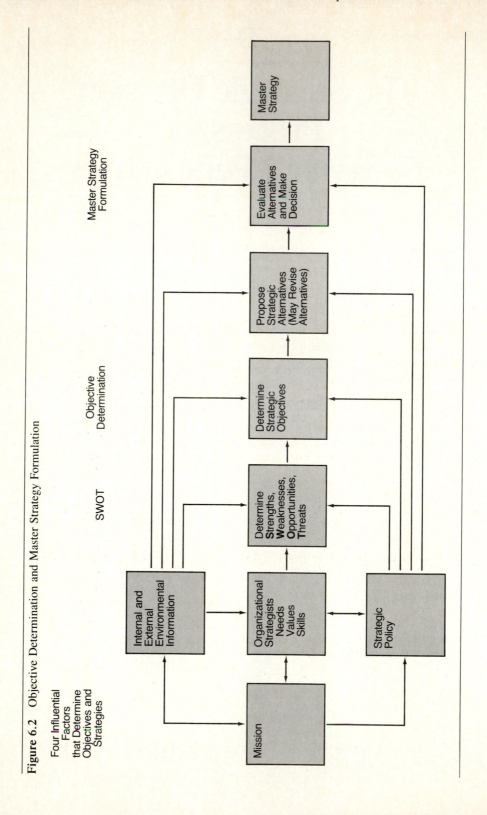

Four Influential
Factors
that Determine
Objectives and
Strategies

SWOT

Objective
Determination

Master Strategy
Formulation

Mission

Internal and
External
Environmental
Information

Organizational
Strategists
Needs
Values
Skills

Strategic
Policy

Determine
Strengths,
Weaknesses,
Opportunities,
Threats

Determine
Strategic
Objectives

Propose
Strategic
Alternatives
(May Revise
Alternatives)

Evaluate
Alternatives
and Make
Decision

Master
Strategy

Figure 6.3   Basic Decision Process Model

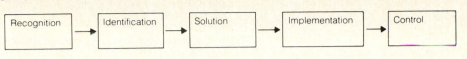

when what is falls short of what should be. Problems result from many factors, but primarily from internal weaknesses or external threats. An opportunity exists when what is falls short of what could be. Opportunities result primarily from favorable environmental circumstances and are almost always expressed in terms of market/profit potentials.

In the recognition phase, problems and opportunities are not well understood. The decision maker simply becomes aware that a problem or an opportunity exists. In the identification phase, these problems or opportunities are better defined. In the solution phase, alternative objectives or plans of action are generated to solve problems or to take advantage of opportunities. The decision maker evaluates these alternatives by using information; the constraints of policy; and for strategy, the constraints of the objectives. Finally a decision is made, followed by implementation of the decision. This decision will then be subject to control efforts that are intended to assure its effectiveness.

The five-part decision process model, while appealing because of its simplicity, understates the complexity of the organizational decision process. Decision making occurs within constraints, which include psychological, environmental, and decision-related factors. Psychologically, the decision maker is constrained by his or her own personality—primarily needs, but also knowledge, risk propensity, information processing, aspirations, values, skills, experience, perceptions, and various skill levels, especially those related to analysis and intuition. Environmental constraints include organizational factors such as objectives and policy, organizational environment and structure, reference groups and group dynamics, and roles. Decision-related factors include the importance of the decision, the time in which the decision must be made, the information available, and the involvement of multiple decision makers. As a result of these and numerous other factors, the decision process is much more complex than classically conceptualized. The following statements provide a more realistic view of decision making in an organization:

1.   Objectives are often vague, conflicting, and not agreed upon.

2.   Too frequently, managers are unaware that problems or opportunities exist.

3.   When problems are recognized, managers often react to symptoms and not to causes. J. Mitroff has labeled this phenomenon as "error of the third kind"—solving the wrong problem.[1]

4.   Since decisions are based on models, rationality, if applied at all, can only be applied to the aspects of the situation perceived to be most important. Omission of vital data, variables, and relationships is not infrequent.

5.   Since it is normally impossible, both mentally and physically to observe all or even

[1] J. Mitroff, "On Helping a Large Governmental Organization to Do Research on Planning on Itself: A Case Study" (Unpublished working paper, University of Pittsburgh).

most alternatives in complete detail, actual search behavior is much less extensive than that conceptualized. The decision maker's knowledge of the situation is limited.

6. Few managers have a maximizing criterion in mind. Most will settle for an alternative which satisfies minimal, and minimally considered, objectives. These are known as "satisficing" criteria.

7. Managers make decisions based on rules of thumb and frequently do not evaluate alternatives even by the satisficing criteria. They apparently believe that whatever worked last time will work this time.

8. Social relationships greatly affect the decision maker's rationality.

9. There is often an overemphasis on rationality at the expense of other processes that also contribute substantially to the success of strategic decision making.

The Strategic Decision Process

The role top management most often plays in strategy formulation is usually twofold: first, to review both policy and (empirical) information related to internal factors and the external environment, and second, through rational decision making, to translate mission into more specific objectives and to establish major plans of action to reach those objectives. Often, the information indicates a need to reformulate strategy, thus triggering the strategic decision process. More often than not, the information indicates the need to change only certain objectives or certain elements of strategy.

Very importantly, research indicates that the role of the strategist in strategy formulation includes not only rational strategy formulation using empirical data, but formulation from an intuitive and creative perspective as well. The research further suggests that the strategist must build consensus for the strategy throughout the organization in order for the strategy to be successful. To this end, politics and the use of power are often employed.[2] Finally, while the use of models may cause the strategy formulation process to appear as a rapid, one-step process, a substantial amount of research suggests that strategy formulation in many firms, and in most very large firms, occurs incrementally as a series of small steps, rather than as grand leaps forward.

The strategic decision process is characterized by the five phases common to other decisions. Research related to the first four phases, especially the solution phase, will be explored here in more detail. The control phase parallels that in Figure 6.1 and is not discussed in detail here, but is in Chaper 9. The remainder of this chapter focuses on describing the actual strategic decision process as opposed to the classical conceptualization.

Most discussions of decision making focus on problem solving. We also believe that recognition, identification, and implementation are of vital interest. (Note that in the strategic situation, decision making occurs not only as the result of problems but also as the result of opportunities. The discussion in this chapter treats both opportunities and problems as initiators of the strategic decision process. While it is questionable whether

---

[2] R. E. Quinn, J. Rohrbaugh, and M. R. McGrath, "How to Improve Organizational Decision Making: A Report on Automated Decision Conferencing" (Paper presented to Academy of Management, New Orleans, 1983). Summarizes strategic decision making as involving rational, empirical, consensual, and political perspectives. While these perspectives address intuition and creativity, they are not direct parts of their model.

smaller businesses engage in opportunity searches, larger businesses clearly treat strategy as an exercise in opportunity exploration, and routinely employ various portfolio management techniques.

A Strategic Decision Process Model

Examining the strategic decision process is important to actual organizational experiences because it leads to a better understanding of organizational objectives, plans, structure, and resulting everyday operations. This examination of the actual decision process will help you gain a better understanding of the objectives, plans, structure, and operations of organizations you may be required to analyze, for example, in case studies, or as top managers.

The behavioral aspects of strategic decision making are somewhat complex, but they can be modeled. Figure 6.4 presents a model for the first four components of the strategic process. The model incorporates the available research evidence and normative/descriptive literature.

The Component Phases of Strategic Decision Making: A Closer Examination

Let us now examine each of the four component phases of the strategic decision process model presented in Figure 6.4. (Again, the control phase will be discussed in Chapter 9.) For the following discussion, the terms decision maker, manager, and strategist may be used in the singular, even though there may well be more than one in an organization.

Recognition

Diagnosis [recognition and identification] is probably the single most important routine, since it determines in large part, however implicitly, the subsequent course of action. Yet researchers have paid almost no attention to diagnosis, preferring instead to focus on the selection routines. . . .

■ *H. Mintzberg, D. Raisinghani, and A. Theoret* ■

In order to know if a problem exists, the decision maker must know what *problem* means. A problem, as suggested earlier, occurs when objective accomplishment differs negatively from established objectives. (This implies that objectives have been established.) In theory, it is the function of information systems to alert the manager to such situations. Indeed, information systems should be designed to discover problems before they become serious. But while we might assume that problems are precisely defined at this stage, recognition more often involves a vague feeling or intuition that something is not right. In the identification phase, more precise modeling of the problem occurs.

One of the weaknesses of the decision-making/problem-solving process as it actually occurs is the fact that too few organizations and too few decision makers have seriously approached the question "How do we know when we have a problem?" A study by W. E. Pounds, one of the few studies which has analyzed the problem recognition process, re-

Figure 6.4   Strategic Decision Process Model

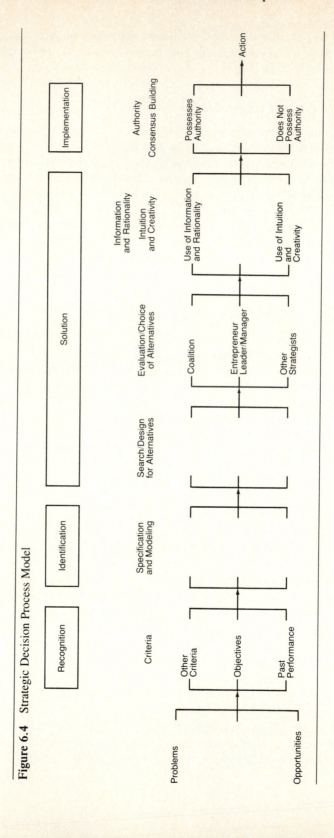

veals that business managers do not utilize objectives to establish the existence of problems.[3] Theoretically, managers should know they have a problem when performance does not equal objectives. In fact, objectives should be the benchmark against which progress is measured. But Pound's study revealed that managers most frequently use previous performances as a reference instead of using current objectives, even though this approach often results in problems not being recognized. Some managers may also compare their firm's performance to the performance of other organizations doing similar tasks or to some other external model. Of these four possible performance comparisons—objectives, previous performance, similar organizations, and external models—the first is the most appropriate for determining whether organizational goals have been accomplished. Yet, it is apparently seldom used.

In another study of 33 case histories of strategic problem and opportunity recognition and identification (they used the term *problem formulation* to identify these two stages), Marjorie Lyles and Ian I. Mitroff found that 80 percent of the managers involved believed themselves to be aware of the problem before formal indicators, such as financial figures, indicated the existence of a problem, or before a superior or a subordinate brought the problem to their attention. Their study supports the view that much decision making occurs as the result of: first, the use of informal information sources, and second, the use of intuition for recognition. They reported significant human behavioral factors being involved in the recognition and in the identification phases of decision making, including commitment, political maneuvering, denial, etc. They suggest that such factors may reduce the utilization of rational approaches to problem recognition and identification.[4]

Alice M. Sapienza, in a limited study of the strategic decision process, found that where multiple decision makers exist, there is first an individual realization, and then a collective realization that a problem exists. There must be not only a shared perception, but also a shared vocabulary describing the problem (or opportunity). It may take some time, and perhaps even considerable effort on the part of some, before several decision makers arrive at essentially the same perceptions. However, the evidence is not clear in her report whether or not the organization in question ever identified the actual problem, or bypassed identification and moved to solution.[5]

As stated earlier, an opportunity exists when a firm determines that what is falls short of what could be. First, of course, a firm must establish what could be. Organizations must scan their environments as suggested in Chapter 2 in order to be able to recognize opportunities. But thus far, little research has examined how firms determine opportunities. The comments by H. H. Stevenson referred to in that chapter are especially relevant; not all managers use the same criteria for identifying the various parts of SWOT.[6] Entrepreneurial ability plays an important role here; although many might assess the same information, only one might see the opportunities revealed.

---

[3] W. F. Pounds, "The Process of Problem Finding," *Industrial Management Review*, Fall 1969, pp. 1–19.

[4] M. A. Lyles and I. I. Mitroff, "Organizational Problem Formulation: An Empirical Study," *Administrative Science Quarterly*, March 1980, pp. 102–119.

[5] A. M. Sapienza, "A Cognitive Perspective on Strategy Formulation: Six Steps in the Development of Institutional Response" (Paper presented to *The Academy of Management*, New Orleans, 1983.)

[6] H. H. Stevenson, "Defining Corporate Strengths and Weaknesses," *Sloan Management Review*, Spring 1976, pp. 51–66.

Identification

Once it is known that a problem or opportunity exists, then the causal factors must be identified or the opportunity more clearly defined. With the problem-solving system most managers employ, the real problem or opportunity is often overlooked. Managers often jump right in, assuming they know what the problem or opportunity is. Like recognition, identification has been little researched or considered. However, information again plays an important role in this process.

C. Kepner and B. Tregoe, in one of the few discussions of problem identification, suggest that the process of specification is helpful.[7] In specification, decision makers must determine exactly what the specific problem is, where and when it occurred, whom or what it affected, and the extent of its effect. The decision maker must distinguish differences between the problem's consequences and other events in similar situations. This occurs as a result of examining the situational data.

Specification aims at factually separating what the problem is from what it is not. Uncovering the real problem then becomes a matter of deduction from what should be to what is. This process is not simple; it is at least partly intuitive and it also relies partly on experience. The decision maker must learn to ask a series of questions which aid in this process; for example: What is the urgency and severity of each problem? How are these problems related? Which problems result from other problems? What could uniquely produce these consequences? The end result of this phase will be a model of the problem. The model routinely summarizes and conceptualizes the situation under examination. Importantly, processes such as competition analysis (Chapter 4) and portfolio management (Chapter 5) help in the identification process.

Continued analysis by Lyles of the 33 case histories, discussed in the previous section on recognition,[8] revealed that many organizations initially identify the problem incorrectly, or avoid it all together. This suggests a slowness to "trigger" identification processes even though there is clear recognition of the problem. Interestingly, she found that in 75 percent of the situations reviewed, a problem was explicitly identified, only to have the identification process reinitiated and a new definition begun.

Based on additional findings in her research, Lyles suggests several propositions:

1.   The more ill-defined the nature of the problem, the more political will be the problem formulation process.

2.   The more political the problem formulation process, the more debate should be used as a method of confrontation.

3.   The more debate that is used, the more accurate will be the problem definition.[9]

Her propositions are especially relevant to strategic problems and opportunities, since many, if not most, strategic situations are typically ill-defined and thus "open to divergent interpretations."

---

[7]C. Kepner and B. Tregoe, *The Rational Manager* (New York: McGraw-Hill, 1965).

[8]M. A. Lyles, "Formulating Strategic Problems: Empirical Analysis and Model Development," *Strategic Management Journal*, January–March 1981, pp. 61–75.

[9]Ibid., p. 74.

The mere formulation of a problem is often far more essential than its solution, which may be merely a matter of mathematical or experimental skills. To raise new questions, new possibilities, to regard old problems from a new angle requires creative imagination, and marks real advances in science.

▪ *Albert Einstein* ▪

Finally, Omar A. El Sawy, in examining how executives searched for threats and opportunities, describes the recognition and identification stages as having an additional component—the "threshold" of realization. Confirmation must occur once this threshold of recognition has been reached. This is identification.[10]

Solution

As suggested in Chapters 3, 4, and 5, in the solution component of the decision-making process, the decision maker first searches for alternative solutions, procedures, or courses of action to solve the problem or exploit the opportunity, and then arrays these alternatives in some fashion that will facilitate making a choice among them. The search for alternatives can be extremely time consuming and complicated. This section will examine in detail the social processes involved in the solution process. The emphasis will be on the nonrational aspects of decision making displayed by each of the three types of decision makers identified in Chapter 1.

Organizational outcomes—both strategies and their effectiveness—are viewed as reflections of the values and cognitive bases of powerful actors in the organization.

▪ *Donald C. Hambrich and Phyllis A. Mason,* ▪
Academy of Management Review, April 1984, p. 193.

Entrepreneurial Leader/Manager.   Managers cannot separate their personalities from their decisions. Their needs, their values, their emotions, their ethics, their feelings, their risk propensities, their approaches to problem solving, their attitudes toward people, their attitudes toward life, and numerous other personality factors influence the decisions they make. Of all these behavioral variables, however, the most frequently discussed behavioral determinant of organizational success or failure has been values.

Values conceptualize what their holders view as desirable. They reflect an individual's, a group's, an organization's, or a society's history of experiences. For, while the perception processes trigger decision-making actions, values enter into perceptions. Thus values play a critical role in decision making. Many times, managers are not consciously aware of utilizing values in making decisions; values nonetheless may greatly affect their decisions at the subconscious level.

William D. Guth and Renato Taguiri have identified six primary types of value orientations:[11]

---

[10]O. M. El Sawy, "Understanding the Process by Which Chief Executives Identify Strategic Threats and Opportunities" (Proceedings Academy of Management, 1984), pp. 37–41.

[11]W. D. Guth and R. Taguiri, "Personal Values and Corporate Strategies," *Harvard Business Review*, September/October 1965, pp. 125–126.

1. *Theoretical:* interested in the discovery of truth, in rationality, in reason.

2. *Economic:* practical; interested in what is practical; interested in the accumulation of wealth.

3. *Aesthetic:* values the artistic aspects of life; enjoys each event for its own sake, for its beauty.

4. *Social:* loves people; is sympathetic, unselfish, kind.

5. *Political:* oriented toward power; sees competition as vital.

6. *Religious:* has a "mental structure permanently directed to the creation of the highest and absolutely satisfying value experience"; seeks relationship with the universe.

Guth and Taguiri found that the business managers they sampled had values strongest on economic, theoretical, and political scales and weakest in aesthetic and social areas, and that their religious value scores were moderately strong relative to the other values.

How are each of these values reflected in decisions? We can't be sure; but it seems likely that values enter into virtually every decision and that more than one value is usually involved. For example, when L. M. Clymer resigned as president of Holiday Inns in protest of the directors' decision to establish a gambling casino, he may have been motivated by "religious" values.[12] When resort owners hire Peter Dye to design a golf course, they do so, it would seem, primarily for his ability to create a course that is aesthetically pleasing as well as economically successful.[13] When Philip Friedman and Mickaell Keiser founded Recycled Paper Products Inc. in 1971, they did so to help keep trees from being cut down to make greeting cards. They were satisfying a social or perhaps aesthetic value.[14] Many more examples could be cited; the point is that since values underlie managerial decisions, they have important impacts on these decisions.

Other managerial personality traits play an important role in strategic decisions as well. A study by Danny Miller suggests that top-management traits such as conservatism or extremely arbitrary risk taking are significant in determining whether a firm is successful or unsuccessful.[15] Unsuccessful firms did not employ techniques such as environmental scanning, environmental analysis, or analysis of any kind in terms of strategic formulation as often as did successful firms. This study suggests that the human variable may be an important predictor of strategic success and that therefore strategy may be contingent upon this variable. For example, Miller's study described one firm's scenario as characterized by a bold and reckless entrepreneur who was proactive and a high risk taker.

Top-Management Coalition.   While the entrepreneurial leader/manager guides most organizations, not all such leaders are sufficiently strong to cope with all the forces they encounter. Where weaker chief executives head an organization or where especially strong

---

[12] "Holiday Inns Sets its First Hotel-Casino, Prompting Clymer to Resign as President," *The Wall Street Journal*, October 2, 1978, p. 16.

[13] Pete Dye is known for his dramatic use of water and sand in combination with wood retainers. Among his courses are the Campo de Campo in the Dominican Republic; Amelia Island in Jacksonville, Florida; Oak Tree in Edmond, Oklahoma; and Harbor Town on Hilton Head Island, South Carolina.

[14] S. Graham, "I Think that I Shall Never See a Greeting Card Lovely as a Tree," *The Wall Street Journal*, September 3, 1980, p. 29.

[15] D. Miller, "Towards a Contingency Theory of Strategy Formulation" (Proceedings: Academy of Management, 1975), pp. 64–66.

power centers exist, one or more coalitions are the dominant factors in strategy determination. This is especially true of larger organizations.

R. Cyert and J. March first noted the existence of the coalition.[16] Organizational objectives and strategies are determined in the coalition process through a bargaining mechanism—essentially a trading process involving exchanges of what have been termed "policy side payments" for alliance on some particular strategic objective or plan. These payments may take the form of money, a promise of agreement on some future policy matter or objective, personal favors, authority, and so forth.

Objectives set by this process tend to be vague and to vary over time and reflect the aspirations of various coalition members. Conflict within the organization is never fully resolved (because of the bargaining, compromising, and vagueness involved). This latter characteristic Cyert and March referred to as the "quasi-resolution of conflict." As an example of this phenomenon, there often exists a constant struggle among marketing, accounting, and production subunits regarding the amount of inventory that should be maintained. The marketing director seeks high inventories of all items in order to be able to satisfy customers. On the other hand, the comptroller seeks low inventories to reduce carrying costs. And depending on how each manager's performance is judged and the rewards to be received for alliance, the production manager may be aligned with either. This problem is usually quasi-resolved; that is, no party achieves a clear victory. As a result, the issue remains as a roadblock to organizational mission achievement. However, if, say, the marketing manager finally wins and the company agrees to maintain in inventory a great number of products across a diversified number of product lines, then a policy side payment will be forthcoming. What emerges is a view of strategy formulation as an exchange process based on power.

While much of the following discussion on coalitions focuses on internal coalitions, organizations, their subunits, and individual members may also form coalitions with major stakeholder constituents, especially when they are dependent on these constituents. Additionally, coalitions with unions, government, competition (restraints of trade), and various pressure groups may exist. For example, many business organizations have attempted to work "with" environmentalists and minority interest groups rather than fight them. In so doing, they are forming coalitions, exchanging increased social responsibility commitments for decreased protest.

Surprisingly, there has been little research attempting to verify the coalition concept, perhaps because most practitioners and researchers have experienced this phenomenon, or because the concept seems so intuitively valid. Following are brief descriptions of the major studies which have dealt with this process.

J. D. Thompson was the first to elaborate on the coalition in his discussion of organizations. He observed that the relationship of the organization to its environment was important in determining coalition functioning. He also expressed the view that the future of the organization's objectives depended on the perceptions of the dominant coalition.[17]

E. E. Carter empirically tested Cyert's and March's behavioral theory of decision making. He examined six different but related major decisions for a small computer firm. Carter's results essentially verified the Cyert and March hypothesis. However, he suggested

---

[16] R. Cyert and J. March, *The Behavioral Theory of the Firm* (Englewood Cliffs, N.J.: Prentice-Hall, 1963).

[17] J. D. Thompson, *Organizations in Action* (New York: McGraw-Hill, 1967), pp. 127–128.

certain changes in their theory. One such change was that, instead of a single, large, dominant coalition which resolved conflicts within itself, there existed a series of small groups engaged in bargaining at each level of the organization. As a decision passed through each level of the organization on its way to final executive approval, a new coalition might exert its influence on the eventual decision.[18]

C. B. Saunders reported that, in an eight-year study of the planning process in a single firm, observed behaviors did not differ significantly from those described by Cyert and March. In reviewing the coalition process, he concluded that in complex organizations strategy formulation was a highly diffuse and highly political process. He viewed environmental factors as important determinants of an organization member's efforts to influence the firm's activities. His research also supported the concept of a dominant coalition.[19]

H. Mintzberg, D. Raisinghani, and A. Theoret closely scrutinized twenty-five strategic decisions—nine in service firms, five in quasi-governmental agencies, five in government agencies, and six in manufacturing firms. The results of their study also support the coalition concept. Coalition bargaining behavior was reported in over half the decisions they observed.[20]

Finally, a study of strategic energy policy decision making in six large multidivisional firms by Liam Fahey supports the previous views of researchers related to the significant impacts of behavioral and political processes on strategic decision making. Several tentative propositions include the following: strategic decision making is predominantly political; it is iterative and interactive; it is more "problematical" than rational; the search process for alternatives is multilevel and highly political; and a structured process of decision making does not necessarily lead to a "rational" decision.[21]

With the exception of these studies, much of what is known about the coalition results from studies of power relationships within the organization. The coalition is, after all, a power concept. In recent years, interest in power in the organization has increased as its significance has been recognized.

Power and the Political Aspects of Strategic Decision Making.   The use of power (politics) to further one's own interests is not new to the organization. Its use in planning is certainly not new, nor is the recognition of its importance. Anthony Jay addressed this aspect of corporate life in his book *Management and Machiavelli*. He observed that while controlling this problem is not too difficult at the lower levels of organization, it is quite difficult at the higher management levels—the strategic decision levels.[22] According to a study by R. Stagner, business executives reported that key (strategic) decisions in their

---

[18] E. E. Carter, "The Behavioral Theory of the Firm and Top-Level Corporate Decision," *Administrative Science Quarterly*, December 1971, pp. 413–429; "A Behavioral Theory Approach to Firm Investment and Acquisition Decisions" (Ph.D. dissertation, Graduate School of Industrial Administration, Carnegie Mellon University, Pittsburgh, 1970).

[19] C. B. Saunders, "What Should We Know about Strategy Formulation" (Proceedings: Academy of Management, 1973), p. 32.

[20] H. Mintzberg, D. Raisinghani, and A. Theoret, "The Structure of Unstructured Decision Processes," *Administrative Science Quarterly*, June 1976, p. 258.

[21] L. Fahey, "On Strategic Management Decision Processes," *Strategic Management Journal*, January–March, 1981, pp. 43–60.

[22] A. Jay, *Management and Machiavelli* (New York: Holt, Rinehart and Winston, 1967).

"OK, Accounting agrees to bigger inventories,
but we get to keep our offices in the upwind wing . . . !"

organizations were often settled by power rather than by rational maximization criteria.[23] Another study, this one by L. J. Bourgeios III and J. V. Singh, confirms that power and the availability of power definitely affected strategic decisions in the 24 organizations they examined.[24] Thus, while rationality may be a formally proclaimed method of making strategic decisions, power and personality clearly play important roles in this process.

Much of the coalition phenomenon results from competition among organizational subsystems. Operationally these subsystems are interdependent: a problem for one is a problem for another. But relative power among these subsystems is determined by such factors as how well each subsystem can help the organization to cope with uncertainty, how well each subsystem can directly contribute to the organization's ability to generate revenue, and on how important each subsystem is to the organization. Accordingly, the composition of the dominant coalition and its power distribution largely result from the effects of environmental change.

The coalition or coalition member who is best able to provide the means for coping with change, who has lower substitutability, or who is more central to the work flow gains power. The implication is obvious: the subunit manager is in a position to gain power.

[23]R. Stagner, "Corporate Decision Making: An Empirical Study," *Journal of Applied Psychology*, February 1969, pp. 1–13.

[24]L. J. Bourgeois III and J. V. Singh, "Organizational Slack and Political Behavior among Top Management Teams," *Academy of Management Proceedings*, 1983, pp. 43–47.

Coping with uncertainty is one obvious basis for the increasing power of planning units in larger organizations. This power can lead to dominance by the planner.

While research regarding the coalition is not abundant, as indicated earlier, that which does exist supports Cyert's and March's postulations. And though more research is needed (especially to sample behavior across many firms of varying sizes in several industries and in nonprofit organizations), we must not overlook the abundant informal group research that is available. This research mainly examines groups at lower levels of the organization, and also concludes that power is relative and is bargained for. It also suggests that an informal group at lower levels can counteract the power of the formal managerial leader. These findings support the coalition concept.

The effect of power (and politics) on an organization cannot be overemphasized. Remember that one subunit of an organization the size of General Electric may be larger than several entire companies against which it competes. Consequently, considerable resources of a larger organization may be allocated to the coalition process. Much additional evidence of the importance of power can be found. Even the president of a large strategic-planning consulting firm indicates that organizational politics often prevents his firm's adoption of recommended planning models. Indeed, the recognition of the correlation between political behavior and success in the organization has been increasingly discussed in the strategic management literature. For example, F. F. Gilmore has outlined a four-stage strategy for assisting the executive in efforts to have plans adopted by the organization.[25] A. P. Brief and A. C. Filley have outlined a similar series of propositions for selling proposals for change before committees.[26] Several books are also available which offer advice to the aspiring manager in the political organization.

To summarize, coalition activity, power, and politics in strategic decision making are interdependent. As coalition power centers develop, admission to them becomes partially a function of politics. As objectivity in decision making is reduced, power and politics become increasingly important to those who aspire to and have a high need for achievement. Success becomes a function of power.

> *It's not so much what you know, but who you know that counts.*
>
> ▪ *Anonymous* ▪

Other Strategists.   Other strategists make decisions as would the top manager, except for the differences in authority and related roles between them. Our earlier discussion of how values and other personality traits influence the individual top manager are relevant here; the coalition may also have an impact on these decision makers. Additionally, there exist certain subtleties of organizational structure and, hence, position power that might affect these strategists as well. Certainly professional planners are affected by their power and this, in turn, affects their position in the organization.

In summary, evaluation and choice normally involve either a single entrepreneurial leader/manager, a coalition of top managers, or other strategists. Returning to Figure 6.4,

---

[25] F. F. Gilmore, "Overcoming the Perils of Advocacy in Corporate Planning," *California Management Review*, Spring 1973, pp. 127–137.

[26] A. P. Brief and A. C. Filley, "Selling Proposals for Change," *Business Horizons*, April 1976, pp. 22–25.

you can see that each of these decision makers may or may not utilize information and follow a rational choice process; they may or may not be intuitive and creative. Note that this is not an either/or situation. Decision makers ideally should be both rational/empirical *and* intuitive/creative.

Implementation

When decision makers do not possess the authority to approve the decision, they must seek it if the decision is to be implemented. Decision-making processes may be repeated as an issue progresses upward through the decision levels of the organizational hierarchy. Often, however, the higher-level decision process is abbreviated as decisions are based on lower-level recommendations. Here we find what is known as incremental decision making. Once authority is possessed, implementation action ensues. However, since various interruptions and delays to this process may occur and may result in variances in the exact decision process in any particular situation, consensus building with subordinates, coalitions, or top management is essential.

Incremental Decision Making. Examination of the strategic decision process reveals that, in many organizations, decisions are made in a series of small steps—hence the term *incremental*. As portrayed by C. E. Lindblom and by Lindblom and D. Braybrooke, incrementalism is based on the belief that a rational approach does not account for people's limited problem-solving capacity, their lack of information, the impact of their values on decisions, the openness of systems, the high cost of total rationality, the need for sequencing of decisions, or the variations in policy problem situations. Lindblom's and Braybrooke's idea of incrementalism is based on the concept that most governmental policy decisions involve small changes not guided by a high level of understanding.[27] Political decisions indeed proceed by small steps—a preliminary solution is attempted, performance is measured, and perceived shortcomings are corrected. Such an approach is best, because it allows for the recognition of the problems associated with the rational approach to decision making. Related research supports the existence of the incremental process in business, but not necessarily all of Lindblom's and Braybrooke's assumptions about it.

Y. Aharoni observed the foreign investment decision processes of 38 U.S. firms. His research suggests that incremental decision making is at least partially a function of organizational structure. His research is important because it substantiates the observations of Lindblom and Braybrooke as well as the coalition propositions of Cyert and March. He concluded that decision making in large, complex organizations was a continuous social bargaining process composed of many small parts. He observed that different people were involved at different points in the organization and at different times. Personal interests were found to play a key role in decisions.[28]

[27] C. E. Lindblom, *The Policy-Making Process* (Englewood Cliffs, N.J.: Prentice-Hall, 1968); *The Intelligence of Democracy* (New York: Free Press, 1965); "The Science of 'Muddling Through,'" *Public Administration Review*, Spring 1959, pp. 79–88; C. E. Lindblom and D. Braybrooke, *A Strategy of Decision* (New York: Free Press, 1963).

[28] Y. Aharoni, *The Foreign Investment Decision Process* (Boston: Division of Research, Harvard Business School, 1966).

Two additional studies supporting both bargaining and incremental decision making are those of J. L. Bower and R. W. Ackerman. Both studies were concerned with investment decisions. Bower examined one firm's decisions extensively.[29] Subsequently, Ackerman, testing Bower's decision model, observed four firms extensively.[30] A third effort, by S. C. Gilmour, examined simultaneously the work of Cyert and March and Bower and traditional capital budgeting theory.[31] As the result of his study of divestiture in three large U.S. businesses in different industries, Gilmour postulated a revised theory which focused on the concept of individual commitment. He proposed that an individual would become committed to a self-generated solution and would implement the decision if he or she had the power. If not, he or she would attempt to persuade others to follow the recommended course of action. E. W. Trevelyan, in researching strategic decision processes in two large organizations, substantiated the concept of incremental decision making.[32] Trevelyan found that each successive commitment to a course of action reinforced others of a similar nature.

Finally, James Brian Quinn, in a key study of 10 major multinational firms, found extensive support, not only for the existence of, but also for the need for, incrementalism. He argues convincingly that politics are a part of organizational life and should not be ignored. Indeed, according to Quinn, a considerable amount of time is spent legitimizing the strategy, building support for it, and coping with opposition. He also suggests that more attention be paid to the behavioral aspects of strategy formulation and implementation.[33]

The incremental decision process in business organizations appears to result from reviews of strategic decisions, taking place at every organizational level. Figure 6.4 reflects this process under the Implementation Component. When the individual does not possess authority (or has not gained support), he or she refers the decision upward in the organization (or attempts to build support). Additional repetitions of the strategic decision process are then necessary. However, incremental decision making for governmental decisions, while resulting partially from structure, appears to result primarily from the desire of the politician "not to rock the voter boat." Several repetitions of the model occur, but not necessarily because the decision maker did not possess the proper authority. In business, the initial impetus for strategic incrementalism (which, importantly, is not characteristic of all decisions) is the initiation of strategic commitments at lower levels, which, once approved by successively higher levels of management, leave little room for rejection at the highest level. But in government, incrementalism allows the politician who does not make waves to be reelected.

[29] J. L. Bower, *Managing the Resource Allocation Process: A Study of Corporate Planning and Investment* (Boston: Division of Research, Harvard Business School, 1970).

[30] R. W. Ackerman, "Influence of Integration and Diversity on the Investment Process," *Administrative Science Quarterly*, September 1970, pp. 341–352; "Organization and the Investment Process: A Comparative Study" (Ph.D. dissertation, Boston: Harvard Business School, 1968).

[31] S. C. Gilmour, "The Divestment Decision Processes" (Ph.D. dissertation, Boston: Harvard Business School, 1973).

[32] E. W. Trevelyan, "The Strategic Process in Large, Complex Organizations: A Pilot Study of New Business Development" (Ph.D. dissertation, Boston: Harvard Business School, 1974).

[33] J. B. Quinn, "Formulating Strategy One Step at A Time," *Journal of Business Strategy*, Winter 1981, pp. 42–63.

The Decision Stages from a Political Perspective.

V. K. Narayanan and Liam Fahey examined the political processes involved in strategic decision making as portrayed in the above-discussed research and in additional research findings. Their work led them to suggest that in organizations where coalitions are an important part of the decision process, distinct stages related to political behavior are identifiable. These stages, in their sequence of occurrence, include: activation, mobilization, coalescence, encounter, and decision. Activation and mobilization parallel recognition and identification respectively in Figures 6.3 and 6.4. Coalescence appears to occur across the identification stage, and perhaps early in the solution process, in those same figures. The encounter and decision stages of the Narayanan and Fahey model occur during the solution and implementation phases of Figures 6.3 and 6.4.

In their model, activation is the stage in which individuals become aware (recognition) of the existence of strategic problems. As awareness of the problems heightens and shifts from an individual to an organizational level, mobilization (identification) occurs. Mobilization is crucial to strategic decision making, because it is in this stage that political commitment is made to various potential decisions. During coalescence, a coalition of interested parties develops, and an impetus towards problem solving evolves. This coalition proposes and sponsors solutions, and as it does, it enters the encounter stage, where it must "encounter" others in the organization in order to present those solutions. The coalition must justify its choices to others through interaction with individuals, other coalitions, organizational subunits, and so on. Eventually, the organization must make a decision. Though the positions of various parties have crystallized, consensus must occur nonetheless. To this end, bargaining, negotiation, and compromise are employed.

This model of the political decision illustrates more distinctly the political process than does the more inclusive, political/rational process model described earlier in this chapter. Understanding how this political process occurs is important because of its significant impact on the rational process.[34]

Three Common Strategic Planning Modes

With respect to the solution and implementation components of the planning process, Henry Mintzberg suggests that three common modes of planning exist. These modes summarize most of the research presented in this chapter.

The first mode he labels the entrepreneurial mode. The traditional concept of strategy formulation holds that it is the entrepreneurial leader who guides the organization to its destiny through strategic decision making. This view of the entrepreneurial leader resulted primarily from the classical economic literature, which saw the entrepreneur as the risk taker, the decision maker. When corporations became the dominant form of enterprise, the characteristics were transposed to the CEO, who normally does not start the enterprise but rather manages it. Certainly many organizations, especially smaller business organizations, are headed by chief executives who fit this model and who do indeed

[34] V. K. Naranyanan and L. Fahey, "The Micro-Politics of Strategy Formulation," *Academy of Management Review*, January 1982, pp. 25–34.

guide almost single-handedly their organizations' fortunes. Among the characteristics of this mode Mintzberg lists the following:[35]

1. *Strategy-making is dominated by the active search for new opportunities.*
2. *Power is centralized in the hands of the chief executive.*
3. *Strategy-making . . . is characterized by dramatic leaps forward in the face of uncertainty.*
4. *Growth is the dominant goal.*

This model is congruent with how most conceptualize strategic management; but, as the material presented earlier in this chapter has shown, other modes exist. Another mode Mintzberg identifies is referred to as the adaptive mode, which is characterized by the coalition and by incremental decision making. Mintzberg characterizes this mode as follows:

1. *Clear goals do not exist . . . strategy-making reflects a division of power among members of a complex coalition.*
2. *The strategy-making process is characterized by the "reactive" solution to existing problems rather than the "proactive" search for new opportunities.*
3. *The adaptive organization makes its decision in incremental, serial steps.*
4. *Disjointed decisions are characteristic of the adaptive mode.*

Mintzberg also suggests a third mode—the planning mode. At the center of this mode are rationality and the analyst. Mintzberg characterizes this mode as follows:

1. *The analyst plays a major role in strategy-making.*
2. *[It] focuses on systematic analysis, particularly in the assessment of the costs and benefits of competing proposals.*
3. *[It] is characterized above all by the integration of decisions and strategies.*

Mintzberg summarizes the key characteristics and conditions of these modes in Table 6.1. What appear to distinguish these three modes are: the source of power, especially single versus multiple decision makers; the decision process utilized, especially the use or absence of systematic planning and planning information; and the number and types of decisions made. While the planning mode was earlier dominated by the professional planner, it would now appear to be dominated by other types of strategists, especially those that are extremely rational in their approach.

Managerial Comprehension of the Behavioral Process

Top management must be attuned to the behavioral aspects of the organization's strategic process—formulation, implementation, and control. Strategy simply cannot be successfully implemented without organizational support. And, as this chapter demonstrates, the

---

[35]H. Mintzberg, "Strategy Making in Three Modes," *California Management Review*, Winter 1973, pp. 45–51.

Table 6.1   Characteristics and Conditions of the Three Modes

Characteristic	Entrepreneurial Mode	Adaptive Mode	Planning Mode
Motive for decisions	Proactive	Reactive	Proactive & reactive
Goals of organization	Growth	Indeterminate	Efficiency & growth
Evaluation of proposals	Judgmental	Judgmental	Analytical
Choices made by	Entrepreneur	Bargaining	Management
Decision horizon	Long-term	Short-term	Long-term
Preferred environment	Uncertainty	Certainty	Risk
Decision linkages	Loosely coupled	Disjointed	Integrated
Flexibility of mode	Flexible	Adaptive	Constrained
Size of moves	Bold decisions	Incremental steps	Global strategies
Vision of direction	General	None	Specific
Conditions for use			
Source of power	Entrepreneur	Divided	Management
Objectives of organization	Operational	Nonoperational	Operational
Organizational environment	Yielding	Complex, dynamic	Predictable, stable
Status of organization	Young, small, or strong leadership	Established	Large

Source: © 1973 by the Regents of the University of California. Reprinted from *California Management Review*, volume XVI, number 2, p. 49, by permission of the Regents.

actual content of strategy will be affected by this process. Decisions reflect their decision makers. Strategies reflect their formulators, their implementers, and those who control them. The top manager who wishes to have strategies succeed must work within the behavioral/political environment as well as within the rational one. Information Capsule 6.1 provides an additional insight into one manager's understanding of this process.

Summary

The strategic decision process follows the classic decision model consisting of recognizing the problem, identifying the problem, solving the problem, implementing solutions to that problem, and controlling for results to make certain that the actions taken did solve the problem. But the behavioral factors involved make the strategic decision process much more complex, much less easy than it might first appear. Figure 6.4 and its accompanying narrative revealed just how complex the process can be. We discovered that both recognition and identification may be complicated by the availability of information and by the use of decision rules of thumb and decision criteria (last year's performance, for example) which may not be appropriate. We also observed that intuition and creativity are necessary parts of the process. Rationality alone is insufficient. The solution phase was characterized as dominated by three types of decision makers—the entrepreneur, the coalition, and other strategists. Each type may or may not make use of information and rational thinking in the decision-making process. Coalitions tend to make decisions in a series of small steps, known as increments, rather than making larger, grander-scale decisions. The values held by the decision makers were found to have significant impacts on strategic decisions, especially those in which a coalition dominated the organization's strategic decision-making process. Mintzberg has shown that three common strategic planning modes exist. These modes are: the entrepreneurial modes, the adaptive mode, and the

INFORMATION CAPSULE 6.1
Commitment to Excellence in Aerospace

When the president of one of the United States's premier aerospace firms appraised the company's strategic situation, he identified two primary issues. First, the future of the aerospace industry was almost certain to hinge on a "fixed-price" contract as opposed to the prevailing "cost-plus" contract. Second, he foresaw significant competitive advantages accruing to foreign competitors, principally the Japanese, in nonproprietary domestic and in virtually all international contract situations because of their abilities to produce high-quality products.

High quality had become an absolute necessity in this industry where a single product unit, for example a missile, might cost $50 million. Encouraged by his operations vice-president, who directed the efforts of two thirds of the firm's 10,000 employees, and who was confronted with the tremendous task of managing the firm's manufacturing efforts for its five current major contracts, the president determined that a commitment to excellence (CTE) program was necessary. This program would require "zero defects" in all products, a gigantic undertaking when one considered the thousands of parts involved in individual product units. With the approval of the firm's top eight managers, the president sent the company's 200 foremost managers to the leading quality management educational institution. This represented an initial investment, in out-of-pocket expenditures, of more than $200,000. Each of these 200 managers attended a three-day seminar on the basics of quality management.

However, these seminars were only the beginning of a major educational process intended to ensure that all levels of management "signed up" for the CTE program. The major problem that the president foresaw with this quality management strategy was that many of the top managers in the firm remembered earlier, largely unsuccessful, attempts at similar programs. And, he was rightfully concerned that many managers within the organization would not support the program for any number of reasons. For example, the firm had been recently restructured into a matrix structure at the macro level. Project managers had responded less than enthusiastically to this new structure since in the former project-based structure they had been more powerful. Consequently, programs initiated from the president's office were often viewed as suspect by some, regardless of their actual, long-term value to the firm. In addition, a number of powerful coalitions existed within the company, while the president had only recently become president. Furthermore, since he had come from another division of the firm and had replaced most top managers within the firm, there existed a coalition of old-line top managers who felt that "outsiders" ran the firm. And though he was an engineer, there were those that felt the new operations emphasis of the firm was less than desirable; after all, for the past ten years, this had been a research and development firm based on engineering. Too, there were always those who thought they "had been passed over." Combined with the inevitable resistance to any change that occurs within organizations, much less a change of such major proportions, challenges to the CTE program were plentiful. The president recognized that he faced considerable opposition in moving forward with his desire to change the organization. He knew that virtually all of this opposition was based on power and other behavioral factors, while, to him, the changes certainly made rational, empirical sense.

Because of this behavior resistance, the president encouraged key managers at all levels of the organization to take part personally in the educational process. He was especially careful to include those top managers whom he felt might not be totally supportive. He believed that by giving them active roles in the process, he would further their personal stake in its success. He was also careful to solicit their advice in developing the specifics of this process and the actual operational mechanisms to be employed. And, when necessary, he twisted a few arms to gain support for the CTE program. These actions occurred within the first six months of what he anticipated to be a three- to five-year program before total implementation would occur and zero defects would become a reality.

Source: This incident was related to one of the authors by several of the firm's top managers.

---

planning mode. These three modes are dominated by the entrepreneur, the coalition, and various strategists and the analyst respectively, and are comprised of varying degrees of objective setting, incrementalism, political maneuvering, use of information, and rationality.

Key Terms and Concepts

Before you complete this chapter, you should become familiar with the following key terms and concepts: the classic five-part decision model; the definitions of and problems associated with recognition, identification, solution, implementation, and control; the differences between problems and opportunities; the role of criteria in decision making; the uses of information and rationality in decision making; the three major types of decision makers; Mintzberg's three types of decision modes; the impacts of values on decision making; the coalition and how it functions; and the nature of incrementalism.

Discussion Questions

1. How might social relationships among organizational strategists play a role in determining strategy content?

2. What are the four major component phases of strategic decision making as contained in Figure 6.4?

3. Describe the coalition, incremental decision making, and the adaptive mode.

4. Think of an organization with which you are familiar. Imagine a strategic decision of this organization. Now follow the route you think this decision might take through the model in Figure 6.4.

5. Which of the three modes of strategic planning do you suppose is most common? Why?

References

Alexis, M., and Wilson, C. Z., eds. *Organizational Decision Making*. Englewood Cliffs, N.J.: Prentice-Hall, 1967.

Astley, W. Graham. "Toward An Appreciation of Collective Strategy." *Academy of Management Review*, 1984, Vol. 9, No. 3, pp. 526–535.

Bauer, R. A., and Gergan, K. J. *The Study of Policy Formation*. New York: Free Press, 1971.

Bourgeois, L. J. III, and Singh, Jitendra V. "Organizational Slack and Political Behavior Among Top Management Teams." Academy of Management Proceedings, New Orleans, 1983.

Bourgeois, L. J. III. "Strategic Management and Determinism." *Academy of Management Review*, 1984, Vol. 9, No. 4, pp. 586–596.

Chittipeddi, Kumar, and Gioia, Dennis A. "A Cognitive Psychological Perspective on the Strategic Management Process. Proceedings of the Academy of Management, New Orleans, 1983.

Dess, Gregory G. "Consensus in the Strategy Formulation Process and Firm Performance." *Academy of Management Proceedings*, New Orleans, 1983.

Dutton, Jane E. "The Influence of the Strategic Planning Process on Strategic Change." Paper prepared for the Symposium on "Linking Organizational Strategy and Organizational Change." Division of Business Policy and Planning, Academy of Management, Boston, 1984.

Fredrickson, James W. "Rationality in Strategic Decision Processes." Academy of Management Proceedings, New Orleans, 1983.

Hall, Trish. "Executive Style—for a Company Chief, When There's a Whim There's Often a Way." *The Wall Street Journal*, October 1, 1984, pp. 1, 21.

Hambrick, Donald C., and Mason, Phyllis A. "Upper Echelons: The Organization as a Reflection of Its Top Managers." *Academy of Management Review*, 1984, Vol. 9, No. 2, pp. 193–206.

Hickson, D. I., et al. "A Strategic Contingencies Theory of Intraorganizational Power." *Administrative Science Quarterly*, June 1971, pp. 216–229.

Hill, W. "The Goal Formation Process in Complex Organizations." *Journal of Management Studies*, May 1969, pp. 198–208.

Hinings, C. R., et al. "Structural Conditions of Intraorganizational Power." *Administrative Science Quarterly*, March 1974, pp. 22–44.

Karda, M. *Power: How to Get It, How to Use It*. New York: Random House, 1973.

Kelley, George. "Seducing the Elites: the Politics of Decision Making and Innovation in Organizational Networks." *Academy of Management Review*, July 1976, pp. 66–74.

Kipnis, David. "The View from the Top." *Psychology Today*, December 1984, pp. 30–36.

McMurry, R. N. "Power and the Ambitious Executive." *Harvard Business Review*, November/December 1973, p. 140.

"Machiavellian Tactics for B-School Students." *Business Week*, October 13, 1975, p. 86.

March, J. G., and Simon, H. A. *Organizations*. New York: Wiley, 1958.

Mason, R. O. "A Dialectical Approach to Strategic Planning." *Management Science*, April 1969, pp. B403–B414.

Mintzberg, H. "Planning on the Left Side and Managing on the Right." *Harvard Business Review*, July/August 1976, pp. 49–58.

Narayanan, V. K., and Fahey, L. "The Micro-Politics of Strategy Formulation." *Academy of Management Review*, January 1982, No. 1, pp. 25–34.

Ramaprasad, Arkalgud, and Mitroff, Ian I. "On Formulating Strategic Problems." *Academy of Management Review*, 1984, Vol. 9, No. 4, pp. 597–605.

Rondinelli, D. A. "Public Planning and Political Strategy." *Long Range Planning*, April 1976, p. 76.

Quinn, J. B. *Strategies for Change: Logical Incrementalism*. Homewood, Ill: Irwin, 1980.

Shrivastava, Paul. "Enhancing Organizational Research Utilization: The Role of Decision Makers' Assumptions." *Academy of Management Review*, 1984, Vol. 9, No. 1, pp. 18–26.

Simon, H. A. "Theories of Decision Making in Economics and Behavioral Science." *American Economic Review*, June 1959, pp. 253–283.

———. *Administrative Behavior*. New York: Free Press, 1957.

Soelberg, P. "Unprogrammed Decision Making." Research toward Development in Management Thought: Proceedings of the 1966 Annual Meeting of the Academy of Management. Eds. H. P. Hottenstein and R. W. Williams, 1976, pp. 3–16.

Taylor, Ronald N. "Organizational and Behavioral Aspects of Forecasting." *Handbook of Forecasting: A Manager's Guide*. New York: John Wiley & Sons, 1982, pp. 519–534.

Watson, Charles E. "Managerial Mind Sets and the Structural Side of Managing." *Business Horizons*, November/December 1983.

Wu, F. H. "Incrementalism in Financial Strategic Planning." *Academy of Management Review*, January 1981, No. 1, pp. 133–143.

Zalesnik, A. "Power and Politics in Organizational Life," *Harvard Business Review*, May/June 1970, p. 47.

7

Implementation through Management of Structure

The proof is in the execution.

▪ *Robert H. Waterman, Jr.* ▪

The most elegantly conceived, most precisely articulated strategy is virtually worthless unless it is implemented successfully. Far too many firms and far too many managers forget this vital component of the strategic management process. Braniff chose a grand strategy of growth through market development, to be carried out by opening numerous new routes upon deregulation of the airline industry. It forgot that it did not have sufficient staff (pilots, cabin attendants, service and maintenance personnel) to execute that strategy successfully. Coleco, wanting to become a major force in the personal computer market with its Adam, chose a grand strategy based on a price lower than the competition's. To employ this strategy required incorporating consumer-acceptable hardware and software design features and efficient, technologically oriented manufacturing capabilities. Selling the product was not difficult at the projected price. But meeting the requirements of design, price, and quality at that price was. As of May 1985, the firm had failed to achieve its strategic objectives, withdrawing the "Adam" from the marketplace because it did not recognize its limitations in the design and manufacturing of this type of product. Fortunately, Coleco did know how to make toys, and the "Cabbage Patch" proved to be a bountiful garden in 1983 (and to some extent, in 1984), saving the company's beleaguered financial statements. These two firms and thousands of others, large and small, discover each year that setting objectives and formulating strategies is one thing, and making those strategies work to achieve their objectives is another.

This chapter examines implementation—the means by which strategy is translated into successful accomplishment. There are any number of approaches to achieving implementation. Most authorities, however, point to the matching of organizational structure to strategy, to the development of appropriate systems for implementation, to the proper management of the organization's human resources, to the creation of a dominant shared value system, and to the management of the organizational culture, as the key ingredients in successful implementation. The first of these topics, organizational structure, is the principle subject of this chapter.

Organization and Implementation

A great many administrators and managers carry in their heads a pattern of the "ideal" organization. That pattern is the classic hierarchy, the family tree; one man at the top, with three below him, each of whom has three below him, and so on with fearful symmetry

Figure 7.1   The Organization—a Strategic Management Process Model

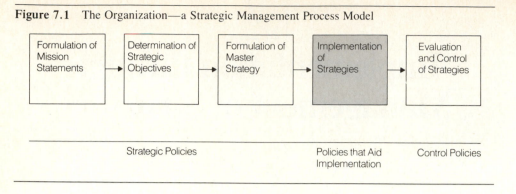

unto the seventh generation, by which stage there is a row of 729 junior managers
and an urgent need for a very large triangular piece of paper.

▪ Anthony Jay ▪

Once strategy has been formulated, it is necessary to design an organizational structure to
carry out that strategy as portrayed in Figure 7.2. In the organizational structuring process, the tasks and jobs required to achieve objectives and enact plans are determined, and
authority is delegated to perform these tasks. This structuring process has a significant
impact upon mission accomplishment:

1. *Because structure defines the specific actions to be taken in implementation.*
2. *Because structure establishes the degree of autonomy each individual has in perform-
    ing implementation activities.*

Organization and implementation are highly interdependent processes. For example, the
amount of authority a manager has places limits on his or her ability to lead—a critical
managerial implementation process. Because organizations are normally ongoing, they
are not concerned with organizing for the first time, but rather with achieving an appropriate combination of strategy and structure in order to ensure the proper implementation.
The components of the organizational process model discussed in this chapter are indicated in Figure 7.1, and the components of the implementation model to be discussed here
are indicated in Figure 7.2.

Organizational Structure

An organization's structure is the combination of its formal and informal structures. Most
perceive the organizational structure as those boxes and connecting lines depicted on the
formal organization chart. But, if the actual concept and relationships portrayed there are
to be realistically envisioned, then the informal organization must also be considered. The
primary dimensions of formal structure include

1. Roles as required by plans and successive divisions of labor (defining the task).
2. Delegation of authority to various individual roles and groupings of roles to enable

Figure 7.2 Implementation

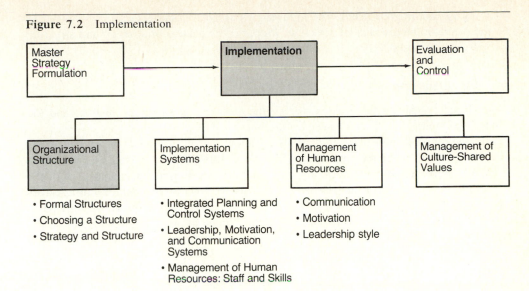

people who fill the roles to accomplish them (delegating the authority to accomplish the task).

Other major structural dimensions include

1. The manager's span of control.
2. Departmentation—the grouping of roles and spans of control into departments on a functional, product, customer, project, geographic, or SBU-division basis.
3. The formalization of processes as revealed in records and reports.
4. The existence of written policies, procedures, and rules governing behavior.
5. Written communications.
6. The number of levels of authority in the organization.
7. The amount of authority delegated—centralization versus decentralization.

A formal, rationally organized social structure involves clearly defined patterns of activity in which, ideally, every series of actions is functionally related to the purposes of the organization.

■ *Robert K. Merton* ■

The informal organization consists of all that is not formal, primarily

1. The personalities of the individuals who fill the roles prescribed by the formal structure.
2. The informal groups which develop within the formal structure.

While much of what follows in this chapter is primarily related to formal structure, the individual and the group as determinants of structure will also be discussed where relevant, though not in great detail. The following paragraphs examine factors considered to be the primary determinants of structure. Proper combinations of strategy and structure will also be discussed.

Formal Structures

Three basic organizational structures exist: the classical pyramid, the matrix, and the team. (See Figure 7.3.) Each displays a different distribution of authority.

The pyramidal form is found in most organizations and is the product of classical organization theory. It is common in both single- and multiple-SBU firms. Note that staff positions may be added throughout the pyramid without changing its basic shape. Both the team and the matrix forms are normally found as part of a pyramidal structure, rather than constituting a firm's entire structure. Figure 7.4 indicates the major types of basic pyramidal forms. The simple structure is normally found in the small organization in the early stages of its existence, or in later stages if it does not grow. The economic functional structure is usually the next structure, to be employed as an organization grows as the result of one major product, or only a few products. The third structure presented is the product structure, which occurs as firms reach certain sizes and various products become significant in terms of contribution to the firm. It then becomes desirable to structure on the basis of products. Once enough product lines in a specific industry or major target market area become sufficiently large, the organization will normally proceed to some type of SBU structure, such as indicated in Figure 7.5. Within any of these four major types of pyramids, departmentation of jobs may occur on the basis of geography, client, or by task specialization. The very large complex organization, pictured in Figure 7.5, often has all of these types of departmentations and basic structures as components. Additional comments on these structures occur later as we discuss in more detail the relationships between and among strategy, structure, and size.

The exact shape of a particular organization's pyramid is primarily a function of the spans of control which exist in the organization. A flat pyramid indicates large spans of control and a high degree of delegation of authority. A tall, slim pyramid indicates small spans of control and little delegation of authority. But shapes can be deceiving. Actual delegation may far exceed what the shape indicates; decentralization is a matter of interpersonal relationships, not simply a matter of line drawings on an organization chart.

Figure 7.3   The Shapes of Organization Structures

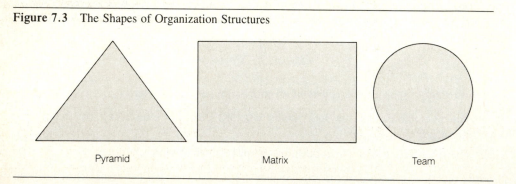

Pyramid   Matrix   Team

Figure 7.4 Types of Pyramids

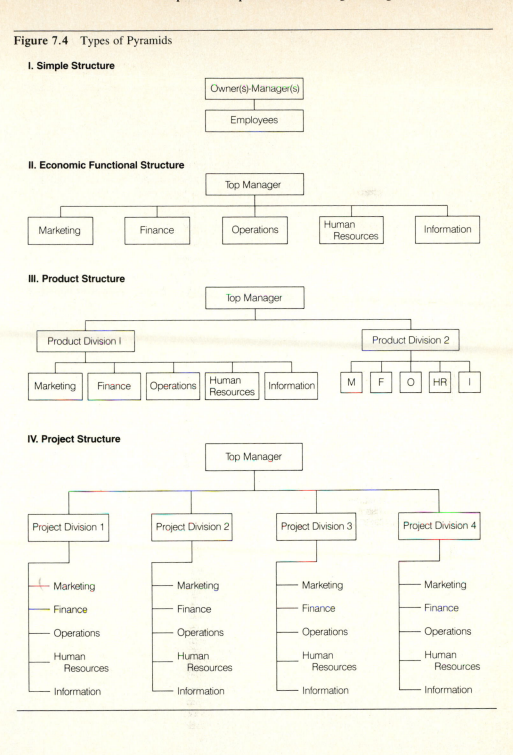

I. Simple Structure

Owner(s)-Manager(s)

Employees

II. Economic Functional Structure

Top Manager

Marketing | Finance | Operations | Human Resources | Information

III. Product Structure

Top Manager

Product Division I

Product Division 2

Marketing | Finance | Operations | Human Resources | Information

M | F | O | HR | I

IV. Project Structure

Top Manager

Project Division 1 | Project Division 2 | Project Division 3 | Project Division 4

Project Division 1:
- Marketing
- Finance
- Operations
- Human Resources
- Information

Project Division 2:
- Marketing
- Finance
- Operations
- Human Resources
- Information

Project Division 3:
- Marketing
- Finance
- Operations
- Human Resources
- Information

Project Division 4:
- Marketing
- Finance
- Operations
- Human Resources
- Information

Figure 7.5 Typical Multidepartmental Organization

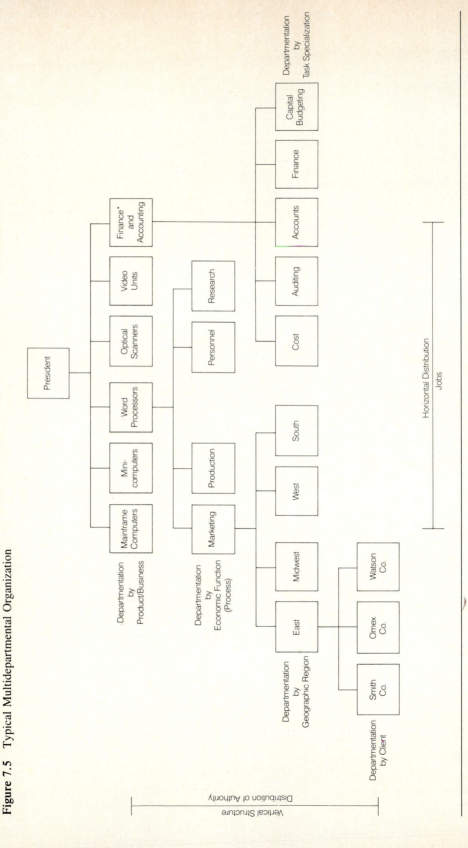

*This particular staff job is normally centralized, that is, operating divisions do not usually have their own finance department.

Source: J. M. Higgins, *Human Relations Concepts and Skills*. Copyright 1982, Random House, Inc., p. 237.

Figure 7.6 The Matrix Organization

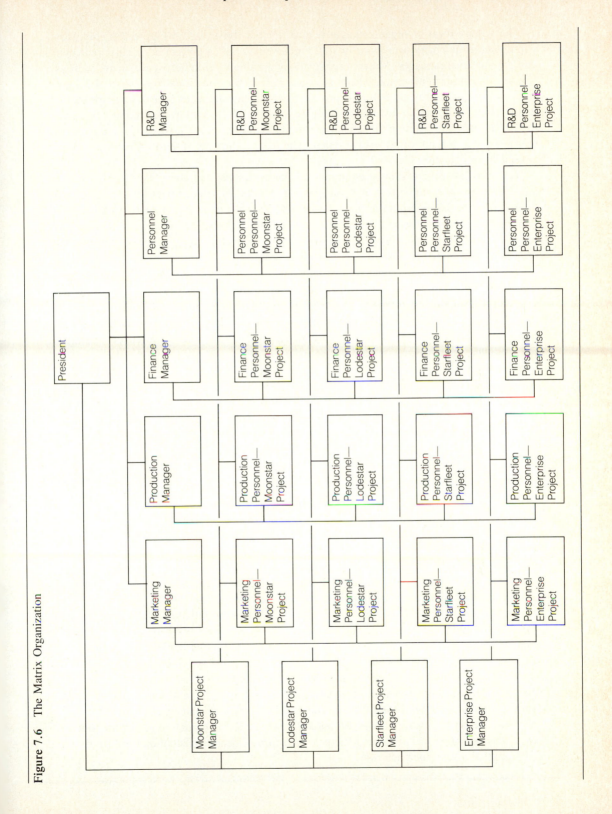

The matrix form of organization structure, further illustrated in Figure 7.6, involves simultaneous authority over a line or staff employee by both a project or product manager and a functional manager. Matrix organizations are common in aerospace firms such as Lockheed or Martin Marietta, where it is necessary to use functional specialists for a period of time on a project, SBU, or product. Matrix management is also appropriate to firms where assignments by functional specialty are made within continuing organizational subunits and where both subunit and functional control are desired; for example, a loan officer at a Bank of America branch. The use of a matrix system in banking is discussed in Information Capsule 7.1.

The matrix organization is used in many organizations to overcome the complex problems of business diversity of either projects or products. A strict project form of management structure differs from the matrix form in that the project structure is principally a temporary pyramidal form of management, with line and staff personnel assigned to the project for a limited time period. (See Figure 7.4.) In a matrix, the project is ongoing and the individual employee has two quasi-permanent bosses.

The team management concept, as illustrated in Information Capsule 7.2, emphasizes the sharing of authority among team members—hence the circle in Figure 7.3 to indicate an equal distribution of authority. The term *team* implies an attitude as much as a structure. The actual distribution of authority depends upon numerous factors: but the essence of team management is participation—the sharing of authority between leader/manager and followers/subordinates in an effort to increase both productivity and employee satisfaction. Teams are usually found as part of a pyramid or matrix. Each work group can be viewed as a team as long as the attitudes utilized in the work force favor participation. More and more organizations are adopting one type of team approach or another in an effort to achieve their objectives. In any organization, some chain of command must exist; but how the subordinates participate within that chain is the vital issue.

INFORMATION CAPSULE 7.1
The Sun Comes Up Matrix

In 1980, Sun Banks, the then third-largest bank group in the state of Florida, found itself with numerous operational problems. Many of its branches had been acquired through purchase. As a result, numerous differing policies and practices existed in the Sun system. Especially troublesome were the reporting relationships in acquired banks, as loan officers and other operating personnel reported to their former presidents, who were now branch managers. Additionally, lending limits varied substantially, and often were not acceptable to higher headquarters. But changes were slow to come through branch managers, many of whom naturally wanted to protect their individual banks since they had a personal interest in them. As Sun reviewed what systems other major banks had employed to overcome these problems, it became obvious that the matrix system was the solution. Loan officers and operations officers were consequently placed in a dual reporting relationship. They were controlled through the headquarters loan and operations officers in terms of loan and operational policies, but still reported to the branch manager for routine day-to-day operations. This arrangement proved to be extremely beneficial in improving Sun's control over branch activities.

INFORMATION CAPSULE 7.2
The Quality Control Circle

The quality control circle is a team-management approach being utilized increasingly in the United States and Canada today. The quality control circle is a voluntary group of employees meeting periodically on company time to analyze and solve work-related problems. Major features of the group include their heavy usage of statistical quality control methodologies and their use of participation in decision making. The supervisor of the work group participates in these meetings, but is more of a facilitator and resource person than a traditional "boss."

The quality control circle was started in Japan, but has been imported to the United States and Canada in an effort to improve sagging quality and productivity. It remains to be seen whether or not this approach can work well in these countries, but reported results in companies such as Lockheed, Quasar, Martin Marietta, and others have been impressive.

In addition to the three structures described above, another form exists—the venture. Ventures are basically partnerships between two distinct organizations which allow firms to combine their strengths and mitigate their weaknesses to accomplish jointly a task neither could achieve singly. Many times, resolving capital or cash flow problems may lead to a venture agreement. The need to enhance technology and management skills may also bring two firms together. Quite often, a smaller, technologically innovative firm will combine with a larger, cash-rich, marketing-oriented firm to market a particular product, often for a set period of time. Edward B. Roberts suggests that two major problems occur in joint ventures.[1] First, both partners may misread the match; each may think the other is better suited to the joint purpose than it is. Second, there is often what Roberts calls an impedance mismatch; the firms simply do not manage the same way. The smaller firm, for example, may find itself ready to make decisions, while the larger firm's representatives must carry back information from meetings to supervisors, who will ultimately decide on strategic matters. Nonetheless, the rewards from ventures can be great, and ventures are an increasingly popular form of organizational structure.

Choosing a Structure

Most decisions regarding structure are concerned with

1. What division of labor is appropriate for a given situation (defining the task).
2. Whether, how, and to what degree the organization should be centralized or decentralized (delegating authority to accomplish the task).

The determinants of structure have been examined extensively in both the normative and the empirical literature. It is evident that no single factor determines structure. Rather, multiple factors are responsible for the structures used by organizations, and the primary

[1] E. B. Roberts, "New Ventures for Corporate Growth," *Harvard Business Review*, July/August 1980, pp. 134–142.

determinants appear to vary from situation to situation. However, the available information points to the following seven factors as the most important determinants of structure in most situations. Since these factors and related research should be familiar, they will not be reviewed here in depth.

1. *Size (Growth)*. Organizational size is a significantly structural determinant. As organizations grow to certain sizes, they encounter various structural problems. The product or SBU division is a natural consequence of growth.

2. *Technology*. The types and complexity of the technology employed to accomplish an organization's tasks have been shown to be significantly related to structure. This complexity is not only an issue at lower organization levels, where much of the research has been performed, but also at upper levels, where the complexity of tasks facing top management often requires structural solutions. Computers are having a substantial impact on structure, allowing simultaneously for greater centralization or decentralization depending on management prerogative.

3. *Environment*. Several environmental factors seem to help determine structure, but the amount of change in the environment appears to be the most important. Decentralized firms respond faster to environmental flux than do centralized firms, and are thus preferable in changing environments. Centralized structures, in turn, fare well in stable environments. Information systems may soon allow centralized structures greater flexibility in changeful environments.

4. *Top-Management Prerogative/Philosophy*. Top management may intentionally choose to structure the organization in a certain manner for reasons related to technology, size, or environment. For example, in order to develop its managers' decision-making abilities, some firms may require large spans of control. Or, in order to cut overhead, middle management may be virtually eliminated.

5. *Geographic Considerations*. As organizations expand geographically, either within a single country or into different countries, certain divisions of labor must obviously occur. Geographic decentralization does not necessarily require decision decentralization, although the latter often follows. However, geographic decentralization does require new divisions of labor. Martin Marietta, for example, has three SBU group divisions, one of them an international division.

6. *Informal Organization*. The people who fill positions in the organization may, in fact, demand a particular type of formal structure. For example, professionals—engineers, accountants, and scientists—may not tolerate a mechanistic, formalized work situation.

7. *Strategy*. A. D. Chandler, in his classic book *Strategy and Structure*, was the first to expound the relationship between these two concepts.[2] His examination of the histories of General Motors, Dupont, Standard Oil of New Jersey, and Sears Roebuck & Company showed that their decentralized, multidivisional structures resulted largely from trial-and-error attempts to meet environmental conditions. He believed that outside market opportunity was the primary variable affecting structure, since structure

---

[2] A. D. Chandler, *Strategy and Structure* (Cambridge, Mass.: MIT Press, 1962). D. J. Hall and M. A. Saias, "Strategy Follows Structure," *Strategic Management Journal*, April–June, 1980, pp. 149–165.

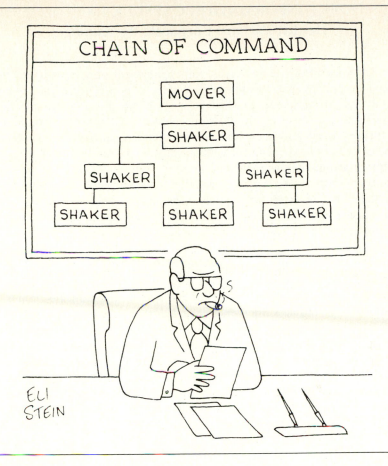

followed strategy. Also, while supporting the view that size contributed to variations in structure, he observed that task complexity at top-management levels also accounted for a significant amount of variation in organizational structure. It is logical that what an organization wishes to become and how it goes about accomplishing that goal, while managing its interactions with the environment, would to a great extent decide most of the other structural determinants as well—technology, size, environment, and geographic dispersion. Strategy, by definition and as discussed in relation to the organizational process model, leads to structure. It has been observed that structure can lead to strategy as well. Indeed, certain structures prohibit certain strategies as Information Capsule 7.3 reveals.

Little further research has been performed strictly on the strategy and structure relationship. However, both Parsons and Selznik have argued that a very definite relationship exists between organizational charter (mission) and structure.[3]

---

[3]T. Parsons, "Suggestion for a Sociological Approach to the Theory of Organization: I and II," *Administrative Science Quarterly* June 1956, pp. 63–85 and September 1956, pp. 225–239; P. Selznik, *TVA and the Grass Roots* (Berkeley: University of California Press, 1949).

INFORMATION CAPSULE 7.3
Hewlett-Packard Corporate Revamping

In July 1984 Hewlett-Packard announced the appointment of a chief operating officer (COO) and a major corporate reorganization. Widely acknowledged for an organizational culture which valued innovation and which utilized a highly decentralized operating mode that had spawned a series of highly successful products, HP's announcement came as a surprise. It even prompted some analysts to suggest that the reorganization was an indication of the company's disappointment with its early forays into personal computers and other high-tech and high-growth markets. Dean O. Martin, the newly appointed COO, refuted these observations and suggested that it was not a reflection of any kind of dissatisfaction. Rather, he suggested that the reorganization had been discussed over a long period of time and would be an orderly process. (H-P has a reputation for being one of the nation's most well-managed companies and had had only one previous change in top management. In fact, Peters's and Waterman's *In Search of Excellence* had noted H-P as one of their "excellent" companies.)

Hewlett-Packard reorganized "according to market areas rather than along product lines", creating three main areas: the medical and analytical instruments groups; a group selling computers for business use (which included personal computers); and the instruments group (which included computer-aided engineering [CAE] and computer-integrated manufacturing). Prior to this reorganization, Hewlett-Packard had operated as a loose agglomeration of small, autonomous businesses, each focused on its own product line. One analyst suggested that this had worked wonderfully as long as Hewlett-Packard pursued hundreds of niche markets. But as customers began to demand systems of Hewlett-Packard products that could work together, the organization's autonomous structure turned into a liability.

To the astonishment of Hewlett-Packard executives restructuring to a centralized operating structure proved extremely difficult, as it required the (previously) fiercely autonomous divisions to cooperate in the new structure in order to establish effective product development and marketing activities. An example of this difficulty is the Computer-Aided Engineering (CAE) division, which was established in early 1983. The CAE industry is a fast-growing market totaling approximately $275 million in 1984 and expected to double in 1985. Hewlett-Packard had previously announced that a line of CAE hardware and software designed to speed the development of electronic systems would be marketed beginning in November of 1984. To this end, the CAE Division was given a special franchise to build systems out of hardware drawn from at least six other Hewlett-Packard divisions. In fact, Hewlett-Packard didn't launch any CAE products in 1984, and according to a *Fortune* magazine article of October 29, 1984, Williams Parzybok, general manager of the design systems group, "prefers not to talk about introduction dates."

What's Happened?   With reorganization in July of 1984, most of the CAE division was assigned to two design groups in Colorado, far from their old home in Cupertino, California. Many CAE division engineers and managers were reported to be embittered about the reorganization and were reluctant to transfer. Many began to move to other companies, including a 23-year Hewlett-Packard veteran, Richard Moore, who had headed the division. In fact by the time Hewlett-Packard closed the division in late 1984 many top managers and engineers were gone. Why? People who left are reported to have complained that they had trouble getting rival fiefdoms to cooperate.

Sources: Carrie Dolan, "Hewlett-Packard Corporate Revamping Seen; Adding of Operating Chief Expected," *The Wall Street Journal*, July 16, 1984, p. 2; "Who's Excellent Now?", *Business Week*, November 5, 1984, p. 76–88; Bro Utal, "Delays and Defections at Hewlett-Packard," *Fortune*, October 29, 1984, p. 62.

Structure follows strategy.

▪ *Alfred Chandler* ▪

Strategy follows structure.

▪ *David J. Hall and Maurice A. Saias* ▪

These seven factors are not mutually exclusive. In fact, their interdependence has made scientific analysis difficult, though not impossible. Clearly, strategy and top-management prerogative are primary determinants. However, once these commitments are made, the other factors also have varying impacts on the eventual structural pattern. Only in recent years, as multivariate techniques have been utilized, has the relative importance of these factors been better understood; and what has become apparent through extensive research is that their relative importance is situational. The following summary observations can be made:

1. All of these factors (plus some not mentioned) contribute to structure, but structure begins with strategy. As Chandler has noted, "Unless structure follows strategy, inefficiency results."[4] (See above exceptions.)

2. Within departments (whether based on product, function, customer, project, or geography), operational technology usually plays a significant role in determining structure specifically impinged on by the work flow. Supportive technology (and knowledge) may also play an important role in determining structure. Technology has more of an impact on smaller organizations than on larger ones, on manufacturing organizations than on service organizations. Operational technology has little impact on administrative structures or decentralization, but computers do.

3. Organizations vary substantially in their structures. Subsystems' structures also vary substantially, both within and among organizations. These differences result from the processes of differentiation and integration—coping with the environment while accomplishing mission.

4. Both size and task complexity affect structure. The more tasks, and the more specialized the tasks, the greater the need for structured arrangements of coordination and control—that is, formalization. Size and complexity of tasks affect top-management levels and result in the need for decentralization, except where information systems allow for centralization.

5. The routineness, predictability, or certainty of environment, tasks, or problem-solving

---

[4]Chandler, *Strategy and Structure*.

orientation have all been depicted as the underlying factor that explains much of the variation in structure. These terms appear to describe the same phenomenon.

6.   The classic pyramidal structure model, while common and useful, is limited in its utility as a description of certain types of situations.

7.   An organization is not independent of its environment. The degree of interaction and dependency varies, but no organization completely escapes bargaining or accountability. Structure changes as a result.

8.   Structure is not and cannot be static in a changing environment.

9.   The structure of staff as well as line components is governed by these factors, but in different degrees.

Designing organizations to meet the demands of the situation is not an easy task. There are few authoritative guidelines, and the research is only now beginning to suggest what separates effective from ineffective organizations. It has often been assumed that for a given environment or technology a certain structure was appropriate. However, empirical evidence to date does not support this view. Rather, many factors result in the selection of structure and in the proper combination of strategy and structure. The next few paragraphs review some of the more common problems associated with organizational structure.

Never formalize, print, and circulate them (organization charts). Good organizations are living bodies that grow new muscles to meet challenges. A chart demoralizes people. Nobody thinks of himself as 'below' other people. And in a good company, he isn't.
Yet on paper, there it is.

■ *Robert Townsend, Former President of Avis* ■

Strategy and Structure:
Size, Growth, and Environment—a Discussion

Given the results of research and the nature of the strategy formulation process, the organization's primary concern with structure becomes one of matching strategy to structure and structure to size and environment. Size is invariably a direct result of growth. The importance of growth as a factor in structure determination is obvious, since most organizations, especially businesses, grow and have growth strategies. Growth has, of course, been discussed at length, and several theories of resultant structural relationships have emerged. Examining these theories and other data reveal several commonly occurring problem areas in the relationship between growth, size, and structure.[5]

[5]R. R. Blake, W. E. Avis and J. S. Mouton, *Corporate Darwinism* (Houston: Gulf, 1966); N. C. Churchill and V. L. Lewis, "The Five Stages of Small Business Growth," *Harvard Business Review*, May/June 1983, pp. 30–50; L. E. Greiner, "Evolution and Revolution as Organizations Grow," *Harvard Business Review*, July/August 1972, pp. 37–46; J. R. Montanari, "Operationalizing Strategic Choice" (Paper presented at the Academy of Management Meeting, Kissimmee, Florida, August 1977); R. P. Rumelt, *Strategy, Structure and Economic Performance of the Fortune "500"* (Cambridge, Mass.: Division of Research, Harvard School of Business, 1974); M. Salter, "Stages of Corporate Development," *Journal of Business Policy*, Autumn 1970; B. R. Scott, "The Industrial State: Old Myths and New Realities," *Harvard Business Review*, March/April 1973, pp. 133–149; Scott, *Stages in Corporate Development: Part II* (Cambridge, Mass.: Harvard School of Business, 1971); D. H. Thain, "Stages of Corporate Development," *Business Quarterly*, Winter 1969, pp. 32–45.

In its most rudimentary form, a firm begins as an individual entrepreneur with an idea. After starting a business, the entrepreneur soon realizes that one person cannot perform all of the tasks related to the product or service. Hence, the first structural problem arises. To solve it, the entrepreneur must institute a division of labor and hire additional employees on a functional basis. Often he or she must seek professional managerial assistance. Soon, however, a second structural problem arises—the entrepreneurial leader has not delegated any authority to the functional area personnel. They are not allowed to manage; they have no autonomy. At this juncture, the leader must delegate and/or the recently hired professional managers must delegate. And, as the firm continues to expand, the amount of authority delegated usually increases. With continued growth, the organization arrives at a point at which geographical expansion is desirable. The third structural problem arises. If the expansion occurs entirely within one country, geographic decentralization (division of labor) follows, with the possibility of increased decision decentralization ensuing. If the expansion involves entering other countries, then a somewhat different pattern of actions is employed. The fourth structural problem (or third, if it occurs before geographic expansion) then occurs, and is related to diversification. The organization may decide to offer additional product lines or services. But the size and task complexity may become too much for one leader to manage closely. As a result, a decision-decentralized product, project, or SBU division structure normally emerges, though sophisticated information systems may allow for centralization. Thus arises a fifth problem, control, associated with all acts of decentralization. When authority is delegated, results must be assured. To ensure those results through formalization may cause the organization to become mechanistic and unadaptive. Eventually, the organization must develop a means of control by specific objectives, with the division or functional area managers delegated authority to proceed within policy to accomplish those objectives. Other approaches, such as team management or the matrix, may be added to the organizational structure, depending on various factors, such as complexity. Various forms of departmentalization also become necessary as the organization grows.

While this model is a simplification, it does point to the major problems normally encountered as organizations grow. Next, each of these problem situations will be discussed in more detail.

Entrepreneurial Start-Up—The Need for Functionalization.   In practice, most firms begin with some type of simple structure which quickly evolves into a functional structure (see Figure 7.4). The problem at this stage of organizational growth is to determine the exact division of labor among the employees. Smaller organizations have difficulty in fully utilizing the efficiencies associated with the division of labor because these firms do not have the resources to take full advantage of all of the possible task simplifications. For a smaller organization, the cost-benefit trade-off of hiring additional personnel to perform more efficiently is often not sufficiently positive to justify this action. The recruitment of a work force with multiple-task skills is therefore required and unfortunately not easily accomplished.

Another problem encountered in this stage is the need for professional management. Entrepreneurs must either learn how to manage as a professional would or must hire professional managers.

A Crisis of Autonomy—A Solution of Delegation.   Some entrepreneurs never can relinquish authority. One clothing manufacturer who had 250 employees and annual sales of

$6 million could be found working at 10 p.m. on weekends on the accounts payable ledger, even though he had an accounting staff. Six months after he was advised to use his time better, he was still performing this activity. In another case, an Air Force missile wing commander personally inspected Montana State Highway bridges for tonnage requirements because a bride had collapsed under a truck carrying a missile. He also personally sanded the base gymnasium floor to make certain a good job was done. And he personally approved every purchase order over $50.

The syndrome is a common one. The question is: who will inform the leader of his or her faults? Just as importantly, how can his or her behavior be changed? A change agent (a consultant) may be requested, but often only after a catalyst, usually a serious downturn in organizational fortunes, has taken place. It is normally the catalyst that calls attention to the need for delegation. This pattern occurs in the largest multidivisional organizations as well as in smaller organizations. Managers have a natural propensity for holding onto power. Indeed, one of the major value orientations of managers is the political orientation, the desire for power, as discussed in Chapter 6.

The Problem of Geographic Expansion—A Solution of Decentralization.   When expansion occurs within a single country, the structural patterns routinely include some decision decentralization as well as geographic decentralization. The greater the physical distance, the more the amount of decision decentralization that would seem naturally to follow. When expansion occurs into new countries, a somewhat different pattern of events normally transpires, as discussed in Chapter 10.

Diversification—Decentralization with the Product/SBU Divisionalized Structure.
When the business firm diversifies into additional products and services, the characteristic structure utilized is one known as the product/SBU division structure. (See Figures 7.4 and 7.5.) In this structure, the product/SBU division is the first level of the corporate hierarchy below the CEO. These divisions usually have functional internal structures. Making the transition from an organization operating on a functional basis to an organization operating primarily on a product/SBU basis is apparently called for by the complexity of the top-management process in highly complex situations.

A. H. Walker and J. W. Lorsch identified three criteria for choosing between product (SBU) and functional structures.[6]

1.   Which approach permits the maximum use of special technical knowledge?
2.   Which provides the most efficient utilization of machinery and equipment?
3.   Which provides the best hope of obtaining the required control and coordination?

Recognizing, however, the extent of the problem, the behavioral aspects, and the significance of information obtained through research since the first set of criteria was formulated, they offer the following as more relevant criteria:

1.   How will the choice affect differentiation among specialists? Will it allow the necessary differences in viewpoint to develop so that specialized tasks can be performed effectively?

---

[6] A. H. Walker and J. W. Lorsch, "Organizational Choice: Product versus Function," *Harvard Business Review*, November/December 1968, pp. 131–132.

2. How does the decision affect the prospects of accomplishing integration? Will it lead, for instance, to greater differentiation, which will increase the problems of achieving integration?

3. How will the decision affect the ability of organization members to communicate with each other, resolve conflicts, and reach the necessary joint decisions?

L. Wrigley found that among larger, diversified firms, the product/SBU divisionalized structure is quite common; it is the dominant form (approximately 90 percent) among *Fortune* 500 companies.[7] A whole series of studies performed at the Harvard School of Business reveals that the divisional form has in the past 15 to 25 years become the dominant form in the largest firms in the United States, Europe, and Japan.[8] L. G. Franko, in a separate survey, found similar results among European firms. However, he suggested that the divisional structure in Europe resulted primarily from competition and not from product diversification strategies, which seems to be the common cause in the United States.[9]

It may very well be that there is a point of diminishing returns with regard to size. As suggested previously, the product/SBU division structure may become tangled by mechanistic control systems which attempt to ensure that all activity is congruent with overall objectives. Commonly, people refer to these controls as red tape. Red tape is found in business, in government, and in nonprofit private sector organizations. Various means of removing it have been suggested. The best at this time appears to be autonomy for the decision-decentralized divisions. Broad policy guidelines and specific objectives exist for the company, but plans of action are formulated by the divisions themselves. In this process, information and control systems play significant roles.

Team management has been offered as another solution to the problem. If team management should prove to be the appropriate device for controlling large, multidivisional organizations, then presumably another structure problem would result. Only time will tell what problems will result from team management.

In summary, organizational structure does not seem to depend on any one factor. Rather, several factors act as determinants. The relevance of each is situational, although strategy begins with structure and management prerogative—two considerations often neglected in current research. Organizations pass through various stages of growth, each of which results in certain structural problems. Finally, it should be observed that we cannot yet determine what problems may be associated with growth beyond the team-managed stage of organization. There are sufficient problems dealing with earlier stages of structure, as Information Capsule 7.3 reveals.

[7] L. Wrigley, "Divisional Autonomy and Diversification" (Ph.D. dissertation, Cambridge, Mass.: Harvard School of Business, 1970).

[8] D. F. Channon, "Strategy and Structure of British Enterprise" (Ph.D. dissertation, Cambridge, Mass.: Harvard School of Business, 1971); R. J. Pavan, "Strategy and Structure: The Italian Experience," *Journal of Economics and Business*. Spring/Summer 1976, pp. 254–260; R. J. Pavan, "Strategy and Structure of Italian Enterprise" (Ph.D. dissertation, Cambridge, Mass.: Harvard School of Business, 1972); G. Pooley, "Strategy and Structure of French Enterprise" (Ph.D. dissertation, Cambridge, Mass.: Harvard School of Business, 1972); H. Thanheiser, "Strategy and Structure of German Enterprise" (Ph.D. dissertation, Cambridge, Mass.: Harvard School of Business, 1972).

[9] L. G. Franko, "The Move toward a Multidivisional Structure in European Organizations," *Administrative Science Quarterly*, December 1974, pp. 493–506.

Current Trends in Organizational Structuring

Five factors had a major impact on organizational structure in the early 1980s. First, a recession from 1981 to 1983 caused many firms to cut staff and middle-management positions. The "lean-and-mean" look became a popular objective as firms trimmed employees to save money. Second, a philosophical management change regarding structures transpired. Spurred on by books such as *In Search of Excellence*, many top managers began to believe that running "lean and mean" was a better structural approach regardless of the condition of the economy. Financial success, in fact, began to be considered as a consequence of that approach. Thus, staff and middle management became less desirable. Third, there arose a disenchantment with the process and results of strategic planning, and with the role of professional strategists. Influenced by the various proponents of intrapreneurship, top management decentralized in many firms, making line management more responsible for strategic decision making and implementation. Fourth, the personal computer and related software have enabled almost anyone with information access to engage in strategic planning. These innovations further reduce the need for middle-management and professional advisory personnel. Note that the options include not only increased decentralization, but also increased centralization due to information availability. The computer will, in fact, process the information, a function that middle management and staff used to perform. Finally, the continued demands of employees for a quality work life provided an impetus for increased worker participation in decision making.[10]

Summary

Organizational structure has several major determinants, whose importance varies with the situation. Organizations have a choice among three basic structures: the pyramid, the matrix, and the team. The decentralized pyramid is the most common structure in larger organizations. The product/SBU division structure is the most common structure in diversified firms. The choice of structures depends on seven key factors: size, technology, environment, top-management prerogative/philosophy, geographic considerations, the informal organization, and strategy. Once structured, the organization must implement its plans, a process that is discussed in depth in the next chapter. The relationships between organizational structure and implementation are of critical importance.

Key Terms and Concepts

By the time you have completed this chapter, you should be familiar with the following key terms and concepts: strategy follows structure, structure follows strategy, major structural dimensions, three major formal structures, ventures, seven factors upon which choice of structures depends, and common major problems and current trends in structure.

---

[10] "A New Era for Management," *Business Week*, April 25, 1983, pp. 50–86; "Here Comes the 'Intrapreneur,'" *Business Week*, July 18, 1983, pp. 189–190; "Office Automation: Savvy Executives Can Use New Technologies to Flatten the Bureaucratic Pyramid—by Cutting Management Layers and Redefining Work Patterns," *Business Week*, October 8, 1984, pp. 118–121; L. McGinley, "Despite the Expansion, Many Companies Trim Their Labor-Force Size," *The Wall Street Journal*, October 26, 1984, pp. 1, 14.

Discussion Questions

1. Describe for each of the seven major determinants of organizational structure a situation in which that determinant plays the major role in determining structure.

2. What did Chandler mean when he said that structure follows strategy?

3. How are size (growth) and structure related?

4. Walker and Lorsch identified three criteria for choosing between product (SBU) and functional structures. Discuss the usefulness of these criteria.

5. Has Hewlett-Packard resolved satisfactorily the problems of reorganization noted in Information Capsule 7.3?

References

Abrams, Bill. "Sperry Planning to Write Down Its Trilogy Stake." *The Wall Street Journal*, July 16, 1984, p. 2.

Aldrich, H. B. "Technology and Organization Structure: A Reexamination of the Findings of the Aston Group." *Administrative Science Quarterly*, March 17, 1972, pp. 23–43.

Blois, K. J. "The Structure of Service Firms and Their Marketing Policies." *Strategic Management Journal*, 1983, Vol. 4, pp. 251–261.

"Delays and Defections at Hewlett-Packard," *Fortune*, October 29, 1984, p. 64.

Dewar, R. D., and Simet, D. P. "A Level Specific Prediction of Spans of Control Examining the Effects of Size, Technology, and Specialization." *Academy of Management Journal*, March 1981, pp. 5–24.

Ford, J. C., and Slocum, J. W., Jr. "Size, Technology, Environment and the Structure of Organizations." *Academy of Management Review*, October 1977, pp. 561–575.

Franklin, J. L. "Relations among Four Social-Psychological Aspects of Organization." *Administrative Science Quarterly*, September 1975, pp. 422–433.

Fredrickson, James W. "The Effect of Structure on the Strategic Decision Process." *Academy of Management Proceedings*, New Orleans, 1983, pp. 12–16.

Grinyer, P. H., and Ysai-Ardekani, M. "Strategy, Structure, Size, and Bureaucracy." *Academy of Management Journal*, September 1981, pp. 471–486.

————, "Dimensions of Organizational Structure: A Critical Replication." *Academy of Management Journal*, September 1980, pp. 405–421.

Hax, Arnoldo C., and Majluf, Nicholas S. "Organization Design: A Case Study on Matching Strategy and Structure." *The Journal of Business Strategy*, Fall 1983.

Lorange, Peter. "Organizational Structure and Management Processes, Implications for Effective Strategic Management." *Handbook of Business Strategy*, eds. William Guth, Warren, Gorham & Lamont, Inc., Boston, October 1984.

Peters, Thomas J. "Strategy Follows Structure: Developing Distinctive Skills." *California Management Review*, Vol. 26, No. 3, Spring 1984, pp. 111–125.

Pugh, D. S. "The Context of Organizational Structures." *Administrative Science Quarterly*, December 1969, p. 91.

Watson, Craig M. "Leadership, Management and the Seven Keys." *Business Horizons*, March/April 1983, pp. 8–13.

"Who's Excellent Now?" *Business Week*, November 5, 1984, pp. 76–88.

Implementation through Management of Systems, Human Resources, and Culture

We are in the process of reinventing the corporation. The rules are rapidly changing. And today's planners must consider several surprising new factors as they enter the work place.

■ *John Naisbitt,* Defining the New Workplace ■

Probably less is understood about successful implementation, once structure is determined, than about any other phase of strategic management. Fortunately, the amount of relevant conceptual and research literature is growing rapidly because strategists have realized the importance of this complex topic. Much has also been written with regard to the topics embodied in the remaining process of implementation.[1] Almost all the management functions—planning, controlling, organizing, leading, directing, integrating, communicating, decision making, and representing—are to some degree applied in these processes.

However, this text is not the appropriate medium for a long discourse on the nature of successful implementation. The focus of the following discussion, then, is only on those aspects of implementation considered to be the most essential and which may not have been covered extensively in other courses. Where the reader is expected to be familiar with the topic, the discussion will be brief, with emphasis on how these familiar topics relate to successful implementation. Figure 8.1 indicates that component of the strategic process discussed in this chapter.

I used to keep a sign opposite my desk where I couldn't miss it if I was on the telephone [about to make an appointment] or in a meeting in my office: "Is what I'm doing or about to do getting us closer to our objective?" That sign saved me from a lot of useless trips, lunch dates, conferences, junkets and meetings.

■ *Robert Townsend, Former President, Avis* ■

---

[1] M. Jelinek, "Implementing Corporate Strategy—Theory and Reality" (Paper presented to the Strategic Management Society, Paris, October 1983).

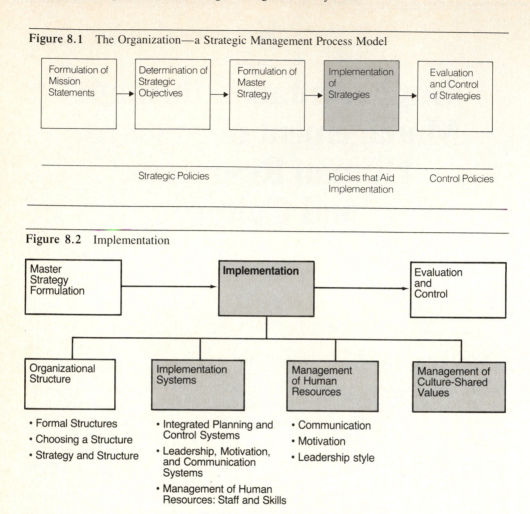

Figure 8.1   The Organization—a Strategic Management Process Model

| Formulation of Mission Statements | Determination of Strategic Objectives | Formulation of Master Strategy | Implementation of Strategies | Evaluation and Control of Strategies |

Strategic Policies   Policies that Aid Implementation   Control Policies

Figure 8.2   Implementation

Implementation Systems

Implementation is the process of translating strategic plans and policies into results. It is the summation of activities in which people use various resources to accomplish the objectives of the strategy. In conjunction with the choice of structures (discussed in Chapter 7), four other key elements are necessary in order for strategy to be successfully implemented. First, as portrayed in Figure 8.2, management systems must be adequate to the task. Integrated planning and control systems; appropriate leadership, motivation, and communication systems; and relevant human resources management systems (to provide a staff with skills) must be utilized. These systems function to ensure that implementation activities—for example, decision making or physical labor—are in accordance with strategy. Vital to this end are objectives, plans, and policies. In most organizations, the strategy is first further spelled out in terms of intermediate plans/programs, later in terms of operational plans, and finally in individual and work group actions. Operational planning is especially critical to successful implementation, since, in this planning effort, the exact actions to be taken by first-line employees are delineated. One of the major operational plans (a financial plan) is the budget, which guides the year-to-year expenditure of funds in pursuit of mission accomplishment. Second, once resources—human, financial, and capital—are committed to the tasks established in organizing, they must be properly managed. Appropriate human resources management by individual managers is the essence of this phase of implementation. Third, corporate culture must be managed in a manner that is congruent with mission. This often leads to the additional concern of implementation, a dominant sense of shared values for organizational members.

Integrated Planning and Control Systems

Integrated planning and control starts with master strategy formulation and is of concern in the formulation of all plans derived from the master strategy. Successful implementation requires that precise objectives be stipulated for strategies and for the intermediate and operational plans derived therefrom. This is accomplished through the use of an MBORR-type system, as was discussed in Chapter 3. Precise objectives, by clarifying role prescription for executives, managers, and first-line employees, achieve the following:

1. They assure that these individuals will know what is expected of them.

2. They provide built-in standards against which performance can be compared for control purposes.

3. They assume that each action taken is in pursuit of mission.

Integration of the efforts of the organization's subsystems is assisted by these systems and by network planning models such as the now-familiar Program Evaluation Review Technique (PERT), Critical Path Method (CPM), and Gantt Charts. Since control is the subject of the next chapter, this chapter focuses on the planning aspects of these systems. The following sections discuss the following planning and control systems: intermediate planning programs, operational planning, and budgets.

Intermediate Planning Programs.   In the intermediate planning phase, the broader plans of strategy are more specifically delineated in what are often referred to as programs. Large, diversified organizations make these more refined plans on an SBU/product division basis. The business/product divisions themselves, as well as firms that make a single product or few products, formulate these plans on a functional (marketing, production, finance, personnel) basis. Some firms attempt to skip the intermediate phase entirely, going directly from strategy to operations. This usually results in ineffective operations, since strategies are so broad and operations so specific that additional intermediate planning is necessary for a smooth transition. Intermediate plans vary greatly in scope, time, horizon, comprehensiveness, and degree of detail. Normally, several successive intermediate plans are required to translate strategy into operations. For example, in a large multinational firm, the master strategy might consist of a corporate strategy and several SBU/product division strategies. These in turn might consist of competitive, supportive, and strategic issues strategies. Each of these components has several substrategies, all requiring intermediate plans/programs. (Some prefer to use the term *program* as a designation for an SBU division grand strategy only.)

As an example, let us examine the production substrategy. An intermediate plan is required to translate the production strategy into requirements for the various countries involved. Another intermediate plan is required to allocate objectives and actions to plants within those countries. Yet another intermediate plan is required to allocate objectives and actions to departments within each plant. Finally, operational planning occurs to allocate objectives and tasks to individuals. At each of these levels, coordinated policies are generated to aid managers in decision making.

Planning—setting objectives and determining plans to reach those objectives—is what connects mission with individual performance. Intermediate plans play an important role in this process. By establishing successive levels of objectives, plans to reach those objectives, and coordinated policies to ensure proper implementation of those plans, organizations greatly improve their chances of success. After all, the individuals who must perform operational tasks can do so correctly only if they know precisely what they are supposed to do. The intermediate planning process aids in forming proper individual role prescriptions by parceling strategic objectives, plans, and policies into more manageable dimensions at each successive level of the firm. Note that what is strategic to divisions or an SBU will be an intermediate plan/program to the total organization.

The strategy is nothing until it degenerates into work.

▪ *Peter Drucker* ▪

Operational Planning.   Operational planning is a key component of implementation. Operational plans normally cover a period of one year, although the period varies among organizations. General Electric and many other organizations label these one-year operating plans Profit Plans. Profit Plans are used to translate intermediate plans into definite, result-producing actions. The descriptions of these actions and their objectives are normally referred to as procedures, rules, or job descriptions. It is these operational plans that give substance to strategy. Profit plans have the most detailed objectives and the most specific activity requirements of any plans. They specify the exact resources needed and the precise manner in which to obtain and utilize those resources. Operational planning involves the middle and lower levels of management. But sometimes these plans don't work out as the cartoon suggests.

As observed by T. A. Anderson, operating plans emphasize automatic decision-making rules, procedures, and integrative activity.[2] These plans deal with adjusting production, marketing, and financial capacity to the levels of operation. They aim to increase the efficiency of operating activities, and provide specific details of short-term operations. In short, operational planning focuses on the ways and means of accomplishing strategic objectives.

Budgets.   The most common of the specific operational planning and control systems is the budget. The budget is usually referred to as a financial operating plan. It translates plans of action, usually operating plans, into dollar commitments. Through the budget,

---

[2]T. A. Anderson, "Coordinating Strategic and Operational Planning," *Business Horizons*, Summer 1965, p. 51.

"I must have heard you wrong, Winfield. I thought you said this little
$100 million pension liability just appeared out of nowhere."

Source: Buck Consultants, Inc., Two Pennsylvania Plaza, New York, New York 10121.

the organization determines whether an operating plan is acceptable on the bottom line
(anticipated profit). It is also the primary means by which funds are committed.

There are normally two major types of budgets: the operating budget and the financial
budget. The operating budget consists of various functional budgets. This budget begins
with a revenue forecast. For business, this is the sales forecast; for government, it is the
tax receipt estimate and the monetary manipulations forecast; and for nonprofit private
sector organizations, it may be a forecast of contributions. In budgeting, when estimated
expenditures are matched against anticipated revenues, role expectations emerge. Usually, some provisions are made for unforeseen variations in budgeted performance expectations. The operational budget's impacts upon the financial health of the firm are portrayed in the financial budget, composed of various cash and capital budgets. These, in
turn, are used to develop pro forma financial statements. Figure 8.3 details the relationships between the major types of budgets.

Real live businessmen have learned that the big challenge
isn't concocting strategy but making it work.

▪ *Walter Kiechel III* ▪

Figure 8.3   The Budget

```
                    ┌──────────────────┐
                    │  Operating Plan  │
                    └──────────────────┘
                             │
                             ▼
                    ┌──────────────────┐
                    │ Annual Profit Plan│
                    └──────────────────┘
                             │
                             ▼
                    ┌──────────────────┐
                    │ Income Objective │
                    └──────────────────┘
                   ┌─────────┴─────────┐
                   ▼                   ▼
        ┌──────────────┐        ┌──────────────┐
        │ Sales Budget │        │ Other Income │
        │              │        │ Budget       │
        └──────────────┘        └──────────────┘
              └──────────Less──────────┘
                             ▼
                    ┌──────────────────┐
                    │ Estimated        │
                    │ Total Costs and  │
                    │ Expenses         │
                    └──────────────────┘
            ┌────────────┼────────────┐
            ▼            ▼            ▼
    ┌──────────┐  ┌──────────────┐  ┌──────────────┐
    │Production│  │ General and  │  │ Other Income │
    │Budget    │  │ Administrative│ │ Budget       │
    │          │  │ Budget       │  │              │
    └──────────┘  └──────────────┘  └──────────────┘
            └────────────┼────────────┘
                         ▼
                ┌──────────────┐
                │ Financial    │
                │ Budget       │
                └──────────────┘
                         │
                         ▼
                ┌──────────────┐
                │ Balance Sheet│
                │ Cash Budget  │
                │ Capital Budget│
                └──────────────┘
```

Leadership, Motivation, and Communication Systems

Strategists must lead and channel their subordinates' motivations in order to have successful implementation. Top-management's leadership style has a tremendous impact on the success and failure rates of corporations. There are now only beginning to emerge a number of theories related to top-management styles and their impact on successful implementation. These theories are as yet too preliminary for discussion here, but comments on leadership made later in this chapter are generally relevant.[3] Equally as important as leadership are the motivation/compensation approaches employed to motivate managers to implement strategy. Part of Chapter 5 addressed this issue in terms of motivating SBU managers in multiple-SBU firms. On a broader scale, the strategists and the organization must provide some reason, normally monetary in nature, for the top managers (and all

[3]For example, see J. G. Wissema, H. M. Van Der Pol, and H. M. Messer, "Strategic Management Archetypes, *Strategic Management Journal*, 1980, Vol. 1, pp. 37–47.

others) to want to implement strategy. Participative types of management also apparently motivate managers (and others) to want to implement strategy. Therefore, careful thought and attention must be given to the development of these systems. (More detailed commentary, relevant here as well, follows on motivation as it applies to implementation in general.) Finally, an entire range of communication systems—policies, rules, procedures, memorandums, marketing plans, program plans, bulletin boards, periodic meetings, company newspapers, retreats, action lines, and so forth—must be carefully employed in order to assure successful implementation. (Note that plans not only serve the function we normally envision, but also serve as communication devices as well.)

Management of Human Resources

From the systems perspective, much of these areas are managed through the personnel, or human resources management function, which, in most organizations, has assumed a much more significant role than it did years ago.

Human resources officers now play a key role and command top dollar.

▪ Business Week ▪

A note on the Personnel Function.   The personnel department—or, as it is often called today, the human resources management department—is charged with two primary series of functions. The first series focuses on placing the employee and includes:

- *Personnel Planning.* Determining the jobs necessary to carry out the mission; determining the number of people needed and where and when they will be needed, and with what capabilities, to fill those jobs.
- *Recruiting and Attracting.* Obtaining a pool of applicants for those jobs.
- *Selecting.* Choosing from among the applicants those best suited to perform those jobs.
- *Training and Developing.* Preparing employees to perform those jobs.
- *Orienting.* Integrating the individual into the work unit.

The second series of functions occurs once the employee has been placed in the job; it includes:

- *Training and Developing.* Training and development occur both before and after placement as employees continue to grow and seek new jobs.
- *Providing Compensation, Benefits, Motivation.* One of the major functions of the personnel department is to motivate employees, most often through compensation and benefits systems but increasingly through other programs—for example, through improving managerial styles.
- *Ensuring Employees' Health and Safety.* Monitoring and improving the work environment and providing insurance are included in this category.
- *Helping Group Relations.* Group relations relates to unions and other specific groups, such as employees protected by equal employment opportunity laws, professional employees, and so forth.
- *Evaluating and Controlling.* Evaluation and control are typically accomplished at the

individual level through performance appraisal and disciplinary systems. Promotion, termination, and transfers, for example, are resolved by this function. The ultimate objective is to assure that organizational behavior leads to mission accomplishment. Human resource managers design the systems to do this.

- *Managing Change.* Increasingly, the human resources management department is assuming the function of managing change through organizational development and related approaches for treating people within the organization.

- *Improving Productivity.* In the United States and Canada, there is increasing concern for improving productivity. Through various systems, such as work redesign, changes in managerial styles and organizational structures, and improvements in technology, the personnel department is leading this effort in many organizations.

- *Improving Organizational Communication.* Numerous programs to improve communication have been attempted. Among them are employee assistance programs, listening posts, company newspapers and magazines, bulletin boards, television broadcasts, discussion groups, meetings, and so forth.

The purpose of all of these functions is to assure that organizational behavior accomplishes strategic objectives. In order to be effective, the organization must have the correct staff with the proper skills. Personnel's role is an increasingly critical one in this area, one which goes far beyond its traditional staffing functions. The organization's systems for managing organizational behavior are to a great extent designed and controlled by this department.

As a result, human resources departments, in conjunction with and as influenced by the strategist(s)'s managerial style(s), determine to a great extent the nature of the organization's culture. In reexamining the factors under the jurisdiction of a human resources manager, such as motivation, the management of groups and change, and the management of productivity, you will see that these factors have a tremendous influence on organizational culture. These factors will be discussed in more detail shortly.

> *Business performance therefore requires that each job be directed*
> *toward the objectives of the whole business.*
>
> ▪ *Peter Drucker* ▪

Human Resources Management, Organizational Behavior, and the Individual Manager

After operational planning has been accomplished, what remains is to ensure that resources are appropriately utilized. The following paragraphs focus on how individual managers manage human resources, because if these resources fulfill their roles effectively and efficiently, then the remaining resources will be effectively and efficiently managed as well.

An exhaustive treatment of organizational behavior is beyond the scope of this text. Organizational behavior is the subject of other texts and other courses. However, a brief review to relate its importance to strategy will be helpful.

Once the organization is committed to a course of action, communication, motivation, and leadership are needed to assure successful implementation. Therefore, a brief review of the major facets of these three important concepts is relevant here. Moreover, the other functions of management should not be ignored. Lower-level managers, those primarily responsible for this phase of implementation, must plan—to an appropriate degree, organize, control, communicate, and make decisions. Also critical to this process are the actions of the personnel division as it recruits human resources for the organization and provides organizational systems to aid the individual manager in motivation and leadership efforts.

Communication

Some 30 to 70 percent of an individual manager's time in the organization may be spent communicating. Communication occurs verbally and nonverbally; nonverbal communication may account for as much as 70 percent of the process. Not only sending, but listening is critical to successful communication. It is evident that more and more organizations will train their employees in this vital but often misunderstood practice.

Motivation

Motivation, in an organizational context, concerns the managerial influencing of subordinates to accomplish the objectives of the organization. This is accomplished by providing an environment in which the employee can satisfy needs and, in so doing, accomplish organizational objectives. Motivation begins with an individual's perception of needs. The organization may provide need satisfiers; so may the manager. But, because of organizational motivation systems, managers often have limited latitude in providing need satisfiers. The manager's motivation dilemma may thus evolve into attempts to build satisfaction into a particular job and to provide rewards where no organizational opportunities exist. For example, to reward superior performance when no merit compensation is given by the organization, the manager may have to develop some enterprising recognition techniques.

The number of needs, and hence need satisfiers, is substantial. Typical needs include physiological, safety, social, esteem, self-actualization, power, achievement, objective accomplishment, and role fulfillment. And while needs appear to be ordered in a hierarchy, evidence points to a different hierarchy than that proposed by Maslow. Needs may also be classified as intrinsic or extrinsic with respect to a particular position, but are not readily stereotyped into motivators or hygienic factors as originally proposed by Herzberg. Motivation is further complicated by the fact that individual needs are multiple, change over time, and vary from situation to situation. As need satisfiers are offered, certain moderator variables may impinge and prevent the need satisfiers from having the desired impact. Managers must be alert to these processes. For example, employees ask themselves questions before and after rewards are offered such as: Can I do the job? If I do the job, will I get the reward? What's the reward worth to me? Was the reward tied to performance? Were the rewards equitably distributed? Furthermore, the process itself seems to have a major impact on continued motivation in terms of how the individual's self-image was affected.

The individual manager's role in motivation is to diagnose the situation correctly, determine the appropriate need satisfier or need satisfiers, offer them or effective substitutes, and ensure that consequences of the motivation process are congruent with expected results—all within organizational and nonorganizational constraints. This is obviously not an easy undertaking, but it is essential if employees are to fulfill their tasks. If individuals work to only a small part of their capabilities, then the organization will fall short of mission accomplishment. It is motivation that causes employees to work nearer their full potentials. The role of leadership is to strengthen and channel motivation.

Leadership

Management is situational; therefore leadership, a major function in the total management process, could hardly be otherwise. The situational approach to leadership proposes that managers identify the major factors in each situation and adjust their leadership techniques to match those factors. The difficulty lies in identifying the most critical factors. Some critical factors for the manager to consider in choosing a leadership style are the subordinates' needs and personalities, the nature of the subordinates' work groups, the types of tasks the subordinates perform, and the organization's structure and climate.

Having acknowledged the situational aspects of the leadership function, it is important to note that leaders then have a choice from among many types of leadership behaviors. The more or less continual pattern of these choices and resultant actions is known as leadership style. The major areas within which managers must make leadership choices are[4]

- **Task.** How much should I emphasize goals, objectives, the job, and how much should I control this person's, or this groups's performance?

- **Relationship.** How much do I want to attempt to build strong social friendships with subordinates; how much do I do to satisfy their social needs?

- **Rewards.** How much should I and can I reward behavior?

- **Attitude.** What type of attitudinal approach do I want to use with this person, this group?

- **Participation.** How much do I let this person or group participate in decision making?

Obviously, not all behaviors are appropriate in all situations or for all managers. Again, leadership style is to a great extent explained by organizational climate. The individual manager's propensity for authoritarian versus democratic management style is tempered by how the organization prefers to be led. Organizational leadership style preferences are defined in policy and become a part of structure.

> *Not only is it difficult to effect changes in the styles of managers overnight, but the question that we raise is whether it is even appropriate.*
>
> • *Paul Hersey and Kenneth H. Blanchard* •

The Management of Corporate Culture

An organization's culture is that pattern of behaviors and values that separates one organization from another similar organization operating within a society and industry. Because

---

[4]J. M. Higgins, "The Management TRRAP" (Unpublished working paper).

of books such as *Theory Z*, *The Art of Japanese Management*, *Corporate Cultures*, *In Search of Excellence*, and *American Spirit*,[5] there is a widespread belief that a powerful corporate culture leads to outstanding financial performance. Despite the substantial anecdotal evidence that this belief is true, strong empirical evidence is lacking.[6] Nonetheless, as with shared values, organizations are pursuing the management of corporate culture full steam ahead.

There exist numerous obstacles to the management of culture, the first of which is defining it. A working definition acceptable to all is elusive, but that presented above is representative of, and a combination of, the more commonly employed definitions. Depending upon which definition is used (whose book the company is relying on), the corporation would ultimately emphasize one aspect of culture management over another. Maintaining the culture is another major problem, especially in an environment changing both internally and externally. Charles J. Fombrum suggests that culture evolves from the interplay of a host of variables related to the overall society, the industry, and the organization itself. Consequently, he states that "managing corporate culture is therefore an awesome if not impossible task," and observes that as organizations continue to expand into multiple industries and multiple societies, the task is further complicated.[7] In that sense, managing culture is much like shooting at a moving target. It requires constant reaiming.

Another barrier to successful culture management is its strategic relevance. The culture, to be supportive of strategy, must be in tune with it. The Hewlett-Packard example cited previously shows how a strong set of values—a strong culture—can in fact prohibit, at least in the short term, the satisfactory implementation of strategy. What appears to occur initially is agreement that a set of strongly supported, centrally shared values must exist, that employees must commit to these, and that these values must be in consonance with all else that is happening in the firm. In *American Spirit*, Lawrence M. Miller has identified what his research (interviews and observations) leads him to believe are the key values that organizations are adopting: purpose, excellence, consensus, unity, performance, empiricism, intimacy, and integrity. (See Information Capsule 8.1.)

It is clear that a change is taking place in the cultures of American corporations. It is also evident that managers are, many for the first time, attempting to "manage" corporate culture in the best interests of the firm. And many of the beliefs that are the focal point for this culture management process have been brought to our attention by the books mentioned previously. Thus, excellence, performance, intimacy, concern for employees, participation, and other major beliefs espoused by these books are going to have a major impact on the cultures of our organizations.

[5] W. G. Ouchi, *Theory Z: How American Business Can Meet the Japanese Challenge* (Reading, Mass.: Addison-Wesley, 1981); R. T. Pascale and A. G. Athos, *The Art of Japanese Management: Applications for American Executives* (New York: Warner Books, 1981); T. E. Deal and A. A. Kennedy, *Corporate Cultures: The Rites and Rituals of Corporate Life* (Reading, Mass.: Addison-Wesley, 1982); T. J. Peters and R. H. Waterman, Jr., *In Search of Excellence: Lessons from America's Best-run Companies* (New York: Harper & Row, 1982); L. M. Miller, *American Spirit: Visions of a New Corporate Culture* (New York: William Morrow and Company, 1984).

[6] R. Keating and K. E. Aupperle, "Culture and Climate: A Search for Strategic Relevance" (Paper presented to the Academy of Management, Boston, 1984).

[7] C. J. Fombrum, "Corporate Culture, Environment, and Strategy," *Human Resource Management*, Spring/Summer 1983, p. 152.

INFORMATION CAPSULE 8.1
Key Values Organizations Are Adopting

The Purpose Principle

We all have a need to confirm our self-worth. Self-worth cannot be achieved in the absence of a sense of contribution to some higher purpose. Leaders fulfill this need. They communicate purpose to those who follow. The ability to communicate a valued purpose is a rare art among corporate managers. Achieving return on equity does not, as a goal, mobilize the most noble forces in our souls. The most successful companies have defined their aims in terms of product or service and benefits to customers in a manner that can inspire and motivate their employees. Most corporations do serve a worthy purpose. Individuals seek to identify with it. The competitive leader will make the connection between our souls and our work, and will benefit from the energies released.

The Excellence Principle

Our culture values comfort, both material and psychological. We feel we should achieve personal satisfaction and fulfillment. We not only value this comfort, but feel that it is our due. We do not welcome personal tests and trials, we seek to avoid them and view them as contrary to satisfaction. Satisfaction and excellence are inherently in conflict. Satisfaction implies acceptance of things as they are. Dissatisfaction is the source of motivation. It leads to actions to change that which is the source of discomfort. The achievement of excellence can occur only if the organization promotes a culture of creative dissatisfaction.

The Consensus Principle

Managers are stuck in the culture of command. They feel an excitement, an exhilaration when they are able to command. Unfortunately, command behavior is what was successful in the crisis climate of battle. The leader of old marched ahead of his troops because he was the strongest and the most brave. He exemplified the values that were important to that organization. The future corporation will not march into battle. It will succeed by its ability to bring ideas together, to stimulate the employees and managers to think creatively. The employee will not be asked to risk life and limb for his superior. He will be asked to risk sharing his thoughts and feelings. He will be asked to focus not his physical energies, but his mental energies. This change in task necessitates a change from command to consensus.

The Unity Principle

Our corporations maintain the traditions of a class society. We maintain the distinctions of management-labor, salary-hourly wage; exempt-nonexempt, thinker-doer. They are all false distinctions, the old, useless baggage of a deceased society, carried forward into a new world. We live in an age of unity, of integration, when distinctions that disunite and limit people are inherently counterproductive. There are other traditions from our past to which management must return. There was a time when ownership and identity with the job was a source of pride. The industrial age, with the anonymity of mass production, swung the pendulum from ownership to alienation. The electronic age, with its emphasis on information, the flexibility of information technologies, and the psychological needs for community, identity, and a source of personal worth, will swing the pendulum back toward ownership. The competitive corporation will accept the value of fully involving the individual in its workings and decision making so that he or she again feels in unity with and ownership for his work.

The Performance Principle

In Western society the corporation is the agency that metes out more rewards and punishments than any other. The prevalent principle by which it distributes its rewards is power. Those who organize, those who are in short supply, those who can control have power and are rewarded in proportion to that power. The distribution of rewards according to power is as old as our civilization. However, this system contains within itself the seeds of its own destruction. When rewards are granted without regard to performance, productivity suffers. When they are tied to performance, individual and corporate performances improve. If the corporation is to succeed in the new era we are entering, it must reevaluate the values by which it distributes its rewards. In the future rewards must be granted according to the value of performance, a value not currently exhibited at the level of the chief executive or the union apprentice.

The Empiricism Principle

We are not skilled thinkers. Much of the explanation for the poor performance of American industry in recent years can be found in the sloppy mental habits at every level of our organizations. It is a myth that American managers manage by the numbers. Most of them have little understanding of data, statistical methods, the use of empirical analysis. However, this is only a reflection of the larger culture. We are a nation of sloppy thinkers. In the school, in the supermarket, and in the executive suite we make decisions based on gut reactions that are often easily manipulated. Intuition is most useful when it is founded on a sound knowledge of the facts. Intuition in the corporate culture is more often an excuse for lazy and undisciplined analysis. If we are going to improve our corporate performance, we must begin to teach the value of statistics and their appropriate use at all levels of the corporation.

The Intimacy Principle

The military model of management was necessarily impersonal. In battle the cost of personal involvement in the psychological world of another individual presented too great a risk to the emotional well-being of the leader. This is our tradition. Strength is represented as a detached, masculine absence of emotion and intimacy with fellow human beings. Management style will inevitably change because the future corporation is faced with a different challenge. The new challenge will be to tap not the physical labor of the individual, but his inner thoughts, his emotional and spiritual energies. This will require an intimate culture. Tasks will be accomplished when individuals are able to share openly without risk of emotional punishment, when managers have intimate knowledge of their subordinates' thoughts, feelings, and needs. But intimacy requires a strength and security that are not promoted in most American corporate cultures.

The Integrity Principle

Decision making in our organizations has become dominated by a concern for legalisms, regulations, and precedents. Integrity is the foundation upon which must be built all other values, and upon which rests the trust and relationship between individual and corporation. The ability to discriminate between what is honest and what lacks honesty is a skill that is critical to the establishment of the new corporate culture. We live in a society of law and legalism in which the lawyer has become the corporate high priest of right and wrong. That which is honest has become confused with that which is permissible by law. Our managers and corporations generally adhere to what is legal. However, the law does not specify what is right, and it is a poor guide to making the decisions that will establish trust and unity between individuals and organizations, between customers and suppliers. These relationships have deteriorated to the point where they represent a drag not only on productivity within major corporations but also on their ability to market their products in this country. When managers are able to discern and act on that which is honest in spirit, trustful business relationships will be reestablished.

The American corporation is not dearly loved by the populace. The corporation is viewed as an impersonal edifice of materialism. It neither inspires man to achieve his highest aspirations nor inspires the loyalty and devotion that would contribute to its own purpose. American managers have a tradition of pragmatism which is a traditional source of strength. However, this pragmatism may require the balance of new values that are lofty, that do inspire the imagination, engage the loyalty and devotion of the common man.

Source: Lawrence M. Miller, "Introduction," *American Spirit: Visions of A New Corporate Culture* (New York: William Morrow & Company, 1984), pp. 15–19. Copyright 1984 by Lawrence W. Miller by permission of William Morrow & Company.

The Creation of Shared Values

One of the most important cultural characteristics of successful firms, as described by Peters and Waterman,[8] is the existence of shared values among organizational members. In their research, they have found that successful companies first established a set of beliefs or values, and then gained commitment to them from their employees. Typically, a company adopts one dominant value. At IBM it's service. At Ford it's quality. At Chrysler it's becoming the best there is because—"what else is there?" At GE, "We bring good things to life." However, there needs to be more than one shared value, and typically there is. In Chapter 1, we reviewed the corporate objectives of Hewlett-Packard, which drive the organization. These are shared values, as is H-P's now-famous "management by walking around," in which managers are seen as coaches helping employees make decisions.

[8] T. J. Peters and R. H. Waterman, Jr., *In Search of Excellence* (New York: Harper & Row, 1983).

Similarly, the Coca-Cola Inc. objectives and strategies, also noted in Chapter 1, set the tone for its employees.

Many times these values are unspoken, but known. Many times these values are neither unspoken nor known; thus the values a firm has are, in fact, not shared. Many times management wants to change those values, but they remain nonetheless, and changing the firm's strategic direction becomes impossible as a result. This has happened to some extent at Hewlett-Packard, where as we saw in the previous chapter, interactive information processing products were necessary for the market, but were not created because of a highly autonomous product/market structure. It's also much more difficult to share values among the many businesses in a holding company conglomerate corporation such as Allegeny Ludlum than it is in a single-industry firm such as McDonald's. (Some would argue that there need to be shared values only at the business level of multi-SBU firms and not at the corporate level.) But one factor is certain. As a consequence of believing in the findings of Peters and Waterman, a large number of organizations are attempting to create a set of shared values.

A Note on Implementation Policies

Just as the organization establishes strategic policies to aid in formulating strategy, it must also establish implementation policies to aid in implementing strategy. The nature of implementation policies varies with the level of the organization at which they occur. Those at the top-management level deal largely with management philosophies of staffing, leading, and motivating. By the time these policies reach the operational level of the organization, they may be quite detailed in terms of how employees will be developed, how managers will treat employees, what reward systems will be employed, how employees may progress in a career within the organization, how employees are recruited and selected, how groups should work together, what control measures can be expected to be utilized, and so forth. In addition, specific task instructions and procedures, detailed budget methodologies, and performance evaluation systems would sometimes be included among these policies.

An Additional Perspective on Strategy/Implementation Relations—The 7-S's Framework

McKinsey and Company have developed a model known as, "the seven elements of strategic fit," or the "7-S's." The 7-S framework is indicated in Figure 8.4. The 7-S's are: strategy, structure, systems, style, staff, skills, and shared values. These 7-S's are defined briefly in Table 8.1. The underlying concept of the model is that all seven of these variables must "fit" with one another in order for strategy to be successfully implemented. The idea of "fit" is that successful strategy implementation depends on a proper "culture," and that only if all 7-S's are working in coordinated fashion, will this culture exist. A number of McKinsey clients have adopted this framework as a model for attempting to implement strategy.[9] And, from the conceptual viewpoint, the framework is appealing. On

[9] R. H. Waterman, Jr., "The Seven Elements of Strategic Fit," *Journal of Business Strategy*, Winter 1982, pp. 69–73; also see R. H. Waterman, Jr., T. J. Peters, and J. R. Phillips, "Structure Is not Organization," *Business Horizons*, June 1980, pp. 14–26.

Figure 8.4   McKinsey 7-S Framework

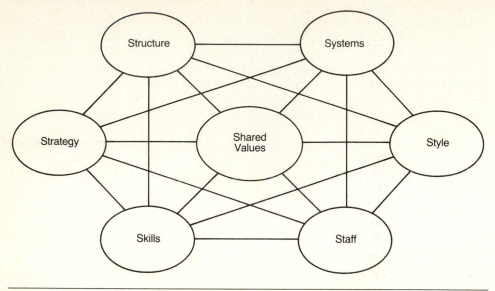

Source: R. H. Waterman, Jr., "The Seven Elements of Strategic Fit," p. 71. Reprinted by permission from the *Journal of Business Strategy*, Winter 1982. Copyright © 1982, Warren, Gorham & Lamont Inc., 210 South Street, Boston, Mass. All Rights Reserved.

Table 8.1   A Summary of the 7-S's

1. *Strategy.* A coherent set of actions aimed at gaining a sustainable advantage over competition, improving position vis-à-vis customers, or allocating resources.
2. *Structure.* The organization chart and accompanying baggage that show who reports to whom and how tasks are both divided up and integrated.
3. *Systems.* The processes and flows that show how an organization gets things done from day to day (information systems, capital budgeting systems, manufacturing processes, quality control systems, and performance measurement systems all would be good examples).
4. *Style.* Tangible evidence of what management considers important by the way it collectively spends time and attention and uses symbolic behavior. It is not what management says is important; it is the way management behaves.
5. *Staff.* The people in the organization. Here it is very useful to think not about individual personalities but about corporate demographics.
6. *Shared values (or superordinate goals).* The values that go beyond, but might well include, simple goal statements in determining corporate destiny. To fit the concept, these values must be shared by most people in an organization.
7. *Skills.* A derivative of the rest. Skills are those capabilities that are possessed by an organization as a whole as opposed to the people in it. (The concept of corporate skill as something different from the summation of the people in it seems difficult for many to grasp; however, some organizations that hire only the best and the brightest cannot get seemingly simple things done while others perform extraordinary feats with ordinary people.)

Source: R. H. Waterman, Jr., "The Seven Elements of Strategic Fit," p. 71. Reprinted by permission from the *Journal of Business Strategy*, Winter 1982. Copyright © 1982, Warren, Gorham & Lamont Inc., 210 South Street, Boston, Mass. All Rights Reserved.

the basis of research, however, it has yet to be shown whether or not successful implementation or failure in implementation can be predicted using this model. This model generally agrees with the major elements presented in this chapter and their components—structure, systems, the management of human resources by individual managers, the creation of shared values, and the management of culture. Thus the 7-S's are in general agreement with much of the strategic management literature as to the key factors for successful implementation.

Evolving Approaches to Implementation

The classic model of strategic management, such as presented in Figure 8.1, states that strategy is formulated, implemented, and controlled, in that order and in a very segmented manner. But as suggested in Chapter 7, strategy occurs incrementally, and the power and political realities of most organizations are such that acceptance of a strategy by many strategists and nonstrategists alike is often necessary in order for it to be implemented. Consequently, in numerous situations when strategy is being formulated, the first steps of implementation are already being taken, or should be. (Additionally, the standards by which control may be accomplished are evolving and being defined during formulation.) With regard to these preliminary implementation actions, David R. Brodin and L. J. Bourgeois III, have suggested five models of strategy formulation and implementation that form a continuum ranging from a very separated sequence of formulation and implementation to a very integrated approach: the commander, the organizational change, the collaborative, the cultural, and the crescive.[10] Table 8.2 further describes these five models.

It is important for your understanding of formulation and implementation that you realize that, while the strategic management process model used here (Figure 8.1), separates the stages, it does allow for the more integrated formulation/implementation approaches.

Matching Strategists to Strategy

In recent years, it has been proposed by many that the skills of a strategist (most often directed at implementation skills) must be matched to the strategy of the firm.[11] Chase Manhattan Bank, Heublein, Texas Instruments, Corning Glass, and General Electric are among those companies that select top managers on the basis of linkage with strategic requirements.[12] The reality seems to be that the "universal manager" does not exist. Yes, some are more skilled than others at managing, and can transfer those skills from situation

---

[10] D. R. Brodwin and L. J. Bourgeois III, "Five Steps To Strategic Action," *California Management Review*, Spring 1984, pp. 176–190.

[11] A. D. Szilagyi, Jr. and D. M. Schweiger, "Matching Managers to Strategies: A Review and Suggested Framework," *Academy of Management Review*, Winter 1984, pp. 626–637; J. G. Wissema, H. W. Van Der Pol, and H. M. Messer, "Strategic Management Archetypes," *Strategic Management Journal*, January/March 1980, pp. 37–47; M. Gerstein and H. Reisman, "Strategic Selection: Matching Executives to Business Conditions," *Sloan Management Review*, Winter 1983, pp. 33–49; A. K. Gupta, "Contingency Linkages between Strategy and General Manager Characteristics: A Conceptual Examination," *Academy of Management Review*, July 1984, pp. 399–412.

[12] "Wanted: A Manager to Fit Each Strategy," *Business Week*, February 25, 1980, pp. 166–173.

Table 8.2   Comparison of Five Approaches

Factor	Approach				
	Commander	Change	Collaborative	Cultural	Crescive
How are goals set? Where in the organization (top or bottom) are the strategic goals established?	Dictated from top	Dictated from top	Negotiated among top team	Embodied in culture	Stated loosely from top; refined from bottom
What signifies success? What signifies a successful outcome to the strategic planning/implementation process?	A good plan, as judged on economic criteria	Organization and structure which fit the strategy	An acceptable plan with broad top management support	An army of busy implementers	Sound strategies with champions behind them
What factors are considered? What are the kinds of factors, or types of rationality, used in developing a strategy for resolving conflicts between alternative proposed strategies?	Economic	Economic, political	Economic, social, political	Economic, social	Economic, social, political, behavioral
What is the typical level of organization-wide effort required?					
during the Planning phase	Low	Low	High	High	High
during the implementation phase	N/A	High	Low	Low	Low
How stringent are the requirements placed on the CEO in order for the approach to succeed?					
Required CEO knowledge. To what extent must the CEO be able to maintain personal awareness of all significant strategic opportunities or threats?	High	High	Moderate	Low	Low
Required CEO power. To what extent must the CEO have the power to impose a detailed implementation plan on the organization?	High	High	Moderate	Moderate	Moderate

to situation. But the evidence also proscribes a knowledge of the industry and the situation as prerequisites to successful strategic decisions. Managers may, however, be able to adapt their management styles to varying situations (although the evidence suggests that though they should, they often do not).

Thus it becomes important that organizations choose managers for their abilities in various strategic circumstances. Most of the literature keys proposed strategist/strategy

Table 8.2   *continued*

The Five Approaches in Brief

Approach	The CEO's Strategic Question	CEO's Role
Commander	"How do I formulate the optimum strategy?"	Rational actor
Change	"I have a strategy in mind; now how do I implement it?"	Architect
Collaborative	"How do I involve top management to get commitment to strategies from the start?"	Coordinator
Cultural	"How do I involve the whole organization in implementation?"	Coach
Crescive	"How do I encourage managers to come forward as champions of sound strategies?"	Premise-setter and judge

1. The Commander Approach—the CEO concentrates on formulating the strategy, applying rigorous logic and analysis. He either develops the strategy himself or supervises a team of planners. Once he's satisfied that he has the "best" strategy, he passes it along to those who are instructed to "make it happen."
2. The Organizational Change Approach—once a strategy has been developed, the executive puts it into effect by taking such steps as reorganizing the company structure, changing incentive compensation schemes, or hiring personnel.

The next two approaches involve more recent attempts to enhance implementation by broadening the bases of participation in the planning process:

3. The Collaborative Approach—rather than develop the strategy in a vacuum, the CEO enlists the help of his senior managers during the planning process in order to assure that all the key players will back the final plan.
4. The Cultural Approach—this is an extension of the collaborative model to involve people at middle and sometimes lower levels of the organization. It seeks to implement strategy through the development of a corporate culture throughout the organization.
5. The Crescive Approach—in this approach, the CEO addresses strategy planning and implementation simultaneously. He is not interested in strategizing alone, or even in leading others through a protracted planning process. Rather, he tries, through his statements and actions, to guide his managers into coming forward as champions of sound strategies. (Since this involves "growing" strategies from within the firm, our label comes from the Latin *crescere*, to grow.)

Source: David R. Brodwin and L. J. Bourgois III, "Five steps to Strategic Action," *California Management Review* Spring 1984.

matches to the stage of the product life cycle or related grand strategies. Table 8.3 provides a representative matching scenario. Figure 8.5 offers a framework for making those matches. While the research is at best categorized as preliminary, there is sufficient information available to suggest that, yes, strategists should be matched to strategies, and/or must adapt their management styles to the situation.

One of the by-products of change is "culture shock." For example, AT&T has found itself having to compete, and in culture shock because of its previous situation as a monopoly. Neither it nor its employees have been fully prepared for the consequences of deregulation.[13] (See Figure 8.2.)

---

[13] "Culture Shock Is Shaking the Bell System," *Business Week*, September 26, 1983, pp. 112–116.

Figure 8.5   A Suggested Framework for Strategy—Manager Matching

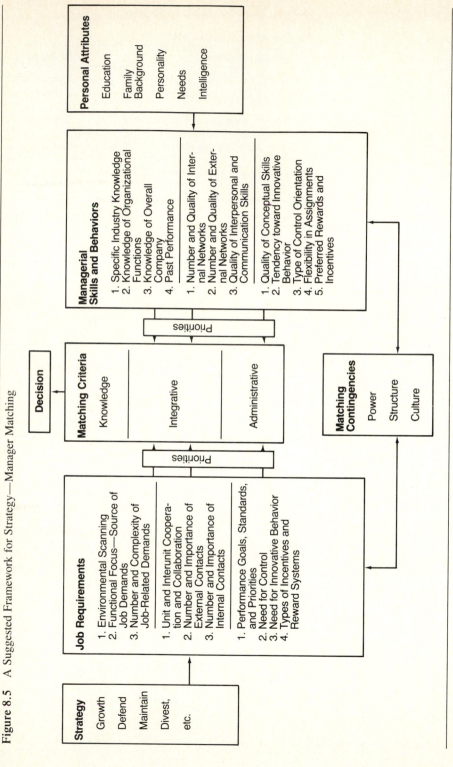

Source: Andrew D. Szilagyi, Jr. and David M. Schweiger, "Matching Managers to Strategies: A Review and Suggested Framework," *Academy of Management Review,* Winter 1984, p. 633.

Table 8.3   General Management Requirements for Various Strategic Situations

Situation	Major Job Thrusts	Specific Characteristics of Ideal Candidates
1. Start-up	Creating vision of business Establishing core technical and marketing expertise Building management team	Vision of finished business Hands-on orientation: a "doer" In-depth knowledge in critical technical areas Organizing ability Staffing skills Team-building capabilities High energy level and stamina Personal magnetism: charisma Broad knowledge of all key functions
2. Turnaround	Rapid, accurate problem diagnosis Fixing short-term and, ultimately, long-term problems	"Take charge" orientation: strong leader Strong analytical and diagnostic skills, especially financial Excellent business strategist High energy level Risk taker Handles pressure well Good crisis management skills Good negotiator
3. Extract profit/rationalize existing business	Efficiency Stability Succession Sensing signs of change	Technically knowledgeable: "knows the business" Sensitive to changes: "ear-to-the-ground" Anticipates problems: "problem finder" Strong administrative skills Oriented to "systems" Strong "relationship orientation" Recognizes need for management succession and development Oriented to getting out the most: efficiency, not growth
4. Dynamic growth in existing business	Increasing market share in key sectors Managing rapid change Building long-term health toward clear vision of the future	Excellent strategic and financial planning skills Clear vision of the future Ability to balance priorities, i.e., stability vs. growth Organizational and team-building skills Good crisis management skills Moderate-high risk taker High energy level Excellent staffing skills
5. Redeployment of efforts in existing business	Establishing effectiveness in limited business sphere Managing change Supporting the "dispossessed"	Good politician/manager of change Highly persuasive: high "interpersonal influence" Moderate risk taker Highly supportive, sensitive to people: not "bull in a china shop" Excellent "systems thinker": understands how complex systems work Good organizing and executive staffing skills

continued

Table 8.3   *continued*

Situation	Major Job Thrusts	Specific Characteristics of Ideal Candidates
6. Liquidation/divestiture of poorly performing business	Cutting losses Making tough decisions Making best deal	"Callousness": tough-minded, determined—willing to be the bad guy Highly analytical re: cost/benefits—does not easily accept current ways of doing things Risk taker Low-glory seeking: willing to do dirty jobs—does not want glamour Wants to be respected, not necessarily liked
7. New acquisitions	Integration Establishing sources of information and control	Analytical ability Relationship-building skills Interpersonal influence Good communication skills Personal magnetism—some basis to establish "instant credibility"

Source: Reprinted from Marc Gerstein and Heather Gerstein, "Strategic Selection: Matching Executives to Business Conditions," *Sloan Management Review*, Vol. 24, No. 2 (Winter 1983), p. 37, by permission of the publisher. Copyright 1983 by the Sloan Management Review Association. All rights reserved.

We are caught constantly in a time warp, implementing a plan on a certain set of assumptions and developing another plan on a different set.

▪ *Jeffrey N. McCollum, Division Manager at AT&T Consumer Products* ▪

Summary

Organizational structure has several major determinants. However, once structured, the organization must implement its plans. Successful implementation depends on proper integrative planning and control techniques and on appropriate managerial functioning—especially motivation and leadership. Relationships between organizational structure and implementation are critically important.

What can be said with certainty with regard to organization and implementation is that there is no one best way to organize or to implement. Various factors moderate the effects of actions taken. The primary factors affecting each individual situation should be determined and a course of action taken based on this analysis. Sound human resources management policies are critical to implementation, as are proper communication, motivation, leadership, shared values, and organizational culture. A continuum of five models of strategy formulation and implementation ranging from very separated to very integrated suggests that an integrated formulation/implementation approach is possible, as is the matching of strategists to strategy.

Key Terms and Concepts

By the time you have completed this chapter, you should be familiar with the following key terms and concepts: key elements in successful implementation; the roles of resource management and organizational behavior; the basic personnel functions; the basics of communication, motivation, and leadership; the 7-S's framework of strategic fit, corporate culture, and shared values; five approaches to implementation—the commander, the organizational change, the collaborative, the cultural, and the crescive; and matching strategists to strategy.

Discussion Questions

1. What is the relationship of structure to implementation?

2. Why are systems so important to successful implementation?

3. Why is human resources management so critical to successful implementation?

4. Compare the collaborative with the crescive approach to strategy formulation and implementation.

5. Contrast the CEO's role as coach in the cultural approach to strategy formulation and implementation with the rational actor role in the commander approach.

6. The suggested framework for strategy–manager matching as summarized in Figure 8.5 highlights which matching criteria?

References

"A New Era For Management." *Business Week*, April 25, 1983, pp. 50–86.

Barrow, J. C. "The Variables of Leadership: A Review and Conceptual Framework." *Academy of Management Review*, April 1977, pp. 231–245.

Bourgeois, L. J., III, and Brodin, D. R. "Strategy Implementation: Five Approaches to an Elusive Phenomenon." *Strategic Management Journal*, July/September 1984, pp. 241–264.

Fombrun, Charles. "Strategic Management: Integrating the Human Resource Systems into Strategic Planning." *Advances in Strategic Management* (Greenwich, Conn.: JAI Press, Inc.) 2, pp. 191–210.

Hall, Trish. "Demanding PepsiCo Is Attempting to Make Work Nicer for Managers." *The Wall Street Journal*, October 23, 1984, p. 31.

Herbert, T. T., and Deresky, H. "Creating the Conditions for Effective Implementation of Strategies: Preliminary Evidence on Strategy–Manager Fit" (Working paper #83-004, Concordia University).

"Here Comes the 'Intrapreneur.'" *Business Week*, July 18, 1983, p. 188.

Jelinek, M., and Amar, P. "Implementing Corporate Strategy Theory and Reality," Paper presented to the Strategic Management Society, Paris, October 1983.

Kiechel, Walter, III. "Corporate Strategists." *Fortune*, December 27, 1982, pp. 32–40.

"Kodak's New Lean and Hungry Look." *Business Week*, May 30, 1983, p. 33.

Miner, J. B., and Dachler, H. P. "Personnel Attitudes and Motivation." *Annual Review of Psychology*, 1973, pp. 379–402.

"Office Automation." *Business Week*, October 8, 1984, pp. 119–121.

Oliver, Alex R., and Garber, Joseph R. "Implementing Strategic Planning: Ten Sure-Fire Ways to Do It Wrong." *Business Horizons*, March/April 1983, pp. 49–51.

Tichy, Noel M., Fombrun, Charles J., and Devanna, Mary Anne. "Strategic Human Resource Management." *Sloan Management Review*, Winter 1982, pp. 47–61.

Trice, Harrison M., and Beyer, Janice M. "Studying Organizational Cultures Through Rites and Ceremonials." *Academy of Management Review*, 1984, Vol. 9, No. 4, pp. 653–669.

Walsh, Mary Williams. "Company-Built Retreats Reflect Firms' Cultures and Personalities." *The Wall Street Journal*, August 16, 1984, p. 27.

Wu, Frederick H. "Incrementalism in Financial Strategic Planning." *Academy of Management Review*, 1981, Vol. 6, No. 1, pp. 133–143.

9

The Evaluation and Control of Organizational Strategy

The best laid schemes o' mice an' men gang aft agley.

▪ *Robert Burns* ▪

There are three primary types of organizational control: strategic control, management control, and operational control. Strategic control, the process of evaluating strategy, is practiced both after strategy is formulated and after it is implemented. The organization's strategists evaluate strategy once it has been formulated to ascertain whether it is appropriate to mission accomplishment and again once it has been implemented to determine if the strategy is accomplishing its objectives.

Management control is the process of assuring that major subsystems' progress toward the accomplishment of strategic objectives is satisfactory. For example, is SBU/Product Division A's ROI performance acceptable? Or, is the Production Department meeting its quality control objectives? Operational control is the process of ascertaining whether individual and work group role behaviors (performance) are congruent with individual and work group role prescriptions. (Is Tom reaching his sales quota?)

Like the phases of planning, the types of control are not distinct entities. Rather, in various organizations, one type of control may be almost indistinguishable from another. Furthermore, the devices used in one type of control may also be employed in another. For example, management control devices such as ROI may be used to measure not only the performance of organizational components but the total organization as well. Finally, while most operational and many management control systems may incorporate automatic correction activities, the evaluation of strategy requires executive judgment.

This chapter is concerned with those parts of the strategic management process indicated in Figure 9.1. The chapter begins with a discussion of control, followed by some observations on how to evaluate strategy. Next, some of the more common types of strategic/management control techniques are reviewed. Certain of the more relevant of these are discussed at length. Finally, the dysfunctional consequences of control are presented, followed by some concluding remarks on control.

At ITT we used everything available to us to get results. We used everything we had learned at school, everything we had learned from our own experience in business, everything we could learn from one another. We used our intuition. We used our brains. And we always used the numbers.

▪ *Harold S. Geneen, former CEO of ITT* ▪

Figure 9.1   The Organization—a Strategic Management Process Model

| Formulation of Mission Statements | → | Determination of Strategic Objectives | → | Formulation of Master Strategy | → | Implementation of Strategies | → | Evaluation and Control of Strategies |

Strategic Policies   Policies that Aid   Control Policies
                                                Implementation

Control and Strategy

Strategic, management, and operational control systems perform an important integrative function, since the measurement of performance as related to objectives accomplishment coordinates activity. Experience and research have revealed that any number of variables may cause performance to be incongruent with strategy. For example, the assumptions under which strategy was formulated may change. Or, strategy, plans, and policies may not be adhered to. As deviations from either assumptions or guidance lead to unsatisfactory results, the successful strategy must have control as one of its dimensions.

What is controlled varies from level to level in the organization. The organization's strategists are responsible for strategic control, as are the stockholders, theoretically. Management control is principally the function of top management, especially the CEO, while operational control is primarily the concern of lower-level managers. Traditionally, strategic control and management control focus on perspectives broader than the details examined in operational control. Note, however, that modern strategic information systems allow top management to view the details of operations if necessary. Also note that, while much of what follows is related to formal control systems, informal control systems may suffice in the smaller organization, especially for operational control where personal observation is possible.

Control may be depicted as a six-step feedback model as follows:

1. *The Establishment of Standards of Performance.* Standards are specific points against which actual performance will be judged. As such they are more detailed expressions of strategic objectives and are the bases of role prescriptions. Establishing standards for organizational subcomponents is the first step in management control, and establishing them for individuals is the first step in operational control.

2. *The Statement of Acceptable Tolerances.* The standard is a single point on a continuum of possible behaviors, but it is not always necessary to perform exactly to that point. Normally, deviation from standards will be tolerated within certain control limits.

3. *Measurement of Actual Performance.* Measurement is the third step in management or operational control. It involves the identification of role behavior either for components or individuals. Measurement techniques vary from situation to situation and are often imprecise.

Figure 9.2   The Organization as a Processing System

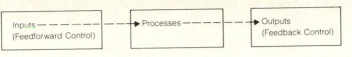

4. *Comparison of Standards and Performance*. While comparing standards and performance might appear to be a simple task, it is quite complex in the more qualitative performance areas because of the inability to quantify either standards or performance.

5. *Action*. Where performance is satisfactory—that is, congruent with standards—no action is necessary. But where it is not, corrective action must be taken.

6. *Preventive Action*. As Bill Greenwood has observed, it is insufficient simply to correct problems. Rather, action must be taken to assure that these problems do not occur again.[1]

This model focuses on results (outputs). In fact, most control systems—strategic, management, or operational—focus on results. Often, the consequence of utilizing these feedback control systems is that the unsatisfactory performance continues until the malfunctioning is discovered. One technique for reducing the problems associated with feedback control systems is "feedforward control." First suggested by Harold Koontz and Robert W. Bradspies, feedforward control focuses on inputs to the system and attempts to anticipate potential problems with outputs.[2] (See Figure 9.2.)

With respect to strategy and planning, feedforward control has wide applicability. For example, the feedforward principle underlies the concept of simulation modeling. "What-if" questions are, after all, examinations of hypothesized inputs to determine resultant effects on system outputs. Simulations of performance can be made in any number of strategic situations to test for changes in basic assumptions. In fact, any situation with identifiable inputs which can be modeled can and should utilize the feedforward approach.

Strategic Control: The Evaluation of Corporate Strategy

Once strategy has been formulated, it should be evaluated. Several criteria for evaluation have been suggested. The best known of these, the Tilles model, can be summarized as follows:[3]

1. Is the strategy internally consistent—for example, is it consistent with mission and consistent among its own plans (other strategies in the master strategy)?

2. Is it consistent with the environment (constituent demands, competition, economy, product/industry life cycle, suppliers, customers)?

[1] W. T. Greenwood, *Business Policy: A Management Audit Approach* (New York: Macmillan, 1967); Greenwood, *Decision Theory and Information Systems* (Cincinnati: South-Western Publishing, 1965); Greenwood, *Management and Organizational Behavioral Theories* (Cincinnati: South-Western Publishing, 1965).

[2] W. H. Koontz and R. W. Bradspies, "Managing through Feedforward Control," *Business Horizons*, June 1972, pp. 25–36.

[3] S. Tilles, "How to Evaluate Corporate Strategy," *Harvard Business Review*, July/August 1963, pp. 111–121.

3. Is it consistent with internal resources?

4. Does it have an appropriate amount of risk?

5. Does it have a proper time horizon?

6. Is it workable? Implementable? (The McKinsey 7-S approach discussed in Chapter 8 is applicable here.)

E. P. Learned and others, building on the Tilles model, suggest that the following are also proper evaluative questions:[4]

7. Is it identifiable? Has it been clearly and consistently identified and are people aware of it?

8. Is it appropriate to the personal values and aspirations of key managers?

9. Does it constitute a clear stimulus to organizational effort and commitment?

10. Is it socially responsible?

11. Are there early indications of the responsiveness of markets and market segments to the strategy?

J. Argenti adds[5]

12. Does it rely on weaknesses or do anything to reduce them?

13. Does it exploit major opportunities?

14. Does it avoid, reduce, or mitigate the major threats? If not, are there adequate contingency plans?

Intuitively, these questions seem sound. More importantly, they relate directly to the strategic management process model constructed in Figure 1.1. In fact, these questions, when considered in total, comprise a checklist to determine if the strategic management process model has been properly followed. All these questions can be applied as the strategy progresses through its various stages, including implementation. Progress and changes can thus be observed, and specific standards of performance can be established by the strategic objectives of the master strategy and subsequent component objectives.

Once implementation occurs, measurements will be taken to determine if the objectives have been reached. Varying from firm to firm, the tolerances established in Step 2 of the model are primarily judgmental—they tell how much deviation from the standard management can live with. Corrective and preventive actions may require that strategy be changed.

Management Control

Management control becomes a distinct concern when decentralization occurs. Where management control is imposed, it functions within the framework established by the strategy. Management control focuses on accomplishing the objectives of the various substrategies comprising the master strategy and accomplishing the objectives of the inter-

---

[4]E. P. Learned et al., *Business Policy: Text and Cases* (Homewood, Ill.: Irwin, 1969), pp. 22–25.

[5]J. Argenti, *Systematic Corporate Planning* (New York: Wiley, 1974), pp. 266–267.

mediate plans. Normally these objectives (standards) are established for major subsystems within the organization, such as SBUs, projects, products, functions, and responsibility centers, with allowable tolerances varying from organization to organization. Typical management control measures include ROI, residual income, cost, product quality, efficiency measures, and so forth. These control measures are essentially summations of operational control measures. When corrective or preventive action is taken, it may involve either very minor or very major changes in the strategy. Often, top-management strategists may be removed from their positions as the consequence of poor performance as indicated by these control measures.

Operational Control

Operational control systems are designed to ensure that day-to-day actions are consistent with established plans and objectives. Operational control is concerned with individual and group role performance as compared with individual and group role prescriptions required by organizational plans. Such control systems are normally concerned with the past (unless feedforward systems are being utilized). Focusing on events in a recent period, operational control systems are derived from the requirements of the management control system. Specific standards for performance are derived from the objectives of the operating plans, which are based on intermediate plans, which, in turn, are based on strategy. Performance is compared with objectives at the individual and group levels, and corrective or preventive action is taken where performance does not meet standards. This action may involve training, motivation, leadership, discipline, or termination.

When all else is lost, the future still remains.

▪ *Christian Nestell Bovee* ▪

Strategic and Management Control Measures of Performance

Step 3 of the control process involves measurement of implemented strategy. For most firms, strategic and management control techniques that follow the implementation of strategy are identical. The most commonly used measures of strategic and management performance are financial statements and analyses of them. Included are considerations of profit, ROI, return on equity, ratio analyses, trends in the financial statement items, and several additional factors. Inspection of these factors may occur in routine reporting cycles, as the result of consulting efforts, or as the result of internal or external audits. Budgets, program planning budgeting systems, and zero-based budgets and planning systems also serve as important financial indicators of strategic and management performance, but most often only for a specific operating period. The objective of all of these endeavors is financial control. Financial control features include information on revenues, costs, profits, and funds flows within the control of responsibility centers and for the organization in total.

But financial control is only part of the total strategic or management control process. Why? Because much of the activity that affects financial performance is nonfinancial in nature. Recognizing this, firms have recently widely employed more comprehensive mea-

Table 9.1 Summary of Financial Ratio Analysis

Ratio	Formula for Calculation	Calculation	Industry Average	Evaluation
Liquidity				
Current	$\dfrac{\text{Current assets}}{\text{Current liabilities}}$	$\dfrac{\$\ 700{,}000}{\$\ 300{,}000} = 2.3$ times	2.5 times	Satisfactory
Quick, or acid test	$\dfrac{\text{Current assets—inventory}}{\text{Current liabilities}}$	$\dfrac{\$\ 400{,}000}{\$\ 300{,}000} = 1.3$ times	1.0 times	Good
Leverage				
Dept to total assets	$\dfrac{\text{Total debt}}{\text{Total assets}}$	$\dfrac{\$1{,}000{,}000}{\$2{,}000{,}000} = 50$ percent	33 percent	Poor
Times interest earned	$\dfrac{\text{Profit before taxes plus interest charges}}{\text{Interest charges}}$	$\dfrac{\$\ 245{,}000}{\$\ 45{,}000} = 5.4$ times	8.0 times	Fair
Fixed charge coverage	$\dfrac{\text{Income available for meeting fixed charges}}{\text{Fixed charges}}$	$\dfrac{\$\ 273{,}000}{\$\ 73{,}000} = 3.7$ times	5.5 times	Poor
Activity				
Inventory turnover	$\dfrac{\text{Sales}}{\text{Inventory}}$	$\dfrac{\$3{,}000{,}000}{\$\ 300{,}000} = 10$ times	9 times	Satisfactory
Average collection period	$\dfrac{\text{Receivables}}{\text{Sales per day}}$	$\dfrac{\$\ 200{,}000}{\$\ 8{,}333} = 24$ days	20 days	Satisfactory
Fixed assets turnover	$\dfrac{\text{Sales}}{\text{Fixed assets}}$	$\dfrac{\$3{,}000{,}000}{\$1{,}300{,}000} = 2.3$ times	5.0 times	Poor
Total assets turnover	$\dfrac{\text{Sales}}{\text{Total assets}}$	$\dfrac{\$3{,}000{,}000}{\$2{,}000{,}000} = 1.5$ times	2 times	Poor
Profitability				
Profit margin on sales	$\dfrac{\text{Net profit after taxes}}{\text{Sales}}$	$\dfrac{\$\ 120{,}000}{\$3{,}000{,}000} = 4$ percent	5 percent	Poor
Return on total assets	$\dfrac{\text{Net profit after taxes}}{\text{Total assets}}$	$\dfrac{\$\ 120{,}000}{\$2{,}000{,}000} = 6.0$ percent	10 percent	Poor
Return on net worth	$\dfrac{\text{Net profit after taxes}}{\text{Net worth}}$	$\dfrac{\$\ 120{,}000}{\$1{,}000{,}000} = 12.0$ percent	15 percent	Poor

Source: From *Managerial Finance*, 5th edition, by J. Fred Weston and Eugene Brigham. Copyright © 1981 by CBS College Publishing. Reprinted by permission.

sures of strategic and managerial performance not normally found on traditional financial statements. They include considerations of labor efficiency and productivity (especially important to competing internationally); production quantity and quality; human resources factors such as absenteeism, turnover, and tardiness; on a very limited basis, human resources accounting and personnel satisfaction measures; more commonly, management by objectives systems; social performance measurements (social audits); cost benefit analysis; operational audits of any functional, divisional, or staff component; distribution cost and efficiency; network planning models; Gantt charts; market share analyses; inventory analyses; management audits; modeling; and so forth. The list is almost endless and there is not time to discuss each item here. In most instances, these measures stress short-run results. The obvious consequence is that managers will place their emphasis on "looking good" in the short run rather than the long run, as would be appropriate. One notable exception is at General Electric, which as part of its operational control standards for executives (and for the company and its components), emphasizes a balance between long-range and short-range objectives and emphasizes personnel development as well.

Most of the above-mentioned measures are familiar. However, in order to provide a common analytical base, a review of a few of the more important or promising of these measures follows.

Ratio Analysis

Ratios of financial statement items (here, balance sheets and income statements) are widely used to measure strategic and management performance. With the exception of the current and quick ratios, few generally acceptable and appropriate ratio values exist. The exact number of ratios to use, the circumstances in which to use them, their components, and their exact meanings often are not agreed upon. Every financial analyst seems to have a preferred system.

Fortunately, there is common support for several ratios, which are presented in Table 9.1. These ratios are divided into four main subdivisions, each of which tells the analyst about a specific facet of corporate performance. Appendix 3 to this text explains each of these ratios in more detail. As Table 9.1 shows, a firm's ratios are normally compared with the ratios of other firms in the same industry. A firm's ratios may also be compared with its own historical ratios. Trends or deviations are the primary consideration. Comparative industry figures are often difficult to obtain, although certain organizational figures are available through the services provided by Dun & Bradstreet and Robert Morris Associates. (While your library may have Dun & Bradstreet, you may find your local bank the only source for Robert Morris.) In addition, *Dun's Review* publishes annually (usually in November) "Ratios of Manufacturing"; annually in May and June, *Fortune* publishes selected ratios and financial statement items and evaluations thereof for the *Fortune* 1000 and the *Fortune* 50s; annually (in January) *Forbes*, in "The Annual Report on American Industry," provides evaluative commentary and analysis; *Business Week* reports selected large firms' financial information quarterly; the major investment banking firms provide studies on industries and individual firms; individual firms' annual reports and 10Ks often yield useful information; Standard and Poor's *Industry Surveys* are helpful; and finally, Compustat and several other financial information firms will provide financial information on most large corporations.

The major problem with using these sources is finding the exact industry or group of firms against which to compare the subject firm. While data on large organizations is abundant, the multiplicity and diversity of products among firms make comparisons suspect. Data on small firms is available only from Robert Morris, and not all industries are covered. Data on intermediate-sized firms is virtually nonexistent. Even where comparative ratios are available, they must be used with caution. Financial statement information is subject to varying accounting practices which hamper comparisons. Footnotes to these statements often make significant differences as to the true value of certain items.

Return on Investment (ROI)

As a result of its positive aspects, decentralization has become a popular organizational design technique. As indicated in an earlier chapter, the need arises to control the resulting subsystems. Two primary types of control systems exist to exert financial control over these decentralized units: those that control projects and those that control responsibility centers. Anthony, Dearden, and Vancil describe five types of responsibility centers:[6]

1. Standard cost centers are those for which standard costs can be computed. By multiplying this cost times units, an output measure is devised.

2. Revenue centers are those for which revenues can be determined.

3. Discretionary expense centers are organizational units, normally staff units, whose output is not commonly measured in financial terms.

4. Profit centers are subsystems for which both costs and revenues can be measured and where responsibility for the difference—profit—has been assigned.

5. Investment centers are profit centers for which the assets employed in obtaining profit are identified. (These are SBUs or major project divisions.)

ROI (net income divided by total assets) is the performance measure most frequently used for the last of these responsibility centers—the investment center. As suggested in Chapter 8's discussion of top-management motivation, ROI is a critical issue in large organizations. For inappropriate division control systems, which reduce executive motivation, can and usually do result in reduced profits. Indeed, while ROI analysis has several advantages, it also has several limitations.

Advantages of ROI analysis include the following:

1. ROI is a single comprehensive figure influenced by everything that happens.

2. It measures how well the division manager uses the property of the company to generate profits. It is also a good way to check on accuracy of capital investment proposals.

3. It is a common denominator that can be used to compare many entities.

4. It provides an incentive to use existing assets efficiently.

5. It provides an incentive to acquire new assets only when such acquisition would increase the return.

---

[6]R. N. Anthony, J. Dearden, and R. F. Vancil, *Management Central Systems* (Homewood, Ill.: Irwin, 1972), pp. 200–203.

Limitations of ROI analysis include the following:

1.   ROI is very sensitive to depreciation policy. Depreciation write-off variances among divisions affect ROI performance. Accelerated depreciation techniques reduce ROI, conflicting with capital budgeting discounted cash flow analysis.

2.   ROI is sensitive to book value. Older plants with more depreciated assets and lower initial costs have relatively lower investment bases than newer plants (note also the effect of inflation on rising costs of newer plants and on the distortion of replacement costs), thus causing ROI to be increased. Asset investment may be held down or assets disposed of in order to increase ROI performance.

3.   In many firms that use ROI, one division sells to another. As a result, transfer pricing must occur, with the expenses incurred affecting profit. Since in theory the transfer price should be based on total impact on firm profit, some investment center managers are bound to suffer (equitable transfer prices being difficult to determine).

4.   If one division operates in an industry with favorable conditions and another in an industry with unfavorable conditions, one will automatically "look" better than the other.

5.   The time span of concern is short range, while the performance of division managers should be measured in the long run. This is top-management's time-span capacity—how long it takes for their performance to realize results.

6.   The business cycle strongly affects ROI performance, often despite managerial performance.

Despite these criticisms, ROI will likely continue as the leading index of management performance if for no other reason than its simplicity. Importantly, though, ROI must be supplemented with other decision information.

ROI is an important concept in terms of both total organizational control and subsystem control. As noted, it is the most widely used measure of a firm's operating efficiency. While ROI represents net income as a percentage of total assets, it is a function of many variables (see Figure 9.3). ROI results from two key factors, profit margin on sales and assets turnover. Factors that contribute to these two ratios are outlined in the figure. These factors will not be discussed here at length, since most of you should already be familiar with the concept. You might want to work through the numbers given in the figure as a review process, relating the results to the contributive factors surrounding the model.

Strategic and Management Audits

One of the major questions confronting organizations today is how to evaluate the performance of the top-management team. In order for this end to be achieved, several factors must be considered:

1.   Did top management accomplish the objectives it established?

2.   How good were the objectives it established? How good were the strategies it employed to accomplish these objectives?

3.   What factors beyond the control of top management affected its performance?

4.   How well has it responded to and how well has it anticipated these factors?

Figure 9.3 Financial Analysis Using ROI

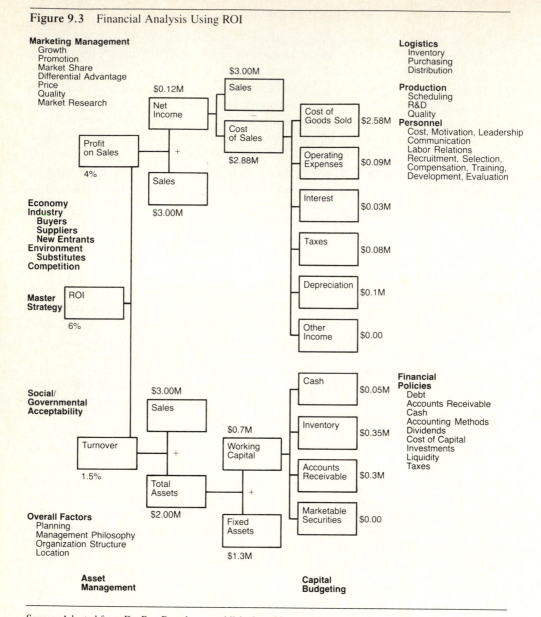

Source: Adapted from Dr. Ray Bressler, unpublished working paper.

These questions are operational control criteria for top management. Note, it is strategy that is at issue.

Several systems have attempted to measure top-management's performance. One of the more promising is the management audit which examines all facets of organizational activity. A management audit familiar to many management practitioners is the one developed by the American Institute of Management (AIM). This audit examines ten categories perceived by AIM's founder, Jackson Martindell, to contribute to strategic success.[7]

The AIM audit consists of a questionnaire containing about 300 questions, each related to organizational performance in one of the ten categories. The questionnaires are completed by a team of AIM auditors. Questions are answered and additional information provided through interviews with organizational managers, analyses of reports, and third-party sources. At the end of the audit process, point values are assigned to the organization in each of the audit categories. An excellent rating is given if enough points are achieved. The audit has been widely used in many of the largest corporations and in smaller firms as well. Importantly, the audit can be adapted to organizations with missions other than profit, such as commonweal, service, and mutual benefit organizations.

Several additional approaches to the management audit have been suggested. Of interest is William Greenwood's management audit.[8] He suggests that a management audit should examine:

1.   Strategy and strategy determinants, especially environmental factors.

2.   The major functional activities of a firm—marketing, operations (production), personnel, and accounting and finance.

3.   Whether managers are performing the major functions of management—planning, organizing, staffing, directing, and controlling.

Finally, Greenwood recognizes the need for an annual organizational policy audit. In this audit Greenwood has followed a management theory approach more traditional than Martindell's.

More recently, Robert J. Thierauf, Robert C. Klekamp, and Daniel W. Geeding have developed an extensive, almost exhaustive, management audit questionnaire as an approach to the teaching of the introductory management course, as well as to the analysis of a firm. This audit is quite extensive and examines virtually all facets of organizational functioning.[9]

Management audits may also follow a format parallel to the content of the master strategy (see Table 3.5). Such an analysis is divided into four major parts: those for enterprise, corporate, business, and functional strategies. This approach includes recognition of product divisions but examines strategy on the basis of functional activities within divisions if they exist.

In observing any technique, it is important to note its weaknesses. While the strength of the management audit is that it often has been able to predict corporate performance successfully, it is not always accurate. Such audits have predicted success for some companies that failed miserably. Why? First, and probably most important, the environment may have changed drastically. Strategic issues management must be monitored for surprises. Second, observing the manner in which ratings are assigned reveals that the process is rather arbitrary. There are no specific point values for responses to the questions, and such strict values would probably not be feasible. The auditors who audit a company and obtain responses to audit questions often disagree on the rating of the firm.

---

[7] J. Martindell, *The Appraisal of Management* (New York: Harper & Bros., 1962).

[8] W. T. Greenwood, *Business Policy: A Management Audit Approach*.

[9] R. J. Thierauf, R. C. Klekamp, and D. W. Geeding, *Management Principles and Practices: A Contingency and Questionnaire Approach* (New York: Wiley, 1977).

Regardless of its weaknesses, the audit serves an important function in its comprehensive examination of the organization. While examination of the "bottom line" indicates problems, the auditing of other areas is vital in explaining the causes of these problems. The audit is primarily effective because it looks beyond financial information and systematically appraises the performance of top management.

A brief example of a management audit that follows the master strategy format appears as part of Appendix 2. This appendix should be a key part of your analyses of companies and their situations. Importantly, this management audit is part of a more comprehensive strategic audit. A strategic audit goes one step past the management audit and examines the external environment in which the organization finds itself. This allows for a full SWOT analysis. Furthermore, the questions employed in the management audit have been couched in such a way as to emphasize the firm's relationships with its environment. Many of the questions seek responses that require an examination of the firm's relationship to its external environment before they can be answered. This approach to performing a management audit was used in the Martindell, Greenwood, and Thierauf et al. audits referenced earlier. The strategic audit is becoming an increasingly utilized technique in the formulation and in the evaluation and control of strategy.

Human Resources Accounting (HRA)

The evaluation of human assets offers great promise, but to date this promise has been largely unfulfilled. The relevance of human resources accounting to strategic management is connected principally to evaluating the worth of the abilities, skills, knowledge, aspirations, and so forth, of the strategic decision makers. But, in addition, the evaluation of corporate strengths and weaknesses requires an assessment of all employees and their potentials related to threats and opportunities.

To date, much of the implementation of HRA has involved calculations of the historical cost of human "assets" to the organization. A typical cost model observes the cost of recruiting and acquisition, formal training, orientation, development, familiarization, and related human resources expenses. Other HRA cost models exist. One might calculate opportunity cost, for example, and replacement cost, based on historical cost with operation costs added. In addition to cost models of HRA, one other major model—the economic value approach—exists in aggregate or on an individual basis. Ultimately, this latter is the information sought, but the difficulties, and even impossibilities of estimation, in the authors' opinion, severely limit the applicability of the approach. The main problem with the economic value approach is one of validity. Such approaches require estimation of the worth of individuals to the organization. The question is, how can one be sure these estimations are meaningful?

In spite of the difficulties involved, the number of firms attempting HRA is growing and includes such firms as American Telephone and Telegraph, GTE in Michigan, and Texas Instruments. The increased emphasis on people and productivity which is anticipated in the 1980s should spur additional development of HRA systems.[10]

The Social Audit

In recent years, business's critics have demanded that social audits of corporations be conducted. The term *social audit* refers to any device that attempts to evaluate an organization's social performance. Areas that might be audited include environmental protection, equal employment opportunity, consumer satisfaction, governmental relationships, energy usage, and employee job satisfaction.

Ultimately the aim is to determine the social impact of the firm on its stakeholders. While some social areas are readily definable, a quantitative measure of both requirements and performance for many of these areas is extremely difficult, if not impossible, to obtain. Furthermore, it is difficult to obtain agreement as to exactly what business should accomplish. Each pressure group seems to have its own set of demands. Obviously, business cannot respond to all of them. Nevertheless, many corporations have audited their activities in several of the social responsibility areas, and the scoring systems used were somewhat quantitatively oriented.[11]

Other Aspects of Control

Several additional factors should be considered with respect to control. The following paragraphs examine them.

---

[10]P. H. Mirvis and B. A. Macy, "Human Resources Accounting: A Measurement Perspective," *Academy of Management Review*, April 1976, pp. 74–83; P. Ogan and S. Matulich, "Human Resource Accounting: Dead or Alive," *Atlanta Economic Review*, July/August 1976, pp. 13–16.

[11]For example see J. M. Higgins, "A Social Audit of Equal Employment Opportunity Programs," *Human Resource Management*, Fall 1977, pp. 2–7.

Control Policies

Just as organizations establish strategic and implementation policies, they must also establish policies which guide control of the organization. Control policies naturally evolve from the objectives and standards established for performance. The organization must simply indicate to its managers and other employees what the specific objectives are, how performance against these will be measured, what comparisons will ensue, and how differences between expectations and performance will be handled. Rewards must naturally be tied to results.

The organization needs policies establishing total performance measurements, intermediate organizational-level performance measurements, and work group and individual performance measurements. Of principal concern is that the "what" and "how" of control is sufficiently definitive to motivate employees to perform.

A Note on the Role of Information in Control

A decision can be only as good as the information upon which it is based. In strategic control, management control, and operational control situations for both feedforward and feedback control systems, comparison and adjustment occur as information is received. The absence of information, such as is the rule in management-by-exception control systems, is also important. There are differences in the characteristics of the information required in strategic control, management control, and operational control. These differences are portrayed in Table 9.2. The mass of information at operational levels must be meaningfully reduced before top-management reports are prepared.

Integrated Planning and Control Systems

In a previous chapter, the importance of integrated planning and control was stressed from a planning perspective—objectives provide direction and motivation. As objectives are anticipated results, they provide, for control purposes, standards against which to compare performance. Program Evaluation Review Technique (PERT); Critical Path Management (CPM); Management by Objectives (MBO); Planning Programming Budgeting Sys-

Table 9.2   Information Requirements by Type of Control

Characteristics of Information	Operational Control	Management Control	Strategic Control
Source	Largely internal	Internal, partly environmental	Internal and environmental
Scope	Well defined, narrow	Moderately broad	Broad in scope
Level of aggregation	Detailed	Aggregated	Aggregated
Time horizon	Historical	Historical	Future and historical
Frequency of use	Very frequent, continuous	Periodic	Occasional, but with increasing frequency

Source: Reprinted from "A Framework for Management Information Systems," by G. Anthony Garry and Michael S. S. Morton. *Sloan Management Review*, Fall 1971, p. 59, by permission of the publisher. © 1971 by the Sloan Management Review Association. All rights reserved.

tem (PPBS); budgets, and other planning and control systems can and should be applied to ensure successful mission accomplishment. It is essential that implementation be controlled if it is to be effective.

Dysfunctional Consequences of Control Systems

A certain amount of tension is desirable, but at many companies, the pressures to perform are so intense and the goals so unreasonable that some middle managers feel the only way out is to bend the rules, even if it means compromising personal ethics.

▪ *Paul Lawrence* ▪

Control systems are sometimes formulated without consideration of the human beings who will be controlled by them. The behavioral results are often dysfunctional. For example, in business it is often observed that divisional managers may intentionally not invest in a needed new plant(s) and equipment in order to improve ROI results by reducing the size of total assets, the divisor in the ROI calculation. Or, managers may not expend monies for the development of personnel, thereby increasing the dividend of the ROI calculation—net profit. Budgets have also been shown to result in undesirable consequences. In fact, pressures associated with budgets may be resented by managers and their subordinates, resulting in inefficiency. Pressure from the staff agencies requiring budget preparations may lead to staff-line conflicts. Examples of these dysfunctional consequences may be found in even the "best-managed" firms, such as Heinz, Ford, GM,[12] and Pepisco.[13]

Other examples could be cited. The point is this: if organizations have control systems, they must recognize that individuals can find ways to beat them, and will do so when the systems are unsound. Furthermore, control systems may often be so poorly designed that they are activity centered and not performance centered. Much of the behavioral literature addresses the identification and removal of such dysfunctional activities. Results, not activity, should be controlled.

What Should Be Measured?

There is a growing suspicion that the more relevant criterion of organizational effectiveness is not as it used to be, that of efficiency, but rather that of adaptability to changes in the environment.

▪ *Dennis Organ* ▪

Having just said that "it's results that count," it is appropriate to question if that is indeed all that should be considered in evaluating the success of a strategy. Or are there other factors that are just as important as results? If so, what are they? We believe that results-oriented systems are somewhat less applicable to service organizations and to nonprofits than they are to manufacturing and sales-type situations. Even there, results do not always tell the whole story. This, for example, is a major reason that management audits typically

[12] G. Getshow, "Overdriven Execs: Some Middle Managers Cut Corners to Achieve High Corporate Goals," *The Wall Street Journal*, November 8, 1979, pp. 1, 34.

[13] A. Hershmen, "Cooking the Books," *Dun's Business Month*, January 1983, pp. 40–47.

incorporate process questions, and that strategic audits include external environmental questions.

In the sense that an organization's effectiveness is in major part a measure of the effectiveness of its master strategy, the following conceptualization is highly contributive to our understanding of the evaluation of strategies. J. Barton Cunningham, after reviewing the relevant literature, concluded that seven major ways of evaluating organizational effectiveness existed. These are defined as follows:[14]

1. The rational goal approach evaluates the organization's ability to achieve its goals.

2. The systems resource model analyzes the decision maker's capability to distribute resources efficiently among various subsystem's needs.

3. The managerial process model assesses the capability and productivity of various managerial processes—decision making, planning, and the like—for performing goal-related tasks.

4. The organizational development model appraises the organization's ability to work as a team and to fit the needs of its members.

5. The bargaining model measures the ability of decision makers to obtain and use resources for responding to problems important to them.

6. The structural functional approach tests the durability and flexibility of the organization's structure for responding to a diversity of situations and events.

7. The functional approach relates the usefulness of the organization's activities to its client groups.

It is evident that this text has stressed the first of these, but you may also observe that specific applications or examples of the others are noted throughout, and/or are queried in the strategic audit in Appendix 2. Tables 9.3 and 9.4 provide additional information on Cunningham's analysis.

The Emergent Strategy

Henry Mintzberg has cautioned us to recognize that there is quite often going to be a difference between our intended strategy and our realized strategy. He suggests, in fact, that the strategy that is formulated is more properly entitled an "intended strategy," and the realized strategy is the actual strategy that results and is, in fact, "a pattern in a stream of decisions," sometimes deliberate, sometimes simply happening. His concept is pictured in Figure 9.4. The basic viewpoint expressed here is that many intended strategies become unrealized, and emergent strategies take their place. Intended strategies that were realized Mintzberg terms as deliberate. In analyzing the success of strategies, we typically seek to measure performance related to deliberate, realized strategies. But we must be alert to the fact that many times we are in effect measuring something that was not planned, but that just happened along the way . . . that pattern of decisions over time that emerged.[15] This is not a critical point in most cases, but when it comes to measuring the performance of a specific unit or a specific manager, those involved should, in terms of their own corporate security, be quite concerned with this distinction.

---

[14] J. B. Cunningham, "Approaches to the Evaluation of Organizational Effectiveness," *Academy of Management Review*, July 1977, p. 464.

[15] H. Mintzberg, "Patterns in Strategy Formation," *Management Science*, 1978, p. 945.

Figure 9.4   Types of Strategies

Source: H. Mintzberg, "Patterns in Strategy Formulation," *Management Science*, 1978, p. 945.

Growing Concerns in Strategic Control

One of the issues of grave concern to many stockholders, lenders, suppliers, and government is the accuracy of accounting information provided by firms to interested parties through their financial statements. For, despite the existence of generally accepted public accounting principles and practices, financial statements can be constructed in any number of ways. There is also concern about the impacts of a host of environmental variables, such as inflation and taxes. A number of alternatives, most of these aimed at improving balance sheet accuracy, have been proposed by the Financial Accounting Standard's Board, signaling a trend away from historical concerns for income statement accuracy.[16]

But perhaps of greater concern are those deliberate attempts by organizations and/or their managers to distort the information they provide to interested parties. (This problem was previously discussed to some extent in the section related to the dysfunctional consequences of control.) But in addition to misstatements induced by the pressures of managerial control are those occurring for more disconcerting reasons, such as fraud or the intentional misstatement of company position to temporarily protect the stock holdings of insiders. Seeking to reduce the number of such "cooked books," the Securities and Exchange Commission launched a campaign in late 1984. Apparently, the practice of misstatement is much more widespread than it is normally thought to be, for a number of well-known companies have been found guilty. Tandem computers, for instance, overstated its revenue in 1982, as did the holding company of the nation's largest savings and loan, Financial Corporation of America, for its 1983 income.[17] Many companies have been found to actively "hide" certain information, such as that related to loans or other debts, in order to make their books "look" better than they really are.[18] Some of the occurrences of misstatement, though extremely significant were not detected by the firm's CPAs. One such case, that of the Frigitemp Corporation, is highlighted in Information Capsule 9.1. As of early 1985, it is not yet clear what additional courses of action the government may take to halt these practices, besides arm twisting with the threat of litigation and litigation itself, but it is evident that stronger actions may be necessary to protect interested parties in the future.

---

[16] D. F. Hawkins, "Toward the New Balance Sheet," *Harvard Business Review*, November/December 1984, pp. 156–163.

[17] "The SEC Turns up the Heat on 'Cooked Books,'" *Business Week*, September 3, 1984, pp. 63, 64; "Tandem Computers Overstated Revenue Report, SEC Charges," AP wire story, October 3, 1984.

[18] L. Berton, "Many Firms Hide Debt to Give Them an Aura of Financial Strength," *The Wall Street Journal*, December 13, 1984, pp. 1, 12.

Table 9.3   Criteria Appropriate to Specific Applications of Evaluation Approaches

Organizational Effectiveness Approach

Evaluating the Performance of the Organizational Structure		Evaluating the Performance of the Organization's Human Resources	
Rational Goal	**Systems Resource**	**Managerial Process**	**Organizational Development**
Accomplishments: goals of the Esso Standard Oil Company for preparing employees for retirement: 1. Increasing industrial efficiency, prestige, worker satisfaction; reducing costs; increasing public good will. 2. Aiding the nation and the community to solve problems of the aged. 3. Helping the worker be well adjusted in retirement.[a]	*Efficiency and satisfaction criteria for the systems need of adapting to a changing and turbulent environment:* 1. Adaptability—the ability to solve problems and to react with flexibility to changing internal and external circumstances. 2. Identity—knowledge and insight on the part of the organization of what it is and what it is to do. This involves (a) determining to what extent the organizational goals are understood and accepted by the personnel and (b) ascertaining to what extent the organization is perceived vertically by the personnel. 3. Capacity to test reality—the ability to search out, accurately perceive, and correctly interpret the real properties of the environment.[b]	*Productivity and capability criteria (managerial principles):* 1. Planning—shaping the future direction of the organization. 2. Organizing—recognition of the organization's personal needs, obtaining people to meet these needs, and attempting to place people so that individual and organizational needs are in harmony. 3. Staffing—recognition of the organization's personnel needs, obtaining the people to meet these needs, and attempting to place people so that individual and organizational needs are in harmony. 4. Leading—motivation of people to teach goals without deterioration of morale both of themselves and the organization. 5. Controlling—activity that checks actual progress against planned progress and suggests ways of modifying activities falling below expected levels of performance.[c] The principles are John G. Hutchinson's suggested redefinition of Henri Fayol's ideas using more modern terminology.	*Interpersonal competence and job satisfaction criteria:* 1. Improvement in interpersonal competence. 2. Development of the norm that human factors and feelings are legitimate. 3. Increased understanding between and within working groups in order to reduce tensions. 4. Development of more effective team management. 5. Development of more rational and "open" methods of conflict resolution rather than suppression, compromise, and unprincipled power. 6. Development of organic rather than mechanical systems.[d]

[a] Bass, Bernard M., "Ultimate Criteria of Organizational Worth" in Jaisingh Ghorpade, *Assessment of Organizational Effectiveness* (Pacific Palisades, Calif.: Goodyear, 1971).

[b] Bennis, Warren, "Toward a Truly Scientific Management: The Concept of organizational Health" in *Changing Organizations* (New York: McGraw-Hill, 1966), pp. 32–63.

[c] Gross, Bertram H., *The State of the Nation: Social Systems Accounting* (London: Tavistock, 1966).

[d] Bennis, Warren, *Organizational Development: Its Nature, Origins and Prospects* (Reading, Mass.: Addison-Wesley, 1969), p. 15.

Table 9.3   *continued*

Organizational Effectiveness Approach

Evaluating the Impact of Organizational Functions or Activities

Bargaining	Structural Functional	Functional
Resource utilization criteria (dimensions of exchange):	*Structural viability—performance (functional) elements:*	*Functional criteria:*

Bargaining

Resource utilization criteria (dimensions of exchange):

1. The parties to the exchange—their affiliation, function, prestige, size, personal characteristics, and numbers and types of clients served.

2. The kinds of quantities exchanged—the actual elements exchanged (consumer, labor services, and resources other than labor services), and information on the availability of these organizational elements and on rights and obligations regarding them.

3. The agreement underlying the exchange—terms explicitly defined by one party or mutually defined by a number of parties.

4. The direction of the exchange—the direction of the flow of organizational elements (unilateral, reciprocal, or joint).[e]

Structural Functional

Structural viability—performance (functional) elements:

1. Satisfying the interests of members and clientele groups.

2. Producing a quantity, quality, and mixture of outputs.

3. Investing in the system through hard goods, people, subsystems, and external relations.

4. Using inputs efficiently to achieve potential and profitability.

5. Acquiring resources such as money, people, goods.

6. Observing codes of laws and organizational rules.

7. Using relevant technical knowledge and administrative methods to behave rationally.

Structural elements:

1. Number and character of people.

2. Physical and monetary assets of nonhuman resources.

3. Type, location, form, and differentiation of subsystem.

4. Conflict, conflict resolution, superior/subordinate relations, bargaining procedures, formal and informal communications defining the organization's internal relations.

5. External organizations, agencies, roles, and environment characterizing the organization's external relations.

6. Values describing the organization's orientation; i.e., competitive, active.

7. The internal structure support base defining the guidance system.[f]

(These criteria, although defined in Bertram Gross's social systems model, are appropriate within Philip Selznick's definition of structural-functionalism.)

Functional

Functional criteria:

1. Goal attainment—planning, programming, scheduling, rule making.

2. Adaptation—procurement, property management, office services, budgeting, personnel.

3. Integration—work flow procedures, internal rule-making process, informal organizational status system, wage determination system.

4. Pattern maintenance—consideration given to agency's legal mandate, clientele needs, public interest, professional and mission-oriented values of the organization, employee satisfaction and morale, social norms of informal groups within the organization.[g]

[e] Jaques, Elliot, *Equitable Payment* (Heinemann Educational Books, 1961).

[f] Growler, Dan, and Karen Legge, "Stress, Success, and Legitimacy," in Dan Growler and Karen Legge, *Managerial Stress*, 1975, pp. 34–51.

[g] Fremont, James Lyden, "Using Parsons' Functional Analysis in the Study of Public Organizations," *Administrative Science Quarterly*, 1975, Vol. 20, pp. 59–70.

Source: J. B. Cunningham, "Approaches to the Evaluation of Organizational Effectiveness," *Academy of Management Review*, July 1977, p. 464. Reprinted by permission of the Academy of Management.

Table 9.4 Summary of Organizational Effectiveness Approaches

Organizational Effectiveness Model	Organizational Situation	Central Focus or Purpose	Assumption	Limitations
Rational Goal	Evaluation of performance of organizational structures.	Determine degree to which organizations are able to achieve their goals.	An organization is rational if its activities are organized to achieve its goals.	The model frequently shows that organizations do not reach their goals. There is also a difficulty in identifying and defining organizational goals.
Systems Resource	Evaluation of performance of organizational structures.	Determine decision maker's efficiency in allocating and utilizing resources for fulfilling various systems needs.	An organization, in order to survive, must satisfy some basic needs: 1. Acquiring resources, 2. Interpreting the real properties of the external environment, 3. Production of outputs, 4. Maintenance of day-to-day internal activities, 5. Coordinating relationships among the various subsystems, 6. Responding to feedback, 7. Evaluating the effect of its decisions, 8. Accomplishing goals.	Measures of all systems needs are difficult to develop.
Managerial Process	Evaluation of performance of organization's human resources.	Determine capability or productivity of managers or managerial processes.	An organization can be considered rational when its various managerial processes and patterns enhance the individual's productivity or capability to obtain objectives.	Measures of productivity and capabilities pinpoint personal problems and limitations.

Organizational Development	Evaluation of performance of organization's human resources.	Determine organization's ability to work as a team and fit the needs of its individual members.	Work which is organized to meet people's needs as well as organizational requirements tends to produce the highest productivity.	Emphasis on the informal organization takes precedence over the formal. Individuals may be reluctant to accept interpersonal feedback supplied by the model.
Bargaining	Evaluation of impact of decisions.	Determine use or uses which various decision makers make of their resources in achieving organizational goals.	An organization is a cooperative, sometimes competitive, resource distributing system.	The model deals with a very specific part of the organization's activities.
Structural Functional	Evaluation of impact of organization's structure on performance.	Determine organization's ability to develop structures to maintain and strengthen performance.	A system's survival is equated to satisfying five basic needs: 1. Security of organization in relation to environment, 2. Stability of lines of authority and communication, 3. Stability of informal relations in organization, 4. Continuity of policy making, 5. Homogeneity of outlook.	The model deals with a very specific part of the organization's activities.
Functional	Evaluation of impact of organizational activities.	Provide information on social consequences of organizational activities and on organization's ability to meet needs of key client groups in its environment.	Every system must define its purpose for being (goal attainment), determine resources to achieve its goals (adaptation), establish means for coordinating its efforts (integration), and reduce strains and tensions in its environment (pattern maintenance).	The model deals with a very specific part of the organization's activities.

Source: J. B. Cunningham, "Approaches to the Evaluation of Organizational Effectiveness." *Academy of Management Review*, July 1977, p. 464. Reprinted by permission of the Academy of Management.

INFORMATION CAPSULE 9.1
Frigitemp: A Chilling Experience for Arthur Andersen & Co.

The nation's largest public accounting firm, Arthur Andersen (AA), failed to detect irregularities at Frigitemp, a company that ultimately succumbed to "dirty deeds." It is reported that AA has paid out over $7 million to settle related lawsuits, and that it still has at least three more sizable suits pending. Frigitemp's abuses included bribing federal government officials, misusing federal funds, flagrantly and chronically overstating earnings, and taking sizable bribes at the top-management level. Some have suggested that, in aggressively seeking to achieve new business and maintain its current clients, Arthur Andersen may have become too close to its clients to see the existing problems. (No evidence of compromise on the part of AA has been found, however.)

Gerald Lee, the company's chairman, and Mervyn Silver, the company's president, admitted to conspiring to "loot the company." They have admitted to kickback schemes and embezzlement. Virtually millions of dollars were fraudulently taken from the firm. They even conspired to murder two other Frigitemp officials to keep them from talking, but these actions were never carried out.

From the control perspective, what was even more incredible was that according to Silver's testimony, Arthur Andersen's assigned project auditor to Frigitemp, Michael Gorin, encouraged the company to use a "creative accounting" technique known as "cost-to-cost percentage-of-completion accounting." This approach allows a firm to report long-term construction project income that has not yet actually been received. Its use hinges on the purchase of materials, so that if 40 percent of a project's materials have been purchased, then 40 percent of the project may be assumed to have been completed for revenue-reporting purposes. Frigitemp used this approach to its fullest extent, even having its lead contractors (where it was a subcontractor) pay for the materials.

Frigitemp officials also established false accounting trails to cover up some of their looting schemes in the event that Gorin's audit team should inquire about certain matters. Moreover, some evidence suggests that the accounting situation was so irregular that Silver and Lee were not even knowledgeable about how much inventory they had, nor about how to stop continual in-house thefts other than their own. Yet, apparently AA never substantially questioned the Frigitemp books prior to their receipt of an "anonymous" letter alleging all sorts of misdoings in the firm. Two months after Arthur Andersen received that letter, Frigitemp declared bankruptcy.

How can those that must interact with a firm—creditors, suppliers, customers, and stockholders—be protected? Does the CPA's statement of certification of financial statements mean that much? We often think it does, but CPA firms emphasize that the statement means only that, given accepted practices of auditing and accounting, the books *appear* satisfactory. To what extent are practices acceptable? One AA official revealed that, as an auditing case, Frigitemp was especially trying because it was primarily a defense contractor and subcontractor. The AA officer also noted that federal agencies seldom respond to auditor requests for information. One must assume then that the auditors rely on their own efforts and their clients' word as to the validity of many numbers. When asked about changes in auditing procedures as a consequence of this case, Arthur Andersen's final comment was, "We have a continuing commitment to quality of service. There has not been a change as a result of this case because there was none needed." It is not clear what actions will be taken to prevent further abuse of those who depend on certified, audited statements as a major input to their decisions.

Source: John J. Fialka, "Why Arthur Andersen Was So Slow to Detect Chicanery at Frigitemp," *The Wall Street Journal*, September 21, 1984, pp. 1, 18; Edward T. Pound, "How Frigitemp Sank After It Was Looted by Top Management," *The Wall Street Journal*, September 20, 1984, pp. 1, 20.

Summary

Control techniques are employed to ensure that mission is accomplished. Three principal types of control systems are created to that end: strategic control, management control, and operational control. Strategic control is concerned with the appropriateness of strategy to mission accomplishment. Such control is ongoing. Management and operational control systems control extensions of the strategy. That is, once the strategy has been more specifically defined and implemented, it must be ascertained whether the planned results, or objectives, have been achieved, both at the major component or total organizational level (via management control), and at the individual or group level (via operational control). Management and operational control systems, then, are designed to control the more articulated objectives and plans of action which emanate from strategy. These systems also indicate changes in the premises upon which the strategy was formulated, an important contribution.

Much of the organizational control system depends on financial information—information provided by the accounting system. The most sophisticated of the techniques are financial, ROI, and profit related, but other types of control measures such as management audits are being increasingly utilized and are proving essential, especially the objectives-oriented techniques. The essence of the various control systems is accountability and responsibility, though there is growing concern about their accuracy.

An organization can survive so long as it adjusts to its situation.

▪ *James D. Thompson and William J. McEwen* ▪

Key Terms and Concepts

By the time you have completed this chapter, you should be familiar with the following key terms and concepts: control, strategic control, management control, operational control, measures of performance, ratio analysis, ROI, advantages of ROI, limitations of ROI, management audits, human resources accounting, social audit, strategic audit, role of information in control, integrated planning and control systems, intended strategy, and emergent strategy.

Discussion Questions

1. What is controlled by each of the three types of control? Why are three different types of control necessary?
2. Describe each of the strategic and management control measures mentioned in the chapter. Why is each necessary?

3. How can the dysfunctional consequences of control be overcome?

4. What are the six steps of the feedback model?

5. What is "feedforward" control?

6. What are the three aspects of an organization that should be examined in a management audit?

7. How would you explain "human resources accounting" to someone who was unfamiliar with the term?

8. What is the role of information in control?

References

"The Anatomy of RCA's Videodisc Failure." *Business Week*, April 23, 1984, p. 89.

Anthony, R. N. *Planning and Control Systems: A Framework for Analysis*. Boston: Harvard University Graduate School of Business Administration, 1965, pp. 24, 27, 29.

Anthony, R. N., Dearden, J., and Vancil, R. F. *Management Control Systems*. Homewood, Ill.: Irwin, 1972, pp. 200–203.

Argyris, C. "Human Problems with Budgets." *Harvard Business Review*, January/February 1953, pp. 97–110.

Bales, C. F. "Practice of Business Strategic Control: The President's Paradox." *Business Horizons*, June 1977, pp. 17–28.

Berkwitt, G. J. "Do Profit Centers Really Work?" *Management Review*, July/August 1969, pp. 15–20.

Cammann, C., and Nadler, B. A. "Fit Control Systems to Your Managerial Style." *Harvard Business Review*, January/February 1976, pp. 65–72.

Casey, Cornelius J., and Bartczak, Norman J. "Cash Flow—It's Not the Bottom Line." *Harvard Business Review*, July/August 1984, pp. 61–66.

Cunningham, J. B. "Approaches to the Evaluation of Organizational Effectiveness." *Academy of Management Review*, July 1977, pp. 463–474.

Dalton, G. W. "Motivation and Control in Organizations." In *Motivation and Control in Organization*, edited by G. W. Dalton and P. R. Lawrence. Homewood, Ill.: Irwin, 1971.

Dearden, J. "Appraising Profit Center Managers." *Harvard Business Review*, May/June 1968, pp. 80–87.

———. "The Case Against ROI Control." *Harvard Business Review*, May/June 1969, pp. 124–135.

deNoya, L. "How to Evaluate a Long Range Plan." *Long Range Planning*, June 1978, pp. 36–40.

Garry, G. A., and Morton, M. S. S. "A Framework for Management Information Systems." *Sloan Management Review*, Fall 1971, pp. 55–70.

Giglioni, Giovanni B. "A Conspectus of Management Control Theory." *Academy of Management Journal*, June 1974, Vol. 17, No. 2, pp. 292–305.

"How Bob Pritzker Runs a $3 Billion Empire." *Business Week*, March 7, 1983, pp. 64–70.

Kaplan, Robert S. "Yesterday's Accounting Undermines Production." *Harvard Business Review*, July/August 1984, pp. 95–101.

Lengnick-Hall, Cynthia A., and Futterman, Dorothea Hardt. "Control in Complex Systems: How to Manage What You Cannot Understand." Presented at the 43d Annual Academy of Management Meeting in Dallas, Texas, August 1983.

Mintzberg, H., and Waters, J. A. "Tracking Strategy in an Entrepreneurial Firm." *Academy of Management Journal*, Vol. 25, No. 3, pp. 465–499.

Rumelt, R. "Evaluation of Strategy: Theory and Models." In *Strategic Management: A New View of Business Policy and Planning*, edited by D. Schendel and C. Hofer. Boston: Little/Brown 1979.

"TRW Leads a Revolution in Managing Technology." *Business Week*, November 15, 1982, pp. 124–130.

Zammuto, Raymond F. "A Comparison of Multiple Constituency Models of Organizational Effectiveness." *Academy of Management Review*, 1984, Vol. 9, No. 4, pp. 606–616.

10

Strategic Management in the International Arena

The introduction of the five-day working week in Japan has been blamed for a rise in neurotic illness among employees, who are not used to lying in bed on Saturdays.

▪ *News item in the* Economist. Fortune, *November 26, 1984, p. 171* ▪

Strategic management in the international arena follows the same basic patterns established earlier for domestic management, as revealed in Figures 10.1 and 10.2. The conceptual processes are essentially the same, but the operating environment is often so different that the resultant actions are frequently unrecognizable, especially in terms of implementation. Multinational corporations (MNC), firms that conduct business across national boundaries (MNCs have multinational sources of capital, markets, manufacturing and suppliers), find themselves confronted with four major problems:[1]

1. The international marketplace is highly competitive. Firms in France, Hong Kong, Germany, Great Britain, Brazil, Japan, Korea, Taiwan, Canada, the United States, and numerous other countries have forged substantial, internationally competitive operating units. Many of these firms have significant strategic advantages, such as those involving labor costs or technology, that make competing with them very difficult.

2. Operations are conducted in widely varying economic, legal, political, social, and cultural environments. For example, a wide range of economies exist, from developing to mature. Also, many of the customs so common to the parent country of the MNC are virtually unknown in the host country in which the MNC will do business.

3. The relative values of currencies vary rapidly, and currency translations can quickly turn a profit into a loss. As the result of currency transaction losses, one major U.S. multinational recently lost one-third of its profits. Some lose all their profits. Due to the strong value of the dollar, virtually all U.S. MNCs have had to alter their strategies in the mid-1980s.

4. Government-to-government relationships and government-to-MNC relationships have a significant bearing on results. For example, the U.S. government often encourages U.S. firms to enter into international business, but then places severe restrictions on their rules of operation.

---

[1] Y. N. Chang and F. Campo-Flores, *Business Policy and Strategy* (Santa Monica, Calif.: Goodyear Publishing Company, 1980), Chapter 17; Y. L. Doz, "Strategic Management in Multinational Companies," *Sloan Management Review*, Winter 1980, pp. 27–46.

245

Figure 10.1   The Organization—a Strategic Management Process Model

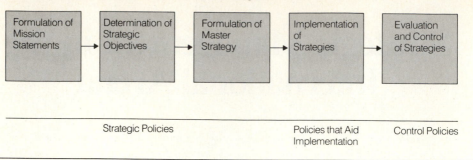

| Strategic Policies | Policies that Aid Implementation | Control Policies |

An additional factor is that management, and in particular strategic management, may often be in a different stage of development in a country other than one's own. Therefore, adjustments in management practices (strategic management practices in particular) become necessary.

The evolution of multinational companies (MNCs) over the last decade has been characterized by a growing conflict between the requirements for economic survival and success (the economic imperative) and the adjustments made necessary by the demands of host governments (the political imperative).

▪ *Yves L. Doz, 1980* ▪

The Four Influential Factors

Strategic management is every bit as important in the international business situation as it is in the domestic market. Strategists must learn to cope with the variables in this environment just as they would in any other. Let us examine how competition in the international arena affects the four influential factors for objectives determination and strategy formulation depicted in Figure 10.2: mission, strategic policy, strategists, and information.

Mission

The four types of basic missions listed earlier remain; but in much of the world outside the United States and Canada, the service and commonweal missions are more often legally required for business than they are in these two countries. Outside North America a close tie more often exists between business and government. There is an even closer alignment in many cases between business and labor; thus, the mutual benefit mission is sometimes more pronounced. For example, in much of Europe, it is illegal to terminate employees for other than the most grievous offenses, because government wishes full employment for the commonweal (apparently whether the firm remains productive or not). In France, Great Britain, Italy, and many other European countries, the government owns many major businesses. Thus, business assumes a commonweal mission. And in Japan, the firm is, in a sense, viewed by most of its employees as a mutual benefit organization. For example, the biggest firms guarantee male workers lifetime employment. On the other hand,

Figure 10.2   Objective Determination and Master Strategy Formulation

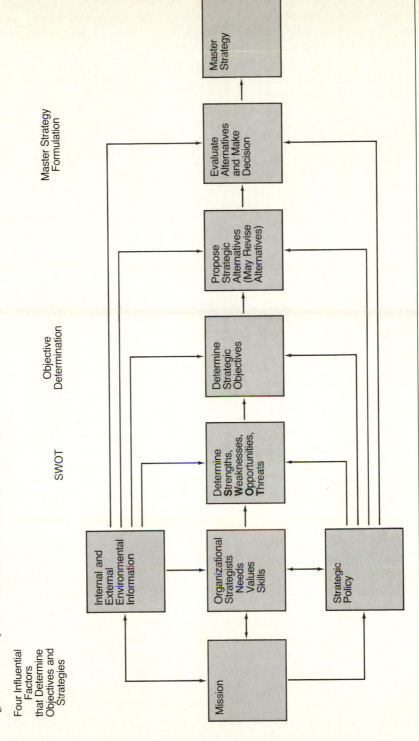

Four Influential
Factors
that Determine
Objectives and
Strategies

Japanese employees work within the firm not so much to further their own interests but rather to further the interests of the organization for the benefit of society. In England, profit and service missions are apparently much more subordinate to the commonweal mission than they are in the United States and Canada. Service and quality have all but disappeared from many English industries as a result. Again, then, we see the priorities of the missions change. The results are most dramatically displayed in the marketplace and in the management of employees.

Strategic Policy

Because missions vary, strategic policy mixes (and, indeed, operational and control policies as well) must vary. For example, in most of the world, concern for employees and employee development is very low. The essential question in developing nations is how to make any profit. Organizational climate and management philosophy policies are therefore quite different from what they might be in the United States and Canada and are most often not even addressed as strategic policies. Product quality is often of less concern in countries (for example, England) with close government/business ties, because in such countries protected internal markets exist. On the other hand, in Japan, another country with close business/government ties, quality is important, because the Japanese seek to be highly competitive in the international marketplace even though they also protect their home markets.

The Strategists

Again, because of varying mission significance and the related closer or more distant business/government relationships, variances exist in the composition of the strategist group. In countries with closer business/government relationships and more commonweal-oriented objectives, the government is often a full partner or even a managing partner in business endeavors. This is true to some extent in Germany and Japan, to a great extent in England, France, and Italy as well as in Yugoslavia and most of the Soviet-bloc countries, and to a limited extent in Brazil. It is increasingly true in the United States. And because of mutual benefit arrangements, unions and frontline employees may be in a position, usually elected, to aid in the strategic decision process. For example, in Germany, a law requires that approximately half of the board of directors of each of the larger business firms be composed of elected frontline employees.[2] In Poland, until the imposition of martial law in late 1981, the labor union Solidarity—uncharacteristically for a communist country—played a major part not only in strategic business decisions but in governmental decisions as well. And in the United States, there is a limited trend toward worker participation at the strategic level.

In most countries, governments have established policies demanding that a certain percentage of the MNC's top management be residents of the host country. Thus, the importation of management talent from the parent country of the MNC is often restricted, and in some cases even forbidden. The composition of the group that formulates strategy there-

[2]K. E. Agethe, "Mitbestimmung: Report on a Social Experiment," *Business Horizons*, February 1977, pp. 5–14.

"Let's see, Pitcairn, if my ears don't deceive me, you say the 3rd quarter 1.3 million dollar loss in our overseas division is due to an act of Satan!"

Source: from *The Wall Street Journal*. Reprinted with permission by Cartoon Features Syndicate.

fore varies and often includes people who do not speak the same language, further compounding an already complex problem. In terms of impact on organization and implementation, these laws are especially significant, because they virtually always require that all frontline, supervisory, and middle-management positions be filled by host-country residents.[3]

Internal and External Environmental Information

The information requirements are greater for multinational firms than for domestic ones, because the multinational firm must know about more economic, cultural, social, political, legal, and monetary systems. Sources of this information vary, and are often less accessible than in the parent country. Furthermore, because the transmission of information depends on language, language differences also present problems. Unfortunately, management information systems elsewhere are often less sophisticated than managers might be used to or might desire. Informal sources must often be relied upon.

Research shows that many multinationals historically have not always performed a thorough environmental analysis.[4] Indeed, they often attempt simply to replicate "back-home" strategies in lieu of assessing external environmental situations and developing strategies accordingly. That such practices are foolhardy has been reflected on many an income statement and balance sheet.

The overriding purpose of obtaining information—identifying SWOT in order to better formulate objectives and strategies—remains the same in the international arena. The

[3]R. Hal Mason, "Conflicts between Host Countries and the Multinational Enterprise," *California Management Review*, Fall 1974, pp. 5–14.

[4]"A Survey of International Research Practices by American International Corporations" (New York: International Research Associates, 1969).

problem with fulfilling this purpose is twofold: first, SWOT changes; second, the appropriate strategies often differ. Fundamental marketing approaches must be altered, as suggested above. Leadership and motivation strategies must also be changed, because underlying basic cultural motivations differ.[5] Even more fundamentally, the choice of basic action strategies and their combinations must be altered to meet the demands of the situation. The variances that occur in mission, policy, and the composition of strategist groups; the resultant differences in objectives and strategies; and the differences in the environment require that information be gathered beyond or instead of that which would routinely be gathered if the organization were operating only in the parent country.

Typically, multinationals possess some resource advantage, either capital, technology, or managerial expertise. Depending upon host-country and parent-country requirements, the multinational corporation's capital may or may not be invested in foreign countries, its technology may or may not be fully shared with others, and its managerial expertise may or may not be exported. Typically, licensing and joint ventures have replaced the capital investment and direct-ownership basic action strategies of the 1950s and 1960s. The primary causes for this shifting of strategies are the potential for expropriation and the demands of host countries.

As a result of the potential for expropriation, assessing political instability is a critical strategic step, but the information needed for this assessment is complex and difficult to obtain and assimilate. Many foreign governments have political structures different from those of the parent country; and most governments are quite secretive about internal affairs. F. T. Haner has developed one useful system for classifying investment risks abroad. He uses a series of factors rated from 1 to 5, with total points being accumulated for the series. Acceptable levels of risk are defined and then compared to the estimates for various countries.[6] Investing is quite risky in some countries; on the other hand, stable countries such as the United States and Canada offer sound investments for firms from other nations. Table 10.1 provides a checklist for evaluating the investment climate in a foreign country.

In summary, the information requirements are greater at the international level than at the domestic level, because they involve learning the basic economic, cultural, social, political, and legal structures for each country in which business is transacted. The purpose and process of information gathering remains the same, but differing SWOT and strategies may result. We will now continue examining the processes described in Figures 10.1 and 10.2.

Strategic Objectives and Master Strategy Formulation

Objectives and strategies result from the strategists' considerations of mission, strategic policy, and information. It follows that, since each of these factors is usually changed to some degree as the result of operating in a country other than the organization's parent country, strategic objectives and the master strategy will also be different. They usually are.

---

[5]S. H. Robock and K. Simmons, *International Business and Multinational Enterprises* (Homewood, Ill.: Irwin, 1973).

[6]F. T. Haner, "Rating Investment Risks Abroad," *Business Horizons*, April 1979, pp. 18–23.

All organizations depend on some strategic advantage for their existence. Multinationals are no different. Typically, multinationals rely on some form of resource superiority. These resource advantages usually include superior capital, technology, or management expertise. Sheer size, in terms of ability to provide markets for certain products or raw materials, may also be a strategic advantage in and of itself. The multinational business must convert one or more of these advantages into strengths to help it overcome weaknesses, such as an absence of host-country management talent; to take advantage of opportunities, such as a developing economy; and to overcome threats, such as international competition. So far, so good. But the rules by which the game is played are often different in the international arena; and hence, objectives and strategies must be altered.

In further examining some of the constraints which face multinationals, Hal Mason reported that host countries often place restrictions on the following:

- Ownership—typically, the host country or a firm from the host country must own a major or controlling interest.

- Employment—almost always, host countries demand that certain positions in management and technological areas be held by host-country nationals.

- Profits and fees—typically, profits and fees are set at some maximum level.

- Internal debt capital—often, internal debt capital is set according to a preestablished formula.

- Training and development—insistence on training and development for host-country nationals is common.

- Host-country markets—most host countries demand development of their exports.

- Technological bases—most host countries seek technologically based industry rather than extractive industry.[7]

As you can imagine, the impacts on objectives setting may be significant. Reexamining the objectives noted in Figure 3.3, we find, for example, that growth may be legislatively limited; efficiency may be governmentally held to a lower level than desirable because of extra costs such as those for extensive training and development; utilization of resources is often set at certain levels; contribution to owners (profits) is almost always set at certain levels, as is the ownership itself; contribution to customers may be modified to meet government-set levels; contribution to employees focuses on technical training and often on guaranteed employment as opposed to true development; and finally, contribution to society is stressed through the government involvement outlined above. But this latter concern does not take the forms, such as emphasis on pollution control, that dominate in the United States and Canada, despite the fact that in many communist-controlled countries, such as Poland, pollution is devastating.

Similarly, if we review some of the major basic action strategies, we find, for example, that in Japan, diversification occurs earlier in the firm's history than in the United States, while in Europe, it tends to occur later.[8] In Japan, the supportive strategy of quality in production probably is emphasized more than in any other country. Firms in much of the

---

[7] R. Hal Mason, "Host Countries and the Multinational Enterprise," pp. 5–14.

[8] Y. Suzuki, "The Strategy of Top 100 Japanese Industrial Enterprises, 1950–1970," *Strategic Management Journal*, July/September 1980, p. 285.

Table 10.1   Checklist for Assessing a Nation's Investment Climate

Market Characteristics
Size of market and growth rate.
Key market characteristics.
Industry structure and competitive position.
Product adaptation needs.
Any price controls?
Level and type of price competition.
Channels used, controls and availability.
Media used, costs and availability.
Advertising controls, spending patterns.
Tariff position. Is protection available?

Macroeconomic Factors
Size of GNP and growth rate.
Inflation rate.
Attitude to private enterprise?
Fairness and honesty of administration of accepted standards of morality; corruption present or not?
Fairness and honesty of legal system.
Efficiency and operating speed of bureaucracy.
Details of corporate law affecting the MNC; monopoly control? Restrictions on ownership? Legal obligations? Consumer law? Product liability? Pollution control?

Infrastructure Characteristics
Geographic distribution of industry and population.
Availability, cost, and efficiency of transport systems.
Availability, cost, and efficiency of port facilities.
Availability, cost and reliability of raw materials.
Availability, cost, and reliability of energy and utilities.
Site location prospects and proximities to raw materials? Markets?
Site costs? Building costs?
Climatic conditions?
Housing, educational, social/cultural facilities?
Ease of foreign trade imports? Exports?

Labor Factors
Availability of managerial, technical, linguistic, and skilled and unskilled production labor.
Labor productivity, historic? Expected?
Educational and skill levels.
Level of unemployment, historic and expected trends.
Degree of union membership.
Balance of payments position, historic? Future?
Stage of economic development.
Income per capita, historic? Future?
Size and demographics of population.
Number of households; percentage home ownership.

---

rest of the world, including the United States, lag behind in this regard. The Japanese have also emphasized management philosophies different from those used in much of the rest of the world. These management styles are very work group/team oriented. And the Japanese have emphasized market share as opposed to profit strategies. On the other hand, firms from the United States have historically emphasized production and research technologies and new products. Foreign-country marketing of such products as Coca-Cola, McDonald's restaurants, and Kentucky Fried Chicken have, however, usually followed standard approaches found in the United States. Finally, in virtually all the countries of the

Table 10.1 *continued*

Political Factors

Type and stability of government.

Any dangerous internal strife?

Any particular ethnic, social class problems?

Economic ideologies of major political parties.

Historic attitude toward MNCs. Any nationalization? Unfair discrimination?

Trade union structure and attitudes.

Record of industrial relations.

Labor laws affecting the MNC; trade union participation? Employment protection? Social security payments? Hire and fire regulations? Redundancy costs? Other fringe benefits expected costs?

Wage rates, historic? Trend?

Attitudes to profit sharing?

Financial Considerations

Stage of development of local capital market.

Sources and type of funds available; costs?

Stability of local currency, historic? Future?

Exchange of control regulations.

Treatments of leads and lags.

Investment incentive schemes available.

Stability of investment incentives.

Depreciation treatments.

Accounting and financial reporting requirements.

Availability and cost of risk insurance locally? In home country?

Fiscal Considerations

Tax rates (corporate and personal, income capital gains, withholding, excise duties, payroll tax, value-added tax rates, other direct and indirect taxes).

Tax treatments on dividends, interest payments, technology, management fees, transfer policies, and other means of extractions.

Tax incentives for investment.

Customs and tax-free zones.

Joint tax treaties.

Treatment of losses.

Import-export tax drawbacks.

Attitudes to avoidance? Evasion?

Source: D. F. Channon with M. Jalland, *Multinational Strategic Planning* (New York: AMACOM, 1978), pp. 193, 194.

world, negotiations with governments are becoming increasingly more critical than they have been historically in the United States and Canada.

From these few examples, you can see that both objectives and strategies will vary. Most of these differences are the result of cultural/historical factors, including many nations' negative experiences with colonialistic MNCs. Regardless of the cause, the multinational strategic manager must be alert to the necessity for changing strategic standard operating procedures.

International Master Strategies at the SBU Level

The fundamentals of the master strategy at the SBU level are applied internationally as they would be domestically, but the specifics of application and the bases upon which these applications occur are again significantly modified by multinational operations.

Each of the five major factors involved in the marketing mix is affected in some way by the international situation. For example, the size of the target market, its purchasing capabilities, and its identification are often much more difficult to determine because of varying demographic and socioeconomic factors. S. Majaro indicates that numerous potential problems exist with respect to the other factors: product, promotion, price, and distribution.[9] He emphasizes the impacts of environment, competition, institutions, and the legal system on the components of the marketing mix.

Some of the major impacts of these four factors on the product, including its aesthetic design, branding, and packaging, are as follows: special needs for sizes, dimensions, and standards; attitudinal constraints; available supportive resources; attitude of local consumers to colors, shapes, and appearances; local tastes and traditions; acceptability of proposed product name and its pronounceability, recall-ability, and message conveyance; availability of desired packaging materials; compliance with various bodies that set standards for product and packaging; compliance with laws affecting the use of the product; safety rules; pollution rules; registration of design; constraints on shapes; registration of trademark; legal constraints on name; and requirements for labeling of packages.

Among the major factors relating to promotion are the following: language; literacy levels; readership details; attitudes towards advertising, sales personnel, and sales promotions; influencer patterns; demography; symbolism; media availability and other situational aspects of media; legislative bans on certain advertising; sales promotion or personal selling practices; and laws limiting expenditures on marketing.

Majaro goes on to suggest that many local market factors must be considered in pricing. Among them are: whether social and cultural taboos affect the amount of money that can be spent on a product; whether it is customary to overprice in anticipation of reducing the price; whether institutions exist that must be consulted before the price is set; whether there are legal constraints on price changes; whether legal limitations on margins exist; and finally, whether there is a legal requirement to print price details on the product or package.

Among the major factors relevant to distribution are: availability of roads and other transportation channels; customer buying habits; use of local agents versus a company sales force; whether channels are government controlled; what red tape must be managed before and during distribution; and whether special packaging, safety, size, material, or other rules exist.

These are lengthy lists, but critical ones. A few examples will show that firms have not always taken these factors into account and have suffered as a result. One U.S. auto manufacturer, exporting its sporty model to a Spanish-speaking country, chose a name for the car to replace its English name. The company wanted something that sounded sporty and chose one that sounded sporty to them, but which meant slow or sluggish in Spanish. Another U.S. firm attempted to sell its razor blades in one foreign country in drugstores and supermarkets just as they had in the United States. Sales failed to materialize; people in that country at that time bought their razor blades in hardware stores. One fried-chicken firm scored an instant success in Japan. Apparently thinking that the Far East market was homogeneous, the firm attempted to sell its "finger lickin' good" chicken in Hong Kong. But several problems arose. The Chinese apparently expected to be served a

---

[9] S. Majaro, *International Marketing* (London: Allen & Unwin, 1977), pp. 88, 111, 178.

towel with their meal, and they tended not to eat with their fingers. Finally, one U.S. cereal manufacturer attempted to sell its cereal in Brazil, where people do not eat breakfast. Not to be outdone, another division of the same company attempted to sell its gelatin dessert to a population of which only 3 percent owned refrigerators. Similar examples are numerous, although multinationals are improving in this regard.

With respect to the other functional strategies, many differences exist. Financial strategies must of course include some concern for currency translations. For example, most U.S. MNCs are seeking to manufacture overseas in light of the U.S. dollar's strong showing in the mid-1980s. Production strategies must cope with numerous logistical problems resulting from differing and often inadequate transportation systems, the absence of suppliers, and the frequent absence of necessary skills in the work force. Personnel strategies must cope with differing laws and local customs regarding work and authority. For example, in much of Europe little work is accomplished in the summers as workers take their holidays, since vacations in Europe range from four to eight guaranteed weeks. Other external factors may influence personnel matters. For example, in parts of Ireland, there exists a cultural necessity for segregating the work force along religious lines, and firebombings of plants sometimes result from religion-related labor disputes.

With respect to behavioral and contingency theories of strategy formulation, there is no reason to believe that approaches similar to those employed in the United States for determining what strategies might be appropriate could not also be performed for other countries. For example Timo Santalainen and Risto Tainio studied 80 of the largest banks in Finland (some of which were multinational in their operations) in order to isolate factors which distinguished high performers from low performers. Of ten factors (and an indeterminate number of processes and mechanisms) studied, the following three were deemed most important: labor force and effort; attributes of top executives; and leadership orientation and management-development endeavors.[10] But in another study by Tainio and Santalainen,[11] they seriously question the universal validity of the opinion that American organizational models generate controllable and beneficial changes in other cultural settings. However, the amount of reported research in this vein has been limited. Santalainen and Tainio's research is examined in some detail in Information Capsule 10.1.

Finally, management functions differ in other countries. Managers often find themselves confronted with differing expectations about motivation and leadership styles. In much of Europe and Japan, participation in decision making by firstline employees is much greater than in the United States and Canada. Yet, in the Middle East, Central and South America, and most of the rest of the world, the manager's word is law and is seldom disputed. Long-range planning is important in Japan, where it is viewed as critical to the success of the organization; but it is not much practiced in China. Another factor, motivation techniques, varies primarily with need levels; and the need levels of people outside major industrialized countries tend to be much lower on Maslow's scale than the needs of people in industrialized nations, who often seek high-level need satisfiers in their jobs. Control strategies are of special importance in the multinational enterprise because of the

---

[10]Timo Santalainen and Risto Tainio, "Factors and Mechanisms Affecting Business Performance of Banks" (Helsinki School of Economics, Working Paper F-39, October 1982).

[11]Risto Tainio and Timo Santalainen, "Some Evidence for the Cultural Relativity of Organizational Development Programs," *The Journal of Applied Behavioral Science*, 1984, Vol. 20, No. 2, pp. 93–111.

====================== **INFORMATION CAPSULE 10.1** ======================
A Study of Cultural Relativity in
Organizational Development Programs

Two Finnish researchers, Risto Tainio and Timo Santalainen, in attempting to understand the transferability of American-developed management methods to other cultures, compared the effects of two prepackaged organizational development (O.D.) programs: the well-known Management Grid program and the Finnish Results Management Program (ReMa). Both organizations where these programs were applied were multiunit service organizations.

The Grid and ReMa programs are both based on a conceptual managerial frame of reference and on a change process for implementing the conceptual frame. Both contain management-development and organization-development elements, providing methods of planned change intended to produce organizational excellence by increasing managerial effectiveness. Excellence is measured by gains in material and financial wealth, profitability, and productivity.

The Tainio and Santalainen study's main interest was to determine the extent to which the Grid program might reflect culture bound "individuality" and "masculinity" dimensions in their management methods and how/if the ReMa program results might differ from the Grid along these two dimensions.

Findings.   The most striking differences between the programs related to significant development of individual managers in the Grid program, but not in the ReMa program. Conversely, the benefits of the Grid did not carry over into the organization as a whole, but the ReMa program seemed to benefit the organization as a whole in a substantial way.

Tainio and Santalainen concluded that the Grid program more closely resembled typical American individualistic and masculine values than did the Finnish ReMa program. They stated that differences between the two were found to be so extensive and consistent that they could not be totally explained by methodological inadequacies. The Grid program generated early visible and strong changes in management but the results were short lived and didn't transfer to the total organization. Thus the extent to which American management methods can be transferred is viewed to be limited by Tainio and Santalainen when considering cultural factors impacting on the transferability process.

The researchers suggest that when the business success of the firm is the transfer target of management and organizational development programs, culture takes on a more profound meaning. Not only management, but also labor and the sociotechnological factors, regulate the value formation of the enterprise. On this basis Tainio and Santalainen seriously question the validity of the belief that American organizational models generate controllable and beneficial changes in other cultural settings.

Source: Risto Tainio and Timo Santalainen, "Some Evidence for the Cultural Relativity of Organizational Development Programs," *The Journal of Applied Behavioral Science*, 1984, Vol. 20, No. 2, pp. 93–111.

multitude of factors already noted, especially geographic separation and, in many cases, the absence of a manager familiar with the multinational's operation (the manager may be a host-country national rather than a parent-country employee). Communication habits, decision-making skills and habits, and a host of other functional strategy factors vary as well. The multinational organization must be extremely adaptive if it is to survive and prosper.

The Master Strategy at the Corporate Level for Multinational Multiple-SBU Firms

The master strategy for multinational multiple-SBU firms is conceptually similar to the master strategy for other organizations. It is the specific content that varies. With respect to the utilization of the techniques of matrix and portfolio management, the process for multinational use appears essentially the same as the process outlined in this chapter. However, the specific factors to be considered vary. Derek F. Channon and Michael Jalland suggest that the following are often of critical importance when multinational enterprise is being considered:

- Market characteristics.
- Macroeconomic factors.
- Political factors.
- Infrastructure characteristics.
- Labor factors.
- Financial considerations.
- Fiscal considerations.

Table 10.1 presents each of these important factors in more detail for the direct investment alternative.

Channon and Jalland also suggest that, in addition to direct investment, both licensing and joint ventures are sound methods for entering new geographic areas. Licensing, for example, usually requires very little capital investment and fewer parent-country managers; is a relatively cheap method of marketing to a given market; involves fewer problems of exchange risk; is the only way to enter certain countries (for example, in Eastern Europe); and may be an important component of an overall strategy. Licensing does have its drawbacks: every licensee is a potential competitor; control is more difficult to maintain than over a direct investment operation; the licensee usually comes out better than the licensor with regard to factors such as inflation; and fiscal problems such as taxes or even refusal of the licensee to pay royalties are not uncommon.

Behavioral Aspects of Strategic Decision Making for Multinational Firms

For multinationals, behavioral aspects of decision making are conceptually the same as for other firms; but the degree of incrementalism and the degree of power sharing and usages of power may differ significantly. Recall from the discussion earlier in this chapter that in many countries, the government takes a much stronger role in business decision making than in the United States or Canada. Thus, for firms operating in such countries, the strategic decision process is often slowed by bureaucracy; and a fourth strategist—government—is added to the process.

The Soviet government, for example, is extremely slow to decide about foreign business or even domestic business investment. In Europe and South America, the process takes less time, but can still be quite involved. In particular, the desire of persons in many South American countries to socialize for long periods of time before making a business decision often causes problems for multinationals attempting to conduct business there. Throughout much of the Middle East, a similar socializing requirement exists; and many locals will not do business except with well-established friends.[12] In Europe, where unions often play a strategic role in the organization, there is frequent use of politics and power. For example, in England, unions have nullified the efforts of both business and government to arrive at strategic business decisions. The Triumph motorcycle essentially disappeared from the marketplace largely because of a union strike that negated a strategic decision jointly determined by business and government.[13] Finally, in most major Japanese firms everyone who has any stake in a decision must be consulted before the decision is made. This requirement adds a tremendous amount of time to the decision process. However, it does aid in implementation, since it ensures commitment. Thus the total time of decision and implementation is probably no greater in Japan than elsewhere.[14]

In summary, the multinational's decision processes are essentially the same as those of other organizations; but the number of strategists is often greater, the incrementalism more pronounced, the usages of power more frequent, coalitions more abundant, and the time taken for making decisions is often much greater than in the United States and Canada. Multinational managers must be alert to these differences and not expect to be able to make decisions as independently of social and political stakeholders as they otherwise might.

Multinational Aspects of Implementation

The basics of structure are the same for multinationals as for other firms; but various macrostructures may be employed in different countries for different reasons.[15] Typically, multinationals add a "foreign subsidiaries" or "foreign business" division as one of their

---

[12] J. Higgins, *Human Relations Concepts and Skills* (New York: Random House, 1982), Chapter 14.

[13] W. R. Sandberg, "Norton Villiers Triumph and the Meriden Cooperative," in W. F. Glueck, *Business Policy and Strategic Management* (New York: McGraw-Hill, 1980), pp. 436–442.

[14] W. J. Ouchi, *Theory Z* (Reading, Mass.: Addison-Wesley, 1980).

[15] A. Chandler, Jr. and H. Daems, "The Rise of Managerial Capitalism and Its Impact on Investment Strategy in the Western World and Japan" (Working paper, European Institute for Advanced Studies in Management, 1974); L. E. Fouraker and J. M. Stopford, "Organizational Structure and the Multinational Strategy," *Administrative Science Quarterly*, March 1968, p. 62; T. T. Herbert, "Strategy and Multinational Organization Structure: An Interorganizational Relationship Perspective," *Academy of Management Review*, April 1984, pp. 259–271; A. R. Neghandi and B. C. Reimann, "A Contingency Theory of Organization Reexamined in the Context of a Developing Country," *Academy of Management Journal*, June 1972, pp. 137–147; H. Schollhammer, "Organization Structures of Multinational Corporations," *Academy of Management Journal*, September 1971, pp. 345–365; J. L. Simonetti and F. L. Simonetti, "The Impact of Management Policy and Organization Structure on the Management Effectiveness of Firms Operating in Italy," *Journal of Business and Economics*, Spring/Summer 1976, pp. 249–252. Also see footnotes 6, 7, 8, 9, and 10 earlier in this chapter.

major SBUs. Then, depending upon growth, size, and other structural determinants, other departmentations, such as geographic subdivisions or product subdivisions, may occur. It is almost always necessary to have special departments within the major staff functions of finance and personnel to cope with the problems encountered. With respect to delegation of authority, management styles, job design, and other microstructural phenomena, the multinationals find themselves subject to a set of rules quite different from those governing domestic firms.

When you go to a foreign country, much that you have learned at home about the meanings of people's behaviors will not apply. Not only the verbal languages but also the non-verbal languages are different. Furthermore, cultural patterns vary significantly among countries. Multinational managers are confronted with a bewildering array of changes. The following pages provide insights into a few of the problems which may be encountered.

Time.   Probably nowhere is time so critical as in the United States and Canada. The Japanese use time especially well with Americans because they know our weakness for it. "A Japanese once stated that Westerners have a most convenient weakness: if they are kept waiting long enough they will agree to almost anything. Consequently, negotiators visiting Japan will often be asked how long they have planned to stay. Once that is known, they will be pleasantly entertained, while negotiations are kept inconclusive until a couple of hours before they are scheduled to leave, when the real business starts."[16] In much of Eastern Europe, in China, in parts of South America, and in much of Africa, time is of little consequence. People may seem to take forever to make decisions and, indeed, may feel their esteem raised as the result of the time it takes them to decide.

Aspirations.   In some countries, to strive for one's own objectives is discouraged. It is the community, the state, the religion that must be served first. Traditional Western motivational systems may fail.

Authority.   In much of South America, in much of the Soviet Union, and in much of the Middle East, the manager has absolute authority and no subordinate would ever dare practice participative management or even question the manager's orders. On the other hand, in Japan, there is much more participation than in the United States and Canada.

Rank and Social Status.   Rank and status play a much more important role outside the United States and Canada than they do in these two countries. The ramifications are significant in terms of forms of address, the amount of social space allowed between persons, the right to speak one's opinions, and so forth.

Role of Women.   Women play more important roles outside the home in the United States than in most of the rest of the world. Women cannot drive cars in Saudi Arabia. They cannot own property in many countries. Women have virtually no managerial roles in Japanese society. Indeed, women are seen and not heard in much of the world. They cannot therefore be multinational managers in many countries.

---

[16]H. K. Arning, "Business Customs from Malaya to Murmansk," *Management Review*, October 1964, p. 11.

Discussion Topics.   Europeans love to philosophize and analyze issues. Americans typically are not prepared for such discussions in social situations. Furthermore, Europeans are much more likely to accept communistic and socialistic economic philosophies than Americans. Again, problems may result.

Nonverbal Communications.   In Greece, a nod of the head means no, not yes. In Italy, one must learn literally hundreds of hand gestures in order to assure that one understands the language. In Europe, it is common for men to embrace upon meeting, a traditionally unacceptable behavior in the United States.[17]

The examples are numerous, but by now, you have probably got the point. The task of implementation is compounded greatly in the multinational operation.

Evaluation and Control

Control is absolutely critical in the multinational enterprise. The vagaries of this marketplace cannot be overestimated. Control of the multinational enterprise depends, as does all control, upon information. However, when language, distance, politics, and a host of other exotic variables intervene, the difficulty of obtaining valid information is heightened.

James Hulbert and William Brandt suggest that the multinational is interested in achieving two objectives with its control systems—first to assure that its investment provides adequate returns, and in that same sense, is therefore protected; and second, to be able to coordinate all multinational marketing, production, financial, personnel, distribution, and related strategic processes. They suggest that the primary tool for achieving these ends is the budget, combined with standard total organizational performance measures such as ROI and cash flow. Hulbert and Brandt also believe that control policies and requirements must be built around the organization's structure, with the amount of centralization and decentralization in foreign subsidiaries playing a major role in the development of control systems.[18] Michael Brooke and H. Lee Remmers, in examining the control systems of 30 American multinationals, found no fundamental differences between their systems for their multinational operations and those they used domestically. These authors caution, however, that several major differences in operating environments cause the specifics of reporting systems to vary. The major factors they identify include

1.   Wide variations in rates of inflation encountered from country to country.

2.   Changes in the valuation of the currency of a country of investment.

3.   The influence of intercompany transactions on the short-run performance of an operating unit.

4.   Wide differences in cost structures among affiliates in different countries.[19]

---

[17] These and numerous other cross-cultural human relations examples may be found in J. Higgins, *Human Relations Concepts and Skills*, Chapter 14.

[18] James M. Hulbert and William K. Brandt, *Managing the Multinational Subsidiary* (New York: Holt, Rinehart and Winston, 1980), p. 112.

[19] Michael Z. Brooke and H. Lee Remmers, *International Management and Business Policy* (Boston: Houghton Mifflin, 1978), p. 179.

The Global Nature of Change

The preceding discussion has addressed the issues of how organizations that do business internationally, many of them multinationals, would proceed through the accepted stages of the strategic management process. But in addition, of special concern to U.S. and Canadian firms must be the changing environment for business. These changes include: a decline by most measures in the relative competitiveness of the United States and Canada in the international arena; new entrants into the capitalistic structure, including China; and a host of changes in world demographics, world politics, world governments, world military situations, and so on. The next few paragraphs examine some of these major issues to provide some insight into the changing global situation.

> *If Japan had manufactured the Columbia, the tiles would never have fallen off.*
>
> ▪ *Yoshihide Hiraiwa, Mitsubishi Electric* ▪

Only a Rip van Winkle could have failed to notice that both the United States and Canada (and most of Europe) have lost much of their competitive edge in many industries: autos, appliances, cameras, steel, and so forth. Several Asian nations, notably Japan, Korea, Singapore, Hong Kong, and Taiwan, have made substantive inroads into many industries formerly dominated by North American firms. Even competition between Canadian and U.S. firms has intensified, as, for example, Canada's ALCAN now challenges the United States's once undisputed ALCOA for the number-one position in aluminum production.[20] There is growing concern that the United States is losing much of its competitive ability. Two Harvard professors are attempting to convince U.S. business and government leaders of this fact, and they apparently have strong supporting evidence for their arguments.[21] Perhaps the "good news" is that cultural response to economic progress often runs in cycles. An example of this is that the famous and often-heralded Japanese work ethic shows some serious signs of erosion,[22] while U.S. firms, due to lost competitive position, have made strong efforts in recent years to improve productivity and quality. More good news is that U.S. firms are still viable and often dominant in Europe, especially in technological areas. But the reality of the situation is that American firms must become more competitive if they are to stay in certain businesses. And as the evidence gathered by Professors Lodge and Scott implies, the United States as a nation may need to counter other nations' greater relative strategic support of their businesses.

> *"Marx died 101 years ago. There have been tremendous changes since his ideas were formed . . . So we cannot use Marxist and Leninist works to solve our present-day problems."*
>
> ▪ *The* People's Daily *of Peking, in a front-page editorial, reported in* Fortune, *January 7, 1985, p. 11* ▪

[20] "ALCAN Goes Toe to Toe with ALCOA for the No. 1 Spot in Aluminum," *Business Week*, August 27, 1984, pp. 95–96.

[21] D. Wessel, "Harvard Professors Market Their Belief That U.S. Is Losing Its Competitive Edge," *The Wall Street Journal*, December 12, 1984, p. 24.

[22] L. Smith, "Cracks in the Japanese Work Ethic," *Fortune*, May 14, 1984, pp. 162–168.

INFORMATION CAPSULE 10.2
China Turns toward Capitalism

Although China still has a state-owned economy and is by no means going capitalist, China's supreme leader, Deng Xiaoping, is introducing elements of capitalism: privately owned businesses, profits, prices determined by market forces, and unearned income from stock dividends. At an October 1984 meeting Mr. Deng surprised many observers by delivering a speech to the Central Advisory Commission, a grouping of the Chinese Communist party's elder statesmen, in which he said, "No country can develop by closing its door. We suffered from this, and our forefathers suffered from this. Isolation landed China in poverty, backwardness, and ignorance." It was during this speech that Mr. Deng proposed a landmark economic plan aimed at the gradual abandonment of most Soviet-style central planning. Over the next several years more than a million state enterprises and factories are to be cut loose from governmental planning and protection to fail or succeed on their own economic merit and efficiency. Of great importance is that their workers will succeed or fail right along with these enterprises. Mr. Deng is reported to have said several times, "It cannot harm us. It cannot harm us."

Some China observers point out that this is just another step in Mr. Deng's economic reform begun eight years ago when he became the supreme leader. He seems to have rewritten Karl Marx's dictate, "From each according to his abilities, to each according to his needs," to read "From each according to his abilities, to each according to his work." Mr. Deng's reforms began in rural China, where 80 percent still live, when he dismantled agricultural collectives by restoring family farms and introducing production and free-market incentives. Agricultural production drastically increased as a result, the grain harvest alone rising from 320 million tons in 1980 to 400 million by 1984, and in so doing the average peasant income more than doubled to approximately $112 in 1983.

Mr. Deng is now intent on economic reforms for the remaining 20 percent of China's population, the urban dweller. Earlier reforms did not extend to the large and generally inefficient state-owned industry generally located in urban areas. The new program calls for virtual managerial autonomy, the institution of a corporation-type tax, and a cutback in central planning. For example, state-owned enterprises can only count on 70 percent of their raw materials and supplies to be guaranteed from state sources. The remaining 30 percent must be bargained for from other sources. But, after paying the state levy of taxes, the resultant profits are for the enterprises to use as they wish. Thus, production incentives for workers and special arrangements with suppliers and other capitalistic types of activities are occuring.

In ongoing reforms, Mr. Deng, in January of 1985, also loosened the rigid wage system for government workers in order to reflect "individual merit." Also with the new year, the workers' traditional two-hour lunch break was cut back to one hour. However, individual enterprises are being encouraged; as Mr. Deng has said, only by foreign investment and trade can China achieve its paramount goal of quadrupling its gross national product to $1 trillion by the year 2000.

The riskiest economic reform for Mr. Deng has yet to begin. That is the plan for price decontrol through the removal of state subsidies. Controls have kept the costs of food, housing, clothing, transportation, utilities, education, and medical care at artificially low levels—in fact, below the costs of providing these goods.

Source: James P. Sterba, "Peking Turns Sharply Down Capitalist Road in New Economic Plan," *The Wall Street Journal*, October 25, 1984, p. 1; James Kelley, "It Cannot Harm Us," *Time*, January 14, 1985, pp. 36–37; Dorothy E. Jones, Dorinda Elliott, Edith Terry, Anne Catta, Charles Guffney, and Bruce Nussbaum, "Capitalism In China," *Business Week*, January 14, 1985, pp. 53–59.

The participants in the rapidly growing global economy are changing, not only in relative size and strength, but with respect to who they are. It is indeed noteworthy that China, with one-fourth of the world's population, has done an apparent about-face in 1985, declaring in favor of capitalism over communism. However, there is no anticipation of a great immediate and complete Chinese embrace of capitalism, nor is there any great danger of immediate competition from them either. For rather than a true 180-degree turn in philosophy, China's new outlook may be considered more of a 135-degree turn. And, even that could change with the often-shifting political situations characteristic of China. All "ifs" and "buts" aside, though, this is still a significant development, which foreshadows a very great potential strategic change in the global economy. Information Capsule 10.2 provides a more detailed review of this change.

In early 1985, many changes transpired internationally. We saw a potential OPEC dissolution and at worst, reduced oil prices. There were some 40-plus wars or military conflicts of various types and sizes going on in the world, some ending, some starting, some stalemating. There were citrus freezes in Florida that resulted in increased Brazilian citrus market shares. Canada's new prime minister welcomed U.S. investors, in contrast to his predecessor. Much of the debt of economically depressed nations such as Mexico, Argentina, and Poland was carried by U.S. banks, with further downturns in their economic situations potentially leading to serious problems for the U.S. banking industry, and for the U.S. economy as a whole. Many countries in Europe, especially France, showed renewed interest in reducing socialism and in attempting to create new jobs—something the United States has done well in recent years. Japanese firms sought to become more innovative as opposed to continuing to adapt the technologies of other countries' firms. Europe's unemployment remained high. The U.S. dollar became a very strong currency. Changes. The world is full of changes.

Summary

The international ball game is different than the one back home. It's not really a whole new ball game, although some of the rules are different. It's more like playing in a different ball park, where you have to learn the factors unique to the field. Thus, the tasks of the MNC's strategists are essentially the same as those of domestic strategists, but they must learn to cope with numerous variables not frequently found in their own domestic environments.

In the international arena, different missions may be emphasized, varying strategists will exist, strategic policies may cover a host of dissimilar concerns, and information systems are usually less sophisticated in a situation when the need for sophistication is greater than it is domestically. The objectives set will necessarily reflect variances in mission, strategists, policies, and information. The strategies formulated will depend upon these. Typically there are numerous restrictions upon both objectives and strategies that are not encountered domestically. The international investment decision requires careful analysis of social/political considerations not often evaluated domestically. In addition, the behavioral aspects will often be contrary to what one might be familiar with. The implementation of strategies, and their formulation as well, must be uniquely suited to the cultures of the societies entered. Control of strategy is often more difficult, although the same hard dollar issues are the principal concern.

Key Terms and Concepts

After you have completed this chapter, you should be familiar with how the following key terms and concepts vary in an international arena from the domestic (U.S. and Canadian) mission; strategic policy; strategists; information; objectives setting; strategy formulation; the master strategy at the SBU level; the master strategy in multiple-SBU firms; and the behavioral aspects of strategic decision making, implementation, evaluation, and control.

Discussion Questions

1. How does establishing the master strategy for a multinational multiple-SBU firm differ from establishing a master strategy for a multiple-SBU firm which only operates domestically?

2. List the external environmental operating differences which would be of concern to the international strategist planning for operations in Japan and West Germany as compared with operations in the United States.

3. Would government-to-government relationships be of concern to the strategist in Question 2? Would government-to-MNC relationships?

4. How do the four influencing factors for objectives determination and strategy formulation (detailed in Figure 10.2) change in the international arena?

5. Table 10.1 lists a number of factors which should be utilized in assessing a nation's investment climate. Which factor(s) is most important?

6. Should organizational development models developed in the United States be utilized in other cultural settings? If so, why? If not, why not?

7. Is "control" important for an MNC? Is it any more important for an MNC than for a firm operating only domestically?

References

Alexander, Charles P. "A Global Money Machine." *Time*, January 14, 1985, pp. 48–50.

———. "That Threatening Trade Gap." *Time*, July 9, 1984, pp. 61–64.

Alm, Richard. "How 'Perk Packages' Keep Foreign Executives Happy." *U.S. News & World Report*, October 8, 1984, pp. 71–72.

Alm, Richard, and Collins, John. "U.S. in the World Economy: The Changing Role." *U.S. News & World Report*, September 10, 1984, pp. 63–65.

Anders, George. "Europe's Answer to Harvard Business School Becomes a Mecca for Multinational Recruiters." *The Wall Street Journal*, October 30, 1984, p. 34.

Anderson, Charles A. "Corporate Directors in Japan." *Harvard Business Review*, May/June 1984, pp. 30–38.

Berlew, F. Kingston. "The Joint Venture—A Way into Foreign Markets." *Harvard Business Review*, July/August 1984, pp. 48–50, 54.

Bonfante, Jordan. "The New Refrain: 'Vive l'Amerique.'" *Time*, January 14, 1985, p. 40.

Boyer, Edward. "Restarting Europe's Job Engine." *Fortune*, August 20, 1984, pp. 183–186.

Byrne, Harlan S. "Caterpillar, Facing Japanese Competition in Earth-Movers, Tries to Regain Footing." *The Wall Street Journal*, December 9, 1983, p. 60.

Csath, M. "Strategic Planning—a New Arrival in Hungarian Industry." *Long Range Planning*, 1983, Vol. 16, No. 2, pp. 85–94.

Daniloff, Nicholas. "Who Says Free Enterprise Is Dead in Soviet Union?" *U.S. News & World Report*, June 25, 1984, pp. 35, 36.

Dennis, Darienne L., and Wolfe, Royce D. "The International 500." *Fortune*, August 20, 1984, pp. 200–221.

"Employee Involvement Pays Dividends in France." *Business Europe*, September 7, 1984, p. 281.

"Europe Learns to Love the Dollar." *Business Week*, September 24, 1984, p. 35.

"The Europeans Come Over to the Supply Side." *Business Week*, October 1, 1984, pp. 52, 54.

"Europe's Unions Are Losing Their Grip." *Business Week*, November 26, 1984, pp. 80–88.

Frederick, Glenn D. "The State of Private Sector Strategic Planning in Canada." *Long Range Planning*, 1983, Vol. 16, No. 3, pp. 40–46.

"The Furor over America's Ability to Compete." *Business Week*, September 10, 1984, pp. 89, 90.

Hegarty, W. H., and Hoffman, R. C. "Strategic Decision Making among European Firms." Paper presented to the Strategic Management Society Conference, Paris, October 1983.

"How U.S. Companies Guard Their Flanks." *U.S. News & World Report*, January 9, 1984, p. 25.

Huey, John. "Executives Assess Europe's Technology Decline." *The Wall Street Journal*, February 1, 1984, p. 28.

Ingrassia, Lawrence. "Situations Wanted—Persistent Joblessness Still Troubles Europe in Wake of Recession." *The Wall Street Journal*, November 13, 1984, pp. 1, 19.

Jones, Dorothy E., Elliott, Dorinda, Terry, Edith, Robbins, Carla Anne, Gaffney, Charles, and Nussbaum, Bruce. "Capitalism in China." *Business Week*, January 14, 1985, pp. 53–59.

Kathawala, Yunus, and Busch, Edgar. "Management of an International Portfolio." Paper presented and published in the proceedings of the Southern Management Meetings, Atlanta, November 1983.

Kelly, James. "It Cannot Harm Us." *Time*, January 14, 1985, pp. 36–37.

Kempe, Frederick. "Modified Marx—Hungary Takes a Flier in Private Ownership of Business Enterprises." *The Wall Street Journal*, March 26, 1982, pp. 1, 16.

Koten, John, and Ingrassia, Lawrence. "Parts That Fit—British Car Maker's Tie to Honda Shows Why Auto Linkups Increase." *The Wall Street Journal*, December 12, 1983, pp. 1, 23.

Lohr, Steve. "The Japanese Challenge—Can They Achieve Technological Supremacy?" *The New York Times Magazine*, July 8, 1984, pp. 18–27, 33, 39.

McAvoy, Clyde. "Asian Airlines Buck U.S. Free-Market Turbulence." *The Wall Street Journal*, October 29, 1984, p. 33.

Migdail, Carl J. "Will Mexico Show the Way for Latin Debtor Nations?" *U.S. News & World Report*, September 10, 1984, pp. 41–42.

Murphy, Jamie, Munro, Ross H., and Ungeheuer, Frederick. "Canada—Hanging Out the Welcome Sign." *Time*, December 24, 1984, p. 31.

Newman, Barry, and Cohen, Roger. "Obscure Giant—Italy's IRI Pervades Economy, but the Firm Baffles Many Italians." *The Wall Street Journal*, July 10, 1984, pp. 1, 19.

Pascale, Richard T. "Perspectives on Strategy: The Real Story behind Honda's Success." *California Management Review*, Vol. 26, No. 3, Spring 1984, pp. 47–72.

Pearson, John, and Helm, Leslie. "For Multinationals, It Will Never Be the Same." *Business Week*, December 24, 1984, p. 57.

"Pernod Ricard's Recipe for More U.S. Profits: Add a Big Splash of Soda." *Business Week*, December 3, 1984, pp. 69–71.

Pitts, Robert, Daniels, John, and Tretter, Marietta. "The International Division: Temporary Phase or Permanent Institution." *Proceedings, Academy of Management*, New Orleans, 1983, pp. 81–85.

"Play It Another Way, Sam." *Time*, July 23, 1984, pp. 66–68.

Port, Otis, Sabin, Margaret, and Jones, Dorothy E. "The King of Knockoffs Rushes to Go from Imitation to Innovation." *Business Week*, November 26, 1984, pp. 188–194.

"A Powerful Call to Loosen the State's Grip on Industry." *Business Week*, November 14, 1983, p. 60.

Putka, Gary, Thurow, Roger, and Ricklefs, Roger. "Backlash Abroad—U.S. Economic Surge, a Source of Pride Here, Causes Envy Overseas." *The Wall Street Journal*, October 8, 1984, pp. 1, 24.

"Samurai Spirit Lives On in Japan's Economic Drive." *U.S. News & World Report*, November 19, 1984, pp. 47–48.

Sanders, Sol W. "Reaganomics Is No Longer a Dirty Word in Europe." *Business Week*, September 24, 1984, p. 56.

Scherer, Ron, Dudney, Robert S., Kaylor, Robert, and Taylor, Walter A. "Pacific Rim—America's New Frontier." *U.S. News & World Report*, August 20, 1984, pp. 45–48.

Schlender, Brenton R., Manguno, Joseph P., and Leung, Julia. "Detailed Sino-British Agreement on Future of Hong Kong Appears to Allay the Capitalist Enclave's Apprehensions." *The Wall Street Journal*, September 27, 1984, p. 34.

Sease, Douglas R. "Gearing Up—South Korea Will Vie in U.S. Auto Market to Spur Its Economy." *The Wall Street Journal*, November 16, 1984, pp. 1, 21.

Sesit, Michael R. "Money Game—Funds Blocked Abroad by Exchange Controls Plague Big Companies." *The Wall Street Journal*, December 3, 1984, pp. 1, 24.

Shreeve, Thomas W. "Be Prepared for Political Changes Abroad." *Harvard Business Review*, July/August 1984, pp. 111–118.

Smith, Lee. "Creativity Starts to Blossom in Japan." *Fortune*, October 29, 1984, pp. 144–153.

"A Spark of Militancy in the Land of Loyalty." *Business Week*, September 5, 1983, pp. 96–98.

Sterba, James P., and Bennett, Amanda. "Deng's Tune—Peking Turns Sharply down Capitalist Road in New Economic Plan." *The Wall Street Journal*, October 25, 1984, pp. 1, 29.

Taylor, Alexander L. III. "The Gathering Storm." *Time*, July 2, 1984, pp. 38–40.

"The Superdollar." *Business Week*, October 8, 1984, pp. 164–176.

"A Way for U.S. Companies to Make 'Free Money.'" *Business Week*, October 29, 1984, p. 58.

Wheelwright, Steven C. "Japan—Where Operations Really Are Strategic." *Harvard Business Review*, July/August 1981, p. 67.

Wilson, Ian. "The Current State of Planning in North America: Introduction to the Special Issue." *Long Range Planning*, Vol. 16, No. 3, pp. 2–3.

"World Bank Calls for Birth Control." *The Orlando Sentinel*, July 11, 1984, p. A-10.

Zanker, Alfred. "Why World May Be Near Another Economic Boom." *U.S. News & World Report*, August 20, 1984, pp. 54–57.

Strategic Management in the Not-for-Profit Organization

Our responsibility is not discharged by the announcement of virtuous ends.

▪ *John F. Kennedy* ▪

Strategic management in the not-for-profit organization follows much the same pattern as indicated in Figures 11.1 and 11.2, at least conceptually. However, a number of factors serve to alter that process, and indeed to alter the manner in which economic and management functions are practiced within not-for-profits as well. The following paragraphs first identify the nature of the not-for-profit organization and then indicate in general terms how the strategic management process varies in a not-for-profit from that process in a for-profit organization. The remainder of the chapter discusses strategic management in not-for-profit organizations in more detail, using Figures 11.1 and 11.2 as the basis for this discussion.

The Not-for-Profit Organization

Philip Kotler advises that four major types of organizations exist when classifications of private, public, for-profit, and not-for-profit are considered:

1. The private for-profit includes private corporations, partnerships, sole proprietorships.
2. The public for-profit includes state-owned airlines, utilities, and so forth.

Figure 11.1 The Organization—a Strategic Management Process Model

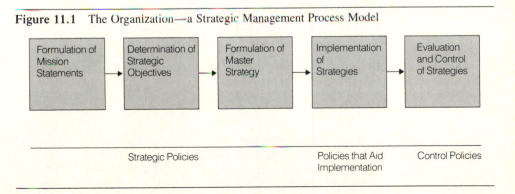

| Formulation of Mission Statements | Determination of Strategic Objectives | Formulation of Master Strategy | Implementation of Strategies | Evaluation and Control of Strategies |

Strategic Policies   Policies that Aid Implementation   Control Policies

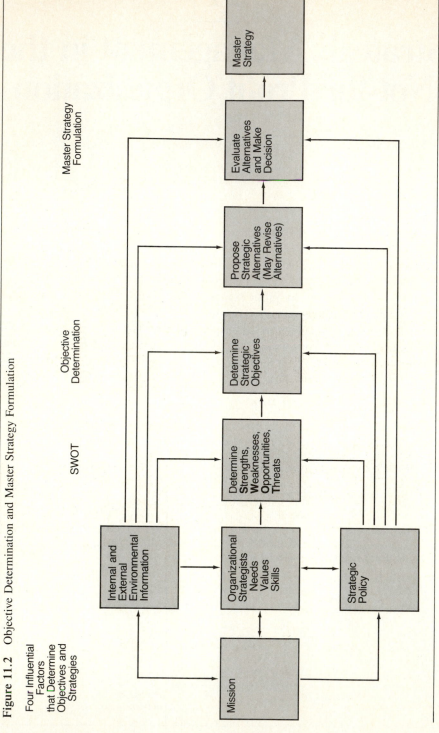

Figure 11.2   Objective Determination and Master Strategy Formulation

3. The private not-for-profit includes private museums, charities, universities, associations, hospitals, and so forth.

4. The public not-for-profit includes government agencies, public schools, public hospitals, and so on.

The private, nonprofit organizations, are often referred to as the third sector (of the economy), not being for-profit nor government based. These may be broken into eight major groups as follows:[1]

1. Religious organizations
    a. churches
    b. church associations
    c. evangelical movements

2. Social organizations
    a. service clubs
    b. fraternal organizations

3. Cultural organizations
    a. museums
    b. symphonies
    c. opera companies
    d. art leagues
    e. zoos

4. Knowledge organizations
    a. private grade schools
    b. private universities
    c. research organizations

5. Protective organizations
    a. trade associations
    b. trade unions

6. Political organizations
    a. political parties
    b. lobbyist groups

7. Philanthropic organizations
    a. private welfare organizations
    b. private foundations
    c. charity hospitals
    d. nursing homes

8. Social cause organizations
    a. peace groups
    b. family planning groups
    c. environmental groups
    d. racial rights groups
    e. consumerist groups
    f. women's rights groups
    g. anti-vice groups

Not-for-profits comprise a major portion of the national economy. Various forms of government collectively account for a third of the U.S. GNP.[2] Indeed, few would argue that government in its various forms is the most pervasive of all institutions. On the other hand, it is not monolithic; but as E. S. Savas observes, is actually comprised of some 80,000 units within the United States,[3] albeit, one—the federal government—seeming monolithic to many. The number of private not-for-profit organizations is also extremely large and their impact on GNP is also highly significant.

Perhaps the most distinguishing feature of not-for-profit organizations is the separation which exists between their clients or users and their resource contributors.[4] Marketing in this environment serves the same dual function as in a for-profit organization—to market

[1] Philip Kotler, *Marketing for Nonprofit Organizations*, 2d ed., (Englewood Cliffs, N.J.: Prentice-Hall, 1982), pp. 12–14.

[2] E. S. Savas, *Privatizing the Public Sector: How to Shrink Government* (Chatham, N.J.: Chatham House Publishers, 1982), pp. 7, 8.

[3] Ibid.

[4] E. Greenburg, "Competing for Scarce Resources," *Journal of Business Strategy*, Winter 1982, p. 82.

"Why don't we just look at ourselves as a nonprofit organization?"

Source: Copyright 1984. Reprinted by permission of *Success Magazine* and Joseph Farris.

the product or service, and to raise funds. But in the for-profit organization, marketing accomplishes both at the same time (except for contributed stockholders' equity or debt); while in the nonprofit, these are usually accomplished separately. In the for-profit organization, the client or user pays for the product or service, thus providing cash flow and hopefully profits. This is not true typically of the user or client in nonprofits and, therefore, that type of organization must seek financial resources elsewhere.

Now let us examine the ways in which the various major factors in the strategic management process are affected by the nonprofit situation.

Mission

Two major problems in a nonprofit organization are the absence of a clearly defined mission and the absence of related clearly defined objectives. While it seems a simple matter to establish these, it is not in nonprofits—at least partly because of the political nature of most such organizations, and at least partly because of the aforementioned separation of users and clients from resource contributors. The political process affects their missions and subsequent objectives in a number of ways. First, in government and in many of the other nonprofits, top management is continually changing, and with that change, mission and objectives change. Second, it is more politically expedient not to have a specific mission and measurable objectives if one wants to retain an elected position. Then too, there are always numerous constituents seeking to have a nonprofit organization satisfy their particular needs. This leads to a series of conflicting objectives which may never be resolved. For example, a hospital is typically required by law (federal and often municipal) to provide care to indigent patients. It is also expected to provide paying patients with the lowest-cost care. Yet, because of one constituent's demand (that of government), as much as 30 percent of a hospital's patient costs are written off, thus raising the price of a paying patient's care. Obviously, this angers paying patients—who may be represented by insurance companies, consumer groups, and even state agencies seeking to lower hospital costs. Finally, many of these organizations are subject to a charismatic leader, who may substitute mystique for substance.

The separation of providers of funds from clients and users contributes to imprecisely defined missions and objectives in two major ways. First, the influence of the resource contributors on decisions related to mission is often great. Unfortunately, however, they are often not qualified to be setting mission and objectives. And since their time and interest are limited, they may react to, rather than think through, the problem. And frequently, customer influence in these same decisions is limited. Therefore, market-driven (customer-influenced) mission statements are not typical of nonprofits. Indeed, one might question if they should be, since in many cases, services, especially government services, are provided at less than cost or are free, clearly biasing rationality from the perspective of the taxpayer or other contributor.

Another factor posing problems in determining mission and objectives is that service (which most of these nonprofits provide) is intangible and difficult to measure. This does not mean that it is impossible to establish measurable missions and objectives, but that it is frequently difficult. (Information Capsule 11.1 illustrates this point very well.) Efforts have been made in recent years to improve the measurability of service organization objectives, for example, establishing specific percentages of welfare clients that should be taken off the welfare roles for a given period. Nonetheless, it is still difficult to use quantified objectives in many instances and, therefore, qualitative objectives abound in nonprofit organizations.

Finally, one must always be conscious of how success is measured in these organizations. Many of these organizations have multiple missions (as do many for-profit organizations). The mutual benefit mission noted earlier in Chapter 1 can therefore play an important role in determining their missions and objectives. For example, since these organizations often work on a budgetary basis, for which there are many demands, an external pressure usually exists to reduce the spending level. If a unit is too successful in achieving objectives, jobs may be lost—even those of top management. And who would rationally opt to work oneself out of work? Too, survival is a measurement of success for many of these organizations. Therefore, the focus often is "breaking even," not accomplishment. Another measure of success is spending the budget—not exceeding it, but spending it. Because of the historical trend in many of these nonprofits to base next year's budget on last year's budget, most make certain that this year's budget disappears.[5]

[5] Based loosely on the following: W. H. Newman, and H. W. Wallender, III, "Managing Not-for-Profit Enterprises," *Academy of Management Review*, January 1978, pp. 24–31; M. L. Hatten, "Strategic Management in Not-for-Profit Organizations," *Strategic Management Journal*, April–June 1982, pp. 89–104; E. L. Greenberg, "Competing for Scarce Resources," *Journal of Business Strategy*, Winter 1982, pp. 81–87; and M. W. Dirsmith, S. F. Jablonsky, and A. D. Luzi, "Planning and Control in the U.S. Federal Government: A Critical Analysis of PPB, MBO, and ZBB," *Strategic Management Journal*, October–December 1980, pp. 303–329.

INFORMATION CAPSULE 11.1
United Way Mission and Objectives

United Way Mission Statement

To increase the organized capacity of people to care for one another.

Goals and Objectives:

- Provide the focus for a single community campaign at the workplace.
- Distribute funds to agencies in the community through the "citizens review" process using volunteers to allocate monies after reviewing agencies.
- Unite diverse elements of a community by building partnerships and coalitions.
- Serve as a catalyst to link together people with common concerns and interests.
- Deal with government at all levels so the public and private sectors work together to meet community needs.
- Promote the values of voluntary service and raise the profile of programs that are dependent on volunteers for their success.
- Recruit and place volunteers in the United Way campaign and in all other principal areas of activity within the United Way organization as well as in the agencies it supports.
- Operate programs of information and referral aimed at helping people locate and use services they need.
- Match management assistance from companies and organizations to social service agencies that need expert help.

Source: United Way internal documents.

Strategic Policy

The strategic policies are often vague for many of the same reasons that mission and objectives are vague. Clients keep changing, if only by political decree. The service's quality is difficult to define—i.e., should a person be out of the hospital in six days or seven for a particular operation? (The federal government has defined the quality of service for all major diagnostic-related groupings with respect to how much they will pay for Medicare services.) The roles of these organizations in society are not always well understood. Top managers often change, so there is a lack of consistency in management philosophy. The basic actions in which these organizations can engage are often limited by law or other factors (a charity, for example, seldom diversifies into another charitable cause). And, finally, performance criteria are hazy, and as noted earlier, difficult to define. Though it would be easy to say that the profit motive gives for-profits an advantage in establishing strategic policies, perhaps, as noted above, other factors, such as politics, increase the complexity of the strategic process in nonprofit organizations.

The Strategists

The strategists vary. They may be contributors, top managers, board members (who are often chosen for their financial contributions), professional staff, clients, members of various coalitions which may develop, and finally society at large through various pressure groups or the electoral process. Critically, the motivations of the members of the management group may vary. For example, professional salaried managers often work with volunteer managers. The volunteer wants certain objectives accomplished and has certain preferences for plans that often are in conflict with those of the professional manager. And volunteers, though often well intentioned, are not particularly well trained nor skilled in management. Also, because board members are often chosen for their financial capabilities and not their management skills, their inputs to strategy formulation may be less than adequate as well. Characteristically in many of these organizations, government especially, bureaucracies arise and any strategic decision must be approved by numerous layers of managers whose personnel are affected by the decision. One study of more than 100 NFPs shows clearly that their trustees are not functioning as well as they should with respect to strategy formulation.[6]

Finally, many of these organizations are very small. The top manager's time is limited. He or she is stretched thin, yet expected to perform strategic management functions as well as many others. The task becomes almost impossible—to be a specialist in many areas, such as accounting and marketing, and yet also plan strategy.

Nonprofits and Their Usages of Information to Determine SWOT

Nonprofits examine themselves for strengths and weaknesses and assess their environments for threats and opportunities. But the nature of what is examined, both internally and externally, will vary from what for-profits might consider. Because the organizational category of nonprofits encompasses such a wide spectrum of organizations, in terms of size and purpose, it is virtually impossible to characterize their situations specifically. Rather, what can be done is to make some very general observations about common characteristics of certain of these nonprofits, and to make some observations about their usages of information in determining SWOT.

Internally, most nonprofits would seem to consider much the same factors as appeared in Figures 2.3 and 3.3 (pages 000 and 000). The target groups, the techniques, the processes, however, will be somewhat different for the economic functions such as marketing, and some of the management functions, such as leadership. In smaller nonprofits, as in smaller for-profits, the performance of these functions is likely to be less sophisticated than in larger organizations. And, it is generally recognized that most nonprofits have less sophisticated management systems and fewer skilled managers than for-profit organizations. In another area, significant differences would probably occur with respect to major power/influence groups. Only on limited occasions would there be stockholders. Rather, contributors, taxpayers, or members (in cases of dues-collecting associations such as unions) would be more appropriate persons to examine for their expectations and influ-

[6]I. Unterman, and R. H. Davis, "The Strategy Gap in Not-for-Profits," *Harvard Business Review*, May/June 1982, pp. 30–40.

ence. Similarly, as previously discussed, the nature of the management group will be somewhat different in that nonpaid volunteers will often serve in upper management and on the board of directors or similar governance unit. Government will be an internal factor to consider for all government organizations. Those governments external to a particular government organization will, of course, need to be monitored. Finally, though employees may not be members of organized labor groups; bureaucracies nonetheless tend to dominate the everyday decision process in larger nonprofits, and often, the strategic one as well.

Externally, major differences include the role of government, the definition of "competition" and "the industry," relationships with society and the reaction to societal pressure groups, the role of labor, and the influence or absence of influence of the client group. Here the role of government significantly increases. (Many nonprofits actually are, of course, governmental units, so government may be an internal factor to assess.) For most governments, other governments will still remain an influence to consider—the city must consider the state and federal governments, and so forth. For nonprofits such as health care institutions, governments of all types, but especially the federal government, are a major force in determining proper actions. Administrators must carefully monitor federal legislative action and federal agency interpretations thereof, for the impacts of these. For example, hospitals in 1983 encountered significant changes in federal government Medicare payment procedures. Payments were standardized for any procedure in a given area according to diagnostic-related groupings (DRG). Many hospitals found that their costs exceeded these standard payments. For unions, charities, and several of the other nonprofits, government plays an important regulatory, if not an administrative, role. Thus in most cases, nonprofits must carefully consider government in strategic decisions. The definition of competition and the industry changes somewhat for nonprofits as well. While for-profit competition does not exist, there is competition for resources, for personnel, for clients, for expertise and experience, and for prestige and influence.[7] The competition for funds is especially intense. There are only so many contributors, so many tax dollars available. Known charitable sources, such as business corporations, receive multiple donation requests daily (at all of their geographic locations). Most sources can only give so much, and thus the competition for funds becomes very intense among nonprofits.

A specific example of factors that a not-for-profit (or for-profit) hospital would consider in competitor analysis is indicated in Figure 11.3. This figure suggests that a number of competitors exist in each of a hospital's three major, traditional client service areas. Hospitals must develop strategies for coping with such competition, just as any business would. Other types of nonprofits are also extremely market-oriented and responsive to paying customer demands, as Information Capsule 11.2 reveals.

Normally, nonprofits are very sensitive to societal demands and to emerging pressure groups. Government at all elected levels is responsive, if slowly, to pressure groups, although it would appear that only the "squeakiest wheels" get greased. (But because the internal bureaucracies that emerge are not particularly responsive, strategic managers must be attuned to this problem. One such group, labor, is highly unionized in public education, in certain municipalities in the lower-paying jobs, and in many health care in-

[7]E. Greenberg, "Scarce Resources," pp. 83–86.

Figure 11.3   Competitive Alternatives to Hospital Care

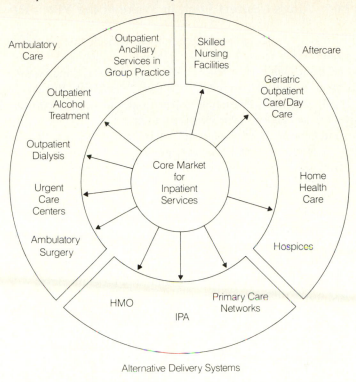

Source: Jeff Charles Goldsmith, *Can Hospitals Survive?* Homewood Ill.: Dow Jones, 1981, p. 17. Reprinted by permission of Jeff Charles Goldsmith.

stitutions. But for most nonprofits, organized labor does not pose the same threat that it does to many for-profits. This is especially true of the federal government. Although some federal employee unions do exist, their powers are significantly less than their for-profit counterparts. Among other things, they do not have the right to strike legally, as President Reagan demonstrated to members of PATCO, the air traffic controller's union during his first term as president. Finally, the client, if a member of a strong pressure group, may have tremendous influence on the organization. If not, then clients typically have little influence since they would normally receive services free or at below cost.

The consequence of the above differences is that the strategists must incorporate their knowledge of these differences into their strategic information systems and into their strategic decision processes. They must monitor more closely various factors depending upon the importance of each strategic factor. As would any strategist, they must consider those factors that will have the most impact on their futures. Perhaps one of the most important points to be made in this section is that for those of us who are not as familiar with nonprofit organizations as we are with for-profit organizations, we need to keep these differences in perspective when examining nonprofit situations.

INFORMATION CAPSULE 11.2

Boston Pops Alters Concert Look in Wake of the Video Revolution

New York—The video revolution has shaken, rattled and rolled one of the most venerable musical institutions on television—the Boston Pops.

Now don't get the idea that Mick Jagger will swagger on stage and swing the baton, nor will the Pops shoot a sexy video for MTV (Music Television). But the 14th season of "Evening at Pops" on public television will open Sunday night with a format that includes rehearsal sequences and photographic essays set to music.

"We wanted to break the traditional concert format on TV," says William Cosel, who has been executive producer of "Evening at Pops" since its inception in 1970. "Instead of a straight performance show, we decided to experiment with one visual show. With most of the symphony shows drying up on TV, somebody had to be the guinea pig."

The first of six new "Pops" broadcasts opens with pastoral scenes of the quaint New England towns and Berkshire Mountains around Tanglewood, the orchestra's summer home. The montage is set to music composed by John Williams, who is in his fourth season as Pops conductor.

There's also a behind-the-scenes look at Williams, as harpsichord player, rehearsing Vivaldi's Concerto for Four Violins and Orchestra. The program closes with the only visual segment that works well. It's a tribute to painter Norman Rockwell, whose classically American faces gain emotional zest from the lyrics of "America the Dream Goes On," which also has music written by Williams.

By focusing on the abundant talents of Williams, the first program becomes "The John Williams Show." It's been four years since the death of the Pops' most famous maestro, Arthur Fiedler, and this program intends to familiarize audiences with the more shy Williams.

Williams is this era's most successful movie musician. He has scored the music for Hollywood's biggest box-office hits, including *Star Wars*, *Superman*, *Raiders of the Lost Ark*, *Jaws*, and *E.T. the Extra-Terrestrial*. Music from the last is performed Sunday by the Pops.

The *E.T.* music conveys the spirit of flight, and it desperately needs some supporting footage on the "Pops" show. The same thing with "The Sorcerer's Apprentice" and its recognizable brooms-and-water sequence from Walt Disney's *Fantasia*.

"We ran up against ourselves because we couldn't visually treat everything," Cosel says. "We created a bigger appetite than we were able to fill. Ignorance is bliss. Once we started to do things visually, we created a monster."

Cosel was interested in matching footage from *Fantasia* with "The Sorcerer's Apprentice," but found it was too expensive and did not synchronize properly with the Pops' version. He also put in a request to Steven Spielberg for clips from *E.T.* but never heard from him.

"We may have been too naive in thinking we could easily change formats," Cosel says.

For the rest of the season, "Evening at Pops" will have more conventional broadcasts—concert performances featuring the Pops' lightly classical and popular music that is familiar and appealing to broad audiences shopping around during the summer's network reruns. These are "the audiences that Fiedler said wouldn't be caught dead in symphony halls," Cosel says.

Other shows, hopefully more joyous, will feature singers Steve Lawrence and Eydie Gorme in a salute to Irving Berlin, pianist-composer Marvin Hamlisch performing his own music, singer-dancer Gregory Hines performing some works of Eubie Blake, and folk singers Peter, Paul and Mary.

"To me the Pops is still an event, an opportunity for classical performers to let their hair down," Cosel says. "In the future, I still would like to occasionally do more interpretative, visual pieces—and do them better."

Source: AP wire story, July 16, 1983.

Impacts of The Not-for-Profit Situation on Strategic Objectives and Master Strategy Formulation

If you will reexamine the objectives in Figure 3.3, you will find that most of these are quite applicable to nonprofits. Among nonprofits there is, of course, more orientation towards budgets than sales and profits, there are problems posed by identifying units of service (that is, specific objectives). And, one would have to substitute contribution to resource providers in place of contribution to owners. But beyond that, the objectives could, not necessarily would, be similar. The priorities will probably vary, however. One would anticipate less emphasis on objectives concerned with resource contributors (as opposed to this very necessary concern in a corporation or other business). There would probably be more stress on contributions to customers (users), employees, and society. And, historically, there has been less concern for efficiency and proper utilization of resources (in budgetary terms) in nonprofits than in for-profits. Most nonprofits are labor intensive, though they seem to take labor for granted rather than making it the subject of efficiency analysis. And, since nonprofits are often managed by politically motivated individuals, the opportunities for mismanagement of employees, especially in terms of inefficient empire building (growth objectives), are substantial. In addition, because of the nonprofits' tendency to manage by budget, there has been a widely observed waste of resources in government, for example, in the military and in numerous state and federal civilian agencies. The point here is that, historically, it is likely that efficiency objectives were not established or perhaps were not stressed.

One group of authors even questions whether objectives-based management systems such as MBO (Management By Objectives), ZBB (Zero Based Budgeting), or PPB (Program Planning and Budgeting) would work in the federal government. They feel that such systems require a tolerance for uncertainty that government officials simply do not have and cannot afford to project.[8] On the other hand, government seems to have responded to societal demands for better planning, and if anything, such systems reduce uncertainty. It would seem to us to be better to force changes in administrator's behavior than to accept an abdication of responsibility for strategic management.

[8] M. W. Dirsmith, S. F. Jablowsky, and A. D. Luzi, "Planning and Control in the U.S. Federal Government: A Critical Analysis of PPB, MBO, and ZBB," *Strategic Management Journal*, October–December 1980, pp. 303–329.

With respect to the strategies identified in Table 3.5 on page 000, it is apparent that nonprofits employ very similar strategies. Nonprofits have societal-response strategies, mission-determination strategies, mission-competitive strategies, and mission-supportive strategies. Because not-for-profit missions are more service, mutual benefit, and commonweal in nature (see above) than a business would be, their mission-competitive strategies reflect nonprofit-type concerns for gaining not only clients and customers, but also resource contributions—tax dollars, donations, or member assessments. Looking more specifically at government, intentional growth strategies are fewer (except as an individual manager would want growth for power reasons). Similarly, acquisition, divestiture, and turnaround have comparatively little meaning, but market and product/service development strategies are likely. Support strategies in government have not always been as likely to focus on quality or efficiency of labor utilization as they might in business, although that seems to be changing. Labor is somewhat of a given, determined in the bureaucracy somewhere outside the manager's control, another reason that labor efficiency is probably not stressed more. Motivation and leadership strategies also differ somewhat, because organizational members are not as likely to be money motivated as their for-profit counterparts (though many are).

In most other nonprofits, one would probably find an absence of intentionally formulated strategies. Rather, most strategies would simply be made on the spur of the moment, as needed, with the probable exception of the financing strategy. This is especially true in the many smaller nonprofit organizations. If you will recall, survival is a major objective, so sophisticated strategies seem out of place in that type of environment. One exception, the hospital industry, has made rapid advances in recent years in terms of strategy formulation. Acquisition, divestment, conglomerate growth, and other strategies common to for-profit organizations are common in that industry as well. Figure 11.4 details some of the ways in which hospitals might in fact tailor basic action growth strategies to their particular situation. Terms such as vertical and horizontal diversification take on whole new meanings when "captured" doctors in HMOs, MD office buildings, satellite clinics, and so forth are added to more typical patient sources such as physician solo practices. Affiliated hospitals that provide horizontal diversification also provide referral patients and thus serve vertical diversification purposes as well. Service objectives are frequently quantified in hospitals and thus strategies are typically more well defined. Marketing strategies are also more sophisticated than in any of the other nonprofits, exclusive of government and a few large charities such as United Way. Finally, the motivation and leadership strategies in hospitals must focus on the higher need levels that employees possess, but also must satisfy their basic needs.

A good example of strategy formation in nonprofits is found in the Equal Employment Opportunity Commission (EEOC). The EEOC has as its mission the enforcement of Title VII of the Civil Rights Act of 1964, as amended. To that end, the EEOC developed a grand strategy to solve the problem of discrimination in employment. As a major objective, it sought to ensure that as many jobs as possible were opened to equal employment opportunity. Pressure, conciliation agreements, and legal suits were used against the largest, most visible employers, such as American Telephone and Telegraph, the entire steel industry, General Motors, and numerous others.[9] The EEOC's strategy recognized that, given its limited man power, it might use the visual evidence of its enforcement efforts to

---

[9] "EEOC Steps Up the Pressure," *Business Week*, February 23, 1974, pp. 87–88.

Figure 11.4 Hospital Feeder System, 1980

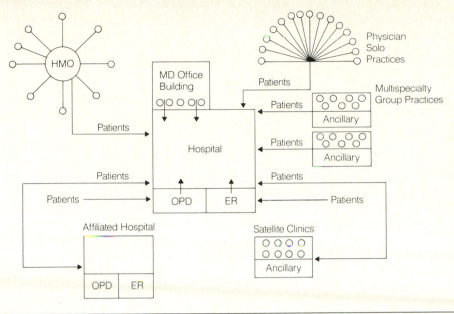

Source: Jeff Charles Goldsmith, *Can Hospitals Survive?* Homewood Ill.: Dow Jones, 1981, p. 143. Reprinted by permission of Jeff Charles Goldsmith.

scare other employers into compliance. This strategy emphasizes the accomplishment of the EEOC's primary mission and strategic objectives; it does not consider other aspects of the organization's external environment.

The above commentary is limited both by space and by the very limited research or even observational analyses that exists with respect to nonprofits, but by now, you probably have the gist of the major differences. The key is that when analyzing any organization's strategies, their SWOT, or their objectives, you must make certain that you recognize the difference in their external environments and in internal organizational profiles.

Nonprofit Strategies at the SBU Level

Since competition and competitive strategies are the primary concerns of the grand strategy—the focal point of the master strategy at the single-business level of strategy—it is appropriate to identify the nature of competition in the nonprofit organization. Ellen Greenberg identifies several key areas in which nonprofits compete: for funding; for personnel and other resources; for users-customers, clients, and audience; for influence and prestige. She suggests that nonprofits have recently entered a more turbulent environment, as there is a related increased taxpayer, contributor, or other fund-provider interest in decreasing taxes, contributions, or dues. Thus there will be an increased competition for funds,[10] and hence an increased need for marketing strategies. Indeed, with federal, state,

[10] Ellen Greenberg, "Competing for Scarce Resources," *Journal of Business Strategy*, Winter 1982, pp. 81–87.

and local government cutbacks, the number of solicitations of business for support for education, for the arts, and for charities has increased substantially. The competition for users would also seem to be quite significant, for in many cases, as governments slash programs, the individual agency will seek to continue to justify funding based on the existence of a significant user base.

> *In short, the nonprofit sector represents a new and virtually untapped area*
> *for research and writing in strategic planning.*
>
> ▪ *Robert C. Shirley* ▪

The absence of related research prohibits this text from identifying specific nonprofit strategies, except for anecdotal evidence or prescriptive strategies. The key factor involved in all of these is much the same as it would be in a for-profit organization—identification of the proper target market. With respect to federal, state, and local government, it is apparent that a large number of publics must be satisfied, and that society at large, political interest groups, legislators, and members of various government agencies all have major concerns regarding taxes and uses of funds. These groups must be marketed to, often a substantive effort. Television, radio, and various forms of printed media may be utilized in order to secure approval and programs and their respective budgets. Millions of various mail pieces may be involved in one single campaign at the federal level, with numerous issues being attacked in campaigns at various times throughout the year. The president, various legislators, lobby groups, and various societal constituents may attempt to influence each other and the general public on a host of issues. Similar efforts may take place at the state and local level.

In other nonprofits, marketing is also critical. In hospitals, for example, the marketing manager's position is vital. There are tremendous needs to raise funds, primarily from sources other than clients, largely to pay for the services provided to many clients at no cost to them. Similarly, most sizable colleges or universities have a professional fundraiser and/or staff serving in the marketing capacity to a host of various target markets. This is especially true of the private institution, but increasingly true of public institutions as well, due to ever-tightening state budgets. With respect to those budgets, most major public institutions must maintain lobbyists in order to preserve funding needs as they proceed through the legislature. In most states, education is the single-biggest expenditure in the budget, and is coming under closer scrutiny. Other nonprofits, such as religious institutions, museums, clubs, and unions also have carefully selected target markets at which they aim their marketing strategies. Many of these strategies play upon historical ties, such as having graduated from a particular educational institution; many focus upon the individual's ethical or moral beliefs; and many focus on the individual's particular needs—for example, the need to help others. Some strategies, such as those employed by clubs and unions, focus on needs for certain activities or factors such as security. These latter organizations, which depend on dues for funds, must of course market heavily the services they provide to users and to potential users in order to create funds. Unions, which especially find themselves losing power in the 1980s, are primarily aiming their marketing efforts at new target markets, such as geographically in the South, or in different jobs, such as those held by white-collar employees (for details see Information Capsule 11.3). Obviously, a tremendous amount of personal selling is involved in virtually all of the marketing strategies of these nonprofits.

INFORMATION CAPSULE 11.3
Decreasing Union Membership and Power

Union membership was estimated at below 18 million in 1983 or under 20 percent of the nonfarm work force versus a 28 percent figure in 1965. The once-formidable power of organized labor seems to have fallen to levels significantly lower than at anytime in the last 20 years, maybe even lower than at anytime since the end of World War II.

Organized labor has suffered from a variety of circumstances:

- High unemployment in the early 1980s brought about by the recession, when combined with upheavals in basic industries, has drastically reduced union membership.

- Unions are finding it harder to organize new groups; for example, in 1981, unions won only 43 percent of representation elections as opposed to 53 percent in 1971.

- The new high-tech industries are not fertile targets for unions, who were defeated in 30 of 37 supervised elections during the period from 1971 to 1982.

- Many unions, especially in the automotive and airline industries, have had to grant concessions related to wage freezes or roll backs as well as other give backs.

- Federal legislative priorities related to the huge budget deficits have not favored massive public works programs.

Union vs. Union.   One indication of the continuing difficulties facing organized labor is the August 15, 1984, incident that placed one union, the United Food and Commercial Workers (UFCW), against another union, the United Steel Workers (USW). UFCW organized and sanctioned a demonstration outside of USW's headquarters building in Pittsburgh to protest USW's invasion of UFCW's retail food territory. This was not just poor fraternal behavior. Rather it indicated the surfacing of a basic problem—the need to organize new members to replace recent losses. Competition for members is so keen that interunion rivalry has begun.

1984 Election Results.   The 1984 election results were not favorable for organized labor. Labor's endorsed candidates in the House, Senate, and gubernatorial elections won 62.7 percent of the campaigns despite Walter Mondale's overwhelming and highly visible defeat. On the surface this 62.7 percent success rate may seem good but, compared to 71.3 percent in 1976, it was a severe disappointment to most labor leaders.

Other Indications.   Other indicators of the erosion of union power often cited by observers are: (1) the decreasing average annual rate of negotiated pay raises, which dropped from 7.9 percent in 1981 to 2.8 percent in 1983, and are estimated at 2.8 percent for 1984; and (2) the decreasing number of strikes involving 1,000 or more workers, which stood at 235 in 1979 but fell to 81 in 1983, and is estimated at under 60 for 1984.

At least one labor economist (Aubrey Freeman of the Conference Board) has been quoted as saying that it is very clear that union power over wages has been smashed.

Source: Leonard M. Apcar, "Labor Talks in '85 to Stress Benefits and Making Concerns Competitive," *The Wall Street Journal*, December 11, 1984, p. 31; Carey W. English, "Bruised Unions Dig in for an Uphill Fight," *U.S. News & World Report*, November 19, 1984, p. 48; English, "Embattled Unions Get Their Act Together," *U.S. News & World Report*, October 17, 1983, pp. 95–96; Carey W. English and Jack A. Seamonds, "A 'Year of Moderation' for Nation's Unions," *U.S. News & World Report*, December 31, 1984/January 7, 1985, pp. 99–100; "It's Union vs. Union in the Scramble for Members," *Business Week*, September 3, 1984, p. 27; Christopher Redman, "Labor's Hard Day's Night," *Time*, October 1, 1984, pp. 46–47; "Showdown in Detroit," *Business Week*, September 10, 1984, pp. 102–110. Alexander L. Taylor, "Showdown at General Motors," *Time*, September 24, 1984, pp. 52–54.

Figure 11.5   Levels of Strategy in a College or University

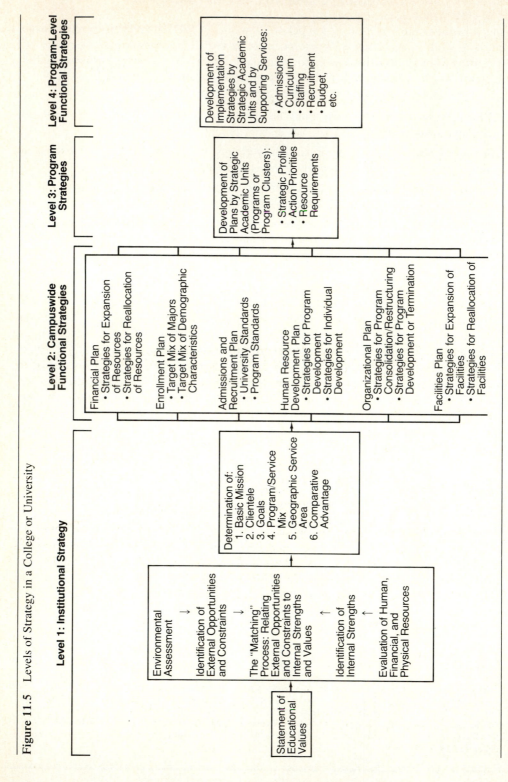

Source: Robert C. Shirley, "Identifying the Levels of Strategy for a College or University," *Long Range Planning*, June 1983, p. 94.

Philip Kotler has suggested that marketing for nonprofits has four distinctive characteristics:[11]

1. Multiple publics—clients and funders, both of whom must be marketed to.
2. Multiple objectives—difficult to find strategies that will satisfy all simultaneously.
3. Services rather than physical goods—these tend to be intangible, inseparable, variable, and perishable.
4. Public scrutiny—observed and pressured externally.

Yet, despite these and several other differences in major strategies, most not-for-profit organizations carry out Figures 11.1 and 11.2 much as do for-profit organizations. Figure 11.5 portrays the various stages of planning for one very representative non-profit, a college or university. As you can see, there is a value-derived purpose, a matching of strengths and weaknesses (implied) against opportunities and threats, a classic mission statement, and an apparent grand strategy seeking some competitive advantage. There are functional strategies, organizational strategies, and implementation strategies as well. All are adapted to the specific environment as they should be. Compare this process then to Figures 11.1 and 11.2 and you will see a significant number of similarities.

The Master Strategy for Multiple-Primary-Mission Nonprofits

In reviewing the contents of the master strategy portrayed in Table 3.5, in light of the context of this chapter, we are concerned with the primary mission strategy. The focus of our concern is with nonprofit organizations that have various divisions, each possessing differing missions—defined as we would define them for businesses, in terms of product or service, target market, characteristics of product or service, and geographic location. As a consequence of these differences in missions, the manner in which these divisions' basic actions are conducted also varies. It is clear that primary mission strategies will vary with each agency. It is also clear that, in government, much of the resource allocation process is political. A rationally derived portfolio process does not exist per se, but rather, based on factors such as the power of coalitions, the strength of various leaders, the demands of society, and the requirements of the law, resources will be allocated among the various divisions of a government, in a typically slow, bureaucratic fashion. Thus, in addition to the local, state, and federal agencies you might normally think of—those assisting in community or individual health and welfare, such as the military, police and fire departments; the commerce department; the transportation or highway department, and so forth; most schools including most major colleges and universities; hospitals; museums; and other public institutions—will allocate resources, or will have their resources allocated to them, on the basis of the aforementioned, often politically inspired bases.

The Behavioral View of Strategic Decision Making in Nonprofits

Much of what we know about the impacts of behavioral factors on the strategic decision process has in fact been learned from examining nonprofit organizations. Indeed, the concept of incrementalism, later identified as existing on business, was first conceptualized

---

[11] Kotler, *Nonprofit Organizations*, p. 9.

and researched in government. (Consequently, much of the discussion in Chapter 6 was based on the nonprofit environment.) Our remarks here are thus limited only to the observation that nonprofits tend to have multiple, major constituents, imprecise missions and objectives, and inherent bureaucracies. All of these factors typically lead to political rather than rational decisions. These characteristics frequently encourage the development of coalitions, of incrementalism, and of decisions based on personality rather than on information. To the extent that these same factors might characterize business, we would expect them to have less rational and more political decision making.

Everything having to do with the government and everything the government does is political, for politics is the art and science of government.

▪ *Paul H. Appleby* ▪

Implementation in the Nonprofit Sector

The basic organizational structures are the same in nonprofits as in for-profit organizations. The choice as to the appropriate levels of centralization and decentralization is also the same. However, in very large government organizations, there is more a tendency to become bureaucratized and overrun with red tape than commonly occurs in business. There are also frequent differences in management systems and human resources management at the individual managerial level. In nonprofits money can seldom be used as an extrinsic motivator.

Management systems in small nonprofits are often nonexistent, even more so than they are in small business. Because funding seems to be a problem in many nonprofits, management systems and management development often suffer. Similarly, there would appear to be an insufficient amount of funds to allow for a compensation reward for performance-type motivation systems. Since budgetary supervision is often used as a justification for administrative salary levels, empire building may result. In terms of managing the culture, there are many more constituents to satisfy, typically, than one would find in business. Thus, any major vested group may sabotage implementation efforts. And, there are probably differences in dominant needs between most nonprofit employees and most for-profit employees. This fact alone leads to very distinct changes in leadership, motivation and communication systems, and individual managerial styles. In summary, there are some very distinct differences; yet, there are numerous similarities.

Strategic and Management Control in Nonprofit Organizations

Chapter 9 addressed the issues involved with control in the profit-oriented organization. Normally, these techniques are also appropriate for nonprofit organizations. However, management control measures—especially financial control measures, specifically profit and ROI—are not very relevant to the nonprofit organization.

The problem of control is made more complex by the nature of the planning system employed by nonprofit organizations. Such organizations generally have vague objectives and ill-defined plans of action. Because of their inability to quantify objectives, and on many occasions their unwillingness to do so, these organizations employ the budget as the principal control device. Unlike the business firm, however, the nonprofit organization has far too little linkage between objectives and the budget. This budget approach, then, is often unsound. The nonprofit's primary concern should be objectives accomplishment—not expenditure, for when activity is equated with achievement, the results are often inefficiency and waste. Anyone who has experienced military service or been employed by the federal government is familiar with the rush to spend as much as possible at the end of each fiscal year (whether the items are needed or not) in order to assure that the budget amount is not reduced for the next fiscal year.

Planning Program Budgeting Systems (PPBS) are designed to eliminate some of these problems by requiring that programs be matched more closely to budgets and that the need for programs and budgeted amounts be verified each year. Several states have adopted the zero-based budgeting programs normally associated with PPBS. But the inescapable truth remains—it is virtually impossible to delineate what it is that many of these organizations are supposed to accomplish. Therefore, it is difficult to control performance towards this nonentity. Responsibility, one of the keys to control, is difficult to affix in such situations.

While it is encouraging that public management is now being accepted and even taught in the major universities (with some significant successes reported), the major problem—how to establish measurable objectives—remains. Until this problem can be solved, improvements will be limited. Furthermore, the problem is not one which many politicians in the public nonprofit sector seem eager to solve. It is vague objectives and reactive decisions that allow politicians to be reelected. And some government agencies have never established objectives before. The coalitions which form and the political promises to various power groups which must be kept often prohibit meaningful plans of action and objectives accomplishment as well as suitable administration. If performance measures were available and accountability became possible, performance would be more common. However, if tax revolts continue, demands for accountability, and use of managerial skills, should increase.

Summary

Based on their missions, there are two major types of organizations: for-profits (business) and not-for-profits. The latter may be further subdivided into government and all other types of nonprofits. Each of these three resulting classifications may be either public or private. Because the number of nonprofits is so large, so is their diversity. This chapter indicated, more specifically than this summary can, the nature of not-for-profits' strategic management processes. Generally speaking, mission in nonprofits is often vague, as are objectives. The number of constituents and their influence on mission determination compounds the difficulty of the situation. The fact that revenue sources and clients are often not the same constituents leads to additional problems: strategic policies are often vague, and the strategists vary—they are often revenue providers, not professional managers.

Information is employed in a SWOT analysis, but to what degree is another issue. It is generally believed that nonprofits' information systems are not as sophisticated as those in business. Certainly their hardware, in many cases, is not. However, the SWOT-analysis process is largely the same. It is primarily the external factors to be analyzed that differ. The objectives that not-for-profits would set are essentially the same that business would

Table 11.1   Comparison of Business and Not-for-Profits

Strategic Characteristic	Business	Not-for-Profits
Dominant missions	Profit	Service, mutual benefit, commonweal
Strategic policies	Usually precise	Often vague
Strategists	Usually few	Many, often outsiders
Information systems, usage	Financially based, many	Budget based, few
SWOT environment	competitive	Increasingly competitive, often monopolistic
Objectives	Quantitative, qualitative	Qualitative, quantitative
Master strategy	Complex	Often not articulated, but increasingly is
SBU strategies	Marketing-oriented	marketing, but to client and source of funds
Strategies for multiple-SBU organizations	Portfolio	Politically determined budgets
Behavioral aspects	Often authoritative	Often coalition, political
Implementation	Compensation-based	Other-satisfier based
	Often strong systems	Often weak systems
	Often decentralized	Often centralized and very bureaucratic
Control systems	Many, results-based	Comparatively few, budget-based

establish; the difference is in the precision of these objectives. Nonprofits tend to have more vague objectives and hence, less precise performance standards. Their master strategies also vary in composition. A nonprofit's chief concerns remain to market, and to finance operations, but the target markets are often different. Mission determination, basic action, and primary mission strategies are emphasized in different degrees than with business. Portfolio analyses have little meaning for most not-for-profits, although some, for example, those in health care, can balance various SBUs using these approaches. The behavior processes in nonprofits are often coalition based, most often incremental in nature. Their implementation depends very much on structure. The term *bureaucracy* is appropriate for nonprofits, and red tape ensues in the larger organizations. The structures of many nonprofits are very similar to those in the average business, though some are more centralized, and often they have more staff. However, systems, especially reward systems, often differ. Typically, money is not readily available as a reward, as it is in business. Thus, control systems are often budget based. Performance criteria are often vague, which relates back to the vagueness of mission.

Table 11.1 portrays some of the major differences between for-profits and not-for-profits. Remember that these organizations are no more homogeneous than are all businesses. Rather, numerous exceptions exist. The table merely suggests average variances between the two types of organizations.

Key Terms and Concepts

By the time you have completed this chapter, you should be able to discuss how the following key terms and concepts apply in the not-for-profit organization: strategic management process, mission, strategists, information, information systems, strategic policies, SWOT analysis, objectives setting, master strategy formulation, SBU strategies, master strategies for multiple-SBU nonprofits, the behavioral aspects of strategic decision making, implementation, and control.

Discussion Questions

1. Choose two not-for-profit organizations with which you are very familiar, for example a church you attend or a social organization. Now contrast how each of these organizations' mission statements compare with a for-profit organization such as IBM. Also compare each not-for-profit with the other not-for-profit. Which of the three has the most specific mission statement? Which the most vague?

2. Using the same three organizations as in Question 1 above, try to list as many constituents as possible that influence each of the organizations' mission statements. Which list of constituents is longest? Why?

3. Now take each of the not-for-profit constituent lists developed in Question 2 and identify the revenue-source constituents versus the client constituents. Which group is more numerous for each not-for-profit organization? Which group is more important to each not-for-profit organization?

4. Can you identify any not-for-profit organizations that have utilized a portfolio analysis approach in any of their activities? If this list contains few organizations, why do you think few not-for-profit organizations are known to utilize portfolio analysis?

5. If money is typically not available as a reward in not-for-profit organizations, what reward systems are available?

References

Andreasen, Alan R. "Nonprofits: Check Your Attention to Customers." *Harvard Business Review*, May/June 1982, pp. 105–110.

Apcar, Leonard M. "Labor Talks in '85 to Stress Benefits and Making Concerns Competitive." *The Wall Street Journal*, December 11, 1984, p. 31.

Bryson, John M. "A Perspective on Planning and Crisis in the Public Sector." *Strategic Management Journal*, 1981, pp. 181–196.

Bryson, John M., and Boal, Kimberly B. "Strategic Management in a Metropolitan Area." Presented at the Academy of Management Proceedings annual meeting, Dallas, August 1983, pp. 332–336.

"Budget Anguish—Reagan's Plans to Cut Deficit Draw Outcries from Affected Groups." *The Wall Street Journal*, December 26, 1984, pp. 1, 8.

Bulkeley, William M. "Churches, Congregations Increasingly Use Personal Computers to Enhance Worship." *The Wall Street Journal*, December 12, 1984, p. 33.

Calonius, L. Erik. "The Rivals—Competition for Glory and Money Is Fierce in Big-Time Science." *The Wall Street Journal*, December 28, 1984, pp. 1, 8.

"The Election Leaves Labor in the Lurch." *Business Week*, November 19, 1984, p. 42.

English, Carey W. "Bruised Unions Dig In for an Uphill Fight." *U.S. News & World Report*, November 19, 1984, p. 98.

English, Carey W., and Seamonds, Jack A. "A 'Year of Moderation' for Nation's Unions." *U.S. News & World Report*, December 31, 1984/January 7, 1985, pp. 99–100.

English, Carey W. "Embattled Unions Get Their Act Together." *U.S. News & World Report*, October 17, 1983, pp. 95–96.

"It's Union vs. Union in the Scramble for Members." *Business Week*, September 3, 1984, p. 27.

Malabre, Alfred L., Jr. "Tracking a Trend—Record Surpluses at the State and Local Levels Ease Worry over Washington's Budget Deficit." *The Wall Street Journal*, December 6, 1983, p. 60.

Mauriel, John J. "Major Strategic Issues Facing Public School Executives." Paper presented to the Public Sector Division of the Academy of Management 44th annual meeting, August 14, 1984.

Newman, William H., and Wallender, Harvey W. III. "Managing Not-For-Profit Enterprises." *Academy of Management Review*, January 1978, pp. 24–31.

Nielsen, Richard P. "SMR Forum: Strategic Piggybacking—a Self-Subsidization Strategy for Nonprofit Institutions." *Sloan Management Review*, 1982, pp. 65–69.

Ramanathan, Kavasseri V. *Management Control in Nonprofit Organizations: Text and Cases*. New York: Wiley, 1982.

Redman, Christopher. "Labor's Hard Day's Night." *Time*, October 1, 1984, pp. 46–47.

Rider, Robert W. "Making Strategic Planning Work in Local Government." *Long Range Planning*, Vol. 16, No. 3, 1983, pp. 73–81.

Ruffat, Jean. "Strategic Management of Public and Non-Market Corporations." *Long Range Planning*, 1983, Vol. 16, No. 2, pp. 74–84.

Scherschel, Patricia M. "Why Postal Service Faces Bleak Future." *U.S. News & World Report*, December 1, 1980, pp. 39, 40.

Sease, Douglas R., and Simison, Robert L. "UAW Switch on Revision Contracts Reflects Growing Concern for Jobs." *The Wall Street Journal*, December 21, 1981, p. 23.

"Showdown at General Motors." *Time*, September 24, 1984, pp. 52–54.

"Showdown in Detroit." *Business Week*, September 10, 1984, pp. 102–110.

"The Time Bomb Set to Go Off at the Veterans Administration." *Business Week*, November 19, 1984, pp. 132–139.

Unterman, Israel, and Davis, Richard Hart. "The Strategy Gap in Not-for-Profits." *Harvard Business Review*, May/June 1984, pp. 30–36, 40.

———. *Strategic Management for Not-For-Profit Organizations*. New York: Praeger, 1984.

Perfumery on Park, Inc.

■ *David M. Currie* ■

In January 1985, Anna Currie was deciding what direction her perfume business should take. She had been approached by representatives of several shopping malls about opening a shop, but she was not sure which malls were appropriate. More basically, she was not sure whether the first six months' experience of Perfumery on Park justified plans for expansion.

History

Perfumery on Park, Inc., was established in May 1984 by Anna and David Currie. It was the first attempt at retailing for either of them, although Anna had been interested in perfumes as a hobby for several years. Anna was the Director of Personnel at a college located in the same town as Perfumery on Park, Winter Park, Florida. She gradually reduced her involvement with the college after the shop opened in July 1984; by January 1985, she worked full-time at the perfumery. David taught finance at the graduate school of business of the same college; his involvement with the perfumery was on a part-time basis.

Winter Park was an affluent community adjacent to Orlando, the tourist center of Florida. Its main street, Park Avenue, was bordered on one side by Central Park and on the other side by numerous small boutiques and specialty shops. *The New York Times* recently had run an article on Winter Park because of its efforts to preserve the original brick streets. The ambience of the town was comparable to that of Carmel, California, Palm Beach, Florida, or the Hamptons of Long Island.

There had been a perfumery on Park Avenue a decade earlier, but it closed when its lease was purchased by a department store seeking to expand. The perfumery operation had been successful according to the owner, who consulted with Anna. In her explorations, Anna heard a rumor that someone else was considering opening a perfumery, but she believed that there was not a market sufficient for two shops; if she could be first into the market, the threat of that competition would be erased.

After preparing a business plan, Anna and David approached a bank about financial support. The bank offered a loan of $155,000 with a 15-year amortization at prime plus 1 percent and a 5-year balloon payment; collateral was to be the inventory of the shop and a second mortgage on their house. (See Exhibit 1.1.)

Anna purposely decided to open in July, traditionally a slow month in retailing and also in a winter resort community. However, she wanted several months of experience and exposure prior to the Christmas shopping season beginning at Thanksgiving. The decision proved to be prudent, as it allowed time to gain knowledge of the products and to work out the management systems used in operation of the shop.

Exhibit 1.1   Perfumery on Park Balance Sheet

Perfumery on Park
Balance Sheet, July 4, 1984

Cash	$ 1,595	Accounts Payable	$ 11,247
Inventory	50,939	Current Maturing Long Term Debt	18,000
Total Current Assets	52,534	Total Current Liabilities	29,247
Furniture and Fixtures	10,785	Note Payable	56,051
Leasehold Improvements	1,022		
Lease Rights	35,000		
Organization Costs	454	Common Stock	100
Preoperating Costs	4,698	Additional Capital	19,095
		Total Liabilities and	
Total Assets	$104,493	Owners Equity	$104,493

The Perfume Industry

The manufacture and application of fragrances has been an occupation of mankind for thousands of years. Fragrances have been linked with medicine as well as with religious and social rituals, and the search for fragrances has been a basis for economic and cultural change throughout history. The modern perfume industry can be separated into three segments: (1) manufacture of the essential oils, (2) packaging, and (3) marketing of fragrance products. This note examines each of these segments, focusing on marketing in the United States, the major world market for fragrances.

Manufacture of Essential Oils

Raw Materials.   The raw materials of perfumery are the fragrant chemicals occurring naturally in plants and animals, or synthesized in the laboratory by chemists. In some cases, as with certain flowers and mosses, the natural fragrance is so weak that it is not detected by the human nose, so it must be concentrated. In other cases, as with animal products such as musk or ambergris, the natural fragrance becomes appealing only when it is diluted. The natural oils must be separated from other tissues, usually by distillation.

Odor properties of plants depend on several factors, including from which part of the plant the fragrant oil originates, when the plant is harvested, and where the plant is grown. Because of this lack of substitutability, the price of fragrant oils is highly dependent on economic, social, climatic, and logistical conditions in the area where the plants are grown. Since it often requires a ton of petals to manufacture one ounce of fragrant oil, the absolute price of fragrances normally is quite high, even though many countries produce the raw materials in commercial quantities.

Odor properties of animals are more dependent on the number of animals available, since some animals must be killed in order to obtain the fragrant oil. Many of the animals, such as whales and musk deer, cannot be bred commercially and have been harvested in such quantities that they have become endangered. Thus limited quantities of these animals as raw material has kept upward pressure on the absolute price of animalic fragrances.

In modern perfuming, natural materials satisfy less than half the worldwide demand for fragrance products. A major effort of perfume chemists has been to duplicate synthetically the oils occurring in nature. In many cases, the synthetic oil is so similar to the natural oil as to be undetectable by the average person. Most modern perfumes contain synthetic imitations of some oils, particularly animal oils. Synthetic versions of amber and musk have reduced the pressure on musk deer and whale populations.

Another effort of perfume chemists has been to develop original oils which do not necessarily duplicate natural odors. So many synthetics have been developed over the past five decades that a separate classification of perfumes had to be developed for them. The first commercially successful perfume to use synthetics as the basis of the fragrance was Numero Cinq (No. 5) by Chanel in 1921.

One system of classification separates perfumes into seven categories, depending on the essential oils which serve as the basis of the perfume. Those categories are: grassy, floral, aldehydic, mossy, oriental (spicy), fern, and tobacco/leather. Although distinctions are somewhat blurred, all perfumes can be classified into one of these seven categories depending on the types of oils composing the fragrance.

Creating a Fragrance.   The goal of the perfumer is to create a fragrance which not only is attractive in itself, but enhances the natural scent of the wearer. Since each person has a different natural scent, the perfume which enhances that scent will be different. By 1980 there were more than 400 fragrances available in the U.S. market, more than half of which had been created within the past 20 years.

Perfumes have three different scent characteristics. The top note is the initial scent to reach the olfactory organs. The middle note is the scent which originates after the oil has been applied to the skin and has mixed with body chemicals and body heat. The bottom note is the scent which remains after prolonged wearing and the more-volatile oils have evaporated.

The creator of a perfume is much like a painter, except that the medium is smell rather than sight. Using a knowledge of organic chemistry, the creator selects oils from the palette and attempts to blend them into a pleasing final product. Since the human nose can recognize scents as dilute as $1/10^{(13)}$ ounce, small quantities of the oils can contribute to the final product. However, chemicals have bonding properties which differ according to other chemical ingredients and according to the medium in which the fragrance is to be carried. Mixing rose oil with musk oil, for example, may not be a pleasing combination, and a pleasing combination in perfume form may not be retained in a lotion or soap.

Another property of chemicals is that fragrant oils are volatile and evaporate quickly, so if a fragrance is to be retained for a length of time the fragrant oil must be bonded to a medium which does not evaporate as quickly. Some oils which have greater fixative power also detract from, rather than enhance, the pleasantness of the final product, making the creative process even more of an art.

Once the composition is completed, the oils are diluted in a mixture of water and ethyl alcohol; perfumes usually contain proportions of 30 percent fragrant oils, 70 percent dilutants, although that is not a rule. The manufacturing cost of a perfume thus depends almost entirely on the cost of essential oils which constitute the fragrance. Since the selection and combination of oils is the task of the creator, one constraint which can be imposed is the cost of ingredients. In this respect, the creator can be viewed as operating under constrained optimization—maximizing the quality of the final product subject to physical constraints imposed by properties of chemicals and to monetary constraints imposed by the client.

Once a fragrance is created, the creator has nothing more to do with the perfuming process. Although they may gain great renown among their peers, creators of perfume fragrances do not enjoy public acclaim. Most fragrances are developed by the few firms which specialize in the creative process. Some of the great perfumes of history were developed by the same individuals or firms, even though the fragrances were marketed under separate couturiers.

Packaging of Perfumes

Packaging.   Presentation is perhaps the most important aspect of marketing a perfume. The cost of packaging, including bottle and box, has the most influence on retail price of the final product. The look of the package, including bottle and box, influences the initial reaction by the consumer.

Prior to the late nineteenth century, bottles had to be manufactured individually. By the late 1800s, experiments with manufacturing wine bottles in France had created the technology for mass manufacture of small containers such as perfume bottles. At the same time, the introduction of railroads allowed lower-cost distribution of bottles, which also could be composed of more delicate materials. The result was wider availability of perfume products at lower prices, which led to greater market penetration. Francois Coty was the first to take advantage of the ability to penetrate the existing market, as well as to extend the market into the United States.

The Couturier.   Of the almost 400 fragrances available in the U.S. market in 1985, only a small fraction were sold under the name of a firm specializing in manufacture and distribution of perfumes. Firms such as Guerlain, Molinard, and Caron were established for the purpose of creating and marketing fragrances. Other firms, such as Hermes, were in fields complementary to fragrance production. (Hermes started in leather goods and originally created fragrances which would disguise the smell of uric acid used in the tanning process.) The majority of today's fragrances are marketed under the names of fashion designers, a trend that began at the turn of the century.

Couturiers began selling fragrances as accessories to their fashions, and the two have become closely linked. Over time, the mass marketing of fragrances became a separate industry, but the link of fragrances to designers persists today. Most designers market at least one fragrance under their name, and many have several fragrances. Firms such as Chanel, Jean Patou, and Worth evolved because designers created fragrances to accompany their fashion lines.

Products.   The final result of all these factors is a bottle of perfume which sells usually in multiples of ¼ ounce. Because packaging is the largest component of production cost, the consumer price depends largely on the cost of packaging. Economies can be achieved in larger sizes, so that one ounce is not priced at four times the ¼-ounce price (unless the container is specially created). In 1985 prices, most ¼-ounce perfumes are priced in the neighborhood of $40.

American consumers have not always used perfumes in their more-concentrated forms, either because of price or because of preference for less-concentrated products. Diluted forms of fragrances are available as eaux de toilette, containing approximately 15-percent fragrant oils. Because they are less concentrated, their price points are lower, but they require more frequent and liberal application. The fragrance of the perfume is not exactly duplicated in eaux de toilette, since chemical properties change with dilution.

The range of products containing fragrance has broadened beyond perfumes and eaux de toilette. Soaps, lotions, creams, powders, gels, and bath oils have been added as bath lines to complement fragrances. They also allow "layering," the process suggested by perfumers as a means of maintaining a fragrance on the body for extended periods.

Marketing of Fragrances

Industry Structure.   Although there are numerous manufacturers of fragrance products in the United States, France remains the locus of the perfume industry. To market their products, French firms maintain subsidiaries or agents in the U.S. Control of marketing channels and programs is more effective with subsidiaries. Sometimes, marketing efforts of U.S. agents may not be commensurate with the goals of the French parent firm; there have been cases where products were withdrawn from the U.S. market because of these differences. More typically, the French parent firm finds another agent for the U.S. market or establishes a subsidiary.

Most representatives are located in Manhattan, but most products are distributed through a large warehouse in New Jersey. The fragrance itself can be mixed and bottled in France and shipped to the U.S. in that form; alternatively, the fragrant oil is shipped to the U.S., then mixed with U.S. water and ethyl alcohol. The latter method is less expensive because it avoids import duties on ethyl alcohol, but it creates subtle differences in fragrance because the alcohol and water differ in each country.

Products are distributed directly to department stores, the main channel of sales for fragrance products in the United States. More than 98 percent of total sales of fragrance products take place through department stores. Many manufacturers restrict their U.S. distribution to department stores, to the exclusion of discount stores, boutiques, and drugstores. Outlets which are not able to purchase products directly sometimes are able to obtain products by purchasing through diverters, who act as unauthorized wholesalers. Manufacturers believe they can maintain quality better by controlling distribution channels and restricting price competition.

Competition.   Price competition does not occur frequently in the perfume industry. Discount stores, which usually deal in diverted goods, offer reduced prices on selected items, but they generally are able to obtain only portions of a fragrance line. Department stores reduce prices only when they have excess inventories or are closing out a line. Most French manufacturers are so conscious of their quality image that they will not sell to retailers who discount the price.

Nonprice competition occurs more often, usually in the form of gift-with-purchase, purchase-with-purchase, or special sizes of products. GWPs and PWPs can be unrelated to the fragrance (umbrellas, briefcases, purses), but the trend in recent years has been toward products related to the fragrance (eau de toilette, bath gel, powder) in smaller sizes of the fragrance itself. These products are made available to department stores but are not always made available to nondepartment stores, resulting in a competitive advantage. Even when they are made available to nondepartment stores, their availability must be conveyed to the public, imposing large costs for advertising.

Competition also takes the form of testing and sampling. Manufacturers sell direct-supply retailers with samples of the fragrance and with testers for showing the fragrance. Both items allow the consumer to determine whether the product forms a pleasing fragrance when worn. These items normally are not available through diverters.

Advertising.   Fragrance manufacturers have used traditional advertising outlets for several years. National campaigns have emphasized television and magazines, while local campaigns have emphasized newspapers. Manufacturers typically share the cost of a local ad with the retailer. In a national ad the manufacturer will "tag" one or a few stores which carry its fragrance. The amount, type, and financing of an advertising campaign is negotiable and can be a big influence on a national launch.

Introductions which are new to the United States market usually are sold only at selected outlets for a period of time. The larger New York department stores, such as Bloomingdale's or Saks, often are the first major outlet. The product then is distributed nationally through selected outlets, with one door in a market given an exclusive for a period of time. After the introduction period, the product is made available to other retailers.

The introduction process creates a competitive advantage for stores carrying the product on an exclusive basis. Not only are they monopolists in the sale of the product in that market, but they also benefit from advertising by the manufacturer, since the store is tagged in any ads.

A major technological innovation has led to an entirely new form of advertising of fragrances over the past decade. Advertising in print or video media always has stressed the image of a fragrance, but the fragrance itself could not be advertised. It was necessary for a consumer to visit the retailer to test a fragrance. Efforts at making the fragrance available in an ad were not initially successful because of the volatility of the chemicals. The fragrance often was gone before the magazine was in the hands of the consumer.

Recent work with polymer chemistry has led to microencapsulation, where the fragrance is captured and retained in small capsules. A strip of the capsules is glued to a printed card which is inserted into a magazine. When the consumer wants to sample the fragrance, the scent strip is scratched, breaking open the capsules and releasing the fragrance. The fragrance can be applied to the body, allowing the consumer to perform the same test that would occur at a retailer. The manufacturer, in effect, has gotten the fragrance into the nose of the consumer.

Marketing Perfumery on Park

Market Niche

A primary consideration for Anna was whether a market existed for a perfume boutique. There was no question that Central Florida was growing, or that Winter Park was an affluent community with a relatively sophisticated clientele for perfumes. The real issues were whether a niche existed for a small boutique and whether the boutique could compete successfully against department stores, the main sales channel for fragrances.

To answer this question Anna did background research on the perfume industry and on the market in Central Florida. She found that there were almost 400 fragrances on the market as of 1984 and that consumers tended to be brand loyal—once an individual had found a fragrance, there developed inertia about changing fragrances. Since each department store carried perhaps 15–20 fragrances and those fragrances tended to be in fashion at the time, it seemed that there existed a market for a shop which specialized in traditional and hard-to-find fragrances.

Another competitive advantage available to a boutique was personal service. Many people preferred sales personnel who knew histories and ingredients of fragrances, who could fulfill a customer's preferences, and whose shop was dedicated strictly to fragrances and related articles of toilette. These criteria were especially relevant to Winter Park, which had a large percentage of retired professionals.

In her discussions with the owner of the previous perfume shop on Park Avenue, Anna's suspicions were confirmed—once a reputation had been established for personal service and availability of traditional and hard-to-find fragrances, a steady flow of clients could be maintained. Results of the first six months further confirmed the idea. Perfumery on Park's sales volume of several prestige products exceeded that of any other individual store in the area, including department stores.

Products and Pricing

Since there is little price competition in the perfume industry, pricing was not a major consideration in the decision to open the shop. Anna did believe there could be an advantage in building on the quality image promulgated by most perfumers. By emphasizing fragrances of high quality and consequently higher price, Anna's perfumery would further differentiate itself from department stores.

Most perfume manufacturers in recent years had expanded product varieties beyond perfumes and eaux de toilette. Items such as lotion, cream, dusting powder, soap, and bath oil were means of carrying fragrances. It was decided to carry complete lines where they were available. Since it would not be practical to carry all products and all sizes in each line, it would be necessary to order products for customers who desired an item that was not on hand. This was viewed as an advantage rather than a disadvantage because it further enhanced the image of service to customers.

Shortly after opening, it became apparent that Anna had seriously underestimated one aspect of pricing—gifts with purchase. Many perfumers offered gifts, such as handbags, wallets, or smaller sizes of fragrance products, as inducements to purchase their fragrance. Since these reduced the effective price of a product, they could be an important marketing tool. After several attempts at obtaining these items, Anna discovered that they usually were made available only to department stores. Even if Anna could obtain them, it would be necessary to communicate their availability to the public, and that entailed an advertising campaign. One factor in favor of expansion was to increase the bargaining position of Perfumery on Park with regard to obtaining these special promotions.

Anna had been aware all along of a problem concerning product availability. Since department stores accounted for such a large portion of fragrance sales, some manufacturers distributed only through department stores. Anna was precluded from obtaining some fragrances unless she purchased them from diverters. However, it was decided that the store's policy would be to purchase only those items which were available directly from the manufacturer. This dilemma became painfully apparent with the national introduction of Giorgio in fall 1984. It quickly became the most successful introduction in perfuming history, but was available locally only through one department store, which had acquired exclusive rights to Giorgio.

A final product consideration was whether to carry cosmetics. Anna decided that although they were indirectly related to perfumes, she did not possess expertise sufficient to sell cosmetics successfully. Moreover, she wanted the image of Perfumery on Park to reflect only perfumes and closely related articles of toilette.

Advertising

Sales prior to January 1985 had been passive—they depended on reputation, word-of-mouth, and walk-by traffic. No advertising had been done in any media. Although it was encouraging to think that $50,000 in sales was achieved without advertising, it was obvious that higher levels of sales would require greater exposure to the Central Florida community. For that reason, Anna began planning her marketing campaign for the coming year.

Advertising would occur through six channels. First, newspaper ads would feature products available almost exclusively at Perfumery on Park. Anna began contacting representatives of perfume manufacturers concerning availability of funds for local advertising, since many manufacturers would co-op on local ads. Second, ads would be placed in magazines prior to special occasions such as Christmas, Mother's Day, and Valentine's Day. Magazine ads were especially effective when they contained scent strips, which allowed someone to smell a fragrance by peeling back a scented piece of paper.

A third method would be to use scent strips in special mailings. Anna already had acquired a large list of visitors who filled out cards listing their fragrance preferences. A relatively new advertising technique had been suggested as the fourth method—video terminals. Many hotels in Central Florida had begun installing computer terminals containing advertising and other information. If terminals were installed in appropriate hotels, Anna considered using video terminals as a means of attracting tourists to the shop.

The two remaining advertising methods involved gifts of the actual product. The most effective means of selling a product once consumers know about the shop is to invite clients for a presentation by the sales representative. At these presentations the client is shown how to apply the fragrance and is provided with a sample. Samples also could be given to selected target audiences such as women's clubs, charitable boards, or service organizations.

Financing Perfumery on Park

Initial Financial Structure

When the idea of opening a perfumery first occurred to Anna, she met informally with a banker to discuss the bank's interest in lending to such a business. Her efforts encountered quick rejection, as the banker said that the bank would not normally make a significant loan to a new business such as the perfumery Anna was suggesting.

As her ideas took shape, however, Anna and David prepared a business plan (Appendix 1A) to help organize their thoughts and to offer to a prospective lender. The next time they approached the bank with a definite proposal about the amount of the loan and possible sources of collateral, the bank responded positively. In fact, several banks approached them soliciting the perfumery's business.

The Curries decided they would commit most of their financial reserves to the perfumery, including drawing down cash invested in a money market account and selling securities. In their initial proposal to the bank they offered inventory of the perfumery as collateral, but the bank was adamant about requiring the inventory plus a second mortgage on the Currie's residence as collateral.

The major cash flow other than purchases of inventory was to buy out the existing leaseholder. A very desirable location for the perfumery was offered by First One In Ltd., a tennis shop. Both owners were tennis professionals who would rather tour than be tied to a retail business. Three years remained on their very favorable lease. Under terms of the agreement, the Curries would purchase the existing lease for $35,000. Although this was higher than prices for spaces which recently had been on the market, the per-square-foot rent was at a more-favorable rate. An accountant told David that the lease could be amortized over the remaining term of the lease, implying a significant tax effect from owning the perfumery.

Armed with the business plan and potential location for the shop, Anna and David negotiated a loan of $155,000 from a local bank. The president of the bank offered them a choice between a fixed rate loan at 2 percent over the then-current prime rate of 14.5 percent or a variable rate loan at 1 percent over prime. In either case, the loan would be secured by inventory and by a second mortgage on their house. The loan would have a 15-year term but would have a balloon payment due after 5 years. (That is, the loan would be amortized as it was to be repaid over 15 years. After 5 years the loan would be paid off by negotiating a new loan.) Interest would be charged only on the amount borrowed and principal could be prepaid without penalty. Since there already was a second mortgage on their house, approximately $30,000 of the new loan would be used to retire the existing second mortgage.

Normal credit terms in the industry were net 30 days. Since the perfumery was new and had no established credit record, several firms insisted on prepayment or COD on initial orders, but credit would be available on future orders. Anna and David established the policy of paying all invoices on the last day due, taking discounts where offered. For planning purposes, David assumed that purchases would be on the books for 30 days.

Form of Organization

Several organizational forms were available, but an early decision was made to incorporate because it offered limited liability. The remaining question was whether to use Subchapter S, under which income from the perfumery would be taxed at personal income rates rather than corporate rates. Because of losses expected over the first few years, Subchapter S would allow more of the losses to flow through to their personal tax liability; the Curries chose Subchapter S as the initial form of organization. The question still remained whether that form would be appropriate for future expansion.

Financial Forecasts and Actual Results

Forecasts for the first year of operation are contained in the Business Plan (Appendix 1.A). The significant question was, what level of sales could be expected during the first year? Anna was not able to locate statistics just for perfume boutiques, but she did find

Exhibit 1.2   Perfumery on Park

Month	Projected Sales	Actual Sales
July	$ 7,500	$ 4,565
August	7,500	5,360
September	7,500	6,940
October	7,500	5,805
November	50,000	8,855
December	50,000	24,420
Total	$130,000	$55,945

Projected and Actual Sales, July 1, 1984–December 31, 1984

statistics for retail specialty shops, which included perfumeries. This research indicated that the typical specialty shop realized sales of $350,000 per year. Since the perfumery was new, it was not expected to achieve that level in the first year. Instead, a sales level of $200,000 was assumed.

Several sales representatives had told Anna that half of the year's sales would occur during the holiday season from Thanksgiving to Christmas. Other peak retail periods in perfuming were during February (Valentine's Day) and May (Mother's Day). Despite its recent growth, Central Florida still was a winter resort, which would make peaks and troughs even more drastic.

Results of the first six months of operation, although encouraging, did not meet projections (see Exhibit 1.2). The Christmas retail season was not outstanding nationally and especially in Florida. In fragrances, the introduction of Giorgio had adversely affected sales of other fragrance lines as it captured a significant position in the market. Anna wondered if she should be encouraged at achieving sales of $60,000 in the midst of a poor sales season. Perfumery on Park had sold more of the higher-priced fragrances than some department stores, and several sales representatives were pleasantly surprised at the sales volumes in their lines, expressing encouragement to Anna.

Financial Implications of Growth

Any attempt at growth would hold increased financial dangers for the Curries. The growth options which would lessen the financial impact were not always available or desirable, and the options which were available had severe financial implications. Someone had mentioned the idea of franchising. Upon investigation, David found that franchising required registration with the state of Florida and submission to its regulations regarding franchises. Essentially, franchising implied that the franchisor had something valuable which the franchisee was willing to purchase; David was not sure what they had to sell a franchise, nor what value to attribute to a franchise. The financial advantage to franchising was that no more of the Curries' funds would be committed to expansion. Instead, they would receive a franchise fee and a portion of any franchisee's sales.

Other alternatives were more practical but involved additional financial commitment by the Curries. Whether they owned the new stores outright or entered into partnership agreements, they would have to provide additional financial support. Not only were they cautious about risk exposure, they also wondered to what extent the bank would continue to support their endeavors.

Operations

Management Control Systems

Both Anna and David entered the perfume business with no retail experience. However, they both had a good feel for the issues involved in management control. As Director of Personnel, Anna had gained a solid reputation for not letting things "slip between cracks" by installing good monitoring procedures in her office. She had a good feel for the checks and controls necessary for a smoothly functioning work environment. Even if these controls were not mandatory for a small retail operation, they would be necessary if the decision was made to expand. One of her inventions was a stock control book which incorporated and expanded upon the books furnished by each fragrance company. Several sales reps were impressed at her innovation.

What Anna lacked was experience in finance, and David had that. Not only did David teach finance, he practiced it as well—in a previous position he had supervised a $50 million budget. He also knew computer applications in business, which would help the firm minimize the amount of time devoted to recordkeeping and free time for planning and analysis.

David knew of several software programs designed to help small businesses maintain a general ledger and subsidiary ledgers such as payroll, accounts receivable and payable, cash, and inventory. Once these programs were purchased and installed, bookkeeping would become fairly routine. Cash registers were available which tied into a computerized inventory system. As an item was sold and recorded by the register, it was immediately deducted from inventory and the proper entries were made into sales, cost of sales, and any ancillary accounts. Since an antique register fit the decor of the shop, however, the Curries decided not to install the computerized register. Because the prices of computer hardware had been decreasing lately, David postponed a computer purchase; as of January 1985, all recordkeeping was done manually.

Inventory Control

A good example of the need for controls was in inventory management. Since gross profit margins were the same for all stores, net income depended on sales volume and on controlling expenses. A major expense was inventory carrying costs. Since it had been decided to carry complete lines of products, each decision on a fragrance implied a significant investment in inventory. The only ways to hold carrying costs down were to carry fewer fragrances or to carry fewer duplicate items of each product.

One thing Anna learned early on was that academic formulas for economic-order quantities and reorder points had little bearing on her business. Some items went for weeks on the shelves with no activity, then would be sold in a few days. Once stockouts occurred they had to be renewed or customers would look elsewhere for the fragrance.

Placing Christmas orders was especially difficult. Anna preferred a bias toward too much of an item—it was better to have an ounce of perfume than not to have it when a customer requested it. The difficulty was in predicting how much of an item was enough. Christmas orders had to be entered during October, but the shop had been in operation for slightly more than three months by that time. There wasn't much experience to base an order on, so inventories for the busiest period of the year were based strictly on educated guesses.

Exhibit 1.3   Perfumery on Park, Inc.: Income Statement and Balance Sheet

Perfumery on Park, Inc.
Income Statement
6 Months Ended
December 31, 1984

Sales	$55,944
Cost of Sales	31,463
Gross Profit	24,481
Operating Expenses[a]	29,974
Net Operating Income	(5,493)
Interest Expense	9,391
Transfer to Retained Earnings	(14,884)

Perfumery on Park, Inc.
Balance Sheet
December 31, 1984

Assets		Liabilities & Equity	
Cash	$ 12,819	Accounts Payable	$ 3,233
Inventory	64,229	Miscellaneous	21
Miscellaneous	1,310	Total Current Liabilities	3,254
Total Current Assets	78,358	Notes Payable	106,217
Net Fixed Assets	8,634	Equity:	
Lean Rights	29,000	Capital Stock	100
Organization Costs	754	Paid-in Capital	122,278
Miscellaneous	219	Retained Earnings	(14,884)
Total Assets	$116,965	Total Equity	7,494
		Total Liabilities & Equity	$116,965

[a] Includes depreciation of ˟6,200
   amortization of 6,000

Sales during the Christmas season confirmed the problem of inventory management. Stockouts occurred in some items, particularly the prestigious lines, while other lines remained on the shelves. It also was obvious that delivery had been scheduled too early. Anticipating a substantial sales upswing following Thanksgiving, deliveries had been scheduled for late November and early December. It was a mistake. Deliveries could have occurred during December without having an adverse effect on sales, since most sales occurred the two weeks prior to Christmas. (Exhibit 1.3 provides detailed financial results for the 6 months ending December 31, 1984.)

One problem David decided to focus on after Christmas was determining optimal order sizes. Some firms prepaid freight on invoices above a certain amount, which could save as much as 1 percent of the wholesale cost on some items.

Control Systems and Growth

Anna knew that whatever problems were encountered with one shop would be magnified if the business expanded. Monitoring and control procedures would need to be established for sales, costs, cash, personnel, and inventory. Anna and David would have to give a great deal of thought to what control systems were required and how they would be set up. By January 1985, these problems were just becoming obvious.

Personnel

Personnel was not a significant issue in the existing shop. David's aunt worked daily. She was retired, experienced in operating a business, and did not want to be paid because of the tax implications. Anna's duties at the college decreased to the point that she worked half-time in the shop, and David filled in occasionally. Christmas season turned out to be a family affair, with children, parents, and grandparents performing specialized tasks.

Personnel would become an issue if a decision was made to expand. Neither Anna nor David could work at a new shop, so it would be necessary to hire new people. Anna was worried about finding qualified people to manage and work in the new shop, and about structuring incentives so they would maintain the quality image while still selling the product. Anna also had a personal conflict in that she had just left a job in personnel management and wasn't sure she wanted to get back into it; after all, one of the main reasons she opened the shop was to gain independence from those problems.

Growth Prospects

Locations

Several locations were available for expansion. Locally, the Altamonte Mall was one of the largest and busiest in Florida. A location in the hub of Altamonte Mall would be expensive, but could lead to a high volume of business. Two other malls were under construction south of Orlando—Florida Mall and the Galleria. Both had approached Anna about leasing space, which would probably be less expensive than in Altamonte Mall. (See Exhibit 1.4.)

One advantage to expanding within the Orlando area would be economies of scale. Newspaper advertising was particularly expensive. If two or more stores could be mentioned in the same ad, there would be an economy. Expanding into a different city meant two separate ads would have to run. Another economy could be gained in inventory, since safety stocks would not be duplicated for each store. A new store also would not have to carry all the fragrance lines of the parent store.

Three areas away from Orlando also offered potential locations. The Tampa/St. Petersburg area was a larger metropolitan area than Orlando/Winter Park. At present, there

---

Exhibit 1.4 Perfumery on Park

Rental price (estimated)	$22.00
Property tax (actual)	1.50
Merchant fee (actual)	1.00
Common area fee (actual)	2.50
Total	$27.00

Data Relevant to Mall Location (all data on per-square-foot basis)

was one perfume kiosk in a mall and one perfume boutique in a suburb of Tampa. Many of Perfumery on Park's customers were Tampa residents who had come to Winter Park to shop. However, Tampa was not a wealthy area and the clientele would not be as sophisticated as the clientele in Winter Park. Several sales reps had cautioned Anna to look closely before going into the Tampa market. The advantage to Tampa was the large population base. If an appropriate location could be found, a boutique could gain a great deal of exposure.

Another potential location was in Naples, a resort community on the southwest Florida coast. A small perfume boutique already was there, but the owner was anxious to sell. Naples was a wealthy community but was very seasonal. Most of a firm's yearly sales would occur from November through April. A shop could close during the summer months, as had been the custom in most Florida resort communities until recently.

The third alternative was potentially the most promising, and also the greatest risk. West Palm Beach was one of the wealthiest and most sophisticated markets in Florida. West Palm Beach's busiest mall did not have a perfumery, even though several sales reps reported that a department store's perfume counter in West Palm Beach was the busiest of all its stores throughout the state. A boutique in Palm Beach Mall would stand a high probability of success. The danger was competition from other perfume boutiques. Two boutique chains were expanding northward from the Miami area. Each chain already had 5–10 stores; one store had recently opened at a mall only 20 miles south of Palm Beach Mall. Neither chain was afraid of competition—in some malls they competed directly against each other.

Strategic Considerations

A major trend in the perfume business in Florida was formation of boutiques. Although Perfumery on Park was the first in Central Florida, two others preceded it in South Florida. Each of those boutiques had expanded into other locations, so it appeared there was a market in Florida for perfume boutiques.

In the long run, many of those boutiques would merge. Anna wondered where she wanted her firm to be when this consolidation took place. Would it suffice to stay a small boutique and be content with the more-relaxed lifestyle of a small retailer? Would it be better to be a larger fish in a different pond by expanding throughout Central Florida, leaving the lucrative South Florida market to the chains which already had a foothold? If consolidation took place, did Anna want to be in a position to purchase or sell? She had no answers to these questions, but she knew she would have to address them.

CASE APPENDIX 1A
Business Plan

Business

The business will be a quality perfume shop, selling only upper-middle and high-priced items.

Competition

No other perfume shops exist in Winter Park. One shop is at Walt Disney World, but it has only a limited variety of perfumes. Because we will specialize in high-priced items, the only stores which are potentially competitive are department and specialty stores; even these carry only a limited variety. There will be no direct competition from discount stores because they do not carry expensive lines. Perfume is as close to being a fair-trade item as any on the market because manufacturers refuse to sell to retailers who discount the price.

There was a perfume shop in Winter Park approximately a decade ago, but the manager decided to change to a dress shop. She reported that the perfume shop was successful but she wanted to enter a different line of business. One distributor with whom we discussed the opportunity said that there was a potential competitor considering entering Winter Park; if we can be the first into the market, it should preclude that competition.

Market

The target market is natives and tourists of medium- to upper-income levels. Winter Park is ideal in both these respects. There are similar shops in most resort communities in Florida; the shop on North Avenue, Palm Beach, is especially successful.

The Product

The product sold will be quality perfume in assorted sizes. In addition to carrying lines of famous manufacturers, we plan to develop a fragrance specifically for Winter Park and a fragrance attractive to young people.

Perfume has a long shelf life (more than two years when unopened). If it becomes necessary to liquidate inventory, it can be sold to other retailers, to the manufacturer, or to wholesalers (known in the trade as diverters).

We plan to carry approximately 70 lines from 30 manufacturers. The minimum suggested inventory level is $100,000. A level below that would not provide the variety necessary for a successful shop.

Customer Relations

Advertising will be directed to magazines catering to the upper-income clientele; examples are the *Florida Symphony* magazine, *Central Florida Scene*, and *Central Florida Magazine* from public television. Prior to opening we will make individual mailings to the

Towers and to selected Winter Park residents, announcing the opening and inquiring whether they have a specific fragrance they would like to purchase. We also will keep a roster of names and fragrances so gifts can be purchased for a specific customer.

Volume

We are budgeting for sales of $200,000 during the first full year of operation. This compares favorably with statistics of franchised operations, which report yearly sales in excess of $300,000. Industry studies have shown that the average sale is $40 to $50 per customer per visit. This would require 5,000 purchases during the year; given the shop's location and the tourist traffic along Park Avenue, this figure does not seem unreasonable.

Location

The location is a prime Park Avenue location. The shop space of 400 square feet is located directly on Park Avenue, not in one of the arcades. It is located between Morse Boulevard and New England Avenue, the most exposed section of Park Avenue.

Labor

The shop will be owned by Anna and David Currie, who will work at the shop on weekends and at various times during the week. The primary labor force will be David Currie's mother, Mary Currie, and aunt, Caroline Powers. Both are recently retired and anxious to remain active. Both are responsible adults who refuse to work for wages due to tax considerations.

Anna, Mary, and Caroline all have retailing experience. David has significant financial management experience, while Anna has significant personnel and administrative experience. Both Anna and David will retain their present positions at Rollins College, providing a financial cushion during the early period of the shop's operation.

Finances

Equity for the shop will be provided by David and Anna Currie, who will be sole owners. Based on the projected financial statements (Exhibits 1.5 and 1.6), we request two types of bank financing.

1. Term loan to finance inventory. Inventory will be maintained at a constant $100,000; inventory reductions due to sales will be replaced by new orders.

2. Line of credit to finance fluctuations in working capital. Because of the seasonal nature of the business, cash flows occur during specific months of the year. Other months create a deficit cash position, so a line of credit is requested as a draw during those months. The line will be replenished during high-volume months. The months of expected higher volume are: November and December (Christmas), February (Valentine's Day), March (Sidewalk Art Festival), May (Mother's Day).

Exhibit 1.5 Perfumery on Park Proforma Income Statement

	June	July	Aug.	Sept.	Oct.	Nov.	Dec.	Jan.	Feb.	Mar.	Apr.	May	Total
Sales	$7,500	$7,500	$7,500	$7,500	$7,500	$50,000	$50,000	$7,500	$20,000	$7,500	$7,500	$20,000	$200,000
Cost of sales	4,500	4,500	4,500	4,500	4,500	30,000	30,000	4,500	12,000	4,500	4,500	12,000	120,000
Gross profit	3,000	3,000	3,000	3,000	3,000	20,000	20,000	3,000	8,000	3,000	3,000	8,000	$ 80,000
Rent	400	400	400	400	400	400	400	400	400	400	400	400	4,800
Utilities	300	300	300	300	300	300	300	300	300	300	300	300	3,600
Wages	2,000	2,000	2,000	2,000	2,000	2,000	2,000	2,000	2,000	2,000	2,000	2,000	24,000
Advertising	200	200	200	200	200	200	200	200	200	200	200	200	2,400
Insurance	250	—	—	—	—	—	250	—	—	—	—	—	500
Depreciation	250	250	250	250	250	250	250	250	250	250	250	250	3,000
Amortization	292	292	292	292	292	292	292	292	292	292	292	292	3,504
Total expenses	3,692	3,442	3,442	3,442	3,442	3,442	3,692	3,442	3,442	3,442	3,442	3,442	$41,804
Operating income	−692	−442	−442	−442	−442	16,558	$16,308	−442	4,558	−442	−442	4,558	38,196
Interest	1,300	1,300	1,300	1,300	1,300	1,300	1,300	1,300	1,300	1,300	1,300	1,300	15,600
Taxable income	−1,992	−1,742	−1,742	−1,742	−1,742	15,258	15,008	−1,742	3,258	−1,742	−1,742	3,258	22,596
Taxes	−598	−523	−523	−523	−523	4,577	4,502	−523	977	−523	−523	977	6,774
Net income	−1,394	−1,219	−1,219	−1,219	−1,219	10,681	10,506	−1,219	2,281	−1,219	−1,219	2,281	$15,822

Exhibit 1.6 Perfumery on Park Proforma Balance Sheet

	June	July	Aug.	Sept.	Oct.	Nov.	Dec.	Jan.	Feb.	Mar.	Apr.	May	Total
Cash	500	500	500	500	500	500	500	500	500	500	500	500	
Inventory	100,000	100,000	100,000	100,000	100,000	100,000	100,000	100,000	100,000	100,000	100,000	100,000	
Fixtures	14,750	14,500	14,250	14,000	13,750	13,500	13,250	13,000	12,750	12,500	12,250	12,000	
Goodwill	34,708	34,416	34,124	33,832	33,540	33,248	32,956	32,664	32,372	32,080	31,788	31,496	
Total assets	149,958	149,416	148,874	148,332	147,790	147,248	146,706	146,164	145,622	145,080	144,538	143,996	
Accounts payable	10,000	4,500	4,500	4,500	4,500	4,500	30,000	30,000	4,500	12,000	4,500	4,500	
Bank loan	100,000	100,000	100,000	100,000	100,000	100,000	100,000	100,000	100,000	100,000	100,000	100,000	
Equity	39,106	37,886	36,667	35,447	34,228	44,909	55,414	54,195	56,475	55,256	54,037	56,317	
Total liability	149,106	142,386	141,167	139,947	138,728	149,409	185,414	184,195	160,975	167,256	158,537	160,817	
Excess (need)	-852	-7,030	-7,707	-8,385	-9,062	2,161	38,708	38,031	15,353	22,176	13,999	16,821	
Cash flow	-852	-677	-677	-677	-677	11,223	11,048	-677	2,823	-677	-677	2,823	$22,326

The assumptions underlying the projected financial statements in Exhibits 1.5 and 1.6 are:

1. **Sales.** Estimated at $200,000 per year, with higher volumes in months indicated above.

2. **Gross profit.** Estimated at 40 percent of sales, the industry standard.

3. **Wages.** Estimated at $24,000 per year; because the shop will be staffed initially by family, the wages category is an upper estimate. It was included to provide a more realistic picture of the shop's cost of operation.

4. **Depreciation.** Depreciation of fixtures of $15,000 on straight-line basis over five years.

5. **Amortization.** Amortization of goodwill of $35,000 on straight-line basis over ten-year period; goodwill arose from payment to the current leaseholder for purchase of her lease.

6. **Interest.** Interest on $100,000 at 16 percent yearly.

7. **Taxes.** Tax rate on 30 percent of taxable income.

8. **Inventory.** Maintained at $100,000; stock reductions due to sales are replaced by new orders.

9. **Accounts payable.** Equal to previous month's purchases.

10. **Equity.** Initial equity of $40,500.

11. **Excess (need).** Shows monthly fluctuations in working capital. Early months of operation will require additional infusions of funds, which will be repaid from later operation in higher-volume months.

12. **Cash flow.** Net Income + Depreciation + Amortization = Net Cash Flow. Provides a more accurate picture of cash changes in the firm. The cash flow of $22,321 for the year can be used to repay principal on the term loan of $100,000.

Creative Dance Ensemble

- *Carla Litvany* -

On Thursday, November 5, 1981, a quorum of 10 board members of the Creative Dance Ensemble (CDE) voted unanimously not to dissolve the dance company despite incredible odds against success. By 5:00 p.m. on Friday the company had to raise $14,000 to pay a visiting dance company and the salaries of all employees on contract. If successful, the company then had to raise a minimum of $75,000 by January 31, 1982, to erase most of the current deficit.

The company met the immediate crisis by securing an emergency grant of $10,000 from the Sarah James Foundation, given under the condition that no future funds would be available to the company until it eliminated its deficit. Another $4,000 was raised by contributions from three board members. It was now up to the board members to plan for the ultimate survival and future viability of the company.

History

The Creative Dance Ensemble grew out of the Clark's School of Dance in Colorado Springs. It was founded by Ted and Laura Clark and Ted's sister, Sharon Geiger.

While Laura was only interested in teaching dance, Ted and Sharon wanted to choreograph works for performance. In 1975 all three became the founding directors of the newly incorporated nonprofit organization, the Creative Dance Ensemble.

During the next four years, the company performed locally, building audiences and developing dancers. An amateur company, most dancers came from Clark's School of Dance and most of the board was comprised of their parents.

During this time, Ted and Sharon choreographed several pieces and experimented with new methods of expression. Two filmed dances were choreographed by Ted and shown on local public TV. One of these, *Mountain Dance*, was shown twice nationally on PBS.

In 1978, Sharon produced the ballet, *Cinderella*, which performed locally for a week to sellout crowds. This was the culmination of all their efforts of the past three years. Sharon and Ted felt that the enthusiasm of the audiences demonstrated a strong need for Colorado Springs to have its own professional dance company. The Creative Dance Ensemble was in a perfect position to fill this need.

Converting CDE into a professional dance company required an all-out effort. First they hired a business manager. Because of their limited budget, they could not afford to hire a professional, so they hired former actor Jerry Langley. For their first season (1979–1980) they hired six professional dancers (former students) and organized two other unpaid companies of younger dancers. To meet their objectives, they would present an annual subscription series of four productions. Each year they would include at least one well-known guest ballet company in the series, exposing Colorado Springs audiences

---

*A disguised case. All names and locations have been changed. This case does not indicate effective or ineffective handling of an administrative situation. Rather, it is to be used for class discussion purposes. Reprinted with the permission of Carla Litvany.

to the many different styles of dance. To accommodate these companies and the full-scale ballets envisioned by Ted and Sharon, they decided to run the series in the 2,500-seat City Performing Arts Center. (See Exhibits 2.1 and 2.2.)

They did not consider the first season a success. The company performed in three productions. One was to feature two well-known dancers of the Oakland Ballet, Sally Michaels and John Toole, but they cancelled at the last minute and had to be replaced by company dancers. The Cleveland Ballet was the one guest company for this series and received rave reviews. At the same time, arrangements were made with the Laredo County School System for 52 paid lecture/demonstrations.

During this year, program expenses jumped over 200 percent and total income doubled, leaving a deficit of over $20,000. (See Exhibit 2.2.) Other problems in administrative management led Jerry Langley to resign. Ellen Leland, a highly qualified nine-year veteran of a dance company and an arts council member, replaced him.

She encountered an exceptionally difficult situation. Jerry had left an inflated budget for the next fiscal year (FYE 1981) and had made commitments for the company that would be difficult to meet; the office records were poorly organized; and the company's credit record was very bad. Ellen set about correcting these problems, but others kept mounting.

Although the contract for the dancers had been reduced from 40 weeks to 36, the number of paid dancers had been increased by seven. This meant much higher production costs compared to the previous year. The season was to include three CDE productions plus one by the Houston Ballet. For the first fall performance, only one-quarter of the auditorium was filled for both presentations of the mixed repertory; the losses were high.

Exhibit 2.1   Creative Dance Ensemble—Company and Performances

	Projected FYE 1982	FYE 1981	FYE 1980	FYE 1979	FYE 1978	FYE 1977
Dancers' contract						
Total weeks	22	36	40	—	—	—
Dancers						
Paid	14	13	6	—	—	—
Unpaid	—	15	15	32	27	30
Apprentices	14	20	17	—	—	—
Youth company	18	—	—	—	—	—
Performances						
Subscription	1	6	6	—	—	—
Lecture/demonstration	4	11	52	25	11	14
Other performances	28	17	13	24	19	8
National/state	5	—	1	1	1	1
Television, local[a]	1	1	1	—	1	—
Television, national[a]	—	1	—	—	1	—
Total	39	36	73	50	33	23
Total audiences[a]	40,000	38,000	67,756	27,925	22,000	9,850

[a]TV audiences are not included in total audience figures.

Exhibit 2.2   Creative Dance Ensemble—Income Statement

	FYE 1981	FYE 1980	FYE 1979	FYE 1978	FYE 1977
Earned income:					
Ticket sales	$ 67,065	$ 94,164	$22,493	$ 8,710	$ 4,012
Nonseries	12,495				
Total performance	79,560	94,164	22,493	8,710	4,012
Nonperformance earned income	9,196		6,865		3,647
Total earned	88,756	94,164	29,358	8,710	7,659
Unearned income:					
Tax support	26,905	46,662	48,941	31,016	4,116
Private support	64,186	58,258	8,290	1,150	8,052
Total unearned	91,091	104,920	57,231	32,166	12,168
Total income	179,847	199,084	86,589	40,876	19,827
Expenses:					
Programs	149,213	144,493	43,181	13,097	n.a.
Fund-raising	3,887	13,647	3,071		
General administration	41,172	61,198	42,033	24,398	
Total expenses	194,272	219,338	88,285	37,495	15,226
Net surplus (deficit)	(14,425)	(20,254)	(1,696)	3,381	4,601
Earnings gap (total expenses less earned income)	105,516	125,174	58,927	28,785	7,567

Additionally, other sources of earned and unearned income were not productive. The costs of the second production, the ballet, *Coppelia*, placed the company deeper in debt. Only an all-out campaign by the directors succeeded in raising sufficient funds to perform the ballet. This campaign also promoted the production, and large audiences attended.

Financially, however, the company was in difficulty. Forced to break the contract and lay off the dancers for six weeks, the board and management tried to regroup. The available grant money was not enough to bring the dancers back after the six-week furlough. To meet the company's artistic obligations, the dancers were paid on a per performance basis for the remainder of the year. Several times the company was unable to meet its administrative payroll.

The guest production with the Houston Ballet and the final spring concert were presented. This last concert was a mixed repertory of new works choreographed by Ted and Sharon. Thrown together on a low budget and performed without adequate rehearsal, the performance was lackluster.

After the 1980–1981 season, the board voted to continue the subscription series the following year, bring in two guest companies rather than one, to tour the state to generate more revenue, and have a three-day home season in one of the smaller auditoriums in the area. It voted to increase the number of paid dancers to between 14 and 16 and add a ballet master. To accomplish these objectives, Ellen had to prepare a budget almost double the actual expenditures of the previous year. (See Exhibit 2.3.)

Exhibit 2.3   Creative Dance Ensemble—Statement of Income and Expenses as of October 31, 1981

	Actual 1980–1981	Actual 1981–1982	Budget 1981–1982	Budget (Under)Over
Income:				
Advertising	$ 6,756	$ 400	$ 8,000	$ (7,600)
United capital fund	—	—	3,250	(3,250)
Contributions:				
Corporate	10,433	7,749	50,000	(42,251)
Individual	19,904	16,987	50,000	(33,013)
Foundations:	1,500		34,000	(34,000)
Sarah James: Challenge grant	25,000	10,000	10,000	—
Media grant	—	983	6,000	(5,017)
Grants:				
Colorado State	14,580		18,000	(18,000)
Colorado State NEA	6,075		—	—
City of Colorado Springs	4,000		—	—
County cultural committee	2,250		—	—
Balance of government grants, 1980–1981	2,000	750	2,370	(1,620)
Interest	277	474	1,000	(526)
Miscellaneous	651	2,667	500	2,167
Performance fees	3,196	2,050	50,000	(47,950)
"Raise"	3,424	16,381	20,000	(3,619)
Sales, retail	935	868	3,000	(2,132)
Sales, tickets:				
Home season	—	1,406	8,000	(6,594)
Series	67,065	9,238	85,000	(75,762)
School	—	2,210	25,000	(22,790)
Special events	9,298	131	15,000	(14,869)
Total income	$ 177,344	$ 72,294	$389,120	$ 316,826
Expenses:				
Administration	14,614	11,971	33,550	(21,579)
Payroll and benefits	78,779	49,047	186,456	(137,409)
Production:	60,204			
New		244	9,000	(8,756)
Repertory		3,827	28,900	(25,073)
Promotion	3,861	4,554	24,000	(19,446)
Series	33,144	15,545	76,300	(60,755)
Travel	1,641	496	21,050	(20,554)
Contingency fund	—	—	9,864	(9,864)
Total expenses	$ 192,243	$ 85,684	$389,120	$ 303,436
Net surplus (deficit)	$ (14,899)	$(13,390)		$ 13,390

By the beginning of the second performance of the 1981–1982 season, these plans had proved unrealistic. Financially, the company was losing ground fast, which led to the November 5, 1981, board meeting.

Objectives

CDE's mission is to promote an understanding and appreciation of various forms of dance (including ballet, modern, and jazz) among central Colorado residents by creating a resident professional dance company. This company would provide a viable cultural institution offering works that were both entertaining and artistic and provide dancers the opportunity to live and work in their home state. The objectives as stated in the bylaws are "to produce programs stimulating public interest and involvement in dance, drama, theater and performing arts; to provide an opportunity for study and participation in dance, drama, theater and performing arts; to sponsor, produce and assist in the presentation of performances of all performing arts."

CDE promotes dance through various vehicles. It is one of three dance companies in Colorado to offer an annual subscription series at the City Performing Arts Center. The series normally includes four productions. Beginning in 1979, each production was performed twice, once in the evening and one matinee, the latter to accommodate children and the elderly. Two performances also gave the dancers experience in consecutive appearances. The 1981–1982 season saw a reduction to one performance per concert.

CDE also presents lecture/demonstrations, miniperformances and full concert performances to schools, festivals, civic and cultural organizations, and universities. A home season has been added for the 1981–1982 year to include a series of three mixed repertory concerts to be held in January at the Santa Fe auditorium. CDE plans to tour the state to generate more revenue and develop more audiences.

Organizational Structure

CDE's organizational structure is shown in Exhibit 2.4. Ultimate authority for the operation of the company lies with the Board of Directors. Administrative and artistic management report directly to the Executive Committee.

Board of Directors

The 1980–1981 Board of Directors was composed of an administrative board with 16 directors and an advisory board with 8 directors. Carol Blackway was president and George Conover past president. Blackway had reluctantly agreed to take this position because no one else had expressed an interest. Board meetings during 1980–1981 were held frequently (sometimes twice a month) because of the repeated crises during the year. Normally, about one-third of the directors attended each meeting. Although agendas were prepared, meetings were informal, with discussions frequently straying to other items.

The community was aware of the problems at CDE and, occasionally, an interested party would attend the meetings and offer advice. Blackway, interested in all possible help, would allow these visitors to take over the meetings even when other items were more pressing.

Exhibit 2.4   Organizational Structure of the Creative Dance Ensemble

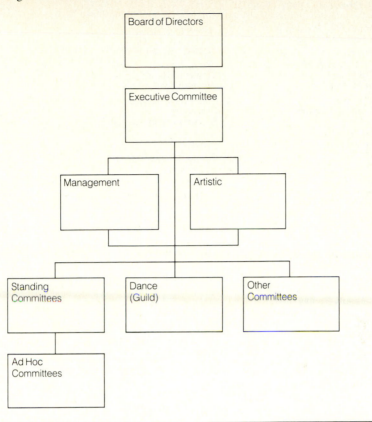

Traditionally, board meetings had no time limits and lasted two or three hours. Because the company was plagued with so many problems, key issues frequently were glossed over and little was accomplished. Further, personality conflicts led to board members acting independently on behalf of the board. The crisis often prevented either Ellen Leland or Carol Blackway from being fully prepared to discuss the topics on the agenda.

The nominating committee for the 1981–1982 Board of Directors consisted of Carol Blackway, President; Emily Briscoe, Treasurer; George Conover, Past President; and Bart Somers, Director. According to the bylaws, the new board members of the following season are to be elected at the annual board meetings in May. Since there was none in 1981, the new members (Exhibit 2.5) were elected at the first board meeting of the next season.

Mike Chamberlin, the 1981–1982 president, knew very little about dance or fundraising but enjoyed leadership.

In general, the board is responsible for setting policy for the company. The bylaws list the responsibilities and duties of the board. They were to "(a) hold meetings at such time and place as it thinks proper; (b) admit members and suspend or expel them by ballot; (c) recommend members of the company to the officers for appointment to committees on

Exhibit 2.5
Board of Directors, 1981–1982

*Mike Chamberlin, President
Assistant Sales Manager
KBCT Radio

*Dr. Morris Winekoff, Vice-President
Chief of Radiology
Mossinger Hospital

Lyle Clausen
retired business executive
Arts Consultant

*Leslie Porter
Travel Consultant
Colorado Travel

*Charles Simwell
Executive Director
Mossinger Hospital

*Paul Klein
Director of Marketing and Sales
Ski Magazine

*Sam Perkins
Textile Representative
Cloth Manufacturers, Inc.

*Kathy Price
Sales Representative
Mountain Beauty Supply

*Ralph Torrence
Public Relations Director
Smith, Blair and Marchman

*Lawrence Spears
Secretary/Treasurer
Waldrop Enterprises

*Peter Maxwell
Vice-President
Western Liquors

*Darren Sycamore
President
Sycamore and Associates

*Pam Stearns
Realtor
Colorado Real Estate

Kirk Giovanni
Vice-President
Warren Ski Lift Services

*Martin LaPaz, Treasurer
Treasurer and Comptroller
Colorado Springs Times

Carla Lopez
Colorado Springs

George Gardner
Attorney
Wassen, Wassen and Farmer

*Susan Larsen
Manager
High Point Apartments

*Sarah Barker
Colorado Springs

Founding Directors

Sharon Geiger
Artistic Director
Creative Dance Ensemble

Ted Clark
Artistic Director
Creative Dance Ensemble

Laura Clark
Owner
Clark's School of Dance

*New members of the board.

particular subjects; (d) audit bills and disburse the funds of the company; (e) print and circulate documents and advertisements to promote the purpose of the company; (f) detail officer actions and decisions; and (g) devise and carry into execution such measures as are proper and legal to promote the objectives and purposes of the company and to best protect the interest and welfare of the company."

The various committees include fund-raising, long-range planning, finance, nominating, advertising, building and grounds, personnel, and Dance (the volunteer organization). By the end of November 1981, none of the 1981–1982 committees had met.

Management

The administrative positions are filled by permanent staff while the artistic positions, with the exception of the directors, are either contractual or paid on a performance basis.

General Manager

Ellen Leland, General Manager of CDE, has nine years of experience in the arts. She has complete responsibility for the day-to-day administration of the company, assisted by a secretary and an administrative assistant (bookkeeper). She receives little assistance from the board. A complete list of her duties is given in Exhibit 2.6.

Artistic Directors

Ted Clark and Sharon Geiger choreograph for the company, teach the dancers, and serve as spokespeople. Their vision keeps the organization alive. Both are voting members of the board. When there is a cash-flow problem, frequently they will arrange for a loan from friends or relatives. They first received a salary in the 1981–1982 season; after years of providing financial support, they can no longer support themselves without some income.

Exhibit 2.6   Position Description

Position: General Manager
                   Effective Date: May 1, 1980

Reports to: Executive Committee

Description of Position:
   Responsible for overall administration of company's activities, including business and financial affairs, program planning and direction, public relations, and staff supervision.

Duties:
1. Represents the company in all contractual and other business activities.
2. Develops an annual budget in cooperation with the Executive Committee.
3. Controls all expenditures in accordance with the operating budget and sound fiscal policies.
4. Oversees the development and presentation of grant proposals.
5. Coordinates all aspects of the performance schedule, including booking, touring, technical aspects, and production.
6. Directs all public relations and promotion of company activities.
7. Supervises the work of staff in accordance with effective management principles.
8. Coordinates all volunteer activities.
9. Reports regularly to the Executive Committee.
10. Assumes other duties as assigned by the Executive Committee.

Salary:
   $14,000–18,000, based on qualifications and experience.

Qualifications:
1. Experience in arts management required.
2. Degree relevant to arts management preferred.
3. Demonstrated management skills.
4. Grant-writing experience desirable.
5. Willingness to adapt to irregular hours as required.
6. Ability to work well with people.

Artistic Staff

There are three dance companies in one. The core comprises 14 paid dancers. In addition, there are 14 talented young dancers in the apprentice company, most between the ages of 14 and 17. The youth company is made up of 18 younger dancers. Of the paid dancers, 9 are new to the company and few come from central Colorado. CDE is considered a stepping-stone to larger regional dance companies, such as might be found in Denver. The dancers are strong and enthusiastic, with good potential. In 1981–1982 the dancers' preparation has been greatly enhanced by the instruction of the new ballet master (a former dancer with American Ballet Theatre), who also has maintained high morale among the dancers. Exhibit 2.2 shows the progressive changes in dancers and performances for the company.

Volunteers

The volunteer organization, Dance, has several responsibilities. Its only substantial contribution to the company, however, has been a boutique, which earned $935 in the 1980–1981 season and is raising items to be sold at the Raise auction (a cultural fund-raising group). Many past volunteers have been parents of the dancers.

Marketing

The Product

CDE presents classical and romantic ballet, modern dance, and American jazz. Sharon Geiger has selected such classical ballets as *Coppelia* and *Cinderella* and has choreographed several, including *Vermila*, to an original and costly musical score. Many pieces selected for concert require more technical strength than evidenced by the dancers in the company. Ted Clark favors modern dance and has choreographed many pieces for the company, including a 40-minute modern ballet. CDE also has contracted with outside choreographers to set dances for the company. Currently, the company has 13 pieces (between 7 and 40 minutes long) and 3 full-length ballets in its repertory. Of these, 11 were choreographed in the 1980–1981 season at a low average cost of $2,000 each. (By contrast, the Cleveland Ballet recently presented *Coppelia* at a cost of $150,000.) Artistic selection and execution in the dance field is a constant trade-off between high artistic quality and cost.

Perhaps the performance that received the most audience exposure was *Mountain Dance*, choreographed by Ted Clark in 1977 and filmed for television. The film had an estimated viewing audience of more than 1 million. In 1979, Ted choreographed a second filmed piece entitled *Perpetual Motion*.

In the 1981–1982 season, both the Dan Wagoner Dancers and the Merce Cunningham Dance Company are scheduled in the series. Two CDE productions were scheduled— *Coppelia* and *Vermila*; however, the cost of reproducing the music was so high that *Vermila* has been cancelled and will be replaced by a guest company.

As a result of the "Help Our Dancers" campaign, CDE sold a record 2,258 tickets to its December 1980 *Coppelia* concert, with gross revenues of $25,135. For the fall 1981 concert, combined ticket sales for the performance and dress rehearsal were only 1,520, with a gross revenue of $10,386. Production costs amounted to $41,232. A total of 1,374 tickets were sold for the Dan Wagoner concert, grossing $13,742. Total production costs were $16,899. The next two productions have been budgeted at $19,075 each. Most performing arts companies strive for 100 percent subscription sales; at 631 series tickets sold, CDE is only 25 percent subscribed for FYE 1982.

Several problems in recent years have contributed to the disappointing attendance at CDE concerts. Performances conflicted with other scheduled major events; the arts center box office has been uncooperative; and the quality of the performances has varied. The 1980–1981 presentation of *Coppelia* was plagued with injuries, inadequate shipments of programs, and insufficient money and man-hours to promote the series. The company's financial struggles were well publicized; consequently, few people wanted to risk subscribing to the 1981–1982 series.

Price

Subscription prices for the 1981–1982 series ranged from $20 to $50 with 50-percent discounts given for senior citizens, students, and military. Season tickets may be purchased by mail or phone but hard-copy single tickets can only be purchased at the auditorium box office. Vouchers are available at various outlets. As CDE personnel have no access to tickets, board members can only take blocks of tickets to sell if they are paid for in advance.

Publicity

A formal publicity program for CDE has been hampered by a lack of manpower and funds. The "Help Our Dancers" campaign was perhaps the most successful, having full cooperation and participation from the board. Because of arrangements of the local arts council, CDE receives a one-third discount off all advertisements placed in the local newspaper.

Occasionally, just prior to a performance, one of the artistic directors or the general manager is interviewed on local radio or television. To announce an event, CDE relies primarily on posters distributed throughout the community.

Recently, Ellen Leland decided to publish a monthly newsletter in a local cultural magazine. Each month she buys a page of advertising (with the help of a $3,000 media grant from the Sarah James Foundation) and prints current information about the company. The magazine has a circulation of 42,300, but few live in Colorado Springs.

Facilities

Since the 1979–1980 season, CDE has performed in the City Performing Arts Center, which has the only proscenium large enough to accommodate full-scale ballets. It seats 2,534 people. Exhibit 2.7 shows this and other possible locations.

The City Center is a city-run facility that also hosts the symphony, opera, broadway series, and big-name music concerts. Neither the opera nor the ballet may handle its own tickets. Except for season tickets, only vouchers may be sold, which allow the holder to pick up tickets at concert time. Regardless of discounts offered, City Center demands

Exhibit 2.7   Available Facilities in Central Colorado

	Number of Seats	Width of Proscenium Opening (ft.)	Rental Cost per Day ($)
City Performing Arts Center	2,534	50	500[a]
Sarah James Theatre	350	35	300
Santa Fe Auditorium	588	40	350
Stueben College Theatre	375	26	375
Rice Hotel Auditorium[b]	2,000	48	1,250

[a] The minimum stay for CDE in the City Center for one performance is four days. The fee is 10 percent of revenues or $500 per day, whichever is less and not to exceed $2,000.

[b] The Rice Auditorium is located about 11 miles south of Colorado Springs. The per-diem fee includes many benefits that are extra in the other facilities.

10 percent of the full price of every ticket sold. Relations between the facility's manager and CDE are very strained.

At City Center, CDE must hire union stagehands, who receive $0.30 less an hour for nonprofit, than for profit, productions.

Until the summer of 1980, CDE offices were in the same building as Clark's School of Dance. Office and studio space were donated to the company temporarily. The donor was trying to sell the building and allowed the CDE to use it until it was sold. One potential buyer wanted to use it as part of a major arts complex, and would have allowed CDE to rent the space permanently; however, the purchaser defaulted. During the next five months, CDE staff had to be ready to move at a moment's notice but had no place to go. Also, there were two electrical fires and several power outages. Concomitantly, another closing was imminent, and building maintenance was being neglected, so CDE employees did all janitorial work. Minimal heat during the winter and no air conditioning in summer made conditions dangerous on the one hand and unbearable on the other. At the end of the summer of 1981, the Sarah James Foundation bought the building as a cultural complex, housing offices of the ballet, visiting symphony, and opera. CDE will now have to pay an annual rent of $12,000 for its space.

Financial Information

The income statements, balance sheets, and relevant percentages are presented in Exhibits 2.2, 2.8, and 2.9, respectively. The deficit for the last three fiscal years was financed mainly with accounts payable and loans from friends.

The company suffered from severe cash-flow problems in the 1980–1981 season. The dancers, initially on a 36-week contract starting in September, had to be laid off December 21. The layoff was intended for six weeks, but when cash flow did not improve, the dancers were placed on a per performance basis for the remainder of the year. During the 1981–1982 season, the dancers were on a 22-week contract with a built-in three-week layoff. Although the contract had an extension clause to be implemented if the company is in a healthy financial position, the board chose not to use it.

Exhibit 2.8   Creative Dance Ensemble—Balance Sheet

	FYE 1981	FYE 1980	FYE 1979	FYE 1978	FYE 1977
Current assets:					
Cash	$ 2,795	$ 1,015	$2,574	$5,073	$1,196
Restricted funds[a]	2,640	6,552			
Accounts receivable	85	2,532	4,591		
Prepaid expenses		164			
Total current assets	$ 5,520	$ 10,263	$7,165	$5,073	$1,196
Other assets					
Utility deposit	1,130				
Fixed assets					
Equipment	8,585	5,339			
Less accumulated deposits	(3,104)	(992)			
Total fixed assets	5,481	4,347			
Total assets	$ 12,131	$ 14,610	$7,165	$5,073	$1,196
Current liabilities					
Notes payable (due within one year)	18,237[b]	20,112	3,000	496	
Accounts payable	13,380	2,770	122		
Accrued interest	2,197				
Accrued payables/receivables taxes	2,115	419	57		
Deferred income[a]	2,640	6,552			
Accrued salaries			1,105		
Total current liabilities	$ 38,569	$ 29,853	$4,284	$ 496	
Long-term liabilities					
Notes payable	5,362	2,133			
Total liabilities	$ 43,931	$ 31,986	$4,284	$ 496	
Fund balance					
Invested in equipment	3,924	1,751			
Unrestricted	(35,724)	(19,127)	2,881	4,577	1,196
Fund total	$(31,800)	$(17,376)	$2,881	$4,577	$1,196
Total liabilities and funds	$ 12,131	$ 14,610	$7,165	$5,073	$1,196

[a] Funds paid for next year's season.

[b] $13,500 are past due.

Cash-flow problems also prevented the company from meeting its administrative payroll several times during the spring and summer of 1981. Since December 1980, the board has been especially unresponsive to the critical cash needs of the members, who already have contributed to the limit both financially and emotionally. Just prior to the December 1980 production of *Coppelia*, it had appeared that the company would not survive. Only the "Help Our Dancers" campaign raised the amount required to keep the company going. Just prior to the 1981 Dan Wagoner production, the company was forced to take an emergency loan and received substantial assistance from several board members. Ellen has commented that, "every time financial matters are brought up at board meetings, someone changes the subject."

Comments made by a local museum administrator reflected the community's attitude

Exhibit 2.9   Creative Dance Ensemble—Relevant Percentages

	FYE 1981	FYE 1980	FYE 1979	FYE 1978	FYE 1977
Percent distribution of earned income					
Ticket sales	76	100	77	100	52
Nonseries performance	14				
Nonperformance	10		23		48
Total earned income	100	100	100	100	100
Percent distribution of unearned income					
Tax support	30	44	86	96	34
Private support	70	56	14	4	66
Total unearned income	100	100	100	100	100
Percent distribution of total income					
Earned income	49	47	34	21	39
Unearned income	51	53	66	79	61
Percent distribution of expenses					
Program expense	77	66	49	35	
Fund-raising expenses	2	6	3	—	100
General and administrative	21	28	48	65	
Total expenses	100	100	100	100	100
Percent of total operating expenses met by income earned	46	43	25	23	26
Percent of program expenses met by program income	53	65	52	67	26
Percent of total expenses met by total income	92	91	98	109	130

toward the financial crisis: "Maybe this area is not ready for a professional ballet. There are a lot of large cities in this country that can't support a professional dance company."

There are several major sources of funds locally. The Sarah James Foundation contributes more than $200,000 annually to the arts in central Colorado, occasionally providing emergency funds to organizations. It does not anticipate any increased funding to the arts in the next several years. Corporations are another source that has been somewhat neglected by local arts organizations. Colorado Power and Light and Denver Oil have long supported the arts. Also, several major corporations have moved to Colorado Springs recently and may be looking for ways to enhance their public images.

CDE's fiscal year ends May 31; a preliminary budget for 1981–1982 was prepared in February 1981, totaling $470,050, but was never given final approval by the board, primarily because it never took the time to review it. When, by July, it was obvious that some of the anticipated government funds would not be available, Ellen Leland began revising the budget. It was not ready for final approval by the first meeting of the new board in July, but was finally approved at the second meeting in October 1981. Exhibit 2.3 compares this budget to actual expenditures and revenues for the previous year.

Several comments should be made about this budget. Each board member is required to contribute $1,000 annually, which was budgeted into the individual contributions. A single donor had already contributed $13,000. There were guaranteed funds from the Sarah James Foundation of $13,000. By July, corporate contributions totaled $11,050.

Raise is a local fund-raising organization from which $15,000 had been received already. Performance fees were budgeted for a state touring program; however, because of the constant attention required in the office and the lack of funds, no one had arranged it. As of August, not a single paid performance had been arranged. The fee for these performances was to have been $1,000 each.

The Future

The board now faces the awesome task of making the company financially stable. The Sarah James Foundation will not rescue the company again. While it is feasible for 15 board members to raise $5,000 each by the end of January, past history makes this unlikely.

Several bright spots were on the horizon. Ted and Sharon planned to open a school of the Creative Dance Ensemble in January, which would be accessible to anyone interested in classes. Initial indications suggested considerable community interest. Because many of the costs involved are fixed costs that would have been incurred anyway, the profit potential was quite high.

A local chapter of the Jaycettes has pledged to take on CDE as a project and raise $200,000 to pay the salaries and insurance for 20 dancers next year. The Jaycettes propose to mount a campaign from May to August 1982 to raise the first $100,000 for start-up salaries. The second half would be raised between September and December. However, as the dancers' contract should be signed by July 31, the company would be signing for contracts without the money in hand.

Ted (now divorced) is selling his interest in the Clark's School of Dance and plans to loan the $40,000 proceeds to the company.

Ted and Sharon are planning to tour the state. Also, Sharon plans to stage *The Nutcracker Suite* next Christmas.

CASE APPENDIX 2A

Colorado Springs has a rapidly growing cultural community with nine major nonprofit arts organizations and the Mountain Council of Arts and Sciences, which exists to provide support services to the cultural community. Exhibit 2.10 presents budget comparisons for these organizations, Exhibit 2.11 analyzes the sources of funds for the Central Colorado cultural community.

Fund-raising is critical for nonprofit organizations because of the large gap between earned income and expenses. The national average of earned income of total expenses for dance companies is between 55 percent and 60 percent. Baumol and Bower have theorized on the increasing gap. In industry, as costs have risen with inflation so has productivity,

Exhibit 2.10　Budget Comparisons

	1980–1981 Budget ($)	Surplus (deficit) ($)	1980–1981 Earned Income (%)	1981–1982 Budget ($)	Change in Budget (%)
Mountain Civic Theatre	$ 167,000	$14,250	61%	$ 201,000	20%
Mountain Art Center	155,000	(30,000)	50	212,000	37
Central Symphony	1,000,000	(17,000)	57	1,000,000	—
McCann Science Center	350,000	14,000	46	360,000	3
Laredo Art Center	463,300	46,000	n.a.	352,515	(24)
James Tyler Art Center	74,000	—	46	72,000	(3)
Western Opera	162,700	(5,000)	52	240,000	48
Community Center of the Arts	106,000	(7,000)	41	126,000	19
Creative Dance Ensemble	194,000	(14,000)	46	386,750	99

Exhibit 2.11　Income Sources for the Arts in Central Colorado, 1980–1981 Fiscal Year

	Estimated Dollar Amount	Percent of Total
Total expenditures of the arts	3,187,500	100
Total earned income	1,346,672	42
Federal funds	58,903	2
State funds	62,774	2
County funds	91,000	3
City funds	35,950	1
Foundation funds	220,000	7
Ski resort funds	5,000	—
Corporate funds	170,000	5
Total income	1,990,299	
Total individual contributions	1,197,201	38

that is, technology has made man-hours more productive. Consequently, more products are made and sold at higher prices to compensate for the higher costs. However, by their very nature the performing arts cannot increase productivity. While the same number of dancers and the same amount of time are required to perform *Coppelia* in 1981 as it would have in 1951, production costs have since skyrocketed. Compensating increases in ticket prices have been restricted because of the risk of decreased demand. If the arts are considered overpriced, many consumers will find less expensive substitutes, such as television or movies.[1]

Although most organizations in central Colorado do not have sophisticated development programs, several of the nine organizations have well-organized fund-raising events. An analysis indicates that the most successful were those that have become traditional in the community. The most successful is the opera's fashion show, which has become a tradition in Colorado Springs and probably can be credited with the current financial stability of the opera. CDE never has had a very successful fund-raising campaign.

Until recently, it has been assumed that the very wealthy, older population provided the primary support for the arts. However, recent trends in the past several years indicate that the new audience comprises the younger, professional segment.

One market most culturals have not penetrated is the tourist market in central Colorado. The McCann Science Center is perhaps the only organization to solicit the tourists actively. In 1980, it attracted about 20,000 to the planetarium.

Underserved segments of the population are normally given exposure to the arts through outreach programs. All nine organizations purport to have them, but most are confined to schoolchildren. There are some notable exceptions. Mountain Art Center has its "Reach with Art" program, which provides art therapy to the elderly, handicapped, and exceptional children. Community Center of the Arts has a special program for the blind. The Pre-Columbian Collection at the Laredo Art Center has attracted a large number of Hispanics, although it is not clear that this was by design. The Central Symphony's chamber series was an unsuccessful attempt to reach the elderly. The mixed success of the outreach programs perhaps reflects the half-hearted attitude of some of the organizations because frequently they are obligated to promulgate them to comply with government and funding agency requirements. Substantively, however, most of these programs provide little exposure to the underserved segments of the population.

Competition permeates the cultural community of central Colorado on a number of levels, the most divisive being for local funding. The larger, older organizations resent the smaller, younger ones eating into their portion of locally available funds. The smaller organizations feel the larger organizations are trying to squeeze them out of the market. After recent budget cuts by the county commission, the three major organizations (each of which stood to lose $25,000) urged that all nine present a united front to the community; however, this lasted only as long as it benefited those major organizations.

Most performing arts groups are supportive, rather than competitive, of each other's programming. The symphony frequently accompanies the ballet and opera and, occasionally, CDE's dancers will perform in opera productions. Additionally, there appears to be substantial overlap of audiences. Interestingly, competition seems to exist among all non-

---

[1] W. J. Baumol and W. G. Bower. *Performing Arts, The Economic Dilemma* (Cambridge, Mass.: The M.I.T. Press, 1968), pp. 161–180.

profit performing arts organizations and the profit-making entertainment industry in the community.

CDE competes not only with other professional organizations, but also with the local dance schools, which resent CDE, especially the Williams Ballet School, the oldest in central Colorado. The Clarks attended this school in their childhood. Bret and Joanne Williams, the owners, feel their position in the community has been usurped and refuse to cooperate with CDE. Their school presents *The Nutcracker Suite* annually at Christmas to provide a showcase for all their students and always performs to a full house at the City Performing Arts Center.

The economic environment for the arts in 1981 was grim, with President Reagan wanting to cut funding to the National Endowment for the Arts by more than 50 percent. While most of the cultural organizations in central Colorado are not direct beneficiaries of these funds, they are affected indirectly. State funding to the arts, partially funded by the federal government, has been cut back. Locally, city and county governments are trying not to raise taxes. This, combined with reduced federal revenues, is reducing the funding for the arts on a local level. Although CDE had received funds from the local government in the past, it was given no funds in 1981–1982 because of lower city revenues and because its stated emphasis was placed heavily on touring out of the area.

George Monihan, Director of the Sarah James Foundation, summed up the future difficulties faced by the arts in obtaining private funds. He said that the foundation will be unable to take up the shortfall in federal monies as its revenues are generated from dividend income, which is not anticipated to increase in the next several years because of the current recession. Inflation has cut into the disposable income of most Americans, leaving people less willing to contribute to nonprofit organizations. While not all local corporate sources have been tapped, it is unlikely that current corporate supporters will increase their cultural contributions.

CASE APPENDIX 2B
Primary Liabilities and Responsibilities for Boards of Directors of Nonprofit Organizations

1. When an organization incorporates as a nonprofit agency:
    a. all profits must be reinvested in the corporation;
    b. the organization is entitled to receive federal and state funding; and
    c. the members individually take on the responsibility of the public good and can be sued individually as, among other things, they are individually liable for the debts incurred by the organization and for the failure of the organization to comply with the law.

2. The board of directors has ultimate responsibility for the success or failure of an organization. It makes top policy decisions within the framework of the stated mission and objectives of the organization. It is responsible for preparing and implementing long-range plans to achieve the stated objectives by either establishing committees within the board or delegating authority to the staff.

3. The most critical responsibility is fund-raising. While the staff works toward maximizing the earned income, the board must close the income gap (discussed in Appendix 2A) through fund-raising.

4. The board is responsible for hiring and firing senior staff and for developing and maintaining an effective volunteer organization.

5. The board has ultimate responsibility for the marketing effort on two levels: effective marketing is essential for attracting audiences; and the organization must be marketed as a whole for fund-raising purposes. Members must advocate the arts in general and the organization specifically, creating a favorable image in the community.

6. The board must provide professional guidance and support to all staff, continuously balancing the artistic needs of the organization with financial considerations.

7. The board should control all fiscal matters. Each director on the executive committee should fully understand and review the budget before giving final approval and should closely monitor the organization's performance in relation to it. By approving a budget, members essentially are verifying that the budget is a realistic fiscal plan for the following year.

Software Architects (A)

▪ *Tom Kosnik* ▪

Harvey Mayerowicz, the president and founder of Software Architects, was in the process of reviewing the business strategy for 1982–1983. Software Architects (SA) was a data processing consulting firm which provided customized computer programming services and technical seminars on various topics to companies in the Chicago area. A small, entrepreneurial enterprise, SA had enjoyed modest growth and profitable performance in the 2½ years since its founding. Harvey's concern was to develop a clear understanding of the factors which had contributed to SA's past success, and to position the company for continued success in an industry that was experiencing rapid growth, increasing competition, and technological change.

Company Background

Software Architects was founded by six individuals in late 1979. Harvey Mayerowicz was the president, elected by his colleagues on the board of directors. The other five directors were Gloria Petersen, Gene Petrie, Ed Wroble, Bruce Parello, and Fritz Wolf. All of the directors were experienced system programmers, who performed technical consulting tasks in addition to their duties of managing the company.

Decision making at SA was a consensual process, with each of the six directors contributing ideas and opinions at the meetings held every one or two weeks. An idea which was of interest to a particular director was often explored outside of the meetings so that he or she was able to make recommendations and advocate a particular position to the others.

Responsibility for business functions was shared among the directors in the following way. Harvey and Gloria were responsible for marketing and new client development. Bruce, who had developed the automated accounting systems used by SA, was concerned with the financial side of the business. Fritz, Gene, and Ed focused their attentions on the conduct of consulting projects themselves, including technical work, supervision of SA employees, and managing the delicate relationships with SA clients.

In addition to the six founders/directors of SA, there were five other technical consultants who performed project work. Harvey anticipated that these employees might be groomed to take on additional responsibilities in marketing or project management as SA grew. They were encouraged to take initiative and to accelerate the timetable for their development, in an effort to provide challenge and stimulation on the job.

Prepared by Tom Kosnik under the supervision of Robert A. Burgelman, Assistant Professor of Management, Stanford University, Graduate School of Business. Reprinted from *Stanford Business Cases 1983* with permission of the Publishers, Stanford University Graduate School of Business, © 1983 by the Board of Trustees of the Leland Stanford Junior University. This case shows neither effective or ineffective handling of an administrative decision. Rather it is to be used as the basis for classroom discussion.

Financial Performance

Harvey and the other directors took pride in the fact that SA had been profitable since the time the firm was established. Exhibits 3.1 and 3.2 provide the balance sheet for SA at the end of June 1981 and the income statements for the 1980 and 1981 fiscal years. The results for the first six months of the 1982 fiscal year (July through December of 1981) showed revenues of over $400,000 and before-tax income of over $140,000.

The accountants who reviewed SA's financial reports had given Harvey a set of financial performance ratios for firms in the computer programming and software services industry. The results of high-, average-, and low-performing companies are provided in Exhibit 3.3. It appeared to Harvey that SA was doing reasonably well, especially in view of the fact that it was a new venture in a fairly competitive marketplace.

Services Offered

SA provided services to clients in three main areas:

1. *Systems programming:* the design and programming of systems software to augment that provided by the hardware manufacturer. Examples included programs for measuring systems efficiency, compilers, utilities, and report generators.

2. *Applications programming:* the design and programming of software to perform specific applications for the client, such as accounting, inventory management, and planning systems.

3. *Technical education:* the development and presentation of training seminars for employees in client organizations on a variety of technical subjects in which SA had special expertise.

Additional descriptions of systems and applications software are provided in Appendix 3A. SA had also done a project on a microcomputer network in the last year. It was possible that there might be other opportunities for SA related to microcomputers in the future, but it was not clear what form those opportunities might take.

SA's costs and revenues for the services it provided were largely based on the time spent by SA consultants to complete design and programming tasks on each project. The custom development of software was usually broken down into several phases. Although the tasks performed in each phase varied depending upon the methodology that was being used, most of SA's projects consisted of:

1. *General design*—in which the overall framework for the new system was developed and the needs of the users which were to be satisfied by the system were identified.

2. *Detailed design*—during which the general guidelines from the previous phase were elaborated to provide a clear, explicit blueprint for subsequent programming.

3. *Implementation*—during which programs written, tested individually and as an overall system, and the final system was introduced into a "live" environment for use in day-to-day operations.

SA spent more time than many of its competitors in the detailed design phase. However, they were convinced that extra effort there allowed even greater time savings during

Exhibit 3.1   Software Architects Inc., Balance Sheet, June 30, 1981

Assets

Current assets:

Cash:

Demand deposits	$ 29,550	
Money market fund	17,023	$ 46,573

Receivables:

Customers	135,458	
Interest	362	
	135,820	
Less allowance for uncollectible accounts	(3,500)	132,320
Prepaid expense		173
Total current assets		$179,066

Equipment:

Computer and office equipment—net of accumulated depreciation of $3,480		3,097

Other assets

Security deposit		66
Total assets		$182,229

Liabilities and Stockholders' Equity

Current liabilities:

Note payable		$ 620
Loan payable—stockholders		943
Accounts payable		12,596
Profit-sharing contribution payable		22,000
Payroll taxes withheld and accrued		448

Income taxes:

Current	$ 4,300	
Deferred	12,895	17,195

Accrued expenses:

Interest	76	
Salaries	58,411	58,487
Total current liabilities		$112,289

Noncurrent liabilities:

Note payable		8,668
Total liabilities		120,957

Stockholders' equity:

Common stock:

Authorized 1,000 shares at no par value; issued 100 shares at stated value, of which 85.7142 shares are outstanding	1,000	
Retained earnings	60,415	
	61,415	
Less Treasury stock—14.2858 shares at cost	(143)	
Total stockholders' equity	61,272	
Total liabilities and stockholders' equity	$182,229	

Exhibit 3.2   Software Architects Inc. Statement of Income and Retained Earnings Years Ended June 30, 1981, and 1980

	1981		1980		
	Amount	Percent of Revenues	Amount	Percent of Revenues	Increase (Decrease)
Revenue	$343,373	100.00%	$326,530	100.00%	$16,843
Operating expenses	(298,264)	86.86	(299,788)	91.81	(1,524)
Operating income	45,109	13.14	26,742	8.19	18,367
Other income (expense):					
Interest income	2,987	.87	704	.21	2,283
Interest expense	(1,457)	(.42)	(431)	(.13)	(1,026)
Total other income (expense)	1,530	.45	273	.08	1,257
Income before income taxes	46,639	13.59	27,015	8.27	19,624
Income taxes	10,800	3.15	5,700	1.74	5,100
Net income	35,839	10.44%	21,315	6.53%	$14,524
Retained earnings:					
Beginning of year	24,576		3,261		
End of the year	$ 60,415		$ 24,576		

Exhibit 3.3   Key Financial Ratios for Firms in the Computer Programming and Software Service Industry

Financial Performance Measures	Industry Performance in 1981		
	High Performers	Average Performers	Low Performers
Percent profit before tax/sales	n.a	8.4%	n.a
Percent profit before tax/net worth	73.5%	45.2%	20.8%
Percent profit before tax/assets	22.1%	14.2%	5.7%
Sales/receivables	7.7	5.7	3.8
Sales/assets	3.0	2.2	1.5
Debt/worth	1.1	2.0	3.6
Current ratio	1.8	1.4	1.0

n.a = Not applicable.
Source: Robert Morris Associates, 1981.

implementation. In essence, their detailed planning allowed a smoother, faster execution and much less time in testing and debugging programs.

Keys to Success

Harvey and Gloria were aware that in a consulting relationship, technical competence was a necessary but not sufficient condition for success. There were other essential ingredients as well. Harvey believed that a programming consultant had to have three qualities to satisfy most clients and earn an invitation for follow-on work. The individual had to be honest, competent, and personable. Gloria felt that the most important characteristic was the ability of the consultant to be empathetic with the client, understanding and listening to the client's business and personal concerns.

Their continuing discussions had yielded a list of factors which they believed were important to a prospective client in deciding whether or not to accept a proposal from a particular software consulting firm:

1. *Availability:* the ability of the consultant to meet staffing levels, start dates, and completion dates required by the client.

2. *Cost:* measured both in terms of an hourly billing rate and an estimate of overall project costs.

3. *Honesty:* the willingness of the consultant to admit he/she either does not know the answer or has made a mistake. In addition, the unwillingness of the consultant to make promises in a proposal that the firm may not be able to keep, e.g., the promise to meet a deadline desired by the client.

4. *Professionalism:* the consultant's respect for the client's work environment rules, punctuality, neatness, and personal appearance.

5. *Quality of past work:* as evidenced either by the recommendations of other satisfied clients or the quality of sample programming documentation, articles, technical papers, etc., provided by the consultant for review by the client. The quality of the analysis supporting the proposal was also important.

6. *Rapport:* a combination of what Harvey had identified as the personable quality and Gloria had called empathy. The sense of shared understanding, values, and personal friendship between the client and the consultant.

7. *Technical fit:* the match between the consultant's areas of competence and the client's needs for specialized expertise. It was possible for a highly technical individual to be undesirable to a client if the expertise was out-of-date or was not relevant in the client's problem situation.

Harvey and Gloria wondered whether their clients saw the keys to success in software consulting the same way that they did. They were also curious about how potential clients perceived SA in each of the areas above. In what respects was SA's position strong relative to its competitors? What were the major areas needing improvement? Were there other considerations in the decision to hire a firm like SA that the two of them had overlooked?

It seemed that getting answers to the questions above was crucial to understanding what SA had done right in the first two years. They were also critical to keeping SA well positioned for the future.

Software Architects' External Environment

Prospective Clients

As suppliers of customized programming services and technical education, SA had a wide variety of potential clients. However, the realities of the marketplace and the values of the SA principals both served to focus attention on a reasonably small group of companies.

The cost of custom programming was prohibitive for many organizations. Harvey believed that the size of the data processing budget was related to the annual revenues of a company, and SA's main targets were therefore the largest industrial firms. Because SA had only one office and the professional staff preferred not to travel out of town, Harvey generally restricted his clients to those in the Chicago metropolitan area. SA did not attempt to specialize in a particular application area (such as general ledger systems) or industry group (such as banking or forest products). However, it did try to concentrate on its areas of primary technical expertise. As a result, potential clients were screened based upon the hardware and systems software that they had in their data processing centers. SA preferred to work with IBM hardware and software and rarely competed for projects in other hardware/software environments.

SA's potential clients, then, included large businesses in the Chicago area with IBM computer equipment. Most of the 19 clients for which they had worked in the first two years had all three of these characteristics. There were almost 50 prospective clients which met the three criteria and showed high potential for future SA work. Harvey and Gloria had identified approximately 50 other firms which were large enough and were based in Chicago. They had not yet found out what hardware and software was in place in each of the second group of companies.

The Chicago area was not a center of high-technology manufacturing like the areas outside Boston, Massachusetts, and San Jose's Silicon Valley. As a result, few of SA's potential clients made computer-related products. Most used computers for their internal administrative, accounting, inventory, and planning systems. Their data processing departments varied in size from a few to several hundred people. Nearly every organization suffered from a shortage of skilled programming personnel. In fact, the shortage of people and technical skills was what provided the principal raison d'être for the hundreds of systems consulting firms which operated in the Chicago area.

The data processing departments of most organizations had at least three separate groups. One was responsible for systems programming and maintained the technical environment in which the other two groups worked. The technical skills required to work as a systems programmer were greater than those of other data processing personnel. The second group was responsible for applications development. This group designed and tested programs for accounting, planning, or other functions which had been requested by nontechnical users in the organization. The third group was responsible for operations. They "ran" the hardware and software in order to process information and produce reports desired by management of the business for planning and control purposes. Computer operators were typically the least technically skilled of the three groups.

The decision to acquire consulting services from a firm like SA was sometimes made by the manager in charge of the systems programming group. At other times, the person in charge of the entire data processing operation was the final decision maker. Occasionally, and especially when a manager from another part of the potential client company had requested that an application system be developed to meet his or her needs, nontechnical management were involved in the process. If the contract was for a large dollar amount (greater than $50,000) or was for a project of critical importance to the organization, senior management approval was usually required.

No matter who was involved in the process of choosing the consultant, SA's client was almost always a member of management in the data processing organization. This individual was often under a great deal of stress to develop a new system under tight budget and deadline constraints. If the project timetable slipped or there were cost overruns, the manager's job could be in jeopardy. With billing rates between $30 and $120 an hour for outside programming support, a small error in estimating the scope of the project resulted in a large increase in cost.

The stories of projects that had been placed in the hands of data processing consultants and had subsequently gone awry were many. There were also frequent accounts of outsiders who had installed a system and left when the initial contract had expired. When the client later found "bugs" during the day-to-day operations of the system, there was often no one in-house who knew enough about the system to make the necessary repairs. The consultants were seldom available for assistance. The programmers were immersed in other projects with new clients. Frequently, the people who had actually worked on the system had moved on to other employers. Turnover among software programming houses was notoriously high.

Thus, the potential clients of SA shared two major concerns about the use of consultants: the fear of project delays and budget overruns in the short run, and the worry about being left "high and dry" when the project was over. Many companies had policies against the use of outsiders for system development. Unfortunately, that rarely offered protection from the two key risks. Inability to meet deadlines was at least as much a problem for internal programmers as it was for firms like SA. So was turnover. The competition for technical people was fierce enough that programmers were often lured away by other employers.

Harvey believed that if SA were able to demonstrate its technical competence and its ability to meet deadlines to a client, the chances for follow-on business were good. Firms who could deliver on promises made at the time of the initial proposal were rare. Repeat business also served to reduce the client's second area of risk. If the SA programmer were working on another project in the same firm, he or she was accessible to answer questions or provide a "quick fix" if problems arose.

The problem for Harvey was how subtly to address what he thought were the two areas of concern for most clients. He was unsure of how SA might demonstrate its competence and its willingness to provide continuity in a way that sounded like an honest promise, rather than a sales pitch.

The clients for SA's technical seminars were sometimes the same individuals as for the programming services. At other times, people in the organization's professional training and development staff got involved. Although the risk of a poorly conceived and executed seminar did not appear to be as great as those for a computer system, the two groups shared something in common. They had to commit money and their reputations in advance to an outside supplier of a product which did not yet exist. This often made the criteria for selection difficult to articulate. The decision was rarely clear-cut. Usually, the client had to rely on "gut feeling" and hope for the best.

Competitors

Harvey and Gloria were not certain who their closest competitors were in the systems and applications programming area. One study (see Appendix 3A) had estimated that there were thousands of firms providing custom design and programming services in the United

Exhibit 3.4 Estimated Hourly Billing Rates of Software Architects' Competitors

	Estimated Hourly Rates for:			
Competitor Name	Programmer Analyst	System Designers	Project Leaders	Partners/ Principals
Arthur Andersen	$38–$40*	$45–$55	$50–$85	
Consumer Systems	$27–$31	n.a.	$38	n.a.
Farlow Associates	$25–$28	n.a.	n.a.	n.a.
Giles Associates	$24–$32	$26–$36	$35 and up	n.a.
McAuto	$46–$58	$66–$83	$109–$136	$127–$159

*For every five programmer/analysts, Arthur Andersen provided an experienced consultant as supervisor at no charge to the client.

States. Of these, there were only about 2,000 competitors nationwide who generated more than $250,000 each in annual revenues. There was no market research data available on the firms in the Chicago area. Harvey had found over 200 names of data processing consultants in the Chicago Yellow Pages. However, neither SA nor several of the firms against which they had bid on past projects were listed in the Yellow Pages. He was not sure how many firms were actually providing a similar type of service to the same target clients.

Harvey and Gloria had developed a list of potential competitors which included those against whom SA had prepared bids for work in the past, as well as those about whom SA had heard from clients and other contacts. Exhibit 3.4 contains information about billing rates of SA's major competitors on past projects.

SA's known competitors included several very large, national firms, such as Arthur Andersen and McAuto. There were also a number of smaller companies. It was unclear what the best strategy might be for SA's positioning relative to this wide variety of opponents. How did potential clients perceive SA relative to a company with the resources and reputation of Arthur Andersen? Where were the client's sensitive spots in dealing with an entrepreneurial company that Harvey had to address? Further, did SA appear to be special in the eyes of the client, or was it one of a myriad of small, nondescript "body shops" that abounded in the marketplace?

Learning where SA was from the client's point of view was an important first step. Creating an image for the firm as a high-quality, high-price source of services was the next item on the agenda.

Industry Facilitators

Although software consultants typically marketed their services by direct sales calls on potential clients, there were other institutions in the marketplace which could aid in the spread of reputation and the generation of leads for new business. Harvey considered at least three types of "industry facilitators":

1. *Hardware vendors*—who often provided purchasers of equipment with the names of several software consulting firms if there was a need for help in setting up new applications.

2. *User groups*—who met to discuss new ideas and common problems with hardware or software that they all had at their respective sites.

3. *University MIS professors*—who provided consulting firms with programmers and who also referred technical consulting business that they could not handle because of time commitments to software houses that they considered "top notch."

It seemed that SA should have a coherent strategy for its dealings with each of these industry groups. Harvey also wondered whether there were other "facilitators" that he might have overlooked.

Growth and Technological Change

Appendix 3A provides growth rates for different segments of the software industry. Professional services for custom software development showed a 20-percent annual growth forecast for the 1981–1986 period. Harvey had no data for the growth in demand for software services in the Chicago area.

Technological change was an important and troublesome issue for SA's future planning. The manufacturers of hardware and systems software improved their products and developed new technologies at a breakneck pace. As a result, technical expertise became obsolete almost as fast as the products did. There was always a lag in the decline in demand for services, because clients who already owned older hardware did not discard it as rapidly as the technology changed.

Harvey had developed a list of three technological changes which offered the greatest risk of obsolescence (and opportunity for new business) for SA:

1. Changes in systems software technology.

2. Development of application generators.

3. Proliferation of microcomputers.

There were two impending changes in systems software technology that threatened SA: (1) IBM's promise of operating systems that eliminated the need for systems programmers and (2) new database management software. SA's special expertise was in system programming for IBM mainframe computers. That firm (IBM) had recently announced a new operating system called the SSX system, which it claimed made it unnecessary to hire system programmers. The software was supposed to allow a nontechnical user to start and operate the system without programming commands in job control language (JCL). Harvey was a bit skeptical about IBM's claims but felt that in the future, systems software might become more "user friendly." In fact, some of the minicomputer manufacturers had made great strides in that area.

SA's experience with database management systems was with a pair of competing technologies known as hierarchical and network architectures. Most of the database packages that had been sold in the last ten years had been one of those varieties. While extremely powerful, these systems were known for their technical complexity, and database design and programming skills were in short supply. SA had a wealth of experience in several of these products, including IBM's flagship IMS, Cullinane's IDMS, and Software AG's ADABAS.

There had been a great deal of interest in the trade press in a new, simpler technology called rational database management systems. There were two or three new products that were actually on the market, and IBM had been working for several years to develop a relational DBMS of its own. If and when the new software came into widespread use, the threats to SA were twofold. First, it was a technology in which SA did not have expertise to differentiate itself from competitors. Second, the systems were supposed to be much simpler and user friendly, reducing the need for specialized systems programming experience.

The shortage of skilled programmers and rising salary costs for technical personnel had provided the incentive to reduce the labor intensity of systems development. Many suppliers had developed application software packages which a client could buy "off the shelf" and use with little or no additional programming. A more radical solution to the problem was the concept of a product known as an application generator. This was an off-the-shelf package that a nontechnical person could use to translate English-like commands into machine-readable code. In essence, the idea of the application generator was to eliminate the middleman between the nontechnical user and the machine. If such a product were perfected, the need for application programmers would all but disappear.

Thus far, no one had succeeded in developing the concept of the application generator to its full potential. Nevertheless, products which vastly improved programmers productivity had been introduced. For example, Cullinane Corporation had recently advertised a package which it claimed reduced the time required for programming by 90 percent.

Most of SA's past experience had been with large IBM mainframes. IBM's share of the data processing industry's total revenues was almost 40 percent in 1980. Its nearest competitor, NCR, had 5-percent share of market in 1980. The large installed base of IBM mainframes made it the obvious choice of hardware in which to develop specialized expertise.

However, there were considerable differences in the growth trends for different segments of the hardware industry, as shown in Exhibit 3.5. In particular, sale of microcomputers had grown 85 percent from 1979 to 1980. Many industry observers believed that microcomputer sales might grow at a faster rate in the 1981–1986 period, as new suppliers entered the marketplace, the technology improved, and the selling price per unit declined.

The massive influx of microcomputers was both a threat and an opportunity for SA. If users moved away from dependence on large mainframes and centralized data processing departments to meet their needs, SA's traditional clients might be faced with less work, lower data processing budgets, and less power in the decision to bring in consultants. On the other hand, many of the users of microcomputers were nontechnical people who preferred not to write their own programs. SA might be able to develop application software for micros and sell it to a large number of users.

Harvey was confident that SA had the technical skill to develop such software. In fact, SA had a TRS-80 microcomputer, and Bruce Parello had written programs to do the company's project accounting, accounts payable and receivable, and general ledger in his spare time. However, SA had no idea how to market microcomputer software once it was developed. They [the directors] had deferred discussion on diversification into that area until they learned more about the marketing channels for microcomputer software.

Harvey knew that SA could not expect to be writing systems and applications programs for IBM mainframes in 20 years. But how fast would the technology change? What could

Exhibit 3.5   Selected Data Processing Industry Growth Rates, 1979–80

Revenues of Top Ten Data Processing Manufacturers ($ millions)

	1980	1979	Percent Growth Rate
1. IBM	21,367	18,338	16.5%
2. NCR	2,840	2,528	12.3
3. Control Data	2,791	2,273	22.8
4. Digital Equipment Corp. (DEC)	2,743	2,032	35.0
5. Sperry	2,552	2,270	12.4
6. Burroughs	2,478	2,442	1.5
7. Honeywell	1,634	1,453	12.5
8. Hewlett-Packard	1,577	1,147	37.5
9. Xerox	770	570	35.1
10. Memorex	686	658	4.3
Total top 10	39,438	33,711	17.0
Total	55,626	46,220	20.4
Top 10 as a percent of total	70.9%	72.9%	

Revenue Growth Rates in Top Twenty Firms ($ millions)

	Total DP% Growth Rate	U.S. DP% Growth Rate	Foreign DP% Growth Rate	1980 DP Revenue	1980 Earnings
1. Sanders Associates	208.5%	91.5%	NM*	$145.0	$49
2. Apple	175.1	163.4	224.7%	165.2	47
3. Philips Information Systems	100.0	100.0	NM*	50.0	98
4. Tandem	93.9	58.7	179.4	128.8	53
5. Intergraph	91.3	80.1	153.7	56.5	90
6. Dysan	86.1	79.9	127.7	62.9	85
7. Computervision	85.5	72.7	108.3	191.1	41
8. Paradyne	83.2	74.0	108.9	75.9	77
9. Prime	75.0	59.9	95.8	267.6	27
10. Teletype	72.4	62.1	NM*	250.0	29
11. CPT	68.9	44.7	157.7	76.4	76
12. Wang Labs	66.1	68.8	61.5	681.8	11
13. Lanier	64.1	60.6	129.7	128.0	54
14. Triad Systems	61.0	61.6	NM*	60.2	87
15. Anacomp	60.1	60.1	60.0	57.0	89
16. Commodore International	54.1	-13.2	105.2	98.7	66
17. Applicon	51.4	35.2	136.6	68.5	82
18. Auto-trol Technology	51.3	58.5	27.1	50.8	97
19. AM International	49.0	49.0	49.0	98.8	65
20. Printronix	48.8	37.7	93.0	48.9	99

SA do in 1982 to anticipate these changes and to build a viable niche in the future data processing arena? With limited time and financial resources, he wondered where he should place his bets in the next two years. The alternatives were almost too numerous to list, much less scrutinize in detail. And it seemed imperative that SA move quickly to establish its position for the future.

Exhibit 3.5   *continued*

Data Processing Revenues by Product Segment ($ millions)

	1980		1979		Percent Growth Rate
Systems:					
Mainframes	$15,148	27.2%	$13,312	29.0%	13.8%
Minicomputers	8,840	15.9	6,916	15.0	27.8
Microcomputers	769	1.4	416	0.9	84.9
Word processing	881	1.6	538	1.2	63.8
Total systems	25,638	46.1	21,182	46.1	21.0
Oem peripherals	3,968	7.1	3,128	6.8	26.9
End-user peripherals	6,910	12.4	5,943	12.9	16.3
Data communications	1,141	2.1	927	2.0	23.1
Software products	1,738	3.1	1,347	2.9	29.0
Maintenance	8,888	16.0	7,372	16.0	20.6
Service	6,432	11.6	5,329	11.6	20.7
All other	911	1.6	772	1.7	18.0
Total	$55,625	100.0%	$46,000	100.0%	20.9%

*NM = Not meaningful.
Source: P. Wright, "The Datamation 100," *Datamation*, June 1981.

Software Architects' Business Objectives

The business objectives which Harvey established for Software Architects were:

1. Preserve the quality of life of the SA employees and directors.

2. Recruit additional consultants to support the growth in revenues and earnings without sacrificing SA's requirements for technical competence and the potential ability to deal effectively with clients and others in the firm.

3. Maintain exceptional quality of SA's work product.

4. Differentiate SA from competitors by demonstrating a perceptibly higher quality of work to existing and potential clients.

5. Charge a premium price based on the value of higher-quality work to the client.

6. Increase annual billings to $700,000 in 1982 and $1.2 million in 1983.

7. Achieve a target percentage of before-tax income to total billings of 30 percent in both 1982 and 1983.

8. Explore new products and services for SA to introduce in order to meet its targets for growth and profitability, and to position the firm favorably in a rapidly changing technological environment.

The projected billings by category of service and staffing levels for SA are included in Exhibit 3.6. SA's performance for the first five months of the 1982 fiscal year made the targets for billings and income seem reasonable. Year-to-date billings were $411,000, with before-tax income of over $147,000. This performance had been achieved with minimal requirement for overtime work.

Exhibit 3.6   Projected Billings, Income Before Tax,* and Staffing Levels for Software Architects

	Period Ending		
Billings by line of business:	**June 1981** **(actual)**	**June 1982** **(Projected)**	**June 1983** **(Projected)**
Systems software	$203	$245	$ 240
Custom application software	75	335	600
Education/training programs	60	105	360
Microcomputer systems	5	15	0
Total billings	$343	$700	$1,200
Income before tax	$ 47	$210	$ 360
Staffing levels:			
Number of consultants for SA	7	15	25
Number of support staff	0	1	2
Number of subcontractors	½	1½	2½

*Billings and income are in thousands of dollars.

Software Architects' Business Strategy

A strategy was under development to address each of SA's eight business objectives. While not yet completed and approved by the board of directors, most of the elements of the plan had fallen into place.

Quality of Life

The six founders of SA had all worked previously for other employers. They had left those organizations because they were dissatisfied with the stress, red tape, and sluggishness they had encountered. Each of them wanted to learn more in the technical area. They also shared the desire to develop their interests outsides of their careers, and wanted to avoid the frenetic pace of tight deadlines and 60-hour weeks that were the rule in many software consulting firms. Therefore, the quality of life for SA personnel was of tremendous concern to Harvey, Gloria, and the other directors. They had adopted the following policies to demonstrate their commitment in this area:

1. The billable hours targeted for each employee were 1,680 a year, considerably lower than targets in other firms. This helped to prevent excessive overtime on projects.

2. Each employee was allowed 12 days of vacation, 12 days of sick leave, 2 weeks for training/development, and 10 holidays a year.

3. To prevent the stress of out-of-town travel, SA limited its marketing activities to the Chicago area. The directors had occasionally turned down lucrative contracts that required prolonged travel to other locations.

Recruiting and Staff Development

Harvey's strategy for preserving quality of service was closely tied to his staffing plans. Every professional at SA was a graduate of a rigorous program in computer science at Northern Illinois University. The school had achieved a prominent reputation in the Midwest for producing graduates of unquestioned technical competence who also had an appreciation for the needs for practical data processing solutions to business problems. Harvey planned to recruit Northern Illinois University students on campus, as well as graduates who had been in industry for a year or two. He also provided funds for continuing development of the technical and interpersonal skills of current SA employees. They were encouraged to take seminars in state-of-the-art technical subjects, as well as those which might refine their skills in marketing, managing subordinates, and interacting with clients.

SA had planned to add several members to the staff in late 1981. They had not yet been brought on board. Several people who had been made offers accepted jobs elsewhere. One indicated that he did not feel technically qualified to "measure up" to the current SA staff. Although there was some concern that SA might be too selective in its recruiting criteria, the directors were convinced that maintaining high standards of technical competence was critical to the preservation of the quality of the work on which SA's reputation was based.

Quality of Service

It appeared that the major causes of failure in system development projects were the imposition of unrealistic deadlines, the use of programmers without relevant experience, lack of adequate planning in the design phases, and poor documentation in the implementation phase. Harvey and Gloria felt that their strategy for quality of service addressed each of those problems.

SA refused to commit to completion dates when submitting proposals for new business. They insisted on being able to work on the problem a few days or weeks in order to gain information to make realistic estimates of the elapsed time required to finish the job. This prevented the premature establishment of a timetable that was doomed to failure.

Many of SA's competitors staffed projects with one or two seasoned programmers and a large number of "green troops." SA used smaller project teams and experienced programmers almost exclusively. When a new person joined the firm, he or she was put on a project with several SA veterans to learn the ropes and ensure that the quality of the new programmer's work was consistent with the rest of the firm's.

SA spent more time and energy during detailed design than many of its competitors. Planning and the preparation of detailed specifications reduced the risk of problems and delays during implementation. SA also documented its programs more extensively than did most other firms. Although this was somewhat time-consuming during the first writing of the program, it made it much easier to test the program later on. Also, modifications were simpler once the program was installed. There was less dependence on a particular programmer, because good documentation was easily decipherable by someone who had not written the original code.

Harvey and Gloria agreed that all of these things made SA's work product better than that of most of its rivals. But they were not sure whether their clients perceived a difference in quality. Nor were they confident that such subtle gradations in quality of service could be effectively communicated to a prospect who was unfamiliar with SA.

Differentiation from Competitors

The strategy for differentiating SA from its competitors was still under review. The firm was considering a policy of guaranteeing their custom software work for a period after contract expiration. This practice was rare in the software industry, where the costs of time spent on "free" warranty work rather than billable projects were high and extremely visible. Harvey was not sure how effective a warranty might be in convincing potential clients that SA provided a quality advantage. It was not clear how to assess the potential benefits of new business versus the costs of honoring the warranty if the client encountered a problem.

Harvey and Gloria stressed the fact that SA programmers were all Northern Illinois University graduates in the belief that the school's reputation for data processing instruction might help to distinguish SA from other firms. But they needed to establish other unique advantages for SA which could be communicated to prospective clients. Harvey was trying to generate creative ideas for doing this.

Pricing Strategy

Harvey was not sure whether SA's billing rates were set at a "premium price." This was mainly due to uncertainty over the pricing strategies of competitors. It was difficult to obtain good estimates of what each firm charged for its services, since there were no industry guidelines for billing rates. Moreover, rates quoted by consultants in response to general inquiries were generally higher than those submitted during competitive bidding. Price cutting in order to win new business occurred frequently. The amount of the reductions varied and was impossible to predict.

It was evident that the rates customers would accept varied, depending upon the service performed. System software development skills were in short supply in the industry, and SA had no trouble charging $50 an hour for such projects. SA's hourly rates for application software development, which was less complex and less specialized, ranged from $33 to $37. Database design and application programming in special environments commanded rates between $34 and $44. The development of technical seminars brought $50 to $65 an hour, while giving the seminars to clients often paid $75 to $100 per instructor hour. However, clients typically wanted a more-experienced individual to prepare the technical training than they did for programming tasks, so the higher billing rates were offset by higher salaries and opportunity costs for SA.

Marketing Strategy to Achieve Target Growth and Profits

It appeared to Harvey that the keys to meeting the goals for growth in revenues, profit, and staffing levels were effective recruiting and marketing programs. The recruiting strategy has already been discussed. The marketing strategy consisted of several elements:

1. Concentrate on the largest private-sector enterprises in the Chicago area.

2. Where possible, use the growing network of key decision makers familiar with SA to obtain referrals to new prospective clients.

3. Where referrals are not possible, initiate "cold calls" on key technical managers in target organizations to expose them to SA and discuss current and future needs for services provided by the firm.

4. Concentrate on organizations using IBM hardware and system software because of the specialized expertise of SA consultants in those systems.

5. Wherever possible, adopt the premium quality and price approach. In competitive-bidding situations, if the potential for repeat business is high, reduce the hourly rate

to not less than $33 an hour for the first contract. Increase the hourly rate for follow-on work, once the client has seen the high quality of SA consultants' performance.

6. Stress the links between SA and Northern Illinois University in order to develop the image of SA as a source of updated technical talent and high-quality work.

Development of New Products and Services

While the first seven objectives were addressed by the strategy Harvey had developed, he was uncertain about the best approach to meet the objective of exploring new products and services. There was no shortage of ideas from within the firm about potential areas of new business. Some of the suggestions included:

1. Development of application software for microcomputers, including a project accounting and general ledger system for a company in a service business like SA's.

2. Development of software to collect information on telephone calls made in a company using Bell equipment. The information would subsequently be used to produce accounting and resource usage reports for management.

3. Development of systems software packages for users of IBM computers in many organizations.

4. Preparation and presentation of courses on programming using techniques that SA had perfected.

5. Joint presentation of technical seminars in cooperation with several of the faculty members from Northern Illinois University.

6. Establishment of an institute in which nontechnical personnel provided by SA's clients would be given an accelerated course in programming. Harvey estimated that a bright liberal arts major could be transformed into crack application programmer in four to six months.

These were but a few of SA's potential alternatives. What was missing was a method by which to review these and other alternatives from the strategic perspective. How might one assess the potential of alternative projects to contribute to SA's growth and profitability? How might one discern whether one project or another provided a better hedge against the risk of technological obsolescence? Developing a strategy and a system for the last objective appeared to be the most difficult task of all.

Harvey's First Action Step

As Harvey reviewed the elements of the strategy he had assembled, he had three major concerns:

1. Was the strategy realistic, given SA's resources and the realities of the external environment?

2. Were the elements of the strategy internally consistent?

3. How might the short-term strategy be modified to better equip SA to deal with its long-term prospects?

The issues were important enough that he wanted an outside opinion. He decided to bring in a consultant that Gene Petrie had recommended to help him think them through.

=== **CASE APPENDIX 3A** ===
Dataguide Report on the Future
of the Software Industry*

The software industry is booming! By 1986 it will be a $38-billion industry. Market growth will average 30 percent per year for the next five years. Today companies spend over $10 billion on external software expenditures.

This may seem an extraordinary growth from other market-size estimates of $3.5 billion today and $10 billion at middecade. However, it is important to realize that most estimates ignore the two largest segments of the software marketplace: professional services and turnkey software, each of which is as lucrative as the combined market for applications and systems software packages, as explained below.

Software is provided to users in two ways: standard off-the-shelf packages and customized products. In addition, software may be packaged with computer hardware and called a turnkey system. The software industry can be graphically depicted as shown in Exhibit 3.7

Turnkey systems can use either standard off-the-shelf software products or can be customized for a client (professional services). It is estimated that between 50 percent and 60 percent of all turnkey systems use off-the-shelf software products, while the other 40 percent to 50 percent use software created specially for the client through a professional services arrangement.

Turnkey systems are generally perceived to be a relatively recent product innovation, although the concept is at least 15 years old. Historically, software vendors sold software products and/or professional services, but rarely involved computer hardware in the sale. Today computer manufacturers offer quantity discounts to turnkey system vendors, who can then add software and sell the system to a user, theoretically generating profit from the software as well as the hardware (marked up to the list price for the user). More will be said about this theoretical relationship later.

Software can be separated into two categories. Systems software enables the computer communications system to perform basic operations. Applications software provides solutions to specific user requirements. It is the application software that is most visible to

*Warren N. Sargent, Jr. and Paul Colen, of the Palo Alto Management Group, "Software," *Dataguide*, Fall 1981.

Warren N. Sargent, Jr., a principal of the Palo Alto Management Group, has 17 years' experience in the computer services industry. He has held management and technical positions in both user and computer services vendor organizations. He has a B.S. in Mechanical Engineering, an M.S. in Mechanical Engineering, and an M.B.A. from the University of Connecticut. He is a PhD candidate in International Marketing and Finance at the University of Texas.

Paul Colen, a principal of the Palo Alto Management Group, has more than 25 years' experience. He was president of Advanced Management Systems and was also founder of the Corporation for Information Systems Research and Development. He has held a number of technical and management positions with Burroughs and Honeywell. He has a B.S. from Northwestern University and an M.S. in Business Economics from Claremont Graduate School.

Exhibit 3.7   Software Industry Composition in 1981

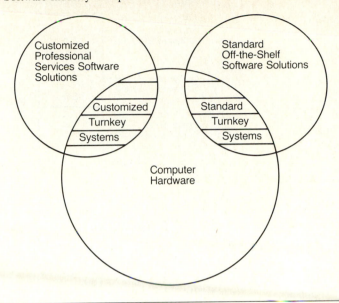

Source: Warren N. Sargent, Jr., and Paul Colen, of the Palo Alto Mangement Group, "Software," *Dataguide*, Fall 1981.

Exhibit 3.8   Computer System Architecture

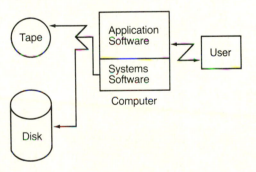

the user, while the systems software supports the functions called for by the application. Exhibit 3.8 depicts a computer system showing the main functions of systems and applications software.

Each of the four elements of the software industry will grow rapidly (see Exhibit 3.9). Turnkey systems user expenditures will grow the fastest: 35 percent per year for the next five years. The practice of computer manufacturers charging separately for systems software products will continue to increase over the next five years and will therefore drive the growth forecast for these products to over 30 percent per year.

Exhibit 3.9   User External Software Expenditures

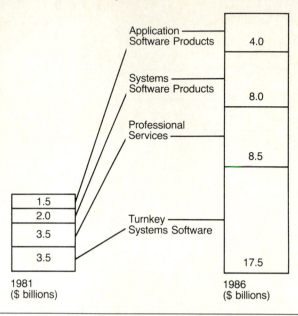

1981
($ billions)

1986
($ billions)

The rate of growth in user expenditures for application software products, 25 percent per year, is deceptive. Turnkey systems use application software products in at least 50 percent of the cases, and turnkey systems user expenditures are growing at 35 percent per year. Therefore, the true growth for all uses of application software (products and turnkey systems) exceeds 30 percent per year. Professional services user expenditure, excluding turnkey systems, will grow at 20 percent per year for the next five years. However, the true growth rate for all types of professional services (including turnkey systems) will be 25 percent per year.

Systems Software

Systems software, which enables the computer communications systems to perform basic functions, is classified by three types—system operation, system utilization, and system implementation.

System operation products manage computer communication system resources during program execution. Examples of such products are operating systems, database management systems, and telecommunication monitors.

System utilization products help manage the computer system operation more efficiently. Performance measurement systems, job accounting systems, and system utilities are examples.

System implementation products prepare applications for execution by assisting application design, programming, testing, and related functions. Examples of such products are assemblers, compilers, software design productivity aids, report writers, and program library systems.

There are probably 4,000 or more systems hardware products, marketed by nearly 1,000 vendors today. It is extremely difficult to count vendors and products because of the changing nature of the industry. Some vendors announce a new product and subsequently drop it because they can't generate sales, or they decide to sell the product and licensing rights for the product to another vendor. Vendors change the name of some products to create a new image even though the product is not actually new. There has been an explosion of new products for personal and small computers. Since many of the vendors of these systems software products are still operating regionally, it is difficult to identify their market presence.

At one time over 80 percent of user expenditures for systems software products were for IBM and IBM-compatible large computers. That percent is decreasing as users of small computers become more sophisticated and realize the value of the systems software products available in the marketplace.

The industry trends of increased use of telecommunications and automation in the office have a positive impact on the market for systems software products. Systems software is the "glue" that joins the computer hardware and application software together. Changing functionality in the computer hardware creates a need for new systems software. Enterprising organizations have recognized this need and have been responding with new and improved products.

Computer manufacturers have historically fostered this industry by their attitude toward independent software vendors, in that they have not "locked out" the independent vendor's software from operating on the manufacturer's computer. Manufacturers have tacitly encouraged independents to develop user-friendly systems that facilitate computer use: the easier computers are to use, the more will be sold.

The future of the systems software market is unclear in the late 1980s and beyond. On the one hand, the computer manufacturer must consider its users and cannot lock out independent systems software products. On the other hand, computer manufacturers could develop similar product capabilities to the independent vendors' products. The investment required to do this is probably prohibitive. The computer manufacturer is left in a precarious position, i.e., how can it maintain control over its customers?

One solution to this dilemma is to combine the systems software and the computer hardware (firmware) together in future computer generations. As users buy these new computers, they will not have a need or perhaps the ability to add additional systems software products to their computers. Will this happen? Intel has stated that software (including applications) will be combined with the hardware in the 1980s. It is unlikely that all systems or application software will be combined with hardware in this decade, but it appears clear that a substantial part of the systems software *could* be combined with the computer hardware in the next 10 years.

Application Software

Application software products perform specific application functions for end-user organizations. These products solve specific user problems.

Application software products can be divided into two types: cross-industry products and industry-specialized products. Cross-industry products perform applications common to many industries, such as payroll, general ledger, fixed-asset accounting, accounts receivable, or inventory management. Industry-specialized products perform applications specific to industries such as banking, medical, or insurance. Examples of industry-specialized applications are demand deposit accounting (banking), shop scheduling (manufacturing), and policy administration (insurance).

Users of application software products are people involved in day-to-day company business. Thus, typical users of an accounts receivable product include clerical personnel who perform data entry, credit managers who use CRT terminals for online inquiry, and the vice-president of finance who uses summary reports. All of the functions described are performed by the application software product. Generally, the people involved with computer operations are not the users of application software products. Computer operations personnel typically use systems software products. However, both groups of people help evaluate application software products for company use.

Nearly 10,000 applications software products are marketed by approximately 2,000 vendors. These numbers grow daily due to the tremendous growth in use of small computers. No vendor, including computer manufacturers, has captured more than 10 percent of this market. At one time the majority of application software products was written for IBM and IBM-compatible mainframes, but this is no longer true today. Over one-half of the application software products and vendors now serve the personal and small computer used by many user markets.

Application software product vendors have penetrated the banking, insurance, and discrete manufacturing sectors with industry-specialized application products to the extent that nearly 60 percent of user expenditures for application software products occur in these three industries. Discrete manufacturing application software expenditures is the fastest-growing section due largely to the need for distributed applications for plant operations in diverse locations. However, other industries, such as retail, process manufacturing, and transportation, will also experience rapid growth in user expenditures for application software products, as these industries have not yet been heavily penetrated by product solutions.

Professional Services

Professional services are used for the design and programming services performed for users who require software tailored to their specifications. In some cases, users want software capabilities that are not available in standard products. In other cases, the user wants very specific functions performed according to set procedures that rule out product solutions. Most professional services are for application software although some systems software is written for mainframes or unique distributed processing projects.

There are thousands of professional services vendors. Every independent consultant who designs software or programs on a custom basis provides professional services. However, probably 2,000 vendors each generate more than $250,000 revenue in professional services per year. The amount of client contact required means these vendors generally serve geographical markets. There are only several hundred firms that offer professional services in more than one geographical area.

The use of professional services is increasing primarily due to the backlog of programming work in data processing departments, the shortage of software designers and programmers, and the lack of specific skills in data processing departments needed to develop certain applications. The backlog of application development in most data processing departments is 24 months and growing. The only way to reduce this backlog without hiring permanent employees (assuming that they could be found) is to use outside professional services. The shortage of software designers and programmers tends to raise the compensation level for people with these key skills. In order to attract and retain these people, professional services firms offer higher salaries and more diverse project experience. This creates a greater personnel shortage in other types of firms, reinforcing the need for outside professional services.

Professional services firms have developed technical skills to handle new applications in distributed processing, telecommunications, database systems, and office automation. Most companies don't have the diversity of needs to have developed these skills in-house. Now that these skills are required, it may be more economical to obtain them from a professional services vendor.

Many professional service vendors have begun offering turnkey systems to their clients. Although it is too early to measure the success of most of these offerings, the professional services firm is extremely well positioned to offer unique turnkey systems because of its established base of technical expertise.

Turnkey Systems

Turnkey systems solve an application problem for a user. The key features are that the computer hardware and software are sold at the same time, and that the problem addressed is an application (as opposed to systems software). Application software not sold at the same time as the computer hardware is considered a product (or professional service) and would be included in the application software product (or professional service) category. User-expenditure data shown in Exhibit 3.9 includes only the software portion of the turnkey system sale. The computer hardware, training, supplies, and computer hardware maintenance components are independent of and not included in Exhibit 3.9.

There are approximately 5,000 turnkey system vendors. Some turnkey system vendors also sell software products and/or professional services. The largest turnkey system suppliers today provide systems for computer-aided design and manufacturing (CAD/CAM). Approximately 15 percent to 20 percent of all turnkey system user expenditures today are for CAD/CAM. The smallest turnkey system suppliers typically serve the general business accounting environment. The supplier sells payroll, accounts receivable, accounts payable, and general ledger software along with the computer hardware. Most of these suppliers are marginally profitable due to intense competition in this market.

The key to successful turnkey systems is offering specialized systems to a narrow audience. Industry-specialized turnkey systems have been successfully sold and serviced and are easily sold by customer referrals. Vendors who have specialized systems have less competition, can command higher prices, and have higher profits. Vendors that offer generalized systems have intense competition (from computer processing services firms and computer manufacturers, as well as other turnkey system suppliers) and generally have to discount list prices of hardware. Thus, it is a myth that the generalized turnkey system vendor will make profit on *both* the computer hardware and software.

The future for independent turnkey system vendors should involve the packaging of small computers with highly specialized software. The more unique the system, and consequently the smaller the market niche, the better for the vendor. The successful vendor will become the leader in serving these market niches and hence move down the experience curve and ultimately raise the barriers of entry to the competition.

Computer manufacturers will concentrate on offering generalized solutions that will appeal to many buyers. However, these solutions will not have the specialization needed to serve small market niches.

Driving Forces

The past five years have shown a dramatic increase in user demand for software. Substantially improved computer hardware cost-performance has lowered the threshold and opened new application areas. A new generation of management is (by education and training) increasingly more aware of the types of applications that can be addressed with computer software. Increased scarcity of software designers and programmers, coupled with the impact of inflation on personnel costs, has forced managers to explore alternatives to in-house software development.

Computer manufacturers have devoted most of their resources to development and marketing of computer hardware and systems software, leaving voids to be filled, particularly in application software. Computer manufacturers such as Atari and IBM are encouraging software developers to write software for the manufacturer's hardware. Government regulation in such industries as banking and insurance, and in such functional areas as human resources and taxes, has had a substantial impact on demand for external software. The net result has been the entry of many small companies, with a corresponding proliferation of software.

New forces are coming into play that will add to the factors influencing the software marketplace in the next five years. Computer manufacturers such as Honeywell and Burroughs and other large companies such as Xerox and Exxon are entering the marketplace. The accompanying buying process—better coordinated, more sophisticated, demanding improved support service—will force greater competition among vendors of software solutions. Advances in technology in areas such as database, microprocessors, image processing, telecommunication network, and distributed processing will furnish new opportunities for new software solutions. Future success will require vendors to excel in software development, sales, marketing, and in customer maintenance and support. Computer manufacturers and selected large companies, together with large independent computer software solution firms, will aggressively acquire smaller vendors, resulting in a market consolidation in which a relatively small number of firms will dominate the profitable market sectors.

Smythe, Klein, Carstairs, Miller and Ping, Professional Association

▪ *James M. Higgins* ▪

Matthew Klein stood gazing out his office window pondering the future of his law firm. He could just make out the silhouette of a fishing boat as it entered the bay, returning home with the day's catch. But he could not keep his mind on that peaceful scene. His mind was forced inevitably back to the problems facing his firm. He had seen it grow from two lawyers and two secretaries, when he and David Smythe had started the firm some 13 years ago, to its current size in January 1984 of 10 lawyers and approximately 25 support staff. There had been plenty of successes and very few setbacks, but the firm had grown so fast in the last three years that it seemed to have outgrown the firm's management capabilities.

Further compounding the firm's management problems was the fact that he had been absent from the firm much of the time this past year, while actively pursuing his other business interests. He knew his absence had had a major impact on the firm because most people in the firm had always looked to him to hold the firm together, and there really had been no one to take his place in that regard. His presence had been missed during this period even more than it might normally have been because of the increased level of intensity of the now continual disagreement between Jack Carstairs and Chuck Miller about how the day-to-day operations of the firm should be conducted. This rift had been accentuated during these past few months as Chuck had spearheaded the conversion of the firm's accounting and management systems from hand-maintained to those using a computer.

Chuck, to put it mildly, did not possess strong positive human relations skills. It was perceived by most members of the firm that he had caused considerable unrest among the legal and support staff during this time period with the way in which he handled this major change program. To make matters worse, Jack had resented Chuck in the computerization effort at virtually every turn. The firm was now apparently divided into two camps, one following Chuck, the other following Jack.

Matthew's firm was the largest in Sarasota, Florida. It faced stiff competition from several other firms seeking to become the largest. The local economy would continue to grow, but not necessarily in the direction that suited the strengths of this firm. The regional economy was prosperous and offered many opportunities for continued growth. Matthew wanted the firm to continue to grow and prosper. It was "his baby." But the exact actions which he should take were at this time, uncertain in his mind. He knew that before he could pursue any additional growth, he had to straighten out the management situation that existed currently.

Entrepreneurship and Law—A History of the Firm

David Smythe had been in practice by himself for almost 10 years when he decided to expand and add a second partner in 1971. He found in Matthew Klein the perfect match for his own skills and personality. Matthew had been in practice for only a few months when David suggested that they become partners. David had not particularly wanted a partner previously, but now sought someone to help handle his very heavy case load. Matthew's reputation had grown quite rapidly in the short time that he had been practicing, and he seemed a likely candidate. The two hit it off immediately. They were both very competent trial lawyers, and their talents suited the needs of the community at that point in time. But more importantly, they were both entrepreneurially oriented, and jointly sought to pursue these interests. They highly leveraged the purchase of a local bank, and soon two more. Everyone was calling them financial wizards, at least for a few months. But the deep recession of 1973–1975 nearly spelled doom for their banks. The law practice fortunately provided sufficient cash flow to keep them afloat. In the spring of 1975, they were able to sell their banks and net about $7 million in profits. David decided, at age 45, to retire and "see the world." He literally did. He purchased a large sailing yacht and commenced a two-year cruise around the world. Matthew, then aged 32, decided to continue his law practice, and chose to dabble in politics—not running for office but helping out various candidates behind the scenes.

It was at this time that Matthew became partners with Jack Carstairs. Jack had been in practice in the area for several years, had a sound reputation, and though flamboyant, seemed to match the skills that Matthew needed to replace those of David Smythe. Shortly thereafter, a third attorney was added, Wade Ping. Wade held much promise, partly because of his outside contacts related to his father's businesses, and partly because of his sharp legal mind. A fourth attorney, Chuck Miller was added to the staff in 1977. He specialized in real estate and the firm then became departmentalized into two major divisions—litigation and real estate. Matthew had used some of his profits from the banks to continue to build his real estate holdings, including a five-story office building which housed the law firm. His interests in real estate and his connections with real estate developers made during his banking days (and retained currently through part of his law practice), had led him to see the increased potential for real estate law as a major part of the firm's services, and thus had caused him to hire Chuck Miller. Wade Ping was made a partner in 1978 and disappointingly, his father's business began to take most of his time so that he no longer was active in the firm. Chuck Miller became a partner in 1978. At this point, only Jack and Matthew held stock in the professional association which was their law firm. An arrangement was made in 1980 to divide the stock into equal one-third shares, with Chuck Miller becoming the third stockholder. In that same year, Matthew's brother Jacob joined the firm, fresh from law school. Between 1980 and the spring of 1983, six additional attorneys were added to the staff. The firm prospered. Real estate began to become a greater part of their business, much of which came as a result of Matthew's personal contacts with various people in the community. In late 1980, Matthew joined two other area developers in a real estate development corporation. As this business grew and took on new dimensions, Matthew began to spend less and less time in the law firm. Various financial adjustments in payments to partners were made to reflect changing contributions, not just Matthew's diminished contributions to the bottom line, but Chuck's

Exhibit 4.1   Income Statement

	1983	1982	1981	1980
Gross fees	$1,318,376	$1,336,131	$1,130,819	$899,644
CGS	0	0	0	0
Gross profit	1,318,376	1,336,131	1,130,819	899,644
Interest	14,998	3,633	4,242	5,412
Gross rents	11,529	12,814	0	7,276 (capital gains)
Other income	0	2,652	0	0
Miscellaneous	14,529	4,153	0	(4,176)
Total income	1,359,432	1,359,383	1,135,061	908,156
Compensation	229,167	201,600	142,712	221,847
Salaries	501,987	467,044	348,224	253,445
Repairs	3,999	22,695	40,146	9,817
Rents	81,009	75,900	63,754	44,639
Taxes	49,946	57,538	37,313	29,925
Interest	52,732	38,659	27,790	26,887
Contributions	0	1,233	2,335	1,729
Depreciation	113,368	109,395	78,374	40,885
Pension/profit sharing	49,379	0	0	0
Other deductions	364,961	328,769	298,108	245,817
Total deductions	1,442,548	1,302,833	1,038,666	874,991
Income	(83,116)	56,550	96,395	33,165
Income Tax	$ 0	$ 25,721	$ 17,141	$ 272
Adjustment to books	(2,272)	36,132	10,681	44,577
Book income	(80,844)	20,418	85,714	(11,412)

increased contributions. In 1983, Jacob was made a junior partner in the firm, buying 10 percent of the total outstanding stock of the PA, 3⅓ percent from each of the three senior partners. Staff had been added slowly as the firm grew until now, when the total number of support personnel was 25. Gross income in 1983 was $1,320,000, but the firm had reported a loss of $83,000 on those gross revenues. (See Exhibits 4.1, 4.2, and 4.3.)

The Cast of Characters

Exhibit 4.4 presents a listing of the individuals within the firm. The following paragraphs provide a brief description of the principal persons involved in strategic management in the firm.

Matthew Klein

Matthew Klein is a man of varied interests, who is co-owner with two other individuals in a large real estate development firm. He has several real estate investment projects which he owns outright in his own name, and others which he shares with David Smythe. And

Exhibit 4.2   Itemized Expenses

Officer Compensation	1983	1982	1981	1980
M. Klein	$ 40,000	$ 37,115	$ 19,013	$ 95,175
J. Carstairs	112,667	84,098	67,481	79,538
C. Miller	76,500	80,387	56,218	47,134

Other Deductions	1983	1982	1981	1980
Auto	$ 22,248	$ 32,402	$ 28,240	$ 13,879
Bank changes commissions	0	0	1,000	0
Dues and subscriptions	7,579	6,210	5,071	2,588
Entertainment/promotion	0	2,049	0	563
Freight				
Insurance	55,057	56,574	45,604	39,827
Legal and accounting licenses	26,548	31,269	14,856	13,100
Miscellaneous	8,946	244	1,354	1,116
Office supplies/expenses	29,020	59,582	51,675	36,838
Postage	12,814	9,692	7,204	6,990
Stationary and printing	6,208	0	0	0
Telephone and telegraph	55,820	54,481	48,901	42,402
Travel and entertainment	5,163	42,086	31,792	34,698
Client costs	14,588	2,661	32,788	1,719
Utilities	0	7,293	2,066	14,457
Computer	14,024	0	0	0
Continuing education	17,173	8,987	5,180	4,647
Equipment maintenance	23,732	0	0	0
Miscellaneous	0	0	2,233	16,822 (Medcal and joint)
Professional books	11,830	15,239	10,869	10,862
Casual labor	0	0	9,185	5,309
Professional fees	48,622	0	0	0
Total deductions	$364,961	$328,769	$298,018	$245,817

then there is the law firm. Everyone who knows him considers him to be a consummate lawyer; he is, above all else, an expert at negotiation and compromise. He has a unique sense of what it takes to have two individuals come to terms. One attorney described him as follows: "He has the ability to take two people who want to kill each other and make them shake hands half-an-hour later." Some of that skill, of course, is necessary sometimes to soothe the ruffled feathers of both Jack and Chuck who do not basically speak to each other except through Matthew.

Matthew really wants to spend most of his time in the real estate development projects because that is where he makes most of his money, but he feels he has to devote at least a couple of days a week now to the law firm. It does, after all, bear his name on the marquee, and he wants to make sure that the quality image of the firm is continued as the firm continues to grow and prosper. His wife, many times, feels that he is spending too much time away from the home, that he is too actively engaged in other interests—so he receives pressure from home as well. He has, in fact, planned a three-week vacation—his first in two years—to begin in a matter of weeks. He also has made a considered effort to spend more time with his children as he realizes that they have grown without his having done very much with them. His children are a boy, age 14 and a girl, age 12. He is a concerned manager, with a background in accounting and finance, so he himself prepares the budgets for the firm. He gets along with everyone in the firm and virtually all look to him for guidance, something he would like to change but feels that he just can't change at this moment in time.

Exhibit 4.3   Balance Sheets

	1983	1982	1981	1980
Assets:				
Cash	(4,925)	(22,771)	1,623	100
Accounts receivable	52,004	15,465		
Other cash assets	19,257	79,019	37,546	35,835
Loans to stockholders	37,161	17,500		
Other investments	250	250		
Buildings and other assets	659,820	674,055	362,304	315,114
Depreciation	313,339	250,208	152,380	85,242
Buildings and depreciable assets	346,481	423,847	209,924	229,872
Land		15,300		
Intangible assets	5,000	7,500		
Other assets	141,635	61,627	73,166	80,262
Total assets	596,863	597,737	322,259	346,069
Liabilities and Stockholders' Equity:				
Accounts payable	0	0	0	0
Mtgs, notes, bonds payable in greater than one year	202,108	52,594	76,318	170,968
Other cash liabilities	26,821	785	2,693	1,517
Mtgs, notes, bonds payable in less than one year	292,142	387,722	107,280	123,330
Common stock	750	750	500	500
Retained earnings	75,042	155,886	135,468	49,754
	596,863	597,737	322,259	346,069
Analysis of Retained Earnings + Equalizing of Books with Tax Return:				
Adjustment to books total	(2,272)	36,132	10,687	44,577
Items:				
Officers' life insurance	6,024	6,700	8,110	0
Contributions carryover	615	0	0	(1,192)
Amortization of goodwill	2,500	2,500	2,500	2,500
Mortgage	0	0	0	22,000
Political contributions	2,725	0	0	0
Installments	0	0	0	12,578
Refunds of federal	(14,136)	25,428	(1,559)	631
Loss	0	0	0	7,260
Penalties	0	1,211	0	0
Nondeductible contributions	0	0	2,550	800
Depreciation	0	0	(1,192)	0

Exhibit 4.4   Firm Members

David Smythe	Retired Partner
Matthew Klein	Managing Senior Partner
Jack Carstairs	Senior Partner, Litigation
Chuck Miller	Senior Partner, Real Estate
Jacob Klein	Junior Partner, Litigation
Wade Ping	Junior Partner—Not Active
Sally	Matthew's Personal Secretary
Rita	Jack's Personal Secretary
Sharon	Chuck's Personal Secretary
Billy	Jacob's Personal Secretary
Margaret	Wade's Personal Secretary
Diana	Head of Computers

Other attorneys, primarily real estate:
Bob Jackson
Denise W. Joyner (does most of the real estate closings)

Other attorneys, primarily litigation:
Frank Rice
Randy Rasmussen
Marty White
Sam Johnson (recently terminated for inadequate client support)

Others
2 Paralegals
6 Computer/filing personnel
1 Excess secretary (was Sam Johnson's)
3 Floating secretaries
1 Receptionist
1 Telephone answerer
1 Half-time bookkeeper
1 Clerk for time-share closings

Source: Firm records.

David Smythe

Although David's name is still a part of the professional association, he has not been active in the firm since 1975. He does, however, jointly own with Matthew, a few real estate investments. He maintains an office in the same building that houses the law firm, and thus Matthew sees him frequently. But, David is no longer a force, not even an informal one, in the firm.

Jack Carstairs

Jack is, without question, the best litigation lawyer in the area. He can win just about any case he takes on. Matthew believes that the firm needs him now, even though he causes a lot of problems. Matthew feels they do not have anyone who could replace Jack—both his experience and his reputation. Jack has several personal problems which affect his work from time to time. One of these is the subject of much company gossip. "The guy is good, but if he grosses $100,000, he spends $125,000. He likes to take in those big American Bar Association conventions, and 'do the town up right' when he does, and that costs the firm a lot of money to no real gain. He sulks. He's very moody. And he burns out, understandably. He works for five months, night and day, seven days a week, but then he has to have three weeks' vacation. So, everyone else has to fit his schedule. That too causes us problems. He has just about quit communicating with Chuck. I think he's jealous of Chuck's becoming a full partner. He has no interest in managing the firm, or in helping anyone else manage properly. He has begun these Sunday-evening sessions for the junior lawyers from 7:00 to 10:00 pm., whereby they schedule the work for the week and go over cases, coverages, etc. That has helped. But that has just about been it. He's usually late to our monthly legal staff meetings. In fact, he's often late to a lot of appointments as well. Jack takes too many nickel/dime cases in the name of client service. He should save himself more for the big ones. He claims the clients want him, not one of the junior people."

Chuck commented, "Jack intentionally keeps clients waiting. He likes them to know how important he is. He refuses to complete the computer sheets we give him. His secretary is a troublemaker.

Chuck Miller

Chuck is a former U.S. Naval officer and thinks in terms of orders, "have-to's" and "do-it-nows," instead of convincing people to do the right thing—explaining to people why things need to be done a certain way. He doesn't believe in participation. He believes in direction. But he's a good manager within his own department. He seems to have a loyal following there. It's just the people in Jack's division, and Jack, that he doesn't get along with. Chuck is now grossing more revenue than Jack, and should continue to do so in the future. Most believe this makes Jack jealous. Chuck gets a lot more of the business that Matthew sends the firm than Jack does, and so there is some question as to just exactly how much business Chuck should be given credit for.

He is famous for his "Z-grams," (named for Admiral Zumalt, a naval admiral of the 1970s, famous for his blunt, directed memos of the same name) during the computer conversion, which still cause trouble. He's a good systems man. He knows how management systems are supposed to work, how they can make the firm more money. He's interested in helping the firm make more money, and in management. The fact that he and his secretary are romantically involved, was at first a negative gossip item, but that is probably no longer a major topic and is probably not affecting the organization much. The computer staff report to Chuck. Jack is opposed to the computer, refuses to use it, and basically wants nothing to do with management. There are some of Jack's subordinates who like Chuck and would rather work for him than for Jack. Several of Jack's support staff also prefer Chuck to Jack, but they fear saying so because of the informal power of Rita, Jack's secretary.

Jacob Klein

Matthew's little brother seems to have adapted well. He gets along with both Jack and Chuck, which is a difficult trick, since he reports to Jack, and works only on litigation cases. But since Jacob is Matthew's brother, no one is going to press him much. Jacob is still feeling his way around as a partner and more basically, as an attorney. In another few years, most believe he'll be as good as Jack is now. Most perceive this as good, because Jack won't be able to keep up his current pace for many more years.

Wade Ping

Wade Ping is a former football star at one of the state universities whose personal life has interfered with his ability to maintain an active partnership in the firm. His father is a multimillionnaire, and dangles the family fortune in front of Wade, demanding that Wade serve him first and the firm second. Wade is an outstanding attorney, primarily a litigation attorney. He takes cases for Smythe, Klein, et al., when they are overloaded, and even though he maintains an office with the firm, he pays for his secretaries' time, the contractual arrangement he has with Matthew being that he must earn at least as much money for the firm as the cost of the office. He prefers to keep his office away from his father's place of business in order to have a refuge from his father, who is a virtual tyrant. Wade is disliked very much by Jack and Chuck but is very well liked by Matthew and hence remains.

The Partners' Secretaries

Sally.   Matthew's secretary, Sally, actually engages in little interaction with others within the firm. She primarily handles Matthew's personal business interests, most of which are outside the law firm. She tries to remain uninvolved in the firm's interoffice politics.

Rita.   Jack's secretary, Rita, is the greatest admirer that Jack has. Rita is a recently divorced, somewhat bitter-against-life individual who actively engages in subterfuge, gossip, politics, and a host of other negative interpersonal behaviors. She is principally responsible for keeping Jack stirred up against the rest of the firm and the rest of the firm stirred up against Jack. Rita has gone so far, for example, as to actively campaign to eliminate various staff members. Some attribute the leaving of Sam Johnson, a recently terminated attorney, to her actions. She also campaigns to remove the paralegals from the firm, since she feels she's more qualified but just barely as well paid even though she has more experience.

Sharon.   Chuck's secretary, Sharon, is an extremely shy, quiet, and reclusive individual who tends to her own business and interacts very little with those outside Chuck's immediate office area.

Billy.   Billy and Rita are good friends and cohorts in crime. They continually keep things stirred up, although Billy is not nearly as guilty of this as Rita.

Margaret.   Margaret is an extremely negative person, one who constantly gossips about everybody and everything within the firm and has more complaints about the firm than anyone interviewed in the company.

Diana, who is head of computers, is a pleasant woman whose subordinates follow her. She seems to be doing an adequate job. She satisfies everyone but Jack.

Other Attorneys

Most of the attorneys switch back and forth between real estate, but Bob Jackson and Denise Joyner function primarily in the real estate closing area. In fact, Denise closes more real estate than anyone else in the firm, almost as much as all the other people combined. Frank Rice, Randy Rasmussen, and Marty White primarily function in the litigation area and handle a lot of less-important cases—divorces, for example.

Other Members of the Firm

Several other members of the firm include the paralegals, the various computer filing personnel, several floating secretaries, a receptionist, a telephone answerer, a part-time bookkeeper, and a clerk who does nothing but time-share condominium closings. These individuals are all women and all paid at the going market wage, which in this particular area is reasonably high due to competition for their services in the local job market. All feel they should be paid more but all enjoy working for the firm because of its reputation in the community. They all appreciate the battles that go on in the firm and they all try to stay separate from them. However, those in the computer area are in constant battle, it seems, either with Jack or his secretary, Rita. Rita continually causes problems for those in the computer area and has had several personal run-ins with Diana.

Organizational Structure

An organizational chart does not exist for Smythe, Klein, et al., but if it did, it would look like the one in Exhibit 4.5

Exhibit 4.5   Organizational Structure

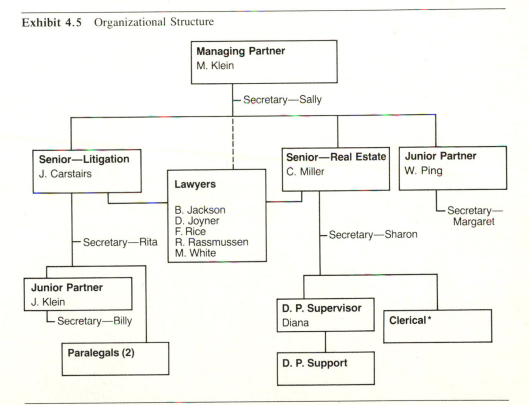

---

*Includes bookkeeper, switchboard operator, and receptionist.

Exhibit 4.6   Attorneys' Climate Survey

Please check that which applies for the following two questions:
1. Paralegal_____ Lawyer's Secretary_____ Other Staff_____
2. Litigation Division_____ Real Estate Division_____
   Data Processing_____ Other Areas of the Firm_____

How important would improvement in the following things be to you?
Please mark the appropriate box with an X.

	Very Little or Not at All	A Little	Fairly Important	Very important	Extremely Important
Longer coffee breaks.	8				
More holidays.	4	1	3		
Flexibility in hours or days off.	4	1	3		
More overtime opportunity.	7	1			
Better insurance.	1	1	3	2	1
Better working conditions.	4	1	3		
Retirement plan.	1	3	1	2	1
Higher pay.	1	3	0	2	2
Education refund.	5	2	1		
Treated more as an individual.	5	0	2	1	
Better way to get complaints heard.	5	0	2	1	
Better/more training.	3	1	2	1	1
More direction from supervisor.	2	2	2	1	1
More opportunity to learn and improve self.	3	0	2	3	
More say in how my department does things.	4	0	2	2	
More opportunity to contribute to company success.	1	3	2	1	1
Better decisions by top management.	4	1	2	1	
More information on what's going on.	1	3	2	2	
Be more in charge of own self.	4	0	2	2	
More company guidance and policy.	3	1	3	0	1

Organizational Culture

Relationships within the firm are hostile. Often there is open sniping between the two groups: the one that supports Carstairs and the one that supports Miller. The two partners often engage in conflict openly in front of others. Members of the groups usually don't speak to each other except to argue. Necessary coordination is brief and tense. Jack and Chuck have gone many weeks at a time communicating only through Matthew. Klein has encouraged them to speak to each other and has talked with each one singly, attempting to appease each one and meet the needs of each. Often he is unable to come to a full agreements between the two. Carstairs is jealous of Miller and Miller's financial success within the firm, because Carstairs has been there longer. Carstairs simply doesn't see that Miller should be making as much as he does even though Miller's division is financially highly productive. There is jealousy, too, because Miller and Klein get along well, and since

Exhibit 4.6   *continued*

What is your opinion on the following statements? Do you agree or disagree?
Please mark the appropriate box with an X.

	Strongly Disagree	Disagree	No Opinion	Agree	Strongly Agree
My pay is fair for this kind of job.		1	2	4	1
My co-workers are good to work with.				5	3
My complaints or concerns are heard by management.		1		5	2
Things are getting better here.		2	2	3	1
The supervisors do a poor job.	1	4	2	1	
Working conditions are bad here.	2	5	1		
I benefit when the company succeeds.			2	4	2
I have all the chances I wish to improve myself.		1		6	1
The company is well run.		2	1	5	
Communications are poor.	1	2	2	2	1
I don't get enough direction from my supervisor.	1	3	2	2	
I enjoy my work.				3	5
I look for ways to improve the work I do.				6	2
I need more of a chance to manage myself.	1	3	2	1	1
Morale is good here.		4	1	3	
Some do only what it takes to get by.	1	2		5	
I like the way my supervisor treats me.			2	5	1
We need a suggestion system.	1	1	2	3	1
I want more opportunity for advancement.	1		4	1	2
My supervisor knows me and what I want.			1	6	1
We are expected to do a good job here.				5	3
There are too many rules.		5	2		1
I feel like part of a team at work.		2		5	1
The company and my supervisor seek my ideas.		2	1	4	1
I know and understand the objectives of my job.				6	2
I know and understand the objectives of the company.				6	2
Some secretaries have too much power.		1	2	4	1
Other.	1		7		

Carstairs and Klein were the original two partners in the firm, there is jealousy for that reason as well. Carstairs is also highly emotional, temperamental, often irrational. A lawyer from a competing firm in the area describes Carstairs as an egomaniac who must be known as the most expensive lawyer in the county. But Carstairs loses very few cases, and is well known for his ability to mastermind strategies for defenses, and has been extremely successful.

His egomania, however, has caused his secretary to be able to wield considerably more influence than her position warrants. She has more than once been responsible for the

Exhibit 4.7 Support Staff Climate Survey

Please check that which applies for the following two questions:
1. Paralegal____ Lawyer's Secretary____ Other Staff____
2. Litigation Division____ Real Estate Division____
   Data Processing____ Other Areas of the Firm____

How important would improvement in the following things be to you?
Please mark the appropriate box with an X.

	No Response	Very Little or Not at All	A Little	Fairly Important	Very Important	Extremely Important	Mean
Longer coffee breaks.	1	17	3	1			1.18
More holidays.		7	6	7	2		2.18
Flexibility in hours or days off.		6	5	2	6	3	2.77
More overtime opportunity.		13	3	4	2		1.77
Better insurance.	1	6	1	7	5	2	2.68
Better working conditions.		3	3	5	5	6	3.36
Retirement plan.		1	3	4	3	11	3.91
Higher pay.		2	0	4	7	9	3.95
Education refund.	1	7	1	5	5	3	2.68
Treated more as an individual.		4	3	6	5	4	3.09
Better way to get complaints heard.		6	0	2	8	6	3.36
Better/more training.		4	2	5	3	8	3.41
More direction from supervisor.		14	3	1	1	3	1.91
More opportunity to learn and improve self.		4	2	5	3	8	3.41
More say in how my department does things.	2	6	3	3	6	2	2.50
More opportunity to contribute to company success.		4	1	6	5	6	3.36
Better decisions by top management.		5	1	3	2	11	3.59
More information on what's going on.		3	0	4	5	10	3.86
Be more in charge of own self.	1	10	1	5	3	2	2.22
More company guidance and policy.		4	2	5	6	5	3.27
Other.					1	1	

firing of innocent individuals whose only real major mistake had been to disagree with her and the actions that she felt might be necessary in the organization. For some period of time she had served as an office manager, and that failed to work out partly because her leadership was not accepted by the other secretarial support staff. The organization is burdened with psychological game playing. The rumor mill is rampant, people try to get other people in trouble, attempt to shaft one person or another, and dwell on the interpersonal relationships of the partners (and the partners with their secretaries), much more than is characteristic of most organizations. It's believed by many of the support staff from Carstairs' side of the firm that they can't be allowed to be seen talking to any of the members of the support staff on Miller's side for fear of retribution by Carstairs' secretary. There is concern for pay and for pension programs, for medical and health care, but mostly for the way in which people are treated. Exhibits 4.6 and 4.7, reveal the results of an organizational climate survey performed by the senior partner.

Exhibit 4.7   *continued*

What is your opinion on the following statements? Do you agree or disagree?
Please mark the appropriate box with an X.

Statement	No Response	Strongly Disagree	Disagree	No Opinion	Agree	Strongly Agree	Mean
My pay is fair for this kind of job.		7	6	5	4	0	2.27
My co-workers are good to work with.		1	4	3	10	4	3.68
My complaints or concerns are heard by management.	1	3	5	2	8	3	3.00
Things are getting better here.		2	5	5	8	2	3.14
The supervisors do a poor job.	1	4	7	6	3	1	2.41
Working conditions are bad here (interviews).	1	2	9	3	6	1	2.64
I benefit when the company succeeds.		1	7	5	8	1	3.05
I have all the chances I wish to improve myself.		2	10	1	7	2	2.86
The company is well run.	1	2	7	11	1		2.41
Communications are poor.		1	3	0	11	7	3.91
I don't get enough direction from my supervisor.	1	5	10	1	3	2	2.27
I enjoy my work.	1	0	1	2	7	11	4.14
I look for ways to improve the work I do.		0	0	0	9	13	4.59
I need more of a chance to manage myself.	1	0	13	3	2	3	2.64
Morale is good here.		7	8	4	1	2	2.23
Some do only what it takes to get by.		1	4	3	7	7	3.68
I like the way my supervisor treats me.		1	1	3	9	8	4.00
We need a suggestion system.		0	1	1	8	12	4.41
I want more opportunity for advancement.	1	0	3	6	4	8	3.64
My supervisor knows me and what I want.		0	2	5	11	4	3.77
We are expected to do a good job here.		0	0	0	7	15	4.68
There are too many rules.	1	3	12	3	3		2.18
I feel like part of a team at work.		9	5	0	6	2	2.41
The company and my supervisor seek my ideas.		5	9	3	5	0	2.36
I know and understand the objectives of my job.		0	0	0	13	9	4.41
I know and understand the objectives of the company.		0	5	4	11	2	3.45
Some secretaries have too much power.	1	0	5	1	2	13	3.91
Lawyers keep us informed as to what is happening.	1	4	12	1	4		2.14
The grapevine is where I get most of my information.		0	1	0	14	7	4.23
Brief weekly informational meetings would be helpful.		0	0	2	10	10	4.36
Other.							

Personnel Relations

The firm has an outdated and very short personnel manual. Many policies are not contained in the manual. Many policies which pose problems with the firm are not clear in the minds of the subordinates. The firm does not at this point in time employ the use of performance appraisal systems for attorneys or for support staff. As one attorney puts it,

"Klein simply waves the magic wand, announces how much you are going to make for the following year and that's it." The junior attorneys complain they don't get credit for much of the work they do because the hours are not billable. One attorney indicated that he did an awful lot of work which he felt was not billed to the company, most of that coming from Klein's real estate firm. Many other unbilled services are also believed to exist within the firm, according to several of the attorneys. Much of this is charity work done for indigent clients according to the county's revolving roles distribution among various firms in the county. The junior attorneys would like to see a better system of timekeeping which recognizes their contributions past those that are billed to the clients.

Marketing

Klein indicates that the way you market a law firm is by making presentations, by being visible in the community, by serving on boards and making yourself known to others; in other words, by exhibiting the quality of your talent. A real problem exists in getting the services of junior staff to the client. When people come to this firm, they either want Carstairs, Miller, or Klein to handle their cases. It is impossible for Klein to handle them and also many times impossible for Carstairs, although he tries to. There is less resistance with referring Miller's cases to others because most of these are real estate closings without any great technical problems involved. But on the litigation side of the firm, many times the client will refuse to have anyone serve them but Klein or Carstairs. Often Klein and Carstairs tell the client that they will supervise but that a junior attorney will do much of the work on their case.

Financial

Were it not for loans, "readjustments" from Matthew's account, the firm would at this time be losing money. It is probable though, that Matthew's "adjustments" are legitimate. He admits that the real estate development firm probably doesn't pay enough in fees to the law firm, but he doesn't know how much this is.

Missions, Plans, and Strategies

The mission of the organization from the viewpoint of the three senior partners is for all of them to be able to retire within six or seven years. Some of the younger people in the firm can be brought into partnership status and, with the increased revenues of the firm that is expected, the partners envision a nice retirement for themselves. Matthew Klein is not as concerned about this as the others. The organization is still his "baby," but he has the income from his substantial real estate interests. But he would like to receive a reasonable amount of pension as well. He owns the building in which the firm now resides and he offers the building at a very low rent rate to the firm. He would like to see the firm eventually purchase the building from him or to purchase condominium suites from him if he chooses to break the building into condominium partials.

The firm operates on an annual budget with projected revenues drawn up by the partners in an annual meeting. However, the objectives which are established are not felt to be very stretching by the senior partner. He feels that essentially they just extrapolate last year's revenues. He would like to see the objectives be more substantial for the future.

Individual attorneys are not actively marketing the firm as the senior partner would like them to. They do not make a sufficient number of presentations to outside parties. In fact, most of them make none. Much of the work that the firm engages in, especially in the real estate area, is brought in through Matthew Klein's contacts. This senior partner is very well known in the community, has additional real estate development interests, and does a sizable amount of business with the law firm—closings for time-share condominium purchasers, and so on.

The organization has no clear-cut plans for diversification into other fields of legal practice nor for growth into the more rapidly increasing southern part of the county, nor for holding the line on costs which are suspected to be too high by the senior partner. Klein would like to see the addition of an office manager to the firm but his goal has been delayed from reaching fulfillment while the firm waits on additional cash resources. Additionally Chuck Miller does not fully accept the idea of an office manager because he doesn't feel the firm is big enough to warrant having one. He feels he is doing a satisfactory job of managing the support staff.

Clermont Builders Supply Inc. and the Florida Concrete and Products Association

▪ *Julian W. Vincze* ▪

Lawson (Speedy) Wolfe, President of Clermont Builders Supply Inc., was enjoying his early Monday morning coffee and planning his week's activities, when a note he was reading triggered his ongoing concern for the validity of the concrete industry in Florida. He wondered if the industry could do more than eek out a marginal existence. He felt he had positioned his company satisfactorily to prosper regardless of what happened in the concrete business, but he hated to see the industry suffer so, as he felt it had in recent years.

Speedy was a very busy person. As president of Clermont Builders Supply (CBS), he had always practiced a "hands-on" style of management. All of his employees were used to seeing Speedy several times each and every day. A desk jockey he was not. As a naturally high-energy person, Speedy liked to feel the pulse of his organization by "being involved." If things were happening in any aspect of the operations, Speedy would be there. Not constantly, necessarily—that is, unless there was an emergency—but there nevertheless, because he would "drop by" several times during the day just to "see that everything was all right." He had always been an active member of, and was past president, of the Florida Concrete and Products Association (FC&PA), and had used a similar "active" style in that organization as well. He made a note to prepare his comments and position for the upcoming Concrete Block Committee meeting where the industry's future was to be discussed. He decided that, more than that, he wanted to find out for himself what was happening in the industry, because no one seemed to know. He thought about his alternatives.

History of Clermont Builders Supply, Inc.

The Clermont Builders Supply Company (CBS) was founded by four investors in 1945. The majority stockholder was Fred Wolfe, who initially owned 70 percent of the stock. Within a short period, however, Fred Wolfe had purchased an additional 20 percent of the stock from two of the others. The remaining 10 percent of the stock belonged to John Lynn.

After World War II, building materials were hard to acquire. However, Fred Wolfe had made many friends and acquaintances during the war and so was able to get these scarce materials. At that time there was one machine in the concrete block plant and that machine produced one block at a time (300 per day, using six people). These men did everything either by hand or by shovel. It is an understatement to say that after World War II the Florida concrete industry was very labor intensive. If one were to compare the above production figures with what a three-man crew could do per machine today, it is rather surprising. Today they can produce 10,000 blocks per shift. Labor costs have actually decreased over the years because of the high volumes being produced with automated equipment.

CBS didn't really have any readily identifiable stages of growth, but rather just gradual and steady growth. In 1950, CBS had one ready-mix concrete truck, which represented an investment cost of $6,000, and one concrete block truck. CBS was primarily involved in commercial work. In 1957, CBS opened their preengineered roof trusses business. However it was not profitable and ceased operating in 1963. CBS seemed to be ahead of its time and the housing industry was not yet ready for preengineered roof trusses. In 1971, Fred Wolfe passed away and his son, Lawson Wolfe, became president, having worked with the company since 1960. During 1971, CBS had sales totaling $800,000. In 1974, the present block plant, located in Clermont, was built. In 1978, the preeningeered roof trusses business was restarted. In 1980, CBS bought Eustis Block and Supply Company (EBSC). The EBSC plant manufactures both ready-mix concrete and concrete block. Also during 1980, CBS sales increased to $4 million. In August 1984, CBS opened a branch location in Orlando. CBS's Orlando facility doesn't manufacture concrete blocks, concentrating instead on handling ready-mix concrete and building materials.

Currently CBS is divided into four separate divisions. Three of these use ready-mix by CBS, such as prehung door units and roof trusses. These three divisions are organized around items that CBS manufactures and sells to contractors, and in total represent 60 percent of CBS's business. The fourth division includes building materials and supplies which represent a resale situation. In general CBS buys these materials and supplies in large quantities and then sells them to contractors in smaller quantities. Approximately 10 percent of CBS's sales volume involves general retail sales mixed among the four SBUs.

In 1982, CBS had $6.5 million in sales. In 1983, CBS had $9.5 million in sales and in 1984 they had $12.5 million in sales. (Please refer to Exhibits 5.1 and 5.2 for complete details.) In fact, the last 25 years represent a huge growth period in the construction industry in Florida and for CBS. This growth is continuing as Florida leads the nation with a 3 to 5 percent annual increase in population. The Orlando metropolitan area is the major market area for CBS's products. About half of its 1983 and 1984 sales came from the sale of concrete block. In 1979, the concrete block industry was estimated to have an 80-percent market share for exterior wall construction in Florida. However, from 1979 to 1984 the concrete block industry experienced a dramatic decline in market share. Exact market share figures aren't available but many operators guessed that it might have dropped to 50 percent by mid-1984.

In 1984, CBS had 24 ready-mix trucks, 9 concrete block trucks, 6 building materials delivery trucks, and 10 forklifts. To understand the changes which have taken place in concrete block production, a person must realize that in 1945 a block machine represented an investment cost of $1,500 and could produce one block at a time, or 300 per day. By 1984, a block machine involved an investment cost of $135,000 but is capable of producing 1,200 blocks per hour. The investment cost for a complete plant is a minimum of $750,000 so that today's Florida concrete industry is extremely capital intensive.

CBS employs six outside salesmen. They call directly on contractors and really could be considered service people rather than salespeople. These salespeople write up and fill orders for a need that already exists; contractors have already decided they need concrete block and the salesmen just write the orders and provide services for them. CBS's current organizational chart is shown in Exhibit 5.3

Exhibit 5.1   Clermont Builders Supply, Inc. Combined Balance Sheet, September 30, 1984

Assets:

Current assets:

Cash and banks	$ 64,037.47	
Notes receivable—current	35,419.06	
Accounts receivable	1,138,248.50	
Employee advances	7,397.68	
Merchandise inventory*	1,068,370.13	
Gas and diesel inventory	18,502.55	
Prepaid insurance	18,516.75	
Prepaid interest	302,363.52	
Prepaid taxes and licenses	8,423.72	
Prepaid income tax	75,793.00	
Total current assets		$2,737,072.38

Fixed assets:

Land		$492,432.32
Buildings	$ 420,257.92	
Automotive	2,187,114.45	
Store equipment	5,200.00	
Machinery and equipment	1,210,757.94	
Office furniture and fixtures	146,627.21	
Other fixed assets	266,739.51	
Less: depreciation allowance	(2,454,855.61)	
Depreciable assets	$1,781,841.42	
Total fixed assets		$2,274,273.74

Other assets:

Notes receivable—long-term	$ 37,971.98	
Stock	411,557.61	
Deposit	120.00	
Other investments	23,008.67	
Total other assets		$ 472,658.26
Total assets		$5,544,004.38

Changes in Direction

After more than 20 years of being a manager, the last 13 of which had been as president and CEO of CBS, Speedy had begun a new stage in his professional management career. He had enrolled in an executive MBA program being offered by a local college. He knew this activity would place a real time constraint on his usual activity schedule. Speedy's dilemma was how to find time for all of his usual activities and still have time and energy for this new commitment. He expected to learn ways in which to better manage his organization from this program, and was looking forward to it. Becoming a student again after so many years was going to be quite a departure for Speedy. He was used to running his own organization and making most of the decisions (and all the really important ones). But Speedy had heard good things about this executive MBA program from several associates. He had even looked up a few of the program's recent graduates. They had all had both good and not-so-good things to say about the program. But the bottom line had al-

Exhibit 5.1   *continued*

Liabilities

Current liabilities:

Notes payable—current	$516,949.82	
Accounts payable	727,147.91	
Employee accounts	(3,694.53)	
Coca Cola machines fund	2,102.61	
Accrued payroll	32,973.81	
Profit-sharing trust	45,980.00	
Accrued payroll taxes	1,033.63	
Accrued unemployment insurance	(6,887.72)	
Accrued property tax	14,636.84	
Accrued sales tax	20,096.78	
Accrued interest	15,027.69	
Accrued emergency excise tax	5,000.00	
Total current liabilities		$1,370,366.84
Long-term liabilities:		
Notes payable—long-term	$1,939,143.55	
Loans from officers	206,267.81	
D. Wolfe—annuity	63,426.75	
Total long-term liabilities		$2,208,838.11
Net worth:		
Capital stock	$ 24,000.00	
Retained earnings	1,880,799.43	
Total net worth		$1,904,799.43
Total liabilities and net worth		$5,544,004.38

*A LIFO inventory is used. LIFO reserve is $67,018.41.

ways been the same: a firm recommendation that they had "learned a lot" and that most of it was "immediately usable" in day-to-day management. Each said he would "do it again," although it was a tough and very time-consuming program.

Although favorably impressed, Speedy had reserved judgment until he had paid a visit to the college. He had talked to the coordinator of the EMBA program for a few hours and had taken away a full set of brochures. He liked what he had seen and heard but he just didn't rush into things. Speedy didn't make commitments lightly. If he was going to enroll in the EMBA program, he was going to give it the time and energy to do it correctly— with a firm determination to do his best and get the most he could out of it.

Personal Style

In fact this was a trait of Speedy's that was recognized by all of his business associates. Speedy didn't do things in half-measure. When Speedy said he'd do the job, it was accomplished on time and in full measure. For example, his active role in FC&PA affairs over the years had been recognized by his election as president for 1983/84. In fact it was his desire to continue his active role in FC&PA, plus his responsibilities as president of CBS, which combined to make this morning's task of planning his week's activities calendar so

Exhibit 5.2   Clermont Builders Supply, Inc. Combined Statement
of Operations, Fiscal Year Ending September 30, 1984

Revenue:		
Sales	$12,538,713.58	
Discounts allowed	161,983.24	
Net sales		$12,376,730.34
Cost of materials sold:		
Beginning inventory	$ 699,466.98	
Purchases	7,977,952.78	
Less: discounts earned	(131,323.02)	
Direct labor	428,949.17	
Mfg. overhead (list attached)	424,220.57	
Less closing inventory	(1,068,370.13)	
Cost of sales		$ 8,330,896.35
Gross profit		$ 4,045,833.99
Expenses:		
Officers' salaries	$ 278,595.22	
Wages and salaries	1,359,965.65	
Payroll taxes	124,808.91	
Group and work compensation insurance	137,787.86	
Employee benefits	30,266.36	
Office expense	58,024.24	
Small tools and supplies	4,661.78	
Utilities	13,460.33	
Telephone	34,518.44	
Administrative expenses	90,000.00	
Repair/maintenance—property	15,473.53	
Repair/maintenance—vehicles	233,752.26	
Repair/maintenance—machinery	18,195.31	
Insurance	24,902.16	
Depreciation	383,310.88	
Taxes	39,240.72	
Rentals	15,296.83	
Bad debts	163,758.92	
Gas, oil, and diesel	298,780.89	
Tires	49,880.21	
Travel and entertainment	17,061.19	
Contributions	5,043.66	
Sales expenses	2,671.36	
Errors and omissions	703.35	
Dues and subscriptions	9,345.29	
Security expense	7,725.37	
Legal and professional	39,466.61	
Deferred compensation	12,999.96	
Advertising	19,202.97	
Miscellaneous expense	20,659.76	
Interest expense	160,737.91	
Profit sharing	45,980.00	
Total expenses		$3,716,277.93
Operating profit		329,556.06
Add: other income		84,268.25
Net profit before taxes		$ 413,824.31

Note: LIFO method of accounting used.

Exhibit 5.3   Clermont Builders Supply—Organization Chart

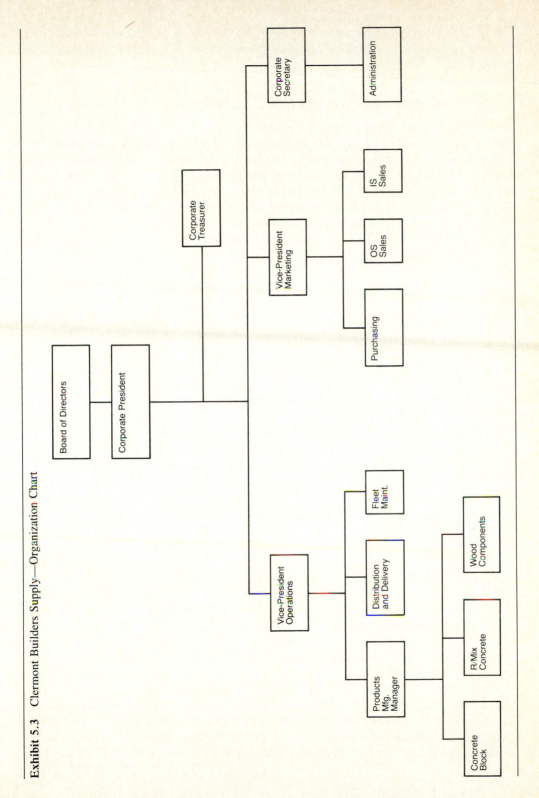

meaningful. He felt the association was moving too slowly on its declining situation. He decided that maybe he needed to prod them a little bit as well as clarify the issues for himself.

Florida Concrete and Products Association

The Florida Concrete and Products Association (FC&PA) was formed in 1955. Its membership numbers 150 companies that do business in Florida. The FC&PA was created to fulfill the needs and mutual interests of concrete and concrete products producers who chose to cooperate in creating an association. Examples of member firms are: Rinker Masonry which is said to have 25 percent of Florida's concrete block production capacity; Lone Star Florida Inc., which employed over 1,400 people in Florida and which was purchased in late 1984 by Tarmac PLC of Wolverhampton, England; and Tarmac PLC, already a member of FC&PA with a currently purported 30 percent of Florida's concrete block production capacity. Completing the list of the three largest (formerly four) producers of concrete block is Florida Mining. In total the FC&PA membership firms represented over 90 percent of all Florida producers and over 98 percent of production capacity.

The FC&PA organization structure is detailed in Exhibit 5.4. The association's charter and bylaws mandate the formation of 15 permanent committees. The purpose of the Accounting and Credit Committee is to annually conduct a seminar for owners and/or accounting/credit personnel, bringing them up-to-date on current topics of general interest relating to accounting practices and credit policies. The Aggregates Committee is required to meet at least semi-annually, or more often if necessary, in order to keep abreast of those activities which relate directly to aggregate producers. Another purpose is to coordinate activities of mutual concern with the Florida Department of Transportation.

The Associate Member Committee is expected to enhance the concrete industry in Florida and to ensure the maximum utilization of concrete, and allied products and services. It also provides a liaison between all associate members and the FC&PA Board of Directors. The purpose of the Building Codes Committee is to meet and coordinate with the Florida Building Codes Commission in their determinations relating to the Florida code. During meetings with this commission this FC&PA committee always attempts to make it known that in the opinion of FC&PA it is impossible for any single building code to satisfy all of the needs in all of the diverse areas of Florida. One of the purposes of the Education and Program Committee is to develop a program of education, short courses, meetings, etc., which will help owners, managers, supervisors, and other personnel of member organizations to do a better job. Another purpose is to determine the number of meetings, courses, etc., to have each year. The ELF/FC&PA Joint Technical Committee is charged with the task of improving the quality of concrete and its inspection and testing, and also to develop solutions in order to reconcile problems and complaints concerning concrete and its inspection.

Based on a decision made by the Board of Directors on October 4, 1968, a Finance and Audit Committee was formed and given the responsibilities of reviewing audits, preparing budgets, financing projects, and so forth, but not to override the treasurer or anyone else's authority. The purpose of the Fire Codes Committee is to monitor the various building codes and to provide for coordination between the FC&PA and other masonry associa-

Exhibit 5.4 Organization Chart
Florida Concrete and Products Association

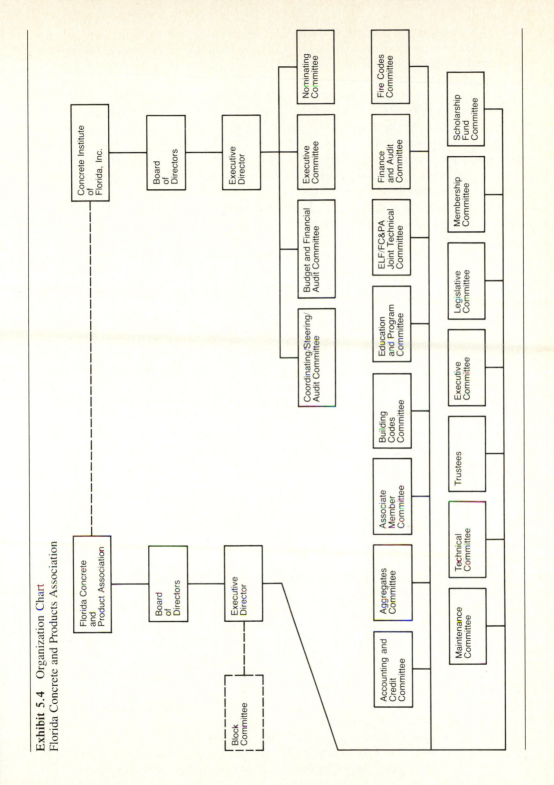

tions, for example the Portland Cement Association (PCA), international associations, various fire marshals, and building officials. This coordination is to ensure that the fire-preventative qualities of concrete and concrete products are known, encouraged, and utilized in multifamily and commercial structures.

The purpose of the Maintenance Committee is to conduct semi-annual seminars for the information and edification of all maintenance personnel in the concrete industry of Florida. The functions of the Technical Committee are to meet as a forum for discussion of industry developments, trends, and prospects of a technical nature, and to bring to the Board of Directors recommendations for the benefit of the concrete and products industry. They are also expected to recommend to the Board of Directors any actions to be taken by the association regarding technical matters.

The remaining committees are: the Trustees, the Executive Committee, the Legislative Committee, the Membership Committee, and the Scholarship Fund Committee. Each of these committees has the responsibilities one would normally expect such committees to have. For example, the Legislative Committee is concerned about any legislational activity which is contemplated by any political entity in Florida and is charged with representing FC&PA's best interests in the political/legislative areas.

Executive Director of FC&PA

The executive director of FC&PA is Mr. Stanley Hand, who has held the position for more than 15 years, since his retirement from the Air Force. Mr. Hand is responsible for the day-to-day operations of FC&PA and is its senior full-time employee. However since Mr. Hand sits on all the FC&PA committees, his actual impact on FC&PA is very important. In many ways the continuity provided by the executive director is the basis of the momentum of the association, or the lack of momentum as the case may be. Mr. Hand then could be described as one of the primary moving forces at FC&PA. In the fall of 1984 Mr. Hand informed FC&PA of his intention to step down in June of 1985.

The Concrete Institute of Florida (CIF)

In 1970, the FC&PA realized that there was a need for promotional activities designed to help sell and spread the word of concrete. As a result the FC&PA formed the Concrete Institute of Florida Inc. It handles any and all promotional activities carried out on behalf of the association, such as supplying technical books and pamphlets on concrete to anyone requesting such information. The Concrete Institute has four committees: the Coordinating/Steering/Audit Committee, the Executive Committee, the Budget & Financial Audit Committee, and the Nominating Committee. (Please refer to Exhibit 5.4.) The concrete industry has always been noted for not spending a great deal on promotion. For example, the budget for promotion was only $100,000 in 1983.

The promotion and advertising themes utilized by the Concrete Institute concentrate on the advantages of using concrete and concrete products. These advantages include: the architect and engineer has enormous versatility available to them because of the endless varieties, sizes, shapes, and strengths of concrete; the builder's job is made convenient because no unnecessary delays need occur to stop or delay construction (all of the proper concrete materials are located locally in Florida); the owner gets a structure which will provide a maximum return for the investment. Other advantages are: that concrete will withstand damage from weather, fire, termites, dry rot, and water; that concrete will afford the lowest-possible insurance rates; that concrete will protect against noise from both outside sources and sources within the building; and that the beauty of a concrete structure will last indefinitely with no costly replacements required. Also, concrete walls store and slow down the passage of heat from the inside out in the winter and from outside in during the summer, providing for lower total energy consumption.

In 1983, the total construction dollar spent on cement use and production for residential and nonresidential building in Florida was estimated at $14,013,000,000. This included 4.8 million tons of cement, 15.5 million cubic yards of concrete, 300 million concrete blocks, 15 million tons of sand, and 25 million tons aggregates.

Executive Director of CIF

The executive director of CIF is Mr. J. E. Paine, who has held the position for many years. Mr. Paine's position at CIF is virtually identical to Mr. Hand's position at FC&PA. Even though CIF was formed by FC&PA, there really were virtually no direct lines of responsibility or authority between the two entities. It seems that Mr. Paine's sole basis of responsibility and authority lies with the CIF Board of Directors. In fact, many members of FC&PA/CIF seem somewhat uncertain as to what, if any, accountability for results exist for Mr. Paine.

Downturn in Block Utilization

As Speedy was grappling with his time dilemma caused by his commitments to CBS, FC&PA/CIF, and the EMBA program, that basic concern he had considered earlier kept interrupting his thoughts. It was during his tenure as President of FC&PA (1983/84) that Speedy had become concerned about an apparent downturn in the utilization of concrete block for constructing exterior walls for the residential segment of the Florida construction industry. Speedy's concern had grown out of many conversations that had occurred over several months with a wide range of the membership of FC&PA.

Traditionally concrete block had been the dominant construction material utilized by Florida builders in virtually all exterior residential walls. This situation was consistent in all but the most northerly regions of Florida where "wood-frame" construction did have a small percentage of the residential exterior wall market. The residential segment of the construction industry was generally understood to include all noncommercial and nonhigh-rise multifamily buildings. As late as 1982 most of the members of FC&PA in conversations would estimate that concrete block held about 80 percent of the residential exterior wall market.

However, beginning in 1982 and by 1983, many FC&PA members were remarking that they had noticed a disturbing trend in tract housing developments. More and more of these developments seemed to be switching to wood-frame construction and away from concrete block. Also noticeable was the trend for the "prestige" residential market segment, which was the premium price market segment, to almost exclusively utilize wood-frame construction. Although these observations were not the same in reliability as a scientifically designed survey, Speedy's concerns stemmed from the frequency with which he heard these observations being voiced by block producers, and by seeing the large increase in his lumber sales and little if any increase in his firm's concrete block sales.

Lack of Statistics

As Speedy's concerns had grown, he had turned to Mr. Hand, the FC&PA executive director, for help in understanding the situation. Mr. Hand seemed somewhat surprised by Speedy's concerns as he pointed out that the statistics gathered by FC&PA indicated the concrete block production levels for member firms had not shown any decreases. In fact, production of concrete block was increasing slightly according to FC&PA figures. (The concrete block production figures were reported to the FC&PA on a voluntary basis by the membership and no efforts had ever been made to verify their accuracy.)

With this response from Mr. Hand, Speedy's concerns turned to puzzlement. How could concrete block production as reported by the membership be increasing while so many members were convinced a downturn in their use for residential exterior walls was occurring? The lack of anything but the most cursory of statistics on concrete block production was definitely a hindrance to really understanding the actual situation.

Because of his many presidential duties, Speedy didn't immediately do anything more about his concern regarding residential exterior wall construction trends. He did examine his own situation at CBS and found that he too had experienced a modest increase in concrete block production over the last few years. (See Exhibit 5.5.) However what Speedy did discover was that the commercial use of concrete block he sold had increased dramatically while the residential use had declined. Thus the slight overall increase was in effect hiding two trends in the use of concrete block—commercial use was increasing and residential use decreasing.

With this better understanding of his own situation, Speedy began to ask other producers if they were experiencing the same two trends. The answers he received were: first of all a surprised "I'm not sure, I'll check on it;" and then later "You're right, Speedy, commercial is up and residential is down." Now Speedy had some general verification of these trends. But what remained an uncertainty was how much exactly had the use of concrete block in the residential market declined. If in 1980 it represented 80 percent of exterior wall residential construction, what had happened to this percentage in 1983 and 1984, and what did the future years hold for continuation of the trend?

Again Speedy approached Mr. Hand, the FC&PA executive director. Mr. Hand's response was once again a statement that total concrete block production as reported to FC&PA had increased over the years and he wasn't at all certain how much of a decrease had occurred in the residential market. Mr. Hand again reiterated that he had no way of knowing what the current percentage had dropped to—although from conversations with members he thought that if the trends continued in 1984 the figures could be as low as 50 percent concrete block and 50 percent wood frame.

Exhibit 5.5   Clermont Building Supply Inc. Block Sales

Fiscal Year	Eustis	Clermont	Total
1981	$ 815,270	$ 860,500	$1,675,770
1982	737,050	974,200	1,711,250
1983	938,370	1,138,500	2,076,870
1984	1,201,350	1,310,600	2,511,950

No one at FC&PA or CIF and no individual member seemed to know with any degree of accuracy what these relative market-use figures for wood frame and concrete block were. And perhaps of equal importance, no one seemed to know how to really find out what these figures were. Speedy knew that without accurate and reliable percentage-of-use figures, the seriousness of the situation was completely uncertain. Perhaps it was a serious trend or perhaps it was not.

After further deliberation about the situation Speedy, as one of his final acts as president of FC&PA (just prior to the end of his tenure), established a temporary Concrete Block Committee at FC&PA. Speedy felt that the FC&PA had a right to be concerned and perhaps to take some action.

Concrete Block Committee

The Concrete Block Committee (not a standing committee at FC&PA) was formed to examine the concerns about downward trends of the concrete block industry and to take necessary actions to rectify them. Since there was a clear perception that existed among just about everyone in the industry that concrete block had lost a significant share of the residential market in the last few years, and since little valid and reliable information was available to substantiate this view, the committee was charged with examining the situation and recommending any action needed.

In order to fund any action which the block committee might recommend, a special concrete block production tariff had been established by FC&PA. This tariff, although on a voluntary basis, was suggested to be $1/10$¢ on each block produced by all members who produced concrete blocks. An approximate figure of $150,000 per year was expected to be collected via this voluntary tariff. In this manner, the block committee fully expected to be able to take specific actions. Another possible and additional basis of funding was being proposed by several members. This source would be to divert the dues currently paid by Florida cement/concrete producers and forwarded to the national Portland Cement Association. If this revenue source did in fact become reality, then an additional maximum of $400,000 per year could become available to the Concrete Block Committee.

The Concrete Block Committee examined two studies, one by the Florida Concrete Institute and one commissioned by the Alabama Concrete Industries Association, in order to provide insights into general trends which existed in the nation and in Florida. The committee found that for the state, the level of concrete block production was not as great in 1984 as it had been in 1973, and that production capacity had not increased during that time period. Some of the estimates and anecdotal evidence suggested to the committee repeatedly was that market share for concrete block may be as low as 50 percent in 1984, while in previous years it was possibly as high as 90 percent. The Alabama study provided interesting evidence that nationwide there were trends of a current downturn in concrete block utilization. These findings and other statements made during the Concrete Block Committee's deliberation seemed to highlight the situation sufficiently that the committee became convinced that a potentially serious situation could arise shortly. However the continuing lack of accurate statistical evidence of actual share percentages seemed to create a feeling of frustration that hindered the committee. This frustration appeared to cause the committee to do nothing but deliberate.

Speedy Takes Action

Because these thoughts about the FC&PA Concrete Block Committee kept interrupting Speedy's attempt to plan his week's activities, he decided to take matters in his own hands. As a concrete block producer, Speedy felt that residential-use trends needed to be taken seriously, especially since for every dollar of blocks sold, he sold an additional $.45 of accessory items. He was convinced that some action to verify the actual market percentages was necessary. He was concerned that the FC&PA Concrete Block Committee would continue to debate the situation and fail to act. He was certain Stan Hand at the FC&PA wouldn't act. Therefore he telephoned two local consultants and asked them to examine the situation and prepare a brief report for him. Because of budget constraints, only a very brief and somewhat cursory examination was agreed upon. Speedy then settled down to finish planning his week's activities.

Examining the Situation

To find out about concrete block utilization, the consultants interviewed Lawson Wolfe, Stan Hand, and Jack Paine. They also examined related federal and state reference materials, and those of the East Central Florida Planning Commission, the Regional and National Home Builders Associations, the Concrete Institute of Florida, and the Florida Concrete and Products Association. While in the middle of this process, Jack Paine of CIF forwarded to Speedy some startling figures which had been prepared by Housing Industry Dynamics. Speedy asked the consultants to examine and verify these figures. Thereafter a discussion via telephone took place with a research staff member of the National Concrete Masonry Association in Washington and a research staff member of Housing Industry Dynamics. A very brief summary of the consultants' findings are as follows.

Consultants' Findings

The sheer absence of information upon which to make decisions was felt to be mind-boggling, and in and of itself, a major problem for the association. Everyone perceived a problem, but the data upon which to make sound decisions were simply not available. For example, it was clear that in the major Florida cities, large developments produce most of the homes, but it was not known what percentage this was of total homes built. One interesting finding was that the National Concrete Masonry Association estimates of annual block production (they are estimates; apparently no state association keeps block data), is based on the application of a 20-year-old factor to Portland Cement Association production figures for that industry. This estimate then goes into various federal information databases. The factor was not originally accurate for any single state, but was aggregate. It does not account for cycles, nor for current conditions.

The Concrete Institute study pointed out several key factors: for example, who apparently makes sidewall building materials decisions in various situations and the factors influencing those choices. This study was found to not need replication, but it appeared advisable to obtain additional information to increase association knowledge of decision variables.

The Alabama Concrete Industries Association study raised issues related to:

1. Who makes decisions—the perception is that architects play the most important role, which is inconsistent with the CIF study.

2. Another issue is how important marketing is. A related issue involves determining the actual marketing activities of FCPA members. Do these members' sales personnel sell or simply provide service? The implication is that, at best, they simply compete with other concrete block manufacturers and not with those in competitive industries, i.e., wood.

3. The ACIA study also indicates that technical and economic criteria are important in the decision process. The question raised is whether this is true in Florida, and if so, what are the perceptions involved and how can concrete producers utilize and/or change these perceptions.

4. The ACIA study suggests that members must increase their marketing efforts, and this is undoubtedly true for FC&PA members as well.

5. Additionally, the ACIA study reveals the need for improved understanding and utilization of management techniques and the acquisition of the strategic ability to react to, and preferably anticipate, market changes.

The NHBA study which provided figures of comparable use of wood frame versus concrete block in residential exterior wall construction signals a dramatic trend. These figures were verified by the consultants and indicated that whereas in 1979 almost 80 percent of residential exterior walls that were constructed in Florida utilized concrete block, by 1983 this figure had shown a startling decline to just over 30 percent. Although the rate of decline was less severe between 1982 and 1983 than it was previously, the question of future utilization trends remains. (See Exhibits 5.6, 5.7, 5.8, 5.9, and 5.10.)

This study was preliminary in nature and designed to determine the extent of available information, the crux of the problem, and future needed actions.

Speedy's Reaction

Upon receiving the consultants' report in early November of 1984, Speedy's worst fears were verified—he was still surprised at the actual percentages and trends in concrete block utilization for residential exterior wall construction. He found it hard to believe that he and the other members of the FC&PA could have believed as late as the fall of 1984 that block still enjoyed at least 50 percent of the market when it actually had dropped below 50 percent in 1981 and was only about 30 percent in 1983. But he could find no reason to disbelieve the figures provided by Housing Industry Dynamics and verified by the consultants. Speedy asked the consultants to present their findings to a meeting of the FC&PA Concrete Block Committee and to also prepare some recommendations for action.

Consultants' Recommendations

A few weeks later the consultants did present their findings to the FC&PA Concrete Block Committee along with the following recommendations (paraphrased and abbreviated).

Exhibit 5.6   Frame Trends

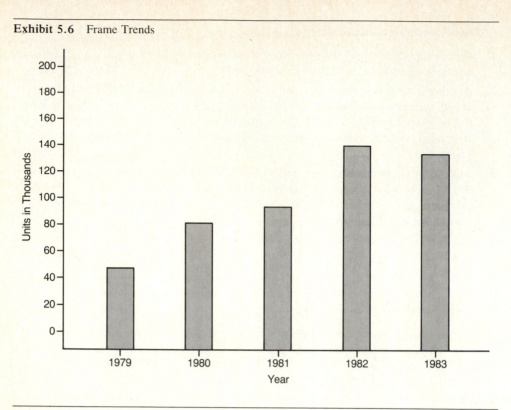

Exhibit 5.7   Frame Trends

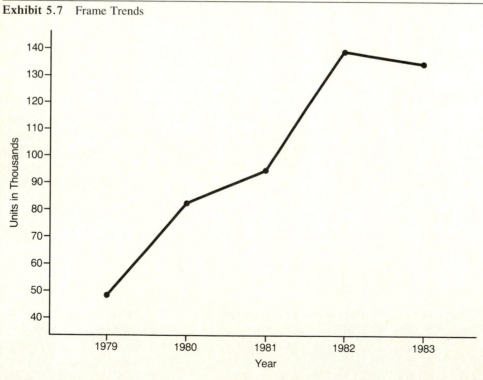

Exhibit 5.8   Masonry Trends

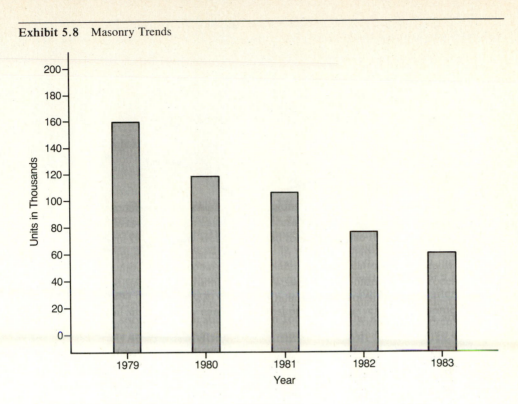

Exhibit 5.9   Masonry Trends

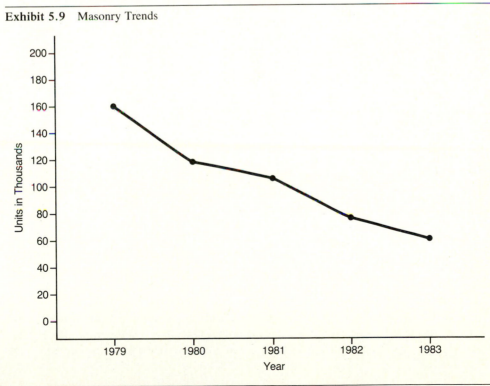

Exhibit 5.10   Masonry Trends

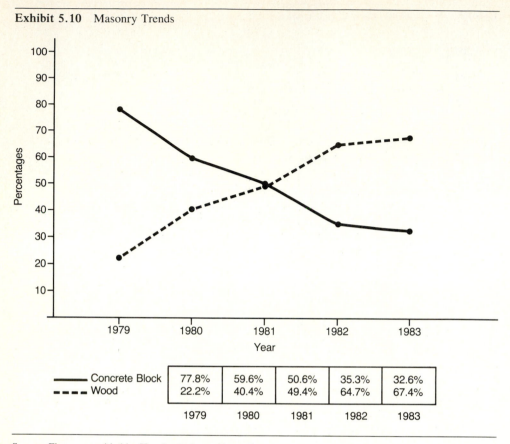

Concrete Block	77.8%	59.6%	50.6%	35.3%	32.6%
Wood	22.2%	40.4%	49.4%	64.7%	67.4%
	1979	1980	1981	1982	1983

Source: Figures provided by Housing Industry Dynamics.

Several actions were perceived as being necessary to first of all obtain information so that appropriate decisions could be made.

▪ Stage 1: Gather data. The consultants suggested that several types of data needed to be gathered from users of concrete block.

▪ Stage 2: Determine strategic alternatives in response to evidence provided by Stage One. Strategic objectives and plans would result.

The absence of decision information was viewed by the consultants as a danger sign. The recommendations made were intended to focus on the major perceived problem areas. The tendency to make decisions without knowing precisely upon what to base those decisions was noted by the consultants, who urged restraint until sufficient information could be gathered to determine several key factors, such as affirming the CIF report regarding who makes the sidewall construction decisions, and very importantly, upon what those decisions are based. Solving an ill-defined problem is really no solution at all, said the consultants. Stage 2 activities would be far more effective if Stage 1 was accomplished first. Information was needed to design the proper strategies, since the available evidence all seemed to indicate that a significant negative impact for concrete block producers had occurred.

Concrete Block Committee Reaction

After receiving the consultants' report, the Concrete Block Committee's meeting lasted several hours. Speedy later recalled that the members of the committee were shocked by the reported decline in concrete block utilization to only 30 percent of residential exterior wall construction. After the initial shock, the next reaction was to demand some action. But what exactly to do wasn't easily agreed to. Many members wanted to mount an immediate marketing program to reverse the decline in block utilization. However no one had an answer for who was going to design the marketing program or what role CIF personnel would have in such a program. In the end the committee decided to ask several consulting firms for proposals similar to the recommendations proposed by Speedy's consultants (as noted above).

Wall Drug Store, 1983

▪ *James D. Taylor and Robert L. Johnson* ▪

The Wall Drug Store is a complex of retail shops located on the main street of Wall, South Dakota, population 770, owned and managed by the Hustead family of Wall. It includes a drugstore, a soda fountain, two jewelry stores, two clothing stores, a restaurant with four dining rooms, a Western art gallery, a bookstore, and shops selling rocks and fossils, camping and backpacking equipment, and saddles and boots, as well as several souvenir shops. Exhibit 6.1. shows examples of the front elevation of the original drug store and a portion of the current mall. In 1983, a major expansion was underway which would add five more shops and a chapel. "The decision, as when you first wrote the case in 1974,[1] is, are we going ahead with our building program or not? That hasn't changed," announced Bill Hustead as he talked about his plans for Wall Drug. The tourist season was just beginning on June 1. The spring had been cool and wet, and sales for the year to June 1 were down considerably from the previous year. Bill continued,

We are still going ahead with the building program. The building program is not necessarily to make more money, but mainly it is to enlarge and enhance the store, so that it makes more of an impression on the traveling public. The church, the art gallery, the apothecary shop—we naturally feel these things will pay their way and make money, but the good part is, when the signs go down, we will have a place that people just won't miss. The place is so crazy, so different—it's the largest drugstore in the world, it may get in the Guiness Book of Records *as the only drugstore with a church in it. People and writers will have a lot to talk about.*

We will continue to seek publicity. We will advertise in crazy places, we will have packets for writers, and we will try to seek national and international publicity.

Wall Drug History

Ted Hustead graduated from the University of Nebraska with a degree in pharmacy in 1929 at the age of 27. In December of 1931, Ted and his wife Dorothy bought the drugstore in Wall, South Dakota, for $2,500. Dorothy and Ted and their four-year-old son Bill moved into living quarters in the back 20 feet of the store. Business was not good (the first month's receipts were $350) and prospects in Wall did not seem bright. Wall, South Dakota, in 1931 is described in the following selection from a book about the Wall Drug Store.

Wall, then: a huddle of poor wooden buildings, many unpainted, housing some 300 desperate souls; a 19th century depot and wooden water tank; dirt (or mud) streets; few

---

[1] Professors James D. Taylor and Robert L. Johnson are coauthors of "Wall Drug Store," a case written in 1974.

Exhibit 6.1

trees; a stop on the railroad, it wasn't even that on the highway. U.S. 16 and 14 went right on by, as did the tourists speeding between the Badlands and the Black Hills. There was nothing in Wall to stop for.[2]

Neither the drugstore nor the town of Wall prospered until Dorothy Hustead conceived the idea of placing a sign promising free ice water to anyone who would stop at their store. The sign read "Get a soda/Get a beer/Turn next corner/Just as near/To Highway 16 and 14/Free ice water/Wall Drug." Ted put the sign up and cars were turning off the highway to go to the drugstore before he got back. This turning point in the history of Wall Drug took place on a blazing hot Sunday afternoon in the summer of 1936.

The value of the signs was apparent and Ted began putting them up all along the highways leading to Wall. One sign read "Slow down the old hack/Wall Drug Corner/Just across the railroad track." The attention-catching signs were a boon to Wall Drug and the town of Wall prospered too. In an article in *Good Housekeeping* in 1951, the Hustead's signs were called "the most ingenious and irresistible system of signs ever derived."[3]

Just after World War II, a friend traveling across Europe for the Red Cross got the idea of putting up Wall Drug signs overseas. The idea caught on and soon South Dakota servicemen who were familiar with the signs back home began to carry small Wall Drug signs all over the world. Many wrote the store requesting signs. One sign appeared in Paris, proclaiming "Wall Drug Store 4,278 miles (6,951 kilometers)." Wall Drug signs have appeared in many places including the North and South Pole areas, the 38th parallel in Korea, and on Vietnam jungle trails. The Husteads sent more than 200 signs to servicemen requesting them from Vietnam. These signs led to news stories and publicity which further increased the reputation of the store.

By 1958, there were about 3,000 signs displayed along highways in all 50 states, and two men and a truck were permanently assigned to service signs. Volunteers continue to put up signs. The store gives away 14,000 6 × 8-inch signs and 3,000 8 × 22-inch signs a year to people who request them. On the walls of the dining rooms at Wall Drug are displayed pictures from people who have placed signs in unusual places and photographed them for the Husteads.

The signs attracted attention and shortly after World War II, articles about Ted Hustead and Wall Drug began appearing in newspapers and magazines. In August 1959, *Redbook Magazine* carried a story which was later condensed in October's *Readers Digest*. Since then, the number of newspapers and magazines carrying feature stories or referring to Wall Drug has increased greatly. In June of 1983, Wall Drug Store files contained 543 clippings of stories about the store. The number by ten-year periods was as follows:[4]

1941–1950	19 articles
1951–1960	41
1961–1970	137
1971–1980	260
1981 through April 1983	exact amount not available

---

[2] Dana Close Jennings, *Free Ice Water: The Story of Wall Drug* (Aberdeen, South Dakota; North Plains Press, 1969), p. 26.

[3] Ibid, p. 42.

[4] Twenty-seven clippings were undated.

The store and its sales have grown steadily since 1936. From 1931 until 1941 the store was in a rented building on the west side of Wall's Main Street. In 1941, the Husteads bought an old lodge hall in Wasta, South Dakota (15 miles West of Wall), and moved it to a lot on the east side of the street in Wall. The building, which had been used as a gymnasium in Wasta, became the core around which the current store is built.

Tourist travel greatly increased after World War II and the signs brought so many people into Wall Drug that the Husteads claim they were embarrassed because the facilities were not large enough to service them. The store did not even have modern rest rooms. Sales during this period grew to $200,000 annually.

In 1951, Bill Hustead, now a pharmacy graduate of South Dakota State University at Brookings, joined his parents in the store.

In 1953, Wall Drug was expanded into a former storeroom to the south. This became the Western Clothing Room. This was accompanied by a 30 percent increase in business. In 1956, a self-service cafe was added on the north side of the store. In the early 1950s sales were in the $300,000-per-year range and by the early 1960s had climbed to $500,000. (A map of the store with the dates of expansion is shown in Exhibit 6.2.)

In the early 1960s, Ted and his son Bill began seriously thinking of moving Wall Drug to the highway. The original Highway 16 ran by the north side of Wall, about two blocks from the store. It was later moved to run by the south side of Wall, about two blocks also from the drugstore. In the late 1950s and early 1960s, a new highway was built running by the south side of Wall, paralleling the other highway. Ted and Bill Hustead were considering building an all-new Wall Drug along with a gasoline filling station alongside the new highway just where the interchange by Wall was located.

They decided to build the gasoline station first, and did so. It is called Wall Auto Livery. When the station was finished, they decided to hold up on the new store and then decided to continue expanding the old store in downtown Wall. This was a fortunate decision, since soon after that, the new interstate highway replaced the former new highway and the new interchange ran through the site of the proposed new Wall Drug.

In 1963, a new fireproof-construction coffee shop was added. In 1964, a new kitchen, again of fireproof construction, was added just in back of the cafe and main store. In 1964 and 1965 offices and the new pharmacy were opened on the second floor over the kitchen.

In 1968, the back dining room and backyard across the alley were added. This was followed in 1971 with the Art Gallery Dining Room.

By the late 1960s and early 1970s, annual sales volume went to $1 million.

In 1971 the Husteads bought the theater that bordered their store on the south. They ran it as a theater through 1972. In early 1973 they began construction of a new addition in the old theater location. This is called the "Mall." By the summer of 1973 the north part of the Mall was open for business. The south side was not ready yet. That year the Wall Drug grossed $1,600,000 which was an increase of about 20 percent over 1972. Bill believes the increase was due to their new Mall addition.

The development of the mall represents a distinct change in the development of Wall Drug. All previous development had been financed out of retained earnings or short-term loans. In effect, each addition was paid for as it was built or added.

Exhibit 6.2   Map of Wall Drug

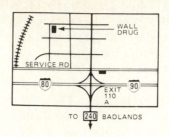

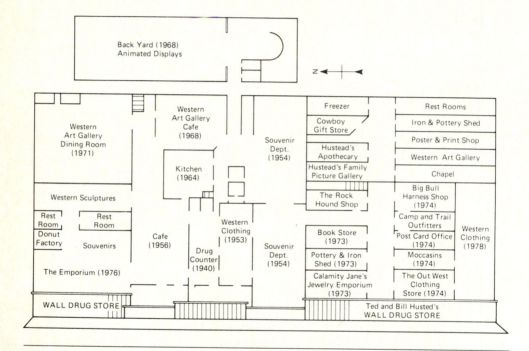

The Mall

The owners of Wall Drug broke with the previous method of expansion when they built the Mall by borrowing approximately $250,000 for ten years to finance the Mall and part of 20 large new signs which stand 660 feet from the interstate highway.

During the last half of the 1960s and early 1970s Bill Hustead had thought about and planned the concept of the Mall. The Mall was designed as a town within a large room. The main strolling mall was designed as a main street with each store or shop designed as a two-story frontier Western building. The Mall is thus like a recreated Western town. Inside the stores, various woods are used in building and paneling. Such woods as pine from Custer, South Dakota, American black walnut, gumwood, hackberry, cedar, maple, and oak are among the various woods used. The storefronts are recreations of building fronts found in old photos of Western towns in the 1880s. Many photos, paintings, and prints line the walls. These shops stock products that are more expensive than the souvenir merchandise found in most other parts of the store beyond the Mall, which had previously been purchased, and furnished expansion for the Western clothing stores, boots, and harness shop.

Currently, in 1983, there is further expansion under construction east of the Mall to the alley. The new area will feature a chapel modeled after a church built by Trapist Monks in Dubuque, Iowa, in 1850. Also featured will be a replica of the original Wall Drug Store, which will be called Hustead's Apothecary and will serve as the Drug Store Museum. The store will sell Caswell-Massey products from the store of that name in New York, which is the oldest drugstore in the United States. Other shops will be a Western art gallery, a poster shop and Western gift shop, an iron and pottery shop, and Hustead's Family Picture Gallery. The shops will be modeled after famous old Western establishments. There will also be a new set of rest rooms. In effect, the new addition will be an extension of the Mall.

Store Operation

Wall is a small town of 770 people as of 1980. The economic base of the town is primarily built around Wall Drug and is dependent on tourist business.

Wall is situated right on the edge of the Badlands and 52 miles east of Rapid City. For miles in either direction, people in autos have been teased and tantalized by Wall Drug signs. Many have heard of the place through stories in the press, or have heard their parents or friends speak of Wall Drug. In the summer of 1963, in a traffic count made on the highway going by Wall, 46 percent were eastbound and 54 percent were westbound. Of the eastbound traffic, 43 percent turned off at Wall. Of the westbound traffic, 44 percent turned off at Wall.

When people arrive at Wall, (those westbound usually after driving 40 miles or more through the Badlands) they are greeted by the large Wall Drug sign on the interchange and an 80-foot-high, 50-ton statue of a dinosaur. The business district of Wall is two blocks long and is about three blocks to five blocks from the interchange. The town has 11 motels and a number of gasoline filling stations.

Cars from many states line the street in front of and several blocks on either side of the drugstore. Tabulation of state licenses from autos and campers parked in front of Wall Drug, June 1, 1983, at 12:00 noon are summarized as follows:

South Dakota (not local county)	20%
South Dakota, local county	22
Balance of states and Canada	58

Wall Drug is more than a store. It is a place of amusement, family entertainment, a gallery of the West, a gallery of South Dakota history, and a place that reflects the heritage of the West. Nostalgia addicts find Wall Drug particularly interesting. Children delight in the animated life-size cowboys singing; the tableau of an Indian camp; a stuffed bucking horse; a six-foot rabbit; a stuffed buffalo; old slot machines that pay out a souvenir coin for $.25; statues of cowboys, dancehall girls, and other characters of the Old West; a coin-operated quick-draw game; and souvenirs by the roomful which make up part of the attractions.

The food is inexpensive and good, and although as many as 10,000 people might stream through on a typical day, the place is air-conditioned and comfortable. The dining rooms are decorated with beautiful wood paneling, paintings of Western art are displayed, and Western music plays. One can dine on buffalo burgers, roast beef or steak, $.05 coffee or select wine, and beer from the rustic, but beautiful, American walnut bar.

About one-fourth of the sales in Wall Drug is food, plus about 5 percent to 10 percent for beverages and soda fountain. (This varies with the weather.) About 10 percent to 15 percent is jewelry, 15 percent clothing and hats, 35 percent to 40 percent for souvenirs, and 5 percent to 10 percent for drugs, drug sundries, and prescriptions.

The store is manned by a crew of 201 people, 76 of which are college girls and 25 of which are college boys who work there in the summer. Student help is housed in homes that have been bought and made into dormitory apartments. There is a modern swimming pool for their use, also. The clerks are trained to be courteous, informed, and pleasant.

Orders for the following summer season begin being placed in the preceding fall. Orders begin arriving in December, but most arrive in January, February, March, and April. Many large souvenir companies postdate their invoices until July and August. Each year brings new offerings from souvenir companies and other suppliers. Much of the purchasing is done by Bill, who admits he relies on trusted salespeople or their suppliers, who advise him on purchasing. Many of these companies have supplied Wall Drug for 30 years or so. Wall Drug generally buys directly from the producers or importers, including photo supplies and clothing.

Years ago, much of what Wall Drug bought and sold was imported or made in the eastern part of the country. In recent years, much of the merchandise is being made regionally and locally. Indian reservations now have small production firms and individuals who make much handicraft which is sold through Wall Drug. Examples of such firms are Sioux Pottery, Badlands Pottery, Sioux Moccasin, and Milk Camp Industries.

The Husteads rely a great deal on the department managers for buying assistance. The manager of the jewelry, for instance, will determine on the basis of last year's orders and her experience with customer reaction and demand, how much to order for the next season. All ordering is centered through Bill.

Highway Beautification and Promotion

In the year 1965, Congress passed the Highway Beautification Act, which was designed to reduce the number of roadside signs. Anticipating the removal of the many Wall Drug advertising signs, Bill Hustead invested in new signs that were allowed under that legislation. These signs were to be placed no closer than 660 feet away from the road. To be read, these signs must be larger than the older signs, and cost close to $9,000 each. Now even these large signs are included in the laws for regulation or removal.

There has been slow compliance with this legislation by many states including South Dakota, since many states in less-populated areas have many tourist attractions, and find road signs the only practical way to advertise these attractions. Since the administration of President Reagan has been in office, there has been little enforcement of the sign legislation since there has been less money available for federal enforcement. There is new legislation being proposed by the Federal Highway Administration of the Department of Transportation as of 1983 that could have an impact on Wall Drug and other tourist-dependent establishments.

Exhibit 6.3   Article about Wall Drug Ad Campaign

Wall Drug ads mystify New Yorkers

By Ruth Hamel
Argus Leader **Staff**

SoDak is a long way from SoHo, where west can mean New Jersey and Wall Drug could reasonably be thought to exist near Wall Street.

But, as usual, mere distance has not deterred Wall Drug owner Bill Hustead from advertising his business. Off and on for the past 20 years, Hustead has bought advertising space in the *Village Voice*, a New York City weekly based in Greenwich Village.

In every recent issue, a Wall Drug advertisement can be spotted between the columns devoted to Manhattan's vegetarian lunchspots and sushi bars. The small box may advertise petrified wood clocks one week, flying jackalopes on another, and free ice water on another.

The tiny advertisements do not tell *Voice* readers where Wall Drug is, nor that it is more than a subway jaunt away for any New Yorker who might want to shop around for a petrified wood clock on a Saturday afternoon.

And the *Voice*'s accompanying Manhattan map that shows where various restaurants are located denotes Wall Drug with a small arrow that simply points west from New York's Hell's Kitchen.

All of which adds to the Wall Drug mystique.

"We do get inquiries from time to time," Katherine Rogers, *Village Voice* restaurant sales coordinator, said. "'What is that?' We give them the address."

Once told where Wall Drug is, people respond with the same question, she said: "'Why?'"

But the baffling ads work. Over the July 4th weekend, Wall Drug served five busloads of New York-area youth, some of whom knew of the drugstore from reading the *Village Voice*, Hustead said.

"One time, late at night, a guy from Massachusetts called" after spotting one of the *Voice* ads, Hustead said. "He wanted to know, 'What is a horse hitch?'"

New Yorkers passing through South Dakota will stop at Wall Drug to read the copies of the *Village Voice* Hustead receives every week and advertises on Interstate 90.

(Wall Drug signs, of course, are legendary. The small-town drugstore with the multinational advertising campaign has placed signs in Amsterdam, London, and along the French Riviera, among other places.)

Hustead's account with the *Village Voice* began about 20 years ago.

Always a fan of New York City, the drugstore owner was sitting in a Greenwich Village coffeehouse reading the paper when "I thought it might be a good move to advertise in the *Voice*," he said. "I knew that a lot of writers take that paper."

So Hustead placed an ad that emphasized the reasonable price of Wall Drug food compared to New York food.

Eventually, the *Village Voice* ads led to a *Newsweek* article about Wall Drug.

Ms. Rogers said a recent ad for Wall Drug's rattlesnake bite kits prompted many calls to the *Village Voice* offices.

Another recent ad boasting of free ice water hit a chord when New York was in a drought and its restaurants would only give customers a glass of water if they asked for it, Ms. Rogers said.

Hustead is proud of the *Village Voice* ads but has reservations about the paper itself.

"I'm a little conservative," he said. "I feel it's not as wholesome a paper as it used to be. The language . . . it isn't something you want to lay around and let your 10-year-old girl read."

On a given week, Wall Drug may share *Voice* advertising space with naughty bakeries and naughtier film houses. And the newspaper that Hustead said used to resemble the paper in Wall now contains articles that might make some South Dakota jaws drop.

But the *Voice* association has allowed Hustead to meet interesting people between his forays to New York and New Yorkers' forays to Wall.

Wall Drug, Hustead says, "is a stop that those New Yorkers will make" as they pass through the state.

Sioux Falls *Argus Leader*, July 8, 1981, p. 1.

Bill and Ted also decided that they must gain as much visibility and notoriety as possible, and to help achieve this, they began using advertising in unusual places. In the 1960s, Wall Drug began taking small ads in unlikely media such as the *International Herald Tribune*, and *The Village Voice*, in New York City's Greenwich Village, advertising $.05 coffee and $.49 breakfast as well as animal health remedies. (See Exhibit 6.3 for additional details.) This brought telephone calls and some letters of inquiry. It also brought an article in the *Voice* and probably attracted the attention of other media. On

January 31, 1971 (Sunday), *The New York Times* carried an article about Wall Drug. This article may have led to Bill Hustead's appearance on Garry Moore's television program "To Tell the Truth." In the year 1979, there were 75 articles in newspapers and magazines about Wall Drug. In the August 31, 1981, edition of *Time*, a full-page article in the "American Scene" featured the store and the Husteads. Also, in 1981, Wall Drug was featured on NBC television's "Today Show" and Atlanta Cable's "Winners."

For a while, Wall Drug was advertised in the London city buses and subways, the Paris Metro (subway) in the English language, and on the dock in Amsterdam where people board sight-seeing canal boats.

Finances

Exhibits 6.4 and 6.5 present summary income statements and balance sheets from 1973 through 1982. The Wall Auto Livery was consolidated into Wall Drug Store Inc. in May 1975. Had this transition occurred prior to 1973, sales for 1973, 1974, and 1975 would have been about $192,000, $248,000, and $52,000 larger, and net profit would have been about $19,000 larger in 1973, and $21,000 larger in 1974, with a negligible effect in 1975. The value of the acquired net assets was about $180,000.

The company's growth and expansion has been financed primarily by retained earnings, temporarily supplemented at times with short-term borrowings. A major exception was a $250,000, ten-year installment loan in 1973 used to help finance the Mall and some large signs located 660 feet from the highway. In 1975, this loan was prepaid through 1980. At the end of 1982, only $34,500 remained to be paid on this loan. Other long-term debt at the end of 1982 includes installment contracts for the purchase of real estate and a stock redemption agreement (occurring in 1979) for the purchase by the company of some Class B, nonvoting stock. As indicated on the December 31, 1982, balance sheet, current maturities of long-term debt were $43,436. Of this amount, $34,496 is the final payment on the 1973 loan due in 1983.

Both the growth and the volatility of the business should be apparent from the income statements presented in Exhibit 6.4. Exhibit 6.6 presents the income statements as a percentage of sales. Exhibit 6.7 is an analysis of the rate of return on equity broken into the component parts using the format:

$$\frac{Sales}{Assets} \times \frac{Gross\ Profit}{Sales} \times \frac{Operating\ Income}{Gross\ Profit} \times \frac{Net\ Income}{Operating\ Income}$$

$$\times \frac{Assets}{Equity} = \frac{Net\ Income}{Equity}$$

Between 1973 and 1982, prices, as measured by the Consumer Price Index, increased by about 115 percent. Percentage increases in some balance sheet and income accounts for Wall Drug over this period are:

Sales	163%
Total general + administrative expense	145
Net income	159
Total assets	115
Equity	169

Exhibit 6.4 Income Statements (in thousands) Wall Drug

	1982	1981	1980	1979	1978	1977	1976	1975	1974	1973
Sales	$4,733	$4,821	$3,970	$3,552	$4,125	$3,777	$3,464	$2,679	$1,991	$1,607
Cost of sales	2,644	2,676	2,230	2,072	2,228	2,098	1,879	1,484	1,100	806
Gross profit	2,089	2,145	1,740	1,480	1,897	1,679	1,586	1,195	891	801
General + administrative expenses	1,802	1,857	1,473	1,433	1,578	1,453	1,312	1,000	754	691
Income from operations	287	288	267	47	319	226	274	195	137	110
Other income expense	36	81	43	–8	35	23	2	3	–8	–10
Income before tax	323	369	310	39	354	249	276	198	129	100
Tax	120	144	125	6	148	94	111	80	54	41
Net income	$ 203	$ 224	$ 185	$ 33	$ 206	$ 155	$ 165	$ 118	$ 75	$ 59

Note: Slight discrepancies may be noted due to rounding to nearest thousand.

Exhibit 6.5 Balance Sheets on December 31 (in thousands)

	1982	1981	1980	1979	1978	1977	1976	1975	1974	1973
Cash and short-term investments	$240	$282	$449	$ 11	$ 82	$ 65	$ 51	$ 93	$145	$ 74
Inventories	631	547	369	403	338	276	249	248	174	144
Other current assets	60	57	53	99	51	58	50	32	26	26
Total current assets	$931	$886	$871	$513	$471	$399	$350	$373	$345	$244
Property, equipment	2,907	2,591	2,380	2,297	2,230	1,960	1,739	1,484	1,234	1,130
Accumulated depreciation	–1,355	–1,254	–1,147	–1,030	– 906	– 790	– 674	– 576	– 496	– 428
Other assets	24	25	27	53	55	33	29	31	34	34
Total assets	$2,507	$2,248	$2,131	$1,833	$1,850	$1,602	$1,444	$1,312	$1,117	$ 980
Current maturities of long-term debt	$ 43	$ 40	$ 46	$ 8	$ 11	$ 5	$ 8	$ 7	$ 21	$ 20
Notes payable	0	0	0	68	20	0	0	5	70	20
Accounts payable	56	58	63	47	43	64	36	42	31	23
Accruals + other current liabilities	252	244	310	124	232	167	178	193	136	110
Total current liabilities	$ 351	$ 342	$ 419	$ 247	$ 306	$ 236	$ 222	$ 247	$ 258	$ 173
Long-term debt	191	149	179	238	133	130	133	136	222	244
Deferred tax	7	1								
Stockholders' equity	1,958	1,756	1,533	1,348	1,411	1,236	1,089	929	637	563
Total liability + equity	$2,507	$2,248	$2,131	$1,833	$1,850	$1,602	$1,444	$1,312	$1,117	$ 980

Exhibit 6.6 Percent of Sales Statements

	1982	1981	1980	1979	1978	1977	1976	1975	1974	1973
Sales	100.0%	100.0%	100.0%	100.0%	100.0%	100.0%	100.0%	100.0%	100.0%	100.0%
Cost of sales	55.9	55.5	56.2	58.3	54.0	55.6	54.2	55.4	55.2	50.2
Gross profit	44.1	44.5	43.8	41.7	46.0	44.4	45.8	44.6	44.8	49.8
General + administrative expense	38.1	38.5	37.1	40.4	38.3	38.4	37.9	37.3	37.9	43.0
Income from operations	6.0	6.0	6.7	1.3	7.7	6.0	7.9	7.3	6.9	6.8
Other income expenses	.8	1.7	1.1	-.2	.9	.6	.1	.1	-.4	-.6
Income before tax	6.8	7.7	7.8	1.1	8.6	6.6	8.0	7.4	6.5	6.2
Tax	2.5	3.0	3.1	.2	3.6	2.5	3.2	3.0	2.7	2.5
Net income	4.3	4.7	4.7	.9	5.0	4.1	4.8	4.4	3.8	3.7

Exhibit 6.7 Components of Rate of Return on Equity

	1982	1981	1980	1979	1978	1977	1976	1975	1974	1973
$\dfrac{\text{Gross profit}}{\text{Sales}}$	.441	.445	.438	.417	.460	.444	.458	.446	.448	.498
$\dfrac{\text{Income from operation}}{\text{Gross profit}}$	.137	.134	.153	.032	.168	.135	.163	.163	.154	.137
$\dfrac{\text{Sales}}{\text{Assets}}$	1.89	2.14	1.86	1.94	2.23	2.36	2.40	2.04	1.78	1.64
$\dfrac{\text{Income from operation}}{\text{Assets}}$	.114	.128	.125	.026	.172	.141	.190	.148	.123	.112
$\dfrac{\text{Net income}}{\text{Income from operation}}$	.707	.778	.698	.702	.646	.686	.602	.605	.547	.536
$\dfrac{\text{Assets}}{\text{Equity}}$	1.28	1.28	1.39	1.36	1.31	1.30	1.33	1.41	1.75	1.74
$\dfrac{\text{Net income}}{\text{Equity}}$	.103	.128	.121	.025	.146	.126	.152	.126	.118	.105

These percentages are based on combining Wall Auto Livery with Wall Drug in 1973 as if the merger occurring in 1975 has taken place.

Given below are percentage changes in some of the general and administrative expenses from 1976 through 1982:

Total general + administrative	37%
Utilities	137
Officers' salaries	2
Other salaries	42
Depreciation	5
Advertising	116
Profit-sharing contribution	49

The items mentioned accounted for 77 percent of total general and administrative expenses in 1982 and 76 percent in 1976. These same items as percentages of sales were:

	1982	1976
Utilities	1.7%	1.0%
Officers' salaries	2.9	3.8
Other salaries	18.5	17.7
Depreciation	2.3	2.9
Advertising	2.1	1.3
Profit-sharing contributions	2.0	1.8

Depreciation methods on various assets vary from straight line to 200 percent declining balance, and over lives of from 15 to 40 years for buildings and improvements to 5 to 10 years for equipment, furnitures, and fixtures. Although not evaluated or recognized on the financial statements, it is likely that some assets, such as the Western art and the Silver Dollar Bar, have appreciated.

Store Management

Recruiting and training the seasonal work force is a major task at Wall Drug. College students are recruited through college placement services. Training is of short duration but quite intense. Summer employees are tested on their knowledge of store operations and their ability to give information about the area to tourists.

Bill Hustead commented:

I really think that there isn't anything more difficult than running a business with 20 to 30 employees in the winter and then moving into a business with 180 to 200 employees, and you have to house 100 of them and you have to supervise them and train them. This lasts through June, July, and August, then the next year you start all over. It's kind of exciting and fun for the first 25 years, but after 30 years you begin to think its a tough racket.

The store had a permanent nucleus of 20 to 30 employees. While the business could operate with fewer employees during the winter, the Husteads believed that they needed the experienced employees to give stability to the operations in the summer. Permanent employees with seniority could get as much as six weeks' paid vacation. Commenting on this policy, Bill said:

We probably go through the winter with more employees than we really need, but we give them time off in the winter because a seasonal business is so demanding. When the Fourth of July comes, you're working; when Memorial Day comes, you're working; when all those summer fun times come, you're working six days a week and it's quite a sacrifice. So, we try to be very generous with our paid vacations.

Dependence on seasonal tourists for the major portion of Wall Drug's business has inherent risks, and uncertainty over the future of the roadside signs, which have brought customers to the store for nearly 50 years, is a grave concern to the Husteads.

We will try to have ideas to modify our outdoor advertising program to adapt to changes in the law which we are sure will be forthcoming. If there are drastic changes, they could put us out of business. If they nail it down so there isn't a sign on the Interstate, that will do the job.

Asked about diversification as a hedge against this risk, Bill replied,

We will try to diversify within our own community. By that I mean probably on our highway location in and around our Auto Livery. We have several hundred acres there (in sight of the Interstate), and a motel and a modified drugstore would be our last straw if we were wiped out in town.

The Husteads hoped to be able to create a fund to provide self-insurance for their dormitory houses. This fund would then also provide some measure of security from business risks as well.

Although over 80, Ted Hustead is still active in the management of the store, involved in everything from physical inspections of the premises to acting jointly with Bill in making policy decisions. Ted can frequently be seen on the grounds picking up litter. Dorothy, Ted's wife, comes to the store every day, summer and winter, helps with the banking, and spends from two to six hours each day on various chores. Bill's son Rick, 33, joined the store in 1980 and now shares in the management. Rick has a master's degree in guidance and counseling and spent four years as a guidance counselor and teacher in high school. Rick also spent two years in the real estate business and one year in the fast-food business before returning to Wall. During his school years, Rick spent ten seasons working in Wall Drug. His wife, Kathy, is a pharmacist and also works in the store.

Bill Hustead expressed his continuous concern with the future of Wall Drug in light of future action concerning roadside sign advertising. Can the store expansion continue; should diversification be attempted in the community; should diversification be considered away from being affected by the tourist? Will Wall Drug be able to continue to gain publicity as they have in the past to keep people aware of their "attraction" characteristics? The costs of doing business are rising, such as the increase in utilities, which is sizable. How can they plan for a bad year or two given the increasing uncertainty in the tourist industry? With these thoughts in mind, the 1983 tourist season at Wall Drug was underway.

Kitchen Made Pies

■ *James J. Chrisman and Fred L. Fry* ■

As 1982 approached, Paul Dubicki, owner and President of Kitchen Made Pies, realized something needed to be done to strengthen his company's competitive market position. Company sales had stagnated since 1975, and the firm was about to suffer its fourth straight year of losses. Competitive forces were strong, the local economy was in bad shape, and Kitchen Made was experiencing a number of difficulties with a big customer and with its bank financing. To further compound things, the firm's financial condition had deteriorated to the point where options for turning the situation around were limited. Nonetheless, Mr. Dubicki was dedicated to returning his business to profitability and, in fact, was confident that the task could be accomplished if he could only get enough relief from the press of day-to-day decision making to attend to the company's future direction and strategy.

In commenting on the current situation at Kitchen Made, Mr. Dubicki emphasized volume as the key to the company's success: "We must increase our customer base, and we must somehow encourage our present distributors to provide the promotional support retailers need to sell our products. One well-publicized special can sell more pies in one day than can be sold in a normal week without one. That's what I'd like to concentrate on, but every day something else comes up around here."

Company History

Kitchen Made Pies produced a wide variety of pies and other bakery products for distribution in the Midwest. Its offices and baking facilities were all located at a single site in Peoria, Illinois. The firm was founded in the 1950s by Frank Dubicki, Paul's father, and was run like most family businesses.

As a youngster, Paul Dubicki often worked at odd jobs in the plant, but he was not really very interested in the family's baking enterprise. After leaving the business for a while to pursue other activities, Paul returned to the company in 1968 and later became, along with David Dubicki, a minority stockholder. During this time, he often found himself frustrated by the never-ending details associated with the operational and administrative aspects of the business. In 1981, however, Paul became owner-manager of the business. Earlier that year, the elder Dubicki had been persuaded to sell out, though he did retain ownership of the company's land and facilities. The sale took the form of a redemption of Frank Dubicki's stock by the corporation and an elimination of his debt to the corporation. During the same period, David exited from the business, leaving Paul as the sole owner.

Upon assuming control, Paul immediately set about changing and updating the firm's operations and, for the first time in the firm's recent history, made a commitment to devote top-management time (mainly his) to charting a course and strategy for the company. Un-

James J. Chrisman and Fred L. Fry are from Bradley University. This case portrays neither effective or ineffective handling of an administrative situation. Rather, it is intended for classroom discussion.

Exhibit 7.1   Pie Categories at Kitchen Made Pies

4-Inch	8-Inch	9-Inch	Other
Apple	Apple	Apple	Shortcake
Pineapple	Applecrumb	Applecrumb	10-inch cakes
Cherry	Peach	Peach	
Blackberry	Pineapple	Pineapple	8-inch cakes
Lemon	Lemon	Blackberry	Sheet cakes
Coconut	Coconut	Black raspberry	
Chocolate	Chocolate	Walnut	
Peach	Black raspberry	Cherry	
	Pumpkin	Lemon meringue	
	Cherry	Coconut meringue	
	High-top meringues	Chocolate meringue	
	Regular meringues	Pumpkin	
		Chocolate Boston	
		Boston	
		Lemon whip	
		Coconut whip	
		Chocolate whip	
		Banana whip	
		Pumpkin whip	

fortunately, at the same time, problems building up over a long period of time began to surface, and Paul's commitment to his role as chief entrepreneur took a backseat to wrestling with daily operations.

Product Line

Kitchen Made Pies makes a full line of pies, some on a regular basis, some seasonally, and a much-more-limited variety of cakes. Exhibit 7.1 lists all major sizes and flavors of pies currently produced by Kitchen Made, as well as the cake products which the firm makes.

Kitchen Made sells both fresh and frozen pies, though the former is preferred due to better turnover and more predictable ordering on the part of the customers. Another problem restricting frozen pie sales is limited freezer space. Kitchen Made can currently freeze and store only 3,500 pies per day.

Kitchen Made takes pride in its long-standing use of only the highest-quality ingredients in its products. Many customers have reported that Kitchen Made pies are better than competitors' products. However, Kitchen Made's emphasis on quality results in its pies being priced above competitors' products. Mr. Dubicki views the quality of Kitchen Made's pies as a major strength, especially to maintain repeat business. Still, he concedes that many buyers are price conscious and select lower-priced pies over Kitchen Made's products. On balance, though, Mr. Dubicki believes quality counts for more than lower price insofar as his company's business is concerned.

Markets/Customers

The majority of Kitchen Made's sales are to food/bakery distributors who basically supply two major market segments. The first is the institutional segment which consists of restaurants, as well as university, hospital, corporate, and government cafeterias. The second is the retail segment which includes supermarkets and convenience food store outlets. The institutional segment accounts for the majority of Kitchen Made's cake and 9-inch pie sales, while sales to the retail segment are mainly comprised of 4-inch and 8-inch pies. Most distributors concentrate on one market segment or the other, thus determining the type of products they buy. Buying motives for both markets vary depending upon the customer and market area involved. Kitchen Made's distributors report that some of their institutional customers are very price conscious in their selection among pies and brands. However, restaurant users are usually quality conscious, and many grocers, while price and quality conscious, are quite concerned about having strong promotional support for the brands they choose to stock (to help achieve higher turnover and self-space productivity).

Most of Kitchen Made's products are sold in the Peoria and St. Louis areas, but the firm also serves customers in other parts of Missouri and Illinois, as well as in Iowa and Wisconsin. Major distributors of Kitchen Made products, as well as their served markets, are included in Exhibit 7.2.

Besides the differences in buying motives and the type of products purchased by the two end markets, there are several other distinguishing features which differentiate them from each other. Institutional users frequently prefer frozen pies, partly because of their tendency to buy supplies on a monthly basis and partly because of the lower risk of spoilage. On the other hand, in the grocery business, where purchases are made weekly or bimonthly, the economics favors fresh pies because they can be put directly on the shelf, they do not require more-expensive freezer storage, and handling costs are lower—although there is greater risk that the products will lose their freshness before they are sold to shoppers. Generally, fresh pies sell best in those supermarkets with in-store bakeries because of the "freshness" connotation perceived by shoppers.

Unlike institutional users, grocery retailers depend heavily upon promotional assistance for sales. One reason Dean's Distributing has become a less-important customer for Kitchen Made is because of its policy of not offering grocers promotional support. As a result, Dean's and Kitchen Made (as Dean's supplier) have lost much of the retail grocer business in recent years in the Peoria area. Today, most of Dean's pie distribution business done in the Peoria vicinity, as well as in other markets, is institutional.

Some distributors sell to grocers on a guaranteed basis, with unsold products returned to the dealer at no charge. Others sell products unguaranteed, where grocers take full responsibility for all products they buy. Naturally, profit margins for the methods differ. Grocers usually make about 23 to 25 percent on guaranteed sales, while unguaranteed sales

Exhibit 7.2   Distributors of Kitchen Made Pies

Distributor	Type of Segment Served	Percent of Kitchen Made's Sales
Dean's Distributing	Institutional/retail	40%
McCormick Distributing	Institutional	10
Lowenberg	Retail	11
Eisner's	Retail	8
Master Snack & New Process	Retail	13
Edward's	Retail	4
Other (including Schnuck's)	Retail	16

yield margins of approximately 35 to 40 percent. However, because of the inherent risks involved in unguaranteed purchases, most grocers prefer the lower-but-safer profit margins of guaranteed arrangements when dealing with "door-to-store" distributors such as Dean's. Nonguaranteed sales work well through efficient drop-shipment techniques customarily used by bread bakers.

Door-to-store distributors accumulate individual orders on a daily basis, pick up what they need from the pie baker, and deliver merchandise direct from the pie baker to the grocer. On the other hand, drop-shipment distributors order large supplies of pies from the pie baker, take them to warehouses, and fill individual customer orders from their warehouse inventories. In some cases, drop-shipment distributors, such as Eisner's, sell direct to their own or an affiliated grocery chain and, thus, enjoy profits on both the wholesale and retail end. This can be an important competitive advantage since 40–50 percent of the product cost is in distribution.

Mr. Dubicki has expressed a desire to expand Kitchen Made's sales to drop-shipment distributors because they operate on a lower margin of markup than door-to-store distributors, thus helping to hold down the prices retailers charge for Kitchen Made pies. This, he feels, could help circumvent the higher prices Kitchen Made charges distributors. Furthermore, since drop shippers order larger quantities, longer production runs and, therefore, lower pie-baking costs are possible.

In addition to sales to bakery wholesalers, Kitchen Made also operates its own delivery truck to handle specialty or rush orders. No plans have been made to expand this portion of Kitchen Made's operations.

The Baking Industry

Though the outlook for the baking industry has been helped by scalebacks in flour and sugar prices, overall prospects have been unfavorable and should continue to be so until economic conditions pick up. The baking industry, and particularly the pie and cake segment, is more susceptible to cyclical economic variabilities than other foodstuffs due to the discretionary nature of purchases. Pies and cakes are more or less luxury foods and are readily cut from household shopping lists when times are hard.

Further dampening the outlook for the industry is the national swing toward nutrition. Sweets and sugar intake have decreased because too much is considered unhealthy, besides, of course, being very fattening. Additionally, younger individuals account for a large portion of the consumption of pies, cakes, and other desserts.

The frozen segment of the bakery industry currently is in even worse condition, owing to the higher prices of frozen-food items, including pies. Frozen-food items, given the effects of recession and consumer budget tightening, are not expected to assume a bigger role in grocery budgets until shoppers are in a mood to spend more money on more expensive types of food items.

In addition to the conditions previously cited, other developments were changing in the industry's makeup. Between 1972 and 1977 the number of firms included under SIC Code 2051 (bread, cake, and related products) dropped from 3,323 to 3,062, but at the same time, the number of establishments employing less than 20 workers increased. A major contributor to this trend was the economic impact of higher gasoline prices; the industry's transportation costs, already high due to the perishable nature of bakery products, became a big distribution factor. The transportation cost advantage went to the large-volume

Exhibit 7.3   Comparative Changes in Price Levels of Cereal and Bakery Products

	1975	1976	1977	1978	1979	1980
Retail						
Cereal and bakery products	11.3%	−2.2%	1.6%	8.9%	10.1%	11.9%
All foods	8.5	3.1	6.3	10.0	10.9	8.6
Consumer price index	9.1	5.8	6.5	7.7	11.3	13.5
Wholesale						
Cereal and bakery products	4.0	3.3	0.1	9.8	10.5	12.2
All foods	6.7	3.8	4.4	10.5	9.6	8.2

Source: U.S. Department of Labor.

national-brand firms with internal delivery capabilities and to the smaller firms which emphasized local business. Medium-sized firms which did not have the volume to support their own delivery function and which depended on a more diffuse range of customers were hurt most by rising distribution and shipping costs.

Other factors likely to affect the performance of the industry in the future were recent trends toward eating out and the emerging popularity of pre-prepared foods. With more women in the work force and more working couples, the food-away-from-home segment was expected to grow. Dessert sales to restaurants and fast-food outlets were viewed as having growth potential. However, many fast-food chains had a policy of using standard desserts supplied from central sources rather than each unit making its selections and purchases from local dessert manufacturers. As of yet, Mr. Dubicki had not investigated the opportunities of Kitchen Made making desserts to meet the specifications of area fast-food chains.

Overall, the bakery industry was giving every sign of being very mature. There had been little real growth in sales over the past few years. However, prices and costs had risen substantially, reflecting inflationary conditions and shortages of certain ingredients. Since ingredient costs represented a major expense (approximately 50 percent of the manufacturer's selling price), recent declines in the prices of baking ingredients (e.g., sugar prices fell from $.55 per pound in November 1980 to $.26 per pound in October 1981) had given bakers the opportunity to improve profit margins. Changes in cereal and bakery prices, both wholesale and retail, as well as the consumer price index for the past six years, are provided in Exhibit 7.3.

The Local Economy

Changes in the local retail market, prompted by changing demographics and a fluctuating economy, were threatening to have a dramatic effect on Kitchen Made's pie sales. Even though the Peoria area, like most Midwestern cities, had shown little or no population growth in the past decade, the economy in Peoria had traditionally been solid due to the dominant impact of Caterpillar Tractor Co., a Pabst Brewing plant, a Hiram-Walker distillery, a number of other medium-sized manufacturing facilities, and a host of small plants—many of which are suppliers of Caterpillar. Peoria wage rates had consistently ranked in the top 20 cities in the nation, and local people were fond of saying "Peoria doesn't have recessions." But this was changing rapidly.

Exhibit 7.4   Kitchen Made's Major Rivals in the Peoria-St. Louis Market Area

Company	Headquarters Location	Geographic Area Served	Product Lines	Market Segments Served
Lloyd Harris (div. of Fasano)	Chicago	East of Rockies	Fresh 9-inch pies	Institutional and retail
Chef Pierre		Nationwide	8-inch and 10-inch frozen	Institutional and retail
Mrs. Smith	Pottstown, Pa.	Nationwide	8-inch and 10-inch frozen	Institutional and retail
Bluebird Baking	Dayton	Midwest	4-inch and 8-inch fresh	Retail
Shenandoah Pie	St. Louis	St. Louis	Full line fresh	Institutional and retail

Caterpillar endured a 12-week strike in the fall of 1979 that idled many of the 30,000 Peoria-area Caterpillar workers and did far more damage to the many suppliers and other businesses that depended either directly or indirectly on the firm. In addition, the Hiram-Walker plant closed in 1981, and the Pabst plant was scheduled to close in March 1982. Caterpillar, for the first time in 20 years, laid off substantial numbers of workers in 1981 and 1982. These events posed a significant threat to the sale of pies and other desserts in the Peoria area. For instance, Caterpillar's cafeteria was now using less than half as many pies compared to 10 years ago.

Competition

Kitchen Made was the only pie manufacturer located in the Peoria area, although it did face competition from food-service firms which had their own in-house baking capabilities. The biggest competitors were other regional and national firms which sold their products in the same areas as did Kitchen Made (see Exhibit 7.4).

Some of Kitchen Made's rivals made a full line of pies, and several were diversified into breads and other bakery products. Some of the smaller rivals concentrated on specific sizes or types of pies to allow longer production runs, permit lower inventories, and help contain production costs. Mr. Dubicki felt, however, that Kitchen Made's full line of pies gave the firm an advantage over competitors in attracting new customers and protected sales from changes in customer taste.

Production

Baking and production techniques at Kitchen Made are relatively simple, though not without their own special problems. In most instances, pie crusts and fillings are made via the assembly line method. One person operates the dough machine which flattens the dough and rolls enough out to make one crust. The dough is passed to a second person who places it into a pie pan. The machine then presses the dough into the pan. Afterward, the crust passes under a filling machine which is set according to the size of pie being made. After the crust is filled with the desired ingredients, the pie passes under another station where the top crust is molded onto the sides of the pie pan and the excess dough removed. This excess is transported by conveyor back to the dough machine. Once the pies are assembled, they are placed on racks and wheeled over to the ovens for baking. All fresh pies are baked; frozen pies may or may not be baked, depending on the type of pie and filling.

A major problem associated with production is the frequent conversions required each time the size or the flavor is changed. It takes approximately 15–20 minutes to change over pie size and 4–5 minutes to change the type of ingredient. Size changes usually occur twice a day (from 4-inch to 8-inch to 9-inch), but ingredients must be changed from 20 to 25 times per day depending upon the production schedule.

All fruit pies are put together by the method described above, but currently cream pies are filled by hand. Mr. Dubicki intends to go to automated pie assembly for both fruit and cream pies in the near future. He is also studying the purchase of a more efficient pie machine; the drawbacks are the $150,000 purchase price and the long production runs needed to maintain peak efficiency with this type of machine.

One way to cut production costs is to limit the numbers of different types of pies made. Substantial savings in changeover time and production efficiency are available by limiting pie varieties. For example, with full crews, Kitchen Made currently bakes about $30,000 worth of pies and cakes per week. Yet, on those occasions where the firm has received a large order for one type of pie, a half crew has been able to produce $10,000 worth of pies on a single eight-hour shift. However, Mr. Dubicki is concerned that a move to fewer varieties could hurt sales since many retail and institutional buyers prefer to buy full lines of products from the same supplier.

Recently, Mr. Dubicki hired a production manager to allow him more time away from the pie assembly operation. The production manager is still in the process of learning all the requirements of the job and Mr. Dubicki has been spending a lot of time giving the new manager on-the-job training. Mr. Dubicki has so far been reluctant to delegate full authority to the new manager even though he is pleased with the progress she is making in taking over the supervison of pie-making activities. The transfer of authority has been hindered by the fact that all aspects of the pie-making operation have not been smoothly worked out and some are in the midst of being changed.

One positive development has been the progress made to reduce inventory. Though done as much out of necessity as out of design, the move has nonetheless helped in many respects. In the past, ingredients were often bought in six-month quantities. Today, the firm tries to buy only what it needs for one or two weeks, except in special cases when supplies are hard to find or favorable price breaks can be obtained.

Financial Situation

Mr. Dubicki believes that with Kitchen Made's current product mix, sales of approximately $35,000 per week ($1,820,000 per year) are needed to break even. Variable expenses are estimated to be about 85 percent of sales revenue. Exhibit 7.5 provides a breakdown of Kitchen Made's sales and gross profits by product line in percentages and dollar amounts. Margins on the 4-inch pies and the cakes are the biggest, with margins on the 8-inch pie and 9-inch pie varieties substantially lower.

The prices of Kitchen Made's pie and cake products have not been changed for approximately 12 months. Exhibit 7.6 shows the prices for the various types of pies made by Kitchen Made.

Kitchen Made's management is particularly pleased with the company's high-top meringue pie. Because of its superior looks and acceptance by consumers, the high-top pies command a $.50 premium over the price of regular meringue pies, yet they cost only a few pennies more to make.

Exhibit 7.5   Sales/Operating Profits by Product Lines, Last 12 Months

Product	Sales Revenues		Gross Profits		Gross Profit Margin
	Dollar	Percent of Total	Dollars	Percent	
4-inch pie	$ 536,000	33.5%	$147,600	61.5%	27.5%
8-inch pie	296,000	18.5	24,700	10.3	8.3
9-inch pie	704,000	44.0	50,400	21.0	7.2
Cakes	64,000	4.0	17,300	7.2	27.0
Total	$1,600,000	100.0%	$240,000	100.0%	15.0%

Exhibit 7.6   Wholesale Pie Prices for Kitchen Made Pies

4-inch pies	$.25	8-inch regular meringue	$.90	9-inch fruit pies	$1.30
		8-inch high-top meringue	$1.40	9-inch whips	$1.30
		8-inch fruit pies	$1.00	9-inch meringue	$1.25
				9-inch specialty	$1.60
				9-inch walnut	$2.00
				9-inch cherry	$2.25

Exhibit 7.7   Kitchen Made Pies' Condensed Operating Results, 1971–1980

Year	Net Income (Loss)			Costs as a Percent of Sales Revenues*				
	Sales Revenues	Dollars	As a Percent of Sales	Materials	Labor	Selling	Administration	Facilities Equipment, and Other
1971	$ 844,000	$14,000	1.7%	51.2%	30.0%	2.9%	9.9%	7.6%
1972	955,000	8,000	.8	50.5	29.3	2.8	9.5	7.1
1973	1,246,000	24,000	1.9	52.7	24.6	2.8	9.2	8.9
1974	1,453,000	18,000	1.2	57.0	22.3	2.5	7.7	9.3
1975	1,604,000	110,000	6.9	53.9	20.7	2.2	6.9	9.4
1976	1,580,000	109,000	6.9	48.8	23.0	2.6	7.4	11.3
1977	1,642,000	7,000	.4	48.9	26.0	2.7	8.5	13.5
1978	1,608,000	−24,000	(1.5)	50.9	26.3	2.2	9.4	12.7
1979	1,601,000	−58,000	(3.6)	50.6	27.0	2.8	10.0	13.1
1980	1,506,000	−91,000	(6.0)	51.3	28.3	3.3	10.3	12.8
1981	1,635,000	−178,000	(10.9)	54.3	27.7	4.1	11.2	13.5

*All of the cost percentages are not completely comparable from year to year due to several changes in how costs were allocated between categories of expenses.

Because of stagnant sales and rising costs over the past several years, the financial condition of Kitchen Made has deteriorated. Exhibit 7.7 provides condensed operating results for the years 1971 through 1981. Exhibit 7.8 shows a condensed balance sheet for 1981. Exhibit 7.9 presents the computable financial ratios for Kitchen Made as compared to industry averages for SIC Code 2051 businesses (i.e., bread, cake, and related products) with sales of under $50 million.

Exhibit 7.8   Kitchen Made Pies Balance Sheet for 1981

Assets		Liabilities and Equity	
Current assets:		Current liabilities:	
Cash	$ 2,000	Accounts payable	$291,000
Accounts receivable	163,000	Unsecured bank note	70,000
Inventory	137,000	Accrued payroll and taxes	25,000
Prepaid expenses	17,000	Note—F. Dubicki	8,000
Total current assets	319,000	Total current liabilities	394,000
Fixed assets: (after depreciation)		Long-term liabilities:	
Leasehold improvements	1,000	Note on truck	15,000
Machinery and equipment	48,000	Note on equipment	12,000
Autos and trucks	28,000	Total long-term liabilities	27,000
Total fixed assets	77,000	Total liabilities	421,000
		Owner's equity	(25,000)
Total assets	$396,000	Total liabilities and equity	$396,000

Exhibit 7.9   Selected Company and Industry Financial Ratios, 1981

	Industry SIC Code 2051	Kitchen Made Pies
Current ratio	.76	.81 (without Dean's .66)
Net profit/sales	3.8%	Negative
Net profit/total assets	6.5%	Negative
Net profit/equity	19.5%	Negative
Sales/equity	7.6x	Negative
Sales/total assets	2.5x	4.1x
Collection period	14 days	36 (without Dean's 23)
Sales/working capital	8.8x	Negative
Sales/inventory	53.3x	11.9x
Fixed assets/equity	131.6%	Negative
Total debt/equity	201.7%	Negative

Source: *Key Business Ratios 1981*, Dun & Bradstreet.

The most immediate financial problem relates to the unsecured $70,000 bank note which has currently come due. Kitchen Made has had an agreement with a local financial institution which allowed the firm to borrow $70,000 on a program resembling revolving credit. Kitchen Made pays only interest on this loan, with the principal due in lump sum at the end of the borrowing period. One option Mr. Dubicki is considering involves trying to refinance the loan and get the borrowing period extended. But he is also considering whether to switch his business to another bank. Mr. Dubicki feels that because Kitchen Made often has a $20,000 to $30,000 balance in its bank account, it is entitled to some relief on the interest rate being paid. Furthermore, in discussions with the bank's loan officers over the possibility of refinancing the loan, Mr. Dubicki has been informed that the bank will insist on a secured note. Since Mr. Dubicki's father holds title to Kitchen Made's property, the bank has mentioned the use of a second mortgage on Mr. Dubicki's personal home as possible security for the loan. This is not attractive to Mr. Dubicki, and he is hopeful that other Peoria banks will be interested in giving Kitchen Made an unsecured loan in the amount of $70,000; Mr. Dubicki is quite willing to establish a business relationship with a different bank in the event satisfactory terms can be worked out. If not, he sees little option but to agree to the second mortgage condition for a secured note at Kitchen Made's present bank.

Another problem causing concern is slow payments by some customers. While such customers as Lowenberg and Eisner's consistently take advantage of discounts for early payment (usual terms are 2%/10 days, net/30 days), Dean's Distributing currently owes over six months' back payments amounting to $60,000. Mr. Dubicki feels most of this account is uncollectible but has not, as of yet, written the amount off as bad debt expense. Mr. Dubicki has expressed a desire to eliminate or substantially cut back on the business done with Dean's Distributing but in an effort to maintain sales levels has continued to supply its pies to Dean's on a strictly cash basis.

In spite of these financial difficulties, Kitchen Made has been able to generate enough cash flow to meet its current obligations and also to make small payments on the amounts owed to creditors of longer standing. Thus, while the situation is far from ideal and the firm is very vulnerable to unforeseen events, liquidity is probably not a life-or-death concern at the moment. However, Mr. Dubicki realizes that any further decline in sales and cash flows could be extremely hazardous and potentially fatal.

Personnel

Most of the managerial activities at Kitchen Made Pies are handled directly by Mr. Dubicki. Besides the production manager, Ms. Barbara Britt, the only other management personnel are Ms. Charolette Watson, Office Manager, and Mr. Lonnie Beard, the Sales Promotion Manager. Mr. Beard is responsible for making sure products are stocked and advertised properly at local retail outlets, which he visits periodically. Mr. Dubicki, besides being president and owner, acts as sales and distribution manager, prepares cash-flow projections, searches for new accounts, and, of course, oversees all day-to-day activities. He also is really the only person who completely understands all aspects of the business. About the only activity he is not directly involved with is the actual assembly of the pies.

Kitchen Made currently employs about 30 production workers, 6 office workers, several maintenance workers, and a truck driver. The shop is unionized and pays wages comparable to other like-sized area firms.

Future Prospects and Outlook

Though the current situation at Kitchen Made Pies is far from ideal, Mr. Dubicki believes the situation is not hopeless and that a turnaround in his company's fortunes is manageable. As he put it, "I'm optimistic about our future, but then again, isn't that the only way I can feel?" He thinks good progress is being made in solving internal operating problems, and he has established good rapport with his work force; he feels the latter will facilitate making many of the remaining internal changes he is considering. Yet, Mr. Dubicki recognizes the need to address several nagging issues:

- Would lengthening production runs reduce costs enough to justify a move to narrow Kitchen Made's product line?
- How important to Kitchen Made's competitive position is a broad product line? What product mix really makes the most sense?
- Would it be economical for Kitchen Made to purchase more equipment to automate its pie assembly operations, and how could such equipment be financed in the event it would improve Kitchen Made's efficiency?
- Should Kitchen Made continue to position itself at the high end of the price/quality range?

Mr. Dubicki also realizes that plain old hard work and dedication on his part, while helpful and necessary, will not be sufficient—improved operating results and a workable strategy are, of necessity, high on his agenda.

Bordados Maty, S. A.

▪ *Lincoln W. Deihl* ▪

Twenty years ago Carolina Garcia turned out a child's dress on her home Singer sewing machine and sold it. Today that machine is ensconced in her plush, feminine, pink-upholstered, vice-president's office.

Based in Aguascalientes, Bordados Maty is one of the largest apparel manufacturers in Mexico. "Maty Group" includes a number of product line divisions including unconsolidated subsidiaries for tax purposes. Approximately 85 percent of revenues come from the apparel division. The basic product line has always been dresses for little girls, and the firm remains dominant. Other lines include women's style dresses as well as clothing for little boys. These two lines are active but have never been fully developed and promoted.

Garcia today, as founder and vice-president, spends much of her time walking through production facilities and communicating to her son and executive vice-president, Carlos, on matters that need to be corrected. She also heads a design department of 20 people. One of her subordinates in the design department is Carlos's wife. At least three times a year, the key design people travel to Europe and the United States seeking fashion information.

The design department is considered to be an expensive function which few firms in the industry can duplicate. The department nominally reports to the sales manager, but because of the family relationship of the key design people, it actually reports to the general management level.

The industry consists of hundreds of small producers of limited lines. These producers have no design departments; they openly copy successful designs of others in the industry. Frequently, they do not pay taxes and various fringe benefits which government requires. Only three or four producers in Mexico operate on the scale of Maty Group.

Maty is the name of Carolina's mother and daughter. The latter today is a university student who is frequently seen in temporary jobs at the company.

Carolina's husband, Don Carlos, is president but largely occupies himself in a small, woodworking shop built for him on the ground floor beneath the executive offices.

The family home is near the center of the walled compound which encloses the main plant.

Carlos, at 33 is executive vice-president and general manager. He left school at 13 to work in the factory his parents had founded. He worked in various jobs in the plant, such as cutting and folding. At age 22, Carlos directed production; at 32, he directed marketing. He took on these positions as the respective functions became dominant in the firm. There was little interest at this time in "administracion," the control function.

Gradually, Carlos became aware of the need for expanding the function of general management. Several years ago he took the IPADE course, a high-quality executive program offered both in Mexico City and Guadalajara. As a result, he has become quite a sophisticated general manager. All of his top-level managers currently are taking the IPADE course, flying in a chartered airplane to Guadalajara Tuesday noons and returning Wednesday evenings. Middle-level managers are making plans to attend the course within the next year.

Meetings of Management

On the evening of June 9, 1980, two important meetings were held to implement the new organization structure designed by Carlos and Planning Director, Raúl González. The first meeting at 5 p.m. was attended by the executive committee: the newly named Head of the Human Resources Division, José Antonio Torres (age 27); the Head of the Administrative Services Division, Humberto Salazar (age 30); the Head of the Apparel Division, Rolando Garcia (age 34); the Head of Comarco, the domestic products subsidiary, Francisco Avayo (age 33); the Head of the Bordamex subsidiary, Javier Medina (age 32); the Head of Production in the apparel division, José de la luz Lopez (age 27). The remaining member, the Head of the Industrial Division, had not yet been named. (See Exhibit 8.1.)

Later that evening, lower-level managers were brought into the meeting. Carlos announced that the new structure was designed by him and the planning director. Some questions were asked, particularly about the level of Bordamex. Carlos explained that the capital structure and growth prospects for Bordamex required it on this level. The organization structure and the rationale were apparently well accepted.

Comarco (Domestic Division)

Francisco Avayo, the new head, Comarco, S.A. (domestic division), has been with Maty Group for 10 months. With his marketing degree from Iberro-Americana University, he spent nine years in Mexico City in marketing and organization development positions with Nestle. Originally from Aguascalientes, he accepted the opportunity to return, recognizing the element of risk in his career move.

Francisco has the task of establishing an autonomous profit center. Traditionally called the domestic division, it has been an integral part of the firm from the beginning. But with the economic growth of Mexico, there was a great demand for ready-made clothing; and this is where the firm placed its priorities. Today the apparel division generates 85 percent of revenues, and the domestic division generates most of the rest.

Now, Comarco, SA is being established as a separate profit center to replace the domestic division. The biggest problem is getting production facilities. Arrangements have been made with the governor of the state to set up two new factories in an underdeveloped part of the state. Construction is already underway. Present output for the division is 49,000 items per month. Current demand is for 85,000 items. Product lines include textiles for the home: kitchen, bathroom, bedroom, living room, and dining room; and institutional: hotels, restaurants, hospitals, military. Institutions normally are supplied on a long-term contract basis. Francisco believes there is a vast potential market, virtually untapped, particularly in institutions. He has recently hired a production manager and a manager of administration and finance. He will take care of marketing himself at present; he sees no major marketing problems at present.

Distribution is through the five sales offices of the apparel division. The same physical

Exhibit 8.1   Bordados Maty, S.A.

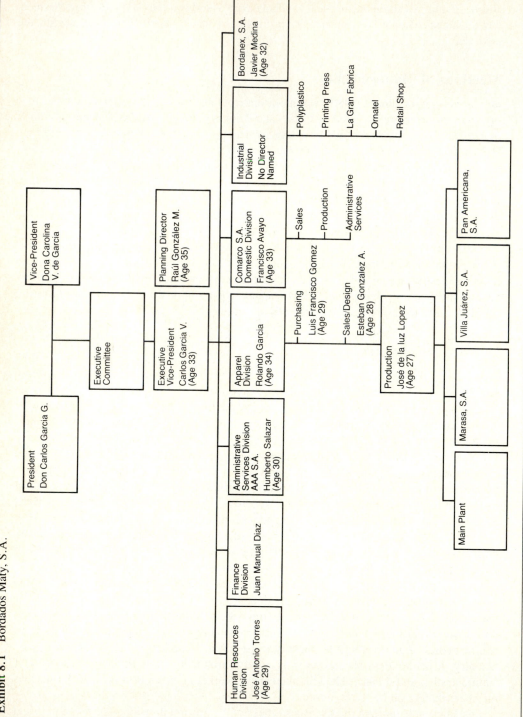

facilities are used in Monterrey, Guadalajara, Mexico City, and Mazatlán. Separate facilities are used in Veracruz. Comarco now has its own people in all these facilities.

Francisco sees no serious problem in obtaining supervisory and middle-management personnel. These people are available in Maty Group and can be transferred. They are frequently willing to come for promotion and added responsibility. It will probably not be possible to find many skilled workers locally as the new plants are somewhat remote. But the firm will provide transportation for workers from Aguascalientes.

Francisco has developed his own control system, relatively simple and economical. He will utilize administrative services division only for data collecting.

Human Resources

José Torres, newly-named head of the division of human resources, has a Business Administration degree with a major in industrial relations from Iberro-Americana University in Mexico City where he was a scholarship holder. While studying, due to financial need, he held a full-time job in industrial relations with Alfa Group, a major Mexican holding company. He found the pace "killing" and went with Famosa, a firm in Monterrey. After two years, he accepted an industrial relations job with Maty Group. He was named head of the division after one year.

José's biggest problem is getting the line managers to recognize that training and development is a line responsibility and that HR is only there to assist and provide resources. He sees a problem in filling new training positions with specialists as these people are scarce. He is uncertain whether his key subordinates can really adapt and change to the new reality of the significance of HR. He believes that top management is now convinced of the importance of developing human resources if the firm is to continue to grow. Marc Rouvroy (age 27) is Belgian and related to the family: his mother was a sister of Carolina. He came to work in the company two years ago as an alternative to military service. The Belgian government permits work in a Third World country as a military alternative.

Marc has worked in human resources, production, administrative services, and the domestic division. Usually, he has been in staff rather than line activities. He has prepared several studies of operations in various units. Currently, he is involved in distribution with some supervisory responsibility for personnel in sales offices. Also, he is concerned with coordination of purchasing and production activities.

The company is sending Marc to IPADE in Mexico City for two years to earn his Master of Business Administration degree. He expects to remain in the company several more years but is uncertain as to his future. He has learned Spanish while in Mexico and is well accepted by others. If the company expands its export activities, he would like to establish a sales office in the United States.

Marc sees possible problems in industrial relations. Traditionally, the company has had good relations as a paternalistic employer. The majority of employees are women at low levels. There is a single labor union—government sponsored—which employees are required to join. Management is on good terms with union representatives. Carlos and the head of the local union are good friends.

Marc sees a number of instances of favoritism, unfairness, and discrimination; and he feels these may cause problems. For example, night watchmen work 13-hour shifts at below-standard wages. He feels the company could face many industrial relations problems in the future as workers become more aware.

Labor Problems at Villa Juárez

Recently, there was a work stoppage for the first time at Villa Juárez, a rural plant. The cause was dissatisfaction over the profit-sharing arrangement. Work resumed after several hours only when Carlos, Carolina, and the labor union representative visited the plant.

The government requires that 8 percent of profits be shared with workers. Each year the plant labor representative and the company sign a document setting forth the agreement for the annual profit distribution. Then, 15 days later the distribution actually takes place. Profit sharing is based on each plant as a profit center.

At the Villa Juárez plant, workers actually received only about 65 percent of the previous year's distribution. This was apparently due to some problems and inefficiencies at the plant during the past year. Operations and piece-rate earnings were very much affected by problems with flow and quality of raw materials.

Two agitators among the workers apparently spread the story that the company was manipulating figures and trying to cheat them. After all, the company is supposed to have been growing and expanding in the past year. So, workers all went out on an illegal work stoppage. The plant manager happened to be in Aguascalientes at the time. Headquarters was notified by radio as this is the only means of rapid communication.

A number of meetings were held at headquarters as the plant manager rushed to Villa Juárez. Carlos and the head of the labor union for the state eventually went to the plant as well. In the first meeting with the workers, the labor union head impressed upon them that the company had always been fair, that the work stoppage was illegal, and that they could be fired. As a result, most returned to work.

In a subsequent meeting with workers who stayed out, the labor union head apparently promised vaguely that the company would provide some additional compensation. Apparently, this had been discussed at headquarters as an alternative; however, several managers had opposed such capitulation as setting a dangerous precedent.

At any rate, everyone eventually returned to work, including the two identified agitators, who showed remorse. The company now has the problem of determining whether and how much additional compensation should be granted.

The agitators have been identified as being affiliated with a socialist party labor union which has been increasingly active in various parts of the country. In particular, in the southern city of Oaxaca, agitation was accompanied by violence. This political party labor union presently has approximately 3,000 families illegally occupying a camp in Aguascalientes. The governor has taken a low-key approach to the problem and avoided violence.

The town of Villa Juárez has near the plant two government-operated but communist-controlled teacher-training institutions. The company feared that instructors at the institutions would attempt to take advantage of the labor situation at the nearby plant, but this has not yet happened.

The Villa Juárez plant manager is the right-hand man of José de la Luz. He has been here for 10 months and expects to be replaced in two months. He will then become a coordinator of plant managers. As such, he will travel to the various plants to try to improve coordination with purchasing and balance the work load among plants. A new plant manager cannot yet be developed internally. The new manager will probably be shifted from the nearby rural plant at Palo Alto.

Presently, the Villa Juárez manager sees no problems with the work force. But he says that management is watching carefully for trouble, especially among the identified agitators. He expects no further labor problems. At the moment he speaks, the plant again is experiencing problems with the water supply for essential worker facilities.

There are problems at Villa Juárez with continuity of supplies. Production workers were laid off the previous week for this reason. They are now trying to contract work from the Pan Americana and the Mara (Palo Alto) rural plants to keep workers busy.

Administrative Services Division (AAA, S.A.)

The administrative services division is organized as a subsidiary to sell data analysis services and systems to clients both within Maty Group and outside as well. As yet, however, there are virtually no outside clients.

A supervisor in the operations research section, Juan Bosco, returned a year ago from Pennsylvania State University with a master's degree in operations research. He took a job for two months with a brewery in Monterrey and has been with Maty Group about 10 months. He admits to personal problems in adjusting on reentry.

Juan sees various problems in transferring systems and management skills—but not technology. Systems require people to make them work; and due to what he calls the "Mexican mentality," transfer requires considerable time and patience to make it work. Juan feels that the people in his group have limited skills, such as in statistics. He has not yet been able to get the support that he feels he needs from the top; probably, he will not stay with the company.

Financial Planning

At 35, Raúl González is the oldest member of management. He is also the most American-oriented member with his Master of Business Administration degree from Eastern Michigan University and Master of Industrial Engineering degree from the University of Michigan. As planning director, Raúl fills the traditional role. He is also a key communication link between middle-level and top management. As the director of the industrial division has not been named, the heads of those five departments and subsidiaries report to him.

Raúl is trying to encourage the planning function within the various functions and divisions. He is trying to set up five-year projections that are realistic. In the past, such projections have been much too optimistic—based on what the various managers want rather than what is possible.

Raúl does not want a separate planning department, but tools and guidance must be provided so planning can be done within the divisions. Progress is being made. There is general acceptance of the need. Managers are now coming up with more realistic projections.

The net profit figures are 4.8 million pesos (22.7 to the U.S. dollar) for 1979 and 2.9 million for 1978. (See Exhibit 8.2.) In actuality, according to Raúl, net profit is probably closer to 20 million pesos due to "tax planning." The difference is in cost of goods sold. Transfer prices are kept deliberately high in order to lower profit for the parent company and raise profit for the subsidiaries. The parent company tax rate is 42 percent while that of the subsidiaries is 30 percent or 20 percent. This tax planning is considered acceptable and within the limits of the law. The government accepts such tax planning in order to encourage industrialization.

Exhibit 8.2   Bordados Maty, S.A., Statement of Results of Operation and Accumulated Profits (in pesos)

	Year Ending December 31	
	1979	**1978**
Net sales	290,209,382	214,463,420
Costs and expenses		
Cost of goods sold	215,318,721	156,768,600
Selling expenses	31,436,623	31,246,255
Administrative expenses	23,823,352	12,621,241
Financial expenses	9,680,724	7,258,570
	280,259,420	207,894,666
Profit before taxes and worker's participation in profit	9,949,962	6,568,754
Income tax	4,356,079	3,096,034
Worker's participation in profit	835,039	600,594
	5,191,118	3,696,628
Net profit	4,758,844	2,872,126
Retained earnings at the beginning of the year	5,191,183	2,319,057
Capitalization of profits	5,191,183	—
Retained earnings at the end of the year	4,758,844	5,191,183
Net profit per share	132.13	159.56

There are only 20 or 30 copies of the audited financial statements. (See Exhibits 8.2, 8.3, 8.4.) Circulation is strictly controlled. The Mexican auditors are affiliated with Touche Ross & Co.; their acceptance of the reports is without reservations.

Raúl points out that selling and administrative expenses (Exhibit 8.3) includes rent of installations—land and buildings. The owners own all facilities and rent them to the company.

The financial reports are only for Bordados Maty S.A.; it is not consolidated. This is not required. Probably by 1985, the firm will "go public" and then be required to publish consolidated statements. The process of going public is a gradual one. Now, partners are being invited in to certain subsidiaries—such as Bordamex, Ornatel, and Polyplastics. These partners are close, well known to the owners, and they have a small financial interest. This process of bringing in partners will be widened over the coming years as the company prepares for the complex task of going public. Inevitably, as the company continues to grow, there is a need for outside capital.

Marketing

There is little need for demand creation. Production is to order and it rarely meets demand. Salespeople take orders several times a year, and the factory normally produces 80–90 percent of what customers order. However, Esteban González, the sales manager, is convinced that some *publicidad* should be undertaken to stress the image of the firm as a quality producer. He feels this would be advantageous as the firm competes with many low-cost producers. Also, he feels it would facilitate adding new product lines in the future.

Exhibit 8.3 Bordados Maty, S.A., Balance Sheet (in pesos)

Assets	December 31 1979	December 31 1978
Current assets:		
Cash	5,877,860	1,665,073
Accounts receivable (it is not considered necessary to estimate bad debts):		
Accounts receivable from customers	64,653,309	43,159,139
Accounts receivable from subsidiaries	5,438,613	—
Advance payment to supplier	1,464,343	—
Other receivables	4,598,982	3,094,827
	76,155,247	46,253,966
Inventories		
Finished goods	11,664,357	4,112,174
In-process goods	19,572,208	18,981,358
Raw materials	42,334,056	30,097,785
In-transit merchandise	3,213,399	127,820
	76,784,020	53,319,137
Advance payments (i.e., insurance and rents)	123,049	622,587
Sum of current assets	158,940,176	101,860,763
Investments (credit union)	804,000	804,000
Plant and equipment		
Machinery and equipment	14,685,163	7,531,981
Office furniture and equipment	8,762,111	3,308,999
Vehicles	1,830,404	1,237,570
Installations (electrical, plumbing)	1,839,887	1,047,887
	27,117,565	13,126,437
Less: accumulated depreciation and amortization	18,596,077	6,141,883
Total assets	178,340,253	108,806,646

Liabilities and Equity	December 31 1979	December 31 1978
Current liabilities:		
Notes payable	26,877,493	4,965,854
Accounts payable to suppliers	71,619,237	52,801,002
Accumulated expenses and taxes, except income tax	6,169,032	7,810,559
Income tax	—	1,116,979
Participation of workers in profits	835,039	641,922
Affiliated companies—accounts payable	5,522,885	4,054,486
Current portion of long-term loan	2,431,244	2,773,193
Sum of current liabilities	113,454,930	74,163,995
Long-term loans—less amount to be paid in one year	24,110,458	11,451,468
Equity		
Capital—42,000 common shares to bearer in 1979 and 18,000 shares in 1978, with par value of 1,000 pesos each	42,000,000	18,000,000
Paid-in capital	(5,983,979)	—
	36,016,021	18,000,000
Retained earnings	4,758,844	5,191,183
	40,774,865	23,191,183
Total liabilities	178,340,253	108,806,646

(22.7 pesos to the U.S. dollar)

Exhibit 8.4   Bordados Maty, S.A., Statement of Sources and Uses of Funds (in pesos)

	Year Ending December 31	
	1979	1978
Sources of funds		
From the operation		
Net profit	4,758,844	2,872,126
Depreciation and amortization	1,599,431	1,214,242
Total funds from the operation	6,358,275	4,086,368
Long-term financing	15,090,232	5,191,862
Sales of fixed assets	—	633,121
Total of sources of funds	21,448,507	9,911,351
Uses of funds		
Acquisition of plant and equipment	1,228,785	3,360,810
Payment of the current portion of long-term loan	2,431,244	3,368,775
Increase in working capital	17,788,478	3,181,766
Total of uses of funds	21,448,507	9,911,351

Distribution is through five regional sales offices, Guadalajara, Monterrey, Mexico City, Pacific, and Surreste. These offices have been operated by independent commission agents. No inventories are maintained.

Recently, the firm has apparently been moving toward staffing the offices with company managers. The company discovered that the agent in Guadalajara was not making visits to service large customers. After lengthy meetings between Carlos and the agent, the contract was canceled and a company manager was placed in charge of the office. As a direct result of the problems in Guadalajara, the agent in Monterrey communicated with Carlos seeking clarification of his relationship with the company. After several communications, that contract was also canceled and a company manager placed in charge. Reportedly, the relationship with the agent in Mexico City currently is shaky.

It appears that the intention of the company is to have employee-staffed sales offices exclusively. The policy in the past had been to have employees in charge of certain functions—such as collections—in the sales agencies. This policy is making the transition to company offices easier as someone is on hand prepared to take charge.

The commission on sales paid to agents was at one time on gross sales, but this has since been related to net sales, which takes into account collections and returned merchandise at end of season. Commissions paid were originally 9.9 percent; then they were reduced to 5.9 percent. Now negotiations are underway to reduce commissions to 2 percent. In a typical case, with 420 million pesos sales, the agent gains 21 million pesos in commissions just for order taking. In negotiations, Carlos is attempting to show agents that with anticipated sales projections their commissions will not drastically change, even at 2 percent. Carlos feels that traditionally agents have been well compensated for doing little.

Sales offices have relatively few customers, large wholesalers, and some major retailers such as Sears Roebuck. Customers have considerable influence over prices and design. There are serious problems in returned merchandise. In the past, customers received perhaps 80 percent of what they ordered, and often substitute colors and designs were included. Consequently, they usually ordered more than they actually expected.

Now, the company supplies closer to 100 percent of what is ordered. Consequently, customers at the end of season are returning large amounts of unsold merchandise; and this presents a problem. Labels are removed, and the merchandise has been sold in a retail shop on the premises of the main plant. Now, the company is considering establishing a network of company-operated retail shops in outlying areas of the state to retail this returned merchandise. Also, an attempt is being made to rationalize selling so that merchandise can be moved to other parts of the republic when the season ends in a particular area.

The planning director recently made a study of pricing in the industry and concluded that Maty's prices were well below average. As a result, there are plans to increase prices significantly, as it is felt that the company should recover its substantial design costs.

Normally, new designs have been produced each season, then discontinued. Then competitors have copied them. Now, Maty will attempt to extend the life of designs to a three- to five-year period.

The current penetration of the total market by Maty's apparel lines is estimated by the planning director as follows:

Women	1.3%
Juveniles (age 15–20)	0.7
Girls (age 1–12)	3.5
Boys (age 5–14)	0.2
Babies (age 0–4)	1.6

It is hoped that by the end of 1980 a start may be made on entering the export market by selling to Costa Rica, a stable country which imports nearly all of its apparel. Such a move would force the company to improve its quality standards in general and would be in line with the government's priorities of increasing exports.

Initially, Maty would simply set up a commission agent in Costa Rica and receipts would be paid into a post office box company to be set up in a tax haven such as the Grand Cayman Islands. Such a triangular relationship is acceptable tax planning, according to the planning director. He and Carlos intend to make a trip to Costa Rica, probably in September. Raúl has had some experience in Costa Rica, having made a number of trips there when he was employed by a Monterrey firm.

The export market is deemed essential as sales are clearly slowing this year. This is due to several factors: consumers have clearly slowed buying, unemployment is rising, wages and salaries have not kept pace with inflation, and a new 10 percent Value Added Tax (VAT) is in effect.

Sales volume was 214.5 million pesos in 1978 and 290.2 million in 1979 (Exhibit 8.2). The sales department estimates 464.0 million in sales for 1980, but Raúl considers this overly optimistic and thinks they will do well to reach 410.0 million, a 36-percent gain. Over the years, the sales managers have tended to overestimate sales.

All materials and supplies, including zippers and fasteners, must be purchased from domestic suppliers in Mexico City. No imports are permitted. Purchasing Manager Luis Gomez utilizes about 40 sources in order to assure continuity, quality, and prices. According to Luis, there are problems in continuity and quality, but these are now being resolved. However, it is not uncommon for work stoppages to occur in the cutting and sewing room due to lack of materials. Luis would like to have earlier and better information from Sales in order to facilitate purchasing, but he understands the problem in providing a longer lead time. Also, Luis would like a narrowing of types of materials needed, but the sales manager clearly wants to provide wide product lines.

Production

Patterns are drawn on large sheets of paper and juxtaposed so as to minimize waste. Cutting is a semiskilled activity. A power jigsaw is manipulated by hand as it cuts through a stack of cloth. Presently, the company is investigating the purchase of computer-guided cutters. There is a problem of matching bolts of cloth with varying shades of color. This is a quality problem with suppliers.

The main plant is to be moved in September 1980 to a building now under construction in the new industrial park. Only a few operations and offices will remain behind: ironing, cutting, packaging, and distribution. The new building has been under construction for two months; it is expected to be finished in September, and production should begin there in October.

The moving of production equipment is to be done in one day and one night to minimize production disruption. The machines are not considered particularly difficult to transport. A possible problem is transportation of employees. Studies have been made and assurances given that transportation will be adequate; it is a municipal function but privately contracted. Public transportation is a chronic problem in Mexico, but the company does not anticipate at this time that they will have to provide transportation.

Ornatel

One of the units in the industrial division reporting to the planning director is Ornatel, a woven garment label subsidiary in which he has a financial stake. A newly organized subsidiary, Ornatel appears to have ample back orders. Just now, however, the general manager and supervisor need to spend considerable time in Guadalajara visiting old customers of the plant from which machinery was bought, assuring them that their needs will be met. This is a task that can only be accomplished in person—perhaps over lunch—not by telephone or by mail.

Only in its second week of operation, the plant is operating more smoothly than in the previous week. The designer is acting supervisor at the moment, and Raúl looks in a couple times a day.

A personal project which also requires that Raúl look in several times a day is a small tortilla-producing plant. His partner is a relative who handles deliveries to small groceries in his car. Another relative and partner is the young supervisor who has been able to cope thus far with the numerous breakdowns of the secondhand equipment as well as supervising the unskilled young women in the labor-intensive operation.

Rural Plants

Bordamex makes sewn ornaments for apparel. Equipment includes two large automatic programmed machines for making fancy emblems. Each machine cost 8 million pesos. Two more machines are on order. The present prefab building will be extended to accommodate them.

Presently, 80 percent of Bordamex output is sold to Maty and the balance is sold outside. The goal is to reverse this within a year or two.

The Pan Americana plant receives textiles from Maty's centralized cutting room and sells its entire output to Maty. Management acknowledges some problems with continuity of supplies. The plant has some training problems as workers are accustomed to field work and must adapt to operating sewing machines. But they do fairly well, with the help of human resources people from Maty. The plant has had some experience in utilizing the Japanese concept of quality control circles in an effort to resolve quality problems.

Home for the Aged

Rising not far from the Villa Juárez rural plant is Carolina's favorite social project, the home for the aged (Rouvroy Hogar Para Ancianos). It will have a total cost of 40 million pesos. The foundation now is in place as well as facilities for pigs and chickens. In one year, the first stage should be in place with accommodations for 20 persons.

A rural plant, La Gran Fabrica, should generate net revenues of 2,500,000 pesos a year which is to be used to cover operating expenses of the home. The señora and the planning director are now actively seeking 1 million pesos from six local banks for fixed assets. Local suppliers have been persuaded to furnish building supplies at lower prices, free in some instances. The well digger and the pipe line supplier have donated services and supplies. The architect often asks local merchants to sell supplies and materials at lower prices. The state and federal governments are expected to provide some support. Plans have been made to solicit contributions from individuals and to raise funds through such activities as lotteries and movies.

Marc Rouvroy opposes the home for the aged even though the project bears his family name. He feels that the need for such an institution in Mexico is limited due to the extended family system which takes care of its own. At one time, Marc says he raised some questions regarding the project's feasibility with Carolina; and she would not speak to him for weeks. He feels that sponsoring a primary school or training school for Maty workers or a literacy program would be better.

La Gran Fabrica, the rural plant which is to cover operating expenses for the home, is managed by Lupita, Carolina's daughter. Lupita is an efficient, capable manager. A walk through the plant convinces one that she organizes well and is respected by workers.

Lupita's husband is manager of Polyplasticos, S.A., a company subsidiary which produces mostly plastic garment hangers. The two operated a dry cleaning business in Guadalajara until it went bankrupt.

Meeting with the Consultants

Rather unexpectedly, two consultants arrived from Kurt Salmon Associates, an international textile industry consulting firm based in Atlanta. Presumably, this was to be an exploratory visit. The purpose apparently was to find ways and means of increasing plant productivity. There was a general feeling that productivity was low and that this could have substantial impact on profitability. It was also felt that equipment was being underutilized.

First, the consultants toured production facilities with Production Head, José de la Luz. OR Supervisor Juan Bosco was enlisted to translate. While this was taking place, several executives with the planning director were sitting together to determine where to focus efforts of the consultants. Rolando was anxious to have the study focus on production within his division. There was some feeling that the study ought to focus on recurrent efforts at standardization and extension of models in the product lines. Unfortunately, Rolando had to leave the meeting to fly to Guadalajara for the weekly IPADE course.

The group then met with the consultants as efforts continued to determine the direction of the proposed study. The planning director understood the importance of the readiness of the organization for the consultants. He was aware that the client needed to focus the effort and that the consultants had a product line—a package—to sell.

Carlos, who had apparently instigated the exploratory visit by the consultants had gone off to Spain a week earlier on a business trip of several weeks. Next morning, a beaming Carolina came through the offices to report that Carlos had just telephoned from Spain where he had arrived safely.

A second meeting with the consultants included the human resources director, the sales manager, the planning director, and the production head. The purchasing manager was too busy elsewhere. The OR supervisor was again included because of his language skills, as the sales manager and production manager spoke little English.

Bob Langley, the senior consultant, spoke some Spanish while his colleague, Gary Ratliff, spoke none.

The consultants were told that growth is to be based on contracting out production to small shops in the area. It is recognized that this is more expensive than in-house capability, but it is essential as capital is needed for growth. Small shops exist in the area with unutilized capacity.

The group was convinced that strategic planning is necessary as well as ambitious objectives. What do we want and what do we need to get there? It is also necessary to have people who will make decisions to see that we reach the goals.

The group felt that in addition to use of contractors, productivity must be optimized in present plants. The production head stated that solving his loading problem would increase productivity 5–7 percent.

The consultants felt that productivity could be increased 50 percent in Cutting and 25–40 percent in other areas. These were cited as "ballpark figures." With 180 sewing machines in Plant #1 and 2,300 square meters, 100 machines could be added. Each operator now had 13 square meters; she should have 7–8.

Another problem cited was that of direct labor to supervisors, now 40–1. The consultants felt that a good look should be taken at the new arrangement, where cutting, ironing, packaging, and shipping are to be centralized in the new building at the industrial park. The consultants felt this is probably "a good fit."

Near the end of the meeting, the consultants proposed a detailed study of production operations as well as direct and indirect labor and the effect on gross margins with a view to improving return on capital. The managers present expressed doubt as to whether this direct-indirect labor ratio can be reduced.

Also, the consultants felt they should look at operational systems and subsystems including work scheduling and process controls as well as manufacturing in general. They assume that product design is adequate and that the company is meeting its sales objectives.

In the diagnostic stage, a project manager would be assigned. This would be a person with experience and background and would be responsible for coordinating the project. It is estimated that four people in all would be needed. Probably they should be at the principal (manager) level rather than staff-consultants. One or two people should be in manufacturing as material utilization is highly technical. Estimated calendar time: 3–4 months.

Fees were not proposed yet. Billing is to be every two weeks; due in 30 days. The fee rate depends on the number of people. For implementing, staff-consultants are used—60–80 hours for staff, 90–125 hours for principals. Added to fees would be travel, transportation, and report preparation costs as well as living expenses, apartment, and car. The report would provide a sequence of priorities which would include evaluating the sales organization and its method of operating.

The consultants left at 7 p.m. for the 2-hour drive in a rented Dodge Dart to the airport in Leon. The complete proposal was promised for the following week's mail.

Most of the managers met early the following morning to evaluate the consultants' visit. It was tentatively decided that at this point they really do not need a full-scale study. The managers have only been in their jobs a few months on the average. Most of them feel they have a "pretty good handle" on the problems they face and have been developing plans to cope with them. They feel they already know their problems and can solve them. It is a little like the farmer who told the county agricultural extension agent: "I only farm half as well as I know how now."

The managers calculated that a full-scale diagnostic study, including apartment and car, would cost 1,500,000 pesos; and resources seem particularly scarce this year. The general feeling of the group was that a limited study might be recommended on how to improve the loading factor and eliminate line-of-balance delays. This would involve improved coordination with suppliers, economic lot inventories, and ways and means to keep production lines functioning smoothly.

Comshare Inc.

■ *Donald W. Sotton, Allan D. Waren, and Bernard C. Reimann* ■

Strategic Actions in the Computer Services Industry

Comshare Inc. was a computer service firm that began operations in 1966. It was a "high-tech" company offering time-sharing services to industry, government, and other non-profit organizations. These services included network access to computers owned and operated by Comshare. Users were able to communicate with the Comshare computers, located at Ann Arbor, Michigan, via sophisticated communication networks of telephone lines. The system was designed to provide very rapid, apparently instantaneous, response to most simple requests. It appeared to users that they had access to their own computer. All of the usual data processing and accounting functions could be performed on data stored at the computer center. Users could access their data from any of their plant locations for use in dealing with organizational problems.

During the period from 1966 until 1982, many advances occurred in the use of time-sharing and in the services offered by Comshare. These included the addition of sophisticated data bases, better methods for retrieving information, and the development of modeling methods for solving business and financial problems. Comshare was a leader in the industry in developing concepts and products to make possible this advanced technology for problem solving.

The latest, and most significant of these developments was System W, an advanced decision support system (DSS) software product, which Comshare introduced late in 1982. This software made it possible for executives to enter or retrieve data from either mainframe or personal computers, build models to simulate their business, make forecasts, do statistical analyses, test assumptions or alternative "scenarios," and even display their results in customized reports or graphs. While a substantial number of competitive products existed, Comshare executives considered System W to be a technological breakthrough in that it greatly facilitated modeling in multiple dimensions. Most of the competitive products were either limited to two-dimensional "spreadsheets," or required extremely complex programming to achieve multidimensional modeling and analysis.

Comshare had recently signed a marketing arrangement with IBM concerning System W. IBM was interested in making highly sophisticated software available to its customers to complement its offerings of mainframe and personal computers. The arrangement included the agreement for IBM salespeople to recommend that users and prospects interested in DSS software consider System W. When feasible and desirable, IBM representatives could make joint sales calls with Comshare salespeople.

Shortly after this arrangement was made, Comshare executives were reflecting upon this action and its implications. Richard L. Crandall, President of Comshare, indicated:

We will utilize our complete organization to make this arrangement successful; and we will modify and adapt System W to the changing needs of users. We are no longer only a computer-based time-sharing corporation. An important part of our future lies in the development of decision support systems that permit business executives to make better decisions through the interactive use of mainframe and personal computers.

The Industry

Product Evolution

Initially computers were developed primarily for scientific computing. Their ability to store and manipulate any information was recognized, and led to more and more business-oriented applications. Information could be stored, processed, and returned to users in manageable and meaningful reports and graphs. The rapid acceptance of computers led to the development of improved computers and ancillary equipment, such as terminals for entering data and calling it out, printers and plotters to provide "hard-copy" output, and supporting networks and hardware to transmit and receive information. A vital complement to the hardware configuration was the appropriate software (program) to tell computers how to process the information.

An early trend toward specialization in the computing industry occurred in the mid 1960s, at which time it was recognized that not every firm or branch operation needed its own large mainframe computer. Rather, access through a communications network to a remote computer could meet user needs more economically, with little or no capital investment. Specialists developed the time-sharing concept whereby many different firms, as well as the many branches of each firm, could share a common computer in such a fashion that it appeared to each individual user as though he or she had sole access to the machine. Initial reception of this approach was best among the scientific and engineering community, and these groups were initially seen as the natural market for time-sharing.

Concurrent with this phase was the development of communication networks that utilized telephone lines and supporting hardware to transmit and receive data.

By the late 1960s, it was recognized that it was the business needs of private firms, nonprofit groups, and government that comprised the most significant market for computer services. There was a growing requirement for better ways to record, store, retrieve, and manipulate information about organization functions such as accounting, finance, production, personnel, marketing, and research. Therein lay the challenge for developers of software packages: to provide the means to perform these functions with the aid of computers. Software specialist firms emerged to supplement the efforts of the large hardware developers such as IBM and Digital Equipment Corporation.

Since hardware manufacturers tended to focus their efforts on systems software, a profitable and growing niche became available in the area of applications software. As a result, a variety of "software houses" emerged to provide high-quality applications software with an emphasis on "user friendliness," or ease of use, as well as on efficiency. Typical applications included material requirements planning, accounting and financial reporting, and data base management.

Another important factor contributed to the accelerating growth of this specialized software market in the 1970s. This was the inability of the data processing function, in most firms, to keep up with the burgeoning demand for its services. The resulting backlog of data processing projects led to an urgent need for highly sophisticated software which would be so easy to use that nonprogrammers, such as financial or marketing executives and their staffs, could develop their own, custom-made applications.

At the same time, the increasing competitiveness and uncertainty of the business environment were creating a growing interest in strategic planning. This in turn led to a strong need for information systems to help top executives and strategic planners make decisions. One answer to this need was DSS (decision support system) applications software. This highly sophisticated software made possible the bringing together of relevant information from both internal and external data bases, and the use of complex models to simulate and analyze strategic alternatives before they were implemented.

The Market

There were less than 2,000 international computer software and service firms as reported in the 1982 Comshare Annual Report. Comshare Inc. was one of the largest of these firms involved in the marketing of DSS software, which included data management, financial modeling, forecasting, analysis, reporting, and graphics. These DSS products were used by time-sharing customers via a worldwide computer network, as well as by customers who licensed the products for use on their mainframe computers/or microcomputers.

The market for corporate and financial planning DSS software and processing services was reported as follows in the 1983 Comshare Annual Report:

1981 sales	$549 million
1982 sales	729 million
1987 forecast	3.1 billion

The report also indicated that 1981 industry sales of all types of software totaled $4.2 billion. Richard L. Crandall, President of Comshare, reported in an interview for this case that 17 percent, or $714 million, came from data management and financial software sales, the two main predecessors of DSS. He indicated also that "in 1975 barely one-half million dollars of industry sales were in software." *Business Week*, in its February 27, 1984, issue, published a special report on "Software: The New Driving Force." In it they forecast that software sales in the U.S. would "keep on growing by a dizzying 32 percent a year, topping $30 billion in 1988."

Competition

Mr. Kevin O. N. Kalkhoven, Group Vice-President, estimated that the 1983 DSS industry leaders, their products, and sales were as follows:

Firm	Product Name	1983 Sales
Execucom	IFPS	$20 million
Management Decision Systems	Express	7–8 million
Comshare Inc.	System W	7–8 million
EPS Inc.	FCS/EPS	6–7 million

It should be noted that, prior to the introduction of System W, Comshare had been a vendor of FCS/EPS on its time-sharing service. It still supported those time-sharing customers who were not willing to switch to System W.

There were more than 60 other competitors, at least 20 of whom had entered the business in the last two or three years. Two software products were identified as being particularly significant to Comshare. These were IFPS, a product originally developed for financial risk analysis, and Express, which was originally developed for marketing research functions. Both products had subsequently been enhanced and were being marketed as full-function DSS systems. Comshare viewed IFPS as being particularly easy to use but lacking integrated functionality in areas such as data management, whereas Express was seen as a very hard-to-use product which was functionally well integrated and quite powerful.

In order to compete effectively in this market, Comshare felt it was essential to develop a product which was easier to use than IFPS and had more capabilities and was better integrated than Express. Thus System W was designed to take advantage of this opportunity for product positioning relative to the industry leaders.

Kevin Kalkhoven was confident that the most recent release of System W (including DATMAN) was much easier to use than any competing product. He pointed out that: "James Martin, an expert on applications software, has just completed his most recent comparative evaluation of financial planning software products. He ranked System W second only to Visicalc in user friendliness, ahead of IFPS and even Lotus 1-2-3." Visicalc was a limited spreadsheet program for personal computers and not considered as a competitor in the DSS software area.

Another potential threat that Comshare management had noticed was that a number of other firms were waking up to the huge potential of the market. These firms were redoubling their efforts both in improving their products and in marketing them. Several firms had decided to "unbundle" their prices for total systems in order to be more competitive. Thus a customer interested only in modeling, for example, could buy a "starter" system for as little as $10,000. If other capabilities, such as forecasting or graphics, was desired, each of these additional modules could be purchased separately for $5,000–$15,000 each. Another aspect of product pricing was the increasing willingness of some vendors to discount the prices of their software, especially for multiple purchases.

Another trend in competition concerned the way in which vendors handled the consulting portion of their DSS software business. Some, such as Management Decision Systems (Express Software) and Chase Interactive Data Corporation (Xsim Software), focused on selling a package of DSS software combined with their management consulting expertise. The consulting services were designed to help the users customize the products for their individual decision support requirements. As a result, the vendors' focus was less on the "user friendliness" of their products than on developing a staff of highly effective and personable consultants and technical specialists. These consultants and specialists were important adjuncts to the vendors' personal selling efforts to large corporations.

At the other end of the spectrum, as Mr. Crandall described it, "Firms like Integrated Planning (Strategem) and GemNet (Fame) chose the strategy of developing and selling DSS products that allegedly required minimal consulting or technical support after the sale." They emphasized product development to make their software so "friendly" and flexible that nonprogrammers, such as financial or marketing executives, could use the software to create their own DSS with minimal outside assistance. Integrated Planning used the services of professional DSS consulting firms, such as Real Decisions Corporation, to assist customers in adapting Stratagem to their needs.

The degree of centralization of selling and technical support was another area in which strategies varied among competitors. Some of the newer and smaller vendors were highly centralized in these functions, due primarily to resource constraints. However, some of the larger firms that could afford to decentralize had concentrated their sales and technical support organizations in a central location. MDS, producers of Express Software, housed all of its consultants and technical support personnel at the headquarters in Waltham, Massachusetts. A toll-free 800 number "hot line" was available to users with problems. This hot line was staffed about 12 hours each working day by rotating shifts of experienced technical people. MDS believed that this allowed better use of their high-quality, specialized technical personnel. They felt that a decentralization strategy using local offices would spread these resources too thinly and result in a reduction of the quality of their customer services. However, a number of firms, such as Boeing Computer Services, Chase IDS, and Comshare chose the decentralized option of serving their users personally from a large number of geographically dispersed offices.

Another contrast in product-market strategies concerned the firms' focus on hardware compatibility. Some, such as Execucom, with its IFPS software, prided themselves on the fact that their software would run on almost every popular brand of hardware and type of operating system, i.e., DEC, HP, IBM, Prime, etc. Even some of the smaller vendors chose this strategy of making their software compatible with as many different types of hardware as possible. GemNet, for example, was in the process of developing Fame (its DSS software) simultaneously for three different operating systems.

Although the degree of competition had increased considerably by 1984, there were signs that rivalry could become more intense in the future. It was still relatively easy for a new firm to enter the DSS industry. Little start-up capital was needed. A few intelligent and hardworking programmers could produce a new DSS software product within a year or two. A number of the most aggressive and successful new firms were founded by former employees of the older and more-established firms. For example, Integrated Planning, the developer of Strategem, was founded by several former employees of Automated Data Processing who had become dissatisfied with that company's supposed lack of effort to improve its products, TSAM and FML, to meet changing customer needs. Similarly, GemNet, developer of Fame software, was started by former members of Chase Interactive Data Corporation's technical staff. Software firms had become attractive acquisition targets for hardware manufacturers and others who were eager to share in the software boom. Acquisitions were of interest also to other software producers as a means to expand their product lines. For example, GemNet had recently received an acquisition offer from Citibank. The new ownership of GemNet would provide increased capitalization and staffing to permit the organization to realize its potential. In so doing it would be regarded as a competitive threat to other members of the industry.

There was also a trend for hardware manufacturers to become more interested in the highly profitable field of applications software. IBM and others seemed to be satisfied with cooperative ventures with software suppliers. However, firms such as Hewlett-Packard were making every effort to produce their own software.

One result of these competitive activities was a downward pressure on prices of applications software and some price discounting was observed in the DSS software industry as well. However, the potential benefits of the "right" software to users could outweigh the initial cost. The "wrong" product could cost several times as much as the acquisition cost in terms of extra implementation problems.

Another competitive threat arose through the actions of time-sharing firms such as Automated Data Processing and Data Resources International, a subsidiary of McGraw-Hill. These firms had developed software for use by their time-sharing customers. At the present time, they were exploring the possibility of selling and/or licensing these DSS products to other users who owned mainframe and personal computers. Data Resources International, for example, announced that it would release its DSS product, EPS, for sale in the fall of 1984.

Life Cycle

Time-sharing sales were of continuing importance to Comshare. A recent issue of *Data Communications* revealed that time-sharing expenditures in the United States were $3.1 billion in 1982 and $3.8 billion in 1983. Projected expenditures in 1984 were $4.2 billion. The bulk of Comshare's revenue continued to be realized from time-sharing services.

Mr. Kalkhoven made the following comments about the time-sharing portion of the industry:

In the mid- and late 1960s there were 800 time-sharing companies and now there are less than 100. There are 600 microcomputer manufacturers today and they will follow the same pattern as time-sharing. There will be a very few in the future. I have been involved in this industry (high computer technology) since 1970. It has undergone an interesting life cycle pattern.

Then he described the three phases in the life cycle of a high-technology computer-oriented firm as follows:

1. *Entrepreneurial Phase.* Normally the computer high-tech firm remains in this phase for about 5 years. It takes from 3 to 5 years to realize a profit. There is a fast change in products; and a heavy capital investment is required. Management is largely drawn from technological people who are involved in the innovation of the products and concepts, for example, from engineering. A large number of firms fail and drop out because they run out of capital and cannot meet the rapidly changing technology.

2. *Growth Phase.* This period extends from about year 6 through 12. Market leaders evolve. The number of competitors is reduced dramatically. For example, in the time-sharing portion of the computer field, the number of firms was reduced from approximately 800 to 100. During this period, technical and management stabilities emerge. The firms begin to develop corporate missions and policies; they establish planning and marketing management approaches to guide their destinies.

   However, signs of what will happen later also emerge. These include a technological slowdown where profit is realized on existing technology rather than on new product developments. As an example, Comshare enjoyed profits and the fruits of a number of innovations associated with time-sharing networks. The need for significant capital becomes urgent in this phase. Furthermore, the economic climate is likely to suffer a recession at some point over this period of years. By the latter 1970s time-sharing technology had passed its period of rapid development, and the onset of a recession confronted young management with new and unanticipated conditions.

3. *Corporate Phase.* During the corporate phase the strategic management and marketing process, initiated in the growth phase, is implemented fully. Marketing opportunities are identified more specifically. Strategic and tactical planning reach maturity. Operational programs and controls are developed as the bases for achieving objectives. At this stage the firm must pick a product and go . . . you must pay for its

development and introduction with the cash cows. The initial mission, technology, and products may change. For many members of the industry, the corporate phase is just emerging. They must decide whether they will be hardware manufacturers, specialists in mainframes and/or microcomputers, time-sharing providers, systems consultants, limited software developers and purveyors, or decision support systems businesses.

Comshare Background

Antecedents

The firm was founded in 1966 at Ann Arbor, Michigan. The founding president was Robert F. Guise, an independent consultant. He was joined in this venture by Richard L. Crandall, at that time a graduate student at the University of Michigan, and by four other persons.

Mr. Crandall studied computer applications under Professor Westervelt and taught computer courses at the university. In 1965, he learned about some exciting developments at Berkeley involving the design of a time-sharing operating system. He joined a group with members from Tymshare and from the University of California at Berkeley to work on this project. Crandall said: "This was a stimulating group with which to work. We completed the operating system development and then I returned to Ann Arbor in 1966 to rejoin Comshare." (He returned as research director).

Time-sharing was the first service to follow Comshare's consulting activities. Their first network consisted of direct-dial access from customers to the Comshare computer. Mr. Crandall was involved in the technical aspects of developing time-sharing and the facilitating network hardware. In 1967 he became vice-president of research and development and also assumed operating responsibilities, including marketing. Mr. Crandall continued his remarks:

We went public in 1968 and took in over $5 million. It was used within one year to open offices around the country. By January 1970 we had $3–$4 million sales volume but were losing so much money that there was concern about the employees and the future of the firm. At the time of our March 1970 board meeting, I was chief operating officer and serious discussions took place as to the survival of the company. In August 1970 I was given the presidency. We were $6 million in debt and losing $3 million a year.

Acquisitions and Divestitures

Comshare reacted to its changing environment through a variety of strategies. First there was a series of acquisitions and divestitures as indicated in Exhibit 9.1. These were carried out in the desire to gain new, related products, market entry, and knowledge about technical products and this adaptation to the markets.

Opportunities and complexities occurred with some acquisitions. Mr. Crandall commented:

Computer Research Company was acquired in 1980 to learn about their use of IBM equipment and software. They were essentially a vendor of raw computer time and we did

---

Exhibit 9.1   Chronological Activities Comshare Inc.

1965   Start-up and time-sharing operating system development.

1966   Incorporation as a Michigan company.

1968   Public offering of stock (traded over the counter).
Start-up of Canadian affiliate (Comshare Ltd.).

1970   Start-up of European operations as Canadian subsidiary (Comshare International B.V.).

1974   Purchase of 30-percent interest in Comshare International B.V.
License agreement to provide services in Japan (Japan Information Service Ltd.).

1977   Acquisition of Systematic Computer Systems Inc. (individual income tax processing services).

1978   Acquisition of Valuation Systems Corporation (consultants in current measurement systems).
Acquisition of Trust Management Systems Inc. (bank trust department services).
Acquisition of 100-percent Comshare International B.V.

1979   Acquisition of Digitax Inc. (individual and fiduciary tax return processing services).
Stock split (three for two).

1980   Acquisition of Computer Research Company (supplier of large-scale IBM computer processing services).
Expansion into France with a wholly-owned subsidiary (after receiving French government permission).
Start-up of Hardware Systems Division (to provide services to users of large-scale Xerox computer systems).
Secondary public offering of shares (net $10.1 million).

1981   Sale of individual income tax processing services (including those of Systematic Computer Systems and Digitax).
Acquisition of Advance Management Strategies Inc. (microcomputer software now sold as Comshare Target Software).
Increase in ownership of Comshare Ltd. (now owns 37.3 percent of Canadian affiliate).

1982   New product release: Planner Calc and Target Financial Modeling (microcomputer-based DSS products).
Sale of the fiduciary income tax processing services.

1983   New flagship product release: System W (DSS system for large-scale IBM computers).
Sale of Trust Management Systems (accounting software for bank trust departments).
Sale of Trilog Associates (balance of bank trust department services).

1984   Consummation of marketing agreement with IBM.

Source: Comshare Inc., *Annual Reports.*

---

not understand the myriad of implications and options, including such items as pricing and IBM operating systems. Initially there was a culture shock between the two firms. Integration was difficult and eventually was achieved by absorbing the entire operation into the main business of the parent, Comshare. We finally learned the IBM environment, from the executive office through to the salesman. In the meantime, Computer Research Company has been completely integrated.

T. Wallace Wrathall, Group Vice President, Finance and Administration, discussed some of the acquisitions and divestitures as follows:

The 1978 acquisition of Valuation Systems Corporation gave us their software for computing the current values of assets based on replacement costs. These financial systems products fit into the Comshare family of products and thus made the merger attractive. The corporation was eventually merged in Comshare. Currently these specific financial reports are no longer required by the Securities and Exchange Commission. However, the merger was successful.

Trust Management Systems Inc. was bought to tie into our human resources (personnel) product lines. Later it was evaluated as belonging to the bank market rather than in the domain of human resources, and it was sold.

We were in the tax processing business and had purchased Systematic Computer Systems Inc. to add to our line of services for CPA firms and their needs. To provide national coverage for our income tax processing services we then acquired Digitax in 1979. These firms were then sold in 1981. They were not profitable and, to offset this trend, more product development effort would have been required."

Mr. Crandall commented that the acquisitions of the Canadian, British, and European affiliates had been highly beneficial in extending markets, integrating operations, and furthering innovation and product development. As shown in Exhibit 9.1, this effort has extended from 1968 forward.

Strategy Leading to System W

Comshare had been a planning-oriented company since the early seventies. In 1972 they first formulated a long-range strategic plan. This plan enumerated corporate goals in broad terms and specified detailed objectives that were as quantified as possible. Strategies were developed to meet these objectives and thus the corporate goals. In general terms these goals were: (1) to be a profitable growth company, and (2) to be the best firm in their market segment.

As a direct result of this planning process, Comshare changed its emphasis from general-purpose time-sharing sales to providing more specialized, business problem-solving assistance. This was achieved by (1) making appropriate software tools available on their time-sharing network and (2) utilizing their customer support representatives to help customers solve business problems using these software tools. As Kevin Kalkhoven stated, "It was no longer appropriate to be everything to everyone."

In 1979 Comshare undertook a major review of their current plans and strategies. Mr. Kalkhoven further commented:

We saw three important things in 1979: (1) we had not changed—we were still primarily a time-sharing company; (2) we had not anticipated the rapid changes in hardware costs and performance; and (3) we had not anticipated the marketplace being dominated by the demand for microcomputers and software. Moreover, Comshare was experiencing the effects of the recession and the accompanying reduced revenues. Although we were one of the market leaders, we were in a period of technological stagnation.

Richard L. Crandall, reflecting on the results of this review, said "We were satisfied that the corporate goals spelled out in 1972 were still valid; however, the environment had changed and we needed to reassess it and its impact on our strategies."

Environmental Review

The environment and company position was reviewed in terms of strengths, weaknesses, opportunities, and threats, and the following were found:

1. Strengths.
   a. The firm was well developed and represented on the international market. Its international sales force provided a strong competitive advantage.
   b. The talent existed to solve business problems. Experienced people had worked on these problems in the sale of time-sharing services.
   c. Market position was established in time-sharing.
   d. A product gap in inquiry and analysis software had been identified, and Comshare had the research and development capability to resolve it.
   e. The firm had a good cash flow and cash position. It could operate at a break-even position for several years.

2. Weaknesses.
   a. Comshare had no identifiable image in software.
   b. The marketing organization did not have selling skills in software.
   c. The business recession and lack of a software product prevented Comshare from taking immediate market action.

3. Threats.
   a. As software firms and products became more prevalent for in-house computer use, the demand for time-sharing services diminished.
   b. Service firms reduced prices to compete for market share.
   c. The advent of personal computers caused both computers and software to become available to users at lower costs.

4. Opportunities.
   a. There was an increased demand for productivity software. Certain packages were available for data management applications. Also there were "first-round," relatively unsophisticated financial modeling packages. There was a need for a more functional product to solve a variety of problems for a broader group of users.
   b. Existing software was relatively difficult to use and not as integrated and functional as it could be. Thus, Comshare had a market opportunity for a more functional and easier-to-operate DSS.

New Strategies

The environmental review led to a number of conclusions that were significant for the development of new strategies to achieve corporate goals. Comshare realized that:

1. Its value and importance to the customer was based on the skills of the Comshare employees and on the capabilities of the software it provided.

2. Time-sharing was only a delivery mechanism for providing access to software, which was used to solve business problems.

3. Software could also be delivered to the customer by selling mainframe software for use on customers' computers.

4. Personal computers were potentially important software delivery vehicles.

As a result of further analysis, Comshare decided that decision support software was its primary product and should be delivered to customers in as many ways as possible. Time-sharing, as a delivery mechanism, remained an important aspect of the business; however, future development emphasis would be on DSS software.

To provide a finer focus for these efforts, Comshare determined that its best approach lay in the development and marketing of DSS software specifically designed for IBM computers. Thus the decision was made to develop a comprehensive, easy-to-use decision support system optimized to run on IBM systems.

The developmental work was carried out in the European headquarters in London and resulted in a software product named Wizard. Presently this DSS is marketed in Europe under the name of Wizard and in the United States as System W. Comshare had planned to use the name Wizard in the United States. However, they discovered that a small software vendor had obtained an earlier trademark of Wizard for his product. To avoid infringement, Comshare was forced to change the name at considerable expense, because sales brochures and other documentation had been printed bearing the designation Wizard.

Complementary Marketing Arrangement with IBM. A letter was received from IBM in September 1982 in which an invitation was extended to approximately 100 computer firms to attend an IBM-hosted conference. The purpose of the conference was to consider strategy for dealing with end users of computers and related services. The emphasis was on application software rather than data management and operating system software. Mr. Crandall attended the conference and noted that most representatives of attending firms did not seem to take the new IBM direction seriously.

However, he felt that IBM was very serious in its desire to have outsiders provide application software, while IBM concentrated on further developing its hardware—both mainframe and personal computers. This was a central part of IBM's new "Information Center" strategy, conceived to meet the pent-up demand among executives to use computers to satisfy their needs for relevant information. This concept required the development of "user-friendly" software which would allow nonprogrammer executive users to develop their own decision support systems. Since IBM did not itself have any strong offerings in this type of DSS software, Mr. Crandall envisioned a desire on the part of IBM to work closely with a firm capable of developing and marketing superior DSS software.

Discussion continued between IBM and Comshare, and in early January 1984 a two-year complementary marketing arrangement was reached. As indicated in the January 9, 1984, issue of *Computerworld*, IBM would recommend System W for use in information centers using IBM 4300 computers. IBM and Comshare sales representatives would refer prospects to each other. In addition, provision was made for joint sales calls of IBM and Comshare personnel to prospective users of DSS. The potential advantage to IBM was the prospect of increased hardware sales resulting from the availability of Comshare's DSS software. Finally, Comshare would continue its responsibility to users to install System W and conduct training programs.

Marketing Mix Strategies
Guiding Strategy

Richard L. Crandall said that "when we decided to develop a DSS software package, it was clear that we would be the new kid on the block as far as software sales were concerned. To be successful it was necessary to carve out a specific niche and to be easily distinguished from our competitors." The firm's strategic plan provided guidance in achieving these objectives.

The plan called for Comshare to develop the best possible DSS software product, and, furthermore, to develop it specifically for IBM computer systems. In order to have the best DSS software, it had to be more functional than the rest of the competition as well as being easier to use. In order to best fit with IBM systems, it was necessary to take advantage of as many of the IBM hardware and software features as possible.

Product

It was observed that purchases of more than $100,000 usually required a series of approvals associated with major capital expenditures. Thus, the executive or group electing to purchase a DSS package must receive higher approval, which could be time consuming. This practice appeared to have imposed an average industry price ceiling of $75,000 for DSS packages.

Comshare conducted research with the use of videotaped focus groups to obtain customer and prospect reaction to System W. A number of considerations were examined such as price and acceptance of the product as to quality, concept, performance, and competition. Current environmental forces were examined and the following price strategies were selected for the introduction of System W in January 1983:

1. Competitive pricing would be utilized. For example, a scaled-down version of System W would be sold for $50,000 to meet Execucom's price on its IFPS product.

2. Elements of target pricing would be employed so that profits would be realized within two years. This was consistent with the dynamics of product innovation and rapid changes in the competing firms.

3. System packages would be priced from $75,000 to less than $100,000.

4. The average price per package would be $80,000 as compared to the industry average of $75,000.

5. The policy of charging for consulting to adapt System W to specific user requirements would be continued.

6. Maintenance charges would be set at an annual rate of 15 percent of the purchase price. This would include program updates and related support services.

Promotion

System W was available in time-sharing applications before the end of 1982. However, the marketing plan called for the development of the "in-house" market. This segment was comprised of organizations owning and operating mainframe computers. In addition, some were using personal computers or were likely to own personal computers in the near future. The firm implemented its program of in-house sales and supporting advertising as of January 13, 1983.

Promotion of the product was carried out in several ways. First, news stories and product information were made available to the media through the public relations activities of the firm. System W reports appeared in *Computerworld*, *The Wall Street Journal*, and other computer and financial journals.

Colleges and universities were viewed as influencers. Comshare executives made themselves available for lectures and consultation about DSS and System W with universities and professional groups. Several universities were given System W packages for use by students. Another group of influencers was identified as business executives who might have use for System W in their positions and to recommend it to others. This group was approached through conferences and "in-house tests."

Comshare's time-sharing customers provided another valuable avenue for product promotion. During the development of System W, it was tested by 100 time-sharing customers. This test served to familiarize these potential users with the product. An additional purpose served by these customer trials was the testing of product modifications and adaptations to the specific user groups. Conferences were held with these time-sharing users to obtain their approvals of the product modifications, as well as their recommendations for use by others.

An advertising program was planned for the Spring of 1984 under the theme of "Safe Harbor." The relationship of Comshare and IBM under the marketing agreement provided the basis to inform potential users that purchasers would be in a safe harbor through the use of IBM in-house mainframes and personal computers with System W. Schedules were developed for advertising to appear in selected business journals. The advertising was to be selective and addressed to financial, marketing, and other senior executives. Not all senior executives would be contacted through the media. The conferences with senior executives mentioned above were viewed as one way to obtain coverage not presently affordable in the media coverage considered. It was recognized that the mass market of knowledge workers would be contacted presently through media advertising. Influencers were to be relied upon until sufficient revenues supported additional advertising.

Kevin Kalkhoven commented as follows about changing advertising requirements: "We used very limited advertising before System W since the time-sharing market does not require much advertising. However, the multitude of potential users for DSS software makes it necessary to communicate about System W through advertising.

Personal Selling.   Comshare executives felt that improvements were needed in sales strategy and performance. Although some experience had been gained in the sale of software, it was believed that the sales organization did not really understand the best way to sell System W. Mr. Kalkhoven believed that the firm was very good in many other aspects of marketing such as promotion, publicity, and time-sharing sales, but that concerted effort was needed in the DSS software personal selling program.

Before System W was introduced, Comshare had initiated a five-year strategic plan for sales activity. That plan was applied to the major product lines, and System W was to be integrated fully. A one-year tactical plan was initiated under the five-year strategic plan for each product line. Every 6 months the yearly plan was updated to "roll over" the plan for the following 12 months. The directors of the product lines developed sales support action plans to include:

1. *Product and Market Development*. Plans for moving products through the markets were made and included things such as identification of users' and prospects' needs and adaptation to them; ways of identifying needs and presenting solutions; sales and revenue plans; and management control of activities. Provisions were made for updating plans as the market and customer needs changed.

2. *Marketing Materials*. Brochures, advertising reprints, and training manuals for salespeople and customers were developed.

3. *Consultants and Technical Support*. Consultants trained in adaptation of products to customer needs were made available to work with salespeople in meeting customer needs.

4. *Training*. Comshare developed an innovative computer-aided instruction system called the Commander Learning Station. This combined the Apple IIe microcomputer and a videotape in such a way that potential users could learn System W in self-paced interactive learning modules. Two versions were offered: a two-day "novice" program, and a half-day refresher program for infrequent, but experienced users.

Because time-sharing would continue to be the most significant portion of revenue for some time, salespeople would be involved in selling both time-sharing and System W. So salespeople were trained to work with and be supported by technical and local branch representatives in the sale and service of time-sharing.

Additional training was initiated to deal with Comshare time-sharing customers who were using FCS/EPS software originally recommended by Comshare salespeople. Comshare had offered support services for this software and felt obligated to continue to do this. However, they would not be able to support new releases of FCS/EPS. Salespeople were trained to explain this situation and also to persuade customers to switch to System W. In addition, Comshare salespeople were informed of the possibility that clients might (1) seek a time-sharing service which supported new versions of FCS/EPS or (2) decide to purchase the FCS/EPS software outright for in-house use.

Distribution.   Distribution of goods was of less importance in the time-sharing and software industry than others. Time-sharing operated through communication networks. Some hardware was required for adapting terminals to telephone lines. However, these were installed on a one-time basis and repetitive shipments of equipment were not required. Inventories were minimal and required little capital investment and management control.

This situation could change in the future. Richard L. Crandall said that it was possible that the vendors of decision support software might consider a new channel of distribution whereby software for microcomputers, personal computers, and mainframe computers would be sold through computer stores. Comshare was examining this possibility and considering the impact of such changes in distribution. For example, a marketing segmentation plan was considered in which Comshare salespeople would call on certain classes of customers and the remainder would be serviced by the computer stores. Another possibility was that other vendors could sell System W to market areas not covered by Comshare.

Financial Considerations

Comshare was founded much as other entrepreneurial firms. Capital contributions by the six founders and the Weyerhauser family provided the impetus for the firm's start. There was a public offering of the firm's stock in 1968 and it was followed by a secondary offering in 1980 which netted $10 million. Exhibits 9.2 and 9.3 contain income and balance sheet data from 1978 through fiscal year 1983. These data reveal revenue increases until 1981, at which time recessionary influences were evident.

T. Wallace Wrathall, Group Vice President, Finance and Administration, commented:

Exhibit 9.2   Comshare's Six-Year Trend Selected Financial Information*

	1983	1982	Year Ending June 30 1981	1980	1979	1978
Revenue	$76,337	$78,453	$79,837	$68,579	$46,049	$23,404
Income from operations	$ 2,453	$ 1,406	$ 8,163	$10,672	$ 8,292	$ 3,791
Interest expense	$ 1,039	$ 1,240	$ 1,291	$ 1,486	$ 752	$ 450
Interest income	$ 1,052	$ 1,278	$ 370	$ 156	$ 116	$ 70
Income before taxes	$ 2,458	$ 1,591	$ 7,535	$ 9,146	$ 7,711	$ 3,943
Income from continuing operations	$ 1,331	$ 829	$ 4,374	$ 5,346	$ 4,383	$ 2,682
Per share	$ .31	$ .18	$ 1.03	$ 1.41	$ 1.31	$ 1.00
Average number of shares outstanding (thousands)	$ 4,340	$ 4,542	$ 4,251	$ 3,791	$ 3,334	$ 2,675
Research and development	$ 6,135	$ 6,109	$ 5,916	$ 4,539	$ 3,289	$ 1,857
As a percentage of revenue	8.0%	7.8%	7.4%	6.6%	7.1%	7.9%
Working capital	$ 9,378	$12,350	$12,244	$ 5,584	$ 3,208	$ 1,107
Capital expenditures	$ 6,377	$ 8,684	$10,516	$13,685	$11,277	$ 3,081
Total assets	$59,381	$66,842	$70,919	$62,581	$47,275	$21,663
Long-term debt	$ 2,067	$ 9,960	$ 8,485	$14,415	$ 9,553	$ 3,825
Shareholders' equity	$38,192	$37,745	$40,735	$27,736	$22,086	$12,537
Number of employees at year-end	1,084	1,164	1,215	1,282	1,100	538

*Dollar amounts in thousands of dollars except per share data

In fiscal 1982, the company, in compliance with Statement No. 52 of the Financial Accounting Standards Board, changed its method of accounting for foreign currency translation adjustments. Financial data for periods prior to fiscal 1982 has not been restated for this change in accounting principle.

Information regarding Results of Operations excludes discontinued operations.

The average number of shares outstanding and income-per-share data have been adjusted to reflect a three-for-two stock split in July 1979.

Source: Comshare Inc., 1983 Annual Report.

There are notable differences in the financial management of Comshare versus industry at large. Some of these include:

1. *We have no inventory—only software tapes with low unit production costs. (This does not include the cost of research and development.)*

2. *There is a short life cycle of plant and products because of the rapidly changing technology.*

3. *Investment decisions have a short life cycle. So we need a high rate of return.*

4. *Research and development expenditures are high compared to other industries.*

5. *Capital requirements are declining and are relatively low compared to the remainder of industry.*

6. *Operating, selling, and development costs are largely people costs and will go up more rapidly than industry averages.*

Mr. Wrathall reflected on other aspects that affect the firm:

1. *Accounting rules can cause us to buy rather than make—the manner in which we are required to report research and development costs is all-important.*

2. *One-third of our sales are in markets outside of the United States. Because of the declining value of the British pound sterling, transferred earnings and investments are reduced. Continued decline in the value of the pound could result in a real loss.*

3. *System W was developed in the United Kingdom (under the name of Wizard) and sold to Comshare in the United States. This developmental policy can result in the parent firm paying less for R&D because of favorable exchange rates and possibly more favorable tax rates.*

Mr. Kalkhoven spoke on the necessity for a combination of product and financial policy to finance the marketing of System W and other new products. He alluded to the Boston Consulting Group's explanation of classifying products according to their growth and market share rates. Those products that no longer have a high growth rate but have retained a favorable market share can be marketed successfully for revenues to support the introduction and market development of new products under the so-called cash cow strategy. The executives of Comshare had its time-sharing product line as a cash cow that would be useful in supporting the introduction of System W, its development, and the development of other DSS products as well. Moreover, Comshare's substantial time-sharing customer base gave it an easily accessible and somewhat captive market for System W and related products.

Management Considerations

Early in 1984, the top-management group consisted of the following relatively young, but highly qualified executives:

Richard L. Crandall, 41, became president and chief executive officer in 1970. He was one of the original six founders of the firm in 1966. In 1978 he had served as president of the Association of the Data Processing Service Organizations. He was also a frequent speaker and author of numerous articles related to issues pertinent to the computer industry.

Kevin O. N. Kalkhoven, 39, was group vice-president in charge of marketing product development and sales. He had been with the company since 1971. Prior to that he worked for IBM as an analytical services manager, and in sales management for SIA Ltd. in the U.K. He lectured frequently on the subject of decision support systems to such groups as the American Marketing Association and the Planning Executives Institute.

T. Wallace Wrathall, 47, Group Vice-President of Finance and Administration, had joined Comshare in 1975. Prior to that he had 17 years of broad experience in finance and accounting. His previous employer, Varian Associates, was also in the computer high-technology business and also had extensive foreign operations. Other employers included Del Monte Corporation, Optical Coating Laboratory, and Eldorado Electrodata.

Ian G. McNaught-Davis, 54, became group vice-president in 1978 and managed the European operations. He was also a director of Comshare Ltd. Mr. Davis was the founding chief executive of Comshare Ltd. (U.K.) in 1970. He was employed earlier for nine years with General Electric Information Systems. His last position with G.E. was director of marketing. He had been the moderator of approximately 20 one-hour television programs for the British Broadcasting Corporation concerning computers and their uses. Also, he lectured throughout the United Kingdom and Europe at universities and professional conferences.

Exhibit 9.3   Comshare Inc. Consolidated Balance Sheet

	As of June 30	
	1983	1982
Assets		
Current assets:		
Cash	$ 3,407,500	$ 3,059,300
Temporary investments, at cost	4,413,800	7,507,000
Accounts receivable, less allowance for doubtful accounts of $570,700 in 1983 and $550,400 in 1982	13,221,900	13,301,000
Prepaid expenses	2,154,200	2,512,900
Total current assets	23,197,400	26,380,200
Property and equipment, at cost		
Land	964,400	999,200
Computers and other equipment	42,983,700	42,408,200
Building and leasehold improvements	6,221,800	6,152,000
Property and equipment under construction	2,518,800	3,530,700
	52,688,700	53,090,100
Less accumulated depreciation	26,605,200	23,694,200
Property and equipment, net	26,083,500	29,395,900
Other assets		
Investment in affiliate	1,905,700	2,020,500
Goodwill, net of accumulated amortization of $766,200 in 1983 and $567,300 in 1982	6,242,800	6,486,300
Purchased software, net of accumulated amortization of $1,101,600 in 1983 and $496,000 in 1982	1,521,100	1,948,600
Deposits and other	430,600	610,700
Total other assets	10,100,200	11,066,100
Total assets	$59,381,100	$66,842,200

These men exercised management and intellectual leadership throughout the organization. They were innovative in the development of solutions to everyday business problems and issues. During the early years the overriding concern was bringing together people who were innovative, self-reliant, and results oriented. In this way, computer services and software could be developed by a group of imaginative and dedicated people.

Richard Crandall was a leader and model for personnel involved in this activity. He became involved at the age of 18. He was president at the age of 26. This was a young man's sphere of activity populated by those who shared common levels of intelligence, curiosity, innovativeness, and the pleasure of working diligently to achieve results to be enjoyed psychologically and materially. At the present time the average ages of Comshare employees were:

Nonmanagers	26 years
Managers	32 years
Executives	38 years

Exhibit 9.3   *continued*

| | As of June 30 | |
	1983	1982
Liabilities and shareholders' equity		
Current liabilities		
Current portion of long-term debt	$ 345,200	$ 1,039,000
Notes payable	1,857,700	1,151,700
Accounts payable	3,709,600	3,437,200
Accrued liabilities		
Payroll	2,722,600	2,391,600
Taxes, other than income taxes	992,400	1,162,400
Discontinued operations	98,500	1,720,500
Other	3,186,100	2,601,300
Total accrued liabilities	6,999,600	7,875,800
Accrued income taxes	907,500	526,300
Total current liabilities	13,819,600	14,030,000
Long-term debt	2,067,300	9,959,900
Deferred income taxes	5,302,500	5,086,900
Deferred credits	—	20,900
Shareholders' equity		
Common stock, $1.00 par value; authorized 10,000,000 shares; outstanding 4,281,414 shares in 1983 and 4,599,604 shares in 1982	4,281,400	4,599,600
Capital contributed in excess of par	24,368,400	25,871,200
Retained earnings	12,624,200	10,415,200
Currency translation adjustments	(3,082,300)	(2,377,200)
	38,191,700	38,508,800
Less treasury stock, at cost (119,000 shares in 1982)	—	764,300
Total shareholders' equity	38,191,700	37,744,500
Total liabilities and shareholders' equity	$59,381,100	$66,842,200

Source: Comshare Inc., 1983 Annual Report

It was found that successful persons were totally adept, got on well with others, and had excellent senses of humor. They had a natural curiosity about management practices. This led them to study and adapt business management approaches to planning, programming, operating, and controlling the firm's activities.

Mr. Crandall summarized the management philosophy and direction of Comshare as follows:

The future of our business is in knowledge-based software, and we must organize and operate properly to maintain success. We are a marketing-oriented company. Our research and development effort is directed to meeting market needs in creative ways. New technology can spur innovation and creativity. We must attract talented people to Comshare who can work successfully in our environment. Top management is the key to innovation and the strategic management and marketing process. The approach and philosophy must permeate from the top of the organization.

Johnson Products Company Inc.

■ *David L. Daughtry* ■

The Cosmetics and Hair Care Industry, 1979

Consumption

Retail sales of cosmetics and toiletries will exceed $14.5 billion in 1985, more than double the 1973 level of $6.2 billion, according to a study by Predicasts Inc.[1] Thus, the annual growth rate in the industry, over a 10-year period (1975–1985) was expected to be nearly 8 percent. In 1979, a Standard and Poor's industry survey reported that the cosmetics industry outpaced growth in the overall economy.[2] In that year, the value of manufacturers' shipments expanded by 12 percent, with the same gains expected annually for the next five years. The reasons for the above-average progress include (1) demographic changes in the female population, and (2) the increasing percentage of females in the work force. The heaviest users of beauty aids were said to be women in the 25 to 44 age range. The size of this age group was expected to expand at the rate of 2.8 percent annually, versus 1 percent for the overall female population. The expansion in the female work force would be 3–4 percent.[3] Thus, as more women entered the work place, they would have more discretionary income and would want to enhance their looks; therefore, cosmetics sales would continue to increase. Exhibit 10.1 shows the growth in retail sales of cosmetics and toiletries from 1975 to 1978.

Retail sales of hair care products increased at a rate of nearly 18 percent in 1978. This growth was partially due to a shift to more active lifestyles (as in sports), which required more frequent hair care, and also because of the consumer's desire to use professional hair care products, previously available only through beauty or barber salons.

Of particular interest was the consumption of cosmetics and hair care products by the black consumer. In 1977, The Johnson Products Company (JPC), which markets primarily to black consumers, described the black consumer as America's last untapped market. The Johnson Company reported that they spend about the same share of personal income for health and beauty aids as the general population. This factor was complemented by favorable demographic changes in the black population, including (1) a greater proportion of blacks than whites growing into the prime consumer age range, (2) the black population growth rate being 1.5 times that of whites, and (3) about 60 percent of all U.S. blacks living in urban areas (vs. 25 percent of whites), where store outlets are plentiful.[4] According to analyst Grayson Mitchell, a recent consumer survey found that 35.4 percent of Black American females were regular users of perfume, as compared to 31.1 percent of

---

[1] "Cosmetics Charted to 1985," *Chemical Marketing Reporter*, Vol. 206, December 23, 1974, p. 5.

[2] "Health Care: Drugs and Cosmetics—Basic Analysis," *Standard & Poor's Industry Surveys*, August 16, 1979.

[3] Ibid.

[4] "Unlocking the Black Market," *Chain Store Age* (advertisement), Johnson Products Co. Inc., December 1977.

This case was written by David L. Daughtry. This case does not indicate effective or ineffective handling of an administrative situation. Rather it is to be used for class discussion purposes. All rights reserved to the contributor. Reprinted with permission.

Exhibit 10.1   Retail Sales of Selected Toiletries and Cosmetics (in thousands of dollars)

Product	1975	1976	1977	1978
Hair products				
Shampoos	$632,320	$693,660	$732,380	$906,800
Rinses, tints, dyes	313,910	335,150	364,270	410,820
Men's aerosol sprays	27,969	25,730	13,430	12,830
Men's nonaerosol sprays	55,690	57,650	69,470	72,770
Women's hair sprays	268,420	279,160	161,441	164,400
Home permanent kits	49,750	55,720	57,230	75,550
Hand products				
Lotions	71,900	87,720	107,230	111,480
Nail polish and enamel	138,040	155,990	198,240	235,970
Cosmetics				
Face creams	299,340	371,180	404,040	456,120
Makeup base	—	—	440,411	446,310
Face powder	112,960	122,120	119,290	123,390
Eye makeup	—	—	701,653	955,930
Talc and body powder	61,080	59,860	59,690	59,600
Lipsticks	388,520	458,450	552,400	681,700
Liquid facial cleansers	75,660	81,180	85,370	82,500
Fragrance preparations				
Perfumes	96,930	107,030	113,390	114,120
Toilet water and cologne	429,140	427,210	426,690	430,580
Other toiletries				
Toilet soaps	557,920	578,170	722,270	927,500
External personal deodorants	619,350	616,940	612,600	561,790
Shaving products				
Shaving preparations	441,131	497,890	538,280	557,830
Aftershave lotions	149,038	159,570	179,860	181,570
Men's cologne	141,718	181,690	188,160	203,110
Shaving accessories	775,189	805,810	840,690	952,090

Source: *Standard & Poor's Industry Surveys*, August 16, 1979.

white females. For bath oil, the disparity was 56.3 percent to 49.6 percent and, for cleansing creams, 61.4 percent to 57.6 percent.[5]

Sources and Types of Products

Exhibit 10.2 is a partial list of the major cosmetics manufacturers. Some of the smaller (black) producers (not listed in Exhibit 10.2) of cosmetics and hair care products include Johnson Products Company, Fashion Fair (Johnson Publishing Co., not related to Johnson Products), Pro-line, and Barbara Walden Cosmetics.[6] Of the companies listed in Exhibit 10.2, the recognized leading producers of cosmetics and toiletries were Avon, Gillette, and Revlon. Of the black producers, Johnson Products was the recognized leader. The types of products made by most of the firms are shown in Exhibit 10.1. Key industry statistics are shown in Exhibits 10.3–10.5.

[5] "G. Mitchell, "Battle of the Rouge," *Black Enterprise*, Vol. 9, August 1978, pp. 22–26.
[6] Ibid.

Exhibit 10.2   Product Line Sales and Profits (in millions of dollars)

Cosmetics-Toiletries		Sales	Profits
Alberto-Culver	Hair care products, men's and women's boots, and health and beauty aids	$ 131	3.8%
	Antiseptic spray, furniture polish, special food items, and cleaning products	32	4.2
	Other manufacturers' beauty and barber products to supply houses	7	0.3
Avon Products	Cosmetics, fragrances, and toiletries	1,612	354.9
	Costume jewelry	363	91.0
	Mail order apparel and housewares through party plans	40	9.1
Chesebrough-Pond's Inc.	Health and beauty	203	37.2
	Packaged foods	184	29.5
	Children's apparel	155	17.1
	Perfumes and other beauty aids	107	23.3
	Base	29	6.2
	Hospital products	29	3.1
	International	262	38.8
Faberge Inc.	Cosmetics, fragrances, and other beauty products	250	24.0
	Entertainment	5	3.5
Gillette Co.	Blades and razors	564	186.5
	Toiletries and grooming aids	428	33.7
	Braun electric shavers and household and personal care products	410	33.7
	Writing instruments	137	15.5
	Disposable and luxury lighters	171	10.4
Helene Curtis Industries	Beauty and hair care	108	n.a.
	Sealants and adhesives	22	n.a.
International Flavors and Fragrances	Flavors	250	n.a.
	Fragrances	116	n.a.
Mary Kay Cosmetics	Skin care products for men and women	28	n.a.
	Makeup items	11	n.a.
	Toiletry items for men and women	8	n.a.
	Hair care	2	n.a.
	Accessories	5	n.a.
Revlon Inc.	Beauty products	943	182.4
	Ethical pharmaceuticals	261	57.0
	Ophthalmic and proprietary drug products and diagnostic labs	247	45.6

Source: *Standard & Poor's Industry Surveys*, August 16, 1979.

Distribution

About 75 percent of all cosmetics are retailed through department stores, drugstores, and home-to-home organizations (about 25 percent each), with mass merchandisers, food stores, and other outlets accounting for the remainder.[7] However, as of late 1979, the mass merchandisers and food stores were growing in importance. This trend began because

[7] "Health Care: Drugs and Cosmetics—Basic Analysis," *Standard & Poor's Industry Surveys*, August 16, 1979.

Exhibit 10.3   Statistics for the Cosmetics Industry, 1970–1978[a]

	1970	1971	1972	1973	1974	1975	1976	1977	1978
Sales	$23.49	$27.48	$30.83	32.27	$35.73	$38.79	$39.29	$44.85	$53.56
Operating income	$4.64	$5.36	$6.07	$6.35	$6.03	$7.03	$7.77	$8.94	$10.56
Profit margins (%)	19.75%	19.51%	19.69%	19.68%	16.88%	18.12%	19.78%	19.93%	19.72%
Depreciation	$0.29	$0.36	$0.41	$0.43	$0.50	$0.55	$0.59	$0.64	$0.75
Taxes	$2.08	$2.38	$2.73	$2.79	$2.74	$3.08	$3.48	$3.95	$4.69
Earnings	$2.26	$2.54	$2.81	$3.02	$2.75	$3.23	$3.65	$4.22	$5.04
Dividends	$1.27	$1.39	$1.48	$1.52	$1.62	$1.69	$1.78	$2.16	$2.51
Earnings as a % of sales	9.62%	9.24%	9.11%	9.36%	7.70%	8.33%	9.29%	9.41%	9.41%
Dividends as a % of earnings	56.19%	54.72%	52.67%	50.33%	58.91%	52.32%	48.77%	51.18%	49.80%
Price (1941–43 = 10)—high	$98.77	$110.50	$136.70	$137.47	$71.68	$65.07	$64.03	$60.76	$75.56
—low	$68.39	$90.68	$101.95	$69.54	$28.56	$39.44	$52.21	$53.81	$55.73
Price-earnings ratios—high	$43.70	$43.50	$48.65	$45.52	$26.07	$20.15	$17.54	$14.40	$14.99
—low	$30.26	$35.70	$36.28	$23.03	$10.39	$12.21	$14.30	$12.75	$11.06
Dividend yield (%)—high	1.86%	1.53%	1.45%	2.19%	5.67%	4.28%	3.41%	4.01%	4.50%
—low	1.29%	1.26%	1.08%	1.11%	2.26%	2.60%	2.78%	3.55%	3.32%
Book value	$9.55	$10.75	$12.64	$12.94	$14.01	$15.55	$16.44	$18.41	$21.02
Return on book value %	23.66%	23.63%	22.25%	23.34%	19.63%	20.77%	22.20%	22.92%	23.98%
Working capital	$7.17	$7.72	$9.73	$9.90	$10.71	$13.23	$13.14	$14.45	$16.06
Capital expenditures	$0.80	$1.01	$1.10	$0.82	$0.95	$0.94	$1.03	$1.12	$2.22

[a]The companies used for this series of composite data are Alberto-Culver (added 3-3-71); Avon Products; Chesebrough-Pond's; Faberge Inc.; International Flavors and Fragrances (added 3-3-76); and Revlon Inc. Helene Curtis & Factor (Max) "A" were deleted on 2-28-73.

Source: *Standard & Poor's Industry Surveys*, August 16, 1979.

Exhibit 10.4   Profit Margins (percentage)

| | Composite Data | | | Cosmetics and Toiletries | | | | |
	Cosmetics	Alberto-Culver	Avon Products	Chesebrough-Pond's	Faberge	Gillette	International Flavors and Fragrances	Revlon
1978	19.7%	4.9%	22.6%	16.0%	8.0%	15.1%	29.3%	19.6%
1977	19.9	4.1	23.1	16.4	7.5	15.7	30.3	19.6
1976	19.8	4.0	23.2	16.1	7.8	15.8	28.8	19.9
1975	18.1	3.4	22.5	15.8	6.5	15.9	23.3	18.4
1974	16.9	2.1	20.0	16.3	7.5	16.5	29.7	17.9
1973	19.7	5.9	24.6	16.6	11.6	17.3	31.7	17.9
1972	19.7	6.8	26.6	17.4	12.8	18.8	32.0	16.9
1971	19.5	7.0	26.7	17.0	11.9	19.2	30.2	16.3
1970	19.8	10.4	27.2	16.7	5.7	20.4	29.7	15.6
1969	20.9	10.9	27.9	17.2	15.9	22.2	30.9	16.6

Source: *Standard & Poor's Industry Surveys*, August 16, 1979.

Exhibit 10.5   Net Income (% of sales)

| | Composite Data | | | Cosmetics and Toiletries | | | | |
	Cosmetics	Alberto-Culver	Avon Products	Chesebrough-Pond's	Faberge	Gillette	International Flavors and Fragrances	Revlon
1978	9.4%	1.8%	11.3%	7.2%	2.4%	5.5%	15.4%	8.9%
1977	9.4	1.5	11.6	7.4	3.0	5.0	14.5	8.6
1976	9.3	1.3	11.7	7.2	2.8	5.2	13.7	8.5
1975	8.3	1.1	10.7	7.1	1.9	5.7	11.0	8.3
1974	7.7	0.8	8.9	7.7	7.6	6.8	14.4	8.5
1973	9.4	2.8	11.7	8.1	5.5	8.1	15.5	8.5
1972	9.1	3.2	12.4	8.0	5.6	8.6	15.6	8.6
1971	9.2	3.1	12.5	7.8	5.4	8.6	15.0	8.8
1970	9.6	4.5	13.0	8.0	2.0	9.8	14.7	7.5
1969	9.9	4.2	12.8	8.7	6.9	10.8	14.4	8.0

Source: *Standard & Poor's Industry Surveys*, August 16, 1979.

beauty aids are typically among the higher-margined items carried by such outlets, an example of which was Hanes's (Consolidated Foods) introduction in 1979 of its L'Erin line of cosmetics in food stores. Hanes was said to be trying to duplicate its earlier success with L'Eggs panty hose.

In the case of beauty aids produced by black-owned firms, distribution usually is limited to stores in traditional black neighborhoods. When stores in the suburbs and predominantly white neighborhoods do sell ethnic products, the shelf space permitted is limited.

The stores usually are supplied by distributors (jobbers), who service retailers and the professional market (beauty salons and barber shops).

Regulations

In 1974, the Food and Drug Administration (FDA), Consumer Products Commission (CPC), and Federal Trade Commission (FTC) all began to take strong positions on the need to regulate the cosmetics industry. The most important areas considered for regulation were:[8]

- Assurance of the safety of chemical compounds used in products and truthful labeling of ingredients.
- Safety of aerosol packaging for personal-use products.
- Substantiation of advertising claims.
- The question of whether treatment cosmetics should be classified as proprietary drugs.

By 1978, the General Accounting Office (GAO) began suggesting to Congress that the Food, Drug and Cosmetic Act be amended to give greater powers to FDA in controlling the cosmetics/hair care industry. A GAO study had reported that some 125 ingredients available for use in cosmetics were suspected of causing cancer, while 25 others may be causes of birth defects. An amended act would provide FDA authority for:

- Premarket approval of certain products.
- Registration of manufacturers and their products.
- Collection of product safety data.
- Establishment of test requirements.
- Collection of consumer complaints.
- Collection of data on cosmetic preservatives.
- Access to manufacturers' productions and control records.

At that time (1978), the Department of Health, Education and Welfare (HEW) did not agree to such extensive controls, believing that the plan would require "an extensive expenditure of resources" (public funds) to regulate the industry.

In 1979, a draft document entitled "Analysis of FDA's Authority and Performance in the Regulation of Cosmetics with Some Legislative Options," remained to be accepted by the FDA. The document listed options that included proposals made in 1978 by the GAO. Standard & Poor's reported that with the pressing issues facing Congress there was little chance of an early legislative overhaul of the industry.[9]

The Economics of the Industry

Until 1974, cosmetics had been categorized as a business that ran counter to downward economic cycles. This recession-proof reputation was lost during the 1973–1974 recession, after which the industry was labeled "recession-resistant." [10] Industry observers ar-

[8] "Cosmetics Charted to 1985," *Chemical Marketing Reporter*, Vol. 206, December 23, 1974, p. 5.

[9] "Health Care: Drugs and Cosmetics—Basic Analysis," *Standard and Poor's Industry Surveys*, August 16, 1979.

[10] A. G. Mottus, *Product Marketing*, Vol. 7 (October 1978), p. 1.

gue that demand for cosmetics remains high in recessionary periods; however the industry is more dependent on the good graces of the retailers than on the desires/demands of the consumer. A typical retailer sells off inventory in preparation for a drop in the consumer's general interest and traffic through the store.

In April 1980, most cosmetics companies were reported to be in excellent financial condition. The firms (Exhibit 10.2) had strong balance sheets, which would allow them to maintain peak operating efficiencies during the coming recession.

Exhibits 10.4 and 10.5 show the performance of the seven largest cosmetics manufacturers from 1969 to 1978.

The Johnson Products Company Inc.

Background/Situation

In 1979, The Johnson Products Company (JPC) was the industry leader in manufacturing and marketing ethnic health and beauty aids. The company produces more than 50 professional and retail hair care and cosmetic products.[11] Net sales for 1979 were nearly $32 million (Exhibit 10.6). JPC is located on a 23-acre site on Chicago's south side, with 422,000 square feet of offices, laboratories, manufacturing and warehousing facilities, and employs more than 500 people.[12]

In 1976, sales and other revenues had totaled more than $40 million, nearly 7 percent more than in 1975. The increased revenues were said to be due principally to increased sales of a new fragrance, Black Tie, and to earnings from several beauty schools that had been purchased in 1975.[13] Despite increased sales, JPC's 1976 net income declined 25 percent from that of 1975. A review of its balance sheets for 1975 and 1976 revealed that, while sales had increased, sales costs, general and administrative expenses, and advertising had increased 10 percent, 30 percent, and 25 percent, respectively (Exhibit 10.7).

In 1977, JPC's overall performance declined even more. Sales and operating revenues dropped to 17 percent below the 1976 level. The downturn was attributed mostly to competition from larger companies, such as Revlon, Avon, and Alberto-Culver.[14]

A turnaround in 1978 saw JPC's sales increase to within 3.8 percent of its peak year (1976). President George E. Johnson attributed the upturn to increased sales of domestic hair care products.[15]

The turnaround was short-lived. Sales and other revenue for 1979 declined to completely offset gains made the year before. As in 1977, President Johnson cited increased competition as one of the causes, with others being a yearlong interruption of sales to Nigeria and severe winter-related problems.[16]

[11] Johnson Products Company Inc., "Johnson Products Company History," 1980.

[12] Ibid.

[13] Annual Report for the Fiscal Year Ended August 31, 1977, Johnson Products Company Inc., 1977.

[14] Ibid.

[15] Annual Report for the Fiscal Year Ended August 31, 1978, Johnson Products Company Inc., 1978.

[16] Annual Report for the Fiscal Year Ended August 31, 1979, Johnson Products Company Inc., 1979.

Exhibit 10.6 Johnson Products Company, Inc.—Financial Review
(In thousands of dollars except per-share data)

	Years Ended August 31				
	1979	1978	1977	1976	1975
Summary of operations:					
Net sales	$31,337	$37,246	$32,380	$39,428	$37,660
Other operating revenue	1,801	1,416	920	703	—
Total net sales and other operating revenue	33,138	38,662	33,300	40,131	37,660
Cost of sales	12,291	14,854	13,071	14,327	12,993
Selling, general and administrative (exclusive of advertising and promotion)	14,657	13,776	12,182	12,232	9,431
Advertising and promotion	6,019	6,211	5,731	5,608	4,498
Interest income	(450)	(416)	(237)	(234)	(372)
Income before income taxes	621	4,237	2,553	8,198	11,110
Income taxes	300	2,000	1,150	3,950	5,460
Net income	321	2,237	1,403	4,248	5,650
Net income per share	0.08	0.56	0.35	1.05	1.40
Dividends per share	0.36	0.36	0.36	0.30	0.25
Other financial data:					
Working capital	15,669	17,122	16,776	17,626	15,418
Capital expenditures	1,008	864	1,508	2,082	2,184
Long-term debt	—	—	—	—	—
Shareholders' equity	26,355	27,433	27,018	27,038	23,415
Shareholders' equity per share	6.63	6.87	6.67	6.67	5.79
Ratios					
Net income to sales and other operating revenue	1.0%	5.8%	4.2%	10.6%	15.0%
Return on shareholders' equity	1.2%	8.2%	5.2%	16.8%	27.0%
Advertising and promotion to net sales and other operating revenue	18.2%	16.1%	17.2%	14.0%	11.9%
Average common and common equivalent shares outstanding[a]	$3,976,000	$3,995,000	$4,051,000	$4,051,000	$4,044,000

[a] Adjusted to give retroactive effect to a 2-for-1 split in January 1973; common equivalent shares consist of class B common shares and outstanding stock options.

Source: Company annual reports to shareholders.

Exhibit 10.7 Johnson Products Company, Inc. and Subsidiaries—Consolidated Balance Sheets

| | Year Ending August 31 | | | |
	1979	1978	1977	1976
Assets				
Current assets:				
Cash (including certificates of deposit of $994,000 in 1979 and $1,780,000 in 1978)	$ 1,915,000	$ 2,161,000	$ 2,022,000	$ 1,920,000
Commercial paper	2,654,000	5,325,000	4,775,000	2,815,000
Receivables				
Trade, less allowance for doubtful accounts of $275,000 in 1979 and $300,000 in 1978	7,149,000	8,648,000	7,610,000	9,670,000
Other	605,000	204,000	82,000	188,000
Refundable income taxes	749,000	—	—	—
Inventories	4,727,000	5,423,000	4,523,000	6,185,000
Prepaid expenses (1976: including future tax benefit)	859,000	871,000	1,014,000	973,000
Total current assets	18,658,000	22,632,000	20,026,000	21,751,000
Property, plant, and equipment	14,363,000	13,355,000	12,567,000	11,059,000
Less accumulated depreciation and amortization	4,963,000	4,009,000	3,034,000	2,152,000
	9,400,000	9,346,000	9,533,000	8,907,000
Other assets:				
Cash value, officers' life insurance	1,226,000	1,023,000	845,000	710,000
Investments, at cost	395,000	244,000	244,000	64,000
Miscellaneous receivables	86,000	120,000	92,000	9,000
Unamortized excess cost over net assets of business acquired	121,000	140,000	160,000	180,000
	1,828,000	1,527,000	1,341,000	963,000
Total assets	$29,886,000	$33,505,000	$30,900,000	$31,621,000
Liabilities and shareholders' equity				
Current liabilities:				
Accounts payable	$ 1,994,000	$ 2,510,000	$ 1,934,000	$ 2,643,000
Due to profit-sharing trust	325,000	540,000	465,000	450,000
Dividends payable	357,000	357,000	365,000	229,000
Accrued expenses	313,000	710,000	434,000	402,000
Income taxes	—	1,393,000	52,000	401,000
Total current liabilities	2,989,000	5,510,000	3,250,000	4,125,000
Deferred income taxes	542,000	562,000	632,000	458,000
Shareholders' equity				
Capital stock:				
Preferred stock, no par, authorized 300,000 shares; none issued				
Common stock, $.50 par; authorized 7,504,400 shares; issued 4,052,722 shares	2,027,000	2,027,000	2,027,000	2,027,000
Additional paid-in capital	634,000	603,000	561,000	524,000
Retained earnings	24,132,000	25,241,000	24,434,000	24,491,000
Treasury stock, 81,000 shares at cost	(438,000)	(438,000)	(4,000)	(4,000)
Total shareholders' equity	26,355,000	27,433,000	27,018,000	27,038,000
Total liabilities and shareholders' equity	$29,886,000	$33,505,000	$30,900,000	$31,621,000

Source: Company annual reports to shareholders.

The History of the Johnson Products Company

The Johnson Products Company was established in 1954 by its current president and principal owner, George Ellis Johnson, and incorporated in 1957. Its first product was "Ultra Wave Hair Culture," a chemical hair straightener and first-year sales totaled $18,000.[17]

Based on his initial success, Johnson made a 15-year projection, aiming for $1 million in sales by the end of 1964, at least $10 million by the end of 1969, and $50 million by 1975.[18] JPC met Johnson's objectives through 1969 and became, in 1971, the first black-owned corporation to be listed on the American Stock Exchange. Two years earlier (1969), Johnson went public with an offering of 300,000 shares of common stock. The underwriter for the offering was Hornblower & Weeks-Hemphill, Noyes, and the stock was sold quickly for as much as $28 per share. The offering was made on behalf of George E. Johnson, and none of the proceeds accrued to the Johnson Products Company.[19]

By 1974, JPC had 50 percent of the black hair care market. Sales had swelled to nearly $32 million, with a net income of close to $5 million, representing a profit margin of nearly 16 percent.[20] The profitability of JPC and the black grooming aid market aroused the interest of the cosmetics industry because the average profit margin for the industry was far less than that of JPC. Typically, Helene Curtis and Alberto-Culver's margins were less than 3 percent in 1974. Revlon, Alberto-Culver, and other large firms began to target their products at the black consumer. Revlon, sensing the profitability of JPC in 1970, even attempted to buy the company, offering nearly $100 million.

According to Robert Metz,[21] JPC's market share and profitability dropped as competition grew within the industry. From 1975 to 1977, JPC's market share descended from the high of 50 percent to a low of 32 percent of the black hair care and cosmetics market. He reported that investors responded by selling Johnson's stock, which fell to a low of 4¾ on the American Stock Exchange after selling at a high of 38.

George E. Johnson has stated that JPC's declining fortunes were compounded by an FTC consent decree the company had signed in 1975. The FTC had begun a crackdown on hair care products marketed to black consumers, and charged that an active chemical ingredient (sodium hydroxide) in JPC's Ultra Sheen Permanent Creme Relaxer, straightened hair by weakening cells in individual hair shafts, thus causing partial or total hair loss. Johnson was required to place an expanded warning on its products stating that misuse could damage the skin and eyes. According to Mitchell's report, Johnson believed that his competitors, especially his arch-rival (Revlon), would be required to follow suit. The FTC did not legally require Revlon to place such warnings on its products until 20 months later. Johnson believed that failure by FTC to apply the standards industrywide at the same time resulted in his competitors' gaining a substantial portion of the black hair care market.

In the same report, Johnson stated that international conglomerates were targeting black consumers, while black companies were limited in their ability to "cross over" into

[17] "Johnson Products Company History," Johnson Products Company Inc., 1980.

[18] "From an Idea for a New Product has Grown a Giant Cosmetics Empire," *Famous Blacks Give Secrets of Success* (Chicago, Ill.: Johnson Publishing Co., Inc., 1973).

[19] "Johnson Products Offering Sold," *The Wall Street Journal*, December 11, 1969.

[20] R. Metz, "Grooming Aids and Profits," *New York Times*, July 28, 1978.

[21] Ibid.

the general market. JPC attempted to do this with its introduction of Black Tie. In 1975, the product was introduced with heavy "racially neutral" promotion but never returned more than a meager profit. Johnson reported that drugstore chains and supermarkets refused to display the product in white neighborhoods.[22]

During the era of JPC's declining profits (1975–1977), the president considered some industry-related expansion moves. For example Johnson planned to establish "the first franchised Ultra Sheen Beauty Boutique," and envisioned franchises that would employ more than 42,000 blacks. The first boutique was opened in May 1977.[23]

Another attempt at expansion was JPC's acquisition (December 1975) of Debbie's School of Beauty Culture, which trains beauticians. According to JPC's 1979 annual report, five of the schools were located in Chicago, with one each in Montgomery, Alabama; East St. Louis, Illinois; and Detroit, Michigan. The latter two were just opening in August and September 1979. The report also revealed that Debbie's managers had assumed responsibility for the Ultra Sheen Beauty Boutiques. At the time of the report, only two boutiques were being readied for business. Three years after its inception, the franchise package (program) was termed as still being in its basic stages.

By 1978, industry observers were estimating JPC's share of the black hair care market to be between 30 percent and 40 percent. According to Grayson Mitchell,[24] the late 1970s saw JPC encounter greater competition from other black cosmetics and hair care businesses, some of which were Fashion Fair (Johnson Publishing Company), Pro-line, and Barbara Walden Cosmetics. Their combined sales were near $33 million in an estimated $120 million black consumer market.

In his 1979 annual report, Johnson explained that JPC continued to be affected by intensified domestic competition and that more companies had entered the cosmetics and hair care field, with many products vying for limited shelf space in retail outlets. He also reported that the company had completed a manufacturing facility in Nigeria and hoped that such expansion would improve the company's failing fortunes (Exhibit 10.8).

JPC Products

The company has three groups of products.

Hair Care.   The company's two principal hair products are conditioner and hair dress, and creme relaxers. Other hair products include sprays, shampoos, and hair conditioners sold under the trademarks Ultra Sheen, Afro Sheen, Ultra Wave, and Bantu, and they accounted for 89 percent of net sales and other operating revenue for the fiscal year ended August 31, 1979. The most important group of hair care product (in terms of sales) is Ultra Sheen, which consists of conditioners and hair dress, shampoos, rinsers, and creme relaxers. The conditioner is JPC's major selling product. Afro Sheen was introduced in the late 1960s to accommodate the faddish Afro hair styles but declined in the 1970s due to

---

[22]G. Mitchell, "Battle of the Rouge," *Black Enterprise*, Vol. 9, August 1978, pp. 22–26.

[23]R. E. Johnson, "The Prodigal Returns to His First Love: The Beauty Industry," *Jet*, Vol. XLIX, November 6, 1975.

[24]Annual Report for the Fiscal Year Ended August 31, 1979, Johnson Products Co Inc., 1979.

Exhibit 10.8   Johnson Products Company, Inc. and Subsidiaries—
Consolidated Statements of Changes in Financial Position

	Years Ended August 31			
	1979	1978	1977	1976
Source of funds:				
Net income	$ 321,000	$2,237,000	$1,403,000	$4,248,000
Charges (credit) to income not affecting working capital:				
Depreciation and amortization	981,000	1,024,000	902,000	675,000
Deferred income taxes (plus other, for 1976)	(20,000)	(70,000)	174,000	250,000
Working capital provided from operations	1,282,000	3,191,000	2,479,000	5,173,000
Restricted employee stock options (for 1976: acquisition cost = 250,000)	31,000	42,000	37,000	288,000
Total source of funds	1,313,000	3,233,000	2,516,000	5,461,000
Application of funds:				
Expenditures for property, plant, and equipment, net	1,008,000	864,000	1,508,000	2,082,000
Dividends on common stock	1,430,000	1,430,000	1,460,000	913,000
Purchase of treasury stock (1976: goodwill cost: acquisition)	—	434,000		195,000
Investment in Nigeria	151,000	—	180,000	—
Other	177,000	159,000	218,000	63,000
Total application of funds	2,766,000	2,887,000	3,366,000	3,253,000
Increase (decrease) in working capital	(1,453,000)	346,000	(850,000)	2,208,000
Summary of net change in working capital:				
Increase (decrease) in current assets:				
Cash and certificates of deposit	(246,000)	139,000	102,000	(522,000)
Commercial paper	(2,671,000)	550,000	1,960,000	372,000
Receivables	(1,098,000)	1,160,000	(2,166,000)	1,003,000
Refundable income taxes	749,000	—	(199,000)	199,000
Inventories	(696,000)	900,000	(1,662,000)	2,226,000
Prepaid expenses	(12,000)	(143,000)	240,000	(327,000)
Total summary	(3,974,000)	2,606,000	(1,725,000)	2,951,000
Increase (decrease) in current liabilities:				
Accounts payable	(516,000)	576,000	(709,000)	898,000
Due to profit-sharing trust	(215,000)	75,000	15,000	50,000
Dividends payable	—	(8,000)	136,000	60,000
Accrued expenses	(397,000)	276,000	32,000	(65,000)
Income taxes	(1,393,000)	1,341,000	(349,000)	(200,000)
Total increase (decrease)	(2,521,000)	2,260,000	(875,000)	743,000
Increase (decrease) in working capital	$(1,453,000)	$ 346,000	(850,000)	$2,208,000

Source: Company annual reports to shareholders.

changing hair fashions.[25] In 1979, JPC acquired the Bantu line of hair care products to serve the professional market (beauty and barber salons). It was described as not a significant part of the business.

Cosmetics.   JPC describes cosmetics as the most exciting and challenging segment of its business. As of 1979, the company reported seven cosmetics groupings under the Ultra Sheen label. It had introduced more than 20 new cosmetic products in fiscal 1979.[26] Nail enamel, liquid and eye makeup, lipsticks, powders, and other facial makeup are sold under the Ultra Sheen name. A reorganizing and upgrading of the line started in 1977 and continued into 1979. Emphasis was placed on strengthening sales to drugstore chains and mass volume retailers.

Fragrances.   Men's cologne and splash-on fragrance products and gift sets are sold under the name Black Tie.

Marketing

Retail selling is "pushed" through in-store promotions and product demonstrations, which are conducted by trained JPC representatives. Other marketing techniques include "clustering" a product line in one section of a store, away from other brands. Professional sales are pushed to gain acceptance and endorsement of products by beauty and barber salon operators. The belief was that once the customer has been "sold" on a product by the salon operator, the customer was more likely to buy it at retail outlets.

Noticing a slowdown in sales and marketing performance (1975–1977), Johnson completely restructured his marketing group in 1977. He added a new vice-president (marketing), a new director for marketing cosmetics, and a new advertising manager.[27]

In 1979, the sales organization was restructured into two divisions: professional and retail.[28] The professional division was to sell through national distributors to beauty and barber salons. The major part of the business was to be handled by the retail division which sold to retail establishments, rack jobbers, and distributors. In 1979, John J. Taylor (appointed in 1977) was not continued as vice-president for marketing.

By 1979, JPC's largest international market was Nigeria, comprising 10 percent of sales ($4 million) in 1978. Its established distribution network covered both professional and retail markets in all of Nigeria's major regional centers. This marketing effort was bolstered by newly finalized arrangements to manufacture products in that country. In addition to the Nigerian business, JPC's new marketing manager was looking forward to further expansion into the African continent, a market with high growth potential.

Research and Development (R&D)

JPC's R&D department consisted of about 40 professionals, including chemists, bacteriologists, and technicians. Their work space included a 6,500-square foot laboratory.

[25] Ibid.

[26] Ibid.

[27] Annual Report Fiscal Year Ended August 31, 1979, Johnson Products Co. Inc., 1979.

[28] "Johnson Products Company History," Johnson Products Co Inc., 1980.

R&D encompassed three areas: new product development, quality control, and salon test-ing. JPC had encountered problems in its R&D program up to 1978, the major one being the lack of new products. Thus, in 1978, the president added a new vice-president (R&D), who substantially increased new product output. In 1979, George E. Johnson stated that "for the first time in several years, a backlog of items is waiting to be introduced at appro-priate times."[29] The company termed R&D as the key to its continued growth.

Social Responsibility

According to management,[30] JPC often is described as the "company with a conscience" because it frequently returns part of its earnings to the surrounding community through the George E. Johnson Foundation (established 1972). The foundation supported pro-grams and organizations designed to improve the quality of life in black America through jobs, housing, health, education, youth services, legal justice, and family services. In addition, JPC established the George E. Johnson Educational Fund (1972), designed to "create opportunities for inner city youths who have the potential for success in school and business, but who are excluded by most scholarship selection processes."[31] JPC re-ported in 1979 that more than 500 youngsters had benefited from the fund.

The firm is also a major supporter of the Independence Bank of Chicago, which Johnson helped to organize in 1964. He became chairman of the board and saw it grow to have $20 million in assets by 1972.[32]

Ownership

The George E. Johnson family and JPC directors own 66 percent of common stock shares of the company and no one else is known to own more than 5 percent of the company's common stock.[33]

---

[29] Annual Report Fiscal Year Ended August 31, 1979, Johnson Products Co., Inc., 1979.

[30] "Johnson Products Company History," Johnson Products Co. Inc., 1980.

[31] "From an Idea for a New Product has Grown a Giant Cosmetics Empire," in *Famous Blacks Give Secrets of Success*, Vol. II (Johnson Publishing Co., Inc., 1973).

[32] Ibid.

[33] "Annual Report Pursuant to Section 13 or 15(d) of the Securities and Exchange Act of 1934; Form 10-K," Johnson Products Co. Inc., August 31, 1979.

Marion Laboratories, Inc.

▪ *Marilyn L. Taylor and Kenneth Beck* ▪

Michael E. Herman, Senior Vice President of Finance for Marion Laboratories, had just received word that the Board of Directors was planning to meet in three days to review the company's portfolio of subsidiary investments. In particular, he and his senior financial analyst, Carl R. Mitchell, were to prepare an in-depth analysis of several of the subsidiaries so the board could be better positioned with respect to these subsidiary's compatibility with Marion's overall strategic objectives. The analysis was part of a continuing process of self-assessment to assure future growth for the company. At the upcoming meeting the board was interested in a review of Kalo Laboratories, Inc.,* a subsidiary that manufactured specialty agricultural chemicals.

Kalo was profitable and in sound financial shape for the fiscal year just ended. (See Exhibit 11.1—Sales, Profits, and Assets of Major Industry Segments). But Kalo, in the agricultural chemical industry, was unique for Marion and Mr. Herman knew that Kalo's long-term status as a Marion subsidiary would depend on more than just profitability.

Marion's future had been the subject of careful study following the first two years of earnings decline in the company's history. In fiscal 1975 net earnings for the company were 12 percent lower than in 1974. In fiscal 1976 Marion faced a more serious problem as earnings fell 30 percent below 1974 levels while sales decreased 4 percent and cost of goods sold rose by 12 percent above 1974 levels.

As a result of the interruption in the earnings growth pattern, Marion has sought to reexamine its corporate portfolio of investments. By fiscal year 1977 some results from the reappraisal were seen as earnings rose 28 percent from the previous year. Although sales continued to climb, earnings had not yet recovered to the 1974 level by the end of fiscal year 1978. Marion's long-range planning was an attempt to define what the company was to become in the next ten-year period. Current analysis of subsidiaries and investments were analyzed within this ten-year framework. As part of this long-range planning, a statement of Marion's corporate mission was developed.

Statement of Corporate Mission

1. Achieve a position of market leadership through marketing and distribution of consumable and personal products of a perceived differentiation to selected segments of the health care and related fields.

---

*Kalo Laboratories Inc. was utilized as the case subject due to the singular nature of the segment information available in Marion Laboratories Inc. SEC Submissions, and does not reflect Marion's intentions as to its investment in Kalo or any of its other subsidiary operations. Materials in this case were generally gathered from publicly available information.

This case was prepared by Professor Marilyn L. Taylor and Kenneth E. Beck, M.S.–Finance, of the University of Kansas. The development of the case was supported in part by a grant from the University of Kansas Fund for Instructional Improvement. The research and written case information were presented at the 1980 Case Research Symposium and were evaluated by the Case Research Association's Editorial Board.

Copyright © 1981.

Exhibit 11.1   Marion Laboratories Inc. Sales, Profits, and Identifiable Assets by Industry Segments (Thousands of Dollars)

	Year ended June 30				
	1978	**1977**	**1976**	**1975**	**1974**
Sales to unaffiliated customers:					
Pharmaceutical and hospital products	$ 84,223	$ 72,299	$ 59,236	$ 64,613	$ 54,165
Specialty agricultural chemical products	9,302	5,227	2,880	4,522	4,044
Other health care segments	23,853	22,605	18,722	14,961	13,569
Consolidated net sales	$117,378	$100,131	$ 80,838	$ 84,096	$ 71,778
Operating profit:					
Pharmaceutical and hospital products	$ 27,900	$ 23,439	$ 18,941	$ 28,951	$ 25,089
Specialty agricultural chemical products	905	382	(328)	881	620
Other health care segments	929	1,251	(593)	686	871
Operating profit	29,734	25,072	18,020	30,518	26,580
Interest expense	(1,546)	(1,542)	(898)	(97)	(83)
Corporate expenses	(5,670)	(4,474)	(3,106)	(2,795)	(2,475)
Earnings before income taxes	$ 22,518	$ 19,056	$ 14,016	$ 27,626	$ 24,022
Identifiable assets:					
Pharmaceutical and hospital products	$ 75,209	$ 69,546	$ 60,376	$ 43,658	$ 35,103
Specialty agricultural chemical products	3,923	3,805	1,801	1,942	1,790
Other health care segments	14,635	14,875	13,902	14,229	12,217
Corporate	5,121	3,424	4,518	3,928	3,770
Discontinued operations	—	—	—	3,370	6,865
Consolidated assets	$ 98,888	$ 91,650	$ 80,597	$ 67,127	$ 59,745

Source: 1978 Annual Report.

2. Achieve long-term profitable growth through the management of high risk relative to the external environment.

3. Achieve a professional, performance-oriented working environment that stimulates integrity, entrepreneurial spirit, productivity, and social responsibility.

In addition to these more general goals, Marion also set a specific sales goal of $250 million. No time frame was established to achieve this goal, as the major emphasis was to be placed on the stability and quality of sales.

Mr. Herman realized, however, that even though there was no written timetable for earnings growth it was well understood that to meet stockholder expectations, the company must grow fairly rapidly.

On June 8, 1978, in a presentation before the Health Industry's Analyst Group, Fred Lyons, Marion's president and chief operating officer, emphasized Marion's commitment to growth. In his remarks he stated:

We expect to grow over the next ten years at a rate greater than the pharmaceutical indus-try average and at a rate greater than at least twice that of the real gross national prod-

uct. Our target range is at least 10–15 percent compounded growth—shooting for the higher side of that, of course. Obviously we intend to have a great deal of new business and new products added to our current operations to reach and exceed the $250 million level. Our licensing activities and R&D expenditures will be intensified. . . . At the same time we'll undertake some selective in-house research business into Marion through the acquisition route. It is our intention to keep our balance sheet strong and maintain an "A" or better credit rating, to achieve a return on investment in the 12–15 percent range, and to produce a net after tax compared to sales in the 8–12 percent range.

To finance this growth in sales Marion was faced with a constant need for funds. Most of these funds in the past had come from the company's operations. To finance a $25-million expansion in its pharmaceutical facilities, the company, in fiscal year 1976, found it necessary to borrow $15 million in the form of unsecured senior notes. The notes were to mature on October 1, 1980, 1981, and 1982 with $5 million due on each of those dates.

In regard to possible future financing, Mr. Herman made the following comments before the Health Industry's Analyst Group. "Most of you realize that industrial companies have debt-equity ratio of 1:1 and, if we so desired to lever ourselves to that level, we could borrow $66 million. However, we would keep as a guideline the factor of always maintaining our "A" or better credit rating, so we would not leverage ourselves that far."

Although Marion was fairly light on debt, the potential for future borrowing was not unlimited. Besides maintaining an "A" credit rating, it was felt that a debt to equity ratio greater than 4:1 would be inconsistent with the pharmaceutical industry.

To analyze Kalo's future as well as the futures of the other nonpharmaceutical subsidiaries, Mr. Herman realized that he and his analysts would have to consider the impact of these financing constraints on Marion's future growth. With unlimited financing in the future he would have only had to make a "good" investment decision. However, to balance the goals of a strong balance sheet and a high growth rate, Mr. Herman was faced with making the optimal investment decision. It was with these constraints that Mr. Herman would eventually have to make his recommendation to the Board of Directors.

Company History

In 1979, Marion Laboratories Inc. of Kansas City, Missouri, was a leading producer of ethical (prescription) pharmaceuticals for the treatment of cardiovascular and cerebral disorders. (See Exhibit 11.2—Marion's Major Ethical Products.) Marion also owned subsidiaries which manufactured hospital supplies, proprietary (non-prescription) drugs, eyeglasses, optical accessories, electrical home stairway elevators, and specialty agricultural chemicals.

Marion Laboratories was founded in 1950 by Ewing Marion Kauffman. Prior to establishing his own company, Mr. Kauffman held a job with a field sales force of a Kansas City pharmaceutical company. After four years on the job Kauffman's sales efforts were so successful that he was making more money in commissions than the company president's salary. When the company cut his commission and reduced his sales territory, Kauffman quit to establish his own firm.

In its initial year of operation the new company had sales of $36,000 and a net profit of $1,000. Its sole product was a tablet called OS-VIM, and was formulated to combat chronic fatigue. The company's three employees, counting Mr. Kauffman, worked from a

Exhibit 11.2   Marion Laboratories Inc. Major Ethical Pharmaceutical Products

Product	Product Application	Estimated Market Size (in thousands)	Marion's Product	Share of Market (Percentage)
Cerebral and peripheral vasodilators	Vascular relaxant to relieve constriction of arteries	$90–$100	Pavabid[R]	22
Coronary vasodilators	Controlled-release nitroglycerin for treatment of angina pectoris	90–100	Nitro-Bid[R]	12
Ethical and OTC plain antacids	Tablets for relief of heartburn	37	GAVISCON[R]	26
Andogens-estrogens	Product for treatment of calcium deficiencies	12	OS-CAL[R]	46
Topical burn antimicrobials	Ointment for prevention of infection in third-degree burns	8	SILVADENE[R]	57
Urologic antispasmodics	Product for treatment of symptoms of neurogenic bladder	10	DITROPAN[R]	10

Source: Smith, Barney, Harris, Upham and Co. Research Report, January 19, 1978.

13′ × 15′ storeroom that served as manufacturing plant, sales office, warehouse, and headquarters.

From the company's inception, the major emphasis for Marion was on sales and marketing. Mr. Kauffman was successful in developing an aggressive, highly motivated sales force. During the mid-1960s the company's sales effort was concentrated on developing Pavabid, introduced in 1962, into the leading product in the cerebral and peripheral vasodilator market.

While other drug companies were spending large amounts on research and development, hoping to discover new drugs, Marion concentrated on the sales effort, spending very little on basic research. Nearly all of its research expenditures were directed at improving its current products or further developing products licensed from other drug companies. This particular approach to product development was still being followed in 1979.

Beginning in the late 1960s, Marion decided to reduce its dependence on Pavabid which accounted for more than half of Marion's sales. In the pharmaceutical area, the company continued to minimize basic research and worked to develop new drug sources. Marion also began diversifying into the hospital and health products' sector primarily by acquiring existing firms in those areas. (See Exhibit 11.3 for a summary of Marion's acquisition and divestiture activities.) Taking advantage of the high market value of its common stock,[1] the company acquired several subsidiaries engaged in businesses other than pharmaceuticals.

Organization

Marion's operations, in 1979, were divided into two separate groups, the Pharmaceutical Group and the Health Products Group. (See Exhibit 11.4—Marion Organization Chart.)

[1] Price earnings ratios for Marion in 1968 and 1969 were 46 and 52, respectively.

Exhibit 11.3   Marion Laboratories Inc. Summary of Subsidiary Acquisitions and Divestitures

Name of Subsidiary	Type of Product(s)	Date Acquired	Date Divested
Marion Health & Safety	First-aid and hospital products	1968	—
American Stair-Glide	Manufacturer of home stairway lifts and products to aid the handicapped	1968	—
Kalo Laboratories	Manufacturer of specialty agricultural chemicals	1968	—
Rose Manufacturing	Industrial fall-protection devices	1969	Sold: 1978
Mi-Con Laboratories	Manufacturers of opthalmic solutions	1969	Merged into MH&S: 1973
Pioneer Laboratories	Manufacturer of sterile dressings	50% in 1970	Sold out: 1971
Signet Laboratories	Vitamin and food supplements	1971	Discontinued operations, selling some assets: 1975
Optico Laboratories	Eyeglasses, hard contact lenses, and related products	1973	—
Certified Laboratories	Manufacturer IPC products	1969	Sold: 1978
IPC	Marketed IPC products	1969	Merged into Pharmaceutical Division: 1979
Marion International	Distributor of pharmaceutical products	Incorporated 1971	—
Inco	Industrial creams	1972	Merged into MH&S: 1974
Occusafe	Consulting services; re: OSHA regulation and compliance	Incorporated 1972	Discontinued operations: 1973
Nation Wide	Specialty AG-Chem products	1973	Merged into Kalo
Marion Scientific	Manufacturer and distributor of	Acquired by MH&S: 1973	—
Colloidal	Specialty agricultural products	1973	Merged into Kalo 1974
WBC	Holding company for IPC	Incorporated 1976	Sold: 1978
SRC	Specialty AG-Chem products	1977	Merged into Kalo

The Pharmaceutical Group's operations were a continuation of the original ethical drug line of the company. The Health Products Group was composed of subsidiaries purchased by Marion in hospital and health-related fields.

Fred W. Lyons, 41, was president, chief executive officer, and member of the Board of Directors. As president, Lyons was responsible for the total operation and performance of the corporation. This responsibility included the company's pharmaceutical operating group as well as all subsidiary operations, corporate planning functions and corporate supportive activities.

Lyons joined Marion in 1970 as vice-president and general manager, and director. He came to Marion from a similar position with Corral Pharmaceuticals Inc., a subsidiary of Alcon Laboratories Inc. Lyons was a registered pharmacist and had received an MBA from Harvard University in 1959.

Also serving on the Board of Directors was Senior Vice President and Chief Financial Officer, Michael E. Herman, 37, who joined Marion from an investment banking firm of

Exhibit 11.4   Marion Laboratories Inc. Organization Chart

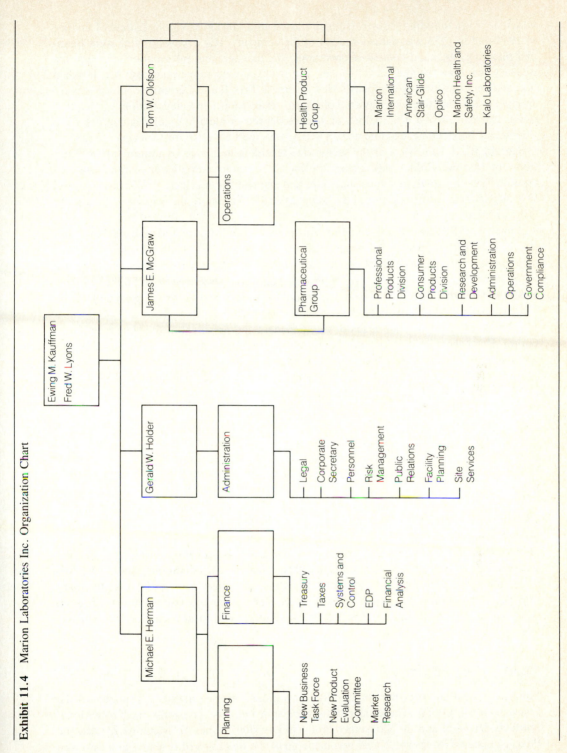

Organization Chart as rendered by authors

which he was a founding partner. Herman started with Marion as vice-president of finance in 1974 and in 1975 was named director of the company. His responsibilities were financial planning, financial control of operations, the management information systems, the treasury functions, product development, and strategic long-range planning. Mr. Herman was also chairman of the company's New Business Task Force Committee which was responsible for the financial review, planning, evaluation, and negotiation of acquisitions. Herman earned a bachelor's of science degree in metallurgical engineering from Rensselaer Polytechnic Institute and an MBA from the University of Chicago.

Gerald W. Holder, 48, was the senior vice-president in charge of administrative functions for Marion. Holder was responsible for all corporate administrative functions, including Marion's legal, personnel, facilities and engineering services, public relations and risk management staffs. He joined the company in 1973 rising to the senior vice-president level in March of 1978.

James E. McGraw, 46, was senior vice-president of Marion Laboratories Inc. and president of the company's Pharmaceutical Group. He was responsible for the manufacturing, marketing, quality control, and accounting functions within the two operating units of the Pharmaceutical Group: the Professional Products Division and the Consumer Products Division. McGraw joined Marion in 1974 from a position as president of the General Diagnostics Division of Warner-Lambert Company.

Tom W. Olofson, 36, was a senior vice-president and president of the Health Products Group. His responsibilities included financial and planning aspects for each of the subsidiaries in the Health Products Group.

Within the described organization, Marion made some of its operating decisions in small group or task force settings that brought together corporate personnel from several different disciplines. The process of approving certain capital expenditures was an example of the review and analysis process.

Marion had a formal capital expenditure review program for expenditures on depreciable assets in excess of $10,000. At the option of the group president, the review program could also be applied on expenditures of less than $10,000 with the modification that in these cases only the group president was involved in the review process.

A form that forced the requesting individual to discount the cash flows of the project was required to be completed and submitted, if the net present value of cash flows was positive, to a corporate planning group. This group consisted of corporate accounting and facilities planning personnel who, since the company was operating with limited funds, decided which projects, based on financial and strategic considerations, should be forwarded to Fred Lyons for final approval or rejection. This process occurred after the planning period and prior to the purchase of the asset. The capital expenditure review program was used for expenditures in both the Pharmaceutical Group and the Health Products Group.

Pharmaceutical Group

Marion's ethical and over-the-counter drug operations were the major components of the Pharmaceutical Group. These operations were split into two divisions, the Professional Products Division and the Consumer Products Division. James E. McGraw headed the Pharmaceutical Group which also was made up of the functions of research and development, administration, operations, and government compliance. Although Marion had been exclusively an ethical drugmaker prior to diversification efforts, the company had recently increased its operations in the proprietary drug area.

In 1978, Marion formed the Consumer Products Division from what had been International Pharmaceutical Corp. (IPC) to market its growing nonprescription product line. This market area, previously untapped for Marion, was expected to be a major ingredient for near-term growth. To aid in the marketing of its nonprescription line, Marion hired a full-scale consumer advertising agency for the first time in the company's history.

Sales for the Consumer Products Division were boosted when, in fiscal 1978, Marion purchased the product Throat-Discs from Warner-Lamberts' Parke-Davis division. In addition, Marion also purchased two Parke-Davis ethical products, Ambenyl cough-cold products and a tablet for the treatment of thyroid disorders. Because of the timing of the acquisition, most of the sales and earnings were excluded from that year's earnings results. Sales for these three lines were expected to be nearly $8 million in 1979.

Marion's ethical pharmaceutical products were marketed by its Professional Products Division. The company sold its ethical product with a detail sales force of about 200 that called on physicians, pharmacists, and distributors within their assigned territories. The sales force was very productive by industry standards and was motivated by intensive training and supervision and an incentive compensation system. There was very little direct selling to doctors and pharmacists, the main purpose of the sales person visits being promotion of Marion's products. In addition, Marion had an institutional sales force that sold directly to hospitals, institutions, and other large users.

In fiscal 1978, 80 percent of Marion's pharmaceutical products were distributed through 463 drug wholesalers. All orders for ethical drug products were filled from the Kansas City, Missouri, manufacturing plant. Marion's pharmaceutical distribution system is diagramed in Exhibit 11.5.

During 1978, the company decided to use its improved liquidity position to aid its wholesale drug distributors. Many wholesalers used outside financing to purchase their inventory and were unable to maintain profit margins when interest rates rose. By extending credit on key products, Marion helped its distributors maintain higher inventories and gave the company a selling edge over competitors.

One of Marion's major goals for each of its products was for the product to hold a market leadership position in the particular area in which it competed. This goal had been accomplished for most of the company's leading products. (See Exhibit 11.2.)

Capturing a large share of a market had worked particularly well for Marion's leading product, Pavabid, which in 1978 accounted for 18 percent of the entire company's sales. Marion was decreasing its reliance on Pavabid (see Exhibit 11.6) which, since its introduction in 1962, had been the company's most successful product. Through the 1960s Pavabid had been responsible for almost all of Marion's growth. In recent years, as the product's market matured, sales growth had slowed, forcing the company to become less dependent on Pavabid. The decrease in sales of 3.9 percent in fiscal year 1976 was due primarily to previous overstocking of Pavabid and the subsequent inventory adjustments at the distributor level.

In April of 1976 the Food and Drug Administration (FDA) had requested that makers of papaverine hydrochloride (sold by Marion as Pavabid) submit test data to support the safety and efficacy of the drug. Many small manufacturers were not able to submit the data and dropped out of the market. Marion complied with the request and had not yet been notified by the FDA of the outcome of the review by early 1979. A negative action by

Exhibit 11.5 Pharmaceutical Distribution

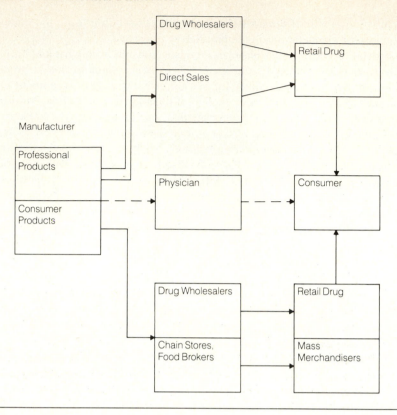

Exhibit 11.6 Marion Laboratories Inc. Changing Product Mix

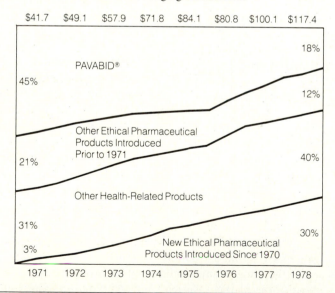

Source: 1978 Annual Report.

the FDA was not expected since it had taken so long for a decision and papaverine had been used safely for decades. However, if the FDA ruled that compounds such as Pavabid could not be marketed, either because they were not safe or were not effective, Marion would lose its leading product.

In August 1977, the FDA requested that manufacturers of coronary vasodilators, including nitroglycerin compounds like Marion's Nitro-Bid, submit test data to prove product safety and efficacy. This review was the same process that Pavabid was subject to and a negative ruling, although not expected, would adversely affect the company.

Proving its products to be safe and effective was only one area in which the company dealt with the FDA. Before any ethical drug product could be marketed in the United States, Marion had to have the approval of the FDA. Under the system effective at that time, the company was required to conduct extensive animal tests, file an Investigational New Drug Application, conduct three phases of clinical human tests, file a New Drug Application, and submit all its data to the FDA for final review. With the FDA's approval, the drug firm could begin marketing the drug.

The approval process from lab discovery and patent application to FDA approval took from 7 to 10 years. Often a company had only 7 or 8 years of patent protection left to market its discovery and recover the average $50 million it had taken to fully develop the drug from the initial discovery stages.

To avoid the R&D expenses necessary to fully develop a new drug entity into a marketable product, Marion's source for new products was a process the company called "search and development." Marion licensed the basic compound from other drug manufacturers large enough to afford the basic research needed to discover new drugs. Generally the licensers, most notably Servier of France and Chugai of Japan, were companies lacking the resources or expertise necessary to obtain FDA approval and marketing rights in the U.S. Marion's R&D effort then concentrated on developing a product with an already-identified pharmacological action into a drug marketable in the U.S. By developing existing drug entities, Marion was able to shorten the development time required to bring a new drug to market at a lower cost than discovering its own drugs. This enabled Marion to compete in an industry dominated by companies many times its own size. (See Exhibits 11.7 and 11.8 for drug industry information.)

In addition to the FDA, the federal government was also affecting the drug industry with its activities that promoted generic substitution. In early 1979, 40 states had generic substitution that allowed nonbranded drugs to be substituted for branded, and often more expensive, drugs. The U.S. Department of Health, Education and Welfare and the Federal Trade Commission had also recently proposed a model state substitution law and a listing of medically equivalent drugs. Under other federal programs, the maximum allowable cost (MAC) guidelines, reimbursement for Medicaid and Medicare prescriptions was made at the lowest price at which a generic version was available.

Generics accounted for 12 percent of new prescriptions being written and were likely to increase in relative importance. To combat the decreasing profit margins that were expected, the industry was looking to its ability to develop new drugs to offset the expected shortfall that was expected in the 1980s caused by a loss of patent protection on many important drug compounds.

The effect that generic substitution laws would have on Marion was unclear. The company had always concentrated on products with a unique pharmacological action rather than those that were commodity in nature. Generic substitution required an "equivalent"

Exhibit 11.7   Selected Ethical Drug Companies, 1977 (in thousands of dollars)

	Net Sales	Cost of Goods Sold	R & D Expenses	Net Income*
Pfizer Inc.	$2,031,900	$978,057	$ 98,282	$174,410
Merck & Co.	1,724,410	662,703	144,898	290,750
Eli Lilly & Co.	1,518,012	571,737	124,608	218,684
Upjohn Inc.	1,134,325	—	102,256	91,521
Smith Kline Corp.	780,337	299,338	61,777	89,271
G. D. Searle & Co.	749,583	345,224	52,645	(28,390)
Syntex Corp.	313,604	132,710	27,648	37,643
A. H. Robbins Co.	306,713	122,374	16,107	26,801
Rorer Group Inc.	186,020	59,606	5,174	18,143
Marion Laboratories	100,131	37,330	5,907	10,652

*After tax.

Source: "Drug and Cosmetic Industry," *Standard & Poor's Industry Survey*, June 1978.

Exhibit 11.8   Marion Laboratories, Inc. Ethical Drug Industry Composite Statistics

	1978	1977	1976	1975
Sales (millions $)	$12,450	$10,859	$10,033	$9,022
Operating margin (%)	22.5%	22.2%	21.9%	22.1%
Income tax rate (%)	36.5%	36.4%	36.2%	36.7%
Net profit margin (%)	11.8%	11.7%	11.7%	11.6%
Earned on net worth (%)	18.5%	17.9%	18.2%	18.4%

Source: Computed from company annual reports.

drug be substituted for the brand-name drug and there were uncertainties about how equivalency would be defined.

Marion's pharmaceutical operations had not produced a major new product for several years. Products that were in various stages of development were diltiazen hydrochloride, an anti-anginal agent; sucralfate, a nonsystematic (does not enter the bloodstream) drug for the treatment of ulcers; and benflourex, a product that reduced cholesterol levels in the blood.

Health Products Group

Subsidiaries selling a wide range of products used in health care and related fields made up Marion's Health Products Group. The company had bought and sold several subsidiaries since beginning to diversify in 1968 (see Exhibit 11.3). By 1978 the group of subsidiaries was responsible for 39 percent of total company sales and 22 percent of earnings before taxes.

Several times after purchasing a company Marion had decided to sell or discontinue operations of a subsidiary. The divestment decision in the past had been based on considerations such as a weak market position, low-growth position, excessive product liability, or a poor "fit" with the rest of Marion.

In his presentation before the Health Industry's Analyst Group, Fred Lyons noted the importance of a subsidiary fitting in with the rest of Marion when explaining the company's decision to sell Rose Manufacturing. "You may have noticed that during this past year we determined through our strategic planning that Rose Manufacturing, in the fall-protection area of industrial safety, did not fit either our marketing base or our technology base. Therefore we made a decision to spin Rose off, and we successfully culminated its sale in November of 1977. Rose, like Signet Laboratories three years ago, just did not fit."

In adjusting its corporate profile Marion was always searching for companies that provided good investment potentials and were consistent with the company's goals. To provide a framework within which to evaluate potential acquisitions and to avoid some of the mistakes made in past purchases, Marion developed a set of acquisition criteria to be applied to possible subsidiary investments.

Search Criteria for Acquisitions

- Product Area: health care
- Market: $100 million potential with 8 percent minimum growth rate
- Net Sales: $3–30 million
- Tangible Net Worth: not less than $1 million
- Return on Investment: not less than 20 percent pretax
- Method of Payment: cash or stock

The Board of Directors made the ultimate decision on the acquisitions and divestment of Marion's subsidiaries. At the corporate level, Mr. Herman was responsible for evaluating changes in the corporate portfolio and, based on his analysis, making recommendations to the board. Since Mr. Herman was also on the Board of Directors his recommendations were heavily weighted in the board's final decision.

In early 1979 Marion had four subsidiaries in its Health Products Group, Marion Health and Safety Inc., Optico Industries, American Stair-Glide, and Kalo Laboratories. Following is a brief description of each:

Marion Health and Safety Inc.   sold a broad line of hospital and industrial safety products through its Marion Scientific Corp. and Health and Safety Products Division. Recently introduced, Marion Scientific products (a consumer-oriented insect bite treatment and a device for transporting anaerobic cultures) both showed good acceptance and growth in their respective markets. Distribution is generally through medical/surgical wholesalers and distributors who in turn resell to hospital, medical laboratories, reference laboratories, etc. Health and Safety Division manufactures and/or packages primarily safety-related products (hearing protection, eyewash, etc.) and first-aid kits and kit products, such as wraps, band-aids, and various OTC products. Sale of these products is made to safety-equipment wholesalers/distributors who resell to hospitals, industry, institutions, etc. Sales of Marion Health and Safety Inc. were estimated to have increased about 17 percent by outside analysts, to a level estimated at $19 million. Pretax margins were about 10 percent in this industry. Marion Health and Safety Inc., was headquartered in Rockford, Illinois.

Optico Industries Inc.   participated in the wholesale and retail optical industry. Its main products were glass and plastic prescription eyeglass lenses and hard contact lenses. Out-

Exhibit 11.9   Kalo Laboratories Sales, Investment, and Expense Information

	1978	1977	1976	1975	1974	1973
			(in millions of dollars)			
Sales	$9.0	$5.0	$2.0	$4.0	$3.0	$2.0
Total assets	5.0	4.0	2.0	2.0	2.0	1.0
Total investment*	3.0	3.0	1.0	1.0	1.0	0.5
			Expenses as Percent of Sales			
COGS	43%	54%	61%	53%	55%	48%
R&D expense	8	7	7	5	5	3
Marketing, selling and general administrative expenses	37	31	42	23	24	27

*Includes Marion's equity in Kalo and funds lent on a long-term basis.

Authors' estimates.

side analysts estimated this subsidiary recorded sales gains of about 26 percent for 1978 for sales estimated to be about $8 million. Optico had reduced profitability during 1978 due to expansion of its retail facilities. Pretax margins for 1978 were estimated at 6 percent, but this was expected to improve when the expansion program was completed. Optico's headquarters were located in Tempe, Arizona.

American Stair-Glide Corp.   manufactured and marketed home stairway and porch lifts and other products to aid physically handicapped individuals. These products were principally sold to medical/surgical supply dealers for resale or rental to the consumer. In some instances distribution is through elevator companies. Sales were estimated at about $5 million annually by outside analysts. This subsidiary was expected to grow slowly and steadily and it had a very stable historical earnings pattern. The trend for greater access to buildings for the handicapped was expected to impact favorably on this Grandview, Missouri-based subsidiary.

Kalo Laboratories Inc.

Kalo Laboratories operated in the specialty agricultural chemical market and provided products to meet specialized user needs. In the past, Kalo had been successful in marketing its line of specialty products. (See Exhibit 11.9—Kalo's Past Earnings Information.) In assessing Kalo's future there were many risks to consider. These risks included competition from large chemical companies, governmental regulatory actions, and uncertain future product potentials.

Competition and Industry.   The United States and Canadian agricultural chemical market was estimated to be $3.2 billion in 1978 and growing at more than 15 percent a year.[2] The industry was dominated by large chemical manufacturers including Dow Chemical, DuPont, Stauffer Chemical, and Gulf Oil. The market was also shared by large ethi-

[2]1979 DuPont Annual Report and 1979 Upjohn Annual Report.

Exhibit 11.10   Marion Laboratories Inc. Total and Agriculture-Related Sales Selected Companies, 1979

| | Total Sales (millions) | Agriculture Related | |
		Sales (millions)	Earnings (before tax)
Eli Lilly	$2,520	$920*	28.6%
Pfizer	3,030	480*	9.8
Upjohn	1,755	280*	9.2
Marion (1978)	100	9	9.0

*Includes international sales.

Source: Company annual reports.

cal drug manufacturers including Eli Lilly, Pfizer, and Upjohn. (See Exhibit 11.10 for agriculture-related sales.) Economics of scale allowed the larger companies to produce large amounts of what might be perceived as a commodity product (herbicides, insecticides, and fungicides) at a much lower cost per unit than the smaller companies. Diversification of and within agricultural product lines assured the larger manufacturers even performance for their agricultural divisions as a whole.

Since smaller chemical companies like Kalo could not afford to produce large-enough amounts of their products to match the efficiency and prices of the large companies, these firms concentrated on specialty markets with unique product needs. By identifying specialty chemical needs in the agricultural segment, Kalo was able to produce its products and develop markets that were very profitable but weren't large enough to attract the bigger firms.

Products.   Since the larger chemical companies dominated the large product segments, Kalo's products were designed to meet the specialized needs of its agricultural users. Kalo's product line was divided into four major classes: seed treatments, adjuvants, bactericides, and herbicides.

Seed treatments for soybeans accounted for the majority of Kalo's sales. One product in this area was Triple Noctin. Products in the seed treatment class were intended to act on soybean seeds to increase their viability once in the ground. Kalo manufactured seed treatments for soybeans only.

Adjuvants were chemicals that, when added to another agricultural product, increased the efficacy of the product or made it easier to use. For instance, Biofilmo prevented liquid fertilizer from foaming, which made it easier to apply, and Hydro-Wet enhanced the soil's receptiveness to certain chemicals, which reduced runoff into surrounding areas.

The newest product for Kalo was the adjuvant EXTEND, a chemical compound added to fertilizer that made it bind chemically with the soil or the plant. The binding process helped retain the fertilizer where it was applied, making each application longer-lasting and more effective. EXTEND was only recently introduced and its success was difficult to assess at such an early stage. Kalo's management was planning to build a family of products around EXTEND. Sales projections showed EXTEND contributing between 60–70 percent of Kalo's future growth through 1987.

Bactericides and herbicides were the final two product classes at Kalo. Bactericides were applied to the soil to either inhibit or encourage the growth of selected bacteria. One product, ISOBAC was used to control boll rot in cotton. Herbicides, mainly for broadleaf plants, were used to control or kill unwanted weeds, leaving the desirable crop unharmed.

In the past, Kalo had acquired several of its products by acquiring the company that manufactured the product. When it purchased a going concern intact, Kalo was able to gain both manufacturing facilities and an existing distribution system. In the future Kalo expected to diversify its product line in a similar fashion. To enlarge its existing product lines Kalo was planning to use both internal and contract R&D. An example of enlarging the product family was the planned adaptation of its products to different numerous crop applications.

Because Kalo did not have a well diversified product line, its operations were more cyclical than the overall agricultural sector. Two major factors beyond Kalo's control made its annual performance extremely unpredictable, the weather and spot prices for commodities.

Kalo's operating results were seasonal as its products were primarily intended to be applied in the spring months. It was not unusual for the subsidiary to show a net loss from operations for the nine months from July until March and show a large profit in the three months April, May, and June, when the products were being purchased for immediate application. If the spring months were particularly rainy Kalo's profitability was adversely affected. Heavy farm equipment couldn't operate on wet fields without getting stuck and application was impossible until the fields dried out. Once the fields were dry, Kalo's agricultural users often did not have time to apply the herbicides or other products even though it would have been economically advantageous to do so.

The other factor that affected the demand for Kalo's products was the spot pricing of commodities. The price of commodities relative to each other had a large effect on the total amount of each type of crop planted. Because the producer was free to switch crops yearly based on the spot prices, Kalo's demand for the upcoming planting season was uncertain and variable. Kalo was particularly vulnerable to swings in demand caused by the substitutability of crops since many of their products were applicable only to soybeans.

Distribution and Marketing.   The end user of Kalo's products was usually the individual farmer. Kalo and the rest of the agricultural chemical industry had a distribution system like the one shown below.

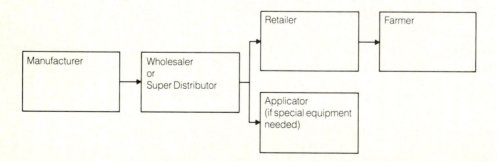

Kalo promoted its products with a sales force of about 30 salesmen. The main task of these salesmen was to call on and educate wholesalers/distributors on the advantages, unique qualities, and methods of selling Kalo's products. In addition some end user infor-

Exhibit 11.11   Kalo Laboratories Forecasted Sales and Asset Turnover

	1979	1980	1981	1982	1983	1984	1985	1986	1987
Net sales $MM (current dollars)	$12	$16	$20	$25	$30	$35	$40	$45	$50
Asset turnover	1.8x	1.8x	1.9x	1.9x	1.9x	1.9x	1.9x	1.9x	1.85x

(Note: After-tax margin expected to increase to 7 percent by 1984.)

Authors' estimates.

Exhibit 11.12   Kalo Laboratories Balance Sheet, June 30, 1978 (in millions)

Current assets	$2.5	Current liabilities	$1.4
PP&E (net)	1.9	Long-term debt	1.0
Other	.2	Capital	2.2
Total	$4.6	Total	$4.6

Authors' estimates.

mation was distributed to farmers, using "pull" advertising to create demand. A limited amount of promotion was done at agricultural shows and state fairs but because of the expense involved, this type of promotion was not used often.

Kalo's Future.   Sales forecasts prepared by the staff analysts for Mr. Herman looked very promising as they predicted sales gains of from $4 to 6 million in each of the next nine years. (See Exhibit 11.11.) There were, however, some important assumptions on which the forecasts were based.

As mentioned earlier, 60–70 percent of the forecasted growth was to come from a product family based on the new product EXTEND. A great deal of uncertainty surrounded the product, however. Since it was new, the current success of EXTEND was difficult to measure particularly in determining how current sales translated into future performance. If the market evaluation for EXTEND and related products were correct, and if a family of products could be developed around EXTEND, then the sales potential for the proposed product family was very promising provided Kalo was able to exploit the available sales opportunities.

Additional growth projected in the sales forecasts was to come from existing products and undefined future products that were to be developed or acquired. Approximately 20 percent of the growth was to come from the existing products in the next 4–5 years. Ten to 20 percent of the growth in the later years of the forecast was expected to come from currently unknown products.

For Kalo to realize the forecasted growth it was going to be necessary for Marion to provide financing. It was going to be impossible for Kalo to generate all the required funds internally. Kalo had been a net user of cash, provided by Marion, since 1976. (See Exhibit 11.9—Kalo's Sales and Earnings Information, Exhibit 11.12—Kalo's Balance Sheet at June 30, 1978, Exhibit 11.13—Balance Sheets, and Exhibit 11.14—Ten-Year Financial Summary for information about Marion's investment in Kalo.) Marion's management did

Exhibit 11.13   Marion Laboratories, Inc. Consolidated Balance Sheet 1977 and 1978

Assets		June 30	
		1978	1977
Current assets:	Cash	$ 381,116	$ 961,588
	Short-term investments, at cost which approximates market	2,561,660	10,028,297
	Accounts and notes receivable, less allowances for returns and doubtful accounts of $1,845,466 and $2,305,793	28,196,199	20,576,412
	Inventories	19,640,945	15,568,170
	Prepaid expenses	2,305,403	1,461,367
	Deferred income tax benefits	757,585	895,110
	Total current assets	53,842,908	49,490,944
Property, plant, and equipment, at cost:	Land and land improvements	2,832,588	2,935,671
	Buildings	24,458,746	25,224,652
	Machinery and equipment	19,671,607	18,110,907
	Aircraft and related equipment	1,670,904	1,670,904
	Construction in progress	365,311	357,338
		48,999,156	48,299,472
	Less accumulated depreciation	(10,725,533)	(8,585,190)
	Net property, plant, and equipment	38,273,623	39,714,282
Other assets:	Intangible assets	4,774,055	2,042,762
	Notes receivable (noncurrent)	890,692	11,589
	Marketable equity securities, at market value	688,914	—
	Deferred income tax benefits (noncurrent)	318,434	249,647
	Miscellaneous	99,597	141,232
	Total other assets	6,771,692	2,445,230
Total assets		$98,888,223	$91,650,456

not consider the amount of cash provided through the first part of 1979 to be excessive so long as Kalo maintained adequate profitability and steady growth rates. In addition to the long-term funds provided by Marion, Kalo also required short-term financing of inventory during each year due to the seasonality of its sales.

Government Regulation.   Another major uncertainty in Kalo's future was an unpredictable regulatory climate. Regulation of agricultural chemicals was under the jurisdiction of the Environmental Protection Agency (EPA). Compliance with the EPA was a similar process as with the FDA. The process of developing and introducing a new chemical product took from 8–10 years which included 2–5 years necessary to obtain EPA approval. The costs of developing and bringing a new product to market were generally from $5 to 10 million.

Once a product was on the market the EPA had powers of recall similar to the FDA and could require the company to do additional research after the product was introduced. The

Exhibit 11.13   *continued*

Liabilities and Stockholders' Equity		June 30	
		1978	**1977**
Current liabilities:	Current maturities of long-term debt	$ 82,102	$ 95,004
	Accounts payable, trade	3,979,341	4,224,105
	Accrued profit-sharing expense	1,752,515	243,096
	Other accrued expenses	3,864,168	3,008,238
	Dividends payable	1,260,612	1,198,938
	Income taxes payable	4,391,252	5,030,219
	Total current liabilities	15,329,990	13,799,600
Long-term debt, excluding current maturities		15,580,072	15,661,399
Deferred income taxes payable		1,107,000	733,000
Deferred compensation		177,975	172,889
Stockholders' equity:	Preferred stock of $1 par value per share authorized 250,000 shares; none issued	—	—
	Common stock of $1 par value per share authorized 20,000,000 shares; issued 8,703,346 shares	8,703,346	8,703,346
	Paid-in capital	3,474,358	3,475,443
	Retained earnings	58,358,925	51,604,550
		70,536,629	63,783,339
	Less: 293,153 shares of common stock in treasury, at cost (189,500 shares in 1977)	3,819,243	2,499,771
	Net unrealized loss on noncurrent marketable equitable securities	24,200	—
	Total stockholders' equity	66,693,186	61,283,568
Commitments and contingent liabilities			
Total liabilities and stockholders' equity		$98,888,223	$91,650,456

Source: 1978 Annual Report.

prospect of having a product removed from the market was an added element of risk for Kalo if any of its products were affected. No problems were expected for Kalo although several of the subsidiary's products (particularly its herbicides and bactericides) had a relatively high potential for environmental problems, if not applied correctly.

The Decision

Mr. Herman knew that in making his recommendation he would have to balance the immediate and long-term resource needs and the goals of Marion. Although Kalo looked promising from the forecasts, there were many uncertainties surrounding these subsidiaries' futures that had to be considered.

Exhibit 11.14 Marion Laboratories Inc. Ten-Year Financial Summary

(Dollar Amounts in Thousands Except per Share Data)
Years Ended June 30

		1978	1977	1976	1975	1974	1973	1972	1971	1970	1969
Sales:	Net sales	$117,378	$100,131	$80,838	$84,096	$71,778	$57,937	$49,066	$41,692	$35,322	$30,188
	Cost of sales	43,177	37,330	29,315	26,078	21,715	18,171	14,932	12,262	10,622	8,985
	Gross profit	74,201	62,801	51,523	58,018	50,063	39,766	34,134	29,430	24,700	21,203
	Operating expenses	51,718	43,397	37,292	31,699	26,991	21,155	19,164	17,181	13,828	12,453
	Operating income	22,483	19,404	14,231	26,319	23,072	18,611	14,970	12,249	10,872	8,750
	Other income	1,581	1,194	683	1,404	1,033	722	709	599	630	328
	Interest expense	1,546	1,542	898	97	83	109	116	88	198	260
Earnings:	Earnings from continuing operations before income taxes	22,518	19,056	14,016	27,626	24,022	19,224	15,563	12,760	11,304	8,818
	Income taxes	10,804	8,404	5,628	13,295	11,791	9,297	7,730	6,364	5,899	4,493
	Earnings from continuing operations	11,714	10,652	8,388	14,331	12,231	9,927	7,833	6,396	5,405	4,325
	Earnings (loss) from discontinued operations	—	—	—	(3,617)	(120)	76	488	—	—	—
	Net earnings	$ 11,714	$ 10,652	$ 8,388	$10,714	$12,111	$10,003	$ 8,321	$ 6,396*	$ 5,405	$ 4,325
Common share data:	Earnings (loss) per common and common-equivalent share:										
	Continuing operations	$ 1.38	$ 1.23	$ .96	$ 1.65	$ 1.40	$ 1.14	$ .90	$ .76	$ .65	$ .52
	Discontinued operations	—	—	—	(.42)	(.01)	.01	.06	—	—	—
	Net earnings	$ 1.38	$ 1.23	$ .96	$ 1.23	$ 1.39	$ 1.15	$ .96	$ .76*	$ .65	$ .52
	Cash dividends per common share	$ .59	$ .53	$ .52	$ .48	$ .28	$ .21	$ .20	$ .16	$ .12	$ .12
	Stockholders' equity per common and common-equivalent share	$ 7.87	$ 7.09	$ 6.63	$ 6.29	$ 5.52	$ 4.16	$ 3.16	$ 2.52	$ 2.01	$ 1.47
	Weighted average number of outstanding common and common share equivalents	8,475	8,640	8,707	8,708	8,689	8,715	8,651	8,396	8,377	8,354

*Before extraordinary charge of $916,000, equal to $.11 per common share resulting from the disposition of investment in affiliated companies.

Source: 1978 Annual Report.

Since Marion had no new drug products ready to be introduced soon, the company would have to rely on other areas of the company to reach its growth goals. Kalo was growing, but it was also requiring a constant input of funds from its parent.

One possibility for growth was to purchase another drug manufacturer and add its products to Marion's taking advantage of any distribution synergies that might exist. To make such a purchase, the company would need more resources. To sell a subsidiary could provide needed resources, but to do so quickly under less-than-optimum conditions would surely result in a significantly lower price than could be realized under normal conditions. The income and cash-flow impact of this approach would be undesirable.

With the board meeting so soon, Mr. Herman was faced with analyzing the complex situation quickly. In three days he would have to make his recommendation to the Board of Directors.

Hewko Supply, Inc.

▪ *Pamela R. Buckles and Juan Carlos Torrealba* ▪

On March 20, 1981, Hewko Supply Company released the following bulletin: "Hewko Supply, Inc. announces that its Board of Directors has approved an amendment to the previously announced merger agreement with the Richfield Company of New Orleans, Louisiana. There are 29,340 Richfield shares outstanding which have been valued at $156 per share and the value of the purchase transaction will be approximately $4,580,000.

"The agreement gives Richfield shareholders the choice of receiving cash and notes or Hewko stock in exchange for their shares, but in no instance would less than 30% nor more than 45% of the transaction be for cash and notes. For those shareholders who choose to receive Hewko stock, the exchange ratio of Hewko shares to Richfield shares will vary between 10.4 to 1; to 6.5 to 1 depending on the price of Hewko common stock prior to the date of consummation.

"Examples of the transaction, assuming 30% of Richfield shareholders choose cash and notes, would be as follows:

HEWK at $21 per share	
Cash and notes	$1,399,000
Additional HEWK shares	152,000
HEWK at $18 per share	
Cash and notes	$1,399,000
Additional HEWK shares	177,000
HEWK at $24 per share	
Cash and notes	$1,399,000
Additional HEWK shares	133,000

It is anticipated that the transaction, which must be approved by Richfield shareholders, will be consummated by the end of May."

The original announcement of the merger released December 1, 1980, concluded: "The results of the proposed merger will be that Richfield Company will survive as a wholly-owned subsidiary of Hewko. The proposed merger is subject to the execution of a definitive agreement and approval thereof by the Boards of Directors of Hewko and Richfield; approval by the shareholders of Richfield; receipt of satisfactory opinions that the exchange will be tax-free; and to the satisfaction of certain other approvals and conditions."

The Company

Hewko Supply Company is a wholesale distributor of electrical fixtures and supplies; plumbing, water heaters, waterwork and industrial fixtures and supplies; electrical utility

---

supplies; construction materials and contractors tools and mobile home supplies for building and mechanical trades.

Hewko operates 22 sales branches in 20 Texas cities and 3 supporting manufacturing operations of Southwestern Lighting Manufacturing Company, a wholly-owned subsidiary. Hewko purchases 92 percent of its products sold from other manufacturers and suppliers. Although industry statistics are not available, Hewko believes they are ranked among the five largest suppliers in the field operating within its marketing area.

Hewko began as a family-run proprietorship. The family continues to play an active role in the management of the company with five out of eight members of the Board of Directors belonging to the Hewko family.

History

Company origins date as far back as 1921 when Clarence Hewko, along with his son Russell, formed an electrical contracting firm, Hewko & Son, that operated successfully in Dallas, Texas, until 1928. Because of the difficulty of obtaining supplies for their operation, Hewko & Son decided to enter the electrical supply business in 1928. Russell was joined by his brother Harry in 1928; together they managed the firm through the depression years and eventually grew large enough to open their first out-of-town branch in Ft. Worth, Texas. Since most of Hewko's competitors in Ft. Worth handled plumbing as well as electrical supplies, the brothers decided to expand their product line into the plumbing area in Dallas as well as Ft. Worth. The name of the firm was changed to Hewko Supply and additional branches were opened throughout the state of Texas in the 1950s and 1960s.

In 1970, Hewko Supply went public, a move that was prompted by estate planning needs, the need for additional capital for growth, and as a means to reduce a third-party outside ownership by Simpson Wire and Cable Company.

The early 1970s were marked by strong residential and commercial building starts in the Central Texas area. Sales reached $45 million in 1970 the same year that David Hewko, Harry's son, joined the firm after completing a law degree from the University of Texas. In 1972 David assumed the presidency from his father.

1975–1976 marked a recession in the housing market despite the strong showing of the oil companies, and Hewko sales fell to $72 million. The company survived the recession by cutting inventories and reducing employees from 1,125 in 1975 to 750 employees in 1976. From 1976 until the present the firm has enjoyed consistent growth; sales amounted to $176.1 million in fiscal year ending January 31, 1981. (See Exhibit 12.1.)

Management Philosophy

The two most important management philosophies are the idea of service to the customer and promotion from within for all employees. Specifically, "You can't do business out of an empty wagon," reflects Hewko's basic idea that service to customers begins with a full and complete inventory. David considers the supply business a "people business" and attributes Hewko's success to the ability of the employees to provide service through the availability and prompt delivery of products at a fair price. Diversification over the years can be attributed to meeting the needs of their customers as well as providing an opportunity for individual employees' growth within the company. Commitment to employees is

Exhibit 12.1   Financial Information by Segments (in thousands)

	Year ended January 30, 1981	Year ended January 25, 1980	Year ended January 26, 1979	Year ended January 27, 1978	Year ended January 28, 1977
Sales and operating profit					
Sales to unaffiliated customers:					
Wholesale division	$169,928	$145,352	$124,614	$ 98,891	$78,128
Manufacturing division	6,194	6,622	3,743	2,850	2,352
Total sales to unaffiliated customers	$176,122	$151,974	$128,357	$101,741	$80,480
Intersegment sales:					
Wholesale division	$ 31	$ 26	$ 25	$ 63	$ 87
Manufacturing division	4,088	4,428	4,158	4,321	3,228
	$ 4,119	$ 4,454	$ 4,183	$ 4,384	$ 3,315
Total sales:					
Wholesale division	$169,959	$145,378	$124,639	$ 98,954	$78,215
Manufacturing division	10,282	11,050	7,901	7,171	5,580
Subtotal	180,241	156,428	132,540	106,125	83,795
Eliminations	(4,119)	(4,454)	(4,183)	(4,384)	(3,315)
Total sales	$176,122	$151,974	$128,357	$101,741	$80,480
Operating profit:					
Wholesale division	$ 10,880	$ 10,114	$ 7,466	$ 4,787	$ 2,977
Manufacturing division	776	1,179	696	84	96
Eliminations	95	(73)	(12)	(20)	(8)
Total operating profit	11,751	11,220	8,150	4,851	3,065
Interest income (expense), net	288	106	(133)	(256)	(218)
Income before taxes on income	$ 12,039	$ 11,326	$ 8,017	$ 4,595	$ 2,847
Asset information at year end					
Identifiable assets:					
Wholesale division	$ 61,580	$ 54,201	$ 45,936	$ 35,556	$32,070
Manufacturing division	4,239	3,298	3,997	2,970	2,817
Corporate	15,635	6,287	6,376	8,912	8,817
Eliminations	(123)	(59)	(103)	(112)	(70)
Total assets	$ 81,331	$ 63,727	$ 56,206	$ 47,326	$43,634
Sales by Product Group (in thousands)					
Electrical fixtures and supplies	$ 74,394	$ 60,966	$ 52,867	$ 43,268	$38,250
Plumbing, water heaters, industrial fixtures and supplies	71,239	63,729	51,400	40,156	28,453
Electric utility supplies	17,594	16,463	14,872	12,562	9,830
Construction materials and contractors' tools	12,942	11,104	9,542	5,905	3,969
Mobile home supplies	1,959	1,414	1,016	860	743
Total gross sales	178,128	153,676	129,697	102,751	81,245
Less cash discounts	2,006	1,702	1,340	1,010	765
Total net sales	$176,122	$151,974	$128,357	$101,741	$80,480

reflected in the following statement by R. V. Hewko, Vice-President of Cost Control: "Our people made Hewko different from our competitors. This is our main advantage."

Promotion from within is an extremely important part of management philosophy and has been strictly adhered to throughout Hewko history. The "President's Message" appearing in the March 1, 1981, issue of *Hewko News*, the company newsletter, indicates that the average age of branch managers is 42 with an average of 17 years of service, and the 12 members of the executive management group average 45 years of age and 21 years of service. The majority of employees are not college graduates and according to David, "In four years it takes to get through (college) we can teach them (employees) more about our business than they can get in school." The internal growth philosophy is not only strongly supported by management, but is also heavily endorsed by employees.

Their management philosophy toward customers and employees is reflected in the organizational structure. The 22 branch stores are autonomous units; each manager is responsible for the total operation in his store. The central purchasing warehouse literally "sells" its inventory to branches passing on low purchasing costs due to volume orders to the branch store.

Diversification and growth strategies have been geared to providing more service to customers. Where needed, manufacturing divisions have developed. Southwestern Lighting Company was acquired to provide high-quality fluorescent lights; PVC manufacturing was begun at a time when PVC pipes were difficult to obtain, and prestressed concrete poles were manufactured to meet the needs of utility customers.

Finally, efforts to acquire Richfield Company is viewed from a management perspective as a geographic as well as product diversification attempt. Hewko policy towards acquisitions restricted investment consideration to similar-type businesses that will provide either vertical or horizontal growth. In addition, similar management philosophy is an important consideration in assessing an acquisition as well as location. By entering the Louisiana market, Hewko can obtain a larger customer base and possibly increase its product line to include air conditioning—a line currently carried by Richfield Company.

Industry and Economic Forecast

The building supply industry is heavily dependent on economic conditions since sales are directly related to housing starts. Although housing starts hit a low of under a million units in 1980, the January 1981 *Fortune* "Business Roundup" indicates that by "spring (the housing industry) will be on a smoother track toward a 1.75 million rate in mid-1982." *Fortune* has identified a strong underlying demand for shelter; this factor along with a mounting shortfall in housing since 1978 should add substantially to the coming economic recovery. The April 20, 1981, *Fortune* "Forecast" updated its earlier forecast to include the influence of continuing high mortgage rates. *Fortune* feels that housing starts aren't likely to fall as far as they did in 1980 because of high interest rates, but that they aren't likely to explode either—although mortgage rates will decline, they will do so grudgingly. In summation, *Fortune* projected that it will be a couple of years before housing starts regain the million-a-year pace that they feel is needed.

Perhaps more important to Hewko however, is the impact of housing starts relative to their geographic location. According to the *U.S. Industrial Outlook 1980*, "one mainstay of the new housing demand making for the early recovery of starts is the population shift to the Sun Belt. These areas cater to a growing number of elderly and retired households, who are attracted to condominium living within so-called adult communities. More basic is a high rate of household formation expected through the mid 1980s. These factors assume a relatively strong housing market over the next few years." The industry survey also cites high rate of household formation, a tendency to view home ownership as the best-available hedge against inflation, a growing number of two-income families, and a rapid increase of owner's equity in older homes as occurrences that have helped keep new homes affordable and have helped offset the impact of extremely high interest rates and steeply rising prices.

The commercial construction area has enjoyed strong growth throughout 1979–1980 and is projected to continue. According to the *U.S. Industrial Outlook 1980*, "over the 5-year period, the construction mix will be greatly influenced by energy requirements and constraints. This means that industrial as well as public utilities construction will be encouraged to expand and improve the energy distribution system and provide new industrial plants that are more energy efficient, productive and cost competitive in both domestic and foreign markets."

Hewko's construction supply sales are directly affected by housing and commercial construction discussed above. Hewko electric and plumbing lines are also directly affected by housing starts but are also impacted by styling trends, the development of water and energy-saving technology, and the use of plastics in fixtures and fittings. The continuing trend toward more bathrooms per new housing unit is beneficial to plumbing supply distributors. This trend will also influence the nature of the future replacement market.

In the electrical lighting supply area, new residential and commercial construction starts greatly influence the future market; in addition, the "worldwide emphasis on energy conservation dictates a continued examination of the efficiency of the lighting industry. From the standpoint of energy construction, the highly efficient high-intensity discharge luminaries look promising." The *U.S. Industrial Outlook 1980* continues "the value of shipments of the lighting fixture industry should increase by a compound annual rate of 9.5% from 1979 to 1984. In real terms shipments are expected to advance approximately 2.5% per year. This estimate is based on 2 to 2.5% growth of new construction expenditures during the 5 year period."

As is indicated by industry projections, sales in construction plumbing and electrical equipment products have been consistently strong in Texas—a reflection of the growth of the state and the Sunbelt in general. Although residential housing starts were down 3 percent in 1980, Hewko sales revenues have continued to grow because of strong commercial and industrial construction starts. Hewko's core group has consistently been in plumbing and electrical sales. With the opening of a new branch for construction materials division in Dallas, Hewko is featuring a complete line of building materials for the general contractor. According to David, this store will serve as a prototype for similar stores to be opened in the future.

In summary, Hewko Supply is in an extremely volatile industry; however, they feel their geographic location is a prime safeguard against risk within the industry. The firm has great faith in the continued growth in Texas and throughout the Sunbelt.

Marketing

Customers and Sales Force

Customers currently number over 8,000 with approximately 3,500 forming a core group. General contractors constitute 4 percent of the total customer base; 80 percent are subcontractors and 16 percent are utilities. No single customer accounts for more than 3 percent of total sales volume. In order to track new business both in customers and construction starts, the company relies on the close association of their sales force with their customers and a publication called the *Dodge Report* and the *Dodge Scan* (microfiche) that lists all specifications for every job currently under construction in a specific area.

Ninety-five outside and 210 inside salespeople service the needs of customers. According to John Oldham, Vice-President of Marketing, the salesperson "is the company to the customers." Accordingly, Hewko places great emphasis on its sales force; outside salespeople are responsible for bringing their "expertise in products, new code requirements, money saving practices in the use of new or adaptations of old materials (to their customers)." A salesperson represents either plumbing, electrical, or construction supplies, but not all three product lines. Dan Clemenza, an outside electrical salesman, estimates that he writes an average of 50 percent–75 percent of his 13 clients total electrical supply orders. Dan feels his competitive advantage over firms such as Graybar, GE, and Raybro is his product knowledge; the quality of inside salespeople actually writing the orders from his sales calls; the large inventory that it has to offer; their shipping and delivery facilities; and the pricing freedom he is allowed to use. Dan indicates that his customers buy on price and service. His biggest problems in the sales area are maintaining high profit levels, inventory limitations, and errors due to high personnel turnover in the shipping and delivery departments. Sales goals are set by management based on past history. Outside salespeople are paid a salary plus escalating commission. An annual award for top salespeople is a week trip with their spouses to a vacation spot chosen by the spouse. In 1981, top performers and their spouses were flown to Munich, Germany. Hewko feels it is necessary to involve spouses in the sales promotion because of the demands and strains placed upon the marriage by the nature of the sales job (i.e., long hours, customer entertaining, etc.). In addition, management feels that spouses are one of the best motivators for a salesperson in improving performance. The average outside sales representative in the building supply industry sells $368,000 annually; Hewko outside salespeople average $1,500,000 annually.

Inside salespeople are the actual point-of-sale representatives. These salespeople work on salary plus an "incentive" commission based upon gross profit of operations. A percent of gross profit for the month is assigned to a pool of funds to be distributed to salespeople according to their competitive rank within the branch sales force. Because of the incentive plan, Hewko may pay two commissions (inside and outside sales for one sale).

The completion of a customer order involves the following sequence of events:

1. Sale originates from an outside or inside salesperson.
2. Invoice is written.
3. Account and invoice are approved for credit by the cashier.
4. Order is pulled from stock.
5. Order is checked against the ticket and checked for product condition.
6. Order is loaded onto the delivery truck.
7. Order is delivered to customer.
8. Customer signs for receipt.
9. Invoice is processed through the manual inventory control system.
10. Invoice is costed, priced, and entered at the terminal.
11. Data processing invoice is generated and mailed to customer.

Product Line

Major product groups can be broken down as follows:

1. **Electrical supplies** (such as wire, cable, cords, boxes, covers, wiring devices, conduit, raceway duct, safety switches, motor controls, breakers, panel, fuses, and related supplies and accessories), electrical fixtures (such as residential, commercial and industrial fixtures, and other special-use fixtures);

2. **Plumbing fixtures** (such as lavatories, bathtubs, toilets, shower stalls, sinks, urinals and related fittings, and hardware) and supplies (such as galvanized steel, plastic and cast iron, pipe and copper tubing, and related fittings); water heaters (residential, commercial, and industrial); related plumbing accessories and supplies (such as valves, pumps, tanks, and softeners); and cast-iron pipe, fire hydrants, water meters, valves and related hardware, and accessories.

3. **Electrical utility supplies** (such as transformers, conductor cable, insulators, prestressed concrete transmission and distribution poles) and related hardware, accessories and tools.

4. **Construction materials** (such as reinforcing wire, reinforcing bars, plyform, expansion joint, lumber, masonry, and other products); and tools (such as carpenters', plumbers', and electricians' tools, and other tools and equipment for the mechanical and building trades).

5. **Mobile home fixtures and supplies** including certain plumbing and electrical fixtures designed to meet the size and other specification requirements of modular and mobile homes.

There has been no significant change in the products distributed or services rendered during the last five fiscal years. Exhibit 12.1 indicates the distribution of total dollar sales among each of the five general classes of products listed.

The average-size sales branch carries a product line of approximately 9,000 items. Most additions to product lines are the result of customers' suggestions to salespeople, although infrequently new items are carried as a result of construction code changes. Manufacturers often request that Hewko carry new lines but it generally carries less than 5 percent of what manufacturers solicit. In dealing with manufacturers Hewko will attempt to secure the right of exclusive representation. According to John Oldham, their salespeople let the competition "sell the new product and then they move in for the order." Dan Clemenza indicates that the only instance where they are restricted from adding a new product is when a manufacturer desires national distribution from a distributor which it cannot offer.

The decision to drop a product is rare; it can stem from a change in construction codes or from slowdown in sales. Inventory is conducted twice a year and once a year the inventory is used to determine and discontinue slow-moving products.

Pricing

Hewko has a set pricing range for sales from stock and direct shipments from manufacturers. The guidelines allow for third-degree price discrimination between branches; that is, an identical item may sell for $3 to $5 more in the Port City branch than in the Dallas branch. Since there are very few leaks from the separate target markets, and the markets are easily divisible, this has worked relatively successfully.

The sales force is given latitude in quoting prices or submitting bids. When a sales representative goes over or under pricing guidelines, the branch manager must give final approval.

Promotion

The promotion mix includes advertising, trade show participation, the publication of an annual catalog, customer entertainment, and a "unique return policy." The advertising schedule includes display ads in all trade journals, outside display billboards, and cooperative (with manufacturers) advertising on radio and TV. Hewko participates in approximately 15 trade shows a year and offers substantial door prizes at conventions and related customer meetings. John Oldham regards Hewko's return policy as a form of advertising since it is unique and is generally regarded by competitors as the "scourge of the industry." The policy specifically allows customers to return unused and resalable merchandise with 10 percent return charge. In essence Hewko returns 90 percent of the purchase price for returned goods including especially built materials. John Oldham considers the expense incurred as a result of this policy as a portion of his advertising budget.

Another customer promotion that they have attempted in the past but found unsuccessful is giving customer premiums or gifts. Customers were generally found to be nonreceptive to such techniques although they are adamant supporters of the sales force's internal promotional programs discussed earlier.

Distribution

Hewko has its own fleet of delivery trucks that deliver from either the central warehouse or a branch to a customer's job site. Hewko's 22 branches are strategically located throughout Texas to ensure maximum efficiency in sales and distribution.

Interview with a Hewko Customer

An interview with a Hewko customer of 20 years began with the following statement by the customer: "(We) used to have a standing order in our organization, just buy from Hewko—that's changed today, we don't have that edict any longer."

The customer continued stating that his dealings with Hewko construction division in the 1960s consisted of an extremely workable and amiable relationship; however with the growth of Hewko in the 1970s and 1980s, the personal service the company had offered earlier disappeared. The customer felt that the salespeople had evolved into "glorified order takers" and "if they go beyond order taking all they do is hand you a brochure and that's it." The customer felt that the new personnel at Hewko were its major weakness—their lack of expertise, ineptness, and failure to meet the customers' needs. The two major complaints from the customer's superintendents ordering from Hewko were that they were usually out of products, and that if they did have it, the superintendent was left waiting on his order for three days. In many instances up to three inquiry telephone calls were necessary to receive an order. The customer continued: "I've had enough complaints from superintendents that I've said look, you don't have to buy from Hewko anymore, order from Kelly Lumber, Walton Supply, wherever you can get it at a reasonable price . . ." The customer indicated that his company growth has been substantial over the past 20 years but the percentage of his business conducted with Hewko has grown in an inverse proportion to a very insignificant level.

When asked how the salesperson responded to this occurrence, the customer indicated that he did not talk to the salesperson, due primarily to bad feelings resulting from an error that was indirectly related to a bid given by Hewko.

Another problem area for the customer with Hewko was in their billing. It took four telephone calls before the customer was able to resolve a billing problem that was a result of an error by Hewko. When asked how Hewko could improve their relationship with their customers, the customer indicated (1) service to the job and (2) if they are out of an item, let the customer know.

The customer summarized his dealings and attitude toward Hewko in the following statement:

"They are shortsighted, they have lived off this tremendous boom in Texas industry and the contractors are so desperate to get these materials they don't care . . . and they have good prices, no doubt about it, they are hard to beat as far as their pricing is concerned . . . that's the only thing that's kept them going—the big boom and their pricing, and when one of those two things fall out of bed they're going to have some big problems. If they don't get some management and make some investment in personnel then they better be prepared to sell out if a good price comes along because I don't think ten years from now, they're going to exist."

Personnel

The central office maintains all personnel records for branch offices although hiring is a function of the branches only. Jim Clarkson as director of personnel prepares all EEOC reports and records, develops orientation and training programs, and updates the employee handbook.

When asked about the success of the promotion-from-within policy strongly advocated by management, Jim's response was "I think that the record speaks for itself." The promotion-from-within career path for an employee is as follows:

1. Hired as a stock clerk on the desk.
2. Driver.
3. Inside stock assignment.
4. Electric or plumbing counter sales.
5. Inside sales.
6. Purchasing agent or outside sales.
7. Top management.

Hewko does not hire in sales or management positions from outside the firm except in specific instances such as an engineering sales position or as in the case of the Controller and Finance Officer, Victor Mendelson. Clarkson indicated that Hewko has no problem generating enough applicants but does have a problem finding quality people who are willing to start at the bottom and work up. When R. V. Hewko was asked what kind of effort was being made to attract good people at the bottom level, his response was "Nothing. We hire whoever comes to us." When questioned further about the promotion ladder, he indicated "Time puts the people where they should be. The best education for our people (is to) start at the back door."

Hewko has a formal training program for branch employees that is given in one-week sessions in the Dallas office. The program involves extensive product training in the plumbing and electrical area. The purpose of the program is to prepare employees for sales or management positions. Hewko had a tuition remission program but discontinued it because of lack of employee use and the fact that employees that did use the plan did not stay with the company.

There is no formal salary structure. Everyone is hired at an entry level position at a standard overall starting wage for the wholesale industry, $3.50/hour. Raises from this point are based strictly on merit—that is performance, attitude, and ability. Ninety-nine percent of all promotions are accompanied by salary increases. A formal salary structure is avoided because it has an "odor of unionism" according to Jim Clarkson.

In a similar vein, there are no formal job descriptions given to the employees—instruction is by word of mouth. Written job descriptions are kept on file at the central office. Performance appraisals are conducted once a year (see Exhibit 12.2) and are kept on file at the central office.

Hewko's orientation program includes an audiovisual slide presentation detailing the history of the company, major medical and life insurance policies, and the profit-sharing and ESOP plans. Part of Jim Clarkson's goals for the personnel office is to push the orientation program for new employees, to make employees aware of their benefit package, and to place more emphasis on the needs of Hewko people. A group automobile insurance policy is currently being considered to increase the employee benefit package.

Because of the bottom-up prerequisite at Hewko, most new employees are in the 18–20-year age bracket. Most people that come in and terminate do so within 2.5 to 3 years. The turnover rate for entry-level positions is 60 percent compared to an industry average of 80 percent.

The latest report to the Equal Employment Opportunity Commission (EEOC) is shown in Exhibit 12.3.

Profit Sharing and ESOP

The profit-sharing plan is available to employees with six months of service to the company prior to January 31 and who have attained the age of 18. The program is funded by the company and is designed to act as a retirement fund for employees. A committee of elected representatives of the firm make the investment decision although the fund is administered by the First National Bank. A diagram indicating the breakdown of investments is attached (see Exhibit 12.4). In regard to the 119,112 shares of Hewko stock in the profit-sharing portfolio, Stewart Halldorson, Vice-President of Credit and Director of Employee Relations, commented at the March 31, 1981, Employee Benefits Annual Meeting:

I think one of the things that we will be looking at over the course of the next couple of years is reducing our exposure in the Hewko stock. But, when we all set out in the program a number of years ago we felt like we needed that stock in there for a number of reasons, and we were aggressive about buying it over a period of a couple years. But we have at this point discontinued any further buying of our own stock particularly with the ESOP now being available. We'll be looking to the next few years for reducing our position in the Hewko stock.

Exhibit 12.2   Employee Job Performance Evaluation

EMPLOYEE JOB PERFORMANCE EVALUATION

NAME _____ BRANCH _____ DATE _____

JOB TITLE _____ HIRE DATE _____ DAYS ABSENT SINCE _____

PRESENT WAGE _____ DATE OF LAST INCREASE _____

INSTRUCTIONS: PLEASE COMPLETE THIS EVALUATION BY CHECKING THE BOX WHICH YOU FEEL BEST DESCRIBES YOUR RATING OF THE EMPLOYEES JOB PERFORMANCE.

PLEASE DISCUSS THIS EVALUATION WITH YOUR EMPLOYEE.

FACTOR	CHECK ONE	ADDITIONAL COMMENTS
1. QUALITY OF WORK How do you rate employees performance in meeting your quality standards.	☐ UNSATISFACTORY ☐ MARGINAL ☐ GOOD ☐ VERY GOOD ☐ EXCEPTIONAL	
2. QUANTITY OF WORK What is your opinion of employees quantity of satisfactory work.	☐ UNSATISFACTORY ☐ MARGINAL ☐ GOOD ☐ VERY GOOD ☐ EXCEPTIONAL	
3. INITIATIVE To what extent do you consider the employee uses initiative in job performance.	☐ UNSATISFACTORY ☐ MARGINAL ☐ GOOD ☐ VERY GOOD ☐ EXCEPTIONAL	
4. COOPERATION How do you rate employees courtesy and attitude toward fellow employees and supervisor.	☐ UNSATISFACTORY ☐ MARGINAL ☐ GOOD ☐ VERY GOOD ☐ EXCEPTIONAL	
5. DEPENDABILITY How do you rate the employees reliability to perform without constant supervision.	☐ UNSATISFACTORY ☐ MARGINAL ☐ GOOD ☐ VERY GOOD ☐ EXCEPTIONAL	
6. ATTENDANCE & PUNCTUALITY Consider number of absences and late arrivals.	☐ UNSATISFACTORY ☐ MARGINAL ☐ GOOD ☐ VERY GOOD ☐ EXCEPTIONAL	
7. Does employee have potential of developing into supervisory or management position in the future.	☐ YES ☐ NO ☐ MAYBE	

OVERALL JOB PERFORMANCE
☐ BELOW AVERAGE   ☐ AVERAGE   ☐ ABOVE AVERAGE   ☐ OUTSTANDING

_____
SIGNATURE—RATING SUPERVISOR

_____
DATE OF RATING

Exhibit 12.3   Report to the EEOC

Class	Black Female	Black Male	Hispanic Female	Hispanic Male	White Female	White Male	Total	Others
Managers	0	7	0	0	23	155	185	
Professional	0	0	0	0	0	10	10	
Technical	0	1	0	0	0	4	5	
Sales	0	5	0	3	16	226	251	
Office and Clerical	4	0	1	2	195	21	223	1
Crafts	0	11	0	2	1	42	56	
Operators	0	31	0	7	5	229	272	
Laborers	0	5	0	0	1	18	24	
Service	1	2	0	0	0	5	8	
Total	5	62	1	14	241	710	1,034	

The ESOP plan initiated in 1980 was announced at the meeting; 45,000 shares of Hewko stock were invested by the company to assure a sound start for the plan—as a result there was no contribution to profit sharing in 1980. A comment was raised in regard to the eligibility requirements for ESOP that an employee must be 23 years of age and have 30 months of service. Since 22 employees were eligible for profit sharing but were not eligible for ESOP, these employees did not receive any contributions for 1980. Stewart Halldorson responded to them indicating that the age and service eligibility requirements were instituted to make the benefit package progressive and "reward people who have made a commitment to Hewko." The ESOP plan is fully (100 percent) vested at time of distribution.

Accounting and Finance

Credit

Credit is an extremely important area for Hewko Supply because it enables them to do business with 98 percent of their customers. Credit policy (10th prox) is standard for all customers regardless of size—10th prox meaning that payment for merchandise purchased in one month is due the 10th of the following month. If manufacturers allow Hewko a 2 percent cash discount, the discount is passed on to customers.

About 80 percent of the accounts are current. The credit goal is to keep 95 percent of all accounts current or within 30 days past due at every branch. Bad debt in 1980 amounted to $487,000 which represents approximately ¼ of 1 percent (.0027). The average for the last five years was about ²/₁₀ of one percent.

Qualifying criteria for a new customer account includes a credit application, trade references, bank references, and the requirement that the account be personally guaranteed by the customer. Hewko will also consult Dunn & Bradstreet and the NACM (National Association of Credit Managers) when reviewing an application for credit.

All collection work is performed within the firm unless Hewko chooses to take a customer to court. No outside collection agency is used. Finally, a historically tight credit policy is expected to remain tight in the future; however Hewko intends to be flexible in

Exhibit 12.4   Account Structure January 31, 1981

	Amount	Percent of Total
Reserves	$ 344,334	8
Fixed income	653,407	15
Real estate	216,500	5
Common stocks		
Hewko Supply Inc.	2,710,025	63
Other	333,738	8
Accrued income	23,048	1
	$4,281,052	100

working out credit arrangements if periodically a customer should run into a tight cash-flow squeeze. Sales and credit work very closely at Hewko to help control the possibility of bad debts.

Financial Policies

The goal in cash management is to limit investment in securities such as commercial paper, treasury bills, certificates of deposit, all with a limit of under 360 days cash investment. Victor Mendelson also participates in bank repurchase agreements (almost on a daily basis) and depending on the rate structure, can overnight rewrite 30 or 60 days of paper.

Financial control over profit centers is maintained by individual profit statements for each branch location. Financial planning may not coincide exactly with profit performance—financial planning takes into consideration the overall performance of the branch. Review of profit and financial plans is done on a monthly basis.

Accounts payable are controlled centrally; daily sales reports indicate purchasing commitments. All accounting activities are centralized and computerized.

Long-term debt is restricted to up to 50 percent of stockholders' equity. Liquidity ratio is maintained at no less than 2.25:1 (in the wholesale business anything less than 2:1 indicates financial problems). The capital budget is divided into 60 percent maintenance and 40 percent expansion and amounts to about $5 million annually. Hewko uses a 15 percent cost of capital. When new projects are considered, the effect on EPS is determined as well as return on investment.

The dividend policy has been very conservative since its inception in 1977. According to Victor Mendelson, "We have a very conservative Board of Directors controlled by the Hewko family and they don't need dividends." Mendelson continues, "My own feeling is that we should be paying 20–25 percent of earnings in dividend to maintain stockholders' interest. If you study the market you will see that investors want a minimum return in addition to the growth aspect."

An outside source commented on the dividend policy: "For years, as far as I'm concerned, the existing management of Hewko Supply has run that company to the benefit of the management and the family and not to the benefit of the stockholders. Mainly, for years they refused to pay a dividend on the common stock, even a penny. Why? If I have a lease and I have that income coming in I have all the income I need, I don't want any more income, specially when this income will be taxed at the same rate."

The income referred to by the outside source is indicated on the balance sheet (Exhibit 12.5). The firm is currently leasing properties that are owned by the family.

Inventory

Inventory varies with the individual branches. Each branch has a purchasing agent who does the plumbing and electrical purchasing. Although each branch is autonomous, 30 percent of purchases for inventory are done through the central warehouse—a procedure that allows Hewko to take advantage of quantity discounts.

Hewko uses a manual ABC inventory system and has established a two to two and one-half-month-minimum reorder point.

Information Systems

The accounting function is now on computer. Sales invoices are entered at terminals and the information is used to create sales reports, inventory reports, and billing invoices. The inventory system as discussed earlier is not on computer. Bill Wise indicated that a computerized inventory system was attempted in 1958 but was discontinued in two months because of poor performance.

The overall management attitude with respect to computers can be summarized in R. V. Hewko's statement: "They're (computers) a necessary evil." When John Oldham was asked about an on-line system for the sales area, his response was "(An) order will never go on-line before it's shipped; we will never have that. It puts the computer between you and your customer." Vincent Hewko was even more adamant in regard to this issue. Vincent felt that computer systems in the sales area were not only ineffective but had contributed to the downfall of many of their competitors. The most favorable management attitude toward computerized sales/inventory came from Victor Mendelson: "I think com-

Exhibit 12.5   Consolidated Balance Sheets

	January 30, 1981	January 25, 1980
Assets		
Current assets:		
Cash	$ 437,130	$ 420,074
Short-term investments, at cost which approximates market value	15,362,695	6,056,057
Accounts receivable, less allowance for doubtful accounts of $437,065 in 1981 and $389,047 in 1980	18,993,335	16,973,098
Inventories, at lower of cost (first-in, first-out method) or market	32,861,333	27,711,105
Prepaid expenses	917,311	840,183
Total current assets	68,571,804	52,000,517
Property, plant, and equipment:		
Land	2,221,312	2,181,452
Buildings and improvements	3,584,498	2,547,867
Transportation equipment	6,221,689	5,419,919
Furniture, fixtures, and equipment	4,431,400	3,928,423
Total, at cost	16,458,899	14,077,661
Less accumulated depreciation	6,853,894	5,890,166
	9,605,005	8,187,495
Leased property under capital leases, less accumulated amortization	2,567,672	2,914,442
Net property, plant, and equipment	12,172,677	11,101,937
Other assets:		
Deferred income taxes	459,199	504,401
Other	127,159	120,221
Total other assets	586,358	624,622
Total assets	$81,330,839	$63,727,076

puterized inventory won't increase the profitability of the company. It will help to foresee where the company is going to be five to ten years down the line, and also it will help to handle the paperwork."

The Acquisition

The company's policy regarding acquisitions is based on the premise that they will only consider firms that meet the following criteria: the firm must be in the same or similar business; the management philosophy of the firm must be similar to Hewko's management philosophy and finally, the firm must be located in the Southwestern portion of the U.S. An acquisition must be either a vertical or horizontal investment. The firm must be in the wholesale construction supply area, since that is where their management expertise lies. In addition, they feel a geographical proximity is important so that they can maintain control. They also feel a Southern location guarantees growth in the future.

Exhibit 12.5   *continued*

	January 30, 1981	January 25, 1980
Liabilities and stockholders' equity		
Current liabilities:		
Current portion of long-term notes	$ 402,314	$ 932,831
Current portion of obligations under capital leases	176,239	200,219
Accounts payable	17,195,191	14,215,349
Income taxes	160,550	1,600,227
Accrued salaries and wages	1,682,516	1,512,811
Accrued employee-benefit-plan contributions		331,000
Other accrued expenses	2,389,468	1,330,704
Total current liabilities	22,006,278	20,123,141
Long-term debt:		
Long-term notes, less current portion	12,994,959	3,397,273
Obligations under capital leases, less current portion (Note 6)	3,284,949	3,608,708
Total long-term debt	16,279,908	7,005,981
Total liabilities	38,286,186	27,129,122
Stockholders' equity:		
Common stock, par value $1 per share—authorized 10,000,000 shares; issued 2,093,404 shares in 1981 and 2,351,508 shares in 1980 (including shares held in treasury)	2,093,404	2,351,508
Capital in excess of par value	4,700,105	5,188,852
Retained earnings	36,251,144	30,471,111
Common stock held in treasury, at cost—306,000 shares in 1980		(1,413,517)
Total stockholders' equity	43,044,653	36,597,954
Commitments and contingencies		
Total liabilities and stockholders' equity	$81,330,839	$63,727,076

The management team is convinced that the Richfield company meets the criteria established in their acquisition guidelines. Victor Mendelson feels the merger will provide financial strength for Richfield. That firm has expanded rapidly and as a result has heavy short-term debt and is paying high interest rates. Victor expects no less than 15 percent return on investment within the next two to three years.

Details of the merger were drawn up (see Exhibits 12.6–12.10) and the merger was announced to employees in the March 1, 1981, issue of *Hewko News* (Exhibit 12.7).

Exhibit 12.6   Consolidated Statements of Stockholders' Equity

	Common Stock Par Value $1 Per Share	Capital in Excess of Par Value	Retained Earnings	Common Stock Held in Treasury
Balance, January 27, 1978	$1,544,822	$4,969,227	$21,997,933	$(1,413,517)
Net income for the year			4,120,079	
Common stock sold under stock option plan	11,007	113,346		
Cash dividends–$.16 per share			(323,604)	
Balance, January 26, 1979	1,555,829	5,082,573	25,794,408	(1,413,517)
Net income for the year			5,942,006	
Common stock sold under stock option plan	14,122	106,279		
50% stock dividend at par value	781,557		(781,557)	
Cash dividends–$.22 per share			(450,746)	
Loss on common stock contributed to profit-sharing plan			(33,000)	
Balance, January 25, 1980	2,351,508	5,188,852	30,471,111	(1,413,517)
Net income for the year			6,405,273	
Common stock sold under stock option plan	17,896	93,770		
Common stock issued to employee stock-ownership plan	30,000	525,000	(6,072)	
Treasury stock retired	(306,000)	(1,107,517)		1,413,517
Cash dividends–$.30 per share			(619,168)	
Balance, January 30, 1981	$2,093,404	$4,700,105	$36,251,144	$

Exhibit 12.7   Comparative Per Share Data

The following table reflects the net income, dividends and book value per share of Hewko Supply Inc. and Richfield Company, and the pro forma equivalent per share amounts under two alternative sets of assumed conditions—those which would cause Hewko to issue the minimum number of shares of its common stock, and those which would cause Hewko to issue the maximum such shares. (These conditions are further described in the headnote under "Capitalization" included elsewhere in this proxy statement.) The pro forma information contained herein is derived from the pro forma combining statements of income and balance sheet appearing elsewhere in this proxy statement.

	Hewko Supply Inc.		Richfield Company	
	Year Ended January 25, 1980	Year Ended January 30, 1981	Year Ended December 31, 1979	Year Ended December 31, 1980
	(Per Share of Hewko)		(Per Share of Richfield)	
Historical:				
Net income	$2.92	$ 3.12	$ 9.74	$ 4.65
Dividends	.22	.30	—0—	—0—
Book value at end of period		20.56		113.18
Pro forma equivalent:				
Minimum Hewko stock issued:				
Net income	2.83	2.94	18.40	19.11
Dividends	.22	.30	1.43	1.95
Book value at end of period		20.70		134.55
Maximum Hewko stock issued:				
Net income	2.71	2.82	28.18	29.33
Dividends	.22	.30	2.29	3.12
Book value at end of period		20.03		208.31

Exhibit 12.8 Richfield Company Summary of Earnings

The following summary of earnings of Richfield Company, with respect to 1976, 1977, and 1978, have been derived from unaudited financial statements. In the opinion of management, all adjustments, consisting only of normal recurring accruals and those adjustments described below, necessary for a fair presentation have been included. The amounts for 1979 and 1980 were derived from financial statements which were examined by independent certified public accountants. The financial statements as of December 31, 1979, and 1980 and for each of the three years in the period ended December 31, 1980, and the report of the auditors on the 1979 and 1980 financial statements are included elsewhere in this proxy statement.

	Year Ended December 31, (in thousands except per share data)				
	1976	**1977**	**1978**	**1979**	**1980**
Net sales	$17,837	$20,623	$22,581	$23,993	$23,455
Cost of sales	14,010	16,243	17,292	18,418	18,131
Interest expense	104	117	174	247	430
Income taxes	126	186	259	219	88
Net income	160	246	321	280	136
Weighted average number of shares outstanding	28[a]	30[a]	29[a]	29	29
Per share data:					
Net income[b]	$5.77	$8.29	$11.11	$9.74	$4.65
Cash dividends	0	0	0	0	0
Book value at end of period[c]					113.18

[a] Restated for three-for-two stock split effected in the form of a 50% dividend on non-voting common stock, declared in 1979.

[b] Based on weighted average number of shares outstanding as restated for stock splits.

[c] Based on shares outstanding at the balance sheet date.

[d] Significant accounting policies are described in Note 1 of Notes to Financial Statements.

[e] Certain expenses previously charged to retained earnings have been reclassified in the above summary. The effect was to decrease previously reported net income by $1,285; $1,420 and $25,645 in 1977, 1978 and 1979, respectively. In addition, the years 1976 through 1979 have been restated to reflect revised inventory costing methods. The effect was to decrease previously reported net income by $4,000; $10,000; $15,000 and $23,000 in 1976, 1977, 1978 and 1979, respectively.

Exhibit 12.9   Pro Forma Combining Statements of Income–Continued (Unaudited)

	Year Ended January 30, 1981 (in thousands except per share data)					
	Historical			Pro Forma Combined		
	Hewko Supply, Inc.	Richfield Company (2)	Adjust-ments	Minimum Hewko Stock Issued	Adjust-ments	Maximum Hewko Stock Issued
Revenues:						
Net sales	$176,122	$23,455	$	$199,577	$	$199,577
Interest and other income	1,873	119	(126)[c]	1,866	40[c]	1,906
Total revenues	177,995	23,574		201,443		201,483
Costs and expenses:						
Cost of sales	140,857	18,131		158,988		158,988
Selling, general and administrative	23,830	4,741	47[a]	28,618		28,618
Interest	938	430	123[b]	1,491	(40)[b]	1,451
Provision for bad debts	331	47		378		378
Total costs and expenses	165,956	23,349		189,475		189,435
Income before income taxes	12,039	225		11,968		12,048
Income taxes	5,634	89	(102)[e]	5,621	39[e]	5,660
Net income	$ 6,405	$ 136		$ 6,347		$ 6,388
Weighted average number of shares outstanding	2,052	29		2,157		2,264
Per share data:						
Net income	$3.12	$4.65		$2.94		$2.82
Dividends	.30	0		.30		.30

(2) Represents Richfield data for the year ended December 31, 1980.

Adjustments:

[a] Additional depreciation on adjustments to cost of Richfield assets (straight-line, 25 years).

[b] Additional interest expense on Hewko's short-term notes issued.

[c] Reduced interest income on Hewko's short-term investments, due to cash distributed for Richfield shares.

[d] Transactions of Tom's Realty Company acquired by Richfield Company in 1979.

[e] Tax effects of interest income, interest expense, Tom's Realty Company adjustments, and elimination of surtax exemption.

Exhibit 12.10   Pro Forma Combining Balance Sheets (Condensed) (Unaudited)

The following pro forma combining balance sheet gives effect to the transaction contemplated in the Agreement and Plan of Merger between Hewko Supply Inc. and Richfield Company, under two alternative sets of assumed conditions—those which would cause Hewko to issue the minimum number of shares of its common stock, and those which would cause Hewko to issue the maximum number of such shares. (These conditions are further described in the headnote under "Capitalization" included elsewhere in this proxy statement.) The transaction is assumed to have occurred as of the balance sheet date, but costs have been assigned based on current estimated fair market values of Richfield's net assets. The statements should be read in conjunction with the other financial statements and related notes of Hewko and Richfield included elsewhere in this proxy statement.

	Year Ended January 30, 1981 (in thousands except per share data)					
	Historical			**Pro Forma Combined**		
	Hewko Supply, Inc.	Richfield Company*	Adjustments	Minimum Hewko Stock	Adjustments	Maximum Hewko Stock
Cash and short-term investments	$15,800	$ 185	$(1,030)[a] (50)[c]	$14,905	$ 331[a]	$15,236
Accounts receivable	18,993	1,866		20,859		20,859
Inventories	32,862	5,214		38,076		38,076
Other current assets	917	191		1,108		1,108
Total current assets	68,572	7,456		74,948		75,279
Land	2,221	280	67[d]	2,568		2,568
Buildings and improvements	3,585	1,424	365[d]	5,374		5,374
Property under capital leases	4,783	—		4,783		4,783
Other	10,653	521		11,174		11,174
Subtotal	21,242	2,225		23,899		23,899
Accumulated depreciation	9,069	822	(822)[d]	9,069		9,069
Net property, plant, and equipment	12,173	1,403		14,830		14,830
Other assets	586	18	2,060[a] 2,517[b] (4,577)[d]	604		604
Total assets	$81,331	$8,877		$90,382		$90,713
Current portion of long-term debt	$ 579	$ 434	$	$ 1,013	$	$ 1,013
Short-term notes payable	—	668	1,030[a]	1,698	(331)[a]	1,367
Accounts payable	17,195	2,331		19,526		19,526
Other current liabilities	4,233	322		4,555		4,555
Total current liabilities	22,007	3,755		26,792		26,461
Notes payable	12,995	1,799		14,794		14,794
Capital lease obligations	3,285	—		3,285		3,285
Total long-term debt	16,280	1,799		18,079		18,079

Exhibit 12.10   *continued*

	Historical			Pro Forma Combined		
	Hewko Supply, Inc.	Richfield Company*	Adjust-ments	Minimum Hewko Stock	Adjust-ments	Maximum Hewko Stock
Common stock	2,093	2,936	105[b] (2,936)[d]	2,198	107[b]	2,305
Capital in excess of par value	4,700	197	2,412[b] (50)[c] (197)[d]	7,062	555[b]	7,617
Retained earnings	36,251	190	(190)[d]	36,251		36,251
Total stockholders' equity	43,044	3,323		45,511		46,173
Total Liabilities and Stock-holders' Equity	$81,331	$8,877		$90,382		$90,713
Shares outstanding	2,093	29		2,198		2,305
Book value per share	$20.56	$113.18		$20.70		$20.03

Year Ended January 30, 1981 (in thousands except per share data)

*Represents Richfield data as of December 31, 1980

The Lincoln Electronic Company, 1984

Arthur Sharplin

The Lincoln Electric Company is the world's largest manufacturer of welding machines and electrodes. Lincoln employs 2,400 workers in two U.S. factories near Cleveland and approximately 600 in three factories located in other countries. This does not include the field sales force of more than 200 persons. It has been estimated that Lincoln's market share (for arc-welding equipment and supplies) is more than 40 percent.

The Lincoln incentive management plan has been well known for many years. Many college management texts make reference to the Lincoln plan as a model for achieving high worker productivity. Certainly, Lincoln has been a successful company according to the usual measures of success.

James F. Lincoln died in 1965, and there was some concern, even among employees, that the Lincoln system would fall into disarray, that profits would decline, and that year-end bonuses might be discontinued. Quite the contrary, 18 years after Lincoln's death, the company appears stronger than ever. Each year, except the recession years 1982 and 1983, has seen higher profits and bonuses. Employee morale and productivity remain high. Employee turnover is almost nonexistent except for retirements. Lincoln's market share is stable. Consistently high dividends continue on Lincoln's stock.

A Historical Sketch

In 1895, after being "frozen out" of the depression-ravaged Elliott-Lincoln Company, a maker of Lincoln-designed electric motors, John C. Lincoln took out his second patent and began to manufacture an improved motor. He opened a new business, unincorporated, with $200 he had earned redesigning a motor for young Herbert Henry Dow, who later founded the Dow Chemical Company.

Started during an economic depression and cursed by a major fire after only one year in business, Lincoln's company grew, but hardly prospered, through its first quarter-century. In 1906, John C. Lincoln incorporated his company and moved from his one-room fourth-floor factory to a new three-story building he erected in east Cleveland. In his new factory, he expanded his work force to 30, and sales grew to over $50,000 a year. John Lincoln preferred being an engineer and inventor rather than a manager, though, and it was to be left to another Lincoln to manage the company through its years of success.

In 1907, after a bout with typhoid fever forced him from Ohio State University in his senior year, James F. Lincoln, John's younger brother, joined the fledgling company. In 1914, he became the active head of the firm, with the titles of general manager and vice-president. John Lincoln, while he remained president of the company for some years, became more involved in other business ventures and in his work as an inventor.

One of James Lincoln's early actions as head of the firm was to ask the employees to

---

This case does not indicate effective or ineffective handling of an administrative situation. Rather it is to be used as the basis for classroom discussion.

elect representatives to a committee which would advise him on company operations. The advisory board has met with the chief executive officer twice monthly since that time. This was only the first of a series of innovative personnel policies which have, over the years, distinguished Lincoln Electric from its contemporaries.

The first year the advisory board was in existence, working hours were reduced from 55 per week, then standard, to 50 hours a week. In 1915, the company gave each employee a paid-up life insurance policy. A welding school, which continues today, was begun in 1917. In 1918, an employee bonus plan was attempted. It was not continued, but the idea was to resurface and become the backbone of the Lincoln management system.

The Lincoln Electric employees' association was formed in 1919 to provide health benefits and social activities. This organization continues today and has assumed several additional functions over the years. In 1923, a piecework pay system was in effect, employees got two-week paid vacations each year, and wages were adjusted for changes in the Consumer Price Index. Approximately 30 percent of Lincoln's stock was set aside for key employees in 1914, when James F. Lincoln became general manager, and a stock purchase plan for all employees was begun in 1925.

The Board of Directors voted to start a suggestion system in 1929. The program is still in effect, but cash awards, part of the early program, were discontinued several years ago. Now, suggestions are rewarded by additional "points," which affect year-end bonuses.

The legendary Lincoln bonus plan was proposed by the advisory board and accepted on a trial basis by James Lincoln in 1934. The first annual bonus amounted to about 25 percent of wages. There has been a bonus every year since then. The bonus plan has been a cornerstone of the Lincoln management system, and recent bonuses have approximated annual wages.

By 1944, Lincoln employees enjoyed a pension plan, a policy of promotion from within, and continuous employment. Base pay rates were determined by formal job evaluation and a merit rating system was in effect.

In the prologue of James F. Lincoln's last book, Charles G. Herbruck writes regarding the foregoing personnel innovations.

They were not to buy good behavior. They were not efforts to increase profits. They were not antidotes to labor difficulties. They did not constitute a "do-gooder" program. They were an expression of mutual respect for each person's importance to the job to be done. All of them reflect the leadership of James Lincoln, under whom they were nurtured and propagated.

By the start of World War II, Lincoln Electric was the world's largest manufacturer of arc-welding products. Sales of about $4 million in 1934 had grown to $24 million by 1941. Productivity per employee more than doubled during the same period.

During the war, Lincoln Electric prospered as never before. Despite challenges to Lincoln's profitability made by the Navy's Price Review Board and to the tax deductibility of employee bonuses by the Internal Revenue Service, the company increased its profits and paid huge bonuses.

Certainly since 1935, and probably for several years before that, Lincoln productivity had been well above the average for similar companies. Lincoln claims levels of productivity more than twice those of other manufacturers from 1945 onward. Information available from outside sources tends to support these claims.

Company Philosophy

James F. Lincoln was the son of a Congregational minister, and Christian principles were at the center of his business philosophy. The confidence that he had in the efficacy of Christ's teachings is illustrated by the following remark taken from one of his books:

The Christian ethic should control our acts. If it did control our acts, the savings in cost of distribution would be tremendous. Advertising would be a contact of the expert consultant with the customer, in order to give the customer the best product available when all of the customer's needs are considered. Competition then would be in improving the quality of products and increasing efficiency in producing and distributing them; not in deception, as is now too customary. Pricing would reflect efficiency of production; it would not be a selling dodge that the customer may well be sorry he accepted. It would be proper for all concerned and rewarding for the ability used in producing the product.[1]

There is no indication that Lincoln attempted to evangelize his employees or customers—or the general public for that matter. The current board chairman, William Irrgang, and the president, George E. Willis, do not even mention the Christian gospel in their recent speeches and interviews. The company motto, "The actual is limited, the possible is immense," is prominently displayed, but there is no display of religious slogans, and there is no company chapel.

Attitude toward the Customer

James Lincoln saw the customer's needs as the raison d'être for every company. "When any company has achieved success so that it is attractive as an investment," he wrote, "all money usually needed for expansion is supplied by the customer in retained earnings. It is obvious that the customer's interests, not the stockholder's, should come first."[2] In 1947 he said, "Care should be taken . . . not to rivet attention on profit. Between 'How much do I get?' and 'How do I make this better, cheaper, more useful?' the difference is fundamental and decisive."[3] Mr. Willis still ranks the customer as Lincoln's most important constituency. This is reflected in Lincoln's policy to "at all times price on the basis of cost and at all times keep pressure on our cost. . . ."[4] Lincoln's goal, often stated, is "to build a better and better product at a lower and lower price."[5] "It is obvious," James Lincoln said, "that the customer's interests should be the first goal of industry."[6]

Attitude toward Stockholders

Stockholders are given last priority at Lincoln. This is a continuation of James Lincoln's philosophy: "The last group to be considered is the stockholders who own stock because

---

[1] James F. Lincoln, *A New Approach to Industrial Economics* (New York: The Devin Adair Co., 1961), p. 64.
[2] Ibid., p. 119.
[3] "You Can't Tell What a Man Can Do—Until He Has the Chance," *Reader's Digest*, January 1947, p. 94.
[4] George E. Willis's letter to the author of September 7, 1978.
[5] LIncoln, *A New Approach*, p. 47.
[6] Ibid., p. 117.

they think it will be more profitable than investing money in any other way."[7] Concerning division of the largess produced by incentive management, Lincoln writes, "The absentee stockholder also will get his share, even if undeserved, out of the greatly increased profit that the efficiency produces."[8]

Attitude toward Unionism

There has never been a serious effort to organize Lincoln employees. While James Lincoln criticized the labor movement for "selfishly attempting to better its position at the expense of the people it must serve,"[9] he still had kind words for union members. He excused abuses of union power as "the natural reactions of human beings to the abuses to which management has subjected them."[10] Lincoln's idea of the correct relationship between workers and managers is shown by this comment: "Labor and management are properly not warring camps; they are parts of one organization in which they must and should co-operate fully and happily."[11]

Beliefs and Assumptions about Employees

If fulfilling customer needs is the desired goal of business, then employee performance and productivity are the means by which this goal can best be achieved. It is the Lincoln attitude toward employees, reflected in the following quotations, which is credited by many with creating the record of success the company has experienced:

The greatest fear of the worker, which is the same as the greatest fear of the industrialist in operating a company, is the lack of income. . . . The industrial manager is very conscious of his company's need of uninterrupted income. He is completely oblivious, evidently, of the fact that the worker has the same need.[12]

He is just as eager as any manager to be part of a team that is properly organized and working for the advancement of our economy. . . . He has no desire to make profits for those who do not hold up their end in production, as is true of absentee stockholders and inactive people in the company.[13]

If money is to be used as an incentive, the program must provide that what is paid to the worker is what he has earned. The earnings of each must be in accordance with accomplishment.[14]

Status is of great importance in all human relationships. The greatest incentive that

---

[7] Ibid., p. 38.
[8] Ibid., p. 122.
[9] Ibid., p. 18.
[10] Ibid., p. 76.
[11] Ibid., p. 72.
[12] Ibid., p. 36.
[13] Ibid., p. 75.
[14] Ibid., p. 98.

money has, usually, is that it is a symbol of success. . . . The resulting status is the real incentive. . . . Money alone can be an incentive to the miser only.[15]

There must be complete honesty and understanding between the hourly worker and management if high efficiency is to be obtained.[16]

Lincoln's Business

Arc-welding has been the standard joining method in the shipbuilding industry for decades. It is the predominant way of joining steel in the construction industry. Most industrial plants have their own welding shops for maintenance and construction. Manufacturers of tractors and all kinds of heavy equipment use arc-welding extensively in the manufacturing process. Many hobbyists have their own welding machines and use them for making metal items such as patio furniture and barbeque pits. The popularity of welded sculpture as an art form is growing.

While advances in welding technology have been frequent, arc-welding products, in the main, have hardly changed except for Lincoln's Innershield process. This process, utilizing a self-shielded, flux-cored electrode, has established new cost-saving opportunities for construction and equipment fabrication. The most popular Lincoln electrode, the Fleetweld 5P, has been virtually the same since the 1930s. The most popular engine-driven welder in the world, the Lincoln SA-200, has been a gray-colored assembly including a four-cylinder continental "Red Seal" engine and a 200-ampere direct-current generator with two current-control knobs for at least three decades. A 1980 model SA-200 even weighs almost the same as the 1950 model, and it certainly is little changed in appearance.

Lincoln and its competitors now market a wide range of general-purpose and specialty electrodes for welding mild steel, aluminum, cast iron, and stainless and special steels. Most of these electrodes are designed to meet the standards of the American Welding Society, a trade association. They are thus essentially the same in size and composition from one manufacturer to another. Every electrode manufacturer has a limited number of unique products, but these typically constitute only a small percentage of total sales.

Lincoln's R&D expenditures have recently been less than one and one-half percent of sales. There is evidence that others spend several times as much as a percentage of sales.

Lincoln's share of the arc-welding products market appears to have been about 40 percent for many years, and the welding products market has grown somewhat faster than the level of industry in general. The market is highly price-competitive, with variations in prices of standard products normally amounting to only 1 or 2 percent. Lincoln's products are sold directly by its engineering-oriented sales force and indirectly through its distributor organization. Advertising expenditures amount to less than one-fourth of 1 percent of sales, one-third as much as a major Lincoln competitor with whom the case writer checked.

The other major welding process, flame-welding, has not been competitive with arc-welding since the 1930s. However, plasma-arc-welding, a relatively new process which uses a conducting stream of superheated gas (plasma) to confine the welding current to a small area, has made some inroads, especially in metal tubing manufacturing, in recent

---

[15] Ibid., p. 92.
[16] Ibid., p. 39.

years. Major advances in technology which will produce an alternative superior to arc-welding within the next decade or so appear unlikely. Also, it seems likely that changes in the machines and techniques used in arc-welding will be evolutionary rather than revolutionary.

Products

The company is primarily engaged in the manufacture and sale of arc-welding products—electric welding machines and metal electrodes. Lincoln also produces electric motors ranging from ½ to 200 horsepower. Motors constitute about 8 to 10 percent of total sales.

The electric welding machines, some consisting of a transformer or motor-and-generator arrangement powered by commercial electricity and others consisting of an internal combustion engine and generator, are designed to produce from 30 to 1,000 amperes of electric power. This electric current is used to melt a consumable metal electrode, with the molten metal being transferred in a superhot spray to the metal joint being welded. Very high temperatures and hot sparks are produced, and operators usually must wear special eye and face protection and leather gloves, often along with leather aprons and sleeves.

Welding electrodes are of two basic types: (1) Coated "stick" electrodes, usually 14-inches long and smaller than a pencil in diameter, are held in a special insulated holder by the operator who must manipulate the electrode in order to maintain a proper arc width and pattern of deposition of the metal being transferred. Stick electrodes are packaged in 6- to 50-pound boxes. (2) Coiled wire, ranging in diameter from 0.035 to 0.219 inches, is designed to be fed continuously to the welding arc through a "gun" held by the operator or positioned by automatic positioning equipment. The wire is packaged in coils, reels, and drums weighing from 14 to 1,000 pounds.

Manufacturing Operations
Plant Locations

The main plant is in Euclid, Ohio, a suburb east of Cleveland. The layout of this plant is shown in Exhibit 13.1. There are no warehouses. Materials flow from the half-mile-long dock on the north side of the plant through the production lines to a very limited storage and loading area on the south side. Materials used at each workstation are stored as close as possible to the workstation. The administrative offices, near the center of the factory, are entirely functional. Not even the president's office is carpeted. A corridor below the main level provides access to the factory floor from the main entrance near the center of the plant. A new plant, just opened in Mentor, Ohio, houses some of the electrode production operations, which were moved from the main plant.

Manufacturing Processes

Electrode manufacturing is highly capital-intensive. Metal rods purchased from steel producers are drawn or extruded down to smaller diameters, cut to length, and coated with pressed-powder "flux" for stick electrodes or plated with copper (for conductivity) and spun into coils or spools for wire. Some of Lincoln's wire, called Innershield, is hollow

Exhibit 13.1   Factory Layout

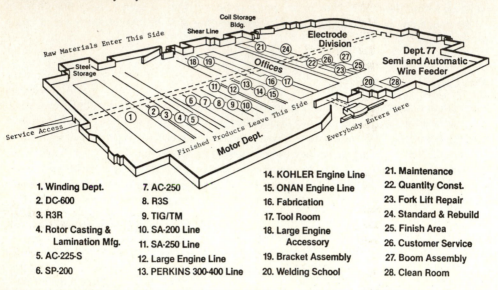

1. Winding Dept.	7. AC-250	14. KOHLER Engine Line
2. DC-600	8. R3S	15. ONAN Engine Line
3. R3R	9. TIG/TM	16. Fabrication
4. Rotor Casting &	10. SA-200 Line	17. Tool Room
Lamination Mfg.	11. SA-250 Line	18. Large Engine
5. AC-225-S	12. Large Engine Line	Accessory
6. SP-200	13. PERKINS 300-400 Line	19. Bracket Assembly
		20. Welding School

21. Maintenance
22. Quantity Const.
23. Fork Lift Repair
24. Standard & Rebuild
25. Finish Area
26. Customer Service
27. Boom Assembly
28. Clean Room

and filled with a material similar to that used to coat stick electrodes. Lincoln is highly secretive about its electrode production processes, and the case writer was not given access to the details of those processes.

Welding machines and electric motors are made on a series of assembly lines. Gasoline and diesel engines are purchased partially assembled, but practically all other components are made from basic industrial products, e.g., steel bars and sheets and bar copper conductor wire, in the Lincoln factory.

Individual components, such as gasoline tanks for engine-driven welders and steel shafts for motors and generators, are made by numerous small "factories within a factory." The shaft for a certain generator, for example, is made from a raw steel bar by one operator who uses five large machines, all running continuously. A saw cuts the bar to length, a digital lathe machines different sections to varying diameters, a special milling machine cuts a slot for a keyway, and so forth, until a finished shaft is produced. The operator moves the shafts from machine to machine and makes necessary adjustments.

Another operator punches, shapes, and paints sheet-metal cowling parts. One assembles steel laminations onto a rotor shaft, and then winds, insulates, and tests the rotors. Finished components are moved by crane operators to the nearby assembly lines.

Worker Performance and Attitudes

Exceptional worker performance at Lincoln is a matter of record. The typical Lincoln employee earns about twice as much as other factory workers in the Cleveland area. Yet the labor cost per sales dollar at Lincoln, currently $.23.5, is well below industry averages.

Sales per Lincoln factory employee currently exceed $157,000. An observer at the factory quickly sees why this figure is so high. Each worker is proceeding busily and thoughtfully about his task. There is no idle chatter. Most workers take no coffee breaks. Many operate several machines and make a substantial component unaided. The supervisors, some with as many as 100 subordinates, are busy with planning and recordkeeping duties and hardly glance at the people they supervise. The manufacturing procedures appear efficient—no unnecessary steps, no wasted motions, no wasted materials. Finished components move smoothly to subsequent workstations.

Worker turnover at Lincoln is practically nonexistent, except for retirements and departures by new employees. Appendix 13A includes summaries of interviews with Lincoln employees.

Organization Structure

Lincoln has never had a formal organization chart.[17] The objective of this policy is to ensure maximum flexibility. An open-door policy is practiced throughout the company, and personnel are encouraged to take problems to the persons most capable of resolving them.

Perhaps because of the quality and enthusiasm of the Lincoln work force, routine supervision is almost nonexistent. A typical production foreman, for example, supervises as many as 100 workers, a span of control which does not allow more than infrequent worker-supervisor interaction. Position titles and traditional flows of authority do imply something of an organizational structure, however. For example, the vice-president of sales and the vice-president of the Electrode Division report to the president, as do various staff assistants such as the personnel director and the director of purchasing. With the use of such implied relationships, it has been determined that production workers have two or, at most, three levels of supervision between themselves and the president.

Personnel Policies

Recruitment and Selection

Every job opening at Lincoln is advertised internally on company bulletin boards, and any employee can apply for any job so advertised. External hiring is done only for entry-level positions. Selection for these jobs is based on personal interviews—there is no aptitude or psychological testing. Not even a high school diploma is required except for engineering and sales positions, which are filled by graduate engineers. A committee consisting of vice-presidents and superintendents interviews candidates initially cleared by the personnel department. Final selection is made by the supervisor who has a job opening. Out of over 3,500 applicants interviewed by the personnel department during a recent period, fewer than 300 were hired.

---

[17] Harvard Business School researchers once prepared an organization chart reflecting the below-mentioned implied relationships. The chart became available within the Lincoln organization, and the present Lincoln management feels that it had a disruptive effect. Therefore, the case writer was asked not to include any kind of organizational chart in this report.

Job Security

In 1958 Lincoln formalized its lifetime employment policy, which had already been in effect for many years. There have been no layoffs at Lincoln since World War II. Since 1958, every Lincoln worker with over one year's employment has been guaranteed at least 30 hours per week, 49 weeks per year.

The policy had never been so severely tested as during the 1981–1983 recession. As a manufacturer of capital goods, Lincoln's business is highly cyclical. In previous recessions Lincoln had been able to avoid major sales declines. Sales for 1982, however, were about one-third below those of 1981. Few companies could withstand such a sales decline and remain profitable. Yet, Lincoln not only earned profits, no employee was laid off, the usual year-end incentive bonuses were paid (averaging $15,600 per worker for 1982), and common shareholders continued to receive about the normal dividend (around $8 per share).

Performance Evaluations

Each supervisor formally evaluates his subordinates twice a year using the cards shown in Exhibit 13.2. The employee performance criteria, "quality," "dependability," "ideas and cooperation," and "output," are considered to be independent of each other. Marks on the cards are converted to numerical scores which are forced to average 100 for each evaluating supervisor. Individual merit rating scores normally range from 80 to 110. Any score over 110 requires a special letter to top management. These scores (over 110) are not considered in computing the required 100-point average for each evaluating supervisor. Suggestions for improvements often result in recommendations for exceptionally high performance scores. Supervisors discuss individual performance marks with the employees concerned. Each warranty claim on a Lincoln product is traced to the individual employee whose work caused the defect. The employee's performance score may be reduced by 1 point, or the worker may be required to repay the cost of servicing the warranty claim by working without pay.

Compensation

Basic wage levels for jobs at Lincoln are determined by a wage survey of similar jobs in the Cleveland area. These rates are adjusted quarterly in accordance with changes in the Cleveland area Consumer Price Index. Insofar as possible, base wage rates are translated into piece rates. Practically all production workers and many others—for example, some forklift operators—are paid by piece rate. Once established, piece rates are never changed unless a substantive change in the way a job is done results from a source other than the worker doing the job. In December of each year, a portion of the annual profits is distributed to employees as bonuses. Incentive bonuses since 1934 have averaged about the same as annual wages and somewhat more than after-tax profits. The average bonus for 1981 was about $21,000. Bonuses averaged $15,500 and $10,400, respectively, for the recession years 1982 and 1983. Individual bonuses are proportional to merit rating scores. For example, assume incentive bonuses for the company total 110 percent of wages paid. A person whose performance score is 95 will receive a bonus of 1.045 (1.10 × 0.95) times annual wages.

Exhibit 13.2 Merit Rating Cards

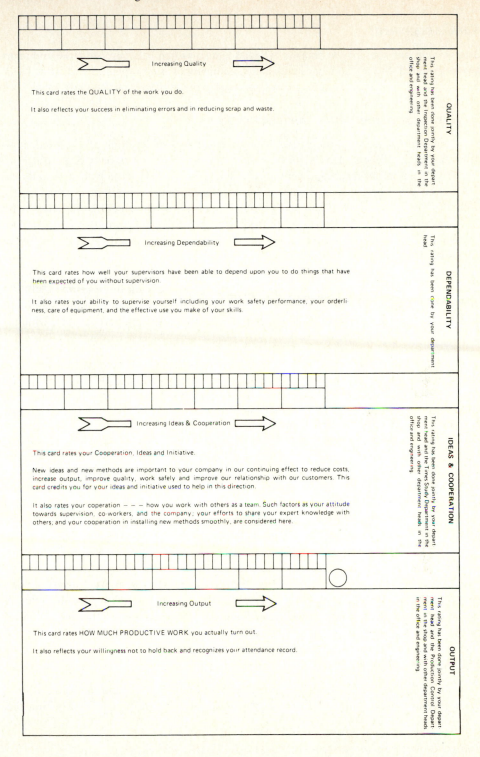

Increasing Quality

This card rates the QUALITY of the work you do.

It also reflects your success in eliminating errors and in reducing scrap and waste.

QUALITY

This rating has been done jointly by your department head and the Inspection Department in the shop and with other department heads in the office and engineering

Increasing Dependability

This card rates how well your supervisors have been able to depend upon you to do things that have been expected of you without supervision.

It also rates your ability to supervise yourself including your work safety performance, your orderliness, care of equipment, and the effective use you make of your skills.

DEPENDABILITY

This rating has been done by your department head

Increasing Ideas & Cooperation

This card rates your Cooperation, Ideas and Initiative.

New ideas and new methods are important to your company in our continuing effect to reduce costs, increase output, improve quality, work safely and improve our relationship with our customers. This card credits you for your ideas and initiative used to help in this direction.

It also rates your coperation — — — how you work with others as a team. Such factors as your attitude towards supervision, co-workers, and the company; your efforts to share your expert knowledge with others; and your cooperation in installing new methods smoothly, are considered here.

IDEAS & COOPERATION

This rating has been done jointly by your department head and the Time-Study Department in the shop and with other department heads in the office and engineering

Increasing Output

This card rates HOW MUCH PRODUCTIVE WORK you actually turn out.

It also reflects your willingness not to hold back and recognizes your attendance record.

OUTPUT

This rating has been done jointly by your department head and the Production Control Department in the shop and with other department heads in the office and engineering

Work Assignment

Management has authority to transfer workers and to switch between overtime and short time as required. Supervisors have undisputed authority to assign specific parts to individual employees, who may have their own preferences due to variations in piece rates.

Employee Participation in Decision Making

When managers speak of participative management, they usually think of a relaxed, non-authoritarian atmosphere. This is not the case at Lincoln. Formal authority is quite strong. "We're very authoritarian around here," says Willis. James F. Lincoln placed a good deal of stress on protecting management's authority. "Management in all successful departments of industry must have complete power," he said. "Management is the coach who must be obeyed. The men, however, are the players who alone can win the game." [18] Despite this attitude, there are several ways in which employees participate in management at Lincoln.

Richard Sabo, Manager of Public Relations, relates job enlargement to participation. "The most important participative technique that we use is giving more responsibility to employees." Sabo says, "We give a high school graduate more responsibility than other companies give their foremen." Lincoln puts limits on the degree of participation which is allowed, however. In Sabo's words:

When you use "participation," put quotes around it. Because we believe that each person should participate only in those decisions he is most knowledgeable about. I don't think production employees should control the decisions of Bill Irrgang. They don't know as much as he does about the decisions he is involved in.

The advisory board, elected by the workers, meets with the chairman and the president every two weeks to discuss ways of improving operations. This board has been in existence since 1914 and has contributed to many innovations. The incentive bonuses, for example, were first recommended by this committee. Every Lincoln employee has access to advisory board members, and answers to all advisory board suggestions are promised by the following meeting. Both Irrgang and Willis are quick to point out, though, that the advisory board only recommends actions. "They do not have direct authority," Irrgang says, "and when they bring up something that management thinks is not to the benefit of the company, it will be rejected." [19]

A suggestion program was instituted in 1929. At first, employees were awarded one-half of the first year's savings attributable to their suggestions. Now, however, the value of suggestions is reflected in performance evaluation scores, which determine individual incentive bonus amounts.

Training and Education

Production workers are given a short period of on-the-job training and then placed on a piecework pay system. Lincoln does not pay for off-site education. The idea behind this

---

[18] Lincoln, *Incentive Management* (Cleveland, Ohio, The Lincoln Electric Company, 1951), p. 228.

[19] Incentive Management in Action," *Assembly Engineering*, March 1967, p. 18.

latter policy is that everyone cannot take advantage of such a program and that it is unfair to expend company funds for an advantage to which there is unequal access. Sales personnel are given on-the-job training in the plant followed by a period of work and training at one of the regional sales offices.

Fringe Benefits and Executive Perquisites

A medical plan and a company-paid retirement program have been in effect for many years. A plant cafeteria, operated on a break-even basis, serves meals at about 60 percent of usual costs. An employee association, to which the company does not contribute, provides disability insurance and social and athletic activities. An employee stock ownership program, instituted in about 1925, and regular stock purchases have resulted in employee ownership of about 50 percent of Lincoln's stock.

As to executive perquisites, there are none. There are crowded, austere offices, no executive washrooms or lunchrooms, and no reserved parking spaces. Even the company president pays for his own meals and eats in the cafeteria.

Financial Policies

James F. Lincoln felt strongly that financing for company growth should come from within the company—through initial cash investment by the founders, through retention of earnings, and through stock purchases by those who work in the business. He saw the following advantages of this approach:[20]

1. Ownership of stock by employees strengthens team spirit. "If they are mutually anxious to make it succeed, the future of the company is bright."

2. Ownership of stock provides individual incentive because employees feel that they will benefit from company profitability.

3. "Ownership is educational." Owner-employees "will know how profits are made and lost; how success is won and lost . . . There are few socialists in the list of stockholders of the nation's industries."

4. "Capital available from within controls expansion." Unwarranted expansion would not occur, Lincoln believed, under his financing plan.

5. "The greatest advantage would be the development of the individual worker. Under the incentive of ownership, he would become a greater man."

6. "Stock ownership is one of the steps that can be taken that will make the worker feel that there is less of a gulf between him and the boss . . . Stock ownership will help the worker to recognize his responsibility in the game and the importance of victory."

Lincoln Electric Company uses a minimum of debt in its capital structure. There is no borrowing at all, with the debt being limited to current payables. Even the new $20 million plan in Mentor, Ohio, was financed totally from earnings.

The usual pricing policy at Lincoln is succinctly stated by President Willis: "At all times price on the basis of cost and at all times keep pressure on our cost." This policy

[20]Lincoln, *A New Approach*, pp. 220–228.

resulted in Lincoln's price for the most-popular welding electrode then in use going from $.16 a pound in 1929 to $.4.7 in 1938. More recently, the SA-200 welder, Lincoln's largest-selling portable machine, decreased in price from 1958 through 1965. According to C. Jackson Grayson of the American Productivity Center in Houston, Texas, Lincoln's prices in general have increased only one-fifth as fast as the Consumer Price Index from 1934 to about 1970. This has resulted in a welding products market in which Lincoln is the undisputed price leader for the products it manufacturers. Not even the major Japanese manufacturers, such as Nippon Steel for welding electrodes and Asaka Transformer for welding machines, have been able to penetrate this market.

Huge cash balances are accumulated each year preparatory to paying the year-end bonuses. The bonuses totaled $55,718,000 for 1981 and about $41,000,000 for 1982. This money is invested in short-term U.S. government securities until needed. Financial statements are shown in Exhibits 13.3 and 13.4.

Exhibit 13.3   Balance Sheets: The Lincoln Electric Company (dollar amounts in thousands)

	1980	1981	1982
Assets:			
Cash	$ 1,307	$ 3,603	$ 1,318
Government securities and certificates of deposit	46,503	62,671	72,485
Notes and accounts receivable	42,424	41,521	26,239
Inventories (LIFO basis)	35,533	45,541	38,157
Deferred taxes and prepared expenses	2,749	3,658	4,635
	128,516	156,994	142,834
Other intangible assets	19,723	21,424	22,116
Investment in foreign subsidiaries	4,695	4,695	7,696
	24,418	26,119	29,812
Property, plant, equipment, land	913	928	925
Buildings*	22,982	24,696	23,330
Machinery, tools, and equipment*	25,339	27,104	26,949
	49,234	52,728	51,204
Total assets	202,168	235,841	223,850
Liabilities:			
Accounts payable	15,608	14,868	11,936
Accrued wages	1,504	4,940	3,633
Taxes, including income taxes	5,622	14,755	5,233
Dividends payable	5,800	7,070	6,957
	28,534	41,633	27,759
Deferred taxes and other long-term liabilities	3,807	4,557	5,870
Shareholders' equity			
Common capital stock, stated value	276	272	268
Additional paid-in capital	2,641	501	1,862
Retained earnings	166,910	188,878	188,392
Equity adjustment from foreign currency translation			(301)
	169,827	189,651	190,221
Total liabilities and shareholders' equity	$202,168	$235,841	$223,850

*After depreciation.

Exhibit 13.4   Income Statements: The Lincoln Electric Company
(Dollar Amounts in Thousands)

	1980	1981	1982
Income:			
Net sales	$387,374	$450,387	$310,862
Other income	13,817	18,454	18,049
	401,191	468,841	328,911
Costs and expenses:			
Cost of products sold	$260,671	$293,332	$212,674
Selling, administrative, freight-out, and general expenses	37,753	42,656	37,128
Year-end incentive bonus	43,249	55,718	36,870
Payroll taxes related to bonus	1,251	1,544	1,847
Pension expense	6,810	6,874	5,888
	$349,734	$400,124	$294,407
Income before income taxes	$ 51,457	$ 68,717	$ 34,504
Provision for income taxes			
Federal	20,300	27,400	13,227
State and local	3,072	3,885	2,497
	23,372	31,285	15,724
Net income	$ 28,085	$ 37,432	$ 18,780
Employees (eligible for bonus)	2,637	2,684	2,634

How Well Does Lincoln Serve Its Public?

Lincoln Electric differs from most other companies in the importance it assigns to each of the groups it serves. Willis identifies these groups, in the order of priority Lincoln ascribes to them, as (1) customers, (2) employees, and (3) stockholders.

Certainly Lincoln customers have fared well over the years. Lincoln prices for welding machines and welding electrodes are acknowledged to be the lowest in the marketplace. Lincoln quality has consistently been so high that Lincoln Fleetweld electrodes and Lincoln SA-200 welders have been the standard in the pipeline and refinery construction industry, where price is hardly a criterion, for decades. The cost of field failures for Lincoln products was an amazing four one-hundreths of 1 percent in 1979. A Lincoln distributor in Monroe, Louisiana, says that he has sold several hundred of the popular AC-225 welders, and, though the machine is warranted for one year, he has never handled a warranty claim.

Perhaps best served of all Lincoln constituencies have been the employees. Not the least of their benefits, of course, are the year-end bonuses, which effectively double an already-average compensation level. The foregoing description of the personnel program and the comments in Appendix 13A further illustrate the desirability of a Lincoln job.

While stockholders were relegated to an inferior status by James F. Lincoln, they have done very well indeed. Recent dividends have exceeded $7 a share and earnings per share have exceeded $20. In January 1980, the price of restricted stock committed by Lincoln to employees was $117 a share. By February 4, 1983, the stated value, at which Lincoln would purchase the stock if tendered, was $166. A check with the New York office of Merrill, Lynch, Pierce, Fenner, and Smith on February 4, 1983, revealed an estimated price for Lincoln stock of $240 a share, with none being offered for sale. Technically, this price applies only to the unrestricted stock owned by the Lincoln family, a few other major holders, and employees who have purchased it on the open market, but it gives some idea of the value of Lincoln stock in general. The risk associated with Lincoln stock, a major determinant of stock value, is minimal because of the absence of debt in Lincoln's capital structure, because of an extremely stable earnings record, and because of Lincoln's practice of purchasing the restricted stock whenever employees offer it for sale.

A Concluding Comment

It is easy to believe that the reason for Lincoln's success is the excellent attitude of Lincoln employees and their willingness to work harder, faster, and more intelligently than other industrial workers. However, Richard Sabo, Manager of Publicity and Educational Services at Lincoln, suggests that appropriate credit be given to Lincoln executives, whom he credits with carrying out the following policies:

1. Management has limited research, development, and manufacturing to a standard product line designed to meet the major needs of the welding industry.

2. New products must be reviewed by manufacturing and all production costs verified before being approved by management.

3. Purchasing is challenged to not only procure materials at the lowest cost but also to work closely with engineering and manufacturing to ensure that the latest innovations are implemented.

4. Manufacturing supervision and all personnel are held accountable for reduction of scrap, energy conservation, and maintenance of product quality.

5. Production control, material handling, and methods engineering are closely supervised by top management.

6. Material and finished goods inventory control, accurate cost accounting, and attention to sales cost, credit, and other financial areas have constantly reduced overhead and led to excellent profitability.

7. Management has made cost reduction a way of life at Lincoln, and definite programs are established in many areas, including traffic and shipping, where tremendous savings can result.

8. Management has established a sales department that is technically trained to reduce customer welding costs. This sales technique and other real customer services have eliminated nonessential frills and resulted in long-term benefits to all concerned.

9. Management has encouraged education, technical publishing, and long-range programs that have resulted in industry growth, thereby ensuring market potential for the Lincoln Electric Company.

Employee Interviews

During the late summer of 1980, the author conducted numerous interviews with Lincoln employees. Typical questions and answers from those interviews are presented below. In order to maintain each employee's personal privacy, the names used for the interviewees are fictitious.

I

Interview with Betty Stewart, a 52-year-old high school graduate who had been with Lincoln 13 years and who was working as a cost-accounting clerk at the time of the interview.

Q. What jobs have you held here besides the one you have now?

A. I worked in payroll for a while, and then this job came open and I took it.

Q. How much money did you make last year, including your bonus?

A. I would say roughly around $20,000, but I was off for back surgery for a while.

Q. You weren't paid while you were off for back surgery?

A. No.

Q. Did the employees association help out?

A. Yes. The company doesn't furnish that, though. We pay $6 a month into the employee association. I think my check from them was $105.00 a week.

Q. How was your performance rating last year?

A. It was around 100 points, but I lost some points for attendance with my back problem.

Q. How did you get your job at Lincoln?

A. I was bored silly where I was working, and I had heard that Lincoln kept their people busy. So I applied and got the job the next day.

Q. Do you think you make more money than similar workers in Cleveland?

A. I know I do.

Q. What have you done with your money?

A. We have purchased a better home. Also, my son is going to the University of Chicago, which costs $10,000 a year. I buy the Lincoln stock which is offered each year, and I have a little bit of gold.

Q. Have you ever visited with any of the senior executives, like Mr. Willis or Mr. Irrgang?

A. I have known Mr. Willis for a long time.

Q. Does he call you by name?

A. Yes. In fact he was very instrumental in my going to the doctor that I am going to with my back. He knows the director of the clinic.

Q. Do you know Mr. Irrgang?

A. I know him to speak to him, and he always speaks, always. But I have known Mr. Willis for a good many years. When I did Plant Two accounting I did not under- **509** stand how the plant operated. Of course you are not allowed in Plant Two, because that's the Electrode Division. I told my boss about the problem one day, and the next thing I knew Mr. Willis came by and said, "Come on, Betty, we're going to Plant Two." He spent an hour and a half showing me the plant.

Q. Do you think Lincoln employees produce more than those in other companies?

A. I think with the incentive program the way that it is, if you want to work and achieve, then you will do it. If you don't want to work and achieve, you will not do it no matter where you are. Just because you are merit rated and have a bonus, if you really don't want to work hard, then you're not going to. You will accept your 90 points or 92 or 85 because, even with that, you make more money than people on the outside.

Q. Do you think Lincoln employees will ever join a union?

A. I don't know why they would.

Q. What is the most important advantage of working for Lincoln Electric?

A. You have an incentive, and you can push and get something for pushing. That's not true in a lot of companies.

Q. So you say that money is a very major advantage?

A. Money is a major advantage, but it's not just the money. It's the fact that, having the incentive, you do wish to work a little harder. I'm sure that there are a lot of men here who, if they worked some other place, would not work as hard as they do here. Not that they are overworked—I don't mean that—but I'm sure they wouldn't push.

Q. Is there anything that you would like to add?

A. I do like working here. I am better off being pushed mentally. In another company if you pushed too hard you would feel a little bit of pressure, and someone might say, "Hey, slow down; don't try so hard." But here you are encouraged, not discouraged.

II

Interview with Ed Sanderson, 23-year-old high school graduate who had been with Lincoln four years and who was a machine operator in the Electrode Division at the time of the interview.

Q. How did you happen to get this job?

A. My wife was pregnant, and I was making three bucks an hour and one day I came here and applied. That was it. I kept calling to let them know I was still interested.

Q. Roughly what were your earnings last year including your bonus?

A. $37,000.

Q. What have you done with your money since you have been here?

A. Well, we've lived pretty well, and we bought a condominium.

Q. Have you paid for the condominium?

A. No, but I could.

Q. Have you bought your Lincoln stock this year?

A. No, I haven't bought any Lincoln stock yet.

Q. Do you get the feeling that the executives here are pretty well thought of?

A. I think they are. To get where they are today, they had to really work.

Q. Wouldn't that be true anywhere?

A. I think more so here because seniority really doesn't mean anything. If you work with a guy who has 20 years here, and you have two months and you're doing a better job, you will get advanced before he will.

Q. Are you paid on a piece rate basis?

A. My gang is. There are nine of us who make the bare electrode, and the whole group gets paid based on how much electrode we make.

Q. Do you think you work harder than workers in other factories in the Cleveland area?

A. Yes, I would say I probably work harder.

Q. Do you think it hurts anybody?

A. No, a little hard work never hurts anybody.

Q. If you could choose, do you think you would be as happy earning a little less money and being able to slow down a little?

A. No, it doesn't bother me. If it bothered me, I wouldn't do it.

Q. What would you say is the biggest disadvantage of working at Lincoln, as opposed to working somewhere else?

A. Probably having to work shift work.

Q. Why do you think Lincoln employees produce more than workers in other plants?

A. That's the way the company is set up. The more you put out, the more you're going to make.

Q. Do you think it's the piece rate and bonus together?

A. I don't think people would work here if they didn't know that they would be rewarded at the end of the year.

Q. Do you think Lincoln employees will ever join a union?

A. No.

Q. What are the major advantages of working for Lincoln?

A. Money.

Q. Are there any other advantages?

A. Yes, we don't have a union shop. I don't think I could work in a union shop.

Q. Do you think you are a career man with Lincoln at this time?

A. Yes.

III

Interview with Roger Lewis, 23-year-old Purdue graduate in mechanical engineering who had been in the Lincoln sales program for 15 months and who was working in the Cleveland sales office at the time of the interview.

Q. How did you get your job at Lincoln?

A. I saw that Lincoln was interviewing on campus at Purdue, and I went by. I later came to Cleveland for a plant tour and was offered a job.

Q. Do you know any of the senior executives? Would they know you by name?

A. Yes, I know all of them—Mr. Irrgang, Mr. Willis, Mr. Manross.

Q. Do you think Lincoln salesmen work harder than those in other companies?

A. Yes. I don't think there are many salesmen for other companies who are putting in 50- to 60-hour weeks. Everybody here works harder. You can go out in the plant, or you can go upstairs, and there's nobody sitting around.

Q. Do you see any real disadvantage of working at Lincoln?

A. I don't known if it's a disadvantage but Lincoln is a Spartan company, a very thrifty company. I like that. The sales offices are functional, not fancy.

Q. Why do you think Lincoln employees have such high productivity?

A. Piecework has a lot to do with it. Lincoln is smaller than many plants, too; you can stand in one place and see the materials come in one side and the product go out the other. You feel a part of the company. The chance to get ahead is important, too. They have a strict policy of promoting from within, so you know you have a chance. I think in a lot of other places you may not get as fair a shake as you do here. The sales offices are on a smaller scale, too. I like that. I tell someone that we have two people in the Baltimore office, and they say "You've got to be kidding." It's smaller and more personal. Pay is the most important thing. I have heard that this is the highest-paying factory in the world.

IV

Interview with Jimmy Roberts, a 47-year-old high school graduate, who had been with Lincoln 17 years and who was working as a multiple drill press operator at the time of the interview.

Q. What jobs have you had at Lincoln?

A. I started out cleaning the men's locker room in 1963. After about a year I got a job in the flux department, where we make the coating for welding rods. I worked there for seven or eights years and then got my present job.

Q. Do you make one particular part?

A. No, there are a variety of parts I make—at least 25.

Q. Each one has a different piece rate attached to it?

A. Yes.

Q. Are some piece rates better than others?

A. Yes.

Q. How do you determine which ones you are going to do?

A. You don't. Your supervisor assigns them.

Q. How much money did you make last year?

A. $47,000.

Q. Have you ever received any kind of award or citation?

A. No.

Q. Was your rating ever over 110?

A. Yes. For the past five years, probably, I made over 110 points.

Q. Is there any attempt to let others know?

A. The kind of points I get? No.

Q. Do you know what they are making?

A. No. There are some who might not be too happy with their points, and they might make it known. The majority, though, do not make it a point of telling other employees.

Q. Would you be just as happy earning a little less money and working a little slower?

A. I don't think I would—not at this point. I have done piecework all these years, and the fast pace doesn't really bother me.

Q. Why do you think Lincoln productivity is so high?

A. The incentive thing—the bonus distribution. I think that would be the main reason. The paycheck you get every two weeks is important too.

Q. Do you think Lincoln employees would ever join a union?

A. I don't think so. I have never heard anyone mention it.

Q. What is the most important advantage of working here?

A. The amount of money you make. I don't think I could make this type of money anywhere else, especially with only a high school education.

Q. As a black person, do you feel that Lincoln discriminates in any way against blacks?

A. No. I don't think any more so than any other job. Naturally, there is a certain amount of discrimination, regardless of where you are.

V

Interview with Joe Trahan, 58-year-old high school graduate who had been with Lincoln 39 years and who was employed as a working supervisor in the toolroom at the time of the interview.

Q. Roughly what was your pay last year?

A. Over $50,000—salary, bonus, stock dividends.

Q. How much was your bonus?

A. About $23,000.

Q. Have you ever gotten a special award of any kind?

A. Not really.

Q. What have you done with your money?

A. My house is paid for—and my two cars. I also have some bonds and the Lincoln stock.

Q. What do you think of the executives at Lincoln?

A. They're really top notch.

Q. What is the major disadvantage of working at Lincoln Electric?

A. I don't know of any disadvantage at all.

Q. Do you think you produce more than most people in similar jobs with other companies?

A. I do believe that.

Q. Why is that? Why do you believe that?

A. We are on the incentive system. Everything we do, we try to improve to make a better product with a minimum of outlay. We try to improve the bonus.

Q. Would you be just as happy making a little less money and not working quite so hard?

A. I don't think so.

Q. You know that Lincoln productivity is higher than that at most other plants. Why is that?

A. Money.

Q. Do you think Lincoln employees would ever join a union?

A. I don't think they would ever consider it.

Q. What is the most important advantage of working at Lincoln?

A. Compensation.

Q. Tell me something about Mr. James Lincoln, who died in 1965.

A. You are talking about Jimmy, Sr. He always strolled through the shop in his shirt-sleeves. Big fellow. Always looked distinguished. Gray hair. Friendly sort of guy. I was a member of the advisory board one year. He was there each time.

Q. Did he strike you as really caring?

A. I think he always cared for people.

Q. Did you get any sensation of a religious nature from him?

A. No, not really.

Q. And religion is not part of the program now?

A. No.

Q. Do you think Mr. Lincoln was a very intelligent man, or was he just a nice guy?

A. I would say he was pretty well educated. A great talker—always right off the top of his head. He knew what he was talking about all the time.

Q. When were bonuses for beneficial suggestions done away with?

A. About 15 years ago.

Q. Did that hurt very much?

A. I don't think so, because suggestions are still rewarded through the merit rating system.

Q. Is there anything you would like to add?

A. It's a good place to work. The union kind of ties other places down. At other places, electricians only do electrical work, carpenters only do carpenter work. At Lincoln Electric we all pitch in and do whatever needs to be done.

Q. So a major advantage is not having a union?

A. That's right.

Nuclear Corporation of America had been near bankruptcy in 1965 when a fourth reorganization put a 39-year-old division manager, Ken Iverson, into the president's role. Iverson began a process which resulted in Nucor, a steel mini-mill and joist manufacturer which reaped national attention and high praise.

In an article subtitled "Lean living and mini-mill technology have led a one time loser to steel's promised land," *Fortune* magazine stated "Although Nucor didn't build its first mill until 1969, it turned out 1.1 million tons of steel last year, enough to rank among the top 20 U.S. producers. Not only has Nucor been making a lot of steel, it's been making money making steel—and a lot of that as well. Since 1969, earnings have grown 31% a year, compounded, reaching $45 million in 1980 on sales of $482 million. Return on average equity in recent years has consistently exceeded 28%, excellent even by Silicon Valley's standards and almost unheard of in steel. The ninefold increase in the value of Nucor's stock over the last five years—it was was selling recently at about $70 a share—has given shareholders plenty of cause for thanksgiving."

The Wall Street Journal in January 1981 commented "The ways in which management style combines with technology to benefit the mini-mill industry are obvious at Nucor Corp., one of the most successful of the 40 or more mini-mill operators." Ken Iverson was featured in an NBC special "If Japan Can, Why Can't We?" for his management approach. As *The Wall Street Journal* commented: "You thought steel companies are only a bunch of losers, with stodgy management, outmoded plants and poor profits?" Well, Nucor and Iverson were different.

In March 1983, Iverson had been one of 52 recipients nationally of the bronze medal from *Financial World*. But the *Charlotte Observer* reported: "Nucor managed to remain profitable in a very weak year for steel producers by watching inventories and keeping costs in line, all without laying off any workers. 'Batten down the hatches—that's what we did,' says Iverson, who won a bronze award for the second straight year." But 1982 had been a horrible year for the steel industry and Nucor; sales had fallen 11 percent and earnings 37 percent. This had been the second year of decreasing earnings and Nucor had been forced to cut wages for its top 12 executives by 5 percent and to freeze wages for its 3,500 employees. (See Exhibits 14.1, 14.2, and 14.3.)

The second quarter of 1983 appeared to be the end of the decline. In October, "We showed some improvement, but we still don't have a good return on equity," said Samuel Siegel, Nucor's vice-president of finance. "Nucor's 9-percent return on equity, as of October 1, is better than last year," Siegel said, "but far below the 30-percent-plus figures achieved in the late 1970s and early 1980s." A steel industry analyst termed Nucor's earn-

The research and written case information were presented at a Case Research Symposium and were evaluated by the Case Research Association's Editorial Board. This case was prepared by Professor Frank C. Barnes of the University of North Carolina at Charlotte as a basis for class discussion and does not intentionally portray either effective or ineffective administration.

Exhibit 14.1   Nucor Corporation Balance Sheet Data 1972 through 1982

	1972	1973	1974	1975
Assets				
Current Assets:				
Cash	3,379,565	5,787,483	6,001,843	3,152,391
Short-term investments	2,250,000	—	2,980,182	3,461,224
Accounts receivable	7,693,499	9,703,612	10,331,819	9,543,570
Contracts in process	4,972,466	6,035,597	5,830,003	2,572,257
Inventories	11,666,772	16,836,235	19,281,168	25,504,684
Other current assets	204,143	146,920	425,461	310,822
Total current assets	30,166,445	38,509,847	44,850,476	44,544,948
Property, Plant and Equipment:				
Land and improvement	1,260,250	1,521,532	1,600,983	2,282,600
Buildings and improvements	6,450,379	9,513,119	10,110,202	14,001,236
Plant machinery and equipment	9,776,614	20,034,462	21,926,174	41,250,517
Office and transportation equipment	440,995	826,345	976,791	1,270,446
Construction in process	1,689,050	1,451,911	9,153,730	156,211
Total Plant, Property, and Equipment	19,617,288	33,347,369	43,767,880	58,961,010
Less accumulated depreciation	3,829,712	5,635,771	8,066,296	11,255,177
Total P.P.&E. less depreciation	15,787,576	27,711,598	35,701,584	47,705,833
Other Assets:				
Deposits for acquisition of plant and equipment	1,578,695	1,323,896	1,477,049	383,814
Other assets	4,531	4,769	9,639	4,818
Total other assets	1,583,226	1,328,665	1,486,688	388,632
Total Assets	47,537,247	67,550,110	82,038,748	92,639,413
Liabilities and Stockholders' Equity				
Current Liabilities:				
Long-term debt due within one year	97,452	100,000	388,462	413,462
Accounts payable	6,051,301	12,366,170	11,557,784	9,217,640
Federal income taxes	2,050,000	969,161	5,547,818	2,121,784
Accrued expenses and other current liabilities	3,465,595	5,829,138	6,531,317	6,123,761
Total Current Liabilities	11,664,348	19,264,469	24,025,381	17,876,647
Other liabilities:				
Long-term debt due after one year	13,224,720	19,850,000	19,461,538	28,251,923
Deferred federal income taxes	539,563	314,563	739,563	1,219,563
Deferred compensation and other liabilities	1,179,091	1,500,883	708,327	741,545
Total Other Liabilities	14,943,374	21,665,446	20,909,428	30,213,031
Stockholders' Equity:				
Common stock	797,660	798,442	838,853	853,592
Additional paid-in capital	5,938,079	5,964,886	7,265,793	7,704,914
Retained earnings	14,193,786	19,903,615	29,097,360	36,090,395
Treasury stock	—	(46,748)	(98,067)	(99,166)
Total stockholders' equity	20,929,525	26,620,195	37,103,939	44,549,735
Total Liabilities and Stockholders' Equity	47,537,247	67,550,110	82,038,748	92,639,413

Source: Company statements.

1976	1977	1978	1979	1980	1981	1982
8,156,215	3,346,196	6,286,583	8,716,950	5,753,068	8,704,859	10,668,165
3,875,000	3,750,000	21,131,652	27,932,854	16,000,000	—	34,224,381
13,493,692	18,897,191	26,580,943	35,203,909	35,537,959	42,983,058	34,685,498
3,428,026	4,494,418	5,316,522	5,004,091	7,985,985	5,719,121	3,656,643
32,643,688	30,410,685	41,548,920	40,007,532	49,599,265	72,996,664	48,831,434
219,423	256,812	245,674	496,854	489,450	978,590	476,527
61,816,044	61,155,302	101,110,294	117,362,190	115,365,727	131,382,292	132,542,648
2,209,289	2,696,502	3,526,812	4,915,078	5,806,711	12,142,613	12,215,375
15,138,400	18,441,047	22,229,110	29,875,783	34,853,546	53,037,722	53,668,523
44,212,629	55,992,359	68,677,667	91,865,271	139,182,579	245,037,510	244,143,769
1,637,493	1,803,511	2,579,600	5,478,870	5,711,199	6,868,069	9,565,667
8,516,708	7,739,163	18,240,643	28,326,555	33,541,819	1,776,106	3,260,329
71,714,519	86,672,582	115,253,832	160,461,557	219,095,854	318,862,020	322,853,663
15,778,779	20,733,060	26,722,157	35,879,558	46,021,581	66,245,946	83,782,273
55,935,740	65,939,522	88,531,675	124,581,999	173,074,273	252,616,074	239,071,390
1,339,259	916,158	3,812,724	1,167,325	2,781,867	783,761	18,903
4,538	—	—	—	—	—	—
1,343,797	916,158	3,812,724	1,167,325	2,781,867	783,761	18,903
119,095,581	128,010,982	193,454,693	243,111,514	291,221,867	384,782,127	371,632,941
438,462	438,462	463,462	1,245,764	1,696,815	1,654,784	1,603,462
16,220,543	12,077,514	24,150,147	26,414,666	36,640,991	32,237,889	22,948,867
5,465,824	4,440,824	15,640,824	15,913,361	4,362,619	10,733,627	12,535,096
8,777,139	13,345,205	15,578,501	19,962,206	23,793,020	28,406,013	29,015,281
30,901,968	30,302,005	55,832,934	63,535,997	66,493,445	73,032,313	66,102,706
31,667,308	28,132,692	41,473,077	41,398,138	39,605,169	83,754,231	48,229,615
1,819,563	2,619,563	4,019,563	4,919,563	7,519,563	15,619,563	25,019,563
621,772	66,317	—	—	—	—	—
34,108,643	31,413,572	45,492,640	46,317,701	47,124,732	99,373,794	73,249,178
885,143	1,261,644	1,795,698	2,721,040	2,758,713	2,797,948	2,802,796
9,211,839	9,855,410	10,743,090	11,125,185	13,353,856	16,531,759	17,696,568
44,088,406	55,497,968	79,934,950	119,891,199	161,952,033	193,355,403	211,921,654
(100,418)	(319,617)	(344,619)	(479,608)	(460,912)	(309,090)	(139,961)
54,084,970	66,295,405	92,129,119	133,257,816	177,603,690	212,376,020	232,281,057
119,095,581	128,010,982	193,454,693	243,111,514	291,221,867	384,782,127	371,632,941

Exhibit 14.2   Nucor Corporation Sales, Earnings and Statistical Data 1972 through 1982

	1972	1973	1974	1975
For The Year				
Sales, Costs and Earnings:				
Net sales	$83,576,128	$113,193,617	$160,416,931	$121,467,284
Costs and expenses:				
Cost of products sold	62,611,109	85,336,598	122,641,020	95,811,251
Marketing and administrative expenses	11,451,950	15,703,147	17,067,469	12,482,924
Interest expense (income)	624,879	1,544,830	1,938,359	1,491,321
	74,687,938	102,584,575	141,646,848	109,785,496
Earnings before federal income taxes	8,888,190	10,609,042	18,770,083	11,681,788
Federal income taxes	4,220,000	4,600,000	9,090,000	4,100,000
Net earnings	$4,668,190	$6,009,042	$9,680,083	$7,581,788
Net earnings per share	.80	1.02	1.64	1.23
Dividends declared per share	—	.05	.08	.10
Percentage of earnings to sales	5.6%	5.3%	6.0%	6.2%
Return on average equity	25.4%	25.3%	30.4%	18.6%
Return on average assets	11.6%	10.4%	12.9%	8.7%
Average shares outstanding	5,830,146	5,865,065	5,920,196	6,153,320
Sales per employee	$ 50,347	$ 60,050	$ 79,218	$ 55,212
At Year-End				
Working capital	$18,502,097	$ 19,245,378	$ 20,825,095	$ 26,668,301
Current ratio	2.6	2.0	1.9	2.5
Stockholders' equity per share	$ 3.57	$ 4.54	$ 6.04	$ 7.13
Shares outstanding	5,862,798	5,858,550	6,142,715	6,250,843
Stockholders	33,000	29,000	28,000	27,000
Employees	1,820	1,950	2,100	2,300

Source: Company statements.

ings "disappointing," noting the industry was deeply mired in recession during 1982's third quarter.

Ken Iverson was a remarkable individual; his accomplishments with Nucor were nothing short of amazing. But as 1984 began it was clear a new era was beginning. He could wonder what it would mean for Nucor.

Background

Nucor was the descendant of a company which manufactured the first Oldsmobile in 1897. After seven years of success, R. E. Olds sold his first company and founded a new one to manufacture the Reo. Reo ran into difficulties and filed for voluntary reorganization in 1938. Sales grew 50 times over the next ten years, based on defense business, but declined steadily after the war. The Motor Division was sold and then resold in 1957 to the White Motor Corporation, where it operates as the Diamond Reo Division. Old Reo Motors planned to liquidate but before it could, a new company acquired stock, and through a proxy fight, gained control. They arranged a merger with Nuclear Consultants

1976	1977	1978	1979	1980	1981	1982
$175,768,479	$212,952,829	$306,939,667	$428,681,778	$482,420,363	$544,820,621	$486,018,162
142,235,949	168,247,627	227,953,309	315,688,291	369,415,571	456,210,289	408,606,641
14,744,882	19,729,586	28,660,033	36,724,159	38,164,559	33,524,820	31,720,377
2,290,757	2,723,024	1,877,476	1,504,791	(1,219,965)	10,256,546	7,899,110
159,271,588	190,700,237	258,490,818	353,917,241	406,360,165	499,991,655	448,226,128
16,496,891	22,252,592	48,448,849	74,764,537	76,060,198	44,828,966	37,792,034
7,800,000	9,800,000	22,600,000	32,500,000	31,000,000	10,100,00	15,600,000
$ 8,696,891	$ 12,452,592	$ 25,848,849	$ 42,264,537	$ 45,060,198	$ 34,728,966	$ 22,192,034
$ 1.36	$ 1.92	$ 3.91	$ 6.29	$ 6.62	$ 5.02	$ 3.18
.11	.16	.22	.34	.44	.48	.52
4.9%	5.8%	8.4%	9.9%	9.3%	6.4%	4.6%
17.6%	20.7%	32.6%	37.5%	29.0%	17.8%	10.0%
8.2%	10.1%	16.1%	19.4%	16.9%	10.3%	5.9%
6,373,223	6,493,822	6,618,404	6,717,638	6,804,703	6,918,861	6,970,859
$ 76,421	$ 88,730	$ 115,826	$ 145,316	$ 150,756	$ 155,663	$ 133,155
$ 30,914,076	$ 30,853,297	$ 45,277,360	$ 53,826,193	$ 48,872,282	$ 58,349,979	$ 66,439,942
2.0	2.0	1.8	1.8	1.7	1.8	2.0
$ 8.34	$ 10.09	$ 13.77	$ 19.73	$ 25.93	$ 30.50	$ 33.20
6,482,559	6,567,315	6,688,419	6,753,877	6,849,997	6,963,507	6,995,941
24,000	22,000	22,000	23,000	22,000	22,000	22,000
2,300	2,500	2,800	3,100	3,300	3,700	3,600

Inc. and in 1955 the stock of Nuclear Corporation of America was first traded. Nuclear acquired a number of companies in high-tech fields but continued to lose money through 1960, when an investment banker in New York acquired controlling stock. The new management he installed proceeded with a series of acquisitions and dispositions; they purchased U.S. Semi-Conductor Products Inc., Valley Sheet Metal Co., an air-conditioner contractor in Arizona, and Vulcraft Corp., a Florence, South Carolina, steel-joist manufacturer. Over the next four years, sales increased 5 times, but losses increased 7 times. In 1965 a New York investor purchased a controlling interest and installed the fourth management team. The new president was Ken Iverson, who had been in charge of the Vulcraft Division.

Ken Iverson had joined the Navy upon graduation from high school outside Chicago in 1941. The Navy first sent him to Northwestern University on an officer training program but then decided they needed aeronautical engineers and switched him to Cornell. This had been fine with Iverson because he liked engineering. When he received his bachelor's in 1945 at age 20 Iverson went into the Navy. Six months later he completed his four-year tour and was discharged.

Exhibit 14.3   Nucor Corporation Financial Position Data 1972 through 1982

	1972	**1973**	**1974**	**1975**
Funds Provided:				
Operations:				
Net earnings	$ 4,668,190	$ 6,009,042	$ 9,680,083	$ 7,581,788
Depreciation of plant and equipment	1,316,583	1,938,913	2,775,493	3,910,766
Amortization of deferred charges	92,055	—	—	—
Deferred federal income taxes	(100,000)	(225,000)	425,000	480,000
Deferred compensation	401,803	322,542	—	—
Total funds provided by operations	6,378,631	8,045,497	12,880,576	11,972,554
Disposition of plant and equipment	11,858	32,546	336,383	8,358
Decrease in deposits for acquistion of plant and equipment	—	254,799	—	1,093,235
Reduction in other assets	13,402	—	—	—
New long-term debt due after one year	11,000,000	6,750,000	4,000,000	9,300,000
Issuance of common stock	368,978	27,589	1,341,318	453,860
Decrease in working capital	—	—	—	—
Other	—	—	—	38,039
Total funds provided	$17,772,869	$15,110,431	$18,558,277	$22,866,046
Funds Applied:				
Purchase of property, plant, and equipment	$ 5,646,134	$13,895,481	$11,101,862	$15,923,373
Deposits for acquisition of plant and equipment	628,005	—	153,153	—
Reduction in long-term debt due after one year	2,286,073	124,720	4,388,462	509,615
Reduction in deferred compensation	—	—	793,625	—
Reduction in other liabilities	2,500	—	—	—
Cash dividends	—	299,213	486,338	588,753
Acquistion of treasury stock	—	46,748	51,319	1,099
Increase in working capital	9,210,157	743,281	1,579,717	5,843,206
Other	—	988	3,801	—
Total funds applied	$17,772,869	$15,110,431	$18,558,277	$22,866,046

Source: Company statements.

Iverson wasn't too excited about an aeronautical engineering career because of the eight years of drafting required for success. Metals and their problems in aircraft design had intrigued him, so he considered a master's in metallurgy. An uncle had attended Purdue, so Iverson chose Purdue. He married during this time. Iverson gave up teaching geometry so he could finish the program in one year and turned down an offer of assistance toward a Ph.D. in order to get to work.

At Purdue Iverson had worked with the new electron microscope. International Harvester's research physics department had just acquired one and hired Iverson as assistant to the chief research physicist. Iverson stayed there five years and felt he was set for life. He had great respect for his boss who would discuss with him the directions business took and their opportunities. One day the chief physicist asked if this was what Iverson really wanted to do all his life. There was only one job ahead for him at International Harvester

1976	1977	1978	1979	1980	1981	1982
$ 8,696,891	$12,452,592	$25,848,849	$42,264,537	$45,060,198	$34,728,966	$22,192,034
5,098,858	5,926,704	7,455,379	9,712,625	13,296,218	21,599,951	26,286,671
—	—	—	—	—	—	—
600,000	800,000	1,400,000	900,000	2,600,000	8,100,000	9,400,000
—	—	—	—	—	—	—
14,395,749	19,179,296	34,704,228	52,877,162	60,956,416	64,428,917	57,878,705
84,386	17,569	1,540,349	225,611	651,862	377,530	2,046,720
—	428,614	—	2,645,399	—	1,998,106	764,858
—	—	—	—	—	—	—
7,250,000	—	13,900,000	1,134,676	—	46,400,000	7,500,000
1,417,516	1,020,072	1,523,910	1,328,548	2,285,040	3,368,960	1,459,008
—	60,779	—	—	4,953,911	—	—
1,467	38,570	—	—	—	—	—
$23,149,118	$20,744,900	$51,668,487	$58,211,396	$68,847,229	$116,573,513	$69,649,291
$13,413,151	$15,948,055	$31,587,881	$45,988,560	$62,440,354	$101,519,282	$14,788,707
955,445	—	2,896,566	—	1,614,542	—	—
3,834,615	3,534,616	559,615	1,209,615	1,792,969	2,250,938	43,024,616
—	—	619,463	—	—	—	—
—	—	—	—	—	—	—
698,880	1,043,030	1,411,867	2,308,288	2,999,364	3,325,596	3,625,783
1,252	219,199	127,178	156,100	—	—	120,222
4,245,775	—	14,465,917	8,548,833	—	9,477,697	8,089,963
—	—	—	—	—	—	—
$23,149,118	$20,744,900	$51,668,487	$58,211,396	$68,847,229	$116,573,513	$69,649,291

and he felt more ambition than that. At his boss's urging Iverson considered smaller companies.

Iverson joined Illium Corporation, 120 miles from Chicago, as chief engineer (metallurgist). Illium was a 60-person division of a major company but acted like an independent company. In the two years there he was close to the young president and impressed with his good business skill; he know how to manage and had the discipline to run a tight ship, to go in the right direction with no excess manning. The two of them proposed an expansion which the parent company insisted they delay three to four years until it could be bought without borrowing.

Iverson joined Indiana Steel Products as assistant to the vice-president of manufacturing with the sole purpose of setting up a spectrographic lab. After completing this in a year, he could see no other opportunity for himself in the company; it was a small group and he could get no real responsibility. He left a year and a half later to join Cannon Muskegon as chief metallurgist.

The next seven years were "fascinating." With only $5–6 million in sales, the small (60–70 people) family company made castings of special metals which were in every aircraft made in the U.S. The company was one of the first to get into "vacuum melting" and Iverson, because of his technical ability, was put in charge of it. After a year the company realized the need for change and hired a new metallurgist. Iverson then asked for and got responsibility for all sales of the company. He wasn't dissatisfied but realized if he was to be really successful he needed broader and managerial experience.

Cannon Muskegon sold materials to Coast Metals, a small, private company in New Jersey which cast and machined special alloys for the aircraft industry. The president of Coast got to know Iverson and needed his technical expertise. In 1960 Iverson joined them as executive vice-president with responsibility for running the whole company.

Nuclear Corporation of America wished to buy Coast but Coast wasn't interested in selling. Then Nuclear's president asked Iverson to act as a consultant to them to find metals businesses Nuclear could buy. Over the next year, mostly on weekends, he looked at potential acquisitions. Iverson recommended they buy a joist business in South Carolina. Nuclear said it would, if he would run it. Coast was having disputes among its owners and his future there was clouded. So he ended his two years there and joined Nuclear in 1962 as a vice-president, Nuclear's usual title, in charge of a 200-person joist division.

By late 1963 he had built a second plant in Nebraska and was the only division making a profit. The president asked him to become a group vice-president, adding the research chemicals (metals) and contracting businesses, and to move to the home office in Phoenix. In mid-1965 the company defaulted on two loans and the president resigned. Over that summer Nuclear sought out some direction. Iverson knew what could be done, put together a pro forma, and pushed for these actions. It was not a unanimous decision that he was made president in September of 1965.

They immediately got rid of some divisions and went to work building Nucor. Iverson stated that the vice-presidents of the divisions designed Nucor in a hard-working, almost T-group-type meetings. Iverson was only another participant and only took charge whenever the group couldn't settle an issue. They identified Nucor's strengths and set the path for Nucor.

By 1966 Nucor consisted of the two joist plants, the Research Chemicals Division, and the Nuclear Division. In 1967 they purchased a building in Ft. Payne, Alabama, to make into another joist plant. In 1968 they began a steel mill in Darlington, South Carolina, and opened a joist plant in Texas. Another joist plant was added in Missouri in 1972. Steel plants were opened in Texas in 1975 and in Nebraska in 1977. The Nuclear Division was divested in 1976. The fourth steel plant was opened in Utah in 1981 and a joist plant was opened in Utah in 1982. By 1984 Nucor consisted of six joist plants, 4 steel mills, and a Research Chemicals Division.

Steel Industry

The early 1980s had been the worst years in decades for the steel industry. Data from the American Iron and Steel Institute showed shipments falling from 100.2 million tons in 1979 to the mid-eighties level in 1980 and 1981. Slackening of the economy, and particularly auto sales, led the decline.

The large, integrated steel mills, such as U.S. Steel and Armco, which made up the major part of the industry, were the hardest hit. *The Wall Street Journal* stated: "The decline has resulted from such problems as high labor and energy costs in mining and processing iron ore, a lack of profits and capital to modernize plants, and conservative management that has hesitated to take risks."

These companies produced a wide range of steels, primarily from ore in blast furnaces. They had found it difficult to compete with imports, usually from Japan, and had given up market share to imports. They sought the protection of import quotas. Imported steel accounted for 20 percent of U.S. steel consumption, up from 12 percent in the early 1970s. U.S. production of raw steel declined from 19 percent to 14 percent over the period. Imports of light bar products accounted for less than 9 percent of U.S. consumption of those products in 1981, according to the Commerce Department. Imports of wire rod totaled 23 percent of U.S. consumption. "Wire rod is a very competitive product in the world market because it's very easy to make," said Ralph Thompson, the Commerce Department's steel analyst.

Iverson was one of the very few in the steel industry to oppose import restrictions. He saw an outdated U.S. steel industry which had to change.

About 12 percent of the steel in the U.S. is still produced by the old open hearth furnaces. The Japanese shut down their last open hearth furnace about 5 years ago. . . . The U.S. produces about 16 percent of its steel by the continuous casting process. In Japan over 50 percent of the steel is continuously cast. . . . We Americans have been conditioned to believe in our technical superiority. For many generations a continuing stream of new inventions and manufacturing techniques allowed us to far outpace the rest of the world in both volume and efficiency of production. In many areas this is no longer true—and particularly in the steel industry. In the last three decades almost all the major developments in steel making were made outside the U.S. There were 13 continuous casting units in the world before there was one in this country. I would be negligent if I did not recognize the significant contribution that the government has made toward the technological deterioration of the steel industry. Unrealistic depreciation schedules, high corporate taxes, excessive regulation and jaw-boning for lower steel prices have made it difficult for the steel industry to borrow or generate the huge quantities of capital required for modernization.

The Mini-Mill

A new type of mill, the "mini-mill," emerged in the U.S. during the 1970s to compete with the integrated mill. The mini-mill used electric-arc furnaces to manufacture a narrow product line from scrap steel. *The New York Times* reported:

The truncated steel mill is to the integrated steel mill what the Volkswagen was to the American auto industry in the 1960s; smaller, cheaper, less complex and more efficient. Although mini-mills cannot produce such products as sheet steel and heavy construction items, some industry analysts say it is only a matter of time before technological breakthroughs make this possible.

Since mini-mills came into being in the last decade, the major mills' market share of all steel products has fallen from about 90% to about 60%, with the loss equally divided between mini-mills and foreign imports.

While the integrated steel companies averaged a 7-percent return on equity, the mini-mills averaged 14 percent, and some of them, like Nucor, had been turning in a 25 to 30-percent return on equity.

The leading mini-mills were Nucor, Florida Steel, Georgetown Steel (Korf), North Star Steel, and Chaparral. Nucor produced "light bar" products: bars, angles, channels, flats, smooth round, and forging billets. They were beginning to make more alloy steels. Florida Steel made mostly reinforcing bar and rebar for construction and dominated the Florida market. Korf Industries had 2 mini-mills subsidiaries, which used the modern equipment to manufacture wire rod.

All of the mini-mills were hurt in the slump. Korf Industries, which owned Georgetown Steel, found its interest charges too much of a burden and sought a reorganization in 1983. In March of 1983 Georgetown followed the historic wage-cutting contract between the United Steel Workers of America and the major steel companies and sought reductions from its union and to defer automatic wage increases.

Florida Steel had about two-thirds of its sales in Florida. At its headquarters in Tampa, a staff of over 100 handled accounting, payroll, sales entry, and most other services for all its facilities. Their division managers did not have sales responsibilities. Florida Steel experienced a sales decline for 1982 of 22 percent and an earnings drop from $3.37 per share to a loss of $1.40. The next year was also a year of losses.

Florida Steel employees had faced periodic layoffs during the recession. They were nonunion, though the Charlotte plant lost an election in 1973, and pay was based on productivity. They could not get a small facility at Indian Town, near West Palm Beach, productive, even with personnel changes, and had to close it. In late 1983 they completed a new mini-mill in Tennessee.

Mini-mills had tripled their output in the last decade to capture 13 percent of domestic shipments. Iverson believed mini-mills could achieve 25 percent by the mid-1980s. But because they could not go beyond 35 to 40 percent because of technical limitations, mini-mills could not produce the sheet steel used in cars and appliances.

Iverson told *Metal Center News*:

We are very interested in the development of a thin slab, which would then allow mini-mills to produce plate and other flatrolled products . . . actually, the thinnest slab that can now be produced is about 6 inches thick. . . . (That results in a plant that is too large.) There are a number of people working to develop the process. . . . We have done some work, but our primary efforts at the moment are in connection with other people who are working on it. . . . The likelihood is it would be developed by a foreign company. There are more efforts by foreign steel companies in that direction than in the United States. . . . I'd say probably a minimum of 3–5 years, or it could take as much as 10 to achieve this.

Iverson foresaw a new generation of mini-mill.

If you go way back, mini-mills got started by rolling reinforcing bars. With the advent of continuous casting and improvements in rolling mills, mini-mills gradually got into shapes. Now they have moved in two other directions; one being to larger sizes, and the other being a growing metallurgical expertise for improved product quality and production of special bar quality in alloys. Both of these represent expansion of markets for mini-mills.

Organization

Nucor, with its 12-person corporate office located in Charlotte, North Carolina, had divisions spread across the U.S. The eight divisions, one for every plant, had a general manager directly responsible to Mr. Iverson, who was also a vice-president of the corporation. (See Exhibit 14.4.) The divisions were of two basic types, joist plants and steel mills. The corporate staff consisted of single specialists in personnel and planning, and then a more-fully-developed financial function under Mr. Sam Siegel. Iverson in the beginning had chosen Charlotte "as the new home base for what he had envisioned as a small cadre of executives who would guide a decentralized operation with liberal authority delegated to managers in the field."

Iverson gave his views on organization:

You can tell a lot about a company by looking at its organization charts. . . . If you see a lot of staff, you can bet it is not a very efficient organization. . . . Secondly don't have assistants. We do not have that title and prohibit it in our company. . . . In this organiza-

Exhibit 14.4   Organization Chart

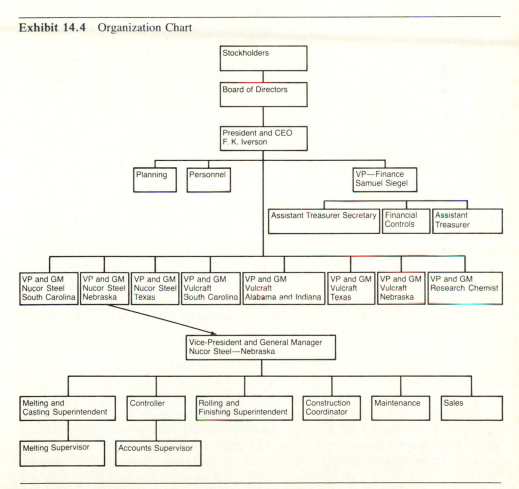

Source: Company Manuals

tion nobody reports to the corporate office, the division managers report directly to me. . . . And one of the most important things is to restrict as much as possible the number of management layers.

Each division is a profit center and the division manager has control over the day-to-day decisions that make that particular division profitable or not profitable. We expect the division to provide division contribution, which is earnings before corporate expenses. We do not allocate our corporate expenses, because we do not think there is any way to do this reasonably and fairly. We do focus on earnings. And we expect a division to earn 25-percent return on total assets employed, before corporate expenses, taxes, interest, or profit sharing. And we have a saying in the company—if a manager doesn't provide that for a number of years, we are either going to get rid of the division or get rid of the general manager, and it's generally the division manager.

A Joist Division manager commented:

I've been a division manager four years now and at times I'm still awed by it, the opportunity I was given to be a Fortune 500 vice-president. . . . I think we are successful because it is our style to pay more attention to our business than our competitors. . . . We are kind of a "no-nonsense" company. That is not to say we don't have time for play, but we work hard when we work and the company is first and foremost in our minds.

He continued:

I think another one of the successes of our company has been the fact that we have a very minimum number of management levels. We've been careful to avoid getting top-heavy and so consequently we put a great deal of responsibility on each individual at each level. It has often been said, jokingly, that if you are the janitor at Vulcraft and you get the right promotions, about four promotions would take you to the top of the company.

Mr. Iverson's style of management is to allow the division manager all the latitude in the world. His involvement with the managers is quite limited. As we've grown, he no longer has the time to visit with the managers more than once or twice a year. . . . Whereas in many large companies the corporate office makes the major decisions and the people at the operating level sit back to wait for their marching orders, that's not the case at Nucor. . . . In a way I feel like I run my own company because I really don't get any marching orders from Mr. Iverson. He lets you run the division the way you see fit and the only way he will step in is if he sees something he doesn't like, particularly bad profits, high costs, or whatever. But in the four years I've worked with him I don't believe he has ever issued one single instruction to me to do something differently. I can't recall a single instance.

The divisions did their own manufacturing, selling, accounting, engineering, and personnel management. A Steel Division manager, when questioned about Florida Steel, which had a large plant 90 miles away, commented: "I really don't know anything about Florida Steel. . . . I except they do have more of the hierarchy. I think they have central purchasing, centralized sales, centralized credit collections, centralized engineering, and most of the major functions." He didn't feel greater centralization would be good for Nucor. "The purchasing activity, for example, removed from the field tends to become rather insensitive to the needs of the field and does not feel the pressures of responsibility. And the division they are buying for has no control over what they pay. . . . Likewise centralized sales would not be sensitive to the needs of their divisions."

South Magazine observed Iverson had established a characteristic organizational style described as stripped down and no-nonsense. "Jack Benny would like this company," observed Roland Underhill, an analyst with Crowell, Weedon and Co. of Los Angeles. "So would Peter Drucker." Underhill pointed out that Nucor's thriftiness doesn't end with its "Spartan" office staff or modest offices. "There are no corporate perquisites," he recited. "No company planes, no country club memberships. No company cars."

Fortune reported: "'Iverson takes the subway when he is in New York,' a Wall Street analyst reports in a voice that suggests both admiration and amazement." The general managers reflected this style in the operation of their individual divisions. These offices were more like plant offices of the offices of private companies built around manufacturing and not for public appeal. They were simple, routine, and businesslike.

Division Managers

The general managers met three times a year. In October, they presented preliminary budgets and capital requests. In late February they met to finalize budgets and treat miscellaneous matters. Then, at a meeting in May, they handled personnel matters, such as wage increases and changes of policies or benefits. The general managers as a group considered the raises for the department heads, the next level of management below them. One of the managers described it.

Once a year all the general managers get together and review all the department heads throughout the company. We have kind of an informal evaluation process. It's an intangible thing, a judgment as to how dedicated an individual is and how well he performs compared to the same position at another plant. Sometimes the numbers don't come out the way a general manager wants to see them, but it's a fair evaluation. The final number is picked by Mr. Iverson. Occasionally there are some additional discussions with Mr. Iverson. He always has an open mind and might be willing to consider a little more for one individual. We consider the group of, say, joist production managers at one time. The six managers are rated for performance. We assign a number, such as +3 to a real crackerjack performer or a −2 to someone who needs improvement. These ratings become a part of the final pay increase granted.

The corporate personnel manager described management relations as informal, trusting, and not "bureaucratic." He felt there was a minimum of paperwork; a phone call was more common, and no confirming memo was felt necessary. Iverson stated:

Management is not a popularity contest. If everybody agrees with the organization, something is wrong with the organization. You don't expect people in the company to put their arms around each other, and you don't interfere with every conflict. Out of conflict often comes the best answer to a particular problem. So don't worry about it. You are always going to have some conflict in an organization. You will always have differences of opinion, and that's healthy. Don't create problems where there are none.

The Vulcraft manager commented:

We have what I would call a very freindly spirit of competition from one plant to the next. And of course all of the vice-presidents and general managers share the same bonus system so we are in this together as a team even though we operate our divisions individually.

The general managers are paid a bonus based on a total corporate profit rather than their own division's profit. The steel manager commented:

I think it's very important for the general managers to be concerned with contributing to the overall accomplishment of the company. There is a lot of interplay between the divisions with a flow of services, products, and ideas between divisions. Even though we are reasonably autonomous we are not isolated.

He continued,

We don't like the division managers to make decisions that would take that division away from where we want the whole company to go. But we certainly want the divisions to try new things. We are good copiers; if one division finds something that works then we will all try it. I think that's one of our strengths. We have a lot of diverse people looking at ways to do things better.

Iverson reveals his view of management in his disdain for consultants:

They must have a specific job to do because they can't make your decision. . . . The fellow on the line has to make decisions. . . . First he has to communicate and then he has to have the intestinal fortitude and the personal strength to make the decisions, sometimes under very difficult conditions.

He continues,

A good manager is adaptable and he is sensitive to cultural, geographical, environment, and business climates. Most important of all he communicates. . . . You never know if someone is a good manager until he manages. And that's why we take people as young as we possibly can, throw responsibility at them, and they either work or they don't work. In a sense it's survival of the fittest. But don't kid yourself; that's what industry is all about.

The Steel Division manager, in comparing the Nucor manager to the typical manager of a large corporation, commented: "We would probably tend to have managers who have confidence in their abilities and, very importantly, have confidence in other people in their division. And people who are very sensitive to the employees of their division." He added: "But, I think if you saw four or five different division managers, you'd have four or five different decision-making styles."

The Vulcraft general manager, in his late 30s, had been promoted to the division manager level four years ago. He commented:

The step from department manager to division manager is a big one. I can't think of an instance when a general manager job has been offered to an individual that it has been passed up. Often it means moving from one part of the country to another. There are five department heads in six joist plants, which means there are 30 people who are considered for division manager slots at a joist plant. Mr. Iverson selects the division managers.

His experience is enlightening.

When I came to this plant four years ago, we had too many people, too much overhead. We had 410 people at the plant and I could see, because I knew how many people we had in the Nebraska plant, we had many more than we needed. That was my yardstick and we set about to reduce those numbers by attrition. . . . We have made a few equipment changes that made it easier for the men, giving them an opportunity to make better bonuses. Of course the changes were very subtle in any given case but overall in four years we have probably helped the men tremendously. With 55 fewer men, perhaps 40–45 fewer in the production area, we are still capable of producing the same number of tons as four years ago.

The divisions managed their activities with a minimum of contact with the corporate staff. Each day disbursements were reported to Siegel's office. Payments flowed into regional lockboxes. On a weekly basis, joist divisions reported total quotas, sales cancellations, backlog, and production. Steel mills reported tons rolled, outside shipments, orders, cancellations, and backlog. Mr. Iverson graphed the data. He might talk to the division about every two weeks. Iverson was known to bounce ideas off the Steel Division Manager in Darlington with whom he had worked since Iverson joined the company.

The Vulcraft manager commented on the communications with the corporate office: "It's kind of a steady pipeline. I might talk to the corporate office once a day or it might be once a week. But it generally involves, I would not say trivial information, but mundane things. Occasionally I hear from Sam or Ken about serious matters."

Each month the divisions prepared a two-page (11″ by 17″) operations analysis which was sent to all the managers. Its three main purposes were (1) financial consolidations, (2) sharing information among the divisions, and (3) Iverson's examination. This was summarized and the performance statistics for all the divisions then returned to the managers.

Vulcraft—the Joist Division

Half of Nucor's business was the manufacture and sale of open web steel joists and joist girders from six Vulcraft divisions located in Florence, South Carolina, Norfolk, Nebraska, Ft. Payne, Alabama, Grapeland, Texas, St. Joe, Indiana, and Brigham City, Utah. Open web joists, in contrast to solid joists, were made of steel angle iron separated by round bars or smaller-angle iron (see Exhibit 14.5). These joists were of lower cost and greater strength for many applications and were used primarily as the roof support systems in larger buildings, such as warehouses and stores.

The joist industry was characterized by high competition among many manufacturers for many small customers. The Vulcraft divisions had over 3,000 customers, none of whom dominated the business. With an estimated 25 percent of the market, Nucor was the largest supplier in the U.S. They utilized national advertising campaigns and prepared competitive bids on 80 to 90 percent of buildings using joists. Competition was based on price and delivery performance. Nucor had developed computer programs to prepare de-

Exhibit 14.5   Steel Joists

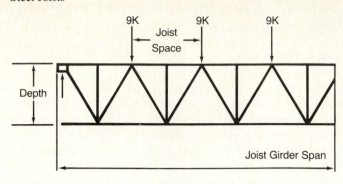

signs for customers and compute bids based on current prices and labor standards. In addition, each Vulcraft plant maintained its own engineering department to help customers with design problems or specifications. The Florence manager commented: "Here on the East coast we have six to seven major competitors; of course none of them are as large as we are. The competition for any order will be heavy, and we will see six or seven different prices." He added, "I think we have a strong selling force in the marketplace. It has been said to us by some of our competitors that in this particular industry we have the finest selling organization in the country."

Nucor aggressively sought to be the lowest-cost producer in the industry. Materials and freight were two important elements of cost. They maintained their own fleet of almost 100 trucks to ensure and control on-time delivery to all of the states, although most business was regional because of transportation costs. Plants were located in rural areas near the markets they served.

The Florence manager stated:

I don't feel there's a joist producer in the country that can match our cost. . . . We are sticklers about cutting out unnecessary overhead. Because we put so much responsibility on our people and because we have what I think is an excellent incentive program, our people are willing to work harder to accomplish these profitable goals.

Production

On the basic assembly line used at Nucor, three or four of which might make up any one plant, about six tons per hour would be assembled. In the first stage eight people cut the angle to the right lengths or bent the round bars to the desired form. These were moved on a roll conveyor to six-man assembly stations where the component parts would be tacked together for the next stage, welding. Drilling and miscellaneous work was done by three people between the lines. The nine-man welding station completed the welds before passing the joists on roller conveyors to two-man inspection teams. The last step before shipment was the painting.

In the joist plants, the workers had control over and responsibility for quality. There was an independent quality control inspector who had the authority to reject the run of joists and cause them to be reworked. The quality control people were not under the incentive system and reported to the engineering department.

Daily production might vary widely since each joist was made for a specific job. The wide range of joists made control of the workload at each station difficult; bottlenecks might arise anywhere along the line. Each workstation was responsible for identifying any bottlenecks so that the foreman could reassign people promptly to maintain productivity. Since workers knew most of the jobs on the line, including the more skilled welding job, many could be shifted as needed. Work on the line was described by the general manager as "not machine-type but mostly physical labor." He said the important thing was to avoid bottlenecks.

There were four lines of about 28 people each on two shifts at the Florence Division. The jobs on the line were rated on responsibility and assigned a base wage, between $6 and $7. In addition, a weekly bonus was paid on the total output of each line. Each worker received the same-percent bonus on his base wage.

Experience had established the time required to make a joist; the manager, with the company 15 years, had seen no time studies in the company. As a job was bid, the cost of each joist was determined through the computer program. The time depended on the length, number of panels, and depth of the joist.

At the time of production, the labor value of production—the standard—was similarly determined. The general manager stated: "In the last five or six years we have not changed a standard." The standards list he was using was eight years old. They adjusted the standard if the bonus was too high. He said the technological improvements over the last few years had been small. He reported that the bonus had increased from about 60 percent four years ago to about 100 percent in 1982. Exhibits 14.6 and 14.7 show data typically com-

---

Exhibit 14.6   Performance: Tons/Man Hour

1977	.163
1978	.179
1979	.192
1980	.195
1981	.206
July 1982	.211

Tons/Man-Hour, 52 Weeks Moving Average

Exhibit 14.7   Sample of Percentage Performance—July 1982

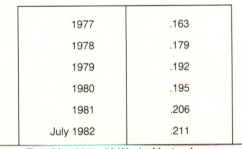

Line	1	2	3	4
1st	117	97	82	89
2nd	98	102	94	107

Shift

puted on performance and used by the manager. He said the difference in performance on the line resulted from the different abilities of the crews. "We don't have an industrial engineering staff. Our engineering department's work is limited to the design and the preparation of the paperwork prior to the actual fabrication process. Now, that is not to say they don't have any involvement in fabrication. But the efficiency of the plant is entirely up to the manufacturing department."

Management

In discussing his philosophy for dealing with the work force, the manager stated:

You believe very strongly in the incentive system we have. We are a nonunion shop and we all feel that the way to stay so is to take care of our people and show them we care. I think that's easily done because of our fewer layers of management. . . . I spend a good part of my time in the plant, maybe an hour or so a day. If a man wants to know anything, for example an insurance question, I'm there and they walk right up to me and ask me questions which I'll answer the best I know how. . . . You can always tell when people are basically happy. If they haven't called for a meeting themselves or they are not hostile in any way you can take it they understand the company's situation and accept it. . . . We do listen to our people. . . . For instance last fall I got a call from a couple of workers saying that the people in our shipping and receiving area felt they were not being paid properly in relation to production people. So we met with them, discussed the situation, and committed ourselves to reviewing the rates of other plants. We assured them that we would get back to them with an answer by the first of the year. Which we did. And there were a few minor changes.

The manager reported none of the plants had any particular labor problems though there have been some in the past.

In 1976, two years before I came here, there was a union election at this plant which arose out of racial problems. The company actually lost the election to the U.S. Steel Workers. When it came time to begin negotiating the contract, the workers felt, or came to see, that they had little to gain from being in the union. The union was not going to be able to do anything more for them than they were already getting. So slowly the union activity died out and the union quietly withdrew.

He discussed formal systems for consulting with the workers before changes were made:

Of course we're cautioned by our labor counsel to maintain an open pipeline to our employees. We post all changes, company earnings, changes in the medical plan, anything that might affect an employee's job. Mr. Iverson has another philosophy, which is, "Either tell your people everything or tell them nothing." We choose to tell them everything. We don't have any regularly scheduled meetings. We meet whenever there's a need. The most recent example was the wage freeze in the spring of 1982.
We don't lay our people off and we make a point of telling our people this. Right now we are scheduling our line for four days, but the men are allowed to come in on the fifth day for maintenance work at base pay. The men in the plant on an average running bonus

might make $13 an hour. If their base pay is half that, on Friday they would only get $6–$7 an hour. Surprisingly many of the men do not want to come in on Friday. They feel comfortable with just working four days a week. They are happy to have that extra day off.

In April 1982 the Executive Committee decided, in view of economic conditions, that a pay freeze was necessary. The employees normally receive an increase in their base pay the first of June. Thus, the decision was made at that time to freeze wages. The officers of the company, as a show of good faith, accepted a 5-percent pay cut. In addition to announcing this to the workers with a stuffer in their pay envelope, a series of meetings were carried out. Each production line, or incentive group of workers, met in the plant conference room with all of supervision, their foreman, the plant production manager, and the division manager. The economic crisis was explained to the employees by the production manager and any questions they had were answered.

Steel Divisions

Nucor had steel mills in four locations: Nebraska, South Carolina, Texas, and Utah. The mills were modern mini-mills, all built within the last 15 years to convert scrap steel into standard angles, flats, rounds, and channels using the latest technology. Sales in 1980 were 677,000 tons, a 25-percent increase over 1979. This was about 65 percent of the mills' output, the remainder being used by other Nucor divisions. In recent years, Nucor had broadened its product line to include a wider range of steel chemistries, sizes, and special shapes. The capacity of the mills reached 2 million tons in 1982 and sales to outside customers were projected to consume this capacity by 1985.

By 1967 about 60% of each Vulcraft sales dollar was spent on materials, primarily steel. Thus, the goal of keeping costs low made it imperative to obtain steel economically. In addition, in 1967 Vulcraft bought about 60% of its steel from foreign sources. As the Vulcraft Division grew, Nucor became concerned about its ability to obtain an adequate economical supply of steel and in 1968 began construction of its first steel mill in Darlington, South Carolina. By 1972 the Florence, South Carolina joist plant bought over 90% of its steel from this mill. The Fort Payne Plant bought about 50% of its steel from Florence. The other joist plants in Nebraska, Indiana and Texas found transportation costs prohibitive and continued to buy their steel from other steel companies, both foreign and domestic. Since the mill had excess capacity Nucor began to market its steel products to outside customers. In 1972, 75% of the shipments of Nucor Steel was to Vulcraft and 25% was to other customers.

Iverson explained:

In constructing these mills we have experimented with new processes and new manufacturing techniques. We serve as our own general contractor and design and build much of our own equipment. In one or more of our mills we have built our own continuous casting unit, reheat furnaces, cooling beds, and in Utah even our own mill stands. All of these to date have cost under $125 per ton of annual capacity—compared with projected cost for large integrated mills of $1,200–$1,500 per ton of annual capacity, ten times our cost.

Our mills have high productivity. We currently use less than four man-hours to produce a ton of steel. This includes everyone in the operation: maintenance, clerical, accounting, and sales and management. On the basis of our production workers alone, it is less than *three man-hours per ton. Our total employment costs are less than $60 per ton compared with the average employment costs of the seven largest U.S. steel companies of close to $130 per ton. Our total labor costs are less than 20 percent of our sales price.*

In contrast to Nucor's less than four man-hours, similar Japanese mills are said to require more than five hours, and comparable U.S. mills over six hours.

Our average yield from molten metal to finished product is over 90 percent, compared with an average U.S. steel industry yield of 75 percent. Increased yield saves energy—our energy costs are about $39 a ton compared with the energy cost for integrated steel producers of about $75 a ton. Newer Japanese mills report productivity in the range of 700–1,000 tons per employee per year. The productivity in older integrated mills in the U.S. is half of that (350–400 tons).

Nucor produced approximately 800 tons per employee and had a goal of 1,000 tons per man per year.

The Steel-Making Process

A steel mill is divided into two phases, preparation of steel of the proper "chemistry" and, secondly, the forming of the steel into the desired products. The typical mini-mill utilized scrap steel, such as junk auto parts, instead of the iron ore which would be used in larger, integrated steel mills. The typical mini-mill had an annual capacity of 200,000–600,000 tons, compared with the 7 million tons of Bethlehem Steel's Sparrow's Point, Maryland, integrated plant.

A charging bucket fed loads of scrap steel into electric-arc furnaces. The molted load, called a heat, was poured into a ladle to be carried by overhead crane to the casting machine. In the casting machine the liquid steel was extruded as a continuous red-hot solid bar of steel and cut into lengths weighing some 900 lbs. called "billets." In the typical plant the billet, about four inches in cross section and about 20 feet long, was held temporarily in a pit where it cooled to normal temperatures. Periodically billets were carried to the rolling mill and placed into a reheat oven to bring them up to the 2,000° F, at which they would be malleable. In the rolling mill, presses and dies progressively converted the billet into the desired round bars, angles, channels, flats and other products. After cutting to some standard lengths, they were moved to the warehouse.

Nucor's first steel mill, employing more than 500 people, was located in Darlington, South Carolina. The mill, with its three electric-arc furnaces, operated 24 hours a day, 5½ days a week. Nucor had made a number of improvements in the melting and casting operations. The former general manager of the Darlington plant had developed a system, involving preheating the ladles, which allowed for the faster flow of steel into the caster and resulted in better control of the steel, less time, and lower capital investment. The casting machines were continuous casters, as opposed to the old batch method. The objective in the front of the mill was to keep the casters working. At Nucor "each strand was in operation 90 percent of the time. A competitor had recently announced a 'record rate' of 75 percent which it was able to sustain for a week."

Nucor was also perhaps the only mill in the country which regularly avoided the reheating of billets. This saved $10–$12 per ton in fuel usage and losses due to oxidation of the steel. In the rolling mill, the first machine was a roughing mill by Morgarshammar, the first of its kind in the Western Hemisphere. This Swedish machine had been chosen because of its lower cost, productivity, and the flexibility it provided. Passing through another five to nine finishing mills converted the billet into the desired finished product. The yield for the billet to finished product was about 93 percent.

The Darlington design became the basis for plants in Nebraska, Texas, and Utah. The Texas plant had cost under $80 per ton of annual capacity. Whereas the typical mini-mill cost approximately $250 per ton, the average cost of all four of Nucor's mills was under $135. An integrated mill was expected to cost between $1,200 and $1,500 per ton.

The Darlington mill was organized into 12 natural groups for incentive pay: two mills, two shifts, and three groups—melting and casting, rolling mill, and finishing. In melting and casting there were three or four different standards, depending on the material, which had been established by the department manager years ago on historical performance. The general manager stated: "We don't change the standards." He further stated that the caster, which is the key to the operation, was used at a 92-percent level, greater than the manufacturer claimed for its equipment. For every good ton of billet above the standard hourly rate for the week, workers in the group received a 4-percent bonus. For example, with a common standard of 10 tons per run-hour and an actual rate for the week of 28 tons per hour, the workers would receive a bonus of 72 percent of their base rate in the week's paycheck.

In the rolling mill there were more than 100 products, each with a different historical standard. Workers received a 4–6 percent bonus for every good ton sheared per hour for the week over the computed standard. The general manager said the standard would be changed only if there was a major machinery change and that a standard had not been changed since the initial development period for the plant. He commented that in exceeding the standard, the workers wouldn't work harder but cooperated to avoid problems and moved more quickly if a problem developed. If there is a way to improve output, "they will tell us."

In the general manager's view,

The key to making a profit when selling a product with no aesthetic value, or a product that you really can't differentiate from your competitors, is cost. I don't look at us as a fantastic marketing organization, even though I think we are pretty good; but we don't try to overcome unreasonable costs by mass marketing. We maintain low costs by keeping the employee force at the level it should be, not doing things that aren't necessary to achieve our goals, and allowing people to function on their own and by judging them on their results.

To keep a cooperative and productive work force you need, number one, to be completely honest about everything; number two, allow each employee as much as possible to make decisions about that employee's work, to find easier and more productive ways to perform duties; and third, be as fair as possible to all employees. Most of the changes we make in work procedures and in equipment come from the employees. They really know the problems of their jobs better than anyone else. We don't have any industrial engineers, nor do we ever intend to. Because that's a type of specialist who tends to take responsibility off the top-division management and give them a crutch.

To communicate with my employees, I try to spend time in the plant and at intervals have meetings with the employees. Usually if they have a question they just visit me. Recently a small group visited me in my office to discuss our vacation policy. They had some suggestions and, after listening to them, I had to agree that the ideas were good.

The Incentive System

The foremost characteristic of Nucor's personnel system was its incentive plan. Another major personnel policy was providing job security. Also all employees at Nucor received the same fringe benefits. There was only one group insurance plan. Holidays and vacations did not differ by job. The company had no executive dining rooms or rest rooms, no fishing lodges, company cars, or reserved parking places.

Absenteeism and tardiness were not problems at Nucor. Each employee had four days of absence before their pay was reduced. In addition to these they were allowed to miss work for jury duty, military leave, or the death of close relatives. After this, a day's absence cost them bonus pay for that week and, if one was more than a half-hour late, they lost the bonus for that day.

Employees were kept informed about the company. Charts showing division results in return-on-assets and bonus payoffs were posted in prominent places in the plant. The personnel manager commented that, as he traveled around to all the plants, he found everyone in the company could tell him the level of profits in their division. The general managers held dinners at least twice a year with their employees. The dinners were held with 50 or 60 employees at a time. After introductory remarks the floor was opened for discussion of any work-related problems. The company also had a formal grievance procedure. The Darlington manager couldn't recall the last grievance he had.

There was a new employee orientation program and an employee handbook which contained personnel policies and rules. The corporate office sent all news releases to the division where they were posted on bulletin boards. Each employee in the company also received a copy of the annual report. For the last several years the cover of the annual report had contained the names of all Nucor employees. Every child of every Nucor employee received up to $1,200 a year for four years if they chose to go on to higher education, including technical schools.

The average hourly worker's pay was $31,000, compared with the average earnings in manufacturing in that state of slightly more than $13,000. The personnel manager believed that pay was not the only thing the workers like about Nucor. He stated that an NBC interviewer, working on the documentary "If Japan Can, Why Can't We," often heard: "I enjoy working for Nucor because Nucor is the best, the most productive, and the most profitable company that I know of."

There are four incentive programs at Nucor: one for production workers; one for department heads; a third for staff people such as accountants, secretaries, or engineers; and a fourth for senior management, which included the division managers. All of these programs were on a group basis.

In the production program, groups ranged in size from 25 to 30 people and had definable and measurable operations. The company believed the program should be simple and that bonuses should be paid promptly. The personnel manager stated:

Their bonus is based on roughly 90 percent of historical time it takes to make a particular joist. If during a week they make joists at 60-percent less than the standard time, they receive a 60-percent bonus. This is paid with their regular pay the very next week. We simply take the complete paycheck including overtime and multiply it by the bonus factor. We do not pay bonus when equipment is not operating. We have the philosophy that when equipment is not operating everybody suffers and the bonus for downtime is zero.

The foremen were also part of the group and received the same bonus as the employees they supervised.

The second incentive program was for department heads in the various divisions. The incentive pay here was based on division contribution, defined as the division earnings before corporate expenses and profit sharing. Bonuses were reported to run as high as 51 percent of a person's base salary in the divisions and 30 percent on jobs in the corporate office.

There was a third plan for people who were not in production nor were department managers. Their bonus was based on either the division return on assets or the corporate return on assets.

The fourth program was for the senior officers. The senior officers had no employment contracts, pension or retirement plans, nor other normal perquisites. Their base salaries were set at about 70 percent of what an individual doing similar work in other companies would receive. More than half of the officers' compensation was reported to be based directly on the company's earnings. Ten percent of the pre-tax earnings over a pre-established level, based on a 12-percent return on stockholders' equity, was set aside and allocated to the senior officers according to their base salary. Half the bonus was paid in cash and half was deferred.

Instead of a retirement plan, the company had a profit-sharing plan with a deferred trust. Each year 10 percent of pre-tax earnings were put into profit sharing. Fifteen percent of this was set aside to be paid to employees in March of the following year as a cash bonus and the remainder was put into trust for each employee on the basis of percent of their earnings as a percent of total wages paid in the corporation. The employees were vested 20 percent after the first year and gained an additional 10-percent vesting each year thereafter. Employees received a quarterly statement of their balance in profit sharing.

The company had an employer monthly stock investment plan in which Nucor added 10 percent to the amount the employee contributed and paid the commission on the purchase of any Nucor stock. After each five years of service with the company, the employee received a service award made up of five shares of Nucor stock. Additionally, if profits were good, extraordinary bonus payments would be made to the employees. In 1978 each employee received a $500 payment.

Iverson had said:

I think the first obligation of the company is to the stockholders and to its employees. I find in this country too many cases where employees are underpaid and corporate management is making huge social donations for self-fulfillment. We regularly give donations, because we have a very interesting corporate policy. First, we give donations where our employees are. Secondly, we give donations which will benefit our employees, such as the YMCA. It is a difficult area and it requires a lot of thought. There is certainly a strong social responsibility for a company, but it cannot be at the expense of the employees or the stockholders.

Nucor had no trouble finding the people to staff its plants. When they built the mill in Jewett, Texas, in 1975, they had over 5,000 applications for the 400 jobs, many coming from people in Houston and Dallas. Yet everyone did not find work at Nucor what they wanted. In 1975 a Harvard team found high turnover among new production workers after start-up. The cause appeared to be pressure from fellow workers in the group incentive situation. The Harvard team found a survival-of-the-fittest situation where those who didn't like to work seldom stuck around. "Productivity increase and turnover declined dramatically once these people left," the Harvard team concluded.

The Wall Street Journal reported in 1981:

Harry Pig, a sub-district director for the USW in South Carolina, sees a darker side in Nucor's incentive plan. He contends that Nucor unfairly penalizes workers by taking away big bonus payments for absence or tardiness, regardless of the reason. Workers who are ill, he says, try to work because they can't afford to give up the bonus payment. "Nucor whips them into line," he adds. He acknowledges, though, that high salaries are the major barrier to unionizing the company.

As 1984 Began

Looking ahead, Iverson said, "The next decade will be an exciting one for steel producers. It will tax our abilities to keep pace with technological changes we can see now on the horizon." He believed the steel industry would continue to play a pivotal role in the growth of American industry. He pointed out comparative advantages of the U.S. steel industry: an abundance of resources, relatively low energy costs, lower transportation costs, and the change in the government's attitude toward business.

The large steel producers were moving to improve their operations. In December 1983, U.S. Steel announced it would reduce its capacity by ⅙ as it closed a number of plants and cut back operations at others. The board approved a plan to spend $300 million to build new continuous casting machines. By 1986, 55 percent of U.S. Steel's production would be through the continuous casting facility. These moves showed U.S. Steel's commitment to remain in the flat roll market, which makes steel for the auto industry. "Rich Carbonara, sales manager of U.S. Steel's 3 person Carolina sales force based in Charlotte, called the company's action 'a giant step forward . . . we just can't be all things to all people,' he said. U.S. Steel is 'being realistic that foreign imports and mini-mills have certain segments of the market.'"

In March 1983, the United Steel Workers of America signed a contract which included wage concessions and reduced benefits to improve the competitiveness of the basic steel industry. Other small steel companies, such as Korf, were expected to gain similar concessions from their unions. At the same time Nucor, which had frozen wages the prior year, announced a 5-percent wage increase. "Most of the plants they are shutting down are making bar products that are similar to the products we produce," said Ken Iverson. "I don't think we are seeing the demise of the steel industry. . . . We are seeing it changing to a high-technology type of industry. . . . Other large steel companies probably will close their antiquated mills in 1984. Nucor has ample capacity in all of its plants and it doesn't have immediate expansion plans."

In the summer of 1982 Iverson had begun to reduce the company's debt to even lower levels. He felt the company's current facilities would be adequate for the next several years. He also felt it would be necessary to slow the company's rapid expansion and allow time for the management to settle down. He was concerned that as sales doubled over the next five years, he would have to add another layer to the management structure. When the *Metal Center News* asked him what scared him most about the future, he responded:

I think probably the biggest concern of all is that we may again experience extremely high interest rates with high inflation and possibly have an economic bust that is even worse than what we experienced in 1982. . . . It could well do a great deal of harm to this company from the standpoint that our philosophies are out of step with that type of economy. Although it's not a written commitment, we say we will not lay off any employee for lack of work unless the survival of the company is at stake. Under that scenario, our survival would be at stake, and that would disrupt the philosophy we had for many, many years.

Iverson now considered other mini-mills to be his primary competition rather than foreign producers. "We are now head-to-head against much tougher competition. . . . It was no contest when we were up against integrated mills. Now we are facing mini-mills who all have the same scrap price, the same electrical costs, and use the same technologies." He believed the easy pickings were over. "The areas of growth opportunities are not as evident or as easy as in the 1970s," Iverson said. "We've said we feel we can maintain growth of 15–20 percent a year. And to do so we are going to have to constantly expand our product line." But it was Iverson's opinion that it would take 2–3 years for earnings to return to the record levels of 1981 because of the historical pattern of recovery in the steel industry. Iverson felt the future would be a new game with numerous challenges, but was confident Nucor was ready.

References

Materials quoted in this case were obtained from the following sources:

Richard I. Kirland, Jr., "Pilgrim's Profits at Nucor," *Fortune*, April 6, 1981.

Douglas R. Sease, "Mini-Mill Steel Makers No Longer Very Small, Out Perform Big Ones," *The Wall Street Journal*, January 12, 1981.

Interview with Iverson.

Lydia Chavez, "The Price of Mini-Steel Mills," *The New York Times*, September 23, 1981.

Don Bedwel, "Nucor's Lean, Mean Management Team," *South Magazine*, August 1980.

"Nucor Corporation," 9-676-078, Harvard University Case Service, Reviewed March 1978.

Allen Joch, "Iverson: Alloys Usher in New Era," *Metal Center News*, August 1983.

Selected articles from the *Charlotte Observer*, August 29, 1982; March 21, 1983; October 26, 1983; December 29, 1983.

Restructuring Playboy for Profits

• *Julian W. Vincze and James M. Higgins* •

The 30th-anniversary annual report (fiscal year ending June 30, 1984) of Playboy Enterprises Incorporated (PEI) heralded a return to profitability of a stronger, leaner PEI. Christie Hefner, the daughter of PEI founder Hugh Hefner, had achieved a remarkable turnaround from the 1982 net loss of over $51 million with a reported 1984 profit of over $27 million.

Many observers were surprised in May 1982, when it was announced that the-then 29-year-old Christie Hefner would assume the president and chief operating officer roles at PEI. Skeptics pointed out that PEI had been a conglomerate for almost 20 years and that 1981 sales revenues had been close to $400 million. Many questioned how a relatively inexperienced person could direct such an organization as PEI, especially a troubled PEI which not only faced significant net losses but several related serious business reverses. However fiscal 1984 results indicated that Christie had steered PEI in a successful direction once again. Thus Playboy continued its up-and-down history, one which evolved over four distinct periods. The first of these is from inception to 1975. Exhibit 15.1 provides financial information related to this first key period in PEI history.

Playboy's History — Growth — FY 1954–FY 1975

Hugh Marston Hefner, Playboy Enterprises' founder and majority stockholder, experienced a puritanical childhood in Chicago. It was the rejection of this background that eventually led Hefner to initiate *Playboy* magazine. After serving two years in the army, Hefner obtained an undergraduate degree at the University of Illinois. He then held several short-term jobs including a stint as a copywriter in the advertising department of *Esquire*, a men's literary magazine. In 1952 Hefner decided to try publishing his own magazine; he modified *Esquire*'s format by adding photographs of female nudes. The result was *Playboy* magazine.

The first issue of *Playboy* was assembled in Hefner's Chicago apartment. To draw attention to his first edition, Hefner bought a nude photograph of Marilyn Monroe. Marilyn became the magazine's first "Playmate of the Month," a unique three-page foldout female nude. This first edition sold 55,000 copies at $.50 each, and the magazine became an overnight success. By the fourth issue, the magazine was solvent, and Hefner was able to open an office in downtown Chicago. As the magazine's circulation and profits grew, maintaining an "image" became important. When he founded Playboy, Hefner adopted a worldly-wise male rabbit in evening clothes, surrounded by a host of admiring female bunnies, as its trademark.

Hefner's empire grew extensively by pursuing not only the expansion of his publishing efforts with new magazines, but also by venturing into movies, television, hotels, records, books, personal items, and other diversifications. These endeavors were grouped together under major divisions: the Publishing Group; Playboy Clubs and Hotels; the Entertain-

Exhibit 15.1   Playboy Enterprises Inc. and Subsidiaries Financed Summary
(in thousands except per-share amounts)

Year	Net Sales and Revenue	Net Earnings	Total Assets	Long-Term Financing Obligations	Earnings Per Share
1984*	$187,144	$27,336	$169,431	$ 3,484	$2.76
1983*	193,672	(17,493)	137,565	152	(1.77)
1982*	210,043	(51,681)	175,182	349	(5.23)
1981	388,870	14,341	291,895	18,806	1.45
1980	363,190	13,078	320,481	19,633	1.31
1979	297,486	9,104	255,668	21,244	.90
1978	246,746	6,269	218,258	16,185	.44
1977	223,402	4,167	181,815	16,271	.62
1976					
1975	197,734	1,046	158,704	17,185	.12
1974	204,268	5,949	154,552	17,684	.64
1973	190,011	11,258	160,599	30,525	1.20
1972	159,450	10,599	148,866	31,968	1.16
1971	131,587	9,221	115,512	34,116	1.07
1970	119,563	8,164			.95
1969	108,488	7,587			.89
1968	89,106	6,779			.78
1967	73,961	5,933			.68
1966	62,303	4,738			.54
1965	46,104	3,107			.36
1964	30,419	2,032			.23
1963	23,880	1,052			.12
1962	18,025	(84)			(.01)

*PEI modified accounting treatment of various items during those years.

Source: PEI annual reports.

ment Group; and Other Operations. All have had a singular dependency upon the Playboy rabbit emblem and the Playboy image. Hefner worked long hours to build his empire, and his thoughts and philosophies guided its destiny for much of its 30 years. Many of his actions were almost whimsical and he had disdain for the business side of PEI, a disdain that cost him millions of dollars because of several ill-founded strategic decisions.

The Publishing Group

Within the publishing group, several magazines had been attempted, but only two have played an important role. *Playboy*, which by 1975 had a circulation of almost 6.5 million (domestic and foreign editions), and *Oui*, which topped 1.5 million in circulation by 1974. Competition entered the field and began to hurt *Playboy*'s sales in the mid-1970s.

Playboy Clubs and Hotels (Leisure Activities)

PEI put its bunny image to good use in its clubs, but did not find that success in hotels.

Clubs.   The clubs offered good food, drink, and entertainment at low prices. By 1971, clubs were located in: Chicago, Miami, New Orleans, St. Louis, New York, Phoenix, Detroit, Kansas City, Baltimore, Cincinnati, Los Angeles, Atlanta, San Francisco, Boston, Denver, and in Montreal and London. The clubs had become famous for mass merchandising a champagne atmosphere at beer prices.

Playboy clubs expanded to Europe, establishing clubs with gaming (gambling) facilities in London (1966), Manchester (1972), and Portsmouth (1973), England. These clubs proved highly successful despite the depressed conditions of the English economy and the failure of similar English establishments.

In the latter 1960s, however, business began sagging in the United States clubs. PEI executives partially blamed this on the poor location of the clubs, and competition from all other forms of leisure activities including restaurants, lounges, movies, theaters, sports, television, and so forth. The clubs were also a victim of the changing sexual mores, a change initiated to a great extent by PEI. The bunnies at the clubs were no longer the only act in town. Singles bars allowed men and women to meet. Bunnies, who could not mingle, became obsolete.

By 1973 the Playboy Clubs Division had sales totaling $33.3 million and had pre-tax profits of 6.7 percent or $5.3 million. However, these impressive figures were only due to the runaway success of PEI's British casinos. The company's 15 domestic clubs operated in the red. In 1975 PEI transferred the operational and administrative controls over its clubs and hotels to its management team in England. It was felt that the British success could be applied to the whole operation. PEI also adopted the policy of franchising clubs and even hotels. Earlier, all hotels and all but three of the clubs (St. Louis, Baltimore, and Boston) had been owned by the company.

Hotels.   In 1968, Hefner ordered diversification into hotels. The company's first purchase was a resort hotel at Ocho Rios in Jamaica. This was followed by the Playboy Plaza in Miami, and Playboy Towers in Chicago. PEI next built two resort hotels at Lake Geneva, Wisconsin, and Great Gorge, in Sussex County, New Jersey.

In 1975 agreements were made with foreign investors to franchise hotels in Tokyo, in Costa Rica, and in Pangkor Laut near Kuala Lumpur, Malaysia. PEI's hotels never fared well in the industry. They seemed to meet substantial resistance from the business traveler.

Other Operations

Playboy Sales Inc.   The sale of miscellaneous accessory items bearing the Playboy trademark was the responsibility of Playboy Sales Inc. Such products ranged from tie clasps bearing the bunny insignia to bunny-tail wall plaques.

Entertainment Group

Playboy Productions.   Playboy also entered into the movie and television production fields, and from 1970 to 1975 lost $6.2 million.

Records.   Despite continuing losses in record and music publishing, Playboy Records in 1975 did earn its first Gold Record.

Limited Interests.   Other smaller investments are Playboy's College Marketing and Research Corporation, model agencies in Chicago and Los Angeles, and a Los Angeles–based limousine service subsidiary.

Playboy Management and the Financial Downturn

Hefner reigned supreme, but severe delays occurred in top-management decision making. For three consecutive quarters, ending December 31, 1974, March 31, 1975, and June 30, 1975, PEI lost money. The financial difficulties were numerous. Revenues from *Playboy* magazine were down. In the last five fiscal years, the hotels had lost $14.4 million. Without the $3.2 million pre-tax profit from the clubs in England, the clubs would have shown a significant loss.

Also over the past five fiscal years, movie production had lost $6.2 million and records continued to lose money. Cash flow was impaired and PEI's line of credit was weakened in 1975 when the First National Bank of Chicago withdrew two lines of credit.

In addition, the Internal Revenue Service was taking an aggressive position on disallowing several million dollars in deductions taken on the two Playboy mansions and the "Big Bunny" (the DC9 aircraft). Concern had been expressed over increases in expenses relative to revenues. Problems seemed abundant.

The Drug Problem.   In December 1974, the national press carried reports that federal investigators were probing drug use at the Playboy mansions in Chicago and Los Angeles. The resulting publicity led to the resignation of the company's two outside directors.

In addition, in January 1975, Bobbie Arnstein, Mr. Hefner's 34-year-old executive secretary who was out on bond while appealing a 15-year conditional sentence for conspiracy to distribute cocaine, was found dead in a North Side Chicago hotel. An apparent suicide, her death stirred up fresh ammunition for those opposing the Playboy life.

The combination of all the above-noted difficulties culminated in the second of the periods in PEI's history—the 1975–1976 reorganization.

The First Reorganization—FY 1976

This first reorganization at PEI occurred in two phases. The first phase in early 1975 involved creating an Office of the President consisting of Mr. Hefner and six top aids. The committee would make operating decisions, a function formerly centered in Robert Preuss, Executive Vice-President. Departments which had reported to Mr. Preuss would be consolidated under five divisions. However it was also announced that this Office of the President would eventually be replaced by a new president and chief operating officer.

Subsequent Actions

In September 1976, Hefner announced he was turning over the title of president to Derick J. Daniels, 47, who would be chief operating officer as well. Hefner would remain as chairman of the board and chief executive officer. Daniels had risen through the editorial ranks to become president of Knight News Service Inc. This marked the first time anyone other than Hefner had held the presidency. Despite PEI's financial condition, the new president was optimistic. A five-man Executive Committee was appointed to report to Daniels and the seven-man Office of the President was abolished. Of the six top men who had formally reported to Hefner, all but Preuss remained. The other five composed the new Executive Committee.

Some of the results of the actions taken were the following:

Publishing.

1. *Playboy.* Circulation increased for six straight months. *Playboy*'s prices were raised, and special efforts were taken to broaden *Playboy*'s distribution through chain stores, with emphasis on supermarkets. *Playboy*'s covers were redesigned to ensure open display at all outlets. Profits rose substantially. But *Penthouse* magazine, beginning late in 1975, started to outsell *Playboy* on the newsstands.

2. *OUI.* The newsstand prices were raised and a new (and cheaper) printing process was employed without a loss in quality. Circulation stabilized. The magazine became profitable.

3. Playboy Book Division. The book club achieved its highest sales level and second-highest profits in its history during fiscal year 1976, becoming the third-largest book club in the United States.

4. Foreign Language Editions of *Playboy*. In fiscal year 1976, the five foreign language editions of *Playboy* more than doubled their circulation to over 1,500,000 copies per month, and royalties became an important source of profit. PEI concluded a license agreement to produce and distribute a sixth version in Spanish. This edition, *Caballero con demejor de Playboy (Gentlemen with the Best of Playboy)*, started in November 1976 for distribution in Mexico, throughout Central America, and in Colombia and Venezuela. Spain and the Philippines were targeted for the future.

Playboy Clubs and Hotels.   The new management team focused on programs to maximize profit. As a result the clubs did show some improvement in fiscal year 1976, but problems remained. Playboy clubs in New Orleans, Kansas City, Montreal, Atlanta, and San Francisco were closed. The greatest successes were in the British gaming clubs, which accounted for $8 million in profit. The United States clubs lost over $4 million. But in December 1976, a franchised Playboy Club opened in Tokyo.

Entertainment Group.   Playboy Productions was responsible for "The Minstrel Man," which appeared on CBS-TV early in 1977. Its "International Bunny of the Year Pageant" was popular. Playboy Records had several hit singles and substantially increased sales. Mickey Gilley was especially prominent in the Country and Western field, winning several major awards for his songs. Barbi Benton's records also sold well.

Other Operations.   Playtique. Opened in August 1976, Playtique, a retail store in the Playboy Building in Chicago, offers a unique mix of designer sportswear for young women, one-of-a-kind items of jewelry, accessories for men and women, and a large selection of albums and tapes.

Financial.   The First Quarter (FY 1977) Report to Shareholders indicated that Playboy was finalizing negotiations with four banks for $2 million each in unsecured open-line credit. Short-term debt had been reduced by $2 million.

Summary

After viewing the substantial improvement in financial performance for 1976 versus 1975, Hugh Hefner remarked,

While we are by no means satisfied with our rate of improvement, we nevertheless are pleased by our ability to report increased earnings. It is heartening as well to realize that our profit improvement was made possible because of the diversification the company has engaged in over the years.

The third major period in the history of PEI ensued, the leadership of Derrick Daniels. Summary financial information for the second and third key periods in PEI's history are shown in Exhibit 15.1.

Playboy — Under Daniels — 1976–Early 1982

After placing Daniels in charge of PEI, Hefner, who owned 70 percent of Playboy's stock and who was still technically considered "the boss," became difficult to reach and all but retired from management of PEI. However he still personally oversaw the magazine operations, most notably the centerfold and cartoon pages. Hefner's detachment led to some disgruntlement among certain top managers. But despite continued losses in several of its major divisions, Hefner's empire held together, even improving profits in the period from 1977 to 1981. However, for FY 1982, PEI reported a $51.7 million loss and found itself at a major crossroads in its history.

In fiscal year 1981, PEI had profits of $14.4 million on $389 million in sales. At that time it held strategic interests in publishing, clubs, hotels, gambling, entertainment, and other areas. But May 1982 found PEI a restructured company, essentially a magazine publishing company. Perhaps most importantly, PEI found itself with a new chief operating officer and president, Christie Hefner, 29, daughter of PEI founder Hugh Hefner. What happened to cause these tremendous changes?

During FY 1982 PEI was confronted with several major problems which resulted in significant changes. Due to legal difficulties, it was forced in the fall of 1981 to withdraw ownership from its major profitable operation, its casinos and betting shops in England. Another profitable operation, its flagship magazine *Playboy*, experienced both a decline in sales volume and a decline in the number of advertising pages. Its domestic clubs were experiencing continued financial difficulties. The company had recently divested or closed nearly all of its hotels. And in April 1982, the company found that its hoped-for big profits from its new casino in Atlantic City, New Jersey, were not likely to materialize. The state of New Jersey had refused to grant PEI a permanent gambling license in April of 1982, forcing PEI to sell its interest to its joint venture partner, Elsinore.

The Details of Playboy Empire's Changes

The principal components of the Playboy empire changed dramatically in FY 1982. At the end of FY 1981, the SBUs were magazine publishing, gaming, clubs and hotels, and other businesses. As of April 1982, hotels and gaming had disappeared as major components, and book publishing had been discontinued from the other-businesses category.

Magazine Publishing

The principal money-maker of this group, *Playboy* magazine, dropped in circulation from about 6 million copies per month in 1975 to 5.2 million copies per month in 1981. Operating earnings from magazine publishing fell more than 50 percent during fiscal year 1981 to $6 million. *Games* magazine, acquired in 1978, didn't live up to its promise. *Oui* magazine was sold in June 1981, due to continuing poor performance.

Clubs And Hotels

At the end of FY 1981, PEI maintained ten clubs in various population centers of the U.S., such as Chicago, St. Petersburg, and Los Angeles; 5 foreign clubs, such as Tokyo; and two hotels. Ten of the 15 clubs were franchised. This division of PEI had been unprofitable for years and many clubs had been closed and hotels sold or closed to reduce losses. The clubs and hotels division lost $5 million during FY 1981. On November 20, 1981, an agreement was reached in principle to sell the Lake Geneva, Wisconsin, and Great Gorge, New Jersey, hotels for $42 million.

Gaming

While the domestic clubs and resorts were losing money, the foreign gaming clubs in Manchester, Portsmouth, and London, England, had become quite successful. In FY 1981, the company's gaming operations were responsible for 87 percent of the company's operating income. But in FY 1982, a crisis struck the gaming SBU.

In early 1981, legal problems occurred in the London casinos. PEI was alleged to have engaged in several credit irregularities. Eventually PEI lost its operating license in England and on November 3, 1981, sold its British gaming interests for $31,400,000.

Equally serious was the situation regarding Playboy's casino in Atlantic City, a hoped-for money-maker, which ran into serious difficulties in the fall of 1981. At first it looked as if Playboy might lose its gambling license in New Jersey strictly because of its problems in England. Finally, after many hours of discussion and several major changes in operations by Playboy, New Jersey allowed PEI to keep its temporary gambling license with another review due in April 1982. PEI's hopes were high, but proved ultimately to be unfounded.

Market Potential—Atlantic City, New Jersey—Casino Site.   Seeing a tremendous potential in Atlantic City and given their successes in casinos in England, PEI had decided to move swiftly into this market. However many expensive and time-consuming delays were encountered between November 1976, when PEI purchased the first parcel of land, and April of 1981, when the casino was actually opened for business. The final total cost for the Atlantic City project has been cited as $135 million, over two and one-half times the original estimate. PEI reportedly invested as much as $60 million in this venture, almost half of its total equity.

PEI had counted heavily on profits from Atlantic City to keep the other facets of the company operating. Hefner wished to keep Playboy a diversified company, with interests in several different industries. Without a casino operation, however, Daniels (who resigned in May 1982) remarked that PEI could, once again, turn into nothing but a privately owned magazine company.

Other Businesses

By 1981 this PEI SBU included the movie and television and records divisions.

Playboy's recording studios had all but closed except to produce special projects for Hefner. The future of Playboy Productions (movies and TV) seemed uncertain, although

TV was the central focus. Costly movies were avoided in order to focus efforts on producing TV scripts and pilot series for consideration by the TV networks. In addition, PEI had been investigating the cable-TV and pay-TV fields hoping to produce a late-night "Playboy Magazine of the Air." Such a series was planned to include nude photo sessions, indepth interviews, and other features that would parallel the printed magazine. PEI was investing heavily in this joint venture.

Keeping with the diversification preferred by Hefner, PEI in 1981 had several other divisions. There was the Playboy Foundation; the Sales Division, which handled a multitude of items carrying the bunny emblem; and other subsidiaries ranging from modeling agencies to insurance marketing. PEI even licensed a Pillsbury Co. unit to market cake pans shaped like the rabbit-head emblem of the company.

More Problems

Problems seemed to compound in 1980, 1981, and 1982 as the company experienced a siege of additional bad publicity. In early 1980 the Securities and Exchange Commission charged Hefner with violating federal securities laws by failing to disclose use of the Chicago and Los Angeles Playboy mansions for personal entertainment. Later in the year, Hefner returned almost $1 million to Playboy. In 1981, Dorothy Stratten, 1980's Playmate of the Year, was murdered by her manager and husband.

Major Misfortune Strikes Again.

Citing a 20-year-old incident involving Hefner's efforts to obtain a New York liquor license, the New Jersey Casino Control Commission refused PEI a permanent gambling license in April 1982. The only alternative to losing the license was for Hefner to divert his 70-percent stock interest in PEI. According to provisions in the joint venture agreement, Elsinore had to purchase PEI's share of the joint venture if the license was refused. PEI had lost its Atlantic City casino and the expected and heavily counted-on profits from it.

PEI under Christie — Restructuring — FY 1982–1984

Christie Hefner joined Playboy in 1975, after graduating summa cum laude from Brandeis University. She moved to the vice-presidential level of the firm in 1980. Derick J. Daniels, who trained Christie for her eventual presidency, declared upon her assuming control, "She's ready." Christie had $100 million to spend on restructuring PEI as a result of recent divestments, but first she had to stop the flow of red ink.

FY 1983–84 Changes

The year 1984 found PEI not "just a private magazine publisher" as was feared by Daniels when he separated from PEI in 1982, but instead an international company with four divisions—Publishing, Video, Clubs, and Products. (See Exhibits 15.2, 15.3 and 15.4.) PEI had 1,050 full-time employees—380 in publishing; 310 in clubs; and 360 in the remaining activities. Employee morale was high and employee relations were very good with no interruptions due to labor disputes. Moreover PEI, on June 30, 1984, had almost $47 million in cash, a current ratio of 2.8, and only $5 million in long-term debt.

Exhibit 15.2   Consolidated Statements of Operations for the Years Ending June 30 (in thousands except per-share amounts)

	1984	1983	1982
Net sales and revenues from continuing operations	$187,144	$193,672	$210,093
Costs and expenses:			
Cost of sales and operating expenses	(156,588)	(179,867)	(194,561)
Selling and administrative expenses	(28,932)	(28,552)	(33,747)
Total costs and expenses	(185,520)	(208,419)	(228,308)
Operating income (loss)	1,624	(14,747)	(18,215)
Nonoperating income (expense):			
Interest income	4,506	4,313	3,989
Interest expense	(741)	(743)	(3,992)
Other, net	4,301	(47)	3,741
Income (loss) from continuing operations before income taxes and extraordinary item	9,690	(11,224)	(14,477)
Income tax expense	(3,392)	(963)	(1,713)
Income (loss) from continuing operations before extraordinary item	6,298	(12,187)	(16,190)
Discontinued operations:			
Loss from operations	—	—	(21,006)
Gain (loss) on disposal	12,433	(5,306)	(14,485)
Income (loss) from discontinued operations before extraordinary item	12,433	(5,306)	(35,491)
Income (loss) before extraordinary item	18,731	(17,493)	(51,681)
Extraordinary item—tax benefit resulting from utilization of loss carryforwards	8,605	—	—
Net income (loss)	$ 27,336	$(17,493)	$(51,681)
Income (loss) per common share:			
Income (loss) before extraordinary item:			
From continuing operations	$ .64	$ (1.23)	$ (1.64)
From discontinued operations	1.25	(.54)	(3.59)
Total	1.89	(1.77)	(5.23)
Extraordinary item applicable to:			
Continuing operations	.34	—	—
Discontinued operations	.53	—	—
Total	.87	—	—
Net income (loss)	$ 2.76	$ (1.77)	$ (5.23)

Playboy Enterprises Inc. and Subsidiaries

Publishing.   Based almost totally on *Playboy* magazine, still the world's best-selling men's magazine, with a reportedly stable 4.1 million domestic circulation and 9 foreign editions with nearly 9 million monthly readers, this SBU reported profits of $17.9 million in 1984, which were more than double the 1983 fiscal results. *Games* magazine, with approximately 650,000 monthly circulation, is the other magazine currently published, and although still operating at a loss in FY 1984, the loss was reportedly narrowed by 25 percent over FY 1983. BOARTS International, which distributes *Playboy* and over 50 other publications in foreign countries, was the other major activity of this SBU.

Exhibit 15.3   Consolidated Statements of Financial Position (in thousands)

	1984	1983*
Assets		
Cash and short-term investments	$ 46,711	$ 26,580
Receivables, less allowances of $2,471,000 and $2,891,000 in 1984 and 1983, respectively	12,467	14,594
Inventories	12,962	12,702
Film production costs	11,680	7,567
Cash in escrow and receivables from sale of discontinued businesses	8,314	2,077
Other current assets	4,574	3,848
Total current assets	96,708	67,368
Property and equipment:		
Land	814	2,174
Buildings and improvements	13,665	12,940
Furniture and equipment	14,607	16,284
Leasehold improvements	10,491	11,367
Capitalized leases	694	461
Total property and equipment	40,271	43,226
Less: accumulated depreciation and amortization	(24,417)	(24,314)
Property and equipment, net	15,854	18,912
Receivables from sale of Atlantic City Venture	36,588	—
Deferred subscription acquisition costs	9,247	7,252
Film production costs—noncurrent	2,999	4,038
Net noncurrent assets of discontinued businesses	—	33,641
Other assets	8,035	6,354
Total assets	$169,431	$137,565
Liabilities		
Current financing obligations	$ 160	$ 647
Accounts payable	17,403	17,894
Accrued salaries, wages, and employee benefits	3,133	4,126
Net liabilities of and reserves for losses on disposal of discontinued businesses	1,039	5,340
Income taxes payable	7,200	8,196
Other liabilities and accrued expenses	6,163	5,405
Total current liabilities	35,098	41,608
Long-term financing obligations	3,484	152
Deferred revenue	41,520	36,730
Deferred gain on sale of partnership interest	3,390	—
Other noncurrent liabilities	3,817	4,505
Commitments and contingencies		
Shareholders' Equity		
Common stock, $1 par value, 15,000,000 shares authorized, 10,099,509 issued	10,100	10,100
Capital in excess of par value	14,903	14,854
Retained earnings	58,356	31,020
Less cost of 177,863 and 201,803 shares in treasury at June 30, 1984, and 1983, respectively	(1,237)	(1,404)
Total shareholders' equity	82,122	54,570
Total liabilities and shareholders' equity	$169,431	$137,565

Playboy Enterprises Inc. and Subsidiaries

*Certain reclassifications have been made to conform to the 1984 presentation.

Exhibit 15.4   Financial Information Relating to Industry Segments (in thousands)

	1984	1983*	1982
Sales to nonaffiliates[a]			
Publishing			
Playboy magazine	$120,067	$122,008	$139,744
Other	27,001	28,182	25,591
Total publishing	147,068	150,190	165,335
Video	19,192	12,383	584
Clubs	12,933	19,801	25,252
Products	7,001	6,479	7,109
Other businesses	950	4,819	11,813
Total	$187,144	$193,672	$210,093
Income (loss) from continuing operations before income taxes and extraordinary item			
Publishing	$ 17,856	$ 6,488	$ 11,923
Video	(317)	(2,269)	(4,372)
Clubs	(2,921)	(2,533)	(2,794)
Products	3,827	2,911	3,292
Other businesses	(227)	(1,135)	(2,511)
Corporate administration and promotion	(16,594)	(18,209)	(23,753)
Interest, net	3,765	3,570	(3)
Other, net	4,301	(47)	(3,741)
Total	$ 9,690	$(11,224)	$(14,477)
Identifiable assets			
Publishing	$ 33,856	$ 32,256	$ 40,140
Video	23,472	17,552	4,186
Clubs	4,271	6,079	12,999
Products	1,822	2,244	2,938
Other businesses	234	623	2,538
Corporate administration and promotion[b]	105,776	45,170	77,700
Total assets of continuing operations	169,431	103,924	140,501
Net assets of discontinued operations	—	33,641	34,681
Total	$169,431	$137,565	$175,182

Video.   This SBU developed and produced programming for pay television (including pay-cable and over-the-air subscriptions television) and home video (videocassettes and videodiscs). This programming is generally short (30 to 60 minutes) original programming or "made-for-television" movies (90 minutes or more).

Most programming was developed for PEI's cable-television channel which was launched with 300,000 subscribers in November of 1982. As of June 30, 1984, this total had grown to almost 720,000, and was available on more than 450 cable systems. The subscription revenues approximated $15,600,000, almost double the FY 1983 figure. However this programming is also repackaged for sale through the variety of licensing arrangements for the over-the-air subscription television and other pay television as well as in the form of videocassettes and videodiscs. Revenues from these licensings approximated $3,400,000, about the same level as in FY 1983.

Exhibit 15.4   *continued*

	1984	1983*	1982
Depreciation and amortization of property and equipment			
Publishing	$ 548	$ 557	$ 505
Video	296	290	99
Clubs	425	757	1,003
Products	51	39	40
Other businesses	20	105	219
Corporate administration and promotion	1,054	1,028	1,299
Total	$ 2,394	$ 2,776	$ 3,165
Capital expenditures			
Publishing	$ 245	$ 1,047	$ 523
Video	33	90	65
Clubs	644	491	418
Products	11	14	56
Other businesses	2	5	114
Corporate administration and promotion	564	345	969
Total	$ 1,499	$ 1,992	$ 2,145

Playboy Enterprises Inc. and Subsidiaries

*Certain reclassifications have been made to conform to the 1984 presentation. The accompanying notes are an integral part of these tables.

ªSales to nonaffiliates include export sales of $21,454,000, $21,367,000, and $24,349,000 in fiscal 1984, 1983 and 1982, respectively.

ᵇCorporate assets consist principally of cash and short-term investments, receivables from the sale of the company's interest in an Atlantic City hotel/casino, and corporate property and equipment.

The videocassettes and videodiscs were distributed to retailers exclusively by CBS/Fox (a joint venture by CBS and Twentieth Century Fox Video). CBS/Fox has in turn made several other agreements including the October 1983 agreement with MGM/UA Home Video which provides for worldwide distribution of many of the PEI produced or co-produced made-for-television movies.

Although this SBU reported a $300,000 FY 1984 loss, after less than two years of operation the Video Division broke through to profitability in the third and fourth quarters of FY 1984. While this achievement was notable, the potential for even greater reward lies in the expanding video market. PEI apparently believes that it is well positioned to take advantage of the expected fast growth in pay-television and home-video markets.

Clubs.   This SBU operated only two clubs (Chicago and Los Angeles), had a new New York City club under construction, and franchised six domestic locations as well as four Japanese clubs and the Manila, Philippines, club. This SBU lost $2.9 million in FY 1984; however a management venture relationship with Lettuce Entertain You Enterprises was formed in May of 1984. Lettuce Entertain You is a Chicago-based company which operates approximately 20 nightclubs and restaurants located in Chicago and Phoenix. The founder and president is Rich Melman. Lettuce Entertain You has established a reputation for marketing effectiveness and for creating entertainment and dining concepts which appeal to the younger, more-affluent consumers. Initially Lettuce Entertain You was expected to concentrate its efforts on the New York City club which was expected to open in early calendar year 1985. In fact several design and operating changes for the New York City club were suggested by Lettuce Entertain You and these were reported to have been rushed into the construction schedule.

The Lettuce Entertain You relationship is expected to provide a rejuvenated Playboy clubs atmosphere and all three PEI-owned clubs will shortly be under their management. PEI reported that moves have been taken to substantially reduce overhead cost in the clubs.

This streamlining of administrative staff is also consistent with the continued strategy of in-hotel franchising. An example of this strategy is the May 1984 opening of the newest franchise—Playboy Club of Omaha. The elements of this new franchising formula include: an in-hotel location, a medium-size city, and the experienced management of an established lodging industry firm. The Omaha, Nebraska, club includes: a social bar area; a guest lounge nestled around a fireplace; a cabaret with live entertainment; and a dining area. The other franchised clubs are located in Miami; St. Louis; Buffalo; Lansing, Michigan; and Des Moines, Iowa.

Products.　This SBU reproted a profit increase of 32 percent to $3.8 million on a 30-percent increase in retail sales by licensees. Worldwide these retail sales total more than $200 million. Much of the improvement is attributed to a shift in the target market to a younger age group (16–26 years of age) while moving toward wider distribution through major chains such as J.C. Penney, and a desire to become mass merchandisers.

Divestitures Continue

With PEI ceasing to operate the leased Bahamian casino earlier in FY 1984, the finalization of the Atlantic City divestiture concluded the company's gaming involvements. PEI also sold its interests in both the partnership owning the Playboy Building in Los Angeles and the adjacent undeveloped land (however PEI leased and continued to occupy the building). In addition the assets of the limousine business were sold in 1983 (although the model agencies in Chicago and Los Angeles continued to operate). (See Exhibit 15.5 for cash-flow information.)

Christie's New Directions

The information contained in Exhibit 15.1 indicates that Christie has indeed "stopped the flow of red ink" noted by Daniels in 1982 as a requirement "if she was to turn PEI around and give it a new direction." But the question that remains is—what is Christie's new direction for PEI? The following few sentences taken from the 1984 Annual Report provide us with Christie's view of the new directions in which she plans to take PEI:

1. *We are justifiably proud of a new and very promising business in video and cable. . . . We hope to dramatically increase the worth of this business by improving our programming and distribution efforts.*

2. *Employing these cash reserves (discussed earlier), we will continue to develop our ongoing businesses while exploring opportunities for expansion consistent with our media and marketing orientation.*

Exhibit 15.5   Consolidated Statements of Changes in Financial Position (in thousands)

	1984	1983*	1982*
Cash flow from continuing operations			
Income (loss) from continuing operations before extraordinary item	$ 6,298	$(12,187)	$(16,190)
Add (deduct) items not affecting cash:			
Depreciation of property and equipment	2,394	2,776	3,165
Amortization and market value adjustment of film production costs	12,624	8,930	359
Gain on sale of properties	(4,489)	(1,001)	(5,388)
Other	471	768	—
Additions to film production costs	(15,698)	(19,349)	(825)
(Increase) decrease in other working capital items	(2,118)	(1,508)	16,829
Increase (decrease) in deferred income, net of deferred subscription acquisition costs	2,468	1,425	(2,038)
Decrease in noncurrent liabilities	(361)	(1,713)	(441)
Other, net	423	222	197
Cash provided by (used for) continuing operations before extraordinary item and other sources of cash	2,012	(21,637)	(4,332)
Extraordinary item—tax benefit, not affecting cash	3,351	—	—
Other sources (uses) of cash:			
Additions to property and equipment	(1,499)	(1,992)	(2,145)
Sales of property and equipment	10,861	2,805	8,791
Payment of cash dividend	—	(593)	(592)
Other, net	—	—	(762)
Cash provided by (used for) continuing operations before financing activities	14,725	(21,417)	960
Cash flow from discontinued operations			
Income (loss) from discontinued operations before extraordinary item	12,433	(5,306)	(35,491)
Extraordinary item—tax benefit, not affecting cash	5,254	—	—
Net proceeds from sale of discontinued businesses	7,145	15,351	46,716
Net (increase) decrease in net assets of discontinued operations	(19,036)	1,819	36,257
Cash provided by discontinued operations	5,796	11,864	47,482
Financing			
Additions to (retirement of) financing obligations	(390)	35	(27,834)
Issuance of common stock	—	86	187
Cash provided by (used for) financing	(390)	121	(27,647)
Increase (decrease) in cash and short-term investments	$20,131	$ (9,432)	$ 20,795

Playboy Enterprises, Inc. and Subsidiaries

*Certain reclassifications have been made to conform to the 1984 presentation.

Advertising Age (AA) in its February 27, 1984 issue reported that in an interview Christie said Playboy's goal was to position itself as a premier marketer of print information and video programming. The AA article suggested that a strategic plan would be prepared over a 12-month period (by Spring 1985) and that Christie's blueprint for PEI would probably call for:

1.   Starting more direct-mail properties designed around *Playboy* and *Games* magazines;

2.   Acquiring small publishing concerns;

3.   Launching new publications;

4.   Enlarging the programming scope of the fledgling video division;

5.   Continuing to attain further product licenses for goods bearing the Playboy and Playmate signatures; and

6.   Moving forward with franchising of the Playboy clubs.

Although some brief additional information about each of these probable areas of activity are included in the article a cautionary point concludes the discussion: during 1984, Christie will have to restructure PEI's top management as Mr. Marv Houston and Mr. Stephen Silverstein, two of the senior managers, will be leaving. Although this will consolidate Christie's position it will compound the difficulties she finds in developing a strategic plan for PEI.

Future Outlook for PEI

As of the time of this case, little factual evidence of what the details of PEI's strategic plan will be have emerged. A *Business Week* article dated February 11, 1985 quotes Christie as remarking that "Rich (Malman of Lettuce Entertain You) is one of the best leaders and motivators I've ever encountered in business," and that "Morale has never been higher" (at Playboy Clubs). However the article's author Jo Ellen Daily notes that Melman's history is of opening one-of-a-kind restaurants not the rigidly controlled corporate restaurant. Daily suggests that many critics believe Melman may be unsuited for Playboy.

The heart of PEI is still *Playboy* magazine according to Jill Bettner of *Forbes* who in the March 26, 1984 issue notes that Christie faces some tough challenges but that video operations look promising. However Bettner asked Christie if video operations which had 650,000 subscribers in early 1984 and which was purported to be adding 1,000 more each day, was profitable yet. Christie's response was "I'm not allowing the incremental revenue to drop to the bottom line. We need to reinvest a substantial portion of it in the business." However the video market is a highly competitive one and Christie is very reluctant to predict when profits might occur. Bettner says Christie's been burned before and responded, "There's no upside in it. And if you're wrong, they nail you to the wall."

In May of 1985 *Playboy* announced that beginning in October of 1985 it would no longer have centerfolds. Instead Miss October will tumble from a triple folded page near the back of the magazine. Dennis Salyers, *Playboy* publicity chief is quoted as saying; "At one time we were on the leading edge of sexual change in this country, nowadays nobody here would want to be on the leading edge of sexual change . . ." * Christie Hefner noted upon taking the presidency of PEI in 1982, that curiosity about sexual explicitness was ending and that those magazines dependent on it would fail. Christie is credited with making the decision to change the centerfold to a foldout and is reported to have said, "It's the end of an era, but the problem always was that we had to work our quality fiction and writing around the centerfold. Now we won't have that problem anymore." * It remains to be seen if *Playboy* will have other problems.

---

* "Nudity Is No Longer The Center of Playboy's Attention," by Joan Ryan, *The Orlando Sentinel*, May 9, 1985, pp. E-1.

References

Annual Reports. Playboy Enterprises Inc., 1982, 1983, and 1984.

Bittner, Jill. "After the Centerfold." *Forbes*, March 26, 1984, pp. 43–44.

Christopher, Maurine. "Hefner Pushing Hard for Playboy Channel." *Advertising Age*, May 16, 1983, p. 52.

————. "Playboy Channel Loses to Bible Belt." *Advertising Age*, November 28, 1983, p. 72.

Daily, Jo Ellen. "Rich Melman: The Hot Dog of The Restaurant Business." *Business Week*, February 11, 1985, pp. 73 and 76.

Form 10-K. Securities and Exchange Commission, 1984.

Johnson, Robert. "Passe in the Big City, Playboy's Ailing Clubs Search for Profits in America's Hinterlands." *The Wall Street Journal*, September 28, 1983, p. 31.

Reed, Robert. "*Playboy* Faces Turnaround Fight." *Advertising Age*, August 1, 1983, pp. 41–43.

————. "Playboy Charts Its Growth." *Advertising Age*, February 27, 1984, pp. 3 and 80.

Reuter, Madelynne. "Playboy Discussing Sale of Book Operations." *Publishers Weekly*, March 1982.

Rosenberg, Hilary. "Playboy: Wornout at 30?" *Financial World*, June 30, 1983, pp. 40–42.

Ryan, Joan. "Nudity Is No Longer The Center of Playboy's Attention." *The Orlando Sentinel*, May 9, 1985, pp. E-1.

Tully, Shawn. "Playboy Makes the Boss's Daughter Boss." *Fortune*, August 23, 1982, p. 105–118.

Walt Disney Productions, November 1983

▪ *Bill Burns* ▪

On Thursday, November 10, 1983, Walt Disney Productions (WDP) released its 4th-quarter/total year-end results for fiscal year 1983. Wall Street responded by providing a direct descent of $11.50 per share of WDP stock, which closed that day at $47.25 (down 20 percent on extremely heavy volume). Institutions, which hold an estimated two-thirds of the 33.4 million outstanding shares, were bailing out of the former "glamour" stock. The major cause for this bailout was that Disney had reported that net income for the quarter (ended September 30, 1983) had declined 13 percent to $24.5 million, or $.70 a share, down from $28.1 million, or $.84 a share, a year earlier. Contrastingly, revenue increased 23 percent to $363 million. For the full year, net income had decreased 7 percent to $93.2 million, or $2.70 a share, down from $100 million, or $3.01 a share in 1982, while revenue for the year had increased 27 percent to $1.31 billion. (See Exhibits 16.1 and 16.2.)

Analysts had predicted that fourth-quarter earnings would lift the full-year net income to between $3.05 and $3.40 per share.[1] They had been wrong. This was the third consecutive year that Disney had experienced an earnings decline. Ray Watson, Chairman of the Board since May 1, 1983, wondered in what direction the company should turn in order to regain its former growth patterns and competitive advantages.

Many observers had been surprised when Mr. Watson, a member of the Disney Board of Directors for more than ten years, was elected chairman of the board at the annual stockholders' meeting in February 1983. It marked the first time that an outside director had held that spot and meant that Ron Miller (Walt's son-in-law) would remain as president and chief operating officer.

Watson holds a bachelor's and a master's degree in architecture from the University of California in Berkeley. He was the former president of and the prime driving force behind the Irving Land Company which developed tens of thousands acres of prime California land in Orange County. The city of Irvine was a rural outpost in the mid–1960s, but today boasts a population of over 75,000.

In 1973 *Professional Builder Magazine* named him builder of the year. "His creative planning and strong management abilities helped turn the Irvine Ranch into a virtual laboratory of ideas for new community development," the magazine said.[2]

Watson, then in his mid-fifties, established his own real estate development company in 1977 with headquarters in Newport Beach. His original intent was to divide his time between Disney and his own firm, but he found himself spending considerably more time in Burbank than Newport Beach.

This case is not intended to show either the effective or the ineffective handling of an administrative situation. Rather, it is intended for classroom discussion. This case was written under the direction of Dr. James M. Higgins. All rights reserved to the contributor.

[1] "Walt Disney Stock Plunges after Drop in 4th Quarter Net," *The Wall Street Journal*, November 11, 1983, p. 2.

[2] *Professional Builder's Magazine*, 1973.

He spent his first few months as chairman visiting with management from every corner of the Disney organization. Each meeting was held on the manager's turf and included a thorough update on current activities and future plans. At first, these sessions were dreaded by the managers, who were used to the volatile reactions of the former Board Chairman, Card Walker. Word soon spread that Watson asked excellent questions, listened attentively to all sides of an issue, and provided rapid feedback on what he felt were the main issues at stake. A thorough memo was usually on the manager's desk within two days of Watson's visit. This memo would summarize the meeting from Watson's point of view and would usually request additional information and opinions from that manager.

At the corporate level, Watson saw his role as that of adviser to Ron Miller. As an outsider, he was careful not to preempt Disney family members or old-time members of the Disney team. He sought to persuade them through Miller. This approach seemed to work well.

Poor earnings performance over the past three years and a general feeling that the book value of the company's Florida land holdings were grossly understated, as was the value of the film library, have led to rumors of takeover efforts. *The New York Times* estimates the value of Walt Disney World property at $700 million, nearly one-half of the company's current market value.[3]

Disney bylaws provide a great deal of protection against an unfriendly takeover by requiring approval of 80 percent of the stockholders. This amendment was added in 1977 as the company began stashing cash for the EPCOT Center project. It was feared that an undervalued stock might lead to a rapid takeover attempt in which the buyer could recoup a substantial portion of the purchase price simply by raiding the cash and marketable securities account.

Nonetheless, everything has its price and Watson felt the company's 7.5-percent return on assets had to be improved. As he reviewed six months of extensive notes, in early November 1983, Ray Watson pondered the courses of action he should recommend to Ron Miller and the Board of Directors.

Walt Disney Productions

Walt Disney Productions is "a diversified international company engaged in family entertainment and operates in three business segments: Entertainment and Recreation, Motion Pictures, and Consumer Products and Other."[4] In mid-1983, these three divisions were changed into four for business operating purposes. Motion Pictures was split into Motion Pictures and Television Production and Marketing (MPTPM), and Telecommunications. The other two divisions remained the same. For financial reporting purposes, Telecommunications are consolidated as shown in the reports in this case. Its major operations are located in Southern California (Anaheim and Burbank) and Orlando, Florida. Major new endeavors include Tokyo Disneyland and the Disney Cablevision Channel. Product and service quality have always been major factors in the success of the company. Creativity

---

[3] "The Troubled World of Disney," *The New York Times*, September 25, 1983; "Disney Profit Dip Stirs Waves on Wall Street," *The Orlando Sentinel*, November 11, 1983.

[4] Form 10K, Walt Disney Productions, 1983, p.1.

Exhibit 16.1 Consolidated Statement of Income 1974–1983 (dollar amounts in thousands, except per-share data)

	Year Ending September 30									
	1983	1982	1981	1980	1979	1978	1977	1976	1975	1974
Revenues:										
Entertainment and recreation	$1,031,202	$725,610	$691,811	$643,380	$571,079	$508,444	$445,165	$401,613	$349,666	$282,514
Motion pictures	165,458	202,102	196,806	161,400	134,785	152,135	118,058	119,133	112,528	90,390
Consumer products and other	110,697	102,538	116,423	109,725	90,909	80,564	66,602	63,150	57,812	57,074
Total revenues	1,307,357	1,030,250	1,005,040	914,505	796,773	741,143	629,825	583,896	520,006	429,889
Costs and expenses of operations:										
Entertainment and recreations	834,324	592,965	562,337	515,848	450,435	402,492	353,103	331,190	288,679	236,517
Motion pictures	198,843	182,463	162,180	112,725	94,556	98,016	71,964	65,332	59,473	44,575
Consumer products and other	53,815	54,706	65,859	54,632	46,087	43,095	35,258	35,450	36,792	35,196
Total costs and expenses of operations	1,086,982	830,134	790,376	683,205	591,078	543,603	460,325	431,972	384,944	316,288
Operating income (loss) before corporate expenses										
Entertainment and recreation	196,878	132,645	129,474	127,532	120,644	105,952	92,062	70,423	60,987	45,908
Motion pictures	(33,385)	19,639	34,626	48,675	40,229	54,119	46,094	53,801	53,055	45,815
Consumer products and other	56,882	47,832	50,564	55,093	44,822	37,469	31,344	27,700	21,020	21,878
Total operating income before corporate expenses	220,375	200,116	214,664	231,300	205,695	197,540	169,500	151,924	135,062	113,601

Corporate expenses (income)									
General and administrative	16,079*	9,964	12,113	16,754	17,212	17,830	21,130	26,216	30,957	35,554
Design projects abandoned	1,285	6,702	3,182	1,740	3,311	2,390	4,294	4,598	5,147	7,295
Interest expense (income)—net	7,266	2,655	(3,570)	(6,341)	(12,468)	(28,413)	(42,110)	(33,130)	(14,781)	14,066
Total corporate expenses (income)	24,630	19,321	11,725	12,153	8,055	(8,193)	(16,686)	2,316	21,323	56,915
Income before taxes on income	88,971	115,741	140,199	157,347	189,485	213,888	247,986	216,980	178,793	163,460
Taxes on income	40,444	54,000	65,600	75,400	91,100	100,100	112,800	95,500	78,700	70,300
Net income	48,527	61,741	74,599	$ 81,947	$ 98,385	$113,788	$135,186	$ 121,480	$ 100,093	$ 93,160
Per-share data	$ 1.58	$ 1.91	$ 2.30	$ 2.53	$ 3.04	$ 3.51	$ 4.16	$ 3.72	$ 3.01	$ 2.70
Cash dividends	$ .12	$ .12	$ .12	$ .15	$ .32	$ .48	$ .72	$ 1.00	$ 1.20	$ 1.20
Other data:									
Stockholders at close of year	30,700	59,000	61,000	65,000	66,000	65,000	62,000	60,000	61,000	60,000
Employees at close of year	15,000	17,000	19,000	19,000	21,000	21,000	24,000	25,000	28,000	30,000

*Accounting change in following years causes different allocation.

Note: Numerous accounting changes over the years result in differences between the numbers reported for certain accounts in various annual reports.

Source: Annual Reports

Exhibit 16.1   *continued*

	Year Ending September 30									
	1973	1972	1971	1970	1969	1968	1967	1966	1965	1964
Operations:										
Revenues	$385,065	$329,437	$175,611	$167,103	$148,367	$137,148	$117,486	$116,543	$109,947	$86,651
Income before taxes on income	85,168	74,393	48,521	43,709	32,504	26,545	20,334	23,463	22,258	12,749
Taxes on income	37,400	34,100	21,800	21,950	16,700	13,440	9,067	11,071	10,877	5,692
Net income	47,768	40,293	26,721	21,759	15,804	13,106	11,267	12,392	11,379	7,057
Working capital provided by operations	93,203	79,314	49,205	31,239	24,508	21,655	19,271	18,517	18,852	13,517
Cash dividends	3,429	2,756	2,361	1,664	1,308	1,261	812	771	787	707
Stock dividends	2%	2%	2%	2%	2%	3%	3%	3%	3%	3%
Retained in business	44,339	37,537	24,360	20,095	14,496	11,845	10,455	11,621	10,642	6,350
Depreciation and amortization	$ 28,982	$ 26,754	$ 7,833	$ 7,880	$ 7,404	$ 6,849	$ 7,854	$ 5,800	$ 7,474	$ 6,459
Net income Percent of revenues	12.4%	12.3%	15.2%	13.0%	10.7%	9.6%	9.6%	10.6%	10.3%	8.1%
Percent of stockholders' equity (beginning of year)	10.4%	12.7%	12.3%	14.9%	17.5%	17.0%	17.2%	23.3%	27.4%	20.2%
Per-common and common-equivalent share	$ 1.67	$ 1.45	$ 1.02	$ .92	$ .81	$ .68	$ .61	$ .69	$ .64	$ .40
Cash dividends per share (on shares outstanding during the year)	$ .12	$ .10	$ .09⅜	$ .07½	$ .07½	$ .07½	$ .05	$ .05	$ .05	$ .05

Year-end financial position

Current assets	$ 69,094	$ 58,487	$ 76,475	$ 75,632	$111,465	$ 65,107	$ 30,117	$ 21,294	$ 28,276	$19,065
Working capital	1,630	6,437	30,486	39,501	79,744	40,076	8,099	115	6,349	5,566
Entertainment attractions and facilities	552,447	519,740	361,199	98,468	96,599	88,366	84,046	62,661	50,274	45,383
Other buildings, equipment, and properties	52,847	41,001	35,523	12,918	12,587	11,565	10,742	10,326	9,351	8,744
Construction in progress	65,220	24,831	46,444	106,271	36,277	13,438	1,173	151		
Accumulated depreciation	113,025	87,278	63,220	55,317	48,199	41,554	35,518	28,687	31,228	26,284
Total assets	678,807	609,335	497,315	267,626	238,174	165,038	118,628	98,466	88,154	67,883
Stockholders' equity	506,446	460,619	318,464	218,116	146,205	90,308	77,210	65,573	53,125	41,494
Per share	$ 17.71	$ 16.55	$ 12.12	$ 9.18	$ 7.47	$ 4.68	$ 4.15	$ 3.63	$ 2.99	$ 2.38
Average number of common and common-equivalent shares outstanding during the year	28,602	27,838	26,288	23,758	19,572	19,298	18,584	18,082	17,776	17,450

Source: 1973 Annual Report

Exhibit 16.2 Consolidated Balance Sheet 1974–1983 (dollar amounts in thousands)

	Year Ending September 30									
	1983	1982	1981	1980	1979	1978	1977	1976	1975	1974
Assets:										
Current Assets										
Cash	$ 18,055	$ 13,652	$ 5,869	$ 9,745	$ 8,790	$ 9,318	$ 10,744	$ 8,567	$ 40,633	$ 16,244
Short-term investments			248,408	318,533	346,100	278,281	164,134	101,118		
Accounts receivable net of allowances	102,847	78,968	69,302	50,711	37,122	26,708	22,832	21,287	23,035	30,605
Income taxes refundable	70,000	41,000	—	—	—	—	—	—	—	—
Inventories	77,945	66,717	59,773	54,640	41,874	32,453	33,680	32,312	30,368	23,392
Film production costs	44,412	43,850	59,079	61,127	38,278	39,404	48,694	25,158	24,024	23,445
Prepaid expenses	19,843	18,152	15,398	11,438	8,977	8,284	9,810	7,434	7,314	7,397
Total current assets	333,102	262,339	457,829	506,202	481,141	394,448	289,894	195,876	125,374	101,083
Film production costs—noncurrent	82,598	64,217	61,561	59,281	47,610	40,822	31,953	45,520	30,224	27,559
Property, Plant, and Equipment at cost										
Entertainment attractions, building, and equipment	2,251,297	1,916,617	968,223	935,152	882,137	853,381	821,875	781,812	751,729	667,824
Less accumulated depreciation	(504,365)	(419,944)	(384,535)	(352,051)	(310,750)	(275,758)	(240,159)	(206,124)	(172,183)	(140,996)
	1,746,932	1,496,673	583,688	583,101	571,387	577,623	581,716	575,688	579,546	526,828
Construction and design projects in progress										
EPCOT Center	70,331	120,585	439,858	141,373	29,889	13,223	—	—	—	—
Other	37,859	39,601	29,404	21,658	30,907	26,151	31,211	31,077	20,528	68,292
Land	16,687	16,379	16,419	16,414	16,264	16,888	17,013	16,777	16,586	16,507
	1,871,809	1,673,238	1,069,369	762,546	648,447	633,885	629,940	623,542	616,660	611,627
Other Assets	93,686	103,022	21,250	19,378	19,226	13,986	12,688	8,987	10,408	11,270
Total assets	$2,381,195	$2,102,816	$1,610,009	$1,347,407	$1,196,424	$1,083,141	$964,475	$873,925	$782,666	$751,539

Liabilities and stockholders' equity:

Current liabilities										
Accounts payable, payroll, and other accrued liabilities	187,641	210,753	148,516	109,047	74,591	65,059	50,891	50,630	47,471	39,122
Taxes on income	50,557	26,560	33,057	36,244	45,177	48,615	35,557	31,090	26,547	19,721
Total current liabilities	238,198	237,313	181,573	145,291	119,768	113,674	86,448	81,720	74,018	58,843
Long-term borrowings, including commercial paper of $118,200 (1983)	346,325	315,000	110,000	—	—	—	—	—	—	55,000
Other long-term liabilities and noncurrent advances	110,874	94,739	61,886	30,429	18,616	11,393	10,781	10,761	6,100	5,801
Deferred taxes on income and investment credits	285,270	180,980	89,432	96,889	96,978	96,839	96,040	89,062	76,868	63,144
Commitments and contingencies										
Stockholders' equity										
Preferred shares, no par—Authorized 5,000,000 shares, none issued										
Common shares, no par—Authorized 75,000,000 shares Issued and outstanding 34,509,171 (1983) and 33,351,482 (1982)	661,934	588,250	540,935	537,689	535,859	534,324	513,307	471,193	423,387	409,777
Retained earnings	738,594	686,534	626,183	537,109	425,203	326,911	257,899	221,189	195,356	150,394
Total stockholders' equity	1,400,528	1,274,784	1,167,118	1,074,798	961,062	861,235	771,206	692,382	618,743	560,171
Total liabilities and stockholders' equity	$2,381,195	$2,102,816	$1,610,009	$1,347,407	$1,196,424	$1,083,141	$964,475	$873,295	$782,666	$751,539

Note: Certain accounts have been combined to provide consistency.

Source: Disney annual statements.

has been one of the major, if not the major, component in the success of the company.[5] Walt Disney's underlying mission was to provide "the finest in family entertainment." Disney feels it represents and happily projects values such as "joy, imagination, brotherhood, integrity, happiness and optimism." The three (four) major divisions are supported by these major units: Marketing, Business Affairs and Legal, Finance, Imagineering (WED), Construction Contract Administration and Purchasing, Employee Relations, Corporate Planning, and Entertainment.

The Company's History

Walt Disney Productions was incorporated as a California corporation in 1929 as the successor to a partnership that Walt and Roy Disney had founded some 16 years prior. The early years were lean as the new animation endeavor of the Disney brothers struggled to create a satisfactory product and to sell it. The Mintz Theatre in Los Angeles was Walt's first customer. Later RKO Pictures picked up the distribution rights to Disney's animated short subjects.

After a decade of having other people handle the distribution of Disney films, Walt and Roy were convinced that they needed their own distribution company. However, a lean financial situation and the impacts of the war years prevented this marketing effort from being undertaken until 1946. Their strong desire to control the product from conception to consumption led WDP founders, Walt and Roy, to seek vertical integration in all company SBUs over the years.

Although small by Hollywood standards, Walt Disney Productions was known as a media innovator from its inception. Innovation in marketing was also sought as a corporate objective, and achieved through a process in which each of WDP's product lines served to promote the other areas of the company. Disneyland and Walt Disney World had many attractions based on Disney movies, while the television anthology series promoted both the films and the theme parks. Character merchandising drew its appeal from the movies and the parks and also served to promote those entities. This strategy continues today. (See Exhibit 16.3.)

Historically, WDP has always plowed its earnings back into the company to reduce debt and finance new undertakings. It wasn't until 1961 that the company cleared its loans with Bank of America (see Exhibit 16.4) and felt comfortable financially. Even then Walt was dreaming of new projects and investments. His involvement in producing the opening and closing ceremonies for the 1960 Squaw Valley Olympics whetted his appetite for the winter recreation business—a hunger not unattempted but still unsatiated at WDP.

On the movie scene, *Mary Poppins* was a huge financial success and helped substantially to clear the company's debt. Walt was intrigued with a new show he had just produced for Disneyland, the Enchanted Tiki Room, which used three-dimensional animated figures in a show featuring music and humor. Some of the proceeds from *Mary Poppins* were used to start MAPO (another acronym derived from *Mary Poppins*) where Disney engineers and designers at WED could have their creations built. At MAPO Walt would create new ride systems for Disneyland and delve into the realm of audio-animatronics, mechanical figures for his shows.

---

[5] These latter two statements are author observations.

Exhibit 16.3   Walt Disney Productions Organization Chart

DISNEY TEAMWORK

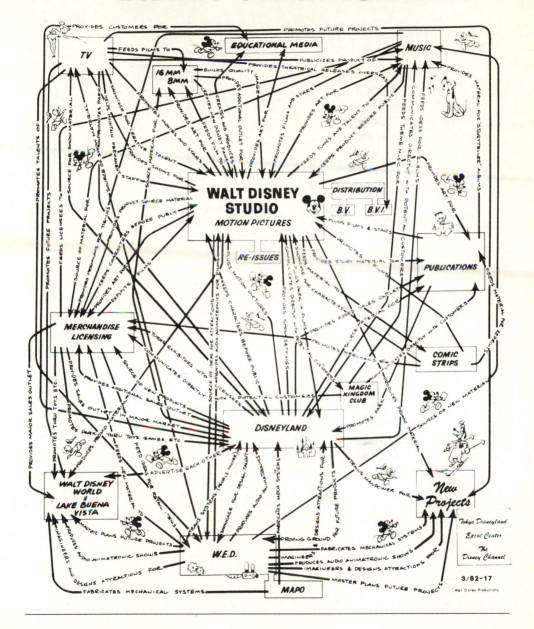

Exhibit 16.4   Milestones in Disney History

1901   Walt Disney born in Chicago—loved art as a child.

1919   Walt becomes a commercial artist. A partnership with Ub Iwerks is formed, but only lasts one month. The Iwerks family later becomes very involved in Disney films, creating special cameras for Walt such as the multiplane animation camera, underwater rigs for *20,000 Leagues Under the Sea*, and special mounting assemblies for time-lapse photography.

Ub and members of his family ran the machine shop at Walt Disney for decades.

1920   Walt creates his own business called Newman Laugh-O-Grams. Working out of his garage he creates and markets his first animated cartoons.

1923   Walt arrives in Hollywood. On October 16, 1923, he and Roy sign a contract for the distribution of six Alice Comedies at $1,500 apiece, six more at $1,000 apiece and an option for two more series. This was the beginning of Walt and Roy's partnership.

1924   Mintz Theatre offers them a contract for more Alice cartoons, offering a share of profits from theater rentals.

1926   They move into a new studio near Los Angeles and change the name of the firm to Walt Disney Studios for more box-office appeal and name identification. Walt realizes that creators, unless they control their own releasing companies, are at the mercy of distributors.

1929   The partnership incorporates, assuming assets of $85,852 and liabilities of $32,813. Walt's family holds 60 percent of the stock and Roy's family holds 40 percent. Thus, from the beginning this was a closely held corporation.

1932   They produce the first color cartoon.

1936   Bank of America establishes a revolving line of credit after screening portions of a new Disney animated feature. The bank agrees to lend money on need, but is to receive all revenues from RKO's distribution of Disney films as collateral.

1937   They produce their first full-length cartoon, *Snow White*.

1940   Despite apparent success, Walt and Roy are in debt to the banks for $4 million. Their first public offering of common and convertible preferred stock yields $3.5 million which eases financial pressures. Walt feels the public might cramp his style since stockholders generally disapprove of experimentation.

1941   Company's animators unionize.

The New York World's Fair in 1964–65 was to aid in this effort. Three major corporations and one state came to Walt seeking his assistance in developing unique presentations for this World's Fair. The funds provided by these groups not only paid for the top four "draws" at New York, they also allowed WDP to develop a whole new generation of shows at someone else's expense. These corporate relationships also led to the sponsorship of several major exhibits at Disneyland and later Walt Disney World's Magic Kingdom and EPCOT Center on the domestic scene, and the 100-percent Japanese corporate investment in Tokyo Disneyland.

The mid-1960s saw WDP faring well in the movies, in television, at Disneyland, and in character merchandising. But Walt was restless to get on with bigger and better things. He and Roy quietly bought up 27,000 acres in Central Florida upon which the company planned to construct the largest destination resort in the world, centered around a new theme park patterned after Disneyland. The Florida property was expansive so as to preclude "intrusion" by a myriad of motels, eateries, and amusements similar to that which had sprung up around Disneyland. Walt died shortly after the property had been assembled for this new effort. Five years later and once again in hock up to its corporate eyebrows, WDP opened Walt Disney World. Another gamble paid off handsomely, and despite huge

Exhibit 16.4   *continued*

1943   War years put WDP heavily in debt once again.

The studio takes on much government work doing training films, propaganda, etc. Some of the work is done free, but it keeps the animators working. The chairman of the board of Bank of America stands behind Walt and continues credit extensions. These years form a close bond between Walt Disney Productions and Bank of America which still exists 40 years later.

1946   Walt realizes diversification is needed. The company was heavily in debt, the world economy was in a shambles, and domestic spending was erratic. A live-action feature is produced and released under the auspices of Buena Vista, a new sales organization Roy sets up. The film, *The Living Desert* earns $4 million against production costs of only $300,000.

1951   Disneyland Inc. is formed to play with idea of doing an amusement park.

1952   WED Enterprises is formed to design Disneyland. WED is an acronym for Walter Elias Disney.

1955   Walt and Roy negotiate arrangement with ABC-TV whereby the network would accept a Disney-produced series for television in return for a $500,000 investment in Disneyland and ABC would guarantee loans on the new park of up to $4.5 million. Walt uses the television show to plug the new endeavor and opens Disneyland in July 1955. Originally projected to cost $11 million, opening day investment is $17 million.

1956   ABC attempts unfriendly takeover but is rebuffed by WDP.

1961   The loan from Bank of America is paid off. WDP is free of debt for the first time in 22 years.

1964   Walt produces four hit shows for corporate sponsors at the New York World's Fair. This paves the way for corporate sponsorship of attractions at Disneyland.

1965   Disney quietly purchases 27,000 acres in Central Florida at an average cost of $200 per acre.

1966   Walt Disney dies of cancer in December

1971   Walt Disney World opens in Florida after an initial investment of over $300 million. Roy Disney passes away.

1982   EPCOT Center opens on Walt Disney World property in Florida after an initial investment of $1 billion. Total investment in Walt Disney World is now over $1.8 billion.

1983   Disney enters the pay-cablevision market with its Disney Channel. Tokyo Disneyland opens. Disney investment is zero in this project as the Japanese bought the land and put up the capital. Disney collects a percentage of admission, food, and merchandise revenues.

---

cost overruns during the initial construction, WDP had once again wiped the debt off its balance sheet and paid for substantial additions to the Walt Disney World resort.

As the mid-1960s had been spent posturing the company for construction of Walt Disney World's hotels, recreation facilities, and Magic Kingdom theme park, so the mid-1970s were spent preparing for EPCOT Center, the company's new amusement park. By 1979 a cash hoard of $350 million had been stashed and several major corporate sponsors lined up for participation in this new project to be constructed on 600 acres of Walt Disney World property. Three years and $913 million later, EPCOT center opened.

Six months after this milestone, Tokyo Disneyland (TDL) opened. While TDL did not require any direct investment by WDP, it did place a tremendous strain on WED and MAPO to design and construct ride systems and shows for two major theme parks at the same time.

During the same month as the TDL opening, Disney also launched its cablevision venture, the Disney Channel. The channel had commenced 18 months previously as a joint venture with Westinghouse's Group W subsidiary, but this effort had collapsed and Disney proceeded on its own.

Back at the Disney studios, live-action movies with the Disney name and a G rating were not being well received at the box office. In 1981 and 1982 the studio took write-downs amounting to nearly $50 million on live-action features. Only the rereleases of Disney animated classics and a reasonable showing by a new-release animation feature helped stem the red ink in this division.

Similar problems with the movies were encountered in 1983, with a $21 million write-down of one movie. Additionally, start-up costs for the Disney Channel resulted in a $28-million loss on that project. Interest costs also accounted for poor profit showings on a corporate basis. As the following sections suggest, each of the major divisions and major new projects have contributed to the ups and downs of corporate fortunes in recent years.

The Entertainment and Recreation Division

The company operates the "Disneyland," amusement theme park, in California and destination resort, the "Walt Disney World," in Florida. In addition to an amusement theme park, the "Magic Kingdom," and the "Epcot Center," the Walt Disney World complex includes three hotels, camping, golfing and other recreational facilities, a shopping village, a conference center and other lodging accommodations. The Company receives royalties on revenues generated by the Tokyo Disneyland amusement park in Tokyo, Japan, which is owned and operated by an unrelated Japanese corporation.

Theme parks have been the principal source for both corporate revenue and corporate income over the past decade, but there is considerable concern that the market has matured. Attendance at both Disneyland and Walt Disney World's Magic Kingdom has fallen slightly over 1982, 1981, 1980, due in part to an unfavorable economic environment and, at the Magic Kingdom, in part to EPCOT. (See Exhibit 16.5.)

Fiscal 1983 results indicated that operating margins slipped somewhat as fourth-quarter revenues for this division were up 32 percent while operating income was only up 3 percent.

Disneyland.   Disneyland mainly services the metropolitan Southern California region within a 100-mile radius of the park. Over 70 percent of the annual attendance is classified as "local." Repeat visitations must be generated to keep attendance stable from year to year. This necessitates opening at least one new major attraction every two to three years and involves capital expenditures varying from $20 to $50 million per project. A slumping national economy hurt Disneyland in 1981–1982. June 1983 saw the opening of a new Fantasyland section in the park, totally replacing the old Fantasyland. As a result, fourth-quarter attendance rose 3 percent.

Disneyland is laid out with guests entering the park and funneling up a "Main Street," patterned after an idealistic turn-of-the-century small-town setting. At the end of this "street" is Sleeping Beauty's castle, separated from Main Street by a circular "hub." Radiating off this hub are pathways leading to various themed areas of the park, i.e., Adventureland, New Orleans Square, Frontierland, Fantasyland, and Tomorrowland. Many of the rides and shows draw their themes from Disney movies or television productions.

Walt Disney World.   Walt Disney World is a resort destination complex located near Orlando, Florida. It consists of the Magic Kingdom theme park, the new EPCOT Center

Exhibit 16.5   Other Financial Data (in thousands)

	1983	1982	1981	1980	1979
Entertainment and Recreation					
Walt Disney World					
Admission and rides	$ 278,320	$153,504	$139,326	$130,144	$121,276
Merchandise sales	172,324	121,410	121,465	116,187	101,856
Food sales	178,791	121,329	114,951	106,404	95,203
Lodging	98,105	81,427	70,110	61,731	54,043
Disneyland					
Admissions and rides	102,619	98,273	92,065	87,066	75,758
Merchandise sales	72,300	76,684	79,146	72,140	60,235
Food sales	45,699	44,481	44,920	41,703	35,865
Participant fees					
Walt Disney Travel Co.					
Tokyo Disneyland royalties and other	83,044	28,502	29,828	28,005	26,843
Total theme park revenues	$1,031,202	$725,610	$691,811	$643,380	$571,079
Theme park attendance					
Walt Disney World	22,712	12,560	13,221	13,783	13,792
Disneyland	9,980	10,421	11,343	11,522	10,760
Total attendance	342,692	22,981	24,564	25,305	24,552
Motion Pictures					
Theatrical					
Domestic	$ 38,635	$ 55,408	$ 54,624	$ 63,350	$ 49,594
Foreign	43,825	64,525	76,279	78,314	57,288
Television worldwide	27,992	44,420	43,672	19,736	27,903
Home video and nontheatrical worldwide	55,006	37,749	22,231	10,565	9,273
Total motion picture revenues	$ 165,458	$202,102	$196,806	$171,965	$144,058
Consumer Products and Other					
Character merchandising	$ 45,429	$ 35,912	$ 30,555	$ 29,631	$ 24,787
Publications	20,006	20,821	24,658	22,284	18,985
Records and music publishing	30,666	26,884	27,358	23,432	16,129
Educational media	10,269	15,468	21,148	21,908	19,967
Other	4,327	3,453	12,704	1,905	1,768
Total consumer products and other revenues	$ 110,697	$102,538	$116,423	$ 99,160	$ 81,636

theme park, three company-owned hotels (total 2,000 rooms), a company-owned campground (1,000 sites), three golf courses, water-oriented recreation facilities, a unique shopping village with themed stores, and a hotel plaza area where outside operators run six (to be nine by late 1983 early 1984) hotels on property leased from Walt Disney World.

Attendance at the Magic Kingdom and EPCOT Center is highly tourist-oriented with 80 percent originating from outside the state. The Magic Kingdom is very similar to Disneyland in layout, but has much more room available for expansion (27,000 acres, most of which Disney plans to retain in its natural state). The Disneyland site is bounded by com-

Exhibit 16.6   EPCOT Center Future World Pavilions

Corporate Sponsor	Topic
AT&T	Communications
Exxon	Energy
General Motors	Motion
Sperry	Computers
Kodak	Imagination
Kraft	Land
General Electric	Future lifestyles
United Technologies	Living seas

mercial development with virtually no expansion possible. EPCOT Center (an acronym for Experimental Prototype Community of Tomorrow) covers over 200 acres (vs. just over 100 for the Magic Kingdom), not including parking or support facilities, and is divided into two main sections—Future World and World Showcase.

The pavilions in Future World are each sponsored by major corporations and range in cost from $30 million to over $70 million for the new Living Seas pavilion currently under construction. Each pavilion covers a topic of scientific or sociological interest. Exhibit 16.6 gives a breakdown of the Future World sponsors and the topics of pavilions. Disney owns and operates all of these pavilions. Although participant contracts differ slightly, the general principle is for the corporate sponsor to pay Disney a small percentage during construction with the remainder spread over 10 or 15 years. This means that while WDP reaps all income from the park admissions and realizes the cash-flow benefits of investment tax credit and depreciation, it must also produce the up-front working capital to facilitate construction.

World Showcase is intended to be a permanent "World's Fair" setting. There are sites for 18 countries situated around a 45-acre lagoon. Each pavilion is intended to present the architecture, culture, food, and merchandise of the particular nation. World Showcase currently has nine nations represented, with one more under construction and at least two more in design. Here, as in Future World, there is some corporate participation, but on a much smaller scale.

Several of the restaurants are operated by nationals of the country represented, with the income going to that operator. Two of the merchandising facilities are under a similar arrangement. In these types of participation, Walt Disney World "leases" the facility to the operator for a set fee and a percentage of the gross revenues. These contracts call for a much larger portion of the participant fee "up-front."

In addition to the shopping village at Lake Buena Vista on Walt Disney World property, the company also operates a series of "vacation villas" and town houses. These facilities are available to the public for nightly rentals. Some units are on long-term leases with corporate sponsors who use them for incentive vacations or business entertaining.

Hotel Plaza lies on both sides of a beautifully landscaped four-lane boulevard which leads from a major Interstate exit to the shopping village. All hotel sites are owned by Disney and leased long-term to the hotel operators. Walt Disney World's reservation service books reservations for these hotels on a commission basis. The average year-round occupancy is close to 85 percent (as opposed to 99 percent for Disney-owned hotels). Guests staying at Hotel Plaza are furnished Disney-operated bus transportation throughout the Walt Disney World complex and the hotels are billed for the service based on a charge per-occupied-room night. Feasibility studies indicate that if Hotel Plaza is expanded by another 1,500–2,000 rooms, it would be practical to extend the existing WDW monorail service to Lake Buena Vista. The additional beamway and trains would be paid for by increasing the current assessment per-occupied-room night.

Disney has saved two prime hotel sites in the LBV area for its own future use. The company would also like to expand the shopping village as more and more hotel rooms in the area lead to a larger captive audience. This expansion would also include adding more Disney restaurants in the village to supplement the five major and several minor dining locations the company already provides at Lake Buena Vista.

Disney-owned restaurants throughout the WDW complex have experienced a decline in dining revenues since the opening of EPCOT Center, as many guests choose to dine at the international facilities available within World Showcase. There is some concern as to how many additional seats can be added within EPCOT Center before there is a dilutive effect on the existing participant operators. Current thinking is that EPCOT Center can only handle another 1,200 "waitress-service" seats at current attendance levels. It is not known what further impact these conditions will have on the other WDW restaurants.

Tokyo Disneyland

Tokyo Disneyland, patterned closely after its California cousin, is estimated to add between $15 million and $20 million to the bottom line at WDP during fiscal year 1984. This has been a riskless investment for the company with no detriment to any Disney-owned facilities.

Entertainment and Recreation—Competition On All Fronts

While Disney was the first to build a theme park, and while the company is still the unquestioned leader in the industry, competition is increasing on all fronts.

During the 1970s, theme parks sprang up in a regional format all across the country. Older parks were refurbished and the quality of each guest experience rose sharply. Former Disney technicians roamed the marketplace and combined their skills with proliferating computer technology to produce animated figures of reasonable quality to enhance show presentations at theme parks and pizza parlors alike.

Restaurants got into the business of "theming" and decided to provide a "dining experience" instead of just a meal.

Video games filled arcades and then migrated to the family television set.

Shopping mall developers also cranked out themed-based, speciality environments.

While none of these efforts alone threatened the appeal of a Disneyland or a Magic Kingdom, they all provided the same, generic-type environment as a Disneyland and they all tapped the same pocketbooks the Mouse was after. Attendance has leveled at Disneyland and was actually declining in the Magic Kingdom before the advent of the EPCOT Center. In light of societal changes and increased competition of the past dozen years, it is probably surprising the Disney parks haven't suffered more attendance-wise.

Direct Competition

Disneyland competes directly with Knott's Berry Farm, Sea World, Magic Mountain, Busch Gardens, Universal City Tours and a host of smaller attractions. None can match its drawing power, however. Most thrive on leftovers, but each takes a few dollars which might have been spent on a repeat visit to Disneyland.

But the tourists and residents in the Orlando area only have a certain number of days to spend. Disney World must compete with Busch Gardens, Cypress Gardens, Sea World, Circus World, Wet 'n Wild (a water recreation area), Kennedy Space Center, and Florida's famous beaches for each day and dollar. Nobody questions that the mouse is the magnet which draws tourists into the area, but he must still compete for tourists' time after they arrive.

The Motion Pictures Division

"The Company produces motion pictures for the threatrical, television and home video markets. The Company distributes its filmed product through its own distribution and marketing companies in the United States and through foreign subsidiaries in certain countries and other distribution companies throughout the rest of the world. The Company provides programming for, and operates, The Disney Channel, a pay television programming service." Revenues declined sharply in 1983 while operating income has been on a steady decline since 1980, thanks mainly to the poor showing Disney live-action features have turned in at the box office (see Exhibit 16.7).

Richard Berger, a former executive with Twentieth Century Fox and CBS, was named as the new head of the studio earlier in 1983, but it will be sometime in 1985 before products bearing his mark hit the theatres. Disney has a long history of producing G-rated movies, but a January release being produced by Ronnie Howard (*Splash*) currently includes obscenities and partial nudity. There is considerable controversy in the organization as to how, or if, this movie is to be marketed. One option would be to set up a separate subsidiary (which would not include the Disney name) to handle the distribution of PG- or R-rated movies.

Exhibit 16.7   Motion Pictures Performance and Write-downs

| | Performance (in thousands) | | | | |
	1983	1982	1981	1980	1979
Revenue	$165,458	$202,102	$196,806	$161,400	$134,785
Operating income	$(33,385)	$ 19,639	$ 34,626	$ 48,675	$ 40,229
Operating margin	−20%	10%	18%	30%	30%
Film Division Write-downs (in millions)	$26.4	$27.7	$20.5	$9.5	—
Total 1980–1983 $84.1 Million					

Walt Disney Productions, *Annual Report, 1983*, p. 20; and Walt Disney Productions, Merrill Lynch, September 29, 1983, p. 3.

The real issue which Watson feels he faces is not the rating of the movies Disney produces, but the quality of the product. The studio has had a long-time aversion to bringing in outside producers. Several years ago George Lucas approached Disney to produce a movie he was working on called *Star Wars*. Lucas had long been a Disney admirer and recognized the high level of skills the Disney studio possessed in both animation and special effects. He was turned down.

Berger is aggressively seeking outside producers and feels a current release, *Never Cry Wolf*, has the potential to be a box office hit. The movie is being released in "stages" in an effort to build strong word-of-mouth advertising prior to general release. Critics' reviews and early box-office revenues have been encouraging.

In a normal year Disney will release four to seven new live-action features. Every three years a new animated feature is released (animation is very slow and meticulous work—high-quality features cannot be turned out any faster). During each year the company also rereleases at least one of the old Disney classics such as *Snow White*, *Bambi*, etc. These rereleases have been fully amortized and their net rentals are carried straight to the bottom line. Classics are generally rereleased on a seven-year cycle.

The Disney Channel has replaced commercial television as WDP's main entry into the individual home. After more than 25 years on the air, ratings had greatly deteriorated for the anthology series on network television. The youngsters of the baby boom were off to bigger and better things.

Failure of the joint venture with Westinghouse meant that Disney either had to pursue the cable venture on its own or totally pull out of the television market. The Disney Channel is a highly leveraged operation with break-even estimated at 2 million subscribers. The service is an "extra cost option" for cable subscribers at a retail cost of $9–$12 per month. As of October 21, 1983, the channel had slightly over 500,000 subscribers and estimated hitting the 2 million mark in the Spring of 1985. This venture is currently (1983) losing $15 million per quarter. The cash drain of the Disney Channel will considerably limit working capital available for other projects in the company over the next two years (1984 and 1985).

The Motion Picture Industry.   Walt Disney Productions has never been considered a major studio by the rest of the industry—their annual production and variety of products has always been limited. Walt staked out a small, specialized market segment and used innovation to hold on. Current management views the Disney Channel and the new Touchstone film label as its innovative answer to the stagnation which has led to disappointing studio results over the past 15 years.

The overall industry is being challenged on a broad front. The old, mammoth studios with their equally mammoth fixed costs are being forced to find new ways to push their products. Weekend movies are no longer the American ritual which supported the industry for 50 years. Studios are going bankrupt, merging, or being bought out. Sky-high production costs and interest rates mean more and more red ink from box-office bombs must be absorbed by fewer and fewer blockbusters. And even blockbusters don't return the kind of profits they did two decades ago because studios have turned to joint ventures with independent producers on many occasions.

Pay-cable television, network television, and videotape machines are some of the animals chewing into studio balance sheets. They are also the markets which most movie-

makers see as the salvation of the industry. These markets represented $.31 of every reve-
nue dollar flowing into the studios in 1983.[6] It is anticipated that this number will grow to
$.36 in five years.[7]

Paramount, Twentieth Century Fox, United Artists, Columbia Pictures, and Warner
Communications have all forged exclusive pacts, semi-exclusive deals, joint ventures, and
innovative licensing arrangements to try to secure a foothold in the nontheatrical distribution of their film products.

These firms are all frustrated by their government-mandated exclusion from direct entry into the pay-television market (applies to all-movie format) and the Justice Department's reading of the First Sale Doctrine in the copyright laws which prevents the studios
from collecting revenues from retailers' tape rentals.

Disney Changes Its Movie Strategy

For its own purposes, Disney has found that the overhead burden at the studio is rather
stiff when applied to only three or four new film productions each year. It is hoped that the
new Touchstone label (which will distribute PG movies) and special productions for the
Disney Channel will help spread those fixed costs over more products, therefore lowering
the burden each film must shed before showing a profit.

Miller and associates do not feel there are enough good G-rated scripts available to
warrant more than three or four releases a year under the Buena Vista/Disney label. By
expanding scripts into the PG range with Touchstone, the company feels more good
scripts will become available. The success or failure of *Splash* and *Country* will probably
determine the future of Touchstone.

The name Touchstone was selected by a consulting firm which specializes in selecting
names and logos for companies. The term means "a test of quality." Anticipated movie
releases are indicated in Exhibit 16.8.

Consumer Products and Other Operations

"The Company licenses the name Walt Disney, its characters, its literary properties and its
songs and music to various manufacturers, retailers, printers, and publishers. The Company also produces and distributes phonograph records, 16mm prints of products developed on education subjects, and a broad range of teaching aids. These activities are
conducted through the character merchandising and publications, records and music publishing, and education media divisions and subsidiaries of the Company."

Revenues for this division were up 15 percent over the prior year largely due to royalties from *TRON*, and from the sale of merchandise in Tokyo Disneyland. Major new
thrusts are being made utilizing the cartoon character Goofy as a symbol for youth sports.
Twenty Gold Records were earned by the Records and Music Division. Two of these
include *E.T.* and *Return of the Jedi*. The remaining 18 were Disney titles, including
Mousercise.

---

[6] "Movie Studios Put More Emphasis on Home-Video, Pay-TV Markets," *The Wall Street Journal*, May 1, 1984.
[7] Ibid.

Exhibit 16.8   Disney Film Releases; (with estimated production costs)

Never Cry Wolf ($12 million)	October 1983
Running Brave (distribution only)	November 1983
Mickey's Christmas Carol ($4 million)	Christmas 1983
Rescuers (re-issue)	Christmas 1983
Splash ($10 million)	February 1984
Jungle Book (re-issue)	Summer 1984
Country ($8–$10 million)	Summer 1984
Baby ($10 million)	Christmas 1984
Return to Oz ($20 million)	Summer 1985
Black Cauldron ($25 million plus)	Summer 1985

Source: Walt Disney Productions, Merrill Lynch, September 29, 1983, p. 6.

Finances

The finance unit of the organization interacts with all aspects of the company. Major sub-unit activities include: treasury, controllership, management audit, foreign financial administration, tax administration, loss prevention, credit and collections, stockholder relations, investor relations, employee pension and stock plans, and management information systems.

The historical philosophy of Disney has been to remain debt free and to finance from current revenues. Only with the EPCOT project has Disney moved into a higher-leveraged position. The historical philosophy appears to be softening somewhat, and would definitely change in the face of a serious threat, such as an attempted takeover.

Exhibits 16.1, 16.2, and 16.3 have provided information on income and balance sheet accounts. Disney revenues are highly cyclical as indicated in Exhibit 16.9. Disney cash flows have reflected the EPCOT buildup and consumeration as portrayed in Exhibits 16.2, 16.3, and 16.10. Future cash-flow projects are shown in Exhibit 16.11.

Update

Revolving Line of Credit and Commercial Paper

The company has available, through December 1985, an unsecured revolving line of credit up to $1.3 billion for general corporate purposes. The company has the option to borrow at various interest rates not to exceed the bank's prime rate. Under the line of credit, the company is required to pay a fee on the unused portion of the commitment, to maintain certain compensating balances, and to meet certain minimum net worth and working capital requirements. Up to $200 million of the line of credit is available as backing for commercial paper borrowings by the company.

Exhibit 16.9   Quarterly Financial Summary (in thousands, except per-share data)

	December 31	March 31	June 30	September 30
Operations by quarter				
1983 Revenues				
Entertainment and recreation	$203,698	$239,741	$288,936	$298,827
Motion pictures	41,338	46,109	40,533	37,478
Consumer products and other	25,106	29,826	29,032	26,733
Total revenues	$270,142	$315,676	$358,501	$363,038
Operating Income (loss) before corporate expenses				
Entertainment and recreation	$ 24,898	$ 44,930	$ 67,438	$ 59,612
Motion pictures	5,780	6,512	(32,226)	(13,451)
Consumer products and other	11,841	17,812	15,793	11,436
Total operating income before corporate expenses	$ 42,519	$ 69,254	$ 51,005	$ 57,597
Income before taxes on income	$ 30,414	$ 54,020	$ 38,230	$ 40,796
Net income	17,214	30,020	21,430	24,496
Earnings per share	$ .51	$ .87	$ .61	$ .70
1982 Revenues				
Entertainment and recreation	$140,794	$150,595	$207,333	$226,888
Motion pictures	44,724	67,906	46,050	43,422
Consumer products and other	26,262	29,174	22,368	24,734
Total revenues	$211,780	$247,675	$275,751	$295,044
Operating income (loss) before corporate expenses				
Entertainment and recreation	$ 12,238	$ 19,157	$ 43,155	$ 58,095
Motion pictures	5,680	8,972	13,716	(8,729)
Consumer products and other	11,832	15,654	10,913	9.433
Total operating income before corporate expenses	$ 29,750	$ 43,783	$ 67,784	$ 58,799
Income before taxes on income	$ 31,009	$ 38,648	$ 58,799	$ 50,337
Net income	17,409	21,648	32,899	28,137
Earnings per share	$ .53	$ .65	$ .98	$ .84
Market price and dividend data*				
1983 price per share				
High	$71½	$78¾	$84¾	$68⅓
Low	$55	$60⅛	$65	$55⅞
Dividend per share	$.30	$.30	$.30	$.30
High	$55¼	$54	$59¼	$59
Low	$46	$47	$52⅝	$49⅝
Dividend per share	$.30	$.30	$.30	$.30

*The principal market for trading Walt Disney Productions common stock is the New York Stock Exchange.

As of September 30, 1983, the company had borrowed $15 million at 13.5 percent under the revolving credit and had issued $18 million in commercial paper. This commercial paper is generally intended to be rolled over or replaced by other long-term debt and, accordingly, has been classified as a long-term liability.

On October 15, 1982, the company received $75 million from an additional Eurodollar offering at 12.5 percent, maturing on March 15, 1989. These notes are redeemable after September 30, 1986. A forward exchange contract concurrently converted $50 million of these notes into the Japanese yen equivalent. The yen debt is due March 14, 1989, and is nonredeemable. The effective rate on the yen debt is 7.4 percent in 1983. In the second quarter of 1983, an additional $62.5 million in debt in Japanese yen was arranged at 8.6 percent. These notes are due in 1983. Long-term borrowings are indicated in Exhibit 16.10.

Debt Structure

The long-term debt currently on the balance sheet stands at approximately $450 million. Of this amount $75 million is denominated in yen to aid the repatriation of royalties collected from Tokyo Disneyland. This move was made to ease the restrictions Japan places on taking funds out of the country. The previous section contains statements from the 1983 Annual Report regarding long-term debt. The relatively short maturity on this debt reflects a company philosophy that projects should be funded with a debt only at "start-up." The belief is that a clean balance sheet makes it easier to raise substantial funds if an attractive venture presents itself.

A significant portion of the earnings swing between the fiscal quarters of 1982 and 1983 was caused by the difference in $14 million in interest income in 1982 as opposed to over $14 million in interest expense in 1983.

As primarily a service-oriented company, Disney is able to maintain a low current ratio. The Disney theme parks generate up to $6 million in actual cash (all parks combined) on a peak attendance day.

Marketing the Mouse

Numerous strategies are employed by the marketing function of the organization. Major marketing activities include: advertising, publicity, promotion, corporate public relations, the Magic Kingdom Club, travel services, participant affairs, and marketing development.

The key to marketing is achieving synergy in overall marketing efforts. Product ideas developed by one direction or subsidiary are picked up by other areas of the company. Coordinated programs occur regularly. The chart in Exhibit 16.3 illustrates the interrelationships within the Disney organization.

A classic example of the Disney synergy is the animated film classic *Snow White*. The original 1939 movie is released every six or seven years. It was the basis for the attraction, Snow White's Scary Adventures, in both the Florida and California themed parks, has appeared in book and comic book form, and has been licensed for use in countless lines of merchandise.

During a several-month period prior to each rerelease of this classic, animated window displays featuring scenes from the movie will appear on Main Street U.S.A. at both Disneyland and Walt Disney World's Magic Kingdom. Joint venture promotions with major merchandising concerns will also raise "awareness" of the impending rerelease. Several Disney Channel programs will also feature segments which are both entertaining in themselves and excellent promotions for the film.

Disney's science fiction movie, *TRON*, which dealt with an adventure inside a computer, was a very expensive production. Although it did well in general release, it failed to show a profit. Ancillary merchandising, including an arcade video game based on the

Exhibit 16.10 Consolidated Statement of Changes in Financial Position (dollar amounts in thousands)

	Year Ended September 30				
	1983	1982	1981	1980*	1979*
Cash provided by operations before taxes on income (see below)	$308,369	$309,431	$316,949	$326,504	$286,256
Taxes paid (received) on income—net	(28,987)	34,649	106,144	121,822	103,399
Cash provided by operations	337,356	274,782	210,805	204,682	182,857
Cash dividends	41,100	39,742	32,406	23,280	(15,496)
Investing activities					
EPCOT Center, net of related payables	250,196	566,428	285,651	102,529	16,666
Other property, plant, and equipment	83,542	47,988	47,756	47,450	39,963
Film production and programming costs	83,750	52,295	55,454	68,409	44,436
Rights to the Walt Disney name	(3,640)	40,000			
EPCOT Center and the Disney Channel preopening and start-up costs	18,253	19,170	1,907	—	—
Long-term notes receivable and other	11,406	26,881	4,023	1,619	6,218
	443,507	752,672	394,791	219,702	107,283
	(147,251)	(517,722)	(216,392)	(38,300)	60,078
Financing activities					
Long-term borrowings	137,500	205,000	110,000	—	—
Reduction of long-term borrowings	(99,925)	—	—	—	—
Common stock offering	70,883	—	—	—	—
Common stock issued (returned) to acquire rights to the Walt Disney name and certain equipment	(3,640)	46,200	—	—	—
Participation fees, net of related receivables	11,169	23,867	24,745	10,361	6,245
Collection of long-term notes receivable and other	35,667	2,030	7,646	1,327	968
	151,654	277,097	142,391	11,688	7,213

movie, was very successful, however. The entire *TRON* effort resulted in bottom line profits at the "Mouse House."

Disney's marketing efforts run a full circle with movies, providing merchandising opportunities which raise awareness of the themed parks which, in turn, provide settings and themes for television productions, which are also used to promote movies. Joint advertising and promotional campaigns with major domestic corporate "participants" in Disney parks have recently made the circle even larger.

A Typical Walt Disney World Campaign. Disney's two domestic theme park locations each require totally different marketing approaches. Disneyland experiences a majority of its attendance from the surrounding local populace. Advertising includes billboards, print media, radio, and television. Promotions are aimed at large local companies which have the ability to sell large blocks of tickets (3,500 and up).

Walt Disney World's Magic Kingdom and EPCOT Center react to a different scenario. Local advertising is generally aimed at influencing the time of day a tourist will visit either

Exhibit 16.10   *continued*

	Year Ended September 30				
	1983	**1982**	**1981**	**1980***	**1979***
Increase (decrease) in cash and short-term investments	4,403	(240,625)	(74,001)	(26,612)	67,291
Cash and short-term investments, beginning of year	13,652	254,277	328,278	354,890	287,599
Cash and short-term investments, end of year	$ 18,055	$ 13,652	$254,277	$328,278	$354,890
The difference between income before taxes on income as shown on the Consolidated Statement of Income (Exhibit 16.1) and cash provided by operations before taxes on income is explained as follows:					
Income before taxes on income	$163,460	$178,793	$216,980	$247,986	$213,888
Charges to income not requiring cash outlays:					
Depreciation	90,184	41,917	38,886	43,093	40,439
Amortization of film production and programming costs	65,575	64,868	55,222	33,889	31,823
Other	15,526	9,950	9,449	6,530	4,151
Changes in:					
Accounts receivable	(25,863)	1,077	(18,591)	(13,589)	(10,414)
Inventories	(11,228)	(6,944)	(5,125)	(12,774)	(2,470)
Prepaid expenses	(1,691)	(2,754)	(3,960)	(2,461)	(693)
Accounts payable, payroll, and other accrued liabilities	12,406	22,524	24,088	23,830	9,532
	144,909	130,638	99,969	78,518	72,368
Cash provided by operations before taxes on income	$308,369	$309,431	$316,949	$326,504	$286,256

*Selected changes in accounting policies may cause differences with other exhibits.

park. It stresses special entertainment and events. Promotional efforts aimed at the local populace (which is defined as about 50 percent of the state of Florida for marketing purposes) are intended to draw Floridians to the complex during the nonpeak tourist months of May, September, October, November, and January. These campaigns are patterned along the lines of "Armed Forces Salutes," "Senior Citizen Days," or "Florida" salutes, and attempt to encourage incremental visits by slightly discounting both EPCOT Center and the Magic Kingdom—usually in a combination package.

Walt Disney World uses regional campaigns and "target markets" to stimulate the tourist trade. A typical target market campaign will zero in on large metropolitan areas in the eastern or mid-western United States with a combination promotional/advertising blitz.

As a first step, the target market is surveyed to determine "awareness" of Walt Disney World and how Walt Disney World influences vacation planning. The next step is to provide a promotional campaign headed by a local radio station within that market. This is followed up with local advertising and a concluding survey to test results.

A planned event for the Kansas City market includes a live radio broadcast from Walt

Exhibit 16.11   Cash-Flow Projections (in thousands)

	1985	1984	1983	1982	1981
Sources:					
New income	$155,000	$125,000	$ 93,200*	$100,093	$121,480
Depreciation	85,000	95,000	90,000	41,917	38,886
Amortization and other	70,000	70,000	75,000	74,818	64,671
	$310,000	$290,000	$258,200*	$216,828	$225,037
Other financing	0	50,000	130,000	277,097	142,391
Total sources	$310,000	$340,000	$388,200	$493,925	$367,428
Uses:					
Dividends	$ 45,000	$ 40,000	$ 40,000	$ 39,742	$ 32,406
EPCOT investments	75,000	100,000	200,000	600,777	301,032
Other	60,000	50,000	65,000	47,988	47,756
Film production	110,000	100,000	90,000	52,295	55,454
Total uses	$290,000	$290,000	$395,000	$740,802	$436,648
Net change in working capital	$ 20,000	$ 50,000	($ 6,800)	($246,877)	($ 69,220)

*Adjusted for actual reported income for 1983.

Source: Walt Disney Productions, Merrill Lynch, September 28, 1983, p. 4.

Disney World for 48 hours and a promotional campaign which will award several family vacations to Walt Disney World as prizes. Advertising expenses concerning the vacation giveaway are picked up by the radio station and include television and newspaper ads.

Disney picks up the tab for meals and park admissions, participant hotel operators in the Hotel Plaza at Lake Buena Vista (on Disney property) donate the rooms, and Eastern Airlines, another Walt Disney World participant, handles air transportation. National Car Rental Company, another participant, handles ground transportation in Florida. The large Hallmark facility in Kansas City will act as a registration center for the promotion. Naturally, Hallmark is also a participant at Walt Disney World.

Other promotional efforts take varying themes, but they are all intended to involve as many agencies and companies as possible with minimal direct expense to Disney. Joint advertising and promotional campaigns with the various participant corporations at Walt Disney World are common. These companies also utilize their unique relationship with Disney to promote their own products and services and provide advertising backgrounds for their print and broadcast ads.

Employee Relations

You can dream, create, design and build the most wonderful place in the world . . . but it requires people to make the dream a reality.

▪ *Walt Disney* ▪

Walt believed that people were his company's most important asset, and current company policies continue to reflect that belief. There are three broad responsibilities which the employee relations support functions assist in: obtaining capable employees, utilizing their abilities fully, assisting them in the accomplishment of the company's goals. These are accomplished in Employee Relations through these activities: manpower and organization planning, employment and placement, personnel and benefits administration, first aid, equal opportunity programs, compensational relocation, labor relations, personnel management, and Disney University.

Employee Relations at WDW—an Example of the Disney Philosophy.   Although Walt Disney World operates everything from machine shops to tree farms in addition to theme parks and hotels, it is primarily a service industry with high guest/employee contact.

Exhaustive efforts are made to establish a "family" feeling among the 20,000 employees in Florida. Pay rates are held above the area averages (though still relatively low as compared to a manufacturing concern) and extra employee benefits are stressed.

All employees receive discounts on merchandise, free park tickets several times a year, and access to Disney films at "Family Film Festivals." A full line of recreational facilities includes a lake with white sand beaches, pool, softball diamonds, and jogging facilities. Company-sponsored employee clubs encourage snow skiing, scuba diving, canoeing, group trips to Europe and the Caribbean, etc.

Each new employee begins with the commpany by attending the Disney University where company history, courtesy standards, and group benefits are stressed. If the employee is working in a high guest contact area, this initial training is followed by in-depth training in the area of guest courtesy when the employee reaches his or her work location.

Training manuals stress safety, show, courtesy, and capacity. Employees, called "cast members" in the Disney vernacular, are taught that their "on-stage" performance should stress the safety of the "guests" (Disney's customers), the maintaining of the "show," and courteous handling of both guests and fellow cast members. If all of these functions are handled properly and operating procedures followed, the "capacity" of the facility will simply happen.

The cleanliness of Disney parks, the attention to design and operational details, the courtesy of the employees, and the efficiency with which large crowds are handled, set this organization apart from their competition.

In the operating areas, most promotions are made from within the company. Areas such as food services, hotel operations, and merchandising hire a certain number of trainees out of college, but those represent only a small portion of the total advancements into management each year. This policy forms a loyalty to the company, builds on Disney experience, but also leads to "inbreeding."

The company tries to counter this by developing management generalists. It rotates key managers between divisions, and sometimes between subsidiary companies, to broaden individual development.

Detailed employee opinion polls are taken twice yearly. Each employee participates once every two years. This provides a large sampling (5,000 per survey) on a frequent-enough basis to detect trend development and hopefully address employee concerns before they grow too large. Opinion poll results are discussed in-depth with managers and remedial action, where it is felt needed, is proposed to the overall Operating Committee on a timely basis. The results are also broken down to the "divisional" level to allow managers to address localized problems which might not affect the entire complex.

Exhibit 16.12   Standards of Disney Courtesy

When Walt Disney opened DISNEYLAND on July 17, 1955, he believed that the friendliness of his staff would reach out and touch his guests in a way that would bring them back year after year . . . and it has. . . .

No matter what role we have, whether we are on stage presenting the show or backstage preparing the show, that tradition of friendliness is what we represent every day of the year. We lay that reputation on the line every time we answer a question or give instructions. It is not easy to answer the same question time after time in the same fresh, friendly manner, nor is it always easy to direct people in a way that is well received. Try to keep in mind that even though you have answered the question 50 times, the person has asked you only once. . . . We are people specialists, presenting a very special show and our skill in hosting is one of the most important parts. Our Disney Difference has proven to be a winning way with people. As a Cast Member at WALT DISNEY WORLD, you are expected to:

- SMILE: It is the most important part of your Disney Look. Put a smile in your voice, too.
- Establish and maintain EYE CONTACT whenever you are speaking.
- Reflect the Disney IMAGE in both your appearance and your attitude.
- Use PLEASE and THANK YOU as often as possible.
- ANTICIPATE the needs of people . . . extend to them the same warm hospitality that you would expect to receive.
- SPEAK FIRST—Reach out and say "hello" . . . ask how things are going. . . .
- You are an information source. . . . KNOW the basics every day. If you don't have an answer—OFFER to find one. . . . Answer more than just the question.
- MAKE SOMEONE HAPPY—You can make someone's day memorable and pleasant just by engaging in a little friendly conversation. . . . Everyone likes to be recognized, it makes them feel important. Remember, everybody is a V.I.P. and when you treat them with that "little extra" they won't forget you or the special treatment you gave them.

Walt Disney World is unionized in most hourly categories and the company maintains reasonably good relations with the various unions. As Florida is a right-to-work state, it is estimated that something less than half the eligible employees actually belong to a union. Disney pays close attention to detail through what are known as standard operating procedures (SOPs). An example of one in the personnel area is contained in Exhibit 16.12. This is one item from an SOP pertaining to expected standards of courtesy.

Management Information Systems

Disney has consistently attempted state-of-the-art technological innovations in its film productions and theme park *audio-animatronic* shows. At EPCOT Center, they have even made a "show" out of the Computer Control Center, which operates all of the shows and facilities in the park.

Management access to computer systems to monitor the overall corporate operations is generally considered to be somewhat below current business standards, though. A large Sperry system installed at the studio over a decade ago is overburdened and in the process of being supplemented and replaced. Most financial reporting must be batch-processed, printed, and hand-distributed. The time delay can be very frustrating to operating managers.

Personnel records, payables, receivables, and inventory are only partially computerized. An ongoing design and capital program is in process to address these deficiencies, but will be several years in implementation. A function "attack" team was formed utilizing MIS managers from throughout the company and charged with overseeing the project. Overall direction is still provided by corporate MIS officials based at the studio in Burbank.

Corporate Planning

This division is recently established at the direction of Ray Watson. It is charged with the development and assessment of business plans and strategies to meet the Company's goals. It will work with all areas of the Company in order to do so. The first iteration of a planning cycle, with a full five-year plan and written objectives, is to be completed Companywide sometime in the spring of 1984.

Historically, Disney has not produced hard-dollar objectives, or engaged in an annual planning process. Walt did not like formalized planning, although many of the strategic actions certainly had their own plans. Walt felt that the major objective was to be the "finest provider of family entertainment," and that the revenues would follow if that objective was met. Ray Watson, formerly president of the Irvine Company and its prime driving force, feels that it's time for a large company such as Disney to begin to plan for specific returns, profits, margins, and so forth.

Business Affairs and Legal

This division's responsibilities include negotiating, reviewing, and writing contracts for the varied and worldwide affairs of the company. It has two major divisions: Business Affairs and Legal.

Imagineering (WED and MPO)

WED is the "master-planning, design, production, and engineering branch of the Disney organization. It was established in 1952 by Walt Disney to design Disneyland park." WED stands for Walter Elias Disney.

MAPO (from Mary Poppins), is charged with bringing WED's designs to life. "Formed in 1965, MAPO produces audio-animatronics figures and control systems, assists in the development of ride vehicles, and supports the development of a variety of prototype systems. MAPO also plays a large role in the installation of new projects.

"WED and MAPO are composed of the following divisions: planning, creative development, engineering, production, administration, WED Florida, and project management."

Construction and Contract Administration

"With offices on both coasts, this area supports the corporation by purchasing materials, equipment, contract services and construction for day-to-day operation and/or special projects." There are two divisions: Construction Contract Administration and Purchasing.

Live Entertainment

This division of the firm is concerned with the live entertainment provided for the theme parks and special events around the world. Division subunit activities include: show development and production, stage shows, parties, premieres, parades, special events, Disney characters, talent booking, fireworks shows, music festival program, convention shows, and international festivals programs.

Organization Structure

There is no organization chart for the total company. No chart exists because Walt "didn't believe in putting people in little boxes." He saw that as limiting. "Everyone cooperates with everyone else in doing their job," is one way of describing the structure. Disney is a team-oriented company. Within some divisions, however, organization charts do exist. These are used primarily for keeping track of jobs, reporting assignments, and so on.

Disney is a decentralized company, but it employs standard control systems, such as performance appraisals, in an effort to be efficient and effective.

Disney Culture, Florida Style

Disneyland, Walt Disney World's Magic Kingdom, and EPCOT Center are the crowned kings of the theme park industry. But why? The answer probably lies in attention to detail and a willingness to spend big bucks on design, construction, and maintenance of a total show. It also has to do with pride. Opinion polls show that Walt Disney World employees take great pride in where they work.

Disney's rides and shows are all themed in overall architecture design to show content. Each piece of the park both stands alone and yet fits with the whole. WED imagineers carefully research each topic, country, or theme to be presented and then carry an uncanny attention to detail down to the smallest level—carpet, titles, costumes, props, etc.

Each presentation is designed to totally involve the guest—it attacks all the senses . . . sight, hearing, feeling, and smelling. It frequently reaches out to stir the emotions, hitting at laughter, fear, patriotism, etc. Whether it be a ride-through attraction or a threater presentation, the show is designed to overwhelm the guest with more activity, sights, sounds, than can be absorbed in one visit. The idea is to keep the individual so busy there is not time to pick out the imperfections in the illustration.

Operation of the parks means the illusion must be maintained throughout the show. Cast members are carefully costumed, and the show and surrounding grounds are carefully costumed, and the show and surrounding grounds are meticulously maintained so as not to distract the guest with something out of character.

Employees are carefully trained to watch over the guest during his/her visit—accidents distract from the total show and impair the ability to process large numbers of people through given segments of the show.

Handling large volumes of tourists per day (it is not unusual for more than 100,000 people to visit Walt Disney World's two theme parks on a given busy day) requires great attention to every detail of the daily operation.

Two-way portable radios are frequently evident as supervisors move about the parks evaluating safety, show, courtesy, and capacity. A crack maintenance force reacts quickly when problems arise during the day and then work throughout the night conducting preventative maintenance.

Hoards of landscapers manicure and shape plants and mulch a rich texture of trees, flowering plants, and ground cover. Large beds of annuals are ripped out several times a year and replanted to provide a particular color or pattern deemed appropriate for each time of year.

Entertainment groups, area background music, and subtle architectural perspectives bring a personality to each area of the park. Careful eyes constantly evaluate the show presentation for consistency and overall appearance. Periodic refurbishments bring fresh life to areas showing signs of wear, and new shows are brought in to enliven old themes whose time has passed.

Custodial crews keep the park spotless by day and then pressure-hose all walkways and promenades by night. Carpets are shampooed by the mile, windows washed by the acre, and brass polished to infinity.

The pressure of this environment is high, but teamwork and cooperation among all divisions at all levels is nurtured. The individual jobs are broken down to small-enough segments so as to be readily learnable and manageable. Training is both thorough and ongoing.

Turnover is fairly high among service employees and entry-level supervision, but this helps bring fresh attitudes into the job on a regular basis. Middle and upper management is very stable and brings a high degree of consistency and many years of experience into the process of maintaining the show. Loyalty to the Disney product is very high among this group.

The Disney Management Team.   Raymond L. Watson, Chairman of the Board—information regarding this very essential formulator of Disney long-range strategy and policy may be found at the beginning of the case.

Ronald (Ron) W. Miller, President and Chief Executive Officer—Miller, age 51, was an All-American tight end at the University of Southern California in the early 1950s. He played some professional ball with the Los Angeles Rams. Ron married one of Walt Disney's two daughters, Dianne, in 1954, and became the sixth person hired for the Disneyland project that same year.

After a two-year stint in the army and his year with the Rams, he rejoined the Disney organization as a second assistant director. Miller served as an associate producer on the Disney weekly television series before entering theatrical production in 1960 in a similar capacity. He worked directly with Walt on ten motion pictures as both an associate and coproducer. After Walt's death in 1966, Ron was the sole producer on a long succession of films.

He was named vice-president, television, in 1968 and joined a four-member Executive Committee in 1971. Nine years later Miller became president and chief operating officer. He succeeded Card Walker as chief executive officer in 1983. Ron is currently a member of the four-man Executive Committee along with Watson, and former Board Chairman Walker and Donn Tatum.

E. Cardon (Card) Walker, Chairman of the Executive Committee—Walker joined Disney in 1983 and proceeded to work his way up through the ranks in the marketing area. He was elected president in 1971 upon the death of Roy Disney, and added the title of chief executive officer in 1976. Card followed Don Tatum as chairman of the board in 1980.

Card felt very strongly about the EPCOT Center project and was a major catalyst in its development and construction. Shortly after this new themed park opened at Walt Disney World, he stepped down as both chairman and chief executive officer, but became chairman of the Executive Committee.

Walker also serves as a director on the board of several major corporations, most notably Greyhound and McDonald's.

Michael L. Bagnall, Executive Vice-President–Finance.

Carl G. Bongirno, Executive Vice-President–Administration—Bongirno joined Disney in 1963 as chief accountant. After the opening of Walt Disney World in 1971 he was named as a vice-president of finance. As the EPCOT Center project heated up, he was transferred from Florida to WED Enterprises in Glendale, California, and named president of that subsidiary. WED is the design and engineering firm which oversees the development of Disney themed parks.

Bongirno has retained his directorship with Sun Banks of Florida Inc., one of the largest and fastest-growing banking companies in Florida.

Barton (Bo) K. Boyd, Executive Vice-President–Consumer Products and Merchandising.

Ronald J. Cayo, Executive Vice-President–Business Affairs and Legal.

James J. Jimirro, Executive Vice-President–Telecommunications—Jimirro sold Card Walker on the Disney Channel venture and pleaded for the company to go it alone when the original joint venture with Westinghouse fell through. It is felt his future is almost totally dependent on the success or failure of this venture.

Jack B. Lindquist, Executive Vice-President–Marketing—as a long-time Disney executive, Lindquist is well respected for his imaginative marketing concepts and his willingness to tread on new ground.

Richard (Dick) A. Nunis, Executive Vice-President–Walt Disney World/Disneyland— Nunis played football at Southern Cal with Miller (he was a defensive safety) but saw his football career limited by injury. He was the first academic All-American at USC in 1952.

Dick joined the staff at Disneyland in 1955 prior to its opening and worked his way through management of the park. In 1968 he was named vice-president in charge of Disneyland. During the last year of construction of Walt Disney World, Nunis assumed direct responsibility for the completion of the financially strapped project and opened it on time in October 1971. In 1972 he was named president of the Walt Disney Outdoor Recreation Division.

Martin (Marty) A. Sklar, Executive Vice-President–WED Creative Development.

Future Projects

Ray Watson continues to feel the Florida properties offer the most attractive ground upon which to sow net investments, but he is very concerned with improving the company's return on those dollars.

The business concept of EPCOT Center was to expand WDW's penetration of the estimated 30 million tourists visiting Florida each year and extend the length of stay on Disney property for all guests visiting there. Based on original estimates in 1979 of a $600–$750 million investment, all was well. The return to Disney, based on estimated actual investment through 1983 of $1.2 billion, is less than satisfactory, even though attendance has exceeded original projections by 25 percent.

WED estimates that any new Disney hotels in Florida will likely cost 20–40 percent more than comparable non-Disney hotels due to the great attention to detail, themed design, and guest facilities the company provides in its hotels. Disney hotels must operate at a very high occupancy level to be profitable. There are at least four potential hotel sites near the Magic Kingdom and Disney's existing hotels in addition to the Lake Buena Vista sites mentioned earlier.

Florida management has indicated to Watson a strong desire for additional company-owned rooms to try to further extend the average length of stay. This strategy is intended to increase utilization of hotel restaurants and recreation facilities. There is some doubt as to what impact on length of stay any additional rooms might have.

Consideration is also being given to concepts which would open up sections of the property to outside developers to do an "economy" version of the Lake Buena Vista Hotel Plaza and shopping village concepts. This would require only a small investment from Disney, who would lease the land and collect royalties from the revenue generated by these facilities.

Of the 27,000 acres at Walt Disney World, approximately 9,500 acres is undeveloped swampland and has been set aside by the company as a wilderness preserve. Existing developments, including service facilities and roadways, occupy approximately 5,000 acres.

The success of Tokyo Disneyland has led to the consideration of developing a similar arrangement in Europe, but nothing serious has arisen to date.

During his visits to WED, Watson was also given presentations on a preliminary concept to develop Disney Centers in several major metropolitan areas across the country. It became apparent that this concept was not backed by sufficient market research, as the designers were unable to pinpoint a target market or exactly identify what mixture of "attractions," food, and merchandising would be required. The chairman was also concerned whether Disney could afford its level of detail in design for these small "nonparks." Disney attractions have never been attempted outside of the large theme parks where some economies of scale can be gained for designing for extremely large audiences. Disney's current theme parks draw five times the annual visitation of their nearest competitors.

While the Disney Channel represents a current commitment for the company and an excellent return if the break-even point can be attained in a "reasonable" period of time, Watson is unsure what constitutes a reasonable period of time. This venture is slated to rack up expenses of $60 million during the 1984 fiscal year.

Two prior efforts by the company to enter the winter recreation field met with failure, but after 20 years many members of management still have a strong desire to see WDP tap this market.

In the mid-1960s Disney reached an agreement with the U.S. Government to build and operate a winter ski resort and summer camping facility at Mineral King in the Sierra Nevada Mountains (on government-owned property) midway between Los Angeles and San Francisco. Several years of litigation between the Sierra Club and the government effectively killed any development in the Mineral King area.

During the 1970s Disney made full-blown preparations to develop a resort at Lake Independence located in the Sierra Mountains near Truckee, California. This time California state agencies presented an effective barrier to successful development. Disney presented detailed "impact" studies to nearly two dozen state agencies and quickly found that complying with the requirements of one agency automatically meant being in non-compliance with another. Several frustrating years later, this project was also abandoned.

One approach not yet tried would be for Disney to buy out an existing resort and re-design it to suit a Disney motif.

References

"Attendance at Theme Parks Down in 1981," *Orlando Sentinel Star*, January 17, 1982, pp. 1 and 11D.

"Disney Gambles on Tomorrow," *Fortune*, October 4, 1982, pp. 63–68.

Consolidated Financial Statements, Walt Disney Productions Annual Reports, 1972–1982.

"EPCOT Puts New Spark Into Tourism," *The Orlando Sentinel*, a series, September 25–27, 1983.

"Growing Pains: Walt Would Wilt," *Los Angeles Times*, October 7, 1983, Calendar, pp. 1, 6.

"Is Disney Rumor A Fairy Tale," *Florida Trend*, October, 1983.

"Walt Disney Productions," Merrill Lynch, September 29, 1983.

"Entertainment Industry," Merrill Lynch, August 19, 1983.

"Leisure/Entertainment," July 1983 and August 1983.

"Never Cry Wolf–Not So Mickey Mouse," *Los Angeles Magazine*, October 1983.

"Survival of the Fittest," *Newsweek*, October 17, 1983, p. 98.

Ron Miller's Report in the
Company's Annual Statement

To Our Stockholders, Employees and Associates:

The Horizons pavilion mural gracing the cover of this year's annual report was selected for reasons beyond its grandeur. I believe it is a symbolic representation of the achievements of your company in 1983. It was a year in which the foundations were built that place Walt Disney Productions on the threshold of exciting new horizons.

- Epcot Center, in its first year of operations, became an international landmark, a magnet for tourists beyond compare. Attendance at Walt Disney World soared to 22,712,000 against 12,560,000 the previous year.

- Tokyo Disneyland opened and became an instant success. On a Single day last summer, more than 94,000 people were at the first international Disney theme park, establishing a new attendance mark in the 28-year history of Disney outdoor entertainment.

- The Disney Channel was launched with a commitment to innovative family entertainment and it became the fastest growing pay television service in the history of the cable industry.

- An all-new Fantasyland was opened at Disneyland with immediate positive impact on attendance. The fairy tale attractions of old were revitalized by Disney "Imagineers" with state-of-the-art technology, including holograms, fiber optics, three-dimensional animation and other new special effects that evolved out of EPCOT Center design concepts.

EPCOT Center, Tokyo Disneyland, the Disney Channel and the new Fantasyland all represent substantial involvements in our future. They involved worthwhile commitments of financial and creative resources that establish a foundation for long-term profitability. We expect our company to flourish because we have created unique value along with competitive and strategic advantage in the marketplace.

Financial results for fiscal 1983, the 60th anniversary of Walt Disney Productions, were a disappointing paradox. Revenues rose sharply for the year primarily because of the opening success of EPCOT Center while earnings declined for the corporation as a whole. In our judgment, this decrease in overall earnings was a sacrifice that was made to position the company for future growth and expansion. In this year of transition, the true inherent strength of the company is best reflected in the public acceptance of our new ventures and the other accomplishments of 1983.

During fiscal 1983 we experienced our 16th consecutive year of record revenues, despite a still-awakening economy, especially on the international scene. Revenues for the year ended September 30, 1983, reached $1.3 billion, a 27 percent increase from the prior year, while net income declined 7 percent to $93 million, or $2.70 per share.

The decline in net income was primarily due to an anticipated $28.3 million operating loss incurred by the Disney Channel, the $21 million write-down of *Something Wicked This Way Comes* to its net realizable value, and net interest expense of $14 million in the current year as compared to net interest income of $15 million in the prior year.

589

The management transition went smoothly during my first year as chief executive officer. It has been most important to have the counsel and expertise of our new board chairman, Raymond L. Watson, and the support of a dynamic and experienced Disney executive management team.

We have also strengthened the Board of Directors with the elections of Robert H. B. Baldwin and Samuel L. Williams. Mr. Baldwin is the former chairman of Morgan Stanley, Inc. while Mr. Williams is an attorney who has served as president of both the Los Angeles County Bar Association and the State Bar of California.

Two of our current directors, William T. Anderson and Richard T. Morrow, will not be standing for reelection in February, although their services will still be available to the board. In accordance with established board policy, Mr. Anderson is taking his retirement and will assume the title of director emeritus while Mr. Morrow has determined that he would best serve the company and the stockholders by narrowing his role to that of vice-president and general counsel, the positions he now holds.

And it is with deep personal sadness that I report the loss of Director Emeritus Gorden E. Youngman, who died in May after serving on the board for 30 years. His contributions to Walt Disney Productions and the community were many and his loss will long be felt.

When Ray Watson assumed the duties of chairman last May, he intended to be available only on a limited basis. As our long-range plans begin to crystalize, it became clear that his full participation in our daily business affairs would be invaluable. He has consequently sacrificed his other personal business interests to dedicate himself to the future of Walt Disney Productions.

His past experience as president and chief executive officer of the Irvine Company, one of the nation's largest and most successful community developers, assumes added significance as we further examine the long-term development of our Florida land holdings. Ray spent a total of 17 years with the Irvine Company, the last four, from 1973 to 1977, as its chief executive.

Ray has already played an instrumental role in guiding the development of a formalized, long-range strategic planning process within our organization. Working closely with Vice-President for Corporate Planning, Frank Stanek, procedures and disciplines have been put in place that will ensure that all units of the company are working in concert toward set corporate goals.

With the enthusiastic public acceptance of Tokyo Disneyland, an area of logical future interest is the potential for another international theme park, now that we have a seasoned team in place, skilled and experienced in all critical areas of exploration, analysis and development.

For the new fiscal year, our paramount goals are to make the motion picture segment of our business profitable again and to provide the Disney Channel with the support required to sustain its thrust toward the profit line. I am confident that we have taken great strides in both areas.

Early in 1983, we formed Walt Disney Pictures as a separate company responsible for the development, production and marketing of all our live-action film and commercial television programming. After an extensive search, we selected Richard L. Berger to direct those efforts as president of the new company.

Dick had a long and distinguished record at Twentieth Century Fox and CBS Television. He has moved quickly to build and strengthen every facet of film and television operations with an experienced and talented team.

We are determined to broaden our theatrical audiences without compromising Disney entertainment values. We know that the Disney name communicates special feelings and values to a substantial, worldwide audience. It's a public trust we cherish and one we will never violate.

As Dick said recently: "We're not going to sacrifice image for expedient, short-term gain. Our direction is quality and we expect to adhere to it. We're definitely not going to use exploitive, violent or tasteless material. We will always be above the common denominator of community standards for decency and sensibilities."

Animation, which continues under my direct supervision, has always been the mainstay of our feature film efforts. We continue to be the unquestioned world leader in this magnificent, imaginative vehicle for entertainment. I am most pleased with the progress we are making in our goal of producing a major feature every two years.

Work is proceeding well on *The Black Cauldron*, scheduled for a 1985 release, while *Basil of Baker Street* moves from development into the production phase. Several other animation projects are in development.

The public response to the Disney Channel has been most gratifying and its growth has exceeded our expectations. The operational losses were anticipated in the start-up of the operation and are in line with current projections that estimate a break-even point by mid-to-late 1985.

We have achieved working agreements with all of the multiple system operators in the country, a vital preliminary step towards entry into all major markets. We are now cable-casting in all 50 states.

The Disney Channel's future has been enhanced by our purchase of two transponders on Hughes Communications' Galaxy I satellite. They will eventually replace the leased space we now have on Western Union's Westar V. The state-of-the-art technology will guarantee the absolute finest in home reception and open new markets. The purchase of transponders is financially advantageous and it demonstrates our commitment to this fast growing new medium.

The centerpiece of this dynamic year of growth was, of course, EPCOT Center. We easily surpassed our own early projections of 20 million admissions for Walt Disney World and the new showplace was firmly established as one of the world's great attractions.

We're not resting on our laurels. Horizons, presented by General Electric, officially opened on October 1, 1983, the first anniversary of EPCOT Center. In its exploration of 21st Century lifestyles, it is a synthesis of all the themes of Future World and its reception has been outstanding.

The day after we opened Horizons, we marked the beginning of one of the most challenging and imaginative construction projects the Disney organization has ever undertaken—The Living Seas Pavilion, presented by United Technologies corporation. We will, in effect, create a miniature ocean in a tank that will be the largest man-made marine environment anywhere in the world.

On the same day, we broke ground on the Kingdom of Morocco showcase, the first major addition to our family of nations. The attraction will feature towering minarets and other landmarks, a bazaar of native crafts, historical artifacts and an authentic Moroccan restaurant.

WED Enterprises is now desiging a Scandinavian showcase under a preliminary design agreement with Norwegian business interests. It will combine the cultures of Norway, Sweden and Denmark in another exciting World Showcase presentation.

In addition, the ethnic restaurants of World Showcase have proven so popular that plans are well underway for additional restaurants in Italy and France and two dining facilities for China.

Our Consumer Products segment continued to grow during the year, paced by the outstanding performance of our music company, despite another difficult year for the record industry.

Your company is financially strong and vibrantly creative as we start our seventh decade. We look to the future with the same enthusiasm, pride and confidence that has contributed so much to our past success.

We know that as long as our vision is measured in terms of generations rather than months or even years, we will always be on the threshold of new horizons.

November 30, 1983

Ron Miller
President and
Chief Executive Officer

CASE 17

Project Fantasy
A Behind-the-Scenes Account of Disney's
Desperate Battle Against the Raiders

▪ *John Taylor* ▪

When Saul Steinberg began buying stock in Walt Disney Productions last spring, he kicked off a lengthy corporate carnival that was at times comic, vicious and—the parties agreed—outrageous. To thwart Steinberg, Disney undertook a frenzied search for acquisitions that was code-named "Project Fantasy." When that didn't succeed, the company bought back Steinberg's stock in one of the most notorious greenmail exercises on record. Although Steinberg then called off the hounds, Disney tried to carry through with its defensive acquisition of Gibson Greetings Inc. That decision infuriated assorted Disney stockholders, including a variety of other raiders such as Sid Bass, Ivan Boesky, and Irwin Jacobs, who themselves then besieged the beleaguered company to prevent the transaction. Ultimately, Disney surrendered and canceled the Gibson deal. Shortly thereafter, Disney president and CEO Ronald Miller resigned.

The whole affair provides a fascinating study—half Clausewitzian tactics, half cartoon hijinks—of corporate behavior and the logic of finance. It ranks with the 1982 Bendix imbroglio as one of the wildest, most controversial business battles ever. In less than four weeks Disney, which traditionally carried little debt and had never made an acquisition, purchased one company for $200 million in stock, proposed acquiring another for $310 million, and then bought back Saul Steinberg's stock for $325 million. If the Gibson deal had not been blocked, Disney's long-term debt would have almost tripled to more than $900 million.

It was a battle in which no quarter was asked and none given. The Steinberg people claim that at one climactic point, when Steinberg's Reliance Group announced its tender offer, Disney's management simultaneously offered greenmail and, if Steinberg refused, threatened a counter-tender offer that would leave Steinberg with 100 percent of the company—but one loaded with $2 billion worth of debt. Late on the night of June 8th, Steinberg says he received a phone call from an old friend, Loews Corp. chairman and chief executive Laurence Tisch. Tisch, who so often can be found in the molten core of a deal, was arbitrating the buyback negotiations. He told Steinberg that if he spurned Disney's offer, its management would do "dangerous and stupid things."

At first glance, this is the story of how a Minneapolis investor (Irwin Jacobs) forced a Burbank corporation (Disney) to drop plans to acquire a Cincinnati card-maker (Gibson) dominated by New Jersey investors (William Simon and Raymond Chambers), a deal that Disney had hoped would deter a takeover attempt by a New York holding company (Reliance). But the tenacles of Manhattan law firms and investment banks guided every move. Disney's investment banker is Morgan Stanley, its attorney Joseph Flom of Skadden, Arps, Slate, Meagher & Flom. Gibson's investment banker is Lehman Brothers (now

Source: "Project Fantasy: A Behind-the-Scenes Account of Disney's Desperate Battle Against the Raiders" by John Taylor, *Manhattan, inc.*, November 1984 ©.

part of Shearson Lehman/American Express). Steinberg's investment banker is Drexel Burnham Lambert Inc.; his PR firm is Kekst & Co. Irwin Jacobs handles the press himself and makes his own investment decisions; his law firm is Weil, Gotshal & Manges. The crucial negotiations were conducted in Manhattan, the challenges issued and the deals struck in offices on Wall Street and in midtown.

What follows, based on corporate records, court documents, and interviews, is a reconstruction of the events from March 8th, when a disgruntled Roy Disney resigned from the board, to August 17th, when the company spiked the Gibson deal.

Chapter I
In which Raymond Chambers and William Simon Have a Bright Idea

Last spring, Raymond Chambers, along with everyone else in the investment community, was tracking Saul Steinberg's omnivorous accumulation of stock in Walt Disney Productions. In late April, when Steinberg had scarfed down 9.3 percent of Disney, Chambers read an article in *The Wall Street Journal* that described Disney's plan to dilute Steinberg's holdings by issuing new stock to acquire other companies. Chambers happened to have a company he thought Disney might want to buy, and he reached for the telephone.

Chambers is president of Wesray Corp., the private investment firm he owns with William Simon, the former secretary of the treasury. The company Chambers had in mind was Gibson Greetings Inc., the Cincinnati greeting card-maker that a group led by Simon had taken privately in 1982 in a leveraged buyout that was either enviable or scandalous, depending on your view. Simon and Chambers took Gibson public again a year and a half later for a plump profit of more than $70 million. Had Disney bought Gibson for the price Chambers was contemplating, he and Simon could have more than doubled that profit, bringing them an ultimate return of over $200 million on an initial cash investment of $1 million (and $84 million of debt).

Chambers called an old acquaintance, Eric Gleacher, a managing director of Morgan Stanley, and suggested that Disney might want to take a sniff at Gibson. The two companies were an ideal fit, Chambers said.

And so they were. One key to the greeting card business is the copyright to the characters that appear on the cards. Gibson controls the copyrights to Garfield the Cat, Kirby Koala, and Sesame Street's Big Bird, to name three. While Disney holds the copyrights to its huge stable of characters, it has no card company. Instead, it licenses Mickey, Minnie, Donald, Goofy, Snow White, and the rest of the gang to Hallmark. Hallmark understandably devotes more energy to marketing cards that feature characters for which it holds the copyrights.

If Disney owned Gibson, the card company could dedicate itself to promoting cards featuring Disney characters. That would not only boost Disney's consumer product revenues, it would create a ripple effect for Disney's movies, cartoons, and theme parks by heightening the visibility of the characters. Gibson, for its part, would benefit enormously from the access to all of Disney's characters. The market shares of both Disney and Gibson could soar.

As Chambers put it, "Created characters are an essential part of the greeting card business, and nobody to my knowledge had a better stable of characters nor a more competent creative department than Disney, and that could really help Gibson Greetings' business. . . . At the same time . . . Disney had no marketing capability of its own, but was a licenser. Gibson, with its accomplished market capability, could be a significant help to Disney."

The fit did have a pleasing symmetry. Gleacher said he would pass Chambers's suggestion on to Peter Kellner, the Morgan Stanley managing partner running the merger and acquisitions team for Disney. Over the next couple of weeks, Chambers had a few brief discussions with Kellner. Almost always it was Chambers who called Kellner, and the banker would utter some noncommittal remark about Gibson being under review. By mid-May, Chambers had the distinct feeling that, despite what he saw as a compelling match, Morgan Stanley and Disney were unimpressed. "I was left with the opinion," Chambers said, "that he [Kellner] wasn't all that interested in pursuing Gibson."

What Chambers had no way of knowing was that at virtually the same time that he called Morgan Stanley, the bank had launched Project Fantasy. Kellner hadn't intended to sound indifferent to Chambers; it was simply that he and his team were swamped with work. Since Project Fantasy was initiated, they had been logging 12 to 20 hours a day, seven days a week, in an against-the-clock quest for acquisition candidates. The team investigated more than two dozen companies in broadcasting, real estate, and consumer products. "We looked virtually at the world as a starting point, and over time narrowed it down," Kellner said.

It was work for which the investment bank was to be richly rewarded. Morgan Stanley was to be paid no less than $3.75 million according to the contract in which the firm agreed "to act as financial adviser to Walt Disney Productions for certain shareholder relation matters and to advise Disney on one or more possible acquisitions." "Certain shareholder relation matters" was an oblique reference to Steinberg's lurking presence.

Chapter II
In which Rumors Fly and Disney Starts to Stock a War Chest

The only real surprise about Steinberg's takeover attempt was that someone hadn't done it sooner. Disney, which had been considered vulnerable for at least 18 months, had immensely valuable assets: its real estate was worth an estimated $2.2 billion, and its film and program library and its cable television channel had a book value of $420 million. But the company's performance had been flat since 1981. Attendance at the theme parks was off and, until the release of the highly successful *Splash*, the Disney film division had not been able to shake the impression that it was making movies for kids growing up in the 1940s.

For the preceding two years, Disney takeover rumors had periodically coursed through Wall Street. "There were comments made about the company that indeed we were not aggressive enough, that we were a sleeping giant," said Disney chairman Raymond Watson. At one point last winter, Disney's skittish president Ron Miller had personally called Coca-Cola president Don Keough to check out rumors that Coke was planning a move on Disney. Keough said it wasn't so. On March 8th, Roy Disney, nephew of Uncle Walt himself and one of the company's largest stockholders, resigned from the board. Rumors flew that Roy, who gave no official reason for his resignation but told other directors that he felt he was unable to exercise any influence at the company, had stepped down to try to take it over from the outside.

That particular rumor "had no hair on it," as they say. But around that time, Saul Steinberg—the Darth Vader of Wall Street—decided to go after the company himself.

Watson had been chairman of Disney for a year and a half. Before joining Disney, he spent 17 years with the Irvine Co., a southern California real estate concern, eventually rising to the presidency. Watson likes to make friends, not enemies. Shortly after Roy Disney resigned, Watson began to hear the rumors that Steinberg was taking a position in Disney. It was disturbing news indeed. Steinberg doesn't care much about making friends. If anything, he seems to enjoy making enemies. Steinberg, who made *his* first fortune in computer leasing, has attempted takeovers of—and earned the wrath of—such companies as Chemical Bank and The New York Times Co. A chunky man with chipmunk cheeks, Steinberg's reputation as a malevolent financier has been enhanced by the silence with which he shrouds his operations. Not once did he talk to Disney executives. Watson set up a meeting with Steinberg, but Steinberg canceled.

Executives get chills when the shadow of Steinberg falls across their companies, when, that is, they hear Steinberg is buying their stock. And so it was with Disney. In mid-March, the week after Roy Disney resigned from the board, senior Disney executives, who were on their way to France to explore the idea of a European Disneyland with Mitterrand government officials, stopped off in New York to discuss the implications of Steinberg with their advisers at Morgan Stanley and Skadden, Arps. An elegant dinner, attended by Watson, Miller, Disney's chief financial officer Mike Bagnell, and Skadden, Arps's Joe Flom, was hosted by Morgan Stanley. The occasion was in part social, because Watson had never met Morgan Stanley's managing director Robert Greenhill. During the meal, Greenhill, who founded Morgan Stanley's merger and acquisition department, began to describe his experience with hostile takeovers. At first his remarks seemed general, but it soon became clear that Greenhill was making points directly related to the Steinberg threat, the most pressing being the impact of a hostile takeover on the target company's credit. Regardless of the strength of your ties with your bank, you would find it almost impossible to extend your line of credit once you became a target, Greenhill said, and a long credit line was vital to fighting off a threat. "He urged us to immediately go and increase our line of credit to whatever we could get it to," said Watson. "He did suggest there was a great deal of urgency."

The suggestion took the Disney people by surprise. Disney had a long, happy relationship with its bank, Bank of America, and Watson had always figured that even if Disney needed $1 billion, he could call James Parsons, who handled the Disney account at B of A, and arrange a loan.

Greenhill argued that it was impossible to anticipate a bank's reaction after a tender offer had been issued. By the time the Disney executives left for France, they were convinced. On their return, they proposed to the board that Disney more than triple its line of credit with Bank of America from $400 million to $1.3 billion. Stocking the war chest was a timely act. On March 29th, two days after the board approved the measure, Reliance announced that it was raising its holdings in Disney to 6.3 percent.

At the time, Disney was publicly playing down the Steinberg threat. It announced that the additional credit was to be used for "general corporate purposes." But behind the doors at the Burbank headquarters, company executives were girding for war. Erwin Okun, Disney's vice-president for corporate communications, wrote a confidential memo to Watson and Miller that said "In the event that we become a takeover target, our counter-attack strategy should immediately involve the services of a topflight financial PR firm knowledgeable in the rules of Wall Street combat." Predictably, Okun suggested that Disney hire Richard Cheney, Chairman of Hill & Knowlton USA and a veteran of many take-over battles. His clients have included Getty Oil, the Continental Group, and Mobil.

In the eyes of Disney management, Cheney's involvement didn't accomplish much. "He did very little," said President Miller. "It is the nature of the situation, I guess, because you have the PR firm who is trying to write speeches and press releases, and you have the law firms and the lawyers who say, 'Don't say anything.'"

Chapter III
In which Ray Watson Calls an Old Neighbor and
Ron Miller Straps On a Golden Parachute

The Disney defense was not limited to hiring a heavyweight to handle the press. Increasingly, Disney officers found themselves dwelling on the prospect of making acquisitions. Chairman Watson, the real estate veteran, thought real estate was a promising direction in which to diversify. Disney owned 44 acres at its Burbank studio, a 691-acre ranch outside Burbank, 80 acres in Anaheim, and 88 acres in Melbourne, Florida. The company also owned 25,000 acres in and around the Magic Kingdom and the Epcot Center in Orlando, Florida. This property is worth around $600 million. Watson began to ponder how to put Disney's real estate to best use.

In late April, he called Roger Hall, president of a unit of Arvida Corp., a Florida land developer. Hall was an old friend of Watson's. They had been neighbors several years earlier in Newport Beach and their children had played baseball together. Watson told Hall he was looking for ways to exploit Disney's undeveloped acreage in Florida. He suggested that Arvida might want to act as a consultant to Disney, and he also broached the prospect of a joint venture. Hall quickly reported the conversation back to the Bass brothers of Fort Worth, Texas, who controlled Arvida.

Along with Steinberg and Larry Tisch, the Basses, led by the eldest brother Sid Bass, are ubiquitous faces on the takeover circuit. The family has parlayed a modest oil and gas fortune into a diversified concern with assets in the billions. They acquired Arvida in 1983 in a leveraged buyout similar to the Gibson deal orchestrated by Ray Chambers and William Simon. But unlike Simon and Chambers, the Basses had not taken Arvida public. In a subsequent conversation with Watson, a Bass executive floated the possibility of Disney acquiring Arvida. "Under the right circumstances we might consider acquiring it," Watson told the Bass man. The Basses grew excited, very excited, at the idea of selling the company lock-stock-and-fence-posts to Disney.

While this feeling-them-out foray was taking place, Steinberg was turning up the heat. On April 25th, Steinberg's Reliance Group announced that it intended to raise its stake in Disney to 25 percent. Publicly, Disney was still sticking to the rather bland statement that Steinberg's proposed move "would not be in the interest of Disney stockholders." The official posture was one of disinterested disdain. Privately, however, the company's managers were growing distraught.

At a board meeting on April 30th at Disney's Burbank headquarters, company President Miller, a former Los Angeles Rams tight end who had married Walt Disney's daughter Diane, proposed that Disney revise its business plan to consider possible acquisitions. The board agreed and the next week Project Fantasy officially took wing. Also at the meeting, the directors handed Miller a golden parachute in the form of a termination contract that would give him the equivalent of his $500,000 annual salary through April 1988, if for any reason he was asked to leave the company. Finally, at the suggestion of Skadden, Arps partner Flom, the board rewrote sections of the corporate bylaws to make it easier for Disney to hold a raider at bay. It was the corporate equivalent of clambering into the bunkers.

Chapter IV
In which the Squawk Box Falters and
Everyone Spends a Lot of Time on Jets

As April gave way to May, the pace of events accelerated rapidly. Project Fantasy had assembled a sizable list of potential acquisition candidates. The list included such companies as the Wrather Corp., which owns the *Queen Mary*, the *Spruce Goose*, the Disneyland Hotel, and the rights to "Lassie," among other things. In early May, the Disney executives flew into New York to begin a review of the companies. It was a grueling, tedious process. Days were spent at the Morgan Stanley offices listening to the investment bankers present candidates. After absorbing the reactions of the Disney executives, the bankers would retire to another room to discuss alternatives, leaving the Disney people to sit for what seemed like hours with nothing to do.

The grind was interrupted by a feverish burst of activity that led to Disney's acquisition of Arvida. Arvida was given the code name "Resort Company" by the Project Fantasy team. By early May, in a series of increasingly flirtatious phone calls, both sides had indicated their interest. During one frenetic, jet-hopping week, Arvida executives flew from Miami to Fort Worth to New York, then back to Miami and back again to New York. Bass family associates flew from Fort Worth to New York twice; over the weekend, Disney executives flew to Miami, then to various Arvida properties around Florida, and then back to New York. The deal was settled during an intense day of negotiations at Morgan Stanley's New York office.

Sid Bass and the Arvida executives, who were sitting in one room, opened at $300 million. The Disney executives, in another room, proposed $175 million. The Morgan Stanley people shuttled between the rooms with the offers and the counteroffers.

After several hours of haggling, Disney came up to $200 million—the most it was willing to pay. When the Basses decided to hold out for more, Watson himself crossed into their room.

"I could not justify more than $200 million," he told the Bass group. He was a real estate man and he had evaluated Arvida's property. "I will be leaving this room in about five minutes. We will either have an agreement for you to sell us the property for that price or we will part friends and maybe be in a month or two we will come back and talk to you again about a joint venture."

Sid Bass and his associate Alfred Checchi stepped out of the room to discuss the Disney chairman's ultimatum, leaving Watson with Arvida Chairman Charles (Chuck) Cobb. Cobb started talking to Watson about management and compensation. It struck Watson as a rather irrelevant subject, but he listened politely.

After five minutes, Sid Bass and Checchi returned and Checchi launched into a speech in praise of Watson's real estate acumen. Watson became suspicious. He thought Checchi was praising his judgment only to disagree with it and that the Bass group would not sell for $200 million. Then came the surprise.

"Whenever we have partners we always back our partners," Checchi said. "Mr. Cobb is our partner. We will abide by whatever his decision is, but we want Mr. Cobb and you to know that if he agrees, we will accept the $200 million."

"Does that mean you have agreed?" Cobb asked Checchi.

"Only if you agree," Checchi said. "It's up to you, Chuck."

Cobb then turned to Watson and started to pick up the thread of his earlier conversation about compensation.

"Well, that's all interesting," Watson said. "But what does this mean?"

"I guess we've made a deal," said Checchi.

The assets of the two companies were to be pooled to limit taxes. The 3.34 million shares of Disney stock to go to Arvida was valued at $64 a share, equivalent to around $200 million. But the deal included a collar: the number of Disney shares to be given Arvida stockholders in exchange for their shares of Arvida would vary, depending on the price of Disney's stock in the 20 days prior to the closing. The agreement contained the stipulation that if Disney undertook another major transaction—such as a second acquisition or the purchase of a large block of stock—Arvida had the right to either terminate the sale or postpone the closing for another 20 days to reevaluate Disney's stock.

Not everyone was elated with the prospective acquisition. Stanley Gold, the chief executive of Roy Disney's Shamrock Holdings Inc., who would be elected to the Disney board in June, opposed Arvida on grounds of corporate strategy. Walt Disney Productions, with 20,000 acres of undeveloped land in Florida already, did not need to be encumbered with the additional undeveloped acreage in Arvida's possession. Gold was quoted in *Business Week* as saying, "Disney needs Arvida's 20,000 acres of land like a hole in the head." "I think the reporter was very kind to me in taking some literary license," said Gold. "I think my quote was that 'They needed those acres like they needed another asshole.'"

Roy Disney, who sees himself as the protector of the Disney family interests, opposed any acquisition at all. While purchasing companies with Disney stock would dilute the holdings of Saul Steinberg, it would also dilute the holdings of every other shareholder, including, of course, the Disneys themselves.

On May 16th, Roy Disney sent the following letter on Shamrock Holdings stationery to Disney President Ron Miller and the members of the Disney board.

Dear Ron:

I am writing to you and each of the other directors of Walt Disney Productions about a matter of urgent and grave concern to our company.

I have been advised recently and continuingly that negotiations are currently underway between the management of Walt Disney Productions and another corporation that could result in a significant change in the ownership or control of our company. Such rumors have included, by way of example, Disney's acquisition of a company with substantial debt, an acquisition which could cause Disney to incur substantial debt, or issuance of significant new voting stock.

As I am sure you are aware, many of these restructuring tactics have come under severe public and regulatory criticism. If the maintenance of current management were its primary or perceived purpose at the expense of shareholders, such a restructuring would be especially detrimental.

I well understand the concern the board might have at this time concerning the recent large purchase of Disney stock by third parties, but as a major stockholder I would like to respectfully caution the board against any action made in haste, frustration or fear that would basically alter the business resources, character, or structure of the business. I am particularly concerned that such restructuring might occur without obtaining share-holders' approval, regardless of whether the technical provisions of the Articles of By-Laws require such approval. Not to submit any such plan for shareholder approval would not be fair or consistent with the best interest of the true owners of the company.

You are well aware of my family's deep and continuing interest in the welfare and suc-cess of Walt Disney Productions and the historic and emotional ties that bind us. It is within this context that I am sharing my views with you at this time.

Sincerely,
Roy

"We considered it," said Miller later. "Denied it." Acquisitions were not matters for shareholders to question. They were management decisions to be approved or rejected by the board.

With Steinberg breathing down its neck, Disney plunged ahead. An emergency board meeting had been called for May 17th. Disney's Finance Committee met for an hour and 20 minutes to consider Arvida, then the full board convened. One member, Caroline Ahmanson, was in the Middle East, but listened to the meeting over a telephone squawk box. The board gave the nod to a recommendation that Disney's 14 top officers be given golden parachutes similar to the one handed Miller in April. The compensation contracts guaranteed them the equivalent of their salaries through April 1988 if they were termi-nated. The board also approved the Arvida deal. The vote would have been unanimous but for the abstention of Ahmanson, who did not vote because the telephone line kept fading out, causing her to miss some of the discussion.

The meeting adjourned in time for lunch. Some companies spend up to a year mulling over possible acquisitions. Disney, which had never made an acquisition, had discovered Arvida, examined it and agreed to buy it in slightly more than two weeks.

Chapter V
In which Morgan Stanley is Besieged with Phone Calls and Bo Boyd Falls in Love

When Ray Chambers read about the Arvida acquisition, he thought Disney had definitely lost interest in purchasing Gibson. Chambers called Peter Kellner at Morgan Stanley, who assured him that a Gibson-Disney deal was still a possibility. Nonetheless, Chambers be-gan to lose hope.

Chambers wasn't the only person trying to sell a company to Disney. Minneapolis in-vestor Irwin Jacobs called Morgan Stanley around the same time that Chambers originally did. Jacobs wanted to offer Minstar Inc., a moving and storage company that Jacobs con-trolled. The word was out that Disney would buy just about anything with legs. "I felt this Disney thing was a great opportunity," Jacobs said.

It was a casual move, but then Jacobs is a casual guy. Amiable and unpretentious, he answers his own phone and likes to tell people he attended college for only three days. The modest offices of his holding company, Jacobs Industries, sit across from an aban-doned brewery in Minneapolis. But don't get the wrong impression. Jacobs Industries has interests in everything from boats to real estate. And Jacobs, best known for his abortive but highly profitable takeover attempts of Pabst Brewing Co. and Kaiser Steel Corp., lives in a mansion on the 48-acre lakeshore estate where *The Heartbreak Kid* was filmed.

Like Chambers, Jacobs was put through to Kellner, who at that point must have begun to feel somewhat like a lottery winner suddenly besieged with callers making have-I-got-a-deal-for-you pitches. Kellner listened to Jacobs's proposal, then promised to get back to him in a day or so. A week later, Kellner called Jacobs and apologized for the delay. Steinberg was keeping them all pretty busy, but Disney believed it was gaining the upper hand. "Things have quieted down," Kellner told Jacobs. "They think they have Saul Steinberg in check."

According to Jacobs, Kellner said Disney was going to gear the pace of its acquisitions to the rate at which Steinberg bought Disney stock. The more stock Steinberg bought, the more companies Disney would acquire. Kellner told Jacobs that they might get back to him if things "heated up" again. "We know how to handle situations like this," Kellner said. "In fact, we have many companies that we are looking at and will continue to look at."

Kellner never did get back to Jacobs. But that was not because Arvida had slaked Disney's thirst for acquisitions. (Maybe it was because moving vans and movies aren't a natural mix.) The Sunday following the May 17th board meeting, the Disney officers flew back to New York to continue their consultations with Morgan Stanley over prospective companies. Morgan Stanley had been in contact with the chairman of a large public company. The chairman believed his company was a potential target for a hostile takeover and he wanted it to be acquired by Disney. The Disney executives met with the chairman for two days. When it became apparent that the talks were going nowhere, Kellner mentioned Gibson.

It was love at first sight. Barton (Bo) Boyd, the head of Disney's consumer products division, which licenses characters for toys and books, excitedly declared that a greeting card company was the ideal vehicle for Disney to increase its market share in consumer products. Phone calls ensued. Gibson's president Thomas Cooney caught the next plane to New York.

Boyd and Cooney waxed ecstatic about the glorious fit between Gibson and Disney and their "synergy"—a word that became the noun of choice for Disney and Gibson executives when describing the deal. "[Cooney and Boyd] likened it to the possibility of one plus one equaling three," said Chambers.

The Gibson deal progressed with astonishing speed. The Project Fantasy team gave Gibson the coy code name Koala Company. Within three days, Ray Chambers was invited out to the Disney studio, where he proposed an outright two-for-one stock swap. Since Disney was trading for around $64, that would give Gibson shareholders $32 a share if they received one Disney share for every two of their Gibson shares. The swap seemed reasonable to the Disney people, who at that point seemed more interested in forging ahead with the deal than in dickering over points. So eager were they to push forward that Watson and Miller wanted to fly to Cincinnati immediately and hunker down with the Gibson people.

Two days later, that's just what they did. Gibson officials arranged for them to tour the facilities on Memorial Day when there would be no need to disclose to employees the identities of these gentlemen. The chemistry that day was dazzling. Watson and Cooney saw immense possibilities in a union of Gibson and Disney. Such was the good feeling that it might have been easy for the Disney executives to forget about Steinberg. For a while. A very short while.

The day after Watson and Miller returned from Cincinnati, Steinberg, who by then had accumulated 12.2 percent of Disney, struck again. Reliance simultaneously announced a proxy fight to unseat the Disney board and sued in California Superior Court in Los Angeles to block the acquisition of Arvida. The suit charged that Disney was paying far too much for Arvida. Steinberg also charged in the suit that Bass Brothers "sold substantial income-producing assets" of Arvida to pay for the company. And, the suit said, "Notwithstanding the diminished value of Arvida, [Disney directors] agreed to pay substantially more for Arvida than Bass had paid only five months earlier, and that Bass would receive a premium of nearly 900% over Bass's actual cash outlay."

Five days earlier, when Chambers was meeting the Disney executives to discuss Gibson, a unit of Steinberg's Reliance had sued Disney in California Superior Court on the grounds that the Arvida transaction had no "proper or valid corporate purpose."

But some of the changes in the Disney corporate bylaws made it more difficult for Steinberg to hold the proxy fight. Reliance had announced that it was seeking "consents" of other shareholders to remove the board and that it believed the record date for which shareholders would qualify was, according to the formula in the corporate bylaws, the previous Friday. But the bylaws had been amended to state that the record date would be 40 days after the filing of the first consent. That amendment provided Disney with additional breathing space.

Chapter VI
In which William Simon Lunches at the
University Club and a Collar Is Proposed

With Steinberg wheeling up the heavy siege weapons, the time had come for Disney to reinforce the barricades at the Magic Kingdom. The strategy continued to be defense by acquisition. A negotiating session between Gibson and Disney was scheduled for June 4th at Morgan Stanley's office in the Exxon building.

The time had come, too, for the Gibson stockholders to square on a price for their shares. Ray Chambers had been talking to Disney about a value on Gibson stock in the $30 to $32-a-share range. But Bill Simon and Gibson President Tom Cooney had said they wanted at least $35 a share for *their* stock. (Earlier, by the way, Simon and Chambers had discussed a leveraged buyout of Disney along the lines of their 1982 LBO of Gibson but, after crunching some numbers, they discarded the idea as overwhelmingly difficult.)

It went without saying that neither Disney nor Gibson was interested in a cash transaction. The taxes on a cash purchase would have been horrendous for Gibson shareholders and would have deprived Disney of the opportunity to dilute Steinberg's holdings in the company.

The Gibson men arranged to meet William Kearns for lunch at the University Club just before the negotiating session at Morgan Stanley. Kearns, a Gibson board member, is also a managing director of Lehman Brothers, Gibson's investment banker. Over lunch, he argued that Gibson could command upwards of $35 a share even though the stock at the time was trading around $19. Kearns based his evaluation on the fact that Gibson was heading for a year when, with its earnings projections, it could command around $30 a share in a controlled auction.

After the luncheon, Simon left to catch a plane. The rest of the Gibson group trooped over to Morgan Stanley. Kearns opened with his argument that the stock was worth $35. The Morgan Stanley bankers countered by pointing out that the stock was then trading at

$19. A two-for-one swap was mentioned. The Gibson group complained about the value of Disney's stock. It had climbed on the strength of the takeover struggle; absent Steinberg, it would fall. A collar on the deal was proposed so that if the Disney stock dropped during a specific period, Gibson shareholders would receive a greater portion of Disney shares in exchange for their Gibson stock. If Disney stock for some reason rose, they would receive less.

Late that night, an agreement was hammered out for a two-for-one swap with a collar providing Gibson shareholders with 6/10 of a share of Disney for every Gibson share if Disney fell to $50 or below. At the upper end of the collar, Gibson shareholders would receive only .443 shares of Disney if Disney climbed above $75. The contract also contained a clause that allowed Disney to cancel the deal by paying Gibson a $7.5 million kill fee.

With time of the essence, the Disney crew hurried back to Burbank to seek the directors' approval. It was given—unanimously—at a board meeting the next day where Saul Steinberg was the overriding preoccupation.

The Gibson deal posed an immediate threat to the Arvida deal because of the clause in the Arvida contract allowing the Florida developer the option to cancel in the event of another Disney acquisition. If Arvida's owners felt that the Gibson deal was going to depress the value of the Disney stock they were to receive, they might pull out. So Disney Chairman Watson and President Miller called Sid Bass and proposed closing the Arvida deal immediately, assigning a value of $60 to each share of Disney regardless of what happened to the stock in the near future. The Bass people said that sounded fine to them.

Thus, Disney was able to announce that it was closing Arvida at the same time that it announced it had agreed to acquire Gibson. On June 6th, the press duly reported that Disney was going to buy Gibson for some $307 million—the rough market value of the up-to 6.2 million shares of Disney common stock the company had agreed to issue in exchange for Gibson's 10 million outstanding shares. (For the record, William Simon, Gibson's largest shareholder with 22.8 percent of the stock, stood to receive about 1.3 million Disney shares worth more than $70 million. Unlike Simon's Gibson stock, for which demand is limited, his Disney stock was extremely liquid; it could easily be converted into cash.)

The acquisition was widely described at the time—and still is today, for that matter—as a defensive maneuver. But Disney executives have always publicly maintained that Steinberg had nothing to do with the decision to buy Gibson. "It was damn fine business," Miller said later.

The acquisition came slightly more than two weeks after Disney's offices first learned Gibson was available. In less than three weeks, the entertainment company had committed itself to investments in real estate and greeting cards worth more than $500 million.

Chapter VII
In which Irwin Jacobs Flies to Greece and
Saul Steinberg Receives an Ominous Call

On June 6th, Irwin Jacobs read about the Gibson deal. The next day he called Ronald Alghini, his broker at the Chicago office of Jefferies & Co., and placed an order for 2,000 call options on Disney stock. Jacobs thought the stock was undervalued and that the Gibson deal would push it further down. "It was just a market play," he says.

Later that morning Jacobs received a call from Michael Milkin, senior vice-president of Drexel Burnham in California. Milken said he represented Saul Steinberg and wanted to discuss Disney. Jacobs interrupted Milken, explaining that before the conversation proceeded he would have to cancel the call options he had just ordered on the company. Putting Milken on hold, Jacobs called Alghini. He had already told him to cancel the balance and went back to Milken.

Milken said DBL was arranging financing for a tender offer for Disney. Would Jacobs be interested in kicking in, say, $25 million? Jacobs said he would think about it. The more he thought the more he liked it. That afternoon he called Milken and said he was good for $35 million.

The next day, when Steinberg called Jacobs to thank him for investing in the tender, they discussed the Gibson deal. "This is nothing more than a defensive move," Steinberg said. He said he had decided to tender for Disney to prevent it from making further acquisitions. "I had to move because they would keep doing this forever and ever," he told Jacobs.

Friday, June 8th, was a black day for Walt Disney Productions—possibly the blackest ever, at least for Disney Chairman Watson and President Miller. That day Steinberg made his tender for 37 percent of the company's stock at $67.50 a share, which would bring his holdings to 49 percent. The group—Steinberg's main partners were Kirk Kerkorian of MGM/UA and the elderly Fisher brothers, who control a New York management and construction firm—stated in the tender that they intended to split up the assets of the company: Steinberg would get the real estate, Kerkorian the studio and cable-TV channel, and the Fishers the right to develop land near the theme parks.

Disney management reacted to the tender with the fear and fury of a cornered animal. Disney's attorney Don Drapkin of Skadden, Arps, called Steinberg's attorney, Robert Hodes of Willkie Farr & Gallagher, to begin negotiations to buy back Steinberg's stock at a premium.

In a deposition taken during a lawsuit filed after the buyback, Steinberg said he received a phone call late Friday night from Laurence Tisch, chairman of Loews Corp.

"I got a call from a personal friend of mine [Tisch] who knows Drapkin well and Joe Flom well, urging me to sell out," Steinberg said. "I listened, and he told me the reasons, which were basically that if we did not sell out, that Skadden, Arps, and Morgan Stanley did really not have control over this client, and this client might do dangerous and stupid things.

"And the dangerous and stupid things that they were threatening, and they had also expressed this to Mr. Hodes [Steinberg's attorney], was that if we completed our tender offer, they would during the tender offer make a tender offer for the remaining shares subject to our tender offer. . . . Assuming our tender offer was successful and theirs was successful, we would have owned 100 percent of a company with well over $2 billion in debt, and it would have been a very serious problem for us. . . . I believe that they indicated that they were prepared—I didn't hear this directly, this came to me secondhand—to pay $80 a share."

In other words, if Steinberg succeeded in buying 49 percent of Disney, the company's managers would then make a tender offer of $80 a share for the remaining 51 percent of the company's stock. If they bought up that stock and retired it, they would leave Steinberg with control of 100 percent of the outstanding shares of the company. But Disney would have sunk $2 billion in debt as a result of management's purchase. Steinberg told Jacobs that he didn't want to accept greenmail and that he had been "blackmailed" into taking it.

Disney's chief spokesman Erwin Okun, said the company has "no comment" on Steinberg's charge.

"Management conducted an utter scorched earth policy," says David Kay, a managing director and head of mergers and acquisitions at Drexel Burnham Lambert Inc., which arranged the financing for Steinberg's tender offer. "They were going to make sure that if they weren't running Disney, it was going to be a company that no one wanted to run. They were a client out of control who did not do what their advisers suggested, and who did things that in the final analysis led to their doom."

Over the weekend, the terms of the greenmail were settled. Reliance originally argued that Disney should pay $80 a share for its stock; Disney offered $73. On Monday the two sides agreed that Disney would pay Reliance $325.5 million ($77.50 a share) for its 4.2 million shares. The price included $297.3 million ($70.83 a share) for the actual stock plus $28 million ($6.67 a share) for "expenses." These included Steinberg's legal and investment banking fees plus the payments he owed to Jacobs, Kerkorian, and the Fisher brothers—so-called "commitment fees"—for pledging money for the takeover. In exchange, Steinberg withdrew the tender and promised not to purchase Disney stock for ten years.

(In the Disney deal and other recent takeovers, investors pledged funds to finance acquisitions in exchange for a fee—up to 1 percent of the money committed. But they did not have to actually give the money to the deal maker. They retained the use of their capital during the negotiations *and* made an additional 1 percent.)

The public outcry over the greenmail was deafening. Editorial writers, politicians, and shareholders heaped calumny upon corporate raiders and railed against the absence of regulations forbidding management to pay premiums to select stockholders. Wall Street poured abuse on Disney in its own way: the company's stock plummeted 10⅞ to 54¼ on the day the buyback was announced. By July 3rd, the price had fallen to 45⅝.

The Steinberg group chuckled all the way to the bank. Jacobs had flown off for a vacation in Greece on the weekend of the buyback—before he knew the outcome of the tender offer in which he had agreed to invest. Later, he received a check from Steinberg for $570,412.48. It was the fee he earned for pledging $35 million. But Jacobs says he came out a loser on the venture. Canceling the call options on Disney cost him $700,000. "By doing what he did [Steinberg] wiped me out," said Jacobs. "Some days you win and some days you lose. I'm a big boy."

Chapter VIII
In which Ray Calls Ray and Irwin Jacobs Tapes Two Telephone Calls

At each step throughout the Disney saga, the company's officers believed they had solved one problem, only to find that another issued from their solution. And so it was with the buyback.

On a Friday night in June, Ray Watson called Ray Chambers. Disney's stock had fallen so sharply, Watson said, that the terms of the Gibson acquisition were no longer feasible. Chambers was stunned. An agreement was an agreement. Once it was struck, you stuck. But Watson said the 6.2 million Disney shares the company would now have to issue to acquire Gibson were too many. It would give the Gibson group control of 15 percent of Disney (prior to the buyback they would have gained control of 13.7 percent of the company). Shareholder approval might be required to issue so many shares—and it might not be forthcoming. Watson suggested scrapping the agreement with the collar and making a straight two-for-one swap. "We never expected the stock to drop to the level that it dropped after we repurchased Mr. Steinberg's stock," said Miller. "It was apparent to both Ray and I that we were giving out too many shares to purchase the Gibson company."

Chambers hung up and called Bill Simon, who was in England. Simon was "outraged." So was Gibson President Tom Cooney. Given the stock price of Disney at the time, Gibson's shareholders would receive about $23 for each Gibson share in a straight two-for-one swap.

Another weekend of frantic negotiating took place. By the middle of the afternoon on Sunday, the two sides were still so far apart that Watson felt the deal would collapse. "At the time it was my mood that we were at a stalemate and that the transaction was going to fall apart," said Watson.

But in late afternoon, Chambers proposed a compromise. He would agree to a two-for-one swap if Disney would pay Gibson's shareholders the equivalent of Gibson's projected earnings for 1984: $30 million. Watson leaped at the solution. By one o'clock Monday morning, an agreement was reached.

The Gibson stockholders still would have preferred a straight stock swap because $30 million was subject to taxation. But their lawyer was able to alleviate the pain somewhat by an imaginative accounting technique that allowed the cash to be reported as a long-term capital gain rather than as ordinary income.

With the new Gibson deal, Disney's executives thought they finally had their problems licked. Then began the Great Revolt of the Shareholders.

In the wake of the Steinberg buyback, Roy Disney had begun to apply pressure on Miller and Watson to readmit him to the board and to make directors of Stanley Gold and Peter Dailey, Vice-Chairman of the Interpublic Group of Cos. Inc., and Disney's brother-in-law. In a board meeting on June 22nd, the three were elected to the board, Roy Disney as vice-chairman. Earlier that month, in the wake of the Arvida acquisition, Arvida's President Cobb was also elected to the Disney board. Disney, Dailey, Gold, and Cobb began to lobby against the Gibson acquisition. Their objections were varied. Cobb thought Gibson was a terrific business fit with Disney but he insisted that the price was too high. Gold did not believe in buying a greeting card company. "They could have started their own if it were a good thing," he said. Disney opposed the deal because it would dilute his family's holdings. He was also suspicious of Chambers and Simon. He did not know the two men and he was unconvinced that a pair of high-rolling East Coast investors should become two of Disney's largest shareholders. A board meeting was held on July 16th to approve the amended Gibson transaction. While it passed by a vote of nine to four, the board's earlier unity-in-the-face-of-adversity had started to crumble.

Meanwhile, Irwin Jacobs, tanned and fit after a two-week vacation in Greece, had begun buying Disney stock. Jacobs mentioned his Disney purchases to his associates. Like Jacobs, they called a few banks, cobbled together a few loans, and invested a few million of their own in Disney. "I thought the market had overreacted to Disney," Jacobs shrugs, explaining why by mid-July he had scooped up some $10 million worth of Disney stock.

When the dissident Disney stockholders began to mutter among themselves about the stubborn and intractable board, they turned to Jacobs. Irv, as his friends call him, was complaining the loudest about the Gibson deal. Jacobs was called by an arbitrageur at L. F. Rothschild who was concerned about Gibson. Ivan Boesky called, too. He told Jacobs that he had a position in Disney and was opposed to the Gibson deal. Jacobs also talked to Sid Bass and Stan Gold, both of whom opposed Gibson. Sid Bass put the word out that he was "outraged," just as Bill Simon had been "outraged" earlier when Disney wanted to cancel the Gibson deal.

There was general agreement that the price Disney intended to pay for Gibson—even under the revised agreement—was simply astronomical. An associate of Jacobs had calculated that if Disney's shares were valued at $77.50 apiece—which Disney's managers, by paying Saul Steinberg that much, seemed to admit they were worth—then the company was paying more than $400 million for Gibson. Jacobs grew even more ticked off when he learned Disney could—but wouldn't—squelch the deal and pay Gibson the $7.5 million kill fee.

With his views shared by a considerable minority of Disney's stockholders, Jacobs called Ray Watson and voiced his opinion about the value of the acquisition. Watson responded with the by-now-familiar "synergy" refrain.

"Why would you go ahead with this transaction when you have so much opposition?" Jacobs asked. "You don't have to worry about Steinberg and the Reliance Group anymore. Why don't you just cut the transaction off?"

Watson said it was too late. The board wouldn't reconsider.

"Are you telling me it's a done deal?" Jacobs asked.

"Yes, it's a done deal," Watson said.

Unbeknownst to Watson, Jacobs had taped their conversation. Later that afternoon he played the tape to his associates so they could digest Watson's comments. Jacobs also taped a second call that he made the following day to Watson. "There was no malice intended," said Jacobs, referring to the taping. During that conversation, Jacobs said the Gibson deal should be put to a shareholder vote. Watson refused, with one of his other refrains: such a decision was the responsibility of the directors, not the stockholders.

After playing that tape back to his associates, Jacobs decided it was time to challenge the board. He flew to New York the following day and met with Sid Bass at the Pierre Hotel. The two men, who had not met before, schmoozed for several hours about investments and investors, buyouts and takeovers, your basic financiers' shoptalk. They also discussed holding a Disney shareholders' meeting and the possibility of suing the board. It was a good head-to-head and the two men and their associates left with warm feelings. (By late September, they were sparring with each other for control of Disney's board.)

After a lengthy discussion the following day with his attorneys at Weil, Gotshal & Manges, Jacobs sent the directors a letter.

Dear Members of the Board,

As you know, my associates and I own approximately 6 percent of the outstanding Common Stock of Walt Disney Productions ("Disney"). I am writing to the Board of Directors to express our strong opposition to the proposed acquisition of Gibson Greetings, Inc. ("Gibson"), which I already have communicated to your Chairman, Raymond Watson. It is my understanding that other substantial stockholders have also advised you of their opposition to the transaction.

Our reasons for believing that the Gibson transaction is wasteful and highly detrimental to the company and its stockholders include the following:

As we understand it, Disney would pay one-half share of Disney stock plus $2.90 in cash for each of the 10.3 million shares of Gibson. Based on the price of $77.85 Disney per share which you authorized paying last month for the Disney shares held by Reliance

Financial Services Corp. ("Reliance"), the total cost to Disney of the Gibson transaction is approximately $430 million and the cost of each share is $41.83.

Gibson is not worth that much. The present major stockholders of Gibson bought 100% of Gibson in 1982 in a "leveraged buyout" in which their total investment was $1,000,000. Gibson's book value on March 31, 1984 was a mere $68,037,000 or $6.61 per share. Gibson's 1983 earnings were $22 million or only $2.16 a share. Hardly enough in either case to justify a $41.83 per share payment.

You authorized the Gibson transaction when Reliance had obtained a substantial block of Disney stock and was rumored to be seeking control of Disney (and just before it announced a hostile takeover of Disney), and the transaction was perceived by the investing community as a defensive measure.

I am advised by Ramond Watson that Disney has the right to decline to consummate the transaction by paying $7.5 million in "liquidated damages." We consider $7.5 million a price worth paying to terminate this transaction.

Mr. Watson has also advised me that several members of the board—including directors who personally own or represent substantial amounts of stock—strongly oppose the transaction and in fact have voted against it.

Under these circumstances, we wish to reiterate our request to Mr. Watson that the directors terminate the Gibson transaction. At the very least, we believe that you would be grossly abusing your authority and discretion as directors unless you first comply with your duty to obtain stockholder approval before proceeding with the Gibson transaction which would dilute the ownership interests of all present Disney stockholders by approximately 15%. We, therefore, request that the board convene a special meeting of stockholders, as promptly as reasonably possible, to vote on the Gibson transaction and that the board abide by the wishes of the stockholders as expressed in the vote at the meeting. That is the only responsible way to deal with an issue that has divided the board and would substantially dilute the holdings of present stockholders and has aroused strong opposition fron major stockholders.

Please advise me by Monday, July 30, 1984 whether the board intends to comply with this request.

Very truly yours,
Irwin L. Jacobs

The board did not reply and Jacobs sued. The complaint, filed in California Superior Court, charged the board with "breach of fiduciary duty and waste of Disney's corporate assets." The pressure on Watson and Miller heightened.

A protracted and costly suit would only draw even more attention to Disney's leadership crisis, extend the company's already lengthy run of bad publicity, and further erode investor confidence. The board's anti-Gibson faction led by Roy Disney gained strength as it was joined by others, including director Philip Hawley, Chairman of Carter Hawley Hale Stores Inc. and himself the recent victim of a hostile takeover attempt by The Limited Co. Disney's officers wavered, then folded.

The end, when it came, was abrupt. Lawyers for the opposing sides in the suit had been taking depositions when, on August 17th, Ray Watson suddenly issued a statement saying that due to the "contentious atmosphere" Gibson had created among the shareholders, the company had decided to cancel the acquisition. "They were afraid of what was going to happen in court," says one shareholder source.

Management still maintained that the acquisition of Gibson was a sound idea. Not that it mattered. By that time Roy Disney was already quietly shopping around for a replacement for Miller. Roy and Hawley played a major role in forcing the resignation of Miller three weeks later, on September 7th. Shortly thereafter, Watson stepped down as chairman, although he remains on the board.

Epilogue
In which the Score Is Tallied and the Spoils Are Weighed

So who are the winners and who are the losers? Ron Miller took the biggest beating. As has happened in numerous other takeover attempts, Disney's chief executive did repel the raiders but in the end was forced to forfeit his control of the company. Disney's corporate ego was bruised by months of distinctly unpleasant media attention and the siege anxiety that pervaded the executive suite. The strike at Disneyland by 1,800 workers in September seemed a final cruel ignominy. But the appointment of Michael Eisner, the former president of Paramount Pictures, as Disney's new chairman and chief executive officer, has already bolstered company morale.

For all these shenanigans, the shareholders are now back where they started. In October, Disney stock was trading in the $55 range, near the $52 a share it was trading at when Steinberg began buying last March. But control of the company has been drastically reallocated. By October the Bass brothers had bought out Ivan Boesky and Irwin Jacobs (his group made a tidy $29 million profit; you win some, you lose some) to assume control of 24.8 percent of Disney. Although the Gibson deal collapsed, the ever-successful William Simon and his group came out ahead. Rekindled investor interest pushed Gibson's stock to $24.75 in October, up from $19 when Ray Chambers first called Morgan Stanley. But the biggest winners were the New York bankers, lawyers, and public relations firms who make a living servicing the companies involved in takeovers. Together they earned more than $30 million for their role in the Disney saga.

The Lodging Industry

• *Julian W. Vincze* •

Total receipts for the lodging industry approximated $29.4 billion in 1983. This represented a 6-percent increase over the 1982 figures. For 1984 the industry was expected to top $31 billion.

What the Industry Does

In very basic terms the lodging industry takes care of travelers' (housing) needs while they are away from home. However in today's society the needs of travelers are very different from those of 1794 when the City Hotel opened in New York City. The City Hotel was proported to have been the first building constructed in the United States specifically for hotel purposes.

Today's travelers are often business travelers who typically occupy more than 60 percent of all lodging rooms, with the remaining 40 percent split almost equally between personal and convention travelers. Business travelers' needs include the basic lodging room plus meal services and communication facilities. However additional needs related to meeting rooms, special stenographic, material-duplicating, and special communication needs, as well as recreational and entertainment, are also frequently desired.

The convention travelers' needs also include the basics of lodging room, meal services, and basic communication facilities. However the obvious additional needs relate to standard convention activities such as meeting rooms (both small and large), exhibit halls, and banquet rooms. But additional expectations may also include appropriate social gathering facilities as well as significant leisure and recreational amenities.

The personal travelers' needs are often more basic and relate to lodging rooms and meal services, unless the location is a destination resort. However destination resorts are expected by the personal traveler to provide extensive leisure and recreational facilities as well as socializing facilities. Personal travel has grown steadily in recent years. Several factors which have encouraged this growth in personal travel include rising disposable personal income, stable gasoline prices, expanded leisure time, and increasing numbers of single-person households. In addition the deregulation of the airline industry, with the resultant fare-reduction situations and the establishing of no-frills regional carriers, have also increased personal travel.

Personal travel is generally viewed as being quickly affected by changes in the economy whereas business travel more typically follows the turns in the economy by three to six months.

Food and beverage sales account for approximately one-third of total lodging revenues. Gross profits are usually about 20 percent, which is substantially narrower than those on room rentals, and although food and beverage sales per room have risen over the last ten years, this rise has been at a slower pace than room rates.

This case portrays neither the effective nor the ineffective handling of an administrative situation. Rather, it is to be used as the basis for classroom discussion.

Innovation in the Industry

Instead of travel to the same location, business people may now hold conferences in different cities using satellite communication. Because an estimated 40 percent of hotel revenues come from corporate business meetings, many hotels originally feared this development. Recently, however, more than one-eighth of the nation's largest hotels have been linked to a teleconferencing system. These hotels are expecting teleconferences to attract new customers and to increase the bar, catering, and meeting room revenues, although it may indirectly hurt the primary room revenues.

Another innovation that has been introduced are in-room computer terminals that provide the occupant with access to a computer that can receive telegrams and telexes, and supply economic news, shopping information, entertainment tips, and even job listings. Users gain access to the computer through the use of a credit card number and will be charged for their time at the terminal on the basis of sliding rates similar to those for long distance calls. Some industry observers predict that within the next few years thousands of rooms may be equipped with these terminals.

Major Subdivisions

More than 50,000 lodging locations are currently operating in the United States. However the industry is fragmented, ranging from small roadside motels to mammoth resort hotels containing 3,000 or more rooms. The lodging industry is usually subdivided into four distinct categories: convention/commercial, resort, roadside, and airport.

Lodging chains may operate through a management contract of a franchise system or have full or partial ownership of their properties. On a franchised system the properties are neither owned nor managed by the lodging company—the company receives an initial fee and a percentage of gross room receipts in exchange for the use of the company's name, reservation services, national advertising, and other considerations. Most of the national chains are franchise operations.

The management contract method has grown in importance over the years. With this method, the facility is managed for its owners for a fee based on gross room rentals.

Factors in Successful Lodging Enterprises

Although a variety of factors influence the operation of every lodging enterprise, the following six are considered the key success factors: an effective reservation system, actual locations chosen, the amenities/facilities available at each physical location, friendliness/efficiency of staff, pricing policies, and aggressive marketing, including customer groups targeted plus advertising and special promotional activities.

It may seem unnecessary to detail the importance of an effective reservation system; however, no other single factor can cause the equivalent ill will in potential customers than lost reservations, incorrect dates, errors in requested room types, and so on. Even if adjustments at the check-in registration can be affected in order to accommodate the customer, the impact is still the same—a negative start to the guest's stay at that location. A negative which may never be overcome.

In a similar manner it seems intuitively logical that the actual physical location chosen for a lodging enterprise would be extremely important to the success of its operations. For example, a resort hotel in Florida located on the beach would be expected to have a more advantageous location than one situated three or four blocks further inland. However locational factors are much more complex than this simplistic example. Various factors must be included in the location decision analysis process. These factors include, but are not limited to, the following: (1) the type of lodging enterprise planned (airport versus midtown commercial); (2) the physical amenities to be included in the actual operation (lounges, cafes, swimming pool, exercise facilities); (3) the types of customer groups expected to be chosen as the dominant group targeted for marketing efforts (business versus personal versus convention traveler); (4) the proximity of the physical location to other desirable amenities and services (for example, golf courses, gourmet restaurants, or after-hours social activities), including proximity to business centers, transportation facilities, convention centers, exhibition halls, and so forth.

A third success factor includes the actual facilities available at each location site, both in-room facilities such as bed sizes, bath and dressing room configurations, cable, color television, and desks and furnishings; and also overall facilities such as swimming pools, tennis courts, exercise rooms, cafes, restaurants, lounges, meeting rooms, recreational and duplicating services, computer hookups, and so on. The list can be very lengthy and is continuing to expand with changing lifestyles and technology.

Several lodging chain operators have quickly suggested that the friendliness and efficiency of the lodging staff is an extremely important success factor. This friendliness and efficiency must be a pervasive staff attitude. It must begin at the initial guest/staff contact point, be in the doorman or reception desk clerk or wherever, and continue through all other guest/staff contact situations for the duration of the guest's stay.

The final few success factors of pricing policies, advertising, and special promotional activities are all related to an aggressive marketing program as an important key to success. Pricing has recently become far more segmented and competitive than in the past. Convention and business as well as other group pricing is only the beginning of the pricing policy variables currently practiced at many enterprises. A basic variable of room amenities and location becomes much more complex when factors related to the type of guest, the length of stay, the days of the week in residence, the frequency of visits, and so forth, are included in a pricing formula approach. In addition these pricing policies must be established to be compatible with and coordinated to other marketing activities such as advertising themes and special promotion programs and activities. To summarize, what is necessary for success in today's highly competitive lodging industry is a well-designed and coordinated aggressive marketing program which stresses promotional activities such as media advertising in conjunction with a relatively sophisticated approach to multiple pricing policies.

In the future all segments of the lodging industry are expected to become more aggressive as they compete in the market. Special promotions will be offered to encourage short stays during holiday periods and weekends. Hotels that cater to a balanced mix between business, convention, and pleasure travelers are expected to fare better than others.

Major Competitors in Integrated Hotels

Listed below are a number of organizations which operate multiple locations and which have thousands of lodging rooms available nightly:

- Best Western Inc.
- Friendship Inns

- Budget Motels and Hotels
- Days Inn of America
- TraveLodge International/Trusthouse Forte Inc.
- Quality Inns

However these organizations are either specialized or concentrated in their types of operations and therefore are not considered major competitors in the integrated hotel segment of the lodging industry.

The major competitors operating in the integrated hotel segment are firms such as:

- Holiday Inns Inc.
- Ramada Inns Inc.
- Sheraton Corp.
- Hilton Hotels Corp.
- Hyatt Hotels Corp.
- Marriott Hotels Corp.

These firms are integrated from the standpoint of operating several types of lodging destinations from resorts to airport to convention to business and commercial locations. And, in addition, a number of these firms have also moved into new areas such as all-suite and mid-priced locations. All are diversified in their operations. Exhibit 18.1 provides details regarding some of these major competitors.

Exhibit 18.1   Competitors in Integrated Hotels*

	Properties		
Name	Number of Hotels	Number of Rooms	Occupancy Rate
Hilton Hotels Corp.	N/A	88,864	60%
Holiday Inns Inc.	1,707	310,337	70.2
Marriott Corp.	131	55,000	69.5**
Ramada Inns Inc.	593	93,592	63.0

	Financial Highlights (in thousands)				
Name	Revenues	Net Income	Earnings Per Share	Return on Equity	Main Businesses
Hilton Hotels Corp.	$ 682,928	$112,637	$4.20	18.7%	Hotels and casinos (international)
Holiday Inns Inc.	1,585,080	124,399	3.28	12.5	Hotels, restaurants, and casinos (international)
Marriott Corp.	3,036,703	115,245	4.15	20.0	Hotels, contract food services and restaurants (international)
Ramada Inns Inc.	573,831	12,597	.38	5.2	Hotels and casinos (international)

* 1983 figures.

**Estimated by author.

Source: 1983 annual reports.

Occupancy Rates

In 1982 the economic downturn adversely affected occupancy levels. This downturn moderated room-rate increases and lowered profit margins. However, despite an increase in the number of rooms available, economic recovery in 1983 and 1984 boosted pleasure and business travel.

An important factor in determining the profitability of any lodging enterprise is the occupancy rate. The break-even occupancy level for a hotel is determined by the property's initial cost, the manner in which the initial cost was financed, the ability of management to control operations costs, the actual occupancy rate, and the average price per room. The average industry occupancy rate in 1983 was 66.5 percent and grew approximately 6.6 percent from 1982. But with economic recovery 1984 was expected to have an even stronger showing.

The average price per occupied room was just over $56 in 1981. In 1982 it rose to $62, and fluctuated around $68 in 1983. In 1984 room rates continued to rise; however the increase was less than the double-digit raises of previous years when several lodging chains boosted rates in line with changes in the Consumer Price Index.

Construction

The construction rate of new hotel facilities is not expected to grow in the near future, mainly because interest rates remain high. In the latter part of the 1970s and the early 1980s, most lodging chains curtailed construction programs. The reasons included: rising building costs, high capital costs, an oversupply of rooms stemming from overbuilding in previous years, and declining occupancy rates for many hotels brought about by unfavorable economic conditions. In recent years the emphasis has been on renovation of older rooms and eliminating marginal locations. When new construction resumes, airport and downtown locations are predicted to have top priority.

Industry Outlook

As the lodging industry enters the mature phase of its life cycle, several analysts believe that major market segmentation strategies will be utilized by the national chains. These segmentation strategies, which have been identified as budget-priced operations, all-suite operations, premium full-service operations, and so forth are necessary if the national chains are to retain their market share percentages and insure future profits. Meanwhile, the smaller industry competitors are intent on creating a marketing niche for themselves—a niche that separates their operations from the other competitors in the industries. In fact, the all-suite hotel and the budget-priced operations were started by small competitors searching for a marketing niche to give themselves a competitive advantage.

References

Moody's Handbook of Common Stocks. Fall 1984.

Standard and Poors. *Industry Surveys, 1984.*

Travel Weekly, May 31, 1983

U.S. Industrial Outlook, 1984

Value Line Investment Survey, 1984

The Marriott Corporation, 1984

▪ *Julian W. Vincze* ▪

J. W. Marriott, Jr., President and CEO of Marriott Corporation, glanced at the calendar clock on his desk and reminded himself that the date was January 7, 1985. But his mind really wasn't on this day's events. Instead he was thinking about the future. He wondered what lay ahead for Marriott in the next five years, and especially in 1985.

J. W. was principally concerned with the overbuilding in the lodging industry and the provisions of the proposed 1985 Tax Act. He could readily recall grimacing at the headlines "U.S. Lodging Industry Is Staggered by Room Glut and Building Boom" which had appeared in *The Wall Street Journal*. The article had confirmed Marriott's own market research. He vividly remembered the quote attributed to Tom Herring, Sr., the president of the American Hotel and Motel Association: "We're on a collision course with disaster if we don't do something about the overbuilding." He had chatted with Tom several times recently and knew that Tom meant what he said. Perhaps more ominous were the proposals by the U.S. Treasury Department to virtually eliminate business deductions for travel. A lot of empty hotels would result. (Exhibit 19.1 contains the proposed changes in the tax laws.) J. W. did not really believe that the proposed revisions would pass, but he felt that you never could tell about such things. He wanted his firm to be prepared for the most likely scenarios.

The Marriott Corporation

The Marriott Corporation is a diversified company organized into four divisions: Hotels and Resorts, Contract Food Services, Restaurants, and, until 1983, Theme Parks/Cruise Ships. Annual sales surpassed $3 billion in 1983 and were estimated to exceed $3.5 billion in 1984 as shown in Exhibits 19.2 and 19.3. Marriott has facilities in 49 U.S. states as well as 25 countries, and employs more than 109,000 people who make an estimated 6 million customer contacts yearly.

Founded in 1927 by J. Willard Marriott, who is still chairman, the company began as a small root beer stand. Marriott is dedicated to taking special care of people away from home. The primary objective of Marriott is "to be the premier company in lodging, food service and related areas." 1984 had been one of Marriott's most memorable years of operation, filled with major events which had made it a very successful year as Exhibit 19.2 reveals.

Distinctive Aspects

One reason for Marriott's success is the relationship between guests and employees. The company provides an environment which stimulates pride and performance. Employees are encouraged to have the hospitable and friendly spirit that has become a Marriott trademark.

Exhibit 19.1   Lodging Industry Braces for Tax Changes

The U.S. Treasury has proposed limiting deductions for out-of-town business trips and for business meals. In addition the Treasury would completely eliminate entertainment expense deductions for such items as club dues, cruise ship travel, and tickets to professional sports events.

If the Treasury's plan becomes law, the proposal is to limit out-of-town business travel expenses to a maximum of $150 per day, and for some areas (cities) of the country this would be a maximum of $100 per day. These maximums do not include the costs incurred in traveling to the destination city from the traveler's home base of business. Instead the limits per day are for lodging, meals, and other business expenses incurred at the destination city.

These limits are very restrictive, says a spokesperson for the restaurant industry. For example, the Florida Restaurant Association says that the meal limits proposed by the Treasury at $10 for breakfast, $15 for lunch, and $25 for dinner, "aren't realistic because they "don't take regional differences into account."

Sources: Vick Vaughan, "Industry Braces for Tax Overhaul," *Central Florida Business*, January 7–13, 1985, pp. 10–15.

Exhibit 19.2   Income Statement

	Marriott Corporation and Subsidiaries Income Statement			
	1984	1983	1982	1981
	(in thousands except per-share amounts)			
Sales				
Hotels	$1,640,782	**$1,320,535**	$1,091,673	$ 860,134
Contract Food Services	1,111,300	**950,617**	819,824	599,050
Restaurants	772,855	**679,375**	547,403	446,475
Theme Parks	—	**86,176**	82,453	94,655
Total sales	$3,524,937	**$3,036,703**	$2,541,353	$2,000,314
Operating income				
Hotels	161,245	**$ 139,706**	$ 132,648	$ 117,561
Contract food services	90,250	**73,300**	51,006	45,552
Restaurants	76,220	**61,634**	48,492	38,533
Theme Parks	—	**13,041**	20,004	17,714
Total operating income	$ 327,715	**$ 287,681**	$ 252,150	$ 219,360
Interest expense, net	48,691	**55,270**	66,666	52,024
Corporate expenses	42,921	**34,309**	31,801	28,307
Income before Income Taxes	240,613	**198,102**	153,683	139,029
Provision for income taxes	$ 100,848	**$ 82,857**	$ 59,341	$ 52,893
Net income	$ 139,765	**$ 115,245**	$ 94,342	$ 86,136
Earnings per share				
Primary	$ 5.18	**$ 4.15**	$ 3.46	$ 3.21
Fully diluted	$ 5.18	**$ 4.15**	$ 3.44	$ 3.20

Source: Annual reports.

Exhibit 19.3 Marriott Corporation and Subsidiaries Balance Sheet

	1984	1983	1982
		(in thousands)	
Assets			
Current assets			
Cash and temporary cash investments	$ 22,656	$ 92,279	$ 89,811
Accounts receivable	242,341	169,630	167,173
Inventories, at lower of average cost or market	111,722	95,806	89,071
Prepaid expenses	53,330	43,655	35,617
Total current assets	$ 430,049	$ 401,370	$ 381,672
Property and equipment, at cost			
Land	141,714	171,984	153,528
Buildings and improvements	245,367	373,593	419,634
Leasehold improvements	658,815	716,461	564,284
Furniture and equipment	415,634	475,003	446,133
Property under capital leases	77,566	86,539	89,297
Construction in progress	668,845	388,025	200,808
Total property and equipment	2,207,941	2,211,605	1,873,684
Depreciation and amortization	(375,108)	(419,823)	(379,457)
Total property and equipment less depreciation and amortization	$1,832,833	$1,791,782	$1,494,227
Other assets			
Investments in and advances to affiliates	268,177	68,412	42,961
Assets held for sale	230,760	81,312	27,979
Cost in excess of net assets of businesses acquired	26,742	26,380	26,929
Other	116,058	132,172	88,880
Total other assets	641,737	308,276	186,749
Total assets	$2,904,669	$2,501,428	$2,062,648
Liabilities and shareholders' equity			
Current liabilities			
Short-term loans	$ 7,486	$ 8,895	$ 9,155
Accounts payable	252,806	194,499	183,043
Accrued wages and benefits	129,452	111,420	91,145
Other payables and accrued liabilities	152,654	149,308	116,903
Current portion of debt and capital lease obligations	31,588	29,799	27,898
Total current liabilities	$ 573,986	$ 493,921	$ 428,144
Debt			
Mortgage notes payable	632,923	491,999	182,455
Unsecured notes payable	420,860	509,144	627,854
Total debt	$1,053,783	$1,001,143	$ 810,309

(continued)

Exhibit 19.3   *continued*

	1984	1983	1982
		(in thousands)	
Capital lease obligations	61,504	70,468	79,016
Other long-term liabilities	259,694	60,009	61,420
Deferred income taxes	280,142	247,683	167,754
Shareholders' equity			
Common stock	29,419	29,422	29,424
Capital surplus	145,756	140,882	135,589
Deferred stock compensation and other	3,141	4,160	6,671
Retained earnings	622,283	494,585	389,524
Treasury stock, at cost	(125,039)	(40,845)	(45,203)
Total shareholders' equity	675,560	628,204	516,005
Total liabilities and shareholders' equity	$2,904,669	$2,501,428	$2,062,648

Source: Annual reports.

The Marriott Corporation became the largest chain of company-operated hotel rooms in America in 1984. They have a strong management training and development system and controls which help maintain an unsurpassed reputation.

The strategic planning, market research, and business development staffs work closely with senior operating executives to develop new opportunities. These new opportunities include the Host and Gino's acquisitions, as well as the internal developments. (See Exhibit 19.4.)

Marriott is one of the largest developers in the country utilizing another key skill—real estate expertise. Each year they develop hotels and restaurants valued at over $1 billion. These are designed and constructed through a fully integrated internal department.

Marriott's management is characterized as strong, stable, and aggressive. The top 100 executives average 12 years of company experience.

Financial Policies

Creative, sophisticated financial skills have been used to repurchase the company's stock, to dispose of nearly $200 million in underproductive assets, and to finance $3 billion in hotels since 1978.

Financial policies which are followed by Marriott and which are important to shareholders involve cash flow, cost of capital, debt maturity, and working capital. These financial policies are important because Marriott's ambitious capital investment and acquisition programs are financed by a combination of retained discretionary cash flow, incremental debt on an expanding asset base, and sales of hotels with management agreements. Careful management of Marriott's highly liquid hotel assets and debt structure has enabled the company to maintain targeted leverage and to minimize capital costs. (Exhibit 19.5 details discretionary cash flow.) Marriott bases target debt levels on cash-flow coverage of four times interest expense. Marriott's coverage objective is reported to be what lenders require to provide the company with debt financing at prime rates.

Exhibit 19.4   Acquisition of Host and Gino's

Host International Inc.

Purchase date:	March 3, 1982.
Purchase price:	Reported at $204,725,000.
Type of business:	Operator of bars and shops in airports (nationwide).
Base of operations:	California.

Gino's Inc.

Purchase date:	February 5, 1982.
Purchase price:	Reported at $112,725,000.
Type of business:	Restaurant operations with a total of 308 locations.
	108 Rustler Steak Houses included in purchase resold in 1983.
	180 of the units acquired were updated and turned into Roy Rogers units (this conversion began in May of 1982 and was estimated to take 20 months).
Base of operations:	Mid-Atlantic market (Baltimore north to northern New Jersey).

Source: The Marriott Corporation 1983 Annual Report, *Business Week*, February 1, 1982.

Exhibit 19.5   Discretionary Cash Flow vs. Net Income ($ in millions)

Year	Cash Flow	Net Income
1984	$278	$140
1983	246	115
1982	192	94
1981	157	86
1980	125	72
1979	118	71

Source: Annual reports.

Despite aggressive expansion, Marriott financing techniques maintained coverage at targeted levels. Total capital spending of $800 million in 1984, $499 million in 1983, and $667 million in 1982 (including Gino's and Host acquisitions) was financed primarily from internal cash-flow and hotel dispositions.

The ability to grow aggressively, yet maintain planned coverage, demonstrate that Marriott's high discretionary cash flow ($8.85 per share versus EPS of $4.15), combined with the declining capital intensity of the company's hotel business, has allowed Marriott to expand hotel rooms 20 percent annually without commensurate capital requirements. As a result, investment capacity has been released to fund additional corporate growth such as the 1982 Host and Gino's acquisitions.

Marriott's objective is to minimize the cost of capital by optimizing a mix of fixed and floating interest rate debt obligations. Marriott believes operating cash flows have a high correlation with inflation and short interest rates. Therefore the desired optimal debt structure requires a significant quantity of floating rate debt to minimize capital cost and risk. In addition, the company requires that construction in progress be financed in the traditional manner with floating rate debt. Excluding construction financing, long-term

Exhibit 19.6   Debt Maturity Schedule ($ in millions)

Year	1984	1983	1982	1981	1980	1979
1	$ 26	$ 25	$ 23	$ 16	$ 9	$ 9
2	36	36	28	17	18	18
3	50	43	36	22	18	24
4	58	50	42	40	34	27
5	72	62	48	43	38	35
Total	$242	$216	$177	$138	$117	$113
Funds provided from operations	$330	$294	$231	$187	$150	$141

Source: Annual reports.

debt with floating interest rates averaged 58 percent of total debt capitalization in 1983, compared to 60 percent in 1982.

Marriott has followed a policy of avoiding new commitments of nonprepayable, fixed-rate, long-term debt since 1980. Rather than speculate on fixed interest rates at relatively high levels, the company has matched capital costs with cash flows, thus attempting to minimize capital cost and risk.

Debt maturity remains within Marriott's conservative policy limits, which require that total debt amortizing in the subsequent five-year period not exceed funds provided from operations of the prior year. The company has met this policy constraint by wide margins since 1979, as shown in Exhibit 19.6.

Marriott has no requirement for positive working capital, since it principally sells services (rather than goods) for cash. Therefore, the company maintains relatively low receivable and cash balances. Negative working capital is a source of interest-free financing. As a result of a company-instituted program to aggressively reduce current asset investment, Marriott increased its negative working capital to $93 million at year-end 1983. Exhibit 19.3 contains a traditional balance sheet.

Lodging

The Hotels and Resorts Division, with annual sales in excess of $1.5 billion, continues to be Marriott's largest and fastest growing. The lodging operations include locations in the United States, Mexico, Central America, the Caribbean, Europe, and the Middle East.

In 1983 sales increased by 21 percent and the trend continued with a 24 percent increase in 1984. Occupancy rates also continued to be among the highest in the industry (up 3 percent in 1983), while average room rates increased by approximately the same rate as inflation.

Marriott is noted for its aggressive marketing program. This program, begun in 1982, stresses strong ties with the airlines' frequent-flier programs but also utilizes extensive promotions at the individual hotel level, the keystone of which is the emphasis on selling skills in all levels of customer-contact employees.

The corporation has excellent employee relations. Marriott reinforces its employees' positive attitudes with recognition and development programs, but also believes in internal promotion/advancement opportunities and the need for strong technological support systems. In 1983 approximately one-third of all new managers were originally hourly paid personnel.

Marriott concentrates ownership of its hotels among outside investors while retaining long-term management contracts. In fact, over 75 percent of Marriott-operated hotels are owned by outside investors. Marriott is also a leader in financing hotel growth utilizing various methods, including private syndications, management agreements, and traditional financing. In fact it has developed and financed more than $4 billion in hotels since 1970 with $800 million in 1984 alone.

Contract Food Services (CFS)

Contract Food Services revenues amount to approximately one-third of Marriott's annual sales. CFS sales increased 16 percent in 1983 and 17 percent in 1984, while operating profit rose 30 percent in 1983 and 23 percent in 1984. CFS is the world's leading airline caterer, serving more than 150 airlines (from 80 flight kitchens located in the U.S. and abroad).

Since 1982, through its Marriott/Host facilities, CFS has been a major operator of airport terminal cafeterias, snack bars, full-service restaurants, gift shops, and newsstands. These airport operations at 39 domestic locations are viewed as complementing CFS's airline catering business and thereby broadening Marriott's ability to serve airline passengers.

A third area of CFS's activities involve providing quality meals and food-service assistance to more than 275 business, educational, and health care facilities nationwide. CFS's services range from management supervision to facilities design, and even to turnkey operations. CFS also manages education and conference center facilities for corporate clients.

In addition CFS does operate a few nonairport merchandise shops and turnpike restaurants. However CFS's strategic growth is attributed primarily to these factors: its relatively large size and depth of experience; its productivity (low costs); and its reputation for quality in operations management, procurement capabilities, and organizational depth.

Restaurants

Marriott's Restaurants Division operates or franchises over 1,800 popularly priced restaurants in 47 states, Canada, and Japan. In 1983 a sales gain of 24 percent was reported with a 27 percent increase in operating income. The sales increase was attributed to gains in both customer counts and average amount of checks, plus the addition of 100 company-operated and franchised units. The increased income was attributed to relatively stable food and labor costs throughout the year. The two largest restaurants (chains) are Roy Rogers and Big Boy.

The Roy Rogers (RR) chain was founded in 1968 and provides premium quality fast-food at more than 500 locations, primarily in the Middle Atlantic region. RR features a varied menu offering roast beef sandwiches, burgers, chicken, salad, and breakfast items. Approximately one-fourth of RR's locations are franchised.

The Big Boy (BB) chain includes more than 1,200 restaurants, making it larger than any of its direct competitors. Although founded in California more than 40 years ago, BB now is located nationwide. Most BB restaurants are franchised but more than 200—operating under the name Bob's Big Boy—are company-owned. During 1983 the Big Boy franchise system received new emphasis via cooperative national programs in marketing, menu development, and procurement, in order that Big Boy might retain its company-perceived leadership in family restaurants.

In addition to Big Boy and Roy Rogers, Marriott operates several other theme restaurants. Over 50 speciality restaurants are in operation in California or the East Coast under the Charley Brown's/Charley's Place dinner house concept or the Casa Maria Mexican restaurant concept.

Theme Parks and Cruise Ships

Marriott's fourth division until 1983 included two Great America theme parks and three Sun Line cruise ships. In total about 5 million people annually were customers of this division. The 1983 sales revenues increased about 5 percent over the prior year but operating income declined some 35 percent.

Located in Gurnee, Illinois (between Chicago and Milwaukee), and in Santa Clara, California (near San Francisco), the theme parks were designed to have strong family appeal. Thrill and family rides, as well as games, stage shows, and restaurants were offered. Attendance rose 9 percent in 1983 due to lower admission prices and aggressive marketing. However 1983's attendance was still 10 percent below the 1981 figure. Both parks were sold during 1984.

The city of Santa Clara purchased the California park for $101 million. The Gurnee park sold for approximately $114.5 million. Neither park will be operated by Marriott in the future.

The three Sun Line Ships—the Stella Oceanis, the Stella Maris, and the Stella Solaris—offer a combined total of about 140 cruises per year. Cruises are offered on the Caribbean, Aegean, and Mediterranean Seas.

Theme Parks and Cruise Ships by the end of 1984 was no longer considered a separate operating division or a "primary business line."

Remarks to Shareholders—1984 Results

J. W. had asked his secretary to bring him a copy of his "Remarks to Shareholders" from the 1983 annual meeting and, as he held the document up to look at it, his memory focused on that day (May 10, 1984).

He remembered beginning his remarks by noting the construction of the New York Marriott Marquis which, at 1,900 rooms, will be Marriott's largest hotel. However, the construction list included Boston's Copley Place and Fort Lauderdale's Beach Resort (both of which opened in 1984) as well as the Atlanta Marriott Marquis (which, with the New York Marquis, was due to open in 1985), the Orlando World Center Resort (1986), and the San Francisco–Yerba Buena Center (1988). These five added a total of over 6,000 more rooms. In fact, by including the international expansions and acquisitions, especially the Vienna, Austria, 1984 opening, the planned additions to hotel rooms totaled 26,000 by 1988.

However the real theme of his remarks had centered on the phrase about Marriott's "five special strengths—(which) are the basis for our growth strategy." J. W. scanned the copy and recalled these five distinctive strengths as:

First, our values and systems.

Number two is our leadership position.

The third strength is our business synergy.

The fourth strength is our technical skills.

Number five, we have a strong management team.

But here, J. W. paused! In his own mind the question formed—are these still our special strengths? Or, does Marriot have more than five special strengths? He didn't want to take the time now to answer these questions, but J. W. knew he would have to come back to answer these questions very soon.

Instead J. W. scanned his copy to recall how he had worded the "strategy for growth." After noting the most visible growth mechanism—"the expansion of our existing business"—which was exemplified in hotel room additions, other operations' "selective expansions" were highlighted in general terms. But perhaps the most important major growth strategy was: "acquisition and development of new businesses . . . to develop, test, and expand a number of new, yet related business opportunities."

Two specific new opportunities for 1984 had been cited, Courtyard Hotels and American Resorts Group.

Courtyard Hotels.   In fact the decision to move forward from a testing of the Courtyard concept into a major expansion mode had occurred in June of 1984, shortly after the annual shareholders' meeting. A statement had been released that Marriot planned to expand Courtyard nationwide. Over the next 18 months between 20 and 30 Courtyards in: (1) New Jersey/New York; (2) Washington D.C./Baltimore; (3) Chicago/Milwaukee; and (4) northern California were planned. The total investment over five years would be between $1 and $2 billion. The statement also noted that, by the 1990s, Marriott could have more than 300 Courtyard locations with more than 5,000 rooms.

The Courtyard hotel concept had developed from Marriott's research (over several years) into the moderate-price segment of the lodging market. The moderate segment's current price range was considered to be between $30 and $60 per night and was referred to as the "largest part of the lodging market." Marriott had found that these customers viewed the following factors as important:

1.   An attractive, comfortable, and functional room.
2.   A relaxed, secure environment.
3.   A relatively simple restaurant with good food.
4.   A well-managed operation.
5.   Friendly, helpful staff.
6.   All the above at "affordable" prices.

To meet these customer needs, Marriott had designed a small 130- to 150-room operation that required "very few employees." The targeted customer group was focused "on the transient guests . . . not the group business of a traditional hotel."

Testing of Courtyard had occurred in Atlanta, Augusta, and Columbus, Georgia, and because of the favorable results, expansion into states adjoining Georgia was planned as well as the eventual nationwide expansion noted above.

American Resorts Group.   The second example of new opportunities, American Resorts Group, was viewed as an extension of Marriott's lodging and management skills. American Resorts Group is a leading developer of vacation ownership condominiums in the time-share industry. Marriott's initial venture into the time-share industry was a 120-unit resort on Hilton Head Island in South Carolina named Monarch at Sea Pines.

J. W. knew he would have to carefully explain to the shareholders why Marriott had moved into the time-share industry. He was well aware of the many negative stories about the time-share industry which had appeared in the press recently. J. W. recognized that some shareholders were likely to hold a poor opinion of the time-share industry and perhaps even the basic concepts of time-sharing. It was even probable that some shareholders could have personally experienced a less-than-successful time-share investment, or at least have close relatives or friends who were unhappy about a time-share investment. He knew he had to think through this "new-opportunity" explanation with more than ordinary care for shareholders' sensitivities.

Recent Developments

As J. W. was pondering the ways of explaining these already-announced new opportunities which Marriott had acted upon, he also realized that other more recent developments had not yet received full disclosure. Three items immediately came to mind.

First there was the sale of the 24-unit Casa Maria Mission restaurant operation to El Torito Restaurants Inc., a subsidiary of W. R. Grace and Company. This divestiture was expected to be completed in early 1985 and was generally reviewed as consistent with Marriott's longer-term strategy related to the purchase of Host in 1982. Casa Maria was acquired as a part of Host in 1982 and since Host's acquisition, many locations which were considered peripheral to the Restaurant Division's main activities had been sold.

A second development related to a new approach to financial management of Marriott's assets. In August of 1984 a wholly-owned but indirect subsidiary had been established to purchase nine existing Marriott hotels for $305 million. The new company would continue to operate these hotels as an integral part of the Marriott Hotels and Resorts Division (via management agreement with Marriott). Interests in Chesapeake Hotel Limited Partnership were offered in private placement to accredited investors in 440 units of $100,000 each.

The third development concerned a recent decision that Marriott would build all-suite hotels. Construction of the first Marriott Suites hotel was announced to begin in the spring of 1985, with about a dozen expected to open in 1988. This new hotel product was designed to compete directly with companies already in the all-suite market. Marriott Suites would be located in suburban areas, and possibly in downtown areas of medium-sized cities. Each would contain 200 to 250 suites as well as limited meeting space.

A few other developments also had occurred. For example, during 1984 Marriott had substantial numbers of its own shares on the open market, 1,475,000 shares during the first six months of the year. Also Marriott had reported "exploring entry into the life care community development." In an approach similar to that used for the Courtyard hotel concept, Marriott had issued a statement that a test of the concept would occur with "two or three life care communities" being established "over the next four years." A decision to proceed on a larger scale would then occur. A typical Marriott life care development was expected to accommodate approximately 300 to 400 people in a complete retirement community. Services offered would include lodging, food service, recreational facilities, and limited health care facilities.

Summary of Items to be Explained

At this point J. W. paused and mentally summarized the items which he felt needed to be explained to shareholders:

1. Full expansion of Courtyard hotels concept (moderate price customer segment);
2. Movement into time-share vacation ownership—American Resorts Group;
3. Continued expansion of major hotels with ongoing construction program;
4. Sales of the two Great America theme parks;
5. The sale of Casa Maria Mexican restaurants and the continued expansion of Big Boy and, to a lesser extent, Roy Rogers Restaurants;
6. The testing of Marriott Suites concept in hotels;
7. The purchase on the open market of Marriott's own stock; and finally
8. The continuation of funding the hotel expansion program through creative financial arrangements, i.e. the Chesapeake Hotel Limited Partnership.

However, in addition to these eight items, J. W. knew he also had the traditional explanation of operating results for 1984 to explain. He knew the stockholders would be pleased with the 1984 financial results but the future role of Marriott in the lodging industry was the key issue.

References

"Bill Marriott's Grand Design for Growth: Upscale and Down in the Lodging Market." *Business Week*, October 1, 1984, pp. 60–62.

Carmichael, Jane. "Full Speed Ahead." *Forbes*, July 5, 1982, pp. 90–94.

Celis, William, III. "U.S. Lodging Industry Is Staggered by Room Glut and Building Boom." *The Wall Street Journal*, November 26, 1984, p. 37.

"Expansion at Marriott Hits a Financial Snag." *Business Week*, June 7, 1982, p. 28.

Form 10-K, Marriott Corporation, Securities and Exchange Commission.

Gamrecki, John. "The 'New Breed': Marriott Design Transformed." *Hotel and Motel Management*, June 1982, pp. 22–23.

Karmin, Monroe W., and Morse, Robert J. "Higher Taxes? Who Would Pay." *U.S. News and World Report*, December 10, 1984, pp. 20–24.

Kordsmeier, Joseph G. "Kordsmeier Analyzes Industry's Growth," pp. 207–208.

Marriott Corporation 1983 and 1984 Annual Reports.

"Marriott's New Deals Defy the Recession." *Business Week*, February 1, 1982, pp. 21–22.

Mikesell, Lillie A. "Marriott International Headquarters." *Buildings*, August 1980, pp. 35–39.

Moody's Handbook of Common Stocks, Fall 1984.

Travel Weekly, 25th Anniversary, Vol. 42, No. 46, May 31, 1983.

Vaughan, Vicki. "Industry Braces for Overhaul." *Central Florida Business*, January 7–13, 1985, p. 15.

Weiser, Mort. "The Rise of Hotel Chains and Expansion of Markets," pp. 189, 192.

Holiday Inns Inc., 1984

▪ *Arthur Sharplin* ▪

Holiday Inns Inc. (HI), headquartered in Memphis, Tennessee, is the world's largest hospitality company, with interests in hotels, casino gaming, and restaurants, having sold its Delta Steamships subsidiary in 1982. For the first half of 1983, 64.6 percent of operating income came from hotels, 32.9 percent from gaming, and 1 percent from restaurants. First-half net income and sales were at respective annual rates of $123 million and $1.5 billion. More detailed financial information is provided in the Exhibits 20.1 and 20.2.

The Holiday Inn hotel system includes 1,744 hotels with 312,302 rooms in 53 countries on 5 continents and produces an estimated $4 billion in annual revenues. Licensed, or franchised, hotels account for 86 percent of total Holiday Inn hotels, 81 percent of total rooms, and 6 percent of HI sales. Franchisees pay $300 a room initially plus a royalty of 4 percent of gross room revenues and a fee for marketing and reservation services of 2 percent of gross room revenues. The company's reservation system is the largest in the hotel industry.

In 1982, less than 3 percent of Holiday Inn customers dropped in without room reservations, down from 95 percent in the fifties. In 1981, the company started to deemphasize highway locations. Virtually all new Holiday Inn hotels are placed near airports, industrial parks, and similar sites.

Business travelers account for about 60 percent of Holiday Inn room nights occupied. The company is launching two new hotel chains aimed at the upscale business traveler. The first, Crowne Plaza hotels, offers fine dining, complimentary morning newspapers, continental breakfasts, 24-hour maid service, bellmen, and free HBO movies. Rates are $15 to $20 higher than the average rate of $44 at existing company-owned Holiday Inns. Crowne Plaza hotels are now located in Rockville (Maryland), San Francisco, Miami, and Dallas. Four more will open in Stanford (Connecticut), Houston, and New Orleans by year-end. The second new chain, Embassy Suite hotels, is targeted primarily at the business traveler near the upper end of the lodging market who stays three or four days instead of the usual two, and will pay for specialized service. Each suite will offer a separate living room with a wet bar and the option of one or two bedrooms. The company plans to have six all-suite hotels in varying stages of development in 1984.

In December 1983, the company announced plans to develop a new budget hotel chain, called Hampton Inn hotels, to include 300 company-owned and franchised units within five years. The first will open in Memphis, Tennessee, in 1984. Room rates at these hotels will average about $30. They will feature rooms for smokers and nonsmokers, free television and movies, local telephone calls, continental breakfasts, and arrangements for children under 18 to stay free with their parents.

The Holiday Inn hotel group spent $60.1 million in 1982 to upgrade and renovate company-owned hotels. Old franchises were eliminated at the rate of about one a week, as

The research assistance of Connie Shum is gratefully acknowledged.

This case portrays neither the effective nor the ineffective handling of an administrative situation. Rather, it is to be used as the basis for classroom discussion.

Exhibit 20.1 Holiday Inns Inc. and Consolidated Subsidiaries Statements of Income (in thousands, except per share)

	Three quarters ended		Fiscal year ended	
	September 30, 1983	October 1, 1982	December 31, 1982	January 1, 1982
Revenues				Restated
Hotel	$ 667,644	$ 651,740	$ 840,698	$ 853,645
Gaming	449,239	360,608	472,792	388,148
Restaurant	71,016	70,865	100,584	96,366
Other	4,183	7,624	11,224	13,616
Total revenues	1,192,082	1,090,837	1,425,298	1,351,775
Operating income				
Hotel	143,552	132,280	150,205	170,944
Gaming	98,576	63,647	74,595	56,291
Restaurant	3,486	2,714	5,029	6,547
Other	2,741	3,424	4,999	10,826
Total operating income	248,355	202,065	234,828	244,608
Corporate expense	(22,058)	(17,860)	(24,487)	(25,736)
Interest, net of interest capitalized	(31,725)	(38,738)	(50,965)	(65,540)
Foreign currency translation gain (loss)	—	—	—	1,889
Income from continuing operations before income taxes	194,572	145,467	159,376	155,221
Provision for income taxes	85,612	58,187	62,157	56,515
Income from continuing operations	108,960	87,280	97,219	98,706
Discontinued operations				
Income from operations, net of income taxes	—	(22,100)	4,671	38,652
Loss on disposition, plus income taxes Payable of $5,505	—	—	(25,910)	—
Net income	$ 108,960	$ 65,180	$ 75,980	$ 137,358
Income (loss) per common and common equivalent share				
Continuing operations	$ 2.86	$ 2.23	$ 2.50	$ 2.68
Discontinued operations	—	(.58)	(.56)	.98
Total income loss	$ 2.86	$ 1.65	$ 1.94	$ 3.66
Average common and common equivalent shares outstanding	38,055	38,305	38,216	39,449

minimum operating standards were raised. So drastic was the pruning that, even with 569 new hotels in the past eight years, there has been a net gain of only 45 in the number of Holiday Inns. At the end of 1982, there were 48 Holiday Inn hotels under construction worldwide. The Holiday Inn sign is being replaced with a new rectangular one bearing the chain's name topped with an orange and yellow starburst on a green background.

In March 1983, Roy E. Winegardner, Chairman, and Michael D. Rose, President and Chief Executive Officer, briefed stockholders on Holiday Inn's preparations for the future. Some excerpts from their comments are on page 630.

Exhibit 20.2 Holiday Inns Inc. and Consolidated Subsidiaries Balance Sheets (in thousands, except share amounts)

	December 31, 1982	January 1, 1982
Assets		Restated
Current assets		
Cash	$ 49,945	$ 39,655
Temporary cash investments, at cost	32,544	20,181
Receivables, including notes receivable of $12,618 and $31,927, less allowance for doubtful accounts of $18,925 and $15,080	73,008	91,782
Supplies, at lower of average cost or market	21,871	23,424
Deferred income tax benefits	13,510	11,190
Prepayments and other current assets	18,101	9,775
Total current assets	208,979	196,007
Investments in unconsolidated affiliates, at equity	108,480	46,535
Notes receivable due after one year and other investments	44,186	49,214
Property and equipment, at cost		
Land, buildings, improvements and equipment	1,635,310	1,496,491
Accumulated depreciation and amortization	(367,434)	(313,947)
Subtotal	1,267,876	1,182,544
Excess of cost over net assets of business acquired, amortized evenly over 40 years	54,314	55,787
Deferred charges and other assets	24,172	31,275
Net assets of discontinued operations	—	111,297
Total assets	1,708,007	1,672,659
Liabilities and shareholders' equity		
Current liabilities		
Accounts payable	77,867	66,375
Long-term debt due within one year	31,267	30,478
Accrued expenses	123,283	133,256
Total current liabilities	232,417	230,109
Long-term debt due after one year	436,356	581,465
Deferred credits and other long-term liabilities	33,938	34,851
Deferred income taxes	62,334	53,857
Shareholders' equity		
Capital stock		
Special stock, authorized—5,000,000 shares; series A—$1.125 par value; issued—491,541 and 576,410 shares; convertible into 1.5 shares of common stock	553	648
Common stock, $1.50 per value; authorized—60,000,000 shares; issued—40,218,350 and 32,909,606 shares	60,327	49,364
Capital surplus	294,517	161,188
Retained earnings	671,609	626,310
Cumulative foreign currency transaction adjustments	(3,804)	—
Capital stock in treasury, at cost; 3,036,081 and 2,439,500 common shares and 72,192 series A shares	(78,660)	(63,170)
Restricted stock	(1,580)	(1,963)
Total shareholders' equity	942,962	772,377
Total liabilities and shareholders' equity	$1,708,007	$1,672,659

With the disposition of our steamship subsidiary, Holiday Inns, Inc., is now strategically focused on the hospitality industry. We also introduced a new sign and logo for our Holiday Inn hotel system, better reflecting the range of property types and level of product quality that will characterize the Holiday Inn hotel system in the decades ahead. Recognizing the increasing segmentation of the lodging market, we also began construction on two new hotel products. We also embarked on an aggressive expansion plan for our core Holiday Inn hotel brand. This represents the most aggressive company hotel development effort in recent years, and reflects our continuing belief in the long-term strength of the lodging market and of our Holiday Inn brand within the large moderate-priced segment of that market.

Our company has prospered with the growth of Atlantic City, as our Harrah's Marina facility there has proven to be the most profitable hotel/casino in that market on a pre-tax, pre-interest basis. We entered into a joint venture to build a new 600-room hotel and 60,000-square-foot casino on the Boardwalk. We believe this should contribute to Harrah's ability to achieve the same brand leadership position in Atlantic City that it now enjoys in Northern Nevada.

As a result of [a competitive] pricing strategy, operating margins suffered in our hotel business. However, this approach enabled us to maintain occupancy levels despite the fact that occupancies declined throughout the rest of the hotel industry. At Perkins Restaurants, Inc., our restaurant subsidiary, this pricing strategy paid off, contributing to substantially higher customer count and improved unit profitability. We also made the decision to dispose of a number of restaurants and hotels which were not performing to our financial standards.

In addition to strengthening our market position, we also strengthened our balance sheet. The company's 9⅝-percent convertible subordinated debentures were called for redemption on March 2, 1982. The result was conversion to $143 million of additional equity, which provides the basis for significant new debt capacity to fund our future expansion. Consistent with our stated intention to reduce floating rate debt, we issued $75 million in fixed-rate, 10-year notes in August. In 1982 we commissioned an update of an independent study of the appreciated value of the company's tangible assets and certain contract rights. This study indicated that the net market value of these assets approximated $2.5 billion. [This] appraisal reflects the value of the company's franchise and management contract income streams as well as the appreciation of our real estate assets. [We have] also made substantial progress in improving the productivity of our most important resource, our people. We undertook a thorough review of staffing levels and programs to assure that we were bringing sufficient resources to bear on those things that matter the most, and not expending time or money on those efforts that yield more limited returns. As a result, we have eliminated significant overhead costs and focused our attention more clearly on those things that are most critical to our success in the future. We deliberately increased our expenditures on training and development. We believe that, in our businesses, people represent the greatest opportunity for competitive advantage.

As we look ahead, the economic picture remains clouded. We cannot accurately predict the impact of the unprecedented massive Federal budget deficits on our economy. We remain confident in our ability to manage our businesses effectively under both good and difficult economic conditions.

The Personal Computer (PC)
Industry, October 1984

▪ *James M. Higgins and Mark Blankenship* ▪

When Steven Jobs and Stephen Wozniak assembled the first Apple computer in 1976, in the garage of Job's parents in Los Altos, California, they could hardly have foreseen the growth industry that their efforts would spawn. As youngsters, Jobs and Wozniak were intrigued by computers. They would send away for the latest specifications of new computers, and study them in great detail. At that time, the only "personal computers" that were available had to be assembled by consumers from kits. Engineers were the primary purchasers of these kits, and the computers suited their needs best. Jobs and Wozniak felt they could produce a better personal computer unit, and one that didn't need assembling. After months of designing and trial-and-error efforts, they developed the prototype Apple I. The device linked a keyboard to a microprocessor, which, when attached to a television set, enabled the consumer, then envisioned primarily as a computer hobbyist, to solve various problems and to play video games. Jobs and Wozniak put together 200 units, selling them to retailers for $666.66 each. They recovered their investment after selling the first 100 units. Selling these Apple Is proved to be quite easy. They found their product to be in great demand.

It was shortly thereafter that they met Armas "Mike" Markkula, Jr., a "retired" millionaire who had made millions by helping to launch the Intel Corporation, where he had been the marketing vice-president. With Markkula's money, and venture capital from both Arthur Rock and Associates and Venrock Associates, the "Appleseed" was planted. The rest is history. PC sales of $14 billion are expected in 1984.[1]

The Computer Industry

The 1984 computer industry is gigantic, and diverse. It is composed of numerous sub-industries. The major of these include: hardware, software, storage, printers, terminals/workstations, data communications, semiconductor manufacturers, CAD/CAM, office automation, services/leasing, distribution, and forms/supplies. 1983 revenues from the major firms in these industries totaled $113 billion. Exhibit 21.1 shows a breakout of sales by major firms within each of these subindustries. Numerous smaller firms in each of these segments contribute several billion more to total computer industry sales. Further, the computer industry is only part of a larger information processing industry, which also includes the office equipment industry and additional related communications industry firms. The information processing industry had total sales in 1983 of $268 billion, and it is estimated by Dataquest Inc. that sales for this more-encompassing industry will total

This case is not intended to portray the effective or ineffective handling of an administrative situation. Rather, it is intended for classroom discussion. All rights reserved to the contributor. Prepared as part of a research project funded by the Roy E. Crummer Graduate School of Business, Rollins College.

[1] How IBM Made 'Junior' an Underachiever," *Business Week*, June 25, 1984, p. 106; estimates by Dataquest Inc.; "Apple's New Crusade," *Business Week*, November 26, 1984, pp. 146–156.

Exhibit 21.1   Major Subindustries of the Computer Industry

	Company	1983 ($B) Revenue	1982 ($B) Revenue	Percent Change	Notes
Main frames	IBM	$40,188	$34,364	17%	
	Honeywell	5,753	5,490	5%	Less than ⅓ revenues from computer systems
	Sperry	4,745	4,928	−4%	55% revenues from computer systems; 38% government
	Control Data	4,583	4,340	6%	25% from commercial credit; 30% peripherals, 30% services
	Burroughs	4,390	4,186	5%	25% revenues from service, 12% from forms
	NCR	3,731	3,526	6%	60% from systems
	Amdahl	778	462	68%	48% owned by Fujitsu
	Cray Research	170	141	20%	
Minicomputers	Hewlett-Packard	4,933	4,358	13%	About 50% from computer systems; year ending January 1984
	Digital Equipment	4,828	4,018	20%	
	Data General	867	804	8%	
	Prime Computer	516	436	18%	
	Tandem Computers	450	335	34%	
	Management Assistance	389	354	10%	45% from maintenance (Sorbus); other includes Basic/4
Personal computers*	Tandy	2,661	2,265	17%	Over 8,000 stores; micros comprise less than 40% revenues
	Apple	1,085	664	63%	
	Commodore Int.	1,042	460	126%	
Software	Informatics	198	170	16%	
	MSA	145	101	43%	
	Cullinet	108	70	54%	
Storage	Storage Tech	887	1,079	−18%	
	Tandon	344	177	94%	
	Seagate	222	57	299%	
Printers	Dataproducts	344	298	15%	
	Centronics	164	138	19%	
Terminals/ workstations	Lear Siegler	1,527	1,460	5%	Most business is aerospace; less than 10% in terminals
	Datapoint	554	506	9%	Also minicomputers and local networks
	Diebold	445	428	5%	
	Mohawk Data	400	361	11%	As of January 1984; includes Qantel Business Systems

$1 trillion by 1990.[2] The information processing industry has some 500 computer hardware manufacturers, 5,000 software companies, and about 430 communications equipment manufacturers.[3]

Historically, the computer industry has been driven by the changing capabilities of hardware, although the associated software has been instrumental in selling most of this

[2]"Reshaping the Computer Industry—For Companies Big and Small, Collaboration Is the Key to Survival," *Business Week*, July 16, 1984, p. 85; estimates by Dataquest Inc.

[3]"Reshaping the Computer Industry," *Business Week*, p. 84.

Exhibit 21.1   *continued*

	Company	1983 ($B) Revenue	1982 ($B) Revenue	Percent Change	Notes
Terminals/ workstations *continued*	Telex	307	256	20%	Also storage systems and communications subsystems
	Docutel/Olivetti	222	147	69%	
	TeleVideo	169	98	71%	
	Convergent Tech	164	97	69%	
	Quotron	154	121	27%	
	Recognition Equip	121	111	9%	
Data communications	Paradyne	209	207	—	
	Micom Systems	114	75	52%	
Semiconductors	Texas Instruments	4,580	4,327	6%	Computers under 25% of revenues; chips about 30%
	Motorola	4,328	3,786	14%	36% semiconductors; 12% information systems
	National Semi	1,385	1,151	20%	35% from digital systems
	Intel	1,122	900	25%	
	Advanced Micro Dev	488	336	45%	
CAD/CAM	Computervision	400	325	23%	
	Intergraph	252	156	61%	
Office automation	Wang Labs	1,793	1,376	30%	
	Harris	1,860	1,734	7%	Restated to include Lanier; also in defense
	CPT	192	159	21%	
	NBI	141	116	22%	
Services/leasing	ADP	816	709	15%	
	Computer Sciences	719	683	5%	75% business is contract services
	EDS	719	563	29%	
	GEISCO	620	585	8%	
	Comdisco	538	491	10%	IDC estimates of computer services/software revenues
	McAuto	376	295	27%	IDC estimates of computer services/software revenues
	Planning Research	319	321	—	About 50% services/software
Distribution	Avnet	1,375	1,100	25%	Includes electronics
	ComputerLand	963	451	114%	Privately held
Forms/supplies	Moore	1,814	1,849	−2%	Canadian; 60% U.S. revenues
	Wallace Systems	229	202	13%	
	Verbatim	149	97	51%	

*IBM's PC sales, as those of other manufacturing firms, are included in their mainframe sales figures.

Source: Advertisement section of *Fortune*, July 9, 1984.

hardware. Some would argue therefore that the industry has really been software driven, but it is more pragmatic to recognize that the various other subindustries have arisen to support the basic hardware and to provide services for various users or manufacturers. Hardware firms typically sell software, and in many cases, provided peripherals and other services. But up to this point in time, independents have often been able to provide these same products and services in a more efficient, lower-cost manner, or in a way that results in more quality for end users.

There are three distinct types of hardware: mainframes, minicomputers, and micro-computers—or, as they are better known, personal computers (PCs). The major mainframe companies include IBM, Honeywell, Sperry, Control Data, Burroughs, NCR, and Amdahl. The largest minicomputer manufacturers include Hewlett-Packard, Digital Equipment Company, Data General, Prime Computer, Tandem Computer, and Management Assistance. The primary personal computer manufacturers include IBM, Apple, Tandy, and Commodore. (IBM's total revenues are indicated in Exhibit 21.1 under the subindustry title of "mainframes," but their micro-subindustry sales volumes are not broken out.)

Major Industry Trends[4]

The industry is undergoing several major changes. First, there is the aforementioned merging of the computer, office equipment, and communications industries into the more all-encompassing information processing industry. Secondly, there is a definite movement in virtually all segments of the computer industry towards an industrywide shakeout. Consumers are demanding increased communications capabilities among information processing machines. This trend will help determine who survives the shakeout. It is also evident that a more complete line of products is becoming necessary to compete in this industry. There is thus a trend towards mergers, joint ventures, letters of agreement, and other forms of collaboration among firms in the industry. There also exists a blurring of products and markets as firms scramble to compete industrywide as well as in their traditional niches. Finally, the pace of technological change is accelerating.

An industry shakeout appears inevitable. While the mainframe portion of the industry, and some of the other major subindustries, have already undergone this phase of development, the industry as a whole is transforming in such a way that it is possible, if not likely, that only a few giant firms will dominate across all segments of the industry, just as there are currently only a few firms that dominate each of the segments. The key to success in the information processing industry in the future is apparently going to be the ability to offer compatibility in a complete line of hardware and software, because most of the industry's main customers are organizations, and organizations want their computers and other office machines to be able to talk to each other. Communication among machines is becoming an imperative. Organizational consumers are thus narrowing their vendor choices to those that have a full product line of compatible machines. Finally, voice-entered data networks and data bases are not that far from reality, further increasing the importance of communication's knowledge and capability in the information processing industry. As a consequence of these trends, traditional communications companies are beginning to play a more critical role in the industry. Thus, while AT&T is a late entrant into the computer marketplace, it may have a leg up on more established competitors due to its intermachine communications capabilities and its research into voice-entered data bases.

One of the major consequences of the anticipated industry shakeout will be the reduction in size and impact of the mini segment of the hardware market. Literally millions of managers, professionals, and frontline employees already have their own micros or have ready access to them. These, and available minis, are being used more and more in the analysis of data supplied by mainframes in larger organizations, as mainframes are more and more being employed as data base storage facilities. Because micros do not yet, and

---

[4] Much of the material in the earlier part of this section is taken from "Reshaping the Computer Industry," *Business Week*, pp. 85–111.

may never have, sufficient memory for storing all relevant information for larger organizations, their utilization as smart terminals for the mainframe from which data is to be withdrawn for analysis by the micros' software will continue to grow. The tremendous advances in technology which have been taking place in this industry are further inducing the collapse of the categories of hardware from three into two—mainframes and micros. However, micro's will shortly be able to supply the same kind of memory and computation power that minis have for the past decade. Improvements in wiring (new glass fiber versus older copper) and raw materials (silicon may be replaced in a few years by materials built atom by atom), the development of 1,000-K chips, and the increased utilization of subroutine chips in microprocessors to ease the workload for the central processor all point to improved capabilities, and the eventual decline of minicomputers as a major force in the industry. This is not to say that they will totally disappear, but they may be found only performing certain specialty functions, or serving as mainframes in smaller organizations.

The mainframe segment of the industry is marching ever onward towards the development of the "fifth generation" of computers which will have artificial intelligence (AI) capabilities. There seems to be a general belief that AI is possible within ten years. There is a race between Japanese, American, and European competitors to be the first with this breakthrough. Consequently, collaborations among competitors within these three geographic regions is occurring as firms attempt to overcome the capital dollar barriers to developing AI. Fifth-generation computers will be so fast, so efficient, so complex, so powerful, yet so user friendly, that they almost defy the imagination.[5]

The collaborations which are occurring are significant in size and potential impact. For example, in 1983, IBM acquired 22.7 percent of Rolm Corp. and 20 percent of Intel Corp., seeking, respectively, to gain expertise in communications equipment manufacturing and in chip making. Also in 1983, AT&T purchased 25 percent of the Italian office equipment firm Olivetti. In June 1984, AT&T entered the personal computer market with a product manufactured by Olivetti. Olivetti will also sell AT&T systems in Europe as part of the purchase agreement. Burroughs and NCR are just two of many companies that acquire their brand name personal computers from Convergent Technologies. Japanese and European firms are also active in reaching agreements with American firms and with each other. For example, 12 European computer firms have agreed to adopt standard computer networking procedures so that their equipment will be compatible. Also, Europe's three largest mainframe manufacturers, Bull, ICL, and Siemens, have sponsored a joint research laboratory.

The move towards the full-product-line firm is progressing rapidly. AT&T, Bull, Burroughs, Control Data, DEC, Honeywell, ICL, IBM, NCR, Nixdorf, Olivetti, Siemens, and Sperry have all managed to obtain expertise across these six major information processing markets: peripherals/components, small computers, medium computers, large computers, software, and communications. The means by which their positions in these markets were developed were either in-house or through acquisition, equity position, joint venture, OEM agreement, technology development, technology exchange or licensing, joint product development, marketing agreement, or a manufacturing agreement.[6] One-stop shopping is the objective.

---

[5] Ibid., pp. 84–91.
[6] Ibid., pp. 85–86.

Much of the American firms' collaboration efforts apparently stem from fears of potential Japanese market supremacy. The Japanese have long employed the collaboration concept and, with the size of investment necessary for hardware developments today, such collaboration appears absolutely vital to survival. However, it is not clear as yet just how much competition the Japanese may provide. In the early 1980s, it was feared that the Japanese would enter the computer industry with lower-cost, higher-quality products than currently available in the marketplace.[7] They have managed to accomplish that objective in the chip segment of the market,[8] but have not done so to date in other segments holding approximately only 2 percent of the U.S. market compared to 1 percent for European firms and a whopping 97 percent for American firms.[9] They do not seem to have the capabilities yet to develop the fully integrated product line and they have definite problems in software, being several years behind their U.S. competitors. This latter area has been a real thorn in their side more recently as IBM has taken several actions to reduce Japanese access to American software expertise, including lawsuits for software thefts by Hitachi.[10]

European firms, of course, have much more to fear from IBM than they do from the Japanese. American firms have 81 percent of the European market compared to only 17 percent for European firms. And IBM dominates the American-held portion of the European marketplace across virtually all segments, with 70 percent of the European market.[11]

Because of this complete-product-line, blurred-market, highly capitalized scenario, the future holds the most promise for the very largest of firms. But even the largest of firms, such as IBM and AT&T, have realized that they cannot currently compete in every segment and are taking actions to correct that situation. Nonetheless, it is obviously "Big Blue," IBM, which stands to gain the most benefits from the envisioned scenario. Its position is likely to become even more dominant. As markets blur and a full product line becomes essential, the firm with the most presence in the marketplace will benefit, and that is IBM. Most experts feel that AT&T will become IBM's major competitor.[12]

The Personal Computer Industry

The nine-year-old PC industry is a growing but maturing industry which has two major segments based on price: the home computer market with hardware units generally selling for under $1,500, and the office market with units typically selling for $1,500 to $5,000. Peripherals and software can substantially increase the cost of units in either segment. It is

---

[7] Bro Uttal, "Reshaping the Computer Industry—Can Japan Ever Be More than an Also-Ran?" *Business Week*, July 16, 1984, pp. 103–104.

[8] Bro Uttal, "Here Comes Computer, Inc.,: *Fortune*, October 4, 1982, pp. 82–90; Ibid., "Japan's Latest Assault on Chipmaking," *Fortune*, September 3, 1984, pp. 76–81.

[9] "Reshaping the Computer Industry—Europe's Computer Makers Realize They Must Band Together to Survive," *Business Week*, July 16, 1984, p. 94; estimates by Infocorp.

[10] Bro Uttal, "Can Japan Ever Be More than an Also-Ran?" *Business Week*, pp. 103–104.

[11] "AT&T Takes Its First Giant Steps into Commercial Computers," *Business Week*, April 9, 1984, pp. 100–102; "Reshaping the Computer Industry—Telecommunications Will Separate the Winners from the Losers," *Business Week*, July 16, 1984, pp. 91–92.

[12] "How IBM Made Junior an Underachiever," *Business Week*, p. 106; and "The Computer War's Casualties Pile Up," *U.S. News and World Report*, August 20, 1984, pp. 37–38; "Apple's New Crusade," *Business Week*, November 26, 1984, pp. 146–156.

estimated that in 1984, the home computer market will have total sales of $2–$3 billion, while the office market will have total sales of $11–$12 billion for this same period. It is estimated that $14 million in PC hardware units of $1,000 to $10,000 will be sold world-wide in 1984.[13]

The PC industry has spawned a plethora of supportive and related industries including: software, training and development, office furniture, publishing (300 PC magazines and 4,200 books), videotex data bases to supply PC users with information of all kinds, floppy disk copiers, software swapping clubs, user networks, graphics, and others. The PC has many diverse uses. In addition to its well-known utilization as a financial analyst's tool, as a word processor, and as a means of data base management, the PC has found numerous other functions. Among these are: as terminals or stand-alone units, as members of the "wired university," as a means of providing the handicapped with more independence, as a way for pastors to keep their eyes on the members of their flocks, for home investment portfolio analysis, for real estate firms to keep track of inventories, for forecasting as used by organizational planning personnel, as a chef's reference source, and so on. PCs are not presently in every home or office, but they may be soon. They are so popular that Club Med features training in their usage at some of their resorts.[14]

Most personal computers employ one or a few chips as a central processing unit (CPU). Home computers use typically an 8-bit processor, office PCs use 16-bit processors with 32-bit processors on the horizon. A complete unit includes a main random-access memory (RAM), a secondary read-only memory (ROM) which provides built-in instructions and subroutines, a keyboard, and some type of video display, usually a cathode ray tube (CRT). The most popular home computers have 64K in RAM, with the more popular office PCs having 128K, 256K, or 512K RAM. Printers are also an essential part of most PCs, especially since the most widely used service of the PC is word processing.

PC Industry History

The PC industry was catapulted towards its current level of prominence by the introduction of the innovative Apple I. This was followed by a host of imitations. Most of the early PC manufacturers aimed their products for the home segment, leaving Tandy's TRS 80 series and Apple's Apple II series to battle for dominance in the office segment. There were many early entrants in the PC field ranging from technological giant Texas Instruments to lesser-known quantities such as Timex, Sinclair, Atari, and Osborne. Most early PCs were aimed at the home video-game-playing market, with some adding a few financial and analytical capabilities. The degree of sophistication has risen rapidly, and these "toys" no longer form the mainstream of the PC market. Once the Apple II, with its larger memory and numerous business software programs, became available, the industry shifted in the direction of becoming office-computer product-line oriented. (The Tandy TRS 80 series was also aimed at the office market and helped point the industry in that direction.)

[13] "Riding the Coattails of the Computer Boom," *U.S. News & World Report*, April 30, 1984, pp. 68–69; "Personal Computers Inspire a Rash of Magazines, but Shakeout Is Seen," *The Wall Street Journal*, April 9, 1984, p. 37; "The Shakeout in Software," *Business Week*, August 20, 1984, pp. 102–104.

[14] Susan Chace, "Personal Computers Find New Roles in Religion: For 'Attunement' Network and Tending the Flock," June 7, 1983, p. 60; Erik Larson, "The Sun Sparkles, Palm Fronds Sway, Disk Drives Whir," *The Wall Street Journal*, July 20, 1983; pp. 1, 12. "The 'Wired University' Is on the Way," *Business Week*, April 26, 1982, pp. 68, 73; Michael B. McPhee, "Harvard Requires MBA Students to Use IBM PC's," *PC World*, 1984.

Exhibit 21.2   Shifting Market Shares in PC Industry Segments

Home Computer Market

1984		1982	
Commodore	38%	Commodore	26%
Apple	25	TI	26
IBM	12	Atari	21
All others	25	Radio Shack	10
		Timex	7
		All others	10

Personal (office) Computers

1984		1982	
IBM	33%	Apple	20%
Apple	17	IBM	18
HP	9	Radio Shack	15
All others	41	HP	5
		All others	42

Source: "How IBM Made 'Junior' an Underachiever," *Business Week*, June 25, 1984, p. 106.

Apple, Tandy, and Commodore dominated the PC market through 1981, although strong runs at industry leadership were made by others in various segments. But in August 1981, the inevitable entry of IBM into the PC industry occurred, and the shape of the industry changed forever, and much more rapidly than anyone had anticipated that it would. It was amazing how quickly IBM became number one. By the end of 1983, just 28 short months after its entry, IBM had displaced Apple as the largest producer of units and easily led the industry in sales dollars due to its higher unit price.[15] Exhibit 21.2 contains related industry information.

IBM's rush to dominance has left a trail of firms in its wake. Victims include Osborne, Victor Technologies, Vector Graphics, Intertec Data Systems, Franklin, Fortune Systems, and Tandy (still active but no longer a major force), to name just a few. Other firms, such as Atari, have seen their situation sour due to the changing emphasis in the PC market from games to analytical capabilities. Still others, such as TI, never did quite figure out how the market functioned and thus they have withdrawn from part of the market—the home segment. And still others, such as TI, DEC, HP, and Xerox, have found their office sales severely reduced from hoped-for levels by IBM's quick dominance of the market. The shakeout is so severe that it is likely that fewer than ten firms will remain in the office segment of the industry by the end of 1985.[16] Even Apple has had to accommodate its strategy to the IBM presence despite its $1.4 billion in sales in 1984. "Building a strategy that took the IBM world into account is more important than we expected," admits Steven Jobs.[17] IBM's success in the marketplace has created a niche for "clones," such as Compaq and Zenith, who make similar machines but sell them for much lower prices. The need for these "compatibles," which are designed to use IBM software, could dwindle if demand

---

[15] "Personal Computers: And the Winner Is IBM," *Business Week*, October 3, 1983, pp. 76–77.

[16] Ibid., p. 77.

[17] Ibid.

slips as IBM production capacity increases.[18] Industry demand, however, is expected to grow. Despite the shakeout and IBM dominance, the larger mainframe producers, such as Burroughs, NCR, and Hewlett-Packard, all quickly entered products into the PC office market, as did DEC (a mini manufacturer), in an apparent effort to maintain that total segment, full-product-line capability perceived to be so critical to survival in the information processing industry in the near future.

The IBM Strategy

Any product or service that is marketed with those three little letters—IBM—attached to it, has a phenomenal chance for success. Furthermore, the fact that IBM is the primary moving force in the computer industry—an industry whose customers are organizations—can only aid its introduction of a personal computer when the PC industry is moving towards an office orientation. If the target market is one where the name IBM is already accepted as an industry standard, then all other competitors are at an immediate disadvantage. And, one cannot help but believe that the prediction of IBM's success by industry analysts could hardly help but become a self-fulfilling prophecy.

But IBM did not become successful in the first place by taking strategically unsound actions. When it came time to enter the PC industry, it had considered its moves well—although IBM showed not only good timing, but benefited from some good luck as well. The key elements in the IBM success story include:[19]

- An Advanced Design. At the urging of outside software firms, IBM moved from the industry standard of the 8-bit processor to the 16-bit processor based on a chip made by Intel.

- Allowed for Software which Could Be Readily Written by Others. In another uncharacteristic move, the first being to listen to outsiders with regard to design features (the 16-bit processor), IBM, which has always written its own software, decided to publish its PC software specifications, having recognized that software was critical to PC sales. Software became much more readily available than it would have otherwise.

- Employed Multichannel Distribution. Many PC customers were outside the normal sales distribution channel that IBM employs. Consequently, IBM used multiple channels including 800 strong computer retailers, including the largest franchise chain—Computer-Land and the Sear's Business Systems Centers.

- Low-cost Manufacturing. Recognizing the PC industry as a maturing one—especially with their own entry into the market—IBM took great pains to build substantial production facilities with high levels of automation in order to produce a low-cost product.

- Aggressive Pricing. In April 1983, IBM cut the price of its personal computer by 20 percent, forcing competitors to do the same or more. This 1983 price cut was followed by another of an additional 23 percent in June of 1984, which made it virtually impossible for many of their competitors to compete on a cost basis.

[18] "Computer Market will be Big: How Big Is Up for Grabs," *Mart*, July 1984, p. 43.

[19] "Personal Computers: and the Winner Is IBM," *Business Week* p. 78; plus information from a collection of other sources.

• New Product Introduction. IBM introduced new products, lowering the prices on older ones. First came the 3270, the PC, then the PC Jr., the PC XT, the portable, and most recently, the PC AT. Introduced in August of 1984, the PC AT is much faster and more powerful than previous models. Its expandable memory is sufficiently large to allow it to serve as a minicomputer for two additional "dummy" terminals. This computer represents a further movement towards the merging of micro and minimarkets.

The success of their PC strategies has caused great concern among competitors. David G. Jackson, President of Altos Computers, observes, "IBM is moving faster than anything I've ever seen. It is being positively predatory."[20] Other factors which helped IBM become so successful include Apple's unwillingness to become IBM-compatible, thus forcing software writers to make the choice of writing for the IBM industry standard or the Apple. As a consequence, the level of software being written by outsiders for Apple's Macintosh is much less than they hoped it would be, and this is affecting sales somewhat as the sales of the highly successful Macintosh begin to slow.[21] Additionally, IBM's choice of MS-DOS as the internal machine operating system forced others to follow if they wished to keep pace with the de facto industry leader. This further compounded the software problem for companies whose machines were not compatible. Most have scrambled to become compatible. Wang computers, for example, is to make available in the fall of 1984 an add-on unit for its older PCs which will make them IBM-compatible. After that point, all new Wang PCs will be IBM-compatible. Competitors must be IBM-compatible because software writers simply are not going to write for noncompatible, non-MS-DOS machines. Only Apple, because it holds a sufficient share of the market, seems to be able to remain noncompatible and yet have a sufficient amount of software continue to be written for its machines, and even they have been affected by noncompatibility. IBM has not been totally successful, however. Part of its strategy was to first attack the office market where it knew it would meet with immediate success, then to go after the home market as well with a second product offering geared to that market—the PC Jr. While it has gained a high share of the office market (estimated 33 percent for 1984), and a substantial share of the home market with its PC Jr. (estimated 12 percent in 1984) IBM's "Junior" has been described as an "underachiever."[22]

IBM did not garner as high of a market share as it felt it should, given its substantive investment and advertising. IBM experienced a number of negative consumer responses to this PC, which though priced at the home market level, is targeted also at small businesses. It had a "toylike" keyboard which apparently turned off many potential consumers. It was because of this keyboard that the PC Jr. was unsuitable for word processing, the number-one office use of PCs, and the number-two use of PCs at home after games.[23] It was priced much too high at $1,000 to compete with traditional "home" computers compared to the market-dominant Commodore 64, which sells for $200. It had a relatively small memory of 128K, which made it less competitive on the upper end of the market, especially since its memory cannot be expanded, unlike that in "PC Sr." As a consequence, the PC Jr. was not able to establish a sufficient niche for itself in the market.

---

[20] "Personal Computers: and the Winner Is IBM," *Business Week*, p. 78.

[21] Ibid.; "The Computer War's Casualties Pile Up," *U.S. News & World Report*, p. 37.

[22] "How IBM Made 'Junior' an Underachiever," *Business Week*, pp. 106–107.

[23] Ibid.

Interestingly, success with the full-size PC contributed somewhat to this downfall. IBM wanted to clearly distinguish Jr. from Sr., not wishing to hurt Sr.'s sales. And, because of the rapid growth of the Entry Systems Division, a committee approach had to be employed to design the PC Jr. Finally, so much secrecy surrounded the development of this product that it was essentially not market tested.[24] IBM corrected the keyboard and memory expansion problems in August 1984, in an effort to overcome sagging sales of this model.

The PC Competition, October 1984

IBM dominates the office segment; Commodore dominates the home market. Apple is the second-strongest firm in both segments. (See Exhibit 21.2.) There are third and fourth target market segments to the PC industry—education and scientific. Officetype PCs are the most frequently used PCs in the education market and when sales figures are shown for the office segment, education sales will be included in these figures. This market was dominated early on by Radio Shack, but now Apple and IBM apparently are the dominant firms. Both have made substantial efforts in 1983 and 1984 to increase their market shares, as well as to give substantial numbers of machines to educational institutions.[25] One must applaud their generosity, but one should also recognize that, from a marketing perspective, such actions are sound. The reason is that if someone learns on a certain type of machine, then he or she is likely to buy that machine for personal or office use, thus expanding the market for these companies' major products. The scientific market at this time seems to be the territory of specialty PC manufacturers, but larger firms, such as Hewlett-Packard, are the major force in this industry.[26]

There are several primary hardware segments to this industry: the standard office PC, the portable office PC, the more-powerful office PC with prices ranging to $10,000, and the home computer. The main thrust of the remainder of this case is on the office PC market segment and the related PCs and PC firms

The personal computer industry was an extremely competitive environment in 1984 for several reasons. First, the number of competitors in the marketplace was fairly large at 185, although many of these firms were in specialized niches. Second, fixed costs had to be a significant portion of a firm's cost structure in order to be competitive. Third, plant capacity was normally increased in sizable increments. Fourth, because technology was constantly changing, the product was highly "perishable." New products could become almost obsolete in a matter of months.

An analysis of competition in the personal computer industry is facilitated by examining the overriding marketing strategies utilized in the marketplace as well as the market segments served. For instance, IBM was the market leader and had attempted to set an industry standard. At the same time, many companies such as Apple and Hewlett-Packard ignored this standard and attempted to tackle IBM head-on. Other companies, such as Compaq Computer Corp., accepted the IBM standard and produced an IBM clone designed to capture some of the excess demand for IBM machines.

---

[24] Ibid.

[25] "Slugging It Out in the Schoolyard," *Time*, March 12, 1984, p. 62.

[26] "Hewlett-Packard Dives into the Mainstream," *Business Week*, October 3, 1983, pp. 90–91.

The Players.   The following paragraphs discuss briefly the situations and strategies of each of the primary market shareholders, plus some perceived to have a chance at survival and prosperity based on a niche strategy. The firms listed are in the order of their anticipated 1984 sales.

1. IBM.   The IBM success story was outlined earlier. The PC division—the Entry Systems Division (ESD), headquartered in Boca Raton, Florida—though nonexistent as a market entity until August 1981, will account for a full 5 percent of IBM's total worldwide sales in 1984. The IBM PC strategy fits nicely with IBM's total integrated approach to the information processing industry. ESD markets six hardware units as detailed earlier. Yet, despite having six machines, ESD does not yet have a unit aimed at the "user-friendly" marketplace.[27]

2. Apple.   As the second-largest manufacturer of office PCs, Apple is following a very clear niche strategy aimed at that segment of the market which requires user-friendly computers. Apple makes, "the computer for the rest of us"—the Macintosh and its older, larger sister—the Lisa. As with IBM, Apple has machines in each of the basic segments, but they generally have certain characteristics that make them more user friendly. Apple's entries include: the Lisa in the $3,000–$5,000 per-unit market (more user friendly than the competition); the Macintosh in the more-powerful standard PC market (more user friendly than the competition); the Apple III in the more-powerful PC niche (almost a nonentity); the Apple IIe in the standard PC market (nearing the end of its product life-cycle), and the Apple IIc portable, aimed at not only the office, but the home computer market (more user friendly than its competition). The latter has a tremendous advantage over most of its competition due to the significant amount of software available for all Apple II computers, plus it has many extras built in, including user-friendly technology (the Apple mouse). Apple continues to lead the industry in innovative technology. They developed the "mouse"—a device for easing the use of the computer for novices; they, of course, had the first true PC; they have a very advanced portable; and the Lisa and Macintosh incorporate other features not available on other PCs. Some argue that their refusal to be IBM-compatible hinders Apple's progress; others argue that it helps them create a very definite niche. Apple's sales exceeded $1.4 billion in FY 1984. Macintosh sold 70,000 units in its first 100 days (introduced January 24, 1984). Apple IIc had 50,000 orders the very first day it was announced as available (April 24, 1984). Production facilities were running as much product as possible in June 1984, but could not meet demand for Lisa, Macintosh, and the IIc.[28] Demand had slowed somewhat by October 1984.

3. Hewlett-Packard.   HP is expected to be the third-largest firm in the industry in terms of sales by the end of 1984. They are anticipated to have a market share of 8–9 percent. HP is also following a total integrative strategy similar to that of IBM. They are very strong in scientific PCs, shipping some $500 million in 1984. HP competes with two primary machines: the MP 150 in the standard PC market, and a portable version of that

---

[27] "How IBM Made 'Junior' an Underachiever," *Business Week*, p. 106; various advertisements for IBM products found in *Business Week* and *The Wall Street Journal*.

[28] "The Computer War's Casualties Pile Up," *U.S. News & World Report*, p. 37; various advertisements for IBM products found, for example, in *Business Week* and *The Wall Street Journal*.

computer for the portable market. HP has gone after the user-friendly market that Apple attacks in a similar fashion. Instead of using a mouse to select computer instructions, the user touches applicable places on the HP video screen, and the computer follows the given instructions. The obvious problem is software. Because of their small marketshare, HP has difficulty attracting a sufficient number of software writers to enable the 150 to compete on the basis of completeness of software.

Hewlett-Packard has run into some production difficulties in their PC line in the summer of 1984, and it is possible that they might finish fourth or lower in sales if that situation is not corrected before the year's end. Recognizing that they have a weak level of consumer awareness, they have launched a sizable media—television and periodical—advertising campaign to increase that level. HP expects to sell about one-half of its 1984 sales through its regular sales force efforts, working with businesses and other organizations. The other half is expected to come in sales to ultimate individual or small-business consumers through arrangements with retail chains.[29]

4. Tandy Corporation.   Radio Shack held 15 percent of the office market in 1982. Now its share is probably under 5 percent. It could conceivably edge HP for third place if it did better than expected and HP fell flat on its face, but its fortunes in the PC wars are definitely on the wane. Tandy's strategy has focused on distribution with a captive audience at its 8,700 worldwide Radio Shack stores, about 1,100 of which carry a full line of computer products, others carrying only some models. It has historically not offered PC product hardware units that competed head-on, but rather sought a differential in some way, offering 80K RAM computers instead of 64K or 128K RAM computers. Now, its model TRS 80-2000 competes head-on with the IBM PC and is IBM-software-compatible, but offers several features that position it fairly well against the IBM models. Its service is an unknown quantity. Software has historically been more limited than IBM's or Apple's, but, with compatibility, that should change. Costs should conceivably be in its favor, given the absence of the middleman profit. However, it has priced generally higher, and slowly reduced its prices according to competition. It has introduced portable models for that market. One key question remains: how is Tandy to capture the office market since it has essentially no sales force. Another issue confronting Tandy is R&D. Tandy has not been a market innovator, but rather a follower. In this industry, innovation is important if you are not IBM or one of its clones.[30]

5. Compaq.   It is likely that Compaq will finish number five in the industry in sales for 1984. Compaq is an IBM clone with four models, all portable, which meet IBM's four major models head-on. These four models are priced $50 to $100 higher than IBM's, which is a unique strategy given the compatibility factor. But Compaq's computers do more than IBM's and have several additional features that Compaq feels justifies the price differential. Time will tell whether they have positioned themselves correctly in the market. The impacts of several additional portables being offered in 1984 (IBM, Apple, HP, Tandy) will have a definite impact on its market share. Plus, IBM's increased production

[29] "Personal Computers: and the Winner Is IBM—Hewlett Packard Dives into the Mainstream," *Business Week*, pp. 90–95; and various advertisements for HP products.

[30] "Personal Computers: and the Winner Is IBM," *Business Week*, p. 76; "How IBM Made 'Junior' an Underachiever," *Business Week*, p. 106; various advertisements for Tandy products.

capacity of 2 million total units for 1984, could render Compaq's future an uncertain one, along with the other compatible manufacturers who have built their markets on IBM's inability to produce enough units. With new, low-cost entrants in the field, Compaq now seems to be stressing features and innovative product design. "The IBM product is behind the times: it is behind our second generation product," comments Compaq's president. Compaq has been increasing its advertising budget to attempt to stay in the race.[31]

6. DEC. Digital Equipment Company entered the market in 1982, and has captured perhaps 3–4 percent of the market. It, too, is following the integrative strategy of IBM and the other mainframe majors. It has almost always followed a low-cost strategy, but that is not an apparent feature of its endeavors in the PC market. DEC seems essentially to have a me-too-type product but has been able to sell at current levels due to its sales force and good relations with prior customers.[32]

7. AT&T. It is very likely that AT&T, through its marketing muscle, omnipresence in industry, and high level of brand identification, will be able to break into the top ten in PC sales in 1984, perhaps even into the top five. Only $250 million or so in sales would be necessary to achieve the sixth or seventh position. AT&T acquired its PC manufacturing capabilities through a partial (25 percent) purchase of the Italian firm Olivetti. The Olivetti machine is essentially a me-too IBM clone, but employs the UNIX communication system to allow for machine-to-machine communication. This communications capability seems to be the cornerstone of the AT&T strategy, along with a heavy amount of advertising. Long-term, AT&T would seem the most suited to confront IBM head-on, but short-term, it faces a definite uphill battle.[33]

8. Others Who Might Break Through.

A. Epson. Using an NEC (Nippon Electric Company) manufactured machine, the Epson QX 10, Epson attempts to merge the best of IBM and Apple. It is simpler to use than IBM, but has much more software than IBM's PC XT and more than Apple's Macintosh because it has CP/M and MS-DOS capabilities and IBM compatibility.

B. Xerox. Xerox has recently restructured its strategy (May 1984) under an umbrella campaign known as Team Xerox. It will, for the first time, use the personal selling of its copier direct sales force to market computers. Previously, the firm had used a separate, much smaller sales force for its direct-selling effort. It also has an office networking program that gives it an advantage over some of its competitors. Some feel

[31] Eleanor Johnson Tracy, "Compaq: An IBM Clone Meets the Real Thing," *Fortune*, April 16, 1984, p. 61; "Compaq's Gutsy Bid to be More than an IBM Copycat," *Business Week*, July 9, 1984, pp. 81–82; "How Compaq's Portable Leaped Ahead of the Pack," *Business Week*, August 15, 1983, pp. 89–90; and various advertisements for Compaq products.

[32] "Personal Computers: and the Winner Is IBM," *Business Week*, p. 76; "The Computer War's Casualties Pile Up," *U.S. News & World Report*, p. 37; "A New Strategy for No. 2 in Computers," *Business Week*, pp. 66–75; "Can DEC's Product Woes be Fixed?" *Business Week*, October 31, 1983, p. 44; and selected brochures on DEC's products.

[33] "Reshaping the Computer Industry—For Companies Big and Small . . . ," pp. 85, 88, 90; "The Computer War's Casualties Pile Up," p. 38; "AT&T Takes Its First Giant Steps into Commercial Computers," pp. 100–102; "AT&T Enters Computer Business and Introduces Family of 6 Models," pp. 2, 29; selected advertisements on AT&T products.

it's too little too late for this strategy, but Robert Adams, President of Xerox's High-Tech Division, observes, "I like to have the mind-set of a long-distance runner. Although I'd like to be out in front of a race at every moment, I believe this race is going to be ten years long, and we've only seen the first couple of laps." [34]

C. Texas Instruments. TI has developed a computer known as "The Professional." It compares very favorably to IBM's PC, and has memory options up to the level of IBM's PC XT. It has speech recognition capability which works only on certain commands. Thus, word processing dictation directly to the machine is not yet possible. It has "better" graphics than the IBM PC. There is significant but not substantial advertising of the product. [35]

D. Wang. Wang's keyboard is generally considered superior to that on the IBM PC, but software availability has been a problem. Wang has announced that by the end of September 1984, it expects to have a unit which will enable its older machines to be IBM-compatible, and that its future machines will have built-in IBM compatibility. This move obviously allows for an instant solving of the software problem. The Wang PC has a dedicated word processor which gives it a competitive advantage against IBM's machines. Wang is attempting to follow an integrative strategy which would put it into hand-to-hand combat with IBM, DEC, and others. [36]

E. Kaypro. Kaypro offers a CP/M machine that has numerous software capabilities. It has significant memory, price, and "free" software advantages over most competitors. Clearly, its competitive advantage lies in its price with inclusive software. For about $500 less than for a competitive machine only (prices vary), the purchaser receives a RAM of 64K built-in plus another 400K on two disk drives, the keyboard, a 9-inch screen, and nine key software packages covering word processing, data management, and spreadsheeting, plus BASIC and games. Compatibility with IBM disks is included, and the system weighs only 26 pounds, making it a "portable," but not as portable as the roughly 9-pound IBM and Apple portables. Kaypro boosted dealer margins in 1984 from 28 percent to 35 percent, attempting to get more shelf space in the major retail computer chains. [37]

F. Seequa. With its Chameleon, an IBM clone, Seequa Computer has a portable that is price-comparable to Kaypro's, offers free software, and provides an extra microprocessor that makes it compatible with thousands of currently available software programs. One very intersting thought about the entire PC market is provided by Seequa President David Gardner: "IBM gives you the opportunity to outperform them in many areas. You can't convince every consumer of that, but you can convince an awful lot of them. Even if IBM dominates 50 percent of the industry, the other 50 percent is still billions of dollars." [38]

---

[34] Dennis Kneale, "Xerox Takes New Marketing Tack to Improve Poor Computer Sales," *The Wall Street Journal*, May 9, 1984, p. 31; various advertisements for Epson and Xerox.

[35] Advertisements for TI's PC.

[36] "Wang Lab's Run for a Second Billion," *Business Week*, May 17, 1982, pp. 100–104; various advertisements for Wang products.

[37] Advertisements for Kaypro products; "The Computer War's Casualties Pile Up," *U.S. News & World Report*, p. 38.

[38] Advertisements for Seequa products; "The Computer War's Casualties Pile Up," *U.S. News & World Report*, p. 37.

G. The Others. The others include Corona Data (which uses a low-cost production strategy and retail store salesperson bonuses); Morrow (which gives $20 retail store salesperson bonuses); Acorn; Columbia Data Products (IBM-compatible with aggressive distribution strategy); Grid (featuring the Compass—the "Porsche" of PCs, a portable, flat-screen, high-powered, high-priced machine); and NCR (which is apparently selling only to its existing organizational customers).[39]

Key PC Industry Success Factors [40]

The major keys to the future in this industry appear to be as follows: cost efficiency and price competition, new products and new features (R&D), advertising dollars to gain or retain brand identity and market share, financial resources, the ability to maintain or increase distribution, software, communication, niches, production capacity, and third party hardware and software capabilities.

Cost Efficiency and Price Competition.   An absolute imperative to survival is cost-efficient production. The future will probably see less emphasis on cost and the resultant lower price as a competitive factor since IBM and Apple have extremely efficient production facilities, as do virtually all currently surviving competitors. However, as new product units are introduced (especially by IBM), there will always be clones which can probably be produced at a cheaper price than the major firms (or firm—IBM) are willing to sell new products for on the first offerings of these products. It is more likely that cost and price will be used as a competitive advantage strategy where extras, such as software or additional RAM memory, can be "thrown in" for the same price that IBM or Apple sells its hardware products. This strategy is currently followed by Kaypro, Seequa, and Grid.

New Products and New Features.   It has invariably been IBM's strategy to introduce new products or product modifications to extend the product lifecycle. Older products in the product line are then reduced in price, and the cycle continues. Many new innovations remain. IBM is expected to release a more powerful, faster PC in August 1984. The flat screen is not far away for most PCs, and is available in some portables. And since most "portables" weigh 25 to 30 pounds, much in the way of portable product improvement is in the offing. Many people feel that Apple is the innovator in this industry and many feel that only through the development of new products will it survive. It has allocated $70 million in 1984 for R&D, a far cry from $6,000 in 1976.

Most of the other competitors probably do not have the research and development funds to stay with these two firms, or, as is likely with Hewlett-Packard, NCR, and some of the other larger firms, they may not be willing to invest significant amounts, being satisfied simply retaining only certain lower-market-share levels. Innovation, new products, and new features alone are not enough. HP was certainly innovative with its "touch" screen but does not seem to have the marketing power to cause its products to attain high market shares. Xerox has created some impressive new products in the PC industry, but has as yet

---

[39] Advertisements for various companies' products; "The Computer War's Casualties Pile Up," *U.S. News & World Report*, pp. 37, 38.

[40] Derived from the materials previously cited, plus several additional background articles which were used to obtain general knowledge.

to sell very many. Third parties must be interested in developing peripheral support products for all competitors.

Advertising Dollars.   IBM is the dominant firm, and to have a chance against a dominant firm head-on, high-dollar advertising is absolutely essential. Smaller firms must fight for brand recognition if they expect the major computer retail chains to carry their products. If you go into a smaller ComputerLand, or Businessland, or into a Sears Business Systems store, you're likely to find all of the IBMs, most of the Apples, the two COMPAQs, maybe HP or AT&T, and that's about it. Until customers demand the product, which is caused by advertising, then one cannot expect the retail chains to respond favorably.

Financial Resources.   Due to the high capital investment for R&D, software development, production plant and equipment, high working-capital requirements, and the intense cost competition, firms must have substantial financial resources to compete satisfactorily.

Distribution.   It is absolutely imperative for the smaller firms to have shelf space in the major retail computer stores. One trend currently seen is that the PC chains are striving to become larger. In doing so, they must have proven winners, which pretty much shuts out new firms and older firms with only marginally successful entries.[41] Having your own distribution centers, as do IBM, Radio Shack, and DEC, definitely helps, but is no guarantee as Xerox discovered, eventually selling its 100 stores to the Genra Group.[42] Computer stores will sell approximately one-half of the dollar value of PCs sold in 1984, so shelf space is imperative. Dealers report receiving numerous pleas from smaller firms for shelf space. Many smaller firms are willing to provide inventory for 90 days without payment in order to prove that their products will sell. Other enticements noted earlier include salesperson bonuses and greater margins to retailers.[43]

Software.   Software is another absolute necessity for high-volume sales. Apple II sold well at least partly because it had abundant software. The IBM PC series sells well at least partly because it has abundant software. The IBM PC compatibles follow the compatible strategy because users want IBM software. But as of September 1984, Apple is beginning to show some signs of fatigue in Macintosh sales, simply because there isn't much software for the machine. While they are still selling all that they can produce, there are some signs of market resistance. While the machine is targeted at both business and home markets, it cannot continue to sell in the office market without additional software. Apple is advertising software on television indicating that much is being written, but obtaining it is clearly another matter. Third-party support is missing.

It's true that there are only three primary software needs: word processing, spreadsheet, and data base management; but the quality and selection alternatives of the software

---

[41] "More Power to the PC Chains," *Fortune*, May 14, 1984, pp. 83–88; John Marcom, Jr., and Frederic M. Biddle, "Computer Dealers that Are Selling Top Brands Gain Big Edge in Market," *The Wall Street Journal*, August 23, 1984, p. 25.

[42] "Computer Friendly: Genra Group Buys Xerox Stores," *Fortune*, November 28, 1983, p. 12.

[43] "The Computer War's Casualties Pile Up," *U.S. News & World Report*, pp. 37–38.

which performs those functions, and a host of minor ones, is going to determine how good the ultimate usage of a machine is. Many experts advise finding the software you need, then buying a machine that will run it. IBM software and hardware are somewhat like the chicken and the egg: does IBM sell so much hardware because there is so much software available for the hardware, or is there so much software available because IBM is selling and is going to continue to sell so much hardware? Clearly, IBM has the software advantage, especially over noncompatibles.

Communication.   At first glance, AT&T would seem to have a major strategic advantage in the communication area, but it remains to be seen if they can convert this into a true strategic advantage. Xerox too possessses the necessary communications network capabilities, but as yet has not turned this into a strategic advantage. As reported earlier in this case, virtually all major mainframe firms have this intermachine capability. Note, however, that Apple and the rest of the PC competitors do not. If Apple and these other firms are to make any inroads into the office market in the future, they need that capability.

Niches.   Firms that can find a niche will survive. Among the many possible niches are: machines designed for user-friendly software; machines that are industry specific or have industry-specific software—for example, that are programmed or hardware-designed to the specific needs of the insurance industry, or the engineering science fields; machines that have improved capabilities and features such as the HP "touch screen," or those that use a mouse device; machines that are capable of semi-artificial intelligence. Price could be a niche for some period of time on any new product.

Third Parties.   Suppling both hardware and software make the task of the manufacturer much easier. IBM's machine allows for this, so does Apple II, but Macintosh is difficult for third parties to work with on both counts.

Buyers

The ultimate buyers of personal computers were divided into two basic groups. The first group consisted of home users, and the second group was the professional users. Almost all home users bought their machines through microcomputer retail stores such as ComputerLand, Entre Computer Center, MicroAge, OnLine Computers Plus, and Radio Shack. On the other hand, large businesses chose to buy both directly from the manufacturer and indirectly through retail stores. However, commercial sales through retail stores had grown considerably in recent years. Some retailers catered specifically to large business needs, because it was more profitable than sales to individual users. In fact, many retailers did not consider their businesses to be a store, but instead a service center which provided consulting to its clients on a continual basis.

Home users functioned independently of one another, and therefore, did not have much power over the manufacturers collectively. Moreover, marketing surveys had found that oversaturation of competitors had confused the home consumer, and accordingly, over 50 percent of potential buyers had no brand preference. The typical computer owner held a college degree, and over 25 percent had a graduate degree. In addition, one-half of these owners had managerial or professional jobs, and 25 percent had household incomes in excess of $40,000 per year. In 1984, about 7 percent of all U.S. households, or 5.8 million homes, had home computers.[44]

In contrast, the corporate buyers were much more concentrated and therefore, much more powerful than individual consumers in relation to the manufacturers. These buyers tended to purchase the more expensive, sophisticated machines, and did so in large quantities. This purchasing behavior tended to be more economical in the long run. However, due to the nature of the product, corporate buyers were not as powerful as they would have liked. First, because the IBM standard had not been completely accepted at the high end of the market, buyers suffered from significant switching costs if they decided to change vendors. Once a particular manufacturer was selected by a customer, that customer would most likely continue to buy from that company. Second, with the highly automated society that existed in 1984, computer operations had become a significant influence on the ultimate outcome of a business's products or services. Thus, many businesses had become extremely dependent on its personal computers. Third, personal computers when properly integrated into a business's operations could prove to be very cost effective. Therefore, demand for personal computers was strengthened. Fourth, in the vast majority of cases, the customer's products and services were not even remotely related to personal computer products. Accordingly, there was almost no threat of backward integration.

Suppliers

The supply of personal computer components had always been tight, and this represented a major problem to computer manufacturers. In particular, microprocessors and data storage devices were in low supply. The computer component suppliers such as Intel Corp. and Tecmar Inc. were caught by surprise when the personal computer market began to proliferate and had been unable to manufacture parts fast enough. This problem was hurting the new computer manufacturers the most, because component suppliers needed to meet obligations with existing computer companies first. An option available to new manufacturers was to buy parts on the spot market and pay a premium. However, that premium may have been as much as ten times the value of the part. Many computer companies were attempting to stockpile parts.

The power of suppliers relative to computer manufacturers tended to be significant. First, only a few large suppliers dominated the marketplace. Second, once a computer manufacturer selected a supplier, a huge dependency could develop. For example, the IBM PC and the IBM clones used an Intel microprocessor. In order to have changed suppliers, IBM and its followers would have had to completely redesign its machines.

However, suppliers' power was mitigated from the standpoint that the personal computer industry represented a major portion of the suppliers' business. Thus, the suppliers had a substantial dependency on personal computer companies.

Finally, suppliers had not posed a threat of forward integration. In fact, the case had been exactly the opposite. For example, Commodore continued its practice of vertical integration by acquiring a microprocessor supplier, MOS Technology, in 1978. Also, IBM had employed a similar tactic by purchasing 18 percent of Intel Corporation's common stock.

---

[44] "Buyers Dazed by Computer Market Study." *Advertising Age*, June 18, 1984, p. 40.

Substitute Products

The utilization of personal computers had rapidly become a well-accepted concept. In 1984, substitute products and services were only a very mild threat to the personal computer industry. However, it is still appropriate to identify and analyze these substitute products.

First, mainframe computers were an alternative to personal computers. Before personal computers became abundant, many individuals used time-sharing services. This service allowed users to access a very large computer through their terminals at home or at the office. The time-sharing company would then bill out charges to its customers each month based on a variety of factors such as processing time and storage space. However, customers began to recognize that the purchase of a personal computer was much more cost effective in the long run. Consequently, time-sharing was becoming less popular, and profits for these companies such as Tymshare Inc. were suffering significantly.[45]

In view of the fact that approximately 59 percent of all personal computers were used by owners to do word processing, typewriters and word processors were legitimate substitute products.[46] After all, not many home users or even business users were willing to pay $5,000 for a personal computer solely for word processing capability when a traditional electric typewriter could be purchased for only one-tenth the cost. However, two additional points need to be mentioned. First, a personal computer could run a myriad of other software in addition to word processing. Second, the prices of personal computers were falling much more rapidly than the prices of typewriters or word processors. Within the near future high-quality personal computers would be available for under $1,000.

A third substitute product was the electronic video games and pinball machines found in amusement arcades. Industry analysts found that 69 percent of computers in homes were used to play video games.[47] However, the general feeling was that video games were becoming a less-significant use of home computers. This was especially true in the high end of the personal computer market where the number-one-selling software package in 1983 was a professional spreadsheet program called Lotus 1-2-3.

Current Trends in the Industry

Predictions were made by some industry analysts that one in every three American households would have a home computer by the end of 1985. At the end of the century, it was forecasted that 80 percent of American homes would have a computer. Office use was expected to accelerate. In sum, most analysts agreed that sales and consumption of personal computers would continue to grow at a rapid rate for the next several years.[48]

Another current trend that was projected to continue into the future was declining prices. This trend would persist for three reasons. First, fierce competition in the industry would encourage price slashing in order to maintain market share. The price leader in the low-end of the market, Commodore, had always followed a strategy of low prices. IBM,

---

[45] "Computer Services Industry," *The Value Line Investment Survey*, February 10, 1984, p. 1129.

[46] "How Computers Are Being Used at Home," *Computers at Home*, Fall/Winter, 1984, pp. 14–15.

[47] Ibid.

[48] Joel Dreyfuss, "What Will Send Computers Home," *Fortune*, April 2, 1984, pp. 71–74.

the high-end price leader, had on several occasions displayed its willingness to compete on the basis of price with cuts as high as 20 percent at a time. Second, those competitors who would survive the price wars would do so by bringing down costs per unit. Reducing costs could be carefully planned in advance by mass-producing, and thus, benefiting from economies of scale. Third, as with all industries, each time the cumulative production of a product doubles the cost per unit decreases by some percentage. This phenomenon is referred to as the experience curve, and given the industry analysts' predictions of tremendous growth in production of personal computers in the future, the manufacturers' experience should also increase rapidly.

In addition to a growing demand and lower prices, another significant trend was advances in technology. The most visible area of these advances could be seen in the improved "user friendliness" of personal computers. Manufacturers were aware that most buyers did not want to spend several weeks trying to make a system work. For example, Apple claimed that a novice could learn how to operate its Macintosh in less than 30 minutes. It was predicted that within five years people would no longer need to become computer literate. Contrarily, computers would be people literate. Also, more features would be added to the home systems. In 1984, personal computers could perform the same functions that mainframe computers did just a few years ago. However, the $1,000 computer systems of the future would have capabilities that in 1984 sounded incredible. For instance, scientists were designing a personal computer called the Dimension 68000 which would be able to run programs from all manufacturers with no compatibility problems.[49] Other potential innovations included voice input capabilities and three-dimensional graphics.

Japanese Penetration

Although Japanese producers only had a 2 percent share of the U.S. market in 1983, there was growing concern that these firms were gaining momentum. At the heart of this concern was the unification of more than ten of Japan's largest electronics companies by accepting a common industry standard called MSX.

MSX was a set of uniform specifications which allowed manufacturers to offer complete compatibility with other participating vendors' machines. This concept differed from the idea of the IBM standard in the respect that the IBM standard evolved through fierce competition and still was not accepted by such major competitors as Apple and Hewlett-Packard. Conversely, MSX stemmed from a common agreement among such major electronics firms as Canon, Hitachi, Toshiba, Sony, Sanyo, Mitsubishi, Yamaha, and Pioneer.

The MSX standard was aimed particularly at the low end of the personal computer market and included the following basic specifications: an 8-bit microprocessor, a video chip, an audio chip, 32K of ROM, Microsoft BASIC resident in ROM, 8K of RAM, a 40-column display, an expansion slot for a disk drive, and a joystick port.

In 1984, MSX had not been released in the United States. Two reasons explained this delay. First, some industry analysts speculated that the demand for MSX machines in

---

[49] Rich Cook, "A Machine for All Software," *Popular Computing*, November 1984, pp. 64–72.

Japan alone was far greater than the Japanese firms' ability to fill the orders. Between the announcement of the MSX standard on June 17, 1983, and the end of 1984, it was estimated that approximately 500,000 systems would be sold in Japan.[50]

The second reason for the delayed introduction of MSX into the United States was the tremendous competition that it would receive from companies such as Coleco, Atari, and Commodore. The Commodore 64, which was the world's largest selling computer, was seen as the most significant barrier to entry. MSX manufacturers forecasted that when MSX machines are introduced into the United States the prices would range from $200 to $400. However, with the eventual use of a very large-scale integration, the price could drop as low as $50 within five years. On the other hand, one of Commodore's primary strategies had always been to maintain low prices. Thus, Commodore was prepared to engage in future price wars if necessary.

Industry Outlook

Although the industry was forecasted to continue growing for an indefinite period of time, many industry observers felt that the nature of competition would begin to change very soon. Some characteristics of a maturing market would begin to appear, and those companies that recognized these signals would be the ones who would prosper.

First, marketing surveys indicated that 13 percent of personal computer owners would be repeat buyers within the coming year.[51] Thus, these buyers would be more selective in the brand they chose. Second, some companies in the near future would be much farther down the experience curve than the less innovative firms, and therefore, would be able to place a greater emphasis on cost. This would enable these competitors to put a squeeze on those companies who had not benefited as much in terms of the experience curve. Third, much more attention would be given to customer service. This would be evident especially at the retail stores. Fourth, the entrance of the Japanese machines with the MSX standard would threaten the market share of U.S. firms. Fifth, although costs would fall rapidly, prices would fall just as fast due to intense competition for market share.

Because most industry analysts felt that both growth and maturity characteristics would be apparent in the future, many possible opportunities existed for the competitors. First, a continued effort should be placed on product innovation. Possibilities existed in several areas including telecommunications capability, voice input, more sophisticated graphics, elaborate built-in software, more "user-friendly" software, faster computing capabilities, and more storage space. Second, mass production was important in order to bring down unit costs. Thus, many companies could benefit by expanding the size of operations. Third, emphasis should be placed on servicing customers. Personal computer firms could improve sales if more training was provided at the retail level in order to properly educate the salespeople. Fourth, manufacturers could find greater profitability by distributing their product internationally. Apple and Commodore had already found this path to be a profitable one. Finally, vertical integration could prove to be a logical strategic move if the supply of microprocessors continued to tighten up. IBM, Hewlett-Packard, and Commodore had all enjoyed the advantages of this strategy in the past.

[50] Paul Freilberger, "The Future of MSX," *Popular Computing*, October 1984, pp. 68–73.

[51] "IBM Joins the Race in Personal Computers," *Business Week*, August 24, 1981, p. 39.

Final Observations on Competition in the PC Industry

Virtually every forecast of industry demand calls for 10–25 percent growth per year for at least the next 4 years. Some predict even higher rates for the 1985 and 1986 period. Within the rosy portrayal, IBM is a virtual juggernaut, but one that does have certain weaknesses that can be and are being exploited. It is clear that, as one ComputerLand salesperson related, "The customer is IBM-brainwashed. That's all they want." (It may very well be that many of the computer stores' sales forces and their managers are "IBM-brainwashed" as well.)[52]

One aerospace executive related an interesting story that nicely summarizes market conditions in late 1983. His firm was planning to standardize all PCs across his firm of 13,000 employees. A committee was formed. They studied the various computers, analyzed their features, compared their prices, and found that the IBM clone by Zenith was clearly the best buy. So they bought IBM . . . because "We knew IBM would be there tomorrow."[53] With decisions like that, it's clear that the IBM success if a self-fulfilling prophecy.

The above two incidents do not mean that IBM will control 100 percent of the market. But they do help point out the problems that all other competitors face in the marketplace.

References

Kneale, Dennis and Erik Larson, "Apple Says Profit to Remain Soft for 2 Quarters," *The Wall Street Journal*, November 8, 1983, p. 3.

Kneale, Dennis, "Apple Pins Macintosh Future on User Friendliness' of Lisa," *The Wall Street Journal*, January 27, 1984, p. 33.

Knowles, Malcolm S., "Malcolm Knowles Finds A Worm in His Apple," *Training and Development Journal*, May, 1983, pp. 12–15.

Larson, Erik and Carrie Dolan, "Apple Stages Elaborate Courtship of Press As It Introduces Its Macintosh Computer," *The Wall Street Journal*, June 23, 1984, p. 25.

Larson, Erik, "Apple's Lisa Spurs Software Makers to Duplicate Its Integrated Features," *Wall Street Journal*, July 8, 1983, p. 23.

MacDonald, Stephen, "As Apple Computer Is Hailing Its Mouse,' Others Find Fault," *The Wall Street Journal*, May 16, 1984.

Miller, Michael W., "Apple Introduces Enhanced Macintosh in Bid for Increased Sales to Businesses," *The Wall Street Journal*, September 11, 1984.

Moritz, Michael, "The Improbable Tale of Apple's Quirky Wizards," *Business Week*, September 10, 1984, pp. 12–13.

Morrison, Ann M., "Apple Bites Back," *Fortune*, February 20, 1984, pp. 86–100.

Nulty, Peter, "Apple's Bid to Stay in The Big Time," *Fortune*, February 7, 1983, pp. 36–41.

Shaffer, Richard A., "Next Apple Computer Blends Old Design, New Technology," *The Wall Street Journal*, March 23, 1984, p. 35.

Wall Street Journal Staff Reporter, "Apple to Double Producing Capacity for Macintosh Line," *The Wall Street Journal*, July 10, 1984, p. 12.

Wise, Deborah and Catherine Harris, "Apple's New Crusade," *Business Week*, November 26, 1984, pp. 146–156.

---

[52] Experienced by the author as I attempted to determine which PC I would like to buy. The three saleswomen with whom I spoke, one each in the aforementioned stores, suggested strongly that I forget Apple, buy IBM, because Apple had no software. One said, "I'm a traditionalist. I like IBM."

[53] As related to the author by a high-ranking executive in that firm.

Apple Computer Company, October 1984

■ *James M. Higgins* ■

John Sculley, President and Chief Executive Officer of Apple Computer Inc., after reviewing the firm's fiscal year 1984 performance (FY ending September 30, 1984), commented: "A year ago at this time people were worrying whether Apple's best years were behind it. We've proven that is not so. We've made it through an industry shakeout in which billions of dollars were lost by computer manufacturers; Apple has emerged battle-tested and toughened." (See Exhibits 22.1, 22.2, 22.3, 22.4, and 22.5.)

Not all, however, share Mr. Sculley's enthusiasm for Apple's future. Apple, which must daily do battle with its arch-rival, International Business Machines Inc. (IBM is often referred to as "Big Blue"), embarked in FY 1984 upon what Mr. Sculley calls "a year of transition" during which two new computers were introduced and new marketing, operations, and distribution strategies were initiated. During that year, Apple sacrificed short-term profit to invest heavily in advertising, research and development, and manufacturing capacity. Consequently, profits in the previous four quarters had fallen sharply. Significantly, however, there was a steep rise in net profits for the fourth quarter of fiscal year 1984, which clearly represents a turnaround for Apple. But officials at Apple, market analysts, and investors all know that only a battle has been won and not the war, for in the fall of 1984, Apple has launched a bold new campaign to make a big push into the office computer market, away from its more traditional small business and individual consumer market bases. The risks are high.

Launched in time for the Christmas buying season, Apple's new campaign features the "test drive" program for its main-line Macintosh computer. Any potential buyer with a major credit card could take the Apple Macintosh home overnight for free. The underlying concept is much like that used in selling cars—a test drive is better than a salesperson's spiel. Mr. Sculley commented: "We intend to change the marketing ground rules for this industry. Apple is launching an era of brute-force marketing." Mr. Sculley expects the test-drive program to generate "thunder and lightening." In coordination with the company's new marketing program were pricing strategy moves, distribution strategy moves, and sales incentives for retail salespeople.

Furthermore, millions of dollars in advertising, including a one-week buyout of the entire 1984 November election issue of *Newsweek* for $3 million, will occur to support this program. Apple also hopes to build on its "event marketing" strategy, such as was used during 1984's Super Bowl. It was then that Apple introduced the Macintosh computer with a unique television advertising theme apparently based around the novel *1984*. In this TV ad, a beautiful female rebel threw a sledgehammer into the projected portrait of a "Big Brother"-like screen character, as numerous android human beings watched Big Brother. The message that this commercial carried was that Macintosh was coming, a new dawn in computer capabilities, and apparently one aimed at freeing androids that follow

Exhibit 22.1   Selected Financial Information

Annual
Five years ended September 28, 1984
(in thousands, except per-share amounts)

	1984	1983	1982	1981	1980
Net sales	$1,515,876	$982,769	$583,061	$334,783	$117,126
Net income	64,055	76,714	61,306	39,420	11,698
Earnings per common and common equivalent share	1.05	1.28	1.06	.70	.24
Common and common equivalent shares used in the calculations of earnings per share	60,887	59,867	57,798	56,161	48,412
Cash and temporary cash investments	114,888	143,284	153,056	72,834	363
Total assets	788,786	556,579	357,787	254,838	65,350
Noncurrent obligations under capital leases	$ —	$ 1,308	$ 2,052	$ 1,909	$ 671

Apple has not paid any cash dividends on its common stock. The present policy is to reinvest earnings to finance future growth.

Quarterly (unaudited)
(Dollars in thousands, except per-share amounts)

	Fourth Quarter	Third Quarter	Second Quarter	First Quarter
1984				
Net sales	$ 477,400	$ 422,144	$ 300,103	$ 316,229
Gross margin	207,063	175,051	121,775	133,401
Net income	30,806	18,295	9,132	5,822
Earnings per common and common equivalent share	.50	.30	.15	.10
Price range per common share	$ 30–$24⅛	$33⅛–$23⅜	$28⅞–$23⅛	$24⅞–$17¾
1983				
Net sales	$ 273,210	$ 267,284	$ 227,982	$ 214,293
Gross margin	115,893	128,310	116,916	115,885
Net income	5,108	24,204	23,883	23,519
Earnings per common and common equivalent share	.08	.40	.40	.40
Price range per common share	$47½–$22¾	$62⅝–$39⅜	$48⅛–$27½	$33⅞–$18⅛

The price range per common share is the highest and lowest closing bid quotation for Apple's common stock during each quarter.

At September 28,1984, there were approximately 43,000 shareholders of record.

"Big (Blue) Brother." Apple clearly faces a difficult task in dislodging the entrenched IBM from its dominant position in the office market, but this type of advertising has apparently helped as sales of Macintosh surged following its introduction. The question is, can these and other strategies enable Apple to survive and prosper in the long term?

Company History

In the now-famous story, the first Apple computer was assembled in 1976 in a Los Altos, California, garage belonging to the parents of Steven Jobs. Mr. Jobs and his associate Stephen Wozniak were early computer hackers, constantly sending off for the latest com-

Exhibit 22.2   Comparative Levels of Performance

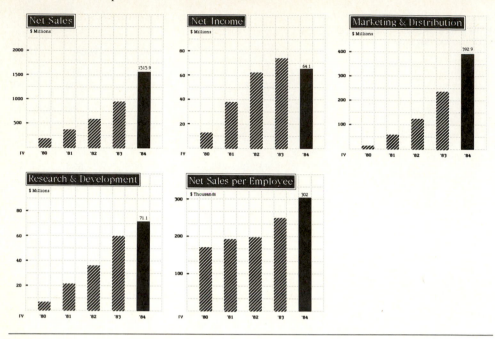

Exhibit 22.3   Consolidated Statements of Income

Three years ended September 28, 1984 (dollars and shares in thousands, except per-share amounts)	1984	1983	1982
Net sales	$1,515,876	$982,769	$583,061
Costs and expenses:			
Cost of sales	878,586	505,765	288,001
Research and development	71,136	60,040	37,979
Marketing and distribution	392,866	229,961	119,945
General and administrative	81,840	57,364	34,927
Total costs and expenses	1,424,428	853,130	480,852
Operating income	91,448	129,639	102,209
Interest and other income, net	17,737	16,483	14,563
Income before taxes on income	109,185	146,122	116,772
Provision for taxes on income	45,130	69,408	55,466
Net income	$ 64,055	$ 76,714	$ 61,306
Earnings per common and common equivalent share	$ 1.05	$ 1.28	$ 1.06
Common and common equivalent shares used in the calculations of earnings per share	60,887	59,867	57,798

Exhibit 22.4   Consolidated Balance Sheets

(dollars in thousands)	September 28 1984	September 30 1983
Assets		
Current assets:		
Cash and temporary cash investments	$114,888	$143,284
Accounts receivable, net of allowance for doubtful accounts of $10,831 ($5,124 in 1983)	258,238	136,420
Inventories	264,619	142,457
Prepaid income taxes	26,751	27,949
Other current assets	23,055	18,883
Total current assets	687,551	468,993
Property, plant, and equipment:		
Land and buildings	24,892	19,993
Machinery and equipment	68,099	51,445
Office furniture and equipment	30,575	22,628
Leasehold improvements	26,008	15,894
	149,574	109,960
Accumulated depreciation and amortization	(73,706)	(42,910)
Net property, plant, and equipment	75,868	67,050
Other assets	25,367	20,536
Total assets	$788,786	$556,579
Liabilities and Shareholders' Equity		
Current liabilities:		
Accounts payable	$109,038	$ 52,701
Accrued compensation and employee benefits	20,456	15,770
Income taxes payable	11,268	—
Accrued marketing and distribution	50,638	21,551
Other current liabilities	63,784	38,764
Total current liabilities	255,184	128,786
Noncurrent obligations under capital leases	—	1,308
Deferred income taxes	69,037	48,584
Commitments and contingencies	—	—
Shareholders' equity:		
Common stock, no par value, 160,000,000 shares authorized, 60,535,146 shares issued and outstanding in 1984, and 59,198,397 shares issued and outstanding in 1983	208,948	183,715
Retained earnings	259,101	195,046
Accumulated translation adjustment	(633)	—
	467,416	378,761
Notes receivable from shareholders	(2,851)	(860)
Total shareholders' equity	464,565	377,901
Total liabilities and shareholders' equity	$788,786	$556,579

Exhibit 22.5   Consolidated Statements of Changes in Financial Position

(in thousands)	Year Ending September 28		
	1984	1983	1982
Working capital was provided by:			
Operations:			
Net income	$ 64,055	$ 76,714	$ 61,306
Charges to operations not affecting working capital:			
Depreciation and amortization	37,963	22,440	16,556
Deferred income taxes (noncurrent)	20,453	35,697	7,625
Total working capital provided by operations	122,471	134,851	85,487
Increases in common stock and related tax benefits, net of changes in notes receivable from shareholders	23,242	44,095	18,399
Increases in noncurrent obligations under capital leases	—	—	1,172
Total working capital provided	145,713	178,946	105,058
Working capital was applied to:			
Purchase of property, plant, and equipment, net of retirements	39,614	52,666	26,470
Other	13,939	11,531	4,421
Total working capital applied	53,553	64,197	30,891
Increase in working capital	$ 92,160	$114,749	$ 74,167
Increase (decrease) in working capital by component:			
Cash and temporary cash investments	$ (28,396)	$ (9,772)	$ 80,222
Accounts receivable	121,818	64,942	29,148
Inventories	122,162	67,089	(22,972)
Prepaid income taxes	(1,198)	25,860	2,089
Other current assets	4,172	9,660	1,156
Accounts payable	(56,337)	(27,576)	1,488
Accrued compensation and employee benefits	(4,686)	(3,996)	(4,015)
Income taxes payable	(11,268)	15,307	(6,686)
Accrued marketing and distribution and other current liabilities	(54,107)	(26,765)	(6,263)
Increase in working capital	$ 92,160	$114,749	$ 74,167

puter specifications from companies such as DEC. These they would scrutinize with great pleasure. At this time, the only personal computers were those constructed by hobbyists from kits. Jobs and Wozniak decided they could improve upon the existing kits and prepare completely preassembled PCs for sale which, from the consumer's viewpoint, would be far superior to kits. After months of designing and building, they developed the prototype of Apple I. The device was a keyboard built around a microprocessor which, when connected to a television set, allowed the user to solve various problems or play a video game. The inventors made 200, selling them to retailers for $666.66 each. They recovered their original investment after selling just 100.

It was at about this point, late in 1976, that they met Mike Markkula, Jr., a retired multimillionaire who had made his millions helping to launch the Intel Corp. where he eventually became the marketing vice-president. With Markkula's money, and venture capital funds from Arthur Rock and Associates and VinRock Associates, Apple began to grow rapidly through the sales of its Apple II computer. By 1980, profits for the company that had begun in 1976 in a garage were up 237 percent over those in 1977, reaching $39.4 million. In 1980, Apple went public with a $96.8 million offering of $22 per share in order to finance its potential growth. For fiscal year 1984, sales reached $1.5 billion with net profits of $30 million or $.50 per share, but the road to glory had not been an easy nor stable one. It had been akin to a roller coaster ride.

Some feel that Jobs and Wozniak were lucky to have been so successful and indeed they may have been, but it is very clear that Wozniak's obsession with building electronic components and Job's fierce determination as a youngster to become financially successful at an early age with a get-rich-quick scheme provided the impetus for their success. If luck is a matter of preparation meeting an opportunity, then indeed these two people were lucky; but the important factor was they were prepared and recognized an opportunity and seized it when it occurred. Neither of the two is a college graduate—both are college dropouts—but they seem to have the right mixture of idiosyncrasies that provides a success story. Both Job's and Wozniak's parents contributed greatly to their child proteges' success. Job's parents indulged his eccentric nature and provided room in their kitchen for the first assembly line once they expanded from the garage. Interestingly, the two Apple founders were never close friends and have in recent years become estranged, partly because they are so different temperamentally and partly because they have different interests. Wozniak works as of the date of the case, as an obscure, though quite wealthy, multimillionaire engineer for Apple. Jobs on the other hand, at 29, is chairman of the board at Apple and active in making management decisions in conjunction with John Sculley.

The Company

Apple Computer Inc. was incorporated on January 3, 1977, and designs, develops, produces, markets, and services microprocessor-based personal computers and related software and peripheral products. Apple Computer is a company whose mission is "to bring technology to individuals. . . . We want to translate highly advanced technology into top-quality, affordable, and easy-to-use products. We are in essence tool builders for individuals; we sell products for people to people, but we can never take off-the-shelf tool technology and merely market it better than anyone else. What we can and will do is to continue to innovate."

Marketing

Much of Apple's marketing program has undergone significant changes in recent months.

Products

In October 1984, the company's principal product line focuses around the Macintosh personal computer system. Macintosh sells for $2,195.00 in the 128K version and $3,195.00 in the 512K version in mid-September 1984. Some stores discounted this price further. The principal comparative advantages that the Macintosh has are its superior graphics and its easy use through a hand-held device known as a "mouse." Extensive additional software capability is built into the Macintosh in order to make it usable by almost anyone.

A second additional major product of the firm is the Apple IIc, a portable version of its famous IIe, selling for $1,195 as of mid-September 1984. This PC is targeted primarily at the home computer market, was introduced in April of 1984—with great fanfare—at a price of $1,295, and has met with considerable success in terms of units sold.

At its current price and a lower one expected in early 1985, the Apple IIc fits well into the $1,000-and-under market, which is typical of the home market. It can compete directly with the PC Jr. but offers the additional feature of portability. A flat screen was promised for the future.

The third major product of the firm is the Lisa series. Part of the Macintosh line, it is a similar but more sophisticated computer than the Macintosh, with additional memory and additional capability, selling in mid-September, 1984 for approximately $3,500–$5,500, depending on features.

The fourth major product of the firm is the Apple IIe—the long-time standard of the firm and industry with 15,000 software programs having been written for it. But this product is in its seventh year of production and despite efforts to increase its memory and capabilities, can no longer sustain the company's growth. Hence Macintosh and Lisa were created.

The firm also has the Apple III. An additional product introduced in 1984 was the Lisa II, a more powerful version.

Apple's products are sold primarily to the business, education, and home markets. The principal method of distribution has been the independent retail dealer, although Apple has recently opened additional channels such as department stores and direct sales. Apple's foreign operations consist of manufacturing facilities in Singapore, and distribution facilities in Europe, Canada, and Australia.

Apple followed a course originally of writing only limited software for its Apple II series, with hundreds of independent vendors having developed the numerous applications for this computer. Similarly, with the Macintosh and Lisa computers, only a limited number of Apple-supplied software has been created. This resulted in a dependence upon external vendors to create a majority of software for this computer as it was with the Apple II series. The difference has been that vendors have not rushed to create software for these computers as they did with the Apple II. These are more complicated computers that require more complex software. And, IBM is now in the marketplace, and its dominance naturally attracts the vendors more than does second-place Apple.

Apple has sold the largest number of PCs in the educational system of any manufacturer. The belief is that once a student uses a certain computer, he or she will want the organization to have the same PC on his/her job when he or she grows up and goes to work.

One area that Apple has been able to really shine in is the educational market. *Future Computing* estimates that over half the computers in use in schools are Apple-manufactured.

The Mac Attack

The Macintosh has been advertised as "so advanced you already know how to use it." The Macintosh, or "Mac" as it is affectionately known in Apple, began life in 1979 when Jef Raskin, who was at that time the writer of the first comprehensive manual for the Apple II, was asked to build a computer that could sell for less than $500 and could work through the average family television set. After producing a cardboard mock-up, Raskin code-named the machine Macintosh, intentionally misspelling the name of his favorite

Apple. With the assistance of just two others, Raskin attempted to make the Macintosh as easy to use as a household television set.

The Macintosh can do a lot of things that no other machine can do. But it is not without its critics. People who are confident in the utilization of computers say that the mouse is really a turnoff, that the Macintosh is not a high-powered machine, that it can't do a lot of things that other machines can, and the fact that it can do a few things really well does not offset that problem. Most authorities will tell you that it is a superior machine to the IBM PC in many ways. But once you get past being a novice in the use of computers, the mouse is really not that beneficial. The mouse is very efficient if you have a limited number of tasks and you want to learn quickly how to do those tasks. But this "plastic rodent" is useless for word processing and not of much use for spreadsheet analysis, two of the major uses of a personal computer. Again, the additional development of software may overcome many of these problems, but perhaps not the perceptions of them as problems. Many people feel there just is no substitute for the keyboard. The bottom line, though, is that the mouse functions very well in one important area—it sells a lot of computers. Another problem with the Macintosh is that its screen is only 60 characters wide, which is not appropriate for most word processing jobs. Most word processing tasks need a screen to be 80 characters wide. Furthermore, even though the Macintosh has built-in word processing, it is not very strong and many people have found it to be too limited for their needs.

It is evident that for at least FY 1985 and 1986, the Macintosh must carry Apple Computers. The company's actions suggest that the company must move ahead into the office market with the Macintosh if indeed it is to continue to successfully sell Macintosh for that period of time. The problem among large business buyers seems to be image. The perception among corporate decision makers appears to be that the Macintosh is not a serious business computer. What Sculley and Jobs want to do is convince those who don't need really strong financial capabilities in their personal computers that the Macintosh is a viable alternative to the IBM PC for data base management and word processing. They want the market to realize that it is so much easier to use—"It's the computer for the rest of us." Their strategy is aimed at changing perceptions and increasing product capabilities. The Macintosh will soon be able to talk to IBM computers. It was anticipated that as early as January 1985, Apple would announce a line of office products that would make the Macintosh not just a standard PC, but an entire office system. A laser printer has been developed. A communication network which is very inexpensive, the Apple Tree, was expected to be available at that time also. Most people do anticipate that this will mean then that the Macintosh will be able to talk to other computers. Sculley states: "What we need is a gateway into the IBM world. We don't want customers put into the position of having to live with two incompatible standards."

Another major focal point of this strategy will be to speed the development of the Macintosh software. Without software, it doesn't matter how good the computer is—it cannot succeed. Apple had in fact reached an agreement with Lotus to develop a Lotus 1-2-3 version in early 1985, possibly as early as mid-March. This will enable Apple to appeal to those who need financial capabilities. Other software writers are being encouraged through various means to write software for Apple. Perhaps one of the most important reasons for these firms to write software for Apple is the fact that IBM is now beginning to develop its own software for its PCs. Software houses do not want to be captive to IBM nor do they want to be displaced by IBM. Therefore, it behooves them to help Apple stay in the market; otherwise there may be no market for their products if IBM, as it apparently intends to do, moves rapidly into software development.

One of the problems that Apple has faced in the past has been its technical writing—that is, the manuals which are produced to assist individuals in learning how to use the computer. Apple has recently undertaken a major program of rewriting these in order to make the computer not only easy to use, but easy to learn to use.

Another action that is being taken is to woo very large corporations such as Honeywell or General Motors. The feeling is that if they can move the Macintosh into a large number of highly visible corporations, others will follow. One of the things that Apple did was to sign up several major universities to high-volume contracts on the Macintosh, thus further increasing their influence in that highly important and visible market. Apple's only real major success to date in the office market was the purchase of 4,500 Macintoshes by Peat, Marwick, Mitchell and Company, the big accounting firm.

Another action is being taken to improve dealer relationships. Apple has increased its distribution points from 1,500 to 2,000 retail centers. It has a 350-person sales force which trains the employees of these distribution centers and services these. Another key point in the strategy is to form strategic alliances. It is reported that efforts are underway to work out a selling arrangement with Wang Computers and maybe even with AT&T.

The Apple IIc

The Apple IIc is an innovative use of a standard product. It has an easy to use 80-column text display and a broad range of colors comes with it. It has 128K characters in memory, a built-in disk drive, and a modem. It promises a flat-screen display which, while not offered at introduction, was expected within a few months. Part of the capability of the Apple IIc flows from the fact that, whereas several chips had been used in the Apple IIe to perform the same functions, only a single chip in the Apple IIc performed those functions. The Apple IIc also employs a technology called complimentary metal oxide semiconductors, or CMOS. CMOS is especially important because it uses very little power, allowing the IIc to be so portable. The technology associated with the CMOS has been considered outdated for many years but, with the advent of portable computers, the product lifecycle of this technology was lengthened. Later versions of this particular chip will allow the computer to work probably ten times as fast as it does now. An interesting product concept has arisen from this technology and that is the theme of "Apple II Forever."

Doing Battle with the IBM PC Jr.

In its initial launching, the IBM PC Jr. was a dismal failure. It was absolutely trounced by the seven-year-old Apple IIe. In fact once the PC Jr. came out, the IIe actually set sales records. One of the key problems was that the PC Jr. had little software available for it, whereas the Apple IIe had over 15,000 programs available. The PC Jr. also had several design feature problems, for example, a "cheap-looking" keyboard and limited memory. While it was advertised at a low price to be effective and was packaged to perform financial analyses, it would cost as much or more than the Apple IIe. The PC Jr., after its reintroduction in August, has been extremely well received, however. Its sales volume has been significantly higher.

Promotion Strategy

It's clear from the Macintosh introduction at the Super Bowl that occurred in 1984, from the nature of the later advertisements, and from the expenditure of $80 million during 1984 for advertising, that Sculley's impact on Apple has been significant. Recognizing the PC as a consumer product, Sculley has transformed the approach taken to advertising at Apple from one of a nuisance to one of paramount importance. It takes a lot of dollars to compete in a maturing market with a higher number of competitors, and Apple, under Sculley, has been willing to commit those dollars.

Apple spent $15 million just to introduce Macintosh between its TV campaign and its tractor trailer sideshow that it took to 1,500 dealers. The $15 million introduction of Macintosh compares less than favorably with the $40 million that was spent promoting PC Jr. in 1984. However, one must note that the effectiveness of this advertising depends upon the style with which it is done and the product itself.

All companies must carefully orchestrate product introductions. Part of that process involves the courting of the press. The press is extremely important in terms of making a successful product introduction in major consumer product markets. It is critical to whom you give information, at what time, and where. Advertising helps, but nothing succeeds like a very strong news article placed in the right journal, magazine, or paper at the right time. An article tells the people in the target market that you want to reach exactly what you want them to know, so it is extremely important that the company cater to, relate to, and work with the press to get them to do the "kind of advertising that you want them to do." Before IBM, this kind of concern for the press wasn't really necessary at Apple. Apple had the market—at least it had most of the market it wanted—but when the IBM PC became the dominant product, it became necessary to change the approach which the company used to reach its target market. Apple was very careful to court the press regarding Macintosh.

Pricing Strategy

As do most computer manufacturers, Apple introduces its products at higher prices, then takes a series of price reductions in order to be more competitive. Having sold to the early adopters with the higher prices, they then reduce prices to attract the mass market. Unlike many products, however, it only takes a matter of a few months in the PC industry to go from the highest price to substantially lower prices.

The Automated Apple Orchard

One Macintosh rolls off the end of the highly automated computer assembly line every 27 seconds in the Fremont, California, factory of today's future. It employs a "just-in-time" system of inventory management, is regulated by a single Macintosh, and has only a few people working within the plant. The plant is designed to last for two years and the new plant, even more automated, will build new Macintoshes or other machines. The plant's manager, Peter Baron, says "We know how to build a better factory in less time, money, and space. We have to be the lowest-cost producer in the world by the time the Japanese figure out how to make a good computer." The Apple Macintosh is a very easy

Exhibit 22.6   The Automated Apple Orchard

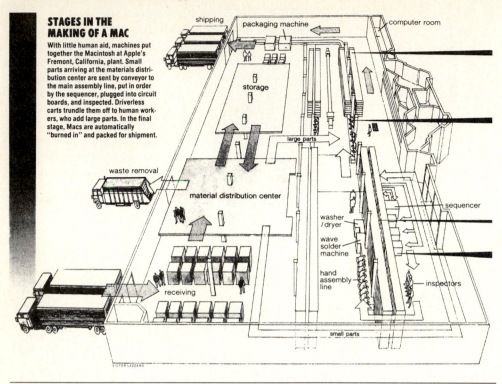

STAGES IN THE MAKING OF A MAC

With little human aid, machines put together the Macintosh at Apple's Fremont, California, plant. Small parts arriving at the materials distribution center are sent by conveyor to the main assembly line, put in order by the sequencer, plugged into circuit boards, and inspected. Driverless carts trundle them off to human workers, who add large parts. In the final stage, Macs are automatically "burned in" and packed for shipment.

shipping

packaging machine

computer room

storage

large parts

waste removal

material distribution center

sequencer

washer / dryer

wave solder machine

hand assembly line

inspectors

receiving

small parts

VICTOR LAZZARO

Source: Victor Lazzaro © *Discover* Magazine, September 1985, Time Inc., p. 80.

machine to mass produce. It goes together quite easily. For example there are only 50 integrated circuits in its main brain, 75 percent fewer than in the IBM PC. The machine was designed so that other machines could assemble it.

Exhibit 22.6 contains a diagram of the Apple PC plant. As soon as materials are received in the receiving area, a computer-driven crane places them in proper cubbyholes, retrieving them as needed for assembly. Another machine called a sequencer picks parts and places them in the order in which they will be needed in assembly. In essence there are two assembly lines—one makes the logic board and another the analogue board. Then a series of additional machines, known as automatic component insertors, plug the various chips and parts into the Macintosh's main circuit board. Little work is performed by human beings. The larger parts, primarily the candy bar-sized Motorola 68000 microprocessor, which is the real brains of the computer, must be inserted by humans; but then the machines take over the process once again. There are automatic solderers to make electrical connections, other devices to clean the boards, and computer-controlled driverless vehicles to take the finished product to another line for final assembly. Disk drives and power supplies are added by hand before the machine is slipped into its plastic case. The machines are then processed for 24 hours in what is known as the "burning tower," where each machine is put through its paces—various tests for temperature, software, and other abuses. (A single Macintosh controls each of the factory's two, seven-tier burn racks.)

After this, the newly manufactured machine is packed in a box for shipping. Total time to manufacture the machine, exclusive of the 24-hour burn-in, is 26 minutes.

The factory is currently capable of handling about 500,000 computers per year with only 300 workers. Debra Coleman, the controller for the Macintosh project, says that Apple did not invest in this automated factory to reduce its labor costs, but rather to introduce automation they felt was essential for quality control. However, as stated earlier, future plants, which will be based on this one, will be designed to lower costs in order to be competitive with the Japanese. Apple's executives, including Jobs himself, toured Japanese factories before the introduction of the Macintosh. They were very very concerned about the ability of Japanese firms to produce products at very little cost and they wanted to learn how to do it.

Because of Apple's sales successes in 1984, it announced in July that it was intending to build a second manufacturing plant similar to the first one. It will be an expansion of the existing plant in Fremont, California. Since the company intended to sell an expanded memory version of the Macintosh, they were selling the 40,000-per-month capacity of the current plant. It was thus necessary to add an additional manufacturing facility.

Management Changes

The historical patterns in Apple's top management reflect its entrepreneurial nature, the fact that the firm has been forced to mature rapidly in face of competition from IBM, and the various power bases within the company. Wozniak never really participated in managing the organization. This left Stephen Jobs and Mike Markkula as the two key top managers. Jobs was always somewhat on the periphery, although he was important in making certain decisions. His inexperience contributed to his being left somewhat on the sidelines as more experienced managers engaged in strategic planning.

It occurred simultaneously to the development of the Macintosh that some rather Byzantine politics were going on inside the company. Apple cofounder, Steven Jobs, who at that time was just a vice-president, wanted in fact to head the development of the Lisa project which the company was engaged in. However, then Apple President Michael Scott and marketing boss Mike Markkula apparently regarded him as purely erratic and inexperienced to handle this major new product introduction. As a consolation, some say Jobs was given the Mac program and Raskin was shoved aside. Gary Martin, who was then an Apple accountant, comments: "Jobs got Mac because it was a small group. Scott and Markkula thought it would keep him out of their hair and he wouldn't bother the Lisa people." As a consequence of the way in which this project situation had been handled, Jobs assumed somewhat of a personal vendetta against the Lisa project and Markkula and Scott. Mac programmer Andy Hertsfeld claims that Steve Jobs said: "I'll get this team that will make a cheap computer and blow the Lisa team off the face of the earth." From that point forward Jobs seemed as though he was driven, sometimes maniacally, to achieve his victory over the Lisa project. He often launched impossible objectives, but his people met them more often than not. There was a tremendous competition which developed between the Macintosh and Lisa projects. In fact, Jobs bet $5,000 with the Lisa Division Director, John Couch, that Macintosh would hit the market sooner than Lisa. That was not to be true. What a situation to occur in a company—two divisions locked in head-to-head battle for market presence! Many foul-ups occurred, probably partly as a result of this conflict. For example, the original disk drive that was intended for Macintosh, and in which the company invested about $6 million in development costs, was ultimately scratched for a disk drive made by Sony.

Eventually Scott and Markkula left Apple, leaving Jobs as chairman looking for a replacement for Markkula as CEO. This he found in John Sculley.

John Sculley

Many felt that Sculley was hired originally because of his marketing expertise. He had, after all, come from one of the premier consumer goods marketing firms in the United States, Pepsi-Co, in May 1983. But it is also evident that Sculley is multidimensional, capable of functioning in all the major areas of the firm. One of the things that Sculley does is immerse himself in the job. Above all, he is a nuts-and-bolts man. He has become capable of talking with Apple's best hardware engineers, he knows the product, he knows what it's all about, he knows how it's designed and engineered and manufactured. He is presently learning the same kind of technical knowledge for software. He, like most really good CEOs, immerses himself in the product.

In his first year he was able to oversee two product launchings, Macintosh and the IIc. He consolidated five product divisions into two. This was an extremely important undertaking on his part. Apple had five products, all of which operated independently, had their own strategic plans, and were not in any way coordinated. So Sculley combined the two more advanced machines, the Lisa and the Macintosh, into one unit. There are reports that the reorganization of Apple, especially the combination of the two divisions of Lisa and Macintosh, caused a lot of morale problems within the company. One insider stated: "There's a lot of anguish at Apple these days." Sculley similarly combined the IIe, the IIc, and the Apple III into one unit as well. He also sought to improve earnings through increased sales of Macintosh and through increased sales of other products. Heavy advertising was part of the strategy. In addition, he began to develop a strategy for competing with IBM head-on in the office market. Sculley also decentralized certain functions: manufacturing, finance, and marketing. He also took efforts to increase accountability. Fifteen division managers who reported to group vice-presidents were instructed to begin reporting to him directly. Seven of these 15 were quickly replaced.

Sculley is an unusual visionary. He actually does see past the current year, a rarity among top executives. He says that he wants Apple to be a role model for the *Fortune 500* in the 1990s. As an example of how he attempted to accommodate to the style of Apple Computer, he enclosed tickets to *Indiana Jones and the Temple of Doom* with everybody's paycheck. He claims: "I'm more a professor than a professional manager; my job has been more coaching the organization than doing it myself. My technique is to get people to do great things." Jobs indicates that one of the real pluses that Sculley brought to the firm was his fresh perspective—the ability to say "This makes sense and that doesn't." Sculley often thinks and plots Apple strategy while he engages in his early-morning three-mile run. Sculley looks at the position of Apple Computer in the industry as extremely critical. He comments: "In a consumer business there is only room for two strong competitors. Nobody remembers number three."

He is also a clear communicator. He initiated a policy that no memo would be longer than one page. When he first came on board he also reduced hiring from 250 people per month to 50 people per month to give the company time to stabilize. Interestingly enough, he successfully pulled off the suspension of the company's generous profit-sharing program. And he engaged many employees in discussions of the mistakes Apple had made and how Apple could be improved. His comment regarding the latter was: "This organization has never been battle-tested to be faced with serious questions about Apple's survival . . . was an incredible shock. The threat that Camelot might not be here anymore made my job a lot easier," he claims. One high-level manager suggested that "He made us respect IBM." Donald Kendall, his former boss at Pepsi-Co, suggests that he's "never heard anybody talk negatively about Sculley. He's very loyal to his people, and he backs them all the way, and he doesn't overmanage." Sculley claims that only one person runs Apple, "Steven and me." Finally, he also added discipline to the company. The results of his efforts have been very impressive. He must be given an A for his performance in his first year as CEO.

Financial Strategies and Performance

The "lean" approach to management is evident at Apple. Labor costs are held low but not solely for the fact of cost control so much as a consequence of their concern for keeping quality high. Nonetheless, the large use of robotics and high-tech manufacturing does keep the cost of manufacturing low, an intentional strategy. The belief is that Apple must be able to compete on cost because of the invasion of Japanese PCs which is expected before too long.

The funds for Apple's early product research and development came previously from the initial offering of stock. The company's current strategy is to use the cash flow that it receives from its sales to fund its necessary capital additions and its research and development. Apple has a standing line of credit of about $125 million with various banks. Apple's $1.5 billion sales in 1984 was a 54 percent increase over fiscal year 1983 sales. Fourth quarter sales were almost a half billion dollars, $477 million, a 75 percent increase over the fourth quarter of fiscal year 1983. Net income in the fourth quarter was $30.8 million or $.50 per share, the highest quarterly profit ever achieved by Apple and in excess of the goal of $.40 per share which Apple had announced earlier last November. (See Exhibits 22.1 to 22.5.)

Corporate Culture

One of the unique features of most of the firms in the Silicon Valley is their corporate cultures. InTel is known, for example, as a very unstructured, highly decentralized, highly participative organization. Tandem Computers, one of the main moving forces in the minicomputer market, has similarly been known for its unique programs of motivation of its employees, its benefits, its flexible office hours, and so on. Apple Computer's culture is very similar to that of these and other high-tech firms. It has what is known as an "open-shirt" culture. Very few ties will be seen in the company, very few people wear business suits. Most people wear jeans and knit shirts. The organization is participative. The office hours are long, often 90 hours per week. The atmosphere at Apple is one of almost religious fervor for the objective of overcoming IBM and putting a computer in the hands of every man, woman, and child in the United States. Apple's rewards are great for its employees, many of whom are millionares because of their early-on stock purchases of the firm. Many parties are held and champagne flows often, but that champagne creates high morale which induces people to work even harder, perhaps to stay all night on a project. Apple's managers use a walking-around management style, meaning that managers, including the president and chairman, mingle with workers on the assembly line, in the cafeteria, and elsewhere, and that managers talk to employees as catalysts, coaches, and facilitators rather than as bosses.

Jobs himself has contributed much to this culture, being a very laid-back person with a lot of ideals that conflict with what you would think of your typical chairman of the board. He himself has said that he probably would be a poet on the Left Bank in Paris if he hadn't discovered the Apple computer.

The workers are dedicated "Blue-busters," a phrase which takes off on the 1984 summer hit movie *Ghostbusters*. This firm really believes that it can defeat IBM. But this culture lacks discipline and many have described Apple as arrogant. Apple employees were astonished to realize that anyone else could develop a personal computer besides themselves. They were open for attack from IBM and this arrogance, combined with the inability to launch successful new products, caused them in 1983 to need someone to demonstrate to them that indeed there was a competitor out there who could succeed. That someone was John Sculley and the competitor was IBM. Even though IBM may have had an inferior product, it still knocked the Apple off its limb. Sculley has modified the culture but he has not changed it dramatically. He simply has attempted to provide more concern for competition and increased awareness of what the opposition is doing. He created an awareness among employees that Apple was not invincible.

One of the major realizations that Apple had to make was that, even though they may be folk heroes to people in the industry, people in the industry don't buy computers. Middle managers, upper-level managers, and purchasing agents make decisions on the computers that will be used in their organizations, and as one purchasing agent said: "No one ever got fired for buying IBM." It's clear that if Apple is to succeed in the office market, it must make inroads into the psychological environment of the decision makers in that market. To do so, it must have a more competitive-oriented, and must be a more goal-oriented, culture. It cannot create products simply for the sake of creating products; products must be salable. Apple IIe, IIc, and Macintosh were tremendous successes. But it could have been otherwise had these not had market appeal.

Jobs had the vision to push for the Macintosh—a low-priced business alternative to the IBM PC. His was a brilliant move and his religious fervor for that product was what carried it to the market so successfully. Sometimes however, Jobs's personality wears thin on those around him. He is known to have fits of temper, and he's often known to move in several directions at one time. It was, in fact, his dislike for the Lisa project that caused him to quit that project and launch the Macintosh. He felt that the Lisa was inappropriately priced—too high for the market—and that it wouldn't sell. He turned out to be correct in that evaluation. But his move to develop a similar but lower-priced product, Macintosh, actually caused marketing problems with the Lisa because the firm announced two products in the same year, one much cheaper than the other one, but both possessing essentially the same capabilities. This caused sales of the Lisa to be not very substantial at first.

Sculley is changing the culture to make it much more performance-based. While Sculley himself has the traditional corner office, he is now moving towards the design of a new headquarters where public areas, and not the executive offices, will have windows.

Sculley himself seldom wears a coat and tie now in the office and looks a lot more like the people he manages than many thought he ever could. It is unique that Steve Jobs and John Sculley virtually manage the company together. Fortunately the two get along well.

Employee Relations

Apple has three various stock options plans. Officers, directors, employees, and contractors may be granted options to purchase shares of Apple's common stock at the fair market value the day of the grant. Several amendments have been made so that employees can exercise options at lower stock prices.

Future Direction

The mission of Apple Computer was described earlier as one of making people computer literate. John Sculley states that he feels "Apple has the chance to become the second-largest computer company in the entire industry by the 1990s." If that came true, Apple would be larger than DEC which is currently (1984) number two, or Burroughs Corporation, a very prominent firm at this point in time. Sculley goes on to say: "We want to be a clear alternative to IBM. We are not content to exist on the edge of a corporate giant." Macintosh is viewed as a low-cost, easy-to-use "computer for the masses." What lies beyond Macintosh is not known at this moment, although several enhancements to the Macintosh system have been proposed, as noted earlier. The product after Macintosh has not been announced. Some wonder if it's being developed.

Sculley indicates:

In 1985 we will not become complacent, we will continue to implement the strategies we put in place during 1984. We are making technology-leading computers which are attractive to people who have never before used computers, thereby opening important new markets and assuring Apple's continued growth.

Sculley observes that IBM's objective is to have the entire business PC market.

References

"A *Newsweek* Full of Apples." *Business Week*, October 15, 1984, p. 88.

Apple Computer, Inc. *Annual Report 1983*.

Apple Computer, Inc. *Annual Report 1984*.

"Apple Computer's Counterattack Against IBM." *Business Week*, January 16, 1984, pp. 78–81.

"Apple, Ford Buy Exclusive Ad Rights." *The Orlando Sentinel*, November 13, 1984, p. D-2.

"Apple Launches A Mac Attack." *Time*, January 30, 1984, pp. 68–69.

"Apple Takes On Its Biggest Test Yet." *Business Week*, January 31, 1983, pp. 70–79.

Bellew, Patricia A., "Apple Is Set To Unveil Bold Ad Campaign In Big Push Into Office Computer Market." *The Wall Street Journal*, November 1, 1984, p. 33.

Bellew, Patricia A., "Apple Says Profit Increased Sixfold In Its 4th Quarter." *The Wall Street Journal*, October 18, 1984, p. 10.

Chase, Marilyn. "Technical Flaws Plague Apple's New Computer." *The Wall Street Journal*, April 15, 1981, p. 31.

Chase, Marilyn. "Test of Time—As Competition Grows, Apple Computer Inc. Faces A Critical Period." *The Wall Street Journal*, November 11, 1981, p. 1.

Dolan, Carrie. "Apple Computer Will Introduce A Portable Version of Popular IIe Model." *The Wall Street Journal*, April 24, 1984, p. 8.

Dolan, Carrie. "Apple Faces Challenge Selling New Computer for Home Use." *The Wall Street Journal*, May 3, 1984, p. 31.

Dolan, Carrie. "Apple's New MacIntosh Computer Is Seen As Critical To Firm's Future." *The Wall Street Journal*, December 8, 1983, p. 33.

Dreyfuss, Joel. "John Sculley Rises In The West." *Fortune*, July 9, 1984, pp. 180–183.

"How Apple Is Bullying IBM's PC, Jr." *Business Week*, April 16, 1984, p. 124.

Hurley, Patricia Galagan. "Apple's Answer: The Worm Is Turning." *Training and Development Journal*, May, 1983, pp. 16–17.

Kisor, Henry. "Macintosh Has Detractors But Also Has Fans." *The Orlando Sentinel*, November 3, 1984, p. G-10.

Kneale, Dennis. "Home-Computer Stores Fear Sales Could Be Slow For Christmas Season." *The Wall Street Journal*, November 5, 1984, p. 35.

The IBM PC, October 1984

▪ *James M. Higgins* ▪

International Business Machines Corporation (IBM) or "Big Blue," as it is more commonly known in the industry, had sales of $40 billion and profits of $5.5 billion in 1983 (See Exhibit 23.1.) In 1984, IBM's stated objectives are to more than double its revenues to $100 billion by 1990, and to nearly double these again by 1994 to at least $185 billion. Sales in 1984 are expected to reach $46 billion. It seeks to become the world's largest manufacturing corporation by 1995. IBM is riding the crest of a wave that is changing America from an industrial society to an information society.

IBM was founded in 1911 as the Computer-Tabulating-Recording Company. It acquired its present name in 1924. In 1984, it employs over 370,000 people worldwide and has approximately 770,000 shareholders. International Business Machines is headquartered in Armonk, New York. (See Exhibit 23.2.) It had assets at the end of 1983 totaling $37.2 billion. It has five major strategic SBU groups: mainframe computers, peripheral devices, PCs and workstations, software, and other products. Sales for these divisions in 1983 were respectively: $10.7 billion, $11.0 billion, $8 billion, $2.3 billion, and $8.2 billion. IBM is the dominant firm in the mainframe computer market, in the peripheral devices market, and in the PC market. It is a dominant force in the mainframe software market but it is not a dominant force in the software market for PCs. IBM is, however, attempting to become a dominant PC software firm. IBM is the leading seller of mainframe hardware in Europe, dominating with some 70 percent of the total market. With such dominance across the industry, IBM is a veritable juggernaut.

Corporate Mission and Objectives

IBM's operations, with very minor exceptions, are in the field of information handling systems, equipment and services to solve the increasingly complex problems of business, government, science, space exploration, defense, education, medicine, and many other areas of human activity. IBM's products include data processing machines and systems, telecommunications systems and products, information distributors, office systems, copiers, typewriters, educational testing materials and related supplies and services. Most products are both leased and sold through authorized dealers and markets.

IBM attributes much of its current success to strategies developed in the mid-1970s. At that time, it anticipated major changes in the use of information systems and perceived that the market would grow tremendously. IBM therefore decided to become a full participant across all product lines in the industry. Central to IBM's strategy are four key business goals: growth, product leadership, efficiency, and profitability. To attain these goals in today's highly competitive environment, IBM has placed an increased emphasis on

This case is not intended to portray the effective or the ineffective handling of an administrative situation. Rather, it is intended for classroom discussion. All rights reserved to the contributor. Prepared as part of a research project funded by the Roy E. Crummer Graduate School of Business, Rollins College.

Exhibit 23.1   International Business Machines Corporation and Subsidiary Companies
Consolidated Statement of Earnings (dollars in millions except per share amounts)

	Year Ending December 31,		
	1983	1982	1981
Gross income:			
Sales	$23,274	$16,815	$12,901
Rentals	9,230	11,121	10,839
Services	7,676	6,428	5,330
Total gross sales	$40,180	$34,364	$29,070
Cost of sales	9,748	6,682	5,162
Cost of rentals	3,141	3,959	4,041
Cost of services	3,506	3,047	2,534
Selling, general and administrative expenses	10,614	9,286[†]	8,383[†]
Research, development, and engineering expenses	3,582	3,042	2,451
Interest expense	390	454	407
Total cost of sales	30,981	26,470	22,978
Net income	9,199	7,894	6,092
Other income, principally interest	741	328	368
Earnings before income taxes	9,940	8,222	6,460
Provision for income taxes	4,455	3,813*	2,850*
Net earnings	$ 5,485	$ 4,409	$ 3,610
Per share	$ 9.04	$ 7.39	$ 6.14
Average number of shares outstanding: 1983—606,769,848 1982—596,688,501 1981—587,803,373			

*State and local income taxes have been reclassified to conform with 1983 presentation.

innovative programs and design, and on the manufacture and distribution of products and services. At the same time, IBM maintains effective cost control and high quality of products.

IBM is reaching these objectives. For example, in 1983 and 1984, they will match and in most areas exceed the industry growth rate. Their continued emphasis on new products in the mainframe and IBM PC areas, for example, shows that they will continue to push for product leadership. The introduction of new products allows them to lower prices on old products, enabling them to gain market share. Their goal is to become the most efficient company in the industry and they have developed many, many programs to achieve that end. Several major programs of quality improvement have been instituted at virtually every IBM location. Many employees have been sent to quality training programs throughout the U.S., but primarily at Phil Crosby's Quality College in Winter Park, Florida. It is their general belief that if they reach growth, product leadership, and efficiency targets, they will consequently become highly profitable. 1983 was a record year for profits for IBM, and it was expected that 1984 would be also. (See Exhibits 23.1 and 23.2) The component divisions of IBM are shown in Exhibit 23.3.

Exhibit 23.2   International Business Machines Corporation and Subsidiary Companies
Consolidated Statement of Financial Position (dollars in millions)

	1983		1982	
Assets				
Current assets:				
Cash	$ 616		$ 405	
Marketable securities, at lower of cost or market	4,920		2,895	
Notes and accounts receivable—trade, net of allowances	5,735		4,976	
Other accounts receivable	645		457	
Inventories	4,381		3,492	
Prepaid expenses	973		789	
		$17,270		$13,014
Rental machines and parts	13,409		16,527	
Less: accumulated depreciation	6,597		7,410	
		6,812		9,117
Plant and other property	15,778		14,240	
Less: accumulated depreciation	6,448		5,794	
		9,330		8,446
Investments and other assets		3,831		1,964
Total assets		$37,243		$32,541
Liabilities and stockholders' equity				
Current liabilities:				
Taxes	$ 3,220		$ 2,854	
Loans payable	532		529	
Accounts payable	1,253		983	
Compensation and benefits	2,450		1,959	
Deferred income	382		402	
Other accrued expenses and liabilities	1,670		1,482	
		$ 9,507		$ 8,209
Deferred income taxes		713		323
Reserves for employees' indemnities and retirement plans		1,130		1,198
Long-term debt		2,674		2,851
Stockholders' equity:				
Capital stock, par value $1.25 per share	5,800		5,008	
Shares authorized: 750,000,000				
Issued: 1983—610,724,641; 1982—602,406,128				
Retained earnings	19,489		16,259	
Translation adjustments	(2,070)		(1,307)	
Total stockholders' equity		23,219		19,960
Total liabilities and stockholders' equity		$37,243		$32,541

Exhibit 23.3   IBM Organization

IBM is organized into the following groups, divisions and wholly owned subsidiaries:

Information Systems Group

Customer Service Division

Provides maintenance, related support and programming services within the U.S. and its territories for assigned products.

Federal Systems Division

Provides specialized information-handling and control systems to the Federal government for seaborne, spaceborne, airborne and ground-based environments. Also participates in applied research and exploratory development.

Field Engineering Division

Provides maintenance and related services within the U.S. and its territories for assigned products, as well as support for specific IBM program offerings. Has overall responsibility for the distribution of all hardware and software products and related publications. Also provides maintenance marketing support and central programming services for assigned products.

IBM Instruments, Inc. (a subsidiary)

Has responsibility for IBM's efforts in the analytical instruments field, including marketing and servicing selected products in the U.S.

National Accounts Division

Has marketing and field administration responsibility within the U.S. and its territories for the full standard line of IBM products. Its assigned customers are selected large accounts with complex information processing needs.

National Distribution Division

Has marketing responsibility within the US. for selected systems and high-volume products delivered through alternate channels of distribution such as IBM Product Centers, value added remarketers and authorized dealers. In addition, the division has responsibility for manufacturing or procurement and marketing within the U.S. of IBM supplies and accessories, as well as for the worldwide supplies business strategy.

National Marketing Division

Has marketing and field administration responsibility within the U.S. and its territories for the full standard line of IBM products. Its assigned customers are large and medium accounts.

Information Systems and Technology Group

Data Systems Division

Has worldwide development and associated programming responsibility for large, complex systems, with primary emphasis on high-performance products, plus U.S. manufacturing responsibility for those systems.

General Products Division

Has worldwide development and U.S. manufacturing responsibility for storage systems, including tap units, disk products and mass storage systems, program products and product-related programming.

General Technology Division

Has worldwide development and product assurance and U.S. manufacturing responsibility for logic, memory and special semiconductor devices and multi-layer ceramics. The division also procures components for the IBM World Trade Americas/Far East Corporation and U.S. operating units.

Systems Technology Division

Has worldwide development and product assurance and U.S. manufacturing responsibility for circuit packaging used in IBM computing systems. Also develops and manufactures intermediate processors and printers and develops programming systems.

Exhibit 23.3   *continued*

Information Systems and Communications Group

Communication Products Division

Has worldwide development and U.S. manufacturing responsibility for telecommunications systems, display products, distribution industry systems and related programming. The division serves as the worldwide architectural and systems focal pont for office systems and Systems Network Architecture activities.

Entry Systems Division

Has worldwide development and product management, and U.S. manufacturing responsibility for IBM's general purpose, low-cost, personal-use computer systems and related software.

Information Products Division

Has worldwide development and related programming and U.S. manufacturing responsibility for typewriters, copiers and systems for the banking industry, and for peripheral equipment, including printers, copier systems, diskettes and associated supplies.

System Products Division

Has worldwide development and U.S. manufacturing responsibility for small and intermediate-sized general purpose systems and related programming, as well as for low-end direct access storage devices.

Other Divisions

Real Estate and Construction Division

Manages the selection and acquisition of sites, the design and construction of buildings and the purchase or lease of facilities for all IBM operations in the U.S. The division has responsibility for assessing real estate projects outside the U.S., as well as for IBM's worldwide energy and environmental programs. It also provides facility services to selected headquarters locations.

Research Division

Brings scientific understanding to bear on areas of company interest through basic research and development of technologies of potential long-range importance.

Other Subsidiaries

IBM Credit Corporation

Offers lease financing of IBM products, either directly or through partnerships, and finances installment receivables resulting from sales by IBM of its information processing systems and equipment to customers in the U.S. It also finances non-IBM equipment.

Science Research Associates, Inc.

Has worldwide development, publication and/or marketing responsibility for a wide range of educational and testing materials and services, including microcomputer software designed for use in schools, colleges, businesses and the home.

IBM World Trade Americas/Far East Corporation

With a territory extending across four continents, this subsidiary is responsible for IBM operations in 46 countries, including Australia, Brazil, Canada and Japan.

IBM World Trade Europe/Middle East/Africa Corporation

Through its subsidiary, IBM Europe, located in Paris, it is responsible for IBM operations in 85 countries.

IBM World Trade Corporation

Provides designated support to IBM World Trade organizational units.

Source: IBM 1983 Annual Report.

Corporate Culture

One of the unique features of International Business Machines has always been its corporate culture. It embodies most of what William Ouchu has described in the Theory organization. For example, one of its primary motivational forces has been its paternalistic management. IBM has never laid off an employee for lack of business. Once an employee comes to IBM, he or she is assured of a job for as long as he or she wishes it and as long as he or she continues to perform. IBM has even gone so far as to move 2,000 people to IBM locations through the U.S. when it closed a plant. These types of actions keep morale high. Additional Theory cultural factors that IBM possesses include a little-bit-slower promotion and evaluation than might occur in many firms, but still, quicker than in many others. There also exists a loose/tight control system for employees. Objectives are well known in advance, and are high. Performances are reviewed formally periodically, but there is also informal supervision from management on a continuing basis. One interesting motivational strategy used by IBM is that of establishing sales and production quotas at levels that most employees can meet. This allows for achievement and success, which then allows for people to build upon that success. This is in direct contrast to the way in which many of its competitors set exceedingly high goals, such that only a few of their sales or production people can possibly meet them. Typically IBM has never engaged in high-visibility marketing promotions.

The classic stereotype of an IBM individual is one wearing a dark gray suit, a white shirt or blouse, and formal shoes. Indeed above certain levels in IBM, this is still the standard uniform, male or female. That appearance is a prerequisite for success is one of their fundamental beliefs. IBM conducts its business in a highly ethical manner and employees are ingrained in that philosophy. For example, professional employees are required to read a 30-page pamphlet on ethics and conduct their business accordingly. Another sign of their culture is the fact that the employee magazine is called *Think*, one of the favorite statements of the late Thomas Watson Sr., IBM's founder.

In recent years, IBM has begun to "loosen up" its culture. There used to be a process known as the oversight process, wherein IBM's corporate operations office observed very closely all actions of subdivisions of the company. Since 1981, IBM has created and allowed loose controls on more than a dozen "independent" business units. This is an effort to provide more freedom to operate. The firm's IBM PC resulted from just such an operation. Another sign of the loosening of IBM's control and the changing of its culture is its willingness to work with second and third parties, in joint ventures, in licensing products, and in the release of competitive details to third parties and the public to allow them to provide products and services for IBM's computers. Other signs of the loosening of the corporate culture, not in the wholesale fashion but in a minor way, includes IBM's willingness now to become more "flashy" with its sales promotions and product launchings.

This change in culture was believed to be necessitated by the-then chairman Frank T. Carey who, in June of 1979, encouraged the development of the more freethinking "intrapreneurship" in the firm. In the 1970s IBM had been unable to establish strong positions in high-growth markets such as distributed data processing (DDP) and office automation. Consequently, Carey's management direction from 1980 and forward was to encourage IBM's managers to explore new high-growth markets such as the PC and to experiment with new distribution channels such as independent retailers. It was believed to be essential by Carey and members of the corporate management committee who designed this strategy in 1979, that not only should low-cost production and low-cost distribution and high-growth markets be targeted, but that the corporate management structure be changed to an independent product-driven structure in order to properly attack various industries segment by segment.

Financial Strategies and Results

Virtually all of IBM's financing comes from current operations. IBM carries very little long-term debt ($2.7 billion in 1983) and only on occasion is its stock sold by the company, much of this coming from stock plans for employees. (See Exhibits 23.1, 23.2, 23.3, 23.4, 23.5, 23.6, 23.7, and 23.8.) Its only major problems in earnings during 1983 and 1984 occurred because of the strong value of the dollar and its large number of overseas operations. (See Exhibit 23.4.) Tremendous amounts of money are being invested in both research and development and land, buildings, and equipment. Some $3.6 billion in 1983 was invested in R&D, $2.6 billion in plant and equipment. Important financial policies are noted in Exhibit 23.4.

Manufacturing Strategies

One of the four principal objectives of the IBM corporation mentioned earlier was efficiency in manufacturing. In 1984, IBM has approximately 113,000 manufacturing employees in some 40 plants working in 24 various countries. Due to federal government pressure, in 1956 the firm moved away from leasing and into sales of its products. In 1956 it had leased virtually all of its products; in 1984 it leased only about 15 percent of its products and sold about 85 percent. As a consequence it had to increase the number and size of its manufacturing facilities; it also had to modify its distribution channels.

Almost all of IBM's plants are at least partly automated, with full automation for most plants. Robots do many of the tasks—virtually all plants have some form of continuous automated manufacturing line, versus only one in three plants in 1980. Edward M. Davis, the Vice-President for Manufacturing, states that two out of three of the IBM plants look like your "classic high-tech." Davis admits that IBM wasn't the first with this approach (the Japanese were) but he says confidently, "But we will be (the leader)."

Because IBM had to become a much more efficient manufacturer, it had to begin buying items from others to use in its manufacturing process and in large quantities. IBM had previously manufactured almost all of its own parts. By 1983 IBM was purchasing as many parts as it was manufacturing. Estimates were that as high as 70 percent of the parts that it uses in its final assemblages would in fact be purchased from others in the near future. IBM has been able to succeed in becoming an efficient manufacturer at least partly because, in the past five years, from 1979 to 1984, IBM had spent $13 billion on land, buildings, and equipment and was only now beginning to realize the return on its investment for that $13 billion. The future holds even more investing. It is likely that the pace in investment is in fact accelerating in IBM with some $56 billion slated for investment in plant and equipment, and research and development, and engineering in the next five years (1985–1989).

There is only one acceptable level of quality in IBM manufacturing—and that is zero defects. IBM's plants are full of bold signs which promote such old-fashioned values as

Exhibit 23.4   International Business Machines Corporation and Subsidiary
Companies Notes to Consolidated Financial Statements:

Significant Accounting Policies

Principles of consolidation: The consolidated financial statements include the accounts of International Business Machines Corporation and its U.S. and non-U.S. subsidiary companies, other than the wholly owned IBM Credit Corporation and similar non-U.S. finance subsidiaries, for which the equity method is used. Investments in joint ventures, and other companies in which IBM has a 20 to 50 percent ownership, are accounted for by the equity method. Investments of less than 20 percent are accounted for by the cost method.

Translation of non-U.S. currency amounts: For non-U.S. subsidiaries which operate in a local currency environment, assets and liabilities are translated to U.S. dollars at year-end exchange rates. Income and expense items are translated at average rates of exchange prevailing during the year. Translation adjustments are accumulated in a separate component of stockholders' equity.

For non-U.S. subsidiaries and branches which operate in U.S. dollars or whose economic environment is highly inflationary, inventories and plant, rental machines and other property are translated at approximate rates prevailing when acquired. All other assets and liabilities are translated at year-end exchange rates. Inventories charged to cost of sales and depreciation are remeasured at historical rates. All other income and expense items are translated at average rates of exchange prevailing during the year. Gains and losses which result from remeasurement are included in earnings.

Gross income: Gross income is recognized from sales or sales-type leases when the product is shipped, or in certain cases upon customer acceptance, from rentals under operating leases in the month in which they accrue, and from services over the contractual period or as the services are performed. Rental plans include maintenance service and contain discontinuance and purchase option provisions. Rental terms are predominantly monthly or for a two-year period. IBM equipment offered under term leases by IBM's financing subsidiaries is accounted for by IBM as outright sales.

Program products: Costs related to the conceptual formulation and design of licensed programs are expensed as research and development. Costs incurred subsequent to a design verification test to produce the finished product are generally capitalized as program products assets. The assets are amortized over the estimated revenue-producing life of the program, but not in excess of five years. Ongoing costs to support or service licensed programs are expensed.

Depreciation: Rental machines, plant and other property are carried at cost and depreciated over their estimated useful lives. Depreciation of rental machines is computed using the sum-of-the-years digits method. Depreciation of plant and other property is computed using either accelerated methods or the straight-line method.

Retirement plans: Current service costs are accrued currently. Prior service costs resulting from improvements in the plans are amortized generally over 10 years.

Selling expenses: Selling expenses are charged against income as they are incurred.

Income taxes: Income tax expense is based on reported earnings before income taxes. It thus includes the effects of timing differences between reported and taxable earnings that arise because certain transactions are included in taxable earnings in other years. Investment tax credits are deferred and amortized as a result of income tax expense over the average useful life of the applicable classes of property.

Inventories: Raw materials, operating supplies, finished goods and work in process applicable to equipment sales are included in inventories at the lower of average cost or market. Work in process applicable to equipment rentals is similarly valued and included in rental machines and parts.

Source: IBM 1983 Annual Report.

Exhibit 23.5   International Business Machines Corporation and Subsidiary Companies
Consolidated Statement of Funds Flow (dollars in millions)

	1983	1982	1981
Funds (cash and marketable securities) at January 1	$3,300	$2,029	$2,112
Provided from (used for) operations:			
Sources:			
Net earnings	$ 5,485	$4,409	$3,610
Items not requiring the current use of funds:			
Depreciation charged to costs and expenses	3,362	3,143	2,753
Net book value of rental machines and other property retired or sold	2,108	1,642	1,212
Amortization of program products	311	249	173
Other	322	85	(189)
	11,588	9,528	7,559
Depreciation of manufacturing facilities capitalized in rental machines	265	419	424
	11,853	9,947	7,983
Uses:			
Investment in rental machines	2,352	4,254	4,610
Investment in plant and other property	2,578	2,431	2,235
	4,930	6,685	6,845
Investment in program products	588	468	348
Increase (decrease) in investments and other assets	1,590	(256)	105
Net change in working capital (excluding cash, marketable securities and loans payable)	725	307	(133)
	7,833	7,204	7,165
Translation effects	(147)	30	(53)
Net provided from operations	3,873	2,773	765
Provided from external financing:			
Net change in long-term debt	(177)	182	570
Net change in loans payable	3	(244)	182
Net provided from external financing	(174)	(62)	752
Provided from employee and stockholder plans:	788	613	423
	7,787	5,353	4,052
Less: cash dividends paid	2,251	2,053	2,023
Funds (cash and marketable securities) at December 31	$5,536	$3,300	$2,029

Exhibit 23.6   International Business Machines Corporation and
Subsidiary Companies Non-U.S. Operations (dollars in millions)

	1983	1982	1981
At end of year:			
Net assets employed			
Current assets	$ 8,294	$ 6,299	$ 5,436
Current liabilities	4,704	4,240	4,108
Working capital	3,590	2,059	1,328
Plant, rental machines, and other property, net	5,622	6,740	7,152
Investments and other assets	904	887	890
	10,116	9,686	9,370
Deferred income taxes	48	—	—
Reserves for employees' indemnities and retirement plans	1,130	1,198	1,184
Long-term debt	466	480	496
	1,644	1,678	1,680
Net assets employed	$ 8,472	$ 8,008	$ 7,690
Number of employees	150,944	150,444	149,794
For the year:			
Gross income from sales, rentals and services	$ 17,053	$ 15,336	$ 13,982
Earnings before income taxes	3,841	3,226	2,664
Provision for income taxes	1,677	1,577	1,123
Net earnings	2,164	1,649	1,541
Investment in rental machines	1,257	1,893	2,451
Investment in plant and other property	730	789	823
	$ 1,987	$ 2,682	$ 3,274

Non-U.S. subsidiaries which operate in a local currency environment account for approximately 85 percent of the company's non-U.S. gross income. The remaining 15 percent of the company's non-U.S. gross income is from subsidiaries and branches which operate in U.S. dollars or whose economic environment is highly inflationary.

For the years 1983, 1982, and 1981, non-U.S. financial results have been impacted by the strength of the U.S. dollar relative to the currencies of many countries. As the dollar strengthens, net assets and net earnings recorded in local currencies are translated into fewer U.S. dollars than they would have been at the previous year's rates.

Undistributed earnings of non-U.S. subsidiaries included in consolidated retained earnings amounted to $8,510 million at December 31, 1983, $7,538 million at December 31, 1982, and $6,565 million at December 31, 1981. These earnings are indefinitely reinvested in non-U.S. operations. Accordingly, no provision has been made for taxes that might be payable upon remittance of such earnings.

Source: IBM 1983 Annual Report.

Do It Right and Excellence Plus. Their history of excellence and service is now being matched by their efforts to have an equal level of excellence in manufacturing.

Marketing Strategies

Historically, IBM has relied upon its "button-down" sales force. Because it operated primarily from the mainframe market perspective, and that of associated peripherals and software, its personnel selling strategy (sales force) functioned more than satisfactorily to meet its selling objectives. This was in fact the firm's distribution channel, not just its promotion mechanisms. Its advertising programs were quiet and conservative, much like the company. Historically, alcohol had been forbidden at any IBM function. It had not been the type of firm to hold sales bashes or market with a "hoopla." But much of that changed in 1984. IBM has begun, especially in the PC segment, to market with more pizzazz. Its introduction of the latest PC was accompanied by alcohol, a barbecue, and hype. IBM has always believed that it was necessary to spend large quantities of dollars in order to gain market share, and its colossal advertising budgets continued to confirm this fact.

IBM's Chief Executives

Many people suggest that the history of IBM is the history of its chief executives. If so, then a new history is about to begin for on February 1, 1985, John F. Akers will become the fifth chief executive of IBM, succeeding John R. Opel, who will continue to serve as chairman of the board. This changing of the guard continues the tradition of retiring chief executives at age 60. (Mr. Opel, who was named chief executive at age 57 in January 1981, turned 60 in January 1985.) Mr. Akers is expected to continue the recent IBM move toward allowing its various businesses and divisions much more freedom to operate autonomously in the intrapreneurship fashion.

IBM's Diversification Efforts

IBM is moving ahead on several fronts. It has purchased Rolm Corporation to cash in on what may be the most lucrative market of all, global telecommunications. It has a joint

Exhibit 23.7   Five-Year Comparison of Selected Financial Data
(dollars in millions except per-share amounts)

	1983	1982	1981	1980	1979
For the year:					
Gross income from sales, rentals, and services	$40,180	$34,364	$29,070	$26,213	$22,863
Net earnings	5,485	4,409	3,610	3,397	3,011
Per share	9.04	7.39	6.14	5.82	5.16
Cash dividends paid	2,251	2,053	2,023	2,008	2,008
Per share	3.71	3.44	3.44	3.44	3.44
Investment in rental machines	2,352	4,254	4,610	4,334	4,212
Investment in plant and other property	$ 2,578	$ 2,431	$ 2,235	$ 2,258	$ 1,779
Return on stockholders' equity	25.4%	23.4%	21.1%	21.1%	21.2%
At end of year:					
Total assets	$37,243	$32,541	$29,107	$26,831	$24,530
Net investment in rental machines	6,812	9,117	9,252	8,390	6,927
Net investment in plant and other property	9,330	8,446	7,545	6,180	5,266
Working capital	7,763	4,805	2,983	3,381	4,406
Long-term debt	2,674	2,851	2,669	2,099	1,589
Stockholders' equity	$23,219	$19,960	$17,676	$16,578	$14,961

*Not restated for 1982 SFAS No. 52 accounting change.

Exhibit 23.8 Gross Income by Industry Segments and Classes of Similar Products or Services (dollars in millions)

	Consolidated		U.S. Only	
	1983	**1982***	**1983**	**1982***
Information-handling:				
Processors:				
Sales	$ 9,046	$ 7,784	$ 4,908	$ 4,203
Rentals	1,692	2,363	711	1,086
	10,738	10,147	5,619	5,289
Peripherals:				
Sales	6,205	3,311	3,669	1,717
Rentals	4,778	5,371	2,533	2,917
	10,983	8,682	6,202	4,634
Office systems/workstations:				
Sales	5,752	3,667	3,667	2,278
Rentals	2,275	2,778	1,295	1,498
	8,027	6,445	4,962	3,776
Program products	2,302	1,693	1,288	935
Maintenance services	4,577	3,940	2,633	2,230
Other:				
Sales	1,181	1,238	778	768
Rentals	485	609	278	372
Services	648	689	135	110
	2,314	2,536	1,191	1,250
	38,941	33,443	21,895	18,114
Federal systems:				
Sales	1,028	753	1,028	753
Services	148	105	148	105
	1,176	858	1,176	858

venture with Etna Life and Casualty Company and Communication Satellite Corporation in satellite business systems. Furthermore, IBM is working with telecommunications agencies in several European countries in an apparent attempt to establish an international IBM network. IBM has also moved more into the consumer market with a joint venture with Sears Roebuck and Company and CBS to develop a nationwide videotex service. This service would enable customers to eventually call up data bases on their televisions or home computers and to shop and bank from their homes. IBM has also entered into a joint venture in the financial service industry with Merrill Lynch and Company. They are attempting to market a stock-quoting desktop computer system.

IBM is also moving rapidly to provide software for its PCs. While the company has always been a major producer of software for large mainframe computers, it has accounted for only about 10 percent of the software sold for PCs in 1983, but it placed over 100 products on the market in 1983. IBM also used its two-year-old IBM Credit Corporation and the $1 billion kitty that it had to finance purchases, obviously at a profit. IBM is

Exhibit 23.8 *continued*

	Consolidated		U.S. Only	
	1983	1982*	1983	1982*
Other business:				
Sales	62	62	55	55
Services	1	1	1	1
	63	63	56	56
Total	$40,180	$34,364	$23,127	$19,028

*Reclassified to conform with 1983 presentation.

While IBM operates primarily in a single industry segment and manages its worldwide business as such, gross income has been categorized into major classes of product.

For purposes of classifying similar products of the Information-Handling industry segment, user programmable equipment having the capability of manipulating data arithmetically or logically and making calculations, in a manner directly addressable by the user through the operation of a stored program, has been classified as Processors, except that small business computers and intelligent workstations are included under Office Systems/Workstations. Typewriters have also been classified under Office Systems/Workstations. Peripherals include printers, copiers, storage and telecommunication devices. Peripheral functions embedded in processors are classified with Processors. Program Products include both applications and systems software. Maintenance Services consist of separately billed charges for maintenance. Other consists principally of supplies and unit record equipment.

Some products logically fit in more than one class and are assigned to a specific class based on a variety of factors. Over time, products tend to overlap, merge into or split from existing classes as a result of changing technologies, market perceptions, and/or customer use. For example, market demand may create requirements for technological enhancements to permit a peripheral product (e.g., printer), to be functionally integrated with a display, telecommunication device and a processor to form an office system. Such interchangeability and technological progress tend to make year-to-year comparisons less valid than they would be in an industry less subject to rapid change.

Federal Systems consists of specialized information-handling products and services primarily for the United States defense, space and other agencies.

Other Business consists of training and testing materials and services for school, home and industrial use.

Source: IBM 1983 Annual Report.

also moving rapidly to further secure its dominant position in Europe. In August 1984, it amicably settled a three-and-a-half-year-old antitrust suit filed by the Commission of the European Community. It was immediately after this that IBM Europe announced its joint telecommunication ventures across the continent. Europe is especially important to IBM because 28 percent of its 1983 sales took place on the Continent. The suit's only real clause calls for the publication within four months of the announcement of a project— information that will enable competitors to design their systems so they will be IBM-compatible. Ironically this is only two months more in advance of when IBM typically announces its plans. IBM Europe employs 9,000 individuals. It paid $1 billion in taxes in 1983. It has 13 plants in 10 European countries and invested $1.2 billion in these nations in 1983. While competition is opening up in Europe, European governments are not insensitive to the positive impact that IBM has. One final note: IBM has indicated to all of its divisions that over the next five years they want compatibility among all machines, especially with the PCs.

The Entry Systems Division

In August 1981, IBM entered a product in the personal computer office market race. At that time Apple and the Tandy Corporation were battling for the lead in market share and some 150 competitors were participating in the industry. By mid-1983 it was evident that the battle was over and IBM was the winner. It had asserted itself in a way not often seen in American industry. In just about two years, it had progressed from being a nonentrant to the most dominant firm in the industry, with 26 percent of the 1983 market for personal office computers. It was anticipated that the firm might sell as many as 2 million units in 1984, more than all the industry had sold prior to 1983. It is generally recognized by most computer experts that the IBM PC is not the best machine on the market; in fact, many say far from it. Nor does it have the best software available; but it still has the most important thing in the world, and that's three little letters on the front of it—IBM. How did IBM succeed so rapidly? How did a division which hardly existed in 1981 account for almost 20 percent of IBM sales in 1984? The answer is severalfold.

The IBM PC Strategy

Any product or service that is marked with those three little letters—IBM—affixed to it has a phenomenal chance for success. Furthermore, the fact that IBM is the primary moving force in the computer industry—an industry whose customers are organizations—can only aid its introduction of a personal computer when the PC industry is moving towards an office orientation. If the target market is one where the name IBM is already accepted as an industry standard, then all other competitors are at an immediate disadvantage. And, one cannot help but believe that the prediction of IBM's success by industry analysts could hardly help but become a self-fulfilling prophecy.

But IBM did not become successful in the first place by taking strategically unsound chances. When it came time to enter the PC industry, it had considered its moves well—although IBM showed not only good timing, but benefited from some good luck as well. The key elements in the IBM success story include:

- An Advanced Design. At the urging of outside software firms, IBM moved from the industry standard of the 8-bit processor to the 16-bit processor based on a chip made by InTel.

- Allowed for Software which Could Be Readily Written by Others. In another uncharacteristic move, the first being to listen to outsiders with regards to design features (the 16-bit processor), IBM, which has always written its own software, decided to publish its PC software specifications, having recognized that software was critical to PC sales. Software became much more readily available than it would have otherwise.

- Employed Multichannel Distribution. Many PC customers were outside the normal sales force distribution channel that IBM employs. Consequently, IBM used multiple channels including 800 strong computer retailers—among them the largest franchise chain, ComputerLand and the Sears' Business Systems centers.

- Low-cost Manufacturing. Recognizing the PC industry as a maturing one—especially with their own entry into the market—IBM took great pains to build substantial production facilities with high levels of automation in order to produce a low-cost product.

- Aggressive Pricing. In April 1983, IBM cut the price of its personal computer by 20 percent, forcing competitors to do the same or more. This 1983 price cut was followed by another of an additional 23 percent in June of 1984, which made it virtually impossible for many of their competitors to compete on a cost basis.

- New Product Introduction. IBM introduced new products, lowering the prices on older ones. First came the 3270, the PC, then the PC Jr., the PC XT, the portable, and most recently, the PC AT. Introduced in August of 1984, the PC AT is much faster and more powerful than previous models. Its expandable memory is sufficiently large to allow it to serve as a minicomputer for two additional "dummy" terminals. This computer represents a further movement towards the merging of micro and mini markets.

This strategy follows the overall total corporate objectives of growth, product leadership, efficiency and extremely high profits. Product innovation and matching price strategies are particularly important. As new products are introduced, prices on old products are reduced, increasing corporate market share. The software strategy of having third parties create software was especially effective in hampering Apple's growth with its Lisa and Macintosh computers. The IBM PC also dominated the market partly because of Apple's difficulties with Apple III. The AT competes extremely well against the Lisa even in its revised version, although Apple is reportedly selling all that it can make.

The success of their PC strategies has caused great concern among competitors. David G. Jackson, President of Altos Computers, observes: "IBM is moving faster than anything I've ever seen. It is being positively predatory."

Other factors which helped IBM become so successful include Apple's unwillingness to become IBM-compatible, thus forcing software writers to make the choice of writing for the IBM industry standard or for the more complex Apple Macintosh. As a consequence, the amount of software being written by third-party firms for Apple's Macintosh was much less than they hoped it would be. This had affected Mac's sales somewhat in late summer of 1984, when the sales of the highly successful Macintosh began to slow. Additionally, IBM's choice of MS-DOS as its internal machine operating system helped make it the industry leader. This further compounded the software problem for companies whose machines were not compatible. Most have scrambled to become compatible. Wang computers, for example, was to make available in the fall of 1984, an add-on unit for its older PCs which would make them IBM-compatible. Its new machines are already compatible. Most feel competitors must be IBM-compatible because software writers simply are not going to write for noncompatible, non-MS-DOS machines. Only Apple, because it holds a sufficient share of the market, seems to be able to remain noncompatible and yet have a sufficient amount of software continue to be written for its machines, and even they have been affected by noncompatibility.

IBM has not been totally successful, however. Part of its strategy was to first attack the office market where it knew it would meet with immediate success, then to go after the home market as well with a second product offering geared to that market—the PC Jr. While it had gained a high share of the office market—(estimates went as high as 33 percent for 1984, while Apple languished in second place with an estimated 18 percent), and a substantial share of the home market with its PC Jr., (estimates went as high as 12 percent in 1984, with Apple still in second place behind Commodore), IBM's "Junior" has been described as an "underachiever".

The Boca Raton Isolation Strategy

In a somewhat unique action for IBM, top management determined that the PC division should be established in a separate facility, where the division culture could be allowed to be more innovative than it might have been otherwise had it been under closer headquarters supervision. The belief was that the division needed to be innovative in order to compete with Apple and other firms in the industry; so a facility was constructed in Boca Raton, Florida, one which could produce an IBM PC every 45 seconds. (Now about one every 7 seconds.) The brain trust assembled there was allowed to be creative and innovative in meeting market demand and, in fact, in creating a market of its own.

The first PC designed was developed in a converted warehouse which had a leaky roof, few windows, and a not very functional air conditioning system. Yet this product changed IBM and the entire computer industry. Phillip D. "Don" Estridge, the project leader whose personal star has risen with that of the product he helped develop, comments that "this unconventional, for IBM, entrepreneurship approach was the key to the PC's phenomenal success. We were allowed to develop like a start-up company. IBM acted as a venture capitalist. It gave us management guidance, money, and allowed us to operate on our own." In August of 1984, Estridge was appointed president of a new seventh production unit for IBM, the Entry Systems Division, and was then given complete responsibility for personal computers and several other small computers and workstations.

Estridge indicates that they felt they had to rely on outside producers, for example with Intel for the chip, in order to get the job done quickly—that is, in order to put out a product in record time so they could compete successfully with Apple and others in the rapidly expanding PC market. They counted on management to run interference for the company with the rest of IBM. David J. Bradley, one of the designers of the PC commented, "If you are going to compete against five men in a garage, you have to do something different." Another necessary part of the strategy was to have everything from manufacturing to marketing and distribution all available at one location at Boca Raton. This is contrary to many of the IBM products which do not have that capability. The PC was really the first time that IBM had gone to outside suppliers.

IBM's PC Family

The IBM PC family includes: PC, the PCXT, the PCAT, and the PC Jr. The PC is the main product aimed at businesses. The XT and AT are faster, more powerful business PC versions. They also have more memory capabilities. The XT has a hard disk available. The PC Jr. is aimed at the low end of the home market.

The PC series has various options in memory; in CRTs—mono or color; in disk drives, e.g., 2 soft, 1 hard and soft; and in other features. Changes in products are continually occurring as are prices. Prices tend to drop at least twice a year, usually in the spring and/or when a new product is introduced. The PC family is in the $3,000−5,000 price range. PC Jr. is less than $2,000, generally. It is IBM's plan that all of its computers eventually have communication capabilities with the PC as the PC has become the workstation standard for the future.

Software

IBM has decided to dedicate itself to PC software in a manner similar to its other product launchings. At the same time it introduced its ATs in May 1984, IBM moved forward with a new $149 program known as Top View which allowed windowing, or splitting the computer screen into several sections for different tasks at the same time. Virtually all the new software and computers that IBM came out with in August make it more difficult for Apple because they copy many of the features that have been Apple's main selling points. The AT system also allowed IBM to move forward into the mini market. While there is some concern that the AT would put pressure on the XT, this original concern has failed to transpire as expected. However, it was necessary to reduce the price of the XT in order to make it clearly distinguishable and marketable compared to its higher-priced but much-more-powerful cousin, the AT.

Pricing Strategy

The pricing strategy followed by the PC division was the same that IBM has followed historically in all of its product lines. A series of products were introduced and, as each new product was introduced, the prices of older products were reduced. A series of products enabled the firm to compete across several different segments of the industry and, indeed, the PC Jr. allowed the firm to enter a new segment of the industry—the home computer market, which it had not previously entered.

The PC Jr.

The PC Jr. was one of those rare IBM mistakes when it was first released. Many claimed it was not aimed at any specific market but was an attempt to quickly capitalize on IBM's PC success with a cheaper model which had no specific purchaser in mind. Introduced in November 1983, the machine looked like it was going to be one of the biggest flops in the history of computers. In spite of a $40 million advertising campaign and IBM's prestige associated with the machine, the PC Jr. moved slowly as retailers built inventory.

Critics of the PC Jr.'s original version say that there were three main problems with it: it was designed in a vacuum, it had limited performance, and there was insufficient market testing before it was sold. From the aspect of being designed in a vacuum, IBM sought little help from the outside as it had with the PC. It failed to do so despite the fact that the PC Jr. was to be the first true consumer product IBM had ever introduced and that IBM was unfamiliar with that market. Secondly, in what industry observers call "true IBM style," IBM was more concerned about differentiating the PC Jr. from the PC than it was in providing a product that would sell. They were concerned about hurting the sales of the PC, so they ignored providing a product that the consumer could afford and use (thus the $1,269 price tag and the toylike keyboard). The product was thrown into the market without really finding out whether anyone wanted the features that the product had. The toylike keyboard, for example, made this home computer unsuitable for word processing, the number-one application for PCs in the office and the number two use for computers in the home. Its lofty price also made it unsuitable for the home market compared to much cheaper computers such as the Commodore 64, which sold for around $200. Essentially, the original PC Jr. had no market niche whatsoever. Many retailers were forced into discounting it to move stock. IBM looked as if it was going to fail to put a computer in every home as it had hoped to do.

Slowly but surely, IBM moved to help beleaguered dealers and to rectify the problems associated with a product whose untimely death was greatly exaggerated. The company allowed dealers to delay payment until the end of August for computers ordered in January, aiding them in clearing inventories and reducing their expenses. Then on July 31, IBM introduced a series of new PC Jr. features and options including a "real" professional-style keyboard which was retroactively provided free to all registered owners of the old-style keyboard. IBM then moved on a massive advertising campaign, having also made the memory expandable and having dropped prices $300 for the single-disk-drive model. In mid-October of 1984, IBM offered dealer rebates of an extra $250 and it was expected that in November a computer and color monitor package would retail for about $900. Some discount houses were selling their packages for even less in October. This pricing package gave the PC Jr. about a $200 undercut below the Apple IIc and provided the user with a full color monitor as opposed to Apple's green screen. Sales, which by mid-July had dwindled to just a few thousand a month, were expected to reach about 90,000 a month in November, maybe 100,000 in December. Anticipation was for about a 275,000-volume year.

Despite all this late success, PC Jr. still has some operating problems. For example, it can only run about 40 percent of the programs written for the PC. New software for the home and school markets was being developed extremely slowly. Plus, the PC Jr. is more difficult to use now that it has more power. IBM had to make a choice between power and ease of use, and chose power. In various configurations, three different versions of the disk operating system, PC-DOS, are required.

The Question

The Entry Systems major concern at this time was how to maintain its momentum.

References

Advertisement. *Business Week*, September 10, 1984.

Advertisement. *The Wall Street Journal*, April 5, 1984, p. 9.

Alexander, Charles P., Thomas McCarroll, Michael Moritz. "Big Blue Aims To Get Bigger." *Time*, October 8, 1984, p. 59.

Businessland, price quote.

Carlyle, R. Emmett. "Tracking The IBM P.C." *Datamation*, February 1984, pp. 75–79.

Elmer-DeWitt, Philip and Thomas McCarroll. "A Flop Becomes A Hit." *Time*, December 24, 1984, p. 60.

Elmer-DeWitt, Philip and Michael Moritz. "Slugging It Out In The Schoolyard." *Time*, March 12, 1984, p. 62.

"How IBM Made 'Junior' An Underachiever." *Business Week*, June 25, 1984, pp. 106–107.

"IBM Joins The Race In Personal Computers." *Business Week*, August 24, 1981, pp. 38–40.

"IBM's Personal Computer Spawns An Industry." *Business Week*, August 15, 1983, p. 88.

"IBM's Second Front." *Fortune*, May 28, 1984, p. 6.

"IBM Strikes Again." *Fortune*, March 18, 1985, p. 8.

Kneale, Dennis. "IBM's AT Computer Puts Pressure On Rivals And Rest Of Its PC Line." *The Wall Street Journal*, October 17, 1984, p. 33.

Kneale, Dennis. "IBM Unveils PC Software For $149 Or Less; Move May Trigger Fierce Industry Battle." *The Wall Street Journal*, May 16, 1984, p. 3.

Kneale, Dennis. "IBM Is Expected To Announce Changes Designed To Increase Sales Of Its PCjr." *The Wall Street Journal*, July 30, 1984, p. 2.

Marcom, John Jr. "IBM Is Lagging A Bit In Rivalry To Set Up Office Data Networks." *The Wall Street Journal*, July 26, 1984, p. 1.

Marcom, John Jr. and Dennis Kneale. "IBM Announces A Broad Range of New Products." *The Wall Street Journal*, September 11, 1984, p. 4.

Marcom, John Jr. and Michael W. Miller. "IBM Introduces Software Series in New Markets." *The Wall Street Journal*, September 26, 1984, p. 3.

Marcom, John Jr. "Dealers Seem Certain IBM's New Products Will Give Them Edge." *The Wall Street Journal*, August 15, 1984, p. 3.

Marcom, John Jr. "IBM's PCjr Computer Is Fulfilling Its Promise After a Faltering Start." *The Wall Street Journal*, December 13, 1984, p. 33.

Marcom, John Jr. "IBM Consolidates Personal Computer Sales in One Unit." *The Wall Street Journal*, January 21, 1985, p. 10.

Marcom, John Jr. "IBM's Hotly Touted PCjr Receives Cooler-Than-Expected Reception." *The Wall Street Journal*, February 21, 1984, p. 35.

Marcom, John Jr. "IBM Plans A Big Party And The Industry Believes Debut Of A PC Is The Reason Why." *The Wall Street Journal*, August 10, 1984, p. 2.

"No. 1's Awesome Strategy." *Business Week*, June 8, 1981, pp. 84–90.

"Personal Computers: And The Winner is IBM," cover story. *Business Week*, October 3, 1983, pp. 76–95.

"Reshaping The Computer Industry," special report. *Business Week*, July 16, 1984, pp. 84–111.

Shaffer, Richard A. "IBM's PCjr Manual Reveals Computer's Strengths, Flaws." *The Wall Street Journal*, January 13, 1984, p. 25.

Schiffres, Manuel. "The Computer War's Casualties Pile Up." *U.S. News & World Report*, August 20, 1984, pp. 37–38.

Schiffres, Manuel. "IBM: Setting Out To Be No. 1 In U.S. Business." *U.S. News & World Report*, June 18, 1984, pp. 61–62.

"The Change In Marketing Style At A Chastened IBM." *Business Week*, August 27, 1984, p. 35.

"The Road Is Clear For IBM's Drive Into Europe." *Business Week*, August 20, 1984, pp. 44–46.

"The Squeeze Begins In Personal Computers." *Business Week*, May 30, 1983, pp. 91–95.

"Will IBM Climb To The Top In Software, Too?" *Business Week*, October 22, 1984, pp. 100–109.

CASE 24
The Airline Industry

■ *Sandra Foster, Steve Keith, and Cathy Shields* ■

In 1978 the airline industry was deregulated. Heralded as a boon to the traveling public, it has meant declining profits, increased competition, and potential disaster for the nation's air carriers. The profits that were realized in the first years of deregulation came to an abrupt halt when, in 1981, the United States's airline industry experienced operating losses of around $300 million. Coupled with rising fuel costs and a weakening economy, deregulation threatened the demise of many air carriers.[1]

In 1982, Pan American World Airways experienced a $485 million loss; whereas Eastern Air Lines, long troubled by small profit margins, had a loss of $50 million. Republic, TWA, and Western each realized losses of $30 million that year.[2] Braniff and Laker Airways each filed for bankruptcy in 1982. Their bankruptcies were followed by that of Continental Airlines in September of 1983. The total industry experienced a loss of $520 million in 1983.[3] On July 3, 1984, Air Florida filed for protection under Chapter 11.[4] 1984 saw Continental, Delta, Northwest, Republic, American, United, and USAir operating in the black; whereas Eastern, Pan Am, TWA, and Western continued to operate in the red. And, although conditions improved for the industry as a whole, the shakeout continued in 1985 with the bankruptcy of Capital Air in February of that year.[5]

As a direct result of deregulation, the threat of new entrants has increased substantially, with the number of carriers rising from 36 to 123 in the past six years.[6] The years since deregulation have seen a rise in fuel prices as well as a weakening of the economy—two more threats with which the industry has had to reckon. In addition to the new entrants, who have been largely responsible for potentially debilitating fare wars, the airline industry has had to deal with the increasing need to reduce labor costs and with the equally increasing challenges by labor to these cost-reduction programs. Finally, the airline industry has witnessed the growing strength of travel agents, who have the power to make or break an airline both through bookings and through very substantial commissions. All of these—deregulation, fuel prices, the economy, labor relations, new entrants, fare wars, and travel agents—are forces which have directed and which will continue to direct the nature of the airline industry.

This case represents neither effective nor ineffective handling of an administrative situation. Rather, it is to be used as the basis for classroom discussion. All rights reserved to the contributors.

[1] Cindy Skrzycki, "Continental Air Soars Above Union Turbulence," *U.S. News & World Report*, July 23, 1984, p. 69.

[2] Craig A. Schmutzer, "An Analysis of the Airline Industry," *The Journal of Commercial Bank Lending*, Vol. 66, February 1984, p. 24.

[3] David Woolley, "Airlines Climb Out of the Red," *Interavia*, October 1984, p. 1035.

[4] Skrzycki, "Continental Air Soars Above Union Turbulence," *U.S. News & World Report*, p. 69.

[5] Woolley, p. 1035.

[6] Skrzycki, "Continental Air Soars Above Union Turbulence," *U.S. News & World Report*, p. 70.

Major Forces Affecting the Industry

Deregulation

On October 24, 1978, President Jimmy Carter signed into law the Airline Deregulation Act of 1978. The objectives of that law were:

1. To make available a variety of economic, efficient, and low-priced services.

2. To place maximum reliance on competitive market forces and on actual competition to provide air transportation.

3. To prevent anticompetitive practices and conditions that would allow carriers to increase prices unreasonably, reduce services, or exclude competition.

4. To maintain systems for small communities and isolated areas.

5. To encourage entry into new markets by existing and new carriers.

By late 1981, the elimination of the control over routes by the Civil Aeronautics Board was affected. By early 1983, CAB control over rates was eliminated. And by early 1985, the CAB itself was dismantled.[7]

A number of things have happened since deregulation. First of all, there has been the very real emergence of national airlines, those carriers which generate less than $1 billion in revenues annually. In 1981, the national airlines experienced a 27.8-percent increase in traffic, whereas the major carriers experienced a 6.9-percent decrease in traffic. Since 1981, the national carriers have continued to expand, primarily through the conservative establishment of hub areas.[8]

Deregulation has also resulted in a number of not-so-conservative expansion efforts. As one New York analyst suggests, ""When they deregulated the industry, it was like putting a 16-year-old out on the street—they were anxious to go." As a result, several airlines have failed since deregulation, largely because they grew too rapidly, they took on too much debt, and they executed their route strategies badly.[9]

One of the most frightening results of deregulation is the amount of debt that has been incurred by the airlines and the effect that debt has had on the industry as a whole. A major factor in the cyclical earning trends of airlines is operating leverage, reflecting the large fixed cost structure and the revenue sensitivity to economic conditions. Since deregulation, the significance of operating leverage has been magnified. Standard & Poors believes that, "prior to deregulation, airline operating risk was no higher than average in American business. Currently, operating risk for the airline industry is well above average, even speculative."[10]

The ultimate dilemma posed for the deregulated airline industry is this: the increased losses experienced by the airlines have placed a premium on efficient operations. However, poor economic conditions and operating performances have resulted in severely lim-

---

[7] Schmutzer, "An Analysis of the Airline Industry," *The Journal of Commercial Bank Lending*, pp. 19–20.

[8] Ibid., p. 23.

[9] Cindy Skrzycki, "Growing Pains for Midsized Airlines," *U.S. News & World Report*, September 17, 1984, p. 49.

[10] Schmutzer, "An Analysis of the Airline Industry," *The Journal of Commercial Bank Lending*, p. 21.

ited financial flexibility with which to initiate the needed changes in operations. And this has created pessimism in the equity investors, which has placed an undue burden of financing on debt—which further limits the financial flexibility of the airlines (the airline industry needs approximately $1 in capital to generate $1 in revenue).[11]

Fuel Prices

In addition to deregulation, the airline industry saw a doubling of fuel prices in 1979 and 1980.[12] In a 22-month period of time, fuel prices increased 128 percent.[13] Since jet fuel accounts for 25 percent of an airline's total operating costs, the increases in fuel prices posed a definite threat to the operating profits of the airline industry.[14]

Three things happened as a result of the escalating fuel costs. The major airlines were forced to phase out older gas-guzzling jets sooner than they anticipated, thus leading to a premature antiquating of existing fleets.[15] The phasing out of the older jets made relatively cheap aircraft available to the new competing airlines. And the major carriers were committed to incurring substantial debts to acquire more fuel-efficient aircraft.

In 1984 fuel prices were 20 percent lower than they were in 1981.[16] Airlines consumed no more fuel than a decade previously, despite a 50 percent increase in seat miles, but the cost of fuel had soared from $.12 a gallon to a peak of $1.05 in 1981 and back down to $.84 in 1984.[17] Despite the 20 percent decrease in fuel prices, the airlines had to continue upon a costly path of fleet modernization. Standard & Poors estimated that $30–$40 billion would be required to replace 40 percent of existing aircraft by 1990. In the interim, airlines were hoping that fuel prices would continue to decline; estimates were that for each $.01 per-gallon decrease in the price of fuel, the airline industry would save an aggregate $100 million in fuel.[18]

The Economy

The economy has always been a major factor in the airline industry, particularly in the field of discretionary travel. Business travelers will choose airline travel no matter what the economy is experiencing. The discretionary traveler—the vacation traveler—however, is extremely sensitive to the state of the economy.

When the U.S. economy softened in the early 1980s, even the largest and strongest carriers experienced huge losses. Delta, for years the carrier with the best results, lost money for five straight quarters. The industry lost a collective $1 billion in the 12 months

---

[11] Ibid., p. 25.

[12] Howard Banks, "Airlines," *Forbes*, January 2, 1984, p. 139.

[13] Schmutzer, "An Analysis of the Airline Industry," *The Journal of Commercial Bank Lending*, p. 22.

[14] Schmutzer, "The Economy," *Fortune*, November 26, 1984, p. 82.

[15] Schmutzer, "An Analysis of the Airline Industry," *The Journal of Commercial Bank Lending*, p. 22.

[16] Woolley, p. 1036.

[17] Schmutzer, "The Economy," *Fortune*, p. 82.

[18] Schmutzer, "An Analysis of the Airline Industry," *The Journal of Commercial Bank Lending*, p. 22.

to the middle of 1983 before things turned around.[19] Although the economy is now re-covering, it is a factor which continues to prompt the airlines to exercise caution in route expansion and fleet modernization.

Labor Relations

Since roughly 60 percent of all operating costs are items such as debt service, fuel, and landing fees, most of the major airlines have attacked labor costs, the area where new entrants have the strong edge.[20] Faced with nonunionized competitors, more than 20 air-lines have made deals with their employees.[21] American Airlines has set up a two-tier wage scale; Frontier has set up a separate nonunion carrier; Continental has reorganized under Chapter 11 into a totally nonunion carrier; and Eastern has led other major carriers in employee give-back programs with its 1984 Wage Investment Program.

Pan Am, too, has asked its employees to participate in a wage give-back program, as well it should. As one industry analyst characterizes it, Pan Am's work rules are "antedilu-vian. A Teamster must collect boarding passes before every flight, though the company swears that the flight attendant who welcomes passengers could do it just as easily. Labor contracts also ban hiring part-timers and farming out work. In April of 1985, at Seattle's Sea-Tac International Airport, Pan Am had 97 full-time employees to service only 14 flights per week. The kitchen staff of 17 included $25,000-a-year dishwashers."[22] Old habits die hard, however, and Pan Am workers have not willingly embraced the give-back program. In fact, the company was beset by a month-long strike by the Transport Workers Union in March of 1985; and the company has recently averted a strike by the flight attendants.

The outlook for the reduction of labor costs seems brighter for the industry as a whole. Despite the fact that the average 747 pilot is paid $125,000 a year,[23] and despite the fact that the average pay in 1984 for all airline workers was 7 percent higher than in 1983,[24] the industry's labor costs as a share of all expenses have dropped from 39.3 percent in 1979 to 35.3 percent in 1984.

There are those people, too, who see a bright horizon in future labor relations. As Continental's President Frank Lorenzo hopes, "I think we'll see much more rational be-havior on the part of the unions." Perhaps that is because, as one industry analyst sug-gests, Lorenzo "perceives with stark clarity the other side of the deregulation equation— that you can't open the skies to free competition if labor, too, isn't subject to the law of supply and demand."[25]

[19] Banks, p. 139.

[20] Kenneth Labich, "Fare Wars: Have the Big Airlines Learned to Win?" *Fortune*, October 29, 1984, p. 27.

[21] Labich, "How Deregulation Puts Competition Back in Business," *U.S. News & World Report*, November 26, 1984, p. 52.

[22] Shawn Tully, "Pan Am's $200 Million Tranquilizer," *Fortune*, November 29, 1982, p. 112.

[23] Schmutzer, "An Analysis of the Airline Industry," *The Journal of Commercial Bank Lending*, p. 21.

[24] Woolley, p. 1036.

[25] Roy Rowan, "An Airline Boss Attacks Sky-High Wages," *Fortune*, January 9, 1984, p. 73.

Fare Wars

Although many people credit the new entrants with the raging fare wars in the airline industry, most people will agree that existing airlines are equally guilty of trying to beat the competition with prices. During the first six months of 1983, 85 percent of all passengers flying received discounts averaging 47.5 percent.[26] In 1984 almost 80 percent of all passengers rode under some kind of discounted fare.[27] The raging fare wars have gotten to the point where Robert Crandall, Chief Operating Officer of American Airlines, jokes about "the adjustable-rate air fare—tell us what you can afford and we'll sell you a ticket."[28]

Interestingly, it is difficult to find someone in the airline industry who can or will make a good case for engaging in fare wars. This is primarily because, despite the fact that fare cutting often stimulates traffic, it also tends toward implosion: discounts increase; passenger yields are driven down; hence higher passenger levels must be attracted.[29] As Robert J. McBride, United's vice-president of marketing, asserts, "The race for lower and lower fares to attract more passengers is not proving beneficial—what is the real elasticity of demand in this business?"[30]

Recognizing the veritable necessity of attracting passengers through low fares in order to spring back from bankruptcy, Continental's Frank Lorenzo is nevertheless very concerned about triggering fare wars. "Always remember the other guy's got to make a buck too. If you don't leave him a profitable option, you'll hit his hot button." For this reason, Lorenzo considers fare-setting an art form. "I'm surprised how many people think you can throw a hand grenade at a competitor and expect he'll stand there and enjoy it."[31]

The major airlines are placing more restrictions on cheap fares than they did two years ago; and they are cutting prices only where the upstarts have challenged them on routes crucial to their overall strategies. They are also limiting the number of discount seats available on each flight. And this is one area where the large airlines can use size to their advantage. Since they fly so many places, at least some of their fares are sure to escape fare competition—as long as the other large airlines cooperate.[32]

New Entrants

The threat of new entrants in the deregulated airline industry is very real; and the possibilities of their continued survival are very good. There is not a great deal of difference between the old and new airlines in terms of revenue yield; it is in the area of cost where the difference is apparent.

The major airlines are carrying heavy historical costs, incurred by underutilized assets, especially airliners acquired over the years. Frequently airplanes are not fully depreciated

---

[26] Rowan, "A Patch of Blue for the Airlines," *Financial World*, No. 153, January 10, 1984, p. 24.

[27] Labich, "How Deregulation Puts Competition Back Into Busines," *U.S. News & World Report*, p. 52.

[28] Labich, "Fare Wars," *Fortune*, p. 24.

[29] Rowan, "A Patch of Blue for the Airlines," *Financial World*, p. 24.

[30] Rowan, "The Airline Business 'Isn't Just Flying Airplanes,'" *Interavia*, April 1983, p. 364.

[31] Rowan, "An Airline Boss Attacks Sky-High Wages," *Fortune*, p. 70.

[32] Labich, "Fare Wars," *Fortune*, p. 28.

and continue to incur amortization charges.[33] The new airlines, however, have much lower costs, despite their miniscule market share. They do not have to shoulder the costs of pensions and seniority benefits. They are able to take advantage of lower costs for equipment by purchasing used airplanes. And they are nonunion, with wage scales roughly half those of union carriers.[34]

As threats, though, the new entrants have probably performed a great service for the flying consumer by forcing the major carriers to operate as efficiently and cost effectively as possible. As Eastern's Frank Borman suggests, "The automobile people have their Japanese. Textile manufacturers have their Taiwans and their Koreas. We happen to have our low-labor-cost airlines. . . . This business is almost a commodity business—the lowest-cost producer inevitably wins."[35]

Travel Agents

The threat of travel agents to the airline industry is insidious. There is no way to eliminate their function; and few ways to minimize their potential effect on the success or failure of a particular airline. C. Edward Acker, Pan Am's CEO, assigns more than half of his company's operating losses in 1982 to "squeamish" travel agents who hesitated to book passengers on the ailing airline because of the inconveniences they experienced following the Braniff and Laker bankruptcies. Travel agents book 78 percent of Pan Am's business, the highest in the industry. The fears of the travel agents have contributed to a 40 percent decline in Pan Am's group reservations, a drop that cut operating profit in 1982 by $60 million.[36]

There are other ways in which travel agents impact the airline industry. Airlines must pay 10 percent commission to agents who book passengers on their flights—when the passengers would have flown some airline even without the agent's help. Additionally, most major airlines offer bonuses of 2–6 percent of ticket prices—on top of the usual 10 percent commission—to travel agents who throw a large proportion of business their way. In fact, bonuses are paid on 15–20 percent of all ticket sales.[37] Obviously, then, what could be seen as an opportunity to one airline would have to be a threat to a competing airline. There is also the very real fear among some airlines that the computerized reservation systems used by travel agents may be prejudicial toward the airline whose system the agent is using.

Competition (Excluding Eastern Air Lines):
Major Airlines/Trunk Carriers

American Airlines (One of the "Big Four").   Headquartered in Dallas, Texas, American Airlines employs 38,700 people; and, in 1983, it carried 31,384,000 passengers. Its

---

[33] Labich, "The New U.S. Airlines: How Their Finances Are Faring," *Interavia*, April 1984, p. 325.

[34] Rowan, "A Patch of Blue for the Airlines," *Financial World*, p. 24.

[35] Thomas J. Billitteri, "Why Eastern Will Go Back to Labor for More Help," *Florida Trend*, November 1984, p. 68.

[36] Tully, p. 110.

[37] Labich, "Fare Wars," *Fortune*, p. 28.

market is the domestic United States; North, Central, and South America; and Europe. In 1983, its passenger load factor was 65 percent. Net profit for 1983 was $348.1 million (up 953 percent), on sales of $5.2 billion (up 19 percent); and its 1983 return on net equity was 23 percent.[38]

American Airlines is indubitably one of the leaders of the airline industry—primarily because of the innovative ways in which management has chosen to deal with labor. The essence of American labor relations, and a direct result of the potentially debilitating effects of deregulation, is its two-tier wage program. Rather than attempting to gain wage concessions from present employees, American has set up an entirely different, and substantially lower, wage structure for new employees. Although the success of this two-tier structure is still to be determined, top management credits it, along with other cost reductions, with the 953 percent increase in profit in 1983. As Bob Crandall, President of American Airlines, characterizes it, "The larger we make the company, the greater average effect we have on overall costs and the more we get from low-cost growth."[39]

It is interesting to note that Crandall does not see labor relations as the sole area in which the profit margin can be impacted. In an industry in which "the newer, the better" has been the battle cry for fleet modernization, Crandall has led American on a cautious path of plane acquisition. In fact, he argues that keeping older airplanes can ultimately be more profitable than acquiring new planes. As he says, "When you sell old airplanes, they don't get ground up and made into tuna cans; they go to a competitor. Instead, now that we can afford it, why not fly them ourselves?"[40] An additional advantage of flying older airplanes is a lower break-even point which, as Crandall asserts, allows American to better compete in smaller markets. And in that, American will achieve an even-greater competitive advantage.

Continental Airlines.   With 9,500 employees, Continental is headquartered in Houston, Texas. It carried 7,791,000 passengers in 1983, with a passenger load factor of 60.3 percent. Its market is the domestic United States, Mexico, Australia, Japan, Micronesia, and the Philippines.[41]

In September of 1983, Continental filed for protection under Chapter 11; but it was back in the air a few days later, paying its employees substantially less than it was before. Pilots and flight attendants went out on strike, accusing Continental of feigning bankruptcy as a ploy to abrogate existing labor contracts; the bankruptcy courts ruled in favor of the corporation.

From the first day of filing for protection, top management of Continental has maintained an air of optimism. As Francisco Lorenzo, President, says, "We filed for bankruptcy not because the company didn't have a future, but because we thought it had a hell of a future."[42]

In its post-Chapter 11 resurgence, Continental has made a conscious decision not to be all things to all people. Because, as Lorenzo puts it, "Deregulation means carving out

---

[38] Woolley, pp. 1056–1060.

[39] Banks, p. 143.

[40] *Ibid.*

[41] Woolley, pp. 1056–1060.

[42] Rowan, "An Airline Boss Attacks Sky-High Wages," *Fortune*, p. 66.

your own special niche." Continental's present niche is to provide all the frills of flying at discount fares. By focusing this formula on high-density markets, Continental can gain many new passengers and become highly profitable—provided it can get costs down by "breaking the stranglehold of the unions."[43]

It seems that Continental has done just that. Flight attendants are now paid $15,000 and pilots are paid $43,000, the same salary Lorenzo is paying himself until Continental becomes profitable. Continental's cost to fly one seat one mile is now $.06, as opposed to the industry average of $.08. Passenger miles on July 8, 1984, hit the highest level in the 50-year history of the airline. With a $7-million profit on operations in the first three months of 1984, Continental could be the first airline since deregulation to turn near-bankruptcy into success.[44]

Looking toward the future, Wayne Parrish, founder of the *Official Airlines Guide* and *Aviation Daily*, rates Continental's chances of success as very good: "It's the first national airline to break the cost barrier. If Lorenzo can make this stick, I can see him running out of equipment—he'll have so many passengers." As Parrish further asserts, "Continental is getting cost down to where it is a tremendous threat even to the biggest trunks."[45] Continental is once again a force with which to reckon.

Delta Air Lines (One of the "Big Four").   Headquartered in Atlanta, Georgia, Delta is one of the few trunk carriers which has managed to emerge from the post-deregulation era relatively unscathed. With 36,000 employees, Delta is alone among the majors because its employees have always been nonunion. In 1983, Delta carried 36,800,855 passengers, with a passenger load factor of 54.02 percent. Its market is the Caribbean, Canada, Europe, and the domestic United States.[46]

In addition to crediting its nonunion employees with the corporation's competitive advantage, Delta also sees its continually changing distribution system as a contributory factor. As Chairman David Garrett says, "You have to have a continuous program, almost, to relook at where you are flying, what cities you go into as new markets, to tie into the schedule."[47]

Despite the fact that Delta has remained profitable for most of the post-deregulation period, there is a caution in its approach to the future, prompting some analysts to call it the most conservative of the "Big Four."[48] This is particularly true in the area of spending. Delta, which has been on an aircraft shopping spree, is cutting back now and has pushed back deliveries of the Boeing 767s and 757s it has on order, reducing its capital spending program over the coming three years to around $500 million a year. The plans are to handle future spending by internal cash flow and the sale of second-hand aircraft.[49]

Northwest Orient (One of the "Big Four").   Serving the market of the Far East, Europe, and the United States, Northwest carried 12,718,000 passengers in 1983. Its 14,187

[43] Ibid.

[44] Ibid., p. 73.

[45] Ibid.

[46] Woolley, pp. 1056–1060.

[47] Banks, p. 142.

[48] Ibid.

[49] Ibid.

employees are headquartered in Minneapolis, Minnesota; and its 1983 passenger load factor was 60 percent.[50]

Not satisfied simply with making a profit in the deregulated air travel market, Northwest is looking to change its image through fleet modernization. "Northwest, with the airline industry's soundest balance sheet, is trying to shuck the image of being a fuddy-duddy, low-cost (poor service) airline. It is going after increased traffic, as well, and has ordered 20 Boeing 757s."[51]

Pan American World Airways.   An airline that is in a precarious position, "loaded with debt and short on cash,"[52] Pan Am has been faced with annual losses which greatly overshadow Eastern's and with labor problems that continue to drive the airline further into debt.

Headquartered in New York, Pam Am serves the largest market among the major carriers: North and Souh America, Europe, Asia, Australia, Africa, and the domestic United States. With 27,587 employees, it carried 14,700,000 passengers, comprising a passenger load factor of 62.4 percent in 1983.[53]

Pan Am has consistently lost money in the last five years. One of the reasons is that Pam Am spends more to fly passengers than it collects from them. In early 1983, it lost $26, or 12 percent, on each ticket sold, over four times the industry average.[54] The total loss for 1982 was $485 million (compared with Eastern's loss of $50 million).[55]

To offset that loss, Pan Am sold the nonairline assets of its New York office building and its Intercontinental Hotel chain for $800 million in cash.[56] Its tenuous survival was further threatened by the month-long strike in 1985 by the Transport Workers Union—a strike which grounded many of its flights and which jeopardized its peak summer travel season because travel agents booked tour groups on other airlines.

Piedmont Airlines.   Headquartered in Winston-Salem, North Carolina, Piedmont entered the ranks of the major carriers on March 1, 1985. With 9,803 employees, it carried 11,701,029 passengers in 1983, with a passenger load factor of 53.8 percent. Its market is the domestic United States.[57]

Piedmont entered the airline market as a regional carrier which primarily served the Carolinas and Virginia. Because of its reasonably strong financial base, Piedmont capitalized on the deregulated conditions by expanding northward and southward without jeopardy. It was this ability to grow, and a management which carefully charted its growth, which helped Piedmont realize a 1984 second-quarter operating profit of $44.8 million and which made Piedmont the newest major carrier in the United States.[58]

[50] Woolley, pp. 1056–1060.

[51] Banks, p. 142.

[52] Labich, "How Deregulation Puts Competition Back in Business," *U.S. News & World Report*, p. 52.

[53] Woolley, pp. 1056–1060.

[54] Tully, p. 111.

[55] Schmutzer, "An Analysis of the Airline Industry," *The Journal of Commercial Bank Lending*, p. 24.

[56] Ibid.

[57] Woolley, pp. 1056–1060.

[58] Skrzycki, "Growing Pains for Midsized Airlines," *U.S. News & World Report*, p. 49.

Trans World Airlines.   Serving the market of the domestic United States, Europe, the Middle East, and Africa, TWA employs 27,299 people. In 1983 this New York-headquartered airline carried 18,634,000 passengers, with a passenger load factor of 64.1 percent.[59]

The deregulated skies have not been kind to TWA; for, as many industry analysts note, it is burdened with high costs and heavy debts.[60] Because of its poor debt structure, TWA has been spun off from its holding corporation to essentially make it on its own. The outlook for TWA is uncertain. Many analysts agree that it is likely that TWA will reduce, by as much as half, its sizable, loss-making domestic routes and concentrate on the international market.[61]

United Airlines (One of the "Big Four").   Headquartered in Chicago, Illinois, United has 45,000 employees. The 38,196,321 passengers it carried in 1983 comprised a passenger load factor of 63.6 percent. Its market is the domestic United States, Canada, Mexico, the Bahamas, Japan, and Hong Kong.[62]

The tremendously successful United Airlines is often paired with American as the two industry leaders. In fact, during the first half of 1984, United and American accounted for 81 percent of the industry's profits. And, as industry analysts assert, both airlines are poised for expansion. The plans for expansion, however, do not include giving away profits through fare wars. Along with American, United is severely limiting the number of discount seats offered on peak-hour flights. United and American have also increased fares $10 each way on routes now flown by the discount airlines.[63]

Analysts characterize United as having the most aggressive mass-marketing campaign in the industry—particularly in seeking new markets. The indication of this change in United's strategy is the fact that it has reentered many small markets in the West which it dropped early in deregulation. In 1984 it operated in 43 of the lower 48 states.[64]

National Airlines/Regional Carriers

Capital Air Lines.   Headquartered in Smyrna, Tennessee, Capital used to employ 1,600 people. In 1983 it carried 1,211,306 passengers in its market of the United States, Europe, and the Caribbean. Despite its passenger load factor of 76 percent, Capital Air filed for protection under Chapter 11 in February of 1985.[65]

Frontier Airlines.   Serving the market of the United States, Canada, and Mexico, Frontier is headquartered in Denver, Colorado. With 5,400 employees, it carried 4,608,333 passengers in 1983, comprising a passenger load factor of 59.9 percent.[66]

---

[59] Woolley, pp. 1056–1060.

[60] Labich, "Fare Wars," *Fortune*, p. 24.

[61] Banks, pp. 141–142.

[62] Woolley, pp. 1056–1060.

[63] Labich, "Fare Wars," *Fortune*, p. 24.

[64] Banks, p. 142.

[65] Woolley, pp. 1056–1060.

[66] Ibid.

Frontier Airlines is noteworthy in that it is the only national airline which has attempted to reduce its labor costs in an innovative way. It has done this by creating a second, nonunion, lower-cost parallel airline to operate in the same market as the parent airline.[67] The formation of the Frontier Horizon, the nonunion associate of Frontier Airlines, represents this corporate reorganization in order to achieve greater freedom in wage negotiations and in order to substantially impact competitive position by greatly reducing operating costs.[68]

Midway Metrolink.   From its headquarters in Chicago, Illinois, Midway serves the domestic United States market. Midway, the first airline begun after deregulation, had revenues of $25 million in 1980, $73.9 million in 1981, $94.7 million in 1982, and over $100 million in 1983.[69]

It began as a no-frills price-cutter, but it has consistently raised prices and has sought out the full-fare business passenger. In 1984 it had net current assets of $15.0 million, net worth of $32.3 million, and stockholders' equity of $32.3 million.[70]

Interestingly, Midway acquired Air Florida after that airline filed for protection under Chapter 11 in 1984. Following that acquisition, Midway did not make a profit in 1984.

Ozark Air Lines.   Headquartered in St. Louis, Missouri, Ozark employs 3,981 people. In 1983 it carried 4,907,810 passengers, with a passenger load factor of 55.8 percent. Serving the domestic United States market, Ozark experienced an operating profit in the second quarter of 1984 of $10.8 million.[71]

Pacific Southwest Airlines.   Headquartered in California, PSA has been quite profitable. Serving the domestic United States, it had revenues of $475 million in 1982 and of $531 million in 1983. In 1984, PSA had net assets of $10.1 million net worth of $165.9 million and stockholders' equity of $165.9 million. It currently achieves revenue yields of 13.4 cents per passenger mile (compared with People Express's yield of 7.89 cents and Eastern's yield of 13.0 cents).[72]

People Express.   If there is an airline which signifies both the opportunities and the threats of the deregulated airline industry, it is People Express. Called the "McDonald's of the Air," People Express was started in April of 1981 with three Boeing 737s traveling from its headquarters in Newark to Buffalo, Columbus, and Norfolk. By the end of the year it had 13 planes flying to 10 cities.[73] It wasn't long before People Express was flying the lucrative East Coast corridor, providing a direct threat to Eastern in its New York-to-Florida lifeline. As Morton Ehrlich, Eastern's senior vice-president of planning, remembers, "Lots of other airlines didn't know how to spell People Express. We sure did."[74]

---

[67] Banks, p. 139.

[68] Labich, "The New U.S. Airlines," *Interavia*, p. 325.

[69] Ibid.

[70] Ibid., p. 326.

[71] Woolley, pp. 1056–1060.

[72] Ibid.

[73] Peter Nulty, "A Champ of Cheap Airlines," *Fortune*, March 22, 1982, p. 127.

[74] Leslie Wayne, "Frank Borman's Most Difficult Years," *New York Times*, February 17, 1985.

The ingredients of the early success of People Express are hardly a secret: rock-bottom fares and savvy marketing. On People Express passengers pay only 9.3 cents a mile for their tickets (compared with Piedmont's 16.1 cents and U.S. Air's 18.6 cents). The only reason that People Express can charge the fares it does is because its costs are so incredibly low. Its 800 full-time employees are nonunionized; and they achieve tremendous productivity for the airline because of their flexibility and versatility. It is not at all unusual for a pilot to be flying one day and working as a ticket agent the next. As Larry Martin, a general manager for the airline, suggests, "You don't keep costs down by counting pencils and paper clips. You have to squeeze massive productivity out of people and planes."[75]

People Express, however, has not succeeded simply because it has cheap employees who will do a variety of different jobs. There is a conscious effort to keep administrative overhead to a minimum; in fact, there are no secretaries anywhere in the company. Additionally, the airline hires independent contractors for baggage handling, maintenance, and other support functions. The company has also profited by buying used aircraft (see American's Crandall's comments), and by continuing to increase its fleet. It is committed to increasing its 56-craft fleet to 81 by the middle of 1986.[76]

A further element of People Express's success has been its recognition of the marketing advantages of the hub-and-spoke system. Rather than set up hubs in areas already dominated by the major carriers, People Express has targeted less-popular, less-expensive, but geographically feasible areas, such as its Newark hub. Future plans call for the establishment of a new hub, probably in the Midwest or the West.[77]

By mid 1985, People Express was flying high. Sales in 1984 were $414.1 million, an increase of 115 percent over the previous year. Net profit for that period was $7.9 million, an increase of 25 percent.[78] The prevailing prediction in the industry, however, was that it would not be long before the great equalizer of a deregulated industry affected the success of People Express. As the airline acquired more debt to finance its expansion and as the major carriers improved their competitive positions, People Express was predicted to become just another airline trying to survive, with the same problems and threats as the rest of the industry (see Industry Outlook).

Republic Airlines.   Headquartered in Minneapolis, Minnesota, Republic employs 14,000 people. In 1983 it carried 17,787,000 passengers, with a passenger load factor of 54.4 percent. Its market is the domestic United States, Canada, Mexico, and the Cayman Islands.[79]

The times following deregulation have not been easy for Republic. In fact, it has frequently been mentioned as the next possible casualty of deregulation. However, in March of 1985 the company announced a record-breaking profit of $29.5 million for 1984. These results represent an improvement of $140.5 million compared with a $111-million loss in 1983. According to Stephen M. Wolf, President and Chief Operating Officer, the profit reflects Republic's emphasis on route realignment, lowered operating costs, and employee commitment.[80]

[75] Nulty, p. 128.

[76] Labich, "Fare Wars," *Fortune*, p. 28.

[77] Ibid.

[78] Ibid.

[79] Woolley, pp. 1056–1060.

[80] A. B. Magary, "Republic Airlines Frequent Flyer Program Update '85," (March 1985).

USAir.   The 12,000 employees of USAir are headquartered in Arlington, Virginia. Serving the market of the domestic United States and Canada, USAir carried 16,352,000 passengers in 1983, with a passenger load factor of 59.5 percent. In 1982, when Pan Am lost $485 million and Eastern lost $50 million, USAir earned $60 million. Its 1984 second-quarter profit was $63.6 million.[81]

Western Airlines.   Headquartered in Los Angeles, California, Western Airlines employs 10,355 people. In 1983 it carried 9,100,000 passengers, comprising a passenger load factor of 56.5 percent. Western's market is the western United States, Canada, Hawaii, Alaska, and Mexico.[82]

Others

There are over 100 airlines in the United States which rank neither as a major carrier nor as a national carrier. They are airlines, such as Florida Express and Air Atlanta, that have sprung up as a result of deregulation. Their fleets may range from three or four prop planes which serve a commuter market to three or four jets that serve a regionalized market whose routes are not covered extensively by the other carriers.

The primary competitive force of these other airlines is in their fares. Because their fares are substantially lower, they represent a potential drain on the load factors of the other airlines. Whereas no one would suggest that they represent a viable threat as far as market leadership, no one can deny their effect in forcing the other carriers to match their fares in the routes served.

1984 Airline Traffic Statistics

The following Exhibit 24.1 contains detailed statistics about the airline industry traffic during 1984.

Industry Success Factors

Quality of Management

A key success factor in many industries is the quality of management. This is particularly true in the airline industry, where deregulation has introduced an entirely different set of rules and subsequent penalties for not playing by those rules. Despite the fact that one can attach blame to any number of extraneous factors as the causes of a particular airline's problems, one must also give credit to top management of those airlines who have and continue to anticipate, plan, react, and manage in such a way as to ensure the survival and the success of their companies.

Deregulation was not a surprise to anyone in the airline industry; it did not suddenly swoop down from the skies onto a totally unsuspecting industry. Because of this, the effects of deregulation should have been anticipated, and strategies and objectives should have been in place before the advent of deregulation. Perhaps no one could have antici-

[81] Woolley, pp. 1056–1060.
[82] Ibid.

pated the exploding effects of escalating fuel prices and a weakening economy on the deregulated airline industry. The fact of the matter is, however, that the management of airlines such as American, Delta, Northwest, United, and Piedmont met those challenges head-on; and their companies flourished because of that management.

Strong Balance Sheet/Strong Capital Base

A strong balance sheet is necessary for essentially four reasons: to withstand fare wars, to expand route systems, to modernize existing fleets, and to attract equity investors. Despite airlines' wishes, fare wars seem to be here to stay. Similarly, as more and more competitors enter the market, route expansion remains a critical strategy for the major airlines. Subsequently, fleet modernization, too, is a critical option and one that must be pursued, albeit cautiously. Finally, a strong balance sheet is necessary to attract desperately needed equity investors so that the airlines can finance their route expansion and fleet modernization without greatly increasing their debt.

In the profit-and-loss equation of the airline industry, capital turnover is a crucial element. As Emile Beekman, formerly the vice-president of finance for KLM Airlines, emphasizes: "Capital turnover is an essential element in return on investment. The more we can turn over our investment, the better the industry can live with small profit margins. . . . Experience has shown that the airline industry needs a strong capital base."[83]

Low Labor Costs/High Productivity

One needs to merely contrast People Express with Eastern Air Lines to realize that the combination of low labor costs and high productivity is a critical success factor in the airline industry. As an industry analyst asserts in *Journal of Commercial Bank Lending*, "lower labor costs are the only answer to the revenue declines for most airlines."[84] It is the substantially lower labor costs of the new entrants which has allowed them to operate cost-effectively and which has made them formidable competitors.

The other side of the coin is high productivity. This is particularly true in the case of the established airlines who, in the face of highly paid employees, must find ways to increase the productivity of their people so they can operate with fewer of them. One of Eastern's managers has identified increased productivity as the key to Eastern's survival. The airlines did not have to worry about productivity during preregulation days; now they must. For, as productivity goes up, costs go down; and Eastern and the other older airlines will be able to compete.[85]

Marketing

Marketing in the deregulated environment has achieved a greater position of importance and a definite place as a key industry success factor. No longer are consumers choosing a particular airline because of convenience of particular flight times. Instead, the flying

[83] Woolley, p. 1035.

[84] Schmutzer, "An Analysis of the Airline Industry," *The Journal of Commercial Bank Lending*, p. 22.

[85] Personal inteview with a manager of Eastern Air Lines, March 18, 1985.

Exhibit 24.1   Airline Traffic Full Year, 1984

	Revenue Passenger Miles (Thousands)	RPM Change (Percent)	Available Seat Miles (Thousands)	ASM Change (Percent)	Passenger Load Factor (Percent)	Freight Revenue Ton-Miles (Thousands)	Freight RTM Change (Percent)
Majors-Domestic							
United	45,308,591	4.8	74,721,209	11.4	60.6	520,109	−7.3
American	33,680,001	7.6	54,297,534	12.6	62.0	419,383	−10.8
Eastern	26,605,279	5.1	46,549,430	9.0	57.2	236,431	17.5
Delta	25,278,743	0.1	48,627,254	2.5	52.0	195,285	−2.9
Republic	8,594,042	−11.2	17,113,169	−3.7	50.2	60,155	22.4
Trans World	14,756,269	−7.7	25,715,695	−1.9	57.4	159,248	9.1
USAir	8,432,890	14.3	14,402,280	16.1	58.6	13,716	22.8
Continental	9,150,804	15.6	14,504,607	10.0	63.1	91,983	−8.0
Northwest	9,823,256	4.0	17,980,534	6.1	54.6	393,350	21.9
Western	8,764,157	−0.1	15,157,953	−2.7	57.8	109,698	−5.1
Pan American	6,009,238	−20.7	10,237,618	−16.9	58.7	113,912	−12.7
Total/Average	196,403,270	2.4	339,307,283	6.1	57.9	2,313,270	0.2
Majors-International							
Pan American	22,396,546	−1.4	33,892,974	−5.0	66.1	527,032	−5.6
Trans World	13,547,448	20.2	29,804,803	21.6	66.1	262,957	38.2
Northwest	10,308,107	19.8	15,059,630	16.4	68.4	576,290	10.5
Eastern	2,803,370	−6.7	5,099,010	−3.7	55.0	31,867	5.2
American	3,025,450	8.3	4,374,559	3.0	69.2	46,641	7.1
Continental	1,773,865	28.5	2,911,823	30.0	60.9	55,397	30.6
Delta	1,776,325	17.8	2,538,317	19.3	70.0	46,146	37.9
United	1,378,596	149.4	2,471,021	50.3	55.8	47,551	51.2
Western	652,813	1.9	1,160,429	7.2	56.3	3,286	36.4
Total/Average	57,662,520	9.9	87,312,566	7.1	66.0	1,597,167	9.9

Nationals

Piedmont	6,254,696	21.0	11,896,134	23.8	52.6	17,321	30.3
Southwest	4,674,428	19.9	7,988,102	26.2	58.5	1,521	26.4
Frontier	4,465,318	14.4	7,025,965	7.1	63.6	9,612	−10.4
PeoplExpress	7,700,945	109.9	11,029,810	124.3	69.8	2,494	N/A
Ozark	2,779,289	3.8	5,067,786	5.5	54.8	5,794	−3.8
Braniff	1,913,541	N/A	4,265,543	N/A	44.9	2,164	N/A
AirCal	1,695,546	11.0	3,004,572	17.8	56.4	2,343	76.3
Transamerica	2,495,708	16.2	2,933,928	9.7	85.1	317,544	15.0
World	4,537,232	21.3	6,725,835	23.4	67.5	67,008	81.2
New York Air	938,260	42.5	1,675,052	45.7	56.0	7	−12.5
Total/Average	37,454,963	36.7	61,612,727	39.9	60.8	425,808	23.1

Large Regionals

Muse Air	931,450	41.0	1,971,918	52.1	47.2	546	24.7
Northeastern	1,674,023	235.4	2,455,533	248.0	68.2	2,207	1067.7
Jet America	881,439	42.4	1,469,599	69.9	60.0	3,419	241.9
Empire	242,898	45.6	561,476	57.8	43.3	60	106.9
Air Wisconsin	163,028	35.2	402,989	42.7	40.5	163	2.5
Total/Average	3,892,838	88.4	6,861,515	95.8	56.7	6,395	252.3

N/A = Figure too small for comparison or not available.

Source: Based on "Aviation Week and Space Technology," April 29, 1985, p. 68.

public is being bombarded with a multitude of discounted fares, with bonuses offered by frequent-flyer programs, and with a variety of connecting flight options.

Because of this, route systems are a critical marketing factor—both in maintaining existing routes and in expanding into new markets. The success of the hub-and-spoke system is undeniable (witness Delta in Atlanta and Eastern in Kansas City). Airlines must continually examine their existing route systems to determine what hubs to remain in or to exit (as Eastern did in Houston and as TWA did in Kansas City); and they must constantly explore the possibility of creating new hubs in order to serve new markets.

Pricing, too, is a critical factor of marketing in a deregulated environment. Given the industry's proclivity for fare wars and the potentially negative impact of discounted fares on the bottom line, fare-setting truly must be an art. More and more airlines are creating MIS departments for the sole purpose of monitoring competitive pricing and of directing their own pricing strategies based on demand (see MIS strategies for Eastern Air Lines). If the Airlines are going to achieve the profits that they must achieve, the planning and control of pricing is crucial.

Buyers

The buyers in the airline industry are comprised of two basic types: the business traveler and the discretionary traveler. The business traveler does not appear to be as price sensitive as the discretionary traveler. Business travelers tend to make reservations based more on convenience of flight times and connections. Service, too, is more important to business travelers—particularly to business travelers who fly frequently and who are likely to remember where and when they have received good or bad service. Because business travel is relatively price inelastic, airlines court the business traveler through private membership airport clubs (e.g., Eastern's Ionosphere and Delta's Crown), and through frequent-flyer programs which offer everything from free flights to discounts on rental cars and lodging. Through these frequent-flyer programs, airlines hope to develop brand loyalty and keep the business traveler flying their airline, without regard to fare. There have been some indications, however, that some types of business travelers, like salespeople, do seek discounted fares. As a general rule, though, flight times, service, and frequent-flyer bonuses are the critical factors to the business traveler.

The discretionary traveler, on the other hand, is the key target of fare wars. If one is planning a vacation, then one has a reasonable amount of latitude as far as flight times and connections go and is most certainly going to shop around for the cheapest fare. This is the traveler whom American is targeting with its recently launched marketing campaign which offers the "ultimate super saver fare," with the restrictions of a 30-day advance purchase and a 25-percent cancellation penalty. Whereas service is occasionally a selling point to the discretionary traveler, price is the key.

Suppliers

Except for the suppliers of jet fuel, the suppliers to the airline industry do not serve as a major threat. As a whole, the suppliers—whether aircraft manufacturers, tire manufacturers, caterers, or tire retreaders—are at the mercy of the airline industry. If the economy is good, people are flying, and airlines are remaining in business, then the suppliers prosper also. It is definitely a buyer's market, except for fuel; and indications are that, because of the recent oil glut, the threat posed by fuel suppliers is diminishing.

Substitute Products

The substitutes for air travel are few: automobiles, buses, and trains. For most business travelers, these modes of transportation are not viable substitutes. And with the tremendous discounting of air fares, they are no longer as viable for the discretionary traveler. In fact, some airlines, like People Express, have launched marketing campaigns in which they sell the advantages of cheap air travel over the substitute modes—a move which has resulted in increased advertising and reduced prices among bus companies and trains.

Industry Outlook

Eleven major carriers in the United States, who account for some 80 percent of the industry's production, began 1984 with a first-half operating profit of $808 million (compared with a $498-million loss in the first half of 1983) and a net profit of $281 million (compared with a $520-million loss in that period in 1983). This improvement has been achieved by a sharp increase of 14 percent in revenue for a modest increase of 3 percent in cost. Yield has increased from 10.71 cents per passenger mile to 12.42 cents.[86] Net on continuing operations for the fourth quarter of 1984 was $155,833,000, a 165 percent increase over 1983. Net income for that same period was $86,266,000, an 86 percent increase over 1983.[87]

Things are definitely improving. One of the reasons is the economic recovery. As a consequence, airline traffic is rising. The increased attention to productivity improvements and cost minimization by the major airlines is reflected in the fact that yield is consistently rising and costs are expected to remain steady. Times are looking better for the airline industry.[88]

Two major problems remain for the industry, however. The first is the "crippling cost" of interest rates, a product of the high ratio of debt to equity in most airlines and the fact that investment continued during the 1982–1983 recession. The second problem is the increasing difficulty of financing future fleets.[89] To further complicate this, Julius Maldutis of Salomon Brothers observes that the industry's profits are deteriorating, primarily because of industry fare wars.[90]

Industry analysts sugggest that the airline industry has passed through two stages since deregulation: experimentation with route structure and pricing experiments. They say that the airlines are now entering a third stage, which will be marked by a growing gap between weak and strong carriers and which will end in a rash of bankruptcies and mergers.[91] Barry Gordon, President of the National Aviation and Technical Corporation, agrees that the shakeout period will continue: "There will be fewer carriers around in a decade, and they will really control the industry."[92]

Which of the airlines flying today will still be flying in 1995 remains to be seen. Most people agree that the discount airlines, like People Express, will ultimately blend into the

---

[86] Woolley, p. 1035.

[87] Woolley, "Industry by Industry Quarterly Earnings," *The Wall Street Journal*, February 19, 1985.

[88] Rowan, "A Patch of Blue for the Airlines," *Financial World*, p. 24.

[89] Woolley, "Airlines Climb out of the Red," p. 1033.

[90] Suzy Hagstrom, "High on Eastern Convertibles," *The Orlando Sentinel*, March 25, 1985.

[91] Labich, "Fare Wars," *Fortune*, p. 24.

[92] Skryzcki, "Growing Pains for Midsized Airlines," *U.S. News & World Report*, p. 49.

industry. If the economy continues to improve and the major airlines begin rehiring, the new entrants will have to increase wages in order to retain their staffs. Similarly, as the economy improves, the surplus of used aircraft will disappear and the new entrants will find their replacement costs increasing. This will erode their competitive advantage, and they will have to rely more on superior productivity to maintain the cost differential.[93]

Additionally, once the costs of the major airlines are more in line with those of the no-frills carriers, the major airlines could profitably cut their prices temporarily and eat into their rivals' business. Airlines like People Express would have no choice but to boost their fares as load factors decline.[94] As one analyst suggests, the two groups of airlines— established and emerging—are on converging trends. As they grow, new airlines will tend to take on more of the characteristics of the established sector; while the latter will have to continue to adopt more of the newcomers' practices to remain competitive.[95]

[93] Labich, "The New U.S. Airlines," *Interavia*, p. 325.
[94] Labich, "Fare Wars," *Fortune*, p. 27.
[95] Labich, "The New U.S. Airlines," *Interavia*, p. 327.

Muse Air Corporation

▪ *Robert McGlashan and Tim Singleton* ▪

En-route to the Love Field airport in Dallas in one of the company's planes, Michael Muse had many things on his mind. He deeply wanted his company, Muse Air Corporation, to be profitable. There was more at stake here than money; it was a matter of pride. "How could anyone have the misfortune to start an airline just a few weeks before the air traffic controllers' strike?" Michael asked his father, Lamar Muse, who was in the next seat. "It's just not possible to control everything at all times. You just have to make the best of things," Lamar responded. "Well it's time we took control again," Michael said firmly. "Let's map out our revised strategy for expansion." Lamar knew that he was going to have to review the major factors facing Muse Air to resolve things in Michael's mind.

The Airline Industry

Regulation

The major issues facing the airline industry today stem from its continuing struggle to adjust to the changing environment created by the Airline Deregulation Act of 1978. Under deregulation, the control of the Federal Aviation Administration (FAA) and the Civil Aeronautics Board (CAB) over airlines was drastically reduced. As controls over routes and fares were lifted, the industry faced rapidly changing market conditions in which competition increased significantly. The immediate result for the major established airlines was a dramatic drop in corporate earnings as new low-priced entrants forced price wars. The industry continues to be plagued by financial losses and excess passenger capacity. From 36 certified carriers prior to deregulation, the industry has mushroomed to about 125 airlines today. But the rate of failure has increased also, as 28 carriers have gone out of business since 1978.

The primary long-term result of deregulation and increased competition is a stronger and more efficient industry. Overall, inflation-adjusted ticket prices, because of discount fares, are now 10–20 percent lower than in 1974. Departures at major hub cities in 1983 were up 15.7 percent, and at medium hubs were up 22.5 percent from 1978. The number of interstate carriers has risen from 36 to 98 with big airlines now controlling 79 percent of the market, versus 91 percent before deregulation. Although, since 1978 the major carriers have reduced their work forces by 24,000 employees, nearly that many jobs have been created by the smaller airlines.

The FAA continues to exercise regulatory authority over airlines in regard to ground facilities, communication, training of pilots and other personnel, and aircraft safety. Air-

The research and written case information were presented at a Case Research Symposium and were evaluated by the Case Research Association's Editorial Board. This case was prepared by Robert McGlashan and Tim Singleton of the University of Houston–Clear Lake as a basis for class discussion. Research was prepared by Sheryl Dawson, Frederick Mullin, David Olson, and Margaret Parish, MBA students at the University of Houston–Clear Lake.

Distributed by the Case Research Association. All rights reserved to the authors and the Case Research Association.

lines must obtain an operating certificate subject to compliance with all regulations in these areas. Environmental regulation is also imposed to control noise and engine emissions. Local pressure groups may exert influence on airports to limit flights over certain areas in order to control noise pollution. One special regulation imposed by the International Air Transportation Competition Act of 1979 is the limitation on flights out of Love Field in Dallas. Destinations from Love Field may include locations only in the four states neighboring Texas—Arkansas, Oklahoma, New Mexico, and Louisiana.

When the CAB is dissolved on January 1, 1985, the regulatory authority over mergers and interlocking relationships will be transferred to the Justice Department, under which the FAA operates. For other businesses, this regulatory authority is the jurisdiction of the Federal Trade Commission. Other responsibilities which the CAB handles, such as selection of carriers for international route operations, have been reassigned to the Department of Transportation. Since both of these departments are in the Executive Branch, there is congressional debate as to whether sufficient control over the airline industry can be retained without the CAB or another congressional agency. Reregulation considerations will continue to surface as the CAB deadline approaches.[1]

Air Traffic Control

Airlines are still dealing with the effects of the August 2, 1981, union strike of the Professional Air Traffic Controllers Organization (PATCO). The air controller's job is to keep airplanes moving at a safe distance from one another as they are passed along from one tower to another. As planes taxi, take off, fly, and land, they stay in touch with the pilots by radio and follow their progress on radar screens. These screens display each plane's location, altitude, speed, and any problems, such as two planes moving too close together. The screens are all computer-generated.

When 12,000 of the 17,000 controllers walked out at the start of the strike, the traffic control system was thrown into confusion. Under FAA emergency controls, which reduced flight frequencies, nearly 75 percent of the 22,000 daily flights were kept flying. All the major airlines experienced a decrease in revenues and available slots, both airport and en route, which reduced flexibility in route structuring despite deregulation. Once the initial pandemonium over the strike abated, the airlines began to tailor their operations to meet the new environment. Steps taken included grounding of the least fuel-efficient planes, concentration on the more important routes, reduction in the work force, and restrictions placed on discount fares. A drop in revenue of 12 percent was reported by TWA and 15 percent by United Airlines. These figures were typical for the airline industry.

Only since October 30, 1983, has the FAA eliminated most slot restrictions, enabling airlines to determine destinations without having to negotiate and trade for landing slots. Because of continued air traffic control problems in Chicago, Los Angeles, New York, and Denver airports, restrictions have not as yet been lifted in these high-density cities. The post-strike rules are slated to expire April 1, 1984, in Denver, but will remain in effect in Los Angeles until after the Olympics. Expiration of the rules in New York and Chicago has been delayed until January 1985, however, based on the FAA's assessment of air control's inability to handle unrestricted air traffic at these airports. The temporary preferen-

[1] Joan M. Feldman, "Deregulation Loose Ends Spark Debate about Regulation after 1984," *Air Transport World*, Vol. 20, May 1983, p. 23.

tial route system requires that aircraft fly specific mandatory routes to circumvent congested airspace, but the routes are often considerably longer in distance than airlines would normally fly. Costing time and fuel, these restrictions have affected airlines' cost-reduction efforts, especially for the majors who serve longer hauls. It is expected that the FAA will finally eliminate the preferential route system early in 1984.[2] The future of air traffic control is enhanced by the long-awaited decision to modernize the system. The FAA has embarked on a ten-year, $10-billion effort to upgrade air traffic control in order to cope with the projected 26.5 percent growth in aviation by the year 2,000

Cooperative Routing

The flexibility in routing brought about by deregulation has given-rise to the hub-and-spoke system with its central exchange point. This system enables airlines to carry passengers to their final destinations without having to share revenues, as is necessary in interlining agreements. This preregulation system of interlining is beginning to fall apart as the majors reevaluate their benefits. Under multilateral, open-ended agreements which have created an integrated national air transportation system, the major airlines provide passengers with interchangeable ticketing and baggage service to final destination. United, American, and Delta are now advising interlining partners that their agreements will be on a bilateral basis with periodic review. The change is contemplated by the majors because of Continental Airlines' action in seeking protection under bankruptcy regulations in 1983. Because Continental did not cease operations completely and resumed service within two days, the bankruptcy court judge ruled that Continental's partners should continue to honor the interline agreement, and yet would not be able to collect money owed for services prior to the bankruptcy. At issue, too, is the industry's default protection plan which protects ticket holders in the event of airline bankruptcy. The end to either system would place new competitive pressures on financially weak airlines.[3]

A new form of cooperative routing has developed in which airlines agree bilaterally to link their route systems in an effort to strengthen their individual hub-and-spoke networks. Muse Air has such an arrangement with Air Cal. Cooperative routing could be achieved by other means, such as arrangements similar to franchise service exchange or outright acquisition of commuter carriers by larger airlines.

Economy

The airline industry is highly affected by the business cycle. The current upturn in the economy has brought increases in revenue passenger miles to help reduce the pressures of overcapacity which plagued the industry throughout the recession of 1981 and 1982. As disposable income grows and air travel increases during the favorable economy, airlines will experience increasing revenues. The temptation in an upturn is to be less vigilant regarding rising costs. Whether these increased revenues translate into increased profits or not depends on the stability of airlines to keep costs down.

---

[2] "FAA Nears Ruling on Preferential Routes," *Aviation Week & Space Technology*, Vol. 119, April 18, 1983, p. 34.

[3] "Airline Cooperation Starts to Break Apart," *Business Week*, November 29, 1983, p. 45.

In fact, cost control is the primary key to profitability in the airline industry. With labor costs representing 37 percent of the total expenses of the established major and national carriers, in contrast to the new entrants' 18 percent, there is a significant disequilibrium in the industry that market forces will inevitably eliminate. Entering into this equation is the labor relations dilemma facing the industry. Recognizing that a favorable employee attitude is essential to high-quality service, how airlines achieve labor cost control directly impacts effectiveness as well as efficiency. Two advantages that new entrants have in labor productivity are: (1) established airline employees and their unions have little understanding or sympathy for the effects of deregulation; and (2) employees of new airlines have no allegiance to the preregulation structure and possess the enthusiasm of sharing in a new enterprise. There have been several approaches to labor cost control including employee ownership programs, establishment of new subsidiary carriers, revocation of labor contracts through declaration of bankruptcy, and a two-tiered wage system for old and new employees.

The second major cost factor is fuel availability. The sporadic shortages, political instability in oil-producing countries, and decontrol of oil prices are uncontrollable external conditions that directly impact profitability of airlines. When fuel costs rose dramaticaly in 1979–1980, competitive pressures prevented airlines from passing on those increases to passengers. Although fuel costs have declined for the past three years, they still represent 25 percent of total airline costs. Fuel-efficient aircraft have become an important consideration as a result of high fuel costs.

Beyond operating expenses, the major cost of airlines is the aircraft itself. The high cost of new aircraft has made their acquisition economically prohibitive in spite of their greater fuel efficiency. At current fuel costs, the savings are not sufficient to cover the cost of buying expensive new aircraft. One of the reasons for the high price of aircraft is the fact that manufacturers produce aircraft on an individual job-order basis rather than by mass production. This nonstandardized production not only increases the original cost but reduces the residual value of aircraft.

Additionally, the fragmentation of the market has reduced opportunities to use larger aircraft. The per-seat cost savings on a 150- vs. 100-seat aircraft, for instance, can only be realized if the extra capacity is utilized. This is difficult to achieve in a competitive market already facing overcapacity. Once again, the impact of deregulation seems to be responsible for setting a new trend. In an effort to reduce capacity, airlines are seeking smaller aircraft. The transition to the downsized transport will be costly to airlines and place new competitive pressures on aircraft manufacturers who have suffered decreased sales for five years. As airlines return to profitability, fleet acquisition will be a priority in order to gain competitive position.[4]

Reservation System

The distribution of airline ticketing is dominated by travel agents utilizing computerized reservation systems. In fact, 65 percent of airline reservations are handled by travel agents. Airlines subscribe to one of the majors' computerized systems, of which American's SABRE is dominant in Texas markets. There are two advantages to the owners, or

---

[4] James Ott, "Airlines Gear for New Challenges," *Aviation Week & Space Technology*, Vol. 118, November 14, 1983, p. 48.

host carriers, of the reservation systems. One is a computer bias in which the host is given priority listing among available flights with more information listed than for other airlines. This tends to encourage the choice of the host by travel agents in reserving flights resulting in increased market share for the host. Secondly, it is commonplace for travel agents to book (or plate) tickets to the servicing carrier, which is the computer host. Since there is a four- to ten-week ticket settlement period, in effect this gives the host utilization of the amounts "plated away" from the airline subscribers, who are denied cash settlement for that period. It is estimated that the float created by this plating process amounts to $3 billion and costs the airlines financing that float $360 million a year in new interest expense. The Justice Department has asked CAB to adopt rules to reduce competitive abuses of the computerized systems.[5]

With agent commissions representing 6.7 percent of total airline operating expenses, the CAB's plan to abolish travel agent exclusivity at the end of 1984 will increase competitive initiatives in retail marketing. By breaking up the travel agent monopoly, new innovations in the distribution of airline ticketing are possible. For instance, direct reservations by individuals through cable television may be implemented, discount houses for airline ticket sales could develop, and business travel departments may gain access to direct reservation systems. New economies may also be realized if the practice of "plating away" from airlines, which attempt to reduce travel agent commission, is eliminated.[6]

Company History

The Beginning

Muse Air Corporation was organized in early 1980 by two ex-Southwest Airlines employees, Lamar and Michael Muse. The airline was organized to provide high-frequency, single-class, low-cost air transportation for the general public. It was one of the many new regional airlines entering the market after deregulation of the airline industry.

Lamar Muse, one of Southwest Airline's founders and former chief executive officers, left Southwest Airlines after a bitter policy dispute in 1978. His two-year, no-competition agreement with Southwest ran out in October 1980, when he joined his son, Michael, to operate Muse Air. Michael was a former chief financial officer for Southwest Airlines.

Muse Air began service on July 15, 1981, with two DC-9 Super 80s flying between Dallas and Houston. The plans were to compete directly with Southwest on their most lucrative route. Muse had an aggressive expansion program laid out for the next several years, planning to become a major airline as quickly as possible. Fate had no intention of allowing Muse's plans to run smoothly.

Air Traffic Controllers' Strike

On August 2, 1981, just 18 days after Muse began service, PATCO went out on a nationwide strike, causing the FAA to place restrictions on landing slots.

With the delivery of two McDonnell Douglas DC-9 Super 80s, Muse Air planned to expand its routes to include Midland-Odessa and Tulsa by May 1982. Even though the

---

[5] Michael Cieply, "Hardball," *Forbes*, Vol. 132, February 28, 1983, p. 33.

[6] James Ott, "House Questions Agent Decision," *Aviation Week & Space Technology*, Vol. 118, May 30, 1983, pp. 57–58.

Exhibit 25.1   Muse Air Corporation Aircraft Delivery Schedule

	Aircraft			
Delivery Date	Type	Quantity	Seating	Cities Served
July 1981	DC9-80 (Super 80)	2	155	Dallas Houston
May 1982	DC9-80	2	155	Midland Odessa Tulsa
October 1982	DC9-80	2	155	Los Angeles
August 1983	DC9-51 (Super 50)	1	130	Lubbock*
November 1983	DC9-51	2	130	Austin
February 1984	DC9-51	1	130	Ontario, CA New Orleans
Projected Delivery Date				**New Cities**
April 1984	DC9-51	1	130	Little Rock** Las Vegas
March 1985	DC9-51	2	130	San Antonio Chicago
March 1986	DC9-51	2	130	Atlanta Florida

*Service discontinued in February 1984.

**Service start-up cancelled February 1984.

Source: 1983 Muse Air Annual Report and Muse Air News Release.

FAA planned to increase the air traffic system's capacity to 90 percent of normal (before strike) by September 1982, no changes or increases in landing slots were authorized for Dallas or Houston. This was at a time when airline officials were expressing strong dissatisfaction with the FAA's continued use of emergency powers to allocate the additional capacity, instead of switching to normal administrative procedures. Many airlines felt the allocation of additional slots and routes was not being handled fairly.

Planned expansion by Muse into these two new markets in May 1982, and two additional markets in July 1982, was being delayed because of Federal Aviation Administration restrictions on operating slots at Love Field in Dallas and Hobby Airport in Houston. Muse Air had applied for permission to provide Houston-Dallas-Tulsa with seven daily round trips and six daily round trips from Dallas to Midland-Odessa. (Refer to Exhibit 25.1.)

The FAA approved Muse Air for operation of one evening off-peak round-trip to Tulsa and denied all other requested slots. The FAA also denied a request for 13 flights daily between Love Field and Austin and 14 flights between Love Field and San Antonio. Muse Air officials argued that the slot restrictions were contrary to the meaning of the deregulation act, tending to favor established carriers over new entrants. Obtaining the slots was vital for Muse Air, not only to prevent grounding of the two DC-9s that were being received, but to boost the load factors systemwide as the result of traffic the new cities would give to its present operation.

The Collapse of Braniff

In May 1982, Braniff Airlines ceased operations and filed for bankruptcy-court protection under Chapter 11 of the Federal Bankruptcy Code. Braniff needed protection from creditors' lawsuits as it tried to work out a plan to repay all debts. This opened up many slots for other airlines to pick up and expand service. Muse Air was one of the first to present its request to the FAA for some of the Braniff slots.

Of all the new slots received by Muse Air, they were able to finally begin service to Midland-Odessa and Tulsa in late May 1982. Attention was then turned toward the next planned expansion, that of Austin and San Antonio. Muse Air felt they still had enough Dallas slots to accomplish this expansion on schedule.

The FAA gave Muse Air seven en-route slots and eight airport slots at Dallas on a temporary basis. These slots were former Braniff slots which the FAA later rescinded and allocated to other airlines by lottery. This left Muse in a position of negotiating for needed slots at Dallas in exchange for slots it did not want, such as at New York's LaGuardia. So, again in August 1982, Muse Air was in a position of having to ground newly acquired aircraft for lack of available slots.

The West Coast

On October 1, 1982, as a way to keep from grounding aircraft, Muse Air began service to Los Angeles, California. This was a complete shift in original expansion plans. While the continuing restrictions on landing rights imposed by the FAA forestalled planned expansion to Austin and San Antonio, the new service to California achieved a break-even level of operations by December 1982.

During the first part of 1983, Muse Air worked very hard at strengthening existing routes and increasing market share. For the first eight months of 1983, passenger traffic, as measured by revenue passenger miles, was up 195 percent. The fact that gains in traffic outpaced any increase in capacity was due to growing passenger-load factors, the percent of seats filled. Growing identity with the traveling public, as much as anything else, was a major reason for these gains. This was accomplished by increasing the number of flights serving a particular market (the Dallas-Houston route was increased to 17 round-trip flights daily), and attracting a larger portion of the business community as passengers, since these are the people who travel most frequently.

Continuing Expansion

In late 1983, Muse Air began the expansion again, with service to Lubbock in August and Austin in November 1983. A major factor that made this possible was the elimination of most FAA slot restrictions on October 30, 1983. Muse's new $3-million terminal at Hobby airport was completed in November 1983, thus adding another large upgrade to the system.

Muse Air continued with expansion in early 1984 with the opening of the New Orleans market in February. With the Mardi Gras festival in the spring and the World's Fair opening in the summer, this means increased traffic to the New Orleans area. Muse Air fully expects to take advantage of this increased traffic flow and become very quickly established in the area.

Service was also begun to Ontario International in California in February 1984. Plus, a selective joint marketing agreement was signed with Air Cal. Through these two "gateway" locations, Muse Air passengers can quickly connect to eight of Air Cal's markets. In essence, this agreement represents a doubling of marketing destinations available to Muse Air customers. All the conveniences of expanded service to eight new West Coast markets was achieved without the costly capital outlays required for opening individual, on-site operations.

In late February of 1984, Muse Air discontinued service to Lubbock as it had proven to be unprofitable for the company. Plans for new service to Little Rock, Arkansas, were abandoned the following month. Southwest Airlines moved into Little Rock first and saturated the market with flights.

In response to this, Muse Air opened up nonstop service between Dallas and New Orleans, began service to Las Vegas from Houston in April of 1984, and began special discount fares and Olympic tour packages. At this time, all eleven of their planes were being fully utilized and earning a profit for Muse Air.

Company Management

Management Organization

The organization of Muse Air's top management is a straightforward top-down style (see Exhibit 25.2). Lamar Muse is chairman of the board and Michael is president and chief executive officer. There are nine vice-presidents that report to Michael Muse, which covers all the major areas of company operation. These people are:

- Vice-President—Flight Operations:
  Mr. Ferguson served as a senior captain for Texas International Airlines and is now responsible for all operations and pilots.

- Vice-President—Maintenance and Engineering:
  Mr. Minter worked previously for Braniff in their maintenance department and as staff vice-president.

- Vice-President—Purchasing and Stores:
  Mr. Lane came from Southwest Airlines as Director of Purchasing.

- Vice-President—Planning and Administration:
  Mr. Thomson is another former Southwest Airlines employee. He was director of treasury operation.

- Vice-President—Finance and Treasurer:
  Mr. Coogan, a former audit manager for Price Waterhouse, has been with Muse Air two years.

- Vice-President—Airport Services:
  Mr. Savage has worked for Texas International, Air Couriers International, and TWA, managing airports and airport facilities.

- Vice-President—Marketing Support Services:
  Ms. Harker was a manager of marketing and financial support for American Airlines previously.

Exhibit 25.2   Muse Air Corporation Corporate Organization Chart

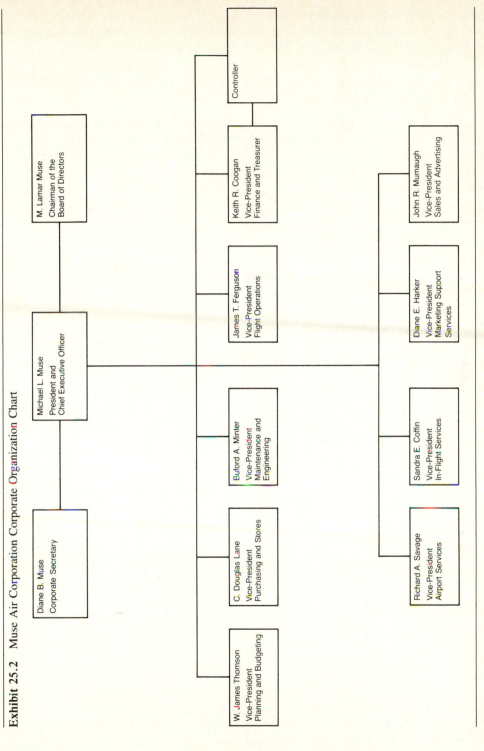

M. Lamar Muse
Chairman of the
Board of Directors

Michael L. Muse
President and
Chief Executive Officer

Diane B. Muse
Corporate Secretary

W. James Thomson
Vice-President
Planning and Budgeting

C. Douglas Lane
Vice-President
Purchasing and Stores

Buford A. Minter
Vice-President
Maintenance and
Engineering

James T. Ferguson
Vice-President
Flight Operations

Keith R. Coogan
Vice-President
Finance and Treasurer

Controller

Richard A. Savage
Vice-President
Airport Services

Sandra E. Coffin
Vice-President
In-Flight Services

Diane E. Harker
Vice-President
Marketing Support
Services

John R. Mumaugh
Vice-President
Sales and Advertising

Source: Muse Air Corporation.

- Vice-President—In-Flight Services:
  Ms. Coffin has worked as a flight attendant and as director of training and support for
  Eastern Air Lines.
- Vice-President—Sales and Advertising:
  Mr. Mumaugh worked for United Airlines previously in sales, marketing, in-flight
  operations, and customer service.

The Muse Air management team contains a great amount of experience and expertise
concerning the airline industry from a wide variety of sources and companies.

Employee Benefits

Muse Air has no pension plan for their employees but does have a profit-sharing plan.
When operating profits exceed a set amount for a quarter, 20 percent of these excess profits are distributed to the employees as cash. This is only for employees who have been
with the company for a set period of time. Muse Air will also adopt a stock purchase plan
for their employees and highly encourage participation in the program. With the employees having a portion of ownership in the company, they will be more inclined to keep
productivity up and costs down.

At present, there is a stock option plan for employees as far down in the company as
mid-management. The employee's position with the company determines how many
shares he or she may purchase and at what price. An employee must have one year of
service with Muse Air to participate and can only purchase one-third of the option shares
within a given year. The employee has five years to purchase all the stocks available to him
or her under the option agreement.

A nonmonetary benefit of Muse Air is the rotation of employees within different
ground operation positions. This allows the employees to become well cross-trained in
various jobs while keeping their interest rate at a high level. Cross-training helps keep
productivity up while keeping costs down for Muse Air, since they do not have to keep
excess people on the payroll.

Aircraft and Facilities

Muse Air uses the McDonnell Douglas DC-9 Super 80, and DC-9 Super 50 aircraft.
These planes both use the cost-efficient, two-engine design and require only two pilots,
instead of three, as needed by other aircraft. All planes are set up for single-class service
with a distinguished, club-style atmosphere. The exterior is white with the Muse Air signature in blue on the side of the plane.

The corporate signature of Muse Air as analyzed by Ray Walker, handwriting expert,
announces strength and character. The backstroke on the letter *M* shows an awareness of
the past, complimented by a powerful forward sweep that indicates confidence in the future. The *A* is an indication of pride. The dot over the *i* is close to the stem, showing an
appropriate caution with emphasis on the safety and well-being of others.

Muse Air has implemented a cost-efficient work force. Employees are nonunion, which
helps keep wage levels moderate. Also, employees are cross-utilized between various
jobs, eliminating the work restriction rules that plague many major carriers and raise their

effective labor costs. Finally, because Muse Air is such a young company, there are no long-time employees, meaning lower overall wage levels.

Within the air terminals, Muse Air uses cash register-type ticketing and standardized check-in and baggage handling procedures. Operating costs are substantially reduced and passenger arrival-departure time kept to a minimun.

Keeping the comfort and convenience of passengers in mind, all flights are nonsmoking. The DC-9 Super 80 carries 155 passengers while the Super 50 carries 130. This, plus the 3–2 style of seating that has been installed, means more room and comfort for the passengers. The DC-9 gives the passenger a very quiet and smooth ride.

Competition

General

The airline industry is divided into three segments: the major airlines, the national airlines, and the regionals, such as Muse Air. The market share of the majors has been declining since deregulation. At the same time, market share for the regionals has been increasing, picking up what the majors have lost. The load factors of the major airlines have stabilized over the past few years, neither growing nor decreasing. Muse Air's competition consists of three types. The first is Southwest Airlines, with whom Muse Air initiated head-on competition. Second are the regionals that have come into existence following deregulation. Last are the majors, who are reestablishing on a much smaller scale, including Braniff and Continental Airlines.

Southwest Airlines

Southwest Airlines provides a single-class, high-frequency air service to cities in Texas and surrounding states. The company concentrates on short-haul markets and stresses high level of aircraft utilization and employee productivity. The principal hubs of Southwest's systems are Dallas's Love Field and Houston's Hobby Airport, with a new hub established in Phoenix. These airports are located substantially closer to downtown business centers than the major airports.

Southwest is considered one of the best-run airlines in the country. Revenues and revenue passenger miles rose all during 1983. The airline has a load factor around 62 percent, well above its break-even point. Southwest will be expanding into the longer-haul routes with the delivery of new Boeing 737-300 aircraft in 1984. With a young and efficient fleet, the company is well positioned to benefit from any improvement in the domestic economic activity.

Regional Airlines

People Express began operating in April 1981, and intends to triple its size by mid-1985 through the purchase of several Boeing 727s. It also began offering transatlantic service during the summer of 1983, with a leased 747-200. People Express services 17 cities domestically, mostly in the Northeast. It flies from its base at Newark, New Jersey, as far as Houston's Hobby. It was one of the few airlines to report a profit in 1982.

New York Air initiated service in late 1980 in the New York-Boston-Washington, D.C., corridor, competing directly with Eastern's shuttle service. Since then it has added cities in the Southeast. The airline experienced an increase of profitability in 1983. New York Air pioneered the concept of business-class service at coach-class rates. Passengers have been lured with such items as two-by-two seating, more legroom, bagels, and the *New York Times*.

In February 1984, Air Atlanta began service between Atlanta, Memphis, and New York. The airline is using fewer seats, bigger chairs, more legroom, shorter ticket lines, and waiting areas with telephones and refreshments to lure full-fare business passengers. Air Atlanta plans to specialize totally in this market. The planes and waiting areas have been completely redesigned for the business passenger to move on and off the plane quickly. Air Atlanta intends to cater to business passengers.

St. Louis-based Air One began operations in April 1983, with flights to Dallas, Kansas City, Washington, D.C., and Newark, New Jersey. Air One is another airline that caters to the business traveler, offering first-class service at coach-class prices. In February of 1984, Air One began service between St. Louis and Houston's Hobby, the first of 22 cities it eventually plans to include in its route system. Air One currently has seven Boeing 727s and will add five more in late 1984.

Rebirths

Like the phoenix that rose from the ashes, Braniff Airlines began flying again on March 1, 1984. It plans to operate a premium-service, low-cost airline, aimed strictly at the business travel market. From its Dallas hub, Braniff will serve 17 cities, including Houston, Austin, Los Angeles, New Orleans, San Antonio, and Tulsa. Braniff is flying from Dallas-Fort Worth Regional Airport and Houston's Intercontinental. Estimates are that it will take several years for the airline to regain the market share it lost in the Houston market.

Braniff restructured itself with the financial backing of the Hyatt Corporation. It has reduced salaries, employees, and operating costs to the bare minimum. Even at these low levels, Braniff needs a 47 percent load factor to break even. The first stock offering by Braniff indicated moderate public confidence in the reborn airline.

Continental Airlines filed to reorganize under Chapter 11 of the Federal Bankruptcy Code during the third quarter of 1983. In February 1984, the airline reappeared with bare-bones pay scales, unrestricted low air fares, and employees with a stake in the airline's profitability. Like many of the new airlines, Continental is aiming for the single-class business market with competitive fares and many special services.

Marketing Strategy

Muse Air endeavors to provide the highest-quality airline service to its target market, primarily business people. The marketing strategy is based on service, price, name recognition, and expansion of routes.

Service

Quality service on Muse Air includes many features; a quiet, comfortable ride on a Super 80 or Super 50 aircraft with comfortable, large leather seats in a clean, smoke-free environment; dependable service with convenient closed-in airport locations and convenient departure times; the convenience of reserved seating to prevent the crush to board; the best service provided by motivated employees; easy booking for travel agents through American Airlines' computerized SABRE system.

Price

The air transportation market is growing as the economy improves. Muse Air must gain its share of this market growth. To accomplish this goal, they use competitive prices to attract customers. In March 1983, Muse Air offered the "lowest" discounted fare to Los Angeles of $88.

Off-peak pricing is used to attract more customers and keep more planes flying at higher occupancy. Muse Air primarily utilizes a two-tier fare structure: business class providing low-cost, first-class air transportation during prime time; and leisure class providing an economically competitive alternative to various forms of ground transportation.

Muse Air has always had to meet or beat the low fares of their major competitor, Southwest Airlines. The recent revival of Continental and Braniff Airlines in March 1984, increased competition on most of the Muse Air routes. This competitive environment may spark another round of price slashing. Braniff has already announced reduced economy fares during March 1984.

The reborn Continental Airlines precipitated fare discounting as a means to fill seats and gain the customers it lost after filing to reorganize under Chapter 11. Additionally, Delta Air Lines, Pan Am, American, Eastern, and TWA have joined in with their own discounting in order to remain competitive. Of these majors, Delta began service on March 1, 1984, from Houston's Hobby Airport to seven cities including Dallas/Ft. Worth, the major market for Muse Air.

Because of deregulation and the Chapter 11 alternative, the airline industry is becoming more efficient. Everyone is trying to keep costs low so their rates can be competitive. It is with Southwest that Muse Air must be competitive in order to gain the needed traffic. Muse Air has a lower average cost than Southwest (5.2 cents a seat/mile against Southwest's 6 cents and the industry average of nearly 11 cents). Since overhead is almost identical, Muse Air must differentiate itself from Southwest in order to "break the Southwest habit" to which the frequent flier has become accustomed.

Name Recognition

Lamar Muse feels that name recognition is critical to success. Therefore, Muse Air devotes a lot of effort to promote a premium product with a reserved and sophisticated image.

To enhance the club-car image, they provide many in-service extras, including drinks on afternoon flights and a complimentary copy of the *Wall Street Journal*.

To encourage repeat customers, Muse Air has developed several packages and clubs that provide benefits for frequent flyers. For example, the Muse Air Club is for travel coordinators, secretaries, and people in business and government who are responsible for travel arrangements. Club members can earn free trips, participate in monthly drawings for special prizes, and receive the Muse Air magazine and invitations to special receptions.

Muse Air continues to spend heavily for advertising. In 1982 expenditures were over $6 million, or 16 percent of all operating expenses, for marketing. The initial ad campaign, "Big Daddy Is Back," emphasized their leader, Lamar Muse, and his experience in the airline industry. The next campaign was testimonials from customers.

The latest advertising effort on radio and television is intended to reach a wider group of potential passengers by using people of various ages and occupations. The campaign also attempts to entice the customer with a mystical, indescribable, beautiful experience. The themes are "You just gotta fly it," and "See how beautiful Muse Air can be." Initial response to this campaign has been very positive.

Route Expansion

The fourth component of the Muse Air marketing strategy is expansion of routes. Muse Air began service in July 1981 between Dallas (Love Field) and Houston (Hobby Airport). As of February 1984, Muse Air flies 17 round-trips daily on the Dallas-Houston route, which is its most popular.

From 1982, Muse Air has expanded service to Midland-Odessas, Texas; Tulsa, Oklahoma; Los Angeles, California; Lubbock, Texas; Austin, Texas; Ontario, California; and New Orleans, Louisiana. As of April 29, 1984, Muse Air will be offering service to Las Vegas. (See Exhibit 25.3 for a map of the expanded service area.) Plans for future expansion include San Antonio, St. Louis, Chicago, New York, Atlanta, and Florida.

Exhibit 25.3   Proposed Expansion of Muse Air Routes Effective April 29, 1984

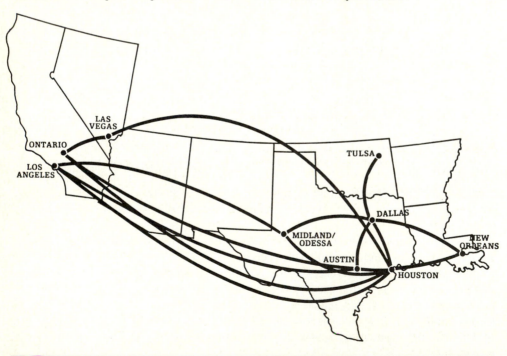

Source: Muse Air Corporation.

Exhibit 25.4 Muse Air Strategic Route Plan 1980

[1] Includes airports at Brownsville, Harlingen, and McAllen, Texas. Long-range plan of Muse Air is to expand its initial Dallas-Houston service to cover a total of 24 markets from hubs at Houston, Chicago, and Atlanta, matching Southwest Airlines' fares in its market and undercutting any other competition.

Source: *Aviation Week and Space Technology*, August 17, 1981.

Originally, Muse Air expansion plans were to fly to the South and Midwest. Exhibit 25.4 is a map of the initial strategic plan of Muse Air as formulated in 1980. There are indications that the westward air travel market is served to overcapacity. Muse may try to return to these original plans to increase profitability. Houston will become the center of operations.

At the end of February 1984, Muse Air had to cancel plans for beginning service to Little Rock, Arkansas. Muse's service to Little Rock had been announced in January and was to begin April 19, 1984. After the announcement, Southwest Airlines flooded the Little Rock market with new flights, forcing Muse Air out before service began.

Exhibit 25.5   Muse Air and Air Cal Routes Effective March 1, 1984

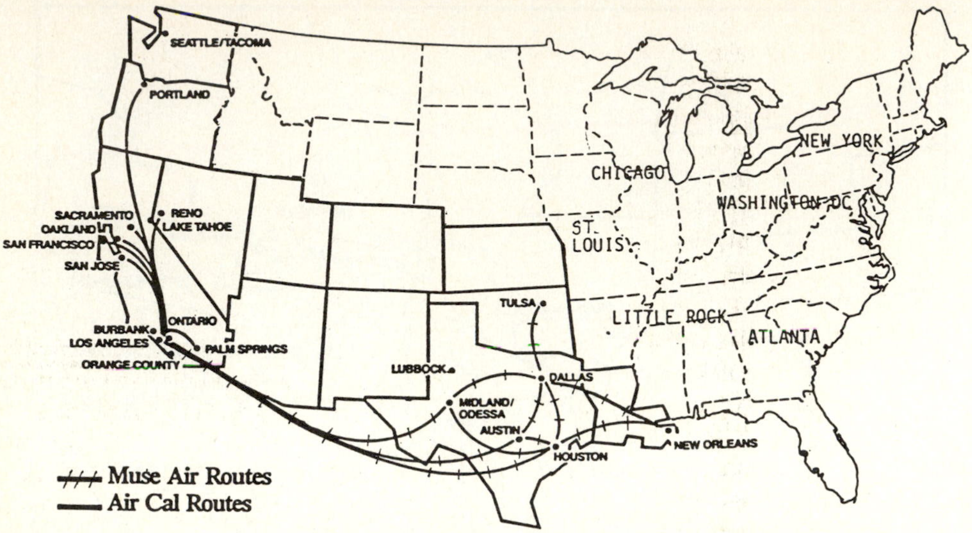

+/+ Muse Air Routes
—— Air Cal Routes

Source: Muse Air Flight Schedule and Fare Summary, effective March 1, 1984.

Muse Air will face other competitors as it tries to expand. Delta has already started service to Atlanta from Houston's Hobby airport, the same route proposed by Muse for service in March 1986.

Not only is Muse Air being crowded out of expansion routes, but existing routes as well. After several months of service, Muse Air discontinued flights to Lubbock, Texas. Delta, American, and Southwest Airlines all service Lubbock. This is the first route that Muse Air has ever had to discontinue.

Besides planned route expansion, an innovative joint marketing program with Air Cal should help Muse Air grow beyond its strictly regional status. The Muse Air/Air Cal joint marketing agreement began February 5, 1984. Muse Air passengers can connect quickly to eight of Air Cal's markets including: San Francisco, Sacramento, San Jose, Palm Springs, and Oakland, California; Seattle, Washington; Portland, Oregon; and Reno, Nevada. (See Exhibit 25.5 for a map of Air Cal routes.)

This selective joint marketing agreement represents a doubling of market destinations available to Muse Air customers virtually overnight. All the conveniences of expanded service to eight new West Coast markets were achieved without the costly capital outlays required for opening individual airline on-site operations. According to John Mumaugh, Vice-President—Sales and Advertising, this joint marketing program illustrates clearly how deregulation has freed carriers to pursue creative marketing techniques in a cost-effective manner to ultimately benefit the traveling public.[7]

---

[7] John Mumaugh, "Executive Corner," *Muse Air Monthly*, October 1983, p. 7.

Finances

Equity

The company was initially capitalized in February 1980 through the issuance of 31,250 shares of common stock to Michael L. Muse for $25,000 in cash. In October 1980, the company issued and sold an aggregate of 318,750 shares of common stock to five members of the Muse family and Cole, Brumley & Eichner Inc. for cash payment of $.80 per share. In October 1980, the company also issued and sold to five members of the Muse family an aggregate of $190,000 principal amount of its 12 percent convertible subordinated debentures at the face amount. In February 1981, 237,500 shares of common stock were issued to the five members of the Muse family upon conversion of the debentures. On March 20, 1981, the company's stock was split five-for-four.

On April 30, 1981, the company made a public offering of 2,200,000 shares of common stock with warrants to purchase 1,100,000 shares of common stock priced at $17.50 per unit (one share of common stock and one-half warrant). The proceeds of this offering were used as a deposit and fee relating to the future acquisition of four new DC-9 Super 80 aircraft, the prepayment of a one-year lease on the two Super 80 aircraft that were in operation, the acquisition of aircraft spare parts and engines, the purchase of ground equipment and leasehold improvements, and the unrestricted addition to working capital. The stock was traded in the over-the-counter market under the symbol "MUSE." The warrants provide for the purchase of common stock at $16.00 per share and expire on April 30, 1986, or as early as January 1, 1984, if certain conditions are satisfied and the company chooses to accelerate the expiration date. No warrants have been exercised to date.

On May 24, 1983, the company made another public offering of 1,540,000 shares of common stock at $16.25. The net proceeds of this offering were used to prepay a secured bank note due in July 1984, and to increase the equity base and working capital position of the company to support future expansion. The common stock commenced trading on the American Stock Exchange under the symbol "MAC" on April 18, 1983, at which time it ceased trading in the over-the-counter market.

With this last equity offering, no further financing is expected in 1984. A cash flow of $12.5 million in 1983 and $25 million in 1984 should pose few difficulties requiring further equity. In addition, the company will likely force the conversion of the 1.1 million warrants at $16 per share if the common stock trades at or above $24 per share for 30 consecutive trading days. Market capitalization on December 31, 1983, stood at 4,030,113 common shares. The company's balance sheet and statement of operations are included as Exhibits 25.6 and 25.7, respectively.

In 1982, Muse sold tax benefits of depreciation and investment tax credits on four of its DC-9 Super 80 aircraft, producing net proceeds to the company of approximately $21.6 million. This item was treated as "other" income and accounted for the net earnings of $3.87 per share during fiscal 1982. Without these tax-related benefits, the company would have reported a 1982 full-year net loss of $3.17 per share.

Capital Stock Valuation

Because of the various crises situations Muse has encountered, the stock's price has fluctuated widely from a high of 19⅜ to a low of 3½ during its short life (see Exhibit 25.8). While the stock price has changed with the outlook for the company's future, the book

Exhibit 25.6   Muse Air Corporation Balance Sheet

	December 31,	
	1983	1982
Assets		
Current assets:		
Cash and temporary investments of $16,931,000 in 1983 and $7,250,000 in 1982	$ 18,404,116	$ 7,488,653
Accounts receivable	6,600,356	3,068,720
Inventories of parts and supplies	513,582	412,833
Prepaid expenses	1,001,455	555,246
Total current assets	26,519,509	11,525,452
Property and equipment at cost:		
Flight equipment—aircraft	130,187,529	109,700,751
Aircraft purchase deposits	8,672,808	
Leasehold improvements	3,454,387	1,026,286
Other flight and ground equipment	14,100,401	9,325,544
	156,415,125	120,052,581
Less: accumulated depreciation and amortization	(10,593,431)	(3,255,798)
	145,821,694	116,796,783
Other assets, net	445,502	2,470,381
Total assets	$172,786,705	$130,792,616
Liabilities and Stockholders' Equity		
Current liabilities:		
Accounts payable	$ 4,352,121	$ 1,081,662
Unearned transportation revenues	1,637,359	681,535
Accrued liabilities	6,957,066	3,389,432
Current maturities of long-term debt	9,615,541	2,460,000
Total current liabilities	22,562,087	7,612,629
Long-term debt less current maturities	83,594,659	76,440,000
Deferred federal income taxes	263,501	715,740
Other long-term liabilities		1,013,790
Total liabilities	$106,420,247	$ 85,782,159
Stockholders' equity:		
Common stock, $1.00 par value; 20,000,000 shares authorized; issued and outstanding 4,636,750 shares in 1983 and 3,100,000 shares, $.10 par value, in 1982	4,636,750	310,000
Additional paid-in capital	56,183,993	37,196,245
Retained earnings	5,545,715	7,504,212
Total stockholders' equity	66,366,458	45,010,457
Commitments and contingencies		
Total liabilities and stockholders' equity	$172,786,705	$130,792,616

Source: Muse Air Corporation 1983 Annual Report.

value has steadily increased. Currently, the stock is selling at a 25 percent discount from book value and about seven times estimated 1984 earnings. As a comparison, Southwest Airlines sells at 3 times book value and 20 times earnings; Midway and People Express sell at comparable or higher multiples. Also, the earnings leverage is considerable because passenger traffic should increase more rapidly than growth in capacity and net-loss carryforwards. Additionally, investment tax credits will be available to offset future income tax.

Based on estimates, Muse Air has the potential to earn $1.50 per share in fiscal year 1984 (see Exhibit 25.9). If these earnings estimates prove correct, and based on a valuation of 12 times earnings, a value for Muse common of $18 per share is possible. The potential for substantial price appreciation is within reason. Since warrants move,

Exhibit 25.7   Muse Air Corporation Statement of Operations

	Year ended December 31,		
	1983	1982	1981
Operating revenues:			
Passenger	$68,976,808	$32,211,861	$ 6,217,593
Other	3,951,150	844,063	78,268
Total operating revenues	72,927,958	33,055,924	6,295,861
Operating expenses:			
Fuel and oil	20,940,064	12,182,590	3,201,335
Flight operations	8,360,307	6,130,036	2,871,844
Marketing	13,292,021	6,112,769	2,251,081
Maintenance	3,827,987	2,211,586	941,113
In-flight service	4,479,305	2,001,974	545,566
Terminal operations	5,109,215	2,889,318	832,069
Insurance and taxes	2,819,025	1,572,725	277,684
General and administrative	2,136,772	1,578,310	714,538
Depreciation and amortization	7,347,628	3,114,827	197,620
Total operating expenses	68,312,324	37,794,135	11,832,850
Operating income (loss)	4,615,634	(4,738,211)	(5,536,989)
Nonoperating income (expense):			
Interest income	1,647,481	897,928	1,569,469
Interest expense (less interest capitalized of $797,967 in 1983 and $1,353,943 in 1982)	(8,556,268)	(4,309,216)	
Other income	499,985	21,835,019	
Other expense	(617,568)	(1,502,186)	
Net nonoperating income (expense)	(7,026,370)	16,921,545	1,569,469
Income (loss) before provision for federal income taxes and extraordinary item	(2,410,736)	12,183,334	(3,967,520)
Federal income tax provision (benefit)	(452,239)	2,540,800	
Income (loss) before extraordinary item	(1,958,497)	9,642,534	(3,967,520)
Extraordinary item—utilization of net operating loss carryforwards		1,825,060	
Net income (loss)	$ (1,958,497)	$11,467,594	$(3,967,520)
Income (loss) per common share:			
Income (loss) before extraordinary item	$(.49)	$3.25	$(1.86)
Extraordinary item		.62	
Net income (loss)	$(.49)	$3.87	$(1.86)
Weighted average shares outstanding	4,030,113	2,963,151	2,136,781

Source: Muse Air Corporation 1983 Annual Report.

Exhibit 25.8   Muse Air Corporation Summary Book Value/Trading Price per Share

Year	Quarter	Book Value Per Share Price Price	Trading Pricer per Share High	Low
1980	4th	$ .81	—	—
1981	1st	—	—	—
	2nd	12.19	15	11½
	3rd	11.26	15¼	7¼
	4th	10.83	12⅝	7⅜
1982	1st	10.35	8⅞	5½
	2nd	9.81	7⅜	3½
	3rd	11.05	9	4⅜
	4th	14.52	13⅝	6⅝
1983	1st	14.09	15	10⅜
	2nd	13.64	19⅜	14¼
	3rd	14.27	17¾	13½
	4th	14.31	16¾	14

Source: 1981, 1982, and 1983 Muse Air Corporation annual reports.

Exhibit 25.9   Muse Air Corporation Statement of Operations
($ in thousands except per-share amounts)

	1984E	1983	1982	1981
Revenues	$135,000	$ 72,928	$33,056	$ 6,296
Operating expenses	110,000	68,312	37,794	11,833
Operating income	25,000	4,616	(4,738)	(5,537)
Nonoperating income	(16,000)	(7,026)	16,922	1,569
Earnings before taxes	9,000	(2,410)	12,184	(3,968)
Tax	2,000	(452)	2,541	—
Earnings before extraordinary item	7,000	(1,958)	9,643	(3,968)
Extraordinary items	—	—	1,825	—
Net income	$ 7,000	$ (1,958)	$11,468	$ (2,941)
Shares	4,640	4,030	2,963	2,131
Earnings Per Share:				
Earnings before taxes	$ 1.95	$ (0.49)	$ 4.11	$ (1.86)
Earnings before extraordinary item	—	—	$ 3.25	—
Net income	$ 1.50	$ (0.49)	$ 3.87	$ (1.86)

Source: 1983 Muse Air Annual Report and Analyst Estimates.

percentage-wise, to a greater extent than does the common, the excellent leverage provided by this vehicle would reward investors even more handsomely.

Muse Air reported its first operating profit of $780,000, or $.17 per share, in the third quarter of 1983. In the 1983 fourth quarter, the company again reported an operating profit of $202,000 or $.04 per share. Both quarters of operating profits helped reduce the 1983 operating net loss to $1,959,000 or $.49 per share. Mr. Michael L. Muse stated that the positive results of the third and fourth quarter "provided Muse Air a solid launching pad for what should prove to be a very successful 1984."[8]

Aircraft Acquisition

The company began service on July 15, 1981, with two Super 80 aircraft leased from McDonnell Douglas Corporation (MDC). The first equity offering in April 1981 provided the funds for the lease of these two aircraft as well as the purchase of four new aircraft. In August 1982, the company repaid the subordinated debt of $4.1 million to MDC from proceeds received from the sale of tax benefits on one of these aircraft.

The company purchased two additional Super 80 aircraft in September 1982, and one in November 1982, with $42 million provided from bank financing and with approximately $14 million of the proceeds from the sale of tax benefits associated with these aircraft. In December 1982, the company leased a sixth Super 80 aircraft under a long-term operating lease agreement from the McDonnell Douglas Finance Corporation (MDFC). As of this date, Muse Air owns five of its Super 80 aircraft and holds a long-term lease for the sixth. Exhibit 25.1 shows the aircraft delivery schedule.

In August 1983, Muse Air negotiated the purchase of ten used McDonnell Douglas DC-9-51 aircraft, five of those from SwissAir and the other five from Austrian Air. The total cost of this acquisition was approximately $100 million. The first two aircraft were delivered in October 1983, the third in February 1984. Two more are to be placed in service during late April or early May 1984. Three additional aircraft are to be delivered in the first quarter of 1985 and the final two in the first quarter of 1986. Muse Air intends to use the smaller aircraft on its shorter hauls with less passenger demand while using the Super 80s on longer and more heavily traveled flights. Approximately $11 million from the second equity offering was used as a deposit on the aircraft with the balance to be financed with bank debt of $65 million as the planes are delivered through 1986.

The Predicament

Lamar and Michael Muse were weary from reviewing all the relevant information pertaining to their situation. The airline industry is going through a time of change. What is the best strategy for Muse Air Corporation to pursue in this rapidly changing environment? Is the time right to expand? Should expansion be regional or national? These were all important questions that Michael Muse felt required definite answers.

References

"Air One Starting Service to Houston's Hobby." *Houston Chronicle*, February 22, 1984.

"Air Traffic Declines Less than Expected." *Wall Street Journal*, September 3, 1981, p. 4.

"Air Transport." *Standard & Poor's Industry Surveys*, Vol. 149, August 20, 1981, A56–A73.

"Air Transport Industry." *The Value Line Investment Survey*, January 6, 1984, pp. 251–252.

"Airline Cooperation Starts to Break Apart." *Business Week*, November 28, 1983, p. 45.

---

[8] "Muse Air Reports Substantial Fourth Quarter Operating Profit; Finishes 1983 with Back-to-Back Quarterly Net Profits as Well," Muse Air News Release, January 1984.

"Airline Labor Costs Increasing Despite Union Concessions." *Aviation Week & Space Technology*, No. 119, October 3, 1983, p. 32.

"Airline Wages Are Set for a Long Slide." *Business Week*, April 9, 1984, pp. 127–128.

"Airlines in Turmoil." *Business Week*, October 10, 1983, pp. 98–102.

Banks, Howard. "Airlines." *Forbes*, Vol. 133, January 2, 1984, p. 139–143.

Banks, Howard. "Fixing Tickets." *Forbes*, Vol. 132, August 29, 1983, p. 42–43.

"Big Daddy's New Airline." *Newsweek*, Vol. 98, November 9, 1981, p. 77.

"Braniff Is Coming Back to Some Tough Competition." *Business Week*, February 27, 1984, pp. 37–41.

"CAB Urged to Reduce Bias in Reservations Systems." *Aviation Week & Space Technology*, No. 119, November 28, 1983, pp. 34–35.

"Can Western Airlines Fly Back to Profitability." *Business Week*, February 27, 1984, pp. 114–116.

Cieply, Michael. "Hardball." *Forbes*, Vol. 132, February 28, 1983, p. 33.

Clifford, Mark. "A Struggle for Survival." *Financial World*, Vol. 152, November 15, 1983, pp. 13–18.

Coogan, Keith R., Vice-President of Finance and Treasurer, Houston, Texas. Interview, March 21, 1984.

Donlan, Thomas. "Turbulent Skies." *Barron's*, October 17, 1983, p. 15.

Donoghue, J. A. "Reservations Systems Likely to be Disciplined." *Air Transport World*, Vol. 20, September 1983, pp. 28–30.

"FAA Nears Ruling on Preferential Routes." *Aviation Week & Space Technology*, Vol. 119, April 18, 1983, pp. 34–35.

Feldman, Joan M. "Deregulation Loose Ends Spark Debate about Regulation after 1984." *Air Transport World*, Vol. 20, May 1983, pp. 23–29.

Harris, William. "Muse Air." *Forbes*, October 26, 1981, p. 200.

Henderson, Danna K. "Muse Air Is Making It." *Air Transport World*, September 1983, pp. 54–57.

Kirkpatrick, John. "High Profile." *Dallas Morning News*, June 19, 1983, p. 4E.

Klempin, Raymond. "Local Airline Activity on the Rise." *Houston Business Journal*, March 12, 1984, p. 8A.

Kliewer, Terry. "Airline Expects Big Demand." *Houston Post*, February 23, 1984.

Kliewer, Terry, and Margaret Downing. "Braniff Will Make Its Mark in Aviation History March 1." *Houston Post*, February 12, 1984.

"Local Airline Activity on the Rise." *Houston Business Journal*, March 12, 1984, p. 8A.

Longeway, Barbara. "Continental and Southwest: Agony and Ecstacy." *Houston Chronicle*, February 26, 1984, Sec. 4, p. 1.

Longeway, Barbara. "Sentimental Journey: Braniff's First Flight Rekindles Memories." *Houston Chronicle*, March 2, 1984.

Low-Beer, Anthony, and Susan Nakada. "Muse Air Corporation." *Rooney, Pace Inc.* August 22, 1983.

McCartney, Scott. "New Braniff Is Ready to Take to the Skies from 18 Cities." *Houston Chronicle*, February 26, 1984, Sec. 4, p. 16.

Meadows, Edward. "The FAA Keeps Them Flying." *Fortune*, Vol. 104, December 28,1981, pp. 48–52.

Mumaugh, John. "Executive Corner." *Muse Air Monthly*, October 1983, p. 7.

Mumaugh, John. "Executive Corner." *Muse Air Monthly*, February 1984, p. 7.

"Muse Air Cancels Plans for Little Rock." Muse Air News Release, March 27, 1984.

"Muse Air Celebrates Inauguration of New Orleans Service." Muse Air News Release, February 5, 1984.

"Muse Air Cites Need for Airport Slots." *Aviation Week & Space Technology*, No. 116, May 17, 1982, p. 41.

Muse Air Corporation 1981 Annual Report.

Muse Air Corporation 1982 Annual Report.

Muse Air Corporation 1983 Annual Report.

"Muse Air Ends Plan for Arkansas Service, Some Fare Increases." *Wall Street Journal*, February 29, 1984, p. 12.

"Muse Air Expands LAX Service." Muse Air News Release, January 22, 1984.

Muse Air Expands Service to Little Rock, Arkansas, on April 29." Muse Air News Release, March 21, 1984.

"Muse Air Expands to Las Vegas April 29." Muse Air News Release, March 21, 1984.

"Muse Air Expands to New Orleans, La. and Ontario, Ca." Muse Air News Release, December 21, 1983.

"Muse Air Reports Substantial Fourth Quarter Operating Profit." Muse Air News Release, January 1984.

"Muse Air to Discontinue Service to Lubbock, Texas." *Wall Street Journal*, February 21, 1984, p. 32.

"Muse Air." *Standard & Poor's*, November 24, 1983, Sec. 8605.

"Muse Air Says Chairman Is Retiring." *Wall Street Journal*, April 2, 1984.

"Muse Air to Terminate Lubbock Service." Muse Air News Release, February 17, 1984.

"Muse Expansion Delayed by Slot Problems." *Aviation Week & Space Technology*, No. 116, April 12, 1982, p. 26.

"Muse Service." *Air Transport Industry* No. 117, October 18, 1982, p. 33.

"New Air Tariff Agreement Drafted." *Aviation Week & Space Technology*, No. 116, February 8, 1982, p. 32.

"New Airline Focuses on Business Travelers." *Houston Post*, February 12, 1984, p. 16E.

O'Lone, Richard G. "U.S. Manufacturers Project Turnaround." *Aviation Week & Space Technology*, No. 119, March 14, 1983, pp. 167–178.

Ott, James. "Airlines Gear for New Challenges." *Aviation Week & Space Technology*, No. 118, November 14, 1983, pp. 48–50.

Ott, James. "Carriers Intensify Labor Cost Drive." *Aviation Week & Space Technology*, No. 118, November 21, 1983, pp. 27–30.

Ott, James. "House Questions Agent Decision." *Aviation Week & Space Technology*, No. 118, May 30, 1983, pp. 57–58.

Robertson, Thomas S. "Management Lessons from Airlines Deregulation." *Harvard Business Review*, Vol. 61, January/February 1983, pp. 40–44.

"The Scramble to Modernize Air Traffic Control." *Business Week*, October 10, 1983, p. 39.

"Service Expansion." *Aviation Week & Space Technology*, No. 116, February 8, 1982, p. 31.

Shifrin, Carole A. "U.S. Airline Traffic Rises by Estimated 8% in 1983." *Aviation Week & Space Technology*, No. 120, January 30, 1984, pp. 35–36.

"Southwest Airlines." *The Value Line Investment Survey*, January 6, 1984, p. 271.

Sylvester, David. "Regional Airline Review." *Wheat First Securities Industries Update*, December 9, 1983.

"Upstarts in the Sky." *Business Week*, June 15, 1981, pp. 78–92.

Wewer, Dan R., Jr. "Muse Air Corporation." *Rauscher Pierce Refsnes, Inc.*, September 26, 1983, pp. 1–8.

Eastern Air Lines
April 1985

▪ *Sandra Foster, Steve Keith, and Cathy Shields* ▪

"I'm tired of being a pincushion for people who keep taking liberties with the truth," mused Eastern Air Lines' Chairman Frank Borman. Whether he was responding to allegations by the doubting press, to allegations by one of Eastern's increasingly angry union leaders, or to allegations by one of the growing numbers of skeptical financial analysts is uncertain; what is certain is that for the past six years Borman has had to respond to any number of allegations about the past mistakes, the present survival, and the future existence of Eastern Air Lines. And it has not been easy—even for a man who has spent much of his life in the public eye.

Many Americans remember Frank Borman as the astronaut who read from the *Bible* on Christmas Eve as he commanded the first manned orbit of the moon. Many more people, however, recognize Frank Borman as the commander of the chronically troubled Eastern Air Lines, the nation's largest carrier. Since he took over as chief executive officer in 1975, Borman has been constantly challenged by an ailing company which has flirted dangerously with financial disaster.

Even in 1975 Eastern was teetering on the edge of bankruptcy. Borman upgraded the aging fleet, improved the airline's service, and effected four straight years of record profits. But, as the impact of deregulation was felt in the early 1980s, Eastern was hit harder than most other airlines. Its highly lucrative East Coast corridor became the first battleground for fare wars, and low-cost entrants threatened its New York-to-Florida lifeline. The effects of deregulation were magnified by escalating fuel prices in the late 1970s and the early 1980s; and Borman directed Eastern on a highly controversial and expensive aircraft buying spree, incurring enormous debt to buy new Airbuses and Boeing 757s—giving Eastern the newest and most fuel-efficient fleet, just as fuel prices dropped substantially.

Eastern has been unprofitable since 1979; and no one, save Mr. Borman, is predicting when it will begin to make money. The airline has accumulated $300 million in losses over the last five years, and its debt has increased to a staggering $2.5 billion. Labor relations are touchy, at best; and despite the fact that Eastern's employees have recently saved the company from default, few people are confident that Eastern can continue to wrest wage concessions from its employees.

Mr. Borman, however, paints a very rosy picture for his company. "I'm confident we will emerge from 1985 and this decade as a tough, competitive, and successful company. The average Eastern employee knows that I care for him and his future. If I didn't think the employees felt that way, I'd leave, and I don't intend to leave." It remains to be seen whether Borman's tenacity and paternalism will be enough to save Eastern Air Lines.

Description of Business

Eastern Air Lines, Inc., is a certified air carrier which provides scheduled air transportation between the peripheral metropolitan areas of the northeastern and southwestern portions of the United States. Although Eastern's route system is predominantly North-South, it also serves major cities in the West. In addition, Eastern provides air service between points in the United States and the Caribbean, Central and South America, Mexico, Bermuda, Canada, and the Bahamas. In its air transportation services, Eastern is subject to competition from other airlines.[1] It is the second-largest airline in the United States in terms of total passengers carried.

History of Eastern Airlines

Harold Pitcairn, born with the proverbial silver spoon in his mouth, was somewhat of a dreamer, tinged with a streak of practicability. Much to his family's dismay, Harold announced his intentions of making a career out of flying and a business out of aviation. After graduation from the University of Pennsylvania's Wharton School of Business Administration, Pitcairn enlisted in the U.S. Army Signal Corps' Aviation Section as a flying cadet. At the war's end, Pitcairn dutifully became treasurer of his father's successful holding company, but his heart and mind were still on aviation. In 1925 Harold Pitcairn won what amounted to his emancipation—his father released him from his corporate position and agreed to finance Pitcairn Aviation as a subsidiary.

Harold joined with a young aeronautical engineer, Agnew Larson, and test pilot James Ray, and built an airfield adjacent to Harold's small factory. After successfully racing a plane which they had built, the name Pitcairn became a new force in aviation. Racing laurels, however, were not on Pitcairn's achievement agenda. Pitcairn's goal was to build a fleet of airplanes with which to start an airline.

Pitcairn was able to secure several contracts to fly mail between various cities and hired several pilots to begin delivery. By 1929 Pitcairn had over 90 employees and was, amazingly, making money and was flying almost a third of the nation's total airmail mileage. Then, without confiding in even his closest friends, Pitcairn mysteriously decided to sell his fast-growing, profitable airline to Clement Keys, owner of National Air Transport. The airlines' headquarters were moved from the Philadelphia area to Brooklyn. The name of Pitcairn Aviation was officially changed to Eastern Air Transport (EAT) on January 15, 1930. Soon to follow, operation headquarters were moved to the more central location of Atlanta, and Key's goal was to start passenger service as soon as possible. On August 18, 1930, Eastern began carrying passengers for the first time on a New York-to-Richmond, Virginia, flight. Plans were made to begin service to Atlanta and, shortly thereafter, Miami. By the end of 1931, EAT had nearly 500 employees and more than 40 aircraft.

The stock market crash hit Keys hard by its overall effect on the general economy and Keys was forced to resign, leaving EAT headed by Tom Doe and Tom Morgan.

Eddie Rickenbacker was a war hero who, after the war joined General Motors as head of their Fokker Aircraft Division. Rickenbacker resigned from Fokker and in less than a month was employed by American Airlines. Rickenbacker came up with the idea to merge

---

[1] Eastern Air Lines Inc. 1983 Annual Report.

with EAT since American was primarily an East-West carrier whose best business was in spring, summer, and fall, and EAT operated North-South with its most profitable traffic in the winter. American management failed to agree and Rickenbacker resigned and joined forces with E. R. Breech, an old friend from GM who was sympathetic to him and was able to gain control over both American and EAT.

On January 1, 1935, Rickenbacker was named general manager of EAT. His first major act was to cancel every pass that had been awarded to various politicians. His second was to fire 19 station managers. In 1934 Eastern had lost $1.5 million, but the following year netted a modest $38,000.

With the help of the Campbell-Ewald Advertising Agency, the "Great Silver Fleet" logo was initiated and was painted on every Eastern aircraft until the 1960s.

Eastern, which had been flying sluggish DC-2s, took delivery on the first two of ten DC-3s in 1936 and also acquired the Wendell-Williams Transport Corporation which operated a small but important route between New Orleans and Houston. This purchase proved to be one of Rickenbacker's most sagacious moves, because it not only gave Eastern its first entry into Texas, but made possible a later expansion into Brownsville, Texas, where Eastern flights would connect with Pan American's service to Mexico, Central America, and South America.

After attempts were made to take over control of EAT by John Hertz, Rickenbacker was able to raise nearly $3.5 million from backers and the new corporation, Eastern Air Lines Incorporated (EAL) was formed. On April 22, 1938, Eddie Rickenbacker became president of EAL.

By 1939 Florida traffic was booming and the company was growing steadily. Eastern was serving 80 percent of the population East of the Mississippi. As 1941 drew to a close, Eastern was serving 40 cities in 17 states with a fleet of just under 40 DC-3s.

World War II caused a virtual moratorium on route expansion and Eastern lost more than 50 percent of its fleet, either selling the planes or leasing them to the Army. By 1944 there were more than 800 EAL employees in uniform. Eastern had an antistewardess policy which had to be abandoned during the war. Women were hired in ever-increasing numbers and assigned to tasks supposedly beyond their female capability. Following the war, EAL was the first airline to introduce the 40-hour workweek.

In most respects the 1950s were the "Golden Decade" for Eastern. It was a ten-year period marked by expansion, continued profits, and fleet modernization. In 1953, Rickenbacker decided to relinquish the presidency of EAL to become chairman of the board and general manager so that he could devote more of his time to high-priority and long-range planning. Tom Armstrong was chosen to become Rickenbacker's successor.

Eastern upgraded its fleet significantly in the 1950s with in excess of $100 million being spent. As of the 25th anniversary Eastern was operating over 13,000 route miles and on September 22 of the silver anniversary year, carried its 25-millionth passenger.

During these years with Rickenbacker in charge, one fault with Eastern seemed to be paramount. Rickenbacker was convinced that scheduling and convenience were far more important than frills to passengers, and thus had a strong disconcern for meeting passengers desires (i.e., hot meals, etc.). This led to the airline's perceived image becoming the same as that of Rickenbacker. Gradually the words "Rickenbacker's airline" had come to mean not efficiency and confidence, but rather poor service and indifference. Such was the dissatisfaction with Eastern that two Pittsburgh businessmen organized WHEAL (We

Hate EAL) as a manifestation of customer resentment against Eastern's attitude toward passengers.

Rickenbacker stunned a staff meeting by announcing that he had ordered 40 Lockheed Electras (propjets) which some executives privately questioned. EAL was buying more Electras than any other carrier. More than one officer wondered if it was wise to buy so many prop planes with the jet age right around the corner.

Rickenbacker finally ordered 16 DC-8 pure jets with options on eight more but was notified that the planes were heavier than expected, making them underpowered. Eastern had the option of either taking delivery of these planes or waiting nearly a full year until a newly developed engine could be completed. Several officers said that it would be fatal to let Delta or National start jet service ahead of Eastern but ultimately the delay was accepted, since neither competitor had ordered a jet yet. Delta found out that Eastern had relinquished its order on six of the jets already committed to the underpowered engines and promptly grabbed them. About a year before EAL could start its own jet service, Delta began operating their jets and Eastern experienced disastrous results in every market involving Eastern-Delta competition.

On October 1, 1959, M. A. MacIntyre, a former American Airlines lawyer and undersecretary of the Air Force, became president and CEO of Eastern. Captain Eddie remained as chairman of the board but without his title of general manager. Things were beginning to change.

MacIntyre was smart enough to recognize Eastern's weaknesses and gutsy enough to do something about it. A "New things are happening at EAL" theme was introduced, emphasizing improved services and scheduling. The first equipment decision MacIntyre made was to order 15 Boeing 720 Jetliners which would be delivered by 1963 and, soon thereafter, a massive purchase of 727s. Eastern was by this time on a downhill slide and at the end of 1961 wound up with a net loss of $9.6 million (a six-day flight engineers' strike had cost $5.5 million in loss revenue).

Toward the end of 1961 with losses growing steadily, EAL attempted a merger with American Airlines which was bitterly opposed by the entire industry. Many factors were responsible for the failure of the merger, not the least of which was Eastern's and American's inability to refute that it would create a giant, controlling one-third of the U.S. air system. 1963 net operating loss would hit nearly $38 million. The only bright spots of 1963 were the introduction of the 727s and the acceptance of Eastern's Air Shuttle, which guaranteed space even if a multimillion-dollar aircraft had to carry a single person. (By all standards the shuttle had been extremely successful. The shuttle has become an institution, unique in its concept. In 1978, the shuttle carried 2.7 million passengers.) Throughout his tenure at Eastern, MacIntyre fought off every attempt to modify the shuttle. When MacIntyre resigned in 1963 there was some sentiment to let the shuttle go with the man so instrumental in its inception.

The next president of EAL was Floyd Hall, Senior Vice-President and General Manager of TWA. Hall was the first to operate Eastern without Rickenbacker's input since he had relinquished his board position. Hall became Eastern's seventh president on December 15, 1963. Surveying the equipment, Hall found that Eastern's fleet consisted of less than 50 percent jets—the lowest percentage in the industry. Realizing that Eastern needed short-range jets, Hall set his sights on the Douglas DC-9 and a contract for these craft was signed in February, 1965. Hall began a program called "Operation Bootstrap" aimed at (1) generating more revenue, (2) improving on-time performance, (3) decreasing passenger complaints, and (4) increasing passenger compliments. By the end of the year, revenues had jumped by $11 million over 1963. The comeback continued in 1965 and EAL ended the year with a net profit of almost $30 million.

On November 11, 1965, Walt Disney announced a plan to build a $750-million "Disneyland of the East," located only a few miles from Orlando, Florida, whose officials let it be known that they would like to choose one carrier to be Walt Disney World's official airline. Eastern put together a package that won them the official airline designation and now carries 50 percent of the Orlando market. Under Hall's leadership, Eastern staged an amazing recovery. Even with a long strike, Eastern still netted $14.7 million in 1966. Also in 1966, Eastern put 65 new DC-9s and 727s into service. Eastern was showing great gains until the disastrous years of 1967–1973—a period in which past gains were wiped out, morale crumbled, and Eastern hovered perilously close to extinction.

Floyd Hall was having difficulties with the directors starting in 1967, and ultimately in 1968, he named Art Lewis as president but retained the CEO position. Lewis became EAL's eighth president, not aware of the difficulties he would face in the forthcoming, unseen recession, and a new menace—hijacking.

Eastern suffered its first hijacking in September 1968 and over the course of the next six years was to experience 29 more. Since Eastern was based in Miami with close proximity to Cuba, it was particularly vulnerable. Once, two groups hijacked the same plane to Cuba at the same time, unaware of each other's existence. Hijacking was one of the biggest headaches Lewis faced. Finally after many disagreements over various policies with Hall, Lewis resigned. At this time, Hall replaced Lewis in early 1970 with Sam Higgenbottom, president number nine. Hall was always a great admirer of men with technical skills and this may be one of the reasons why, in 1969, he hired as a technical consultant a 41-year-old astronaut named Frank Borman. Higgenbottom did not like Borman and even turned in an unfavorable evaluation of Borman to Hall. Borman found EAL's stratified structure repugnant and was able to see many things being done without cost justification.

Friction between Hall and Higgenbottom began to occur but was kept in check during 1970–1972 when Higgenbottom reported net profits of $5.6 million and $19.7 million respectively. In 1972 Eastern became the first airline to fly the new Lockheed 1011. The purchase of these aircraft was the largest purchase in EAL's history ($800 million for 37 firm orders with options for 13 more which was later exercised). The L-1011 commitment was to take much of the blame for Eastern's subsequent financial crisis. At the worst possible time, L-1011s began to develop problems which forced cancellation of scores of L-1011 schedules during most of the 1972–1973 winter season. In 1973, Eastern lost a staggering $51 million.

By mid-1973, Higgenbottom was ready to jump from the helm of Eastern, feeling that EAL was an impossible company to manage. With Sam's departure, Hall resumed full command in Miami.

Eastern managed a modest comeback in 1974, showing a $10.3-million net profit. The black ink was deceptive since it was achieved largely due to a fuel crisis. Losses in 1975 amounted to an unbelievable $88.7 million. At this point, the directors stepped in again. When Higgenbottom left, Borman served as executive vice-president. He was running the airline operationally and learning more every day. He made no bones about the fact that he wanted to be president of EAL and he officially attained this goal and became president and COO on May 27, 1975. As 1975 ended, Eastern still had not been turned around. On

December 16, 1975, the board also elected Borman CEO. Armed with the authority he believed essential to EAL's fate, Borman began moving. His earliest moves jolted EAL to its roots as he thinned out the executive echelons. Hundreds of management jobs were eliminated with many in middle management finding themselves in positions involving sharp salary cuts. The final result showed nearly 800 fewer persons in management, and vice-presidents had been cut from 69 to 38. It is estimated that the reorganization saved Eastern nearly $9 million annually. Borman decided that Eastern must gain some financial breathing room and that he would have to go to labor for voluntary wage freezes. He knew that the unions would not like the idea but felt that if he went to the employees and told them the truth, that "EAL would probably go under" without it, that they would probably accept it. Borman, however, added one vital incentive: the industry's first profit-sharing plan. The unions' eventual acceptance of a wage freeze had the effect of keeping costs down while revenues were climbing, with the result of a $39.1-million net profit in 1976. Borman then instituted a program called the Variable Earnings Plan (VEP). It was another profit-sharing plan but provided for deficit sharing as well. The unions ultimately accepted the VEP and in 1978 Eastern netted a record $67.3 million. In February 1979, each employee got back $1.35 for every dollar they had banked during the previous year.

Even with Eastern's tremendous debt, Borman looked at the age of the Eastern fleet and its oncoming obsolescence technically and also from the standpoint of both maintenance and competition. By 1989, a major portion of EAL's fleet would be 20 years old and it was obvious that the airline was heading for equipment trouble. Rising fuel costs alone demanded more efficient aircraft. Borman finally settled on Boeing 757s as exactly what EAL needed. Borman contracted for 21 757s with an option on 24 more, a total order of $560 million. Eastern will finally have what it has lacked for so many years—a balanced fleet acquired in time to meet future needs.[2]

Finances

Eastern's financial condition has deteriorated since 1979 and remains poor (see Exhibits 26.1 and 26.2). There has been an erosion in net worth of 40 percent since 1979. Eastern has a debt-to-equity ratio of 8 to 1. Last year, the average for all large U.S. carriers—including Eastern's mammoth share—was only $1.12 of debt for every $1.00 in equity.[3] Eastern's debt service took 6 percent of every expense dollar in 1983, compared with an average of 4 percent for the nation's major carriers.[4] However, 1984 marked an important turning point that may lead to further improvement in 1985.

Debt Structure

In May 1980, Eastern Air Lines entered into the 1980 Bank Credit Agreement with a number of major banks. This agreement provides for a standby commitment to lend $400 million to the company, subject to certain conditions precedent to the company's ability to

---

[2] Historical facts on the company were taken from: Robert J. Sperling, *From the Captain to the Colonel* (New York: Dial Press, 1980).

[3] Thomas J. Billitteri, "Why Eastern Will Go Back to Labor for More Help," *Florida Trend*, November 1984, pp. 66–70.

[4] Ibid.

Exhibit 26.1   Ten-Year Financial and Statistical Summary

Balance Sheet*	1984	1983	1982	1981
Assets:				
Current assets	$ 889.1	$ 847.7	$ 712.8	$ 643.6
Operating property and equipment, net	2,796.3	2,805.2	2,419.0	2,237.5
Other assets	84.0	104.8	93.1	53.4
Total assets	$3,769.4	$ 3,757.7	$ 3,224.9	$ 2,934.5
Liabilities:				
Current liabilities	$ 966.3	$ 897.0	$ 774.8	$ 679.0
Current obligations—capital leases	71.0	67.6	73.6	64.3
Long-term debt	1,428.9	1,515.2	1,053.6	815.9
Long-term obligations—capital leases	861.9	803.8	857.3	852.0
Deferred credits and other long-term liabilities	115.9	157.4	70.7	33.8
Total liabilities	3,444.0	3,441.0	2,830.0	2,445.0
Redeemable preferred stock	140.0	139.8	139.6	139.3
Common/nonredeemable preferred stock and retained earnings (deficit):				
Common stock	43.5	35.9	24.9	24.9
Nonredeemable preferred stock	53.6	46.8	—	—
Capital in excess of par value	396.0	380.9	333.1	352.9
Earnings (deficit) retained for use in the business	(324.0)	(285.8)	(101.8)	(26.7)
Employee stock to be issued	17.2	—	—	—
Treasury stock as a reduction	(0.9)	(0.9)	(0.9)	(0.9)
Total common/nonredeemable preferred stock and retained earnings (deficit)	185.4	176.9	255.3	350.2
Total liabilities, capital stock, and retained earnings (deficit)	$3,769.4	$ 3,757.7	$ 3,224.9	$ 2,934.5
Statement of Income*				
Operating revenues:				
Passenger	$ 3,989.3	$ 3,608.3	$ 3,406.0	$ 3,386.7
Cargo, incidental and other	374.6	333.8	363.2	340.4
Total Operating Revenues	4,363.9	3,942.1	3,769.2	3,727.1
Operating expenses:				
Expenses excluding depreciation and amortization	3,886.6	3,772.1	3,563.1	3,547.9
Depreciation and amortization	287.7	270.1	224.9	229.1
Total operating expenses	4,174.3	4,042.2	3,788.0	3,777.0
Operating profit (loss)	189.6	(100.1)	(18.8)	(49.9)
Interest expense	(277.5)	(236.0)	(178.3)	(141.2)
Other nonoperating income and (expense)—net (1)	50.0	152.4	122.2	125.2
(Provision for) reduction in income taxes	—	—	—	—
Income (loss) before extraordinary item	(37.9)	(183.7)	(74.9)	(65.9)
Extraordinary item	—	—	—	—
Cumulative effect of a change in accounting principle	—	—	—	—
Net Income (Loss)	$ (37.9)	$ (183.7)	$ (74.9)	$ (65.9)

1980	1979	1978	1977	1976	1975	1974
$ 810.6	$ 732.3	$ 381.0	$ 338.7	$ 371.6	$ 320.6	$ 361.1
1,964.2	1,675.4	1,486.3	1,281.3	1,254.7	1,249.9	1,321.8
41.4	45.3	41.2	44.0	37.7	50.7	69.7
$ 2,816.2	$ 2,453.0	$ 1,908.5	$ 1,664.0	$ 1,664.0	$ 1,621.2	$ 1,752.6
$ 724.4	$ 624.2	$ 466.2	$ 402.2	$ 420.2	393.7	341.1
56.5	54.6	49.3	41.2	33.3	29.6	26.9
754.2	661.2	399.7	435.8	566.0	622.6	700.2
688.4	591.6	538.9	444.9	379.6	344.9	354.1
17.9	33.3	13.9	8.8	11.9	18.5	22.8
2,241.4	1,964.9	1,468.0	1,332.9	1,411.0	1,409.3	1,445.1
139.3	47.4	47.4	47.3	—	—	—
24.9	24.9	24.9	19.8	19.8	19.0	19.0
—	—	—	—	—	21.7	21.7
355.4	341.0	340.8	298.6	295.7	272.8	272.8
—	—	—	—	—	21.7	21.7
56.3	78.3	27.4	(34.6)	(62.5)	(101.6)	(6.0)
(1.1)	(3.5)	—	—	—	—	—
435.5	440.7	393.1	283.8	253.0	211.9	307.5
$ 2,816.2	$ 2,453.0	$ 1,908.5	$ 1,664.0	$ 1,664.0	$ 1,621.2	$ 1,752.6
$ 3,151.8	$ 2,628.7	$ 2,156.2	$ 1,835.1	$ 1,648.1	$ 1,466.0	$ 1,381.5
300.7	252.8	223.4	200.8	177.4	158.4	148.8
3,452.5	2,881.5	2,379.6	2,035.9	1,825.5	1,624.4	1,530.3
3,250.0	2,595.7	2,116.5	1,830.6	1,592.5	1,475.2	1,312.8
200.6	174.8	166.3	147.2	136.3	129.5	130.3
3,450.6	2,770.5	2,282.8	1,977.8	1,728.8	1,604.7	1,443.1
1.9	111.0	96.8	58.1	96.7	19.7	87.2
(109.8)	(84.3)	(75.0)	(70.0)	(68.2)	(75.1)	(88.9)
61.6	33.7	45.5	39.8	10.6	(5.2)	7.6
4.2	(2.8)	—	—	(9.4)	—	(1.4)
(42.1)	57.6	67.3	27.9	29.7	(60.6)	4.5
24.7	—	—	—	9.4	—	1.4
—	—	—	—	—	(35.0)	—
$ (17.4)	$ 57.6	$ 67.3	$ 27.9	$ 39.1	$ (95.6)	$ 5.9

continued

Exhibit 26.1 *continued*

	Statement of Income* 1984	1983	1982	1981
Earnings per average share of common stock: (2)				
Income (loss) before extraordinary item	$ (1.53)	$ **(7.19)**	$ (3.82)	$ (3.46)
Net Income (Loss)	$ (1.53)	$ **(7.19)**	$ (3.82)	$ (3.46)
Operating statistics:				
Revenue plane miles*	325.7	**302.7**	290.5	303.6
Available seat miles*	51,648.4	**48,020.9**	46,143.8	46,789.7
Revenue passenger miles*	29,408.7	**28,328.7**	26;140.1	26,107.6
Passenger load factor	56.94%	**58.99%**	56.65%	55.80%
Revenue passengers carried*	37.9	**36.8**	35.0	35.5
Available ton miles*	6,248.4	**5,749.4**	5,504.4	5,639.3
Revenue ton miles*	3,359.2	**3,193.5**	2,959.7	2,987.1
Weight load factor	53.76%	**55.54%**	53.77%	52.97%
Percent performance	98.58%	**98.62%**	98.74%	98.04%
Yield per revenue passenger mile	13.53¢	**12.71¢**	13.00¢	12.95¢
Yield per revenue ton mile	124.98¢	**118.72¢**	121.16¢	119.34¢
Total operating expenses per available seat mile	8.08¢	**8.42¢**	8.21¢	8.07¢
Total operating expenses per revenue passenger mile	14.19¢	**14.27¢**	14.49¢	14.47¢
Total operating expenses per available ton mile	66.81¢	**70.31¢**	68.82¢	66.98¢
Total operating expenses per revenue ton mile	124.26¢	**126.58¢**	127.99¢	126.44¢
Aircraft utilization—hours per day	8:53	**8:35**	8:23	8:45
Number of personnel employed at year-end	38,400	**37,100**	39,200	37,700

* All amounts in millions.

(1) Includes impairment in investment of nontransport subsidiary of $2.4 million in 1974 and $16.8 million in 1975.

(2) The company has paid no cash dividends on its common stock since 1969.

borrow, including compliance by Eastern with certain financial leverage, stockholders' equity, and subordinated indebtedness. Under the terms of the agreement, $100 million became available on January 1, 1982, $300 million would be available in 1983, and the full $400 million in 1984. The availability would be reduced by $20 million in each quarter beginning March 31, 1987. $125 million has been drawn and is outstanding at December 31, 1983. Any future borrowings on the undrawn balance are subject to, among other things, review with an approval from the banks party to the agreement. The banks party to the agreement have indicated an unwillingness to provide any additional funds thereunder absent a substantial improvement in the company's financial situation. Eastern has no assurance that any additional funds will be made available under the agreement. However, the company presently believes that it will not be necessary to request the availability of any such funds during the forthcoming year.

During 1982 and 1983, Eastern sought and obtained temporary modifications of certain covenants contained in the indenture and the 1980 Bank Credit Agreement (principally relating to the company's capitalization, minimum stockholders' equity, and net worth) and certain modifications of various conditions precedent to its ability to borrow under the Bank Credit Agreement. Most recently in December 1983, Eastern obtained for

1980	1979	1978	1977	1976	1975	1974
$ (1.96)	$ 2.10	$ 2.91	$ 1.38	$ 1.51	$ (3.23)	$ 0.20
$ (0.97)	$ 2.10	$ 2.91	$ 1.38	$ 2.00	$ (5.07)	$ 0.27
312.7	303.8	288.9	284.3	277.0	266.8	250.9
46,028.4	43,050.7	39,117.5	36,783.5	34,766.2	32,510.8	29,912.4
28,227.0	28,917.7	25,228.2	20,657.3	19,520.5	18,294.2	17,860.3
61.33%	67.17%	64.49%	56.16%	56.15%	56.27%	59.71%
39.1	42.2	37.4	31.3	29.3	27.4	27.2
5,640.8	5,171.3	4,740.9	4,499.2	4,323.1	4,246.0	3,883.0
3,175.6	3,224.4	2,839.7	2,351.4	2,214.5	2,107.4	2,041.2
56.30%	62.35%	59.90%	52.26%	51.23%	49.63%	52.57%
98.55%	97.94%	98.07%	98.68%	98.77%	98.71%	99.01%
11.15¢	9.08¢	8.53¢	8.87¢	8.42¢	8.00¢	7.72¢
104.40¢	85.80¢	80.22¢	82.35¢	78.44¢	73.36¢	71.27¢
7.50¢	6.44¢	5.84¢	5.38¢	4.97¢	4.94¢	4.82¢
12.22¢	9.58¢	9.05¢	9.57¢	8.86¢	8.77¢	8.08¢
61.17¢	53.57¢	48.15¢	43.96¢	39.99¢	37.79¢	37.16¢
108.66¢	85.92¢	80.39¢	84.11¢	78.07¢	76.15¢	70.70¢
9:33	9:44	9:31	9:14	9:05	8:48	8:20
40,000	38,900	37,100	34,300	33,200	32,800	32,600

the year 1984 further modifications of certain covenants contained in the indenture and the 1980 Bank Credit Agreement. Frank Borman and his advisers fully believed that Eastern would be able to comply with the modified covenants during 1984. The covenants were scheduled to revert to their original terms effective January 1, 1985, and the corporate officers believe it will be necessary to obtain additional modifications applicable for periods thereafter. During the past several years, Eastern has periodically sought and received consents to adjust financial covenants and certain other provisions contained in the company's loan agreements.

Minimum repayments of long-term debt outstanding at December 31, 1983, are scheduled as follows (in millions):

1984 (included in current liabilities)	$133.2
1985	166.7
1986	139.6
1987	100.3
1988	97.0
After 1988	1,011.6

Exhibit 26.2   Eastern Air Lines Inc. Statement of Changes
in Financial Position (all amounts in thousands)

	Year Ended December 31			
	1984	**1983**	**1982**	**1981**
Funds provided by:				
Net loss	$ (37,927)	$ (183,667)	$ (74,927)	$ (65,877)
Depreciation and amortization—operations	287,657	270,073	224,882	229,071
Depreciation and amortization—other	13,970	13,612	12,487	9,849
Foreign currency transactions	885	(138)	(66)	(6,052)
Distribution of treasury stock	—	—	—	177
Charge for employee stock under 1984 Wage Investment Program, Net	46,696	—	—	—
Funds provided from operations	311,281	99,880	162,376	167,168
Proceeds from issuance of $3 Cumulative Convertible Junior Preferred Stock, net of expenses	—	46,732	—	—
Proceeds from issuance of common stock, net of expenses	—	76,453	—	—
Proceeds from issuance of Series C Equipment Trust Certificates	—	153,761	15,544	—
Long-term debt financing	107,706	413,911	294,682	135,391
Termination of capital leases (excluding gains of zero, $59 and $33)	—	5,046	160	232
Proceeds from sale of equipment (excluding a loss of $2,944 and gains of $32,676 and $36,529)	18,389	37,877	35,548	44,897
Increase in long-term obligations under capital leases	127,822	18,002	84,715	222,482
Cash advances returned on leased equipment	—	—	25,049	41,830
Working capital components	151,902	127,079	99,797	(64,169)
Total funds provided	717,100	978,741	717,871	547,831
Funds applied for:				
Flight and ground equipment purchases and advances	163,645	668,163	387,503	366,009
Capital lease additions	130,736	21,242	77,378	210,338
Notes payable retired or maturing within one year	191,418	115,654	81,869	75,642
Acquisition of Latin American routes of Braniff	—	—	29,265	—
(Increase) decrease in deferred credits and other long-term liabilities	42,098	(84,733)	(36,974)	847
Obligations under capital leases maturing within one year	69,738	71,011	71,840	58,799
Cash dividends on Preferred Stock	—	17,685	19,780	19,980
Other—net	(1,179)	23,846	23,336	9,842
Working capital components	26,380	50,254	9,525	(26,701)
Total funds applied	622,863	883,122	663,522	714,756
Increase (decrease) in cash and short-term investments	94,237	95,619	54,349	(166,925)
Cash and short-term investments at January 1	266,231	170,612	116,263	283,188
Cash and short-term investments at December 31	$ 360,468	$ 266,231	$ 170,612	$ 116,263

Exhibit 26.2   *continued*

	Year Ended December 31			
	1984	**1983**	**1982**	**1981**
Summary of changes in working capital:				
Funds provided:				
Materials and supplies	3,264	$ 4,953	$ 3,939	$ (18,806)
Notes payable	38,327	50,429	6,090	(8,006)
Accounts payable and accrued liabilities	21,488	49,392	16,441	24,620
Unearned transportation revenues	52,446	22,305	73,327	(61,977)
	115,525	127,079	99,797	(64,169)
Funds applied:				
Accounts receivable	57,732	21,828	9,896	(14,060)
Prepaid expenses and other current assets	1,628	22,435	8,898	(4,841)
Current obligations—capital leases	3,397	5,991	(9,269)	(7,800)
	62,757	50,254	9,525	(26,701)
Net (decrease) increase in working capital, excluding cash and short-term investments	(125,522)	(76,825)	(90,272)	37,468
Increase (decrease) in cash and short-term investments	94,237	95,619	54,349	(166,925)
Net increase (decrease) in working capital	$ (31,285)	$ 18,794	$ (35,923)	$ (129,457)

Export Credit Agreements have provided financing on Boeing 757 and L-1011 engines and spares and on A300 aircraft. The major portion of the export credit includes amounts established for the purpose of providing financing for a portion of the purchase price of the A300 fleet. At December 31, 1983, Eastern had $412.9 million outstanding under these credit arrangements and no additional availability remained as the A300 program has been completed. In addition, approximately 85 percent of the purchase price of all RB211-535 power plants and spares will be financed under a series of Export Credit Agreements arranged for the B-757 program. At December 31, 1984, $59.4 million was outstanding under these agreements and $208.1 million of unused availability remained. Lastly, the export credit also represents amounts outstanding under agreements with a group of British banks which provided financing in British pounds and dollars for a major portion of the purchase price of Rolls-Royce RB211 engines, plus spares, installed on Lockheed L-1011 aircraft. At December 31, 1983, $11.5 million were denominated in pounds sterling and $70.9 million in dollars.

Manufacturers Senior Obligations, which amount to $56.8 million, represent the balance due on certain A300 aircraft purchased during 1980, 1981, and 1982.

Secured Equipment Certificates at 16.125 percent totaling $169.3 million were issued to finance up to 53 percent of ten Boeing 757 aircraft delivered in 1982 and 1983.

There is additional capitalization using subordinate debt totaling $522.9 million as of December 31, 1983.

Basic Action Strategies

Corporate Strategy.   Eastern Airlines is a scheduled air carrier giving full service to all its customers. Its main routes are in the eastern portion of the United States but are not limited to this area.

Natural Strategic Advantage or Innate Interest.   Eastern Airlines was established because Captain Rickenbacker had an interest in flying and saw a customer need for flying between cities in the eastern portion of the United States.

Competition or Niche.   Eastern must compete with the other airlines servicing the same cities as it does.

Concentration on Multiple Products/Businesses.   Eastern only wants to be in the air carrier business, both freight and passengers.

Growth, Stabilization, Investment Reduction, Turnaround, or Combination.   Eastern is definitely concentrating on a turnaround strategy to reduce the indebtedness through cost reduction and modest growth.

Financial Strategy

Eastern has simply been trying to stay alive financially these last five years. The company has a history of heavy indebtedness and is now very highly leveraged.

The company has, on several different occasions, had to go to the lending institutions to ask for a relaxation of certain of the financial tests contained in its loan agreements.[5] Additionally Eastern was required to develop a business plan by the end of January 1985 that would make the carrier profitable that year.

Through effective cost-cutting, wage concessions from unions, and an 18 percent reduction in all nonunion employees' wages, the company was at least able to show an operating profit by the end of 1984. According to a manager at Eastern, it has been able to involve employees in finding ways to save money (e.g., Eastern used to launder all the maintenance employees' uniforms; now, at the employees' request to have the company save money, they each take care of their own uniforms). The company has established participative management through quality circles which have proven to be very effective in bringing waste to the attention of management and to the workers, who then work together to reduce or eliminate the waste.

Eastern's objective financially once it is no longer in danger of defaulting on its loans, is to grow modestly at 2–3 percent growth per year.

Operation Strategies
Fleet Modernization

Frank Borman, upon looking at the existing fleet of EAL aircraft, realized that, in a very few years, major problems would likely occur in the maintenance of an outdated, high-

---

[5] "Eastern in Default on Loans," *The New York Times*, Vol. 134, February 2, 1985, p 31(L), col. 6.

fuel-consuming assortment of aircraft. Even though Eastern was suffering financially, Borman saw the urgent need to begin modernization of the fleet.

As of December 31, 1983, Eastern's fleet consisted of 62 wide-body and 222 narrow-body aircraft, for a total fleet of 284 aircraft. Eastern completed a major phase of its re-equipment program conceived more than five years ago by increasing its jet fleet by 16 units. The increase was a result of Eastern's adding 23 aircraft and disposing of 7. The 23 additions consisted of the acquisition of 13 Boeing 757s, 4 A300s, and 6 Boeing 727 100s.[6]

At the end of 1983, the company had twelve 757s remaining under firm order. As a result of negotiations with Boeing, the company now plans to take delivery on 4 more in 1984, 3 in 1985, 3 in 1986, and 2 in 1987.[7] These 12 aircraft come equipped with an engine which is much more fuel efficient than the first 757s delivered. Eastern has also undertaken an engine retrofit program on the initial fifteen 757s as well as existing 727-225s, which would result in significant fuel consumption reductions.

Eastern was using the 757 at 29 cities by the end of 1983. The 757 is an exceptionally quiet, fuel-efficient aircraft with long-range capabilities and outstanding flight performance. These fuel-efficient aircraft made a very measurable contribution in an area where a $.01 difference in fuel price is worth $10 million a year to Eastern.[8]

Going into 1984, Eastern will be operating a fleet that ranks as one of the most modern of any airline in the world.

The Latin American Market

Eastern's decision to obtain the routes to Latin America when they became available proved to be an excellent one. Bucking the trend of other airlines, Eastern had considerable gains in market share, load factor, and cargo revenue performance in Latin America in 1983 even though the economy there was weak.

The good traffic reflects passenger acceptance of the El InterAmericano service, featuring the finest in airborne dining and other amenities. Eastern is moving to secure permanent authority on these routes.

Improvement of Facilities

Eastern is faced with the challenge of maintaining its high standards in ground facilities despite the competition from low-fare operators.

The largest new facility project undertaken in 1983 was a five-gate expansion at Miami International Airport. Existing gates were also being refurbished at this important hub. Eastern is also working on adding more ticketing and luggage handling ability, increasing the size of the Ionosphere Club at Miami, and expansion of the Customs and Immigration Service facility, which will be a real advantage for international travelers.

Also in south Florida, a major expansion is underway at the Ft. Lauderdale International Airport, which will offer added gate facilities. Construction of a new terminal building is scheduled for completion in 1985, followed by a concourse expansion to be

[6] Eastern Air Lines Inc. 1983 Annual Report.
[7] Ibid.
[8] Ibid.

completed in 1986. As in Miami, Ft. Lauderdale is one of this area's airports showing consistent traffic growth, making improved facilities there essential.

Expansion of Service to More Lucrative Markets

Eastern is increasing flights between Florida and Atlanta and to what Eastern has considered its primary domain, the Northeast, and cutting back its Houston service by one-half because of the strong competition from Delta, American, and even Continental Airlines. The new flight schedule will represent an 18 percent increase in service, EAL said. The Florida-Northeast market represents about one-fourth of Eastern's $4 billion revenues. The number of daily operations to Houston will cut from 46 to 20, and 35 new operations will be conducted in Atlanta. With the new schedule, Eastern will have 339 daily operations in Atlanta compared with Delta's 337. Delta is not expected to surrender its position as the dominant Atlanta airline and is also expected to add flights there.

New Hub in Kansas City

As stated by Frank Borman, "The major service improvement story of the year was our establishment of what some call an instant hub in Kansas City, Missouri."[9]

Because of the heavy encroachment on Eastern's traditional routes by post-deregulation competitors, Eastern sought to capture a new traffic flow. An analysis of the national air service scene revealed Kansas City as a point potentially well-suited to meet Eastern's needs. It was an ideal hub on which to build a schedule pattern linking established eastern cities with Eastern's newer western destinations, forming Northeast-Southwest traffic flow to offset the seasonal character of older routes.

Following Braniff's bankruptcy, Eastern was able to move into ten gate positions there on short notice and at good terms. A detailed market analysis showed that there was a definite service demand on the schedule pattern that Eastern had envisioned.

Human Resources

In the fall of 1983, Eastern Air Lines Chairman Frank Borman appeared on a company-wide videotape and put it to Eastern's 37,000 employees: accept steep wage cuts or risk Chapter 11 bankruptcy proceedings.

Eastern's employees reacted angrily but, in the final analysis, had no choice but to dig deep into their pockets again. A dive into Chapter 11 could have meant the loss of thousands of jobs. So in December 1983, employees agreed to one-year wage reductions of between 18 percent and 22 percent. They also agreed to steps aimed at improving productivity. All of this was designed to save Eastern $371 million. The crisis help, labeled the 1984 Wage Investment Program, did not come cheap. Eastern agreed to fork over a 25 percent equity stake to employees, give labor two more seats on the Board of Directors (two had been granted in an earlier employee bailout plan), let labor participate in the business plans of the company, and to issue 3 million shares of convertible preferred stock that entitles employees to a healthy share of any future profits. Eastern also has several pension plans covering substantially all employees. The company normally makes annual

[9]Eastern Air Lines Inc. 1983 Annual Report.

contributions to the plans equal to the amounts accrued for pension expense. However, in 1983, the company deferred $37 million of 1982 contributions which will be made in three equal annual payments beginning September 15, 1984.[10]

Even so, it appears that Borman will have to ask labor for another round of help in 1985. "For Eastern to be viable in any kind of economic environment next year, there should be an extension of the current wage concessions and preferably a 10 percent reduction as well," says Louis Am Marckesano, Senior Analyst with Janney Montgomery Scott Inc., in Philadelphia.[11]

Eastern is making a strong move toward changing the attitudes of its employees from one of frustration and resentment toward management to one of mutual cooperation and respect. It is recognized that labor unrest impacts in terms of productivity and ultimately, costs; therefore, Eastern has formed the heavy employee ownership program and employee involvement programs, using employees in decision making and by forming quality circles. Eastern feels that these incentives will encourage employees to constantly be looking for ways to cut costs, improve productivity, and ultimately make a profit for themselves. Eastern further feels that 1984 was a good year for cooperation between the union and the company.

Eastern's management now feels that productivity is the key to future success. As part of the 1984 wage freeze, the employees began to participate in—and help direct—a massive productivity program. Employees are encouraged to take suggestions that they believe will save the company money directly to management in an open-door policy which they feel encourages participation. The savings from the wage freeze, plus an estimated $50 million in productivity savings, helped account for a remarkable turnaround in Eastern's 1984 financial performance.[12]

In spite of Eastern's recent successes in terms of labor union cooperation, there still seems to be a number of problems to be dealt with. Borman is repeatedly described as running his operation like a military bureaucracy and of being irritatively direct. Many say that he has lost credibility with his workers. Over the years, Eastern's employees have been asked to participate in a variety of wage reduction programs under the promise of a profitable future that has yet to be seen.[13]

EAL lashed out at its machinists union's novel proposal to be paid a set percentage of revenues, calling it "so outlandish that we can't let employees and the public think it has any merit." Eastern also said it would reinstate last year's 18 to 22 percent wage cuts. "Continuing to apply the 18 percent would be a sure path to destruction," said Richard McGraw, a senior vice-president and the airline's chief spokesman.[14]

Charlie Bryan, head of Eastern's machinists union, is angry at Borman—and that could mean the end of the year-long truce that has brought labor peace and financial progress to Eastern. Bryan is furious that Borman extended wage concessions without employee approval.[15]

[10] Eastern Air Lines Inc. 1983 Annual Report.

[11] Thomas J. Billitteri, "Why Eastern Will Go Back to Labor for More Help," *Florida Trend*, November 1984, p. 66.

[12] Wayne, Leslie, "Frank Borman's Most Difficult Days," *New York Times*, February 17, 1985.

[13] Ibid.

[14] Gary Cohn, *Wall Street Journal*, February 6, 1985, p. 6.

[15] Gary Cohn, *Wall Street Journal*, January 4, 1985, p. 24.

On April 16, 1985, Eastern reported the largest quarterly profit in its history ($24.3 million). Despite the recent upturn in finances, Eastern still must resolve differences with its employees. Flight attendants and ground personnel recently voted to reject labor agreements containing wage concessions for 1985.

If new agreements are not reached by May 15, Eastern will fall into default on its loans. More than 60 creditors that are owed $2.3 billion have required that Eastern obtain new wage concessions from employees.

Because the deadline for obtaining the new contracts was extended from April 15 to May 15, Eastern is not worried about the flight attendants and the ground workers rejecting the agreements, spokesman Mark Wegel said.

"Obviously, we are a little disappointed. It came as a surprise, but we don't look at it as a serious setback," he said. "Keep in mind that leadership of both unions were in favor of the contracts," he said, referring to the Transport Workers Union and the International Association of Machinists. "We think labor and management will work out a proposal." [16]

Information Systems

In the past, Eastern may have neglected management information systems. Information systems did not advance much from the mid-seventies until recently, but, currently such a system is viewed by Eastern management as a resource. It is felt that MIS is an area where Eastern can gain a definite competitive edge.

The MIS at Eastern now consists of an IBM 9083 mainframe and a large Univac system to support the operational areas of the company. Currently everyone involved in pricing and costs has access to a terminal and it is planned that everyone will have a terminal in the future. Though there may be a limited number of PCs purchased, Eastern is not planning at this time to make a heavy investment in this area, as it is felt that their mainframe can satisfactorily be accessed for any necessary information. Eastern is using in-house personnel to develop its own software, when possible. Presently, Eastern has developed a pricing program which other airlines have expressed an interest in purchasing. Republic Airlines is developing software which cuts inventory and order process times dramatically and is expected to save $7 million annually at a production cost of only $250,000. In the meantime, the airline has sold its software package to two other airlines. [17]

Eastern now uses computers in payroll, personnel, and financial applications. In-use MISs also indicate air traffic nationally as well as reporting the load factors on the flights of Eastern's competitors. By studying and evaluating this data Eastern is able to forecast schedules, capacity, expenses, and revenues.

The Department of Transportation is continuing to collect data from airlines with the data being accessed by the various airlines for internal management use, greatly facilitating planning.

Eastern is currently trying to build a true data base and information system which will combine all relevant information. This type of MIS will enable Eastern to forecast full-fare demand as well as look at capacity control, historical data, and future bookings. "What-if" scenarios can then be run, giving spreadsheet analysis, etc.

[16] Suzy Hagstrom, *The Orlando Sentinel*, April 15, 1985, p. B-1.

[17] Margaret Nelson, "Inside Program Saves Millions," *Purchasing*, April 14, 1983, Vol. 94, No. 7, p. 15.

Since deregulation, computerized reservation systems have greatly increased in importance. Currently, American Airlines and United Airlines lead the field in using reservation computers that do a tremendous service for travel agents, who now account for 70 percent of reservations made. Other carriers are attempting to catch up in this area.

As stated by a manager at Eastern: "Given the vast amount of information which must be assimilated, it is becoming almost a requirement that one be computer literate. I can't imagine how we could do the job now without computer support."[18]

Marketing Strategies

Establishment of Kansas City Hub

In an effort to capture more traffic and passengers, to find new customers and more revenue, Eastern opened a mid-continent hub in Kansas City in late 1983 (Exhibit 26.3), initiating a 34-flight pattern of daily departures to 24 cities. They opened with three daily nonstops to Atlanta on November 15, 1983, and expanded to the full pattern on December 15. From a marketing standpoint, Kansas City has proven to be successful. Passenger loads have surpassed forecasts from the day of service inception.[19]

An important part of Eastern's growth in Kansas City has been based on a new spirit of cooperation between union employees and management. Since the planning days of the expansion, Eastern management and the International Association of Machinists have been working together to reduce costs. The IAM has improved productivity by about 40 percent compared with similarly sized Eastern bases. As Frank Borman asserts, "It's been a darn good market for us."[20]

Frequent Traveler Bonus Program

Eastern continues to capitalize on this program, which now has well over 570,000 active members. This project began as a means for travelers to collect bonus points, good for ticket discounts or service upgrades, based on the number of miles flown on Eastern. The program has been developed further by increasing the number of other firms where patronage is good for credits toward travel on Eastern.

Any traveler now doing business with TWA, British Caledonian, SAS, Hertz Rent-a-Car, General Car Rental, or Marriott Hotels is eligible to earn Frequent Traveler Bonus credit on Eastern if certain requirements are met. Additionally, credits come from trips taken on 11 commuter airlines—Air Midwest, Atlantis, Bar Harbor, Command, Mid-South, NewAir, Providence Boston, Pilgrim, Precision, Primair, and Wheeler.[21] (Exhibit 26.4)

---

[18] Telephone interview by authors with an anonymous Eastern Air Lines executive.

[19] Eastern Air Lines Inc. 1983 Annual Report, p. 5.

[20] Billitteri, p. 68.

[21] Eastern Annual Report, p. 5.

Exhibit 26.3   Eastern's Hubs Provide Easy Connections

EASTERN'S HUBS PROVIDE EASY CONNECTIONS

Eastern makes connecting with other flights easy with our hubs in Kansas City, Atlanta and Houston. They smooth your way to points all across the country. So when you have a choice, choose Eastern — and make some great connections.

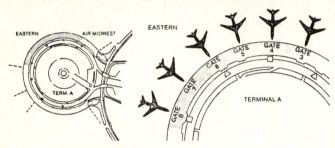

KANSAS CITY. Our new East-West hub is remarkably uncongested. And the terminal is on one level with all Eastern gates in the same concourse. So your connecting times are cut to a minimum. Eastern serves 29 cities East/West from Kansas City.

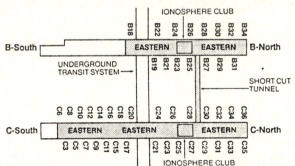

ATLANTA. Our largest hub was designed specifically to move people conveniently. Its underground system is second to none. And Eastern has an exclusive "short-cut" tunnel that saves travel time between our concourses. 340 Eastern flights depart daily from Atlanta. Schedules are coordinated with Eastern Metro Express flights for convenient connections to selected cities.

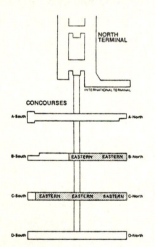

HOUSTON. All our gates are in adjacent flight stations in Terminal A for quick and easy transfer. And Eastern Metro Express flights into Houston are carefully coordinated for convenient connections with our 23 daily outbound flights.

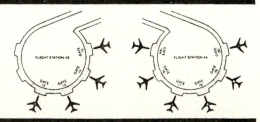

Source: Company records.

Get-Up-and-Go Passport

Recognizing the virtually untapped market of older people with time to travel, Eastern developed this new marketing concept which was introduced during 1983. It was kicked off on November 15 with widespread publicity and advertising on how, for a modest fixed price, a person 65 years or older could travel almost anywhere Eastern flies for a full year with certain restrictions. Also, the person over 65 could buy a second Passport for a companion who need not be 65, but would travel with the elder person. The response to this unique and unmatched marketing program has been very good.[22]

System One Direct Access

Another marketing innovation that is showing marked growth is SODA, Eastern's travel agency automation program. Travel agents are linked directly to Eastern's reservation system, as well as participating airlines' reservation systems, through Eastern's computer. In 1982, there were 1,028 agency users of SODA, but this grew to 2,555 by the first part of 1984. Additionally, four more airlines—Frontier, KLM, Varig, and United—agreed in 1983 to participate in SODA, bringing to 16 the number of airlines, including American, TWA, Pan Am, and British Airways, who have linked their reservation computers to Eastern's.[23]

"Moonlight Special"

This service, which has Houston as the connecting hub for all flights, links the cities of Seattle, Portland, San Francisco, and Los Angeles with the cities of Boston, New York, Philadelphia, Atlanta, and Chicago. Passengers may fly any one-way segment to or from Houston for $49 or connect at Houston and combine any two segments for $98.

All flights depart during late evening or night hours, and all arrivals (except for Houston) are scheduled for early morning. Passengers are permitted two pieces of carry-on luggage. Whereas no luggage can be checked through, up to a maximum of three pieces may be sent (though not necessarily on the same plane) at an additional cost of $10 per bag. Meals are not available on these overnight flights.[24]

This service coincides with the overnight freight service operated in conjunction with CF Air Freight, a freight-forwarding subsidiary of Consolidated Freightways. It uses seven of Eastern's 35 wide-bodied A300 jetliners. The jets' 252 seats are reserved for passengers, but the cargo bellies will be used for CF Air Freight deliveries.[25]

Maintenance of Existing Strategies

1. Business shuttle in Northeast fills niche in dense business market and has proven remarkably resilient to competition by New York Air and other commuter airlines.

---

[22] Ibid.

[23] Ibid.

[24] Russell L. Ray, Jr., "The Country's Brightest Innovation in Air Transportation," *Eastern Review*, April 1985, p. 4.

[25] Ibid., "Eastern Offers Cross-Country Flights for $98," *The Orlando Sentinel*, March 5, 1985.

Exhibit 26.4   Frequent Traveler

Eastern's Frequent Traveler Bonus Program offers people who fly often the opportunity to earn bonus credits based on your Eastern mileage. You can earn free or discounted travel on Eastern, free travel on TWA*, British Caledonian and SAS, free five-year or lifetime memberships to our Ionosphere Club, one-week Hertz or General car rentals, a free weekend at any Marriott hotel—or substantial discounts on Super 7 vacation packages.

On each Eastern flight segment, you will automatically be credited with the actual miles flown or receive a minimum credit of 1,000 miles, whichever is greater. In other words, we'll give you 1,000 miles to help you reach your goal faster. In addition, First Class tickets earn double mileage credits!

AND YOU'LL EARN BONUS MILES ON TWA!

When you fly TWA and submit an Eastern bonus coupon at flight time we'll credit your Eastern bonus account with the actual mileage.* First Class tickets on TWA earn 150% of actual mileage and Ambassador Class (business class) tickets earn 125% of actual mileage.

In order to get credit for travel on any of the airlines in Eastern's program, you must submit your bonus coupon at flight time. We will not be able to give retroactive credit for past flights.

And now, Eastern also offers you more ways to earn bonus miles. Every time you fly British Caledonian between the U.S. and London or SAS between the U.S. and Copenhagen, Gothenburg, Oslo or Stockholm, you will be credited with a minimum of 5,000 bonus miles.* Simply turn in an Eastern bonus coupon when you board one of these British Caledonian or SAS flights. And you can also earn bonus miles when you fly Eastern and rent a Hertz (only applicable at airport locations in the Continental U.S.) or General car by submitting an additional bonus coupon to the rental agent for validation.* Marriott hotel stays in conjunction with Eastern travel will also entitle you to validation of a bonus coupon. Then turn in these coupons to Eastern along with your normal bonus coupon for Eastern travel and we'll credit your account.*

Whenever you fly select commuter carriers including Air Midwest, Atlantis, Bar Harbor, Command, Eastern, Metro Express, Mid-South, New Air, PBA, Pilgrim, Precision, Prinair, or Wheeler and turn in an Eastern bonus coupon, your account will automatically be credited with 500 miles.

There's more reason than ever to fly Eastern and be on your way to great travel awards!

---

*Eastern FTBP participants may earn bonus mileage on all TWA flights through December 31, 1984, except those flights that originate or terminate in Kansas City, or any city in Florida. Certificates for bonus award travel on TWA must be issued by December 31, 1984 and tickets issued by December 31, 1985.

You may earn bonus mileage on all British Caledonian and SAS nonstop and direct flights between the continental U.S. except Alaska and London, Copenhagen, Gothenburg, Oslo and Stockholm. First Class travel earns 7,000 miles, Business Class 6,000 and Coach Class 5,000 miles. Validated Hertz and Marriott bonus coupons will earn 1,000 miles. General will earn 2,000 miles, when submitted directly to Eastern within 30 days.

Eastern's Frequent Traveler Bonus Program Awards Update

10,000 miles	Free First Class upgrade on an Eastern coach ticket.[1]
20,000	25% discount on an Eastern ticket,[1] or a Hertz subcompact Ford Escort or similar car for one week.[2]
30,000	50% discount on an Eastern ticket.[1]
40,000	One free Eastern coach ticket or a 75% discount on an Eastern First Class ticket.[1]
50,000	You may select one of the following:
	a) One free First Class ticket to any Eastern or TWA destination in the continental U.S. or to any Eastern international destination except in South America.[1][8]
	b) A 50% discount for two on an Eastern Super 7 Vacation package.[3]
60,000	A five-year membership in Eastern's Ionosphere Club.[4]
70,000	You may select one of the following:
	a) Two free coach class tickets to any Eastern or TWA designation in the continental U.S. or to any Eastern international destination except in South America.[1][8]
	If you select a destination served by General Rent-a-Car, you may receive a subcompact Chevette or similar car for one week.[2]
	b) One free coach class ticket to any Eastern destination in South America.[10]
80,000	You may select one of the following:
	a) Two free coach tickets to any Eastern or TWA destination in the continental U.S. or to any Eastern international destination except in South America.[1][8]
	1) A Hertz subcompact Ford Escort or similar car for one week.[2]
	2) A free two night/three day weekend stay at any Marriott Hotel.[2]
	b) One free Eastern First Class ticket to South America, with the purchase of a First Class adult fare companion ticket, same flight and date.[5][6]

Exhibit 26.4 *continued*

	c) One free First or Business Class British Caledonian ticket to London or SAS to Copenhagen, Stockholm, Oslo or Gothenburg, with the purchase of an adult fare companion ticket, same flight, class, and date.[6][7]
90,000	You may select one of the following:
	a) Two free First Class tickets to any Eastern or TWA destination in the continental U.S. or to any Eastern international destination except in South America.[1][8]
	If you select a destination served by General Rent-a-Car, you may also receive a Monte Carlo or similar car for one week.[2]
	b) One free First Class ticket to any Eastern destination in South America.[10]
100,000	A lifetime membership in Eastern's Ionosphere Club.[4]
110,000	You may select one of the following:
	a) Two free coach/economy class tickets to any Eastern destination in South America or any TWA international destination.[5][9]
	b) Two free coach tickets to London on British Caledonian or to Scandinavia on SAS.[2]
140,000	Two free Business Class tickets on British Caledonian to London, or on SAS to Scandinavia.[7]
150,000	Two free First Class tickets to any Eastern destination in South America or to any TWA international destination.[5][9]

NOTE:

Awards are subject to change without notice. Travel to international destinations on Eastern, British Caledonian, SAS and TWA is subject to foreign government approvals. Travel awards are valid for one-way or roundtrip travel with one stopover at the outward destination. Tickets, once issued, are valid for one redemption only. All awards are subject to Terms and Conditions as published by Eastern and available on request.

Certain blackout dates prohibit award travel on Eastern, TWA, British Caledonian and SAS. During 1984, travel is not permitted on Eastern (all flights) or TWA (flights within the continental U.S. only) January 1–3, February 17–27, April 20–29, November 20, 21, 25 and 26, December 20–31.

Also during 1984, travel awards on TWA are not permitted internationally January 1–3, April 20–29 or December 14–24. Transatlantic award travel on TWA is not permitted on eastbound flights Thursdays, Fridays or Saturdays June 7–July 7, and August 30–September 15, 1984. TWA transatlantic award travel is not permitted on westbound flights Saturdays, Sundays or Mondays July 1–August 31, and October 1–21, 1984. Travel awards on British Caledonian and SAS are valid for travel through May 31, 1984 and are not available from December 15, 1983 through January 5, 1984.

AWARD FOOTNOTES

[1] Travel on Eastern at this award level is applicable only to Eastern destinations in the U.S., the Bahamas, Bermuda, the Caribbean, Central America, Canada and Mexico. For travel to Canada and Mexico, tickets must be issued and travel originate in the U.S.

[2] Hertz awards may be redeemed at all Hertz corporate and participating licensed locations in the Continental U.S. except the borough of Manhattan, New York City. All Hertz, General Rent-A-Car and Marriott Hotel awards are subject to terms and conditions itemized on the award certificates.

[3] All Super 7 vacation packages include hotel accommodations up to maximum of seven nights. This award includes a 30% discount for two on the Eastern airfare accompanying the package but excludes a 50% discount on extra nights, rental car upgrades and meal plans.

[4] Eastern Ionosphere Club awards do not include spouse membership.

[5] Travel to South American destinations served by Eastern is only valid for travel originating from a city served by Eastern in the Continental U.S.

[6] All ticketing transactions involving the award of a free ticket issued in conjunction with a purchased ticket must be handled simultaneously, including issuance, subsequent change or refund.

[7] Free travel awards on British Caledonian and SAS may include travel on Eastern same class of service originating from an Eastern city in the Continental U.S. (except in Alaska) with a direct connection on either British Caledonian or SAS at the U.S. gateway city. Tickets issued against these awards on British Calendonian and SAS are limited to nonstop and through-flights from the U.S. gateway roundtrip to the termination point of either London, Copenhagen, Oslo, Gothenburg or Stockholm. First Class service is permitted on Eastern when class of service on British Caledonian or SAS is Business Class.

[8] Travel at this award level may include flights on Eastern or TWA on the most applicable or direct routing to the destination city.

[9] International travel at this award level may include flights on Eastern or TWA, same class of service, originating from an Eastern or TWA city in the U.S. (including Puerto Rico and the U.S. Virgin Islands) with a direct connection at the gateway city.

[10] Travel to South America at this award level may include flights on Eastern, same class of service, originating from an Eastern city in the Continental U.S. (including Puerto Rico and the U.S. Virgin Islands) with a direct connection at the gateway city.

2. Atlanta hub.

3. Miami link with El InterAmericano service on Latin American route system.

4. Continued existence in the lucrative North-South market has led to fare-matching with direct competition of People Express. Borman: "We can't afford to have any more dilution in that market or we will really have an enormous problem." [26]

5. Alliance with Walt Disney World in Orlando, Florida, as the official airline of WDW.

6. Expansion of Ionosphere Travel Clubs, which help marketing to business traveler.

7. Continued expansion of MIS to monitor and direct pricing strategies.

Future Miami/London Route

This potentially lucrative route has just been awarded to Eastern. Although the start-up date is uncertain, Eastern will soon be flying this route which could open up the European market with connecting European airlines. The route once belonged to Air Florida, but it was taken away when that carrier filed for bankruptcy. [27]

Top Management

The top management of Eastern Air Lines Inc. is shown in Exhibit 26.5. Frank Borman, Chairman of the Board and Chief Executive Officer, has been with Eastern Air Lines for 16 years. Best known as the commander of the Apollo 8 space flight, the first manned lunar orbital mission in December of 1968, Borman was hired in 1969 by Eastern as a technical adviser for $5,000. In late 1969 he was offered the position of vice-president of maintenance; and, although he had been offered a position with the Nixon administration, he accepted the position at Eastern. Six months later, Borman became senior vice-president of operations; and, in early 1975, he was named executive vice-president. He was named president and chief operating officer on May 27, 1975; and on December 16 of that year, he was elected president and chief executive officer by the board. Borman's sphere of power at Eastern became complete when, in December of 1976, he was named to the additional post of chairman of the board. [28]

It is significant that, for the first five years of his serving as president, Borman recruited no top management from another airline. All the members of his executive staff are "home grown"; they were already with Eastern when he became president, although some were in relatively minor positions. Briefly, the top management at Eastern is as follows (See following organizational chart, Exhibit 26.5):

- William G. Bell: Senior Vice-President of Legal Affairs; with the Campbrell law firm before joining Eastern.

- Thomas Button: Senior Vice-President of Airline Operations; formerly a pilot with TWA.

- Morton Ehrlich: Senior Vice-President of Planning; one of the industry's most respected

---

[26] Billitteri, p. 68.

[27] Kenneth Labich, "Fare Wars: Have the Big Airlines Learned to Win?", *Fortune*, October 29, 1984, p. 26.

[28] All information on top management taken from: *From the Captain to the Colonel*.

Exhibit 26.5   Eastern Air lines Inc. Officers of the Corporation

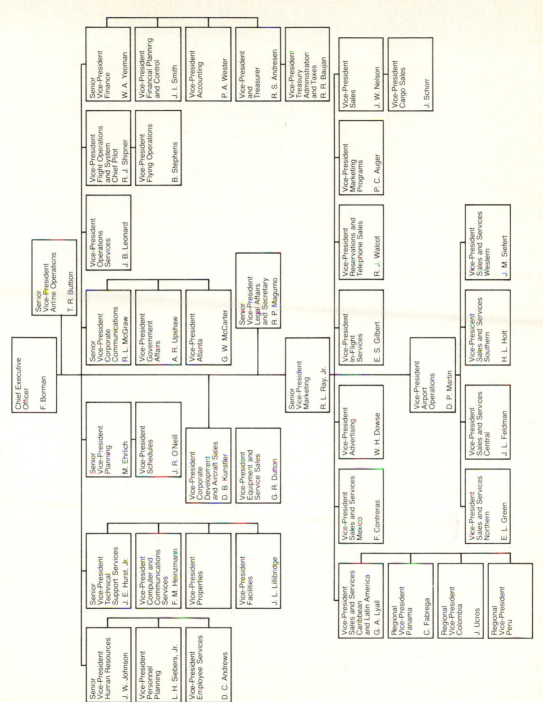

Source: Company records.

economists; became director of economic planning in 1968 and quickly moved up management ladder.

- John Hurst, Jr.: Senior Vice-President of Technical Support; classmate of Frank Borman at West Point; retired colonel in the Army Corps of Engineers.
- Russell L. Ray, Jr.: Senior Vice-President of Marketing; headed the sales team that launched the L-1011; met Borman while at Lockheed.
- Wayne Yeoman: Senior Vice-President of Finance; West Point graduate; retired brigadier general; fighter pilot who flew 53 missions in Korea.

Outlook for the Future

At best, it has to be said that the outlook for the future of Eastern Air Lines is uncertain. Although profits are finally improving, many other factors have to either remain the same or improve if Eastern is going to survive. The economy cannot weaken, and fuel prices cannot again rise. More wage concessions and greater productivity improvements must be accompanied by other cost reduction programs in order to keep the creditors at bay.

Eastern has truly learned the power of its competitors in a deregulated market; and it has taken great strides to satisfactorily meet the competition. But whether or not it will survive, and indeed succeed, is a function of many variables—some of which are beyond the control of Eastern. Things look better, but they still do not look good.

References

"Accent on Managerial Ability in Tomorrow's Industry." *Interavia*, April 1984, p. 290.

"The Airline Business 'Isn't Just Flying Airplanes.'" *Interavia*, April 1983, p. 364.

"A Patch of Blue for the Airlines." *Financial World*, Vol. 153, January 10, 1984, pp. 139–143.

"Air Turbulence Ahead." *Fortune*, September 17, 1983, p. 8.

Banks, Howard. "Airlines." *Forbes*, January 2, 1984, pp. 139–143.

Billitteri, Thomas J. "Why Eastern Will Go Back to Labor for More Help." *Florida Trend*, November 1984, pp. 66–70.

Brayh, Nick. "Marketing in a Competitive Environment: U.S. Carriers Try New Tricks to Attract Passengers." *Interavia*, July 1983, pp. 775–776.

Carter, Craig. "Air Slots for Sale." *Fortune*, August 20, 1984, p. 154.

Clifford, Mark. "A Struggle for Survival." *Financial World*, November 15, 1983, pp. 13–18.

Cohn, Gary. "Angry Union Leader at Eastern Air Lines Feels Betrayed by the Carrier's Chairman." *The Wall Street Journal*, January 4, 1985, p. 24.

Cohn, Gary. "Eastern Airlines Blasts Union Request for Revenue Share, Will Reinstate Cut." *The Wall Street Journal*, February 6, 1985.

"Corporate Performance." *Fortune*, January 7, 1985, pp. 19–22.

Eastern Air Lines 1983 Annual Report.

"Eastern Air Lines Increases Service to the Northeast." *Aviation Week & Space Technology*, September 17, 1984.

"Eastern May Get Route to London." *The Orlando Sentinel*, April 5, 1985.

"Eastern Offers Cross-Country Flights for $98." *The Orlando Sentinel*, March 5, 1985.

"The Economy." *Fortune*, November 26, 1984, p. 82.

Hagstrom, Suzy. "High on Eastern Convertibles." *The Orlando Sentinel*, March 25, 1985.

"How Deregulation Puts Competition Back in Business." *U.S. News & World Report*, November 26, 1984, pp. 51–52.

"Industry By Industry Quarterly Earnings." *The Wall Street Journal*, February 19, 1985.

Interavia, October 1984, pp. 1056–1060.

Labich, Kenneth. "Fare Wars: Have the Big Airlines Learned to Win?" *Fortune*, October 29, 1984, pp. 24–28.

Magary, A. B. Republic Airlines Frequent Flyer Program Update '85. March, 1985.

Maldutis, Julius. "Eastern Airlines, Inc.—An Airline to Start Watching." Salomon Brothers Stock Research: Airlines, March 1985.

Nelson, Margaret. "Inside Program Saves Millions." *Purchasing*, April 14, 1983, p. 15.

"The New U.S. Airlines: How Their Finances Are Faring." *Interavia*, April 1984, pp. 325–327.

Nulty, Peter. "A Champ of Cheap Airlines." *Fortune*, March 22, 1982, pp. 127–134.

Ray, Russell L., Jr. "The Country's Brightest Innovation in Air Transportation." *Eastern Review*, April 1985.

Rowan, Roy. "An Airline Boss Attacks Sky-High Wages." *Fortune*, January 9, 1984, pp. 66–73.

Schmutzer, Craig A. "An Analysis of the Airline Industry." *The Journal of Commercial Bank Lending*, Vol. 66 February 1984, pp. 18–28.

Skrzycki, Cindy. "Continental Air Soars Above Union Turbulence." *U.S. News & World Report*, July 23, 1984, pp. 69–70.

Skrzycki, Cindy. "Growing Pains for Midsized Airlines." *U.S News & World Report*, September 17, 1984, pp. 49–50.

Tully, Shawn. "Pan Am's $200 Million Tranquilizer." *Fortune*, November 29, 1982, pp. 110–112.

Wayne, Leslie. "Frank Borman's Most Difficult Days." *New York Times*, February 17, 1985.

Woolley, David. "Airlines Climb Out of the Red." *Interavia*, October 1984, pp. 1033–1036.

Celanese Mexicana, S.A.

▪ *Lincoln W. Deihl* ▪

Over lunch of filet mignon in the executive dining room on the 39th floor of the headquarters building in suburban Mexico City, Assistant General Manager and Chief Operating Officer, American A. Haisley Lynch, leaned back and chose his words carefully. Celanese Mexicana's biggest problem, he says, is developing human resources. Due to rapid industrialization in Mexico, there is a great demand for trained people. Many of the company's people are being pirated away by other companies, frequently in an unethical manner.

There are many projects Lynch would like to undertake. But, frankly, he asserts, we just do not have the human resources to undertake them. A few years back the company had a group working on possible new product lines in chemicals and fibers. The feeling was that these new areas would be essential when the traditional chemical and fiber product lines mature. However, all new projects have had to be put on the back burner because the company doesn't have the human resources to undertake them. The organization simply is stretched too thinly trying to meet demand for the traditional product lines.

Cost of Money and New Opportunities

A major problem for Lynch is in the area of finance. The company cannot generate the necessary capital funds to undertake the things they would like to do. (See Balance Sheet, Exhibit 27.1; Income Statement, Exhibit 27.2; and Comparative Condensed Data, Exhibit 27.3.) Celanese Mexicana's credit is good. But with the cost of money somewhere between 16 and 23 percent, funding is a major constraint. In a sense, this is an advantage. It makes it much easier for Lynch to say "no" to requests for funds by operating heads.

Lynch sees a real problem to get operating heads to think in terms of new opportunities. They are likely to think in traditional terms and traditional product lines. Their career commitments have been in these terms, and they are not likely to think otherwise. They prefer to see expansion in these terms even though it may be unwise. Therefore, he often has to say "no" to requests for capital expenditures.

Technology and Managerial Skills Transfer

Lynch is seriously concerned about the problems of turning functional managers into general managers. Many of them simply do not develop the necessary breadth to integrate several functional areas. He would be willing to rotate managers to various functional areas, but he feels they just do not have the managerial depth in the various units which would permit managers to be spared.

This case was prepared by Lincoln W. Deihl, Professor of Management, Kansas State University. This case does not indicate effective or ineffective handling of an administrative situation. Rather, it is to be used for class discussion purposes. All rights reserved to the contributor. Reprinted by permission.

Sources: Extensive interviews at company headquarters in Mexico City; annual reports; and the book *Putting Down Roots, 25 Years of Celanese in Mexico*, by Richard W. Hall (New York: Celanese Corp., 1969).

Exhibit 27.1   Celanese Mexicana, S.A. Balance Sheet (consolidated) (in 000 pesos)

	December 31,	
	1979	**1978**
Current assets		
Cash	$ 44,092	$ 36,853
Notes receivable	76,964	213,554
Accounts receivable less allowance for uncollectible accounts	1,637,840	1,357,371
Affiliated companies	43,030	56,573
Inventory	794,015	734,400
Other current assets	133,630	92,255
Total current assets	2,729,571	2,491,006
Long-term accounts receivable	47,603	97,379
Investments	674,651	600,008
Plant and equipment	7,831,877	6,586,601
Less accumulated depreciation	4,047,225	3,729,693
Net plant and equipment	3,784,652	2,856,908
Deferred charges	34,983	22,447
Total net assets	7,271,460	6,067,748
Liabilities and stockholders' equity		
Current liabilities		
Notes payable	5,915	9,198
Accrued expenses payable	118,979	141,659
Accounts payable	1,215,718	1,011,956
Affiliate companies	92,692	77,997
Income taxes	27,213	30,868
Profit sharing for personnel	92,552	84,009
Total current liabilities	1,553,069	1,355,687
Long-term liabilities	1,626,545	1,243,156
Deferred revenues		
Income taxes	197,861	187,439
Others	15,417	5,836
Total deferred revenues	213,278	193,275
Stockholders' equity		
Capital stock	1,557,954	1,286,047
Paid-in value in excess of par value	206,906	118,720
Excess due to reevaluation	605,607	605,607
Legal reserve	211,497	181,492
Retained earnings	130,384	130,384
Unassigned earnings	1,166,220	953,380
Total stockholders' equity	3,878,568	3,275,630
Total liabilities and stockholders' equity	7,271,460	6,067,748

(Approx. 23 pesos to the U.S. dollar.)

Lynch sees no particular problem in technology or managerial skills transfer. The company has had a lot of experience in technology transfer. In the early days, people who could not read or write were adequately utilizing new technologies. Today the company is placing major emphasis on product quality, and they feel theirs can be matched with the best in the United States. Transfer of managerial skills poses no particular problems ei-

Exhibit 27.2   Income Statement (in 000 of pesos)

	December 31,	
	1979	1978
Sales	$9,044,428	$6,860,386
Operating expenses		
Cost of goods sold	7,112,426	5,236,553
Sales and administrative expenses	501,993	409,351
Total operating expenses	7,614,419	5,645,904
Operating income	1,430,009	1,214,482
Other (income) expenses		
Interest income	(92,030)	(63,227)
Interest expense	269,039	194,986
Others—net	87,356	56,328
Total other (income) expenses	264,365	188,087
Net income		
Before taxes and profit sharing by personnel	1,165,644	1,026,395
Income taxes:		
On taxable income	459,732	422,945
Deferred	10,422	14,382
Total income taxes	470,154	437,327
Income before profit sharing by personnel	695,490	589,068
Profit sharing by personnel	92,552	84,017
Net income	602,938	505,051

(Approx. 23 pesos to the U.S. dollar.)

ther. Mexicans, Lynch feels, have done a good job of structuring and administering the organization in the American rather than the European style. (See Organization Chart, Exhibit 27.4.)

In a process industry, Lynch points out, we have to operate 24 hours a day every day of the year. People are not particularly happy about this, but it poses no particular problem. In some ways, he believes, the Mexican is more family oriented than his United States counterpart; but in other ways he is not.

The Mexican is sensitive and proud, Lynch has found; perhaps it is an inferiority complex. The expatriate must be very careful not to offend by something he does or says. If offended, the Mexican is likely not to resort to emotional outburst but may simply become withdrawn and possibly quit.

"He Has Identified with Mexico"

Originally from Pensacola, Florida, Haisley Lynch went to Mexico in 1953 at his own request, after having previously visited Zacapu in 1951 as part of a team to get the first rayon staple fiber line going. He wound up spending seven years in Zacapu—from 1953 to 1960—and it agreed with him, as well as with his wife and daughter. He was promoted to manager of manufacturing in 1960, transferring to Mexico City. He then went on to become director of manufacturing, adding the purchase and planning functions to his chores.

Exhibit 27.3   Comparative Condensed Data (Consolidated)

	December 31,				
	1979	**1978**	**1977**	**1976**	**1975**
Income statement (millions of pesos)					
Net sales	9,044.4	6,860.4	5,795.2	3,854.3	3,054.5
Gross income	1,932.0	1,623.8	1,225.0	744.6	540.8
Operating expenses	502.0	409.3	341.6	249.1	199.5
Other expenses (income) net	264.4	188.1	153.7	136.4	72.9
Reserves for:					
Income taxes	470.2	437.3	337.4	141.7	86.5
Profit sharing	92.5	84.0	66.0	27.9	14.7
Net income	602.9	505.1	326.3	189.5	167.2
Balance sheet (millions)					
Current assets	2,729.6	2,491.0	2,434.9	2,096.0	1,578.2
Current liabilities	1,553.1	1,355.7	1,234.0	981.4	651.4
Working capital	1,176.5	1,135.3	1,200.9	1,114.6	926.8
Current ratio	1.8	1.8	2.0	2.1	2.4
Investments at cost	674.7	600.0	602.3	411.1	362.2
Accounts payable—long-term	47.6	97.4	15.9	52.3	19.7
Building, plant, and equipment at cost	7,831.9	6,586.6	6,092.0	5,758.2	2,890.3
Accumulated appreciation	4,047.2	3,729.7	3,462.0	3,159.1	1,195.8
Net buildings, plant and equipment	3,784.7	2,856.9	2,630.0	2,599.1	1,694.5
Other assets and deferred charges	34.9	22.5	11.5	13.8	11.6
Subtotal	5,718.4	4,712.1	4,460.6	4,190.9	3,014.8
Long-term liabilities	1,626.5	1,243.2	1,359.0	1,330.4	791.2
Deferred income taxes and other	213.3	193.3	176.7	176.2	172.1
Stockholders' equity:					
Capital stock	1,558.0	1,169.1	1,169.1	1,169.1	1,169.1
Paid-in capital in excess of par value	206.9	118.7	118.7	118.7	118.7
Excess due to reevaluation	605.6	605.6	605.6	583.5	—
Retained earnings	130.4	130.4	130.4	130.4	130.4
Legal reserve	211.5	181.5	156.4	140.2	130.5
Cumulative earnings	1,166.2	953.4	744.7	574.9	535.4
Total stockholders' equity	3,878.6	3,158.7	2,924.9	2,716.8	2,084.1
Additional information					
Number of shares	31.159	12,860.00	11,691.00	11,691.00	11,691.00
Net earnings per share	95.350	39.27	27.91	16.21	14.30
Dividend per share		12.00	12.00	12.00	12.00
Dividend in shares of stock		1 for 7	1 for 10		1 for 20
Book value of stock	124.480	254.71	250.18	232.38	178.25
Market value of stock	154.000	338.00	152.00	116.00	115.00
Additions to buildings, plant, and equipment	1,251.900	524.90	141.00	96.10	196.20
Number of employees and operating personnel	8,160.000	7,597.00	7,094.00	6,550.00	7,271.00
Profit (%)					
On sales	6.700	7.40	5.60	4.90	5.50
On total assets	8.300	8.30	5.70	3.60	4.50
On stockholders' equity	15.500	15.40	11.20	7.00	8.00

(Approx. 23 pesos to U.S. dollar.)

Exhibit 27.4   Celanese Mexicana S.A. Organizational Chart

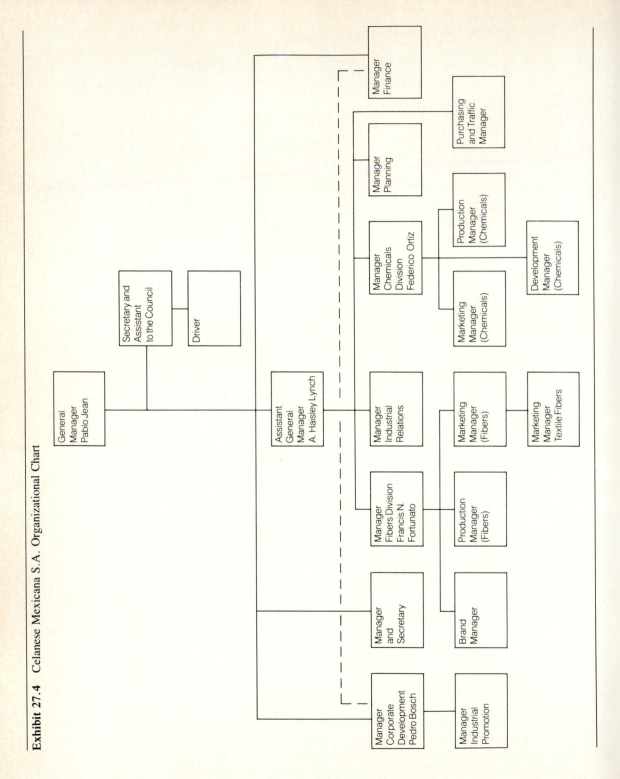

The plants grew appreciably in size during these years also. In 1966, he became executive director of operations and in 1968 he was promoted to assistant general manager.

Lynch has lived in Mexico for nearly three decades, with only occasional visits to the United States. Mexico is his home; his roots go down increasingly deep; and there is no doubt that his commitment to his adopted country is permanent. He has learned to speak excellent Spanish, with the true singsong Mexican inflection; and most of his working day is spent speaking Spanish, not English. As General Manager and Chief Executive Officer Pablo Jean says of Lynch, "He has identified with Mexico and its people."

Decisions and Crises

In the years since Lynch went to work at headquarters, the company has grown immensely. Expansion and diversification, he observes, were the only way to keep ahead of growing competition. Economies of scale could be achieved only through more output and increased productivity, with plenty of innovation.

This formula for growth, however, gives none of the flavor of the decisions and crises that Celanese Mexicana faced through the difficult early years. Guts, good nerves, and a passion for hard work were required to see the company through this critical period. These qualities Lynch and his team had in abundance.

Take the instance of the polyester start-up. The company decided it wanted to begin manufacturing polyester in its staple (or short form). According to Mexican law, a permit for this was required from the Federal Petrochemical Commission, since polyester is a petroleum derivative. The permit was applied for, but denied. Instead, the government granted it to a competitor of Celanese Mexicana. This competitor broke ground for a plant in Monterrey. It became obvious after a while that the competitor was in no great hurry to bring the plant on-stream; in fact, he continued to import polyester from the United States for sale in the Mexican market.

After a year and a half, the polyester plant was still unfinished and Celanese Mexicana decided to reapply for the permit, on the grounds that the present licensee was not living up to his obligations. The government apparently agreed because Celanese Mexicana was granted the permit. Within seven months—more quickly even than might have been possible in the United States—a polyester line was brought on-stream at Toluca by Lynch and his group. The competition, aware of the new development, accelerated its own start-up efforts, but even so was unable to catch up. Celanese Mexicana hit the market with polyester of domestic manufacture first, got a dominant share of the sales, and has held it to this day.

The decisive factor, of course, was planning. By the time the government awarded the permit, Celanese Mexicana had the plant designed on paper and purchase orders ready. On the day of the permit award, the purchase orders went out—not by mail but by telephone and messenger.

Not everything went smoothly. The control panel for the extrusion process was dropped and destroyed on the road to Toluca. This could have been disastrous, since such panels were rare and costly and could be built only in the United States. Fortunately, another Celanese company, Celanese Venezolana, had one on order in the United States and was not in as big a rush for it as was Celanese Mexicana. The panel was shunted to Mexico and disaster avoided.

Marketing, the Response to Competition

When Lynch took over the operations group in 1966, he began to concentrate on the marketing function. He rebuilt and restructured the organization, shifted personnel, and created a more effective balance between commercial and technical marketing. According to Lynch, the restructuring made for a clearer division of responsibilities and more freedom for executives to act. He felt that, as a result, esprit de corps was greatly improved and that customers reacted favorably to the new climate.

The largest single group at headquarters, marketing has been strengthened consistently with more personnel, bigger budgets for advertising and promotion, and more technical assistance to customers. Pablo Jean, General Manager, considers competition the key challenge of the future and marketing the key response to that challenge.

The relatively low degree of marketing sophistication on the part of customers poses a problem. In Mexico, only a few intermediate producers are market-oriented. Most of them do little to build brand identity. They keep their promotion budgets low. Often they are not diversified enough to warrant substantial expenditures.

This has transferred the burden of promoting garments of man-made fibers back to the primary producer of the fiber. For this reason, Celanese Mexicana has one of the largest advertising and promotion budgets in Mexican industry. It includes television time, substantial print campaigns, publicity, fashion shows, point-of-sale promotion, and sales training for department store clerks.

Another form of market support involves technical assistance to customers. A customer service staff of engineers (chemical and textile) provides various kinds of assistance. It might be advice over the telephone to a customer who wants a quick answer to a question—i.e., whether acetate can be blended with wool. It might be a visit to the plant of a customer who is setting up new production and whose engineers need instruction. If Celanese wants to run a market test for a new or improved product, customer service engineers must follow up.

Lack of Transport Restricts Results

Net consolidated sales of the company were 9,044 million pesos for 1979 compared with the year before of 6,860 million pesos, a significant increase of 32 percent. Profits were 603 million pesos, an increase of 19 percent. (See Income Statement, Exhibit 27.2; and Comparative Condensed Data, Exhibit 27.3.)

Sales of the Fiber Division were 6,861 million pesos in 1979; compared with 5,083 the previous year, an increment of 35 percent. This gain was achieved despite work stoppages due to strikes at Ocotlan and Querétaro as well as problems due to availability of raw materials which restricted production.

To take advantage of strong demand for its products, the Fiber Division made capital investments of 851 million pesos in 1979. Part of the production increment resulting from this investment was available in 1979, but the major part of the increment is to be in 1980.

The division produces the widest variety of fiber products in Mexico. Polyester, nylon, rayon, and cellophane are most important.

Sales of the Chemicals Division were 2,387 million pesos in 1979, an increase of 34 percent over the previous year. The division produces a wide variety of chemical products, mostly petroleum based.

The lack of transport facilities, particularly the chronic shortage of freight cars, affected operations in the irregular receiving of raw materials as well as in the distribution of manufactured products to final markets.

Managers on the Move

Many managers at headquarters have spent time at the plants. The policy of promoting Mexicans to key positions establishes a clear line of progression for the man who has ability and wants to stay with Celanese Mexicana. The progression is approximately like this: on graduation from one of the universities with an engineering degree, the young man begins as a shift chief. He is responsible for all product turned out by men in one department for the duration of an eight-hour shift. A promotion would make him department chief, with responsibility for production in one department around the 24-hour clock, with three shift chiefs reporting to him. From there he might progress to a specialized department but with generalized responsibility—like quality control superintendent or engineering superintendent. And with the right combination of skills and personal attributes, he might proceed to managership of the Rio Bravo plant—a plant designated as "a school for budding executives," where they might exercise their first command.

After a stint at Rio Bravo, he might be made a manager at one of the major plants (Ocotlan, Toluca, or Zacapu) or might transfer to Mexico City headquarters, with specific staff responsibilities.

Such a progression might carry a man from modest plant responsibilities to a top job at headquarters. This shifting of managers has made communication easier between headquarters and plant. The men in Mexico City have come up the long way; they have friends at the plants. In many cases, their families consider Zacapu or Ocotlan more home than Mexico City.

Via a regularly scheduled company airplane, visitors from headquarters constantly visit the plants—accountants for a monthly audit, marketing men giving important customers a plant tour, engineering supervisors, top brass, and visitors from Celanese plants in the United States on a technical assignment.

The major liaison, of course, is between the manufacturing staff at headquarters and the plant staffs. The manufacturing staff, with its depth in fiber technology, is constantly on the move to the plants. It may be a routine visit. It may be a trip to check out the installation of machinery being installed for new or increased capacity. It may be in connection with malfunctioning equipment—an air conditioning unit that has failed in a spinning room, for example. It may be to evaluate on-the-spot an engineering study made by plant engineers.

Replacing Managers

Richard Taunton Escobar, Director of Organizational Development at Celanese Mexicana, sees himself as a "generalist." A Colombian, his father is English; he grew up in England. He took his bachelor's degree in animal husbandry at Oklahoma State and studied management at the University of San Francisco. First, Taunton was with Celanese Columbiana, then with Dow Chemical, based both at corporate headquarters in Midland, Michigan, and at Latin American headquarters in Coral Gables, Florida. Then he returned for another stint at Celanese Columbiana before taking on his present job at Celanese Mexicana six months ago. Like so many managers at Celanese, Richard Taunton works long days. His wife sometimes questions the necessity of such a commitment.

In charge of recruiting, training, and development, Taunton sees his main problems as recruiting in this fast-growing company, particularly for the new plant soon to go on-stream in Coatzacoalcas. Mostly local people are being recruited as there is a problem in attracting those from other areas, such as Mexico City.

A continuing problem is that of filling vacant positions for specialists. And there is the problem of developing replacements for managers. Increasingly, the company has to go outside to hire specialists and managers. Taunton himself is directly handling recruiting for several top positions. Search firms—headhunters—are increasingly utilized. These are American firms with Mexican branches; they are fully Mexicanized. It is expensive but worth it. The fee for the company is 30 percent of the first year's salary. Such search firms seem to be doing very well in Mexico these days.

Presently, there are virtually no replacements for top-level managers, except in industrial relations. Only one or two out of nine plant managers have internal replacements identified.

The problem of retaining middle managers was clearly demonstrated that very morning with the casewriter when word came that the area engineering manager who reports directly to the maintenance manager at the Querétaro plant had resigned. Taunton sent back word to find out why. It developed that the manager had left for a job elsewhere at double his wages. As it turned out, a higher engineering job was open at the company, but it was offered too late. Legally, one month's notice is required, but the company permitted him to go on the day of his resignation. "Why try to keep him?"

Salaries for many middle level technical positions are 30 percent below market. This creates a serious problem. Just now, the director of industrial relations is making a presentation at headquarters in New York. He is confident that this salary discrepancy will be rectified.

Even though replacements have not been identified for managers at all levels, the company is not so likely to lose top-level people, Taunton feels, as their commitment to the company is great when they have 20-plus years of service. But at the plant manager level, this can be a serious problem.

The recruiting manager reports to Taunton, who is satisfied with the way the job is being done. The recruiting manager was formerly an organizational development manager who did not seem to be doing a satisfactory job. Taunton is now looking for a head for the organizational development function. It is critical to fill. He is now negotiating with the OD specialist at Kimberly Clark, a multinational firm but small in Mexico and therefore with little opportunity for growth. The candidate is about 35 and well qualified. But he wants more money than Taunton himself is making. Negotiations are continuing.

Taunton wants better performance ratings of managers in order to determine whether suitable replacements for managers are available. He wants more workshops for managers to improve their job ratings. Job ratings have been a problem due to the high number of Very Good ratings. This has been true because in the past they have been used primarily for salary adjustments—merit ratings.

Workshops to improve job-rating techniques are to begin soon. A specialist is coming from Charlotte, North Carolina, to make a presentation to the industrial relations staff. At least six people on the IR staff will then be capable of putting on workshops over the next two months, the training manager estimates.

A serious problem in the organization, Taunton believes, is that of delegating. Many managers tend to centralize decisions. Perhaps they are insecure or they may have subordinates who are not capable of making decisions. Also, many capable subordinates don't want to make decisions as they feel they will be penalized for mistakes. Taunton feels subordinates should be permitted to make mistakes, and he has told Lynch so.

Taunton gets on well with his boss, the director of industrial relations, but feels he does not do a good job of coordinating subordinates' activities. Taunton says he himself does self-coordinate, but he would like to function as a team with his peers. He is considering suggesting to his boss that he have regular meetings with his subordinates—say, every two weeks.

Developing a New Training Philosophy

José Noriega was a trainer whom Taunton made training manager. This was something of a risk as Taunton's superior was unconvinced. But Taunton believes that Noriega is working out well as a manager. He conceptualizes well. Earlier he did not do particularly well in purchasing as he wasn't tough enough. People tended to ride over him. Taunton thinks he may be too nice a guy; he has told Noriega he must sometimes be a SOB.

Initially, Noriega brought every matter to Taunton for decisions and approval. Taunton told him that if he would not make the decisions he didn't want him in the job. Noriega soon got the message and is now doing a good job, Taunton believes.

An enthusiastic, committed company man, Noriega has a background as an English and mathematics teacher. In his 13 years at Celanese Mexicana, he held several jobs in the Purchasing Department before he requested transfer to the Training Department. His department includes training sections for both Fibers and Chemicals divisions.

Noriega has spent the past six months developing a new training philosophy under his newly arrived superior, Sr. Taunton. Training must be related to the specific needs of the individual. It must be tied to the improvement of performance and bottom line results. A contract is made between trainee and supervisor to achieve certain objectives with the training.

Presently, the Training Department has five vacancies for trainers. Noriega optimistically expects to fill them in six weeks' time.

In the past, the Training Department issued elaborate four-color booklets each year listing courses to be offered. Managers could simply choose whatever they liked based on some particular deficiency which they perceived—a problem in X area or whatever the boss wanted them to do. The present attempt to tie course offerings to specific needs is a key part of the philosophic change that Taunton has brought about in six months on the job. He intends to push this now that he has considerable support at the top for human resources development.

Manning a New Chemicals Plant

Federico Ortiz, Director of the Chemicals Division, is quick to say that his biggest problem is in the area of human resources. It takes much of his time and attention at present.

At present, he does not have replacements trained for plant managers, but he expects to make considerable progress in one year and should have the problem resolved in three years' time through rotating managers among various functions.

At the new Coatzacoalcas plant that is about to go on-stream, Ortiz is concerned with the problem of training local operatives and bringing in qualified technicians from outside the area. The first phase of training is going well. He sees little problem in attracting qualified technicians if they can be paid well enough. Younger people can get more responsibility in such a new plant.

A major problem for Ortiz is losing qualified people to other firms. As one of the largest and oldest firms with established training programs, Celanese Mexicana is susceptible to raids. However, the company is able to offer to employees security and prestige which can hardly be matched elsewhere.

The Chemicals Division presently produces 300,000 tons of chemicals per year. New production capacity in the preferential zone at Coatzacoalcas will increase production to 580,000 tons in three years. Locating in the preferential zone means that the government will grant 30 percent discount on petrochemical raw materials from government-owned Pemex. It also means that 25 percent of the plant's production must be exported.

The division is required to buy its petrochemical raw materials from government-owned Pemex at fixed prices. Presently, a full 90 percent of the division's raw materials come from Pemex. Such an arrangement, of course, means inflexibility in supplier relations. However, Celanese Mexicana does have a government-protected captive market in which to sell its products.

Many product lines include basic chemicals approaching maturity. But there is a great amount of pent-up demand for them. The Chemicals Division director does not see a need for demand creation.

Government Intervenes in the Private Sector

In charge of government relations, Pedro Bosch is corporate relations director. He is Spanish in origin and a long-time resident of Mexico. A former professor of economics, many of his former students are at high levels in various ministries.

Bosch stresses that government is a major factor for Celanese Mexicana. There is a tradition of government intervention in Mexico. Particularly following the expropriation of the oil industry in 1938, the government has actively intervened in the private sector. Developments in the private sector have always come about because government has determined a need and approached banks to provide the necessary financing to encourage development in the private sector. This is the way Celanese Mexicana came into being—only because government actively approached banks and Celanese.

Government assures the supply of raw materials through Pemex and assures a captive market to the monopolist by cutting off imports.

Traditionally, the company has not had the capacity to meet demand. When demand is high, they respond by simply raising prices. Celanese Mexicana is still the sole producer of many basic chemicals. However, in fibers they have encouraged competition. With government knowledge, they get together informally with competitors to agree on prices.

Pricing is extremely important. Every month detailed price lists are prepared which show the cost of raw materials, ad valorem duties, actual selling price, and pricing flexibility or excess.

Traditionally, the economy has been dominated by foreigners, primarily Spaniards. Mexicans have had cause to believe there were always foreigners in authority above them. Today, many Mexican groups are forming companies and doing it very skillfully. There are often holding companies which are 100 percent Mexican. Subsidiaries are 60 percent Mexican and 40 percent foreign in keeping with the law. These holding companies are often skillfully able to utilize technology of their foreign partners.

A future problem, according to Bosch, concerns favoritism of Mexican-owned firms by the government. The government will not discriminate, but in a case of an equal situation where the government has to choose, they will naturally choose the 100 percent Mexican-owned firm. This is quite clear.

Other likely future competition is direct investment by the government. Government today owns firms in nearly every industry. This may well squeeze private business. But government would not expropriate. They are able to achieve objectives through intervention.

Government is not likely to encourage production of basic chemicals by the private sector. This would be contrary to the objectives achieved through control of the oil industry. The new plant capacity at Coatzacoalcas will duplicate present capacity for production of basic chemicals but will be able to extend into specialty chemicals at a later time, which is necessary for survival.

Negotiations for the new plant have taken considerable time. Government is providing certain advantages: discounts on raw materials, investment credit for machinery, subsidies for plant payroll, training subsidies.

Social responsibility helps to insure the firm's survival. The firm has always been paternalistic, known as a good employer with good wages and benefits. Local plants must respond to community needs. Managers serve on community committees and provide money for school and community projects. Managerial talent as well as money is provided.

The president of Mexico changes every six years, but this has little impact on economic policy, Bosch points out. In an economy as strong as this which is rapidly growing, adverse economic policies have only a temporary effect. Succeeding presidents may be to the left or right of the previous one. But basic policies continue. Government bureaucrats provide continuity. Presidents have already served as ministers and are well known. President Lopez Portillo does not speak out actively against business as did his predecessor, but the policy of direct government intervention continues.

Bosch is optimistic for the future of the firm. But he believes that the next several years are critical. Government must make some basic decisions regarding economic policies and relations between the public and private sectors.

CASE 28
Club Méditerranée (A)*

▪ *Jacques Horovitz* ▪

Sipping a cognac and smoking one of his favorite cigars on his way back to Paris from New York on the Concorde, Serge Trigano was reviewing the new organization structure that was to be effective November 1981. In the process, he was listing the operational problems and issues that were yet to be resolved. Son of the chief executive of "Club Med," Serge Trigano was one of the joint managing directors, and he had just been promoted from director of operations to general manager of the American zone, i.e., responsible for operations and marketing for the whole American market. Having experienced a regional organization structure that was abandoned some four years ago, he wanted to make sure that this time the new structure would better fit the objectives of Club Med and allow its further development in a harmonious way.

Company Background and History

Club Med was founded in 1950 by a group of friends led by Gérard Blitz. Initially, it was a nonprofit organization, set up for the purpose of going on vacation together in some odd place. The initial members were essentially young people who liked sports and especially the sea. The first "village," a tent village, was a camping site in the Balearic Isles. After four years of activities, Mr. Gilbert Trigano was appointed the new managing director. Mr. Gilbert Trigano came to Club Med from a family business involved in the manufacture of tents in France, a major supplier to Club Med. With this move, and in the same year, the holiday village concept was expanded beyond tent villages to straw hut villages, the first of which was opened in 1954. Further expanding its activities, in 1956 Club Med opened its first ski resort at Leysin, Switzerland. In 1965, its first bungalow village was opened, and in 1968 the first village started its operation in the American zone. Club Med's main activity was, and still is today, to operate a vacation site for tourists who would pay a fixed sum (package) to go on vacation for a week, two weeks, or a month, and for whom all the facilities were provided in the village. Club Med has always had the reputation for finding beautiful sites which were fairly new to tourists (for instance, Moroccan tourism was "discovered" by Club Med) which offered many activities, especially sports activities, to its members.[1] In 1981, Club Med operated 90 villages in 40 different countries on 5 continents. In addition to its main activity, it had extended to other sectors of tourism in order to be able to offer a wider range of services. In 1976, Club Med acquired a 45 percent interest in an Italian company (Valtur) which had holiday villages in Italy, Greece, and Tunisia, mainly for the Italian market. In 1977, Club Med took over Club Hotel, which had built up a reputation over the last 12 years as a leader in the seasonal ownership time-sharing market. The result of this expansion had been such that in

[1] When going on vacation to any of Club Med's villages, one becomes a "member" of Club Med.

1980 more than 770,000 people had stayed in the villages of Club Med or its Italian subsidiary, whereas they were 2,300 in 1950. Most members were French in 1950, and in 1980 only 45 percent were French. In addition, 110,000 people had stayed in the apartments or hotels managed by its time-sharing activity. Actually, in 1980, Club Med sales were about 2.5 billion French francs (FF) and its cash flow around FF170 million. (See Exhibit 28.1 for the last ten years' financial performance.) Exhibits 28.2–28.4 show the number of people who had stayed at the holiday centers of Club Med, the number of beds it had as of 1980, and the nationality of its members. The present case focuses exclusively on the organization structure of the holiday village operations and not on the time-sharing activities of the company.

Exhibit 28.1   Financial Performance
(thousands of French francs)

	1969–70	1970–71	1971–72	1972–73	1973–74	1974–75
Sales	313,000	363,000	427,000	502,000	600,000	791,000
Net income			13,400	22,500	27,300	40,000
Cash flow			25,100	37,000	42,800	56,790
EPS	5.31	5.73	7.41	10.88	12.78	16.08

	1975–76	1976–77	1977–78	1978–79	1979–80
Sales	1,060,000	1,350,000	1,616,000	1,979,000	2,462,000
Net income	51,800	67,870	72,135	85,900	111,600
Cash flow	70,900	103,645	114,578	138,300	173,100
EPS	20.78	20.98	23.78	28.42	36.91

Exhibit 28.2   Growth in Number of Club Members

Year	Number of Members
1950	2,300
1955	10,000
1960	45,000
1965	90,000
1970	293,000
1975	432,000
1980	770,000 (including Valtur)

Exhibit 28.3   Number of Facilities (1981)

	Number of Holiday Centers	Number of Beds
Club Med and Valtur	102	60,500
Hotels	7	1,000
Apartment buildings	24	11,000
Total	133	72,500

Exhibit 28.4   Members of Club Med According to Country of Origin (1979, excluding Valtur)

	Members	Percentage
France	301,000	43.1%
United States/Canada	124,000	17.8
Belgium	41,600	6.0
Italy	34,400	4.9
West Germany	34,100	4.9
Switzerland	18,500	2.6
Austria	6,800	1.0
Australia	18,400	2.6
Others	84,900	12.1
Conferences and seminars	34,700	5.0*
	698,400	100.0%

*Most seminars are in France for French customers.

Sales and Marketing

In 1981 Club Med was international, with vacation sites all over the world, and so were its customers. They came from different continents, backgrounds, market segments, and did not look for the same thing in a vacation package. Club Med offered different types of villages,[2] a wide range of activities to accommodate all the people who chose to go on a package deal. The club offered ski villages, i.e., hotels in ski resorts for those who liked to ski; straw hut villages with a very Spartan comfort on the Mediterranean, mainly for young bachelors; hotel and bungalow resort villages with all comforts open throughout the year, some with special facilities for families and young children. An average client who went to a straw hut village on the Mediterranean usually did not go to a plush village at Cap Skirring in Senegal (and the price was different too), although the same type of person might go to both.

A family with two or three children, who could afford the time and money needed to travel to a relatively nearby village with a baby club, was less likely to go to a village in Malaysia due to the long journey and the cost of transportation. Broadly speaking, a whole range of holiday makers were represented among the club's customers. However, there was a larger proportion of office workers, executives, and professional people and a small proportion of workers and top management. The sales and marketing of the club, which began in Europe, had expanded to include other important markets: the American zone, including the United States, Canada, and South America, and the Far Eastern zone, including Japan and Australia. The club's sales network covered 29 countries; sales were either direct through the club-owned offices, 23 of which existed at the moment (see Exhibit 28.5 for countries where the club owns commercial offices as well as villages and operations) or indirect through travel agencies (in France Havas was the main retailer). Originally, all the villages were aimed at the European market; in 1968 with the opening of its first village in America, the club broke into the American market and opened an office in New York. Since then, the American market had grown more or less independently. Eighty percent of the beds in the villages located in the American geographical

[2]Most villages offered by Club Med are rented by the company or run under a management contract.

area were sold to club members in the United States and Canada. Sixty-five percent of French sales, which represented 47 percent of the club's turnover, were direct by personal visits to the office, by telephone, or letter. However, in the United States, direct sales accounted for only 5 percent of the total, the remaining 95 percent being sold through travel agencies. These differences were partly explained by national preferences but also by a deliberate choice on the part of the club. Until the appointment of Serge Trigano to lead the U.S. zone, all sales and marketing officers reported to a single worldwide marketing director. (The capital structure of Club Med is shown in Exhibit 28.6.)

Exhibit 28.5   Countries of Operations (before new structure)

Country	Separate Commercial Office	Country Manager	Country Manager Supervising Commercial Operations	Villages
Germany	X			
Switzerland	X	X		X
Turkey			X	X
Italy	X	X		X
Venezuela	X			
Belgium	X			X
Mexico			X	X
United States	X	X		
Bahamas		X ⎱ Same as U.S.		X
Haiti		X ⎰		X
Brazil			X	X
Japan	X			
Great Britain	X			
Tunisia			X	X
Morocco		X		X
Holland	X			
Greece	X	X		X
Israel			X	X
Malaysia	X	X		X
France	X	X		
New Zealand	X			
Australia	X			X
Egypt		X		X
Singapore	X			
Canada	X			
Tahiti		X		X
South Africa	X			
Spain	X	X		X
Senegal		X Same		X
Ivory Coast		X		
Mauritius		X Same as Reunion		X
Sri Lanka		X Same as Mauritius		X
Guadeloupe		X ⎱ Same as U.S.		X
Martinique		X ⎰		X
Reunion Island		X		X
Dominican Republic		X Same as U.S.		X
United Arab Emirates				X

Exhibit 28.6   Capital Structure (1981)

Compagnie Financière Group (Rothschild)	7.0%
Banque de Paris et des Pays Bas	6.0
REDEC Group	5.0
Credit Lyonnais	7.5
Union des Assurances de Paris	7.5
The IFI International Group	7.0
The Company Personnel's Common Investment Fund	5.0
	45.0
Public	55.0
	100%

The Village

Club Med had around 90 villages, and it was growing fast. In the next three years (1981–84) about 20 new villages were scheduled to open. At Club Med a village was typically either a hotel, bungalows, or huts in usually a very nice area offering vacationers a series of several activities, among which were swimming, tennis, sailing, waterskiing, wind-surfing, archery, gymnastics, snorkling, deep sea diving, horseback riding, applied arts, yoga, golf, boating, soccer, circuits, excursions, bike riding, and skiing. There were also usually on-site a shop, a hairdresser, even some cash changing, car renting, etc, and a baby- or miniclub in many places. Club Med was well known for having chosen sites which were the best in any country where they were, not only from a geographical point of view, but also from an architectural point of view and the facilities provided. Exhibit 28.7 shows the number of villages which were open during the winter or summer season by type.

Essentially, there were three types of villages: the hut villages which were the cheapest, open only during the summer season, which started Club Med, and which were on the Mediterranean. They did not offer all the comfort that the wealthy traveler was used to (common showers). Then there were bungalows or hotels or "hard-type" villages which were more comfortable, with private bathrooms. Most were still double-bedded, which meant that two single men or women would have to share the same bedroom. In a village, there were two types of people: the GMs or "gentils membres," who were the customers and came usually for one, two, three, or four weeks on a package deal to enjoy all the facilities and activities of any village; the GOs, or "gentils organisateurs," who helped people make this vacation the best; there were GOs for sports, for applied arts, for excursions, for food, for the bar, as disk jockeys, as dancing instructors, for the children or babies in the miniclubs, for maintenance, for traffic, for accounting, for receptions, etc.[3] On average, there were 80 to 100 GOs per village.

There was a third category of people who were behind the scenes: the service people, usually local people hired to maintain the facilities and the garden, to clean up, etc. (about 150 service people per village). They could also be promoted to GOs.

Every season, i.e., either after the summer season from May to September and winter season in April, or every six months, all the GOs would be moved from one village to

---

[3] Although the GOs were specialized by "function," they had also to be simply "gentils organisateurs," i.e., making the GMs' lives easy and participating in common activities, such as arrival cocktails, shows, and games.

another; that was one of the principles of the club since its inception, so that nobody would stay for more than six months in any particular site. The village chief of maintenance was an exception. He stayed one full year; if a village was closed in the winter, he remained for the painting, the repairs, etc. The service people (local people) were there all the year around or for six months, if the village was only open in the summer (or winter for ski resorts). Exhibit 28.8 shows a typical organization structure of a village from the GO's point of view.

Under the chief of the village there were several coordinators: one for entertainment, responsible for all of the day and night activities (shows, music, nightclub, plays, games, etc.); the sports chief who coordinated all the sports activities in any particular village; the maintenance chief who would see to the maintenance of the village, either when there was a breakdown or just to repaint the village or keep the garden clean, grow new flowers, etc., and who was assisted by the local service people; the food and beverage chief who coordinated the cooking in the different restaurants as well as the bar. Usually there was a bazaar for miscellaneous, a garment boutique, and a hairdresser under a boutique's coordinator. There was a coordinator for the baby club (if existent) within the village to provide the children with some special activities; this coordinator was also responsible for the medical part of the village (nurses and doctor). Many times there was a doctor on-site, especially when a village was far from a big town. There was a coordinator of excursions and applied arts. Its services would help the GM to go somewhere or propose accompanied excursions (one, two, three days) for those who wanted it, or try with the help of a GO to make a silk scarf or pottery. There was a coordinator of administration, accounting, and control who dealt with cash, telephone, traffic, planning and reception, basic accounting, salaries for GOs and service personnel, taxes, etc. The services of food and beverages and maintenance were the ones who were the heavy users of local service personnel.

Exhibit 28.7   Number of Villages by Type and Season

	Sea			Mountain	Total
	Huts	**Bungalows**	**Hotels**	**Mountain**	**Total**
Summer season	14	˙31	26	10	81
Winter season	0	19	11	23	53

Source: Club Méditerranée Trident N123/124, Winter 80–81, Summer 81.

Exhibit 28.8   Organization Chart of a Typical Village

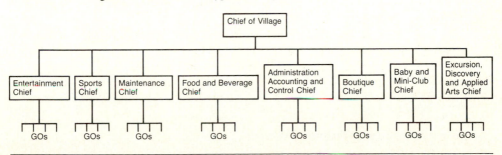

Company Organization Structure

Exhibit 28.9 shows the organization structure of Club Med's holiday village activity just before Serge Trigano's appointment as director of the U.S. zone. (The rest—time-sharing activities—are additional product-market subsidiaries).

There were several joint managing directors who participated in the Management Committee. Essentially, the structure was a functional one with a joint managing director for marketing and sales, another one for operations, and several other function heads like accounting, finance, and tax. Exhibit 28.10 shows how the operations part of the organization was structured.

Essentially the structure was composed of three parts. As there was an entertainment chief in the village, there was a director of entertainment at the head office and the same for sports. There were several product directors who mirrored the structure of the village. There were country managers in certain countries where the club had several villages in operation, and then there were the 90 villages. All reported to Serge Trigano.

The Role of the Product Directors

Product directors were responsible for the product policy. They made decisions with respect to the policy of Club Med in all the villages, such as the type of activities that should be in each village and the maintenance that should be done. They recruited and trained the various GOs needed for their domain (e.g., sports GOs, entertainment GOs, administration GOs, cooks). They staffed the villages by deciding with the director of operations which chief of village would go where and how many people would go with him. They made investment proposals for each village either for maintenance, new activities, extension, or renovation purposes. They also assumed the task of preparing the budgets and controlling application of policies in the villages by traveling extensively as "ambassadors" of the head office to the villages. Each one of them was assigned a certain number of villages. When visiting the village, he would go there representing not his particular product but Club Med's product as a whole. Also, each of them, including the director of operations, was assigned, on a rotating basis, the task of answering emergency phone

Exhibit 28.9   Organization Chart (before November 1981, holiday villages activity only)

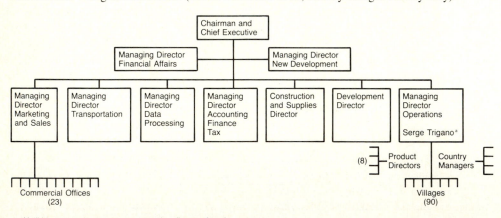

[a] Until his recent appointment as managing director, American zone.

Exhibit 28.10   Organization Chart—Operations Just before the New Move (before November 1981)

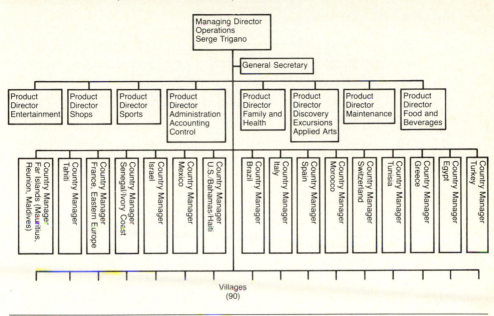

calls from any village and making emergency decisions, or taking action if necessary. Exhibit 28.11 presents examples of product organization. In the new regional structure, their role and place were questioned.

The Role of the Country Manager

Country managers were mainly the ambassadors of Club Med in the countries where Club Med had village(s). Usually they were located in countries with more than one village. They would handle political relations themselves, maintaining lasting relationships with elected bodies, mayors, civil servants, regional offices, etc. They would introduce to the new team coming every six months what the country had to offer, its constraints, local mores, the local people to be invited, local artists to be invited, the traps to be avoided, the types of suppliers, the type of local events that might be of interest for the village (so that the village would not forget, for instance, national holidays). They would try to get Club Med more integrated politically and socially in the host country, in particular in less-developed countries where there was a gap between the abundance and richness of the club as compared to its immediate environment. They also had an assistance role, such as getting work permits for GOs and also finding suppliers; sometimes, in fact, the country manager had a buyer attached to his staff who would purchase locally for the different villages to get economies of scale. In addition, the country managers personally recruited and maintained lists of the service personnel available to Club Med. They would go and negotiate the salaries, wages, and working conditions of the service personnel with the unions so that the village was free of being involved every six months in a renegotiation. Also, they might have an economic role by helping develop local production or culture, as the club was a heavy buyer of local food and products. They could also act as a devel-

Exhibit 28.11   Examples of Product Management

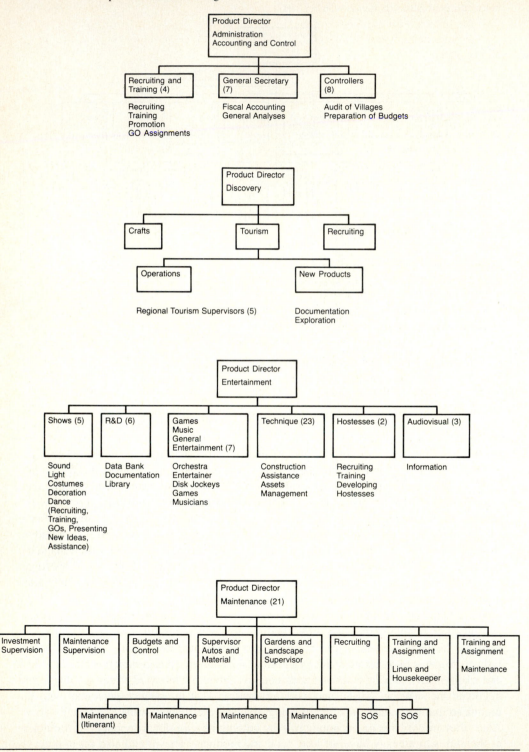

opment antenna, looking for new sites or receiving proposals from local investors and submitting them to the head office. They would also handle legal and tax problems when Club Med had a local legal entity as well as maintain relationships with the owners of the land, hotels, or bungalows when Club Med—as was often the case—was only renting the premises.

Problems with the Current Structure

The current structure had been set up about four years ago. It had also been Club Med's structure before 1971, but in between (1971–1976) there had been a change in the operations side only which had involved setting up area managers; instead of having one director of operations, there had been five directors who had under their control several countries and villages. From 1971 to 1976, there had been no country managers and each of the area managers had had about 10 or 15 villages under his supervision. This structure was changed in 1976 because it seemed to have created several Club Meds in one. The area managers had started to try to get the best chiefs of village and people for their area. As a result, GOs were not moving around every six months from one area of the world to another as was the policy, and also area managers started giving different types of services to their customers so that, for instance, a Frenchman going to one of the zones one year and to another the next year would find a different Club Med. These reasons had led to the structure presented in Exhibit 28.5 for the operations. But until now marketing had always been worldwide.

Of course, the structure in operation until now had created the reverse problem: it seemed to Serge Trigano and others that it was too centralized. In fact, Serge Trigano had a span of control (which is rarely achieved in industry) of 90 chiefs of village plus 8 product directors and 14 country managers, all reporting to him from all over the world. There was an overload of information, too much detail, and too many issues being entrusted to him which would be worse as time would go by, since Club Med was growing and doubling its capacity every five years. Beside the problem of centralization and information overload, another problem seemed to appear because Club Med's operations had not adapted enough to the international character of its customers. Most of the GOs were still recruited in France whereas now 15–20 percent of the customers came from the American zone. France was not even the best location to find GOs, who often needed to speak at least one other language. They had to be unmarried, under 30; they had to change countries every six months, with no roots; and they had to work long hours and be accessible 24 hours a day, seven days a week for a relatively low salary. The feeling was that maybe one could find happier and more enthusiastic people in Australia or Brazil than in France. Too much centralization, information overload, and lack of internationalization in operations were among the big problems in the current structure.

Also, there was a feeling that a closer local coordination between marketing and operations could give better results since customers seemed to concentrate on one zone (American in the United States, European in Europe) because of transportation costs, and a coordination might lead to a better grasp of customer needs, price, product, offices, etc. For example, when Club Med was smaller and only in Europe, departure from its villages was done only once a week. As a result, reception at the village was also once a week. Lack of local coordination between operations and marketing had created arrivals and departures almost every day in certain villages, overburdening the GO's staff and disrupting the organization of activities. As another illustration, the American customer was used to standard hotel services (bathroom, towels, etc.), which may be different than in Europe. Closer local ties might help respond better to local needs.

Centralization had also created bottlenecks in assignments and supervision of people. Every six months everybody—all GOs—were coming back to Paris from all over the world to be assigned to another village. Five or ten years ago this was in fact a great happening that allowed everybody to discuss with the product people, see headquarters, and find friends who had been in other villages, but now with 5,000 GOs coming almost at the same time—and wanting to speak to the product directors—reassigning them was becoming somewhat hectic. It was likely to be even worse in the future because of the growth of the company.

Planning and Control

The planning cycle could be divided into two main parts: first, there was a three-year plan started two years ago, which involved the product directors and the country managers. Each product director would define his objectives for the next three years and the action programs that would go with it, and propose investments that he would like to make for his product in each of the 90 villages. All the product directors would meet to look at the villages one by one and see how the investment fitted together as well as consider the staffing number of GOs and service personnel in broad terms for the next three years. Of course, the big chunk of the investment program was the maintenance of the facilities, since 55 percent of the investment program concerned such maintenance programs. The rest was concerned with additions or modifications of the villages, such as new tennis courts, theater, or restaurant, revamping a boutique, etc. The country managers were involved in that same three-year plan. First of all they would give the product directors their feelings and suggestions for investments as well as for staffing the villages. In addition, they would provide some objectives and action programs in the way they would try to handle personnel problems, political problems, economic problems, cultural and social integration, sales of Club Med in their country, and development.

Exhibit 28.12   The Club Growth in Numbers

	1969–70	1970–71	1971–72	1972–73
Objective	255,000	293,000	299,000	318,000
Villages	25	55	55	60
Beds		33,900	34,300	36,400
Number of hotel nights—winter		881,000	948,000	1,018,000
Number of hotel nights—summer		2,651,000	2,801,000	2,850,000
Occupancy rate percent		68.07%	69.52%	66.81%
Number of permanent employees	793	938	950	978
Number of GOs in villages (summer season)*				
Number of service personnel in villages (summer season)*				
Number of employees in Paris (operations only)				
Number of employees, country management				

---

*Number is approximate.

Besides this three-year operational plan, there was the one-year plan which was divided into two six-month plans. For each season a budget was prepared for each of the villages. This budget was mostly prepared by the product director for administration accounting, and it concerned the different costs, such as goods consumed, personnel charges, and rents. This budget was given to the chief of the village when he left with his team. In addition to this operational budget, there was an investment budget every six months in more detail than the three-year plan. This investment budget was prepared by the maintenance director under the guidance and proposal from the different product directors. It was submitted to the operations director and then went directly to the chief executive of the company. It had not been unusual that, before the three-year plan had been controlled, the proposals that product directors were making to the maintenance director were three times as high as what would in fact be given and allowed by the chief executive.

On the control side, there was a controller in each of the villages (administrator chief of accounting and control) as well as central controllers who would be assigned a region and would travel from one village to the other. But the local controller and his team in fact were GOs like any other ones and they were changing from one village to another every six months. There was a kind of "fact-and-rule book" that was left in the village so that the next team would understand the particular ways and procedures of the village. But mostly speaking, each new team would start all over again each time it was coming with a new budget and standard, rules, and procedures from the central head office as well as with the help of the fact and rule book. These two tools—the three-year plan and the six-month (a season) budgets—were the main planning and control tools used.

Objectives and Policies

Five objectives seemed to be important to Serge Trigano when reviewing the structure. One was that the club wanted to continue to grow and double its capacity every five years, eithers by adding new villages or increasing the size of the current ones (see Exhibit 28.12).

1973–74	1974–75	1975–76	1976–77	1977–78	1978–79	1979–80
339,000	408,000	475,000	540,000	578,000	615,000	698,500
61	69	70	74	74	78	83
37,000	49,300	50,400	53,800	55,600	58,600	64,600
1,044,000	1,240,000	1,628,000	1,790,000	1,940,000	2,011,000	2,250,000
2,920,000	3,210,000	3,400,000	3,550,000	3,710,000	3,970,000	4,265,000
66.76%	69.63%	70.70%	71.19%	71.65%	72.87%	72.88%
977	1035	1157	1132	1192	1286	1297
						6,000
						10,000
						250
						100

Exhibit 28.13   Evolution of GMs by Nationality

	1972–73	1978–79
France	60.0%	47.2%
United States	7.7	17.8
Belgium	8.7	6.0
Italy	7.5	5.6
West Germany	7.4	4.9
Switzerland	2.4	1
Others	6.1	17.5
	100%	100%

The second objective, which had always guided Club Med, was that it would have to continue to innovate, not to be a hotel chain but to be something different as it had always been, and to continue to respond to the changing needs of the customers.

A third objective stemmed from the fact that Club Med was no longer essentially French. The majority of its customers (GMs) in fact did not come from France; as a result, it would have to continue to internationalize its employees, its structure, its way of thinking, training, etc. (see Exhibit 28.13).

The fourth objective was economic. Costs were increasing, but not all of these costs could be passed on to the gentils membres unless the club wanted to stop its growth. One way of not passing all costs to the customer was to increase productivity by standardization, better methods, and procedures.

The fifth objective was to keep the basic philosophy of Club Med: to keep the village concept an entity protected as much as possible from the outside world but integrated in the country in which it was; to keep the package concept for GMs; and, finally, continue social mixing. Whatever your job, your social position, etc., at Club Med, you were only recognized by two things: the color of your bathing suit and the beads you wore around your neck which allowed you to pay for your scotch, orange juice, and so on, at the bar. Part of the philosophy, in addition, was to make sure that the GO's nomadism would continue: change every season.

The Proposed New Structure

With these objectives in mind, the new structure to be effective November 1981 had just been sketched as shown in Exhibit 28.14. The idea would be to move the operations and marketing closer together in three zones. One would be America (North and South); another, Europe and Africa; and the third (in the long run, when this market would be more developed), the Far East. In each area, a director would manage the operations side, i.e., the villages and the marketing side—promotion, selling, pricing, distributing Club Med's concept. In fact, most of the American GMs were going to the American zone villages; most of the European GMs, to the European zone; and most of the Asian GMs, to the Asian zone. As the cost of transportation from one zone to another was increasing, people could not afford to go very far.

This was the general idea, and now it had to be pushed further. Among the main interesting and troublesome aspects of the new structure were the following: how to avoid with this structure that Club Med would separate into three different entities with three different types of products? Should such occurrence be avoided? It seemed that this should not

Exhibit 28.14   The Proposed Structure

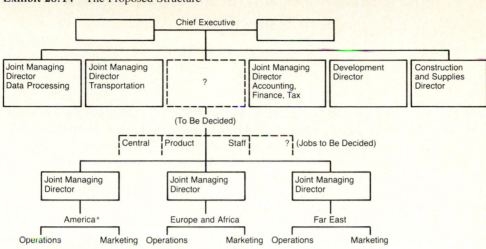

ᵃ Serge Trigano's new position.

be allowed; that's why the structure which had been there four years ago with five regions had failed. It had transformed Club Med into five mini-Club Meds, although even at that time the five area managers did not have marketing and sales responsibility. In addition to this major issue of how to preserve the unity and uniqueness of Club Med with a geographic structure, several other questions were of great importance:

- Who would decide what activities would take place in a village?
- Who would decide the investments to be made in a village?
- Who would staff a village?
- Would there be a central hiring and training of all GOs or only some of them?
- How would the geographic managers be evaluated in terms of performance?
- If they wanted to continue with the GOs and give them the right and possibility to move every six months from one part of the world to another, how would the transfer of GOs be done?
- How should the transfer of GOs be coordinated?
- Should there be some common basic procedures, like accounting and reporting, and in that case, who should design and enforce those procedures?
- How could there be some coordination and allocation of resources among the three regions; who would do it; and how would it be done?

Also of importance was the problem of transition.

- What would happen to the country managers?
- What would happen to the product directors?
- What would happen to central marketing and sales?

These were some of the questions that bothered Serge Trigano on the flight to Paris from New York.

The John Hancock Mutual Life Insurance Company

▪ *Raymond M. Kinnunen* ▪

John G. McElwee, Chairman of the Board and Chief Executive Officer of the John Hancock Mutual Life Insurance Company,[1] asked himself three questions in the spring of 1984 as he prepared the company for the 1990s and beyond: "What is it you want the institution to be? What do you think the world will be like? How do we prepare for that in terms of what business the company will be in and what it will need in terms of talent?" A move to financial services came out of that analysis and, more specifically, an analysis of what McElwee saw as his six criteria: economy, demographics, attitudes and lifestyles, competition, technology, and government action. In McElwee's view, however:

Nobody really *knows what the financial services industry (FSI) will be. We all admit to that. We are all trying to be flexible. We know we all are not doing everything right, and the jury is still out as to which companies will have the right combination and the wisdom and courage to remedy the situation as it evolves. When will this happen? When will the paradigm of the new FSI be in place? In my view it won't be before 1990.[2]*

The John Hancock Mutual Life Insurance Company began its move into financial services in 1968. This case offers some background on the financial services industry, the insurance industry, and the nature of the issues and problems facing the company in 1984.

Trends in the Industry

The late 1970s and early 1980s saw a significant trend toward the provision of fuller financial services being offered by numerous financial-based institutions:

The FSI is a huge amalgam of firms ranging in size from the CitiCorp with well over $130 billion in assets to many small credit unions with a few hundred thousands dollars of assets. In 1980, there were over 40,000 individual firms competing in the FSI with a mix of products including savings accounts, life insurance policies, pension management ser-

---

This case was prepared by Raymond M. Kinnunen, Associate Professor of Business Administration, with the assistance of L. Jake Katz, Research Assistant, with the cooperation of the John Hancock Mutual Life Insurance Company and its Chairman, John G. McElwee and the support of the Instructional Development Fund at Northeastern University. It is intended to be used as the basis for class discussion rather than to illustrate either effective or ineffective handling of an administrative situation.

The research and written case information were presented at a Case Research Symposium and were evaluated by the Case Research Association's Editorial Board.

Distributed by the Case Research Association. All rights reserved to the author(s) and the Case Research Association. Permission to use the case should be obtained from the Case Research Association.

[1] See Appendix A for biographical sketches.

[2] From Gregory L. Parsons, *The Evolving Financial Services Industry: Competition and Technology for the '80s*, 9-183-077, pp. 1–3. Copyright © 1982 by the President and Fellows of Harvard College. Reprinted by permission of the Harvard Business School.

vices, and stock brokering. The size of the FSI as measured by financial assets under control was nearly $4 trillion in 1980, and was experiencing nearly 11% growth [See Exhibit 29.1]

Historically, the various segments of the FSI have been primarily defined by government regulation. In fact, this is the reason many firms in the FSI are considered institutions rather than firms in the economic sense. The institutional segments of the FSI have been controlled and defined by their relationships to regulatory agencies. For example, banks are regulated at the federal, state, and local levels by various agencies. Securities firms are regulated only at the federal level by the Securities and Exchange Commission (SEC). Insurance companies, since 1946, have been regulated by state agencies. The result is an industry where products have been defined by regulation and customer markets have been given access to those products only through specific institutions. Until fairly recently, a customer went to a bank for a loan, to an insurance company for an insurance policy, and to a securities firm to trade stock. In this regulated environment, which defined the channels between customers and the financial products, the FSI was, on average, very profitable. Between 1975 and 1980, the banking industry reported annual profit growth of 18%, the life insurance industry reported 30% annual profit growth, and the securities industry reported 7% profit growth (for a scale of measurement, all U.S. industry reported 12% profit growth during that time).

Competition in the FSI has not been very intense compared to other industries; in fact, the common view of many financial institutions has been that the main objective is not to compete, but to provide public services. This view has been allowed and reinforced by: a) the regulatory environment, b) the web of relationships among financial institutions which required a large degree of coordination and cooperation and c) the historical values and culture which preside in most financial institutions. (The "lean and mean" operation has not been the role model for most financial organizations.) Regulations, severely limiting the dimensions of competition, have sought to create a sort of economic DMZ (demilitarized zone) between the customers and financial markets, reasoning that unlimited competition, by nature, causes behavior and results which are not in the best interest of the customer. The regulatory thinking assumed that unbridled competition would certainly mean more failures of weak and poorly run institutions. This would, over time, create a

---

Exhibit 29.1   Assets

Company	Dollar Amount of Total Assets*
Prudential	$66,707,209
Metropolitan Life	55,731,371
Equitable Life of New York	40,285,559
Aetna Life	28,551,098
New York Life	22,549,386
John Hancock	21,710,494
Travelers	17,440,305
Connecticut General	15,660,054
Teachers Insurance and Annuity	13,519,897
Northwestern Mutual	13,252,835

*Figures do not include assets of subsidiaries.

Source: *Best's Insurance Management Reports*, October 1983.

more efficient marketplace, but the result on the customer of a failing institution could be devastating. Also, it was expected that competition would drive institutions to more predatory and less benign behavior towards their customers and competitors as the scramble for profits intensified.

Traditionally, different types of institutions offered different types of products and services. Banks have concentrated on offering transaction products, and many kinds of loan products to individuals and corporations. Savings and loans (thrifts) have provided savings products and specialized mortgage lending to individuals. Securities firms have tended to specialize to a degree, with different firms offering "wholesale" products to corporations such as underwriting and other investment banking activities (e.g., Goldman Sachs and Salomon Brothers) and other firms specializing in "retail" brokerage and trading for consumers (e.g., Merrill Lynch, Shearson and E. F. Hutton). Insurance companies have generally specialized in either life insurance products (e.g., Prudential, Metropolitan and New York Life), or property and casualty insurance (e.g., State Farm, AllState, INA). To a degree they have also been involved in mortgage and commercial lending. Traditionally, most insurance companies have served both individual and corporate customers. Finance companies have concentrated on consumer lending and mortgage lending primarily to individuals. As noted above, a dominant reason in the traditional product/ institution relationship has been regulation, but institutional thinking has also greatly influenced how the industry has defined itself.[3]

Consolidations Hindered by Sales Force Organization

While the level of merger and acquisition activity within the financial services industry over the last decade seemed to suggest an inevitable fusion of services under one roof, companies found that sales personnel trained to move one service were not necessarily well suited at uncovering client needs for another. For example, Merrill Lynch, the largest marketer of securities, found it inefficient to have their stockbrokers selling insurance policies. "Meanwhile, Merrill has begun experimenting with a more specialized approach to selling. Convinced that the average broker is unable to sell insurance, Merrill last June [1983] began installing life insurance specialists in 32 branches. It plans to hire 100 more this year."[4]

David Koehler, President of Financial Learning Systems, a firm training both securities and insurance personnel to sell new products and to prepare for licensing exams, cites five major barriers insurance agents face when selling noninsurance products. These barriers include: (1) licensing (state licensing exams are relatively easy for the insurance industry but fairly rigorous exams exist for securities); (2) product knowledge (the level necessary for agents to be comfortable selling securities may be underestimated); (3) skills to sell the product (different skills are required to sell a life insurance policy than a mutual fund); (4) commissions (to get a similar dollar-for-dollar commission, an agent has to sell a fund possibly 50 times the "value" of a life policy); and (5) attitude (life agents are accustomed to selling "guaranteed" products).[5]

[3] Ibid.

[4] Merrill Lynch's Big Dilemma," *Business Week*, January 16, 1984, p. 62.

[5] Stephen Piontek, "Securities Products Face Agents with Problems," *National Underwriter, Life and Health Insurance Edition*, July 17, 1982, pp. 28–36.

Others in the industry acknowledge these barriers but conclude that the lines between agents and brokers are becoming blurred. Because of competition, the agent has diversified his product line while the broker has added more service through financial planning.[6]

To make matters more complex, some feel that both agents and brokers will be competing with other brokers selling products based more on price than on service.[7] The vast majority of consumers' liquid assets are held in depository institutions which gives the banking industry an advantage. One way for insurance companies to compete with banks is to offer transaction accounts. To do this, however, they must acquire a bank image.[8]

Total Lines of Services

Standard and Poor's Industry Surveys note the following in regard to the trend toward full service:

The emergence of alternative products, along with general deregulation of the financial industry, has intensified competition in the life insurance industry. The successful life insurance company will be one that adapts quickly to the changing environment. The competitiveness of life insurance will increasingly depend not only on innovations in products and services, but also importantly on the quality of marketing and distribution systems.

Insurers are aware of the need for more effective marketing strategies and some already are making changes. One approach that is taking hold is the combination of insurers and other major financial institutions to form broad-based financial services conglomerates. The goal here is to bring together a variety of financial products and services, provide one-stop access to the consumer, and allow cross-marketing of product and service combinations as financial services packages. This approach to market expansion is evidenced by such recent acquisitions as Bache Group Inc. by Prudential Insurance Co. of America and Shearson Loeb Rhoades by American Express (which owns Fireman's Funds Insurance Co.) among others.[9]

Theodore Gordon, president of the Futures Group, summed it up this way:

The whole marketplace for insurance is becoming very dynamic. It will be increasingly difficult in the future to tell the difference between a brokerage house, an insurance company, a bank, and a large-scale credit card company. To some degree, the functions of these insitutions already overlap.[10]

Are Synergistic Benefits Possible?

A May 1982 article in *Institutional Investor* questions the effects of mergers that result in extended financial services:

[6] Ibid., p. 3.

[7] Ibid., p. 43.

[8] Barbara E. Casey, "Customer Is Key to Insurance-Banking Rivalry," *National Underwriter, Life and Health Edition*, July 17, 1982, pp. 8–9, 36.

[9] *Standard & Poor's Industry Surveys*, July 7, 1983 (Vol. 151, no. 27, sec. 1), *Insurance & Investments Basic Analysis*, p. 155.

[10] Theodore J. Gordon, "Life Insurance Companies in the 80's: A Quiet Revolution,: *Resources*, July/August 1981, p. 3.

While it is too early for a verdict on that, however, there's another critical question at stake here. These firms have also been trumpeting the synergistic *benefits that are supposed to flow from these mergers. American Express, for example, hopes to sell a wide variety of financial services through its credit cards, opening up vast new vistas for Shearson. Sears can envision its millions of customers buying Dean Witter products at its stores. And the Pru can look forward to its agents selling Bache products nationwide. Bache chairman Harry Jacobs Jr. perhaps best sums it up when he says, "We expect the merger to extend the range of services both firms provide."*

Yet, amid all the euphoric talk, no one has really stopped to ask whether these future synergistic wonders will actually come to pass, whether synergy on such a grand scale can really work in the financial services business. Will the vaunted synergy ever materialize to any significant *extent? Will the diverse parts of these financial services conglomerates truly mesh and spur each other on to new heights—boosting sales, cutting costs and adding up to more than the sum of the parts?*

Actually, there's plenty of evidence to suggest these companies may be in for a tougher time of it than most people suspect. For one thing, there's the nagging fact that dozens of previous attempts to create synergy in the financial services industry have, at best, been somewhat disappointing. It was fashionable in the early 1970s, for example, to suppose that retail brokers could sell life insurance as a sideline, thereby increasing their earnings and those of their firms. As it turned out, however, these brokers either lacked the skills to sell insurance or were too busy with stocks to bother with it. No precise figures are available, but Securities Industry Association statistics indicate that Wall Street firms gathered revenues of less than $500 million from insurance in 1980, compared with their total revenues of $16 billion.[11]

The article goes on to detail the experience of Continental Insurance.

Continental Insurance made little progress toward the synergy that was supposed to accrue from its consumer finance subsidiary and its Diners Club credit card operations— both of which have since been sold. Other than the relatively minor business of travel life insurance, Continental found it difficult to sell policies via the credit card. It was hard, says one Continental official, to design a home insurance application form to mail out with bills because it entailed asking so many detailed questions. Nor was it really feasible to sell insurance through consumer finance outlets—local Continental agents would have been annoyed by the competition. Reports Continental chairman John Ricker sadly: "One-stop financial shopping is a buzzword returning to our vocabulary. I am skeptical, not by nature, but by experience. Continental has tried the full financial services approach, and it didn't work."[12]

Robert Beck of Prudential is quoted later in the same article with this view:

"I don't think previous attempts have all *been failures," is the way Prudential chairman Beck shrugs it off. Or perhaps a better way of putting it is that they're persuaded that times have changed dramatically since their previous efforts to achieve financial services*

[11] Neil Osborn, "What Synergy," *Institution Investor*, May 1982, p. 50.
[12] Ibid., p. 52.

synergy were made. Notes American Express chairman Robinson, "The environment to-day is 100 percent different than it was when those (previous) relationships were formed." For one thing, he notes, "there's a trend toward constructing hybrid financial products," begun by Merrill Lynch's CMA account—a trend Robinson thinks multifacted houses may be able to exploit.[13]

Consumer Base

The customer base is also an important factor when it comes to offering financial services.

Sears Roebuck and Company, American Express Company and Prudential Life Insurance Company currently sell their services to some 50 million Americans. The three companies intend to bombard these clients with new financial services products. But according to conventional wisdom in the financial services business, it's not really the quantity of customer that counts, but the quality—how rich the customers are. . . . It's generally assumed that servicing well-heeled folk will be more profitable in years to come than pushing financial products at people of moderate means.[14]

"Well-heeled" is typically defined as meaning an annual family income of $50,000 or more; there are an estimated 3.2 million households in this group. Some experts fear that, with a large number of big as well as small institutions competing, few will make a profit. Given those estimates "the supercompanies plan to concentrate on the vast middle market of families earning $20,000 to $50,000 a year."[15]

Current Actions

The supercompanies (Sears Roebuck and Company, Prudential-Bache Securities, Bank America Corp., American Express, CitiCorp, and Merrill Lynch and Co.) continue to expand into new businesses as fast as the law and technology permit (Exhibit 29.2 compares some financial and product data on the supercompanies with those of the John Hancock). Some large insurers are acquiring small securities firms, money managers, and mortgage bankers. Alexander Clash, President at New York's John Alden Insurance Company, expressed one view that acquisitions are a cheap form of R&D and added, "Buying a foothold in every conceivable financial service is a way of participating in every business because no one is sure what the hot areas will be in 1990."[16]

Obviously, there are considerable mixed feelings in the financial services community concerning recent changes. Movement continues to take place even in light of the questionable results companies may achieve when they offer one-stop financial services, in effect becoming financial supermarkets (see Exhibit 29.3). Part of the reason for this trend may be the estimated $200 billion that Americans spent on financial services in 1982, reportedly earning suppliers of those services $42 billion.[17]

---

[13] Ibid., p. 52.

[14] Ibid., p. 54.

[15] Arlene Hershman, "The Supercompanies Emerge," *Dunn's Business Month*, April 1983, p. 46.

[16] Ibid., p. 47.

[17] Ibid., p. 44.

Exhibit 29.2 Financial Industry Major Competitors Comparative Data

Financial Data (all figures in millions of dollars)	American Express	BankAmerica	Citicorp	Merrill Lynch	Prudential	Sears	John Hancock*
Revenues	7,800	13,112	18,258	4,590	13,200	29,180	4,422
Net Income	559	425	774	220	Not Comparable	735	NC
Assets	27,700	120,498	128,430	20,940	62,500	34,200	**23,714
Customers' deposits	5,700	93,208	77,359	3,930	—	2,300	—
Customers' credit balances	1,200***	—	—	2,700	740	200	—
Money market funds	17,200	—	—	48,900	5,000	9,000	1,125
Commercial loans	4,200	48,800	60,411	400	1,560	—	2,000
Consumer loans	1,000	25,100	22,029	5,000	3,900	4,250	1,900

What They Do	American Express	BankAmerica	Citicorp	Merrill Lynch	Prudential	Sears	John Hancock
Securities brokerage	•			•	•	•	•
Securities trading	•	•		•	•	•	•
Cash management services	•		•	•			
Investment management	•	•	•	•	•	•	•
Commodities brokerage	•			•			
U.S. corporate underwriting	•			•	•		
International corporate underwriting				•	•		
U.S. commercial banking		•	•				
International commercial banking		•	•	•			
Savings and loan operations	•		•				
Small loans offices		•	•			•	
Credit card, charge cards		•	•			•	

What They Do	American Express	BankAmerica	Citicorp	Merrill Lynch	Prudential	Sears	John Hancock
Traveler's checks	•						
Foreign exchange trading	•	•	•	•	•		
Leasing	•	•	•	•	•	•	•
Data processing services	•	•	•	•			•
Property-casualty insurance	•						
Life, health insurance	•			•	•	•	•
Mortgage insurance	•				•	•	•
Mortgage banking	•	•	•			•	•
Real estate development				•	•	•	•
Commercial real estate brokerage	•			•		•	•
Residential real estate brokerage				•		•	•
Executive relocation services				•	•	•	•

Source: *The New Financial Services*, Alliance of American Insurers, Shaumburg, Ill., 1983 (reprinted with permission of Prudential-Bache Securities).

*Source: John Hancock Internal documents.

**Not including subsidiary assets.

***Total assets under management $37 million.

Exhibit 29.3   Financial Services Announcements The First Half of 1983

Travelers owns Securities Development Corporation (securities clearing subsidiary).

President of American Express joins Travelers (hiring said to be influenced by his financial services background).

Equitable Life and First National Bank of Chicago to market cash management services.

Prudential to buy Capital City Bank of Hopeville, Georgia.

Sears to have Dean Witter offices in 100 stores by the end of 1983, 150 by end of 1984, and eventually 400.

CIGNA buys automatic Business Centers, commercial payroll processing centers.

Kemper's regional brokerage houses earned $8.3 million in 1982.

Nationwide to offer insurance in offices of Banc One.

John Hancock's Independent Investment Associates to offer financial services for corporations and institutions.

Prudential to have 30 joint offices with Bache by the end of 1983.

Travelers to offer insured cash management services through its trust company.

Hartford to buy 24 percent of Minneapolis brokerage firm.

Aetna Life & Casualty buys majority interest in Federal Investors.

Mutual of Omaha plans to acquire investment banking and brokerage firm of Kilpatrick, Pettis, Smith, Polian, Inc.

J. C. Penney to buy First National Bank of Harrington, Delaware.

Merrill Lynch to buy Raritan Valley Financial Corporation, a New Jersey savings and loan.

Kemper announces intention to buy a savings and loan.

Chairman of Manufacturers Hanover says much of the euphoria about financial supermarkets may be exaggerated.

Source: Bull, Robert A. "Insurance and the Financial Services Industry," *United States Banker*, August 1983, p. 118.

The decade of the 1980s promises to be an exciting one for the huge American financial services industry, which has, until now, been fragmented. Some uncontrollable factors, such as interest rates, the economic climate, the regulatory climate, and the role of technology, will also affect the industry. Many experts believe that technology (especially computers and telephones), with its costs and unpredictable product breakthroughs, will play such a large part in product cost and delivery that the big competition to worry about may not be other companies in the financial services industry but AT&T and IBM.[18]

The John Hancock Mutual Life Insurance Company[19]

The John Hancock Company began in 1862 when John Hancock started selling life insurance. By 1864 the company had over $500,000 of insurance in force. In less than ten years, the company's insurance in force grew to nearly $20 million. In the early part of the

[18] Ibid., p. 50.

[19] Historical facts on the company were taken from *A Bridge to the Future; One Hundredth Anniversary 1862–1962*, copyright 1962, John Hancock Mutual Life Insurance Company, Boston, Mass.

twentieth century, the company pioneered a number of products, including group life insurance. The John Hancock Company prospered during the boom years following World War I and continued to grow through the Depression. As late as the mid-1960s, the company was still primarily a seller of insurance. A hundred years after its founding, the company's pool of capital had been invested in nearly every imaginable sector of the economy, both private and public.

In December 1983, in an internal bulletin to all home office employees, the John Hancock Mutual Life Insurance Company announced a definitive merger agreement with the Buckeye Financial Corporation of Columbus, Ohio. The merger agreement provided for the acquisition of Buckeye by the John Hancock subsidiary for approximately $28 million in cash, equal to $13.50 per share of Buckeye common shares on a fully diluted basis. Buckeye, a savings and loan holding company in Columbus, Ohio, is the parent of Buckeye Federal Savings and Loan Association. Buckeye Federal, a federally chartered savings and loan association, conducts its business through 19 offices located throughout central Ohio. With assets of approximately $1.2 billion as of September 30, 1983, Buckeye Federal is one of the largest savings and loan associations in Ohio and is the largest mortgage lender in central Ohio. In April 1982, less than two years prior to this merger agreement, the Hancock had acquired Tucker Anthony Holding Corporation, the parent of Tucker Anthony and R. L. Day Inc., a regional brokerage house with 30 offices in the Northeast.[20] These two announcements were the latest of a number of financial services subsidiaries (most developed internally) that had been added since 1968. In a letter dated December 23, 1968, and addressed to home office associates, then-President Robert E. Slater discussed the concept of subsidiaries:

We think of them (the subsidiaries) as a device through which we can develop markets and new products and, as a corollary, other new avenues toward increased compensation for our sales forces. They also provide investment vehicles to enhance the return on total investable funds. Life insurance is still our main business—by a very wide margin—but in the larger view we can use these subsidiaries to augment or supplement our life insurance sales with the marketing of a wide array of financial services.

Background on the Insurance Industry

Today in the United States the insurance industry is divided into three major categories: life, health, and property and casualty. The life and health areas are further divided into group and individual categories. In 1981 new purchases of life insurance in the United States amounted to $812.3 billion.[21]

Commercial life insurance companies are divided into two categories: stock and mutual companies.[22] A company that has stockholders is a stock company, whereas a mutual company is owned by its policyholders. Just over 2,000 life insurance companies were

[20] "Hancock to Acquire Tucker Anthony at up to $47 Million," *Wall Street Journal*, April 15, 1982, p. 16.

[21] Sources of factual data on the insurance industry were: *1983 Life Insurance Factbook* (Washington, D.C.: American Council of Life Insurance, 1983), and S. S. Hubner and Kenneth Black, Jr., *Life Insurance*, 9th ed. Englewood Cliffs, N.J.: (Prentice Hall, Inc., 1976).

[22] For data on the top ten insurance companies, see Exhibit 29.1.

doing business in the United States and accounted for 43 percent of the life insurance in force in 1982.

Stock companies seek to earn the highest possible profits for their shareholders. Policy owners do not benefit from any gains the stock company enjoys nor are they hurt by any losses the company suffers. Because they are not directly affected by the company's financial experience, their policies are called nonparticipating. Because no dividend is expected, the premium paid by a stock company must meet capital and surplus requirements as well as other requirements established by its home state. Having met these requirements and having had its stock subscribed, a stock company may begin doing business. Because a stock company is owned by its shareholders, the first responsibility of the directors is to those shareholders. Because shareholders can vote on major issues and elect the board of directors, control of the company rests with the owners of a majority of the stock. Shareholders may sell their stock or buy more shares at prevailing market prices.

Mutual insurance companies are owned by policyholders. Management's first obligation is to create profit for policyholders, who have the right to vote for directors. When funds available exceed solvency requirements, the directors may pay policyholders a dividend, although such payment is not mandatory. The cost of a policyholders' premium less the dividend paid determines the final cost of the insurance coverage. Because the policyholder may benefit from the favorable financial experience of a mutual company, that policy is called participating. Owners of mutual companies are numerous and scattered and have proportionately small ownership positions. For these reasons, control of a mutual company remains largely with management.

By the end of the 1960s, the rising inflation rate caused a number of people to seek new investment vehicles that offered higher returns than life insurance. The public's attention turned to the stock market. Many viewed life insurance as a high-opportunity cost versus returns they imagined were available through stock market investments. A number of investment firms answered that market's desire by offering mutual fund shares. The public sank dollars into a new breed of mutual fund called money market funds. Securities firms (such as Merrill Lynch) and fund operators (such as Fidelity) invested billions of dollars in low-risk securities offering record levels of income. Banks began offering certificates of deposit (CDs) with very high returns. The insurance industry found itself fighting not only for new business but to retain the reserves that they already held.

To grow and, indeed, to survive, traditional insurance institutions like John Hancock found themselves forced to compete with higher-yielding instruments offered by the federal government, municipal governments, and brokerage houses.

John Hancock Subsidiaries Inc. (JHSI)

In 1980, the structure of the John Hancock Company was changed to incorporate the existence of ten subsidiaries in the form of a downstream holding company (see Exhibits 29.4 and 29.5). Exhibit 29.6 describes the products and services offered by the subsidiaries. Selective financial data on the parent company and the subsidiaries can be found in Exhibits 29.7 and 29.8.

Stephen Brown, Executive Vice-President of Financial Operations of the John Hancock Mutual Life Insurance Company and President and Chief Executive Officer of John Hancock Subsidiaries Inc., had worked for the Hancock for 22 years when he became president of the holding company in 1981. Brown offered the following explanation on the origins of the holding company and its operations. Initially when the individual com-

Exhibit 29.4   John Hancock Mutual Life Insurance Company, Boston, Massachusetts Organization Chart, Effective April 1, 1983

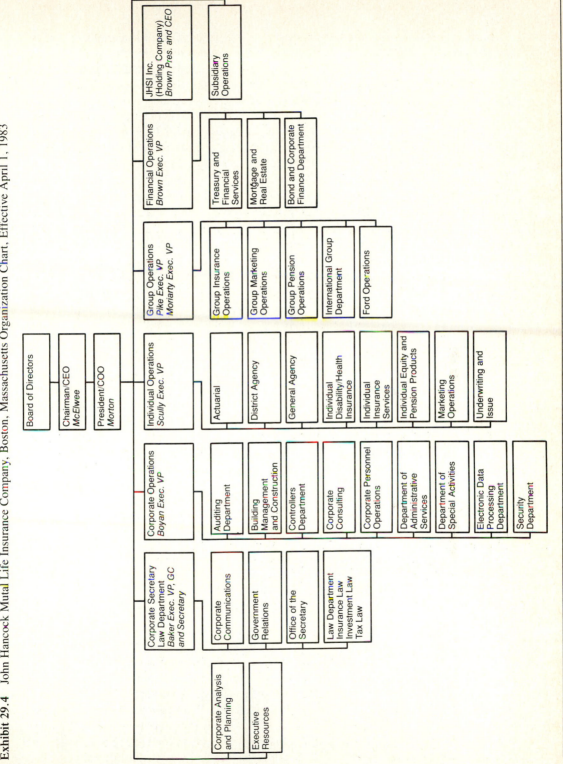

Exhibit 29.5 Subsidiary Organizaton Chart

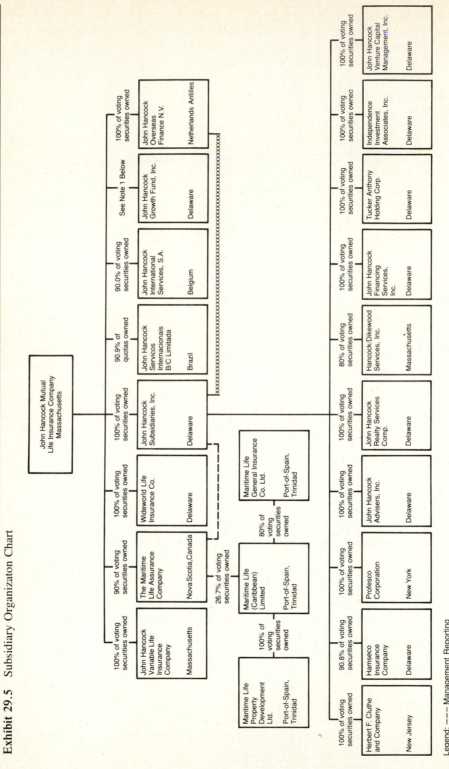

Legend: ———— Management Reporting
xxxx Stockholders' Rights

panies were started (the first in 1968), they became part of an existing department of the company. For example, Hanseco, which offered a line of casualty insurance, operated as a part of the Marketing Department and was expected to attract more revenue to the company by giving insurance agents a larger package of securities to offer. At that time the major objective of a new addition was synergy—or—as Brown described it, "putting more dollars in the agency force." Profit and growth were secondary.

In January of 1980, when the holding company (John Hancock Subsidiaries Inc.) was established, management was charged with the responsibility of overseeing the subsidiary companies and reporting to the Board of Directors of the life company. As control mechanisms, the holding company was to submit to the board quarterly financial statements and yearly presentations on its overall strategy. In addition, various Board committees on organization, finance, compliance, conflict of interest, and auditing could also ask for reports. The individual subsidiaries submitted strategic plans to the board of the holding company. In 1980 the objectives for the subsidiaries had become first profit, followed by growth, and then synergy; and the subsidiaries were expected in the long run to return 15 percent on investment. Brown noted that before this time "profit and return on investment" were not commonplace expectations in the company.

In Brown's view, the major reasons for changing the structure to a holding company were for tax purposes (some subsidiaries were profitable and others were not) and to form more consistent planning and control systems throughout the subsidiaries. Although there were some in the company who felt that various departments should continue to control the subsidiaries, the outcome of the restructuring, according to Brown, was that "there are now clear controls in place with the subsidiaries operating autonomously from day to day."

Each subsidiary has its own board of directors. The holding company decides on the directors and reviews the minutes of meetings. Major capital requirements and any significant change in the type of business performed by a subsidiary also requires approval by the holding company. Personnel selection and compensation are left completely to the subsidiaries. Subsidiaries are welcome, but not required, to use the staff facilities at the life company (for example, EDP, Accounting, Public Relations). Brown stated that, on the average, he visits the subsidiaries once a month. With the major objectives of profitability, growth, and synergy clearly stated, the approach used to run the subsidiaries is, according to Brown, "Now, go do it!"

Mr. Brown commented on the future of the John Hancock:

Profit and return on investment were not common words in the company. In the long run I see us adopting GAAP (Generally Accepted Accounting Principles) instead of statutory accounting and defining profit centers throughout the Life Company as we do in the Holding Company. This is a step toward becoming in the long run a stock company where we can purchase with stock as opposed to cash and offer stock incentives to management and tie a bonus to profits and growth. If in the long run this is where we are headed, the only way to do it is the profit center concept.

The addition of the holding company in 1980, along with the different systems used to measure performance, added a new dimension to the John Hancock and its way of operating. This became clear as people discussed the changes that had taken place inside the Hancock over the past 16 years and the future in the changing financial services industry.

Exhibit 29.6 Subsidiaries of John Hancock Mutual Life Insurance Company (JH)

John Hancock International Services S.A., Brussels, Belgium

1968 Incorporated in Belgium. Established to enable the International Group Department of John Hancock to perform the international employee benefit services expected by multinational companies that participate in the John Hancock International Group Program (IGP).

Maritime Life Insurance Co., Halifax, Nova Scotia

1969 Acquired by JH. Reports to Life Company through JH Subsidiaries, Inc. for management reporting purposes. Offers a full range of life insurance products in Canadian markets.

John Hancock Servicos Internacionais S/C, Ltda., Sao Paulo, Brazil

1973 Organized in Brazil. Established to enable IGP to deliver the same financial results to clients with subsidiaries in Brazil as in all other IGP countries, and to enable funds to be transferred out of Brazil.

John Hancock Variable Life Insurance Co., Boston, Massachusetts

1979 Incorporated in Massachusetts. Provides a vehicle for John Hancock agents to sell individual variable life and universal life insurance products.

John Hancock Overseas Finance N.V., Curacao, Netherlands Antilles

1982 Incorporated in Netherlands Antilles. Raises funds outside the United States and lends such funds to John Hancock and its affiliates.

John Hancock Subsidiaries, Inc., Boston, Massachusetts

1979 Incorporated in Delaware; commenced business in 1980. A downstream holding company organized to provide a means of centralizing the reporting responsibility for the following subsidiaries as a group to coordinate their financial planning and the development of unified policies and strategies.

Subsidiaries of JHSI

Herbert F. Cluthe and Co., Springfield, New Jersey

1968 Acquired by JH.
1980 Acquired by JHSI. Develops total financial plans and group and pension programs for business and trade associations.

John Hancock Advisers, Inc., Boston, Massachusetts

1968 Incorporated in Delaware.
1980 Acquired by JHSI. Manages the portfolios of six open-end investment companies: John Hancock Growth Fund Inc.; John Hancock U.S. Government Securities Fund Inc.; John Hancock Bond Fund Inc.; John Hancock Tax-Exempt Income Trust; John Hancock Cash Management Trust; and John Hancock Tax-Exempt Cash Management Trust, shares of which are sold by its subsidiary broker-dealer, John Hancock Distributors Inc.

Exhibit 29.7 John Hancock Companies—Assets Under Management ($ in millions)

	1972	1973	1974	1975
General account	$10,377	$10,737	$11,232	$12,071
Separate account	818	710	591	730
Guaranteed benefit separate account	0	0	0	0
Subsidiaries (estimated)*	283	488	462	633
Pension advisory accounts	0	0	0	0
Total assets under management	$11,478	$11,935	$12,285	$13,434

*Subsidiary assets are net of Hancock parent equity holdings and contain estimated components.

Source: John Hancock Mutual Life Insurance Company Annual Reports.

Exhibit 29.6 *continued*

John Hancock Realty Services Corp., Boston, Massachusetts

1968   Incorporated in Delaware.
1980   Acquired by JHSI. Invests in income-producing real estate; provides commercial real estate brokerage, mortgage placement and servicing, and appraisal services through its subsidiary, John Hancock Real Estate Finance Inc. Operations are conducted nationwide through a series of regional offices.

Profesco Corporation, New York, New York

1968   Acquired by JH.
1980   Acquired by JHSI. A nationwide organization of franchised specialists providing complete financial services to the professional and business communities.

HANSECO Insurance Co., Boston, Massachusetts

1971   Incorporated in Delaware.
1980   JH ownership transferred to JHSI. In addition to providing a vehicle for John Hancock agents to sell personal lines of Sentry Insurance, the company is actively involved in the reinsurance business through three wholly-owned subsidiaries.

Hancock/Dikewood Services Inc., Albuquerque, New Mexico

1979   Incorporated in Massachusetts.
1980   Acquired by JHSI. Provides data processing and systems analysis services to health care providers. The company also offers a full range of management services to health maintenance organizations and associations.

John Hancock Financial Services Inc., Boston, Massachusetts

1980   Incorporated in Delaware. Provides equipment leasing and financing (tax- and nontax-oriented) and related financial services to the agricultural, professional, and general commercial markets on a national scale.

Independence Investment Associates Inc., Boston, Massachusetts

1982   Incorporated in Delaware. Provides investment management and advisory and counseling services, principally to pension funds and other institutional investors.

John Hancock Venture Capital Management Inc., Boston, Massachusetts

1982   Incorporated in Delaware. Serves as general partner and manager of the John Hancock Venture Capital Fund, a limited partnership with $148,000,000 of committed capital.

Tucker Anthony Holding Corp., Main Offices: Boston, Massachusetts, and New York, New York

1982   Incorporated in Delaware. A holding company offering, through its subsidiary Tucker Anthony & R. L. Day Inc., a broad range of financial services, including stocks and bonds, money management, corporate finance, and tax-advantaged investments.

1976	1977	1978	1979	1980	1981	1982	1983
$13,098	$14,101	$15,212	$16,207	$17,263	$17,824	$18,336	$18,708
898	937	1,016	1,111	1,377	1,448	1,754	2,066
0	0	0	0	121	671	1,633	2,766
708	838	1,014	1,269	1,625	2,365	5,400	6,013
19	24	83	133	161	203	269	398
$14,723	$15,900	$17,325	$18,720	$20,547	$22,511	$27,392	$29,951

Exhibit 29.8   Consolidated Summary of Operations and Changes in Policyholders' Contingency Reserves, John Hancock Mutual Life Insurance Company and Subsidiary

| | Year Ending December 31, | | |
	1983	1982	1981
Income			
Premiums, annuity considerations, and pension fund contributions	$2,489.5	$2,573.4	$2,435.6
Investment income	1,818.1	1,668.1	1,491.2
Separate account capital gains (losses)	118.4	132.9	(106.9)
Other	(346.1)	(562.6)	(552.5)
	4,079.9	3,811.8	3,267.4
Benefits and expenses			
Payments to policyholders and beneficiaries:			
Death benefits	513.3	447.0	405.1
Accident and health benefits	423.9	444.5	496.4
Annuity benefits	182.9	25.0	11.6
Surrender benefits	248.9	90.1	79.1
Matured endowments	15.2	11.6	11.3
	1,384.2	1,018.2	1,003.5
Additions to reserves to provide for future payments to policyholders and beneficiaries	1,560.2	1,599.3	1,187.6
Expenses of providing service to policyholders and obtaining new insurance:			
Field sales compensation and expenses	308.9	292.5	285.6
Home office and general expenses	310.6	279.0	262.5
State premium taxes	30.5	32.2	30.2
Payroll and miscellaneous taxes	27.6	25.2	22.7
	3,622.0	3,246.4	2,792.1
Net gain before dividends to policyholders and federal income taxes	457.9	565.4	475.3
Dividends to policyholders	390.5	326.7	314.2
Federal income taxes	36.0	70.1	50.2
	426.5	396.8	364.4
Net gain	31.4	168.6	110.9
Net capital gain or loss and other adjustments	(52.6)	(50.2)	40.4
Less amounts allocated for:			
Increase (decrease) in valuation reserves	(1.2)	(1.2)	1.2
Additional provision for prior years' federal income taxes		13.9	30.0
Other adjustments	16.0	7.0	15.8
Increase (decrease) in policyholders' contingency reserves	(36.0)	98.7	104.3
Policyholders' contingency reserves at beginning of year	1,002.8	904.1	799.8
Policyholders' contingency reserves at end of year	$ 966.8	$1,002.8	$ 904.1

Exhibit 29.8   *continued*

	Year Ending December 31, 1983	1982
Assets		
Bonds	$ 6,551.5	$ 6,590.2
Stocks:		
Preferred or guaranteed	190.6	197.1
Common	431.3	361.1
Investment in affiliates	342.5	319.4
	964.4	877.6
Mortgage loans on real estate	6,542.0	6,527.3
Real estate:		
Company occupied	161.4	148.6
Investment properties	636.2	530.6
	797.6	679.2
Policy loans and liens	2,041.2	1,890.4
Cash items:		
Cash in banks and offices	40.0	12.4
Temporary cash investments	558.8	789.8
	598.8	802.2
Premiums due and deferred	388.8	341.1
Investment income due and accrued	362.8	344.3
Other general account assets	460.9	283.7
Assets held in separate accounts	4,832.1	3,386.2
Total assets	$23,540.1	$21,722.8
Obligations		
Policy reserves	$11,659.7	$11,442.2
Policyholders' and beneficiaries' funds	4,596.4	4,649.3
Dividends payable to policyholders	429.0	359.5
Policy benefits in process of payment	161.2	99.3
Other policy obligations	161.6	148.3
Indebtedness to affiliate—	74.7	74.4
Commercial paper outstanding—	72.6	0
Mandatory securities and other asset valuation reserves	389.3	272.3
Federal income and other accrued taxes	109.5	148.8
Other general account obligations	101.9	158.1
Obligations related to separate account business	4,817.4	3,367.8
Total obligations	22,573.3	20,720.0
Policyholders' contingency reserves		
Special contingency reserve for group insurance	92.6	87.8
General contingency reserve	874.2	915.0
Total contingency reserves	966.8	1,002.8
Total obligations and contingency reserves	$23,540.1	$21,722.8

Structure, Culture, and Systems

A major concern in the company was the fact that two different entities operate under the name John Hancock Mutual Life Insurance Company. Furthermore, two distinct cultures evolved as a result of defining the subsidiaries as profit centers in 1980 and evaluating them based on profit and return on investment. That change in structure and systems in essence created a new way of operating and, to some extent, a new breed of manager.

Phyllis Cella was president and chief executive officer of Hanseco, a subsidiary spawned in 1971 from within the Hancock and staffed originally with Hancock employees. The expressed purpose of starting Hanseco was to provide products for the Hancock agents. In 1983, Hanseco had approximately $750 million in assets under its management. Up until 1980 they had operated within the Hancock structure. Cella described some of the thinking that went on inside Hanseco as the subsidiary grew. In the beginning:

Hanseco was run according to the Hancock style, and we were all on the Hancock payroll. As we got bigger and began to understand our own business, we began to change that. Having grown up in it you learn how to deal with it, but you also understand how time consuming it is and that you don't always get the answer you want because it is a bureaucracy. Even before the Holding Company officially was formed, we saw ourselves as running a company that was now different from and, in our minds, separate from the John Hancock, even though we were still on the John Hancock payroll. In our minds the paycheck was the only connection. When the world turned [introduction of the subsidiary structure] and the primary objective now became profit, it strengthened the fact that you really are a completely separate entity—it has now been blessed—and you are your own employer.

In 1984 Hanseco had its own payroll that was processed, not on the John Hancock computers, but by the First National Bank of Boston. The subsidiary set its own salaries and had its own retirement plan. According to Cella, the attitude at Hanseco was: "If I can get it cheaper downtown, then I'm going to do that—it's my bottom line. There are still people in the organization that don't understand or accept that fact that maybe we will buy their services—but maybe we won't. There is no question that there now exists two different cultures."

Hanesco's 40th-floor offices are a modular arrangement as opposed to the traditional open concept of the Hancock. Cella's office was on the outside corner of the glass building overlooking the Charles River and the Boston Common. She remarked that she had consciously chosen the modular design and had had to fight for it.

Once you get a taste of it (the profit center concept), I don't think it would be possible to go back and work in the other framework—not at this level or an officer level. Partly because of the size—we still have only 225 employees but are growing every day—but partly because of the need. We all participate very heavily in this organization—all of the officers. We have eight officers, so it is not hard to get eight people together, hammer things out, let everyone have his say, have everyone really go at it, and wide open. How do you do that in the Hancock? You don't—it is impossible. It is much more fun here. A bigger challenge, a lot more sleepless nights than you ever had in the other big organization, but you cannot match the excitement and satisfaction of it and the gratification when it works.

Although officers of the life company were quite aware of the differences, some, like Frank Irish, Vice-President, Corporate Analysis and Planning, viewed the subsidiaries "as indistinguishable from the parent company from the point of view of management control. Standards should be applied equally to subsidiaries and parent company. A lot of my efforts have been designed to achieve this goal, and I think we are close to that."

In response to the issue of transforming units of the life company into profit centers, Irish went on to say: "I can only say that we are very seriously considering it. We obviously can. We know we can." He also had some doubts, however, as to whether the change would accomplish what the Hancock wanted and if, in fact, that change was consistent with their policyholders. "When managing a participating insurance business you are not supposed to be profit maximizing—so why have a profit center concept. There is a conflict."

Phyllis Cella felt as Steve Brown did: "Theoretically, they (the units of the life company) ought to be profit centers and have a bottom line." There was some concern, however, from a practical point of view as to the difficulty of actually getting to the bottom line of some of the units within the life company that really do not have income.

There was also some concern among middle managers within the Life Company concerning the somewhat different nature of the business conducted within the holding company and the way the holding company managers were being compensated. As Irish commented:

What is at this point different about the subsidiaries is their attitude toward things like personnel policies, tenure, compensation, that sort of thing. Not only have they been decentralized, but in theory the subsidiary personnel are working in a more highly rewarded, more risky business than the parent company. . . . I'm not sure how top management views it—and I usually know top management. I know how many middle managers view it—very critically. Subsidiary managers are paid better and have more freedom and have greater opportunities. That's how some people view it, and it's a problem we are going to have to work with. I don't know what the answer is. . . . The other is that you are generally dealing with the kinds of operations where you need risk takers. . . . I think the problem is perhaps made worse by the obvious fact that, despite the statements about profit responsibility, some of the subsidiaries have not produced an adequate rate of return.

Becoming a Stock Company

A related issue was the Hancock's financial restructuring to a stock company. Although this issue was much broader, it related directly to the existing culture within the Hancock. As noted previously, Steve Brown saw the Hancock, in the long run, taking on the structure of a stock company. On that particular issue, Frank Irish pointed out that the thinking had been dominated in the past by having to generate capital internally and that that way of doing things takes away certain possibilities in the way of financial dealings. However, there is less pressure in a mutual company to sacrifice long-term objectives for short-term profit growth.

Irish went on to say that there are other advantages and disadvantages to both forms of business. Some feel mutual companies have more leeway in pricing their products. By adjusting the dividends, mutual companies may much more closely reflect the actual cost of the service provided than their stock company counterparts. Stock companies are constrained to charge whatever the market will bear to achieve the highest possible level of profit for their stockholders.

As insurance companies extend themselves into broader areas of financial service, there is a tendency for firms to make use of holding companies for the management of their subsidiaries. Stock companies typically employ upstream holding companies. An upstream holding company is perched at the top of a corporate organization. The shareholders own it and it owns the subsidiaries. Mutual companies are constrained to use downstream holding companies. A downstream holding company is positioned midway down the corporate hierarchy and is wholly or partially owned by the mutual company. Because the parent mutual company is governed by state insurance laws, the management of a downstream holding company is often more complex than that of an upstream holding company.

As noted earlier, a stock company can raise capital by selling stock. A mutual company does not have this equity option. It may earn revenue from its operations, receive income from its investments, and acquire debt. A stock company may use its stock to acquire other organizations and in merger situations. Frank Irish contends that many of the older and larger mutual companies were able to experience immense growth because at their outset they were not pressured by shareholders to achieve high levels of profitability. Instead, management chose to pursue growth as the company's main objective.

It is possible for a mutual company to convert into a stock company and vice versa. Both processes are complicated, time consuming, and expensive. Conversion from a mutual company to a stock company would typically require the calculation of a policyholder's share of the company and transference of that share to shares of stock. In some instances a stock company, usually motivated by the fear of a takeover, may attempt to mutualize. This conversion would require approval by the company's board, the state insurance commissioner, the stockholders, and the policyholders. All the stock must be purchased and canceled by the company before it can mutualize. According to the *1983 Life Insurance Fact Book*, "In the past 16 years, five companies have converted from the status of a mutual company to a stock company and two stock companies have converted to mutual."[23]

Phyllis Cella commented on moving from a mutual to a stock company:

I think that it is essentially a good idea, because then the whole company has to have a bottom line. Right now mutuals do have a net gain from operations. A stock company has a very different attitude and culture because they have the stockholder that wants a rate of return. But just doing it is not the answer. Just because you become a stock company doesn't suddenly make everything perfect. The old culture is still there.

The Future

Given the recent announcement of a merger agreement with Buckeye Financial Corporation and the 1982 purchase of Tucker Anthony in addition to the other ten subsidiaries,

---

[23] *1983 Life Insurance Factbook*, (Washington, D.C.: The American Council of Life Insurance, 1983), pp. 88–89. Of the seven companies that converted, the council has identified six. Those converting from mutual to stock were: National Heritage Life-Insurance (1966), Brooking International Life Insurance (1966), Viking Life Insurance (1972), West States Insurance Company (1973), and Equitable Beneficial Mutual Life Insurance Company (1977). Farmers and Traders Life Insurance converted from stock to mutual in 1974.

the Hancock has taken some major steps toward competing in the FSI. The strategic thrust behind such moves was that they would result in synergies along such dimensions as offering more products for the sales force, developing multiple service relationships with individual customers, and management synergy—they "knew how to manage financial services."

For E. James Morton, President and Chief Operations Officer and Vice-Chairman of the Board, the question of measuring performance in the life company was at the heart of what he considered one of the Hancock's major problems. What had been done in the past could not be readily identified as bottom-line. They essentially had no measures of profit and had only inconsistent measures of growth. Size as indicated by assets under management had also become difficult to measure. According to Morton: "We have always had some kind of measures that we have tried to be tough about. But I'm not sure they have been the right ones and the ultimate kinds of measures. And they haven't been the kinds of measures that you can really compensate people on."

Morton had some reservations about moving to the profit center concept. He noted that at times they had the feeling that they were a generation behind and that the profit center idea was becoming outmoded. He referred to management journals that indicated that managers spent too much time worrying about short-term results, thus sacrificing long-term objectives.

Part of the problem of moving to the profit center concept was the method of accounting used in mutual life insurance companies. Morton felt, however, that another big piece of the problem was attitude:

Maybe the attitude was not so bad in the days when all we were was a mutual life insurance company being operated with the primary purpose to supply insurance at cost to our policyholders. But now that we are trying to compete in a broader financial services industry we can't do that anymore. We have to operate with the same kinds of efficiencies as our competition.

Morton felt that they had to change the way management and essentially all of the employees of the company look at what the objectives are.

If we do that, we are going to benefit our policyholders a lot more than perhaps we have in the past. We will be forced to cut costs, run things efficiently, be market-driven, and expand the base that expenses can be spread over, resulting in lower consumer costs. We think we are headed in the right direction. But that is not to say that for the first 100 years things were done the wrong way. The times have changed.

Demutualizing, or moving to a stock company, is a very complex issue because of having to deal with 50 state insurance commissions and agreeing on whether a mutual company has equitably treated its existing policyholders.

For Jack McElwee, this was also a complex issue but one that he related to the future environment of the Hancock.

A lot of people feel that it is too complex but you can't possibly afford to feel that way. If the reality of the future is that only a corporation which is the form of a stock company will be able to survive, then you'd better find a way to be a stock company, or at least have all the legal and regulatory characteristics that a stock company has.

Even though the future of the FSI is questionable, there should also be all kinds of opportunities. McElwee noted that capitalizing on those opportunities means "managing ourselves properly. That's what this exercise is all about—it's called management."

Jim Morton expanded on the role of the John Hancock in the FSI:

I am not sure what one-stop financial shopping means. What we hope to do is attract clients. If we attract a client in one piece of the organization, we hope to make that client a target for the other pieces of the organization. I think it would be unrealistic to think that there are going to be a lot of people that get all their financial services from us. We want to see a lot of cross-selling. We want to have plenty of clients in all the sectors and hopefully the rest will take care of itself.

Morton felt that to succeed in the FSI, the important step is to fill out the product line. He went on to say:

"That is why we so badly need a bank. If we can't buy the bank, let's find that out in a hurry because we have to make other arrangements. There is no way we can be a large financial services organization without offering banking services. If you can't do it by owning a bank, you have to do it some other way."

Morton went on to discuss the future of the John Hancock:

We want to end up with an organization that, when people look at it they say, "That's a financial services organization." And if you ask the man on the street, "What is the John Hancock?" he will say that "it is a financial services organization where I can go to do almost anything. I can buy stocks and bonds, house insurance, securities, and tax shelters. I can also get a mortgage for my house and banking services. Furthermore, I get a statement on everything once a month." . . . That is what we would like to be in 1990, and I think we have a reasonably good chance of doing it. There will be maybe 50 large financial organizations at that time and that is the list we want to be on. In order to do that we have to internally become customer-driven, profit-oriented, entrepreneurial, and all those good things you are supposed to be if you are a healthy, growing business. We know what we need to do. The trick is to do it.

It was also clear to Jim Morton that in the next five to ten years the composition of the businesses of the Hancock was also going to change. The assets in the nontraditional ventures were going to become bigger than those in the traditional ventures. According to Morton, "If we succeed in buying the bank that is another billion dollars of assets. Clearly, the nontraditional ventures are where the growth is."

To complicate management tasks in the environment of an evolving FSI, McElwee also had to deal with what he considered an intriguing question, namely, "What is beyond the financial services industry?" To this end he recently put together a study group focusing on the time frame of 2025 and the major questions of "What are the directions that the Hancock should move?" and "To what extent do those directions influence what we do in the way of financial services today?"

APPENDIX TO CASE 29

Officers

John G. McElwee

John G. McElwee was elected chairman and chief executive officer of John Hancock Mutual Life Insurance Co. effective January 1, 1982. McElwee entered the John Hancock administrative training program in 1945 and subsequently served as administrative assistant and in a series of line management responsibilities prior to his election as second vice-president in 1961. He became executive vice-president and secretary in 1974. McElwee then served as president and chief operations officer from January 1, 1979, to his election as chairman. He has been on the Board of Directors since March 1976.

E. James Morton

E. James Morton was elected president and chief operations officer of John Hancock Mutual Life Insurance Co. effective January 1, 1982. Morton entered the company as an actuarial student in 1949. He subsequently held a variety of line assignments within the actuarial area prior to his election in 1967 as vice-president and actuary. In 1971, he was elected senior vice-president, technical operations, and in 1974 executive vice-president, corporate operations. Morton has been on the Board of Directors since March 1976.

Stephen L. Brown

Stephen L. Brown was elected executive vice-president of financial operations of the John Hancock Mutual Life Insurance Co. in December 1981, to the Hancock Board of Directors in January 1982, and served as president and chief executive officer of John Hancock Subsidiaries Inc. until February 1984. Brown joined the company in 1958. He subsequently held various assignments within the actuarial department and was elected second vice-president in 1970 and vice-president in 1973. In 1975, he became vice-president at the Treasury Department and in 1977 was named senior vice-president and treasurer.

Phyllis A. Cella

Phyllis A. Cella of Boston is president, chief executive officer, and director of Hanseco Insurance Co., a subsidiary formed for the reinsurance of Sentry Insurance Co. policies sold by John Hancock representatives. She is also chairman of the board of Hanseco (U.K.) Insurance Company Ltd. and a director of John Hancock Subsidiaries Inc. Cella joined the parent company as a statistician. She advanced to statistical consultant in 1963 and served as assistant to the senior vice-president of field management and marketing from 1968 to 1970, when she was named general director of special projects and research. Cella was elected second vice-president in January 1972, vice-president in February 1975, and senior vice-president in December 1979.

Frank S. Irish

Frank S. Irish was promoted to vice-president, corporate analysis and planning, at John Hancock Mutual Life Insurance Co. in January 1979. Irish joined the company in 1963 as an assistant actuary. He was promoted to associate actuary in 1966 and in 1971 joined the Corporate Analysis and Planning Department in that capacity. Irish was elected second vice-president, corporate analysis and planning, in 1972.

CASE 30

Pacific Telesis Group—New Directions and Challenges

▪ David B. Jemison and Chris Cairns ▪

On January 1, 1984, Pacific Telesis became totally independent of AT&T. Divestiture had been characterized as similar to taking apart a 747 airliner in flight and reassembling it into a 767, all without spilling any coffee on the passengers. The separation occurred on time and the phones kept ringing through it all. In addition, PacTel felt it obtained the right people, assets, and financial status it needed to continue to do the job. Exhibit 30.1 shows the financial improvements made. Exhibit 30.2 shows the position of PacTel in light of other *Fortune* 500 firms.

This case describes the actions taken by the Pacific Telesis Group, formerly the Pacific Telephone and Telegraph Co., during the year immediately preceding divestiture; the organization of the firm after divestiture; and the challenges faced by Sam Ginn, Vice-Chairman and Group President of Diversified Businesses at Pacific Telesis.

Organizing to Meet the Future

After his appointment as strategic planning officer, Sam Ginn set into motion the processes necessary to accomplish the divestiture from AT&T and to develop a strategic plan for the soon-to-be-independent regional company. This included assembling a group to coordinate the divestiture process, establishing a strategic planning group, and organizing to run the businesses after divestiture.

Divestiture Team Set-Up

An experienced team of PT&T managers was quickly assembled to identify, assign, and monitor the myriad of tasks to be accomplished before divestiture on January 1, 1984. These people were selected for their overall knowledge of the firm, their willingness to change, and their commitment to make divestiture work. More than $19 billion in Pacific Telephone assets had to be reviewed and divided between PacTel and AT&T. This included about 3,000 buildings and all the telecommunications equipment they contained. In addition, provisions had to be made to transfer almost 20,000 employees to AT&T. Other key issues that had to be resolved included the financial status of the separated company and use of the Bell symbol. This divestiture team enlisted the support of all the areas of the business. They met regularly in their status room, dubbed the "War Room," to coordinate

This case was prepared by Assistant Professor David B. Jemison and Ms. Chris Cairns of Pacific Telesis as a basis for class discussion rather than to illustrate either effective or ineffective handling of an administrative situation.

Support for the development of this case was provided in part by the Strategic Management Program, Graduate School of Business, Stanford University.

Exhibit 30.1   Financial Highlights and Projections Pacific Telesis Group

Normalized Net Income

(in Millions of Dollars)
Projected improvements in Pac Tel Group cost effectiveness continue the trend of year over year growth.

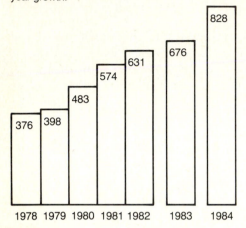

Normalized Pretax Interest Coverage Ratio

With projected 1984 results, Pacific Telesis Group will achieve the highest pretax interest coverage since Pacific Telephone's 1973 performance.

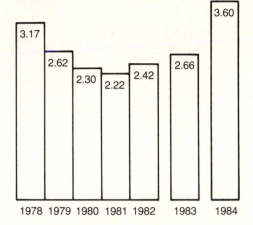

Debt Ratio

(Percentage)
With divestiture, Pacific Telesis will have a debt ratio of 46.5%—a level competitive with other Sunbelt companies.

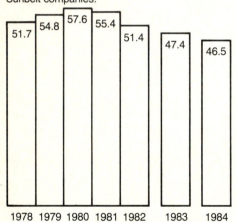

Percentage of Capital Generated Internally

(Percentage)
Pacific Telesis will continue to fund a substantial portion of its construction requirements internally.

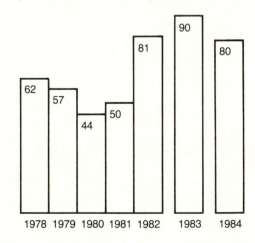

Notes:

• The years 1978 through 1983 reflect financial results for *Pacific Telephone*.

• Normalized results for 1978 through 9 months 1983 net income, pretax interest coverage ratio, and debt ratio have been restated to reflect, in the years to which they are applicable, the impacts of recent congressional legislation (including the effect of the June 1983 closing agreement with the IRS) reducing certain back-tax liabilities and changes to bring the accounting for deferred taxes in line with rate-making practices.

• The 1984 projections are for Pacific Telesis Group for the calendar year 1984.

Source: Annual Reports and Internal Documents.

Exhibit 30.2   *Fortune* 500 Comparisons

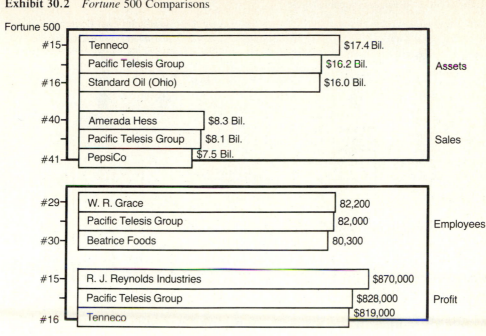

Source: *Value Line*

the divestiture and to track the progress of each task. These tasks were charted on big boards that covered all four walls of the room. The team's efforts were characterized by long, hard hours and a problem-solving, "can-do" attitude.

Strategic Planning Takes Shape

A strategic planning function was established at PacTel with a staff of planners and analysts and the creation of a Strategic Planning Board. Key officers from each major part of the PT&T organization formed the Board. They met regularly to address the major strategic, legal, and regulatory issues facing the corporation. Sam used this forum to discuss, work through, and gain acceptance for the strategic direction that was emerging for PT&T. He saw the Strategic Planning Board as critical to successful operation of the firm after divestiture, since it represented each major portion of the business. During this time, the board met monthly.

The small staff group of strategic planners and analysts provided procedural guidance and analytical support to the board. In addition to PT&T managers, outside experienced planners were hired to minimize the learning period. The group acted in an analytical capacity, as well as independently, identifying the critical issues facing Pacific Telephone that would insure the best outcome from divestiture. They had wide authority to call upon the resources of the entire PT&T organization to resolve the issues they struggled with in very tight time constraints.

Exhibit 30.3   Business Planning Cycle

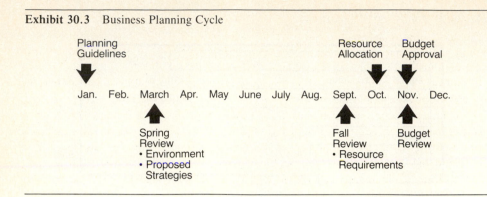

A process was also established to evaluate alternative business plans, allocate resources, and monitor results. The Pacific Management System, as it became known, provided this evaluation, allocation, and monitoring support in the context of a business planning cycle (see Exhibit 30.3) to insure regular review of the business plans from various parts of the company.

Major Outcomes of the Strategic Planning Process

Diversification Strategy Adopted

Sam Ginn and his planners recognized that Pacific Telephone was at an important crossroads. They saw two distinct options. The company could remain a traditional telephone utility. Alternatively, it could adopt an aggressive diversification strategy. There were advantages and risks to both options.

Remaining a traditional telephone utility had appeal because the people in the firm knew this business so well. However, there were substantial risks in standing still as the industry changed dramatically. The traditional revenue stream from regulated services was vulnerable to incursion from competitors who sought to use new technologies to lure selective, profitable customers. This would leave the regulated utility at a continual disadvantage. As competitors skimmed off profitable customers, other customers would be asked to pay more for maintaining service, a scenario that was fraught with regulatory peril.

The company chose to adopt an aggressive diversification strategy, both within and outside the confines of regulation. This would allow Pacific Telephone to explore opportunities for growth in a wide range of enterprises and give it the capability to meet competition in a variety of different arenas. In addition, as it would eliminate the sole dependency on the regulatory process for earnings, it would improve investor perceptions of the firm and, as a consequence, increase financing flexibility.

This diversification was allowed by a provision of Judge Green's Modified Final Judgment on Divestiture. This provision indicated that the regional telephone companies could enter diversified businesses by obtaining waivers from him upon showing that there was no substantial possibility the corporation could use their monopoly power to impede competition in the markets they sought to enter.

New Organization Structure Put in Place

Mr. Donald Guinn, Chairman of the Board, announced a new strategic direction, structure, and name for the firm on August 8, 1983. A holding company, Pacific Telesis, was created with two lines of business: regulated telephone service and diversified businesses (Exhibit 30.4). The regulated telephone business of Pacific Bell and Nevada Bell were structurally separated from the new diversified businesses. This separation was necessary in light of Judge Greene's order and also allowed the companies to compete freely in their respective markets. In addition, it was hoped that this would enhance Pacific Telesis's growing image as a diversified corporation with multiple sources of revenue and profit.

To insure the continuance of the strategic planning process, the position of vice-president, strategic planning, was established. Mr. John Gaulding, who had been managing partner of a consulting firm that had done a significant amount of work for Pacific Telephone, was hired in this capacity. Mr. Gaulding reported directly to the chairman, rather than in one of the two sections of the Pacific Telesis Group.

A key portion of the diversification strategy called for seeking new opportunities in the traditional regulated side of the business, as well as on the diversified business side. With

Exhibit 30.4 Pacific Telesis Group

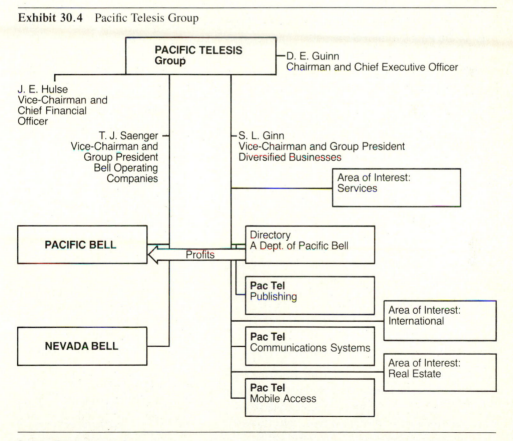

Source: Company records.

this in mind, the telephone company's marketing organization was restructured. John Lockton, previously president of Warner Amex Cable Corporation and a senior officer with Dun and Bradstreet Inc., was appointed to the newly created position of executive vice-president, marketing, for the telephone side of the business. In this position, Mr. Lockton was responsible for developing enhanced regulated services, such as specialized terminals for home banking and shopping, and contracting with municipalities for multiuse cable systems.

New Diversified Businesses

Sam Ginn was appointed vice-chairman and group president—diversified businesses. Several promising opportunities were identified for immediate pursuit, and subsidiary companies were created to develop these businesses. The presidents of each of the diversified subsidiaries reported to Ginn. A brief description of each of the diversified subsidiaries, as well as the major areas of interest for possible future subsidiaries, follows.

PacTel Communications Systems

As part of divestiture, AT&T took responsibility for terminal equipment: maintenance of existing in-place leased telephones and sales of new phones and systems. AT&T also took over all the Phone Center Store outlets and personnel. However, a modification to the final divestiture judgment allowed the local companies to reenter the terminal equipment sales business on January 1, 1984, if they would establish a separate subsidiary for this purpose. PacTel Communications Systems was established by Pacific Telesis to enter this market.

PacTel Communications Systems planned to market a line of technically superior telephone terminal equipment. Beginning operation on January 1, 1984, they contracted with a variety of manufacturers to provide a broad-based line of basic telephones, designer phones, speaker and cordless phones, and telephones combined with other appliances such as clock radios and answering devices. In addition, they targeted small and large businesses for sales of communications systems and data products. Product offerings provided excellent value in terms of warranties and service contracts were designed to position PacTel as the premier service provider in the industry.

The initial revenue projection for PacTel Communications Systems was over $200 million in 1984. The organization began the year with about 250 employees. About 40 percent of these came from Pacific Bell, but a high percentage of the salespeople were hired from other companies, such as IBM, Xerox, and other communications equipment vendors.

Directory

The Directory Department of Pacific Bell (the regulated part of the Pacific Telesis Group) was responsible for producing the *White Pages* and *Yellow Pages* directories. This portion of the telephone business was exempted from regulation in 1978, although the profits were still to be used to support basic telephone service. For 1984, advertising revenue of $508 million was projected. Directory, although a part of Pacific Bell, was managed as a diversified business under Sam Ginn. About 500 management and nonmanagement (sales and production) persons made up the Directory Department, which had been a long-standing department in the telephone company.

The reason that Directory reported to Ginn was that their managers also had responsibilities for managing PacTel Publishing, a completely separate subsidiary. To satisify terms of the divestiture and regulatory requirements, the head of Directory, the vice-president, directory services, and Directory's chief financial officer became holding company employees so that they could report to Sam Ginn and facilitate their additional responsibilities for PacTel Publishing.

PacTel Publishing

A small group, initially composed of six persons, was selected to begin PacTel Publishing. The purpose of this subsidiary was to develop new publishing ventures in four areas.

▪ National directory publications, for example, industrial or trade directories.

▪ Localized publishing products, such as visitors' guides or convention guides.

▪ Directory services under contract for other publishers or telephone companies.

▪ Electronic publishing, such as shop-at-home services.

This group, which except for the marketing vice-president came from the Directory organization, was expected in 1984 to sign contracts that would bring in at least $2 million in revenue in 1985. The group was expected to break even in early 1986 and to become a profit contributor later that year.

PacTel Mobile Access

Originally formed as a nationwide subsidiary of AT&T and called Advanced Mobile Phone Service, AMPS was (as a part of the divestiture decree) split up and assigned to the seven regional holding companies. The California/Nevada portion of AMPS, now part of the Pacific Telesis Group, was named PacTel Mobile Access.

PacTel Mobile Access planned an advanced, high-quality state-of-the-art mobile phone system for use by executives and other people who needed telephone service from their automobiles. They planned to market their services in two ways: on the retail level using their own agents and on a wholesale basis to resellers who would market the service under their own name with their own terminal equipment.

Because of the use of radio waves in this business, the FCC granted franchises for certain areas to partnerships of firms that already provided wire-line telephone services to customers in the area. This business was still in the formative stages nationwide with only a small portion of the major market-area franchises determined. The first service in the Pacific region was planned for the Los Angeles area beginning in May 1984, in time for the Summer Olympics. PacTel Mobile Access was the general partner in providing this service with several other limited partners, including GTE.

PacTel Mobile Access was staffed by about 100 persons and planned to double that size in about eight years. Most employees at all levels in the company had a Bell System background. Revenues for 1984 were estimated at $7 million and were expected to climb dramatically as the service became available in more areas. Estimates of PacTel Mobile Access share of the market approached $200 million in five years.

PacTel Mobile Service

A small group was spun off from PacTel Mobile Access in mid-1984. Their mission was to provide mobile telephone service and equipment sales outside the carrier markets served by Mobile Access. This organizational change was driven by the evolving regulatory environment.

Pacific Telesis International

The international market for telecommunications products and services was exploding. Pacific Telesis International was formed as the vehicle for marketing Telesis's expertise overseas. They would meet international customers' needs with creative solutions to large telecommunications and information problems. Offerings would include services (such as consulting), information systems, telecommunications systems, project management, training, and operational and administrative support systems.

Potential customers would include both governments and private firms; competitors in this business included such well-established firms as ITT, Cable and Wireless PLC, Nippon Electric Company, and AT&T International. If a waiver to enter this business were sought and obtained, a small group of 20–25 persons as a separate subsidiary could be set up. As contracts were obtained, labor and resources from Pacific Bell could be utilized as necessary and charged to the project on a fully distributed cost basis.

PacTel Properties

PacTel Properties was formed to service Pacific Bell and other affiliated companies as a real estate broker and developer. With more than 2,000 owned and leased buildings totaling about 50 million square feet of space, Pacific Bell had in the past generated $1–3 million annually in real estate brokerage commissions and had relied on outside developers for major office complex development. The subsidiary captured some of these commissions and managed project development with favorable financing terms as a result of having Pacific Bell as a guaranteed major tenant. In addition, real estate development had the possibility for certain tax advantages the holding company could utilize. Properties would begin to participate in the broader real estate market when it received a waiver from the court.

A group of about ten persons, primarily from Pacific Bell's Building, Engineering, and Real Estate groups, staffed this separate subsidiary. The president of such a subsidiary might be recruited from outside Pacific Bell, given the specialized expertise required.

PacTel Finance

A small company was formed to provide lease financing for customers of the Diversified Businesses. It had already begun to service PacTel Mobile Services and would be more fully developed in 1985.

PacTel Services

A support group called Services was also considered. This group would provide the administrative staff support needed for the Diversified Businesses Group. With about 20 people, it would assist in strategic planning, budgeting and financial management, and personnel administration in support of the other subsidiaries in the Diversified Businesses Group.

Included in this Services organization would be a small group that would identify and study new ventures that could develop into additional diversified subsidiaries. They would scan a wide range of business possibilities and develop preliminary analyses on promising opportunities. If results of the preliminary analyses were favorable, more in-depth analysis would determine whether or not a new business would be formed. Sam met twice a month with this New Ventures Group to review results and direct their activities.

Management of the New Diversified Corporation

With the decision to diversify came the need to rethink the style of management that had pervaded the Bell System and to decide what was appropriate for the new Pacific Telesis Group. In the past, key strategic decisions were made by AT&T, and the local telephone companies implemented these decisions. As much planning as possible was done on a nationwide basis to ensure uniformity. Compensation plans were similar throughout the Bell System. Pay scales were standard with annual general increases for almost everyone and the possibility of modest individual merit awards for some at the end of the year. The benefit plan was considered by employees to be among the best, partly because of gains made over the years in union contract negotiations.

With the advent of Pacific Telesis as a diversified corporation, there was a need, especially in the Diversified Businesses Group, to develop a management style that best suited these new and varied businesses. In the Diversified Businesses Group, a decentralized management approach was established. Each subsidiary president was now made responsible for attaining certain profit goals.

The Diversified Businesses Group developed monitoring, measurement, and incentive systems, as well as benefit plans that were different from those for the regulated telephone business. Sam Ginn set up a systematic plan for monitoring and controlling the subsidiaries. Regular monthly meetings were scheduled with each subsidiary president. These meetings included reviews of key financial items; discussion of operations matters; possible modifications of strategic direction, such as new markets, products, or channels of distribution; and any current legal or regulatory matters. At the end of each meeting they would decide on the agenda items for the following month. The staff of PacTel Services coordinated the presentation of results and followed up on areas identified for further study. If a major deviation in the business plan results remained uncorrected, Sam could send a task force of PacTel service analysts to visit the subsidiary to assist in problem solving.

With the decentralized management approach came a new measurement system. When Sam had been in charge of Network for Pacific Telephone, he reviewed more than 300 indicators of expense control and quality of service every month. However, with the diversified subsidiaries, he had decided to routinely track three or four key financial measures, (e.g., gross revenue, net income, return on sales, return on equity, asset turnover) together with a few selected "strategic milestones" that indicated how well the new businesses were being established and positioned. These indicators were also the factors on which the managers' compensation was based.

An incentive compensation plan was developed that tied managers' salaries directly to the financial success of each subsidiary, with a portion of each manager's salary placed "at risk" for the possible attainment of a greater incentive award if the financial goals of the subsidiary were exceeded. To accompany this, a new slimmed-down benefit plan was designed for the Diversified Businesses. It was a flexible plan that could be tailored to meet individual needs, while reducing expenses to the corporation as a whole.

Sam Ginn's New Challenges

Sam saw his new role as group president–Diversified Businesses as even more challenging than his last assignment as strategic planning officer. He mused that his recent jobs had coincided with the more critical issues facing the corporation. A few years back, the quality of telephone service had deteriorated in California to the point where the CPUC threatened to withhold needed rate relief. Sam had undertaken the challenge of spearheading the service recovery drive. Next, he had coordinated the divestiture from AT&T, with the attendant development of new strategic direction and organization structure. As a somewhat overlapping assignment, he had introduced strategic planning to the corporation. Now, he was being asked to do what no other telephone company executive had ever done—successfully build a series of diversified businesses in tandem with a regulated telephone utility.

In his new position, Sam had to wear many different hats. He would possibly be a member of seven different boards of directors, including Pacific Telesis, Pacific Bell, and each of the present Diversified Businesses. The number of board meetings Sam Ginn would have to include in his schedule would grow as more new businesses were formed. In addition to being on the Mills College Board of Trustees, Sam Ginn was elected president of the Industry Education Council of California and the Alumni Advisory Board of the Stanford Business School Sloan Program. He also often took time to speak at various industry and educational conferences on behalf of Pacific Telesis.

Sam knew there were some important new activities he had to initiate to fulfill PacTel's strategic direction. For example, to be viewed as truly diversified, a corporation must obtain a significant portion of its revenues and profits from diversified sources. An important part of his charter was to grow the diversified businesses to a point where they made material revenue and profit contributions to the entire PacTel Group. It would take quite a bit to do this when the size of the current diversified businesses for which he was responsible was small compared with the $8 billion in annual revenues on the regulated side. One possible solution would be to acquire other established businesses. But PacTel had never made any acquisitions before. Another avenue for growth was the development and nurturing of new start-up ventures within the firm. They would be an outgrowth of the efforts of the New Ventures Group in the Services Staff.

As Sam reviewed all his efforts, he realized their success hinged on a successful legal and regulatory strategy to obtain waivers to enter new businesses not authorized under the Divestiture Decree and to keep his new businesses from falling under regulatory oversight, with profits taken to support the cost of basic telephone service.

Another factor he saw as crucial to the diversification strategy was the initial success of the first few new businesses. Sam felt responsible for these businesses, although a decentralized form of management had been installed, with the president of each business responsible for its own profitability. However, Sam intensely wanted each to succeed, as that could build credibility for the overall strategic direction of Pacific Telesis. The financial markets and his colleagues in the old Bell System were waiting to see if the ambitious diversification could be managed successfully.

As he jogged through the fog at dawn in the streets near his office in the heart of San Francisco, Sam saw these as the key questions he must address:

1. How do I organize my job and my time to accomplish all my goals?

2. How do I develop a management system that will evolve as the organization grows, so I can understand and manage the group?

3. How do I insure the success of the existing new businesses, with additional ones to come in the future?

4. How should I try to meet my growth goals: by acquisition, by internal development, or by both? How should each be managed? If I try to build the business by acquisitions, how do I develop and implement a successful acquisitions strategy? Should I strictly use consultants and investment bankers to analyze targets, or should an internal capability be developed?

5. Then, if we make acquisitions, how should they be incorporated in our Diversified Businesses Group?

6. What have I missed that I should be wary of?

CASE 31

Hines Industries Inc.

▪ *Robert P. Crowner* ▪

In June 1984, Gordon Hines, the president of Hines Industries Inc., reflected upon the first quarter of the 1985 fiscal year with mixed feelings. His marketing strategy of "niching" had been successful. He had started his second company in 16 years when he began Hines Industries in 1979. The first three years were characterized by rapid growth in sales but the recession took its toll in 1983. (Exhibits 31.1, 31.2, and 31.3 show the balance sheets, income statements, and expense statements for fiscal years 1981 through 1984.) Sales for the first quarter of 1985 looked like they would nearly equal the entire sales of 1984 and a profit of 12 percent to 15 percent should result. He was concerned that this high growth rate might produce a new set of problems.

Gordon Hines is not new to the entrepreneurial ranks. In February 1968, he founded Balance Technology Inc. in Ann Arbor, Michigan, which manufactures and markets balancing equipment and vibration instruments. Bal Tec grew rapidly but Gordon lost absolute control of the company when he needed outside money, a mistake he is determined to not make again. Eventually he was squeezed out of management and finally sold his stock at a considerable profit to an outsider who in turn squeezed out the management that followed Gordon.

Gordon Hines has an unusual background in relation to the businesses he has founded. He has a degree in psychology and at one time was a social worker for the Chicago YMCA. Later, while selling insurance, he successfully sold policies to two partners in a balancing equipment company who really did not have the funds to buy insurance. They were so impressed by Gordon's sales ability that they made him an offer to enter their business. Gordon accepted, and soon was successfully selling machines and became involved in redesigning and improving them as well.

Gordon, who is 54, has a natural aptitude for visualizing how things look and work and can quickly conceptualize his ideas. He is a problem solver. His father was an engineer and took Gordon into work on weekends with him so that Gordon learned early about machinery and the engineering behind machinery. He completed two years of engineering work at the University of Illinois before his intense interest in people drew him toward psychology.

It is certainly a fair statement to say that Gordon Hines *is* Hines Industries. His creativity is in evidence everywhere—marketing, design, manufacturing, and even finance.

The research and written case information were presented at a Case Research Symposium and were evaluated by the Case Research Association's Editorial Board. This case was prepared by Robert P. Crowner, Associate Professor of Management of Eastern Michigan University, as a basis for class discussion.

Copyright © 1984 by Robert P. Crowner.

Exhibit 31.1   Hines Industries, Inc. Balance Sheet

| | Year Ending February 28 | | | |
	1981	1982	1983	1984
Assets				
Current Assets				
Cash	$ 9,005	$ 5,027	$ 11,361	$ 26,707
Accounts Receivable	96,509	124,905	129,413	215,222
Inventories				
Materials	60,448	33,715	83,176	269,268
Work in Process	35,656	135,031	21,794	45,219
	96,104	168,746	104,970	314,487
Loan Receivable, officer				49,935
Total Current Assets	201,618	298,678	245,744	606,351
Property and Equipment				
Leasehold Improvements	7,386	7,386	7,386	7,386
Machinery and Equipment	21,894	38,871	52,358	96,188
Office Equipment	5,451	7,680	13,604	29,557
Transportation Equipment	0	19,933	30,247	58,768
Leasehold Interest in Communication Equipment	5,060	5,060	5,060	5,060
	39,791	78,930	108,655	196,959
Less Depreciation	6,485	20,747	42,084	82,258
	33,306	58,183	66,571	114,701
Intangible Assets	108	81	596	27
Total Assets	235,032	356,942	312,911	721,079
Liabilities and Stockholders' Equity				
Current Liabilities				
Notes payable, Bank	40,000	0	69,300	170,000
Current Portion of Long-Term Debt	6,632	2,626	12,100	27,353
Accounts Payable	77,273	88,765	72,432	181,684
Accrued Expenses	13,896	28,150	29,630	49,047
Accrued Taxes	5,930	8,579	6,748	20,288
Customer Deposits	30,074	117,513	10,000	218,091
Total Current Liabilities	173,805	245,633	200,210	666,463
Long-Term Debt	6,051	67,131	25,178	24,641
Stockholders' Equity				
Common Stock, $1 par Value, 100,000 shares, 70,000 issued	70,000	70,000	70,000	70,000
Retained Earnings	(14,824)	(25,822)	17,523	(40,025)
Total Stockholders' Equity	55,176	44,178	87,523	29,975
Total Liabilities and Stockholders' Equity	$235,032	$356,942	$312,911	$721,079

Exhibit 31.2   Hines Industries, Inc. Income Statement

	Year Ending February 28			
	1981	**1982**	**1983**	**1984**
Net Sales	$394,498	$634,767	$1,114,201	$1,434,912
Cost of Sales				
Material	158,364	269,957	373,713	381,268
Direct Labor	36,345	107,362	174,321	209,747
Subcontract	63,842	27,514	8,288	7,063
Drafting	3,716	7,335	11,078	43,322
Installation	0	2,900	3,567	18,100
Manufacturing Overhead	27,605	80,317	207,173	281,656
Total Cost of Sales	289,872	495,385	778,140	941,156
Gross Profit	104,626	139,382	336,061	493,756
Operating Expenses				
Research and Development	10,945	5,506	25,750	53,449
Selling Expenses	36,498	54,084	131,851	302,048
General and Administrative Expense	68,204	79,000	128,123	173,892
Total Operating Expenses	115,647	138,590	285,724	529,389
Operating Income	(11,021)	792	50,337	(35,633)
Nonoperating Income (Expense)				
Interest Income	0	0	0	790
Interest Expense	(4,473)	(11,790)	(6,992)	(22,705)
Miscellaneous	670	0	0	0
Total Nonoperating Income (Expense)	(3,803)	(11,790)	(6,992)	(21,915)
Income Before Taxes	$(14,824)	$(10,998)	$ 43,345	$ (57,548)

Products

Hines Industries presently has five basic product lines which are shown in Exhibit 31.4. These machines are known as hard bearing balancing machines. They come in a number of different models with different features, as shown in the exhibit. All of the lines are available with microprocessor analyzers. The DL (driveline balancing machine) and the HC (hard crankshaft balancing machine) were the first products developed. The HC500A model has been sold to more than 120 customers in 33 states and four foreign countries. The HC balancer is sold primarily to the automotive aftermarket for high-performance and racing cars.

The DL line is used to balance the drive shaft for cars and trucks. Because of the heavy weights and usage given to trucks, their drive shafts, unlike cars, have to be replaced about every 50,000–75,000 miles and, of course, requiring balancing at that time. Dana Corporation is the exclusive sales agent for the Dana high-tech driveline package. In September 1983, Dana placed a large order for ten units totaling $600,000. Shipments against this order began in February 1984 and $321,000 remains in backlog as of April 30, 1984. A second order from Dana for $600,000 was received in June 1984.

The other three product lines, which are sold in several sizes, are the HO or horizontal overhung machine, the HVR or hard vertical rotator machine, and the HVS or hard vertical static machine. Balancing is important in parts which rotate in order to minimize or eliminate vibration. Parts which are not balanced create noise and excessive wear. These

Exhibit 31.3 Hines Industries, Inc. Expense Statements

	Year Ending February 28			
	1981	1982	1983	1984
Manufacturing Overhead				
Supervisory Labor	$ 0	$ 0	$ 47,103	$ 67,654
Indirect Labor	2,638	2,829	8,635	12,640
Payroll Taxes	2,995	8,827	22,476	43,585
Insurance	2,662	6,469	26,642	37,200
Depreciation	3,469	10,874	15,019	22,710
Freight	4,799	14,118	13,657	30,099
Utilities	2,169	5,288	7,438	9,453
Maintenance	79	272	789	2,117
Tools	1,150	2,414	5,408	12,398
Rent	13,172	36,252	41,404	44,929
Supplies	4,618	4,462	7,885	10,584
Overhead Variance	(10,146)	(11,468)	10,717	(11,713)
Total	27,605	80,317	207,173	281,656
Selling Expense				
Advertising	$ 0	$ 0	$ 0	$ 8,175
Commissions	13,509	33,150	75,082	184,879
Payroll	0	0	20,990	35,747
Sales Promotion	11,616	11,158	18,018	49,460
Payroll Taxes	0	0	2,101	4,382
Travel and Entertainment	11,373	9,776	15,660	19,405
Total	36,498	54,084	131,851	302,048
General and Administrative Expenses				
Auto Operation	$ 8,171	$ 6,275	$ 6,473	$ 2,439
Airplane	510	3,408	3,688	1,876
Bad Debts	0	0	15,616	4,255
Contributions	0	270	394	3,741
Depreciation	1,332	3,388	8,586	17,464
Dues and Subscriptions	32	128	253	434
Equipment Rental	0	647	5,053	6,459
Insurance	1,785	724	8,641	13,956
Professional Fees	3,111	4,990	3,764	12,468
Maintenance and Repairs	0	382	0	1,048
Miscellaneous	942	1,761	2,175	2,511
Office Supplies	3,127	4,047	7,455	7,110
Clerical Payroll	24,781	35,046	39,083	65,275
Payroll Taxes	4,473	4,628	4,509	7,746
Sales Tax	406	273	715	667
Michigan Single Business Tax	219	960	3,900	4,100
Other Taxes	220	185	2,246	1,586
Telephone	8,515	11,888	15,572	20,757
Officer Salary	10,580	0	0	0
Total	$68,204	$79,000	$128,123	$173,892

Exhibit 31.4   Hines Industries Inc. Product Sheet

| HARD BEARING BALANCING MACHINES | Standard features of Hines Balancers: | ELECTRONIC DIGITAL READOUT PERMANENT CALIBRATION DIRECT INDICATION OF ANGLE AMOUNT IN OUNCES OR GRAMS COMPLETE TOOLING PACKAGES |

Hines Industries manufactures a variety of balancers for different applications, all of which are available with **Microprocessor Analyzers.**

HO

ADDITIONAL STANDARD FEATURES:
Single and two plane correction
On machine correction capacity
Automatic cycle
Total enclosure of mechanicals
Handles small and large unbalances
Dynamic braking

OPTIONS AVAILABLE:
• Microprocessor analyzer
• Segmenting
• Tolerance function

APPLICATION:
Specifically designed for overhung part balancing like:

Pump Impellers
Blowers
Fans
and similar parts

CAPACITIES:
8 models available range from .25 to 2500 lbs. part capacities.

HVR

Pure single plane balancing insensitive to couple unbalance
On machine correction capacity
Automatic cycle
Low speed operation
Dynamic braking
• Microprocessor analyzer
• Auto indexing
• Drill countdown
• Complete correction systems
• Tolerance function

Designed for single plane balancing of:

Pulleys
Clutches
Impellers
Flywheels
and similar parts

5 models available range from .1 to 200 lb. part capacities.

HVS

Microprocessor based electronics
Automatic electronic centering
Outstanding sensitivity
• Segmenting
• Tolerance function
• Part lift off device
• Display hold

This nonrotating static balancer is for fast part checking and balancing of:
Grinding Wheels
Fans
Brake Drums
Wheels
and similar parts

7 models available range from .5 to 2000 lbs. part capacities.

HC

Restraint/angle Indicator eliminates end stops
On machine correction capacity
Single and two plane balancing
Simplified belt drive
• Microprocessor analyzer
• Segmenting
• Tolerance function
• Complete correction systems
• End drive

The HC Cradle Balancer will handle a variety of work pieces for job shop or production balancing, any part than can be run on 2 bearing surfaces or mounted on an arbor.

Crankshafts
Rolls
Turbines
Armatures

8 models available range from .2 to 15,000 lbs. part capacities.

DL

The DL driveline balancer is available in several models from 3-3000 lb. capacities.

Digital readout
Direct angle indication
Heavy motorized spindles

FOR MORE INFORMATION ON THESE AND OTHER BALANCERS AVAILABLE CALL OR WRITE.

HINES INDUSTRIES Inc.
661 AIRPORT BOULEVARD, SUITE 2, ANN ARBOR, MICHIGAN 48104
PHONE: (313) 769-2300

machines are sold to industrial customers to balance fans, pump impellers, pulleys, etc. These machines sell for about $22,000 each, but the sales price of the HVR machine can reach $66,000.

Basically, balancing can be done in one or two planes depending upon the size or shape of the part to be balanced. The balancing equipment finds the center of the mass and determines how much weight must be added to or removed from a determined point or points on the part to balance it. Elapsed time for balancing varies between 15 minutes and 1½ hours in the case of engine balancing plus time for leading and unloading the part. The heart of a balancing machine is the microprocessor, which quickly senses and performs the necessary calculations.

Organization

Hines Industries is organized along functional lines. Exhibit 31.5 depicts the organization as of June 1984. Gordon Hines is the president and sole owner of the company. There are 46 employees including 18 temporary or part-time employees. Temporary employees do not receive all of the fringe benefits and are subject to being laid off first should a cutback be necessary. Five of the key employees—Ron Anderson, Ken Cooper, Joann Huff, Mike Myers, and Len Salenbien—were with Gordon Hines at Balance Technology and came to Hines Industries at various times after Gordon organized his new venture.

Marketing

Marketing is managed in an overall way by Gordon Hines through three employees. Joann Huff is responsible for the automotive aftermarket. She joined Hines in June 1980 after being with Bal Tec in secretarial and sales positions for nine years. She supervises 20 manufacturer's representatives employing 45 salespeople who sell the products to the ultimate customers. Mike Myers is responsible for the driveline machines which are sold through several manufacturer's representatives. Industrial sales are handled by John Ramer through three manufacturer's representatives and some direct sales to customers. Bob Edwards was recently hired to cover the Ohio and West Virginia territory directly for the company since it is difficult to get qualified general reps for this market.

Manufacturer's representatives are paid on a commission basis. A 15 percent commission is paid on the basic machine and 10 percent to 15 percent is paid on added components for the basic machine. Advertising support is provided in trade magazines to get inquiries. Exhibit 31.6 shows a typical advertisement which appeared in the June 1984 issue of *Jobber Retailer*.

Products are built to order, so no finished products are stocked. A substantial backlog of orders is considered desirable as an indicator of future sales and as an aid to scheduling production. Exhibit 31.7 is a sales analysis for the 12 months ending in April 1984. It shows the monthly billings and booking by product line and the backlog.

Automotive Aftermarket

The automotive aftermarket for balancing has been primarily for high-performance cars. It is believed to include the potential for 100 to 150 balancers per year. The Hines HC500 balancer for this market sells for about $16,500. The market potential has improved since the EPA and OSHA have backed off interfering with racing.

The automotive aftermarket for balancing has two other competitors: Winona VanNorman, which is a foreign-made copy of Hines equipment, and Stewart Warner, which is now engaging in "puffing" to overcome Hines's advantage. To aid the marketing performed by manufacturer's reps, who also handle other machinery for rebuilding engines, Joann Huff advertises in five trade journals for the performance and rebuilding industry: *Automotive Rebuilder*, *Specialty and Custom Dealer*, *Jobber Retailer*, *National Drag-*

Exhibit 31.5   Hines Industries Inc. Organization Chart

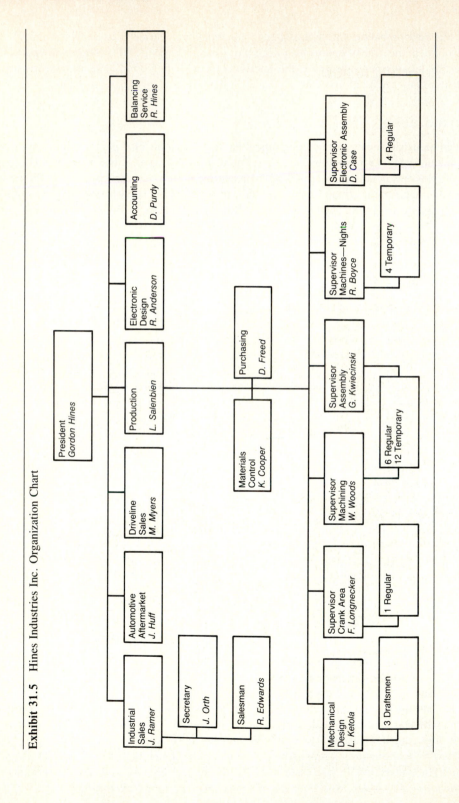

Exhibit 31.6   Hines Industries Inc. Sample Advertisement

Exhibit 31.7   Hines Industries, Inc. Sales Analysis

	Month Ending					
	April 1984	March 1984	February 1984	January 1984	December 1983	November 1983
Billings						
Automotive	$ 74,510	$120,111	$ 191,071	$ 68,368	$ 128,572	$ 112,594
Industrial	112,707	117,705		300	162,725	52,630
Driveline	125,610	124,770	55,555			
Parts and Service	2,373	1,159	2,372	1,281	1,201	1,269
Total	315,200	363,745	248,998	69,949	292,498	166,493
Bookings						
Automotive	96,432	21,019	109,888	(22,942)	280,141	188,781
Industrial	31,808	29,652	132,100	83,470	85,190	114,739
Driveline		4,250	33,725	26,900		
Parts and Service	2,373	1,159	2,372	1,281	1,201	1,269
Total	130,613	56,080	278,085	88,709	366,532	304,789
Backlog	$792,904	$977,491	$1,285,156	$1,256,069	$1,237,309	$1,163,275

ster, and *Circle Track*. Six half-page, two-color advertisements were placed in 1983, costing between $1,200 to $2,000 depending upon the publication. She has increased advertising in 1984 to one ad per month, including some full-page ads which are 1½ times the cost of the half-page ads. She would like to increase advertising to two per month in the latter part of 1984. She gets opinions from respected users as to which journals are most effective and tries to time Hines ads with articles about balancing, editorials about balancing, or issues preceding trade shows. Extra copies of the journals preceding trade shows are often distributed free at the shows. An example of an article about engine balancing is shown in Exhibit 31.8.

Special mailings, using articles such as Exhibit 31.8, and telephone campaigns are conducted to promote to the automotive aftermarket. Mailings typically range from 200 to 600 but have gone as high as 2,500. The membership lists of associations such as the Automotive Engine Rebuilders Association, the Automotive Service Industries Association, and the Specialty Engine Machine Association, are used for the mailings.

The company attends at least six trade shows per year. A balancing machine is displayed and Joann Huff, as well as area manufacturer's reps, are in attendance. Brochures describing the various machines made by Hines are available for use at trade shows as well as for use by manufacturer's reps and company sales personnel. Gordon Hines also attended the important Las Vegas AERA show in June 1984. Seven orders totaling $175,000 were obtained as a result of the show. Other shows of the associations previously mentioned are held in March and October, respectively. The National Dragster show is held in September, the Oval Track show in February, and the Pacific Automotive Show in March. Other wholesaler shows in individual states ares attended by manufacturer's reps and a sample balancer is sent for display.

Joann Huff sees her job as an educational process—first manufacturer's reps and then customers. She said: "The market is there but needs to be made. About half of the rebuilders always balance and the other half never balance." An engine will last 50 percent

October 1983	September 1983	August 1983	July 1983	June 1983	May 1983	April 1983	March 1983
$ 42,305	$ 59,193						
47,070	105,510						
2,231	1,268						
91,606	165,971	111,202	87,012	94,507	10,822	41,224	99,559
78,964	87,560						
129,615	54,310						
	600,000						
2,231	1,268						
210,810	743,138	165,471	114,821	142,277	35,772	182,654	39,444
$1,024,979	$905,775	$328,608	$274,339	$246,530	$198,760	$173,810	$32,380

longer if balanced, which is an important cost factor since the initial cost of engines is causing more and more to be rebuilt rather than replaced.

Diesel engine rebuilding is a new market which the company will be emphasizing. It is estimated by Gordon Hines that 5 percent of all truck engines are rebuilt each year and that 20-million-plus trucks are on the road. Joann plans to use the trade journal *Renews* for advertising which costs $2,600 for a full page. A heavy-duty HC machine with extra bed length will be used for this market. Better driveline tooling has helped the servicing of this market.

Another market which has potential is rebuilding shops which also wish to do some industrial work such as repairing and rebuilding electric motor armatures, pump impellers, fans, and blowers. A microprocessor can be added to the balancers for shops doing this kind of work. The machines are designed and built in a modular form. Therefore, by simply adding or changing certain components, it is possible to "culture whole new products" which can be assembled to satisfy customer requirements. New market segments could be entered in this same way.

The company has a tabletop version of the HC500 called the HC10TC for turbocharger balancing. The machine sells for $10,000. The only competitor is a company which, curiously, is called Heins. One trade show, Automotive Diesel Specialists, can be used to display products.

Another market is the 100 firms making up the Production Engine Rebuilders Association (PERA). A typical firm rebuilds as high as 70 engines per day employing used parts obtained from tearing down used engines. Their business is increasing since the smaller engines used in production cars do not last as long because of higher speeds used in the engines.

Still another market is the clutch rebuilder. An HVR balancer without all of the "bells and whistles" is used for this job and costs about $11,000 versus the normal HVR price of $20,000. The size of this market is not known but is believed to be similar to the PERA

Exhibit 31.8 Hines Industries Inc. Engine Balancing Article

It's high time that the bull stops concerning the area of engine balancing. When many machine shop owners/operators are asked to "balance" an engine, they automatically place the customer at hand into one category: racer/hot-rodder. For years, the only folks who offered balancing services out of their shop were regarded as "specialty speed shops," and out of the realm of the normal or "traditional" machine shop.

Wake up, folks. You cannot offer accurate and truly *complete* engine rebuilding services without including balancing as an integral part of your overall operation. It's called *doing the job right*.

That's right . . . we're suggesting that you go out and buy additional equipment if you don't already have it. That means increased operating bucks, right? Wrong. What it really means is additional profit opportunities.

An internal combustion engine features several moving parts, right? A crankshaft/damper-pulley/flywheel rotates within the engine block; and connecting rods/piston assemblies reciprocate up and down within their respective bores, while attached to the crankshaft. If there are unequal forces at work during engine operation, there is damaging stress being placed on engine bearings, and a loss of overall efficiency. Now, you know you can't dispute that fact, so why in the world are so many shops unwilling to look at balancing as the necessary service that it is? Especially in these days of "downsized" power plants that feature only six or four cylinders, balancing takes on a much more important role during engine rebuilding. Imbalance differences are proportionately more obvious and potentially damaging with the decrease in total number of cylinders. An imbalance condition in a V-8 engine that might go unnoticed has the potential to wreak havoc in a mill with only half the number of cylinders.

Let's take a look at a basic formula which illustrates how to determine the force that an unbalance condition produces. For a given unbalance condition, the force at the bearings is proportional to the speed of the engine *squared*. The relationship for force in pounds to due a given amount of unbalance in ounce inches is as follows: Force = 1.7738 × unbalance × Engine RPM. For example, for one ounce-inch of unbalance at 1,000 RPM, the force is 1.7738 pounds. For 2 ounce-inches at 2,000 RPM, the force is 14.2 pounds (formula courtesy Hines Industries Inc.).

That's 14.2 *pounds* of force applied to the crank bearings *constantly* at 2,000 RPM. With OE factory tolerances being what they are (speaking in generalities), it's not at all uncommon to experience this level of uneven balance in a majority of engines that come into your machine shop. We just can't take balancing procedures for granted as so-called "luxuries" anymore. Our purpose within this industry is to give the end user the *best* and most reliable rebuild that we can possibly achieve. Anything less should not be acceptable.

Let's take a look at the specific items that are included under the broad heading of balancing: the *rotating mass* includes the crankshaft, damper, flywheel, and clutch pressure plate (if any). The *reciprocating mass* includes connecting rods, pistons, and pins.

Rotating mass

Internally balanced engines (where the flywheel and/or damper has no counterweights) offer you a choice: you can either balance the pieces installed on the crankshaft as an assembly, or you can individually balance off the crank.

Externally balanced engines (flywheel and/or damper features counterweights) require these units to be installed on the crankshaft prior to crankshaft balancing.

In-line engines (four-cylinder, straight sizes) allow their crankshaft assemblies to be balanced on the crank balancer machine without the use of bobweights, while V-type engines require bobweights to be installed on the crank prior to balancing (to simulate rod/piston thrusts during crank balancing).

Reciprocating Mass

Here we want to balance piston/pin assemblies and connecting rod assemblies. What we are essentially after here is to make all piston/pin assemblies weigh the same; and for all connecting rod large-ends to weigh the same; and for all connecting rod small-ends to weigh the same. To do this, we basically find the lightest unit and remove metal from other similar units so that they all come down to the weight of the lightest. For example, in balancing pistons, we weigh each piston (clean and dry, with pins), finding the one that weighs less than all the others. We record that lightest weight. All other pistons are then ground carefully in their pin boss areas until they each weigh the same as that lightest unit. Generally, your tolerance is thus: the piston/pin assemblies being lightened should weigh the

Exhibit 31.8   *continued*

same as the light assembly, within +5 gram to .0 gram. Always constantly double-check your weights during and after all machining. Record the finished weight of each piston/pin assembly and mark each with cylinder number (if not already done).

The connecting rods are each weighed on a scale with the use of a special scale pan adapter. The rod ends (small and large) should be set up so that they are "square" with each other. Weigh each rod's large-end and find your lightest end. Carefully grind material from all others to bring them down to this lightest rod-end's weight. The same procedure is followed for small-ends. The tolerance to shoot for is + 1 gram−.0 gram (for automotive engines). For heavy truck engines, the tolerance can be sometimes set at + 2 grams to .0 gram. Most of the time, the very *end* surface of each rod is the area from which material is ground. Be sure to record each rod's end weight as well as double-checking total rod weight. Identify them accordingly.

Recordkeeping (on a bobweight card) is essential, not only for your immediate use, but for any future parts replacements that might be necessary. If you already know what weight a piston/pin assembly *must* be, you can choose an assembly for replacement that will maintain the balance job.

After rods and piston assemblies have been balanced, you can then set up the crank with the correct bobweights (if it's a V-block engine design).

Installation of bobweights, if needed, is critical from a centering standpoint. They must be accurately centered on the crank throws (spacing side-to-side across the bearing surface width). Orientation is not critical, so they do not need to be placed at right angles to each other. Bobweights, for those unfamiliar with this term, are the weights that are attached to the journals of the crankshaft of any V-type engine crank during balancing, on a dynamic crank balancer. They are adjustable, with flowable lead shot inside, and are there to cause the crank to respond to the balancer as if the rods and pistons were attached.

DETERMINING NEEDED BOBWEIGHT

To determine bobweight needed, add up the figures on your bobweight card: add rod rotating weight (large rod end) plus rod bearing weight plus oil allowance (figure average 4 grams) plus piston/pin weight, plus locks (if any) plus piston rings plus the rod reciprocating weight. Add up all of these weight factors that a single rod throw of the crank has to handle, and you've got your total bobweight.

Again, keep in mind that straight-line engine crankshafts do not need the addition of bobweights in order to balance the crank.

Balancing, especially in today's marketplace, is a necessary service and not the grand luxury that some people deem it to be. Just imagine a clothes washer that has had an uneven load placed in it. The resulting vibration causes excessive wear in virtually every moving component in that machine, as well as eliminating the degree of efficiency that the machine is capable of. Translate that into engine operational terms. When a mechanical mass rotates, centrifugal force acts upon the entire mass. If the part is unbalanced, an *excess* of mass exists on one side. Everything is being pulled in the direction of the heavy side, or away from the mechanical axis of rotation. Definitely a no-win situation for main bearings, rod bearings, timing gear setup, transmission input shaft, etc.

TAKE FULL ADVANTAGE OF BALANCING

If your shop is content with simple repair and replacement methods, you are not taking full advantage of the capabilities that balancing equipment offers in terms of *correcting* faulty OE traits, many of which can be traced directly back to unbalance conditions. If you want your customers to be supplied with rebuilt engine assemblies that will perform to the *design* level of efficiency and horsepower *and* offer reliable, extended life service, you must investigate the excellent balancing equipment that is currently available on the market.

Increasing horsepower is not the all-encompassing goal that the traditional machine shop strives towards; rather, it is the *beneficial* by-product of simply *doing it right*. So please, don't just regard balancing as an act performed by the speed-freak seals of the racing world. It should be an integral part of the efficient, quality-conscious machine shop that is concerned with producing the best possible product with currently available methods.

We wish to thank the good folks at Hines Industries Inc. (661 Airport Blvd., Suite #2, Ann Arbor, MI 48104; 313-769-2300) for their valued input for this article.

Source: June 1984. *Jobber Retailer*. Article by Mike Mavrigian.

described previously. The trade group, Automotive Parts Rebuilders Association, puts on one show each year. Hines has three competitors in this business segment.

Driveline Market

The driveline balancer is used primarily to balance the drive shaft for trucks, which have to be replaced frequently because of the heavy weights involved and the many miles of use each year. The current DL balancer was redesigned from the original version to bring it into conformance with the other balancers Hines makes. It is similar to the crankshaft machine, HC series.

Gordon Hines, as he typically does, sold the original concept to Dana Corporation, who is now the exclusive sales agent for the Dana High Tech Drive Line Package. Gordon is intensively involved in the initial design and marketing of a new product for six months or so, often spending long hours at it, and, then, he "eases back so his whole body can come back up." Mike Myers, who sells about one DL balancer to other customers a month, also tries to handle the big Dana account but really needs some help. Mike has a BA degree from the University of Michigan including 2½ years of engineering, and worked at Bal Tec for 15 years in mechanical design, computer programming, and sales before joining Hines in December 1983. Mike is Hines's internal computer expert and often provides help for those using Hines's three computers. He also is somewhat involved in mechanical design although Gordon provides the major mechanical design concepts. Gordon Hines believes the Data account has a potential for $2 million per year, with another $500,000 of DL balancers sold to others.

In addition to the DL balancer, Hines makes two other products which are related to the balancer and sold as part of the package Dana buys for $60,000–$75,000. These are a push-up press and a specialty lathe. This group of machines allows Dana to do eight specific jobs essential to rebuilding shafts—weld cutoff, tube cut and chamfer, push up, pull out, straighten, weld, straighten, and balance. The package includes specialized tooling designed and built to Dana's specifications. Dana, in turn, sells the unit to the ultimate customer.

Industrial Market

The industrial market includes sales of HO, HVR, and HVS products with several size models of each to industrial producers of original equipment (OEM) using impellers, fans, blowers, pulleys, etc. John Ramer heads this sales activity and he and Bob Edwards personally sell the products along with the three manufacturer's reps. John Ramer has a degree in business administration from the University of Michigan and is an artist. He joined Hines in 1982 as his first full-time job. It is believed that there is a great deal of business to be had within a 300- to 500-mile radius and, therefore, company sales personnel can be very effective.

Both John and Bob try to stay "off the road" and do most of their selling by telephone and sending out literature. They use lists of pump and blower manufacturers obtained from their trade association, as well as referrals, to make their calls. Thus they make only "hot calls" in person. Gordon Hines believes the market is too narrow to advertise in publications like the *American Machinist*, so he prefers the "rifle" approach instead of a "shotgun." He believes the HVR market is $4 million per year and, if the balancing could be done automatically, the market could be $20 million. HC balancers are also being sold for industrial use. Hines is successful in this market against established competitors.

Balancing Service

The company offers a balancing service for local customers who need relatively small quantities balanced. The idea behind this venture is to provide a service to smaller customers, gain experience with other items needing balancing and, hopefully, sell balancers to the service customers when they grow large enough to warrant their own machine. For instance, Hines is now balancing 2,000 specialized parts per week for a Ford motor supplier. This activity is managed by Robin Hines, Gordon's daughter. This activity will be housed in a third building, along with demo units, containing 3,200 square feet, which will be available July 1. This move will free up some of the space in the main building.

Manufacturing

Leonard Salenbien, 40 years old, is the manager of production. Prior to joining Hines he served in the same position at Balance Technology. He worked at Bal Tec for eleven years starting as a checkout technician and progressing to head of the service department before he became production manager there.

Hines Industries rents two buildings located in the light industrial area north of the Ann Arbor Airport. The main facility consists of 9,600 square feet located on one floor plus 1,600 square feet located on the second floor. Exhibit 31.9 shows the floor plan of the main plant. The second building which is located nearby contains 3,200 square feet. It is used for painting machines, storage of large parts, lumber storage, fabrication of pallets

Exhibit 31.9 Hines Industries Inc. Floor Plan

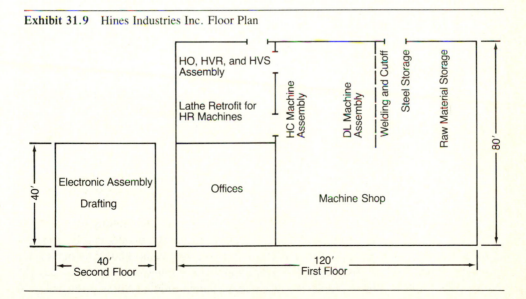

for shipping machines, and storage of concrete bases for machines. Both buildings are quite crowded and thought has been given to the need for additional space. Unfortunately, the present buildings that are available or being built in the area are not big enough to house all of Hines's activities in one area.

The production area uses general-purpose machines for the fabrication work. Most of the machinery was purchased used at auctions at very favorable prices. Later these machines were reworked by Hines to bring them up to the standards required. Some have been converted to numerical control using the microprocessors which Hines produces. The production equipment includes four lathes, two horizontal milling machines, six vertical milling machines, one jig borer, one radial arm drilling machine, one cylindrical ID/OD grinder, one cylindrical ID grinder, one face grinder, a Burgemaster machining center which is being retrofit for numerical control (NC), and a lathe retrofit to CNC. Hines makes many of its own parts and does the mechanical and electrical assembly work. Electronics assembly, including the building of microprocessors, is done on the second floor of the main building, which also includes mechanical drafting.

One of the unique features of the machines produced by Hines is the use of a precision-formed concrete base to provide the mass needed to support and dampen the balancing machines. These concrete bases are purchased locally from a company which uses the forms which were designed and built by Hines. Delivery time on the bases is a week so that it is not necessary to have many of the bulky units in stock.

All machines are thoroughly tested at Hines using customer parts before they are shipped. Len Salenbien is often involved in the testing if trouble is encountered. An automotive-aftermarket-type machine such as the HC takes about two days to assemble and test if all of the parts are available. Hines also trains the customer's maintenance men at the Hines plant so that little field repairs by Hines are required.

Purchasing of standard parts from vendors is the responsibility of Dave Freed who has been with Hines since August 1983. He worked as a refrigeration contractor until three years ago when he was injured while water skiing. He subsequently took training on computers at Washtenaw Community College before joining Hines.

Dave gets verbal or written lists of materials required from seven or eight people who keep track of their own stock and determine what they need. These people and their areas of responsibility are as follows:

- Fran Longnecker—crankshaft machines
- Willie Woods—shop materials and supplies
- Gary Kwiecinski—industrial machines, skidding, and shipping
- Dave Bloom (part-time)—industrial machines
- Keith Kwiecinski—painting
- Larry Ketola—special tooling and special parts for each machine
- Kay Lamay (Doug Case's employee)—electronics

Dave orders all of his parts by telephone. No purchase orders are sent to vendors. Dave maintains a list of purchase orders by number on the computer, including all of the pertinent data on each order. Orders are placed by description of the part. No part numbers have been assigned by Hines and vendor part numbers are not used. Although Engineering is beginning to assign part numbers to mechanical parts required for the company's products, it has not yet been decided if company part numbers will be assigned to standard purchased parts. A bill of material is not generated for each machine although the company wants to do this. In fact, the company does not presently have a comprehensive part numbering system.

Dave does not know how many different parts are in the products but believes there are at least 1,000 purchased parts not counting internally manufactured parts. Partial inventories may be taken every six months or so. Parts are not actually counted but the quantity is estimated. There is no definite stockroom used but rather a series of stock locations by product assembly area. Parts may be stocked in more than one area. Sometimes parts are ordered a second time if an item is on back order. No production schedule is available.

Most of the parts Dave orders are available within a short time. Motors require a week and IC chips (integrated circuits) usually require a month. However, ICs could require four to six months if not in stock. Dave orders from vendors with whom Hines is on good financial terms, based upon price, first, and delivery, second. Quality is important on some items.

Dave believes the company is "moving away from chaos" but not fast enough. He describes the big upswing in business in December 1983 (Dana) like a "cobra trying to swallow a pig." Although everyone knows basically how they fit in, what their job is, and how they do it, they are not aware enough of the company's goals and objectives, Dave believes. Items seem to be ordered on an emergency basis half of the time.

The big upswing in business created some cash-flow problems although Gordon Hines believes the worst is over. Since May, Dave has been required to check the prices before ordering and he may be required to get approval for cash reasons. Sometimes he has ordered smaller quantities at a higher price in order to conserve cash. Sometimes he has delayed orders or challenged the size of orders. Sometimes, if a vendor required COD, Dave has had to find a new vendor, since Gordon has said no COD shipments will be accepted.

Gordon and Len sometimes disagree on product design and ordering. Dave feels caught in the middle. About half of the time Gordon discusses the issue directly with Dave, thus resolving it. Dave would like to see more formal planning. Purchase requisition forms are on order which presumably will be used for preapproval before Dave sees them. The forms will have two parts—one for accounting and one for purchasing. If the originator wants a copy, a Xerox copy will be made.

Dave gets a copy of the sales order information form partial release but is not sure why he gets it, since he cannot order even long-delivery items based on this information. The form is used primarily by Ken Cooper to order outside mechanical items he indicates.

Ken Cooper, whose responsibility is Materials Control, joined Hines in March 1984. He worked at Bal Tec for 13 years and was purchasing manager when he left. Prior to Bal Tec, he worked in the machine shop at Bendix for 20 years. Ken orders some material directly and gets his purchase order numbers from Dave Freed. He subcontracts some of the mechanical parts work to outside firms on a time-and-material basis.

Ken schedules the shop and is supposed to schedule electronics but Doug Case really does it. Ken keeps a cardex inventory system of common manufactured parts. Based upon this information, he initiates orders for parts through Machining and through outside suppliers. The lot size ordered is based on previous experience, with input from Willie Woods and Fran Longnecker. An inventory may be taken on individual items. Ken is trying to set up inventories by production area. He decides whether to make or buy an item.

Ken's goal is to get things running smoothly. He is getting shop costs by using the average actual hours secured from job tickets times $25 per hour, which includes burden. The actual cost of labor is about $7 per hour. If an item has not been made before, he estimates the cost based upon his previous experience. Ken is concerned that production seems to always be behind and is "playing catch-up." He believes the men are learning but are operators and not machinists in that they cannot do setups well. Only Willie Woods and Bob Boyce can do setups. There is not a formal training program. The last thing that gets made is customer tooling, which is what often creates the delays. He also believes more space may be needed soon now that the second Dana order has been received. Under ideal conditions, he estimates two to three Dana Machines, three HCs, and three HVRs or HOs could be assembled simultaneously if parts were available (maybe requiring multiple shifts) and if moves were carefully checked.

Ken describes the delivery commitment process in this way. Len Salenbien makes a tentative commitment to a salesperson who has a potential order. If and when the order is actually received, it may be different than originally described. Also, other orders may have been received subsequent to the tentative commitment and be loaded into the shop. Thus the delivery commitment is frequently a problem. On the average, it takes two weeks from the beginning of assembly until the product is shipped, but shipment could be delayed six to eight weeks because of production planning problems, inadequate pretesting of components, and delays in securing information and samples of customer parts for tooling fabrication.

Electronic Design

The Electronic Design activity is conducted by Ron Anderson who is 49 years old. Ron Anderson, who also worked for Gordon at Bal Tec, began working for Hines on a part-time basis but now is full-time. He has known Gordon personally for many years and began his work at Bal Tec as a consultant. He has a degree in electrical engineering and has specialized in electronic design. He had ten years' previous experience at the University of Illinois as director of electronics for the Chemistry Department, which involved developing specialized instrumentation. Ron tries to use standard techniques and approaches in designing the electronics for the products, so that common modules are used in the various models whenever possible. Ron is happiest when there is some new design to be developed and admits to being bored when things are too routine.

Accounting

Dean Purdy, who is 55 years old, was hired in late March 1984 as controller. Dean had previously worked for Fansteel for 17 years. His last position was controller of their V. R. Wesson Division plant at Ferndale, Michigan, which made tungsten carbide cutting tools. The Ferndale plant had 125 employees and 50,000 square feet of floor area. He also had previous experience with Midwest Machine Company and OEM for the auto industry. Thus Dean's background in the machining business fits well with Hines.

During his three months with Hines, Dean has learned the product line and internal workings of the company. He believes he has made progress in stabilizing the cash flow from receivables to payables. His personal priority is "to establish systems to do things in an orderly fashion" including inventory and production control and cost control.

The company presently uses two Altos computers, one with a 10-megabyte hard disk and one with 1-megabyte dual 8-inch floppy disks. The latter unit, together with a small 64K dual 4½-inch floppy disk computer, is used by Purchasing. Thought has been given to buying a Radio Shack 30-megabyte hard disk computer for additional applications including accounting. Such a computer would cost about $15,000 including software.

Because the equipment for the industrial market and Dana typically have a longer delivery cycle than other products, Hines offers these customers, after receiving their order, a 2–5 percent discount if the customer will make an initial 30 percent down payment and will pay the balance within ten days after delivery. Gordon Hines believes this policy gives the company a competitive advantage in addition to improving the cash flow.

Management

Gordon Hines began to draw a $40,000 per year salary in May 1984. Prior to that he was living off his proceeds from selling his Bal Tec stock. When asked how he spends his time at the company, he estimated the following: sales—20 percent, design—20 percent, general business—20 percent, production—25 percent, and new business planning—15 percent. Gordon expects Dean Purdy will pick up a major share of his general business activities which will free up some of Gordon's time to move into sales/design activities of other products or to develop new large accounts.

Gordon has also contemplated the need for a mechanical engineer who could handle design activities and manufacturing engineering activities. Such a person would be difficult to find and could be quite expensive in salary and relocation expenses. However, such a move would free Gordon from mechanical design activities, which do require a substantial amount of his time.

Gordon also would like to see all of the company's activities in a common location. He would continue to rent since he does not want to put scarce cash into "bricks and mortar." The location would need to be near the present location for the convenience of employees. The airport location is also convenient since Gordon shares an airplane with two other businessmen. Fortunately, the business which occupied the 3,200 square feet immediately adjoining Hines Industries is relocating to another part of the industrial park in July and Hines will be able to rent this space and combine it with the main plant area.

Gordon sees a strong growth potential for the company over the next two years barring another prolonged recession. He thinks fiscal 1985 should see $4 million-plus in sales with the following year increasing another 50 percent. His overall management priorities are to manage cash first and profits second. In his view the October through December 1984 period will set the stage for the following year.

Union Carbide of India Ltd.: The Bhopal Tragedy

▪ *Arthur Sharplin* ▪

December 2, 1984, began as a typical day in the central Indian city of Bhopal. Shoppers moved about the bustling, open-air market; here and there a customer haggled with a merchant. Beasts of burden, donkeys and oxen, pulled carts or carried ungainly bundles through the partly paved streets. Children played in the dirt. In the shadow of the Union Carbide pesticide plant, tens of thousands of India's poorest citizens milled about the shantytown they called home. Inside the plant, several hundred Indian workers and managers went about their duties, maintaining and operating the systems which produced the mildly toxic pesticide, Sevin. Most of the plant was shut down for maintenance and it was operating at far below capacity.

At about 11 o'clock that evening, one of the operators noticed that the pressure in a methyl isocyanate (MIC) storage tank read 10 pounds per square inch—four times normal. The operator was not concerned, thinking that the tank may have been pressurized with nitrogen by the previous shift. Around midnight several of the workers noticed that their eyes had begun to water and sting, a signal experience had taught them indicated an MIC leak. The leak, a small but continuous drip, was soon spotted. The operators were still not alarmed because minor leaks at the plant were quite common. It was time for tea and the crew retired to the company canteen, resolving to correct the problem afterwards.

By the time the workers returned, it was too late. The MIC tank pressure gauge was pegged. The leak had grown much larger and the entire area of the MIC tanks was enveloped in the choking fumes. The workers tried spraying water on the leak to break down the MIC. They sounded the alarm siren and summoned the fire brigade. As the futility of their efforts became apparent, most of the workers panicked and ran upwind—some scaling the chain-link and barbed-wire fence in their frantic race for survival.

By 1 o'clock, only a supervisor remained in the area. He stayed upwind, donning his oxygen breathing apparatus every few minutes to check the various gauges and sensors. By that time, the pressure in the MIC tank had forced open a relief valve and the untreated MIC vapor could be seen escaping from an atmospheric vent line 120 feet in the air.

The cloud of deadly white gas was carried by a southeasterly wind toward the Jal Prakash Nagar shanties, where some of India's poorest citizens lived. Because MIC is much heavier than air, it drifted downward. As the gaseous tentacles reached into the huts, there was panic and confusion. Many of the weak and elderly died where they lay. Many who made it into the streets were blinded. "It was like breathing flame," one survivor said. As word of the gas leak spread, many of Bhopal's affluent were able to flee in their cars. But the poor were left behind. When the gas reached the railroad station, word was sent out along the tracks and the incoming trains diverted, cutting off another means of escape.

Of Bhopal's total population of 1,000,000, an estimated 500,000 fled that night, most on foot. The surrounding towns were simply unprepared to accept the gasping and dying mass of people. Thousands waited outside hospitals for medical care. There was no certainty about how to treat the gas victims and general purpose medical supplies were in hopelessly short supply. Inside the hospitals and out, screams and cries filled the air. Food supplies were inadequate and people were afraid to drink the water, not knowing if it was contaminated.

During the second day, relief measures were better organized. Several hundred doctors and nurses from nearby hospitals were summoned to help medical personnel in Bhopal. Just disposing of the dead was a major problem. Mass cremation was necessary. Islamic victims, whose faith demands burial rather than cremation, were piled several deep in hurriedly dug graves. Bloated carcasses of cattle and dogs littered the city. There was fear of a cholera epidemic. Bhopal's mayor said, "I can say that I have seen chemical warfare. Everything so quiet. Goats, cats, whole families—father, mother, children—all lying silent and still. And every structure totally intact. I hope never again to see it."

By the third day, the city had begun to move toward stability, if not normalcy. The Union Carbide plant had been closed and locked. A decision was made to consume the 30 tons of MIC that remained by using it to make pesticide. Most of the 2,000 dead bodies had been disposed of, however inappropriately. The more than 100,000 injured were being treated as rapidly as the limited medical facilities would allow, although many simply sat in silence, blinded and maimed by an enemy they had never known well enough to fear. For these, doctors predict sterility, kidney and liver infections, tuberculosis, and brain damage. The potential for birth defects and other long-term effects are not yet known.

Company Background

Union Carbide's predecessor, the Ever-Ready Company (of Great Britain) Ltd., began manufacturing flashlight batteries in Calcutta in 1926. The division was incorporated as the Ever-Ready Company (India) Ltd. in 1934 and became a subsidiary of Union Carbide Corporation of New York. The name of the Indian company was changed to National Carbide (India) Ltd. in 1949 and to Union Carbide (India) Ltd. (UCIL) in 1959. The 1926 capacity of 40 million dry cell batteries per year was expanded to 767 million by the 1960s. In 1959, a factory was set up in India to manufacture the flashlights themselves.

By the 1980s, UCIL was involved in five product areas: batteries, carbon and metals, plastics, marine products, and agricultural chemicals. Exhibit 32.1 provides production statistics for UCIL products. The company eventually operated 14 plants at eight locations, including the headquarters operations in Calcutta. Union Carbide's petrochemical complex, established in Bombay in 1966, was India's first. In 1969, UCIL and its American parent reached an agreement with the government of India to set up a pesticide formulation plant at Bhopal. At first, intermediate chemicals were to be imported and only combined and packaged in India. From the first, however, the intention was to manufacture the intermediate products at the Bhopal plant.

UCIL began its marine products operation with two shrimping ships in 1971. The business is completely export oriented and now employs 15 deep-sea trawlers with processing facilities off the east and west coasts of India. The trawlers now harvest deep-sea lobsters in addition to shrimp.

In 1979, UCIL initiated a letter of intent to manufacture dry cell batteries in Nepal. Construction of an Rs. 18-million plant was begun in 1982.

UCIL's assets grew from Rs. 558 million in 1974 to Rs. 1,234 million in 1983. The *Economic Times* of India ranks UCIL number 21 in terms of sales among Indian com-

Exhibit 32.1 Production Statistics

Class of Goods	1982 Capacity	1975	1976	1977	1978	1979	1980	1981	1982
Batteries (millions of pieces)	767	339.0	354.5	363.3	430.3	460.3	458.8	411.3	512.2
Flashlight Cases (millions of pieces)	7.5	3.8	3.3	5.0	5.7	6.4	6.9	7.4	6.7
Arc Carbons (millions of pieces)	9.0	6.1	6.4	6.3	6.1	6.2	6.7	7.0	7.0
Industrial Carbon Electrodes and Shapes (millions of pieces)	2.5	0.5	0.3	0.5	0.2	0.5	0.3	0.5	0.5
Photoengravers' Plates/Strips for Printing (tonnes*)	1,200	440.0	511.0	476.0	506.0	469.0	399.0	431.0	478.0
Stellite Castings, Head Facings, and Tube Rods (tonnes)	150	4.4	10.0	13.7	18.2	15.8	14.5	16.4	12.7
Electrolytic Manganese Dioxide (tonnes)	13,600	11,707	11,563	11,783	8,069	8,511	7,550	6,865	6,331
Polyethylene (tonnes)	20,000	17,151	18,055	15,337	12,059	16,324	19,198	19,928	17,290
MIC-based Pesticides (tonnes)	5,000	—	—	321	367	1,496	1,542	2,704	2,308
Marine Products (tonnes)	5,500	248	420	607	731	648	601	642	649

*1 tonne = 2,240 lbs.

Source: The Stock Exchange Foundation, Bombay, India. *The Stock Exchange Official Directory*, Vol. XVII/29, July 18, 1983.

panies. Union Carbide Corporation of America owns 50.9 percent of UCIL's stock and Indian citizens and companies own the remainder. Since 1967 the chairman of the board of UCIL has been an Indian and foreign membership on the Board of Directors has been limited to four. One expert on Indian industry affairs said, "Though the foreigners on the board are down to four from six in previous years, they continue to hold sway over the affairs of the company."

The Agricultural Products Division of UCIL was started in 1966 with only an office in Bombay. Agreement was reached with the Indian government in 1969 to set up a pesticide plant at Bhopal. Land was rented to UCIL for about $40 per acre per year. The initial investment was small, only $1 million, and the process was simple. Concentrated Sevin powder was imported from the U.S.A., diluted with nontoxic powder, packaged, and sold. Eventually the investment grew to exceed $25 million and the constituents of Sevin, alpha-naphthol—a brown granular material—and the gas MIC, were made at the plant. The insecticide Temik, which also used MIC as a constituent, was made in small quantities at Bhopal.

Operations at Bhopal

On the surface, the UCIL insecticide factory is a typical process plant. A wide diversity of storage tanks, hoppers, and reactors are connected by pipes. There are many pumps and valves and a number of tall vent lines and ducts. Ponds and pits are used for waste treatment. Several railway spur lines run through the plant. Exhibit 32.2 is a diagram of the Union Carbide pesticide factory at Bhopal.

Sevin is made through a controlled chemical reaction involving alpha-naphthol and MIC. When plans were first made to begin production of alpha-naphthol at Bhopal in

Exhibit 32.2   Union Carbide (India) Ltd.

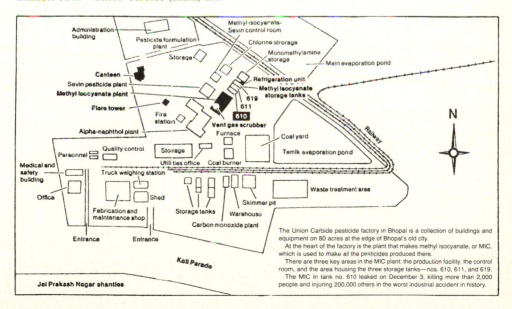

The Union Carbide pesticide factory in Bhopal is a collection of buildings and equipment on 80 acres at the edge of Bhopal's old city.

At the heart of the factory is the plant that makes methyl isocyanate, or MIC, which is used to make all the pesticides produced there.

There are three key areas in the MIC plant: the production facility, the control room, and the area housing the three storage tanks—nos. 610, 611, and 619.

The MIC in tank no. 610 leaked on December 3, killing more than 2,000 people and injuring 200,000 others in the worst industrial accident in history.

1971, a pilot plant was set up to manufacture the product. Because the pilot plant was successful, a full-size alpha-naphthol plant (in fact, the world's largest) was constructed and placed in operation in 1977. Mr. V. P. Gokhale, Managing Director of UCIL, called the alpha-naphthol plant a "very large mistake," but he said the company was forced to build it to keep its operating license from the Indian government.

In the meantime, work had begun on the ill-fated MIC plant. But even before the MIC plant was finished in 1979, problems began to crop up with the alpha-naphthol plant, resulting in a shutdown for modifications in 1978. In February 1980, the MIC plant was placed into service. The alpha-naphthol plant continued in various stages of shutdown and partial operation through 1984. The Bhopal plant was designed to produce 5,000 tons per year of Sevin, but never operated near capacity.

Finance

Exhibits 32.3, 32.4, and 32.5 provide financial facts and figures for UCIL. Union Carbide Corporation U.S.A. holds 49.1 percent of UCIL's common shares. The remainder are publicly traded on the Bombay stock exchange. Most of these shares are held by about 24,000 individuals. However, a number of institutional investors, such as life insurance companies and pension funds, hold substantial blocks. The Indian government does not directly own any UCIL stock. During the months before the Bhopal disaster, the company's common stock hovered around Rs. 25, but dropped to a low of Rs. 15.8 on December 11, recovering only slightly in succeeding weeks.

In 1975, the United States Exim bank, in cooperation with First National Citibank of New York, agreed to grant loans of $2.5 million to buy equipment for the MIC project. Also, the Industrial Credit and Investment Corporation of India (ICICI) authorized a

Exhibit 32.3 Summary of Income Statements (Rs. 000, except per-share data)

	1982	1981	1980	1979	1978
Net Sales	2,075,282	1,854,214	1,615,926	1,449,664	1,111,244
Cost of goods sold	1,720,303	1,518,538	1,307,042	1,190,242	926,958
Operating expenses	136,834	115,550	103,318	83,501	54,592
Profit from operations	218,145	220,126	205,566	175,921	129,694
Other income	27,426	26,955	23,528	13,685	10,187
Profit from operations plus other income	245,571	247,081	229,094	189,606	139,881
Interest expense	57,082	30,950	31,468	19,871	15,131
Depreciation expense	41,614	40,913	36,524	32,016	33,340
Earnings before taxes	146,875	175,218	161,102	137,719	91,410
Provisions for taxes	50,200	80,300	80,000	73,000	41,000
Net earnings	96,675	94,918	81,102	64,719	50,410
Earnings per share	2.95	2.91	2.49	2.98	2.32
Earnings as percent of price	11.73	10.96	10.20	11.46	8.97
Cash dividends per share	1.50	1.50	1.40	1.60	1.60

Average conversion rate for 1978–1982, $1 = Rs. 8.50; for 1985, $1 = Rs. 13.00.

Exhibit 32.4   Summary of Balance Sheets (Rs. 000)

			December 25		
	1982	1981	1980	1979	1978
Assets					
Current assets:					
Cash	52,285	52,173	56,589	53,026	94,482
Receivables	375,672	244,158	169,015	121,718	78,974
Inventories	327,317	368,606	311,612	292,935	231,945
Other current assets	6,088	9,230	9,277	11,237	12,738
Total current assets	761,362	674,167	546,493	478,916	418,139
Net fixed assets	449,546	393,516	405,890	401,422	389,252
Miscellaneous assets	21	21	57	57	57
Intangible assets	3,000	3,000	3,000	3,000	3,000
Total assets	1,213,929	1,070,704	955,440	883,395	810,448
Liabilities and Owners' Equity					
Current liabilities:					
Accounts payable and accruals	530,641	390,990	341,956	320,942	312,116
Provision for taxes	57,739	63,266	60,216	49,000	38,799
Total current debt	588,380	454,256	402,172	369,942	350,915
Long-term liabilities:					
Debentures	29,340	54,823	31,315	20,300	—
Long-term loans	20,836	34,049	40,420	46,306	33,440
Total long-term debt	50,176	88,872	71,735	66,606	33,440
Owners' equity:					
Common stock	325,830	325,830	325,830	217,220	217,220
Retained earnings and surplus	249,543	201,746	155,703	229,627	208,873
Total owners' equity	575,373	527,576	481,533	446,847	426,093
Total liabilities and owners' equity	1,213,929	1,070,704	955,440	883,395	810,448

Rs. 21.5-million loan, part of which was drawn in 1980. Finally, long-term loans were provided by at least seven Indian insurance companies. Some of these loans were guaranteed by the State Bank of India.

The Bhopal facility was designed to produce 5,000 tons of Sevin a year. Profits of several million dollars were predicted by 1984. Several factors kept these expectations from being realized. First, an economic recession made farmers more cost-conscious and caused them to search for less-expensive alternatives to Sevin. Second, a large number of small-scale producers were able to undersell the company because they were exempt from excise and sales taxes. Finally, a new generation of low-cost pesticides was becoming available. With sales collapsing, the Bhopal plant became a money loser in 1981. The prediction for 1984 was for a loss of $4 million based on 1,000 tons of output, one-fifth of capacity.

To forestall what may have seemed inevitable economic failure, extensive cost-cutting efforts were carried out. The staff at the MIC plant was cut from 12 operators on a shift to 6. The maintenance team was reduced in size. Job-entrance requirements were lowered

Exhibit 32.5   Summary of Common Stock Issues

Year	Paid-Up Common Stock			Remarks
	Number of Shares	Paid-Up Per-Share Rs.	Total Amount Rs.	
1959–1960	2,800,000	10	28,000,000	800,000 right shares issued at a premium of Rs. 2.50 per share in the proportion 2:5.
1964	3,640,000	10	36,400,000	840,000 right shares issued at a premium of Rs. 4 per share in the proportion 3:10.
1965	4,095,000	10	40,950,000	455,000 bonus shares issued in the proportion 1:8.
1968	8,190,000	10	81,900,000	2,047,500 right shares issued at par in the proportion 1:2. 2,047,500 bonus shares issued in the proportion 1:2.
1970	12,285,000	10	122,850,000	4,095,000 bonus shares issued in the proportion 1:2.
1974	18,427,500	10	184,275,000	6,142,500 bonus shares issued in the proportion 1:2.
1978	21,722,000	10	217,220,000	3,294,500 shares issued at a premium of Rs. 6 per share to resident Indian shareholders, the company's employees, and financial institutions.
1980	32,583,000	10	325,830,000	10,861,000 bonus shares issued in the proportion 1:2.

and some training programs eliminated. Some jobs which had previously required college science degrees were filled by high school graduates. In a number of instances, faulty safety devices remained unrepaired for weeks. Because a refrigeration unit, designed to keep the methyl isocyanate cool, continued to malfunction, it was shut down. Though instrumentation technology advanced at Union Carbide's other pesticide plants, the innovations were only partly adopted at Bhopal.

Personnel

Until 1982, a cadre of American managers and technicians worked at the Bhopal plant. The Americans were licensed by the Indian government only for fixed periods. While in India they were expected to train Indian replacements. From 1982 onward, no American worked at Bhopal. While major decisions, such as approval of the annual budget, were cleared with Union Carbide USA, day-to-day details such as staffing and maintenance were left to the Indian officials.

In general, the engineers at the Bhopal plant were among India's elite. Most new engineers were recruited from the prestigious Indian Institutes of Technology and paid wages comparable with the best offered in Indian industry. Successful applicants for engineering jobs with UCIL were provided two years of training before being certified for unsupervised duty.

Until the late seventies, only first-class science graduates or persons with a diploma in engineering were employed as operators at Bhopal. New hires were given six months of theoretical instruction followed by on-the-job training. As cost-cutting efforts proceeded in the eighties, standards were lowered significantly. Some operators with only a high school diploma were employed and training was much less rigorous than before. In addition, the number of operators on a shift was reduced by about half and many supervisory positions were eliminated.

The Indian managers developed strong ties with the local political establishment. A former police chief became the plant's security contractor, and a local political party boss got the job as company lawyer. *Newsweek* reports that a luxurious guest house was maintained and lavish parties thrown there for local dignitaries.

In general, wages at the Bhopal plant were well above those available in domestic firms. A janitor, for example, earned Rs. 1,000 per month compared to less than Rs. 500 elsewhere. Still, as prospects continued downward after 1981, a number of senior managers and the best among the plant's junior executives began to abandon ship. The total work force at the plant dropped from a high of about 1,500 to 950. This reduction was accomplished through attrition, with those having the best job prospects tending to leave first.

Marketing

The population of India is over 700 million persons, while its land area is about one-third that of the United States. Three-fourths of India's people depend on agriculture for a livelihood. Fewer than one-third are literate. Modern communications and transportation facilities connect the major cities, but the hundreds of villages are largely untouched by twentieth-century technology. English tends to be at least a second language for most Indian professionals but not for ordinary Indians. There are 16 official languages in the country. The most common official language, and the one supported by the Indian central government, is Hindi, which is dominant in 5 of India's 21 states. Near the borders of the various states, India's working classes speak any of hundreds of dialects, often unintelligible to citizens just miles away.

During 1984, a government program spread TV relay stations at the rate of more than one each day, with a result that 80 percent of the population was within the range of a television transmitter by the end of the year. Still, few rural citizens have access to television receivers.

India's farmers offer at best a challenging target market. They are mostly poor, eking out a living from small tracts of land. They have little more than subsistence incomes and are reluctant to invest what they have in such modern innovations as pesticides. They are generally ignorant of the right methods of application and, given their linguistic diversity and technological isolation, are quite hard to educate. UCIL has used billboards and wall posters as well as newspaper and radio advertising.

Pesticide sales are highly dependent on agricultural activity from year to year. In years of drought, like 1980 and 1982, UCIL's pesticide sales have suffered severe setbacks. In 1981 abundant rains helped spur pesticide sales.

India has a very extensive network of railways. The total track mileage in India is second only to the U.S.S.R. The road and highway system crisscrosses the areas in between railway lines. The railway system is especially significant to UCIL's pesticide operation because Bhopal lies near the junction of the main east-west and north-south tracks in India. Bhopal is also just south of the vast Indo-Gangetic plain, the richest farming area in India. Much of UCIL's pesticide is marketed through government agricultural retailing offices which sell seed, fertilizers, and pesticides. An Indian familiar with the agricultural economy remarked, "Overall, physical distribution of pesticides is not too monumental a task. Getting farmers to use them and teaching them how are the real problems."

Prospects for the Future

The government of India has canceled the license issued to the Bhopal plant, clearing the way for the plant's dismantlement. The likelihood that this would happen provoked a Bhopal leader to remark, "We've lost 2,000 lives, now must we lose 2,000 jobs?"

Manslaughter and other charges have been filed against UCIL executives. And Union Carbide USA Chairman Warren Anderson was briefly detained by Indian officials. Still, the companies continue to enjoy good relations with the Indian government. Many leading citizens and institutions have a financial interest in UCIL. And, except for the Bhopal incident, Union Carbide has an excellent safety record in India.

Warren Anderson has said: "The name of the game is not to nail me to the wall but to provide for the victims of the diaster." Union Carbide USA has begun construction of a hospital to provide treatment to the Bhopal victims. The company has also contributed at least $2 million to a victims' relief fund. Finally, plans have been made for a new plant at Bhopal, one which does not use poisonous inputs and which will provide employment to the workers displaced by the destruction of the Sevin plant.

Union Carbide USA faces lawsuits in amounts far exceeding the company's net worth. A dozen or more American attorneys signed up thousands of Bhopal victims and relatives of victims and filed lawsuits in America purporting to represent them. The Attorney General of India has vowed to sue Union Carbide in an American court, seeking compensation in accordance with American standards. Union Carbide opposes trying the lawsuits in U.S. courts. The company clearly will benefit from Indian trials, where punitive damages are almost never allowed and wrongful death judgments often amount to only a few thousand rupees.

By March 1985, the streets of Bhopal were bustling again. There were cars, cattle, and crowds of people. But everywhere there were reminders of the horror. Many wore dark glasses and covered their faces with shrouds to protect their injured eyes from the sunlight or to keep others from seeing their blindness. At the city's main police station, women and children continued to seek help, anything to help piece together their shattered lives. Vegetables shriveled by the poisonous gas were putting forth green shoots here and there. Occasionally, someone still fell sick from eating fish contaminated by MIC.

In the modernistic masonry-and-glass headquarters in Danbury, Connecticut, Union Carbide officials looked out on the beautiful Connecticut countryside and wondered how best to manage the company's public affairs and how to grapple with the needs in India. Half a world away, in spatial as well as philosophical distance, the poor of Jal Prakash Nagar, now poorer than ever, looked out from their shanties on dusty streets and pondered quite differents questions: From where will tomorrow's food come? How long will the pain inside and the dimming of vision last? And, just as importantly, what source of wealth will replace the Union Carbide plant? And how long will it be before its effects are felt?

References

"Bhopal" (and other related articles). *Chemical and Engineering News*, February 11, 1985, pp. 3, 14–65.

"The Bhopal Disaster" (and other related articles). *The New York Times*, January 28, 30, 31, February 3, 1985.

"Carbide's Anderson Explains Post-Bhopal Strategy." *Chemical and Engineering News*, January 21, 1985, pp. 9–15.

"City of Death" (and other related articles). *India Today*, December 31, 1984, pp. 4–25.

"Gassed" (and other related articles). *The Week*, December 16, 1984, pp. 15–27.

"India's Night of Death" (and other related articles). *Time*, December 17, 1984, pp. 22–31.

"It Was Like Breathing Fire . . ." (and other related articles). *Newsweek*, December 17, 1984, pp. 26–32.

The Stock Exchange Foundation, Bombay, India. *The Stock Exchange Official Directory*, Vol. XVII/29, July 18, 1983.

"Union Carbide Fights for Its Life." *Business Week*, December 24, 1984, pp. 52–57.

"Whose Life Is It Anyway? (and other related articles). *The Illustrated Weekly of India*, December 30, 1984, pp. 6–17.

A number of articles from *The New York Times*, *The Wall Street Journal*, and the Indian newspapers *India Abroad*, *The Indian Express*, *The Financial Express*, *The Times of India*, *The Economic Times*, and *The Hindustan Times*.

A New Version of Pac-Man: The Bendix-Martin Marietta Acquisition Attempt

▪ *Benjamin M. Oviatt and Alan D. Bauerschmidt* ▪

Bendix Corporation had been poised for a major new business acquisition for over a year and a half, and speculation in the business community over what firm would be its target had continued through the summer of 1982. William Agee, 44, the chairman and chief executive officer of Bendix, encouraged the guessing game by indicating only that his firm was looking at candidates possessing sophisticated technology. Bendix was already considered a high-tech firm with 33 percent of its $4.4 billion sales coming from aerospace and electronics during 1981. But Agee seemed aimed at lessening Bendix's dependence on the unhealthy U.S. automotive industry—49 percent of 1981 sales.

The speculation about Bendix's acquisition plan continued until August 24 when the price of the common shares of the Martin Marietta Corporation rose $2.50, and Wall Street rumors indicated that Mr. Agee had found his target. The next day Bendix Corporation announced an offer of $1.5 billion of cash and stock to acquire Martin Marietta, a diversified manufacturing enterprise. The directors and managers of Martin Marietta valued their independence and responded with their own attempt to acquire Bendix. This unusual move, actually aimed at avoiding acquisition entirely, was named the "Pac-Man Defense" because each company was trying to gobble up the other's shares and gain control first. And it ignited one of the most complex acquisition battles in history.

The battle highlighted several unsettling questions concerning U.S. business practices. Some observers found the battle to be a disgusting waste of resources, driven only by the egos of the participants, and involving little thought to corporate or business strategy. Others believed it was an unfortunate, but inevitable, part of the U.S. capitalistic system. Still others said a mismanaged economy made such acquisition activity necessary. Mr. Agee made a strong argument that growth through acquisitions had benefited his firm greatly. However, opponents argued that Bendix's vast liquid assets could be more beneficially invested in internal growth.

An important side issue in the fray involved Mary Cunningham, the developer of Bendix's strategic plan. *Fortune* magazine reported that Ms. Cunningham, 30, resigned from Bendix in late 1980 because of prurient speculations about the means by which she rose in only a year and a half from Harvard Business School graduate to vice-president for strategic planning and close adviser to Mr. Agee. Within four months after her resignation, and after sorting through numerous job offers, Ms. Cunningham joined Joseph E. Seagram and Sons Inc. as vice-president for strategic planning with an annual salary reportedly exceeding $100,000. Later she and Mr. Agee married, and the devoutly Catholic Ms. Cunningham and her husband sought annulments of their previous marriages. She became a close adviser to her husband during his attempt to acquire Martin Marietta, but many participants in the negotiations resented her presence and advice, pointing out that

---

This case portrays neither effective nor ineffective handling of an administrative situation. Rather it is intended to be used as the basis for classroom discussion.

she was an employee of Seagram, not Bendix. Ms. Cunningham was quoted by the *Washington Post* as arguing that she was a continuing victim of sexist attitudes, and she saw herself as knowledgeable adviser simply bringing her strategic plan for Bendix Corporation to fruition.

Mary Cunningham

The previously mentioned *Fortune* articles provided some details of Mary Cunningham's background. She was reported to have been raised in Hanover, New Hampshire, the fourth of five children. When she was six years old, she said she took an I.Q. test that revealed she was a genius with a score of over 160. Her parents divorced when she was five, and she was raised by her mother and a Catholic priest who was curate of the local church and who later became a chaplain at Dartmouth College. Ms. Cunningham believes this platonic relationship between her mother and their priest was misunderstood in the community at that time.

Ms. Cunningham attended Wellesley College in Massachusetts, and the *Fortune* articles indicated that when she was a senior she courted a black man, eleven years older than she, who was attending the Harvard Business School. They were married within a year and moved to New York, where she worked for a year as a paralegal and for three years as a junior officer at the Chase Manhattan Bank. She was the youngest assistant treasurer in the history of the bank. Ms. Cunningham has acknowledged that she and her husband at the time "were much more focused on the message we were sending to society than our marriage." After she began commuting to the Harvard Business School in 1977, their marriage began to dissolve and they were soon separated. At Harvard she built an excellent academic record which won the admiration of her fellow students, although they saw her as making few friends and somewhat calculating and manipulative of associates.

In June 1979, after a three-hour interview with William Agee, she joined Bendix as Agee's executive assistant. In June 1980, she was promoted to vice-president for corporate and public affairs. Gossip about the relationship between Agee and Cunningham gained momentum during that summer, and their references to each other emphasized a close relationship. In August, Agee and his wife of 23 years abruptly divorced. Although Bendix employees complained that Agee was less accessible, Cunningham seemed to be constantly with him. They traveled together, and they stayed in the same two-bedroom suite at the Waldorf Towers. By September Cunningham had been promoted to vice-president for strategic planning. *Fortune* magazine indicated that to some people it seemed that Agee and Cunningham had to be having an affair; it seemed the only explanation for her rapid promotions. However, in private meetings with members of the board and top management, the two denied that there was an affair. Cunningham offered to resign at one point, but noted that it would seem to confirm the rumors, would send a frustrating signal to other potential female executives, and would seem to let rumor dictate decision making at Bendix. Then, at an employee assembly, Agee and Cunningham leaped into the public eye when Agee announced that Cunningham's promotions were justified, while admitting their "very, very close" friendship. A wave of publicity swept over the situation during September and October 1980. The public criticism damaged Cunningham's credibility within Bendix, and after some initial vacillation, both she and the Bendix board agreed that she should resign. Four months later Ms. Cunningham secured the position of vice-president of strategic planning at Seagram.

William Agee and the Bendix Corporation

As the *Fortune* articles indicted, that fall was an eventful time for Bendix Corporation. Not only was there publicity about Mary Cunningham, but Bendix President and Chief Operating Officer, William Panny resigned, apparently because of disagreements with Agee. At the same time Jerome Jacobson, Executive Vice-President for Strategic Planning, resigned, opening the strategic planning position for Mary Cunningham. A week later Bendix announced the sale of its Forest Products Division for $425 million and the desire to sell its 20 percent share of Asarco, a nonferrous metals mining and production operation. Eventually Asarco bought its own shares back from Bendix for about $336 million. A week after those announcements, Bendix unveiled the details of a major program of decentralization involving termination or transfer of almost one-third of the corporate staff.

Business Week and *Fortune* articles revealed certain aspects of William Agee's background and actions in the Bendix Corporation which helped in understanding the strategy of the firm. After graduating from the Harvard Business School in 1963, Agee took a position with Boise Cascade in his native Idaho. By 1967, at the age of 32, he was chief financial officer for Boise. When the real estate investments at the firm soured in 1969 and 1970, Agee says he went through a very difficult period in his life, and in 1972 W. Michael Blumenthal, then chairman of Bendix, hired him away. Four years later when Blumenthal joined the Carter administration, Agee became Bendix's chairman.

As the *Fortune* articles indicated, the atmosphere at Bendix began to change almost immediately. Agee removed the boardroom table and directors found themselves meeting in a circle. Some status symbols such as reserved parking and executive dining privileges were attenuated. Agee invited speakers such as Vernon Jordan and Gloria Steinem to address the Board and top management on controversial social topics. Agee served as co-chair of the National Business Council for the Equal Rights Amendment.

Mr. Agee and Mr. Panny also slowly began changing the businesses at Bendix. They turned around a large French subsidiary that made electrical and mechanical parts by selling substantial assets and cutting the work force. By 1978 Bendix businesses of forest products, machine tools, and auto parts were viewed as satisfactorily countercyclical. Also in 1978 Agee bought 20 percent of Asarco for $127.7 million, viewing it as a turnaround candidate with mineral resources which would quickly appreciate in value. *Fortune* reported he wanted to acquire the whole firm and to move into minerals generally, but Panny and others argued against it, wanting only a limited investment, a board seat, and an opportunity for a quick exit. In 1979 Agee sold a domestic mobile home subsidiary that had performed poorly, and acquired three other businesses.

Bendix served in the capacity of a "white knight" when in 1980 it acquired Warner & Swasey, a machine tool manufacturer, for $300 million in cash and convertible securities worth $83 per share, for shares with a book value of $45. However, the acquired company had $65 million in liquid assets, some $40 million of which Agee sold. Warner & Swasey was approximately equal in size to Bendix's own machine tool business, but the two made different products for different customers, and the combination became the second-largest business in that industry, topped only by Cincinnati-Milacron.

In 1978 Agee had talked of strengthening Bendix's forest products business. In fact, two of the acquisitions made in 1979 had been small wood products marketers. Bendix originally had acquired the forest products business in 1969 with the hope of successfully using Bendix's technological expertise in machine tools to achieve efficiencies unique to the lumber industry. But the effort had been a failure. By spring 1980, Agee was considering the sale of the division.

According to *Fortune* articles, Agee also indicated he might consider having the firm sell its Automotive Division—the original basic business of the company—if it did not measure up to expectations. Insiders were reported to be in agreement that the Automotive Division should be trimmed, and one plant had been sold. But Mr. Panny and others disagreed with Mr. Agee on the amount of trimming needed. The chief operating officer argued that the corporation should not leave a business it knew in order to acquire a business it did not know. In June 1980, Agee asked Cunningham and a staff of seven to prepare a report on Bendix's North American automotive operations. A three-volume study was prepared within 40 days. Bendix's managers resented the newcomer's report on their industry, discounted the value of its results, and objected to Cunningham's unwillingness to coordinate her investigation with them. Eventually, Mr. Agee's desire to emphasize the aerospace operation at the expense of the Automotive Division contributed to the resignation of Mr. Panny and Mr. Jacobson.

Fortune reported that the reorganization which Mr. Agee wanted was another issue which contributed to the resignations. The difference in Panny's measured pace of action and Agee's impatience for completion of tasks had always caused them some difficulties. Mr. Panny was particularly critical of the speed with which the chief executive officer wanted to create organizational decentralization. Within two weeks after the Panny and Jacobson resignations, Agee announced the reorganization.

Some people viewed the eventful September of 1980 as continuing evidence of Agee's lack of strategic thinking. They said that Agee's change of heart regarding the importance of minerals and forest products was a good example of this problem. When Agee said he was accumulating liquid assets through divestitures and was planning to use these assets for acquisitions, critics accused him of inconsistency in spending $265 million of his cash to repurchase 17 percent of Bendix's common stock. When Agee pointed to the $75 million in after-tax profit made on the Asarco sale and to twice that profit level from the sale of the Forest Products Division, the critics accused him of legerdemain with Bendix's assets. But Agee noted the 14 percent increase in Bendix's share price during two days in late September 1980—the month when several major actions were announced and when the Cunningham "affair" became public.

By 1981 the business press characterized Bendix as a one-man show. Former Bendix managers claimed Agee lacked a strategy for Bendix continued. But some outlines of a strategy seemed to emerge. Agee stressed publicly that Bendix would make investments in high technology. Company officials said that in 1981, R&D spending would be at least $100 million, up from $79.2 million in 1980, and an Advanced Technology Center was opened. In 1981 Agee made it clear that he was out for an acquisition involved in high technology. But he would not identify any target industries and the 1981 Annual Report provided only vague acquisition guidelines:

Small ventures to open up new opportunities. . . . Extensions of present businesses to improve market position, increase competitive effectiveness, and expand long range potential. . . . Major new businesses which are sound values in the areas where Bendix skills and marketing capabilities can be fully utilized.

Agee stressed that he was in no hurry. Indeed, the liquid assets which Bendix had accumulated in preparation for an acquisition contributed 17 percent of the company's profits in 1981. Then in September 1981 and again in March 1982, Bendix moved to acquire significant blocks of RCA stock until it owned 7.2 percent of all that company's outstanding shares. However, when the RCA chairman made it very clear that he did not approve of Mr. Agee's stock purchases, the Bendix chief retreated and agreed to buy no more RCA stock for the time being.

Pac-Man, Corporation Style

The press reported that by April of 1982, Mr. Agee had identified Martin Marietta as an acquistion target. *The Wall Street Journal* indicated that Martin Marietta was originally identified during Ms. Cunningham's tenure as Bendix's chief strategic planner. Mr. Agee seemed attracted by the synergies which might be achieved in a merger of Bendix's and Martin Marietta's aerospace divisions. Agee believed that some of their products and services were complementary and that some of Bendix's technology could be used by Martin Marietta. Agee seemed only interested in the Martin Marietta Aerospace Division, and it is generally believed that Agee planned to divest the other Martin Marietta divisions.

From April through July 1982, Bendix quietly acquired 4.5 percent of Martin Marietta's stock (once 5 percent of a firm is accumulated public disclosure is required by the SEC). Yet Bendix managers were apparently unaware that Martin Marietta closely followed movements of its own shares and had detected Bendix's accumulation. Martin Marietta managers could not mistake Agee's intention, and desiring to avoid a takeover, they quietly began arranging a $1-billion credit line to finance a defense.

During August the financial and stock markets suddenly experienced enormous changes as shown in Exhibits 33.1 and 33.2 and Agee decided to make his move. His friendly merger offers were rebuffed by Thomas Pownall, CEO of Martin Marietta, according to the September articles in the *Wall Street Journal*. Pownall was reported to be very leery of Mr. Agee's personality and methods; also the Board and top managers of Martin Marietta wanted very much to retain their independence. On August 25, 1982, Bendix offered $43 per share for up to 45 percent, or 15.8 million of the shares of Martin Marietta Corporation. Bendix anticipated exchanging .82 Bendix shares for each remaining Martin share in

The Bendix Corporation was number 86 on the *Fortune* 500 in 1982. Its automotive division (Fram, Autolite) supplied systems and components, especially brakes, friction materials, cooling fans, spark plugs, air cleaners, and other filters to foreign and domestic manufacturers of autos, light trucks, and heavy vehicles. The division also supplied these products to the automobile aftermarket. The Aerospace and Electronics Division provided products and services for commercial, military, space programs, and general aviation. The main products included brakes, wheels, radar, communication, controls, electric power, instruments, and electromechanical and hydraulic systems. Also Bendix produced electrical connectors, cables, meteorological equipment, and pollution monitoring equipment. Bendix's Industrial Division supplied the metalworking industry with machine tools and accessories.

Exhibit 33.1   The Dow Jones Averages

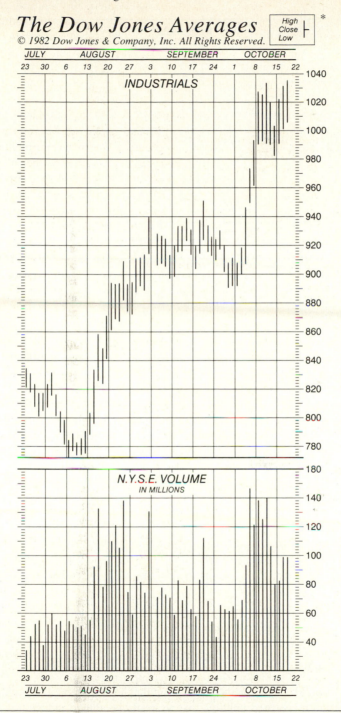

Source: *The Wall Street Journal*, October 21, 1982.

Exhibit 33.2   Prime Rate Changes

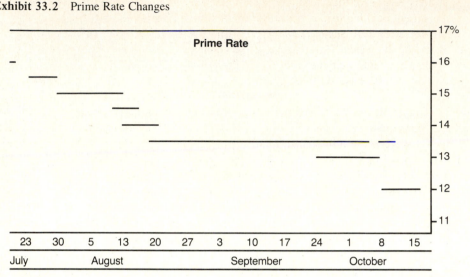

Note: On July 19 the prime rate declined from 16.5 percent to 16 percent. Prior to that date the prime rate had been 16.5 percent for most of the first half of 1982.

Source: *The Wall Street Journal*

a taxfree swap once Bendix took control, but the exact exchange rate was flexible. Bendix had $350 million available in cash and marketable securities, plus $675 million in short-term and revolving credit lines at more than 20 banks, for this purpose.

The $43 offer contained a requirement that promises to deliver the Martin shares (tenders) reach the Bendix agents by midnight, September 4, 1982 (the proration deadline). If, at that time, more than 15.8 million shares were "tendered" each investor would be allowed to sell to Bendix only a prorated amount of his Martin shares, so that a maximum of 15.8 million shares would be sold to Bendix at the offer price, $43. If less than 15.8 million shares were tendered by the proration deadline, Bendix might withdraw its offer and not purchase any Martin shares, or Bendix might extend its offer. The offer also had a withdrawal deadline of midnight, September 16, which meant that investors might change their mind and withdraw their tenders through that date. At that point Bendix could be expected to actually purchase the tendered shares at $43 and complete the transaction by midnight, September 23, when the offer expired. After Bendix acquired what it believed were sufficient shares to use as votes in a shareholder meeting, it could then take operating control of Martin Marietta.

Bendix also began litigation in federal court to block state laws which might hamper or thwart the acquisition. Later this erupted into a number of suits in at least seven state and federal courts, prompting one judge to condemn the actions as a "seven-ring circus." Meanwhile, the Justice Department and the Federal Trade Commission began their routine and antitrust investigations.

In the beginning Mr. Agee seemed convinced that he could obtain a genuinely friendly takeover, although it appeared unlikely that he would be able to induce this by offering a higher price because Bendix earnings per share would be diluted. However, by the next day it became known that Martin Marietta had retained Kidder, Peabody, and Company, an investment banking firm experienced in protecting clients from takeovers.

The day after that, Standard and Poor's bond rating service placed Bendix and Martin on their "credit watch" for possible rating changes. It was estimated that the merger would create a debt/equity ratio for the combined companies of 44 percent. However, the increased revenue base of the unified company could offset the undesirable increase in debt.

On August 30 the Martin Marietta Board of Directors unanimously rejected Bendix's offer as inadequate. They countered with an offer of $75 per share for just over 50 percent of Bendix stock (11.9 million of Bendix's total of 23.7 million shares). Martin would exchange some of its shares valued at $55 for each of the remaining Bendix shares. Martin arranged for a $1-billion credit line without saying how it would be repaid.

Mr. Pownall said that the merger would be better if led by Martin Marietta. This relatively new method of resisting hostile takeover attempts was dubbed the Pac-Man defense, since each company was trying simultaneously to swallow the other. This tactic had never been used in an acquisition of this size, and the legal conundrum of which company controls operations when two corporations own each other had never been settled. Taken to the limit, the tactic could cause both firms to be financially crippled in bidding fights for each others' shares.

The proration deadline for the Martin offer was September 9, the withdrawal deadline was September 21, and the offer expired on September 28. These later deadlines seemed to put Bendix ahead in the Pac-man race. However, Martin was headquartered in Maryland, where state law required a ten-day waiting period before a special meeting of stockholders could be called to vote on a change of directors. Under Delaware law, where Bendix was headquartered, Martin could take control of Bendix almost immediately after acquiring enough Bendix shares. Bendix representatives, however, said that its lawyers would take care of that problem.

The next day the Bendix Board of Directors rejected the Martin offer as inadequate. It

---

Martin Marietta was number 108 on the *Fortune* 500 in 1982. The firm's most important business was the Aerospace Division. It designed, developed, and produced space systems, launch vehicles, missiles, weapons, electronic and communications systems, and aircraft components. It was a primary systems manager and contractor for the Defense Department. In addition, the division was involved in solar energy research and data processing. The Cement Division produced portland and masonry cements for the construction industry. The Aggregates Division made crushed stone, sand, and gravel for the construction, agricultural, glass, and foundry industries. Martin Marietta Chemicals produced dyes, organic chemicals, concrete admixture, grout compounds, floor hardeners, magnesite refractories, and chemical magnesia. The Aluminum Division produced aluminum ingots, sheets, plates, extrusions, and forgings. It also produced ingredients used in the production of aluminum and titanium. In addition it managed a U.S. government ordnance plant in Tennessee for a contract fee.

reiterated its own offer for Martin, and announced the establishment of a "golden parachute" which would provide long-term contracts and financial protection for 27 top employees in case Bendix was acquired by another firm. Bendix representatives seemed surprised that Martin was able to raise the money so quickly to make their counteroffer.

The same day Martin threatened discussions with a "white knight"—a firm that would make a higher and acceptable offer to acquire Martin Marietta. Sometimes such an offer is used to get the original firm to increase its offer, and sometimes it is a genuine attempt to avoid takeover by the original firm.

On September 5, Bendix announced that it held tenders for 58 percent of Martin Marietta shares at the proration deadline. But experts said that Bendix might need to increase its offer to more than $43 per share for Martin in order to avoid too many withdrawals of its tenders. Bendix also announced a special meeting of Bendix stockholders for September 21 to gain approval of a change in the Bendix charter which would make a hostile acquisition of Bendix much more difficult. This was interpreted to mean that Bendix was truly concerned that the Maryland laws might thwart its takeover attempts.

On September 7, United Technologies entered the contest with an offer of $75 per share for 50.3 percent of Bendix stock and proposed a one-for-one stock swap for the remaining shares. Proration and withdrawal deadlines were both September 28, and the offer expired October 5. United insisted that Bendix terminate its offer for Martin and stop the September 21 stockholders meeting. United agreed to buy Bendix only if Martin failed in its own efforts. Martin and United agreed to split up the Bendix divisions between them if they were successful.

With this announcement Martin said it would not seek help from a white knight. With the aid of United, Martin had reduced its cost in taking over Bendix and had put Bendix under a constant threat of takeover unless Bendix dropped its own takeover efforts. If Bendix acquired Martin, it could then be acquired by United. Martin would then be "regurgitated" and Bendix would be split up between Martin and United. Reports in the press indicated the earnings per share of United Technologies would be reduced by its acquisition of Bendix and thus, its stock price declined.

On the same day Bendix increased its offer for Martin stock to $48 per share. Bendix's managers were not surprised that United had become involved, but they had expected the firm to make an offer for Martin. They were surprised by United's unusual offer for Ben-

---

United Technologies was number 20 in the *Fortune* 500 in 1982. The Power Division manufactured aircraft engines and spare parts (Pratt and Whitney), turbo chargers, compressors, steam turbines (Elliott), large electric motors (Ideal), and as a joint venture, it ran two electric power plants. The flight systems products included helicopters and propellers (Sikorsky), rocket motors, radar (Norden), and sophisticated electronic and electrical measurement and control systems for aircraft and spacecraft (Hamilton Standard). Building systems included air conditioning (Carrier), elevators, and escalators (Otis). Industrial products included automotive, electrical, and electronic parts and motors, diesel parts, and varied industrial and military machinery and instruments.

dix, and this surprise was also evident throughout the business community. By the following day, advisers of United Technologies reported that its earnings per share would not be reduced by the acquisition of Bendix.

Two days later it became known that Martin Marietta had written U.S. congressmen portraying Bendix managers as finance specialists without the ability to manage Martin's defense contracts, which were vital to the nation. The press later noted this as one of many small "dirty tricks" which the firms played on each other throughout the acquisition battle.

By September 10 it became known that Martin was having trouble getting the Bendix tenders it needed, partially because nearly 4.5 million of Bendix's shares, or 23 percent of the total shares outstanding, were deposited in an employee stock ownership plan (ESOP). These shares could only be withdrawn on the last day of the month, after 15 days' notice—too late for the acquisition effort. Martin, however, convinced ESOP trustee, Citibank, that it had a fiduciary responsibility to Bendix stockholders to submit its tenders to Martin, since the Martin offer was significantly above the current market price for Bendix shares. Thus, Martin obtained tenders for 63.5 percent (fully diluted) of Bendix's shares by the proration deadline.

Bendix angrily objected to Citibank's move and pointed to possible conflicts of interest—three managers of United Technologies served on the board of Citibank, and the Citibank president was on the United board. Bendix used Citibank in an effort to get the ESOP tenders out of Martin's hands. Citibank responded with the statement that it had merely maintained all available options for the ESOP, its participants, and Bendix.

Also on September 10, Bendix increased the number of Martin shares it sought to 18.5 million in order to gain 55 percent control. They also added First Boston, an investment banking firm, to their list of advisers. With Salomon Brothers Inc. already advising them, Bendix was estimated to be paying at least $7.2 million in fees during the acquisition effort. United and Martin's fees were only slightly lower.

By September 13 Martin had increased its credit line by $700 million. Two days later the Justice Department cleared the Martin Marietta and Bendix merger, but it continued its routine antitrust investigation of the other possible business combinations involved. On that same day United Technologies increased its offer to $85 per share for Bendix stock, but this price would only apply if a merger could be negotiated on a friendly basis. Meanwhile, rumors were flying of a new offer for Martin Marietta by a white knight. By SEC rules this would force a ten-day delay of any purchases of Martin stock by Bendix.

On September 16 a federal judge extended the withdrawal deadlines by ten days for each firm. The judge expressed apprehension that the Pac-Man tactics might cause the firms and their investors irrevocable damage, and he urged a negotiated agreement between the firms. Bendix, fearing its would miss its first chance to actually purchase tendered shares, successfully appealed the judge's ruling.

On September 17 Bendix rejected the new United offer, bought 19.3 million Martin shares, and offered $48 per share for up to 70 percent of Martin's shares. Bendix viewed this increased ownership of Martin as strengthening its legal position. It was speculated that Bendix might also try to gain ownership of 90 percent of Martin's stock, then ask for a court-ordered merger without the need to change Martin's Board of Directors. Experts believed the latter move might be beyond Bendix's financial means. There already were concerns that Bendix was experiencing severe financial strain in trying to consummate the Martin Marietta acquisition.

Martin Marietta was still relying on the difference in the Maryland and Delaware laws to give it the time it needed to win. However, if Bendix won its legal efforts to remove the ESOP shares from Martin's pool of tenders, Martin would probably have less than 50 percent of Bendix stock. Despite this, the United and Martin combination was still considered in a superior position. Although United must have been concerned that Bendix had already spent millions of its assets to buy Martin shares, some Wall Street sources indicated that United could force Bendix's shareholders to pay for this by reducing its offer below the present $75 per share. A lower offer might still be attractive to Bendix investors since the current share price was only about $54.

By September 20 Bendix owned 70 percent of Martin. Federal Judge Edelstein delayed the hearing on whether Citibank could tender the Bendix shares it held in trust. Bendix postponed the special stockholders meeting called to change the Bendix charter.

On the following day Bendix's representatives argued before Federal Judge Joseph Young that Martin should be required to hold a special stockholders meeting on September 30, at which time Bendix would vote its Martin stock to replace the present Martin Board of Directors with its own nominees. However, Judge Young indicated that he was inclined to deny the motion and to let the battle continue. At the same time he condemned the actions of both Martin and Bendix, saying that individual stockholders might be injured by the acquisition attempts. He urged a negotiated settlement.

Actually, the top managers of Bendix and Martin or their advisers had held discussions throughout the merger battle in an unsuccessful attempt to achieve an agreement. On September 21, Mr. Agee and his advisers, which included Mary Cunningham, traveled to the Maryland headquarters of Martin Marietta in a final attempt to reach an agreement. Agee offered to relieve Martin's management and directors of all potential legal liabilities and to buy the remaining 30 percent of Martin's stock for securities that Mr. Agee valued at $55 per share. Mr. Pownall reported that his top management and advisers did not believe it was possible to be relieved of legal liabilities by Bendix. Furthermore, they seemed to doubt that the securities which Mr. Agee offered were truly worth $55 per share. Thus, last-minute efforts to reach an agreement were a failure.

The *Wall Street Journal* reported (and Martin Marietta denied) that Ms. Cunningham's presence infuriated the Martin Marietta top management. It was further reported that her involvement was apparently a factor contributing to the desire of Martin Marietta to remain independent. Later Ms. Cunningham revealed to the press that she had been intensely involved in the decisions made concerning that merger throughout the month-long battle. She maintained that she had an important hand in shaping the Bendix strategy and in choosing Martin Marietta as an acquisition target, and therefore, she had unique expertise.

Also on September 21, Judge Edelstein denied Bendix's suit against Citibank; however, almost all of the ESOP tenders were withdrawn by Bendix employees before the midnight withdrawal deadline. This meant that Martin Marietta had only 42.4 percent of Bendix stock in its tender pool.

Some attorneys were surprised that the federal judges were reluctant to intervene in this merger battle. The results could have led to legal battles lasting years with little settled, while the firms continued to deplete their assets in attempts to control each other. It was even possible that a minority of independent stockholders would decide the final outcome. This was because state laws in Delaware and Maryland said that if the stock of a company is owned by a majority-controlled subsidiary, that stock could not be voted. If Bendix and Martin were deemed subsidiaries of each other, neither could vote the other's stock. It was assumed that there would then be a proxy contest between Bendix and Martin to solicit the shares of the minority of shareholders still eligible to vote.

By September 22 concern had increased that Bendix would be under severe financial strain to complete its acquisition of Martin. Earnings per share would be reduced and its debt might be tripled.

On that day Allied Corporation announced an offer of $85 for each of 13.1 million shares of the Bendix Corporation, and if this 51 percent of the outstanding shares of Bendix were tendered, Allied would offer 1.3 of its own shares plus an additional $27.50 in Allied securities (possibly convertible to common shares) for the remaining Bendix shares. This surprising announcement was a friendly takeover sought by Bendix. Under the terms of the proposal Mr. Agee would become a member of the board and president of the Allied Corporation, and would remain chief executive officer of Bendix. The announcement also included a separate agreement that Bendix would sell its Aerospace and Electronics group to Allied if another company topped Allied's bid for Bendix. This latter provision was designed to deny United Technologies and Martin Marietta the most attractive portion of Bendix if they did not stop their own acquisition efforts.

Although the announcement took the business world by surprise, it was revealed that Allied and Bendix had explored the possibilities of some sort of combination for almost two weeks. Mr. Agee agreed to the merger about midday on the 22nd and the public announcement was made on that date. However, the actual filing with the SEC did not occur until the 23rd because board approval and document preparation could not be completed on the 22nd. This single day of delay allowed Martin Marietta to purchase its first share of Bendix stock shortly after midnight on the 23rd. Had Bendix and Allied been able to file their merger plans with the SEC on the 22nd, SEC regulations would have forced Martin to wait at least ten days before purchasing Bendix stock.

Four outside directors at Bendix quit, apparently because they questioned the wisdom of the merger with Allied and the haste with which the decision was made.

Martin Marietta and United Technologies were initially uncertain how the proposed merger between Bendix and Allied would affect their own acquisition efforts and their

---

The Allied Corporation was number 49 in the *Fortune* 500 in 1982. It was a major producer of chemicals such as sulfuric acid and fluorocarbons used for industrial processes. Agricultural chemicals were also an important segment. Allied was an important manufacturer of man-made fibers, polyurethane plastics, and nylon plastics. Most of the oil and gas Allied produced was sold to companies for further processing, for fuel, or for transmission, but it used some for its own processes and its own retail sales (Texgas). The major electrical and electronic businesses were acquired in 1979 and 1981 (Eltra and Bunker Ramo) and supplied parts, motors, and batteries for a wide variety of industrial, automotive, marine, and communication uses. The business also supplied typesetting equipment (Mergenthaler Linotype), electronic and electrical connectors (including fiber optics, microwave, and cable), and electronic transaction systems for banks, insurance companies, and savings and loan associations. Fisher Scientific supplied scientific laboratory equipment. Allied was the world's largest producer of automotive seatbelts.

ownership of Bendix stock. Therefore, they did not immediately change their publicly stated intentions.

On September 23, Martin Marietta bought the 42.4 percent of Bendix stock in its tender pool and offered to continue buying Bendix shares at $75 each on a first-come, first-serve basis. By the end of the day Martin had acquired 46 percent of Bendix. At the same time, however, Allied and Martin were discussing terms for the exchange of Bendix and Martin stock. Also on that day Allied and Bendix continued to haggle over the details of the terms of their own agreement. United Technologies appeared to be waiting for guidance from its ally, Martin Marietta.

By September 24 all of the parties involved had settled their major disagreements. Agreement in principle was made that Allied and Bendix would merge, that there would be an exchange of Bendix and Martin Marietta stock between Allied and Martin Marietta, that Martin Marietta would retain its independence but would, among other things, accept Allied's ownership of 39 percent of its stock and the placement of two of Allied's top managers on Martin's board. Both Martin Marietta and United Technologies dropped their acquisition bids for Bendix.

On December 3, Allied announced that on December 21 Bendix would swap 19.1 million Martin shares (54 percent of all of Martin shares) for 11.9 million Bendix shares (50 percent) owned by Martin at the time. Bendix would keep 6.5 million shares of Martin, and the shares of its own stock obtained by Martin would be canceled. This would reduce the total number of outstanding Martin shares to 16.4 million, 39 percent of which Bendix would own. Allied had agreed that, after it completed acquisition of Bendix, it would not expand its Martin holdings for ten years without approval from the Martin board. Allied had also set out a schedule of prices at which Martin could buy back its stock from time to time over the ten-year period.

Bendix directors also declared the usual quarterly dividend. The 83 percent per-share payout would be made on December 20. Thus, Martin got a $9.9 million dividend the day before the swap.

On December 6 the Justice Department announced that it would not oppose the Allied-Bendix merger.

On January 31, 1983, stockholders gave final approval for Allied to acquire Bendix. Within one week the president of Bendix, Alonzo L. McDonald, Jr., 54, and Mr. Agee, Chief Executive Officer of Bendix, announced their resignations from Bendix and Allied. Both were under some pressure from Allied Chairman Edward L. Hennessy, Jr., to resign, and the move was not unexpected. Mr. Agee said that he would, however, be a candidate for reelection to Allied's board at the April 25th annual meeting. The *Wall Street Journal* reported that Mr. Agee was leaving his job with considerable resources. His shares of Bendix to be converted to Allied stock were valued at just under $4 million. He was also eligible for five years' pay at $825,004 per year.

Aftermath

Near the end of the month-long Pac-Man game and after its denouement, much was written in the business and popular press concerning this event. It seemed that everyone had an opinion. The opinions of a number of well-known observers appear in Exhibit 33.3. The opinions of the *Wall Street Journal* editorial staff are in Exhibit 33.4. It should be emphasized that a large portion of the attention of the news media was focused on the

Exhibit 33.3   Four-Way Takeover Fight Amuses Some Spectators, Disturbs Others

On Wall Street, they call it the Pac-Man Takeover.

Speculators and traders watch it like Pac-Man, too, on video terminals flashing news and stock prices that signal gainers and losers, and create and decimate large paper fortunes. Two big defense contractors, Bendix Corp. and Martin Marietta Corp., were trying to gobble each other up. Then United Technologies Corp. and later, Allied Corp., joined in, each apparently eager to swallow, in whole or in part, the juiciest and most vulnerable of the contenders.

For businessmen and others on the sidelines, the boardroom battles of the past few weeks at times have seemed amusing—but also disturbing. A steel company executive puts it this way: "Maybe there's something wrong with our system when these four companies can line up large amounts of money in order to purchase stock, when it doesn't help build one new factory, buy one more piece of equipment, or provide even one more new job.

"In fact, some consolidation will probably take place, eliminating some jobs—whereas we in the steel industry have lots of trouble with banks obtaining financing to modernize. We're trying to reindustrialize America, while these other companies want to deindustrialize America."

Many business people were willing to express themselves on the subject, and in talks with reporters for *The Wall Street Journal*, they did. A sampling of their views follows:

This takeover battle has the makings of a beautiful business school exercise. It puts me in mind of the phalarope syndrome—you know, the African bird that spends its entire life chasing its own tail. Does it really matter, and will it result in a more efficient operating unit? I doubt it.

Fred C. Yeager, Professor of Finance, School of Business and Administration, St. Louis University, St. Louis

You don't see these things in closely held companies when the president is spending his own money.

Mar Dillard, Chairman and President, Drillers Inc., Houston

It has all the drama and excitement of a good football game, which maybe is a good thing with the pro football players out on strike now. Allied Corp. kicked a 48-yard field goal with 15 seconds left on behalf of Bendix. I admire Martin Marietta for their spunk. They just simply refused to roll over and play dead. That's part of the drama. . . . I wouldn't characterize it as constructive or destructive, but consistent with free enterprise.

Joseph E. Hall, President and Chief Executive Officer, Flow General Inc., Philadelphia

It's a much easier path to buy a Bendix or a Martin Marietta than it is to create one. I assure you that the chief executives think the battle is for real. One or two of them will wish the battle hadn't happened. We are a very large shareholder in Allied. We own 507,000 shares of its preferred. We are delighted to see Allied get into the fight, because we are going to come out a winner no matter how you slice it.

Joseph S. Gaziano, President and Chief Executive Officer, Tyco Laboratories Inc., Exeter, N.H.

It's not a merger. It's a three-ring circus. If they're really concerned about America, they'd stop it right now. It's no good for the economy. It wrecks it. If I were in the banking system, I'd say no more (money) for conglomerations for one year.

Lee Iacocca, Chairman, Chrysler Corp., Detroit

I don't care what they do. Whatever it is, it won't do any good for the workers.

Douglas Fraser, President, United Auto Workers of America, Detroit

continued

Exhibit 33.3 *continued*

It's cheaper to buy than to make. I wouldn't accuse anyone of setting new standards of corporate statesmanship. (But) competition takes many forms, and competition is to be encouraged. It's a lot more fascinating than watching fluctuations in M1, M2, and M3.

Murray Weidenbaum, economist and former chairman of the Council of Economic Advisers, St. Louis

I frankly confess that I am confused and I'm an attorney. I do think the legal profession will be enhanced greatly by all this.

Nelson G. Harris, President and Chief Executive Officer, Tasty Baking Co., Philadelphia

"What do you tell your son to do when a bully picks on him in school? When somebody hits you, you react in kind. But sometimes these fights aren't productive, whether it's kids in school or corporate management. Shareholder and customer interest often isn't best served by takeover fights. To the extent that management allows itself to be distracted from its job, it's abdicating its responsibility. We managers need to keep our heads screwed on right. Sometimes our egos get in the way.

Cal Turner, Jr., President and Chief Executive Officer, Dollar General Corp., Chicago

What I can't understand is, are they doing it all with a straight face? Are they really serious? The frightening thing we're seeing in the last couple of years is everybody thinks the way to expand is to go out and buy a big company. From a corporate strategy (viewpoint), they're all nuts.

D. E. (Ned) Mundell, President and Chief Executive Officer, U.S. Leasing International Inc., San Francisco

What the hell are those (Bendix) directors thinking of? Why would they let management go out and attack a corporation like Martin Marietta?

William C. Norris, Chairman and Chief Executive Officer, Control Data Corp., Minneapolis

I think it's a shame. It's the kind of thing corporate America ought not to do because the poor stockholder is the one whose interest is being ignored in favor of the egos of directors and executives. And who the hell is running the show—the business of making brakes and aerospace equipment—while all this is going on? I think Martin Marietta has conducted itself well. They haven't dragged the Mary Cunningham business into it, and all of their actions have been taken in quiet dignity in defense of the corporation. I don't think anybody wants to be taken over by Bill Agee.

Robert W. Purcell, retired business consultant and former Bendix Corp. director, Detroit

A chief executive officer is just like anyone else. Once you start something, you don't like to be thwarted. Your personal ego gets caught up in the thing. Now Agee's fighting for his life. He bit off more than he can chew. I would have conducted myself differently if I were in Agee's shoes. But then, I don't have his ego. Or his money. It would be a lot better for Corporate America if this had never started, because it's made the group seem to be avaricious power-hunters.

Charles Haverty, President and Chief Executive Officer, Xonics Inc., Des Plaines, Ill.

One has the sense of capitalism gone mad. Has each of these companies had adequate time to consider what they're getting, the quality of assets, etc.? People are spending too much money too quickly without adequate thought.

Harvey Goldschmid, Professor of Law, Columbia University School of Law, New York

Frankly, we've seen so many of these in the last two years, they're becoming a bore. They're little wars. They're almost like Latin American revolutions. Unless you're one of the generals involved, it's hard to get interested.

Arthur D. Austin, Professor of Law, Case Western Reserve University Law School, Cleveland

continued

Exhibit 33.3 *continued*

Agee perceived a value in Martin Marietta, and the rest is a response to what he did. Martin Marietta should be complimented for its resolve. It strapped itself to the masthead during a hurricane. I don't think there's a moral question here. Business is business. People do the things they feel are in the best interest at the time.
Salim B. Lewis, Chief Executive Officer, S. B. Lewis & Co., New York

These aren't gunslingers or crapshooters. They are responsible businessmen. They're attempting to find value for their shareholders. In the meantime, of course, some of them are protecting themselves, too.
Edward I. O'Brien, President, Securities Industry Association, New York

Fifty percent of it's ego, and 50 percent of it's they probably believe they're doing a good job for their shareholders. (But) it's a waste of shareholders' money, and that's not right.
John Lemke, Secretary and counsel, Amalgamated Sugar Co., Ogden, Utah

I bet you Bill Agee and the rest of them haven't spent ten minutes thinking about running their companies, making better products or serving the public in the past two weeks. Who's minding the store? I have nothing but contempt for the speculators and manipulators. (Agee) started it all, and this whole idea of feathering his nest (with salary guarantees) whether Bendix wins or gets swallowed up, that's the most despicable thing yet. He's taking no risks.
David L. Lewis, Professor of Business History, University of Michigan Graduate School of Business and Administration, Ann Arbor.

Source: *The Wall Street Journal*, September 24, 1982, p. 37.

personalities involved and how these influenced the play of the game by the various firms. This influence is highlighted in the summaries drawn from press reports presented below.

Mr. Agee and Ms. Cunningham

Agee and Cunningham appear to have been the targets of most of the criticism generated by this merger contest. Their relative youth and brash style caused them to be considered outsiders in the business community. Their prominence and previous success in business in the state of Michigan, where business activity was generally poor at the time, may have caused some prejudice. Mr. Agee was accused of allowing his ego to dominate his business judgment in trying to build a large, high-tech, prestigious company through the acquisition of a tenaciously reluctant Martin Marietta. Observers said he misjudged the Martin managers' resolve and strength to resist and should have withdrawn when this became apparent. Ms. Cunningham was criticized for her lack of insight into the emotional reaction which her presence would cause among the opposing negotiators.

Prior to the announcement of his resignation, Mr. Agee implied that he was very pleased with the end result, although he acknowledged that the history of the month-long battle "isn't very pretty." He criticized other managers who had failed to strenghten their firms through acquisition, and accused them of ignoring shareholder value. He noted that share prices were depressed in mid-1982, and that Bendix and Martin Marietta had an opportunity for technological synergy. Agee accepted the label of portfolio manager and pointed to the dangers of diminishing demand in single-business, vertically integrated firms, such as existed in the auto and steel industry.

Exhibit 33.4   Review & Outlook: Pac-Man Economics

Everyone likes a good show, and the Bendix-Marietta-United Technologies-Allied shoot-out has been one of the best Wall Street has seen in years. The pace was fast. The stake-your-company risk-taking was bold and forceful. And the characters! Young Bill Agee and his beautiful wife Mary taking on Marietta's Tom Pownall, a man we're told who once arm-wrestled ex-footballer Jack Kemp to a draw at the cost of several torn ligaments; cagey old Harry Gray, whose United Technologies is the corporate equivalent of "Jaws," edging in to help Mr. Pownall avoid more torn ligaments; and finally Mr. Gray's estranged former associate, Ed Hennessy, maneuvering to gain mastery over Mr. Agee.

Bankers and arbitragers were more than casual bystanders. Then there was the Pac-Man question: When two companies swallow each other, what's left? A black hole? Double acute indigestion? One theorist suggests the little old lady in Dubuque, with 100 shares of the right company and enough stubbornness to resist the juicy offers, could have ended up controlling the whole conglomerate. More serious was the fear that the only winners would be the investment bankers, who collected very large fees.

But as the roundup of corporate opinion on the *Journal's* second front page last Friday made clear, some folks were not amused. A steel company executive said, "We're trying to industrialize America while other companies want to deindustrialize America."

We are deindustrializing America whether we like it or not and it may not be an altogether bad thing. Services account for a large and rising share of the gross national product. In manufacturing, the growth is in high-tech, high-value-added products for the most part. Yet the steel man has a point. Something seems amiss when highly talented executives of four companies that are not low-tech are committing their brains and company resources to corporate cannibalism. Did this Wall Street drama have any redeeming social value?

Perhaps it did, if you believe in morality plays. It may well be true that this whole thing came about because supercharged managerial egos were seeking self-expression, but that would only be part of the story, and not necessarily the most important part in an economic sense. Mr. Agee and his former strategist, Mary Cunningham, did not look toward acquisitions—as opposed to building new plants in Illinios—for no reason. Mr. Gray did not assemble his conglomerate because he loves the ups and downs of Otis elevators. Mr. Hennessy is not on the merger and acquisitions prowl for lack of imagination. They all are simply among that sizable number of executives who, in recent years, have consulted their computers and decided the best place to apply their cash and leverage—and maximize returns for their shareholders—was in the acquisition of existing assets.

In some cases this has involved deindustrializing, as the acquiring management closed old plants and devoted talents and energies to different kinds of enterprises better suited to the needs of consumers and the markets. That process is part of the adaptive and accommodative character of private industry.

But there obviously is something amiss in an economy where corporate assets look more attractive to the investment strategists of other corporations than they look to ordinary investors. The reasons why are fairly complex but inflation has been at the heart of the problem. Not only has it discouraged personal saving and thus stretched very thin the supply of capital, but it also has attracted the available supply of capital to high-yielding debt rather than equities. Corporate assets have been on the bargain counter for anyone who might be able to put them to more profitable use.

The interesting thing about the Bendix attempt, however, is that it proved to be far more difficult than some we were seeing a year or so ago. Martin Marietta did not turn out to be a sitting duck for a company with ready cash. Indeed, the whole pace of merger and acquisitions activity has slowed this year, despite the fact that corporations have been generating liquidity. And as anyone can see, the stock market—that is, the value of existing assets—has been rising. Martin Marietta was an attractive quest but Mr. Agee may have moved a bit too late.

Those who have been decrying the great tender offer fights should note the lesson. The urge to merge is merely one symptom of a mismanaged economy, and the roots of inflation lie with the likes of Lyndon Johnson and Richard Nixon, not with William Agee or Harry Gray. When the economic environment comes under control, our corporate chieftains will quite naturally start to vent their egos not in buying up old assets but in creating new ones.

Source: *The Wall Street Journal*, September 27, 1982, p. 22 (editorial page).

Exhibit 33.5 Daily Closing Stock Prices and Price-Earnings Ratios

Date		Bendix Price	P/E	Martin Marietta Price	P/E	United Technologies Price	P/E	Allied Price	P/E
Aug.	2	$48.75	9	$24.50	6	$42.375	5	$35.25	5
	3	49.875	9	24.375	6	42.25	5	35.25	5
	4	49.00	9	24.50	6	41.625	5	x33.875	4
	5	48.75	9	25.00	6	40.875	5	33.875	4
	6	48.625	9	24.875	6	39.875	5	33.625	4
	9	48.00	9	24.75	6	39.375	5	33.625	4
	10	47.75	9	24.625	6	39.375	5	32.00	4
	11	47.50	9	25.00	6	39.375	5	31.125	4
	12	47.75	9	24.50	6	39.625	5	31.00	4
	13	47.75	9	24.625	6	39.875	5	32.25	4
	16	48.00	9	25.50	6	39.875	5	32.25	4
	17	48.25	9	27.50	6	42.00	5	32.25	4
	18	49.00	9	25.625	6	43.125	5	32.125	4
	19	48.875	9	28.25	7	43.75	5	32.625	4
	20	50.25	9	30.625	7	45.50	6	33.25	4
	23	51.00	10	30.625	7	x46.50	6	34.625	4
	24	52.50	10	33.125	8	45.25	6	34.00	4
BC	25	50.00	9	39.25	9	46.00	6	34.75	4
	26	51.125	10	42.25	10	46.625	6	35.00	4
	27	54.375	10	41.00	10	47.25	6	34.00	4
MM	30	57.00	11	–		47.50	6	34.50	4
	31	56.125	11	x40.00	9	47.875	6	34.875	4
Sept.	1	53.00	10	39.875	9	47.25	6	34.25	4
	2	55.875	10	37.00	9	48.50	6	34.25	4
	3	x58.50	11	37.125	9	50.25	6	34.50	4
UT	7	56.50	11	36.125	8	47.375	6	34.875	4
	8	62.75	12	35.875	8	48.50	6	35.25	5
	9	61.00	11	35.625	8	48.875	6	36.00	5
	10	59.00	11	37.25	9	48.25	6	36.25	5
	13	59.25	11	33.625	8	48.625	6	36.00	5
	14	57.25	11	35.50	8	50.00	6	34.75	4
	15	59.75	11	35.625	8	49.25	6	34.625	4
	16	57.625	11	37.625	9	49.00	6	35.125	4
	17	54.125	10	46.00	11	48.625	6	34.75	4
	20	56.875	11	44.875	11	48.00	6	35.125	4
	21	54.25	10	43.875	10	48.75	6	35.625	5
AC	22	57.50	11	43.50	10	49.00	6	34.875	4
	23	–		–		49.00	6	–	
	24	–		–		48.50	6	–	
	27	74.25	14	35.125	8	48.00	6	32.125	4
	28	75.25	14	35.25	8	47.875	6	32.625	4
	29	73.75	14	36.625	9	47.00	6	31.375	4
	30	73.25	14	36.25	8	47.00	6	31.25	4
Oct.	4	72.125	13	37.375	9	46.00	6	30.625	4
	5	72.625	14	37.875	9	46.50	6	30.625	4
	6	73.625	14	38.00	9	48.75	6	32.00	4
	7	74.50	14	38.25	9	50.375	6	33.00	4
	8	74.75	14	39.25	9	50.375	6	34.00	4

x = ex dividend date.

– = trading of these shares halted because of imbalance of supply and demand or because of price discontinuity.

BC = Bendix announces its initial offer for Martin Marietta.

MM = Martin Marietta announces its initial offer for Bendix.

UT = United Technologies announces its initial offer for Bendix.

AC = Allied Corp. announces its initial offer for Bendix.

Source: *The Wall Street Journal*.

Exhibit 33.6   Consolidated Statements of Income
(millions of dollars except number of shares and per-share dollars)

| | Bendix Corporation September 30 | | | Martin Marietta December 31 | | |
	1982	1981	1980	1982	1981	1980
Net sales	$4,092	$4,393	$3,838	$3,527	$3,294	$2,619
Cost of Goods Sold	3,229	3,509	3,033	3,120	2,792	2,145
Selling, General and Administrative Expense	551	557	468	238	15	111
Noncash Expenses	108	75	81	96	265	133
Other Income	129	242	57	87	71	55
Total Income	333	494	313	160	293	285
Interest and financing charges	100	110	83	68	10	7
Domestic and foreign tax	95	179	95	1	83	90
Net Income before Extraordinary Item	138	205	135	91	200	188
Extraordinary Item	(5)	248	57	0	0	0
Net Income	133	453	192	91	200	188
Preferred Dividend	17	17	9	0	0	0
Net Income Applicable to Common Shares*	$ 133	$ 453	$ 192	$ 91	$ 200	$ 188
Number of Common Shares	22,907,000	24,482,000	24,952,000	31,397,890	37,099,456	37,364,662
Earnings Per Share	5.80	18.49	7.68	2.92	5.39	5.03
Dividends Per Share	3.32	3.00	2.84	1.92	1.80	1.55

*Bendix does not subtract preferred dividends from net income to compute earnings per share.

Mr. Hennessy

Hennessy and his advisers were criticized for acquiring Bendix with too little study. Mr. Hennessy, it was suspected, failed to look far enough beyond personal reasons for entering the Pac-Man game. An investment banker, noting that Allied had tried and failed at a few mergers in recent years, felt that they "needed to do a deal," so they would not be seen as a failure in this area. It was also speculated that Mr. Hennessy wanted revenge against his former boss, Harry Gray, CEO of United Technologies. From 1962 to 1979 he was the senior vice-president for finance and administration at United Technologies, and was considered a possible successor to Mr. Gray, but they disagreed often on business matters and their personal styles were very different. Mr. Hennessy was a devout Catholic and lived in a conservative and reserved manner. Mr. Gray was fond of motorcycles, travel, and had been married three times. Mr. Gray may have been close to firing Mr. Hennessy when the latter accepted the position of CEO at Allied in 1979.

Mr. Hennessy soon changed his new firm's name from Allied Chemical and began acquisitions aimed at diversifying away from chemicals. He indicated he was still shopping for new businesses with high technology when he found a good opportunity in Bendix. In his opinion Bendix's Aerospace and Electronics Division fit well with the Allied elec-

United Technologies December 31			Allied Corporation December 31			
1982	1981	1980	1982	1981		1980
$13,577	$13,668	$12,324	$6,167	$6,407		$5,519
10,790	10,817	9,698	4,743	4,802		4,095
1,674	1,475	1,231	376	198		115
256	367	473	263	336		319
139	97	75	89	21	45	
996	1,106	997	874	1,092		1,035
251	245	230	84	88		81
318	403	374	507	685		637
427	458	393	283	319		317
107	0	0	(11)	29		(28)
534	458	393	272	348		289
70	77	81	68	38		23
$ 464	$ 381	$ 312	$ 204	$ 310		$ 266
53,104,845	49,402,486	42,855,312	32,810,044	33,840,648		32,610,944
8.74	7.71	7.28	6.22	9.17		8.15
2.40	2.40	2.20	2.40	2.35		2.15

tronics businesses. In addition, the Bendix acquisition offered an opportunity to reduce the percentage of Allied's portfolio devoted to oil and gas and to vulnerable commodity products. Furthermore, Mr. Hennessy said that the acquisition would lower Allied's corporate tax rate by increasing domestic income. He admitted that it might seem odd to some that Allied should incur large debts to buy another business when Allied had very recently cut its own production and personnel. He said that the acquisition of Bendix was an investment in the future and was consistent with his increased spending on R&D in recent years. He promised to look for ways of reducing Allied's debt while preserving and creating jobs.

Mr. Hennessy also made it clear that, with a 39 percent ownership of Martin and two board seats, Martin Marietta would not be a passive investment for Allied.

Mr. Pownall

Mr. Thomas Pownall, 60, was CEO of a low-profile firm that had in the past stressed operations management, not portfolio management. He had only been CEO since April 1982, and Mr. J. Donald Rauth, 65, the immediate past CEO, was chairman at the time. Mr. Pownall had joined Martin Marietta in 1963. He had held several top positions for a

Exhibit 33.7   Consolidated Balance Sheets (millions of dollars)

	Bendix Corporation September 30			Martin Marietta December 31		
	1982	1981	1980	1982	1981	1980
Assets						
Current Assets:						
Cash and Marketable Securities	148	572	44	26	84	103
Accounts Receivable	576	622	648	361	292	334
Inventories	765	902	890	507	461	338
Prepaid Expenses, Other	39	43	71	44	47	24
Total Current Assets	1,528	2,139	1,653	938	884	799
Investments	1,347	98	34	92	67	53
Plant, Equipment, Land, Minerals, Net	776	780	706	1,659	1,439	1,078
Goodwill and Intangibles	93	89	91	59	60	61
Other	127	115	440	90	96	78
Total Assets	3,871	3,221	2,924	2,838	2,546	2,069
Liabilities and Owners' Equity						
Current Liabilities:						
Accounts Payable	387	370	411	297	251	219
Short-Term Borrowing and Current Long-Term Debt	585	104	143	79	14	4
Accrued liabilities	514	481	382	161	126	106
Other	2	211	24	159	74	123
Total Current Liabilities	1,488	1,166	960	696	465	452
Long-Term Debt and Capital Leases	832	520	549	1,235	360	163
Deferred Taxes	43	49	37	445	494	330
Other Liabilities	27	33	37	25	27	21
Preferred Stock	71	172	171	115	0	0
Common Equity:						
Stock*	107	97	115	41	41	27
Additional Paid-In Capital	141	43	47	220	222	221
Retained Earnings	1,166	1,145	1,012	1,066	1,034	915
Treasury Stock	(4)	(4)	(4)	(1,005)	(97)	(60)
Total Equity	1,481	1,453	1,341	437	1,200	1,103
Total Liabilities and Owners' Equity	3,871	3,221	2,924	2,838	2,546	2,069

*Par values: Bendix and United Technologies = $5; Martin Marietta and Allied = $1.

**Includes $893-million investment in Bendix Corporation and $301-million investment in Martin Marietta Corporation.

number of years in the Aerospace Division, and he served a short stint as executive vice-president of the corporation before his promotion to CEO. Neither Mr. Pownall nor Mr. Rauth were experienced with mergers, and Mr. Rauth shied from publicity. It is believed that they relied heavily on the advice of their consultants during the contest in September.

Mr. Pownall was described as urbane, aggressive, and extroverted, and he commanded respect from his employees. He was generally praised by the business community for his determined desire for independence from Mr. Agee.

Although Martin Marietta was not taken over by Bendix, the managers of Martin Marietta could expect Allied to be looking over their shoulder, and their firm had taken on a huge burden of debt. Martin had borrowed $892 million to buy Bendix shares and could expect interest payments on that to be $30 million in 1982 and $120 million in 1983. Mr. Pownall predicted his firm would regain its financial strength within a year, but

United Technologies December 31			Allied Corporation December 31		
1982	1981	1980	1982	1981	1980
121	168	147	176	181	189
1,552	1,507	1,586	728	933	785
2,866	2,732	2,778	647	841	601
64	82	66	73	56	74
4,603	4,489	4,577	1,624	2,011	1,649
298	166	151	1,570**	226	388
2,386	2,203	1,963	2,858	2,866	2,384
532	563	—	132	139	60
174	134	645	88	102	57
7,993	7,555	7,336	6,272	5,344	4,538
871	870	913	769	974	673
505	467	689	38	53	33
1,368	1,228	1,237	302	286	430
306	350	379	99	60	46
3,050	2,915	3,218	1,208	1,373	1,182
927	832	867	700	857	885
246	284	204	287	335	311
288	311	312	284	288	236
698	751	855	1,780***	591	260
1,144	1,059	678	669	629	616
—	—	—	—	—	—
1,640	1,403	1,202	1,354	1,290	1,057
—	—	—	(10)	(19)	(9)
3,482	3,213	2,735	3,793	2,491	1,924
7,993	7,555	7,336	6,272	5,344	4,538

*** Includes $1,194 million in adjustable rate Cumulative Preferred Stock held by Bendix Corporation during the interim period until the merger was approved in January 1983. Does not show up in Bendix statements because of differences in the dates of the fiscal years.

Moody's rating service lowered Martin's commercial paper from "prime-2" to "not prime" and senior debt from Baa2 to Baa3.

In an effort to solve these problems, Martin Marietta swapped stock for $10 million of one of its subsidiaries' debt securities in January 1983. In March, Martin sold 2 million shares at $42.75, and avoided spending precious cash by making the required pension fund contribution in $19.2 million worth of shares, also valued at $42.75 per share. Additionally, some of Martin Marietta's assets—the aluminum and cement businesses—were put up for sale. A cement plant, some bauxite holdings, and a chemicals venture had been sold off by March 1983. Unfortunately, the cement and aluminum businesses had suffered losses recently, so severe that Martin expected its first losing quarter in 22 years during the initial period of 1983. Still, Mr. Pownall won praise from Wall Street for chopping his debt by $450 million in such a short time. Martin Marietta's stock appreciated to nearly $44 per share in mid-March. (See Exhibits 33.5, 33.6, 33.7, and 33.8.)

Exhibit 33.8   Composition of Revenues and Income, 1981

United Technologies		Allied Corporation		Bendix Corporation		Martin Marietta	
Net Sales = $13, 668 Mil.		Net Sales = $6,407 Mil.		Net Sales = $4,393 Mil.		Net Sales = $3,294 Mil.	
Other	2%	Health and Science	2%			Instruments	1%
Flight	12	Other and Unallocated	9	Industrial	18%	Data Systems	3
						Aggregates	5
Industrial	19	Electrical	13	Aerospace-Elecronics	33	Cement	6
		Fiber and Plastics	19			Chemicals	8
Building	27	Chemicals	25	Auto	49	Aluminum	19
Power	40			Other and Eliminations	(4)	Aerospace	58
Elimination	(1)	Oil and Gas	32				

United Technologies		Allied Corporation		Bendix Corporation		Martin Marietta	
Total Income = $1,106 Mil.		Total Income = $1,092 Mil.		Total Income = $494 Mil.		Total Income = $293 Mil.	
Other	9%	Health and Science	1%	Industrial	17%	Instruments	9%
Flight	9	Electrical	3			Data Systems	3
Industrial	3	Fiber and Plastics	6	Aerospace-Elecronics	27	Aggregates	10
						Cement	3
Building	26	Chemicals	12			Chemicals	18
		Oil and Gas	78	Auto	28	Aluminum	13
Power	53	Other & Unallocated	(8)	Other and Investments	28	Aerospace	44

Mr. Gray

Mr. Harry Gray, 62, was CEO of United Technologies, a conglomerate much larger than any of the other three firms involved. It appeared that an important motivation for his entering the battle was a friendship with Mr. Pownall of Martin Marietta and a desire to make progress toward his stated goal of making United Technologies a $20-billion firm by the time he retired. Although he is described as easygoing in manner, Mr. Gray was regarded as one of Wall Street's shrewdest and most hard-driving business professionals. Once the Pac-Man game ended, United Technologies escaped with little apparent damage.

CASE 34
Manville Corporation

▪ *Arthur Sharplin* ▪

Asbestos is an insidious poison. Microscopic fibers, as small as a human cell, cause progressive, irreversible, incurable disease. Asbestos causes scarring of the small airways and further scarring of the lung tissue itself, parenchymal asbestosis. Asbestos causes scarring, thickening and calcification of the lung linings, pleural asbestosis. Asbestos causes an always-fatal cancer, mesothelioma, in the tissue surrounding the lungs. Asbestos causes lung cancer. Asbestosis causes an abnormally high level of lung infections which are unusually hard to treat.

For eight years in the boiler rooms of the USS Santa Fe, the USS Antietam and the USS Thomas F. Nickel, Ed Janssens used and repaired thermal insulation. He never knew he was planting a time-bomb deep within his lungs. Twenty years passed before he first felt its toxic effects. He was sick, but he didn't know why.

Ed Janssens has asbestosis. To be more specific, his asbestos exposure from 1943 through 1951 has caused thickening and calcification of the lining of his lungs, small airways disease, complication of his asthma, life-threatening lung infections, and a progressive decrease in lung function. He will require close medical surveillance forever. If Ed Janssens, an asbestotic, does not die soon of cancer, mesothelioma, or massive lung infection, the inexorable march of asbestosis will eventually block his blood flow, swell his heart and cause death by coronary pulmonale.

In 1981, 30 years after his last exposure to its asbestos, Ed Janssens brought Johns-Manville to trial. For ten years, his asbestosis has been stealing his breath, complicating his asthma, retarding treatment for lung infections, keeping him out of work, making him lonely and reclusive, causing him depression and frustration, reducing the length of his natural life, and keeping him from sleeping in even the same bedroom with his wife, Patsy, the mother of his eight children. For years, he had to sit up in a chair to get any sleep; now, under more effective medical care, he can sleep lying down—sometimes.

It was 1978 when Ed Janssens, 35 years too late, first learned of the asbestos hazard. Who knew the death-dealing hazards of the asbestos fibers? Johns-Manville knew. Who knew in 1929, when Ed Janssens was just five years old? Johns-Manville did. Who exercised editorial prerogative over Dr. A. J. Lanza's 1935 United States Public Health Service report entitled "Effects of Inhalation of Asbestos Dust on the Lungs of Asbestos Workers"? Johns-Manville did. And who rushed on Christmas Eve 1934, to make sure "additions, ommissions or changes . . . beneficial from the industry viewpoint" would be included in Dr. Lanza's official report? Johns-Manville did.

When an asbestos manufacturer's health credo was "our interests are best served by having asbestosis receive the minimum of publicity," it is no surprise to learn that no hazard warning besmirched [Manville's] asbestos bags and boxes until 30 years after Dr. Lanza acceded to his benefactor's demands; and, even then, only because Dr. Irving Selikoff had "held the smoking gun aloft"—publicly in 1964.

▪ *Wayne Hogan, Counsel for Asbestos Victims* ▪

The Janssens filed suit in 1979 and were eventually awarded $1,757,600 in compensatory and punitive damages. But Manville moved for a judgment, notwithstanding the verdict, then for a new trial, and then for a return of part of the adjudged damages (none of which had been paid). When all these motions were denied in December 1981, Manville initiated the formal appeal process. The appeal had not been heard—and Ed Janssens had not been paid—when the Manville Board of Directors met secretly on August 25, 1982, to decide whether to file for protection under Chapter 11 of the U.S. Bankruptcy Code.

Manville Corporation (Johns-Manville until 1981) is a diversified mining, timber, and manufacturing company. In 1982, the company employed about 30,000 people at more than 125 facilities (plants, mines, and sales offices), mostly in the United States. For many years, the company had been the world's largest producer of asbestos and asbestos-based products. In 1976, sales of asbestos fiber alone (mostly to manufacturers outside the United States) provided 52 percent of Manville's income from operations, although it constituted only about 11 percent of sales. In addition, asbestos was used by the company in making hundreds of products such as floor tile, textiles, filters, pipe, and roofing materials. Altogether, asbestos and asbestos products clearly account for more than one-half of

---

What Is Asbestos?

This is taken from the *Encyclopaedia Britannica*:

asbestos, mineral fibre occurring in nature in fibrous form. It is obtained from certain types of asbestos rock, chiefly the chrysotile variety of the serpentine groups of minerals, by mining or quarrying. Valued since ancient times for its resistance to fire, asbestos fibre achieved commercial importance in the 19th century.

The fibre is freed by crushing the rock and is then separated from the surrounding material, usually by a blowing process.

This is from an article by Bruce Porter in *Sunday Review of the Society*:

Perhaps no other mineral is so woven into the fabric of American life as is asbestos. Impervious to heat and fibrous—it is the only mineral that can be woven into cloth—asbestos is spun into fireproof clothing and theater curtains, as well as into such household items as noncombustible drapes, rugs, pot holders, and ironing-board covers. Mixed into slurry, asbestos is sprayed onto girders and walls to provide new buildings with fireproof insulation. It is used in floor tiles, roofing felts, and in most plasterboards and wallboards. Asbestos is also an ingredient of plaster and stucco and of many paints and putties. This "mineral of a thousand uses"—an obsolete nickname: the present count stands at around 3,000 uses—is probably present in some form or other in every home, school, office building, and factory in this country. Used in brake linings and clutch facings, in mufflers and gaskets, in sealants and caulking, and extensively used in ships, asbestos is also a component of every modern vehicle, including space ships.

Manville's sales and probably for three-fourths of its operating profit. The ruled insert on page 872 describes asbestos.

In 1957, the Industrial Health Foundation proposed a study on asbestos and cancer to be funded by the Asbestos Textile Institute (made up of asbestos manufacturers). The proposal was rejected by Manville and the other manufacturers at the March 1957 meeting of the institute. "There is a feeling among certain members that such an investigation would stir up a hornets' nest and put the whole industry under suspicion."

In 1963, Dr. I. J. Selikoff of Mt. Sinai Medical Center in New York completed an extensive study of asbestos and health. The minutes of the Asbestos Textile Institute's Air Hygiene Committee meeting of June 6, 1983, noted Selikoff's forthcoming report:

The committee was advised that a Dr. Selikoff will read at the next meeting of the AMA in about 30 days a paper on a study he has made of about 1,500 workers, largely in asbestos insulation application, showing a very large incidence of lung cancer over normal expectations.

Dr. Selikoff's report and the symposia and publications which followed revealed, for the first time to those outside the industry, the magnitude and character of the asbestos problem: Thousands had already died of asbestos-related diseases, and hundreds of thousands more would become disabled and die in the decades to follow. Breathing asbestos dust causes a progressive thickening and stiffening of lung tissue (asbestosis) and sometimes causes the always-fatal asbestos cancer (mesothelioma); either of these diseases may disable the victim 20 to 40 years after exposure.

The dangers of ingesting asbestos fibers began to be widely publicized in the 1960s and 1970s. Beginning in 1978, there were hundreds of newspaper stories, magazine articles, and television documentaries concerning the problem. Joseph Califano, Secretary of the Department of Health, Education and Welfare (HEW), estimated that between 8.5 and 11 million workers had been exposed to asbestos since World War II. In April 1978, HEW announced that it was warning present and former asbestos workers and their doctors about the hazards of asbestos, and the U.S. Surgeon General sent 400,000 warning letters to the nation's doctors. In June, the Environmental Protection Agency established limits for airborne asbestos resulting from building demolition. Then, in December 1978, the Environmental Defense Fund claimed that millions of school children had been exposed to cancer-causing levels of asbestos because of use of the product in school construction.

Manville's Legal Defenses Weaken

The dozens of asbestos injury lawsuits against Manville in the twenties and thirties, scores during the forties and fifties, and hundreds in the sixties and early seventies became thousands in the late seventies. Although the asbestos litigation was not mentioned in Manville's 1977 Annual Report, it was described, as the law required, in the company's 1977 Form 10K, submitted to the Securities and Exchange Commission in April 1978. This form reported 623 asbestos lawsuits against Manville, some of them multiplaintiff cases involving many claimants. The claims for which amounts were given totaled $2.79 billion.

For nearly 50 years, Manville had been able to hide the fact that company executives knew the dangers of breathing asbestos dust from about 1930 onward and suppressed research and publicity concerning asbestos-related diseases. But, in April 1978, plaintiffs in a South Carolina asbestos tort case obtained the so-called Raybestos-Manhattan papers. These documents consist of asbestos industry correspondence and reports from the 1930s and 1940s. Coupled with the publications of Selikoff and other researchers, the Raybestos-Manhattan papers made a compelling case. The ruled insert on page 000 gives excerpts from a few of the papers.

Excerpts from the Raybestos-Manhattan Papers

From a December 15, 1934, letter from George Hobart, Manville's chief counsel, to Vandiver Brown, Manville's corporate secretary and legal vice-president:

. . . it is only within a comparatively recent time that asbestosis has been recognized by the medical and scientific professions as a disease—in fact, one of our principal defenses in actions against the company on the common law theory of negligence has been that the scientific and medical knowledge has been insufficient until a very recent period to place on the owners of plants or factories the burden or duty of taking special precautions against the possible onset of the disease in their employees.

From a 1935 letter to Sumner Simpson, President of Raybestos-Manhattan Corporation, from Anne Rossiter, Editor of *Asbestos*, an industry trade journal:

You may recall that we have written you on several occasions concerning the publishing of information, or discussion of, asbestosis. . . . Always you have requested that for obvious reasons, we publish nothing, and, naturally your wishes have been respected.

From an October 3, 1935, letter from Vandiver Brown to Sumner Simpson, commenting on the Rossiter letter:

I quite agree that our interests are best served by having asbestosis receive the minimum of publicity.

From a report by Dr. Kenneth Smith, Manville physician and medical director, on a 1949 study of 708 men who worked in a Manville asbestos mine (The report shows that only four of the 708 were free of lung damage and that those four had had less than four years' exposure to asbestos dust):

Of the 708 men, seven had X-ray evidence of early asbestosis. . . . They have not been told of this diagnosis. For it is felt that as long as the man feels well, is happy at home and at work, and his physical condition remains good, nothing should be said. . . . The fibrosis of this disease is irreversible and permanent. . . .

There are seven cases of asbestosis and 52 cases in a "preasbestosis group." These 59 cases are probable compensation claims . . . . There are 475 men with "fibrosis extending beyond the lung roots" all of whom will show progressive fibrosis if allowed to continue working in dusty areas.

In ordering a new trial, the South Carolina judge wrote:

The Raybestos-Manhattan correspondence reveals written evidence that Raybestos-Manhattan and Johns-Manville exercised an editorial prerogative over the publication of the first study of the asbestos industry which they sponsored in 1935. It further reflects a conscious effort by the industry in the 1930s to downplay, or arguably suppress, the dissemination of information to employees and the public for fear of the promotion of lawsuits. . . .

On two separate occasions, September 1977, pursuant to subpoena duces tecum, and December 1977, pursuant to a Request to Produce, plaintiff sought to discover the Raybestos correspondence in question. . . . It is uncontroverted that the same documents were produced in April 1977, in a New Jersey asbestos lawsuit. . . .

It is also clear that the defendant, Johns-Manville, upon whom the December Request to Produce was also served, had in its possession since April 1977, the Raybestos correspondence, which also involved its corporate agents.

During the late seventies, asbestos plaintiff lawyers were able to obtain depositions from a number of retired Manville executives. Dr. Kenneth W. Smith (mentioned in the lined insert) had been Manville's physician and medical director from 1945 to 1966 (except for one year). In a 1976 deposition, Dr. Smith testified that he became "knowledgeable of the relationship between the inhalation of asbestos fibers and the lung condition known as asbestosis" during his internship in 1941–1942, before he went to work for Manville. Following are other excerpts from Dr. Smith's testimony:

Q. *Did you [tell other employees of Johns-Manville] of the relationship between the inhalation of asbestos fiber and the lung condition known as asbestosis?*

A. *Many people at Canadian Johns-Manville in supervisory positions already knew about the association of inhalation of asbestos fibers and disease. I just amplified that [and] made much more explicit the disease process.*

Q. *Did you or did you not have discussions with Mr. A. R. Fisher with respect to the relationship between the inhalation of asbestos fiber and the pulmonary lung condition known as asbestosis, both with respect to employees of Johns-Manville and what you defined as the civilian population? [Mr. Fisher had been involved in the asbestos litigation in the 1930s and was president in the 1950s and 1960s.]*

A. *Definitely, we discussed the whole subject many times, about dust and what it does to people, whether they are employed or not employed. . . . The good Lord gave us all the same breathing apparatus and if the asbestos fiber is present and the housewife, and the asbestos worker, and the fireman, and the jeweler, and doctor, and everybody else are all in the same room, they are all going to breath the same dust. . . . So wherever there is dust and people are breathing dust they are going to have a potential hazard.*

Q. *Did you at any point . . . make any recommendations to anyone at Johns-Manville in respect to the utilization of a caution label for the asbestos-containing products?*

A. *Hugh Jackson and I sat down with many people in other divisions suggesting that similar caution labels should be put on products which when used could create airborne dust that could be inhaled.*

Q. *When did you sit down with Hugh Jackson and come to that conclusion?*

A. *It would be late 1952 and early 1953.*

Q. *What was the reason . . . the asbestos-containing products were not labeled with a caution label back in 1952?*

A. *It was a business decision as far as I could understand. . . . Application of a caution label identifying a product as hazardous would cut out sales. There would be serious financial implications.*

Q. *Did you at any time recognize the relationship between the inhalation of asbestos fibers and pulmonary malignancies, as you phrased it, or lung cancer, or pleural cancer?*

A. *Yes, I have recognized the alleged and sometimes factual association of malignancy with the inhalation of asbestos fibers.*

Q. *When would that have been, Doctor, for the first time?*

A. *The first time would be in the late 1940s.*

Q. *Had there been studies in Britain and perhaps even in the United States prior to the beginning of the Saranac Lake Laboratories studies [1936] which had indicated [that fibrous asbestos dust caused lung disease]?*

A. *Very definitely. As I recall, Merriweather and his cohorts studied the effects of the asbestos textile dust many years prior to 1935 and their publications are well-documented and available world wide.*

Dr. Smith died in 1977. In 1981, a Manville lawyer (appealing a $1.9 million damage award to asbestos victim Edward Janssens), argued that the Smith deposition should not have been admitted in court. The attorney said, "J-M made a conscious policy decision not to cross-examine Dr. Smith as fully as it otherwise would have. For example, Johns-Manville decided against examining Dr. Smith regarding the fact that he was an alcoholic and under psychiatric care."

Another Manville executive, Wilbur L. Ruff, who had worked for Manville from 1929 through 1972, much of the time as plant manager at a number of Manville plants, gave an extensive deposition in 1979. Excerpts follow:

Q. *Do you know whether in fact, abnormal chest findings ever were discussed with any employee of the Johns-Manville plant?*

Q. *I know of no specific cases.*

Q. *Was there a policy at that time not to talk to the employees about chest findings, findings that suggested asbestosis, pneumoconiosis, or mesothelioma [asbestos cancer]?*

A. *That was the policy.*

Q. *When did the policy change?*

A. *In the early 1970s.*

Q. *Have you on other occasions, Mr. Ruff, referred to this policy that we have been discussing as a hush-hush policy?*

A. *Yes.*

Q. *Were you aware that it was company policy back in the late forties that if a man had asbestosis or industrial lung diseases that nothing would be said to him until he actually became disabled?*

A. *That's the way it was done.*

Q. *You were aware that was the company policy?*

A. *Whether it was policy or not, it was somebody's decision.*

In 1964 Manville placed the first caution labels on its asbestos products. The labels read:

This product contains asbestos fiber.
Inhalation of asbestos in excessive quantities over long periods of time may be harmful.
If dust is created when the product is handled, avoid breathing the dust.
If adequate ventilation control is not possible, wear respirators approved by the U.S. Bureau of Mines for pneumoconiosis producing dust.

In upholding a landmark 1972 district court decision against Manville and other asbestos defendants, the New Orleans U.S. Court of Appeals stated:

Asbestosis has been recognized as a disease for well over fifty years. . . . By the mid-1930s the hazard of asbestos as a pneumoconiotic dust was universally accepted. Cases of asbestosis in insulation workers were reported in this country as early as 1934. . . . The evidence . . . tended to establish that none of the defendants ever tested its product to determine its effect on industrial insulation workers. . . . Indeed the evidence tended to establish that the defendants gave no instructions or warnings at all.

The court quoted Manville's caution label (above) and continued:

It should be noted that none of these so called "cautions" intimated the gravity of the risk: the danger of a fatal illness caused by asbestosis and mesothelioma or other cancers. The mild suggestion that inhalation of asbestos in excessive quantities over a long period of time may be harmful conveys no idea of the extent of the danger.

New Directions for the 1970s

By the 1960s, several of Manville's older directors had died or retired. Among them were A. R. Fisher and E. M. Voorhees, senior Manville officials since before 1930. (Both Fisher and Voorhees were involved in the early asbestos lawsuits. Also, Fisher was chief executive in the fifties and early sixties.) Compared to the 1966 Board of Directors, the 1969 board contained a majority of new members. Departing from a tradition of promotion from within, in 1969 Manville brought in an outsider, psychologist Richard Goodwin, to fill a top-management position. The next year, the Board of Directors voted

to move long-time President C. B. Burnett to the position of chairman and to install
Goodwin as president and chief executive officer. Goodwin led the company through at
least 20 acquisitions and several divestitures, increasing the company's profit and sales but
also increasing its long-term debt—from zero in 1970 to $196 million in 1975.

Goodwin arranged to purchase the 10,000-acre Ken-Caryl Ranch near Denver in 1971,
moved the company there from New York, and made plans to build a luxurious world
headquarters. The first phase of the project was to cost $182.2 million, 45 percent of
Manville's net worth. The magazine *Industrial Development* called the Manville plan "a
study in corporate environmental concern." *Fortune* magazine quotes Goodwin as saying,
"A company's headquarters is its signature. I wanted a new signature for J-M that, frankly,
would attract attention—that would tell everybody, including ourselves, that things were
changing."

Things did change. When the asbestos problem grew out of control and the company
lost the first of many asbestos lawsuits, Manville turned back to one of its own—its chief
legal officer—for leadership. In what *Fortune* magazine called "the shoot-out at the J-M
corral," the Board of Directors deposed Goodwin without explanation and installed
J. A. McKinney as president in September 1976. McKinney charted the new course in his
1977 "president's review":

*We believe we can further improve the fundamental economics of a number of our opera-
tions and we will be working toward that end in the year to come. . . .*

*Asbestos fiber, while contributing substantially to earnings, has assumed a less impor-
tant position with the earnings growth of our other basic businesses. Although its profitability is expected to improve in the long term with reviving European economies,
we do not expect asbestos fiber to dominate J-M earnings to the extent that it has in
the past. . . .*

*We have also consolidated and repositioned some businesses for more profitable
growth and phased out others not important to the future direction of the company. . . .*

*We have begun aggressively to seek out opportunities for growth. One example is the
previously announced $200 million capital expansion program which will, by 1980,
double U.S. fiber glass capacity over the 1976 levels. . . . We continue seeking still other
growth possibilities that would markedly change the Johns-Manville profile, possibly
through substantial acquisitions. . . .*

*Our main thrust in 1978 will be to continue improving profitability by maintaining our
expense control and pricing vigilance, by adding volume to below-capacity businesses, by
better utilizing existing capacity and by adding capacity in sold-out businesses.*

By that time, Manville had already begun to seek a large merger candidate—a "substantial acquisition"—employing the services of the Morgan Stanley investment banking
firm to assist in the search. Manville quickly identified Olinkraft Corporation, a forest
products manufacturer and timber company (owning 580,000 acres of timberland), as a
likely prospect. After a brief bidding war, Olinkraft and Manville completed their merger
agreement. The purchase price was $595 million. This was 2.24 times Olinkraft's June
1978 book value and over twice the average total market value of Olinkraft's stock in the
first half of 1978.

Approximately half of the purchase price was paid in cash, and the other half with
preferred stock. The preferred stock was described in the 1978 Annual Report:

On January 19, 1979, the Company issued 4,598,327 shares of cumulative preferred stock, $5.40 series, to consummate the acquisition of Olinkraft. . . .

Under a mandatory sinking fund provision, the Company is required to redeem the $5.40 preferred series between 1987 and 2009 at $65 per share plus accrued dividends. The annual redemption requirements will consist of varying percentages applied to the number of outstanding shares on October 20, 1986, as follows: 5% annually from 1987 through 1996, 4% annually from 1997 through 2007, and 3% in 2008. All remaining outstanding shares are required to be redeemed in 2009.

While the Olinkraft merger was being negotiated, Manville common stock declined in market value to a low of $22.125, a total decrease of over $225 million. Olinkraft's stock rose, approximating the proposed acquisition price of $65 a share.

The merger was consummated on January 19, 1979. The purchase method of accounting was used. Essentially, the book values of Olinkraft's assets were adjusted upward by the amount by which the purchase price exceeded the net worth. The adjusted and unadjusted balance sheet values for Olinkraft are shown in Exhibit 34.1

After the mergers and divestitures engineered by Goodwin and McKinney, Manville's mix of businesses (as described in the 1978 and 1979 annual reports) was as follows:

Fiberglass products: Residential insulations account for the largest portion of the product line, with commercial and industrial insulations and fiber glass making up the rest. . . . New home construction represented 55 percent of the total market while [insulation for existing homes] accounted for 45 percent. . . .

Non-fiber glass insulations: This business segment includes roof insulations, refractory fibers, calcium silicate insulation, and a broad range of other commercial and industrial insulating products. . . .

Pipe products and systems: Major products in this business segment are polyvinyl chloride (PVC) plastic pipe and asbestos cement (A-C) pipe. . . .

Exhibit 34.1   Purchase Method Merger Accounting: Olinkraft Balance Sheets (in millions of dollars)

	Adjusted	Unadjusted
Current assets	$137,557	$119,610
Investments in and advances to associated companies	6,886	6,078
Property, plant, and equipment	700,633	372,761
Deferred charges and other assets	799	3,513
Total current assets	$845,857	$501,962
Current liabilities	$ 83,912	$ 67,793
Long-term debt	141,258	141,295
Other noncurrent liabilities	25,159	26,678
Total current liabilities	$250,329	$235,766
Net worth	$596,528	$266,196

Source: December 31, 1978, Manville-Olinkraft joint proxy statement; Manville 1978 Annual Report.

Roofing products: The roofing products segment includes residential shingles and built-up roofing for commercial and industrial structures. New construction accounts for 40 percent of sales. Reroofing represents 60 percent. . . .

Asbestos fiber: Asbestos fiber is sold in markets throughout the world. A major portion of the fiber sold is used as a raw material in products where the fiber is locked in place by cement, rubber, plastics, resins, asphalts, and similar bindings. Products include asbestos cement products, brake linings, resilient flooring, roofing, and other products that require strength and fire protection, heat resistance, dimensional stability, and resistance to rust and rot. . . .

Industrial and specialty products and services: A diverse group of businesses that has as its principal areas: Holophane lighting systems, filtration and minerals [comprised of diatomite, perlite, and fiber glass filter products] and industrial specialties. . . . Perlite is . . . used by J-M in the manufacture of Fesco Board roof insulation. Other uses are in acoustical ceiling tile, horticultural applications, and in cryogenic insulations.

Forest products: Forest products include clay-coated unbleached Kraft and other paperboards: corrugated containers; beverage carriers and folding cartons; Kraft bags; pine lumber, plywood, and particleboard; and hardwood veneer and flooring.

Strategic Management in the 1980s

After Richard Goodwin was expulsed, top-management continuity was maintained through the late seventies and eighties. The Chairman of the Board and Chief Executive Officer, J. A. McKinney, the President and Chief Operating Officer, Fred L. Pundsack, and all ten senior vice-presidents listed in the 1981 Annual Report, were also listed in the 1977 Annual Report. In fact, the five most-highly-paid executives of Manville, as shown on the March 1982 proxy statement, had all been with the company for 29 years or more. Only three of Manville's outside directors joined the board after the sixties. Except for John D. Mullins, former president of Olinkraft, who performed brief service, no new director was added after 1976. Then, in May 1982, the existing directors were renominated.

Manville's asbestos-related health costs were relatively insignificant (less than 0.5 percent of sales through 1981). But asbestos use, especially in the United States, declined sharply after 1978. The U.S. Department of the Interior reported a 36-percent drop from 1979 to 1980 alone. With a virtual U.S. monopoly of asbestos sales, Manville was hardest hit. The loss of asbestos profits was compounded by a deep recession in housing and other construction which began in mid-1978 and was to last through 1982.

Attempts to expand and diversify Manville had begun in 1970, when net sales totaled $578 million. The sixties had seen only a 1.5 percent real rate of growth, less than the rate of gross national product (GNP) growth. Because of the purchases of businesses by Goodwin and McKinney, the company had surpassed $1 billion sales in 1974 and $2 billion in 1978. However, on an inflation-corrected basis, sales declined from 1978 onward, despite the contribution of $500 million in annual sales by Olinkraft. Exhibit 34.2 illustrates Manville's sales and earnings patterns from 1977 through 1982. The corresponding financial statements and a record of Manville's common stock prices appear in Exhibits 34.3 and 34.4.

Six pages of Manville's 1978 Annual Report and over half of J. A. McKinney's "chairman's message" were devoted to the personal injury lawsuits. Excerpts from these documents follow:

Exhibit 34.2   Manville Corporation Sales and Earnings, 1978–1982 (Constant 1981 dollars)

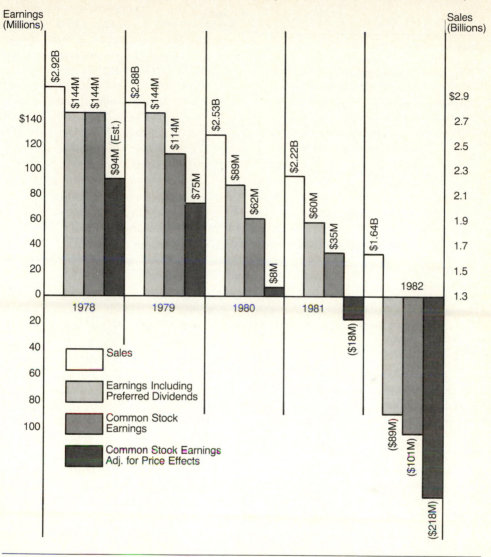

Source: Annual reports.

During the past year a great deal of publicity has appeared in the media about asbestos health hazards—most of it attacking the corporation and nearly all of it needlessly inflammatory. Your corporation has acted honorably over the years and has led the asbestos industry, medical science and the federal government in identifying and seeking to eliminate asbestos health problems. . . .

Individuals exposed to asbestos-containing insulation materials are particular victims of the incomplete knowledge of earlier years. . . . It was not until 1964 that the particular risk to this category of worker [insulation workers] was clearly identified by Dr. Irving J. Selikoff of Mt. Sinai Hospital in New York City. . . .

Exhibit 34.3   Manville Corporation Income Statements (amounts in millions)*

	1982 6 mos.	1981	1980	1979	1978
Sales	$ 949	$2,186	$2,267	$2,276	$1,649
Cost of sales	784	1,731	1,771	1,747	1,190
Selling, general, and administrative expense	143	271	263	239	193
R&D and engineering expense	16	34	35	31	33
Operating income	6	151	197	259	232
Other income, net	1	35	26	21	28
Interest expense	35	73	65	62	22
Total income	(28)	112	157	218	238
Income taxes	2	53	77	103	116
Net income before extraordinary items	(25)	60	81	115	122
Dividends on preferred stock	12	25	25	24	0
Extraordinary item	0	0	0	0	0
Net income available for common stock	$ (37)	$ 35	$ 55	$ 91	$ 122

Revenues and Income from Operations by Business Segment

	1981	1980	1979	1978	1977	1976
Revenues						
Fiberglass products	$ 625	$ 610	$ 573	$ 514	$ 407	$ 358
Forest products	555	508	497	0	0	0
Nonfiberglass insulation	258	279	268	231	195	159
Roofing products	209	250	273	254	204	171
Pipe products and systems	199	220	305	303	274	218
Asbestos fiber	138	159	168	157	161	155
Industrial and special products	320	341	309	291	301	309
Corporate revenues, net	12	9	11	20	12	(22)
Intersegment sales	(95)	(84)	(106)	(94)	(74)	(56)
Total	$2,221	$2,292	$2,297	$1,677	$1,480	$1,291
Income from operations						
Fiberglass products	$ 90	$ 91	$ 96	$ 107	$ 82	$ 60
Forest products	39	37	50	0	0	0
Nonfiberglass insulation	20	27	27	35	28	18
Roofing products	(17)	9	14	23	14	8
Pipe products and systems	0	(5)	18	26	24	(3)
Asbestos fiber	37	35	56	55	60	60
Industrial and special products	50	55	43	36	25	19
Corporate expense, net	(23)	(38)	(23)	(23)	(24)	(49)
Eliminations and adjustments	3	11	(2)	1	3	2
Total	$ 198	$ 223	$ 280	$ 260	$ 212	$ 116

*Totals may not check due to rounding.

Source: Annual reports and June 30, 1982, Form 100.

Media representatives and some elected officials have consistently ignored J-M's inten-sive efforts to solve asbestos health problems and, in fact, have untruthfully portrayed those efforts. . . .

Litigation is based upon a finding of fault, and with respect to asbestos-related dis-ease, there simply is no fault on the part of J-M, a fact increasingly recognized by juries

Exhibit 34.4   Manville Corporation Balance Sheets (amounts in millions)*

	June 30 1982	1981	1980	1979	1978
Assets					
Cash	$ 10	$ 14	$ 20	$ 19	$ 28
Marketable securities	17	12	12	10	38
Accounts and notes receivable	348	327	350	362	328
Inventories	182	211	217	229	219
Prepaid expenses	19	19	20	31	32
Total current assets	$ 576	$ 583	$ 619	$ 650	$ 645
Property, plant, and equipment					
Land and land improvements		119	118	114	99
Buildings		363	357	352	321
Machinery and equipment		1,202	1,204	1,161	1,043
		$1,685	$1,679	$1,627	$1,462
Less accumulated depreciation and depletion		(525)	(484)	(430)	(374)
		$1,160	$1,195	$1,197	$1,088
Timber and timberland less cost of timber harvested		$ 406	$ 407	$ 368	$ 372
	$1,523	$1,566	$1,602	$1,565	$1,460
Investment and advertising to associated companies		0	0	0	0
Real estate subdivision investment and advertising		0	0	0	0
Other assets	148	149	117	110	113
Total assets	$2,247	$2,298	$2,338	$2,324	$2,217
Liabilities					
Short-term debt	$	$ 29	$ 22	$ 32	$ 23
Accounts payable	191	120	126	143	114
Comp. and employee benefits		77	80	54	45
Income taxes		30	22	51	84
Other liabilities	149	58	61	50	63
Total current liabilities	340	316	310	329	329
Long-term debt	499	508	519	532	543
Other noncurrent liabilities	93	86	75	73	60
Deferred income taxes	186	185	211	195	150
Total liabilities	$1,116	$1,095	$1,116	$1,129	$1,083
Stockholders' equity					
Preferred ($1.00 par)	$ 301	$ 301	$ 301	$ 299	$ 299
Common ($2.50 par)	60	59	58	208	197
Capital in excess of par	178	174	164	0	0
Retained earnings	642	695	705	692	643
Cumulative currency translation adjustment	(47)	(22)	0	0	0
Less cost of treasury stock	(3)	(3)	(4)	(4)	(6)
Total stockholders' equity	1,131	1,203	1,222	1,196	1,134
Total liability and stockholders' equity	$2,247	$2,298	$2,338	$2,324	$2,217

*Totals may not check due to rounding.

Source: Annual reports and June 30, 1982 Form 10-Q.

throughout the nation. Litigation is, of course, favored and fostered by lawyers in search of lucrative fees and by "media personalities" in search of sensational stories. . . .

Despite the worsening financial situation and though besieged by thousands of asbestos victims seeking billions of dollars in damages, Manville was publicly optimistic. The 1979 Annual Report stated, "Johns-Manville has a strategy for the early 80's . . . and the commitment to succeed. . . . J-M's strategic plan embraces three major goals." The goals were described as follows:

Goal 1: To rebuild our financial reserves. . . . As expected, the Olinkraft acquisition burdened our financial resources. . . . For this reason, our most immediate short-term goal is to improve and increase the financial strength of J-M's balance sheet. We will accomplish this by increasing productivity and using the better levels of cash flow that result to provide for most of our new capital needs.

Goal 2: To improve productivity and cost efficiencies. . . . We will look for ways to increase the output of our manufacturing processes, concentrating first on those projects promising the shortest payback periods. . . .

Goal 3: To reaffirm J-M's position as a technological leader in terms of product performance and cost of production. . . . to increase the effort and money spent on improving manufacturing methods, enhancing the competitive strengths of present product lines and developing new products.

In 1981 Manville accelerated efforts to avoid the asbestos claims. McKinney wrote to his shareholders, "You can be assured that we will continue to be aggressive in asserting our defenses." By spending millions on the defense efforts, Manville was able to avoid or delay payment of most tort judgments and to settle many for cents on the dollar. The company was reorganized into a parent corporation and a number of operating subsidiaries, with the asbestos businesses in one subsidiary.

The Day of Decision Approaches

It quickly became apparent that courts would see through the new corporate structure and treat the companies as one for asbestos liability purposes. Further, as the numbers and amounts of asbestos tort judgments skyrocketed, Manville's ability to avoid paying them grew increasingly questionable.

Manville's mid-year 1982 form 10Q (submitted to the Securities and Exchange Commission) described the worsening situation with regard to the asbestos injury claims:

During the first half of 1982, J-M [Manville] received an average of approximately 425 new cases per month brought by an average of approximately 495 new plaintiffs per month. . . .

J-M was, for the first time in 1981, found liable by juries for punitive damages in five separate asbestos-related actions. [Punitive damages are payments above the actual damages sustained—intended to punish defendants.] All of these cases are presently subject to posttrial motions or appeals filed by J-M. The average of the punitive damages awarded against J-M in these five cases (one of which involved eleven plaintiffs) and the five cases decided during the first half of 1982 and discussed below is approximately $616,000 per case. . . .

Hansen v. Johns-Manville. *$1,060,000 in compensatory damages and $1,000,000 in punitive damages were assessed against J-M.*

Bunch v. Johns-Manville Corp. *A jury verdict of $420,000 in compensatory damages and $220,000 in punitive damages. . . .*

Dorell v. Johns-Manville Corp. *The jury awarded the plaintiff $100,000 in compensatory damages and $1,000,000 in punitive damages. . . .*

Jackson v. Johns-Manville. *A jury verdict of $195,000 in compensatory damages and $500,000 in punitive damages. . . .*

Cavett v. Johns-Manville Corp. *The jury awarded the plaintiff $800,000 in compensation damages and $1,500,000 in punitive damages.*

Aside from actual and anticipated tort claims, Manville was in much worse condition in 1982 than the financial statements indicated (see Exhibit 34.3). This was true for four reasons. First, $340 million of Manville's net worth resulted from purchase method accounting in the Olinkraft merger. Second, the $300 million in "preferred stock" shown on the balance sheet was essentially equivalent to a 16 percent long-term debt. Third, Manville had endured several years of negative cash flow requiring certain cash-producing strategies which tended to reduce asset values. For example, the 580,000 acres of timber farms obtained in the Olinkraft purchase were converted to a 30-year planned life from a 40-year life. This rationalized immediate cutting of about one-fourth of the timber and continuing removal of one-thirtieth of that remaining each year instead of one-fortieth.

Exhibit 34.5   Manville Corporation Monthly Common Stock Trading Range 1976–July 1982

Finally, the desire of Manville executives to show profits each year had resulted in "creative accounting" which tended to inflate reported earnings (see Exhibits 34.4 and 34.5). The following are examples from the 1981 Annual Report: (1) a $9-million increase in "other revenues" which resulted largely from the sale of mineral exploration rights on 580,000 acres of timberland, (2) a $2.7-million increase in reported earnings due to the "reversal of a portion of the litigation reserves established at the time of the Olinkraft, Inc., acquisition," (3) a $9.8-million increase in reported earnings because of a new way of reporting foreign currency transactions, (4) an unspecified amount due to "the sale during 1981 of eight container plants [which] occurred as part of [the] asset management program," and (5) an $8.4-million increase in reported earnings brought about by "changes in certain actuarial assumptions in computing pension expense."

If Manville were to fail, not only would managers and directors lose their salaries, benefits, and perquisites, but they would also lose their corporate indemnification against personal liability for the asbestos injury claims. Undoubtedly each one would then be subject to hundreds, perhaps thousands, of tort lawsuits.

In December 1981, Manville formed a ten-member committee of inside and outside lawyers, the litigation analysis group (LAG), to study the firm's situation with regard to

Usual Effects of Filing for Reorganization under Chapter 11

All debts are stayed until a "plan of reorganization" is confirmed or special approval of the bankruptcy court is obtained.

The bankrupt corporation, with prefiling management, is declared to be the "debtor in possession" (DIP).

The DIP can carry out the "ordinary course of business," e.g., hiring and firing employees, incurring and repaying debts, making and executing contracts, selling and buying assets.

The DIP is allowed to enforce all claims against others, by filing lawsuits if necessary.

Lawsuits against the DIP are stayed.

Unsecured creditors and common and preferred stockholders are represented by committees appointed by the bankruptcy judge.

The DIP is allowed to cancel contracts, including collective bargaining agreements and leases, to the extent that they have not been carried out.

The DIP is allowed 120 days to file a plan of reorganization and 60 days to seek the required approval of each creditor class (half in number holding two-thirds in amount) and equity class (holders of two-thirds in amount), either of which periods may be extended.

The plan of reorganization typically provides for:

1. Payment of postfiling debt, including costs of administering the case.

2. Payment of secured prefiling debt up to the value of the liened property.

3. Payment of some or all of unsecured debt over some period into the future, with or without interest.

4. Discharge of all claims not provided for in the plan.

the asbestos injury liabilities. LAG employed a number of consultants to research various aspects of the issue and met each month to hear reports and discuss developments. The conclusion of LAG, arrived at in mid-1982, was that Manville would eventually have to pay about $2 billion to present and future asbestos injury victims.

In a subsequent lawsuit it was alleged that the $2 billion figure was contrived so as to be high enough to justify a filing for reorganization under Chapter 11 of the U.S. Bankruptcy Code but not high enough to appear to require liquidation of the company. At a meeting of the Board of Directors on August 4, 1982, J. A. McKinney (Chairman of the Board and Chief Executive Officer) appointed four outside directors to a special committee to determine what Manville should do. Members of the special committee were briefed on Chapter 11 by company executives. A limited overview of the practical effects of a Chapter 11 reorganization is provided in the lined insert.

A special meeting of the Board of Directors was called for August 25, 1982. The special committee was expected to present its recommendation at that meeting.

Introduction to the Case Method

We learn best by doing.
▪ *Anonymous* ▪

The content of strategic management and organizational policy courses may vary substantially given the diversity of the objectives of such courses. (See the Preface for a discussion of these objectives.) This book uses text to teach these subjects. Having reviewed strategic management and organizational policy through the use of text material, it is now time to apply this knowledge to the real world and to cases. For use with cases, an introduction to the case method is in order. The following pages review the case method and explore some of its dimensions to acquaint you as a student with the case method in order that you will be better able to utilize any cases which you are assigned.

The case method has become a popular tool in teaching strategic management and organizational policy because it brings realism to the classroom. Reading theories and concepts is the beginning of knowledge, but in order to complete your education, it is believed necessary that you gain some practical experience. The case method involves the examination of an actual organizational event or series of events. These situations usually involve statements that reveal problems or opportunities. These problems (internal weaknesses or external threats) or opportunities must be recognized, identified, and solved. In short, strategic decisions must be made.

Cases are usually written by management consultants or by other individuals who were involved in the problem. They are almost always derived from real life occurrences, but occasionally cases may be hypothetical. Not infrequently, the identity of the firm involved is disguised in order to protect the firm from unwanted publicity.

While attaining access to internal corporate information is difficult for most students, it is relatively easy to observe an organization through the use of the case method. The case method as a presentation of a real situation does have one weakness, however: the student is not allowed to interact with the data—that is, the student does not change the data, nor does the data change. However, this is not a major problem, and some actions can be taken to reduce its effects—for example, certain assumptions of the case can be changed.

Cases are occasionally accompanied by notes, which are usually industry data and survey information to be used with more than one case.

Objectives

The case method's objectives are

1. To add realism to the classroom.
2. To cause the student to integrate knowledge of the functional areas and to employ principles of strategic management.
3. To improve the decision-making ability of the student, primarily through having the student practice making decisions.

4. To cause the student to see interrelationships of facts and what they mean in a practical as well as a theoretical sense.

5. To encourage students to be self-assertive. This occurs when the student is required to respond in class by attracting the professor's attention through both physical and mental assertion. The student who does not "seize the floor" will probably never be heard from and will not do well in the course.

6. To improve students' communication skills.

Approaches

There are two general approaches to the case method. In the first, students follow a set format in analyzing a case. They read the case and attempt to identify the principal problems and the principal factors involved in these problems by utilizing a specific list of predetermined key factors which are believed relevant to proper management functioning. This is referred to as the structured approach. In the second approach, students are not provided with a particular format but are left to derive their own methodology. This is commonly referred to as an unstructured approach. Individual instructors will indicate which is to be utilized. Case analyses for class may be either written or oral, or a combination.

Types of Organizations Encountered

Three primary types of organizations, according to size, are encountered in cases: large national or multinational firms, medium-sized organizations and entrepreneurships, or small businesses. They tend to have differing types of problems and opportunities, requiring somewhat different types of resultant analyses. And two primary types of organizations, according to mission, are also encountered: profit-oriented organizations, and nonprofit organizations. Again, these types often have differing problems and opportunities.

Planning Level of Problems, Opportunities Encountered

Most of the problems and opportunities which confront the case analyst occur at the strategy formulation level. However, in most texts, a limited number of cases are presented that involve other stages of the planning cycle, so that their interrelationships may be interpreted. In fact, many cases involve multiple stages, since stages are so highly interdependent. For example, control information points to the need to reformulate strategy, strategy leads to structure, and so forth. Cases on international business and nonprofits are often included.

Classroom Pedagogy

Group versus Individual Analyses

Students can engage in preclass and class analysis of a case in two ways. The first is in a group. This method is appropriate when students are able to come together for lengthy periods of time to analyze the case. As with all group activities, there may be those who work on the group's project and those who do not. Appropriate peer group evaluations should be carried out. (Note, however, that working in a group does not require conformity; here too, strength of personality can be developed.) Prior to the group analysis, the individual should go through the recommended steps of analysis which conclude this introduction.

To use the second method, students study the case by themselves and must cover all its facets individually.

Student Classroom Participation

In some classes, students must seize the floor in order to be heard. Here it becomes imperative that the individual become self-assertive. The student must also realize that he or she may make a mistake and must be either willing to learn to accept criticism or able to avoid making mistakes in judgment (a tough task for anyone). The student should anticipate that the instructor will attempt to find people who disagree with the student's position and analyses. The risks of nonassertion (failing grades) are, of course, motivating.

Specific questions may also be asked of a student on a nonvoluntary basis. Finally, analyses prepared by the student may be read and debated in class. Some combination of these three approaches is common.

Instructor's Role

Normally the instructor leads the discussion; he or she may also participate in it. Instructors usually are viewed as resource persons.

Preclassroom Analysis

As in real-life situations, there is never enough data in any case to enable a perfect decision to be made. One of the most important factors to remember is that decision making is a function of time and data availability. No one ever has enough time or enough data. Therefore, the common criticism by students that the case may leave out data is not an acceptable one.

Students are allowed to undertake extra research; but for most cases the decision can and should be made based on the data presented. Furthermore, while students are encouraged to find information, especially industry information, relevant to the time the case was occurring, they should not seek to find out what happened subsequent to the time of the case—for example, when using Appendix 2 to this text.

Answers

There are no right answers in a case situation. There are, however, better answers. The only true test of the decision is in its implementation; and unfortunately, the case method does not allow for implementation of decisions. The right answer, then, is an unknown. Only the better answer can be determined. Students who make decisions based on insufficient analysis usually come up with worse answers and correspondingly worse grades. It is the facts upon which decisions are made that are important; several acceptable solutions may be derived from them.

Degree of Difficulty

Sometimes the point of the case will be obvious. At other times it will be necessary for the individual to read, reread, and reanalyze the case in order to determine what is the major problem or opportunity. Often, cases contain numerous technique problems which are not the major problems, only symptoms of a major problem.

Viewpoint

One factor to be considered is the viewpoint of the student. Should he or she envision himself or herself as a consultant or as a member of the organization? The ease with which solutions might be implemented is related to the choice of viewpoints.

Results

One important factor to consider is this: in many situations, no matter what the decision, the results may be ineffective. There are many factors, especially external environmental factors, which are completely out of the control of the organization. In such situations, the best decisions may be those which allow an organization to minimize the loss it might incur.

Strength of Analyses

Most students will not uncover all the factors which will eventually be revealed in the classroom discussions. This constitutes one of the most important learning factors gained from use of the case method—the realization that there is always something the individual will overlook. This is very much like real life.

Perspective

For both the student and the instructor, the case method is a difficult process. In traditional classroom learning situations, students have been assigned the roles of listeners and non-participants. To be effective, the case method requires that students think, act, and participate. In order for students to receive a good grade, they must achieve these more active levels of learning as opposed to being merely receptive and passive members of a lecturer's audience. The role of a strategic manager, too, demands this kind of behavior.

Case Bias

One must be aware of the inherent bias in a case. The case is related as it is perceived by someone else, the casewriter. The reader of a case does not have the benefit of knowing how the information was obtained or what factors the individual considered in writing the case. What is presented as fact may not be as clear-cut as it seems. How facts are presented, which facts are included, and which facts are left out are critical factors. Occasionally facts may be distorted, especially facts related to statements about the personalities of individuals. Often, individuals' personalities are the key problems in a case; yet the reader can never be sure that the statements about these personalities are exactly accurate.

A Suggested Course of Action

1. Read the case; become familiar with the situation. If possible, put the case aside for awhile.

2. Reread the case and:
   a. Summarize pertinent information.
   b. Pay special attention to information in exhibits—for example, financial statements, sales figures, and the like.
   c. Think of the questions your professor may have given you. Do they give clues as to what to do next? What are these clues?

3. Establish a decision framework:
   a. What is the major area of concern—strategy formulation, intermediate planning, organization, implementation, evaluation, or control?
   b. What are the organization's missions, objectives, policies, and strategies?
   c. What are the decision constraints?

4. If this is a strategy formulation problem, normally you should:
   a. Determine current master strategy.
   b. Identify strengths, weaknesses, opportunities, and threats (SWOT).
   c. Analyze substrategies if necessary.

5. Ask yourself if you really understand what's happening. If not, retrace your steps.

6. Search for and delineate alternatives. If the strategy must be reformulated, follow the strategic management process procedures discussed in the text. Be especially careful to match strengths and weaknesses against threats and opportunities. The alternative generation process involves examining the basic action strategies available and choosing the most appropriate. Next, the marketing strategy should be generated. In both these actions, the product life cycle should be observed for its impacts. Finally, supportive and strategic issues strategies should be formulated. Table 4.1 lists factors which should be considered in formulating strategy, while Table 4.2 lists classical marketing strategies. Both tables provide information for each stage of the product life cycle. Table 4.3 suggests possible supportive strategies by product life cycle stage. Numerous additional possible strategies exist, but these tables are a good place to begin. If the tables fail to yield what you consider to be appropriate strategies, then use your creativity to formulate additional ones.

7. Choose the appropriate alternatives. The evaluation process involves examining proposed alternatives to determine how well they match SWOT, mission, objectives, policies, the dominant planning mode, and other relevant criteria. The GE Strategy Matrix, or Stoplight, is one approach which may be used in this endeavor when multiple alternatives are available. The evaluation process is partly rational, partly intuitive, and partly dependent on skill. In many situations, it is also partly social. Once choices are made, the total master strategy should be viewed for compliance with the strategic control items noted in Chapter 9. Think through its consequences.

8. Set priorities for your solutions.

9. Be prepared to implement these decisions—that is, consider if they would and could be implemented. Eliminate "pie-in-the-sky" solutions and marshal sufficient evidence to defend your solutions. Do your solutions solve the problems or exploit the opportunities? Budget for your decisions.

10. If written or class presentation is required, be professional. Use charts, handouts, slides, and the like.

The list above is a suggested series of general actions. Questions at the end of each case may direct that other actions be taken. The instructor may also choose other courses of action. Use what you have learned; for example,

1. Use the strategic audit in Appendix 2.

2. Use the information in Table 9.1, Appendixes 3 and 4.

3. Determine the stage of the product life cycle.

4. Determine the contingency factors for this stage.

5. Decide what actions are appropriate in this situation.

6. Use a strategy matrix (like the GE Stoplight) where applicable.

7. Make certain you determine what it is your decision is supposed to accomplish.

8. Review the strategic control checklists in Chapter 9.

9. Review the 7-S's and other implementation materials in Chapter 8.

10. Accomplish spreadsheet pro formas where necessary.

INDEX

911